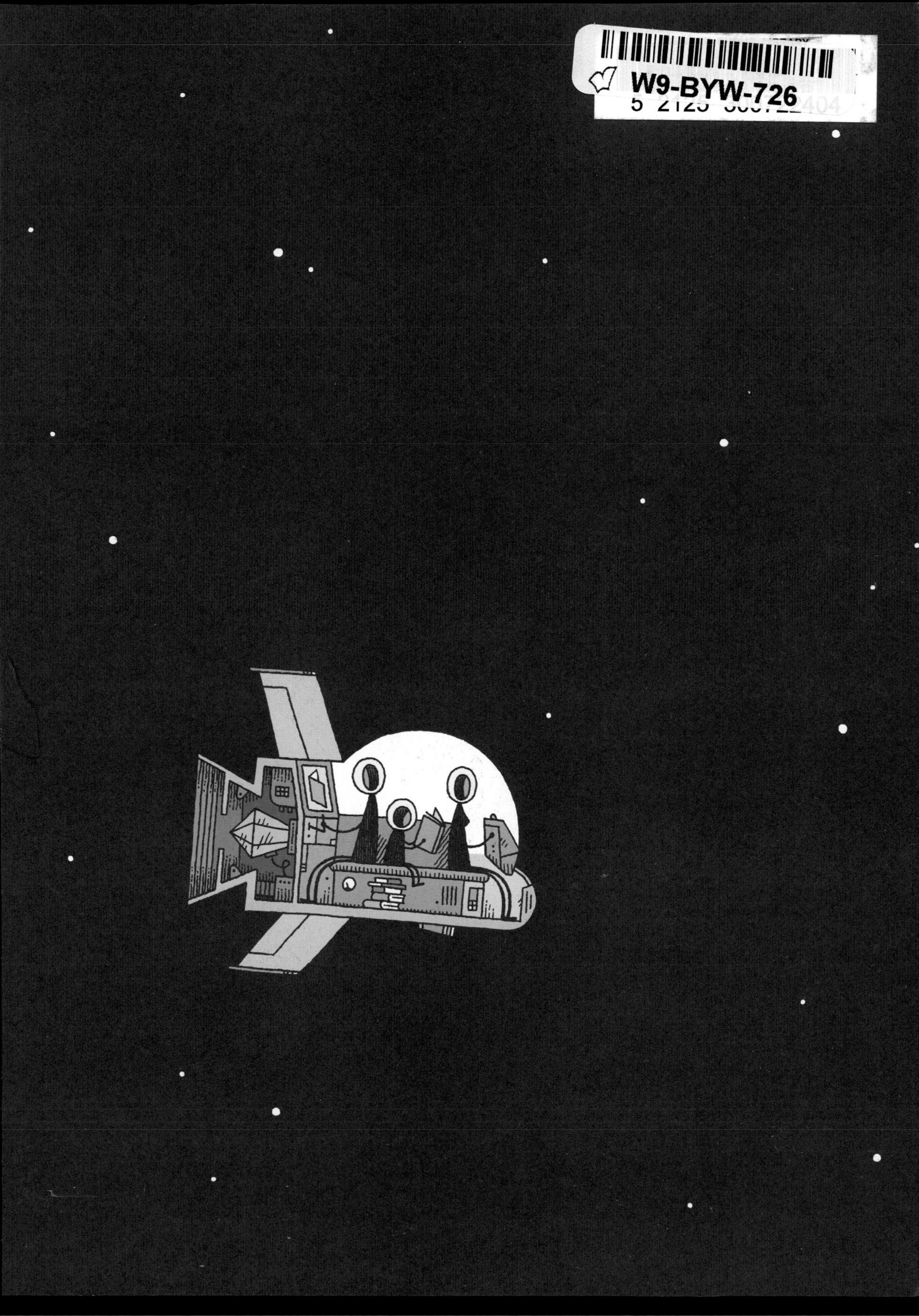

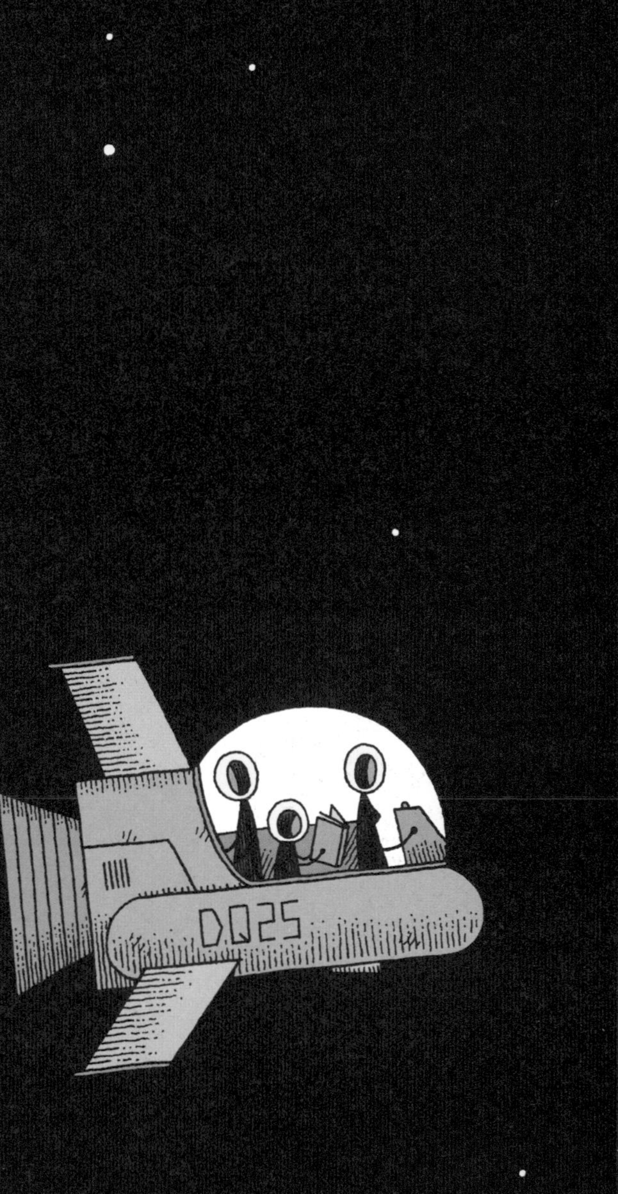
D.Q25

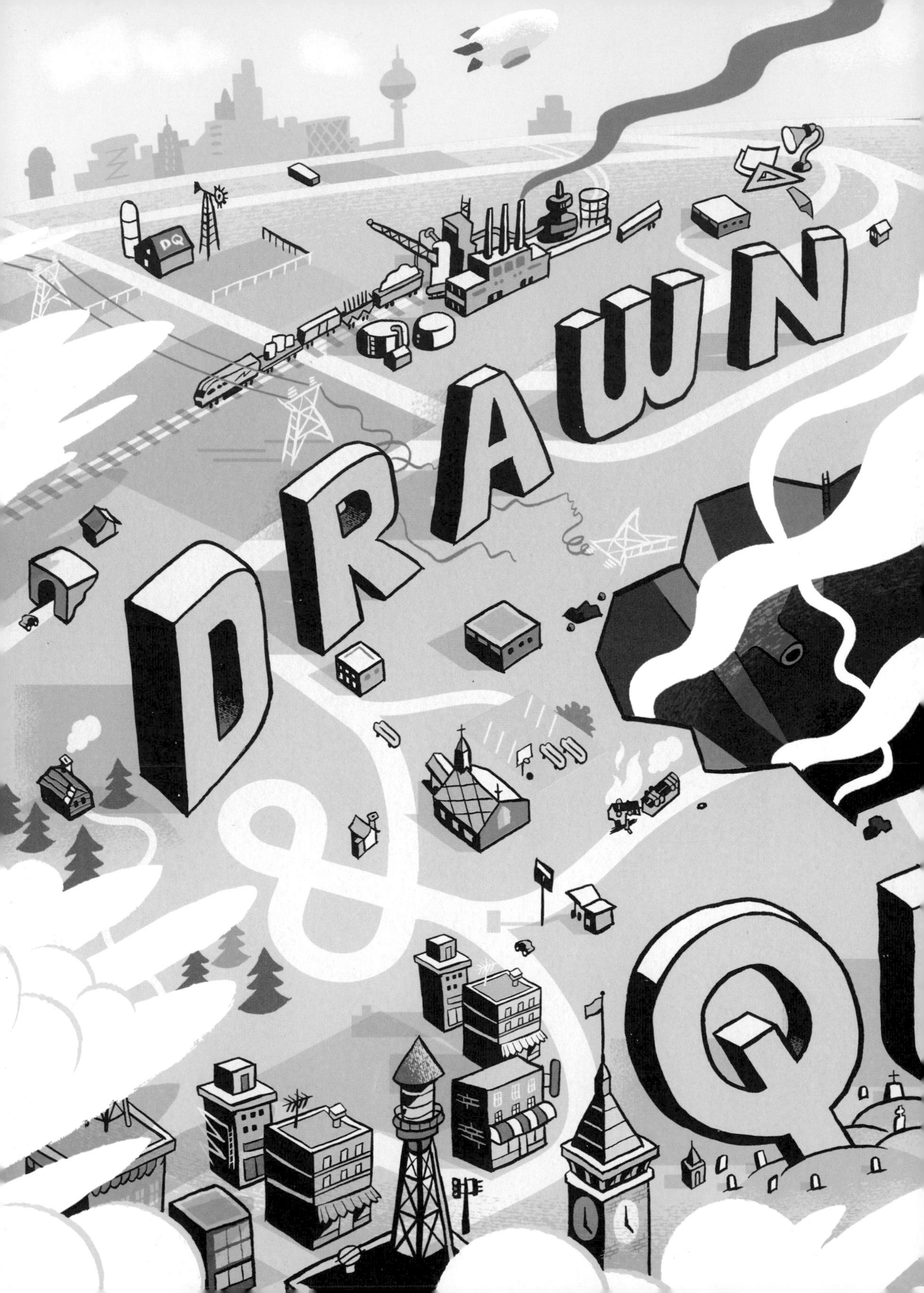
DQ
DRAWN
&

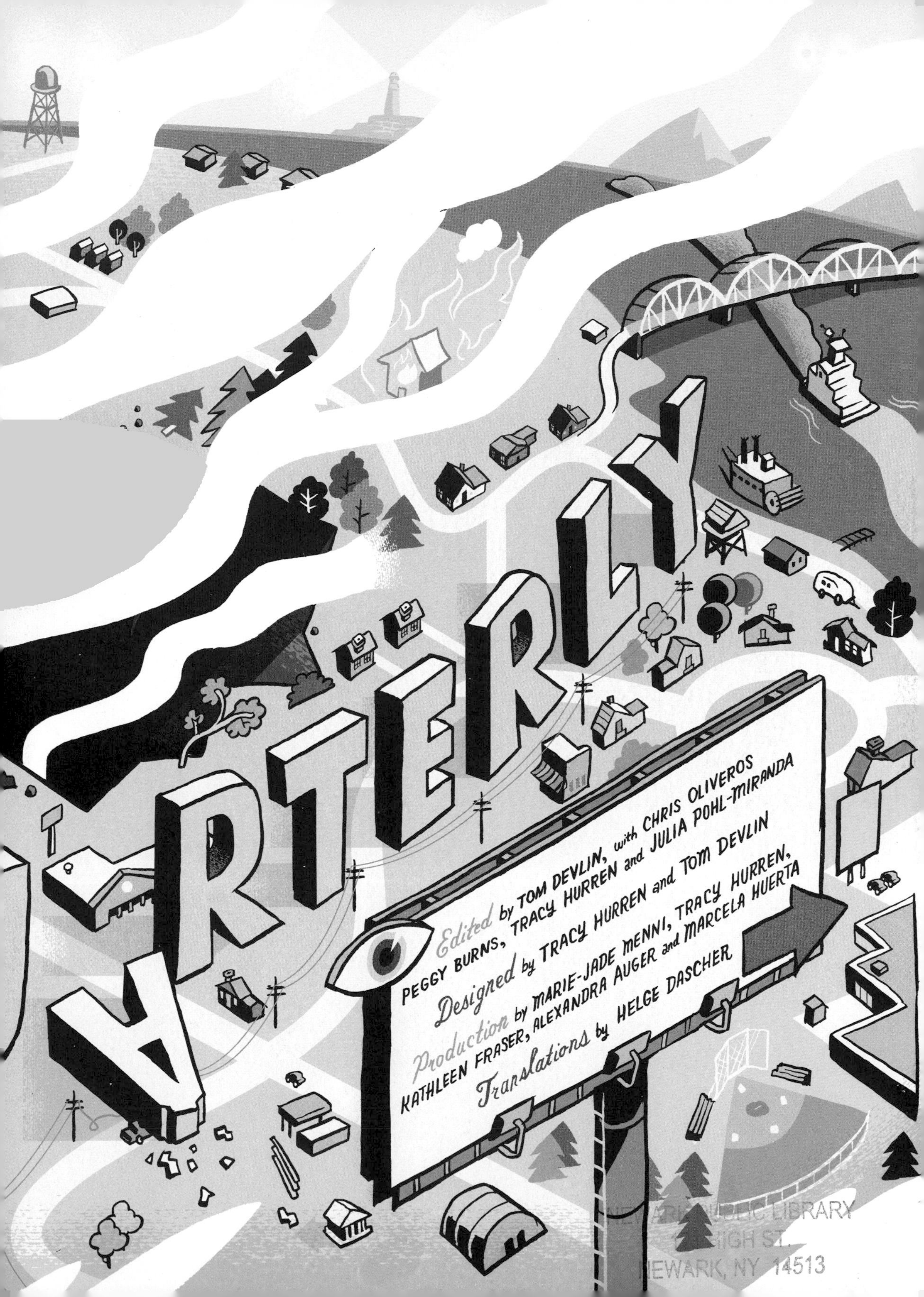
RTERLY
Edited by TOM DEVLIN, with CHRIS OLIVEROS
PEGGY BURNS, TRACY HURREN and JULIA POHL-MIRANDA
Designed by TRACY HURREN and TOM DEVLIN
Production by MARIE-JADE MENNI, TRACY HURREN,
KATHLEEN FRASER, ALEXANDRA AUGER and MARCELA HUERTA
Translations by HELGE DASCHER

CONTENTS

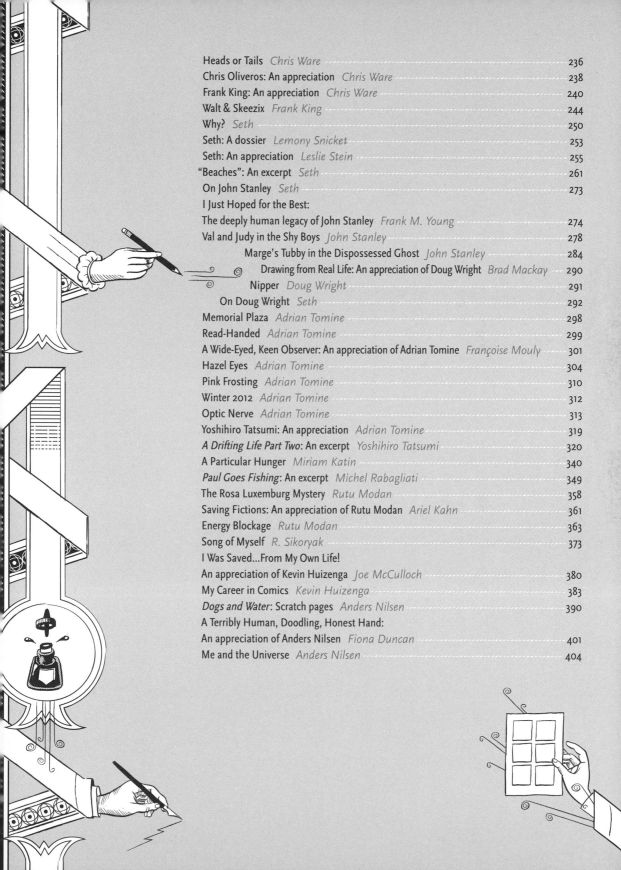

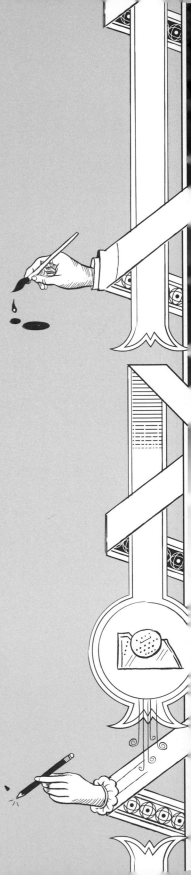

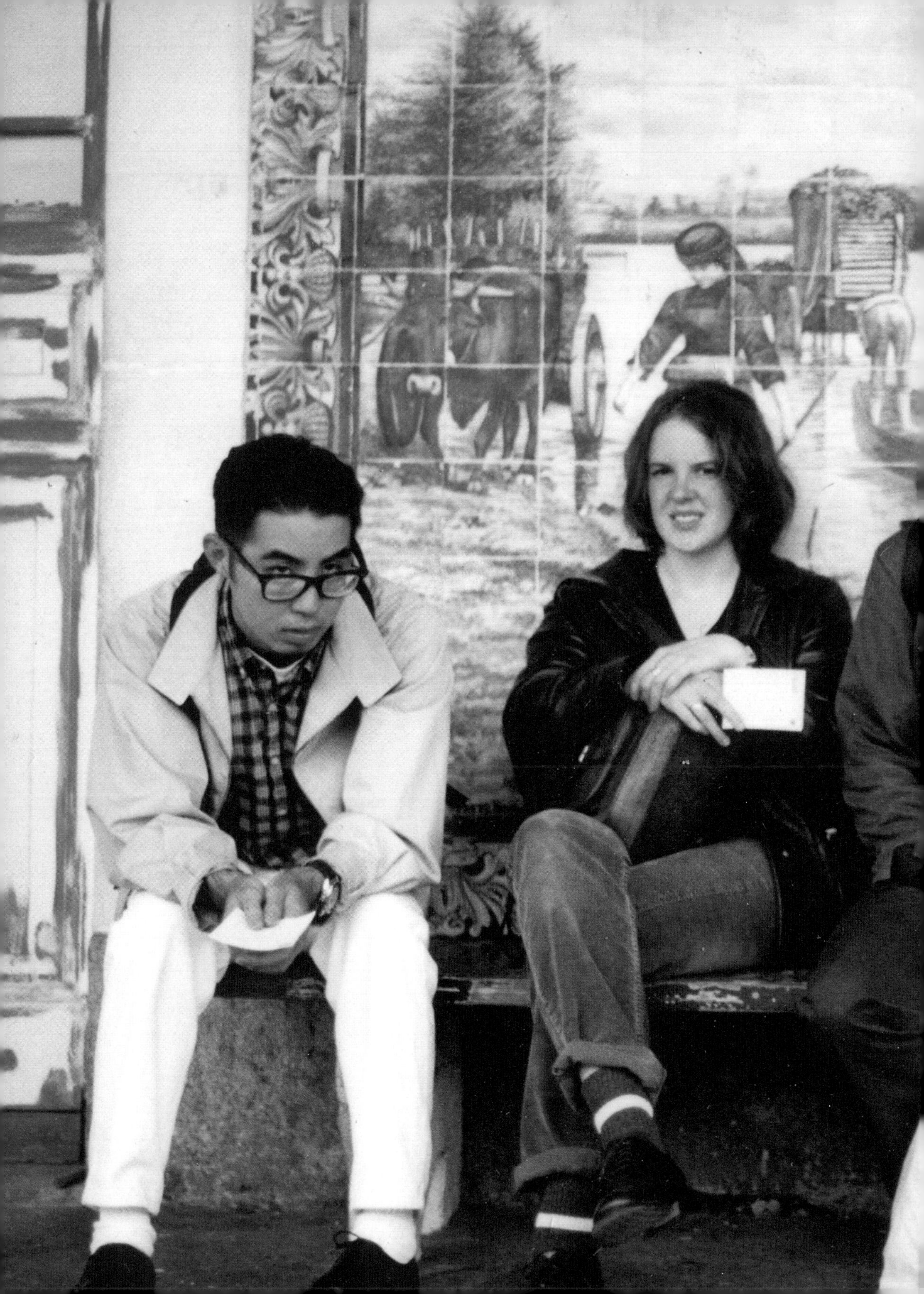

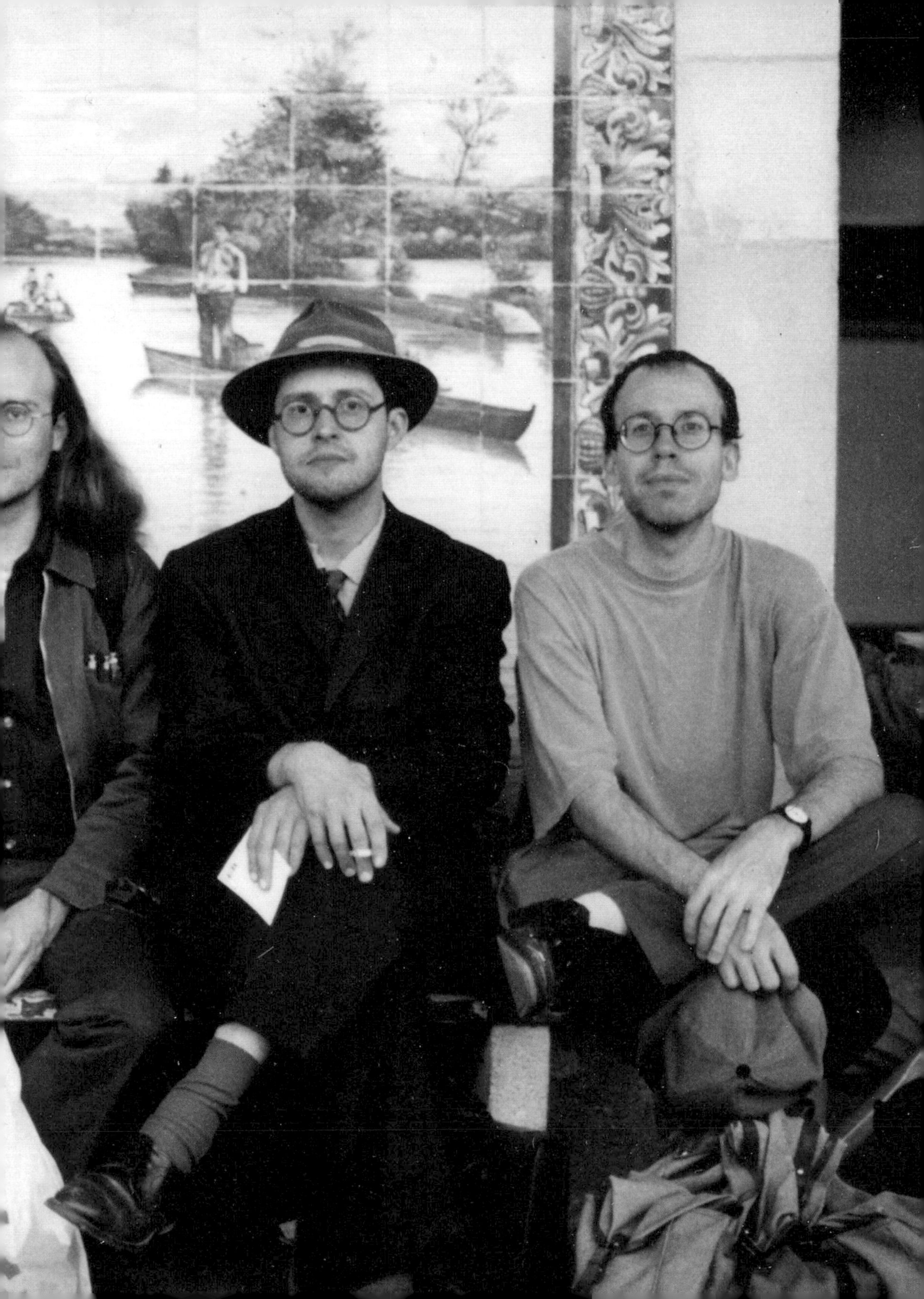

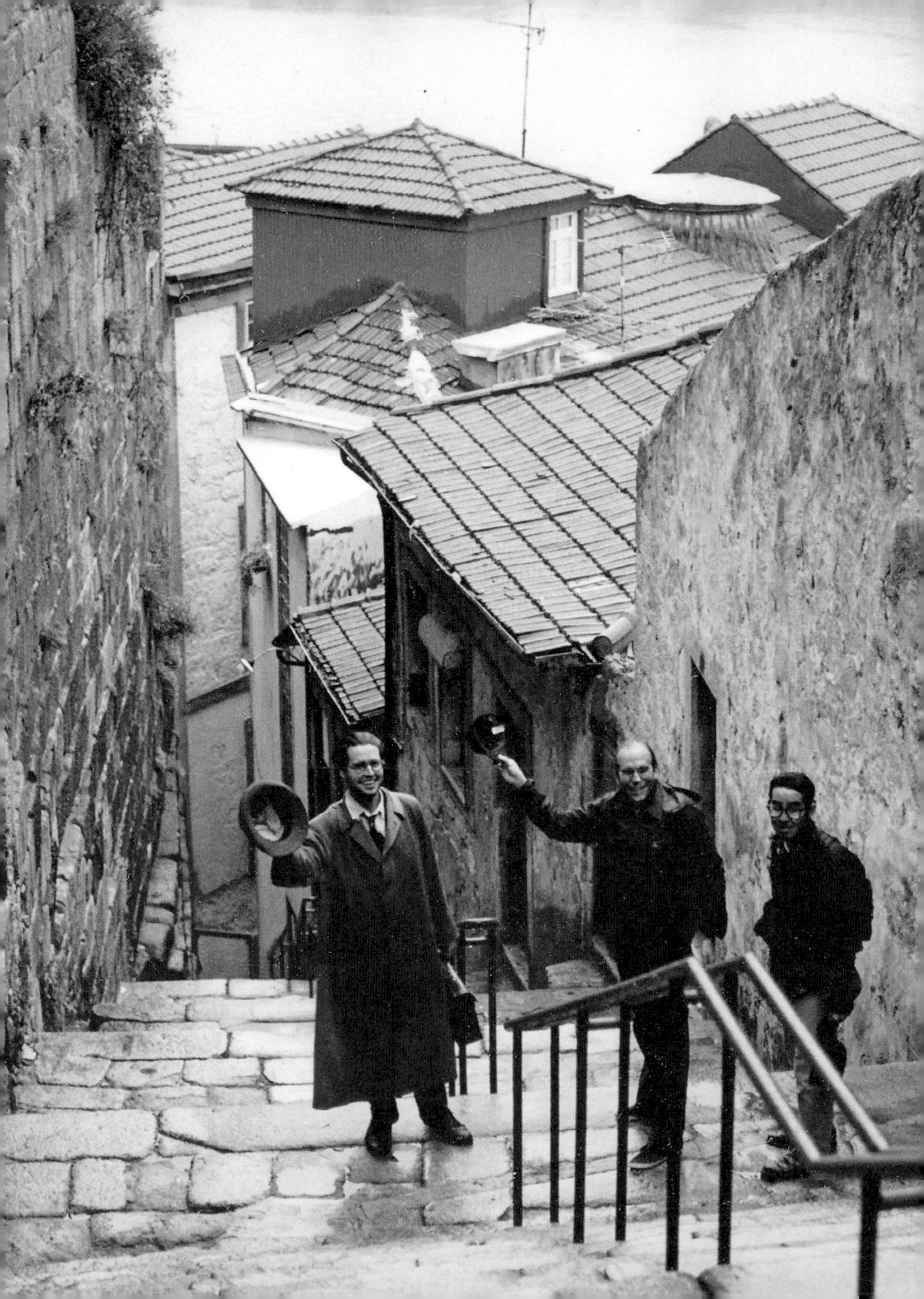

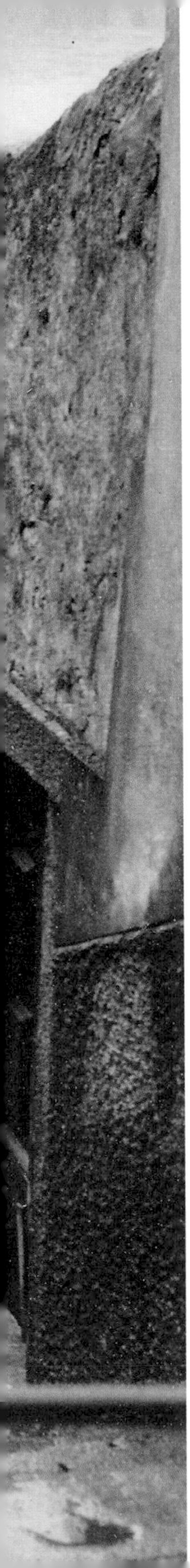

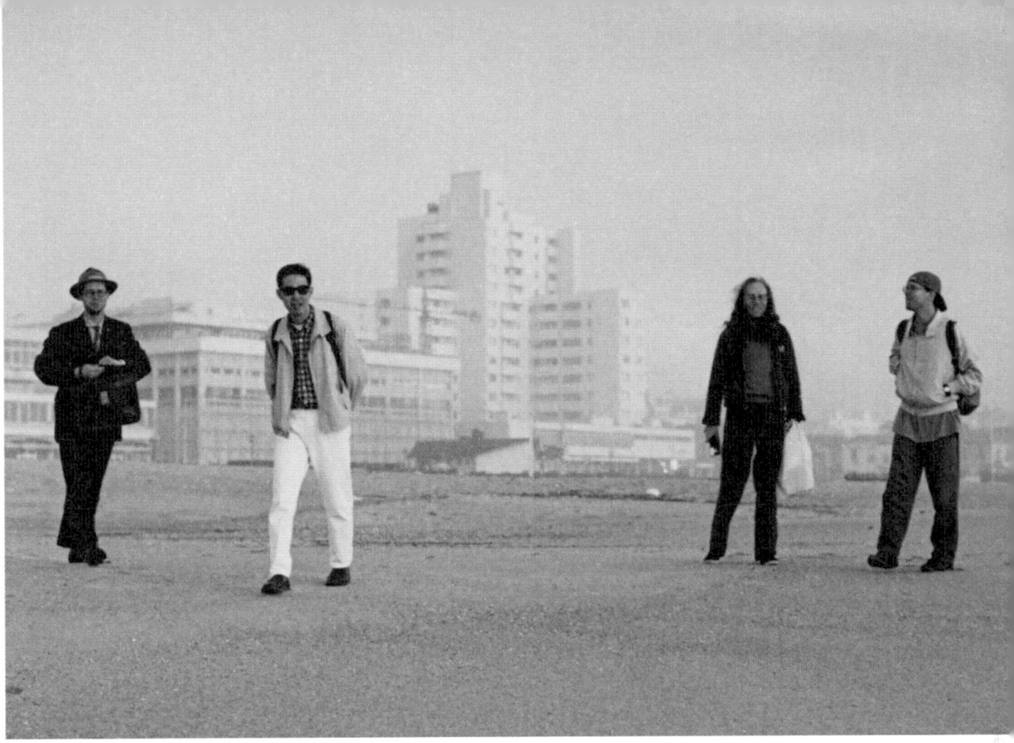

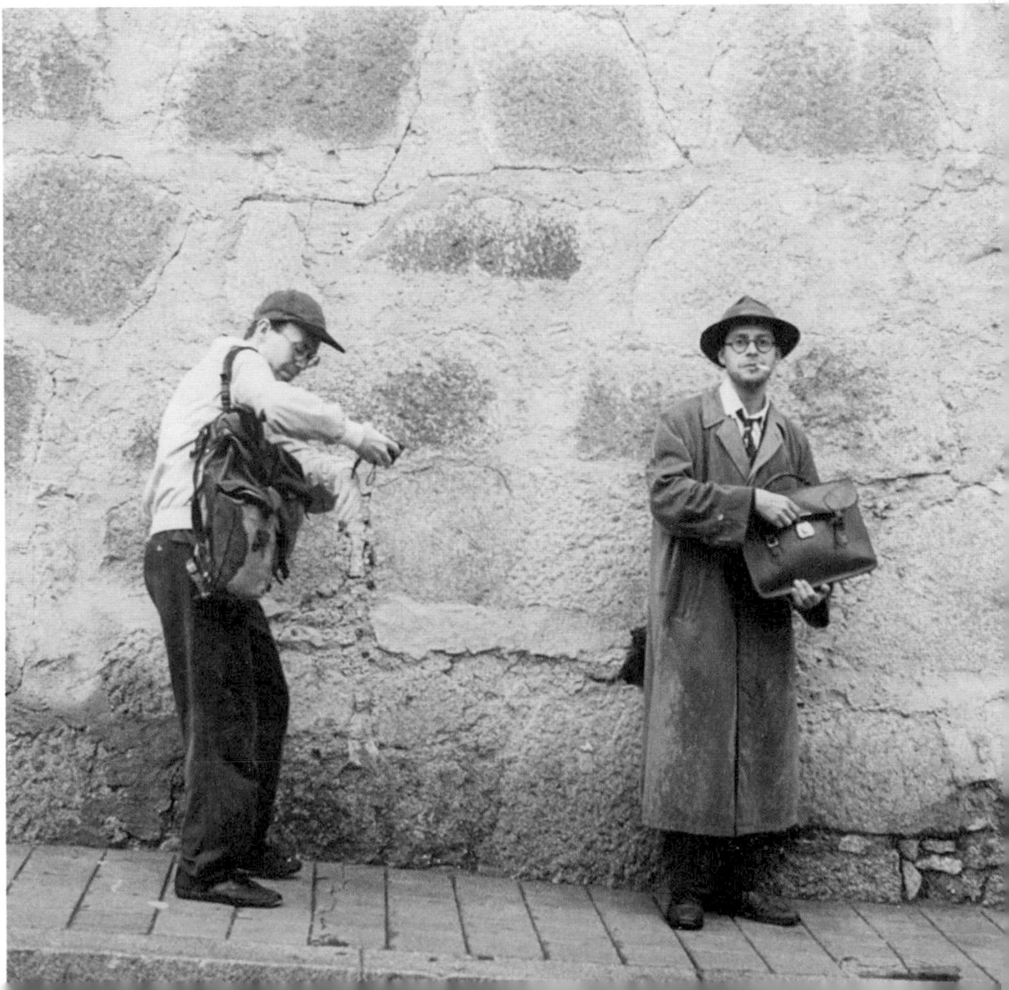

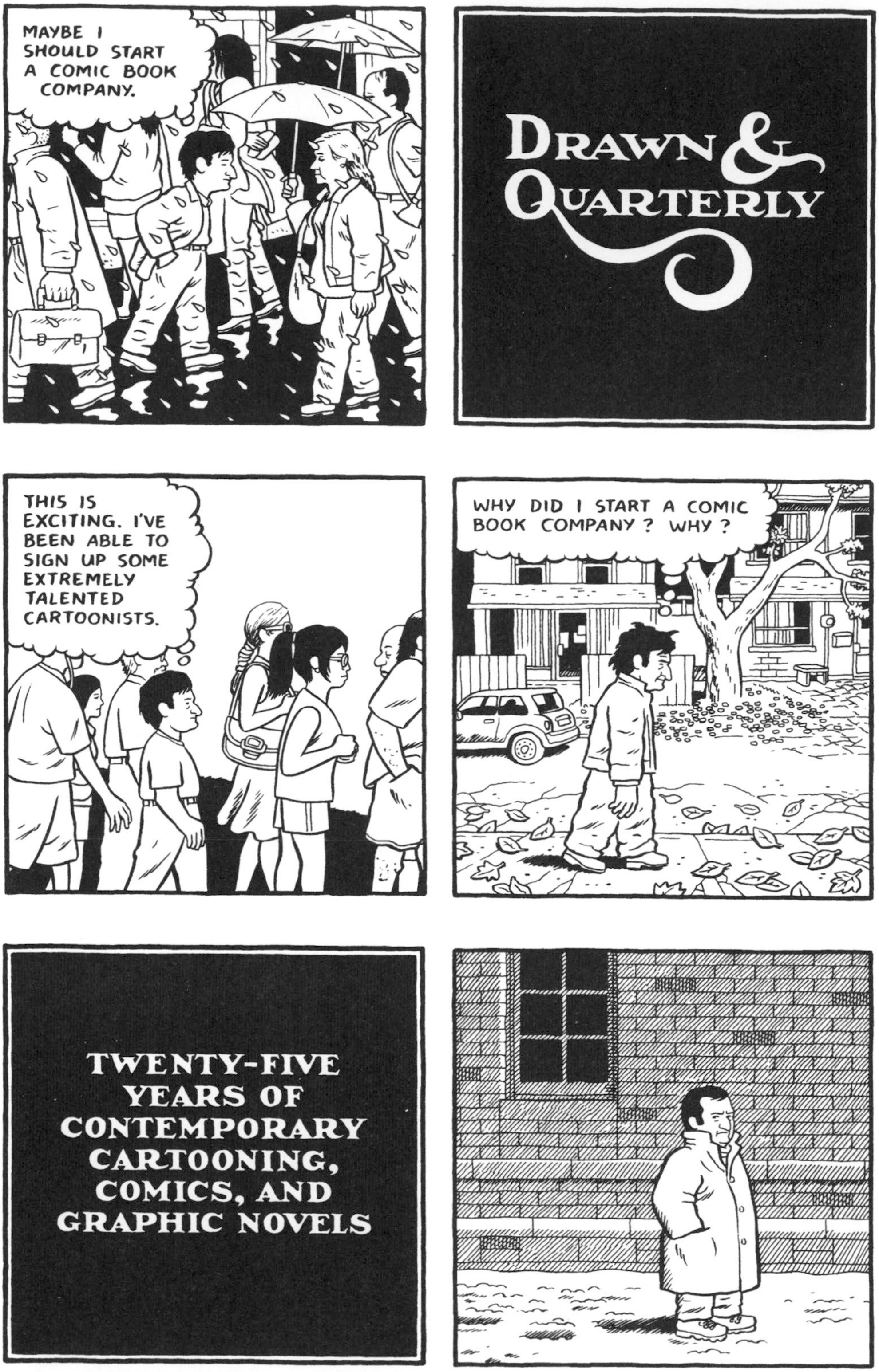
MAYBE I SHOULD START A COMIC BOOK COMPANY.
DRAWN & QUARTERLY
THIS IS EXCITING. I'VE BEEN ABLE TO SIGN UP SOME EXTREMELY TALENTED CARTOONISTS.
WHY DID I START A COMIC BOOK COMPANY? WHY?
TWENTY-FIVE YEARS OF CONTEMPORARY CARTOONING, COMICS, AND GRAPHIC NOVELS

A HISTORY OF DRAWN & QUARTERLY

by Sean Rogers, with additional research by Jeet Heer

Maybe I'm crazy, or maybe I overestimate the tastes of the North American Public, but I firmly believe that an intelligent magazine showcasing a number of quality comic strips can survive and even thrive within our culture.
—letter from the editor,* Drawn & Quarterly *no. 1, spring 1990

In 1989, with the popular perception of comics still largely defined by the superhero genre, it probably did seem more than a little crazy to start a comic-book company with literary and artistic aspirations. And with the burgeoning independent comics scene once again experiencing one of its periodic busts, this was hardly the time to launch a new venture. Still, Chris Oliveros remained undaunted. Twenty-five years on, his belief in intelligent comics looks less foolish than it does commendably far-sighted. Drawn & Quarterly, the company he created, has flourished, and the kind of "quality comic strips" he valued from the start have found an admiring public at last.

At first, the company was very much a one-man (or one-family) affair, headquartered for many years in whatever apartment in Montreal's Mile End Oliveros and his girlfriend and sometime co-editor Marina Lesenko lived in. But today, D+Q is a much more substantial operation, bolstered not just by an international reputation but also by an actual office—housed in part of a century-old, wonky-angled, ten-storey industrial building near a clattering railway line—as well as a storefront that has become a Montreal literary destination. Between the office and the bookshop, the ten full-time and eight part-time employees, and the backlist of hundreds of groundbreaking comics, Drawn & Quarterly today barely resembles the company of even ten or twelve years ago, let alone that crazy endeavour Oliveros dreamed up a quarter century back.

In the 1980s, though, before the thought of D+Q had ever crossed Oliveros's mind, it would have been absurd to predict so much growth and success for an upstart comic-book publisher. At the time, the tradition of underground comix, which thrived in the late 1960s and early 1970s, had lost whatever cultural foothold it once enjoyed. Instead, comics at the outset of the eighties was overwhelmingly a commercial art form, with family humour dominating newspaper strips just as the superhero genre had hegemony over the comic-book field. In that context, it was ridiculous to conceive of cartooning that attempted to explore a personal vision rather than fulfill a commercial imperative: to create or publish comics that aspired to be art was the very height of folly.

Thanks to this mindset, the world of comics was largely a wasteland in the early 1980s; still, if you looked hard enough, a few green shoots could be spotted. New Yorkers Art Spiegelman and Françoise Mouly were then at the helm of *RAW* magazine, a lavish showcase for formalist experimentation and avant-garde comix where Spiegelman serialized his groundbreaking *Maus*, while in California, Robert Crumb launched another iconic anthology, *Weirdo*, which demonstrated that the underground's aesthetic of abrasive outsider art was still vital. Few of the new "ground-level" or "alternative" comic-book companies that emerged to serve the fledgling market of specialty comic-book stores

June 1989
Chris Oliveros begins work on a comics anthology magazine, with the goal of launching the first issue by year-end. At this point the name of the company is not yet set, and "Bleeding Heart" is used in very early references as the working title of the magazine.

July 1989
An ad calling for submissions is placed on the back page of *New York Press*, an alternative weekly newspaper. As a result, numerous submissions arrive in the mail over the next couple of weeks, including a package from James Sturm, then a young student at SVA.

August 1989
Potential names for the company are narrowed down to a short list. Marina Lesenko suggests "Drawn & Quartered" and Chris modifies the last two letters to settle on the final name. Drawn & Quarterly is registered as a company later that month.

September 1989
Contact is made with early contributors, including Joe Matt, Peter Bagge, and J.D. King. (King's contribution to the first issue was a collaboration with writer Alice Sebold, who later went on to renown as the author of *The Lovely Bones*.)

(Photos on previous two spreads) Seth, Chester Brown, Julie Doucet, Joe Matt & Adrian Tomine in Porto, Portugal (1995).

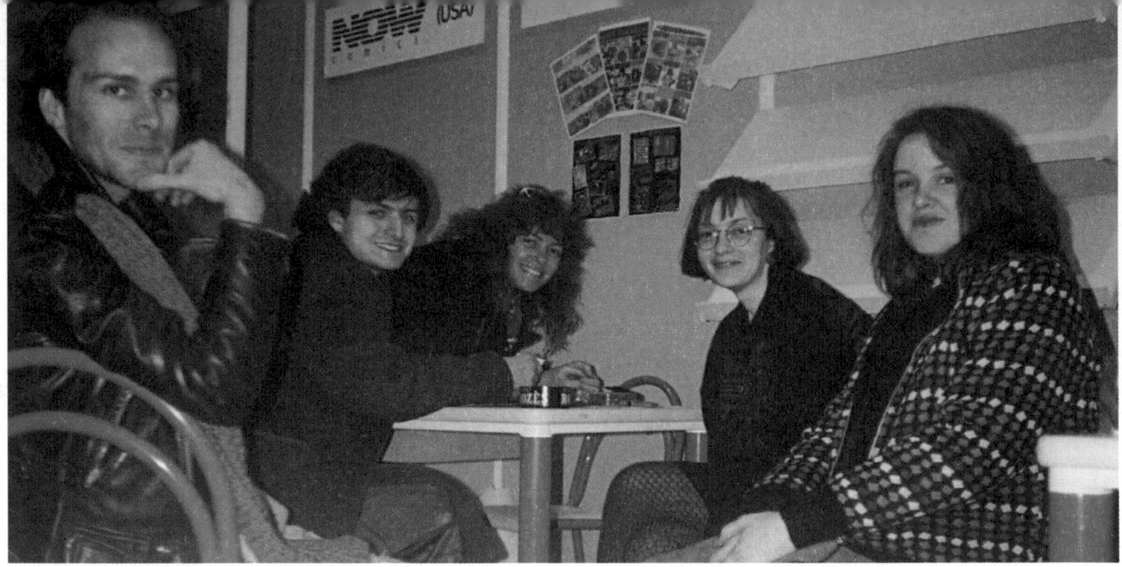

My first encounter with the handiwork of D+Q was in late 1991 or early 1992, when I was going through the back-issue boxes at Fallout Records in Seattle. I found the first five or six issues of *Drawn & Quarterly* magazine and promptly bought them. They were the kind of comics I was hungry for—taking a cue from the precedent set by Art Spiegelman's *RAW* magazine, but stepping out from under the influence of the American underground, which had overshadowed so much of "alternative comics" up to that point. Whenever I visited Fallout after that, I bought all the D+Q stuff I could afford.—***Jason Lutes***

released anything as daring or accomplished as *Weirdo* or *RAW* (after all, "ground-level" comics were so called since they dug nowhere close to as deep or as dirty as undergrounds proper). Perhaps the most notable exception was Fantagraphics, which published the confrontational and contentious *Comics Journal*, a vocal forum for championing innovative work and criticizing compromised commercial fare. Steered most prominently by the sensibilities of Gary Groth and Kim Thompson, Fantagraphics branched out into publishing its own distinctive line of comics, which tried to attain the ideals espoused in the *Journal*, and its flagship title quickly became the Hernandez brothers' soap operatic *Love and Rockets*.

For a critical reader of comics in those dire 1980s, these were the few standards to look up to and emulate. But despite the promise of this small group of comics, much of the energy in the field at that time was inchoate and confused. It was on this disorderly world that Chris Oliveros decided to make his mark. From a tiny apartment in Mile End in Montreal—a bilingual metropolis at the heart of francophone Quebec, far removed from *RAW*'s arty New York, the underground's hippie west coast, or the American offices of any of the black and white indie publishers then flooding comic-book stores—Oliveros made his unassuming start as a publisher.

Born in 1966 in Montreal, the youngest son of a Spanish immigrant psychiatrist and a Manitoba transplant, Oliveros was a comics reader from an early age. His lifelong interest in the medium began in his youth with superhero fare published by Marvel or DC, waned in his teenage years, and matured after he read the first issue of *RAW* in the

December 1989
Seven thousand copies of *Drawn & Quarterly* no. 1 are received at a second-floor apartment located at 95 Bernard Street West in Montreal. It is discovered that the printer made an error; they agree to pulp the entire print run and reprint at their cost.

March 1990
Chris reaches out to Montreal cartoonist Julie Doucet. Up until this point Julie has self-published *Dirty Plotte*, a zine collecting her comic strips. When she states that she is looking for a publisher, Julie becomes D+Q's first "solo author," and a one-page, handwritten contract is signed between her and Chris.

April 1990
Drawn & Quarterly no. 1 debuts in comics stores.

September 1990
Steve Solomos, co-owner of the Beguiling, organizes a comics convention in Toronto and invites D+Q as an exhibitor. There, Chris meets Seth and Chester Brown for the first time. Coincidentally, Seth is nearly finished work on *Palookaville* no. 1 and is about to look for a publisher. By the end of the weekend, *Palookaville* is signed on as D+Q's second comics pamphlet series.

 Chester Brown, Chris Oliveros, Mary Fleener, Marina Lesenko & Julie Doucet in Angoulême (1992).

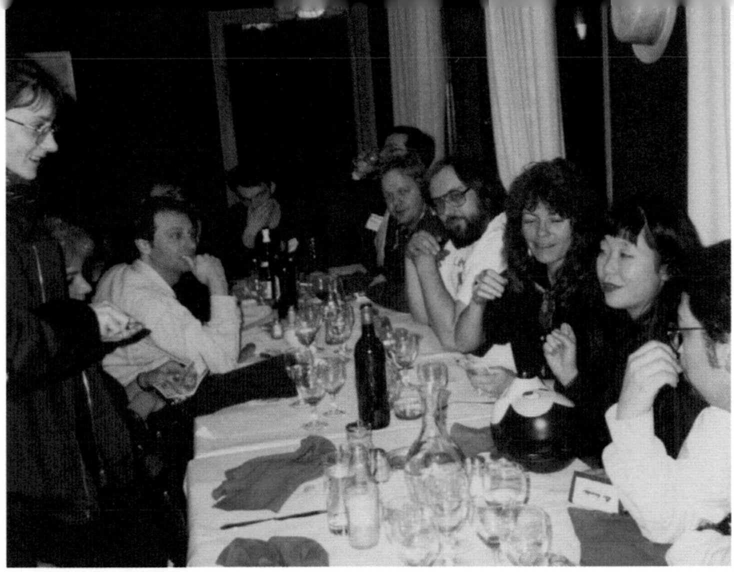

early eighties. Spiegelman and Mouly's cutting-edge anthology demonstrated for Oliveros that comics could become an art form for adults, and he learned many lessons from *RAW*, especially the crucial skill of curating the comics one publishes, selecting the best stories, and presenting them in a physical framework where form and content work together.

Although excited by the artistic possibilities displayed in *RAW*, which he continued to follow throughout the eighties, Oliveros had little contact with other comics until 1986, when the first Fantagraphics issue of *Lloyd Llewellyn* by Daniel Clowes inspired him to investigate the nascent alternative comics scene. Then, in 1988, Oliveros worked with an artistic group on a short-lived comics magazine called *Core*. Unhappy with the indiscriminate editing of the magazine, which was willing to include seemingly any submission, Oliveros still found that working on *Core* gave him a hands-on education in the basics of publishing. He acquired the knack of assembling and distributing a magazine. A seed was planted in Oliveros's mind: what if he helmed an anthology that had a more ambitious agenda than contemporary comics magazines like *Honk!* or *Centrifugal Bumblepuppy* could offer? What if he edited a title that tried to push comics forward the way *RAW* was doing, only with more approachable narratives? Such a magazine could be the comics counterpart to the *New Yorker* or *Harper's*.

To Oliveros, launching a magazine seemed like a feasible enterprise because the so-called "direct market" distribution system in comics was uniquely hospitable to small start-ups. (In comics

October 1990
Julie Doucet's *Dirty Plotte* no. 1 is published. Julie wins a Harvey Award for Best New Talent.

April 1991
Seth's *Palookaville* no. 1 is published.

July 1991
Chester Brown agrees to switch publishers, moving his comic-book series *Yummy Fur* over to D+Q. *Yummy Fur* no. 25 is published.

January 1992
D+Q attends its first international convention: Angoulême's Festival international de la bande dessinée. Chester Brown, Julie Doucet, Mary Fleener, Marina Lesenko, and Chris Oliveros are in attendance.

June 1992
Joe Matt's *Peepshow* no. 1 is published.

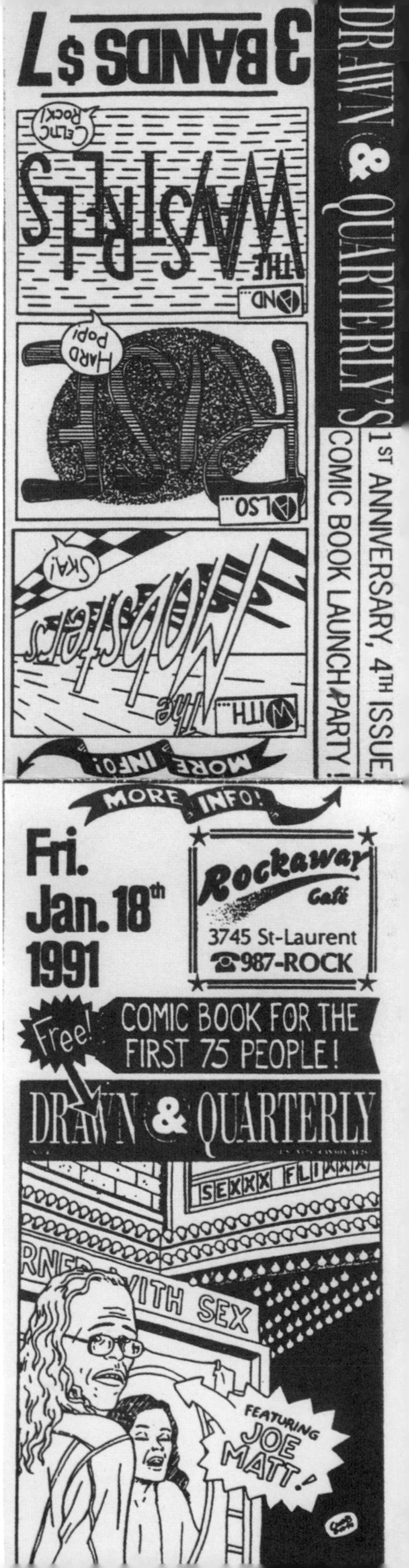
DRAWN & QUARTERLY'S
1ST ANNIVERSARY, 4TH ISSUE, COMIC BOOK LAUNCH PARTY!
3 BANDS $7
AND...
THE WASTRELS
CELTIC ROCK!
ALSO...
HARD POP!
WITH...
the Mobsters
SKA!
MORE INFO!
MORE INFO!
Fri. Jan. 18th 1991
Rockaway Café
3745 St-Laurent
987-ROCK
Free!
COMIC BOOK FOR THE FIRST 75 PEOPLE!
DRAWN & QUARTERLY
SEXXX FLI
WITH SEX
FEATURING JOE MATT!
Flyer design: John Oliveros (1991).

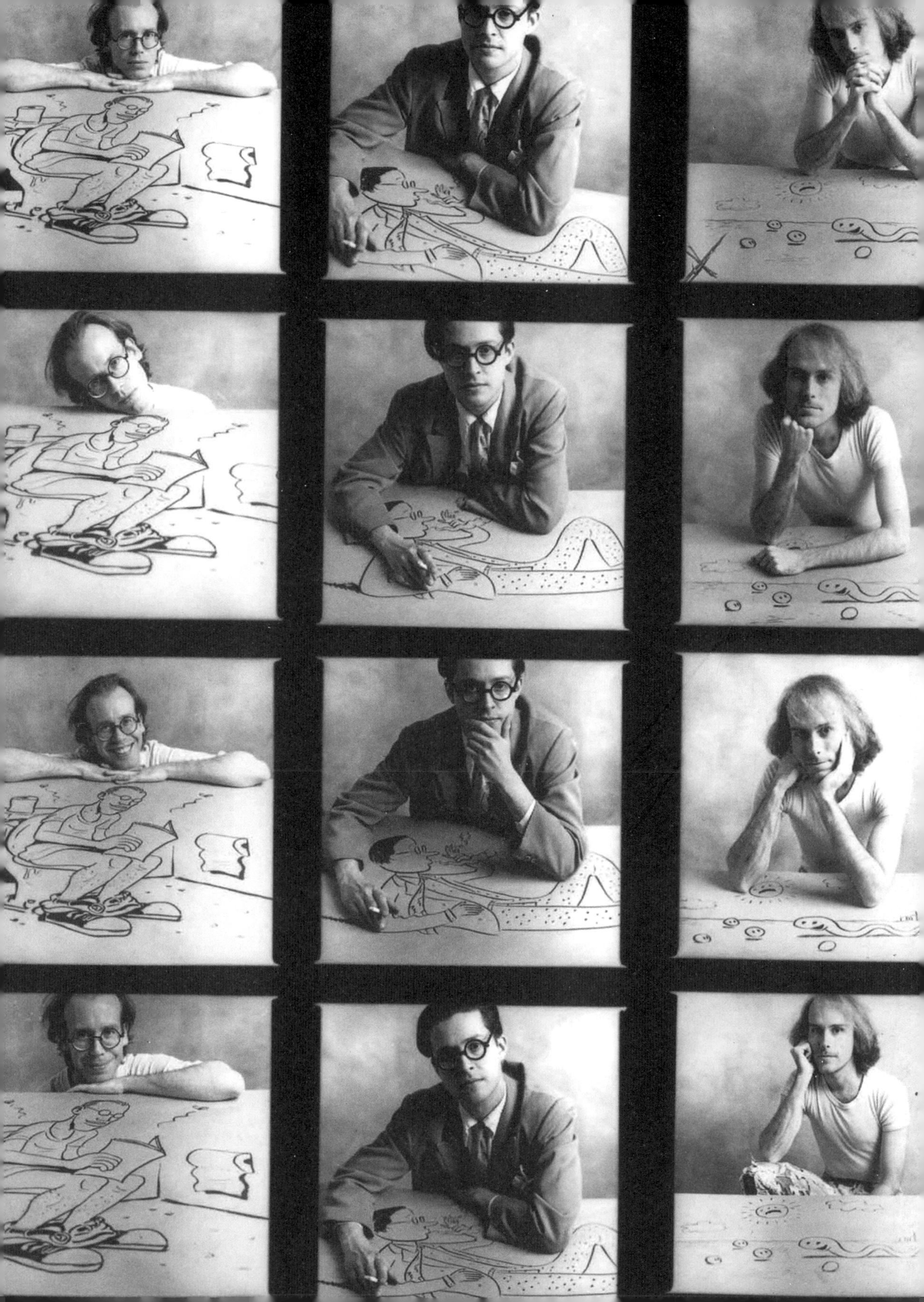

industry parlance, "direct market" describes a method of selling directly to comic-book specialty shops.) Traditional book and magazine publishing allows for unsold titles to be returned, which means that many more copies are published than sold. The returns system also dictates that payment is made many months after publication, meaning that a publishing house needs to be heavily capitalized to succeed. The direct market, on the other hand, catered to collectors who wanted long-term access to out-of-print back issues, with specialty stores buying magazines and books on a non-returnable basis. Therefore, three months after a book was released, the publisher would get paid for all copies bought by stores. And in the 1980s, because "ground-level" titles like *Teenage Mutant Ninja Turtles* were sometimes surprise hits, some stores were willing to buy a few copies of almost any title offered. In those days, the direct market provided a framework that enabled a publisher like Oliveros to get his start: anyone could scare up enough cash to meet a printing bill, package together a plausible-looking comic book, and then reasonably expect to break even (or at least not lose too much money).

By June 1989, Oliveros started working on plans for his proposed magazine. Names like "Bleeding Heart" were booted around. Eventually, Marina Lesenko suggested "Drawn & Quartered," which

Oliveros streamlined to "Drawn & Quarterly" (to reflect the magazine's publishing schedule, four times a year). A call for submissions was issued in the form of an ad in the *New York Press*, which drew several contributions, including a package from cartoonist and future educator James Sturm, then a student at the School of Visual Arts, who would publish several books with D+Q in the future.

As *Drawn & Quarterly* received material from alternative comics mainstays like Joe Matt, Peter Bagge, and J.D. King, the first installment started to shape up. Published in April of 1990, that inaugural issue was a solid anthology, but undistinguished in that it shared several similarities of form and content with earlier comics magazines like *Snarf* and *Prime Cuts*: it was the standard newsstand magazine size (8½" by 11"), with thirty-two black and white interior pages stapled together under a glossy cover. As a publisher, Oliveros was learning on the job, and it took some time before he embarked on the more ambitious designs of later anthologies, comics, and books.

That first issue started off with a defiant editorial from Oliveros, a rare and vocal statement of purpose that laid out an artistic—and feminist—agenda. The new publisher firmly—and perhaps crazily—believed in the potential for intelligent comics of distinguished quality to succeed with a cultured readership.

October 1992
Chester Brown's *The Playboy* is published: D+Q's first graphic novel.

May 1993
A rare early anniversary concert for D+Q happens in Montreal, featuring Jonathan Richman as the main act.

October 1993
D+Q's second graphic novel is published: Julie Doucet's *Lève Ta Jambe, Mon Poisson Est Mort!*

November 1993
Chris writes a letter to then-nineteen-year-old cartoonist Adrian Tomine. Encouraging but at times critical, the letter is handwritten on the back of a Xerox.

May 1994
After receiving the latest self-published issue of *Optic Nerve* in the mail, Chris calls up Adrian Tomine and asks if D+Q can

Contact sheet from shoot with Joe Matt, Seth & Chester Brown. Photos: Rick McGinnis (1992). 17

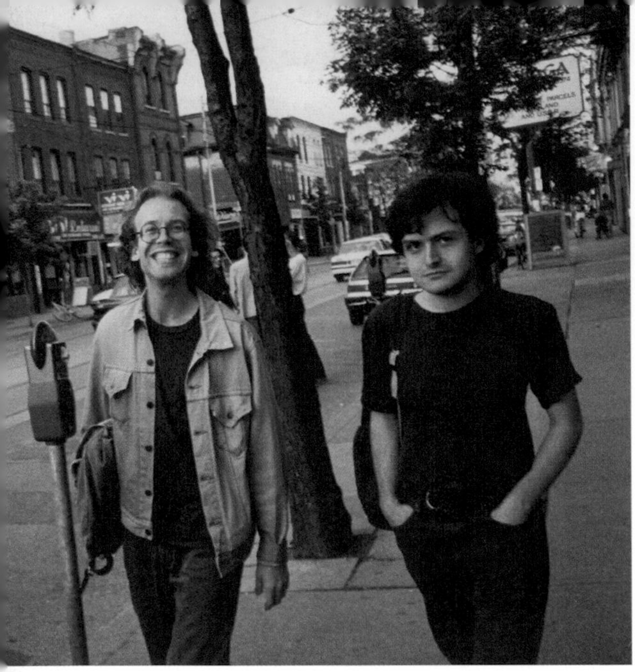

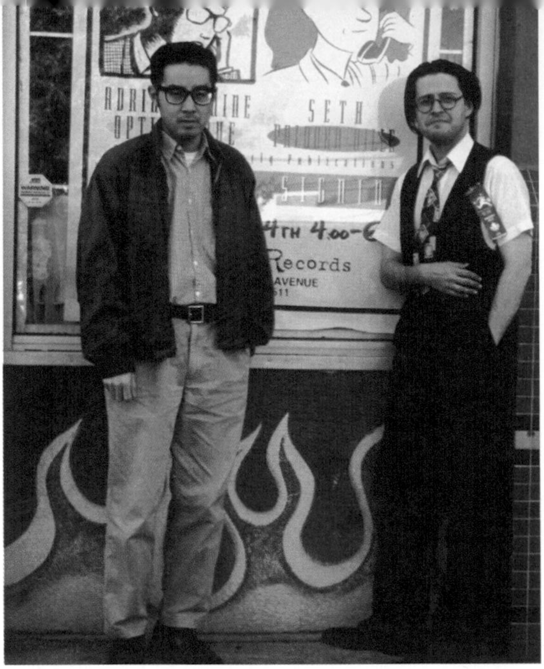
SETH

But the editorial also called out one failing in particular that "severely limited" the audience for comics, lamenting the fact that the world of comics was "a private boy's club" producing work that "very few women actually read." That first issue's cover was an implicit response to this state of affairs, with its portrait of a frenzied but determined woman, pen in hand, at her drafting table, drawn by Anne Bernstein—only one of the issue's female contributors. Soon, too, D+Q would release its debut comic-book series—Julie Doucet's radical *Dirty Plotte*, still a standard-bearer for feminist comics.

Already, D+Q was dedicated to making inroads against the gender imbalance in comics. In the years to come, that effort would only redouble: throughout its existence, the company has published many outstanding new female cartoonists, helped rediscover and rekindle the careers of many more, and built a staff comprising mostly women, making it the most female-friendly company in the history of comics. Many of D+Q's greatest successes have come from the pens of authors like Lynda Barry, Kate Beaton, Rutu Modan, and Tove Jansson, and the company continues to privilege the voices and stories of women authors and readers—just as was promised with that opening shot fired in D+Q's first publication.

In the second and third issues, *Drawn & Quarterly* magazine started displaying a more distinctive editorial sensibility, which lifted it above the ruck of mediocre anthologies crowding the market. A stable of artists emerged as regulars, including Joe Matt and Seth, while the stories themselves tended to hang together cohesively. The magazine had a predilection for autobiographical anecdotes—small, well-shaped tales dwelling on brief incidents. In effect, *Drawn & Quarterly* magazine cut a middle swath between *RAW* and *Weirdo*, featuring work that was more narratively inclined and less formally challenging than most of *RAW*, but moving beyond the underground shock tactics of *Weirdo*.

The turn to autobiography was part of a larger trend in alternative cartooning, inspired by a widely felt need to

---

publish *Optic Nerve* as a comic-book series.

July 1994
D+Q attends first American comics convention: San Diego Comic-Con. The booth costs are shared with fellow Montreal publisher Black Eye Books.

September 1994
Helge Dascher begins a decades-long association with D+Q with her translation of a Dupuy & Berbérian short story.

October 1994
Chester Brown's second book with D+Q is published. He is dissuaded from using "Fuck" as the title of the book and instead goes with his second choice, *I Never Liked You*.

April 1995
Adrian Tomine's *Optic Nerve* no. 1 is published.

September 1995
Adrian Tomine's *32 Stories: The Complete Optic Nerve Mini-Comics* is published.

October 1995
Julie Doucet's *My Most Secret Desire* is published.

October 1995
D+Q's first international exhibition is held in Porto, Portugal. It features the work of Chester Brown, Julie Doucet, Joe Matt, Adrian Tomine, and Seth. Chris Oliveros and the exhibiting artists attend the opening.

(Left) Joe Matt & Chris Oliveros on Queen Street in Toronto (1992). (Right) Adrian Tomine & Seth at Criminal Records, Atlanta, GA (1996).

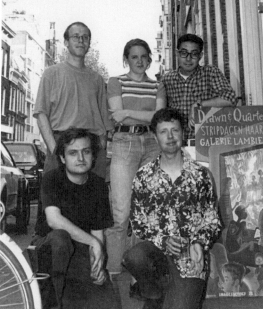

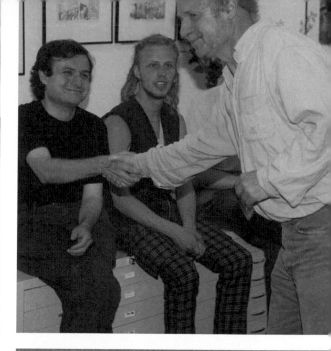

Drawn & Quarterly
STRIPDAGEN HAARLE
GALERIE LAMBIEK

Maurice Vellekoop. (Right) Chris & Kees Kousemaker. Both photos: Rob Becker, Lambiek, Amsterdam (1996).

eschew genre clichés and explore new ground in comics. Perhaps young artists turned to their own lives for subject matter because the material was familiar, and sifting through their own experiences proved less daunting a task than crafting fiction out of whole cloth or deriving stories from history, as more weathered D+Q authors would later do. Regardless, many of the emerging cartoonists of the early 1990s were also influenced by the fact that some of the best comics of the previous decade were autobiographical (as were Harvey Pekar's *American Splendor* and many of Crumb's best *Weirdo* comics), or at least seemed to be convincingly drawn from real life, even if in the end they were indeed fiction (like the stories in Lynda Barry's *Ernie Pook's Comeek*—a significant influence on Seth, if not others).

Even as he was planning the first issue of *Drawn & Quarterly* magazine, Oliveros was also laying the groundwork for a line of single-artist comic books—many of which would end up featuring autobio comics. The single-artist format, originally pioneered by Crumb in the late 1960s, had gained

June 1996
The D+Q exhibition expands to feature Maurice Vellekoop and travels to Holland for the Stripdagen Haarlem comics festival and a show at Galerie Lambiek in Amsterdam.

September 1996
Seth's first graphic novel, *It's a Good Life, If You Don't Weaken*, is published.

September 1996
First incarnation of a D+Q website is launched.

October 1996
Joe Matt's first graphic novel, *The Poor Bastard*, is published.

The modern graphic novel would be virtually nonexistent today if not for the early and ongoing support of a few dozen scrappy, ragtag individuals who own and operate comics shops across North America and Europe. These stores created the environment that allowed cartoonists like Daniel Clowes and Chester Brown, and publishers like Fantagraphics and Drawn & Quarterly, to establish a beachhead of sorts in the early days of alternative comics.

Steve Solomos, co-founder of the Beguiling, supported D+Q right from the beginning, inviting Julie Doucet and me to exhibit at a convention he organized in Toronto. D+Q was barely a company then, in 1990, and it probably didn't make much sense moneywise to pay for our transportation. Anyway, in the end Steve was probably not cut out for the hard, cold world of comics retailing, and he could barely get through a day without taking a sip from the flask he carried with him during business hours. He finally sold the Beguiling to Peter Birkemoe in 1998, abruptly swapping comics for the more lucrative film production business. Peter went on to improve on the initial success of the Beguiling and, if that wasn't enough, he created TCAF (with Christopher Butcher), possibly the best independent comics festival on the continent. Oh, and he went on to become D+Q's best friend and saviour. What more can we ask?

Many comics retailers got their start at an early age. The great Kees Kousemaker founded what is regarded as the world's first comics store, Lambiek, in Amsterdam in 1968. He worked tirelessly for over four decades to make the store an extension of his own eclectic personality. Sadly, he died in 2010, but Lambiek still carries on. We fondly remember the time that he hosted D+Q for an exhibition in 1996. Josh Palmano was still a teenager when he opened Gosh! Comics in 1986 and, over the next three decades, he's managed to make the store a hub of London's comics community. Dirk Rehm worked in Berlin's best comics shop, Grober Unfug, and he was one of the first international retailers to order from D+Q directly before he jumped to the other side of the fence to become a publisher himself with Reprodukt (see his essay on page 70).

There were several other retailers who took a chance on D+Q right from the beginning, stocking some of the very first comics that we published: Jim Hanley from Jim Hanley's Universe in New York; Brian Hibbs from Comix Experience in San Francisco; Chloe Eudaly from Reading Frenzy in Portland; Russ Battaglia from Fallout Books & Records in Seattle; Rory Root from Comic Relief in Berkeley; Eric Kirsammer from Chicago Comics; Bill Boichel from Copacetic Comics in Pittsburgh; Michael Drivas from Big Brain Comics in Minneapolis; Gaston Dominguez-Letelier from Meltdown Comics in Los Angeles (where a D+Q exhibition was held in 1998). And then of course there was Tom Devlin, who called in orders for a few years in the mid-1990s for the Million Year Picnic in Cambridge before starting his own company, Highwater Books, and later moving up to Montreal to join D+Q.

And beyond this support, many retailers have influenced up-and-coming cartoonists by helping to steer them to the "good" material. Gareth Gaudin, of Legends Comics in Victoria, BC, is cited by both Geneviève Castrée and Kate Beaton as having helped shape their comics-reading sensibilities at a crucial age. At another point, Kate lived on the other side of the continent, where Calum Johnston of Strange Adventures in Halifax played a similar supportive role.

While the competition from book retailers and, especially, Amazon has grown exponentially, it's heartening to note that almost all of the stores mentioned here still exist and even thrive, decades later.

—*Chris Oliveros*

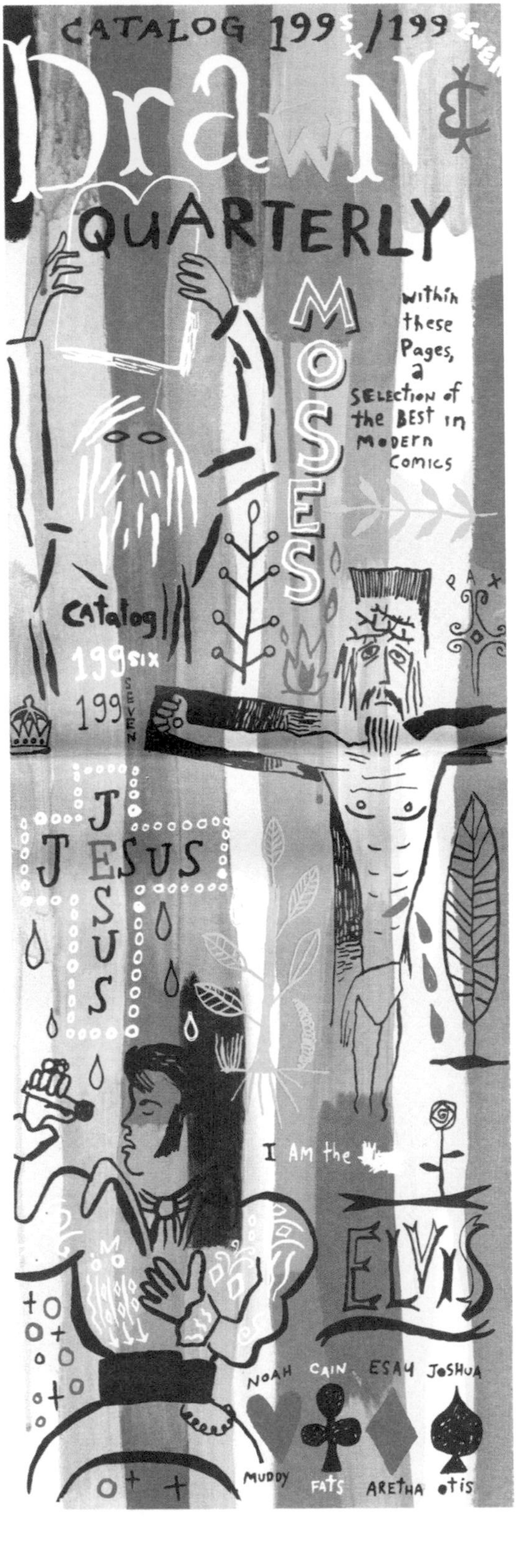

CATALOG 199six/199seven
Drawn &
QUARTERLY
MOSES
within these Pages, a SELECTION of the BEST in MODERN COMICS
Catalog
199six
199seven
JESUS
JESUS
I AM the
ELVIS
NOAH CAIN ESAU JOSHUA
MUDDY FATS ARETHA otis

Josh Gosfield's cover for 1996–1997 catalogue, elements of which were used as the basis of D+Q's first website design in 1996.

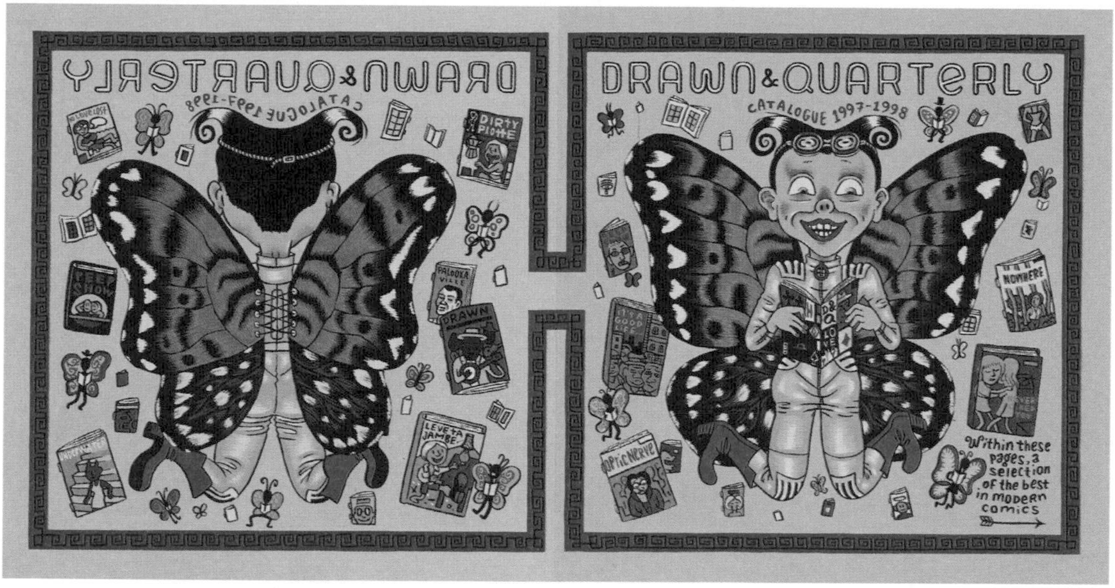
DRAWN & QUARTERLY
CATALOGUE 1997-1998
DIRTY PLOTTE
DRAWN
OPTIC NERVE
Within these pages, a selection of the best in modern comics

a new vitality in the 1980s thanks to Chester Brown's *Yummy Fur* (published by Toronto's Vortex Comics), as well as Fantagraphics titles like Daniel Clowes's *Eightball*, Peter Bagge's *Neat Stuff*, and the Hernandez brothers' two- or three-artist anthology, *Love and Rockets*. The single-artist comic book, filled with short stories and ongoing serials, was set to replace the multi-author anthology as the most important form within comics. Anticipating that change, Oliveros used a combination of geographical good fortune and a shrewd editorial eye to sign talent to do their own comics.

In March 1990, Oliveros met Julie Doucet, who broke into the field by publishing minicomics—xeroxed pamphlets, small in size, sold cheaply by the artist herself. Doucet produced startlingly surrealistic work that broke every known taboo about sex and bodily fluids, and she titled her minicomic and her eventual D+Q series *Dirty Plotte*—a further affront to parents and priests and any other prudes, since "plotte" is a particularly suggestive French-Canadian slang word for the female anatomy. As

The first time I came across D+Q was probably one of the early pamphlet-style anthologies, possibly in a discount bin, in 1991 or so. Having given up on superheroes a few years earlier, I had been exploring a variety of indie anthologies: *Weirdo*, *RAW*, *World War III*, etc. One of the things that set D+Q apart was Joe Matt's work, which I didn't want to like nearly as much as I did. But the stuff that sticks in my mind most from the early anthologies are the short, single-page colour pieces on the inside covers by people like David Mazzuchelli and Luc Giard. Luc Giard did a great, weird Tintin piece. I also remember a great little piece by Maurice Vellekoop depicting the lingering echoes of music in the mind of a listener as he leaves his house and goes out into the world. It was a perfect, unassuming little visual poem that perfectly captured something I could relate to in a way I'd never seen before. It's what D+Q later came to exemplify in my mind: a quiet, understated commitment to quality work.—***Anders Nilsen***

September 1997
Adrian Tomine's *Sleepwalk and Other Stories* is published.

January 1998
Black Eye Books ceases operation. D+Q buys leftover stock of *Jar of Fools*, *Berlin*, and *Hicksville* and becomes the primary publisher for future comics by Jason Lutes and Dylan Horrocks.

May 1998
Joe Sacco's *Soba: Stories from Bosnia* is published.

August 1998
D+Q's first exhibition in North America, at Meltdown Comics in Los Angeles. The exhibit features Chester Brown, David Collier, Julie Doucet, Joe Matt, Archer Prewitt, Joe Sacco, Adrian Tomine, and Seth, all of whom are in attendance for the opening.

November 1998
D+Q exhibition at the Helsinki Comics Festival in Finland. The exhibit features work by many D+Q cartoonists, with Chester Brown, Pentti Otsamo, Seth, and Adrian Tomine in attendance for the opening.

June 1999
Chester Brown's *Louis Riel* no. 1 is published.

September 1999
A D+Q "Year 2000" calendar is released and serves as a tenth anniversary of sorts for the

Julie Doucet's cover for D+Q's 1997–1998 catalogue.

her comic's title indicates, Doucet was a path-breaking artist in her frank inspection of female sexuality. Often inspired by dreams, her early strips were beguiling forays into an untrammeled imagination, rich with fantastic displays of menstrual flow, severed unmentionable body parts, and inanimate objects forced into service for pleasure. One of the most visually impressive cartoonists of the last century, whose drippy Rorschach-test pen line remains inimitable, Doucet has been incomparably daring in making public her fantasies and fears.

According to Doucet, she and Oliveros "met a few times, and at some point we talked about future projects and I told him my fantasy was to have my own comic book, something regular, not too expensive, maybe two dollars,

easily obtainable, things like that." Oliveros drew up a one-page handwritten contract with Doucet, and the first comic-book version of *Dirty Plotte* came out in October 1990.

A month before Doucet's series debuted, Oliveros fortuitously met Chester Brown and Seth at a convention in Toronto. Eager to advance from his work on the generic sci-fi/superhero title *Mr. X*, which he was now embarrassed by, Seth had been assembling the first issue of a solo comic titled *Palookaville* and was looking for a publisher. Oliveros snapped up the title: the first issue of *Palookaville*, featuring lovely melancholy art inflected with the style of the 1930s *New Yorker* cartoonists, premiered in April 1991. Intrigued by D+Q's dedication to the distinctive artistic visions of Doucet and Seth—and convinced by the offer of more sizable

company. The calendar features a cover by Julie Doucet, as well as new illustrations for each month from D+Q cartoonists.

October 1999
Julie Doucet's *My New York Diary* is published.

January 2000
D+Q website is completely redesigned and features extensive author pages for the first time.

April 2000
Drawn & Quarterly vol. 3, a large-format anthology, is released, marking the first time D+Q publishes work by Chris Ware, Frank King, R. Sikoryak, Miriam Katin, Ron Regé, Jr., and Michel Rabagliati. D+Q vol. 3 wins an Eisner for Best Anthology.

June 2000
The first volume of Jason Lutes's Berlin trilogy is published. *Berlin: City of Stones* will go on to have twenty-five thousand units in print with seven printings.

May 2001
For the first time in its nearly twelve-year existence, D+Q is no longer located in a small apartment. The company rents a two-room office space, sandwiched between a lingerie shop and a liquor store.

August 2001
James Sturm's *The Golem's Mighty Swing* is published.

(Left) Chris Ware, Chester Brown, Daniel Clowes, Seth & Adrian Tomine at Comic-Con (1998). Julie Doucet's cover for the D+Q year 2000 calendar.

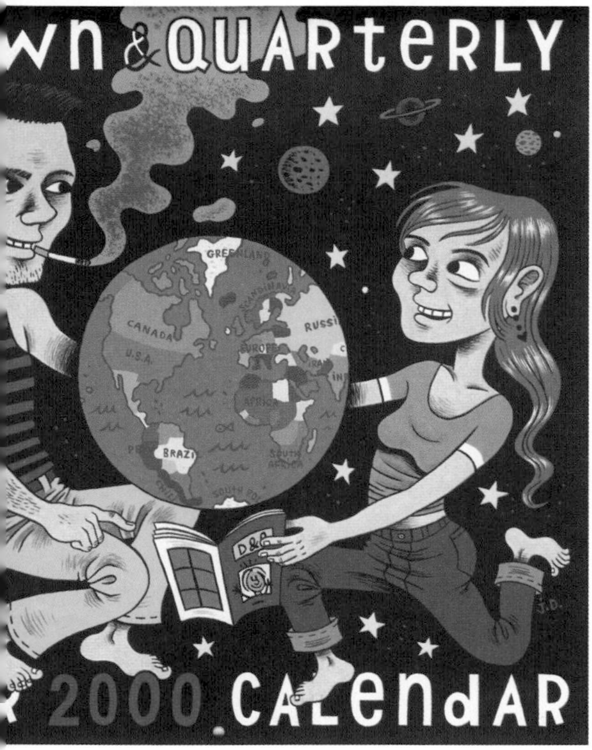
WN & QUARTERLY
GREENLAND
CANADA
U.S.A.
EUROPE
RUSSIA
AFRICA
BRAZIL
SOUTH AFRICA
D&Q
J.D.
2000 CALENDAR

royalties than his then publisher could muster—Chester Brown also jumped on the burgeoning D+Q roster by bringing *Yummy Fur* to the press with issue no. 25, published in the summer of 1991.

While other artists would become part of the list, in the early days the core D+Q artists were Doucet, Seth, Brown, and the shamelessly confessional cartoonist Joe Matt. By this point, Seth and Brown were friends with Matt, who was living in Toronto without a Canadian visa, and whose many-panelled diary strips were a regular feature in *Drawn & Quarterly* magazine (and a profound inspiration for Brown's own warts-and-all cartooning). The first issue of Matt's *Peepshow* hit the stands in June 1992, beginning a hilarious and cringe-packed account of his personal foibles as a bad

September 2001
D+Q publishes its first two hardcover art books: Seth's *Vernacular Drawings* and Julie Doucet's *Long Time Relationship*.

September 2002
D+Q signs on with Chronicle Books for distribution in the book market. On a visit to the Bay Area, Adrian Tomine introduces Chris Oliveros to the work of Yoshihiro Tatsumi, whose English-language editions D+Q would go on to publish under the editorial vision of Tomine himself.

January 2003
Chris spearheads an effort to lobby the Book Industry

I imagine that for a child growing up in Montreal's Mile End neighbourhood today, Drawn & Quarterly publications are as ubiquitous as sesame seeds on the back seat of a gluten-tolerant Mile End family's car. Back when I was running around Waverly Street in short pants in the early 1990s, there was no D+Q store, no Moomin book to read at bedtime, no Melvin Monster–themed game of hide-and-go-yikes; what it is wasn't yet, and finding out about Drawn & Quarterly took effort.

My first encounter with D+Q comics was achieved after considerable scheming and some heavy lifting. Alone at home after school one day, I pushed my father's desk over to his library, hauled myself up, and tilted an unmarked cardboard box off the top shelf. In the tradition of deeply unpopular children everywhere, I was looking for an escape from the childhood at which I seemed to be failing so miserably. From around the age of nine or ten, I had found my way out through the lower shelves of my father's library, through paperback reprints of *MAD* magazine, collections of *Pogo* comics, and compendiums of *Playboy* cartoons from the 1960s. Their outdated political and cultural references, musty vaudevillian humour, and leering sexist sexiness seemed to me to open the door to adulthood, which I pictured as a rowdy cocktail-party-cum-Passover-seder.

But the comics in the unmarked box were different. Joe Matt's self-abuse, Julie Doucet's psychotic dreams, Chester Brown's *Ed the Happy Clown*'s talking penis—these were a far cry from the sloshing martinis, buoyant boobs, and references to *Bonanza* I had come to expect from grown-up comics. The drawings were sort of ugly and the stories didn't always make sense. Were they even supposed to be funny? These comics opened another door into adulthood, which now looked more like an unfurnished room lit by a single bare light bulb. I was fascinated, titillated, terrified. I hid the comics under my mattress for a few weeks, then set them on fire in the alleyway behind our apartment. What else could I do? I had opened a door that couldn't be closed, and the only thing left to do was to cover my tracks.

A few years later and a few blocks away, on a stretch of Saint-Laurent that was still, at that time, more seedy than not, I crouched glowering in Doc Martens, fending off the affections of a Pomeranian named Conrad to dig through back-issue bins for copies of the burned comics. By then, I was on a first-name basis with Joe and Chet and Julie and Marlys and Enid and Maggie; comics were central to my identity as a nerd, a rebel, and a self-proclaimed weird girl. Across the street from the comic-book store was a pornographic movie theatre where, later still (but not a legally appropriate number of years later), I looked Drawn & Quarterly up in the phone book behind the cash register at the urgent prompting of my manager, a writer in his mid-thirties who wanted to see me do something other than ring up Mars bars and tickets to Peter North's *North Pole*. I was surprised to see the Parc Ave. address; I hadn't realized that the D+Q headquarters were just three blocks away from my dad's bookshelf. I called the number.

In those days, the D+Q office was located above an Orthodox Jewish import/export agency with irregular hours and a puzzling window display of fake flowers and plaster statuettes set against a dusty pink velvet background. Clutching my letter of intent, I followed a handwritten sign up a dark staircase, careful not to disturb the boxes of books perched on every step. I knocked on the first door I came to and was beckoned into the kind of small studio apartment generously referred to by Montrealers as a "three-and-a-half." Inside, a small, dark man stood smiling shyly at the centre of a labyrinth of shelves and desks piled high with books, galleys, and unpaid bills. There were comics in drawers, cupboards, and cabinets; comics on the kitchen counter; boxes of comics in the shower stall. There were framed Seth drawings on the wall. The room smelled of coffee and paper. I was in rapture, and would remain there for eight years.

Those eight years covered a period of extraordinary growth in the company's history, and as D+Q grew, so did I. Every work of art that I handled, every line that I wrote or edited, every book that I mailed out, every crumbling Dell comic that I scanned, every artist, boss, employee, and intern that I met there led me further along the road from weird girl to strange woman. College didn't teach me empathy, patience, perseverance, or good taste; I got that training on the job. If Drawn & Quarterly were any other publisher, my time there would have been subsumed into the narrative of my early twenties, slotted between stories about backpacking and broken hearts. But it isn't like that; I grew up with Drawn & Quarterly, and I grew with Drawn & Quarterly, and I grow a little more with every new D+Q book that I read. **—Rebecca Rosen**

boyfriend and chronic masturbator, later collected under the apt title *The Poor Bastard*.

These core artists overlapped in interesting ways. All were doing autobio comics in the early 1990s (while Doucet and Brown had started off as surrealists, they eventually moved to memoirs). They also, to varying degrees, drew one another. Seth created a cartoon afterword to Matt's first book, *Peepshow*, which denounced Matt for his cheapness, sloth, and general ignorance. Seth and Brown are also prominent characters in *Peepshow*, offering the hapless hero Joe Matt good advice that he doesn't listen to. Brown in turn served as a sounding board for Seth's monologues in his first graphic novel, *It's a Good Life, If You Don't Weaken* (1996). And finally, Seth and Matt show up in various Brown comics, most recently in *Paying for It*, where they are aghast at his patronage of prostitutes. Living in Montreal (and later New York, Seattle, and Berlin), Doucet was slightly removed from this game of autobiographical ring-around-the-rosie, but she did draw some excellent caricatures of her fellow artists in her book *Long Time Relationship* (2001), as well as a dream comic on the back of her first D+Q issue starring a killer-whale-riding Chester Brown. All of this gave the D+Q line a weird cohesiveness, as if it were the alternative comics counterpart to the Marvel universe.

D+Q's notoriety as a publisher of autobio comics is based on a few years in the early 1990s. Brown's third book, the quietly devastating *I Never Liked You* (1994)—only strenuous dissuasion by the publisher prevented him from using his original title, "Fuck"—was perhaps the masterpiece of this autobiographical moment. Few at the time, however, noticed that most of the artists who did memoirs were starting to move away from the genre. Seth's *It's a Good Life, If You Don't Weaken* is, in retrospect, a transitional work: on the surface, this tale of the search for an old *New Yorker* cartoonist wears the guise of autobiography, featuring both Seth and Brown as characters, but it is in essence a work of fiction. Debbie Drechsler's *Summer of Love*

Study Group to add "Comics & Graphic Novels" as a recognized category in bookstores.

Peggy Burns joins the campaign and brings DC Comics (her employer at the time) on board as a signatory to the industry letter. Oliveros and Burns also invite Art Spiegelman to the meeting in New York, where BISG ultimately agrees to adopt the new category, making the wide availability of comics in trade bookstores possible.

March 2003

A third incarnation of D+Q's website is launched with a new design.

is another borderline case: a melancholic account of a teenage girl's coming of age, the book has all the knowing details and searing quality of truth but is presented beneath a veneer of fiction, and it was conceived with the purposeful symmetries and cohesive structure of a novel—a self-sufficient graphic novel, before such efforts became *de rigueur*. While a few D+Q artists continue to do autobio—Miriam Katin and John Porcellino have authored recent highlights—many more have branched out into genres like history, reportage, and fiction.

D+Q's turn toward fiction, in particular, was accelerated by the emergence of an astonishingly young and talented newcomer. While still in high school in Sacramento, California, Adrian Tomine ignited intense excitement and scrutiny in the comics world thanks to his minicomic series, *Optic Nerve*, which featured minimalist gems of short stories far more accomplished than many cartoonists of more advanced years were capable of creating. Oliveros wrote to Tomine in November 1993 to encourage his cartooning career (the letter is reproduced, along with all seven issues of Tomine's minis, in an archival box set titled, simply, *32 Stories*). The following May, Tomine, still shy of his twentieth birthday, signed on as a D+Q artist with his full-fledged solo comic-book series, also called *Optic Nerve*. "Before [Oliveros] called, I hadn't even

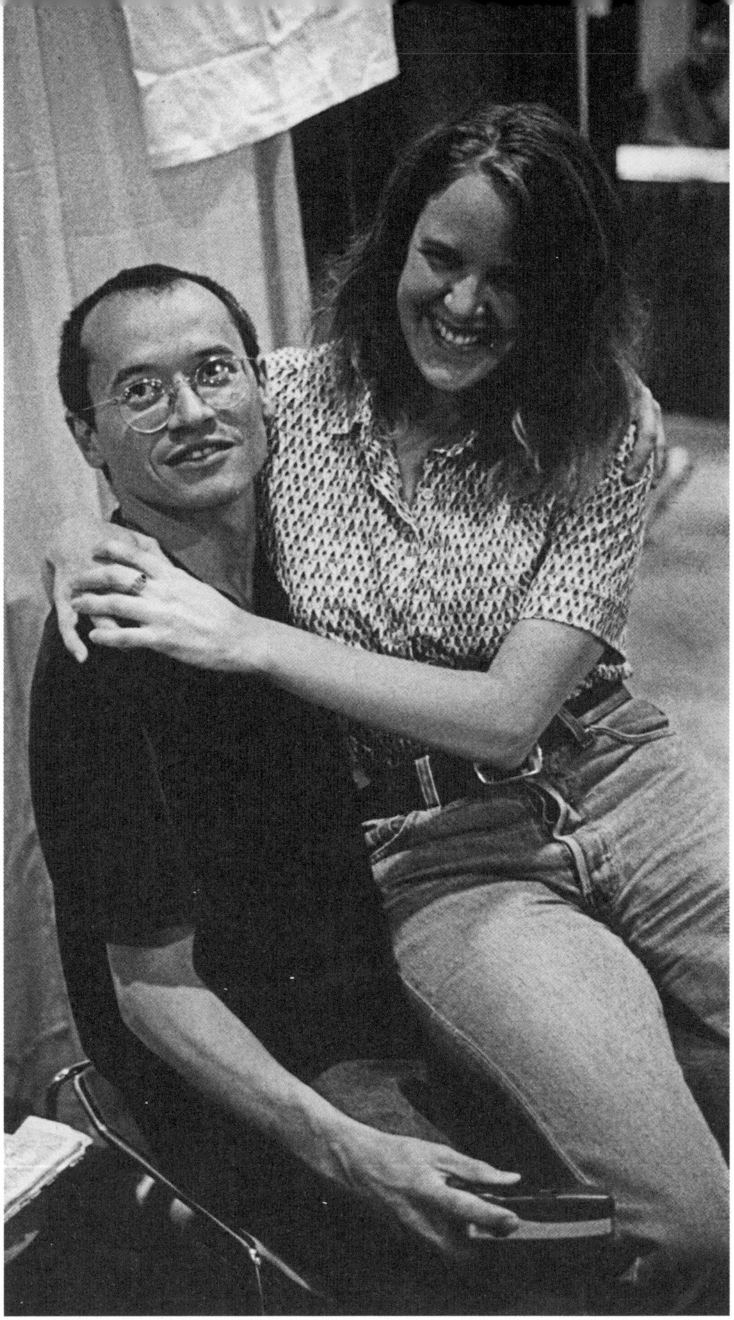

May 2003
Adrian Tomine's *Summer Blonde* is published.

July 2003
Rebecca Rosen, D+Q's first intern, is hired at seventeen. She is later hired as production manager and stays with the company until 2010.

September 2003
Peggy Burns is hired as publicist. She will later go on to be promoted to associate publisher. Chester Brown's *Louis Riel* is published; it's D+Q's first book to hit the *Globe and Mail* best-seller list and will win a Harvey Award. Chris Ware's *ACME Novelty Datebook* vol. 1 is published. Joe Sacco's *The Fixer* is published. Chris Ware, Jeet Heer, and Chris Oliveros travel to St. Louis, MO, to meet Drewanna King Schutte, granddaughter of Frank King, and research ephemera for the *Gasoline Alley* series, *Walt & Skeezix*.

November 2003
Final large-format *Drawn & Quarterly* anthology is released: this marks the first time D+Q publishes work by Rutu Modan and Yoshihiro Tatsumi.

February 2004
Optic Nerve no. 9 is published, and it will later be the first chapter of Adrian Tomine's *Shortcomings*.

(Above) Joe Sacco & Julie Doucet at Comic-Con (1998). (Next page) The *Drawn & Quarterly Manifesto* for booksellers (2003).

considered Drawn & Quarterly an option," Tomine told an interviewer in 1998. "I didn't think I was at that level." Thanks to his work in *Optic Nerve*, collected in D+Q perennials like *Sleepwalk* and *Summer Blonde*, Tomine's resonant, probing stories, graced with precise and lovely art, quickly entered the art comics pantheon, while the artist himself became the final member of D+Q's signature lineup of nineties cartoonists.

Aside from publishing fine cartoonists like Tomine in solo titles, Oliveros returned to anthologies when he relaunched *Drawn & Quarterly* magazine in 1994. While the earlier version of *Drawn & Quarterly* was largely North American (with one or two exceptions), the new series gave ample space to the best European artists, including Jacques Tardi, Pentti Otsamo, and the team of Philippe Dupuy and Charles Berbérian. (As it happens, Berbérian had translated Joe Matt's *The Poor Bastard* into French—further evidence of D+Q's international reach.) The first stirrings of D+Q's global understanding of comics occurred here: contributions by these artists served to anchor each issue of the anthology, rather than appearing as exotic curios imported from unknown and foreign traditions. D+Q's ever-increasing spate of translated work by Québécois, Flemish, Ivorian, Finnish, Israeli, French, German, Spanish, and seminal Japanese authors testifies to the international vitality of comics and helps point toward the extraordinary realms that English-language readers have yet to explore.

In another contrast to its rudimentary predecessor, the new incarnation of *Drawn & Quarterly* was exquisitely designed: the entire magazine in full colour, the cover and endpapers designed by the same artist, the table of contents and indicia often hand-lettered. In the stylish pages of this updated version of *Drawn & Quarterly* magazine, the D+Q sensibility took a new turn, revelling in shapely line work and foregrounding design and the niceties of printing, while placing greater emphasis on the use of controlled colour palettes to convey tone and emotion.

This new aesthetic was influenced in part by a friendly rival, Black Eye, a comics publisher run by Michel Vrana, which in the 1990s operated just over a block away from D+Q in the Plateau neighbourhood of Montreal. As Oliveros notes, "Perhaps Vrana's greatest contribution was as a designer: with the publication of Black Eye's first impeccably designed paperbacks in 1993 and 1994, Michel played an important role in raising the bar in regards to how graphic novels were presented." When Black Eye ceased publication

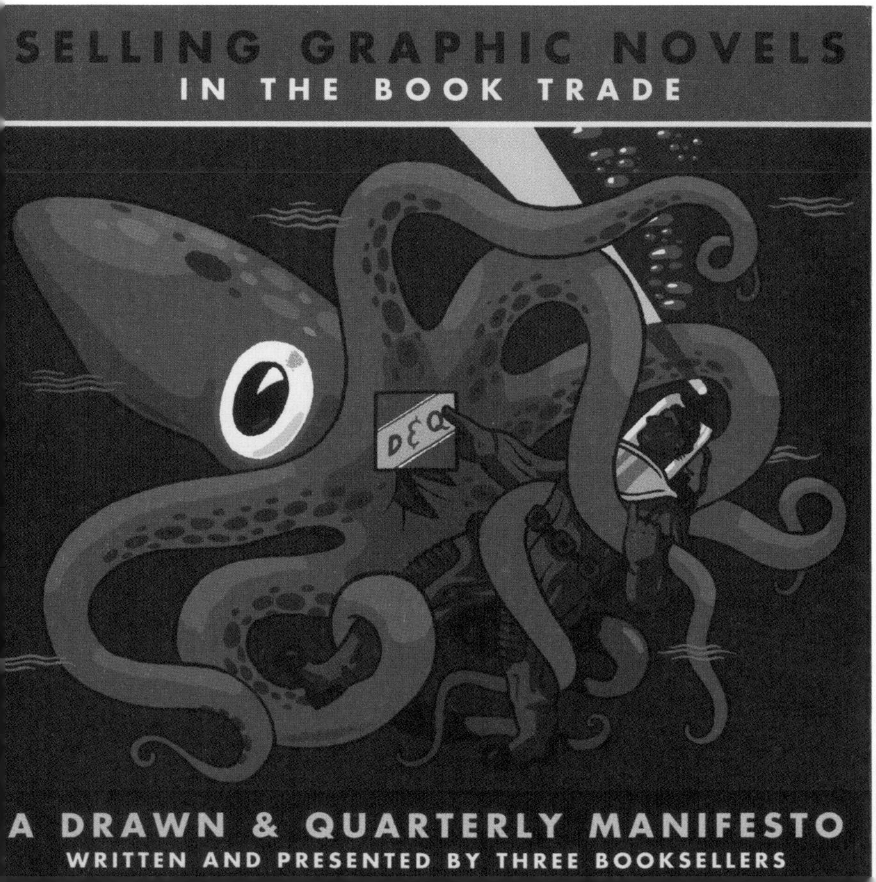

SELLING GRAPHIC NOVELS
IN THE BOOK TRADE
D&Q
A DRAWN & QUARTERLY MANIFESTO
WRITTEN AND PRESENTED BY THREE BOOKSELLERS

"Graphic novels? We sell graphic novels. Those Dilbert and Garfield books sell well. The kids come in for that Japanese stuff, manga. And the guys for the superhero and sorcery rubbish..."

What you have just read is a typical response from a bookseller when it is suggested to them that their graphic novel section may be suffering from neglect, or that it may be missing and not exist at all! Take a look at your section, if you have one. Do you privately consider it an eyesore? No wonder you hide it between humor and sci-fi. Like many booksellers, you think graphic novels are for kids and guys in STAR TREK t-shirts.

You know it doesn't pay to ignore even a fraction of your floor. By cultivating your graphic novel section you can begin attracting new and loyal customers. But it is tough if you've never really taken a good look at your graphic novel section before. Tougher still if you don't even have one. Your sales rep has learned the ropes and can help you out. We've put together this colorful little pamphlet featuring the testimonials of three booksellers from different retailers, and different cities. They have

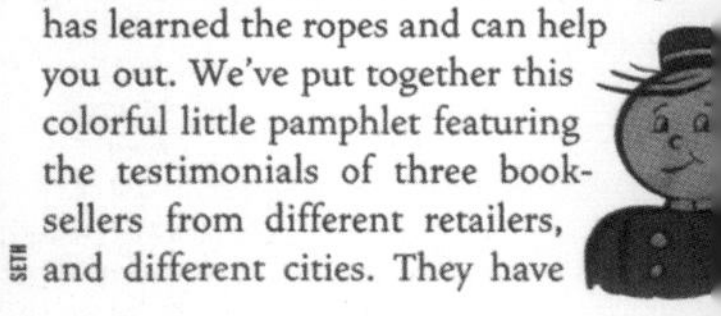

SETH

—1

in 1998, two of the publisher's major artists, Jason Lutes and Dylan Horrocks, migrated to D+Q with their ambitious books *Berlin* and *Hicksville*.

Black Eye's disappearance from the publishing scene is evidence of how challenging it was to print and promote worthwhile comics in the 1990s. By 1994, D+Q was already a pillar of art comics, but its financial position remained precarious. The comic-book industry, rooted in hobbyist stores geared to hardcore collectors, had a punishing boom-and-bust economy. Throughout the 1980s and 1990s, countless independent comic-book companies lived like mayflies, briefly flourishing and then dying.

D+Q managed to survive in this environment thanks to Oliveros's modesty and steadiness of purpose. He resisted the temptation to expand too quickly, never published comics he didn't believe in, and remained loyal to his core artists. Given the economic realities of the comic-book market in the 1990s, Oliveros wisely kept D+Q a micropublishing firm, operating out of his home with very little overhead. Still, finding firmer economic footing—and a wider audience for comics, beyond the direct market's pocket universe—seemed at once eminently desirable, and entirely out of reach.

Chris Oliveros founded Drawn & Quarterly the same year I moved to Montreal's Mile End neighbourhood. Buildings were empty and rents were cheap—a mix of Greek, French, English, Italian, and so much more. It seemed like half the storefronts on Parc Avenue were *à louer* the year I started my publishing house, Conundrum Press. I started off as a prose publisher (I was coming from the spoken word community), added art books, and recently went all-in on comics.

In 2002, I interviewed Chris for an article I wrote for *Maisonneuve* magazine. I found him above the travel agent in a dark two-room former dentist's office crammed with bookshelves—industrial bookshelves, which impressed me somehow. Thankfully, by then, I had some idea of what a publisher does. So mostly we talked shop. The proofs of *Drawn and Quarterly* volume 3 were on the table. Naturally I gravitated toward them, and when we were done I asked about them.

"They're okay," he said. "But I am unhappy about one thing and I am considering a reprint."

xperiences, taking dead
making it an eye catch-
int on their floor.
nber graphic novels are
t from other books. You
itles the exact same way.

MAT, NOT A GENRE.

of comics are different
the past. Diamond
tors has estimated that
then 70% of comics.
ined taste looking for
ovels have to go to the
here garish adolescent
s are the big sellers.
they shop? Your store.
by Zadie Smith, Dave
ael Moore, Chuck
ah Vowell, Michael
oody, Neil Gaiman, and
ey like cult books and
They spend money on
McSweeney's, The
squire, and Vanity Fair.
are loyal to authors and
y are loyal to affordable
ucts with a recogniz-
ng edge design style.
re loyal to stores they
the latest and greatest
classic graphic novels.

BREAKTHROUGH GRAPHIC NOVELS

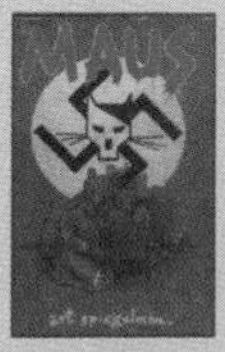

MAUS

MAUS (Pantheon, 1991), by Art Spiegelman. A Pulitzer Prize-winner and over a million copies sold. The story of a family destroyed by the Holocaust.

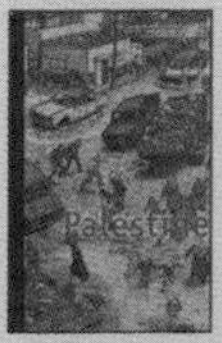

Palestine

PALESTINE (Fantagraphics, 2001), by Joe Sacco. American Book Award winner. Introduction by Edward Said. Gritty and compassionate journalism depicting life in the occupied territories.

GHOST WORLD (Fantagraphics, 1997), by Daniel Clowes. Over 100,000 copies sold. Two teenage girls graduate and begin looking for something real to care about. An Oscar-nominated film adaptation in 2001.

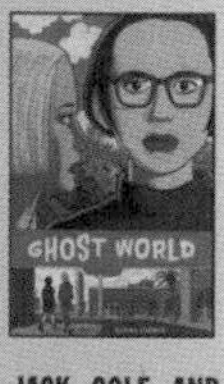

GHOST WORLD

JACK COLE AND PLASTIC MAN (Chronicle, 2001), by Chipp Kidd & Art Spiegelman. A visually stunning tribute to a forgotten hero.

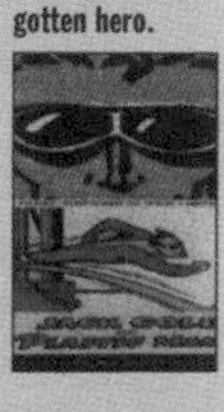

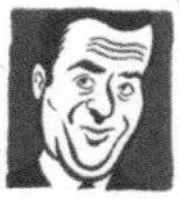

SETH

CARSON HALL
VIRGIN MEGASTORES

"Graphic novels," or comics, have had a difficult time in book stores. There's that misleading moniker—the term is used broadly to describe any comics published in book form, many of which are not, in fact, novels at all. Then, many people associate the comics medium exclusively with super-hero or fantasy material.

This is changing, however. As the book buyer for the Virgin Megastores between 1994 and 2002, I saw graphic novels grow to more than ten percent of the chain's annual book sales. It seems that comics are finally having their day, and it's interesting to note that the titles driving this current publishing boom are not heroic fantasy at all but more personal, literary work. As a sort of illustrated literature, graphic novels have, in my experience, a strong and loyal following among the same customers who buy art and design titles as well as among readers of contemporary fiction. The Princeton Architectural Press customer, as well as the McSweeney's crowd, is definitely hip to graphic novels. (Tip for booksellers: whatever you do, don't file these books with role-playing games or science fiction).

Readers will always return for more once you stock these and (of course) a selection of Drawn & Quarterly titles

Pantheon is having enormous success with their highly-acclaimed series of graphic novels; Doubleday has launched Doubleday Graphic Novels, a new imprint, this fall. W.W. Norton now distributes Fantagraphics Books, one of the two preeminent publishers of great comics, and sales are reportedly stronger than anyone had hoped.

Drawn & Quarterly is the other publisher whose list includes the great talents of the art form, as well as the publisher with the most lavish production values in the comics industry. Under a new distribution partnership with Chronicle Books, D&Q titles are now finally in a position to achieve the wider distribution they deserve.

"Really?" I asked. I pored over the proofs. They were, of course, gorgeous. Full-colour Frank King Sundays, R. Sikoryak, Pentti Otsamo, Michel Rabagliati, Blutch, truly an international and generational effort. I could see nothing wrong. "I give up," I said.

"I'll give you a hint. It's on every page."

"Are the page numbers the wrong font?"

"No, they printed it on the wrong stock of paper."

It really looked fantastic. It was like nothing I had seen before. This book embodied the Montreal conjunction of European and North American. But not just that, it was classy. Mile End at that time was not considered classy. I could not believe he was considering pulping thousands of copies of this book. That was badass. I understood something, then, of his uncompromising high standards.

They say publishing is a vocation, a gentleman's art, and Chris is a stellar example and inspiration. Chris Oliveros is an architect of the graphic novel as a literary artifact. If there is any justice in the world, history will acknowledge him as the pioneer that he is.

—Andy Brown, publisher, Conundrum Press

The bookstore market offered one possible alternative to comic-book stores, but it was difficult to crack. The "graphic novel" (as any book-length comic would come to be known) was still an inchoate form, and bookstores didn't know how to handle such titles, in the rare event that they even stocked them. Confusingly, the few stores that did order graphic novels lumped them all in together, so superhero titles were mixed with books from Fantagraphics and D+Q. Worse, according to comics lore, Art Spiegelman's *Maus* was sometimes placed in the "humour" section of bookstores, so that the harrowing account of surviving the Shoah shared company with *Garfield* and *The Far Side*.

There were a few exceptions to this bleak situation. D+Q did well in a handful of independent bookstores and at chains like Virgin Megastores and Tower Books, as well as online at Amazon, which was not yet the behemoth of today. D+Q also courted a traditional book-buying audience with the design and trim size of each new release. When reprinting material from comics, D+Q was careful to package it in the form of books that actually looked like books, and not just thick comics. D+Q titles, especially Seth's *It's a Good Life*, were models of attention to design, with care being taken when it came to the art that appeared on the

"The breakthrough is happening now. Graphic Nove

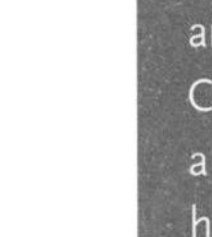
SETH

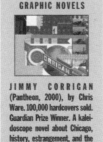

PAUL CONSTANT
ELLIOTT BAY BOOK CO, SEATTLE

When I started at Elliott Bay two years ago, there was no comic book section at all. It was technically the Science Fiction-Art subsection, next to the Boris Vallejo dreck and things like that. Julius Knipl books were shelved in fiction, but were as overlooked as the books in science fiction art. I expressed interest in expanding the section and placing it next to fiction. Much to my surprise, the store owner and the store manager were both very supportive and let me order all the books that I wanted (within reason) and create a new category. We're a bit technical here, so calling the new section "Graphic Novels" didn't really seem like a good idea, what with MAUS, PALESTINE, UNDERSTANDING COMICS, and all the rest of the good non-fiction out there. Non-fiction, quite simply, is not a "novel," and we pride ourselves on being a literary bookstore. Holly Myers, our head buyer, came up with the term "graphica," which we agreed upon as the best option. "Graphica," of course, has its limitations (sounds too much like erotica, is an unidentifiable new word, etc.,) but it was the best of the options. The first thing that I did, essentially, was take out most of the superhero books. I still drag them out for special occasions but the focus is definitely on superhero-less fare. As the fiction head, and bearing in mind the failure of Ben Katchor's work to catch on in fiction, I can tell you that the idea of mixing graphica with the appropriate categories is a dead end. They will not sell from fiction, unless they're faced out and tagged with a staff recommend card, and to suggest that kind of special treatment is ridiculous. What is needed is a subsection, NEXT to fiction, featuring the attractive, sophisticated titles (some Crumb because everyone has heard of him, Chris Ware, Tomine, Clowes, Doucet, Seth, etc) on display. Browsers head into a section with prefabricated ideas and a misplaced romance or graphica book will just put them off. But if you have a subsection prominently placed next to fiction, good literary fiction, it begs people to look at the section. MAUS never did as well in biography as it has in our Non-fiction Graphica section, and PALESTINE was nearly pulled from our Middle Eastern section for lack of sales.

BREAKTHROUGH GRAPHIC NOVELS

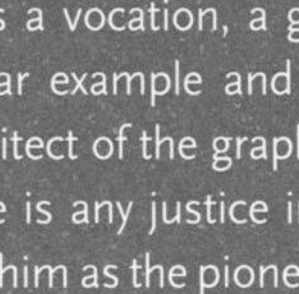
CORRIGAN

JIMMY CORRIGAN (Pantheon, 2000), by Chris Ware. 100,000 hardcovers sold. Guardian Prize Winner. A kaleidoscope novel about Chicago, history, estrangement, and the nature of family. Breathtaking.

What graphica publishers need to dc independent booksellers excited abou books. Handselling is key to starting u tion. I'm of the opinion that every mid-to-large sized independent bookstore has at least one rabid comics fan in their midst. (They're usually the ones in the horn-rimmed glasses, but I digress.) I am definitely of the opinion that graphica can become an important part of any bookseller's inventory. We sold nearly a hundred copies of JIMMY CORRIGAN the Christmas that it came out. MAUS, on display properly, is a perennial seller at a healthy five or six copies a month, in its various hard-cover, soft-cover, boxed, cc formats. That trumps many of our own Bay bestsellers such as Cormac McCa Kurt Vonnegut. It's necessary to keep t four copies of McCloud's UNDERSTA COMICS in stock at all times because intense word of mouth that surroun book like a magnetic force.

And not just booksellers are begin notice, authors are beginning to spea well. At our own bookstore, both Dave endpapers and half-titles, the paper stock chosen, and all the other sundry niceties of book-making.

Despite these slight hints at better things to come, Oliveros wasn't expecting a quick solution to industry troubles, so he was prepared to struggle over the long haul. The publisher's pessimistic temperament served him well, giving him the fortitude to keep working the grindstone in a situation that an optimist would find discouraging. As he told an interviewer in 1996, "I see myself as plugging away at this for years and years, and maybe after ten years I can look back and see we've come this far and managed this much, and maybe after I die things will be a little bit better."

Luckily, Oliveros didn't have to wait that long. At the turn of the twenty-first century, things were about to improve for comics. Pantheon's publication of Chris Ware's *Jimmy Corrigan* in late 2000 marked the beginning of a transformation in the public perception and mainstream marketability of comics—changes that would prove both a blessing and a curse. The sea change initiated by *Jimmy Corrigan* precipitated later waves like *Ghost World*'s success in movie theatres in 2001, as well as the phenomenon of Marjane Satrapi's *Persepolis*, translated in 2003 (and also from Pantheon). While each successive work helped to enhance the stature of the graphic novel in both bookstores and the larger literary culture, the fact that major mainstream houses like Pantheon (a division of Knopf) were becoming interested in comics—one of the only growth markets in all of the struggling book industry—meant that big money now had the potential to poach talent away from smaller publishers like D+Q. Oliveros became petrified that D+Q's authors would find greener pastures. How could a tiny publishing house like D+Q compete against the titans of the publishing world?

The question would prove tough, and the answer long in coming, but one part of the solution might be indicated by D+Q's relationship with Chris Ware himself. While 2000 was the year of *Jimmy Corrigan*'s success, it also marked the beginning of Ware's long association with D+Q. In that year, he designed the cover for another relaunch of the *Drawn & Quarterly* anthology, now a handsome, full-colour bound book. Ware's detailed and intimate sketchbooks would soon become one of D+Q's first big bookstore hits, and he went on to publish his era-defining ACME Novelty Library comics with Drawn & Quarterly, too. Finally, the cartoonist continues to edit and design the *Walt & Skeezix* series, where he lavishes his exacting and loving attention on reprints of Frank

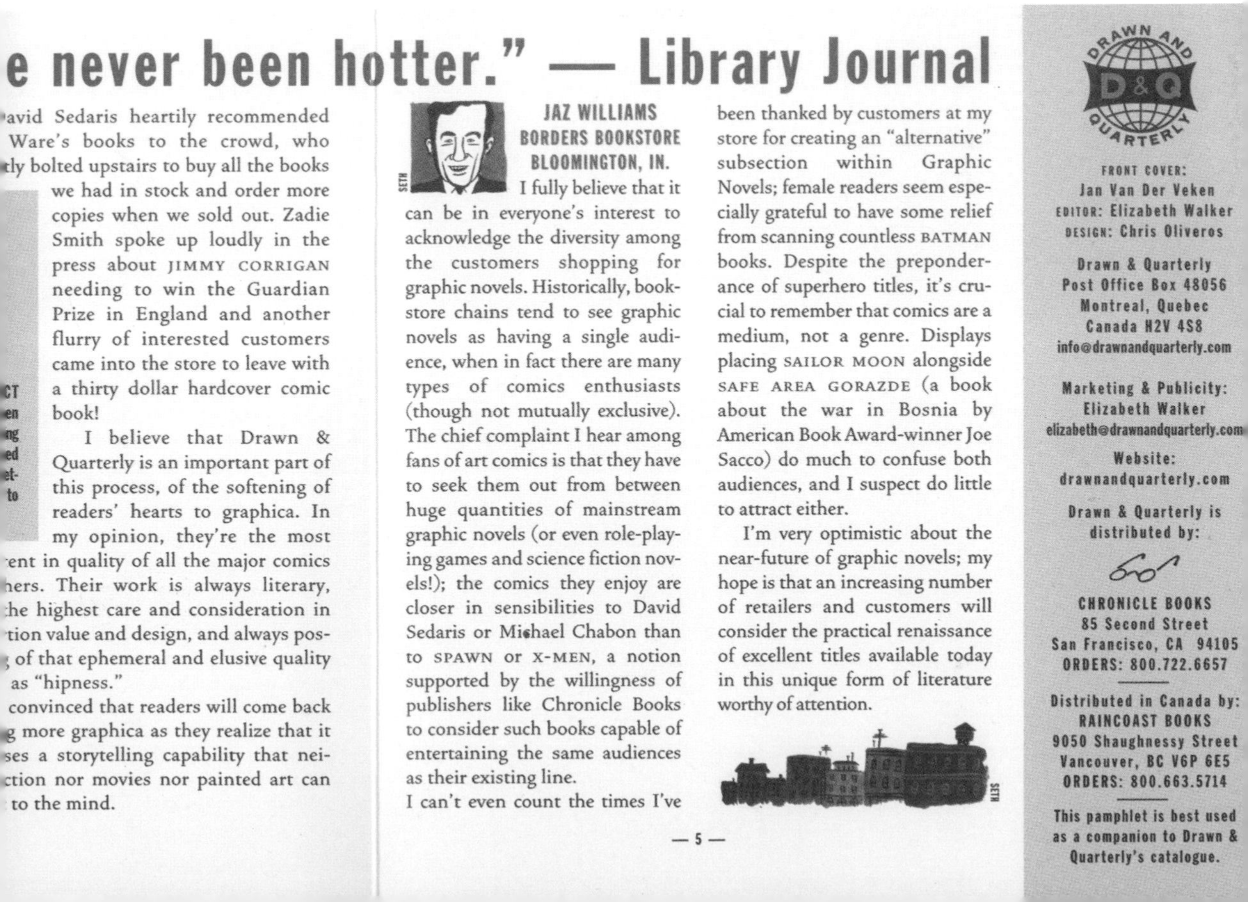

e never been hotter." — Library Journal
avid Sedaris heartily recommended Ware's books to the crowd, who tly bolted upstairs to buy all the books we had in stock and order more copies when we sold out. Zadie Smith spoke up loudly in the press about JIMMY CORRIGAN needing to win the Guardian Prize in England and another flurry of interested customers came into the store to leave with a thirty dollar hardcover comic book!
I believe that Drawn & Quarterly is an important part of this process, of the softening of readers' hearts to graphica. In my opinion, they're the most ent in quality of all the major comics hers. Their work is always literary, he highest care and consideration in tion value and design, and always pos- of that ephemeral and elusive quality as "hipness."
convinced that readers will come back g more graphica as they realize that it ses a storytelling capability that nei- ction nor movies nor painted art can to the mind.
SETH
JAZ WILLIAMS
BORDERS BOOKSTORE
BLOOMINGTON, IN.
I fully believe that it can be in everyone's interest to acknowledge the diversity among the customers shopping for graphic novels. Historically, bookstore chains tend to see graphic novels as having a single audience, when in fact there are many types of comics enthusiasts (though not mutually exclusive). The chief complaint I hear among fans of art comics is that they have to seek them out from between huge quantities of mainstream graphic novels (or even role-playing games and science fiction novels!); the comics they enjoy are closer in sensibilities to David Sedaris or Michael Chabon than to SPAWN or X-MEN, a notion supported by the willingness of publishers like Chronicle Books to consider such books capable of entertaining the same audiences as their existing line.
I can't even count the times I've been thanked by customers at my store for creating an "alternative" subsection within Graphic Novels; female readers seem especially grateful to have some relief from scanning countless BATMAN books. Despite the preponderance of superhero titles, it's crucial to remember that comics are a medium, not a genre. Displays placing SAILOR MOON alongside SAFE AREA GORAZDE (a book about the war in Bosnia by American Book Award-winner Joe Sacco) do much to confuse both audiences, and I suspect do little to attract either.
I'm very optimistic about the near-future of graphic novels; my hope is that an increasing number of retailers and customers will consider the practical renaissance of excellent titles available today in this unique form of literature worthy of attention.
SETH
— 5 —
DRAWN AND QUARTERLY
D&Q
FRONT COVER:
Jan Van Der Veken
EDITOR: Elizabeth Walker
DESIGN: Chris Oliveros
Drawn & Quarterly
Post Office Box 48056
Montreal, Quebec
Canada H2V 4S8
info@drawnandquarterly.com
Marketing & Publicity:
Elizabeth Walker
elizabeth@drawnandquarterly.com
Website:
drawnandquarterly.com
Drawn & Quarterly is distributed by:
CHRONICLE BOOKS
85 Second Street
San Francisco, CA 94105
ORDERS: 800.722.6657
Distributed in Canada by:
RAINCOAST BOOKS
9050 Shaughnessy Street
Vancouver, BC V6P 6E5
ORDERS: 800.663.5714
This pamphlet is best used as a companion to Drawn & Quarterly's catalogue.

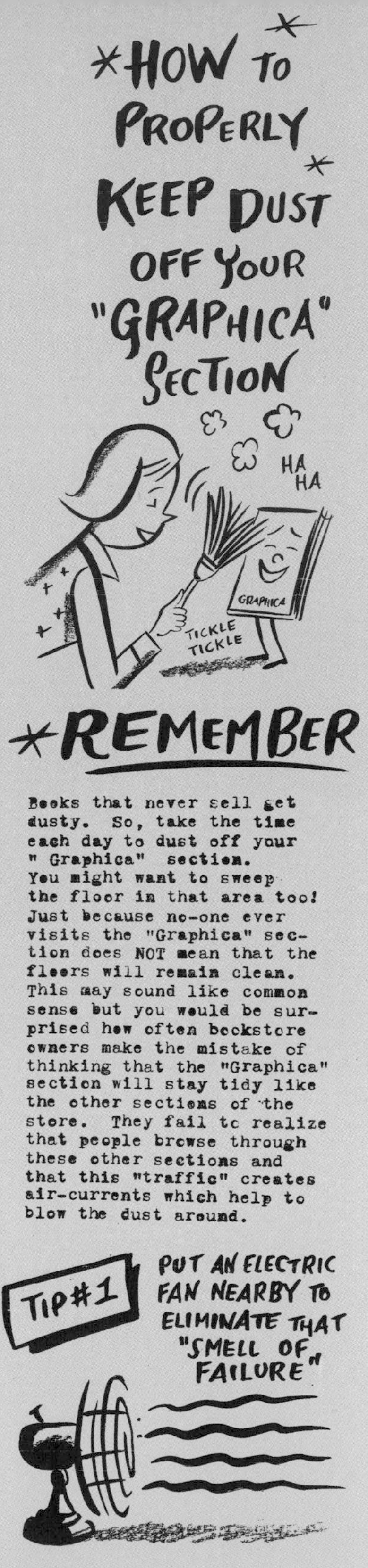
*HOW TO PROPERLY KEEP DUST OFF YOUR "GRAPHICA" SECTION
HA HA
GRAPHICA
TICKLE TICKLE
*REMEMBER
Books that never sell get dusty. So, take the time each day to dust off your " Graphica" section. You might want to sweep the floor in that area too! Just because no-one ever visits the "Graphica" section does NOT mean that the floors will remain clean. This may sound like common sense but you would be surprised how often bookstore owners make the mistake of thinking that the "Graphica" section will stay tidy like the other sections of the store. They fail to realize that people browse through these other sections and that this "traffic" creates air-currents which help to blow the dust around.
TIP#1
PUT AN ELECTRIC FAN NEARBY TO ELIMINATE THAT "SMELL OF FAILURE"

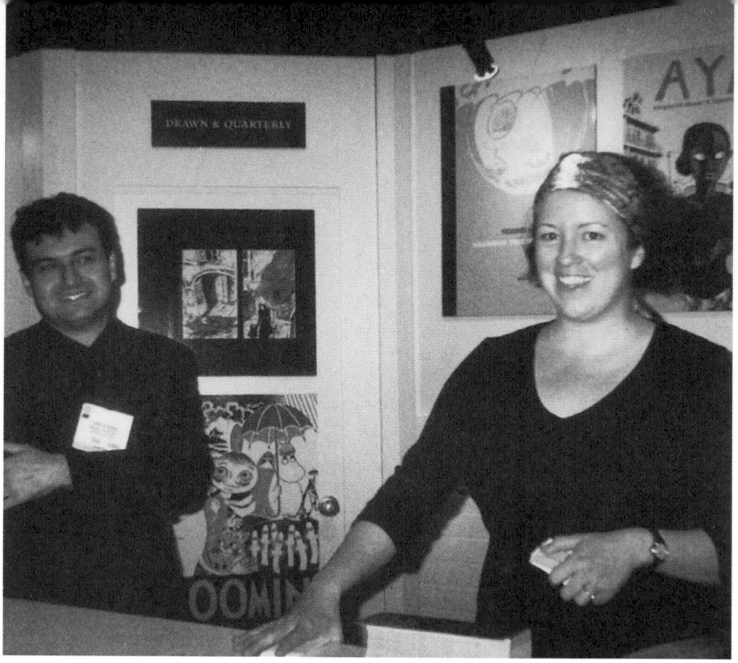
DRAWN & QUARTERLY

I think I first met Peggy Burns at a convention somewhere. Later, we were both living in New York. This was before she joined D+Q and became its promotions queen. In New York she was doing something or other for DC or Marvel, who can remember which? Anyway, I went out to her place for dinner one night. At some point we were in a cab on our way to Times Square. Or was that another time? Anyway, it was very late, and I believe we were both considerably far along the path to inebriation. We were having a good time. Look! There's a peep show! In those days, Times Square still meant something. We each put down five dollars or whatever it was. And then we squeezed into a booth. This was completely against the rules, we were told later when we were kicked out. But before we got the boot, a woman was dancing for us, twirling around. I think we passed dollars through a little slot. We were giggling like schoolchildren. And we were quite cramped in there, but I assure you, nothing happened. Except one of us farted. Does it matter who? But it seemed to add an exclamation point to our fun. There's nothing more to tell. Peggy comes from a fine family, and so do I. We were kicked out and that's that. I put Peggy in a cab or she put me in a cab, and we each went our respective ways. When we meet now, we shake hands. Ask Peggy!—***Joe Sacco***

March 2004
D+Q publishes *Way to Go* by ninety-three-year-old cartoonist Harry Mayerovitch with a launch at Blue Metropolis International Literary Festival. Mayerovitch passes away two weeks later on his ninety-fourth birthday.

June 2004
D+Q and Chronicle Books agree to terminate their distribution agreement, which leaves the publishing schedule for the second half of the year in limbo. D+Q is profiled in *Time* magazine, which calls the company "the most elegant comics publisher in North America." D+Q publishes Adrian Tomine's first art book, *Scrapbook*, for which he tours North America.

July 2004
The *New York Times Magazine* does a comics issue, featuring Daniel Clowes, Art Spiegelman,

(Left) Seth's *D+Q Manifesto* (2003). (Top) Chris Oliveros & Peggy Burns at Book Expo America (2006).

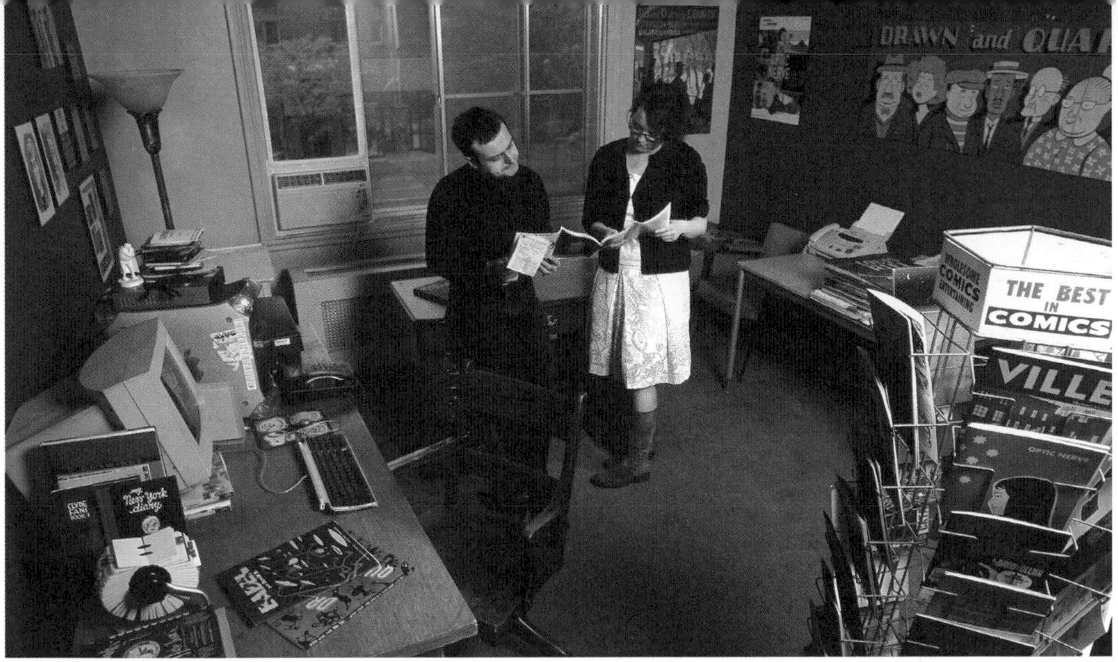
DRAWN and QUA
THE BEST IN COMICS

King's *Gasoline Alley* comics—a strip whose calm, quiet sense of time's passing Ware paid homage to in that initial anthology cover. Thanks to D+Q's longstanding dedication to its authors' visions, its concentration each season on a small but well-defined batch of titles, and its willingness to execute boundary-pushing designs, cartoonists like Ware and many others could find themselves at home, and among kindred spirits, with the company. Another part of the solution lay in the heartening orders for books like James Sturm's 2001 bit of fantastic Americana, *The Golem's Mighty Swing*—an all-original graphic novel that forewent serialization and appeared just a few months after *Jimmy Corrigan* settled in to its bestselling run. It had never been more apparent that an audience was actually developing for this kind of work.

Throughout those early years of the millennium, while bookstores were becoming much more receptive to graphic novels, Oliveros worked with other publishers in an attempt to encourage this new audience to perceive the distinctions between different types of graphic novels. The *Drawn & Quarterly Manifesto*—a somewhat controversial but influential pamphlet released in 2003—helped those outside the comics ghetto understand the field and differentiate the *Dilberts* from the D+Q books.

As these new markets were opening up for comics, Oliveros was also looking for a professional publicist who could make sure D+Q books got attention from book buyers. He had worked with Peggy Burns, a publicist for DC Comics, to help introduce the use of a "graphic novel" category throughout the book industry, so he sent Burns a note asking if she knew anyone who would want the job. As it turned out, she did.

The arrival of Burns as publicist in September of 2003 was fundamental to the transformation of D+Q from a niche press to a full-fledged book publisher. Although not D+Q's first hire, Burns played a pivotal role in making the publishing house into a professional operation with many employees, all while remaining true to Oliveros's vision.

Seth, Adrian Tomine, Joe Sacco, Julie Doucet, Lynda Barry, and more. Chester Brown does the cover (see page 34).

December 2004

The Petits Livres imprint debuts with Marc Bell's *The Stacks* and Julie Doucet's *Lady Pep*. It will go on to feature such authors as Julie Morstad, Charles Burns, Jillian Tamaki, and Royal Art Lodge members Michael Dumontier and Neil Farber. Seth travels to Montreal to visit D+Q. While at dinner, he hands Chris his sketchbook, which contains a brand-new completed graphic novel, *Wimbledon Green*. It will win a Doug Wright Award.

January 2005

D+Q begins a new distribution agreement with esteemed American publisher Farrar, Straus and Giroux.

February 2005

Tom Devlin proposes a collection of Tove Jansson's *Moomin* comic strips to Chris Oliveros, who tells him to go for it.

March 2005

Tom Devlin is hired as D+Q's first production manager. He will later be promoted to creative director.

May 2005

D+Q outgrows its two-room office and moves to an old industrial building at the edge of

Chris Oliveros & Peggy Burns during Peggy's first year on the job. Photo: Marie-Louise Deruaz (2004).

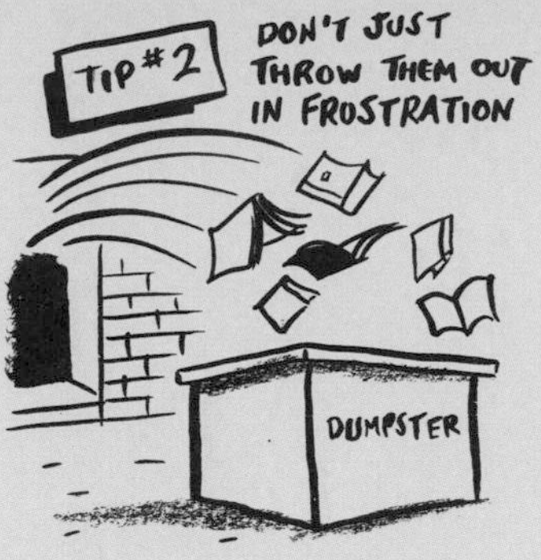
TIP #2
DON'T JUST THROW THEM OUT IN FROSTRATION
DUMPSTER

You might try situating the "Graphica" section near a popular section (such as pornography) in the hopes that the heavy activity of shoppers there will help toblow some of the dust off "Graphica" as well. It might help-- but it is not the full solution.

No. Folks, you will simply have to get in there and dust. Take the books right off the shelf and clean out in between them. Again--just because no-one has ever removed them from the shelf before doesn't mean that there is no dirt gathering there.

Here's a hint from Janice Goldfarb of "Nite-owl books" of Winnipeg:

"Keep an eye out for cob-webs--they form easily in unwatched, deserted areas of a room."

Tim Franklin of "Narwhal Books" of Dominion also warns:

"Watch out for silver-fish--they easily get into abandoned spaces."

If you can keep these books in good shape they may eventually become valuable antiques. (It could happen). At least you don't have to worry about damage from people handling them.

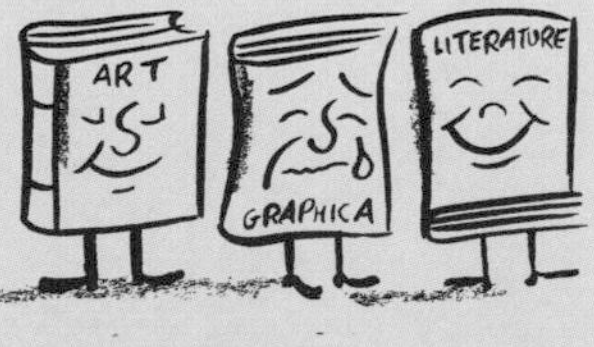
ART
GRAPHICA
LITERATURE

Finally, always remember:

The anguish you feel over mistakenly purchasing these books is in no way equal to that of the publisher who published them or the artists who foolishly produced them.

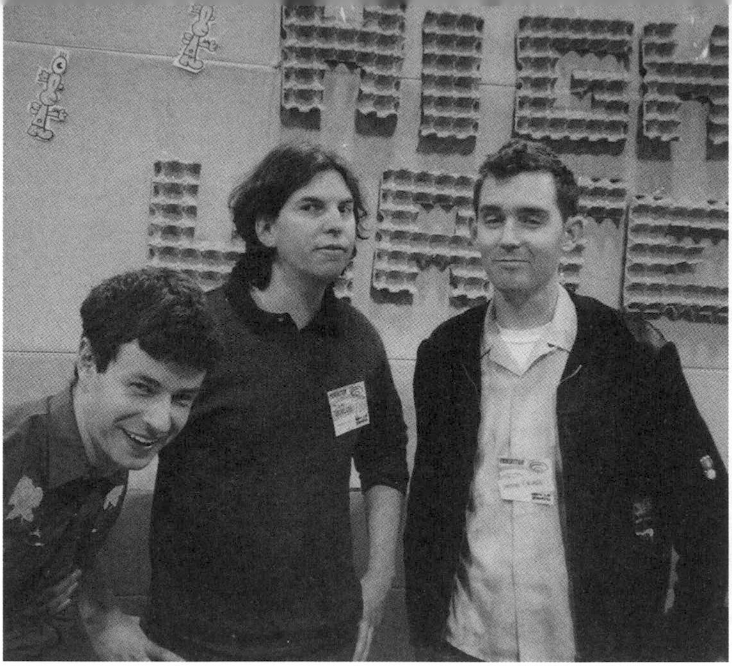

Highwater booth at Wonder Con: Ron Rége, Jr., Tom Devlin & Jordan Crane. Photo: Martin Wong (1999).

Burns was steeped in fashion and publishing culture in a way that was rare in comics. She found her first employment as a publicity coordinator at PolyGram Filmed Entertainment, where she worked under a formidable and demanding boss who taught Burns the basic principles of public relations. Under this corporate tutelage, Burns learned that a publicity campaign had to be planned out step by step, beginning with early prepublication notices in the trade press and ending with write-ups in general-interest papers and magazines.

In 2000, Burns brought her skills as a publicist to DC Comics. Although she did very well at the job, it was a mismatch. Before landing the position, unfamiliar with the bulk of the company's titles, Burns researched DC comics by browsing intently at Forbidden Planet, a large New York comic-book store, whose manager, Jeff Ayers, astutely advised her to note the differences between DC and Marvel—distinctions that, to an outside observer, are minute and academic. Once at DC, she zeroed in on the author-driven Vertigo titles, launching the company's first-ever *New York Times* bestseller with Neil Gaiman's *The Sandman: Endless Nights*. Still, she was less enthusiastic about the gimmicky superhero titles that made up the company's bread and butter, and what's more, as someone who wanted to have a family, Burns wasn't sure what her future would be in the corporate

rail yards. The office will move to a different floor in the same building in 2008.

September 2005

Pyongyang: A Journey in North Korea, D+Q's first book by Guy Delisle, is published. D+Q marks its first sale of UK rights ever to Jonathan Cape and its largest first printing ever with sixteen thousand copies. The book will go on to sell fifty thousand units in all editions. Guy will be interviewed by Steve Inskeep on NPR's *Morning Edition*. Seth interviews Chester Brown at the second annual Doug Wright Awards held at the Gladstone Hotel. *The Push Man and Other Stories*, D+Q's first book by Yoshihiro Tatsumi, is published, edited by Adrian Tomine.

April 2006

D+Q is named Outstanding Canadian Comic-Book Publisher

world of DC, where executives were expected to put in sixty-hour weeks.

As she immersed herself deeper in the world of comics, Burns found that her personal tastes continued to run toward alternative titles like Usagi Yojimbo, *Eightball*, and the *Twisted Sisters* anthology, as well as a couple of new discoveries—comics from D+Q and Highwater Books. Highwater was a small publishing house in Cambridge, Massachusetts, run with an eye for the spare and poetic by cartoonist Tom Devlin. Devlin and Burns met at 2001's San Diego Comic-Con, which Burns attended for her job at DC, and the two would start dating long-distance soon after. Meanwhile, other industry conventions provided occasions for Burns to interact with D+Q's Oliveros. When Oliveros asked Burns for a tour of the offices of DC Comics and *MAD* magazine (both are owned by the same corporation), he was delighted that he got to see original art by *MAD* veteran Al Jaffee, famous for his intricate, highly crafted "fold-in" paintings.

For Burns and Oliveros to work together, though, was a more serious matter. In deciding to move to D+Q, Burns was taking a huge risk. She would be giving up a well-paid job at DC, just when she and Devlin, by then her fiancé, most needed financial stability. Devlin had relocated to Brooklyn in 2002, but in a post-9/11 economic landscape, he was having trouble finding consistent freelance design work. Those difficulties, combined with a pay cut for Burns the size of a middle-management salary, meant that their wedding would have to be postponed. The couple would be moving not just away from New York, but also away from the US altogether, settling down in an entirely new country, in a city that mainly spoke French. Moreover, Oliveros had repeatedly told her that D+Q was on shaky financial grounds and might not exist in six months' time. "I was pretty nervous to tell my parents that we were cancelling our wedding, moving to Canada, and taking a pay cut, but my dad was surprisingly supportive," Burns recalls. He told her, "If you want to take a chance, do it now." Burns and

---

at the second annual Joe Shuster Awards.

May 2006
D+Q publishes Miriam Katin's World War II memoir, *We Are On Our Own*.

July 2006
After verifying that most of Lynda Barry's books are unavailable, Tom Devlin proposes a series of books collecting all of Lynda's comics. Yoshihiro Tatsumi makes his first stateside visit as a special guest of San Diego Comic-Con. He and his editor Adrian Tomine also do an event at the Hammer Museum in Los Angeles.

September 2006
Guy Delisle visits the D+Q office and meets the staff in person for the first time. D+Q signs a new distribution deal with PGUK for the United Kingdom. Seth begins serializing a weekly comic in the Funny Pages section of the *New York Times*. This comic will eventually be collected by D+Q as *George Sprott (1894–1975)* and will win a Doug Wright Award.

October 2006
Chester Brown tours Canada for the paperback edition of *Louis Riel*. In all editions, *Louis Riel* has fifty thousand copies in print. Rebecca Rosen is pulled aside by Canada Customs

NON5 signing, Jim Hanley's Universe: Greg Cook, Tom Devlin, Kurt Wolfgang, Jordan Crane, Brian Ralph, Paul Lyons & Megan Kelso. Photo: Theresa Dillon (2002). 33

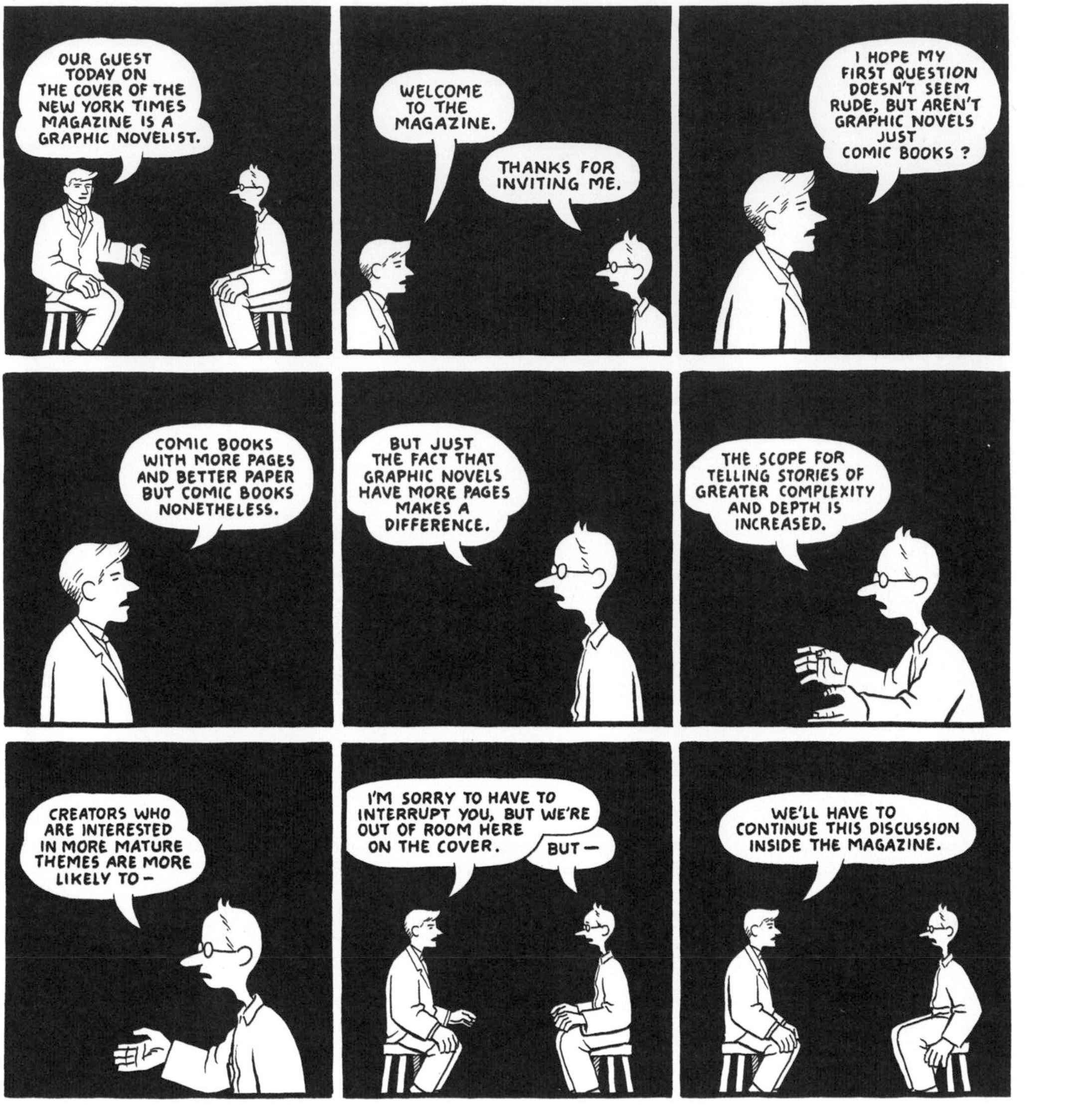
OUR GUEST TODAY ON THE COVER OF THE NEW YORK TIMES MAGAZINE IS A GRAPHIC NOVELIST.
WELCOME TO THE MAGAZINE.
THANKS FOR INVITING ME.
I HOPE MY FIRST QUESTION DOESN'T SEEM RUDE, BUT AREN'T GRAPHIC NOVELS JUST COMIC BOOKS ?
COMIC BOOKS WITH MORE PAGES AND BETTER PAPER BUT COMIC BOOKS NONETHELESS.
BUT JUST THE FACT THAT GRAPHIC NOVELS HAVE MORE PAGES MAKES A DIFFERENCE.
THE SCOPE FOR TELLING STORIES OF GREATER COMPLEXITY AND DEPTH IS INCREASED.
CREATORS WHO ARE INTERESTED IN MORE MATURE THEMES ARE MORE LIKELY TO–
I'M SORRY TO HAVE TO INTERRUPT YOU, BUT WE'RE OUT OF ROOM HERE ON THE COVER.
BUT–
WE'LL HAVE TO CONTINUE THIS DISCUSSION INSIDE THE MAGAZINE.

It was just Chris and me the first year or so that I was with Drawn & Quarterly, and in April 2004 Chris and Marina gave birth to their third son, Charles. So sometime in April or May, I was sitting by myself in the office when the phone rang. I almost plopped off my chair when the caller identified himself as Chip McGrath, and then I double-plopped when he said he was working on a story on graphic novels for the *New York Times Magazine*. I called Chris at home, sorry to interrupt his time with the baby, but this was huge news! It was like if we were in fashion and Anna Wintour called the office, I explained. Surely Chris got that reference?

McGrath's interest was in literary graphic novels, and the article became a cover story. It seemed like the cover would go to Spiegelman, Clowes, or Ware, but the magazine asked Chester. We considered this a harbinger that McGrath understood the richness of the medium beyond the big hits. Chester is one of the few cartoonists who do very few illustrations, no design work, and really not much beyond actual comics—what he would do with a cover for such a large audience, no one knew. When we saw the cover, it was glorious, wonderful, idiosyncratic Chester Brown! All drawn in the *Louis Riel* style, big noses and big hands. Chester panders to no one.

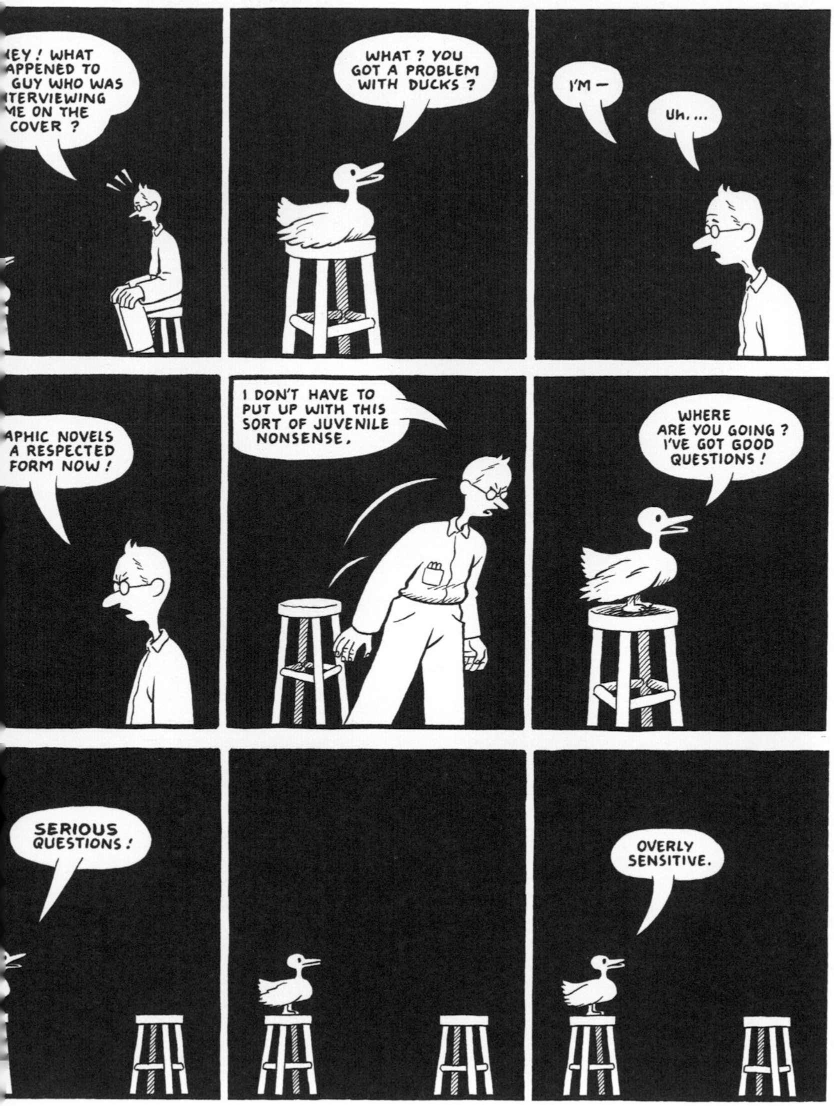
EY! WHAT APPENED TO GUY WHO WAS TERVIEWING ME ON THE COVER ?
WHAT ? YOU GOT A PROBLEM WITH DUCKS ?
I'M —
Uh, ...
APHIC NOVELS A RESPECTED FORM NOW !
I DON'T HAVE TO PUT UP WITH THIS SORT OF JUVENILE NONSENSE.
WHERE ARE YOU GOING ? I'VE GOT GOOD QUESTIONS !
SERIOUS QUESTIONS !
OVERLY SENSITIVE.

The first page of this Chester Brown comic (left) originally appeared as the cover of the July 11, 2004, issue of the *New York Times Magazine*. The second page of the comic (right) appeared inside the issue, along with a feature on literary comics, which included a full-page photo of Chester, Adrian Tomine, Art Spiegelman, Seth, and Joe Sacco, shot on Art and Françoise Mouly's rooftop.

In publicity terms, it doesn't really get better than that article. I have always viewed it, though, as early confirmation that we are in the midst of the graphic novel golden age. Finances were bleak for us that year, and we had recently committed to changing distributors for 2005. Chris refused to release any books that fall for fear they wouldn't get the sales push they deserved, which made our economics even dicier. This article gave us the sincere hope that the fiscal hardship would be worth it.

Now, ten years later, I think of how much D+Q has changed. In 2004, there was no Moomin, no Lynda Barry, Kate Beaton, Rutu Modan, Guy Delisle. If you had told us we would be publishing Art Spiegelman in ten years, it would have been unimaginable, as would having eighteen employees. But when I look at the photo that ran with the article, a group shot of the artists featured, I see how some things have not changed at all—mostly the friendship of the core D+Q cartoonists Seth, Chester, and Adrian. I always love doing festivals with the three of them because you can sit back and just watch them go. They joke, they razz, they tease each other. But they are genuine friends who care deeply for each other. And in those ten years, they have each produced not just one but several successful titles. It truly is the golden age of graphic novels.

—***Peggy Burns***

Devlin agreed that moving to a less financially draining city and working with D+Q could be a risky leap, but it could also pay off much more, artistically, than either of their current situations.

The company that Burns joined in 2003 was struggling against powerful economic headwinds. In 2002, D+Q's book distributor, LPC Group, went bankrupt, resulting in a considerable financial loss. The publisher then briefly hooked up with Chronicle Books as a distributor from 2003 to 2004, but that turned out to be the wrong fit—Chronicle specializes in coffee-table art books, while D+Q's market is more literary. In theory, the relationship with Chronicle should have been ideal since D+Q books are beautiful art objects of the type Chronicle represents. But in fact, D+Q books have a narrative sensibility in addition to their fine-art aesthetic: they're intended to be lovingly pawed over, of course, but they're also meant to be read.

It was Burns who recognized that the partnership wasn't working out. She convinced Oliveros that they had to find a new distributor, even though this meant a short-term financial loss and more insecurity. Oliveros and Burns investigated various options. Book-industry stalwart W.W. Norton was one possibility, but it had already signed a contract with Fantagraphics. For Norton to carry two similar comics presses would have opened up all sorts of potential conflicts of interest. Burns and Oliveros also made overtures to Random House, but a frustrating meeting with an executive at that publishing house focused largely on "the bottom line," rather than on the possibility of working as partners.

After the meeting with Random House, Oliveros and Burns had a much more fruitful conversation with Farrar, Straus and Giroux, the prestigious literary publisher. Burns had long been thinking about FSG, even before she was hired by D+Q. She enjoyed FSG books like Jonathan Franzen's *The Corrections* and Jeffrey Eugenides's *Middlesex*. She had encouraged Tom Devlin to approach FSG as a distributor for Highwater, noting, "they distribute poetry, which is basically what a Highwater comic is."

while crossing the US border from the Alternative Press Expo, as they deem two issues of Chester Brown's *Ed the Happy Clown* comic potentially obscene. Charges are later dropped. **November 2006**

Moomin: The Complete Tove Jansson Comic Strip vol. 1 is published and will go on to have seventy thousand units in print in eight years. D+Q starts to distribute Chris Ware's ACME Novelty Library with issue no. 17 and will distribute nos. 18, 18.5, and 19, eventually publishing no. 20—also known as *Lint*—with thirty thousand copies in print. **January 2007**

Gabrielle Bell, Kevin Huizenga, and Anders Nilsen tour in support of their books *Lucky*, *Curses*, and *Don't Go Where I Can't Follow*. Yoshihiro Tatsumi and Kevin Huizenga make *Time* magazine's Best of 2006 list for *Abandon the Old in Tokyo* and *Curses*. **February 2007**

D+Q publishes the first volume of *Aya*. **May 2007**

Lease is signed for retail space at 211 Bernard West in Montreal. Renovation work goes on throughout the summer.

Rebecca Rosen, Jamie Quail, Ron Rége, Jr., & John Porcellino at Alternative Press Expo. Photo: Chris Anthony Diaz & Graham Willcox (2006).

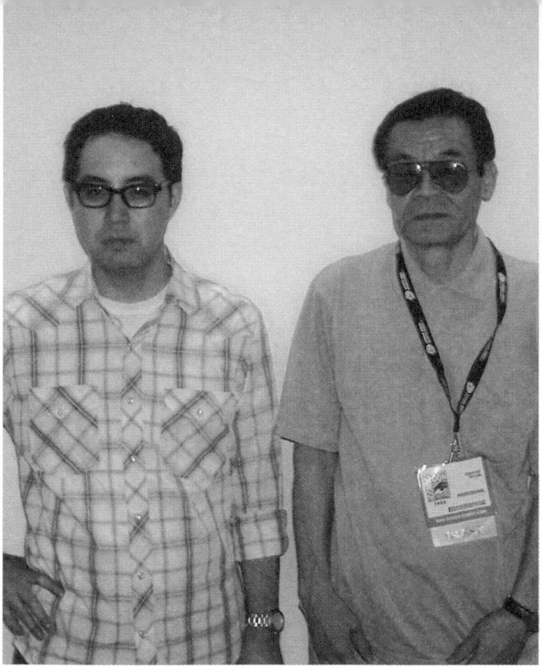

Adrian Tomine & Yoshihiro Tatsumi in LA following Comic-Con, where Tatsumi was a special guest (2006).

The meeting with FSG took place in what Burns describes as a "lovely, messy maze of books," a very different atmosphere from the corporate headquarters of Random House. Oliveros and Burns were asked why they wanted D+Q to be distributed by FSG. Burns responded, "Our cartoonists are the equivalent of your authors. We want people to immediately understand the literary heft of our books, and if we are your client publisher, stores will understand that." The 2005 distribution agreement that D+Q signed with FSG transformed the profile of the smaller press, giving it a much more secure foothold in American bookstores. And thanks to specialized departments at FSG's parent company, Macmillan, D+Q titles also began to appear in libraries and academic settings—huge areas of growth for the company over the last decade-plus.

The deal with FSG was augmented by Burns's considerable talent in public relations. As a publicist, her distinguishing trait has been that she regards each book as unique and carefully tailors its promotional campaign to a specific audience.

June 2007
Exit Wounds, Rutu Modan's debut graphic novel and first book with D+Q, is published. It will become the sleeper hit of 2007 and will be called the best of the year by *Entertainment Weekly*, *Time* magazine, and *New York* magazine, and it will win an Eisner Award. In both hardcover and paperback, *Exit Wounds* will have twenty-five thousand copies in print.

September 2007
Librairie Drawn & Quarterly opens at the end of the month in the Montreal neighbourhood of Mile End, the same neighbourhood a block away from where

In the early 1990s, as a half-formed adult, I wandered the aisles of bookstores trying to figure out my future. I'd go from store to store, scrutinizing the books, asking ridiculous questions about how they were made. The booksellers all looked at me like I was a thief. I decided I was going to be a publisher mostly because I thought publishing would give me a certain professional and financial independence (which goes to show how *really* young I was). But I had a few strikes against me.

First, there was my inexperience. The only thing I knew about publishing came from the thousands of hours I'd spent as a kid reading and drawing comics. My father would take a few pages to the office and make photocopies that I'd then staple together and call a "magazine."

Next was my age, which made me overconfident and arrogant. I rejected the idea of doing what my role models had done. It was either produce something absolutely original or let the earth swallow me up.

And then there was money. I didn't have any, not even enough to pay a Czech printer (the cheapest printers at the time). I thought I could make up for it with crude screen-printing and the cheap local photocopy shop.

For all these reasons, there was no way I could have produced a traditional-style album, created its cover, or even paid to have it made. But in considering the various parameters, I'd come up with a miracle solution: I was going to make French comic books. In other words, serialized comics that would be cheap to produce and absolutely distinct, thanks to their screen-printed covers and content that would be the total opposite of American superhero comics that were everywhere.

Fired up about my great idea, I went to see one of the few booksellers who still tolerated me. I explained my plan, congratulating myself on my genius and cracking up at the thought of the fortune awaiting me. The bookseller simply reached into a box and pulled out a comic book. "Here you go, my friend. It looks good, it's cheap, and it's not about superheroes." I was crushed.

That comic was *Yummy Fur* no. 26. The bookseller had finally managed to sell me something. And so I turned to my role models for inspiration. I've put in years learning the trade. I've yet to get rich. But I have a vocation. And more than twenty years after that day, I've had the pleasure of forging close friendships with the team at D+Q and, to my great astonishment, become Chester Brown's French publisher. Chester, Chris, Peggy, Tom, Julia, and Tracy—thank you.

—Jean-Louis Gauthey, publisher, Éditions Cornélius

The readership for Guy Delisle's *Jerusalem* isn't the same as the one for Lynda Barry's *What It Is*, so for these books, as she does for all other D+Q titles, Burns planned a specific promotional campaign, targeting broad and diverse audiences who might not otherwise have given comics a second thought—timing an excerpt of *Jerusalem* to run in *Foreign Policy* close to its publication date, and asking professors and sex workers to blurb *Paying for It* to provide a historical perspective as well as an insider's. In addition to having a gift for promotions, Burns was always more than a publicist, being involved intimately in shaping the list with acquisitions like Dumontier & Farber, Julie Delporte, Sarah Glidden, *Rookie*, and *WORN Fashion Journal*. In recognition of these indispensable skills, in 2008 she was elevated to the position of associate publisher.

While Burns brought her business acumen and industry savvy to D+Q's operations, Devlin offered his distinctive talents with design, as well as a canon-busting take on comics history and style. When the couple moved to Montreal in late 2003, Devlin was already a major figure in alternative comics as the head of Highwater Books, which he had started in 1997. Following in the tradition of *RAW* and D+Q, Highwater Books was at the forefront of the shift from the comic-book pamphlet to the graphic novel. Highwater titles were created by minimalist and cute-brut cartoonists such as Megan Kelso, James Kochalka, John Porcellino, and Ron Regé, Jr. (the latter two of whom would have their Highwater masterworks, *Perfect Example* and *Skibber Bee Bye*, reissued by D+Q), but also by the high-art metalheads associated with the Fort Thunder movement in Providence, RI. Such diverse offerings were unified by the beautiful design of each Highwater volume, the physical form of the books being integral to the content. The subtle shifts in the colour of ink with which *Perfect Example* was printed conveyed an impressionistic, melancholy sense of youth's passing, while *Skibber Bee Bye*'s wee size belied its overpowering emotional impact. These kinds of fine-grained details would come to define D+Q's output, as well, with Devlin on board.

Just as Oliveros had been shaped by *RAW* comics, Devlin had been shaped by the flourishing alternative comics culture of the late 1980s and early 1990s, as embodied not just by publishers like Fantagraphics and D+Q but also by the vibrant minicomics scene that emerged in those years. Devlin studied computer science at Northeastern University and started working for the music and comics chain Newbury Comics in the late 1980s, where he first encountered Chester Brown's work in *Yummy Fur* no. 1. Like Oliveros, Devlin regularly read the *Comics Journal*, which he credits with helping him sharpen his critical skills and deepen his sense of the history of comics.

After leaving Newbury Comics, Devlin worked for Diamond, the distributor that dominated the direct market. As a Diamond employee, he occasionally talked to Chris Oliveros, and he remembers that *Dirty Plotte* no. 1 had a total of seventy-five sales in the New England area. He then took a job at Million Year Picnic, a tightly packed store serving the Harvard Square neighbourhood in Cambridge. Million Year Picnic would take minicomics on consignment, and while working there Devlin became excited by artists like Ron Regé, Jr., and John Porcellino, as well as other authors who hadn't been picked up yet by the bigger publishers. The spark that

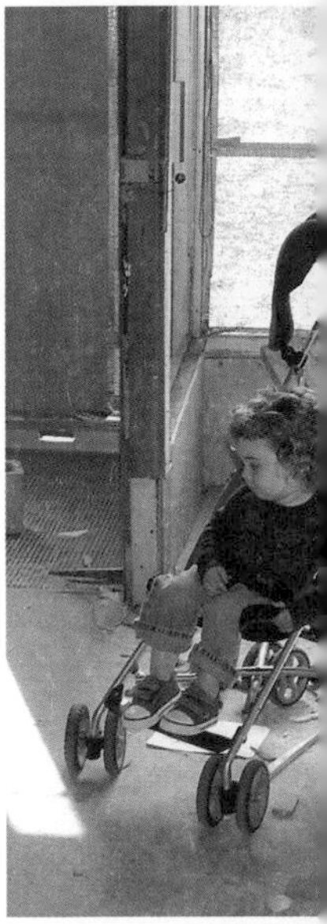

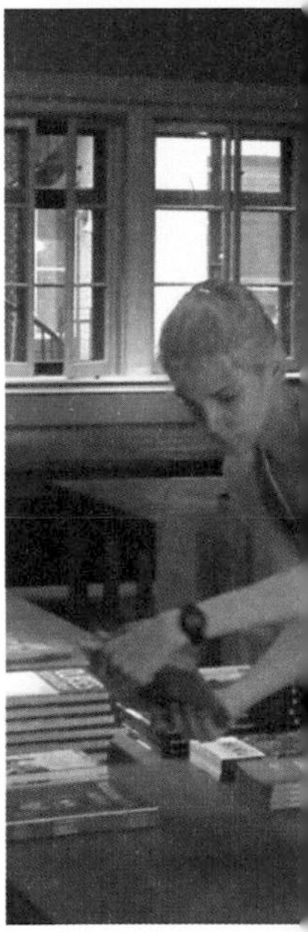

Chris Oliveros founded the company. *Moomin: The Complete Tove Jansson Comic Strip* vol. 2 is published and will go on to have fifty thousand units in print. D+Q will publish nine volumes, with 250,000 units of the series in print.

October 2007

Adrian Tomine's *Shortcomings* is published; it is reviewed in the *New York Times* and is both an editor's choice and a *New York Times* Notable Book. Tomine is also interviewed by Terry Gross on NPR's *Fresh Air*. *Shortcomings* will eventually have fifty thousand units in print in hardcover and paperback formats.

December 2007

The band Lavender Diamond, with drummer Ron Regé, Jr., plays at the Librairie D+Q on a snowy Sunday afternoon.

January 2008

D+Q publishes *365 Days*, Julie Doucet's illustrated diary, which will be her last book with D+Q. It takes three letterers, Dirk Rehm, Rich Tommaso, and Chris Ware, to hand-letter the book as translated from French to English.

February 2008

Librairie D+Q hosts events with Michel Rabagliati for *Paul Goes Fishing* and Adrian Tomine for

 (Top) Gigi Devlin at Librairie D+Q pre-construction (2007). (Bottom) Claudia Eve Beauchesne, Matt Shane & Chris Oliveros preparing to open (2007).

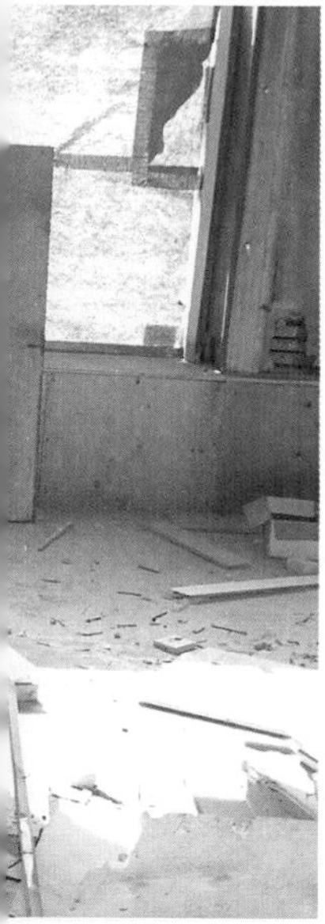

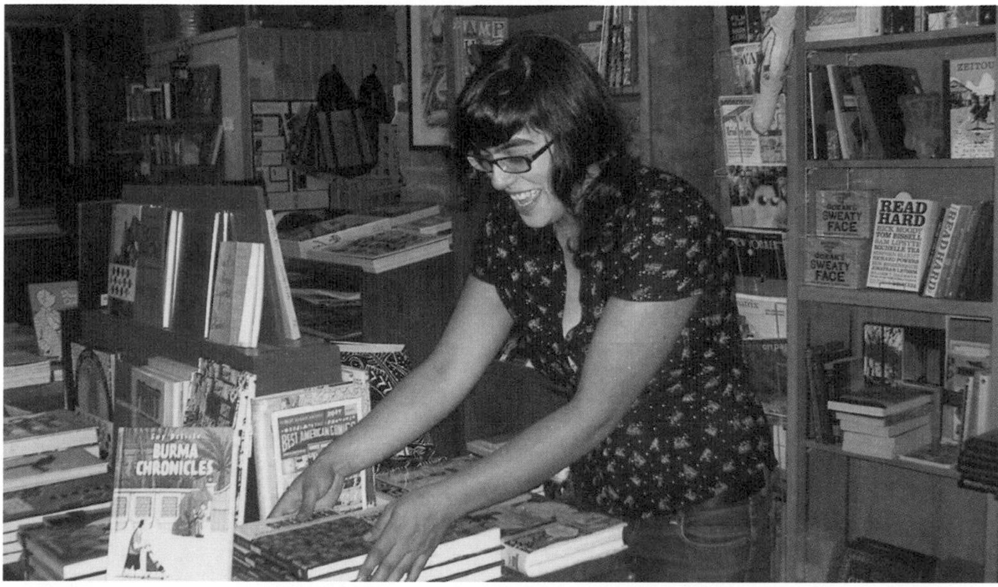
BURMA CHRONICLES
BEST AMERICAN COMICS
READ HARD
SWEATY FACE

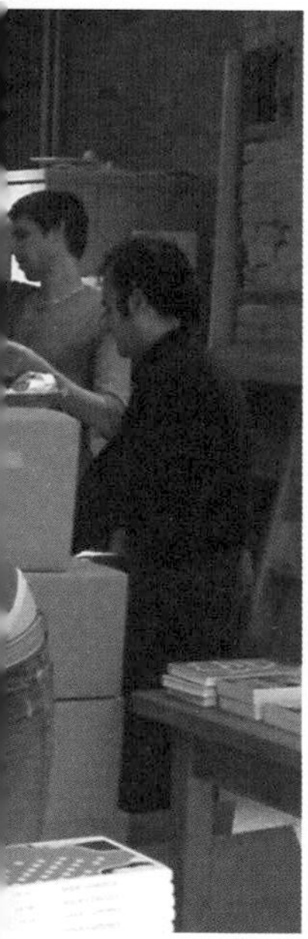

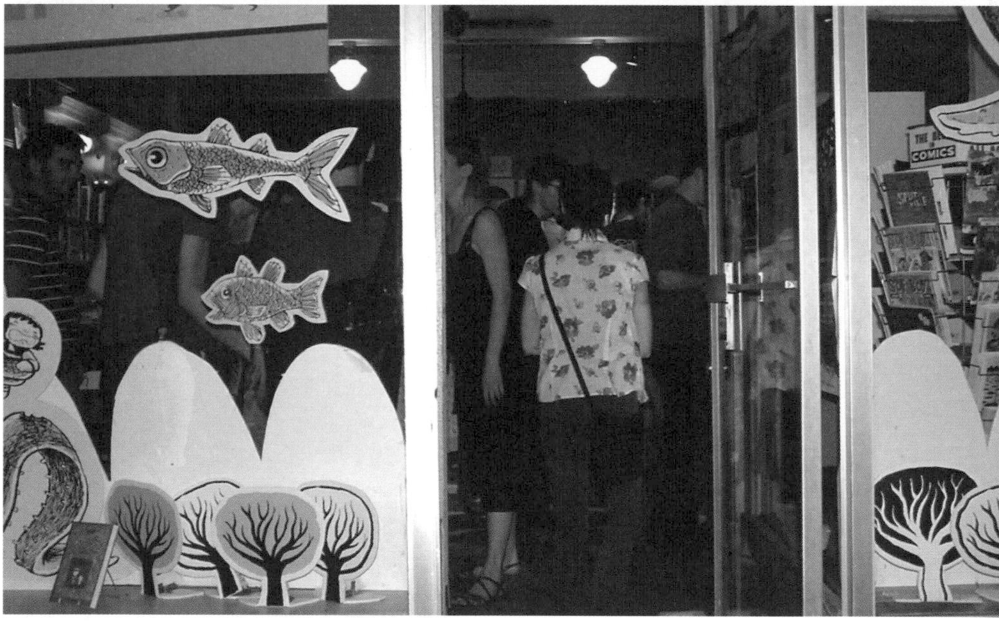
COMICS

Shortcomings. The band Islands plays a secret show at Librairie D+Q.

March 2008

The Handsome Furs play at the Librairie D+Q. A neighbour complains about the noise and the concert series ends. Librairie D+Q hosts an exhibition by local artist Diane Obomsawin, who will later publish *Kaspar* and *On Loving Women* with D+Q.

May 2008

What It Is, Lynda Barry's first book with D+Q, is published; it debuts with a profile in the *New York Times* Sunday Arts & Leisure section. The book will become D+Q's fastest seller in history—three printings in its first year, with eight printings and sixty-five thousand units in print altogether—and will win an Eisner Award.

July 2008

Librairie D+Q hosts a month-long residency with Ron Regé, Jr., with an exhibition and launch for *Against Pain*.

August 2008

D+Q publishes *Berlin: City of Smoke*, the second installment of Jason Lutes's trilogy. Tom Devlin is trapped inside the D+Q elevator for three hours while delivering a fridge he bought on Craigslist. Librairie D+Q hosts a launch for Matt

(Top) Julia Pohl-Miranda. Photo: Ann Pohl (2009). (Bottom right) Window display & crowd for the launch of Matt Forsythe's *Ojingogo* (2008).

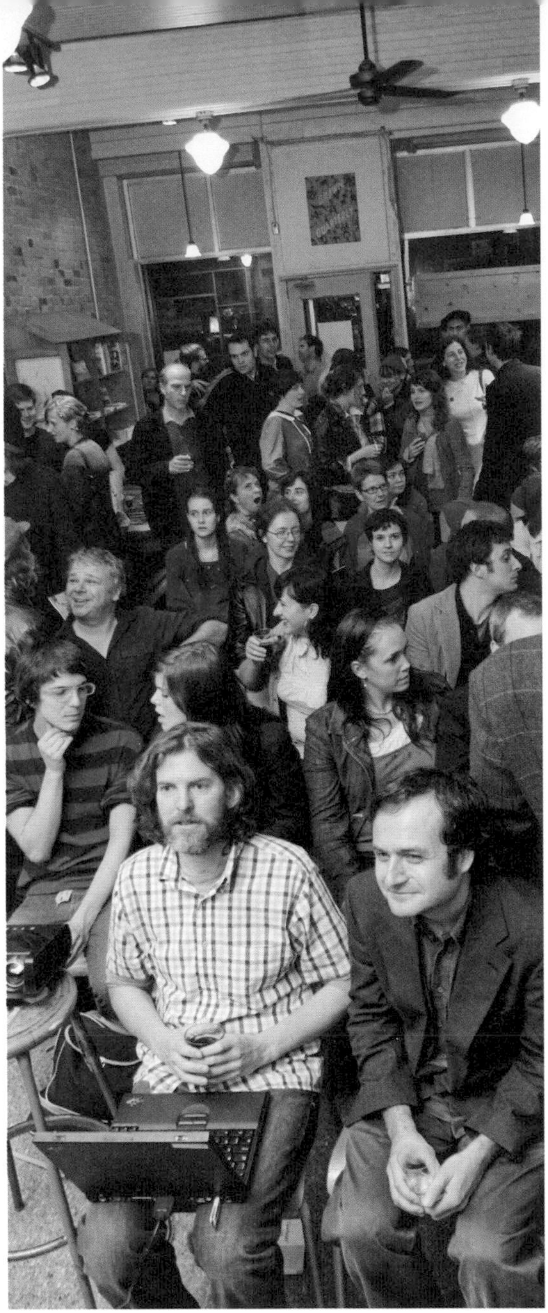

launched Highwater Books was Devlin's conviction that these artists deserved a wider audience, and that they could find it if their often intimately scaled work appeared in books whose design was sensitive to nuance.

Although radically and chronically undercapitalized, Highwater had an enormous impact on alternative comics, pushing a new style of cartooning that more closely resembled poetry than prose, eschewing bluntness in favour of quiet moments of reverie and reflection. Highwater resembled a small record label, and what Devlin published was like DIY indie rock. And when it came to comics' cherished classic rock standards, Devlin was unsurprisingly contrarian: guest-editing a 2001 issue of the *Comics Journal*, Devlin took on the increasingly conventional comics canon, penning a takedown of fan-favourite EC Comics entitled "A Legacy of Mediocrity" and running tantalizing appreciations of long-neglected works like Tove Jansson's *Moomin* and John Stanley's *Thirteen* (both eventually reprinted by D+Q). That issue of the *Journal* boasted atypically elegant design by cartoonist Jordan Crane, with whom Devlin worked closely on Highwater's books, as well. Devlin's own sense of book design was sharpened after a stint at Harvard University Press. Working together, Crane and Devlin elevated the importance of design in comics, producing books that graced any shelf they sat on.

It was natural for Devlin to bring his unique skill set to D+Q. With his background in comics, Devlin had been following D+Q closely from its first publication. "I loved the aesthetic," he recalls. "I was completely on board. I agreed with the literary approach, in contrast to Fantagraphics's more transgressive approach."

He started working for the publishing house on a part-time basis in early 2004, helping with mailings and more elaborate production jobs like the books of Seth. Seth himself was becoming more interested in the expressive possibilities of book design, so he found a kindred spirit in Devlin. By the end of 2004, Devlin was working for D+Q full-time as the primary designer and production person.

Forsythe's *Ojingogo*, where 150 copies are sold.

October 2008

Chester Brown runs for Parliament in his riding of Trinity-Spadina as the Libertarian party candidate and garners a fifth-place showing out of seven candidates. Librairie D+Q hosts an exhibition for Marc Bell's *Illusztraijuns for Brain Police*.

November 2008

Librairie D+Q hosts an event for the Petit Livre *Pohadky* by Pat Shewchuk and Marek Colek. Chester Brown and Seth write an open letter to the Governor General's Literary Awards, protesting how the prestigious Canadian awards split nominated graphic novels into two categories, best writer and best artist. [Editor's note: the Governor General Awards only accepts graphic novel nominations in children's categories. Graphic novels are explicitly denied entrance in adult categories, prohibiting D+Q from ever submitting a book for the national award.]

December 2008

Librairie D+Q hosts an exhibit for Jillian Tamaki, showcasing her drawings for the book *Skim*.

January 2009

Librairie D+Q hosts the launch for Pascal Girard's *Nicolas*, his first book with D+Q.

 Tom Devlin, Chris Oliveros & crowd at Librairie D+Q's inaugural event. Photo: Alison Naimark (2007).

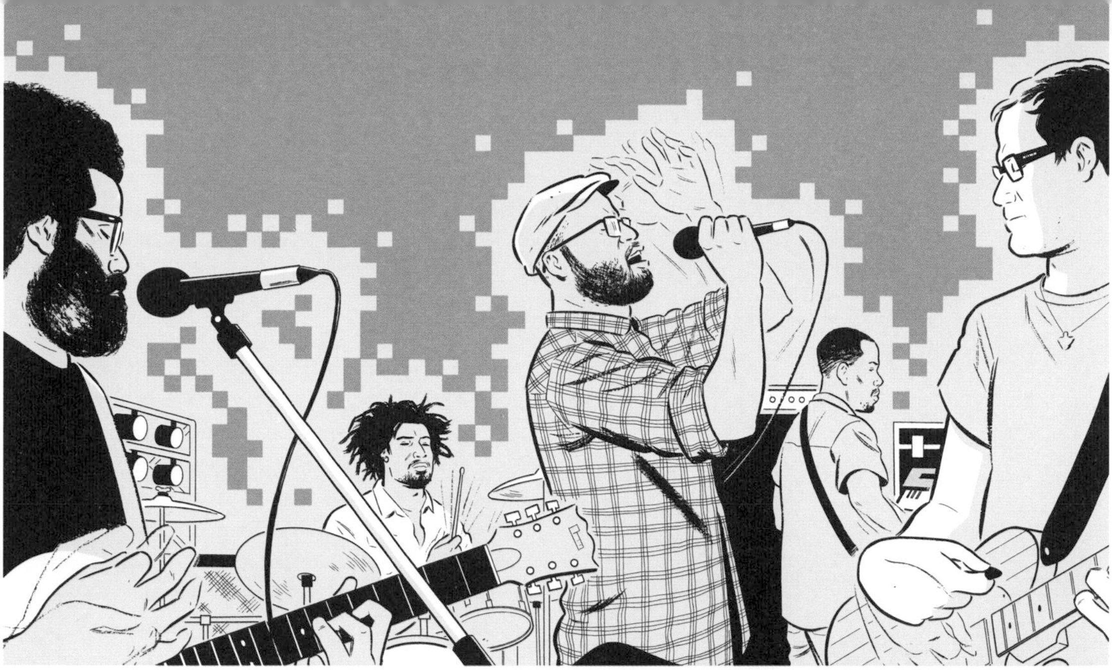

To celebrate D+Q's twentieth anniversary, TV on the Radio & the Dirty Projectors played a show in Montreal. Poster by Adrian Tomine (2009).

Among the gifts Devlin has brought to the company is his strong, revisionist sense of comics history, which has been on display as far back as that *Journal* issue and beyond. Devlin has long and eloquently made the case for preferring cartoony creators like Stanley, Jansson, and Lynda Barry to the more conventional illustrators typically lionized by comics fans, all those Wally Woods and Hal Fosters celebrated for their muscular craft. As a result of Devlin's advocacy, D+Q undertook two of its most successful projects of the twenty-first century, the first major English-language reprinting of Jansson's whimsical *Moomin* strips and the publication of Lynda Barry's experimental textbooks.

Though Devlin's tastes are evident in the D+Q catalogue, the titles he's helped introduce have extended Oliveros's original aesthetic without ever displacing it. Thin-lined, dreamy zinesters like John Porcellino and Ron Regé, Jr., as well as art-schooled eccentrics like Brian Ralph and Marc Bell, might all have got their start with Highwater Books, but their first wave of D+Q books hardly looked out of place next to

February 2009
Librairie D+Q hosts a launch for Diane Obomsawin's *Kaspar*.

March 2009
Librairie D+Q hosts a launch for Pascal Blanchet's *Baloney*.

April 2009
D+Q publishes Yoshihiro Tatsumi's eight-hundred-page memoir *A Drifting Life*, which will go on to four printings and twenty-five thousand units in print; an Eisner Award; and the cover of the *New York Times* daily arts section in a review by critic Dwight Garner. Yoshihiro Tatsumi visits the East Coast of North America with special guest appearances

***Drawn & Quarterly* no. 1, April 1990**

I was sixteen, living in Pittsburgh, and was at my favourite comic store, Phantom of the Attic, with my best friend, Nick Green. Usually we dropped into the Phantom to pick up the requisite superhero mags: *X-Men*, *Batman*, *Punisher War Journal*, etc. We'd go in to pick up our reserved copies, then we'd hover around browsing and chatting with the store owner, Jeff. I really don't know how it happened, but we ended up with a copy of *Drawn & Quarterly* no. 1 in our hands. Nick had a cool uncle who'd shown him *RAW* magazine and various Crumb stuff so he knew that side of comics and thought I'd be into it. I remember looking at the cover (an artist struggling with her work) and the artwork inside and thinking, "Man, this is disgusting. Why is it in black and white? Why is it so big? This guy just said 'fuck.' These drawings are so twisted and great. This weird dog is smoking a joint. Is this Canadian? This definitely looks like something I shouldn't be reading. There's bare genitals all over this thing. What is this? I'm totally getting this."

As an aspiring cartoonist, it was really inspiring to see a book that made me feel better about liking comics. I was at that age when I was losing interest in/embarrassed by mainstream comics and was a little confused as to what I was going to do with all this knowledge of drawing superheroes

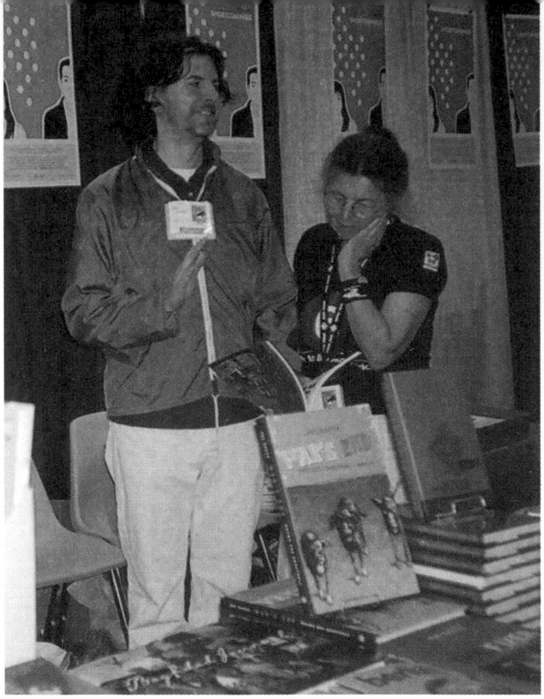

Tom Devlin & Miriam Katin at Comic-Con. Photo: Klara Tobias, Miriam's mother (2008).

This is to be filed as "clueless." My very first comic, a four-page story, was published in *Monkeysuit*, a brave little anthology privately published by the participating artists. It was in 2000. Greg McElhatton reviewed it in *iCOMICS*. He wrote, "Miriam Katin's 'Mittel Europa Rerun' would be just as at home in an issue of *Drawn & Quarterly*." I turned to my colleagues at MTV and asked, "What's *Drawn & Quarterly*?" I was that green. When they told me, I ran out to Borders on Broadway and bought volume 3. Wow. With uncharacteristic chutzpah I mailed the issue of *Monkeysuit* and a copy of the review to Chris. I didn't know you were not supposed to do it that way. Shortly after, I received a phone call from Chris, who asked me if I had anything like this work lying around in twelve pages. I had nothing but I sat down and made damned sure I had that twelve-page story in short order. No. I am not going to say it (the rest is history). Ugh. I did say it.—***Miriam Katin***

Brown's similarly reserved comics or Doucet's *outré* ones. And the new additions Devlin has steered into D+Q's stable of authors—cartoonists like the diagrammatic Dan Zettwoch, the ebullient Vanessa Davis, or Gabrielle Bell, with her deadpan daydreaming—continue Devlin's advocacy for cartoony playfulness while complementing D+Q's tradition of literary stories from everyday life. As with Peggy Burns, then, Tom Devlin has added striking new facets to D+Q's sensibility while still being loyal to the identity of the company.

As Burns and Devlin settled into Montreal, and as D+Q sought just the right distributor, the public's awareness of—and eagerness for—graphic novels was rapidly changing. So were the publisher's standards for success. D+Q's backlist of books from the nineties, when comics were serialized in the direct market first and then collected into book format later, continued to enjoy a prolonged shelf life, as did the small handful of original graphic novels they released at the turn of the century.

D+Q had its successes over the rocky next couple of years—including new books from Tomine, Doucet, and Seth—but it was Burns's first week on the job when the new decade truly began for the company. The roster of new titles included Chester Brown's collected *Louis Riel* (fall 2003); Joe Sacco's Bosnian war reportage, *The Fixer* (again, fall 2003); Adrian Tomine's *Scrapbook* (spring 2004); Seth's *Clyde Fans Book One* (spring 2004)—a murderers' row of cartoonists, and a spate of books that easily number among the decade's very finest. It was Burns's job to help readers find these books—and find them they did. *Louis Riel*, for example, Brown's "comic-strip biography" of the controversial Métis leader, soon became the first graphic novel to appear on Canadian bestseller lists and has since been acclaimed as a national classic, a regular in reading groups and on syllabi. *Louis Riel* had been published for years in the floppy comic-book format, but it was only in its collected edition that readers took notice: the era of the graphic novel was in full swing.

In those early years of widespread bookstore distribution, the books that hit big for D+Q were conceived first

at the PEN World Voices Festival in NYC and Toronto Comic Arts Festival. Librairie D+Q hosts an exhibition with Vanessa Davis and a musical performance by Geneviève Castrée.

May 2009

Chris Oliveros is given a special award "recognizing twenty years of excellence and innovation in the field of comics publishing in Canada" at the fifth annual Doug Wright Awards at the Toronto Comic Arts Festival. In attendance are Adrian Tomine, Yoshihiro Tatsumi, Chester Brown, Seth, Zach Worton, Gabrielle Bell, and Michel Rabagliati.

June 2009

D+Q's twentieth-anniversary concert is held in Montreal, featuring Dirty Projectors and TV on the Radio. Seth and Adrian Tomine go on tour for *George Sprott* and the paperback edition of *Shortcomings*.

July 2009

At San Diego Comic-Con, during Seth's panel, Chris Oliveros is given an Inkpot Award in recognition of his contributions to the industry. Calvin Johnson performs at the Librairie D+Q.

September 2009

D+Q publishes R. Sikoryak's twenty-years-in-the-making *Masterpiece Comics*, which will have three printings. D+Q and foremost as *books*, front to back. The traditional comic-book series was becoming less effective as an income stream for those artists plugging away at lengthy, time-consuming work—though stubborn souls like Tomine and Lutes still do put out the odd issue here and there. In the 2000s, the book was the thing. And so the company's standout authors from this mid-decade period, like Guy Delisle, Michel Rabagliati, Rutu Modan, and Miriam Katin, each went to press with hefty, uncommon, and self-contained books. (Realizing such a focus on labour-intensive, book-length work may have reduced the chances for young cartoonists to hone their skills on short subjects, the publisher introduced the *Showcase* series, where future D+Q authors like Kevin Huizenga, Geneviève Castrée, and Dan Zettwoch tested out astonishingly accomplished but compact material before stretching their legs with full-length releases.)

While Sacco's, Brown's, Tomine's, and Seth's books connected with readers, 2004 was the year that D+Q cut ties with Chronicle and moved to FSG. Changing distributors left D+Q's books in limbo, and it wasn't until more than a year later that the company's next breakthrough came. In 2005, Quebec native Guy Delisle's *Pyongyang* provided readers with a rare glimpse into life in Kim Jong-Il's hermit kingdom, made timely by North Korea's escalating sabre rattling and missile testing. The follow-up, *Shenzhen* (actually published before *Pyongyang*, in French), cemented Delisle's place as one of D+Q's new marquee artists. Thanks to his one-time profession as an animator and his wife's position in Médecins Sans Frontières, the artist has travelled the globe, crafting a series of travelogues that give readers fresh views of remote, contested areas. In *Pyongyang* and *Shenzhen*, as well as subsequent books about Myanmar and Israel, Delisle avoids the glibness of much travel writing by keeping focused on everyday interactions and miscommunications, as well as on the impact of landscape (both natural and human-created). Delisle's journalistic *carnets de voyage* are deservedly international bestsellers because of the honesty and care with which they capture the texture of foreign lands.

celebrates its twentieth anniversary with a party at Rocketship Comics with Guy Delisle, R. Sikoryak, R.O. Blechman, Marc Bell, Adrian Tomine, Ron Regé, Jr., Gabrielle Bell, and Miriam Katin.

October 2009
D+Q's Enfant imprint debuts with the publication of the Tove Jansson classic *The Book About Moomin, Mymble and Little My*. The imprint will go on to feature books by Astrid Lindgren and Ingrid Vang Nyman, as well as Anouk Ricard. Librairie D+Q hosts John Porcellino for *Map of My Heart*.

I'd amassed from middle school up through that point. I got home, experienced Peter Bagge, Dennis Worden, Anne D. Bernstein, Joe Matt. JOE MATT. Who is this person? Is this all true? So many panels. Holy shit. I was hooked. It was illicit, it was bitter, it was hilarious, it was beautiful, and even the trippiest parts of it felt honest. It made the stuff I'd liked until then look stupid and childish. Surprise. Why draw superheroes when you can actively document what you hate about yourself, your friends, your enemies, and your weird-ass reality? This all happened in the same stretch of time I discovered D.C. hardcore, the Violent Femmes, the Hernandez bros., electronic music, the Beats, and the Tao Te Ching, and I was well on my way to being one of the most pretentious young black comic punks in the tristate area. From then on I only wanted to read and make "underground" comics, watch and make "underground" films, listen to "underground" music, and basically soak up anything that seemed even a little bit subversive. You guys got me. Still hooked. D+Q was a formative part of my adolescence and is partially responsible for the creative path my life has taken. Thanks for nothing.

Seth and Adrian Tomine, 1994ish–1996ish
A few years after this I was living in New York and was well into comics like *Dirty Plotte*, *Yummy Fur*, *Palookaville*, and *Peepshow* (as well as a bunch from a popular Seattle-based publisher who yeah yeah yeah whatever...) and was making minicomics and zines myself. I'd come across an issue of the *Optic Nerve* minicomic (I know it was no. 6 because of what happens later in this story) in a zine store called See Hear and was really excited about it. I loved the drawings, the writing, the humour, the jaded worldview. Shortly after, I started seeing Adrian's work in the Tower Records magazine (*Pulse!*) and recognized it immediately. Maybe a year later I saw the Xeric-funded *Optic Nerve* no. 7. I was shocked. It looked so good. Colour cover. Cardstock. Great writing, and the artwork was incredible. So pro. He'd won a Xeric! Of course he did. This is so great. Good for him. I was on my way to my girlfriend's place to show her, and sometime during that subway ride I read something

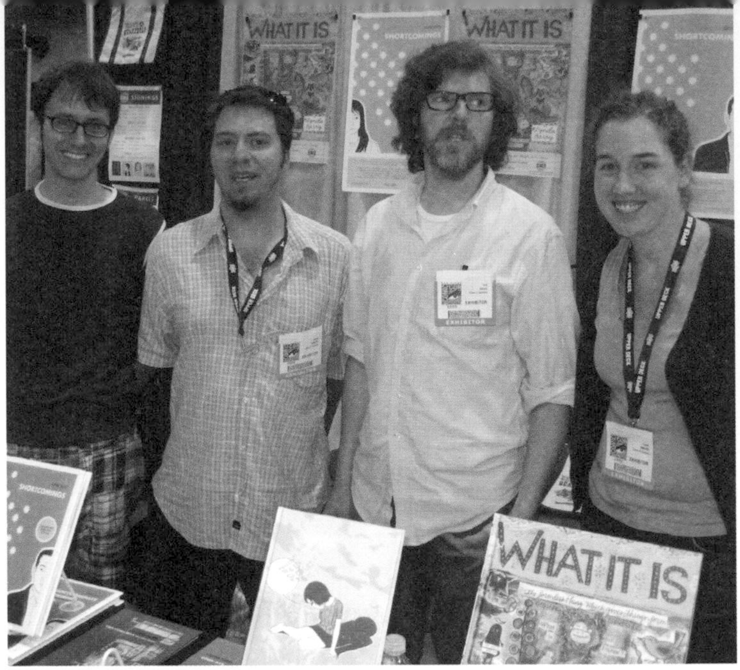
WHAT IT IS
WHAT IT IS
WHAT IT IS

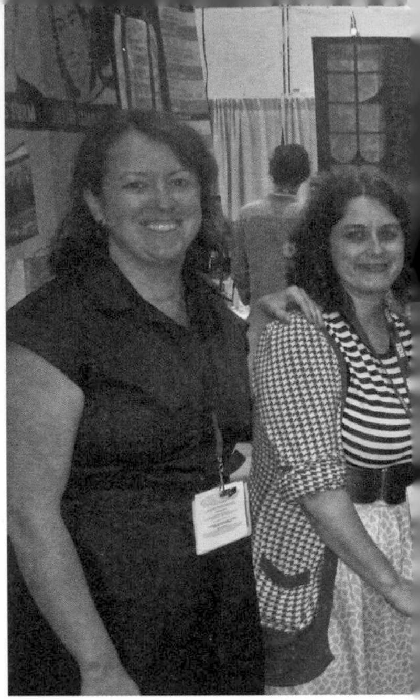

As the decade progressed, D+Q's core line of graphic novels was becoming more and more difficult to pigeonhole—and more and more diverse in both style and subject matter. Delisle's topical *Jerusalem* might have had surface similarities with, say, Rutu Modan's Israel-set *Exit Wounds*—a solemnly picaresque tale of a prickly IDF soldier looking for her lover, who she suspects has been killed in a bombing. But Modan's subtly orchestrated fiction contrasts with Delisle's diaristic observations almost as much as her clear-lined, flat-coloured style sets her work apart from his black and white, cartoony shorthand. You would likewise have to squint pretty hard to see similarities between either of these artists' works and books by Michel Rabagliati—whose Paul series, a veritable phenomenon in Quebec, calmly relates the life lessons learned by the title character in the classical idiom of Franco-Belgian kids' comics—or Miriam Katin, whose *We Are On Our Own* was the debut graphic novel from its sixty-three-year-old author, summoning up her memories of surviving World War II as a Hungarian Jew, sketched out in tentative pencil strokes and occasional delicate colours. With such wide-ranging themes and approaches diversifying D+Q's catalogue, by decade's end, there was no longer such a thing as a "typical" D+Q book.

What defined D+Q, from the 2000s onward, was precisely this kind of growth that resists definition. Perhaps the only constant across D+Q's titles was the company's continued dedication to contemporary, literate, visually distinctive cartooning—and so to its authors' unique voices, too. With these principles rooting the company, D+Q has steadily become more secure, gradually taking on more employees while comfortably increasing its publishing program. So the company's expansion has been organic and sturdy—if also, at times, experimental. Nurtured by a few new and capable hands, D+Q still has the literary graphic novel at its core, but fresh shoots and branches constantly reach off into adventurous areas for the publishing house to explore.

November 2009
Librairie D+Q hosts a double launch for Marc Bell's *Hot Potatoe* and Amy Lockhart's *Dirty Dishes.*

December 2009
Librairie D+Q hosts Guy Delisle at his first event for D+Q in Montreal.

April 2010
The *New York Times* reviews James Sturm's *Market Day* in its Books of the Times column, stating the book is "superb in its uncertainty." *Wilson*, Daniel Clowes's first book with D+Q, and his first graphic novel since his acclaimed *Eightball* series, is published; it lands on the *New York Times* bestseller list. It will go on to have thirty-five thousand units in print and have the most foreign rights deals by a D+Q book ever with deals in thirteen territories. Clowes will go on to win the PEN USA Award and the Eisner.

May 2010
Tom Devlin commissions Dan Zettwoch to draw a *Gilmore Girls* tribute comic; the comic stalls due to licensing issues. Librairie D+Q hosts a double launch for Keith Jones's *Catland Empire* and Seth Scriver's *Stooge Pile.*

June 2010
Librairie D+Q hosts a launch for Sonja Ahlers's *The Selves.*

 A bunch of yo-yos at Comic-Con: (Left) Peter Birkemoe, Jamie Salomon, Tom Devlin & Alison Naturale (2008); (Right) Peggy Burns, Jessica Campbell,

Rebecca Rosen, Vanessa Davis, Gabrielle Bell, Jillian Tamaki & Mimi Pond (2010).

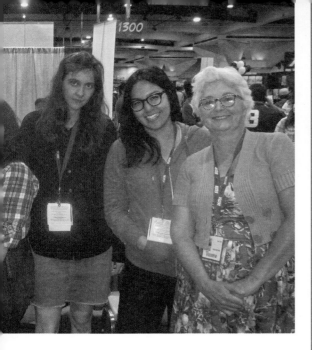

One of these ventures took D+Q well outside the traditional world of publishing proper. After living in Montreal for four years, Burns and Devlin shared Oliveros's frustration with the peculiar predicament of being an English-language company in a French-speaking city. Anglophone comic-book stores focused mainly on superheroes; their Francophone counterparts sold mostly *bandes dessinées*. Montreal had no retail outlet that sold the type of comics and books D+Q's staffers liked to read, which also meant D+Q had no venue suitable for launching its books, except a local coffee shop or the popular rock club Casa del Popolo.

In 2007, though, D+Q opened up its own store to service these needs: Librairie Drawn & Quarterly. Burns and Devlin had toyed with the idea of opening a storefront in Brooklyn for Highwater, but the right location eluded them. They found Oliveros receptive, however, to a similar idea for D+Q in Montreal. Initial searches for an appropriate space proved fruitless, especially because the company was looking for new

July 2010
Librairie D+Q hosts a launch for the god of cyberpunk, William Gibson.

October 2010
D+Q publishes *Palookaville* no. 20, the first hardcover expanded issue of Seth's iconic comic-book series. Librairie D+Q hosts an event for the novelist Tao Lin. Chris Oliveros and then–store manager Rory Seydel will both later appear in his 2013 novel *Taipei*. Librairie D+Q hosts Dylan Horrocks, who was invited to Canada by the International Festival of Authors in Toronto for the reprinting of his graphic

(in the letters page, or one of the stories) that hinted at his age and I realized that this person, whom I so admired, whose talent I aspired toward, who I'd figured was at least a decade my senior, was exactly one year older than me. I was nineteen. A deep, deep existential depression descended upon me and I walked off the N train in a daze. "What's the point?" I asked myself over and over. "I've wasted my life. It's over for me." I Charlie Browned it all the way to my girlfriend's dorm and sat on her bed, wrecked, as she flipped through the mini. "It's good! What are you so sad about?" she asked. I told her, "What's the point? I'm never going to make something this good. He's only twenty! I've wasted my life." She said, "Oh, come on. It's really good, but he's probably never even kissed a girl." At which point I said something like, "What the fuck is so great about kissing a girl? I'd much rather be able to make something like this than waste my time kissing a stupid girl." Actually, that's exactly what I said. I know this because I remember how hurt and angry she got, and how I tried to explain that I absolutely was not talking about her, and how it was way too late for her to believe that, and also how poorly the rest of that relationship played itself out. Awful, but I was nineteen and I cannot stress how badly I wanted to be a great cartoonist. Shameful. I'm still ashamed. Adrian, if you're reading this, you turned me into a monster and ruined my early twenties. Great comic, though.

Last story: Two years later I saw that Adrian and Seth were coming through New York on a book tour. Seth was promoting *It's a Good Life, If You Don't Weaken* and Adrian was promoting a D+Q-published issue of *Optic Nerve*. Number 3, I think. I loved and love everything both of them do, so I went to the signing at Jim Hanley's Universe on Thirty-third Street and waited patiently in line to get my books signed. While I was waiting I overheard Seth answering questions about *It's a Good Life*. It was great to hear him talk in person about the quest detailed in the book. The story of how he travelled all over for months on end to find a long-forgotten cartoonist's origins was really impressive to me, not to mention the fact that he'd laid it all out so simply and eloquently

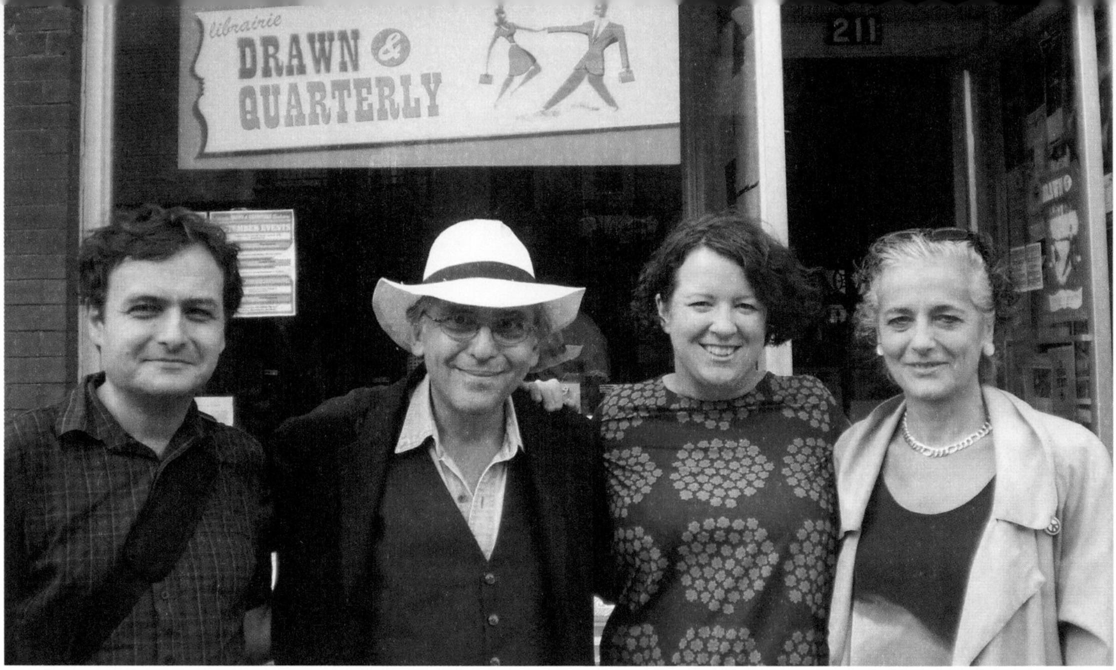
librairie
DRAWN & QUARTERLY
211

office digs, as well. But in early 2007, after successfully moving day-to-day operations to a larger location, D+Q found the right retail space in the newly redeveloping Mile End neighbourhood: 211 Bernard Street West. The new bookstore, which featured a wide selection of French and English prose books and comics, quickly became a hub for literary Montreal. Over the years, authors ranging from Margaret Atwood and Alison Bechdel to Neil Gaiman and Art Spiegelman have launched their work at Librairie D+Q events.

"The most fun we had as a team was opening the store," Burns recalls. "Everyone told us we were crazy—even a person on our staff told us we were crazy—but we knew it would work. We figured we could open a store and just order for ourselves the books that weren't sold in Montreal. So it wasn't even about D+Q—we wanted to be able to buy the McSweeney's, New Directions, Fantagraphics books. Pragmatically, owning a store has been one of the best lessons in publishing. I feel like all retailers should publish a book and all publishers should open a shop."

Another way that D+Q started to branch out, mid-decade, was by releasing books from beyond the reach of typical comic-book publishing. When the publisher debuted the Petits Livres imprint in 2005, the non-linear and purely visual aspects of cartoon art would often get eclipsed thanks to the increased visibility of graphic novels and the lengthy literary stories they could tell. But many cartoonists chose to reject narrative and looked to the gallery world to express themselves, while more and more fine artists, especially in Canada, were making use of cartoon-inspired line art and figuration in their work. Petits Livres would provide a home for this kind of uncategorizable comic/art hybrid. The line launched with D+Q stalwarts Julie Doucet and Marc Bell offering up something unfamiliar to comic-book readers in their books *Lady Pep* and *The Stacks*, respectively—gorgeous but free-form monographs, full of collages and mad doodling. The Petits Livres have proved expansive enough to welcome everything from virtuosic sketchbooks (like Jillian Tamaki's *Indoor Voice*) to vibrant and abstract

novel classic *Hicksville*, which in all editions has had four printings. Librairie D+Q hosts a double launch for Leanne Shapton's *Native Trees of Canada* and Sheila Heti's *How Should a Person Be? Native Trees of Canada* will be D+Q's most successful Petit Livre ever and have four printings.

November 2010

Chris Ware's *ACME Novelty Library* vol. 20 is published, the first *ACME* volume published by D+Q. D+Q publishes *Picture This*, Lynda Barry's follow-up to *What It Is*. Lynda is profiled in the *New York Times Magazine* and the book debuts on the *New York Times* bestseller list.

December 2010

Librairie D+Q hosts a launch for Pascal Girard's *Bigfoot*.

January 2011

Lynda Barry visits Montreal for her Librairie D+Q event at the Ukrainian Federation. Six hundred people attend.

February 2011

D+Q publishes *Scenes from an Impending Marriage* by Adrian Tomine, which debuts on the *New York Times* bestseller list.

March 2011

Librairie D+Q hosts a double launch for Pascal Girard's *Reunion* and Joe Ollmann's *Mid-Life*.

 Chris Oliveros, Art Spiegelman, Peggy Burns & Françoise Mouly outside Librairie D+Q (2011).

Chris Ware, Adrian Tomine & Seth at Toronto Comic Arts Festival (2011).

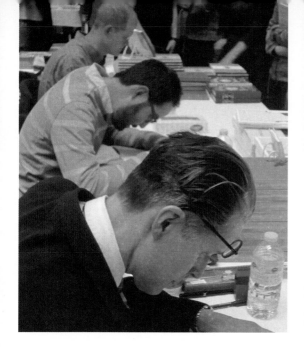

Although I was late to the comics party, when I rediscovered them, I started going to my local comic store, the Beguiling, regularly. My collection began with a number of books published by Drawn & Quarterly. The books and artists I encountered were a wonderful source of inspiration. Pascal made me cry, Lynda gave me permission to be a child again, Adrian and Seth made me see the beauty in being ultra-tidy, Katie made me chuckle, Marc fascinated me, Anders challenged me, and John P. made me appreciate life with all of its warts. I guffawed at Lisa's work and revelled in Brecht's watercolours, and my heart broke for Geneviève.

Over the past few years, I have been fortunate to meet all of these artists in person.

If reading provides a universal escape, then D+Q has been a good companion in my travels.

—Annie Koyama, publisher, Koyama Press

April 2011
D+Q publishes its first book by the acclaimed Japanese cartoonist Shigeru Mizuki, *Onward Towards Our Noble Deaths*, which will win an Eisner. It will be the company's first of many books by the *manga-ka*. D+Q receives a company record eleven Eisner nominations for books by Lynda Barry, Daniel Clowes, James Sturm, John Stanley, Chris Ware, and Brecht Evens. Librairie D+Q hosts Ben Katchor, who is on tour for *The Cardboard Valise*.

May 2011
Paying for It, Chester Brown's memoir of being a john, is published

in two colours. After every answer, I noticed that Adrian, who'd quietly been signing copies of his book, would raise an eyebrow and peer over. Other times, Seth would say something and Adrian would snicker and shake his head. I was confused and found myself hoping that Adrian wasn't a horrible person. It would ruin my life all over again. When I got to the front of the line, Adrian was signing my book and Seth was fielding a question from a fan, something like, "Was it strange to come into contact with Kalo's family? Was it odd for them?" Seth was about to answer when Adrian rolled his eyes, crossed his arms and said kind of loudly, "Oh, YEAH was it WEIRD for them? Tell her how ODD it was for you to meet his FAMILY." Seth shot him a cold and dirty look. Eye-dagger dirty. I had no idea what was going on. An awkward tension locked in for a second, then dissipated, and everyone went back to what they were doing.

I got my books signed and handed them both copies of the comic I'd made, and they traded me the photocopied sketchbook zine they'd brought along. Adrian complimented my lettering and I got a really encouraging postcard from Seth about my work in the mail about a month later. After the signing, they ended up going to dinner with a group of their New York friends and were nice enough to invite me along. Everyone was insanely civil, and it made me like those guys more than I already did. I chalked the earlier face-off up to two fairly introverted people being forced to travel together and interact with large groups of strangers nightly. It would get on my nerves. It *gets* on my nerves.

I don't remember how long after that Seth revealed that *It's a Good Life* wasn't an autobiography. I remember first feeling let down, then being impressed, thinking it was a great stunt to pull. I thought back to what had happened at the signing and wondered what it must have been like doing a book tour with a guy who was openly and audibly threatening to blow your cover. At least I hope that's what was happening, because I think it's pretty punk rock on both ends, and pretty funny.

—Tunde Adebimpe, lead singer, TV on the Radio

In the beginning it was just the Chief. You drew a comic book and sent in the pages, and the Chief phoned you up and gave you feedback. Here is the feedback he gave: "Thanks, it arrived."

That was it. No "I loved it" or "Looks beautiful" or even "I didn't care for it". Just, "Thanks, got it."

The other D+Q cartoonists and I used to joke about this rudimentary feedback. It was kind of a running gag amongst us. Sometimes we even imitated his voice when we repeated that line.

The funny thing is, I liked that system. I was used to the autonomy given me. Oliveros published me because he liked my work and trusted me to find my own way. I doubt he liked everything I produced, but he had faith in me that good work would result. This trust was tremendously important to me and gave me the confidence to become "my own man" as an artist. I've never underestimated that support or taken it for granted. Thank you, Chief.

I also thought that system would never change. I figured if the company endured, then I would be working with the Chief, issue by issue, until I was old and feeble.

So, naturally, I was taken aback when one day it became apparent to me (no one ever told me anything) that the Chief simply never called anymore, and now it was Tom Devlin who was saying, "Yup, the artwork arrived." I can't put my finger on exactly when it happened but a transition occurred, and now Tom was "handling" me. I wasn't sure I liked the idea at first. I was used to the Chief and while I knew Tom as a friend I kind of felt I had been shuffled to the side or something. I missed the Chief.

I must say, though, for a person who doesn't like change, I got used to this transition quickly. Tom was so easygoing, so willing to help me get things done in this new computer age (of which I knew nothing), and so supportive that I rolled with the changes. I liked working with Tom. When I did *George Sprott* for the *New York Times*, he handled all my production work. How could I have done it without him? I developed a real loyalty to him. I mean, he really went the distance for me. He was scanning my overlays for the last installment of *Sprott*, for

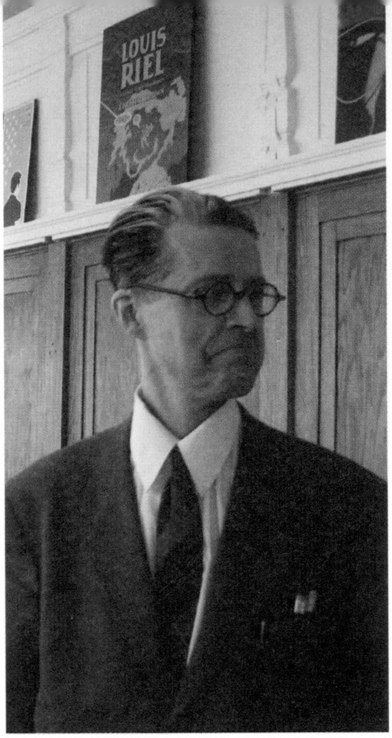
LOUIS
RIEL

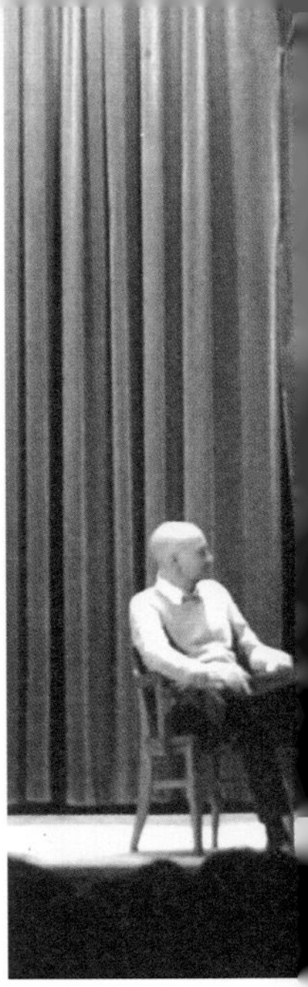

paintings of leaves (Leanne Shapton's *The Native Trees of Canada*), while still making room for traditional comics, as well—though Pascal Girard's regretful and impressionistic *Nicolas*, Matt Forsythe's wordless romp *Ojingogo*, and Anders Nilsen's diaristic, scrapbook-y heartbreaker *Don't Go Where I Can't Follow* are hardly typical graphic-novel fare.

Petits Livres artists like Girard and Tamaki would later make books for the core D+Q line as well, but the imprint's clear purpose and character helped encourage other new and diverse directions for the company. Of course, after D+Q had capably published "petits" art books, large coffee-table tomes like Bell's *Hot Potatoe* (a glorious goof on the genre) or Art Spiegelman's *Co-Mix* (a true career retrospective) were only logical developments. But it was perhaps a less obvious move to make forays into children's publishing or the world of fashion and lifestyle journals. Nevertheless, in 2009 the publisher launched D+Q Enfant, a series of children's books whose compact design, girl-friendly narratives, and recognizable stars from kid-lit classics (Moomin!

and will be D+Q's first book to be reviewed twice in the *New York Times*, first by critic Dwight Garner and second by sex activist Annie Sprinkle. It will land on the *New York Times* bestseller list and will go on to have over thirty thousand units in print. Chester Brown visits Montreal for his standing-room-only Librairie D+Q event. With Chris Oliveros, John Porcellino, and Tom Devlin, he travels to his hometown of Chateauguay, QC, and revisits key sites from his graphic novel *The Playboy*. The film *Tatsumi*, based on *A Drifting Life*, premieres at the Cannes Film Festival.

Seth and Daniel Clowes visit Montreal while on tour for their books *The*

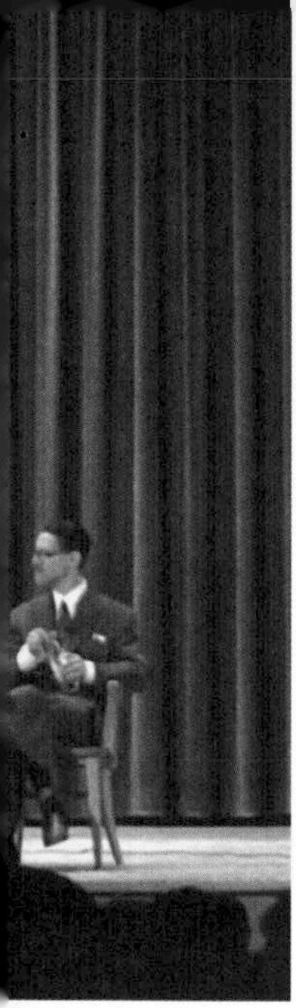

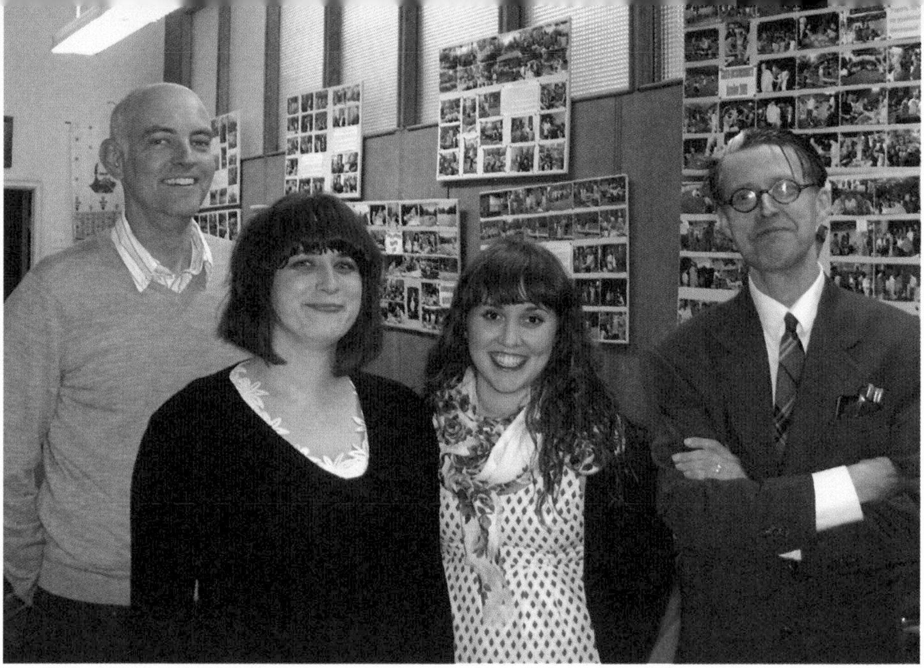

Pippi!) all help to keep D+Q's offerings afloat in the unnavigable sea of children's bookselling. And with the collected editions of the teen-powered feminist online magazine *Rookie*, and the stylish and smart indie-fashion journal *WORN*, D+Q devoted its talents for publication design to entirely new and more inventive ends.

But for all this experimentation around D+Q's perimeters, the company was diversifying its central line of comics, too. The vintage and provenance of D+Q's comics began to vary, as well, casting away from cartooning that's anchored solely in the here and now. For one, with the launch of Frank King's *Walt & Skeezix* series in 2004, D+Q started delving into comics history. As with the graphic novels they published, D+Q brought to comics reprints their own distinct sensibility by carefully linking older works to current artists so that reprinting doesn't seem like an exercise in mere nostalgia or an antiquarian indulgence. The *Walt & Skeezix* books are lovingly designed by Chris Ware, an artist much influenced by Frank King. A similar pairing of older artists with their contemporary counterparts can be seen in the reprints of Yoshihiro Tatsumi's groundbreaking manga (designed by Adrian Tomine), Doug Wright's classic Canadiana strip *Nipper*, and the John Stanley Library (both designed by Seth). In all these cases, old work is carefully recontextualized so that it speaks to contemporary concerns.

The Tatsumi series, which debuted with *The Push Man and Other Stories* in 2005, was especially important in initiating D+Q's efforts to translate key authors from the vast world of Japanese cartooning. While Japanese comics, or manga, aimed at children and teenagers have seen huge commercial success in the West, manga that deals with mature themes is much less likely to be translated. Tatsumi invented the term *gekiga* ("dramatic pictures") to describe these moody, adult-oriented comics that he and his colleagues were publishing throughout the sixties, in the hopes of differentiating such serious work from the frivolous kids' comics people thought of as manga. In the wake of Tatsumi's

June 2011
Shigeru Mizuki conducts a rare interview with PRI's *The World*.

August 2011
Anders Nilsen's collected *Big Questions* is published and becomes a *New York Times* Notable Book, winning the Lynd Ward Graphic Novel Prize and the Ignatz Award.

September 2011
Hark! A Vagrant, Kate Beaton's first book with D+Q, is published; it will spend five months on the *New York Times* bestseller list. It will have sixty-five thousand units in print and will win Harvey, Doug Wright, and Ignatz awards. D+Q publishes Brian Ralph's art-house zombie classic *Daybreak*, which debuts on the *New York Times* bestseller list. D+Q publishes Adrian Tomine's *Optic Nerve* no. 12. Librairie D+Q hosts launches for Anders Nilsen's *Big Questions* and Craig Thompson's *Habibi* in the same week.

October 2011
Art Spiegelman visits Montreal for an event cohosted by the Librairie D+Q and SBC Gallery. D+Q publishes *The Death-Ray*, which debuts on the *New York Times* bestseller list. Daniel Clowes and Seth go on tour together for *The Death-Ray* and *The Great Northern Brotherhood*

Great Northern Brotherhood of Canadian Cartoonists and *The Death-Ray*. (Right) Daniel Clowes, Jessica Campbell, Tracy Hurren & Seth (2011).

goodness' sake, while his child was being born in the hospital.

And then one day, I realized that Rebecca Rosen was taking my calls and emails (I had a computer now). Somehow another transition had occurred without anyone ever telling me. What had I done this time? In retrospect, those years with Tom and the Chief seem like ancient history now. The modern era of D+Q feels like it came about for me with Rebecca. Somehow it feels like we worked together a very long time—though it couldn't have been that terribly long. I adored working with her and came to rely on her expertise. When the time came for her to leave, I didn't think I would be able to get used to anyone else. She was like a third hand for me. No one could replace her. I was sure of it.

And then came Tracy. Beloved Tracy Hurren. I've already used up so many of the appropriate superlatives with her predecessors that it will appear I am repeating myself with Tracy. I'd hate to give a weak impression by merely complimenting her professionalism or her skill or her patience. Tracy is something else to me. She's more than a third hand, even. More a second brain. Or perhaps some image less disturbing.

I cannot praise her enough. Her calm patience with my foolish, ancient production methods (and with me) has allowed me to exist in the twenty-first century. She's really the only person in the world I fully trust to handle my artwork—to deeply understand what I want done and to present me with the options I desire without even asking for them. To make my work look better than it would if it were left only to my decisions. Perhaps the only person I really consider a collaborator—because I generally dislike collaborating. She also knows not to phone me (because I hate talking on the phone). I never had to tell her this, either. She has very good radar. And she is a very lovely individual. Easy to like. Whenever we meet in person, we share an awkward hug. I don't generally hug people. When I hug Tracy it means "thank you."

—Seth, D+Q cartoonist and dear friend

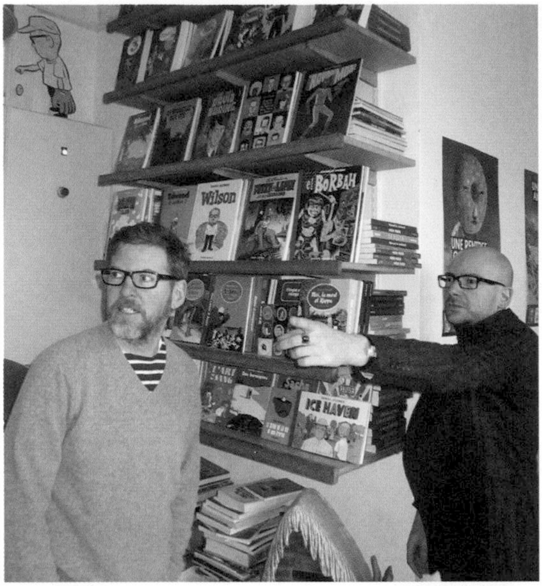

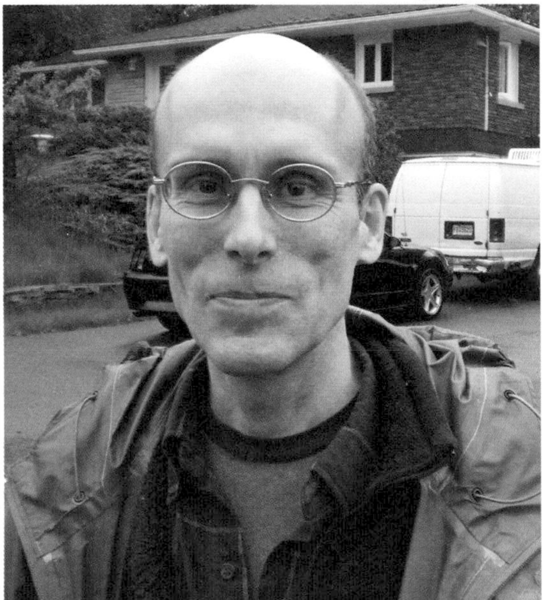

(Top) Tom Devlin & Jean-Louis Gauthey in the Cornélius offices, Paris. (Bottom) Chester Brown in front of his childhood home in Chateauguay, QC (2011)

of *Canadian Cartoonists*. For their stop in Montreal, the Librairie D+Q hosts over four hundred people. Librairie D+Q hosts a launch for Adrian Norvid's *Nogoodniks*.

November 2011

Librairie D+Q hosts a standing-room-only event for Kate Beaton. Chester Brown's *Louis Riel* makes it to the top ten in CBC's Canada Reads shortlist. D+Q publishes the first book, *Blabber Blabber Blabber*, in Lynda Barry's Everything series. On its release date, the *New York Times* profiles her. Seth accepts the success with English-language audiences—especially *A Drifting Life*, his autobiographical account of struggling in postwar Japan and breaking into the manga industry—D+Q has done more than any other publisher to increase the visibility of gekiga abroad and help preserve the legacy and vitality of that movement.

Crucially, D+Q has translated many of the authors who published in the heyday of *Garo*—a magazine as important to comics as *RAW*, and the main venue for boundary-pushing manga throughout the sixties and seventies. Rectifying long decades of neglect, D+Q finally published such works as Seiichi Hayashi's 1971 *Red Colored Elegy*, an aching and lyrical masterpiece of comics poetry, as well as Oji Suzuki's *A Single Match* and Tadao Tsuge's *Trash Market*, landmark collections of dreamlike and harshly realist stories, respectively. D+Q's dedication to the work of Japanese national treasure Shigeru Mizuki, in particular, has resulted in a shelf's worth of his books being translated. These include a massive retelling of his country's turbulent twentieth-century history, the Showa series, as well as his signature *Kitaro* stories, in which the cartoonist's renowned fascination with Japan's folktale monsters and spirits, the *yōkai*, is on full display.

While D+Q has helped shine new light on many older comics in recent years, the company has also brought the work of many women cartoonists back into the spotlight. Just as Tove Jansson's *Moomin* comics had gone unremarked for so long before D+Q's reprints, so too had the history of cartooning overlooked the efforts of other women artists who had never enjoyed the good fortune of having their own alternative comic-book series or golden-age newspaper strip, and so had been left off the male-dominated lists of the usual cartooning greats. But authors like Mimi Pond (*Over Easy*) and Lynda Barry (*The Freddie Stories*) had had long careers cartooning for magazines or alternative newspapers, and an artist like Sylvie Rancourt (*Melody*) had been a pioneering self-publisher and memoirist, while still others like Miriam Katin (*Letting It Go*) and Diane Obomsawin (*On Loving Women*) had excelled in

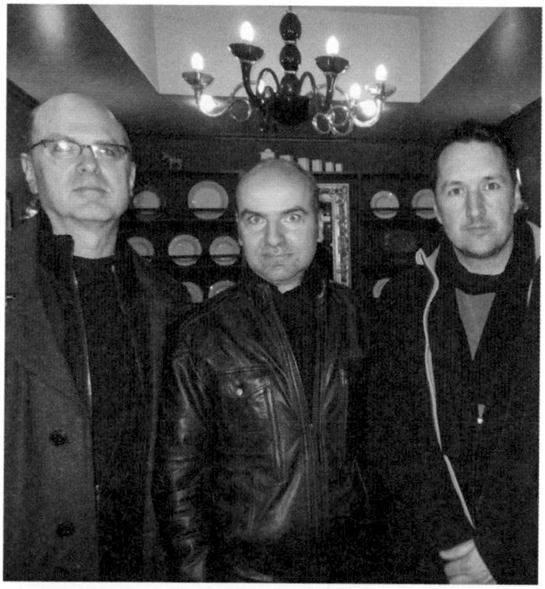

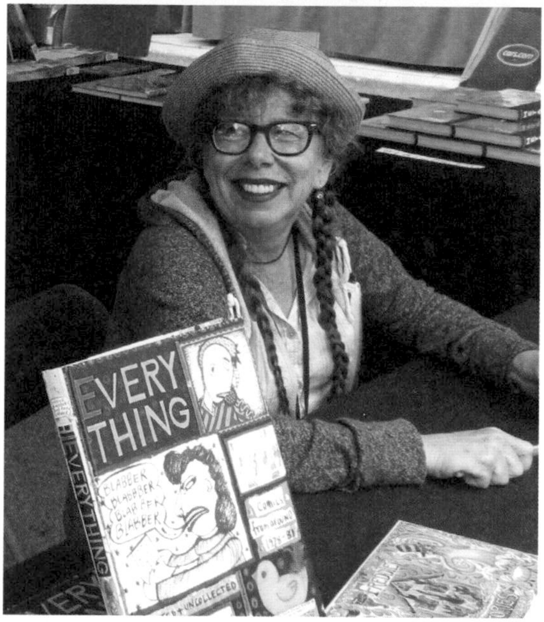
EVERY THING

Harbourfront Prize from the prestigious International Festival of Authors. Librairie D+Q hosts an event for six hundred people at the Ukrainian Federation for Miranda July.

December 2011
D+Q announces digital strategy and releases its first ebook, Chester Brown's *Louis Riel*. *Time* magazine selects *Hark! A Vagrant* and *The Death-Ray* for its top ten books of the year list.

January 2012
Guy Delisle wins the Fauve d'Or at the Angoulême International Comics Festival for the French edition of *Jerusalem*. The English edition will come out in May, supported by Delisle's first North American tour. *Jerusalem* will debut at number one on the *New York Times* bestseller list.

February 2012
Goliath, Tom Gauld's first book with D+Q, is published. Chris Oliveros is a special guest at Comic Con India along with R. Crumb, Aline Kominsky-Crumb, and Gary Groth. Librairie D+Q launches *Jinchalo* by Matt Forsythe.

May 2012
Librairie D+Q hosts Tom Gauld for *Goliath*. The *Montreal Mirror* votes Librairie D+Q the best comics shop in Montreal. Librairie D+Q hosts R. Sikoryak's

(Top) Charles Burns, Lewis Trondheim & Guy Delisle in Angoulême (2012). (Bottom) Lynda Barry at Chicago Printers Row (2013).

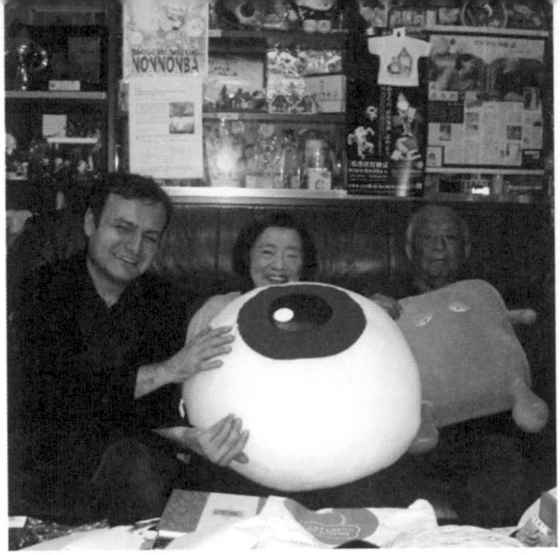

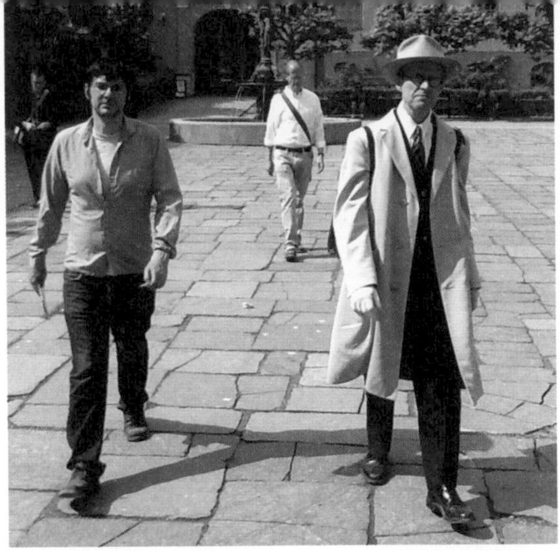

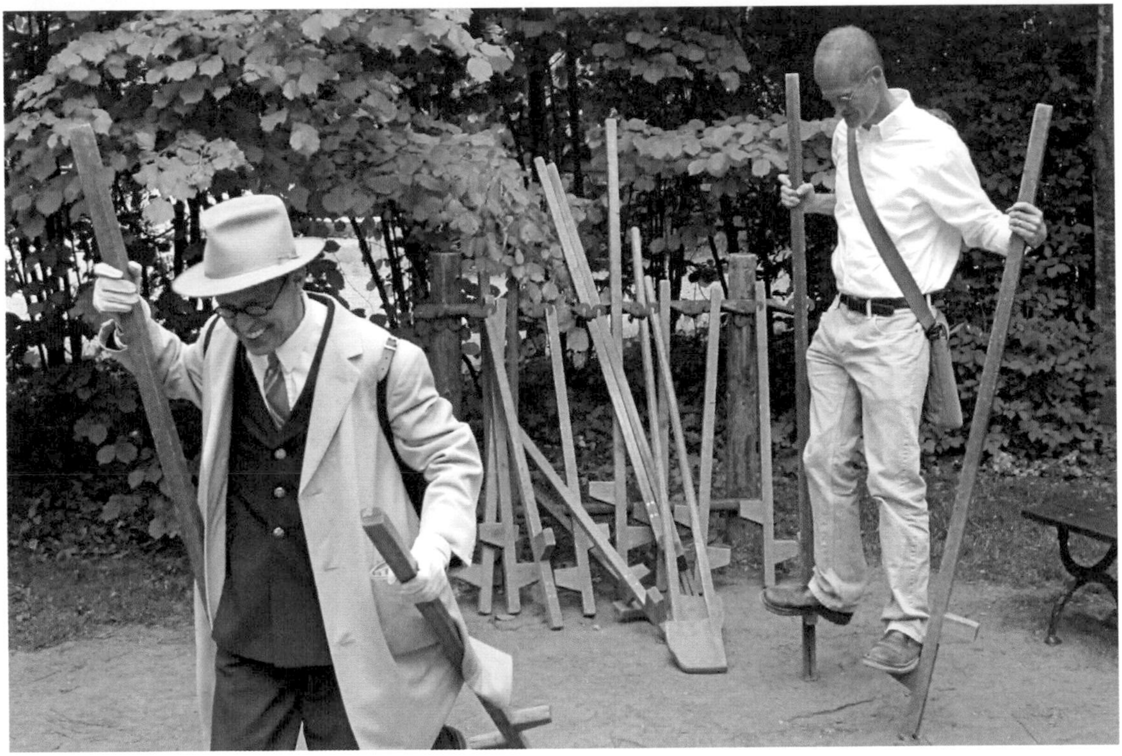

Carousel with Joe Ollmann, Julie Delporte, Howard Chackowitz, Billy Mavreas, and Pascal Girard. Librairie D+Q hosts a launch for Amber Albrecht's *Idyll*.

June 2012

The Oslo Comics Expo celebrates Canadian comics and hosts Marc Bell, Tom Devlin, Pascal Girard, Seth, Jillian Tamaki, and Chris Ware as special guests.

July 2012

Librairie D+Q hosts Guy Delisle for *Jerusalem*.

September 2012

D+Q publishes forty thousand units of *Rookie Yearbook One*, edited by sixteen-year-old Tavi Gevinson, who appears on Jimmy Fallon and Stephen Colbert in support of the book. Librairie D+Q hosts David Byrne and Win Butler in conversation in front of six hundred people at the Ukrainian Federation.

October 2012

D+Q publishes Adrian Tomine's *New York Drawings*, a collection of his *New Yorker* magazine covers; the book debuts on the *New York Times* bestseller list. D+Q publishes original mid-century Pippi Longstocking comics written by Astrid Lindgren and drawn

 (Left) Chris Oliveros, Nunoe Mura & Shigeru Mizuki in Japan (2012). (Right & bottom) Pascal Girard, Marc Bell, Chris Ware & Seth in Oslo (2012).

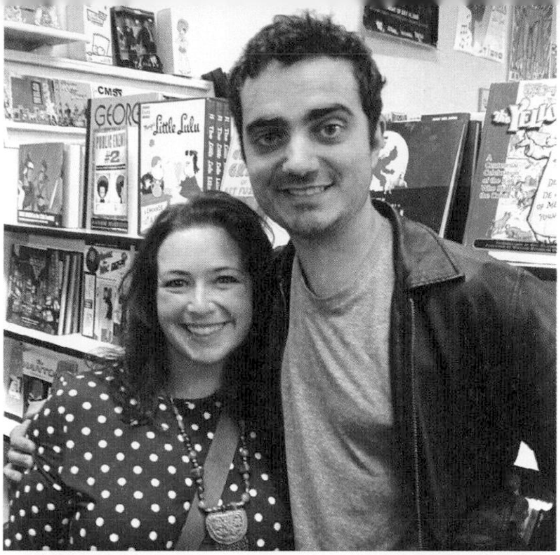
Little Lulu

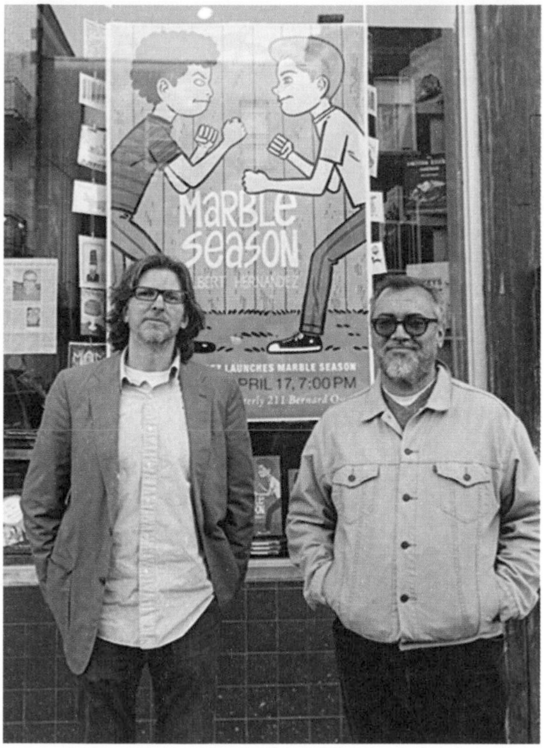
MaRBLE
SeaSON

professions like illustration and animation before thinking the world of graphic novels at all worth exploring.

The case of Lynda Barry is in many ways exemplary of this cohort's struggles. Barry had been a crucial part of art comics going back to the early 1980s, yet by 2006 her career was in trouble: the staple of her income was her weekly strip, syndicated in alternative weeklies, but that market was drying up. Her cartoon books had sold well in the past but were now out of print. What's worse, her new efforts were meeting with resistance from her publisher, a conventional press who could understand neither her darkly comedic graphic novel, *The Freddie Stories*, nor her deeply personal "autobifictionalography," *One! Hundred! Demons!* Both titles—and much more from Barry, including her funky, genre-defying "how-to" manuals—have since been welcomed into the D+Q fold.

"I don't know what I would have done if it wasn't for [Drawn & Quarterly]," Barry told an interviewer in 2012. "After I did *One! Hundred! Demons!* in 2002, I couldn't find a publisher. Nobody would touch my work. It was over! That's when I started to sell stuff on eBay. The comic strip market head was gone, and nobody would publish my work. So there's no place to publish my work—what happens to the work? Nothing. That's when I felt really—that's [when] it's like being a kid again. Because otherwise I'll only write a book if I know where it's supposed to go. Or that it has this place to go. And when I started making the collages for *What It Is*, I mean, I didn't know what they were, or what they were going to become...[*What It Is* and *Picture This*] would not exist without Drawn & Quarterly."

While providing a home for both veteran cartoonists and late-career first-timers, D+Q has made room in the new decade for the latest breed of irreverent Young Turks, as well. Rather than coming up exclusively in the comic-book world, like that first generation of D+Q artists, the new crop of artists has succeeded in the online economy of LOLing and Likes or used their peculiar perspectives and fully formed styles to break into the world of mass-market publications like *Vanity Fair*, the *Guardian*, and the *New*

by Ingrid Vang Nyman. As with *Moomin*, this is the first time the comics have been published outside of Scandinavia. Librairie D+Q hosts Chris Kraus for *Summer of Hate.*

November 2012

Librairie D+Q celebrates its fifth anniversary with a sold-out event featuring Chris Ware, Adrian Tomine, and Charles Burns. Chris Oliveros travels to the Kaigai Manga Festa in Tokyo, where he visits Yoshihiro Tatsumi and meets Shigeru Mizuki. Librairie D+Q hosts a launch for Julie Morstad's *The Wayside* and Anouk Ricard for *Anna & Froga.*

February 2013

D+Q acquires rights to Lynda Barry's classic backlist title *The Freddie Stories* and publishes it in an all-new hardcover format; it lands on the *New York Times* bestseller list. Librairie D+Q launches Geneviève Castrée's *Susceptible.*

April 2013

Librairie D+Q hosts Alison Bechdel at the Ukrainian Federation. *Marble Season*, Gilbert Hernandez's first book with D+Q, is published and lands on the *New York Times* bestseller list. Gilbert will win the PEN USA Award. Librairie D+Q hosts Gilbert Hernandez.

(Top) Vanessa Davis & Matt Forsythe in LA at Meltdown Comics (2012). (Bottom) Tom Devlin & Gilbert Hernandez in Montreal (2013).

D+Q publishes one of Japan's most famous characters with *Kitaro* by Shigeru Mizuki. The Montreal literary festival Blue Metropolis hosts Miriam Katin for her book *Letting It Go*.

May 2013

D+Q publishes Rutu Modan's second graphic novel, *The Property*, which goes on to win the Prix du Jury at the Angoulême festival and an Eisner Award. Librairie D+Q hosts Lisa Hanawalt and Michael Kupperman. Lisa's book *My Dirty Dumb Eyes* will have two printings and she will be the only D+Q cartoonist nominated for a James Beard Award.

June 2013

Tavi Gevinson spends a week in the D+Q office to work side by side with designer Tracy Hurren on *Rookie Yearbook Two*. Tom mystifyingly deejays an entire four-hour set of two-tone-era ska. Librairie D+Q is voted best bookstore and best comic shop by the weekly *Cult Mtl*.

August 2013

Adrian Tomine is invited to the White House for a luncheon honouring the White House Historical Association and American art. He meets Michelle Obama. Librairie D+Q hosts Neil

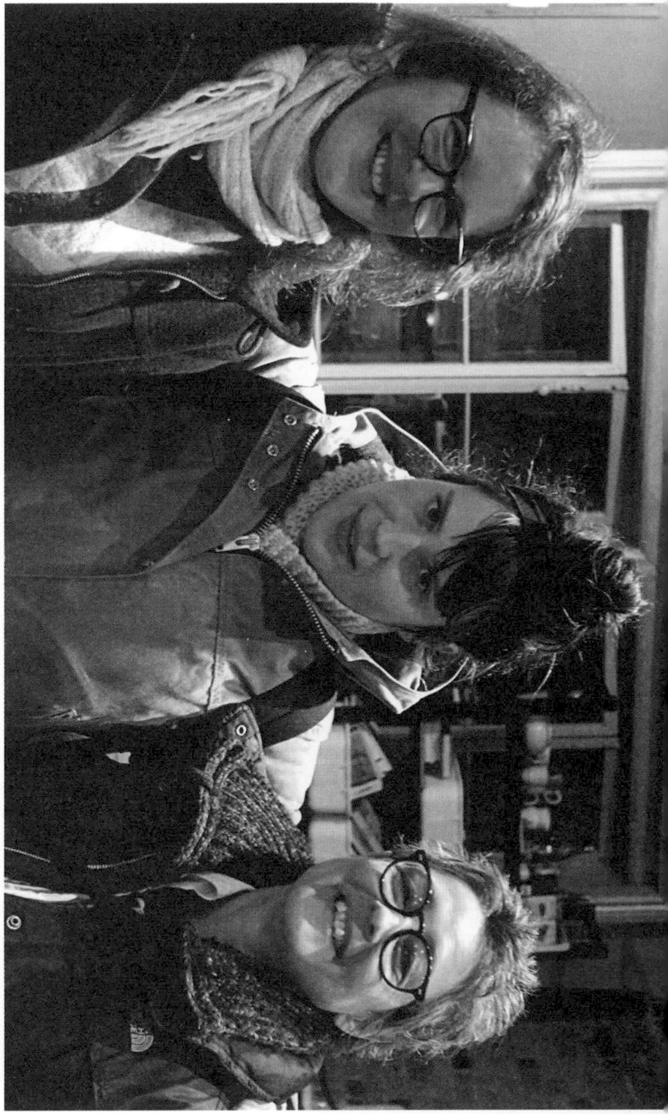

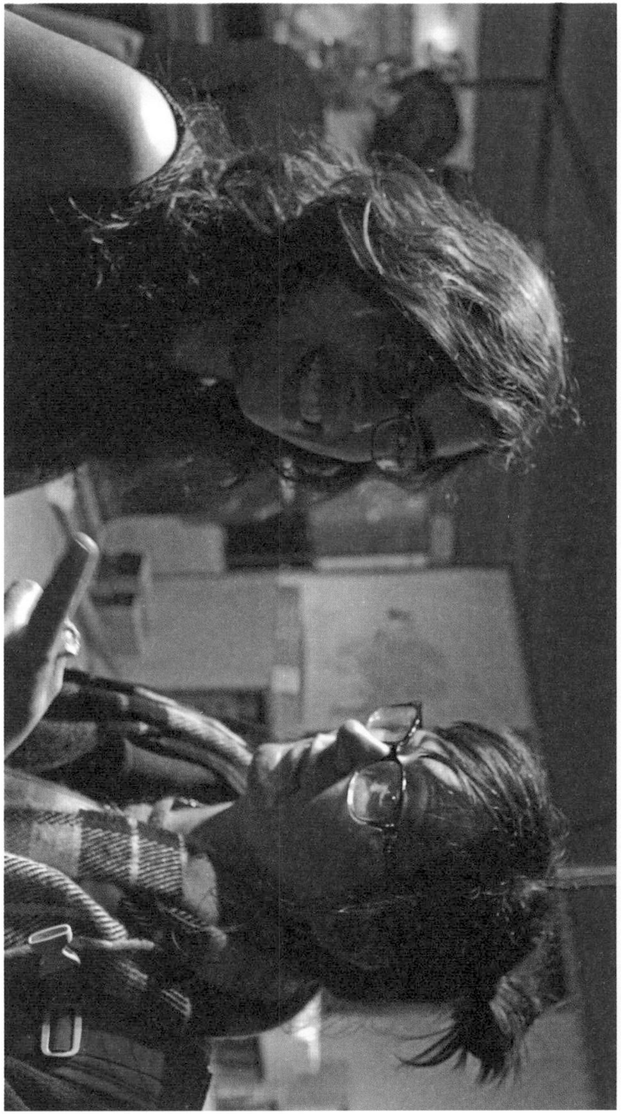

 (Top) Julie Doucet, Geneviève Castrée & Diane Obomsawin at Librairie D+Q (2013). (Bottom) Julia Pohl-Miranda & Anouk Ricard in Angoulême (2013).

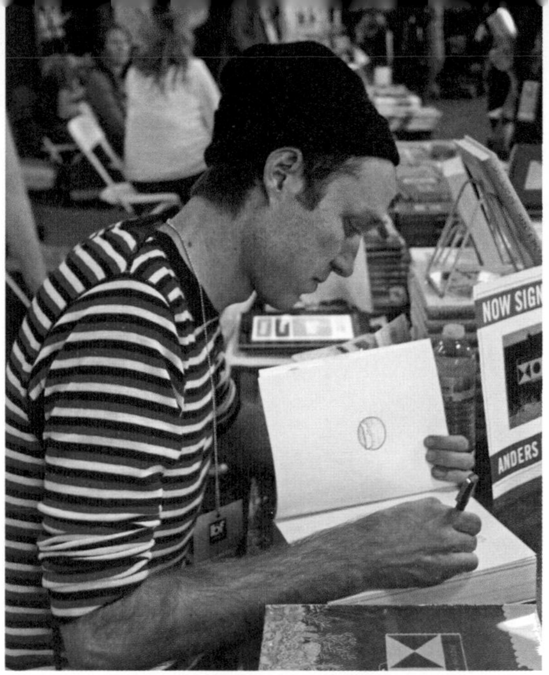

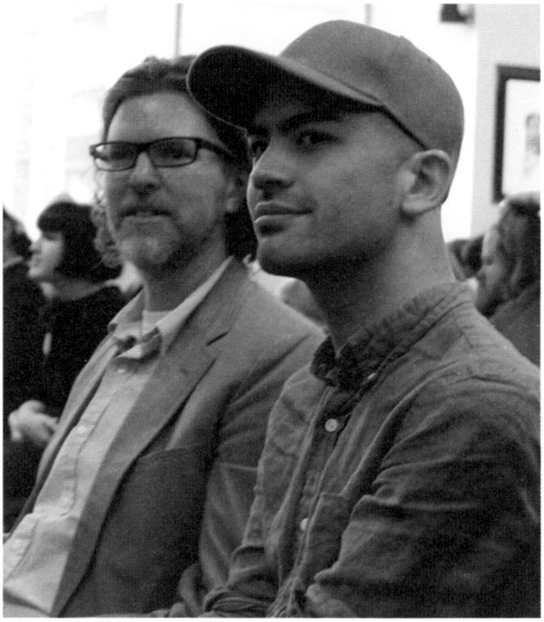

Prose can do a funny and familiar trick. When you're reading a good prose book the book itself ceases to exist, the words you are looking at cease to exist, and you are there on the bright cliffs or reaching out to touch a face, or a sword, or another book, which will cease to exist in its own turn when you start to read it. This is nothing new.

Comics don't work like that, which can feel sad, but it's okay, and maybe it's even part of why we love them. The little drawings demand their autonomy. They are not us and we are not them. Each image exists in its own right as its own world that is held delicately on a page, which is next to other pages holding other images that are worlds as distinct from—and as interconnected with—one another as one moment in time is from the next.

It's because of this that we fall in love with and lust for physical comic books in a way we can't with prose books. Loving a book containing prose is like loving a cup filled with a wonderful drink: the cup and drink are only connected by circumstance. Loving a comic book is different. The content and the form of a comic are connected inextricably. The little autonomous drawings are held tightly in the pages of the book the comic is printed in, and they cannot get away. When you hold the comic book, you hold those worlds. They are yours.

Drawn & Quarterly publishes extraordinary comics. And because they are an extraordinary company they know to make extraordinary books for these comics to live in. Each book is lovely and different and it is perfectly suited to its occupant. The satiny cool gloss of *Exit Wounds*, the welcoming textures of the Moomin books, the warmth and solidity of *The Freddie Stories*, the simplicity and balance of *King-Cat Classix*. The comics live inside these books and they are the books, and we love them in the same way we love our friends and family, who are bodies, who are people, who are moments, who are worlds, and who will always be separate and mysterious to us, because they are them, and we are not.

***—Eleanor Davis, cartoonist of* How to Be Happy**

Gaiman with an audience of 750 people.

September 2013

Co-Mix: A Retrospective of Comics, Graphics, and Scraps, Art Spiegelman's first book with D+Q, is published in conjunction with a travelling retrospective that debuts at the Jewish Museum in Manhattan. The book is profiled in the *New York Times* and lands on the *New York Times* bestseller list.

October 2013

Woman Rebel: The Margaret Sanger Story, Peter Bagge's first book with D+Q, is published and will spend several weeks on the *New York Times* bestseller list. It will be nominated for an Eisner and a Washington State Book Award and make the ALA's Best Feminist Books for Young Readers list. *Rookie Yearbook Two* is published with twenty-five thousand units printed. Tom Devlin turns fifty, making him old.

December 2013

Librairie D+Q hosts Margaret Atwood in conversation with Sheila Heti at the Rialto Theatre with an audience of 650 people.

January 2014

Ant Colony, Michael DeForge's first book with D+Q, is

Anders Nilsen at Alternative Press Expo (2013). Tom Devlin & Michael DeForge at Toronto Comic Arts Festival (2014).

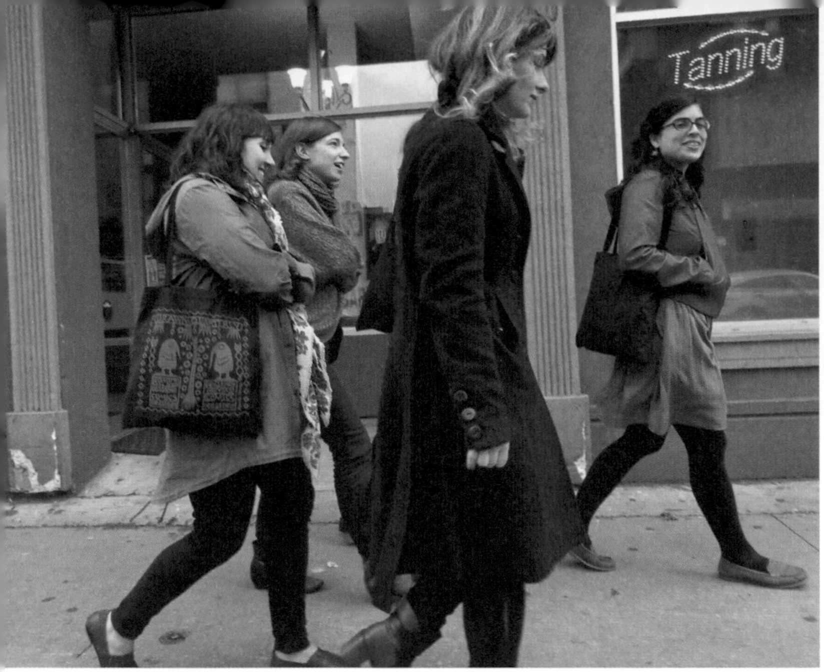
Tanning

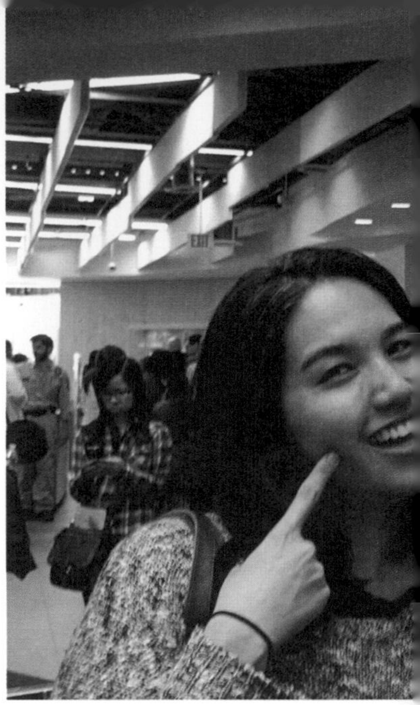

When I worked at McSweeney's, trying (and failing) to figure out how to run a publishing company, I always looked up to D+Q as a beacon of professionalism, a flickering northern light of hope—proof that it's possible to put out great work and still be steady and stable and grown-up. Just good book after good book, with a minimum of fuss or drama. That said, Tom Devlin—a married man and father of children—was forced to sleep on my terrible couch during business trips, so maybe it wasn't always quite as professional as I imagined. Still, though: twenty-five years of classics!

—Eli Horowitz, former publisher of McSweeney's

York Times. Compiled from the pages of such tony venues, *You're All Just Jealous of My Jetpack* features Tom Gauld's smart but silly spoofs of the highbrow book world, while *My Dirty Dumb Eyes* collects Lisa Hanawalt's cockeyed takes on popular culture, from *The Bachelor* to Anna Wintour, along with irresistible drawings of costumed lizards and bare bums. Jillian Tamaki's *SuperMutant Magic Academy* derives from the award-winning illustrator's online homage to the X-Men's soapy teen romances, but it was fellow Canadians Kate Beaton and Michael DeForge who first brought web-based cartooning to D+Q books.

Beaton in particular is an internet success story. Her off-hours doodles, dreamt up while she toiled away in northern Alberta's isolated petrochemical industry, gained her a massive online following—but her work has proven to be far more lasting than the transient debris that litters so much of the web. With the strips on her website *Hark! A Vagrant* (many of which are gathered together in a D+Q book of the same name), the Nova Scotia–born Beaton pioneered a new genre of erudite comics that riff on history and literature. In Beaton's work, we see Jane Austen being harassed to write books about "hunky dreamboats," and a crazy-eyed John Diefenbaker—Canada's thirteenth prime minister—taking all the cabinet positions in his government for himself.

published and debuts on the *New York Times* bestseller list. A second printing is ordered within three months.

February 2014
Librairie D+Q hosts Michael DeForge for *Ant Colony* and Diane Obomsawin for *On Loving Women*. D+Q publishes the English translation of *Beautiful Darkness*, which turns out to be its sleeper hit of 2014.

April 2014
Over Easy, Mimi Pond's memoir of dropping out of art school and working in a diner in the seventies is published and will spend several weeks on the *New York Times* bestseller list. Later Mimi wins the PEN USA Award. A second printing is ordered within four months. D+Q publishes the ebook of the classic Lynda Barry graphic novel *One! Hundred! Demons!*

May 2014
The Stockholm Seriefestival celebrates Canadian comics and invites Kate Beaton, Peggy Burns, Tom Devlin, and Seth as special guests. The Toronto Comic Arts Festival hosts Kate Beaton in conversation with Lynn Johnston of *For Better or For Worse* fame. Librairie D+Q hosts "Secondhand Prom" for *The WORN Archive* at La Sala Rossa.

 (Left) Tracy Hurren, Sarah Glidden, Lisa Hanawalt & Julia Pohl-Miranda at TCAF (2013). (Centre) Jillian Tamaki, Matt Forsythe & Pascal Girard at TCAF (2014).

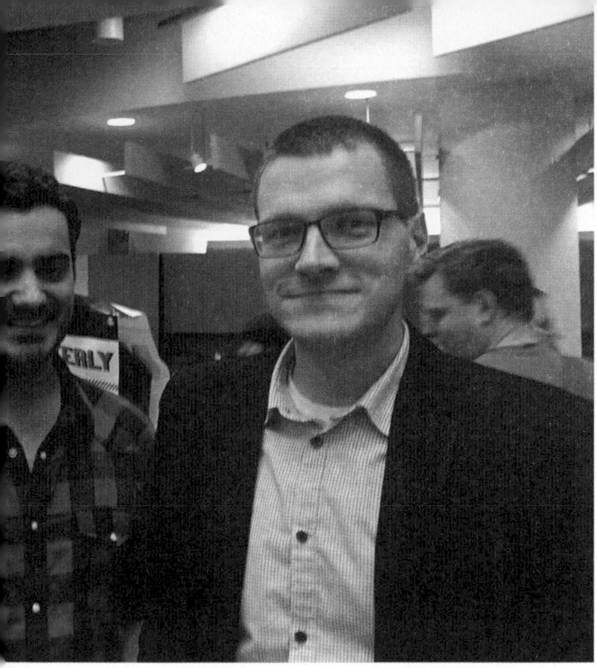

ERLY

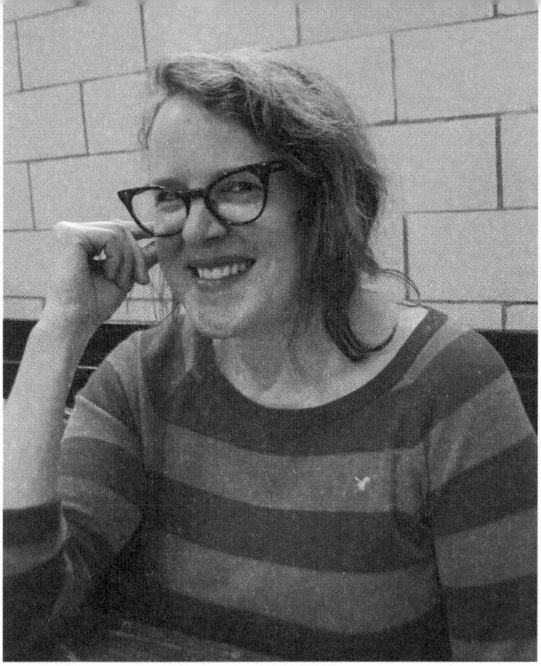

Only slightly more absurd than actual history, Beaton's strips are brought to life by a delightfully free-flowing pen line and an acute gift for caricature.

Along with Beaton, Michael DeForge has emerged as the star Canadian cartoonist of the last decade. His talent for unsettling and disquieting dream imagery calls to mind the early work of Chester Brown. In his first full graphic novel, *Ant Colony*—serialized online before appearing in print from D+Q in 2014—DeForge uses the conventions of anthropomorphism to question humanity's tendency to construct oppressive social systems and rigid gender boundaries. DeForge's ants are all too human in the way they buy into toxic masculinity and consumer culture. In his art, DeForge shows a complete mastery of the language of comics combined with a unique approach to character design and a startling Day-Glo colour scheme that owes much to punk poster art. Still shy of his thirtieth birthday, DeForge shows that the tradition initiated by Brown and other early D+Q artists is still vital and able to inspire new talent.

Beaton, DeForge, Tamaki, and others have helped to keep D+Q connected in the digital era, even while traditionally analogue artists like Lynda Barry and Chester Brown were among the first D+Q authors to have their work published as ebooks. But what's next for the company? Among all these different authors and books and kinds of cartooning, it's as difficult to predict a next step for the publisher as it has been to trace a clear path through Drawn & Quarterly's history.

But such abundant and unpredictable variety is exactly the point: the story of Drawn & Quarterly has always been the story of its artists and the singular visions that they create. It's been that way for the first quarter century of Drawn & Quarterly's existence, and it's sure to be that way for the next twenty-five years, too. Rest assured, Oliveros, Burns, Devlin, and crew are far from crazy, despite Oliveros's worries back in 1990. They've helped Drawn & Quarterly prove beyond a doubt that intelligent comics can "survive and even thrive within our culture."

August 2014
After over a decade in use, the old website is retired. The fourth incarnation of D+Q's website, designed by Tracy Hurren and Tom Devlin, is launched. New website includes a search function!

September 2014
D+Q publishes *The Hospital Suite*, the first all-new John Porcellino book, on the twenty-fifth anniversary of his seminal *King-Cat Comics*. Porcellino embarks on a thirty-one-city North American tour. D+Q publishes its second Gilbert Hernandez book, *Bumperhead*. The National Film Board of Canada releases *Seth's Dominion*, a documentary on Seth, at festivals around Canada.

October 2014
D+Q publishes *Moomin: The Deluxe Anniversary Edition*, collecting all of the Tove Jansson comics.

November 2014
Librairie D+Q hosts Aisha Franz for her book *Earthling*.

December 2014
D+Q graphic novels make forty-three best of 2014 lists.

January 2015
D+Q sends the 776-page book *Drawn & Quarterly: Twenty-Five Years of Contemporary Cartooning, Comics, and Graphic Novels* to press. Somehow.

(Right) Julie Doucet at Comic Arts Brooklyn. Photo: Jody Culkin (2014).

NO PROBLEM

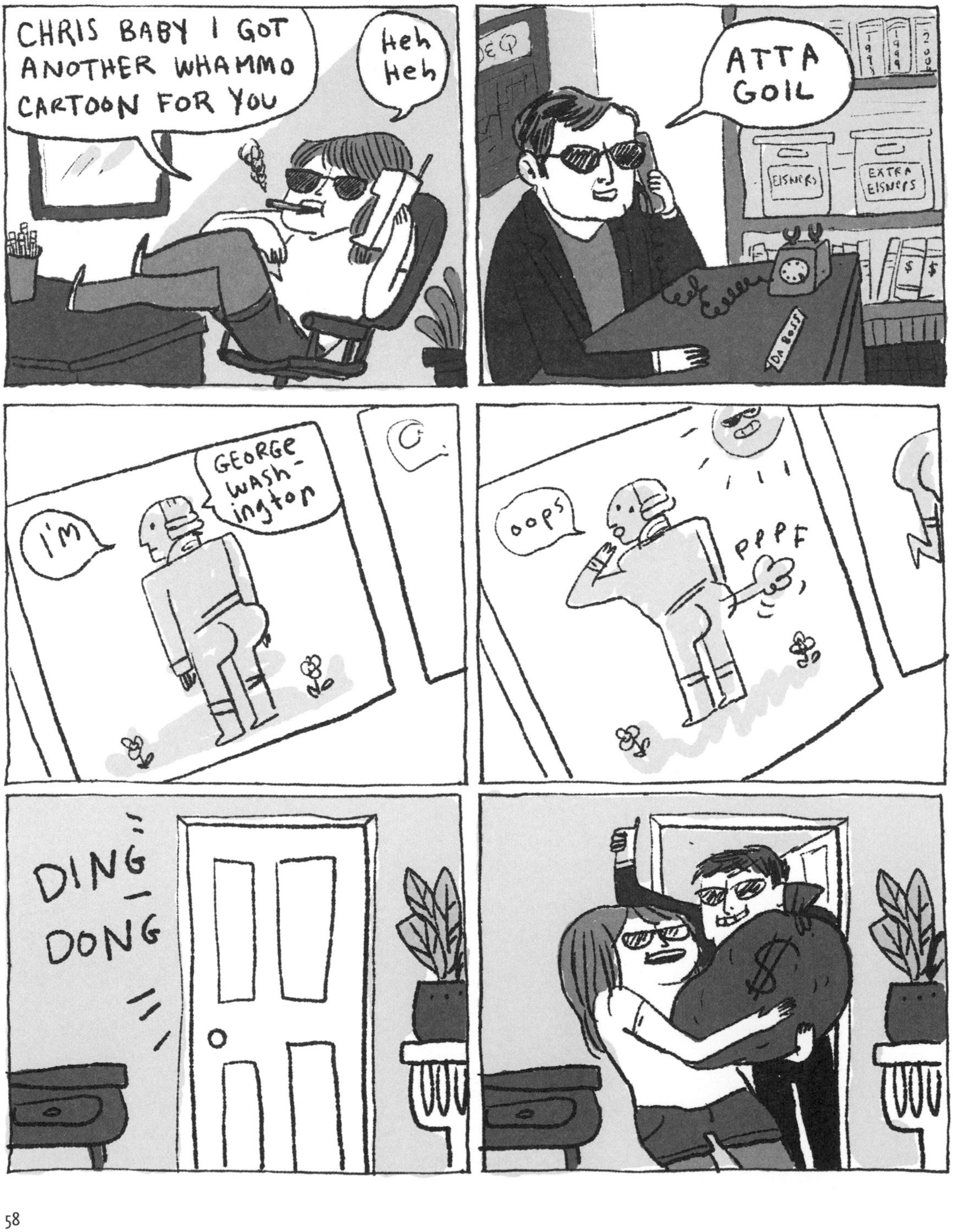
CHRIS BABY I GOT ANOTHER WHAMMO CARTOON FOR YOU
Heh Heh
ATTA GOIL
EISNERS
EXTRA EISNERS
DA BOSS
I'M
GEORGE WASH-ington
oops
PPPF
DING DONG

JUST KIDDING

SO YOU'RE INTERESTED IN PUBLISHING A BOOK
A BOOK. YES. I DON'T KNOW. YES.
OR NOT
YES?
I WANT TO...
COMICS
JESUS TAKE THE WHEEL

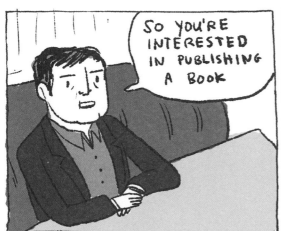

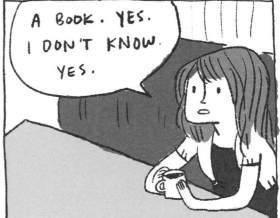

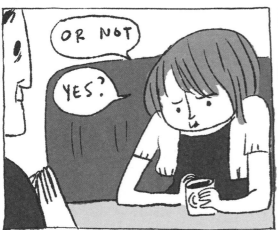

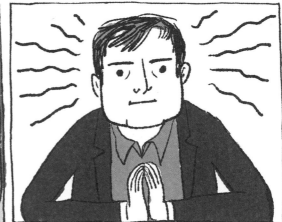

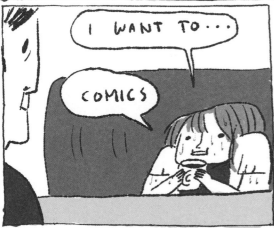

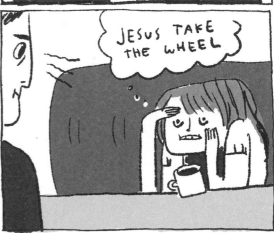

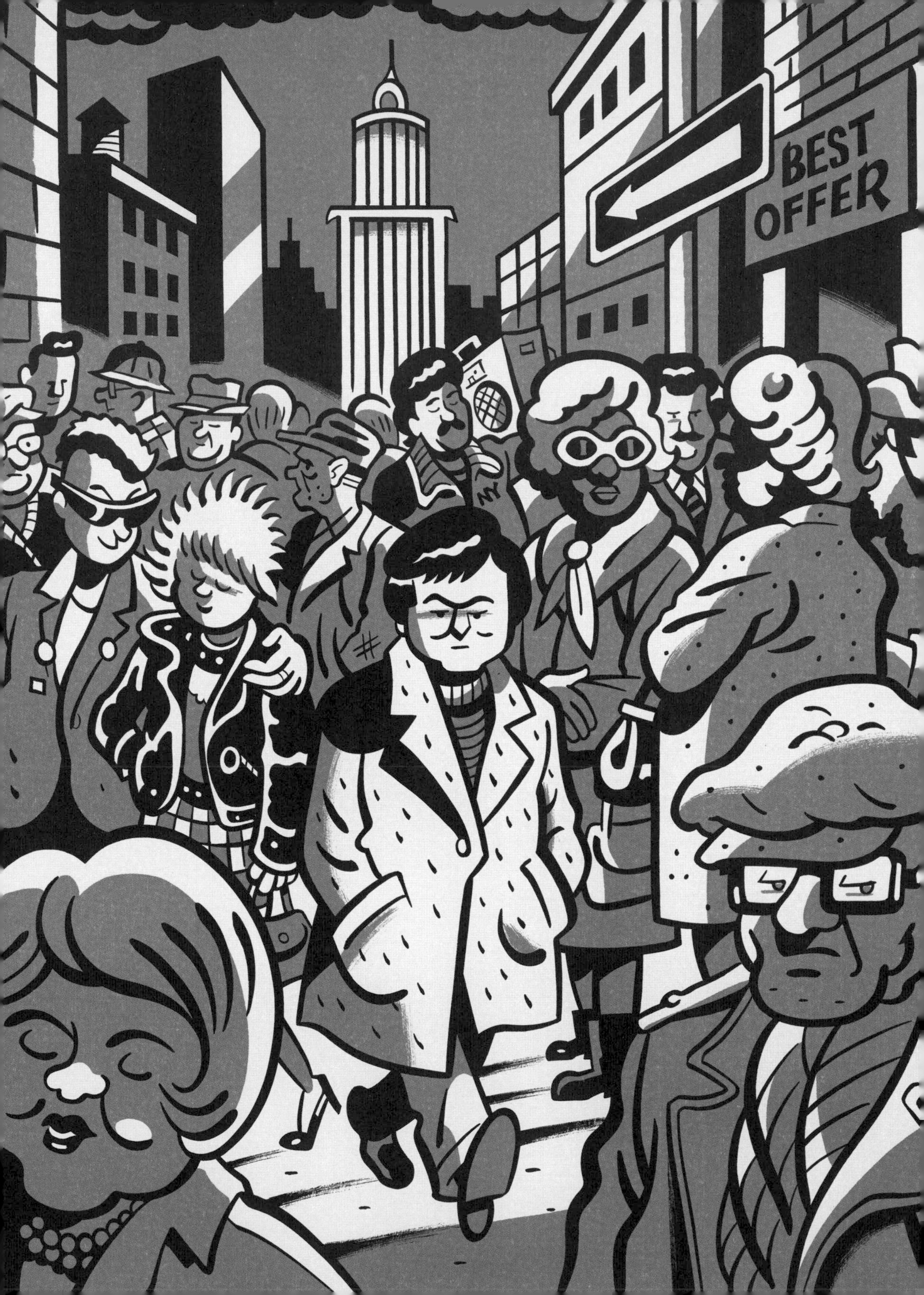
BEST
OFFER

THE COMIC-BOOK MANUFACTURER

an interview with Chris Oliveros by Sean Rogers, images by Seth

Before sitting down in a Mile End café to talk comics with Chris Oliveros, I found Drawn & Quarterly's "Chief" browsing the new wares on display in his company's flagship bookstore, Librairie D+Q. The shop is cavernous but cozy, its high-ceilinged interior crammed invitingly with all manner of prose fiction and poetry, funny books and graphic novels, limited prints and original art, and scads of other eye-catching, uncategorizable doodads and whatsits. Though Oliveros might protest that he's far from the mastermind of the shop, it was hard to resist thinking that, in seeing the man immersed in his element like that, I was also catching a glimpse of what the world of comics had always looked like in the D+Q founder's brain. Here, fully realized on the tables and spinner racks and brick walls of this store, was Oliveros's long-held ideal of what cartooning should be: a diverse selection of voices and languages, a potpourri of styles and approaches, all expressed in the medium of comics, but genially mixed in with new trends in literature and fine art as well.

When he started D+Q, Oliveros could only have imagined this profusion of cartoon art. Now, having helped foster its existence, he's free to revel in how much comics have grown and let unusual little outcroppings surprise and inspire him. Scanning the tables for something new, he reached out and liberated an unassuming, pastel-coloured pamphlet from behind its neighbours. "What's this," he said, almost to himself. "This is great." As he paged through the minicomic—each spread elegantly pencilled, peopled with figures adrift in abstract cityscapes—I got the impression that Oliveros the editor and publisher was at work even here. Quietly appreciative, endlessly inquisitive, and with an instinctive eye for new talent, Oliveros has used that unerring taste and unstinting enthusiasm to establish not just a bookstore, or a publishing concern, but a legacy, as well (though he might protest, once again, the use of that term). It was a privilege to get to talk with him about how his company—and D+Q's comic-book legacy—came to be.

What kind of comics did you encounter, growing up? How did you get interested?

My brother and I grew up in suburban Montreal. We read comics, although we couldn't choose the same type of comics in this odd sibling rivalry we had, so we had to stake our own ground. He was older than me, so he staked out Marvel, and I was left with the only other thing, which was DC. This was in the seventies—a desolate period, by any means. Even for Marvel it was grim, because that was a good decade after their golden age. My father brought home *MAD* magazine, and *Heavy Metal*, and *National Lampoon*, and these awful Warren horror magazines, *Eerie* and *Creepy*. A very strange mix of material was coming into our house. But there really was *nothing* going on at that time—from that base, I'm not sure how I even continued to maintain an interest in comics.

Would you have seen *RAW* at some point?

It was after that period. When I was about fifteen, I encountered Robert Crumb and Gilbert Shelton, whose work was obviously completely different from any of the comics I was familiar with. One day my father brought home this Crumb collection. It's very odd that he would leave it around—I mean, we were teenagers, we weren't really kids at the time, but it was just there in the house [*laughter*]. I was very intrigued by those, and within that year I came across the first issue of *RAW*, a month or two after it was published in 1980. My brother had just moved out of the house, and I remember visiting him in his apartment and he had it lying there. That had a very profound effect on how I saw comics. The undergrounds had an effect as well, but *RAW* was this completely other level.

Were you following the Hernandez brothers and *Weirdo* at that time, or was it basically just *RAW*?

At that point I had stopped reading mainstream comics—that was over—and I really liked *RAW*, but that would have been in 1980, before all the alternative comics started. At one period there was this gap, when the undergrounds had died, and there was just *RAW* and *Weirdo* and that

IT'S CALLED DIRTY PLOTTE.

YOU INTERESTED?

SURE.

When I was first starting out in the early- to mid-1990s, I used to send single-page comics as submissions to D+Q...They were really quite terrible, and not up to the publisher's standards at all. I was just really excited about comics, and on the verge of breaking out...not quite there yet, but I didn't know. So, I'd send the page off and wait very patiently and in a few weeks I would get a polite handwritten rejection letter from Chris Oliveros. Encouraged by the note, I would draw a new submission right away and mail it out the next day! This went on for months until finally Chris suggested that maybe I should stop sending submissions for a while until I got better. Of course I found this fairly embarrassing but also kind of funny, and I really respected his frankness. It was good to know! It helped me realize I had to try a lot harder.

Years later, after I was well established, I asked him if he remembered these early encounters with my work and he did not remember getting any submissions from me at all. Which was kind of a relief.

Now, when talking to young cartoonists who are afraid to send out submissions, afraid that they will embarrass themselves, I tell them this story. There's really nothing to fear from exposing your bad early work to the world because later probably no one will remember it. It's really only the good stuff that makes an impression. That's what makes people take notice. And in the meantime you yourself can learn a lot by gauging people's reactions to your work.

—James Kochalka, cartoonist of American Elf, The Glorkian Warrior Delivers a Pizza, Johnny Boo, and numerous other comics

was it. I guess there was *Cerebus*—that was almost the first independent comic, but I remember for whatever reason never being interested in trying to dive into it.

Soon after that point, would you have gone away to school?

I lived in New York from eighteen to twenty and went to art school there. I continued buying *RAW*—it was obviously easier to get in New York. Then I came back to Montreal, and at that point I was out of comics. I had missed the whole Hernandez brothers thing, and I missed the very beginning of Chester's career—the first few issues of *Yummy Fur*. I became very interested again when I came across *Lloyd Llewellyn* [Daniel Clowes], thinking, "What *is* this?" [*laughter*]. I started buying the *Comics Journal*, which at that point was very important as a doorway into that whole world. It was through the *Comics Journal* that I was able to discover a lot of other books: usually anything that was good was discussed and reviewed in the *Journal*. It was a good base to go on.

After you came back to Montreal, what led up to that first issue of *Drawn & Quarterly*?

There were unusual circumstances. It's funny: sometimes there are things in life where if this one incident didn't happen, your entire future would be different. There's no way I would've wanted to start a comic-book company or a magazine, because I just didn't have the experience. I wouldn't have known what the first step was. But in the summer of 1988, I heard about this group who got a short-term grant from the Quebec government, just to last for that summer, and they wanted to start a comics anthology. Somehow I got connected with this group, and we ended up putting out two issues of this comics anthology that were *terrible*. There wasn't any editorial direction at all—if they had a friend who had something, *anything*, they would put it in; whatever happened to be lying around the table would go in those issues. In private, I referred disparagingly to the editorial direction as the "open slot policy," because any submission that came through the mail slot would find its way into the magazine. Nonetheless, it was a really good learning experience for me. I learned a lot about basic things like distribution. Then all of a sudden it seemed to me that this was a possibility, and I thought, "Well, I can probably do this better on my own. I'd like to start a comics magazine." The original idea wasn't to start with a comics company, but just to start a quarterly magazine. I thought a comics magazine could exist in the same way that *Harper's* or the *New Yorker* did. One thing led to another as

I was contacting people for what was to be the first issue of *Drawn & Quarterly*: a lot of those cartoonists happened to be right at the beginning of their careers, doing longer works.

In short order, you were publishing *Dirty Plotte*, first of all.

I contacted Julie so that she could contribute something to *Drawn & Quarterly*, which she did. But in that first meeting, she said that she was working on this comic called *Dirty Plotte*, and that it was turned down by Fantagraphics, and would I like to publish it? I said, "Sure, that sounds great." The same thing happened with Seth: I contacted him to contribute something to *Drawn & Quarterly* and I met him in Toronto. We were at his apartment, and he said, "By the way, I'm working on this new comic-book series called *Palookaville* and I'm almost finished the first issue. Would you like to take a look at it?" So a lot of it was being in the right place at the right time. I've often thought, if I had started this maybe six months later, none of it would've worked out, because it was so crucial to make all those connections. *Drawn & Quarterly* started pretty fast—it didn't take ten years or even two years to get all these important cartoonists. Within twelve months we got a lot of the crucial people. And if we didn't get Seth and Julie and Joe Matt, then Chester probably wouldn't have come over. And if we didn't have all *those* people initially, then a young teenager named Adrian Tomine wouldn't be thinking, "I've got to get published by Drawn & Quarterly." It was a chain reaction that happened at very key moments.

How did you meet the first handful of Drawn & Quarterly cartoonists? When you began the anthology, were you just asking people out of the blue to submit?

When the anthology started, I put an ad in the *New York Press*. They had a back page that had all kinds of listings and ads, and I thought it would be a good way to get cartoonists from the United States—from New York, in particular. One of the people who responded to the ad was James Sturm, who was just about to graduate from SVA. He sent in comics and they were great, and I wrote to him right away. The comics didn't make it into that first issue of *Drawn & Quarterly*, but they made it into the second one, and a few later issues as well. It was the beginning of a long association: a few years ago, we published his most recent book [*Market Day*]. One of the other people who responded to that ad was an artist named Anne D. Bernstein, who ended up doing the cover to the first issue. That was an example of the way a lot of things worked at that time: you would meet one person, and that would lead to a referral to another person. Anne D. Bernstein introduced me to her friend J.D. King, who then had a piece in that first issue—a collaboration with Alice Sebold, who would later go on to become a very successful novelist. Then J.D. King introduced me to Peter Bagge—that's one of the first contacts I made in comics, calling up Peter Bagge. Now, you just send someone an email. But back then I guess it was fairly normal to cold-call someone—I don't know why he spent so much time speaking to me, this guy calling out of the blue. It seems insane now! But I think having those early associations helped lead to other things.

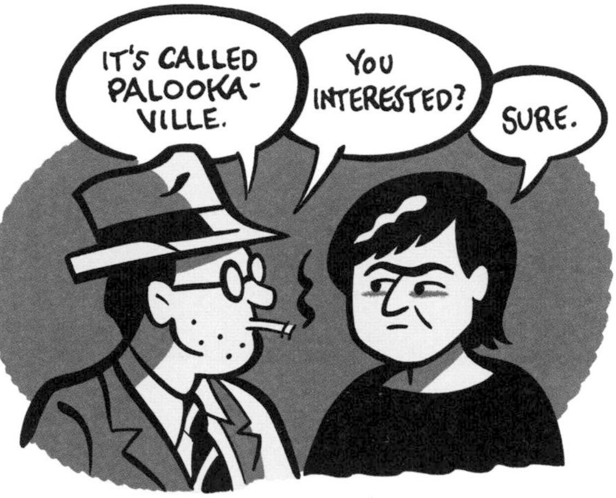
IT'S CALLED PALOOKA-VILLE.
YOU INTERESTED?
SURE.

Those interactions were by mail or telephone—when did you actually start meeting cartoonists?

One of the first cartoonists I met would've been Julie Doucet, locally. I was trying to seek out work in my immediate geographic area, in Montreal, and also trying to seek out work from the rest of Canada and the United States. Julie Doucet had that previous year started self-publishing her minicomics in Montreal, so I mailed her a letter, and then we met in town. Joe Matt had also just started publishing and he was living in Montreal as well, but I didn't know how to reach him. This was of course before the days when you could Google someone, so I sent him a letter in care of Kitchen Sink [Matt's original publisher]. The letter went to Wisconsin, then it was forwarded back to Montreal to Joe, and we met in person. A lot of this stuff was happening before I had anything published at all. I don't know why these people even bothered to call me back or write me a letter—it seems crazy! Chester was one of the people I started contacting once I actually had a magazine—something physical—to mail out. He sent a brief, kind letter in response.

With Seth, it was the same thing: I waited until we had one or two issues of the magazine published, then mailed him a copy. In the summer of 1990 I came to Toronto and met both Seth and Chester for the first time in person, and Joe was there at the time too. I remember meeting Seth at the bus station [*laughs*].

Was he still very dapper?

He adopted his current look slightly before then, maybe about '87 or '88, so it was still pretty new back then. He's frozen in time on two levels: he has this look of someone circa 1947, but it's like he hasn't aged, as well. Every time I see him, he looks the same as when I first saw him in 1990. I don't know what he's got going on, but there's something preserving him [*laughs*]. Chester also looked pretty much the same as he does now, except that he had hair on the top. Except for that detail, he looks very similar.

What kind of conversations would you have with your artists at the beginning?

A lot of the conversations would've been around immediate issues, in terms of what they were working on, when their next issue was due, deadlines, and things like that. But when I would come visit Toronto and spend time with these guys, a lot of the discussions would centre around what we all wanted to achieve in comics, and where we wanted to see comics going in the years to come. In the early nineties, we were all talking about our hope that comics would be distributed to general bookstores, and we were talking about the "collection." Those guys knew that pamphlet comic books were where you would serialize a story, and at the end you would have your collection, and that book would hopefully get beyond the traditional comic distribution channels.

Did you have a close working relationship with Julie, because you were in the same town?

I would see Julie a few times a year. She would have a new issue so she would bring over her artwork, or I would go to her place—she didn't live that far. But by '91 she had moved to New York and in early '92 she moved to Seattle, then afterwards to Germany. So it was really only that first year, probably the first four issues of *Dirty Plotte*, that I would see Julie when she would have a new issue.

At what point did you and Adrian get in touch? At what point did you become aware of his work?

Whenever Adrian would have a new minicomic, he would send in the new issue. I remember reading it and keeping all of his issues of *Optic Nerve*. I didn't realize at the time how young he was—he was only around sixteen years old, and for some reason I just assumed he was in his early twenties. Which is a pretty huge difference: it might only be four or five years, but that's a really important time in anyone's development. For a sixteen-year-old to be doing work on that level almost never happens. I felt really dumb that I didn't realize it much sooner. In theory, we could have lost him; he could easily have gone with another publisher. By the time he sent me his fifth *Optic Nerve* minicomic, I sent him an embarrassingly poorly thought-out reply—just kind of messily scrawled on paper. That was discussed in detail in the 32 *Stories* box that we did. It was an encouraging letter, implying that we'd maybe, probably like to publish him, at some point, but without actually offering him a publishing deal. About three or four months after that, by early 1994, I realized that we really should be publishing him. At that point, I called him up and asked him if Drawn & Quarterly could publish the first issue of *Optic Nerve*.

What kind of negotiating brought Chester Brown on board from Vortex Comics, his original publisher?

It took a while. Around the time that we started publishing Julie and Seth, by the fall of 1990, almost immediately I asked Chester if he would come on board with us. He politely turned me down, saying he had this working relationship with Vortex Comics, obviously. I don't know how many times I tried in the ensuing year and a half, but I think I asked him every three months or something. I was asking him to come on board with Drawn & Quarterly because the sensibility of the company was much more in line with his own sensibility, but also because I felt that his work was out of place at Vortex. In the early- or mid-eighties, Vortex was kind of interesting, but by the late eighties and early nineties they were publishing almost nothing else of interest. They had *Yummy Fur* and that was it—they started getting into these really goofy things, like NASCAR comics and a real hodgepodge of whatever the publisher thought would sell. I also offered Chester a higher royalty, because our royalties were higher then than they are now—in part because our overhead was very low. According to Chester, it was the part about the higher royalty that actually got him to come on board.

Chester's *The Playboy* was Drawn & Quarterly's first graphic novel. What kind of learning experience was publishing that first book? It's got to be different in a lot of ways from publishing a comic-book series.

The market was completely different then—almost unrecognizable from what it is today—so it was very different publishing a graphic novel than it is now. For one thing, there was no bookstore distribution. Of course, without the direct market comics distribution system, you wouldn't have the graphic novels of today—we were all very grateful for that. But at the same time, we also recognized that it needed to go further. The paradox was that there were no bookstores interested in carrying comics at the time. By publishing books throughout the nineties, Drawn & Quarterly and other publishers like Fantagraphics were making small steps. Even though it didn't happen overnight, those were important steps that helped to create awareness and set the foundation for graphic novels in bookstores later on.

***The Playboy* was a book that stayed in print for a really long time—the new edition just came out last year. Was that something that you had overestimated?**
Because everything we published up until that time was comic books, the printing bill would never be that high. All of a sudden, we're doing a book and the printing bill is five times higher than a normal comic book would be! The thing in printing is, the price goes down with volume. I remember getting estimates and seeing that if you print twelve thousand copies, the unit cost was about half the amount it would be if you printed three thousand. So I thought, "Let me print twelve thousand copies, because it's Chester, and it's a good book, and it's going to sell." It eventually did sell, but it took a long time [*laughter*].

The initial batch of artists and works that were being published at Drawn & Quarterly were all pretty solidly autobiographical comics. Do you feel, in that first decade, that that pigeonholed Drawn & Quarterly at all?
I think it did. In the early 1990s, I didn't set out and say, "Drawn & Quarterly is *the* autobiographical comics publisher, and I only like autobiographical comics." It just happened that way. At that moment in time, a lot of the really talented people who were emerging happened to be doing these first-person narratives, and you could see people get influenced by each other—probably the most direct example would be Chester dropping *Ed the Happy Clown* because he was influenced by what Seth and Julie and Joe Matt were doing. On the one hand, it was beneficial, because it made those books distinct from a lot of other things that were going on, and there was a lot of great work that resulted—a lot of perennials and books that are still great now, like *It's a Good Life, If You Don't Weaken*. But at the same time it

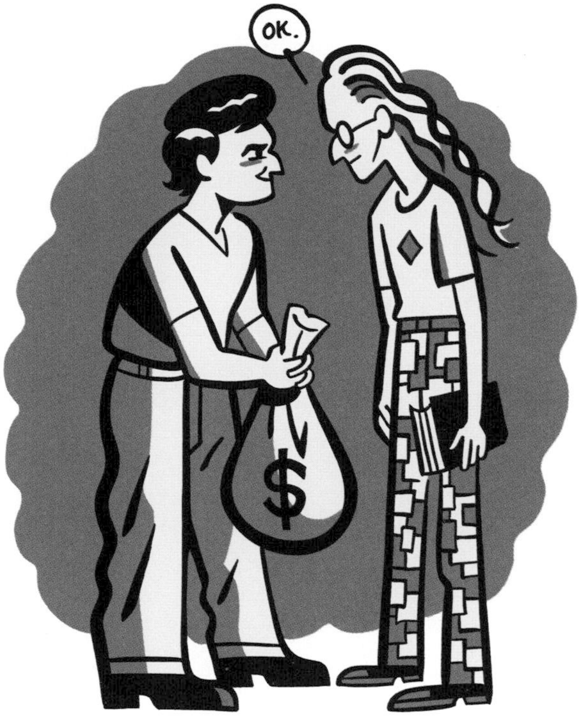
OK.

For the first dozen or so years of its existence, D+Q was run out of the various apartments that Chris and I lived in, all located within a roughly six-block range in Montreal's Mile End neighbourhood. At times the company had its own room, depending on the apartment set-up, but either way, the business had its way of slowly trickling into the rest of our living space, and our lives. In fact, a lot of the work happened at our kitchen table, which is where, in September 1989, Chris and I came up with a list of possible names for the company—I wrote down "Drawn & Quartered," and Chris changed the ending to arrive at Drawn & Quarterly. Our living room was also very often a hub of activity, usually when it came time to pack orders for subscriptions and catalogue mailings. At one point in the pre-internet days, Chris purchased three thousand names and addresses in an effort to go wide with a new catalogue, and together we spent long hours stuffing and sponging envelopes and affixing address labels. By its end, the maze of envelopes created a miniature city, stacks curling around the hallway, beyond our living room, and into our kitchen.

Throughout much of this early period I was busy studying at McGill University and, later on, working as a Spanish and English teacher at a Montreal high was a problem, because Drawn & Quarterly did become pigeonholed really fast. It was very easy for people to dismiss Drawn & Quarterly and say, "They just publish these navel-gazing autobiographical comics." Gradually, things did evolve, very slowly—it didn't happen overnight. Eventually, we took over publishing comics like *Berlin* and a few other books that weren't autobiographical. But it took a long time to get to the point where we are today, where there are so many different types of material we're doing.

With these perennials that started coming out—*I Never Liked You*, *It's a Good Life*, *Sleepwalk*—did you realize right away that those were hits? Were they a success immediately?

They were a success, on many levels, right off the bat. They did sell quite well initially—probably at least three thousand copies, which nowadays would be considered very good. Considering we didn't have bookstore distribution, that actually is *really* good! In all those cases, we knew right away that these books were reaching a certain audience. It wasn't really a surprise because the books were by cartoonists who were really well known, even by then. Chester already had a following; a lot of people were waiting for *It's a Good Life* because they were following *Palookaville*. Even though a lot of people were reading it serialized, when *It's a Good Life* came out in book form it really was one of the important books of the nineties, because it was one of the first books that had this incredible design aesthetic. A lot of people were really amazed by Seth's whole approach, especially if you compare it to its original incarnation in the black and white *Palookaville*.

Those books were also getting written up in places like *Entertainment Weekly* and the *Globe* and *Village Voice* and *Artforum*...

To a small degree. Throughout the nineties, that was just starting to happen, but there really wasn't much writing on comics outside of the *Comics Journal*. Of course, in the last fifteen years, we've become used to it. The way things are now, comics get written about seemingly everywhere. But back then there were, like, three people writing about comics. There was one guy in *Entertainment Weekly*, one guy in the *Village Voice*, and then one guy in some paper in Detroit or something. The *Globe and Mail* had one article in the mid-nineties, and then didn't have another one for almost ten years. So it was a hard period [*laughter*].

What was publicity like back then? Was it mainly going to comics conventions?

It's hard to imagine now, but in the early years there weren't really conventions that were geared toward independent or

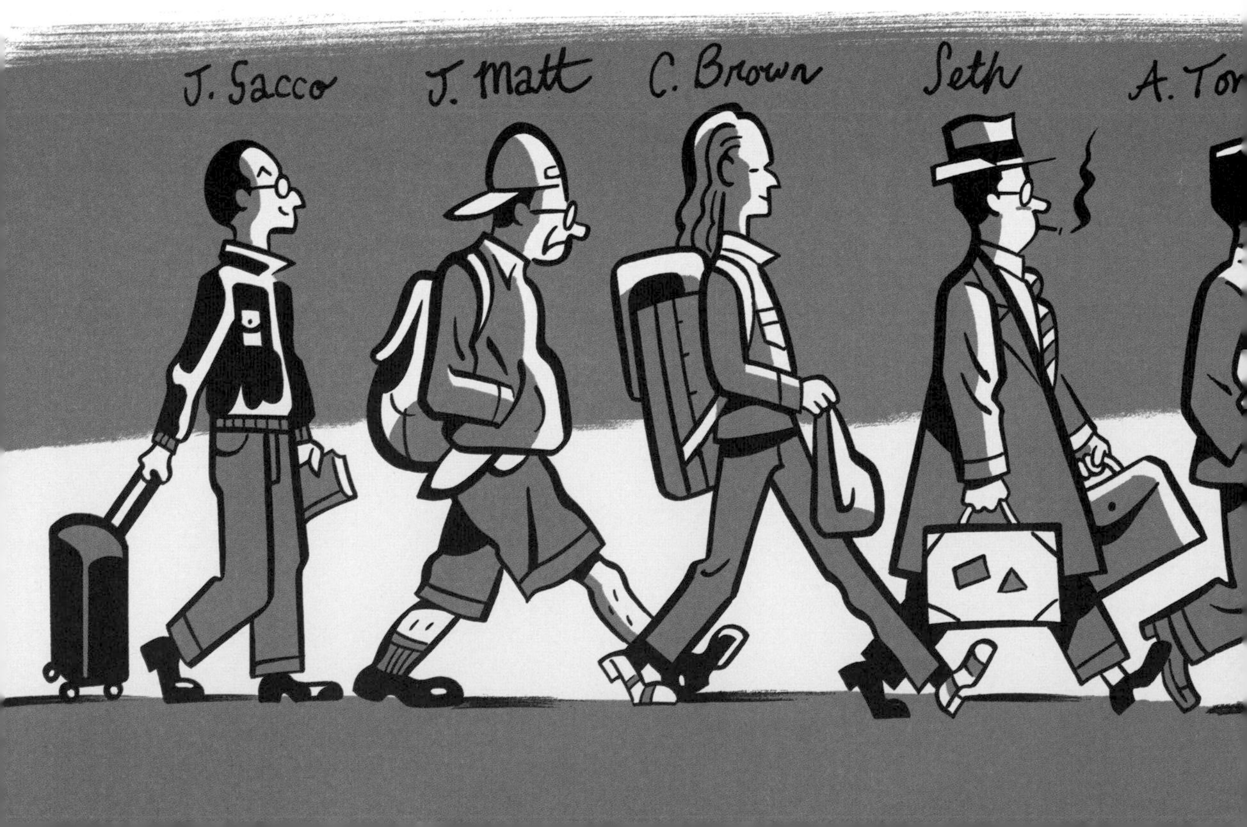
J. Sacco
J. Matt
C. Brown
Seth

alternative comics. That was all decades before TCAF—even years before SPX or APE or anything like that. The only convention option was San Diego—San Diego was *the* convention. I actually didn't go to San Diego for the first time until '94, because in those early years we would've only had a few three-dollar comic books, so there was no way to justify the cost. And back in those pre-internet days, the readership was not as widespread as it is now; it was very focused. You didn't really have to go too far to reach those readers. The readership was so concentrated that by placing an ad in, say, the *Comics Journal*, you could probably reach about 90 percent of it—all of a sudden, everyone would know about this. That's one of the things I've heard from many people over the years, about how Drawn & Quarterly began and picked up so quickly. People would say that in '91 or '92, they had heard all about us: *Dirty Plotte* was known almost immediately, *Palookaville* was known, even the *Drawn & Quarterly* anthology was known and had relatively high sales. You could get to that level without having conventions and without having those big press hits, which you have now.

When you finally ended up going to San Diego, would you bring your artists with you?

In the first two or three years, it wasn't really centred around having the artists there. We would usually try to

school, so my role was never more than part-time, but I still managed to help Chris with a variety of tasks. I sometimes double-checked the bluelines for a book (the term used for proofs of a book, back when printing was done using films), and I often proofread comics before they went to the printer. I proofread *Louis Riel* and I appreciated the research behind Chester's story. For a year or two I prepared D+Q's year-end paperwork, until Chris hired an outside accountant to do what was, even by then, quickly becoming a complicated endeavour.

Our first son, Miguel, was born in 1996, and for the next few years the company continued to evolve and co-exist with our changing personal lives. Book stacks were baby-proofed, and overstock on Chester Brown's *The Playboy* was kept on a high shelf. It was quite literally a family-run operation, with even our then-toddler son receiving a couple of jokey credits in some of the books along the lines of "office boy" or "financial advisor."

By early 2001, when I was pregnant with our second son, Elliot, the company had finally outgrown the confines of our apartment. Boxes and books began to overflow from D+Q's designated room in the apartment, and deliveries left little space in our hallways beyond

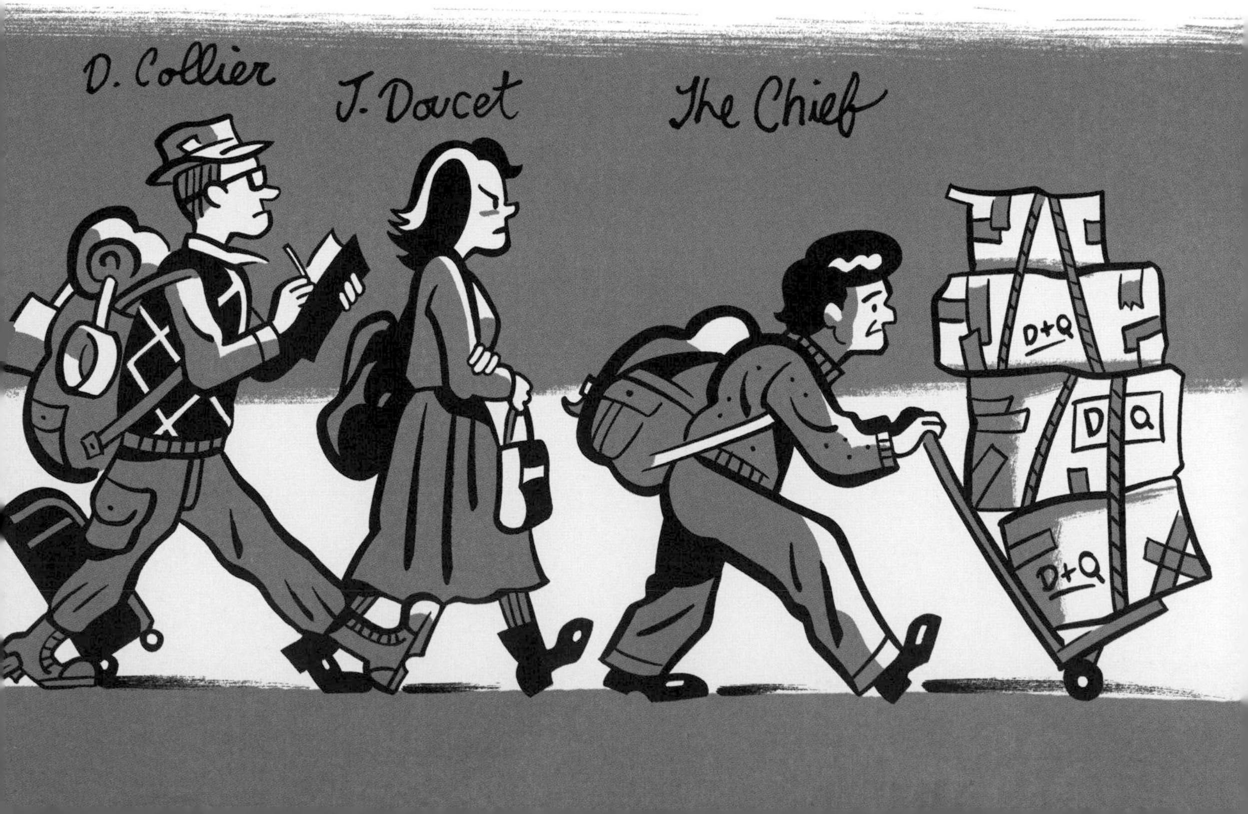

D. Collier
J. Doucet
The Chief
D+Q
D Q
D+Q

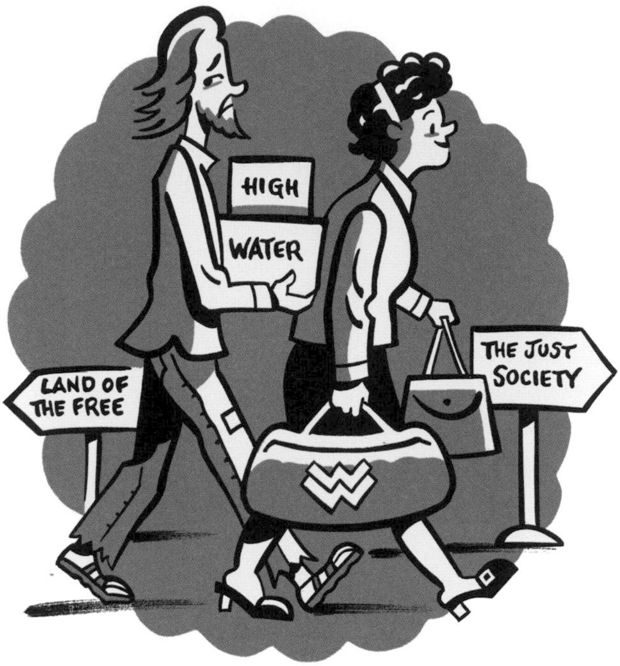
HIGH
WATER
THE JUST SOCIETY
LAND OF THE FREE

have a debut book, but it was tricky because with those three-dollar comic books, there's only so much you could sell. There's no way you could even cover plane fares and hotels, so you would do it in hopes that it would be a very big promotional thing. The first year that we had a very large showing in San Diego was 1998, where we had almost all of our cartoonists at the time there. We brought Chester Brown, Seth, Julie Doucet, Joe Matt, David Collier, Joe Sacco, Archer Prewitt—it was a very large contingent. That was in association with an art show we had at Meltdown Comics in Los Angeles.

Were there any run-ins on that trip, or did everyone get along okay?

I think everyone got along pretty fine [*laughs*]. Julie may have grown tired. I think one of the things that may have driven Julie from comics was that, since around '95 when we went to a show in Portugal, she has complained about how comics were primarily a boys' club, at least at that time, and how certain cartoonists would only want to talk about comics when they would get together. I think that sort of appalled her sensibility. I often wonder if that's what triggered her desire to leave comics. It's also interesting to see how that's evolved, and how there are so many great female cartoonists now that it's gotten to the point where it seems weird to call attention to the fact they're female cartoonists: they're just cartoonists.

That's something you had drawn attention to in the editorial in that first *Drawn & Quarterly*, that there was that boys' club atmosphere. I think your publishing was a corrective to that from the very beginning, putting Anne D. Bernstein on the cover and then printing Julie and Mary Fleener and so on.

Some of the cartoonists from that first decade haven't continued working—great cartoonists, like Debbie Drechsler. It's a real shame that she just fell off the radar. Or Ariel Bordeaux... there've been a few others.

You've got a strip of your own in *Drawn & Quarterly*, and your series *The Envelope Manufacturer* has come out irregularly. Was cartooning something you had intended to pursue longer than you ended up doing?

I had something in that first issue of *Drawn & Quarterly*, and the moment I opened the box when the first issue was out, I realized, "Oh my gosh, what a mistake" [*laughter*]. From that point onward, I knew that I didn't want to publish my own work—or at least not have Drawn & Quarterly publish my own work, for conflict of interest reasons and so on. It's a weird thing, if an editor puts his or her own work in what he or she is editing. I knew that I wanted to separate that right away. Technically, I self-published *The Envelope Manufacturer*. Drawn & Quarterly has an incorporated name, this numbered company, which no one would have known. And I thought, "I can use this name, because no one knows it's Drawn & Quarterly."

***The Envelope Manufacturer* is the story of a man struggling to keep his small business afloat. Is it a veiled autobiography at all?**

No [*laughter*]. There are no autobiographical elements in it. I remember Seth making jokes about that: "This is the story of Drawn & Quarterly!" On the other hand, if I wasn't working at Drawn & Quarterly, I might not have been thinking, "What's it like to have a small business?" Working in the company on a daily basis probably makes me think about these things more than the average person would be thinking about them.

Is that series something that you are interested in continuing?

I did two issues and, again, almost immediately after they came out, I wanted to disown them. I didn't like them. For quite a few years, I completely stopped and didn't do anything at all. Over the last three or four years I've actually been finishing it, but because I disliked the first two installments so much, I decided that I wanted to scrap it entirely. I started from the beginning again, and I'm almost finished it now. There are three installments, but it's all done from scratch, as if the first two didn't exist.

I know back in the early days you would see your family's names pop up again and again—your father, your brother, Marina. To what extent was Drawn & Quarterly a family affair?

My father played an important role in that he helped me start it financially. It wasn't a lot of money—I mean, to start a company like this now you probably would be talking about hundreds of thousands of dollars. But back then, the entry point was fairly easy, in that you could print your book and have it distributed to the comic distributors and get your money back in thirty days. My father was able to front me the money to get those early magazines and comic books out there, and he helped me support myself as well during those early years. My wife, Marina, didn't actually work full-time in the company per se. In the beginning she was a McGill student, so almost all of her time was taken up, but she would still help in a lot of the day-to-day things. Sometimes we would have a catalogue mailing, so we would be stuffing a thousand envelopes, or she would proofread comics—things like that. I would also discuss comics submissions with her, and which artists to commission for stories in D+Q, as I valued her opinion. She also had another important role, in that we both came up with the name Drawn & Quarterly. We had a list of titles, and one of the names on her list was "Drawn & Quartered," and I changed the ending to "Quarterly." And then the other family member would be my oldest son, Miguel: when he was young, as a joke, I would sometimes credit him in the indicia, usually along the lines of "office boy" or "financial consultant."

Were you basically working out of your house?

Yeah, out of our apartment—either in the living room, or later on in its own room. The apartment where Drawn & Quarterly first started is only two blocks away from where the store [Librairie Drawn & Quarterly] is now.

Would it have been very hands-on work, then? When did computers enter into things?

Throughout much of the nineties it was either paste-ups or, for the solo comics like *Palookaville* or *Dirty Plotte*, those would be all hand done, cover to cover, so Seth or Julie would give us the artwork and I would send it to the printer. Even up until the very late 1990s this was still done with a camera

a narrow passageway where we could walk from one end to the other. Chris rented a two-room office in May 2001, just around the corner from our apartment. But even then things were still all in the family, with Chris making our five-year-old son, Miguel, paint the office (okay, maybe it was just part of one wall).

More recently I had a chance to become directly involved in a D+Q book when I translated Pablo Holmberg's *Eden*. Pablo's one-page comics are imaginative and endearing. My love of Spanish came full circle again when I worked on this translation. Coincidentally, Chris and I visited Argentina in the summer of 2010 and we were able to hand-deliver his personal copies just before the book was published.

D+Q became too big for our home, but the clutter was never a nuisance. It deserved all our support, and I am proud to have worked behind the scenes during those early years.

—*Marina Lesenko*

Miguel Lesenko-Oliveros painting the office (2001).

Before I started Reprodukt in 1991, I was closely following what was going on in the North American comics scene. I was struck by the first two issues of the *Drawn & Quarterly* magazine. It wasn't as perfect as *RAW* magazine, nor as far-out or deeply rooted in North American alternative culture as *Weirdo*. But still, the mix of personal and appealing stories, clear artwork, and concept that Chris Oliveros realized in *Drawn & Quarterly* was inspiring to me. It was something I could present to the German comics scene. It was much more universal in approach than what other North American comics publishers were doing. Ultimately, I never did publish this German comics magazine, but I was inspired. I began creating German editions of the North American comics that I loved.

Reprodukt started out with *The Death of Speedy* by Jaime Hernandez and *Blood of Palomar* by his brother Gilbert and then *Like a Velvet Glove Cast in Iron* by Daniel Clowes and then Julie Doucet's *Dirty Plotte*. Reprodukt was still more of an alternative project then, a means to publish the comics I loved most, more an idea I wanted to follow than a means of making a living. We translated Geneviève Castrée, Debbie Drechsler, Adrian Tomine, and many other cartoonists who were previously published by D+Q.

The arrival and success of *Persepolis*—and graphic novels in general—changed the landscape after some difficult years. D+Q revitalized itself by hiring Peggy Burns and Tom Devlin and making marketing a much more important part of its publishing business. Reprodukt began publishing full-colour comics from the new French generation of cartoonists. We also took our cues from D+Q and broadened our distribution into bookstores and hired a staff of salespeople. We too saw success with Guy Delisle's reportage and had a bestseller by adopting D+Q's design for the Moomin series.

Our generation of publishers chose to publish for love, not to make products aimed at youth culture or the movie industry. With D+Q you can easily see the company's passion in the quality of the books they produce—the vision and taste of Chris Oliveros remain a standout for publishing comics worldwide. Reprodukt is honoured to have been sharing titles as well as ideals for nearly twenty-five years.

—*Dirk Rehm, publisher, Reprodukt*

and film. We'd send the original artwork to the printer, who would shoot it with these gigantic old cameras—this was used for, like, a hundred years. Seth would have overlays, so the printer would shoot the art, shoot the overlay, and put the pieces of film together and try to match it up. That all started to change right around the turn of the century. Most artists are scanning their work at this point. Lynda Barry still sends in her original art—she just sent in the art for her new book, *Syllabus*, last week—and Seth of course still does it the same way that artists did it in 1945 [*laughter*].

At what point did you get bookstore distribution?

We first signed up with a bookstore distributor in 1997. At the time there was this company called the LPC Group, who were similar to what Consortium Books is now—probably even larger, actually. We were the first graphic-novel publisher to sign up with them and, funnily, the second one was Marvel [*laughter*]. The first year or two with them our orders were very small—less than 5 percent of all our total sales. In the late nineties, that market grew, but very, very slowly.

The late nineties looked pretty dire for comics. Kitchen Sink went bankrupt, Black Eye stopped publishing, the direct market seemed almost doomed...

It was a pretty shaky period in the second half of the nineties. In the first half, you had all this growth—certainly with Drawn & Quarterly there was growth. In the second half of that decade, things got stalled a little bit. If you look back, there were not as many strong or new works being introduced, and some of the books we tried didn't quite work out in the same way as our others. But the market was changing, too, and in 1996 one of the largest comic distributors, Capital City, went bankrupt. At the time, a lot of us thought, "This is it. This is the end. Things are going to fall apart, now." In a sense, there was kind of a holding pattern. People were just trying to hang on, and there weren't a lot of changes being made—until 2000, when Chris Ware's *Jimmy Corrigan* came out [from Pantheon]. That's when everything started to change: I think that was the key title that really opened the door for graphic novels, and it was almost as important as *Maus* [by Art Spiegelman] was in the late eighties and early nineties.

Did you see a marked difference with the books you released in 2000?

Not immediately, in 2000—it actually was in 2001. *Jimmy Corrigan* was a fall book in 2000, so people were talking about it and so on, but its effect took a few months. In the spring of 2001, we were preparing two art books—*Vernacular Drawings*, by Seth, and *Long Time Relationship*, by Julie Doucet—and we had an original graphic novel that season, as well—*The Golem's Mighty Swing*, by James Sturm. By that summer I was really beginning to see how much things were changing, especially with the Sturm book. Up until that point, I was able to handle things on my own. Part of it was by default: you didn't have to chase down all of these publications to get interviews or reviews, because no one was writing about this stuff anyway. But I was starting to see a lot of demand for press coverage and author tours and things like that. So by the summer of 2001, you could see things were changing.

What did the company look like at that point?

It was still just me, and then that summer I realized that I couldn't do it on my own. D+Q's first hire was Traie Payne in June 2001. He came in part-time on weekends to pack our mail orders and website orders, and later in the decade he came back to work, this time at D+Q's bookstore, for a brief stint. By early 2002 I needed to hire somebody in publicity. A few months later, I did hire someone—Peggy Burns's predecessor, Elizabeth Walker—and then in 2002 we realized that we needed better distribution, because the LPC Group filed for bankruptcy. There was this whole new bookstore market that was developing—but our book distributor filed for bankruptcy. We needed to do something major, something that would change things. I had the sense that this was a moment that could work really well, or that things could really, really collapse at that point—and they almost did. So we contacted Chronicle Books and it took a while but we finally worked out a contract with them. They were our distributor for about a year and a half. The only problem is that things in the book industry move slowly. You're always planning books a year in advance, so even though we signed with them in 2002, our first season with them was spring 2003. So 2002 was devastating [*laughter*]. First of all, there was LPC going under, so we lost some money that we would never recover. Then there's the latter half of 2002: we had no books or distribution, at a time when the bookstore market was taking off. We were in a sort of holding pattern, waiting for 2003 and our first season with Chronicle.

And then 2003 seemed like a big deal.

It was a big deal, in the sense that in our first season with Chronicle we had some strong books that are perennials even now. We had the *ACME Novelty Datebook*—our first Chris Ware title. We had our first original graphic novel by Joe Sacco, *The Fixer*. And then of course, later that year, we had *Louis Riel*. Instead of just two or three book titles a year, 2003 was really the first year when the books became the main thing, and the comic-book pamphlets started dropping off. It was a pretty important year.

The first time I had the pleasure of meeting Chris was in 1992. I had dropped by to show him my portfolio and he ended up commissioning an illustration for the magazine *Drawn & Quarterly*. I was impressed by his kindness and his devotion to comics.

His office was in the kitchen. I met his wife and one of his children. But here's how my memory wants to reconstruct the facts:

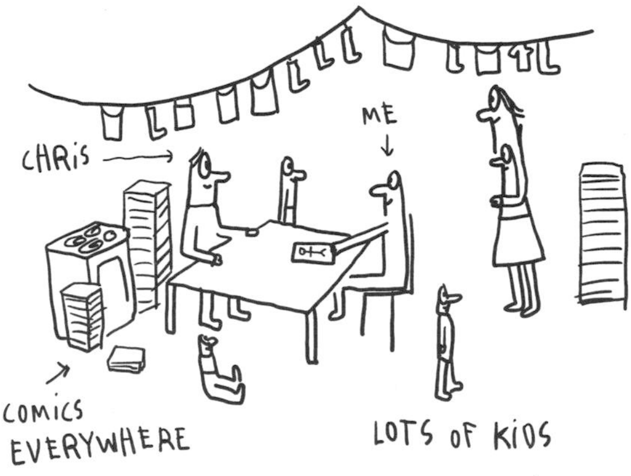
CHRIS
ME
COMICS EVERYWHERE
LOTS OF KIDS

—Diane Obomsawin

At what point did you get the book industry organization to implement the "graphic novels" tag, as a way to categorize books?

When we signed up with Chronicle, they informed me about BISAC [Book Industry Standards and Communications], and I learned that all books have to have a category. I remember looking at their list and seeing that there was a category for *everything*—every obscure subject matter you can think of—but there was no category for graphic novels. That just showed you how low comics were, and why they weren't ever in bookstores—there wasn't even a category for them! So I started contacting other people in the industry, to see if we could all sign a letter to BISAC, to lobby them to add "graphic novels"

Rebecca and I were flying out to a convention and our flight was at some terrible hour like 5:00 a.m. Before heading to the airport, we had to collect suitcases full of books and convention supplies from the office, which meant meeting there at 3:00 a.m. I was grumpy about having to go in to work so early in the morning. I think I was on about two hours of sleep, and Rebecca was on none since she had a tendency to sleep through alarms and wouldn't sleep before an early flight. Not only that, but we were going to have to get off the plane and head straight to a convention centre, put our table together, and then field questions like "Why didn't you include the original covers in the John Stanley reprints?" for the rest of the day. We were both irritated and spent the elevator ride up to the office grousing about having to wake up so early.

Midway through some whining sentence, we got to the office doors and put our keys in, only to discover that Chris Oliveros was in there, working at three o'clock in the morning. He was in the throes of putting the final translations into Julie Doucet's *365 Days* (a book that made at least one letterer quit) and had to meet the printer's deadline. If anything, he was a little apologetic to us for being there so late in the night, laughing a little bit about it. We said good night to him, collected our suitcases, and went outside to get into a cab. We were silent; our complaints no longer felt justified. Sure, it was and is annoying to get up at 3:00 a.m., but when your boss is staying late into the night to finish books, when he could be at home working on his own beautiful comics or spending time with his family, or, well, sleeping, it makes the sacrifice of staying up all night seem slight.

And while finding Chris in the office at 3:00 a.m. was unexpected, Chris making sacrifices for the authors and his employees was and is commonplace. He would readily take the blame when something went wrong and pass on praise when something went well. He didn't even pay himself for the first fifteen years that the company was in operation, but we could always count on being paid promptly, which is something that I've stopped taking for granted. Chris Oliveros is the kindest, most self-sacrificing person I've ever met, and if there were a person whose life I could decide to model mine after, it would be him.—*Jessica Campbell*

as a category. I had met Peggy earlier that year, but this was our first business interaction. She was working at DC Comics, so she got DC to sign on board, which was important because they were one of the biggest mainstream publishers. Fantagraphics signed on, and you had people like Art Spiegelman who signed on as well.

At what point did Peggy join Drawn & Quarterly?

The person who had been with us in publicity was no longer working there by early summer 2003, so for a period Drawn & Quarterly was a one-person operation again. I had known Peggy for barely a year, at that point, but I had corresponded with her a lot and worked with her extensively with this BISAC letter. So when the position in publicity opened, I contacted her right away and said, "Do you know anyone who would want the job?" I thought this was a total long shot, because she was in New York: why would she know someone in Canada, let alone Montreal, who would be qualified for or interested in the job? Within about five minutes, I got a reply from her, and there was nothing in the email except her CV. It seemed so absurd—I was thinking, "As if! She's living in New York and she has this incredible job at DC—as if she'd be applying for a job at Drawn & Quarterly, to move to Canada, in a French-speaking city." I actually thought it was a joke. I didn't reply to her right away, and a couple hours later she emailed me again and asked if I wasn't interested. Then I realized that she wasn't joking. That would have been in June 2003. It's amazing, to think back now, how fast all that happened. It's hard enough moving from, let's say, Toronto to Montreal—that's a really big deal. But to move to another country, with the whole immigration process and everything…So in June we started talking about it, and by July it was solidified and she was making plans, and by mid-September both Tom Devlin and Peggy were here in an apartment. In fact, Peggy's first week on the job was the week that *Louis Riel*, *ACME*, and *The Fixer* were all coming out [*laughter*].

That's sink or swim! Had you been familiar with Tom's work at Highwater at that point?

Definitely. By then I had known Tom for several years, since around '95 or '96. I knew him through his work at the comics store the Million Year Picnic. In those days, because the internet was still pretty new, a lot of people were still used to calling in orders and just chatting. Tom would call in whenever he wanted to place an order for the store, and we developed a friendship through those calls. I remember talking to him when he was just starting Highwater Books, so I had known him for quite a few years by then.

When he and Peggy moved here, to what degree was he involved with Drawn & Quarterly at the start?

I don't think it was official, but we all thought there could be a role for Tom, although we knew it couldn't happen right away. There was barely enough money to pay a second person, being Peggy, let alone a third person. So for the rest of 2003 it was just Peggy, and Tom was still doing design work for other publishers. Then he started at Drawn & Quarterly doing basic things, like packing orders. That didn't last very long, because by early 2004 we would farm out certain design projects to him, and production projects, and that went on for a few months. I would say by mid-2004 he was actually in the company, and not just freelance.

What do you think Tom brought to the company?

Both Tom and Peggy are so important, in that both of them bring their own unique areas of expertise. Tom is one of the great comics editors of this whole era, going back the last twenty years. He has this really fantastic sensibility that you could certainly see with Highwater Books. I always thought Highwater was one of the few other graphic novel publishers that had a really distinct identity—I don't think you could say that for a lot of other comics publishers. Each book had a strong sense of what it was and how it related to the others. So, editorially, he brought a lot of important things with him, but also designwise, too. Especially in the early years that he was at Drawn & Quarterly, he took on a lot of the things that I didn't like doing, like catalogues and ads and so on, and he did a lot of great designs. A lot of the books we do are designed by the authors, but as we've taken to publishing different kinds of books, more and more it requires in-house design. When Tom came on board he was able to work on that—that was the perfect time.

You've talked about Tom as an editor, but I'm curious what you think your own personality as an editor is?

My role has primarily been that of a curator rather than an editor, selecting authors to be published.

Is there a trait that definitively stamps something as a Drawn & Quarterly book?

We've continued to branch out from being a company that was seen, twenty or twenty-five years ago, as just doing autobiographical comics. The kinds of comics we're pub-lishing have really expanded, so now you have books like *White Cube* [by Brecht Vandenbroucke], which is completely different on many levels from what Seth is doing, or Michael DeForge. To me, it's a natural progression: I see all our books blending in together and complementing each other. To me, it's not a big leap to go from, let's say, the Lynda Barry book—a book made up of a lot of collages, which is very different from comics—to the Petits Livres imprint, to the *Rookie* yearbooks. What holds it all together is that everything has a distinct imprint: it has the author's sensibility, a strong vision. We're a very author-driven company, and our authors succeed because their work is unique.

Where do things stand now, as D+Q completes its first twenty-five years in publishing?

It's been difficult to survive and to get to where we are now, but I think at this point D+Q is likely in its strongest position both in terms of what we publish and structurally, as a company. Editorially there's a good mix of veteran cartoonists, many of whom are currently doing some of the best work of their long careers, and new cartoonists doing groundbreaking material. And the organization supporting all of this has really developed, with key staff like Peggy, Tom, Tracy Hurren, and Julia Pohl-Miranda making indispensable and invaluable contributions on a daily basis. As long as you have the right people in place—which I think we do, at this point—things can really flourish.

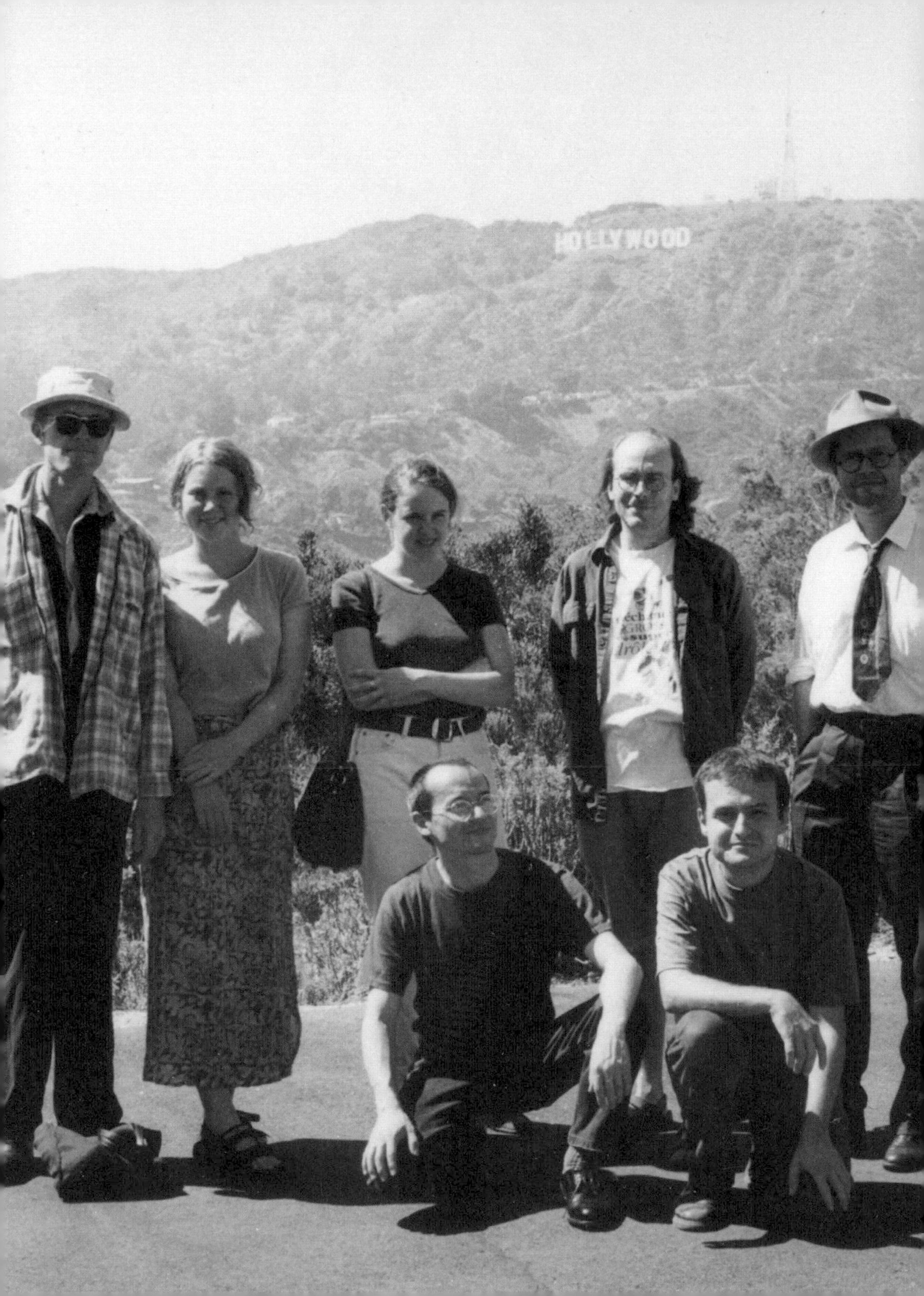
HOLLYWOOD

THE ARTIST'S PUBLISHER: A BRIEF TRIBUTE TO CHRIS OLIVEROS

written by Adrian Tomine for the Doug Wright Awards, 2009

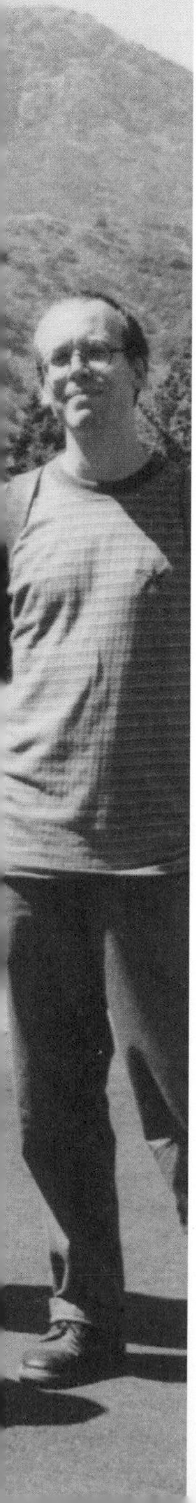

I've been asked to say a few words about the Chief, and I'm going to focus in on the thing that he'd probably least like me to talk about. Sorry, Chris. And that's the fact that he is a cartoonist. Not a lot of people know this, but that's significant as well.

First of all, I should make it clear that Chris isn't just a cartoonist—he's a very good cartoonist. His work is personal without being indulgent, naturally readable and engaging, and his drawing is thoroughly original and beautiful. Like with all my favourite cartoonists, I can spot his style in an instant simply by the way he draws hands. In my opinion, he can run rings around a lot of cartoonists who are riding high on book contracts and movie deals, and yet very few people know his work.

So clearly this isn't a case of "those who can't do, publish." The fact that Chris has an artist's eye is a big part of why everything he's ever published has looked terrific. He's the only publisher I've ever known who is as meticulous, obsessive, and attentive as the artists he works with. Early in our working relationship, there was a situation in which we were struggling to make a printer's deadline. Everything was being held up by some sort of technical glitch, and we stayed up all night, working over the phone, staring into our respective computers until we got it right. I kept expecting him to say something like "Well, it's getting late—I'd better get to sleep," or "Oh well, it's just a minor thing; you're the only one who'll notice," but he never did.

I don't want to put words in Chris's mouth here, but the impression I get is that it's because of his perfectionist streak that he has chosen to devote his life to publishing rather than full-time cartooning. It's as if, with characteristic modesty, he evaluated his own comics work and decided he'd prefer to focus the bulk of his energy on bringing other artists' work to the world. This level of humility is a rare thing, and the respect it shows for his artists is unparalleled.

A lot of us who have worked for D+Q over the years have noticed that Chris isn't always effusive in his praise. He is unfailingly kind, generous, and polite, but his response to something we've turned in can sometimes be...muted. (If people are interested, they might want to check out Julie Doucet's *365 Days* for further discussion.) But I think that when Chris offers to publish your work, he is, in a sense, saying that he loves it even more than his own work, and from one artist to another, that really is the ultimate compliment.

(As a side note, I should also mention that Chris hasn't abandoned cartooning altogether. I've heard through the grapevine that every morning, before his family is awake, before he's expected at the office, he gets up, pulls his drawing board down from a closet shelf, and makes slow, steady progress on the book he's been working on for virtually as long as I've known him. This compulsive endeavour is emblematic of the tireless dedication and commitment he shows toward all his work, and it puts to shame those of us who have fewer obligations and distractions in our life and yet still produce at a less than speedy pace. I'm guessing Joe Matt would argue that he actually has *more* obligations and distractions in his life, but that's another story.)

Chris has been doing this for twenty years, and while I know he's seen D+Q go through some challenging times, I think it can be safely said that his efforts and dedication have paid off. Not only is he responsible for bringing some of the greatest works of the medium into the world, he has also played a significant role in the sea change of respectability and liveliness that comics are presently enjoying in North America. I've known him for around fifteen years, and I consider our working relationship and friendship to be one of the luckiest breaks of my life. He's given me the career that I spent my childhood dreaming of, and he's afforded me a way of life for which I'm grateful every day.

David Collier, Jennifer Hambleton, Julie Doucet, Chester Brown, Seth, Joe Matt, Joe Sacco & Chris Oliveros (1998).

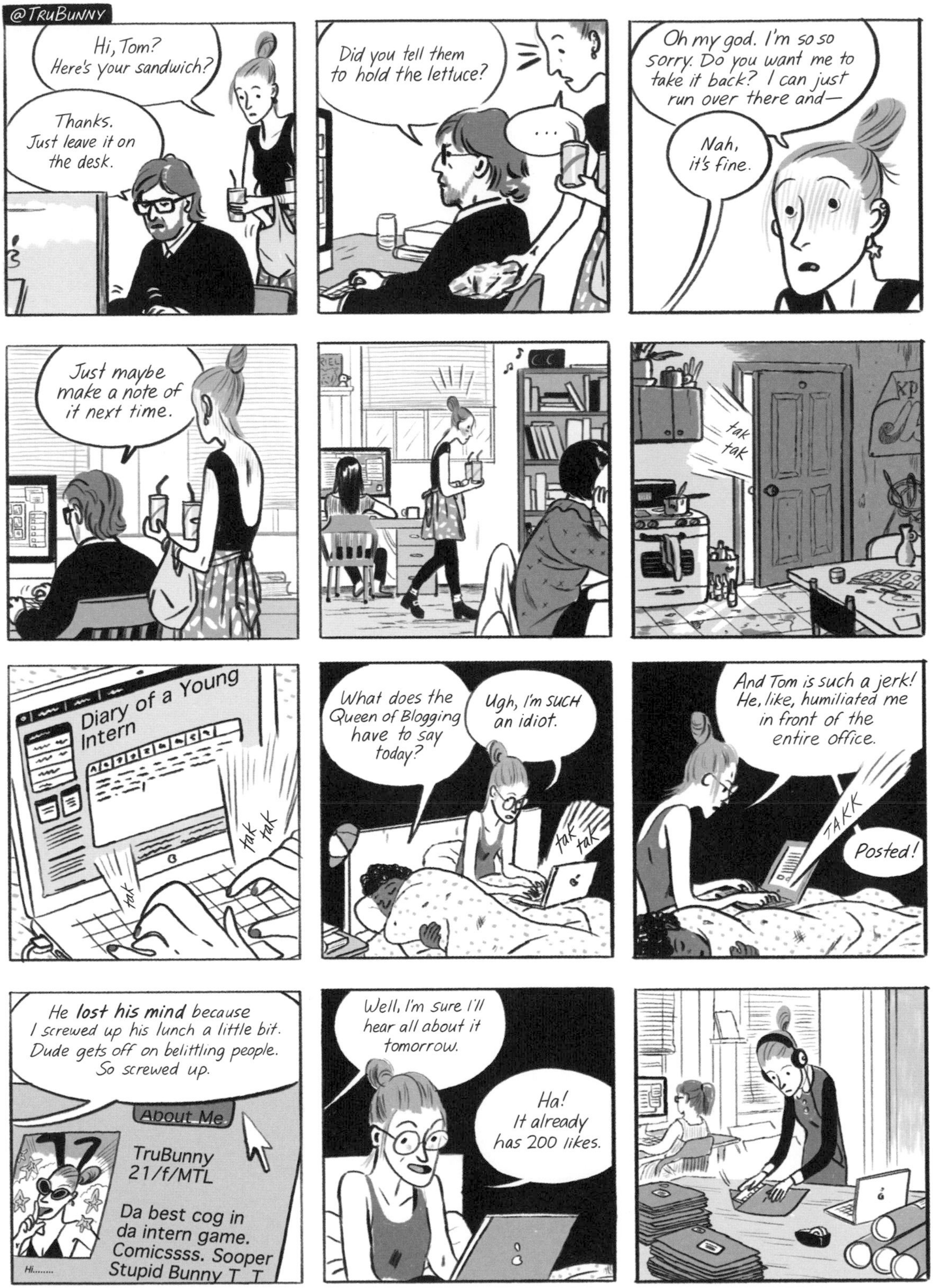
@TruBunny
Hi, Tom? Here's your sandwich?
Thanks. Just leave it on the desk.
Did you tell them to hold the lettuce?
...
Oh my god. I'm so so sorry. Do you want me to take it back? I can just run over there and—
Nah, it's fine.
Just maybe make a note of it next time.
tak tak
Diary of a Young Intern
tak
tak tak
What does the Queen of Blogging have to say today?
Ugh, I'm SUCH an idiot.
tak tak
And Tom is such a jerk! He, like, humiliated me in front of the entire office.
TAKK
Posted!
He **lost his mind** because I screwed up his lunch a little bit. Dude gets off on belittling people. So screwed up.
About Me
TruBunny
21/f/MTL
Da best cog in da intern game. Comicssss. Sooper Stupid Bunny T_T
Hi........
Well, I'm sure I'll hear all about it tomorrow.
Ha! It already has 200 likes.

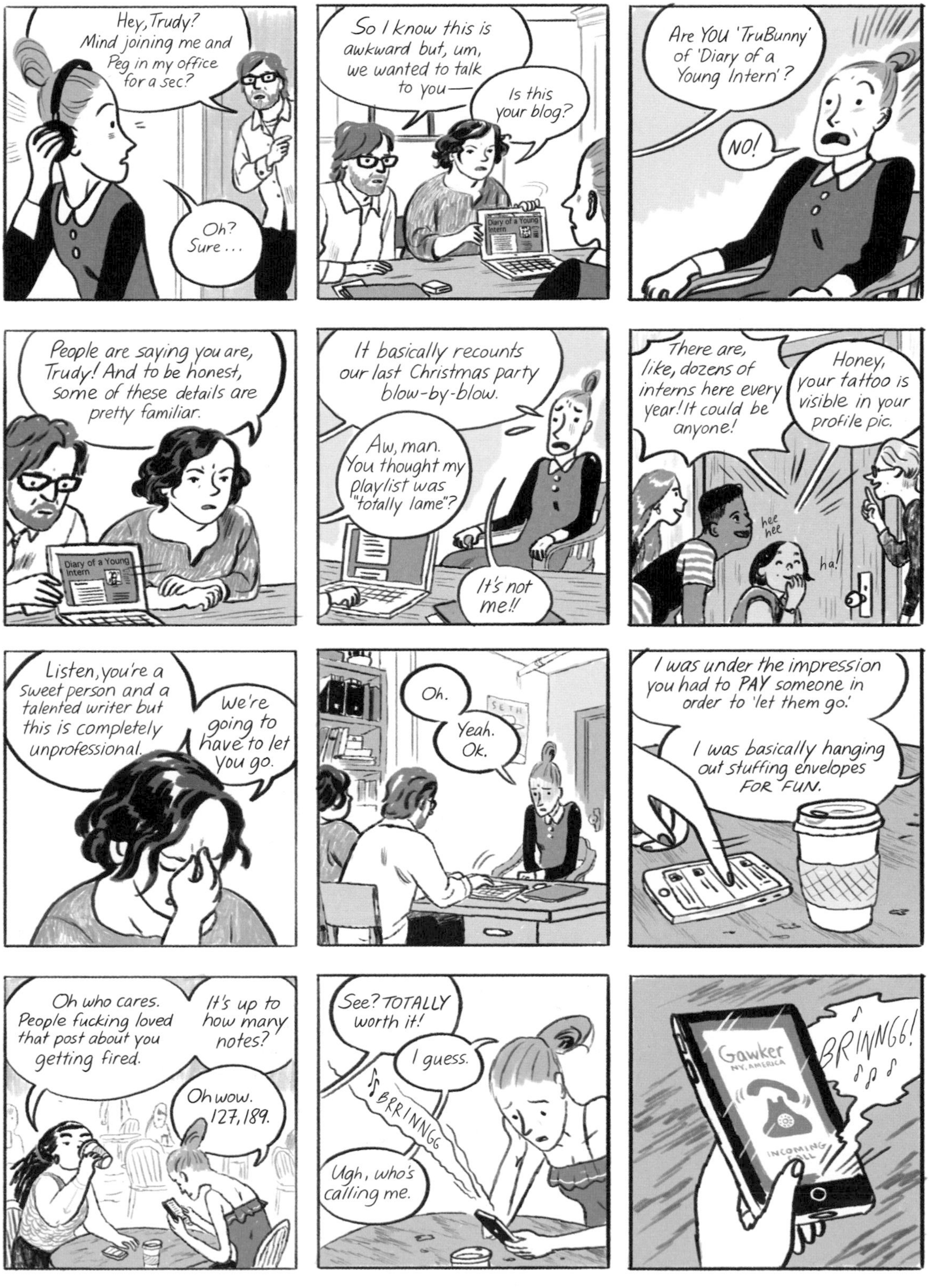

Hey, Trudy? Mind joining me and Peg in my office for a sec?
Oh? Sure . . .
So I know this is awkward but, um, we wanted to talk to you—
Is this your blog?
Diary of a Young Intern
Are YOU 'TruBunny' of 'Diary of a Young Intern'?
NO!
People are saying you are, Trudy! And to be honest, some of these details are pretty familiar.
Diary of a Young Intern
It basically recounts our last Christmas party blow-by-blow.
Aw, man. You thought my playlist was "totally lame"?
It's not me!!
There are, like, dozens of interns here every year! It could be anyone!
Honey, your tattoo is visible in your profile pic.
hee hee
ha!
Listen, you're a sweet person and a talented writer but this is completely unprofessional.
We're going to have to let you go.
Oh.
Yeah. Ok.
SETH
I was under the impression you had to PAY someone in order to 'let them go.'
I was basically hanging out stuffing envelopes FOR FUN.
Oh who cares. People fucking loved that post about you getting fired.
It's up to how many notes?
Oh wow. 127,189.
See? TOTALLY worth it!
I guess.
BRRINNGG
Ugh, who's calling me.
Gawker
NY, AMERICA
INCOMING CALL
BRINNGG!

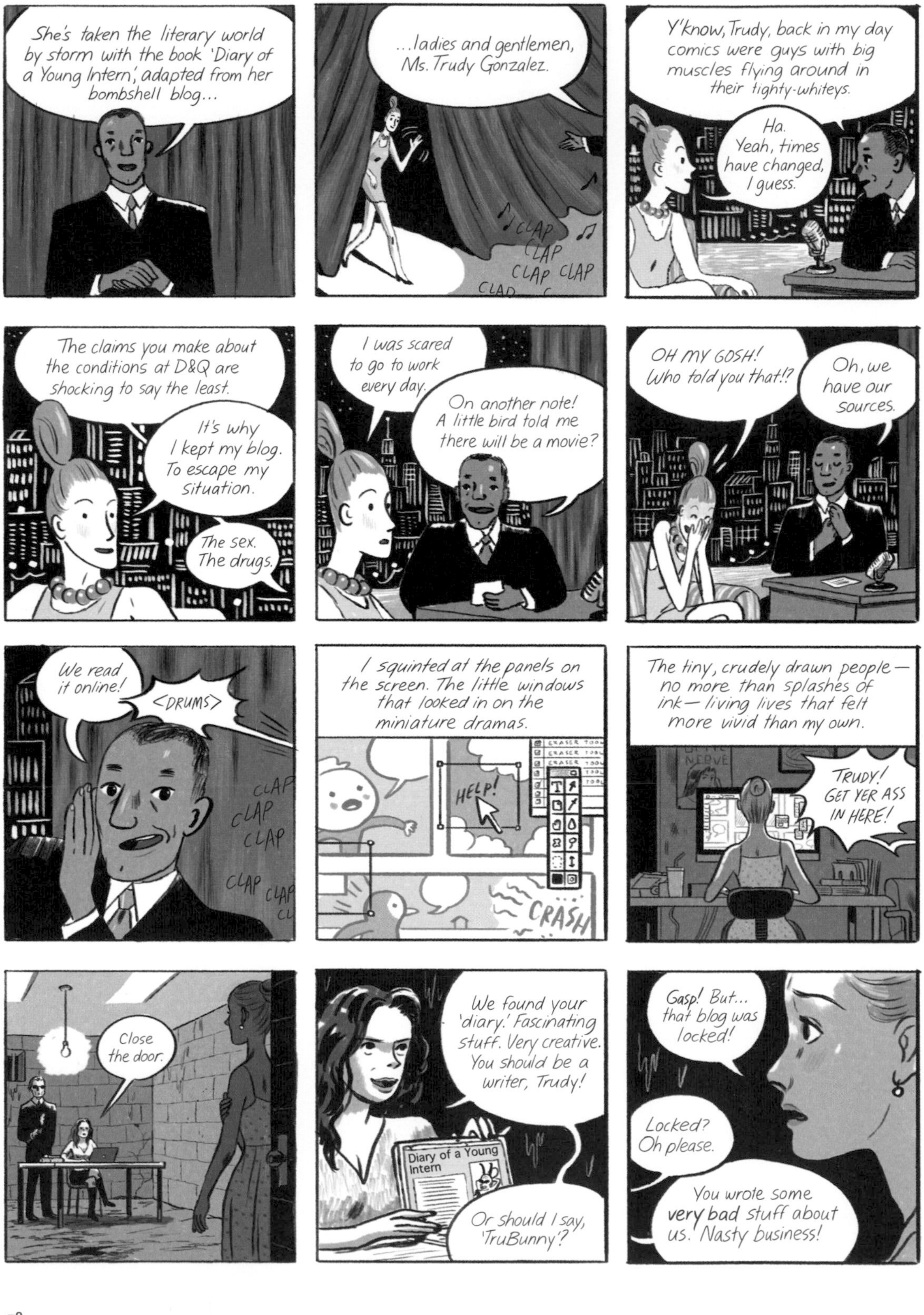
She's taken the literary world by storm with the book 'Diary of a Young Intern,' adapted from her bombshell blog...
...ladies and gentlemen, Ms. Trudy Gonzalez.
CLAP CLAP CLAP CLAP
Y'know, Trudy, back in my day comics were guys with big muscles flying around in their tighty-whiteys.
Ha. Yeah, times have changed, I guess.
The claims you make about the conditions at D&Q are shocking to say the least.
It's why I kept my blog. To escape my situation.
The sex. The drugs.
I was scared to go to work every day.
On another note! A little bird told me there will be a movie?
OH MY GOSH! Who told you that!?
Oh, we have our sources.
We read it online!
<DRUMS>
CLAP CLAP CLAP CLAP CLAP
I squinted at the panels on the screen. The little windows that looked in on the miniature dramas.
ERASER TOOL
HELP!
CRASH
The tiny, crudely drawn people— no more than splashes of ink— living lives that felt more vivid than my own.
TRUDY! GET YER ASS IN HERE!
Close the door.
We found your 'diary.' Fascinating stuff. Very creative. You should be a writer, Trudy!
Diary of a Young Intern
Or should I say, 'TruBunny'?
Gasp! But... that blog was locked!
Locked? Oh please.
You wrote some **very bad** stuff about us. Nasty business!

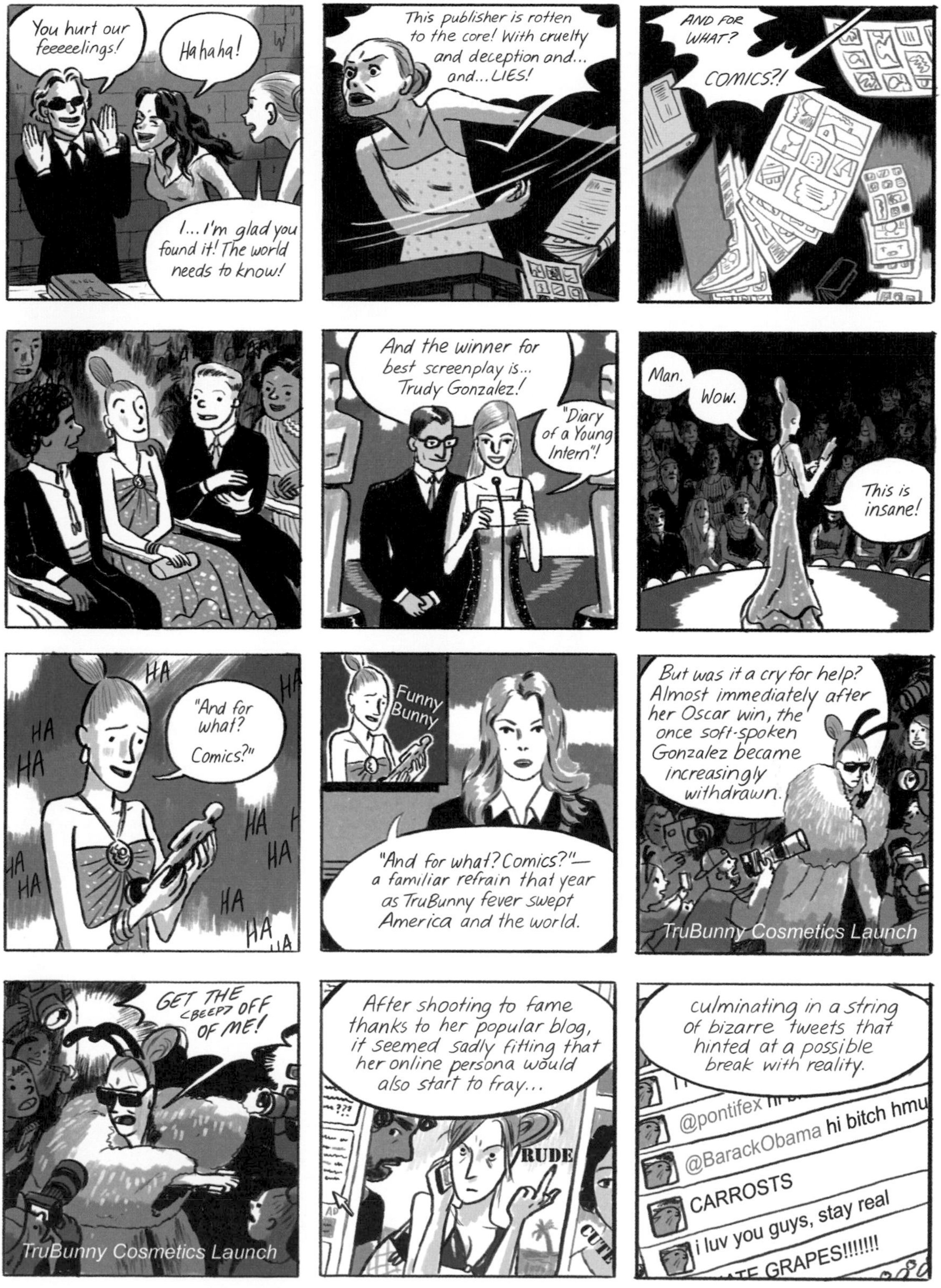
You hurt our feeeeelings!
Hahaha!
I... I'm glad you found it! The world needs to know!
This publisher is rotten to the core! With cruelty and deception and... and... LIES!
AND FOR WHAT?
COMICS?!
And the winner for best screenplay is... Trudy Gonzalez!
"Diary of a Young Intern"!
Man.
Wow.
This is insane!
HA
HA
HA
"And for what? Comics?"
HA
HA
HA
HA
HA
HA
Funny Bunny
"And for what? Comics?"— a familiar refrain that year as TruBunny fever swept America and the world.
But was it a cry for help? Almost immediately after her Oscar win, the once soft-spoken Gonzalez became increasingly withdrawn.
TruBunny Cosmetics Launch
GET THE <BEEP> OFF OF ME!
TruBunny Cosmetics Launch
After shooting to fame thanks to her popular blog, it seemed sadly fitting that her online persona would also start to fray...
RUDE
CUTE
culminating in a string of bizarre tweets that hinted at a possible break with reality.
@pontifex
@BarackObama hi bitch hmu
CARROSTS
i luv you guys, stay real
GRAPES!!!!!!!

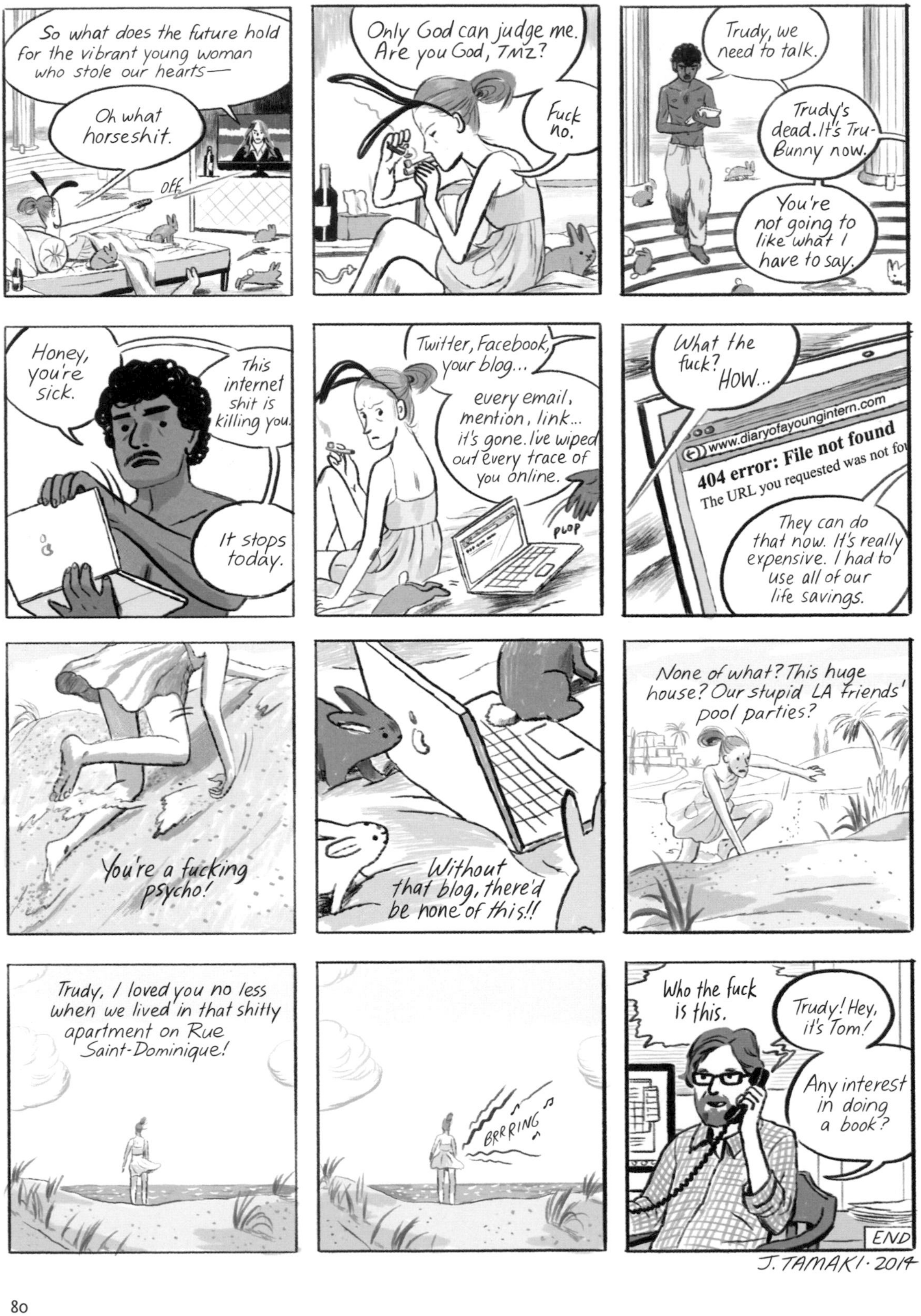
So what does the future hold for the vibrant young woman who stole our hearts—
Oh what horseshit.
OFF
Only God can judge me. Are you God, TMZ?
Fuck no.
Trudy, we need to talk.
Trudy's dead. It's Tru-Bunny now.
You're not going to like what I have to say.
Honey, you're sick.
This internet shit is killing you.
It stops today.
Twitter, Facebook, your blog...
every email, mention, link... it's gone. I've wiped out every trace of you online.
PLOP
What the fuck? HOW...
www.diaryofayoungintern.com
404 error: File not found
The URL you requested was not fo
They can do that now. It's really expensive. I had to use all of our life savings.
You're a fucking psycho!
Without that blog, there'd be none of this!!
None of what? This huge house? Our stupid LA friends' pool parties?
Trudy, I loved you no less when we lived in that shitty apartment on Rue Saint-Dominique!
BRRRING
Who the fuck is this.
Trudy! Hey, it's Tom!
Any interest in doing a book?
END
J. TAMAKI · 2014

I CAN'T IN GOOD CONSCIENCE HIRE YOU

a reminiscence by Peggy Burns, images by Pascal Girard

It is easy to describe Chris and me as opposites. He is reserved; I am extroverted. He is measured; I am impetuous. He is thoughtful; I am, ahem, "unrefined." D+Q has pretty much been his only job in his adult career; I have had several. He was born and raised in Montreal; I moved here after ten years in NYC, two years in Minneapolis, and having grown up in up-state New York. Perhaps most tellingly, he is Canadian; I am American. But for all the obvious differences in our character apparent from the moment you meet us, it is our shared belief that D+Q comes first and foremost that has made our work-ing relationship click over the past thirteen years.

I have come to my contribution to the book kicking and screaming. I was trained as a publicist by an old-school flack of the Edelman/PMK pre-internet variety. The number-one rule was that a good publicist never seeks the limelight. A publicist is neither to be named nor photographed. The cli-ent is always first. In some ways, I think this number-one rule of publicity is how Chris Oliveros has always approached running Drawn & Quarterly. The author is always first to him, and that's the single most important reason Chris has been able to run one of the most successful independent pub-lishing companies of the past three decades.

Like most decisions I make, I emailed my CV and cover letter to Chris in a mad dash of hubris and haste. It was a Friday morning in June 2003. I was in Manhattan at my office at DC Comics while Tom was home, running High-water from our Greenpoint apartment, preparing for the MoCCA festival that weekend (at the Puck Building, be-fore it became an REI). Chris was supposed to come down from Montreal and stay with us. He had stayed with us that spring and regaled us with stories about just "how cheap" Montreal was. He looked around our two-bedroom apart-ment, littered with Highwater boxes posing as furniture, and said this would be a five-hundred-dollar apartment in Montreal. Our jaws dropped. On this trip, he also asked for a tour of DC Comics, which I happily gave him. So that June morning, he emailed to say that he wouldn't be able to come, and did I happen to know any publicists who would be able to work for D+Q? I did what anyone would do. I applied for the job myself.

After pressing "send," I called Tom to tell him that I had just sent my CV to Chris to apply for a job in a city that I had never visited. Tom laughed and said, "Well, I guess we're moving to Montreal." And then I waited. I went to lunch with my friends: Vertigo senior editor Will Dennis; artist Cliff Chiang; Leon Avelino, then a DC comics contracts assistant and now the publisher of Secret Acres. We would spend way too long in the Time Warner cafeteria playing our usual game of casting DC Comics staff: Hollywood blockbuster; indie Sundance film; network original movie; and Lifetime special. The joke was always the same: I would insist Parker Posey play me in each version, and Leon would never cast her as me. I would get mad. "Leon, why won't you give me Parker! I cast Kevin Spacey for you!" Cliff and Will would just laugh. Our lunches would stretch from one to two hours, mostly derailed by me. I loved my job at DC Comics, but my passion did not lie there. I was obsessed with indie comics. I was dating Tom; had devoured comics from Fanta-graphics, Top Shelf, and D+Q; had befriended Joe Sacco and Ivan Brunetti. There was something about the immediacy of the form, and the cartoonists that practised it, that took my life by storm. When my father would come visit me in NYC, he would remark, "The comics in your apartment are much different from the comics in your office."

That afternoon, after returning from lunch and seeing no email from Chris, I emailed him to demand an answer. He immediately called me; he thought it was some sort of a mean-girl joke. "It's not," I insisted. "I'm serious!" He said, "You would have to take an enormous pay cut and move from NYC." I replied, "You said Montreal was cheap!" I was hired that afternoon.

I am often wrongly referred to as Chris's first employee. I wasn't his first (that would be Traie Payne, who came in on weekends to help with scanning), second (that would be Elizabeth Walker), or third (D+Q's first intern, Rebecca Rosen, hired a few months before me when she was just seventeen years old). I was the lacklustre fourth employee in the history of D+Q.

By San Diego Comic-Con that summer, Chris had submit-ted a visa application to hire me. Out of the four Comic-Cons

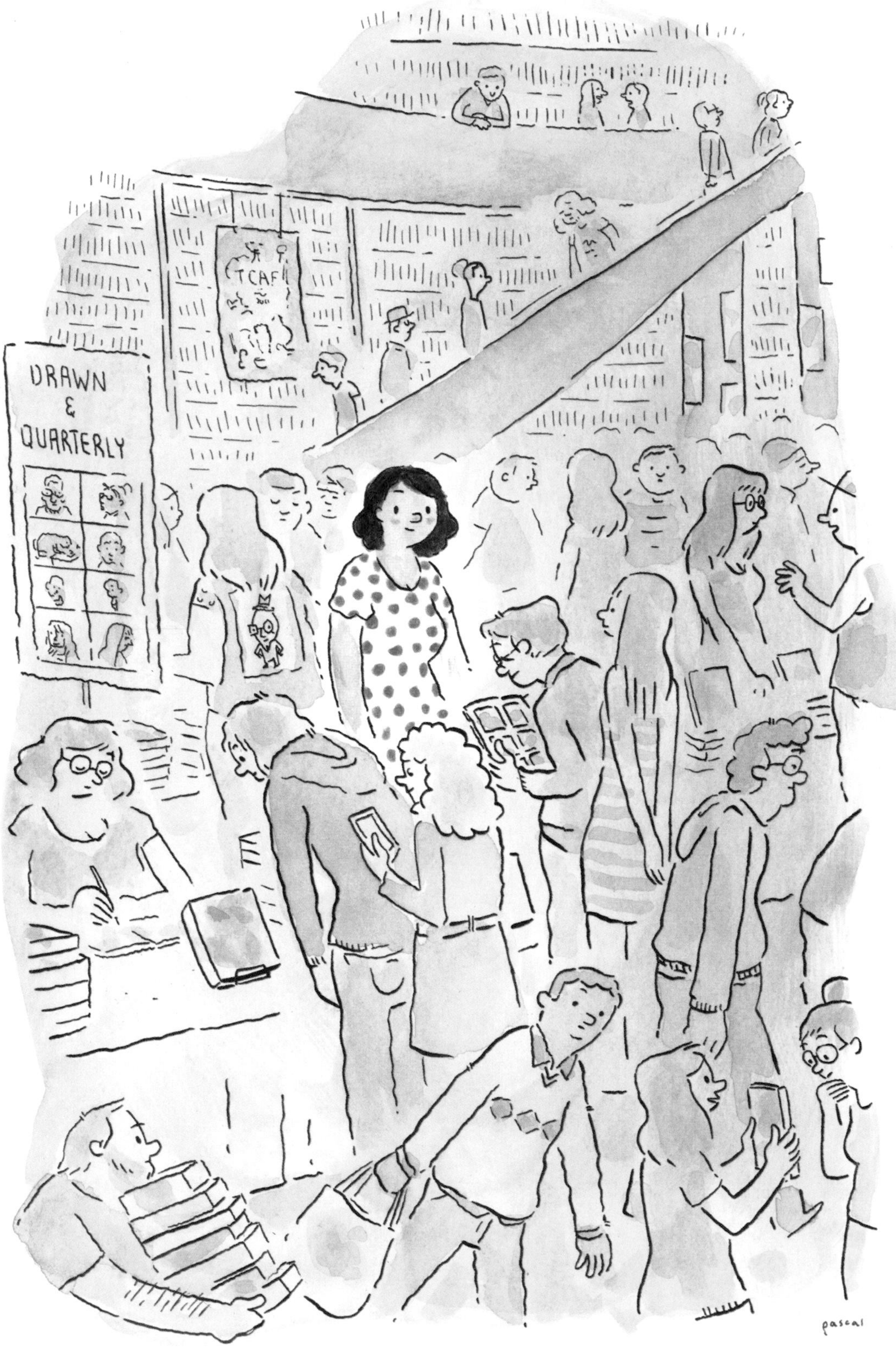
DRAWN
&
QUARTERLY
TCAF
pascal

I attended while working for DC, it wasn't the best—of course, that would be the show when I met Tom—but it was by far the second-best show. Working the DC Comics booth was gruelling. It is the epicentre of the show. It is where the cosplayers meet and take photos. It is the focal point where everyone meets if they get lost. It is where, in the course of an eight-hour day, no one may ever actually ask you about a comic. Knowing this was my last summer was liberating. Knowing that by the next year, I would be working at D+Q—which had just debuted Chris Ware's *ACME Novelty Datebook*—was thrilling.

One morning at Comic-Con, Chris and I met for breakfast to make a plan, but instead he dropped a series of bombshells. After a long, quiet, and steady period of being financially self-sufficient, the company had hit a number of economic setbacks. D+Q was still struggling from the fallout of its original book distributor LPC's bankruptcy, and it was waiting for the fruits of the new distribution deal with Chronicle Books. The company had printed several books in Europe: *ACME Novelty Datebook*, 5 *Is the Perfect Number*, and *Drawn & Quarterly* volume 5. When payment came due, the dollar fell in relation to the Euro and the costs of the print runs tripled. These setbacks were a perfect storm of bad luck for a company just trying to get ahead in the new book market. On a sunny morning at a sidewalk café, Chris Oliveros said, "I don't know if the company will still be standing in six months. I can't in good conscience hire you." I immediately called Tom back in Brooklyn, and we both agreed that we couldn't let Drawn & Quarterly go out of business. We had to move to Montreal.

The visa came through in August. Tom and I travelled up to Montreal that month—it's always a good idea to visit the city you're moving your whole life to, right? Chris was so quiet. He toured us around the city on foot, taking us on a three-mile walk. We walked past a yard sale, and there was a vintage two-hole punch for twenty-five cents. Chris bought it for me, and we still use it in the office to this day. We returned to Chris's balcony, where his wife, Marina, made us lunch. Their kids played in the alley, and Julie Doucet joined us. We drank a Quebecois craft beer, called La Fin du Monde, to our future. On the cusp of my thirtieth birthday, I was not only getting out of NY, I was going to Montreal. I was leaving the corporate world and going to Drawn & Quarterly.

The only thing in our way was the matter of our wedding. Tom and I had sent out save-the-dates for an October wedding in North Adams, Massachusetts, to get married at MassMOCA. We cancelled the wedding the day before our deposit became unrefundable.

When I turned in my notice to my boss, John Nee, he asked what it would take to keep me. I said, "Nothing. I'm taking a pay cut." He asked me how much; I told him. He didn't ask any more questions. I recommended that he hire David Hyde of Vintage Books to be my replacement. Since I had just toured Chris Oliveros around the office that spring, no one was surprised. It was unceremonious. Even in the comics press, no one wrote about the job change. That August, DC Comics and *MAD* magazine took their annual field trip to Six Flags (the trip would form the basis for the yearly D+Q field trip to La Ronde). Paul Levitz, who had always been a very paternal mentor to me, took me aside and gave me the single best piece of advice about moving to Montreal. "It's Ke-Beck, not Kwa-Beck," he said. Prescient that I would be doing more than just publicity, he said not to be shy about going to the McGill bookstore and picking up a textbook on business; then he said, "Good luck at Top Shelf." It seems unfair to include this line, but it is true, and too good not to, and really why should the president of DC Comics know the difference between Top Shelf and D+Q? Since then, Paul has remained a great colleague, stopping by the D+Q booth every summer. He even congratulated me after D+Q landed our client partnership with FSG a few years after I started working there.

When Tom and I moved, we rented pretty much the crappiest U-Haul in all of Brooklyn and packed it to the gills. We lived around the corner from the cartoonist Tom Hart, who later told us that he rescued the Highwater submissions box from the garbage. North of Albany, our gas tank went from half-full to empty in a matter of minutes and we exited off the highway and ran out of gas. Somehow we managed to get to Montreal.

That September, I slowly realized the difference between a D+Q cartoonist and a DC Comics freelancer. At Word on the Street Toronto, I gave Chester, Seth, and Adrian a fistful of sharpies to do their signings. They all politely thanked me and then pulled out their vintage pencil cases and rapidographs and special pens with which to sign. Of course! Working on press simultaneously for *The Fixer* by Joe Sacco and *Louis Riel* by Chester Brown, I learned that the friendly people-person Joe hated to be interviewed and do publicity, whereas the shy introvert Chester loved it and would call me weekly to see if anyone wanted to talk to him. Early the next year, I travelled to NYC to help Adrian launch *Optic Nerve* no. 9 (his first comic after *Summer Blonde*) at Housing Works. When his signing started, I sat six inches away from him, answered all the questions from his fans for him, and would tell each fan, "He's only signing the latest issue." Adrian

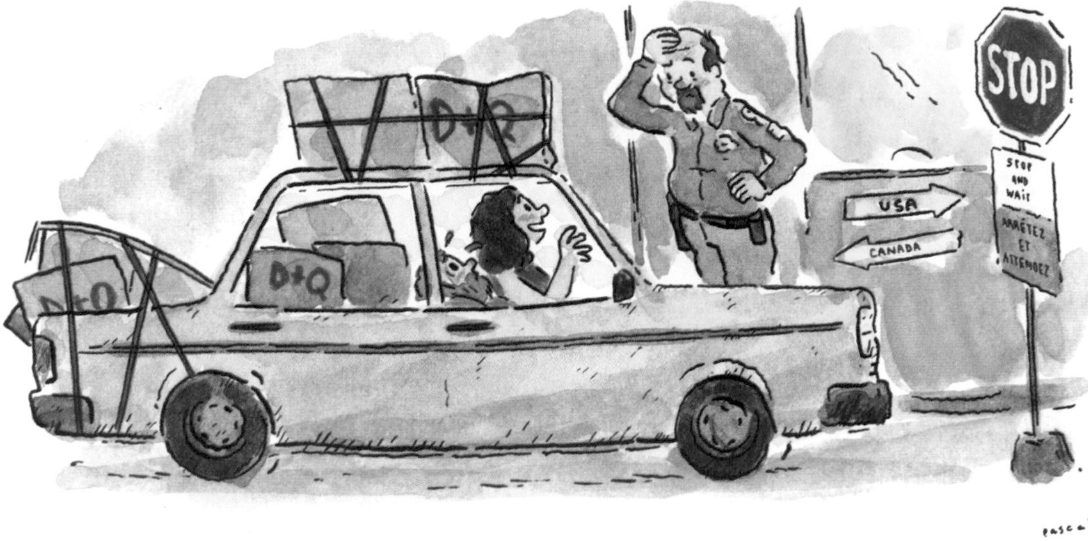
STOP
USA
CANADA
D+Q

was horrified, I'm sure, but politely told me he could do the signing on his own. I backed up, only to watch the nicest, sweetest stream of fans, most of them women, anxiously tell him how much they liked his work and then move on. To me, this politeness was unheard of. At DC, if I wasn't managing every detail of a Gaiman or Miller signing, the fanboys stayed forever, pulling out every issue of *Daredevil* and *Sandman*. Here with Adrian, everyone was just…nice.

I like to think that the cartoonists immediately recognized that my outgoing personality complemented Chris's cool nature. And over the first year, Tom slowly took on more responsibility. Chris had not minced his words at that San Diego breakfast. Editorially, D+Q was the best it had ever been. Financially, there was no money. One of my early paycheques bounced, and cheques bouncing that first year was not a rare occurrence. There was no credit line. I used my own credit card for all travel and mailings. In order to save thousands of dollars by avoiding international postage on press copies sent to the US, I started renting a car monthly and doing the mailings by hand at the post office in Champlain, NY.

Chris was right in other positive respects. Montreal was cheaper. In Brooklyn, rent was $1,650 for a two-bedroom; in Montreal, rent was $625 for a floor in a hundred-year-old triplex. There was no commuting: we lived a block from work. Since Tom and I had no friends, we rarely went out. There were no East Village brunches or happy hours or nights out until four in the morning. Living was cheaper, but not necessarily easier. We didn't speak French, and we had no time to learn, as working at D+Q was a fifty- or sixty-hour week. Chris had his third child, Charles, that year, so I travelled by myself to all shows. If the company could afford it, Tom would come with me. For my first MoCCA for D+Q, Tom and Chris packed our 1984 Volvo with so many books for the drive to NYC, I couldn't see out the back window. The car barely cleared the ground, and we definitely did not clear customs at Champlain. It was laughable until I spent five hours in a dizzy maze of customs brokers and finally threw myself at the mercy of the officer on duty, who let me cross with an "unofficial entry."

The first year was exhausting but thrilling. While the financial aspect was precarious, doing publicity for D+Q was the most satisfying job I'd ever had. Immediately, people took notice. *Louis Riel* became a bestseller. *The Fixer* and *Louis Riel* went back to press. Over one hundred people showed up to the aforementioned launch of *Optic Nerve* no. 9, and Adrian was featured in almost every weekly (there were several back then!). Ten months into the job, Charles McGrath did a cover story on comics for the *New York Times Magazine*, Chester did the cover, and D+Q was front and centre. With the talent of our cartoonists, publicity for Drawn & Quarterly has always been the easiest part of my job.

Sometime during that first year, I audaciously marched into Chris's office and declared that Chronicle was not a good distributor for us. Chris did not laugh me out of his office. He listened to my case and he agreed. He called Random House while I called Farrar, Straus and Giroux, and a month later we rented a car and drove all night to Brooklyn to sleep on the floor in the Brooklyn apartment of one of my girlfriends. We got up the next day and pitched ourselves to the fanciest NYC publishers, asking them to have faith in our two-person operation from Montreal. We put on our song and dance and were back on I-87 heading north by 5:00 PM Even though we landed the deal, switching distributors for the second time in two years wasn't the soundest financial decision we could have made, but we were in agreement that it had to be done for the good of the books and artists.

Why I didn't run for the hills that first year wasn't just to do with the faith that Chris had in me, but the faith that the artists had in me, and in Tom, and in the three of us as a team. Chris and I had a motto that first year. It's embarrassing, but here it is: "What would Pantheon do?" Pantheon, at the time, had all of the bestselling graphic novels, and they had increased the stakes tenfold for independent publishers. We had to give our authors reasons to believe in us. We had to do right by them. We had to show them that their faith in us was not for naught. The first thing was to be able to get publicity: done. The second was to get better literary distribution: we signed up as a client partner of Farrar, Straus and Giroux. The third was to offer foreign rights. When D+Q was a one-man operation, Chris never insisted that his authors give him world rights, because he didn't have the time to properly manage foreign deals. We signed with the Transatlantic Literary Agency and contracted world rights wherever possible with our backlist and frontlist, and our rep, Samantha Haywood, started selling our books all over the world. At the time, we simply viewed this as a way to be competitive, but in hindsight, it gave us another way to make money, which we needed very badly then. During this first year, I was the only one taking a paycheque. I think Tom made something embarrassing for someone of his age and stature, like two hundred dollars a week—it was all D+Q could afford. And who knows what Chris paid himself.

Somehow, over the next few years, it all started to come together, slowly, very slowly. It was a lucky break for Chris to hire me and eventually Tom as a package: we were two employees for the very low price of one. And a luckier break for all of us to have Jamie Quail, Rebecca Rosen, and Jessica Campbell as our part-time support staff a few years later. They never had to be told the various mottos we lived under—"authors first," "what would Pantheon do"—they just got it. They were university students when they worked at D+Q, and they're no longer here. All three are off to greener pastures. If you ever have the chance to hire them, you should—you won't be sorry.

Recently, I said to Chris, "This anniversary book is too painful. The first five years of my being here are too painful to revisit. I can't do it." Chris replied, "The first five? Try the first seven or eight years!" He was right. It was hard for a very long time. Throw in opening a bookstore during the recession, the ascent of the ebook, Tom and me having two kids, various health concerns, living in a city where your entire worth as a citizen is summed up in the question: "When do you plan to learn French?" and it's enough to send you back to the States. I admit, I did keep an eye on the classifieds; however, I never again sent my CV in haste and hubris.

In January 2014, Chris sent Tom and me a flood of emails in regards to wanting to meet with us. The D+Q office is an open loft, so private conversations are a weird covert operation of outside meetings. We met in the lobby of a nearby building, and Chris told us his plan. After twenty-five years he wants to step down as publisher; he wants to draw comics. He and I had spoken about forming a succession plan, but I always thought that Chris would be at D+Q forever. But in a way, this makes perfect sense. He is a true artist at heart.

But to pass your twenty-five years of work to me and Tom?! "Who does this?" I cried to him. Chris has been answering the same question in various ways since he started the comic-book company. Who does that? Who assembles the most esteemed group of cartoonists the world has ever seen with practically no capital, working out of his apartment? Who hires a NYC publicist in Montreal? Who puts his complete faith in his authors and employees? Who opens an English bookstore in Montreal? Who hands over the reins with the utmost faith and confidence?

"Exactly. Nobody does this," he answered.

Only one person does this. It's Chris Oliveros, the Chief, the man with the gentle, selfless fortitude to come out on top in the worst of times. He is one of the kindest, sweetest, most generous people I have ever met. I am proud to call him my best friend.

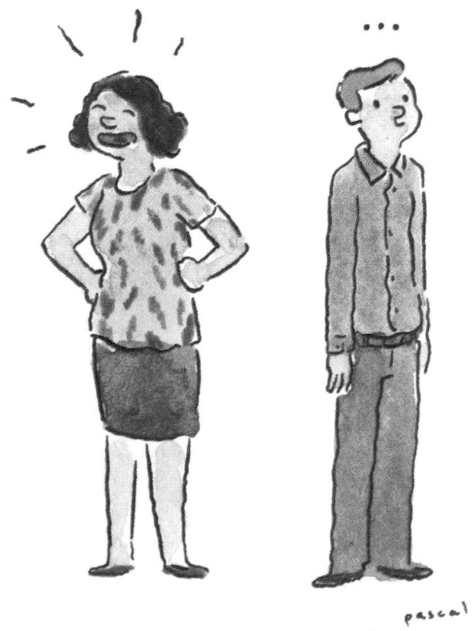

pascal

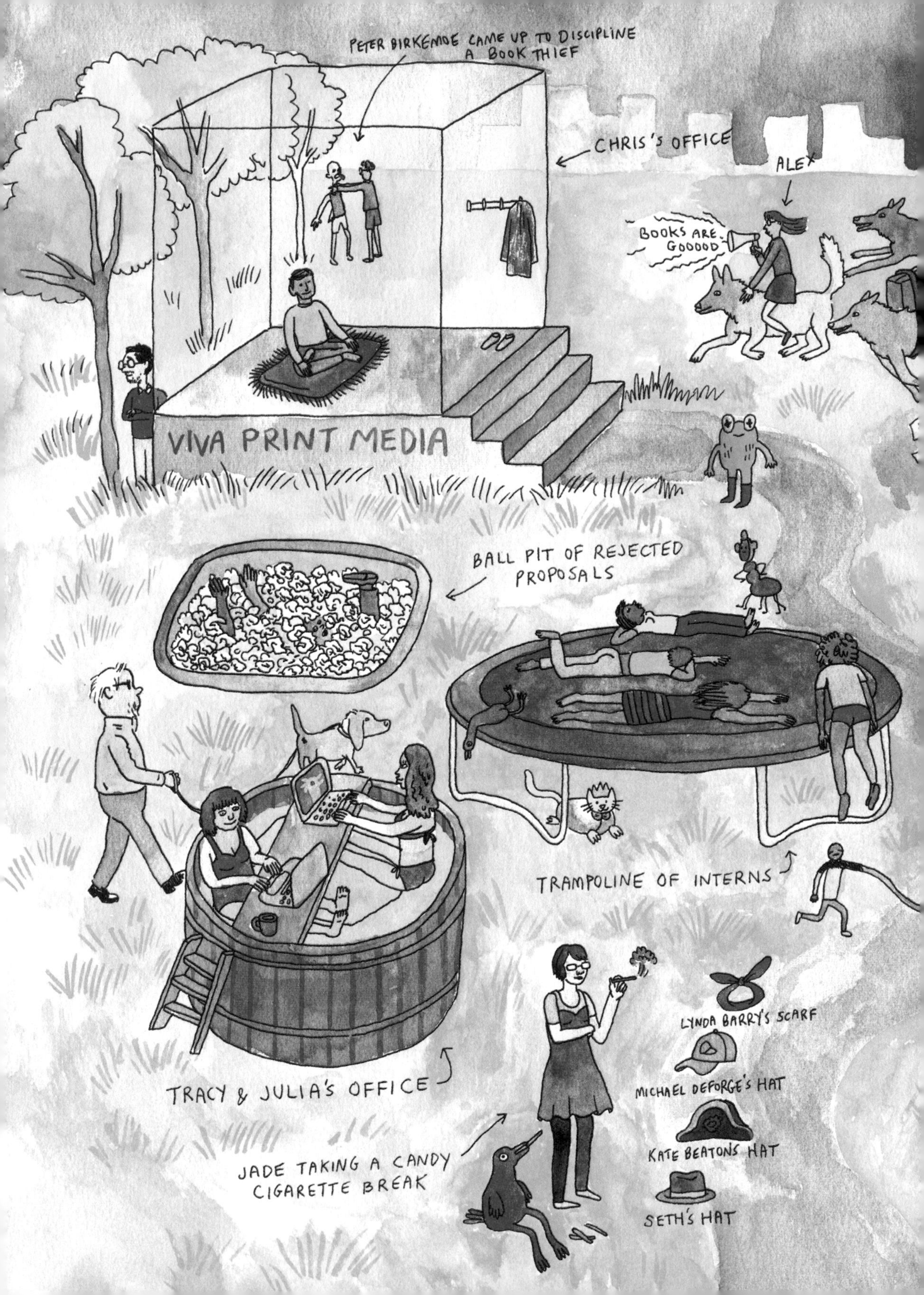
PETER BIRKEMOE CAME UP TO DISCIPLINE A BOOK THIEF
CHRIS'S OFFICE
ALEX
BOOKS ARE GOOOOD
VIVA PRINT MEDIA
BALL PIT OF REJECTED PROPOSALS
TRAMPOLINE OF INTERNS
TRACY & JULIA'S OFFICE
LYNDA BARRY'S SCARF
MICHAEL DEFORGE'S HAT
KATE BEATONS HAT
SETH'S HAT
JADE TAKING A CANDY CIGARETTE BREAK

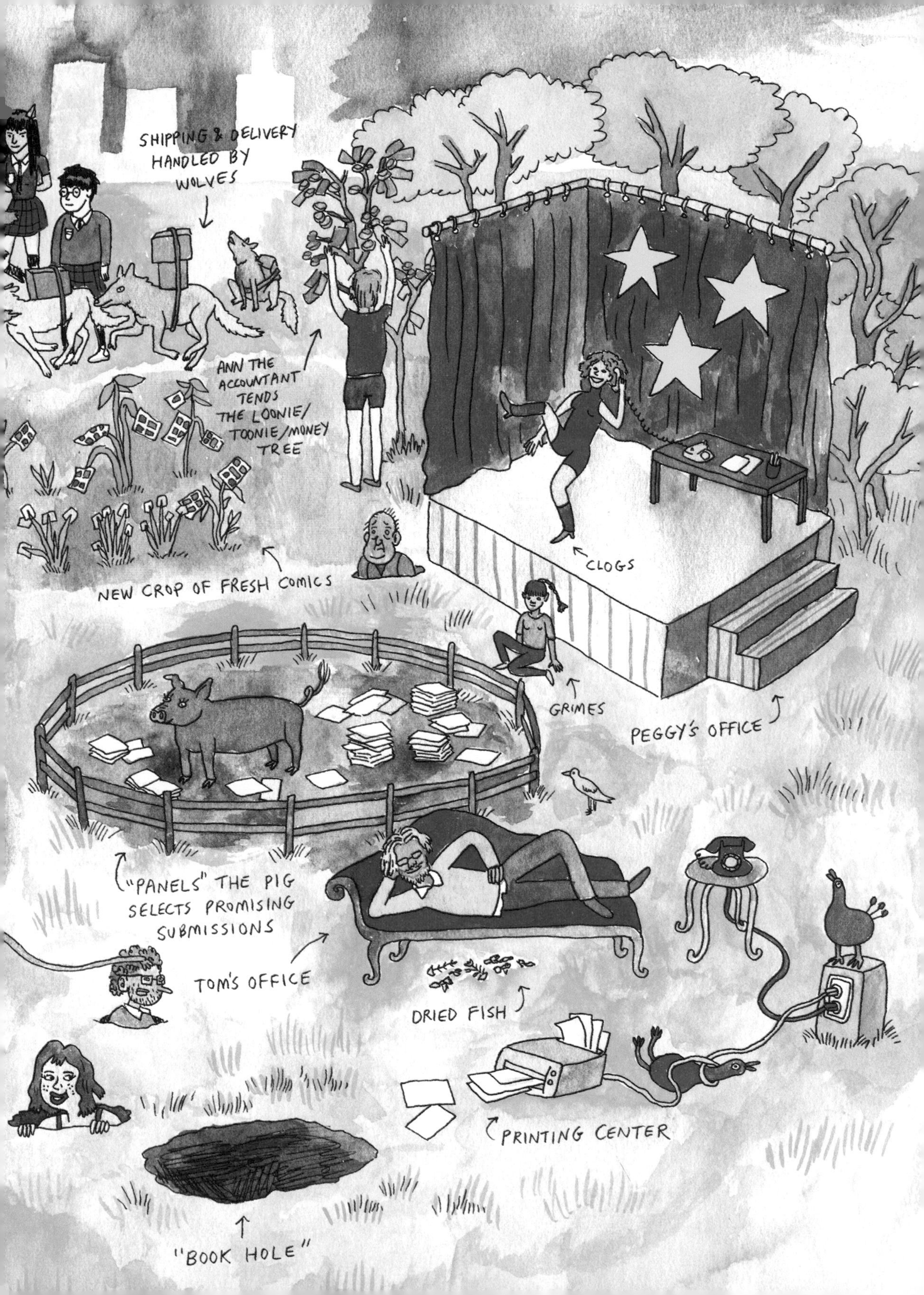
SHIPPING & DELIVERY HANDLED BY WOLVES
ANN THE ACCOUNTANT TENDS THE LOONIE/ TOONIE/MONEY TREE
NEW CROP OF FRESH COMICS
CLOGS
GRIMES
PEGGY'S OFFICE
"PANELS" THE PIG SELECTS PROMISING SUBMISSIONS
TOM'S OFFICE
DRIED FISH
PRINTING CENTER
"BOOK HOLE"

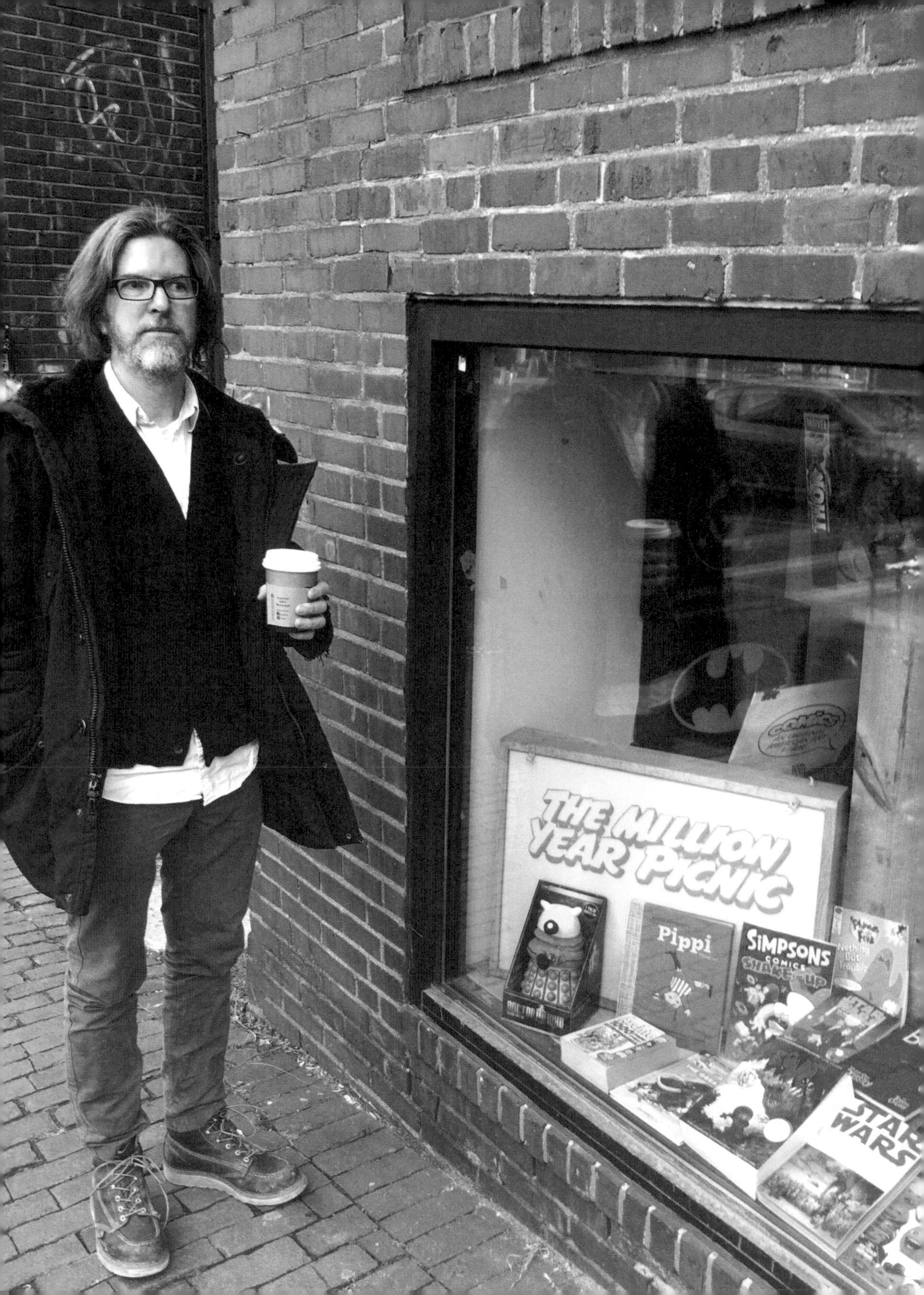
THE MILLION YEAR PICNIC
Pippi
SIMPSONS COMICS
STAR WARS

A COMPLETE MESS OF OVERLAPPING: LIVING THE COMICS LIFE WITH TOM DEVLIN

an interview by Sean T. Collins, images by Vanessa Davis

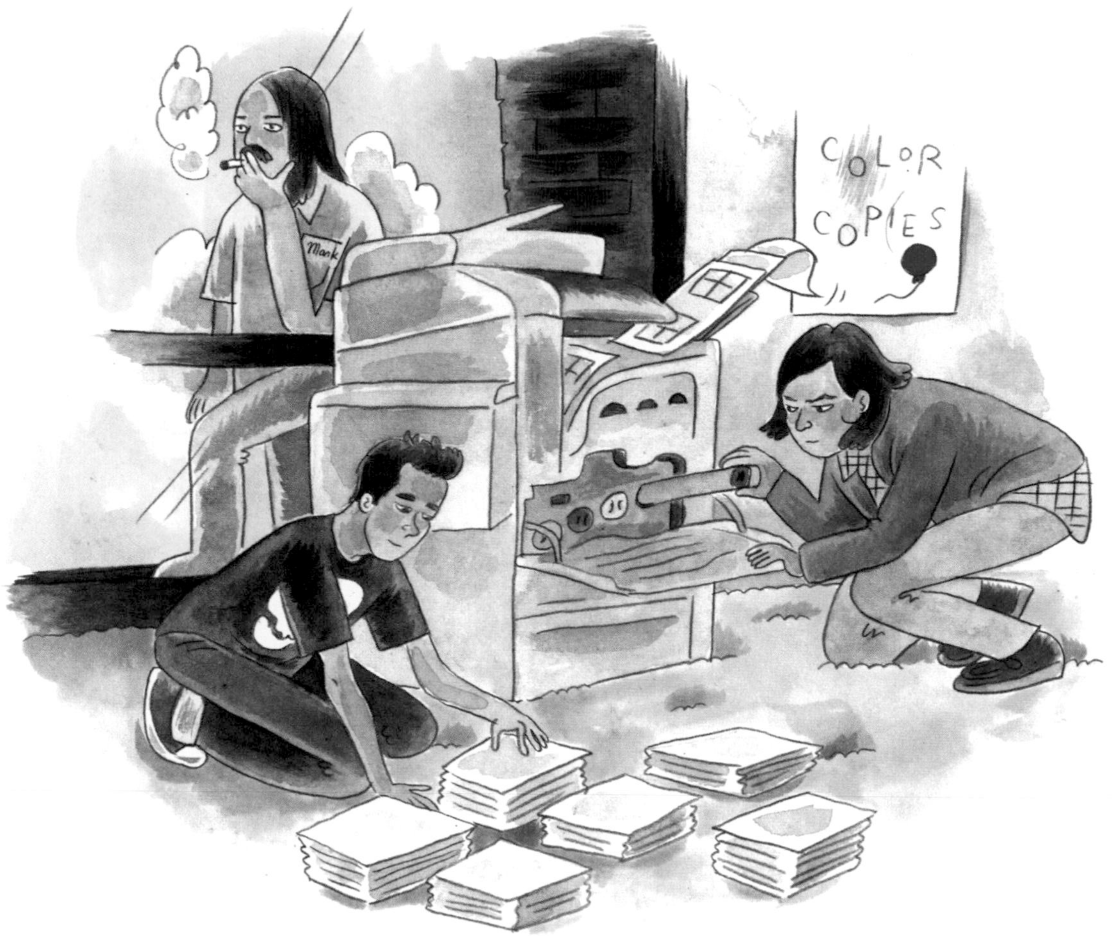
Mark
COLOR COPIES

With his expertise and aesthetic hidden like Russian nesting dolls inside the larger edifice of Drawn & Quarterly, Tom Devlin has helped make D+Q what it is today, following a solo publishing career that helped make comics what it is today in turn. As the founder of the hugely influential early-2000s publishing house Highwater Books, Devlin gave North American alternative-comics audiences their first book-length exposure to a wide range of innovative artists, many of whom have since rejoined him at D+Q: the minimalist John Porcellino, the maximalists Marc Bell and Ron Regé, Jr., Fort Thunder alumnus Brian Ralph and his genre-rooted explorations. The high production values, lovely and thoughtful design work, and bookshelf-ready format he brought to these projects—decisions made in part thanks to hard-earned experience as a retailer and distributor—anticipated the graphic-novel boom that Chris Oliveros's company helped spark. Together with Oliveros and associate publisher Peggy Burns, he now has a hand in most everything D+Q publishes.

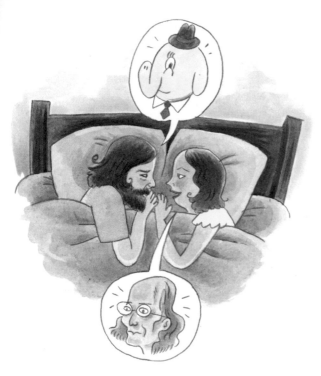

And his shifting duties extend beyond office hours, since he and Burns are married with children, making them arguably the First Family of alt-comix. To hear Devlin tell it, given his overwhelming interest in comics as an art and a business, that kind of overlap was all but inevitable.

How early were you exposed to comics, Tom? And which ones?

Like most people, I read the newspaper comics. This would be the late sixties, early seventies, so I loved *Peanuts*, *Pogo*, *Lil' Abner*, *Miss Peach*, *Tumbleweeds*, *Broom-Hilda*, *B.C.* My mom worked at the town library (still does), so I would go through the magazines there looking for any comics or comiclike things—like *Goofus and Gallant*—I could find. I remember reading a lot of hot rod comics—for some reason the library had a subscription to *CARtoons* magazine. I had no interest in cars but comics were comics. I read a lot of *Archies*, Gold Key supermarket three-packs, and Don Martin paperbacks. Part of this was that I was also drawing and wanted to be a cartoonist, so I was checking out all the books on *How to Be...* from the library that I could find, too.

Eventually, I started reading superheroes. I always figured I didn't care what kind of comics I read—I just wanted to read as many as possible—and there were just a lot of superheroes. There was a newsstand the next town over, so my brother and I would get my mom to drop us off while she went shopping nearby. It's called Out of Town News in Norwood, Massachusetts, and it's still there, or at least it was five years ago. I was a Marvel kid, especially once I was old enough to go into Boston and Cambridge and visit all the places that sold comics like Newbury Comics and Million Year Picnic. A bunch of us in the neighbourhood would go in and buy back issues and swap them. I was really into the oddball teams like *Guardians of the Galaxy* or books like *Deathlok* but lost interest relatively quickly, sometime before high school ended—maybe sophomore or junior year?

By the time I got to college, I wasn't drawing much—comics were frowned upon in high school art classes—and I don't recall reading much at all. I had a friend in college who was into comics, and he got me back into it a bit. I almost immediately got into that new wave of alternative books, most not so good, but they led me right to *Love and Rockets*. And that was that.

What was it about *Love and Rockets* that struck you, versus the stuff you'd read before?

I always loved reading comics, but by then I'd gotten bored a couple of times. When I found *Love and Rockets*, it perfectly matched the punk/post-punk world I was into. And it was just soap operatic enough; the soap opera stuff was always my favourite part of comics, whether it was *Archie* or [John] Romita's *Spider-Man*. It was ambitious, and funny. I wasn't very sophisticated, but I knew *everything* was in that comic.

You wound up spending a lot of time working in comics retail and distribution positions, and my impression is that, almost uniquely among major figures in alternative comics, it really shaped your approach to the medium.

Like many people in their twenties, I worked my crappy retail jobs. I was really into music, though to say all kinds wouldn't really be the truth. I liked punk and some dance stuff. College radio stuff mostly—R.E.M., Echo and the Bunnymen, the Smiths, lots of local garage pop bands. So I worked at a music chain called Strawberries while in university. Afterwards, I applied for a job at Newbury Comics, which had started out as a comics and punk music store and then become like a bigger pop-culture emporium with large comics and music components. I was the assistant comics guy at the Harvard Square store for a few months, and through that job I met the guys who worked at Diamond

Comics, where we picked up our weekly comics for the store. I started working at Diamond myself, off and on, for years. My first boss there was a guy named Ralph Turner, who was transferred there from Baltimore and maybe not always happy about it, but he was a good boss who taught me how to be detail-oriented. He was later replaced by Jeep Holland, who is one of the greatest characters I've ever met. He was part of the music scene in Michigan in the sixties and had great stories about the MC5 and the Stooges; he was famous for giving Iggy Pop the "Iggy" nickname.

While at Diamond, I rewrote the warehouse comics-sorting computer program to make it more efficient, and to install some checks and balances so we didn't mis-pick the comics. I mostly did this to make my own job easier, but also because when I saw something done wrong it drove me crazy until I had to fix it. This might be a personality flaw. I was kind of a lousy employee in my twenties. I was an arrogant know-it-all. I would get angry and quit and go somewhere else for a while but then I would come back because I really only wanted to work in comics.

After Diamond, I started working at the Million Year Picnic in Harvard Square. I learned a lot from [my boss] Tony Davis on what sold, how to rack comics, how to bring people into the store. At the same time, I got deeply into the small press scene—not just doing the ordering of D+Q and Fantagraphics books, but also the minis and some self-published stuff. All this experience made me very aware of the numbers. I saw what comics sold and even had an idea why. For ten years, practically every single comic printed passed through my hands. I saw so many poorly printed comics. So many poorly designed comics. The good stuff really stood out.

I always had an evangelical streak with comics, but working in a store and controlling how many copies were on the shelves really turned that up. I started booking signings with minicomics and alternative artists. I met Ron Regé, Jr., who worked at a nearby copy shop. I eventually met Greg Cook, Jef Czekaj, and Jordan Crane. Jessica Abel and I became friends, and she introduced me to Brian Ralph. I used to sit behind the counter at the store and decide on a cartoonist I wanted to meet, then call them up and chat and invite them to come to the store for a signing. That's how I met folks like Jessica, Adrian Tomine, Chris Ware, Tom Hart, John Porcellino, Dave Cooper, Jason Lutes, Megan Kelso, and Seth.

Were you drawing during these periods? Self-publishing, or publishing anyone else? I'm curious as to how your creative growth dovetailed with your nuts-and-bolts work, and whether you see the two as interrelated.

I would draw off and on, but I was very conscious that I was drawing in a watered-down Gilbert Hernandez or Chester Brown style (depending on my mood). I was not very disciplined. I'd go through periods of intense drawing, but I never worked that hard at it, or not as hard as you need to. I did a minicomic for a bit called *Eyewater*, which is where the High-water Books name came from. But out of that comic grew the first *Coober Skeber* anthology, which was an Angoulême giveaway. That was the first time I published other people. I liked wrangling everyone, and I liked the sense of accomplishment.

There was a copy shop across the hall from the Million Year Picnic, and I would spend hours in there on my break or even my day off cutting and pasting up comics, trying to get them to look just right. This was all sort of pre-computer. It was all scissors and glue sticks then. They used to have different colour cartridges for the black and white copy machines, so I started experimenting with two-colour printing and overlaying colour. I used to bug this one guy to let me come behind the counter and fiddle with the machines when he worked late processing orders for the next day. I have no idea why he indulged me.

So I guess I do see it all as interrelated. I was intensely into *comics*. Nothing else interested me in that way. I liked music a lot, even played in a band, but I wasn't deep into it like I saw other people being. But I was so deeply into comics that I wanted to pull them apart and figure out everything about them, in a really nerdy, scientific way—like how they were printed, actually produced, rather than just written and drawn.

Then came Highwater. Because I came to it so cold, really just discovering alternative comics beyond Chris Ware at the time, I had no real conception of what a miniature miracle it was that you were able to make books that looked like that, featuring artists who drew like that, and sell them everywhere from stores in midtown Manhattan to the San Diego Comic-Con. What were your goals with Highwater? Would you say you achieved them?

I was certain that Highwater would be huge. I knew it was time for the graphic novel format. I deeply felt that comics got no respect because the format was so disposable. So I figured it was just a matter of time before Highwater had a hit book and then everyone associated with Highwater would be taken care of. I tried to make the books have a more general appeal, at least on the surface, so that's where the textured cover stock and endpapers and the thicker interior stock came from. I was also influenced by Black Sparrow Press (they published Bukowski and Bowles and Fante),

Cornélius, and L'Association, as well as the obvious—D+Q, Fantagraphics, and Black Eye. Meeting Jordan Crane was a big deal because he actually knew how to use the computer and had figured out some printing techniques that I wanted to play around with. He also had a crazy work ethic for production that I needed at that time, as I was trying out some marketing ideas. Those marketing ideas definitely came from years of working in the comics shops.

Well, they certainly worked on me. How old were you at this point?

I guess I was in my early thirties when I started on the early beginnings of Highwater, and probably around thirty-four when I published *Tiny Bubbles* and *Queen of the Black Black* [Highwater's first graphic novels]. Reflecting back on whether or not I achieved my goals, I guess it's hard to say. All the artists I published are pretty much struggling to make a living, so I didn't "take care of them" in that regard. But I did really want to advance what people thought a comic book could be and get people to seriously consider the packaging, so I suppose those goals were met. I won't pretend I created any of that, though. Comics was moving in that direction—I just got really loud about it. Chris Ware was well into experimenting with design and format, and the Fort Thunder guys were doing their elaborate silkscreening. I just incorporated all that with the help of Jordan and other friends and pushed it into people's faces.

At the same time I was reading Highwater, I was a journalist working with Peggy while she was doing PR for DC Comics. Those were two worlds I never anticipated colliding. How did you meet? When did you realize, you know, this is the real deal?

Peggy and I met at Comic-Con the year we were assembling [Jordan Crane's anthology] *NON5* behind the table. She was a huge fan of Ron Regé, Jr., and came up on the first day, maybe preview night, and just started talking away. I was busy setting up and had to think about the ten artists

I had there, so I kind of ignored her. But later we saw her at one of the hotel bars, and we talked, and I thought, "This woman is kind of cute." I tried to give her a goodbye kiss and she pushed me down and I thought, "I will never go out on a limb like that again." She told me later that she was mad that I was leaving, so she pushed me when I leaned in. But we had to go back to the hotel to make more *NON5s*!

Living that comics life, man.

A couple days later we ended up at the beach party and finally did kiss. Then we both made excuses to go to Providence the week after Comic-Con because it's between New York, where she lived, and Boston, where I lived. So I guess that weekend after was when I realized she was "the one."

Peggy preceded you at D+Q, right? What was her decision process for that big move like? What was yours?

We'd been dating for a little while by then, and I had moved to New York. But she had been in New York for ten years and was afraid of getting caught in the corporate treadmill and never being able to leave. I was freelancing, and it was just a few months after 9/11, so jobs in New York were scarce. When Chris made the offer to Peggy, it seemed like such an easy choice. I knew Peggy wanted to try it and I knew living in Montreal was an exciting thing to try. We also both figured that we would make Chris hire me as soon as possible. And working for D+Q seemed like an impossible dream.

Ha! What had been your experience with D+Q in the past, as a reader or as a publishing peer? What did you respond to most strongly about what Chris had been doing?

I had felt that the typical comics pamphlet was on the way out for a while, and almost all the D+Q cartoonists were working toward graphic novels, so I could tell Chris felt the same way. And the line was very consistent. It was rare that I didn't agree with a publishing choice Chris made. D+Q was forward-thinking, always working toward books more

than just mismatched collections of shorter comics or strips. When I started doing shows, Chris was very approachable. People always mention how daunting Chris's silence is, but I didn't see that. Of course, I wasn't trying to get published by him. I had also talked to Chris a couple of times on the phone, setting up signings, or he might call me to try an idea out on me as a retailer. I also had called him for printer advice when I started out. I pretty much just wrongly considered myself to be peers with Chris and Michel Vrana right off the bat. I'm sure I was annoying.

So what were you doing when you started at the company? Editing, design, or the management stuff you'd developed skills in during your retail & distro days?

I was packing boxes using the skills I learned from Ralph Turner at Diamond! *Bannock, Beans, and Black Tea*, the one Seth and his dad did together, was the first book I did the production work on. I was freelancing at D+Q but also doing some freelance advertising illustration and design for other people. Sometimes I would just come by D+Q and work for free because I might not be doing much else that day. Eventually D+Q got stronger, and when they could afford to pay me, Chris and Peg hired me. Peggy and I started the intern program where we've trained almost all of our future employees—Julia, Tracy, and Jade were all interns first. I also created some computer programs to keep track of book planning and do some projections.

You have such a strong aesthetic as a designer and publisher. Surely there were some jitters about trying to fold that into Chris's operation.

Oh, definitely. But Chris is very trusting, so it wasn't too hard. I was also very respectful of D+Q, so I didn't do anything too wild like I might with Highwater. Back then, I would do any stupid idea I had, but at D+Q I definitely had to consider the legacy. I didn't suggest things for a couple of years because I didn't want to dilute. Eventually I approached Chris with the Moomin idea and he said yes right away.

What made you think of Moomin? Why did you like it, and why did you like it for D+Q specifically?

I had wanted to do Moomin for years and was even thinking about it when I had Highwater. But I knew I needed to be more stable to pull that off. After being at D+Q for a bit, I just decided to dig into my backlog of ideas and try them out on Chris. Moomin was obvious because the chapter books had a cult following, and people were starting to have some success exploring comics history. *Moomin* comics also had such a great, subdued sense of humour, which I thought of as very D+Q. I do think Tove is one of the best comics drawers of all time. Her character designs are just so simple and perfect.

What are some books that you feel helped you make your stamp on D+Q, or that were your "babies"?

Well, Moomin is the obvious one. And that opened up the idea of trying other kids-focused things like Anna & Froga and Pippi. I never pushed Highwater people on Chris or Peggy—I always let them make that call—but they were fans of Ron, John P., Marc Bell, and Brian Ralph before I even got to D+Q, so signing those guys wasn't hard. But obviously I'm very proud of their D+Q books. I loved designing the Japanese titles—Sakabashira, Hayashi, Suzuki, Katsumata—but those were often arrived at by Chris and me, with early help by Mike Buckley and very obviously Mitsuhiro Asakawa, who was our contact in Japan. I'm very proud of *Birdseye Bristoe*, *Make Me a Woman*, and the Brecht Evens books—Brecht was a blind submission. I love those John Stanley Library books so much.

One of the things about it is that Chris, Peggy, and I all have a hand in selecting the books, so it's tricky. People always think that the Petits Livres series was my doing, but it was Chris's idea...but I suggested a lot of those books, and so did Peg. I don't think people realize how much Peg does editorially. I really pushed for Lynda Barry and got Chris to contact her, but I've done almost no work on those books past that (but I will happily take any credit offered). Other books, I designed the covers but Chris handled the interior editing, or Tracy han-

dled everything after I sent out the contract. Yeah, it's tricky. The store was Peg, Chris, and I together, for example. Chris knew that Peggy and I had looked at a storefront in Brooklyn for Highwater, and the opportunity came up and he jumped on it because he knew he would have us to back him up.

What do you do there now?

A lot of what I do is big-picture stuff, trying to dream up projects that might have an impact like the colour Moomin series or the recent *Deluxe Moomin* box. But I also regularly email authors as they're working on their books to keep them on deadline. I worked pretty closely with Gilbert Hernandez and Mimi Pond as they made their books. I edit a lot of the translated titles after they've been translated, meaning I rewrite a bunch of the text for the translator to get annoyed at. I used to do almost all the design, but now a lot of the time I just do a sketch or select an image for Tracy or Jade to tighten and finish—they're both much better at the basic design stuff than I ever was. I'll sign off on most of the design.

How is the company different for your presence?

Before I got here, the company was just Chris, then Chris and Peg in separate offices. Now in the office there are eight full-timers, one part-timer, and anywhere from one to three interns. It used to be so quiet in the office, but Peg and I are a couple of chatterboxes, so the office can get pretty loud

now—our space is an open loft. And Peg and I were always more social than Chris, so Chris gets out a little bit more now as a result. I don't know if I think the company is radically different because of me. But Chris had some support to try some things that he might not have in the past, like opening a store or increasing the number of titles we publish a year.

You and Peggy also started a family during your time at D+Q. Since you and she work together as well, have the two spheres overlapped more than usual, would you say? How does one shape the other?

Oh, it's a complete mess of overlapping. We talk work at home and personal stuff at work, and we're both pretty bad at separating it all. Often, one of us is dashing off an email or editing something after dinner, or fitting it in while making lunch for the kids in the morning. Our daughter's school is a block away from the store, and she just started leaving of her own accord at the end of the day and going to the store and sitting in the kids section and reading. We're both very dedicated to comics, but yes, it's a bit much. Often we walk or ride our bikes to and from work, and the whole time we're mulling over some sort of work problem. The best of it is us bouncing ideas off of each other outside the workplace and being able to refine them before we talk to Chris. I would never recommend working with a spouse, but we do pretty good, considering that it is such a terrible idea.

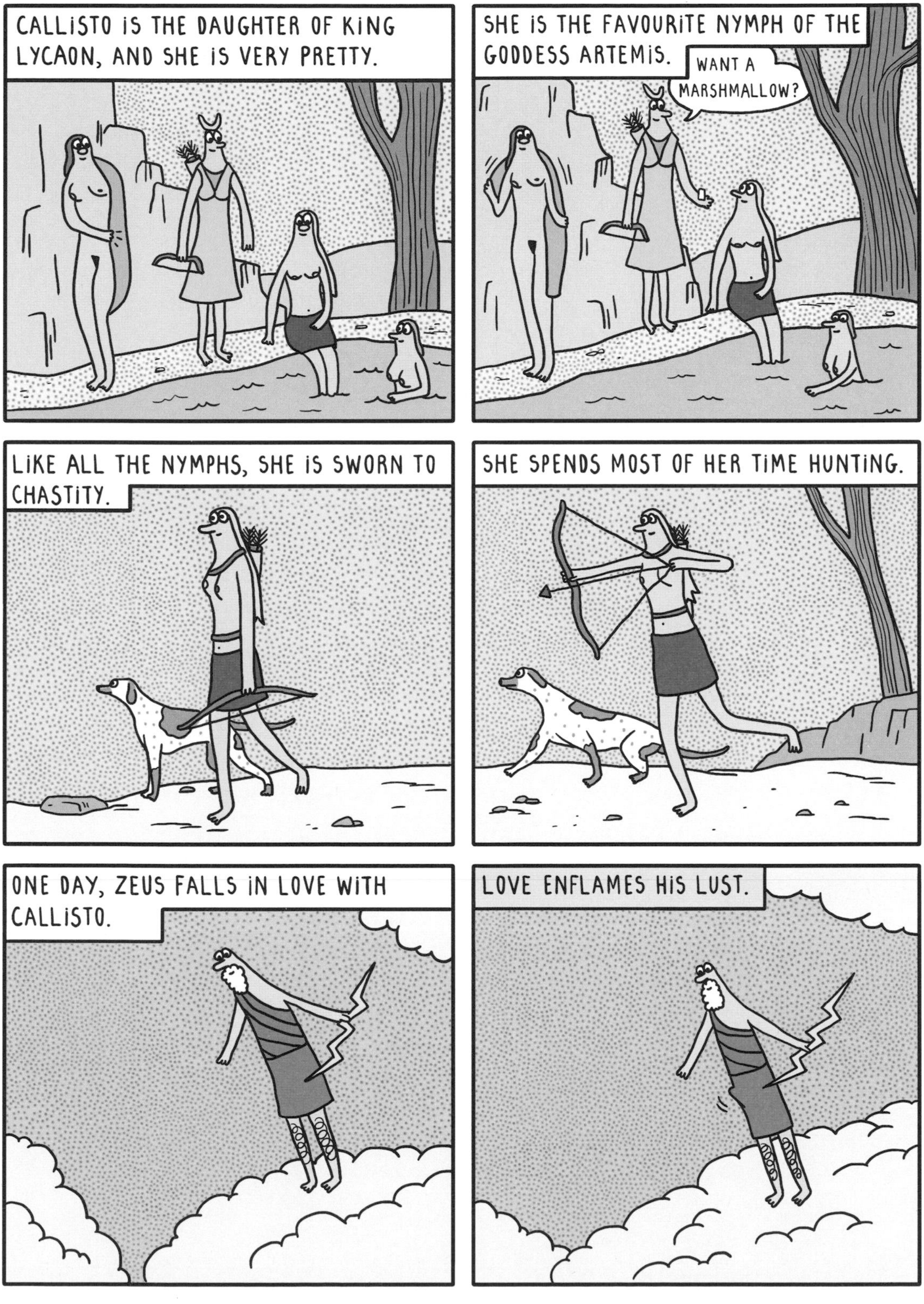
CALLISTO IS THE DAUGHTER OF KING LYCAON, AND SHE IS VERY PRETTY.
SHE IS THE FAVOURITE NYMPH OF THE GODDESS ARTEMIS.
WANT A MARSHMALLOW?
LIKE ALL THE NYMPHS, SHE IS SWORN TO CHASTITY.
SHE SPENDS MOST OF HER TIME HUNTING.
ONE DAY, ZEUS FALLS IN LOVE WITH CALLISTO.
LOVE ENFLAMES HIS LUST.

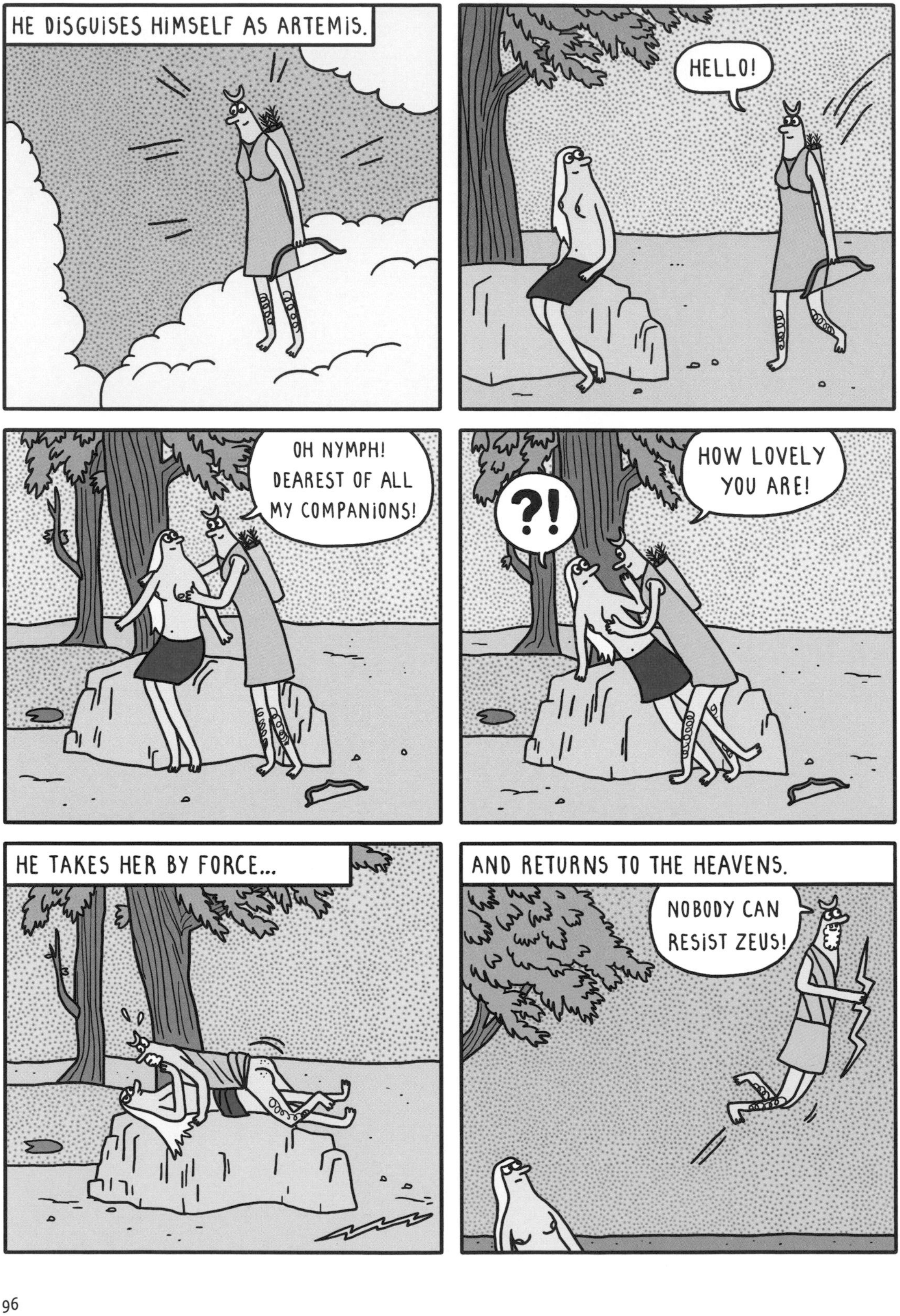
HE DISGUISES HIMSELF AS ARTEMIS.
HELLO!
OH NYMPH! DEAREST OF ALL MY COMPANIONS!
?!
HOW LOVELY YOU ARE!
HE TAKES HER BY FORCE...
AND RETURNS TO THE HEAVENS.
NOBODY CAN RESIST ZEUS!

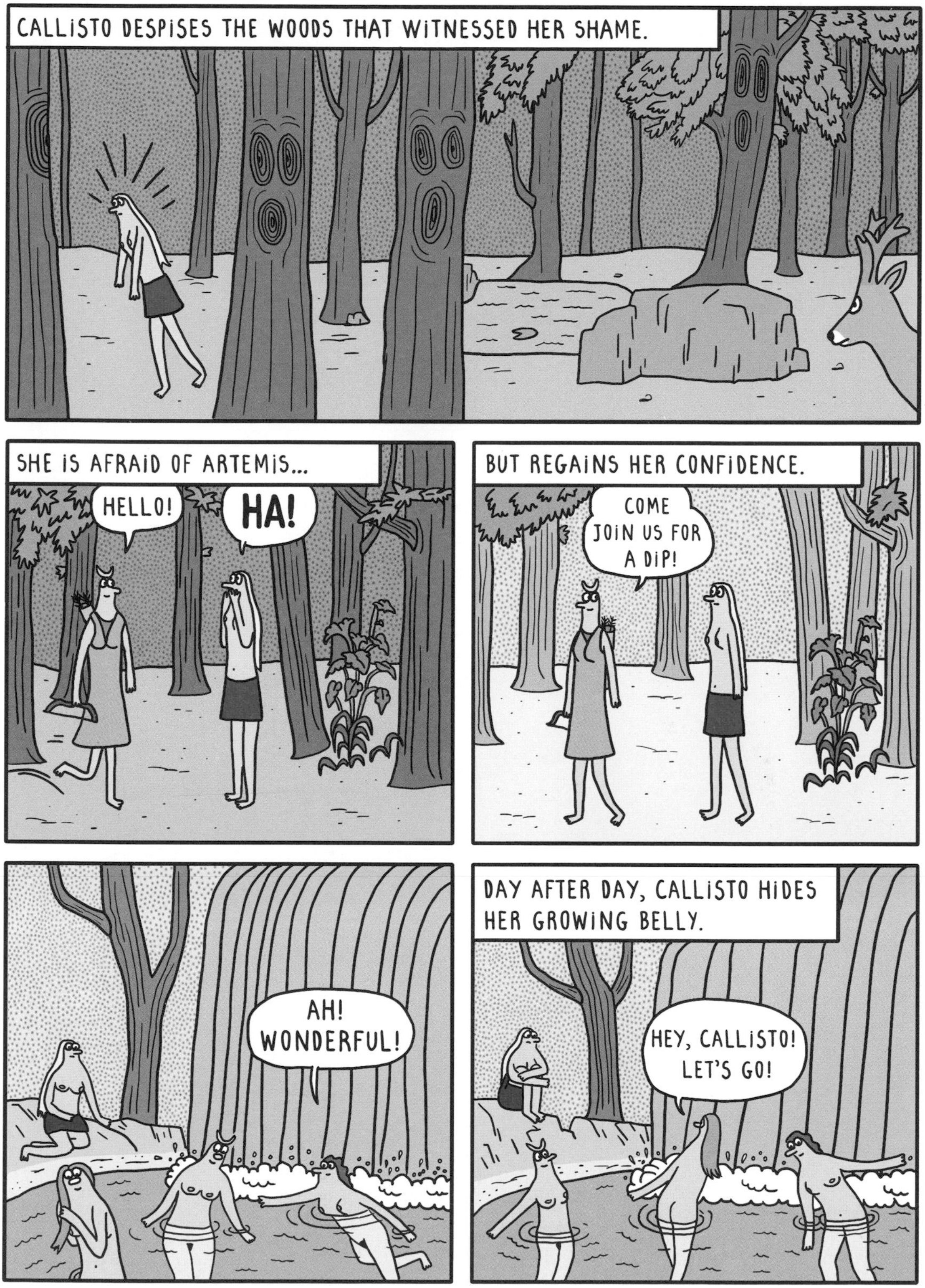
CALLISTO DESPISES THE WOODS THAT WITNESSED HER SHAME.
SHE IS AFRAID OF ARTEMIS...
HELLO!
HA!
BUT REGAINS HER CONFIDENCE.
COME JOIN US FOR A DIP!
AH! WONDERFUL!
DAY AFTER DAY, CALLISTO HIDES HER GROWING BELLY.
HEY, CALLISTO! LET'S GO!

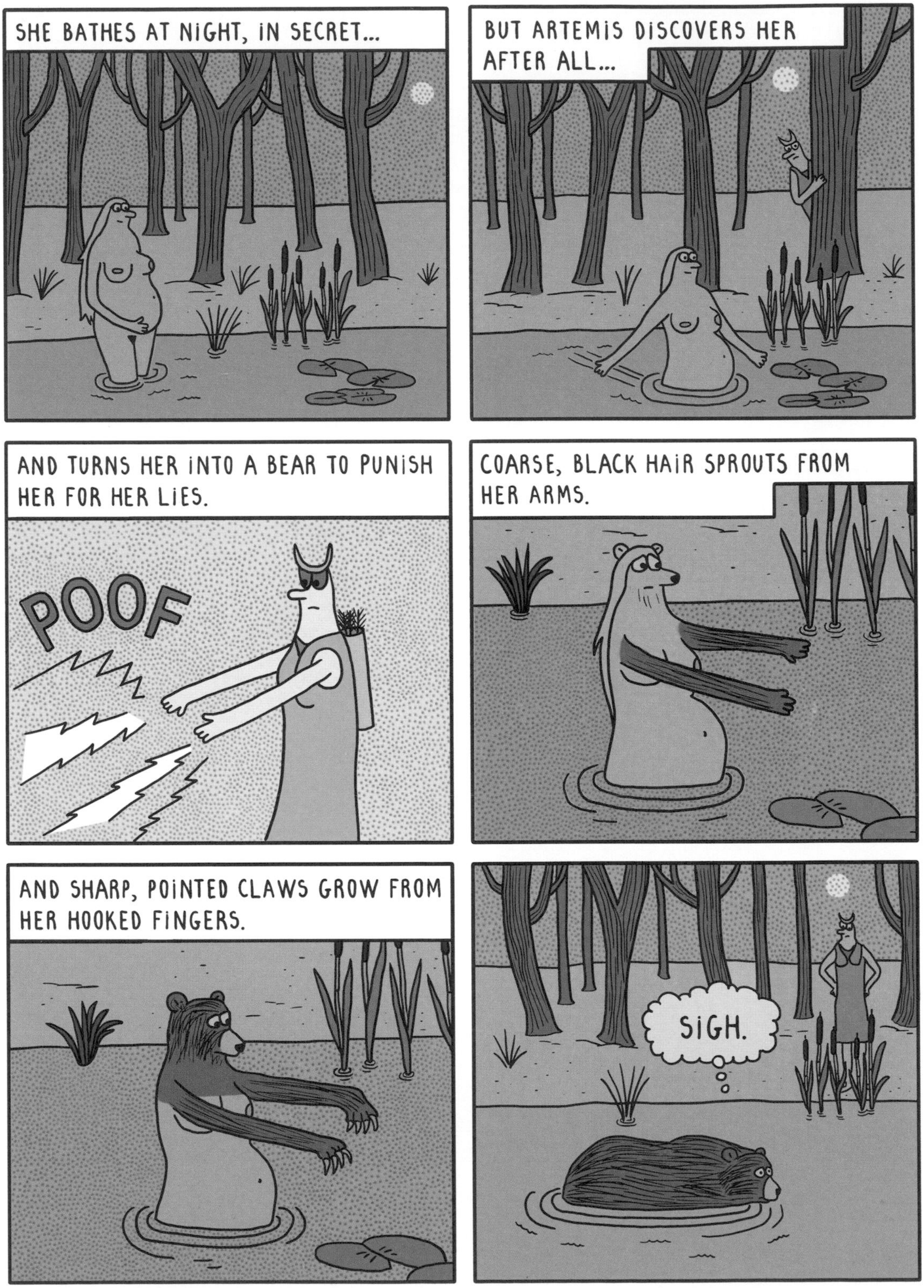
SHE BATHES AT NIGHT, IN SECRET...
BUT ARTEMIS DISCOVERS HER AFTER ALL...
AND TURNS HER INTO A BEAR TO PUNISH HER FOR HER LIES.
POOF
COARSE, BLACK HAIR SPROUTS FROM HER ARMS.
AND SHARP, POINTED CLAWS GROW FROM HER HOOKED FINGERS.
SIGH.

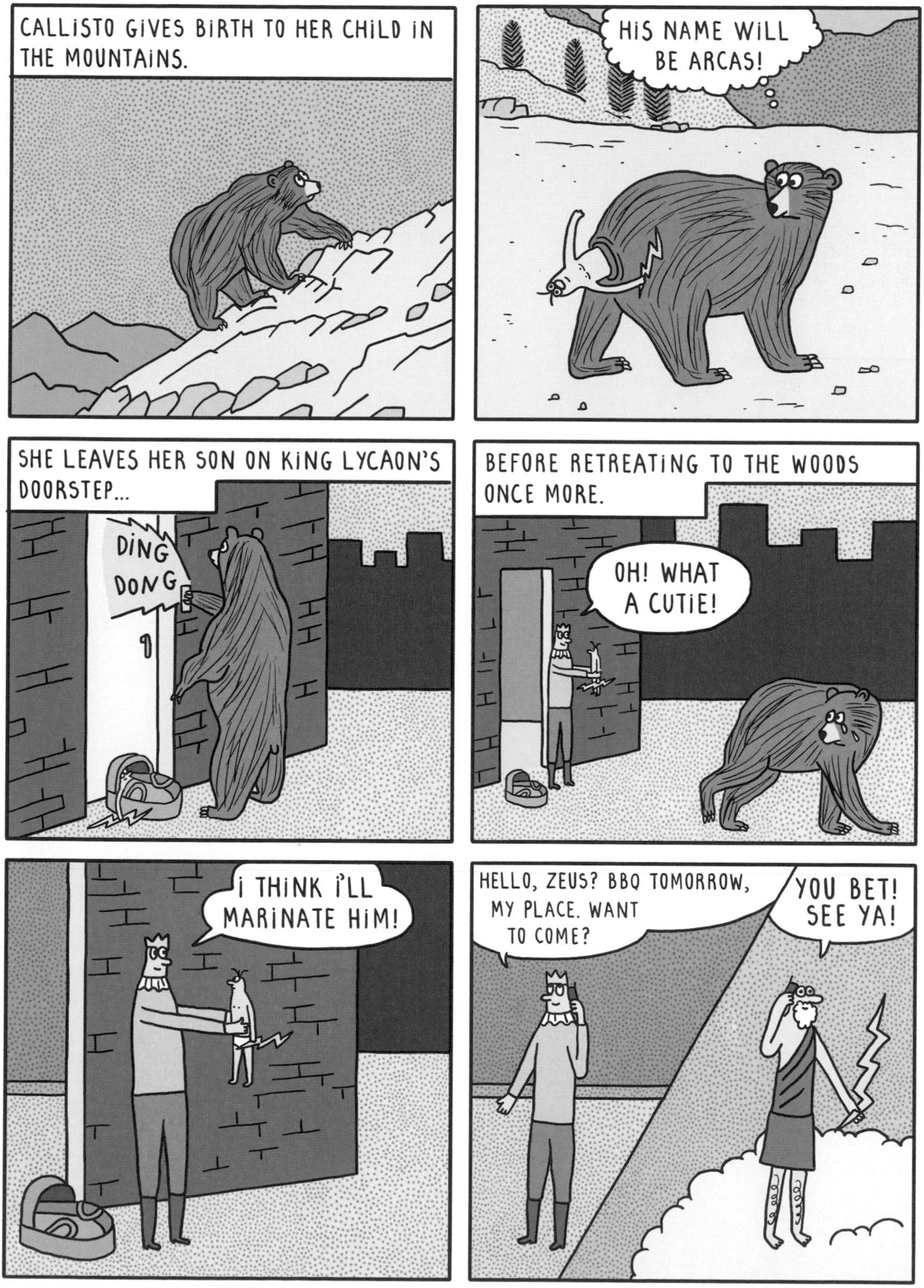
CALLISTO GIVES BIRTH TO HER CHILD IN THE MOUNTAINS.
HIS NAME WILL BE ARCAS!
SHE LEAVES HER SON ON KING LYCAON'S DOORSTEP...
DING DONG
BEFORE RETREATING TO THE WOODS ONCE MORE.
OH! WHAT A CUTIE!
I THINK I'LL MARINATE HIM!
HELLO, ZEUS? BBQ TOMORROW, MY PLACE. WANT TO COME?
YOU BET! SEE YA!

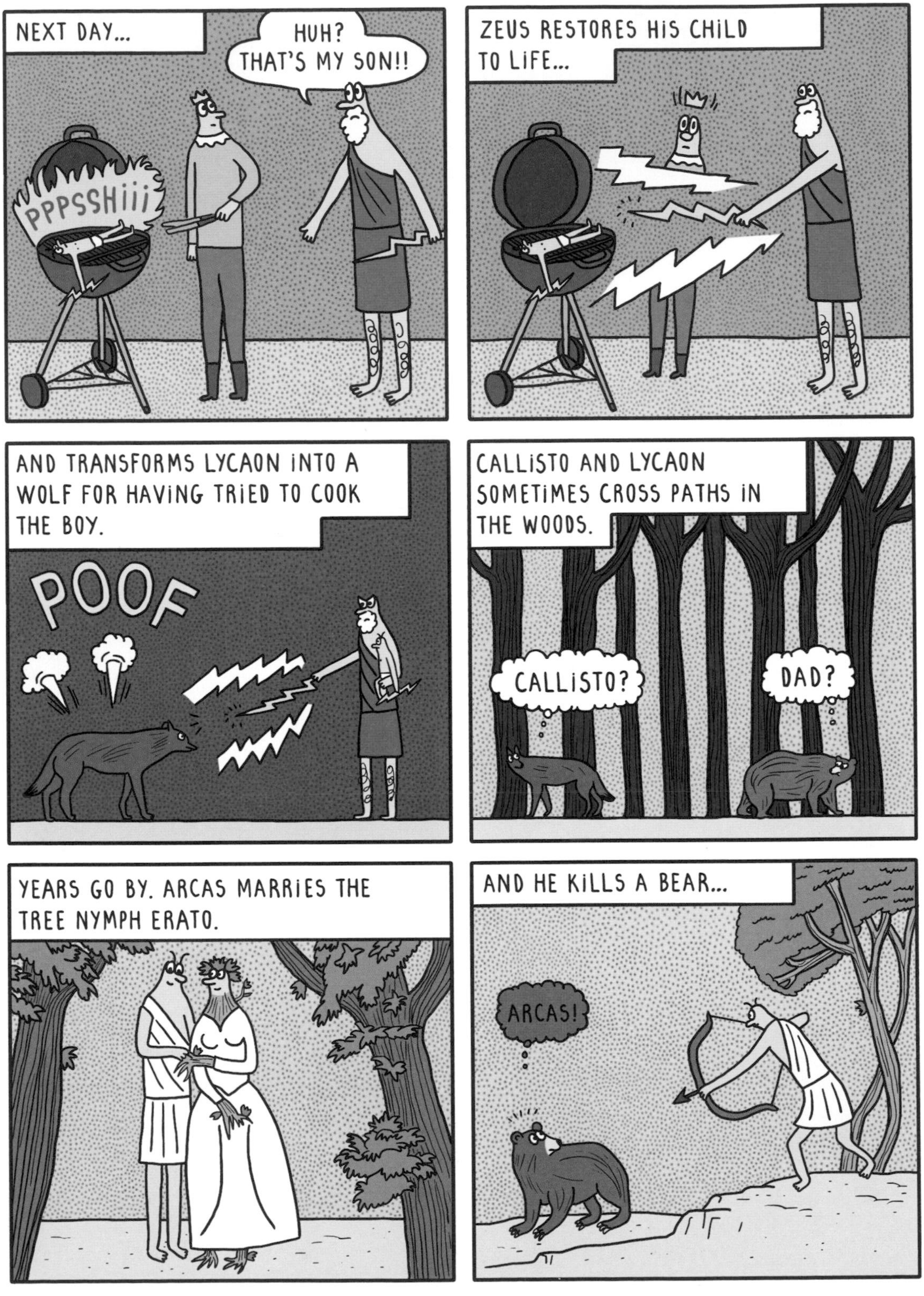
NEXT DAY...
HUH? THAT'S MY SON!!
PPPSSHiii
ZEUS RESTORES HIS CHILD TO LIFE...
AND TRANSFORMS LYCAON INTO A WOLF FOR HAVING TRIED TO COOK THE BOY.
POOF
CALLISTO AND LYCAON SOMETIMES CROSS PATHS IN THE WOODS.
CALLISTO?
DAD?
YEARS GO BY. ARCAS MARRIES THE TREE NYMPH ERATO.
AND HE KILLS A BEAR...
ARCAS!

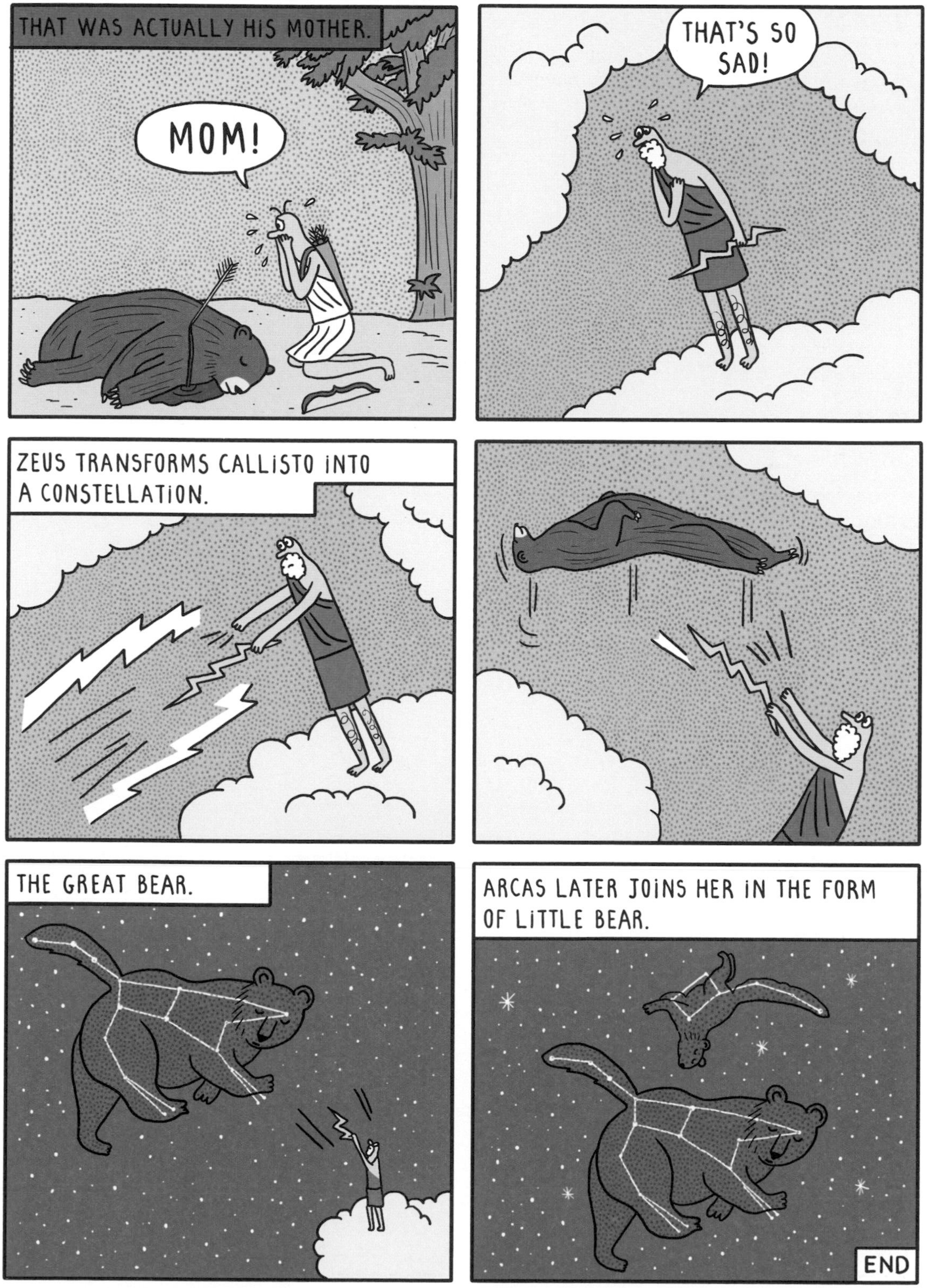
THAT WAS ACTUALLY HIS MOTHER.
MOM!
THAT'S SO SAD!
ZEUS TRANSFORMS CALLISTO INTO A CONSTELLATION.
THE GREAT BEAR.
ARCAS LATER JOINS HER IN THE FORM OF LITTLE BEAR.
END

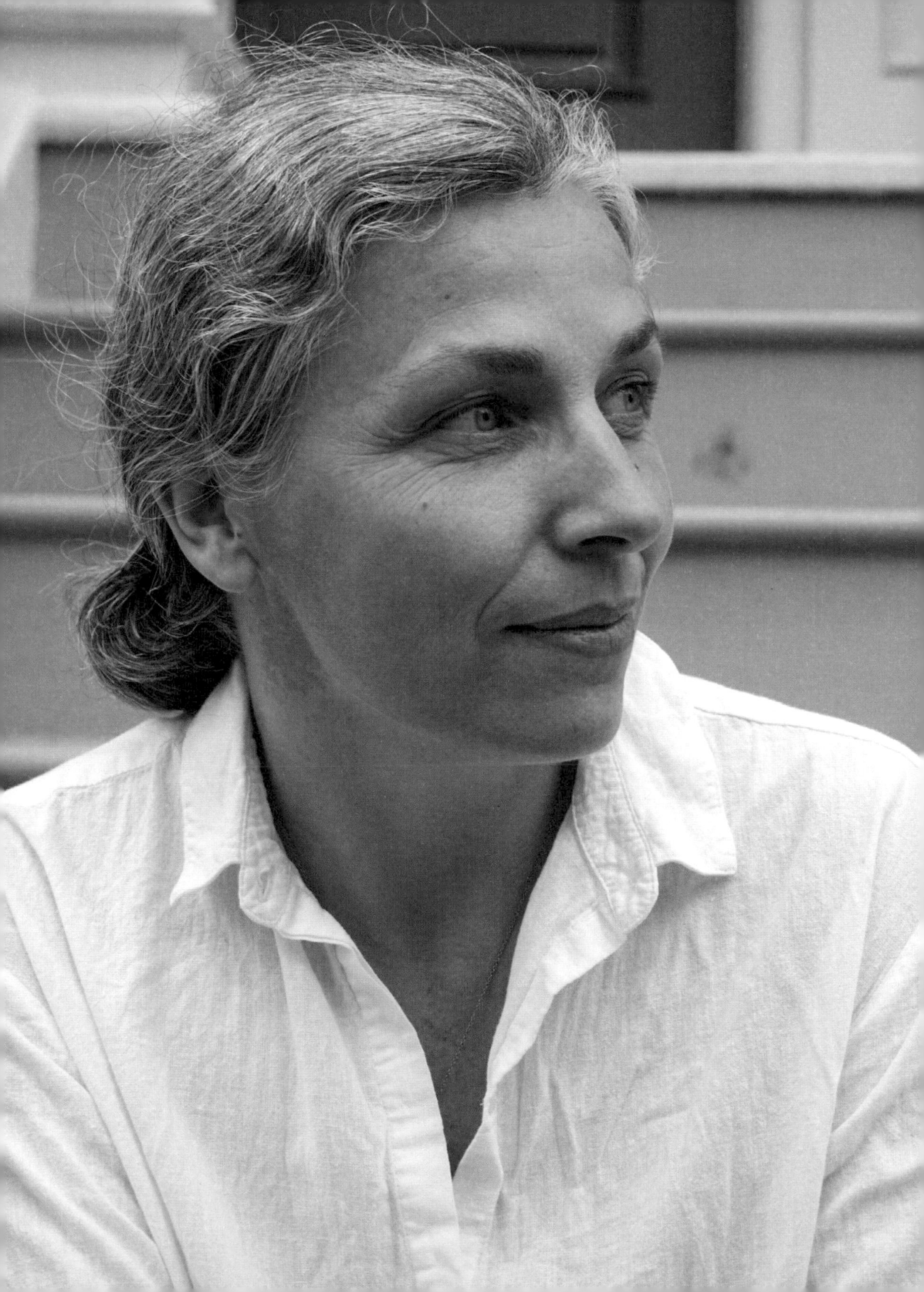

VOICE LESSONS

an interview with Helge Dascher by Emilie Le Hin-Singh

For a while now, as well as being their publicist, I have been translating comics for Cornélius, a company that is in many ways D+Q's French cousin. In the past, I have been fortunate enough to translate a few D+Q authors like Chester Brown, Marc Bell, and Daniel Clowes, and I very much hope that this tradition will continue.

On hearing I was to interview Helge, I felt flattered and exhilarated. Some people give the impression of having lived multiple lives or sleeping very little. While the rest of us were busy making pancakes, Helge put out a magazine (in her twenties) and worked as a curator, a journalist, a teacher, and a translator.

Helge grew up in a German-speaking family in Montreal, therefore already fluent in three languages—German, French, and English—as a child. As an adult, she studied a few more along with art history, history, and, later on, translation. As someone whose best achievement is speaking English—having spent over a decade learning it—I am in awe. But that is just the tip of the iceberg: over the years, she has become a major figure in the comics world. She met Chris when he was publishing his first comic books out of a tiny room in his apartment and that was the beginning of a long friendship and professional collaboration.

These days, when she is not translating museum exhibitions and catalogues, she is hard at work translating the crème de la crème of French- and German-language comics: cartoonists from Michel Rabagliati to Guy Delisle, as well as Anouk Ricard, whose series Anna & Froga is one of my all-time favourites.

If that is not enough, she also has the privilege of getting to hang out with the D+Q team—my cheeks are turning green with envy.

Could you tell us about your background? Did you learn French and German at home?

I was born in Montreal, and until age ten, I lived in a mostly immigrant part of town. We spoke German at home and English and French in the streets. I went to a bilingual school, where all subjects were taught in both French and English. That was excellent, because both were treated as primary languages. Later we moved to one of the more English suburbs, and my French got sidelined for a few years until I came back to the city to study.

Did you study languages/translation at university?

I studied art history, history, and languages—German, Italian, and Spanish, plus two years of Russian that mostly evaporated. Later, after I started translating, I went back and did a graduate certificate in translation, just to get oriented on some of the issues I was coming across.

What was it that first got you interested in comics, in translating them?

I was working freelance as a journalist and I spoke a few languages, so every now and then a translation contract would land on my desk. One day a friend introduced me to Chris Oliveros, who needed someone to translate the introduction to an excerpt from Tardi's *Putain de Guerre*. Back then, Chris had a few other French projects in mind, and things continued from there, first with a story by Loustal, and then books by Baru and Dupuy & Berbérian.

What was the first book you translated?

The first complete book was Baru's *Road to America*. Like any other project, it was full of translation issues. It tells the story of an Algerian boxer in the 1950s whose rise to fame attracts the attention of the French government and the Algerian resistance movement—both wanting to claim him as a symbol of their conflicting causes. Part of the feeling of the book is carried by the language itself. There are the working-class Algerians, the boxer's handlers, French bureaucrats, Parisian thugs—and they all speak a slightly different French. The thugs yell insults that have no direct equivalent in English. I came away from the book with many questions about translation and decided it was time to learn about it—to find out how others deal with those kinds of issues.

Photo: Cora Thornton-Silver (2014).

Were you already working as a professional translator when you worked on your first comics?

I did the occasional translation job. I remember a patent for a device used in bridge building, and another about tobacco stem substrates used to grow mushrooms. Things I knew nothing about. That's an everyday experience for translators, but at the time it seemed surreal. I had done some journalism, and I was teaching a university writing course.

What was the appeal of translating comics for you?

I was always torn between text and image—publishing or writing on the one hand, and curatorial work on the other. I was in my mid-twenties. With a group of women, I had put out a magazine for two years. I had helped put together a touring exhibition for a museum in Vienna and represented a few European artists. And suddenly with comics, the two worlds came together. These days I also translate museum exhibitions and catalogues, and it's the same beautiful combination.

How did you get to know D+Q and how did you meet Chris Oliveros?

I met Chris through a friend who had introduced me to D+Q. Chris was running D+Q out of a tiny room in his apartment on St. Viateur, upstairs from the Bagel Factory. It was just him and Marina. Talk happened at the dining-room table, because—the way I remember it—the office was hardly big enough for the desk and books inside. It was extraordinary: these stunning books—so beautiful and carefully put together—coming out of this very basic setup. I bumped into Traie Payne recently, who handled mail and spent many months of Saturdays scanning the *Gasoline Alley* strips for D+Q at Chris's first out-of-home office. When Traie was out on the sidewalk waiting to meet Chris for a job interview, Chris arrived pulling a kid's wagon loaded with boxes of books, and Traie ended up helping Chris carry the loaded wagon up the stairs. Those stairs were just a bit wider than the door, and there was usually a box of books waiting for Canada Post on every step, so you needed to go up carefully along a narrow path. Traie was a huge D+Q fan, and he'd been expecting to walk into a big publishing headquarters with a company truck parked out back, and here he was carrying the back end of a red wagon up into a little one-man operation…That was D+Q for many years: Chris, a desk, and a computer.

If you think about your relationship with D+Q, how has it evolved over the years?

On a personal level, not much has changed. D+Q started out warm and personable, and it has stayed that way right through its growth.

There have been two production changes that have had an impact on my work as a translator—a positive impact. One was the shift from hand-lettering to fonts. When I first started at D+Q, the translations were all hand-lettered by Dirk Rehm, an amazing letterer based in Germany. The process was labour-intensive, so we made very few changes after layout. These days, a few translations are hand-lettered by the artists themselves, but in most cases, a font is made from randomly recombined samples of the artist's own lettering. The translated text is converted to the font and dropped into the word balloons, and it isn't too complicated to type in revisions. A translation always reads very differently once it's in the word balloons and alongside the artwork, so it's great to be able to revise it once I can see how everything looks on the page.

The second change is that editing has come to play a bigger role in production. I'd say the change came with Tom's arrival at D+Q. Tom lettered a few of the last pre-font translations. Dirk dropped in text as he received it, but Tom would make small fixes—ostensibly to get a better fit in the word balloons, but probably just by inclination, too. The D+Q edition of David B.'s *Babel* got that treatment, and I think it opened the way for more exchange around the translations. I like feedback, and Tom, Tracy, and Julia are all great readers—they make the work shine.

Tom Devlin edits your translations, particularly where humour is involved, like the Anna & Froga series. Could you tell us about this second half of translation, when the editor is editing the text closely in collaboration with the translator?

I'm not sure how Tom goes about it, but I imagine him coming back from lunch and rewriting a bunch of jokes just to get warmed up for the rest of the afternoon. He's very funny. I love what he comes up with, and these days, on some projects, I take into account that he's likely to weigh in. Sometimes I'll push back, sometimes his revisions get a better solution out of me, and many times his changes are perfect.

Collaboration with editors varies. Most stay out of the way; a few like to dig in. One thing an in-house editor can bring is a perspective on how a book will be marketed, or what the market might want from the book. Recently, we were dealing with a joke that seemed unacceptable in English. Tom tried moving it from one character to another, and suddenly the offense was benign, but the humour was still there. An inspired solution…

You had a good working relationship with Kim Thompson. Could you tell us a little about it? How you met, anecdotes you remember...

Kim wrote to me years ago to ask if I'd be interested in translating for Fantagraphics. Kim was able to translate all Indo-European languages, and at the time, with the exception of Max Andersson's books and a few Finnish titles, all of Fanta's European books came straight off his desk. He translated mostly outside of work hours—in the evenings and on weekends. A few years after that first email, he got back in touch and asked if I'd step in. I took on Mezzo & Pirus's *King of the Flies* and invited a friend and writer, John Kadlecek, who has also worked on a few D+Q books, to come on board.

For a Danish-born person—which Kim was—my name, Helge, spelled with an *e* at the end, would be considered a man's name (as opposed to Helga). We never met, and it was a long time before we spoke on the phone, so I think it was a while before he found out that I wasn't another guy in the industry. Maybe that made things easier at the start. I don't know. But in the end, the dynamic was great: our voices and sensibilities were very different, and that worked out well on paper.

Kim was an amazing editor. He could read the source text (which isn't always the case with editors). He was a translator himself and was used to working with other translators and editors. But above all, he'd get totally engaged by the questions that translation raises. He was always interested in taking things a step further, just for the pleasure of it.

Kim was also your peer as one of the best-known translators working in comics, an aspect of his work that has been written about very little. Could you tell us more about it?

Kim translated as somebody with a solid knowledge of many languages, but also with an understanding of publishing, layout, comics, the specific history of European comics, and the community of people producing the work. So his translation decisions drew on many considerations. He thought about the way words *look*. ("No ugly descenders!" was his request for chapter titles in one book.) He got behind projects that probably had no commercial value but were significant for bringing a certain body of work to the attention of English-speaking readers—and he put his sense of what was valuable into the translations. And since he was not just the translator but also the publisher, he was calling all the shots: he wasn't negotiating an approach, but making the decisions as he was going along. That's an interesting position to be in.

He really loved the challenge of translating jokes and any kind of wordplay, and he got a lot of fun out of his solutions. He wasn't shy about improvising accents, period language, and strong voices. He didn't get tied up in a knot about word-for-word equivalence. He once organized a round table of a group of us comics translators, and he talked about Art Spiegelman's approach, which was not so much to translate as to write. That was Kim's approach too: "You junk all the stuff you know is in the way, because it was in that language to begin with, and just go for the spirit, the meaning of it."

I imagine that you have developed your own relationship with some cartoonists whose work you have been translating for a long time. Could you tell us more about it? For instance, do you have a direct correspondence with the authors to discuss their work? Any anecdotes?

I always like working with authors. I like being able to check intentions, and when an author can read English, I always send a draft for an okay. Diane Obomsawin's writing looks very minimal, but there's a lot packed in there, and I often get in touch to let her set a direction. Pascal Girard has a nice ear for dialogue, so I'll send him a draft that includes alternatives in the margins. The depth of author involvement depends on an author's ability to read English, so it goes right across the spectrum.

You also do a lot of commercial translation. How would you compare the different requirements/expectations of commercial vs. literary translation, as well as literature vs. comics translation? What makes comics a unique challenge?

I used to do a lot of commercial translation. These days I'm working mostly on comics, museum exhibitions, and other kinds of art publications.

In commercial translation, I think about accuracy and the reader: the information needs to be right and it needs to be clear and accessible for the person reading it. If a commercial text is unnecessarily complicated or awkwardly simple, for instance, I won't hesitate to move things around or adapt.

In literary translation, on the other hand, I'm thinking at least as much about the author's intentions—and if I can, I'll validate with the author.

Comics translation occupies a middle ground between literary translation and subtitling. It's like literary translation in that it has a kind of authoritative "permanence" on the page, and it's (usually) invisible—unlike the way subtitles stream past, with that disproportion of written to spoken text reminding you of all the losses and approximations going on. But comics translation is also like subtitling or dubbing, in the sense that an effect (a joke, for example) has to happen in no more than the space and time available to it in the original—unlike literary translation, where you can take all the space you need to deliver an idea. In comics, you've got the advantage that you can enlist some of the supports available to literary translations, like introductions, footnotes, endnotes, and glossaries—although, depending on the kind of book and readership you're dealing with, you may be less likely to use them.

In comics, tone is sometimes more important than meaning. How do you juggle accuracy and what actually just sounds good?

You can't always reproduce meaning. You're limited by space and by the resources that the target language has to offer. And generally speaking, you probably don't want to get too academic on the reader. You can use footnotes and endnotes to fill in meaning, but you don't want to rely on them as a crutch in every book.

What you do have to do—every time—is this: you need to fill the word balloon (without overstuffing it or leaving big blanks) and you need to drop in text that matches the communication situation in the panel. If a joke is happening, you need a joke—but because of constraints, you may have to make a slightly different joke. Or maybe the job of the text is to emphasize the mood in the panel—or to pull away from it. Or to colour a character in a certain way.

Comics writing is very economical (after all, the pictures are telling part of the story). So when I'm translating, I'm thinking about what the text is contributing to the panel and the page. When constraints call for sacrifices, I'm more likely to focus on translating function than literal meaning.

The books we've been most "free" with are Anouk Ricard's Anna & Froga comics and her workplace comedy, Benson's Cuckoos. Those books are all about the effect of a panel—the joke or awkwardness it delivers—so we've worried less about literal translation and more about getting the effects right.

Comics translation includes one restriction: one phrase has to fit in one bubble. How do you deal with it?

Right! And sometimes the word balloons are profiled to tightly hug each line of text. One especially difficult instance of that was the Onésime strips by the pioneering Quebecois cartoonist Albert Chartier. Chartier's artwork was all

about curved lines, and the word balloons themselves were all curves—more cumulus clouds than balloons. Dirk did a beautiful job reproducing the lettering, but given the logistics of subcontracted, transatlantic hand-lettering, it just wasn't possible to fiddle each line into place.

These days, I always start a project with a free draft, reading and translating as I go. I don't worry too much about line length at that point—I just want to get a rhythm going. During the second draft, I'm solving issues and looking at line length. I eyeball the lines, or if I'm really worried about line length, I'll type the source text over the English text, with line breaks, to get a sense of how much space I have to work with. All the negotiations in subsequent drafts are between space, flow, meaning, and the function of the text.

Which book do you consider your best achievement and why?

I love that translation brings these books to a larger audience. That's the achievement I care about. It was moving to read the reviews of Diane Obomsawin's On Loving Women—in which she sets down friends' stories of first love and being gay—and seeing this very personal and local book resonate with readers right across Canada and the US. I think it's great that Michel Rabagliati's books about everyday life in Quebec are recommended reading in school libraries all over the continent. Dupuy and Berbérian once told me that all subsequent foreign language rights to their Monsieur Jean books had been sold based on foreign publishers' encounters with the English editions. That's one of the particularities of translating into English (as opposed, say, to Czech): it not only brings a work to English readers but also has the potential to open doors to other international markets. D+Q puts together an extraordinary list of French-language and foreign titles, and it's just a privilege to be able to work on them.

D+Q tends to follow its authors over the years, which implies that it gives you a chance to translate several books by the same authors. As a result, do you feel more at home when translating someone like Guy Delisle or Pascal Girard? Do you have the impression of "hearing" a recurring by voice for some authors?

Yes, definitely. You also get a sense of what matters to the authors. Timing is something that's come up with Guy Delisle—maybe reinforced by his background in animation—so I try to pay attention to it. Atmosphere matters to Michel Rabagliati, so I know I can take liberties to convey the feeling of a panel.

You translate from both French and Quebec French. Is there a difference to you? If so, how do you convey it in English?

I've translated Quebecois and French authors, but also Belgian, Swiss, Algerian, Moroccan, and Ivorian ones, and there are differences in each case. Some books are story-driven: when language is almost incidental, I might aim to take out all speed bumps and let the text read as smoothly as possible. But language is part of what matters in many books, and in those cases it feels relevant to put "markers" in the text. Publishers differ in their views on that, and I like that D+Q is willing to let the source culture come through in its books.

The challenge is biggest when the authors themselves make a point of emphasizing the distinctness of the language they use. Michel Rabagliati's books—especially the earlier ones—aren't about the political situation in Quebec, but they capture it in passing, and language carries most of the political content of those books. In his books, we've generally left street signage as is, so you get a sense of the bilingual reality of the place. French Canadian swears are related to Catholic ritual; in one panel, the protagonist, Paul, strings a few together as symbol swears (with drawings in the word balloon of a host, a tabernacle, a chalice, and Christ at Calvary), and we dropped in a deadpan footnote and an explanatory endnote for context. An incomprehensible English-speaking landlord became an incomprehensible Italian-speaking landlord—that was a shift, but it still reflected a reality of this place.

Marguerite Abouet's Aya books, set in Ivory Coast in the late 1970s, are written in *nouchi*—a street language that originates in Abidjan and mixes French with words and idioms from other Ivorian languages and English. If you're a French reader of the original books, you get the dialogues, but you'd need the glossary at the back of each volume to really understand all the expressions. At Marguerite's request, we did the same thing in English, and I had an Ivorian reader help with placing the nouchi terms into the English texts.

I hear you do a lot of background research (like tracking down all of the Boivin/Rancourt versions of *Melody* and reading them all, just to get a context for the solo Rancourt version). Could you tell us more about it?

I like to understand where a project is coming from and how it fits into the bigger picture. You mention the *Melody* example. When I started working on the book, I knew Sylvie Rancourt had made these "barzines," and that Kitchen Sink had offered to publish them on the condition that her stories be drawn by another artist, Jacques Boivin. It was easy to imagine that she had been dispossessed of her own voice along the way. So it was interesting to read the Kitchen Sink issues, because they left me with a whole other impression: her voice is so distinct that it definitely leads the collaboration. It changed my sense of what we're doing with this edition: she wasn't a victim, and we're not recovering a lost voice, but bringing another facet of this extraordinary production to light in English.

Working on Guy Delisle's books is amazing. His storylines seem driven by coincidence, and his narrating "self" seems slightly blundering and naive, but every detail is highly deliberate. I've never out-researched Guy: I'll read a source for context and realize he's already been there.

Text-based research is one thing. But whenever I can, I also speak with people who have inside knowledge of the worlds I'm looking at. For *Melody*, I've been checking things with the former manager of a strip club. For Aya, I got in touch with an Ivorian studying in the US, Herman Koutouan. For a plumbing joke in Guy Delisle's first bad parenting book, I spoke with a friend and plumber, Rob Aspinall, who was also helpful for some welding situations in a book by Pascal Girard, and who turned out to have such a great sense of timing and humour that I invited him to translate Guy's second bad parenting book with me—since it's a book that's all about timing and jokes.

I also work with people to try to make voices as vivid as possible. I've translated a few dozen authors and hundreds of characters, and I don't want them all to sound alike. I've tried different things to mix it up. For one *Aya* book, I invited my brother, Dag Dascher (who also translated another book in that series), to write some of the men's voices. Friend and writer John Kadlecek has collaborated on many translations. He knows a bit of French, but I like for him to think mostly about the English—to really set his ear to a book and check if the writing seems idiomatic and fresh. And just about everyone I know eventually gets tapped for one character or another. D+Q is kind enough to include my acknowledgements, so the people who've added their voices get thanked. My brother, Dag, has contributed thoughts to almost every book, and so has the painter Mark Lang. The art school professor who ridicules a student as "Mr. Hamfist" in Philippe Dupuy's *Haunted* is 100 percent Mark. There's a character "shakin' the dew off the lily" in another book—that's also thanks to Mark. I love when people bring words or expressions to the translations that are totally outside my own vocabulary. It's one of the things Kim Thompson also liked about having other people translate for and with him: it's like being able to dip your brush into a whole other palette of colours.

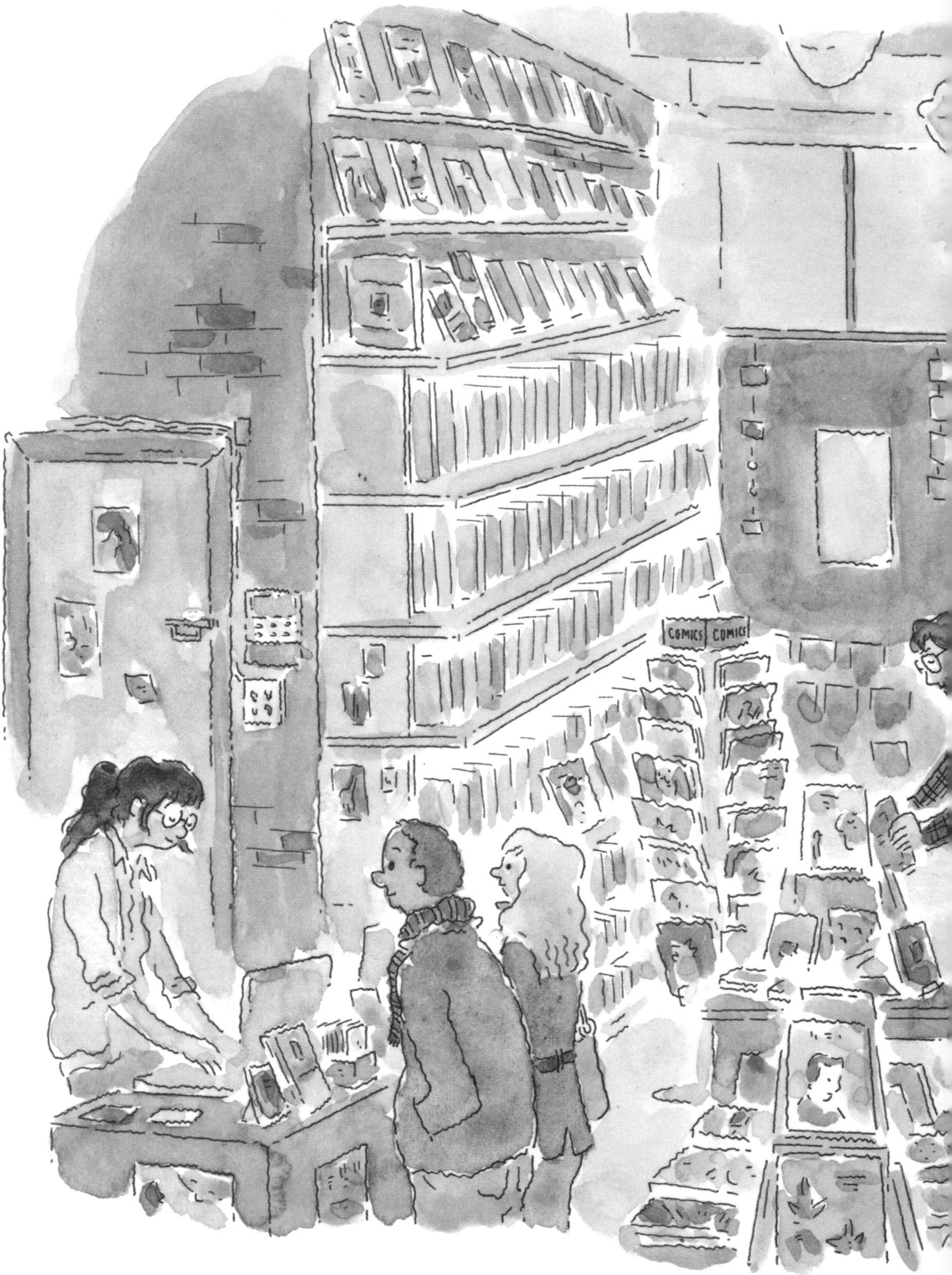
COMICS
COMICS

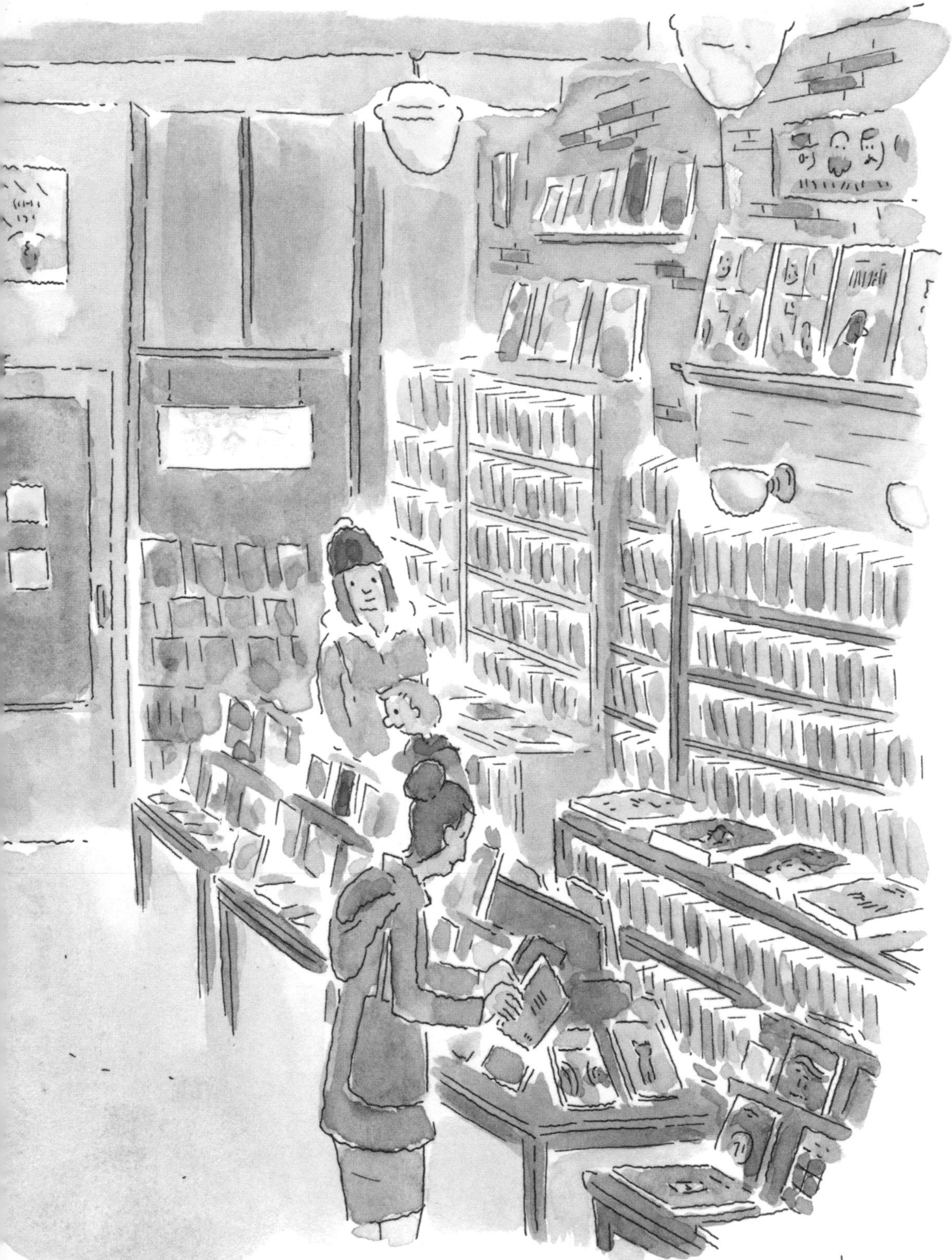
pascal

In 1997, I was fourteen years old and living in Ville Saint-Laurent, an area of Montreal that felt really boring and suburban to me. After school, I would often stop by the public library to borrow tons of books plus some CDs to make mix tapes. One day, I noticed Daniel Clowes's *Ghost World* in the new releases section, took it home, and became completely obsessed with it. After that, I read every comic and graphic novel I could find that didn't involve superheroes or anthropomorphic animals, including early D+Q titles like Adrian Tomine's *Sleepwalk* and Chester Brown's *I Never Liked You*. At some point, I realized that D+Q was located in Montreal—inconceivable! Just knowing that such a cool publisher existed in my hometown made me feel better about being "stuck" there.

Working at Librairie Drawn & Quarterly didn't feel like work. I really thought that people needed our books more than they needed their money and that my job was to make them realize that. I was always super enthusiastic about everything we carried and that probably turned some people off but I couldn't help it.

I worked at the store on the day that it opened—we did a soft opening in September 2007, before the official opening party. There were only a few tables and an antique cash register lying on top of a vitrine. At that point, the store only carried D+Q books (the rest would arrive in the following weeks) but still, a lot of people came that first day. I remember that I wore a T-shirt that said "What would Mr. Miyagi do?" and that I hadn't figured out how to add up the taxes so I probably either overcharged or undercharged every customer who came in that day.

—Claudia Eve Beauchesne

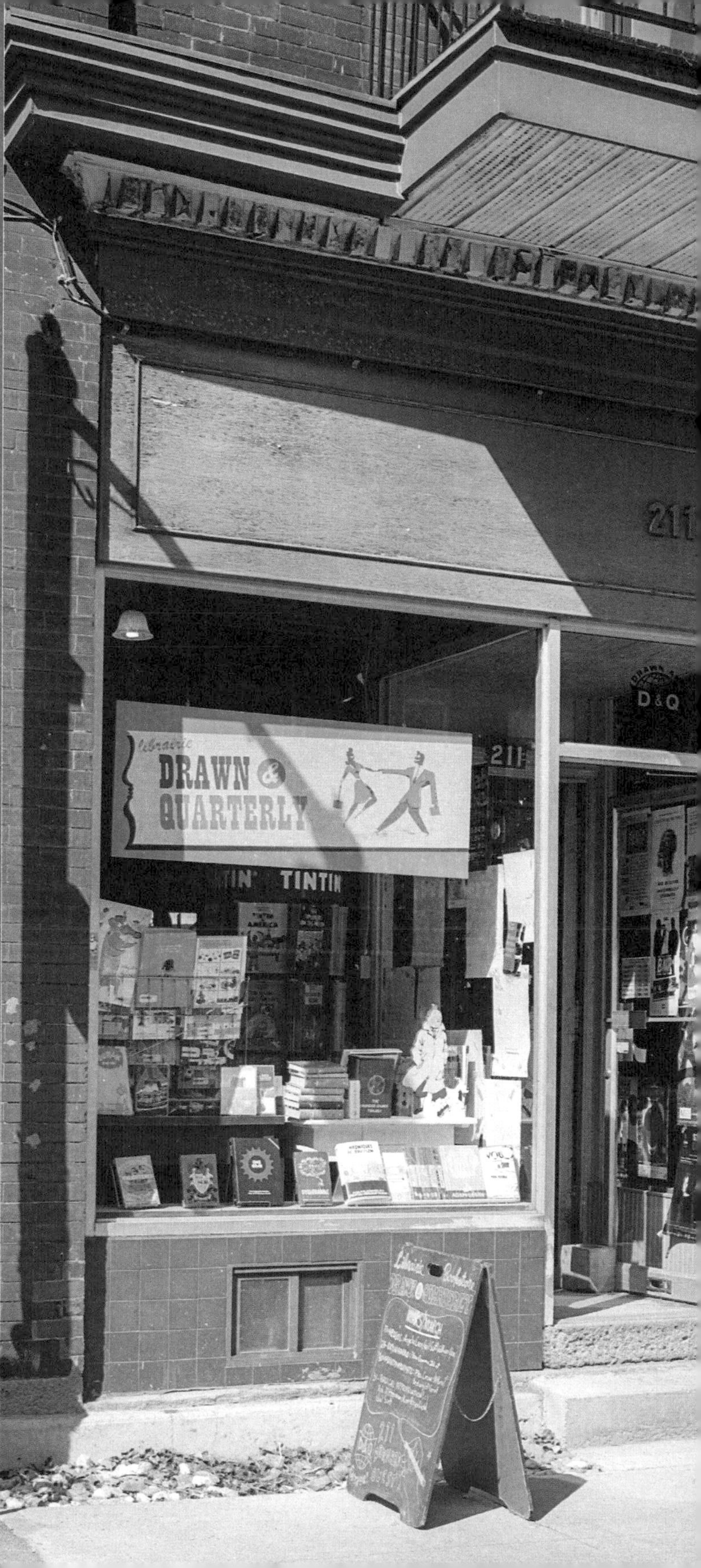
Librairie
DRAWN & QUARTERLY
211
TINTIN
D&Q

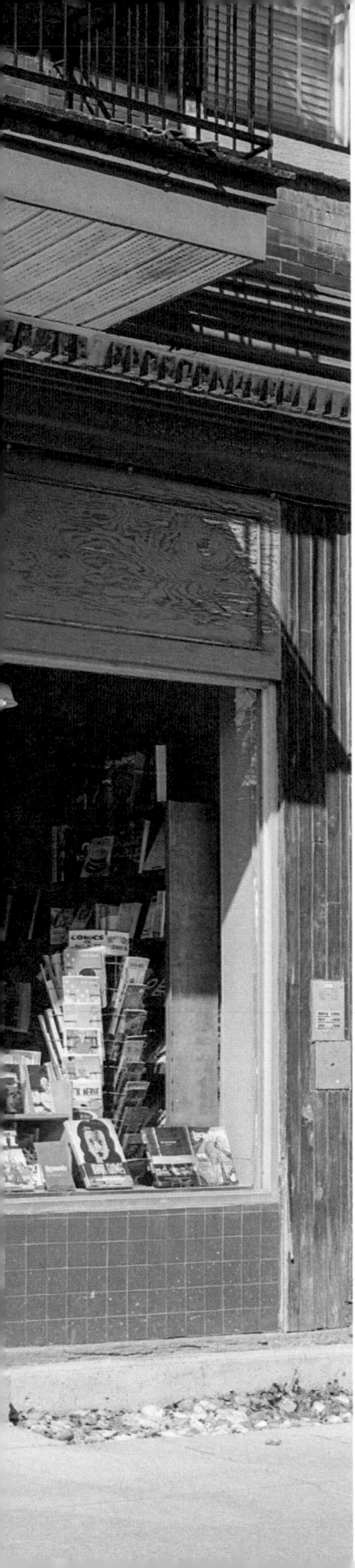

LIBRAIRIE D+Q

an appreciation by Heather O'Neill

Mile End is a small neighbourhood. It's only about six blocks wide and five blocks long. It is the same size that you were allowed to explore on your bicycle when you were a little kid. I moved to Mile End when I was twenty years old and pregnant. I moved to an apartment on the fourth floor of a big building beside a church that had been turned into a library.

I was part of the first migration of artists that crossed north of Mont-Royal Avenue looking for cheaper apartments. We were each of us like Henry Hudson looking for a Northwest Passage. We artists arrived like a group of oppressive fanatics with our extremist views. We had grown up in the 1980s. We had a disgust for consumerism, the way some people have toward a strict religious upbringing. We wore clothes from thrift shops and got our furniture from the trash. Our briefcases were held together with masking tape. We never, ever went to chain stores. We preferred cafés where the gold ceiling was caving in and the waitress had oil paint in her hair.

And a couple of decades later the area is still lousy with artists. There are artists in the backyards making dinosaurs out of sheet metal and old pans. There are writers in all the cafés, staring at their computer screens, typing away like Schroeder from *Peanuts* at his piano. And, yes, of course, there are loads and loads of musicians. They ride around with their trumpets in the baskets of their bicycles. They can occasionally be seen performing in old ballrooms with hitherto unseen musical instruments too, like a drum kit made out of empty coffee tins, or a child's plastic keyboard attached to an amplifier.

The neighbourhood has a Fellini-like quality.

If you expect to open a business in Mile End, you have to accept the rules of the tree house. You can't come to the street unless you accept the culture. You have to be as mad as everyone else.

So one day in 2007, Drawn & Quarterly decided to move into a little empty shop on Bernard Street that had once been a Hasidic business. The spot was near a florist that has fifty tiny bird cages hanging down from the balconies above its door. It was near a messy sports store that sharpens skates and has Christmas lights in the window all year long. It was near an old Greek diner with yellow light bulbs around the marquee and a theatre that La La La Human Steps rehearses on top of.

I was very excited to see a new bookstore, so I decided to go and take a peek. My dog Moppet came along and she stayed close to my ankles as I pulled open the door. The interior was small and pretty. The sunlight beamed through the

(Previous spread) Illustration by Pascal Girard. (Left) Photo: Alexi Hobbs (2012).

windows onto the grey tiled floors. The walls were exposed brick. There were assorted bookshelves in different colours along the walls and piled on top of one another, as though we were in the nursery of a child genius and these were collected books. The tables in the centre were covered with comic books and graphic novels. There were posters on the wall by various Montreal artists. The cash was in a small alcove and there were piles of eccentric birthday cards and bookmarks on the counter.

There were three people inside working, officially or not, I can't say. I asked if they could recommend a good book to me.

A girl with short black hair dressed like a boy leapt up and ran and pulled a book of interviews with Francis Bacon off the shelf. She said that if she were lost on a desert island, this was the one book that she would take with her and she would be happy reading it over and over again for the rest of her life.

That's the sort of hyperbole that is characteristic of the book recommendations at Librairie Drawn & Quarterly and it is invariably charming. I've bought loads of novels there over the years. Whenever someone at the store recommends me a book, I feel as though I'm at a strange apothecary in New Orleans where they are offering me an elixir with impossible qualities, like eternal youth or love.

Another beautiful thing about this independent bookstore is that it is wonderfully curated. They always have a display of the strangest and most beautiful art books.

I bought a giant book by Henry Darger there. I walked home with it in my arms. And when I got home, I opened the book and all the little girls in bloomers and short dresses rushed out on their hobby horses with bayonets to attack my dogs. I once bought a Marcel Dzama book there and now there is a bank robber in a catsuit touching his toes in my kitchen and a bear in the living room playing with the remote control.

I once had a dream that I got trapped in Librairie Drawn & Quarterly. I went through a door at the side that I'd never seen before and there was a room with all these people sitting in cubicles drawing teacups and sad horses whose proportions were incorrect. I was looking through the bookshelves in that room and I found a book that I hadn't written yet.

In the summer there is always a chalkboard outside on the sidewalk advertising upcoming readings. They have a little stage in the back on which Booker Prize winners have conversed about culture and where local residents have waxed poetic about beetles. Librairie Drawn & Quarterly organized my book launch at the theatre next door, and when I arrived they had a group of polite twelve-year-olds working the door and escorting guests up the stairs. Everything about Librairie Drawn & Quarterly is weird and wonderful. And that is why they have come to be beloved by everyone in Mile End.

Heather O'Neill is the author of one book of poetry,* two eyes are you sleeping, *and two novels:* Lullabies for Little Criminals *and* The Girl Who Was Saturday Night. Lullabies for Little Criminals *won the CBC Canada Reads contest in 2007 and was shortlisted for numerous awards. A forthcoming collection of her short stories,* Daydreams of Angels, *will be published in 2015.

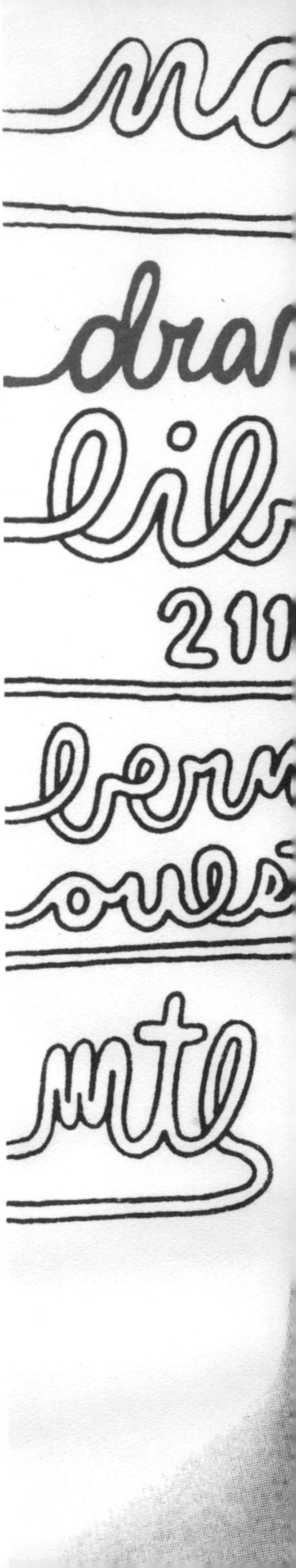

 Julie Doucet's poster for the opening of Librairie Drawn & Quarterly (2007).

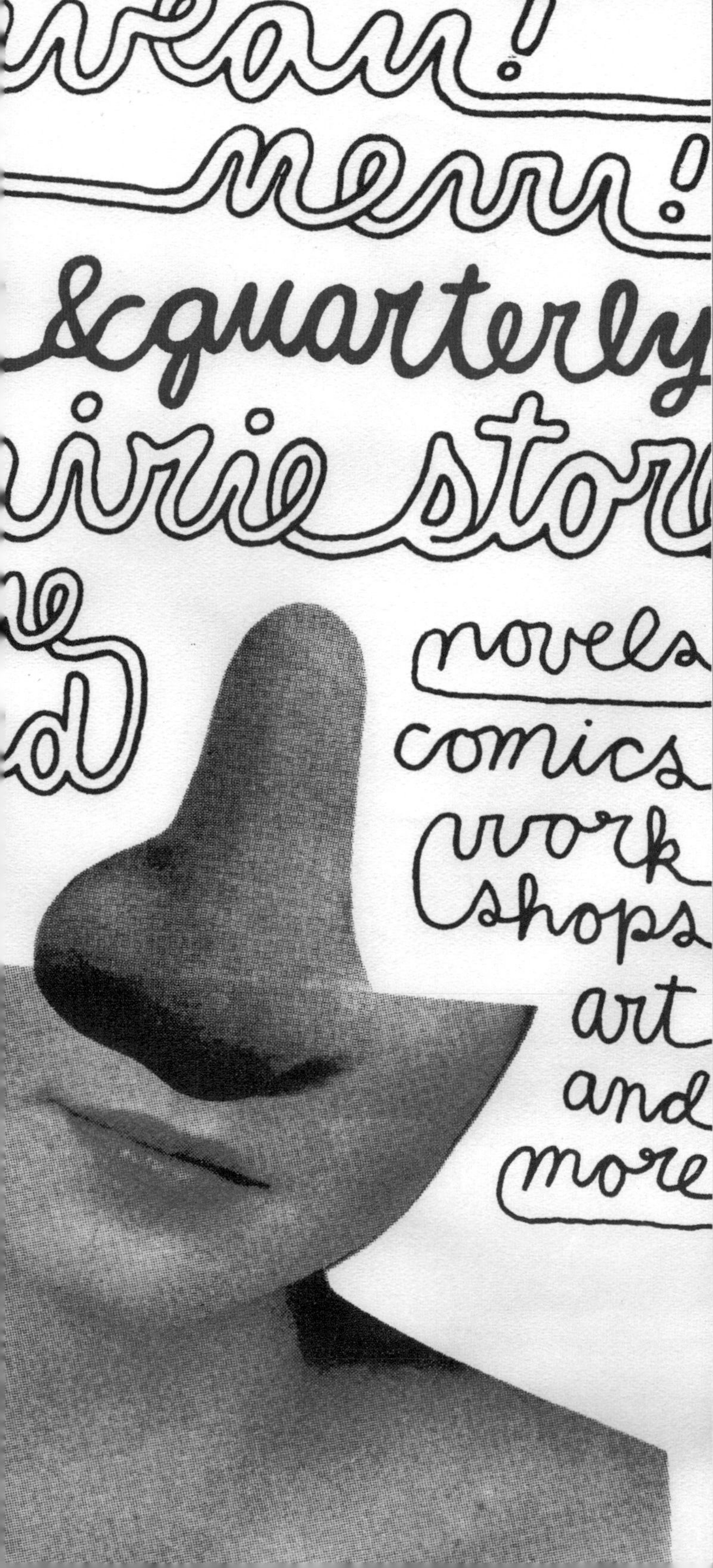
novels
comics
work
shops
art
and
more

I've been at D+Q for almost seven years, and when people ask me what I do, I still struggle with my answer. And that's because one thing I love about D+Q is that the job can be whatever you want it to be. I started as an intern and in the intervening seven years, I've done every job at this company that doesn't require Photoshop or accounting skills. And I've loved it all, but working at the bookstore was a particular sort of delight.

I grew up adoring bookstores, so I was thrilled to find myself working in one where we could order any book we wanted (and were encouraged to!); where one of our duties was to dream up lists of authors we wanted to host (and they often wound up coming—Sheila Heti, David Byrne, Margaret Atwood, Daniel Clowes!); where the customers sometimes brought you snacks or wrote Missed Connections about you. Early on in my employment there, store manager Rory sent an email: somebody had guerrilla-planted tomatoes, corn, and potatoes in our front yard, so we should be sure to water regularly.

Event hosting was a big part of the job: there was the time Kate Beaton came to town and signed a boob (with a fat pony!) and the heart-opening experience of watching a crowd of six hundred wipe tears away at a Lynda Barry talk. It was often magical to work at the Librairie. But really, my favourite thing was that, hip as the books were, the Librairie staff never had an unapproachable, judgy vibe. We were all there because we loved sharing books with other people, a sentiment I still hear about from strangers when I tell them, a little longingly, "No, I don't work at the bookstore anymore. But I used to! I help out with events sometimes."

—***Julia Pohl-Miranda***

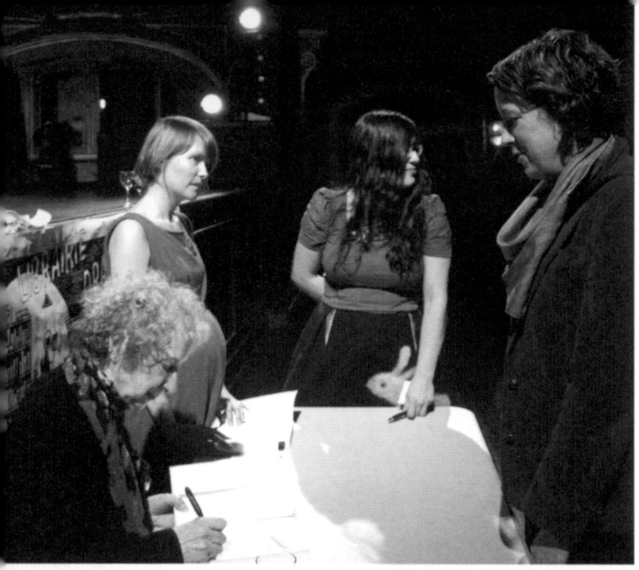
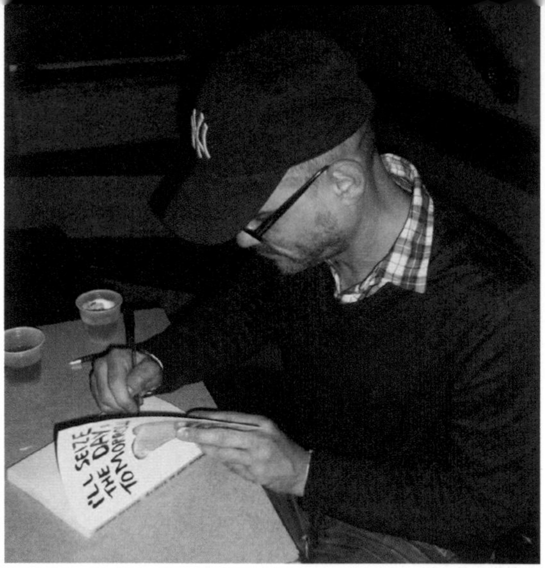
I'LL SEIZE THE DAY
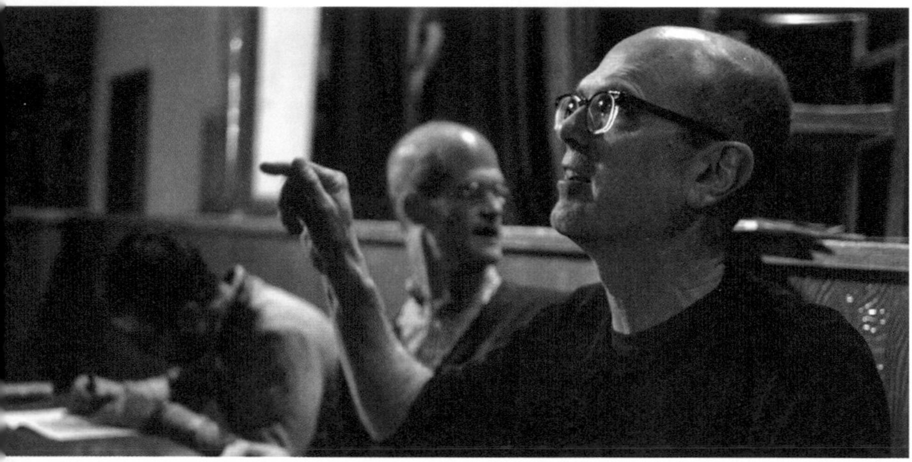
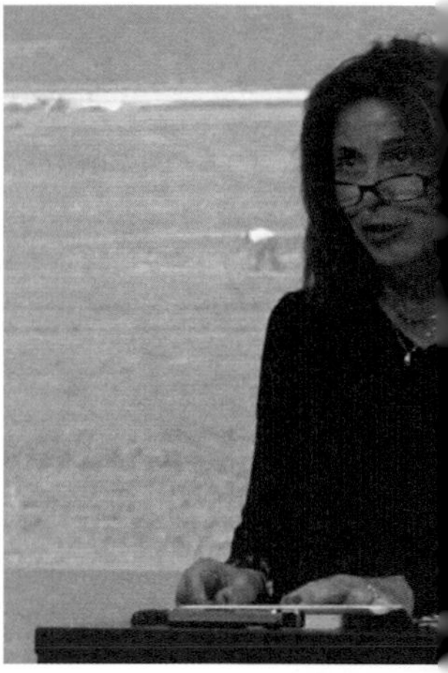
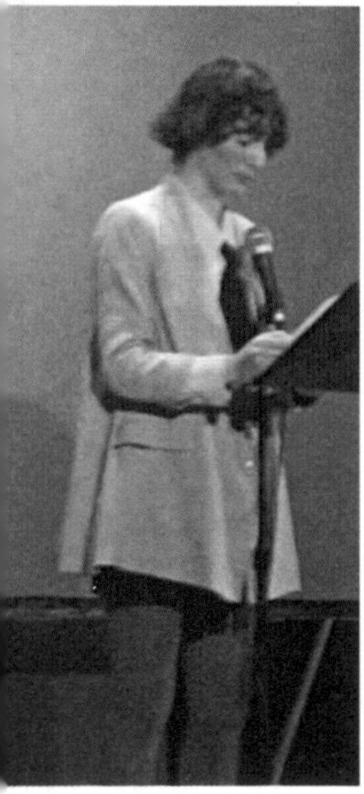
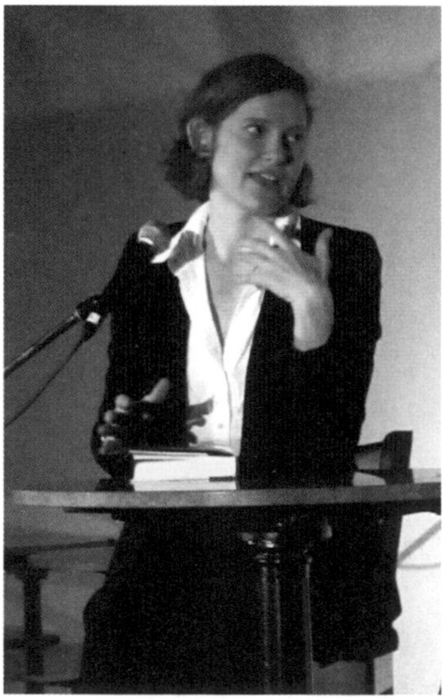
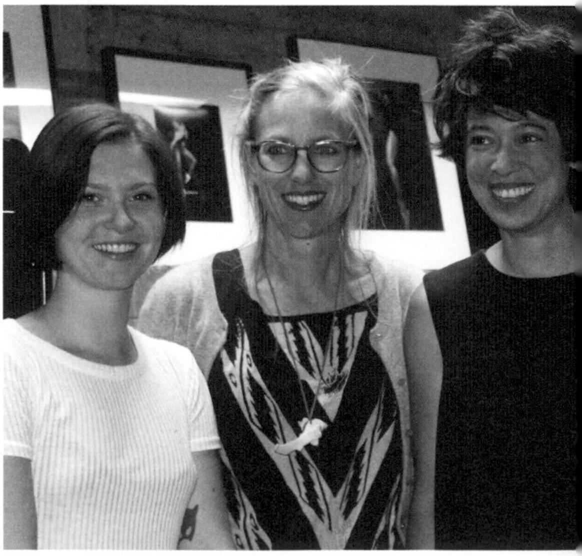

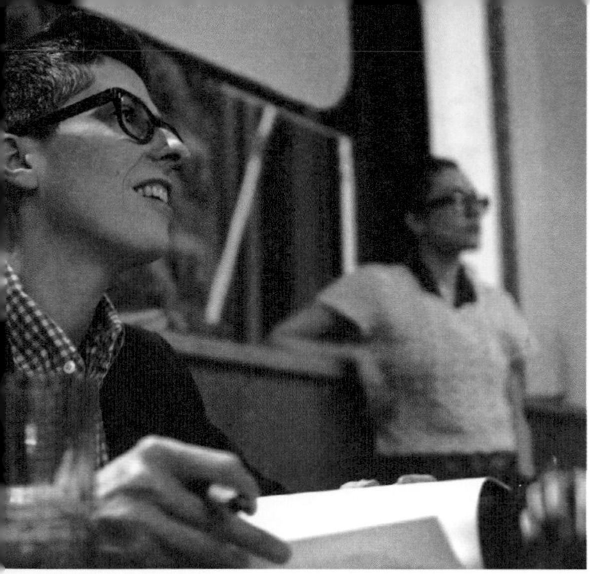

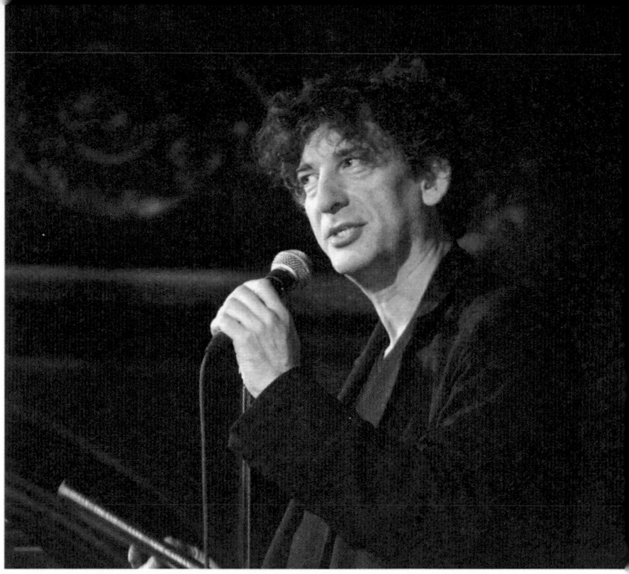

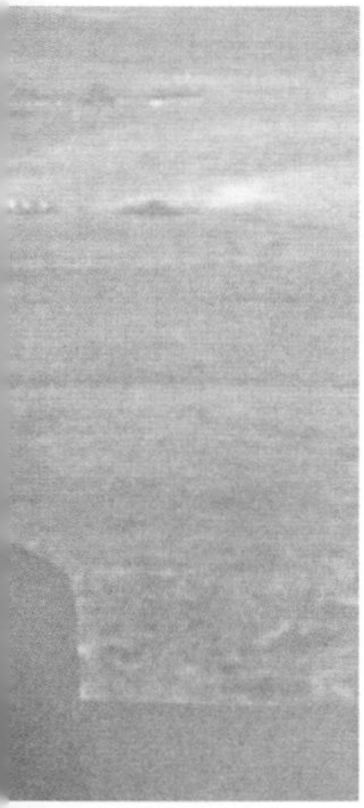

Librairie D+Q events: (Top row) Margaret Atwood chats with Julia Pohl-Miranda, Peggy Burns & D+Q staffer Aleshia Jensen (2013). Jonathan Goldstein at La Sala Rossa (2012). Alison Bechdel & D+Q staffer Helen Chau Bradley at the Ukrainian Federation. Photo: David Smith (2013). Neil Gaiman onstage at the Rialto theatre. Photo: David Smith (2013). (Middle row) Librairie D+Q's fifth anniversary event with Adrian Tomine, Chris Ware & Charles Burns. Photo: David Smith (2012). Chris Kraus reading from *Summer of Hate* (2012). (Bottom row) Miranda July reading from *It Chooses You* (2011). Heather O'Neill in conversation with Laurel Sprengelmeyer (2014). Fiona Duncan, Heidi Julavits, Leanne Shapton & Sheila Heti backstage at the launch for *Women in Clothes* (2014). David Byrne in conversation with Win Butler. Photo: Richmond Lam (2012).

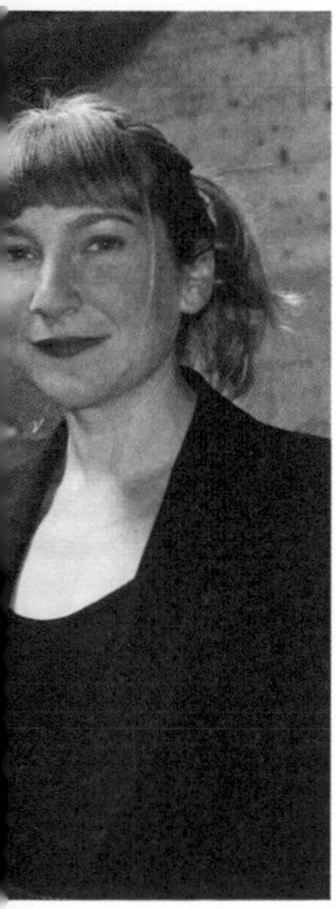

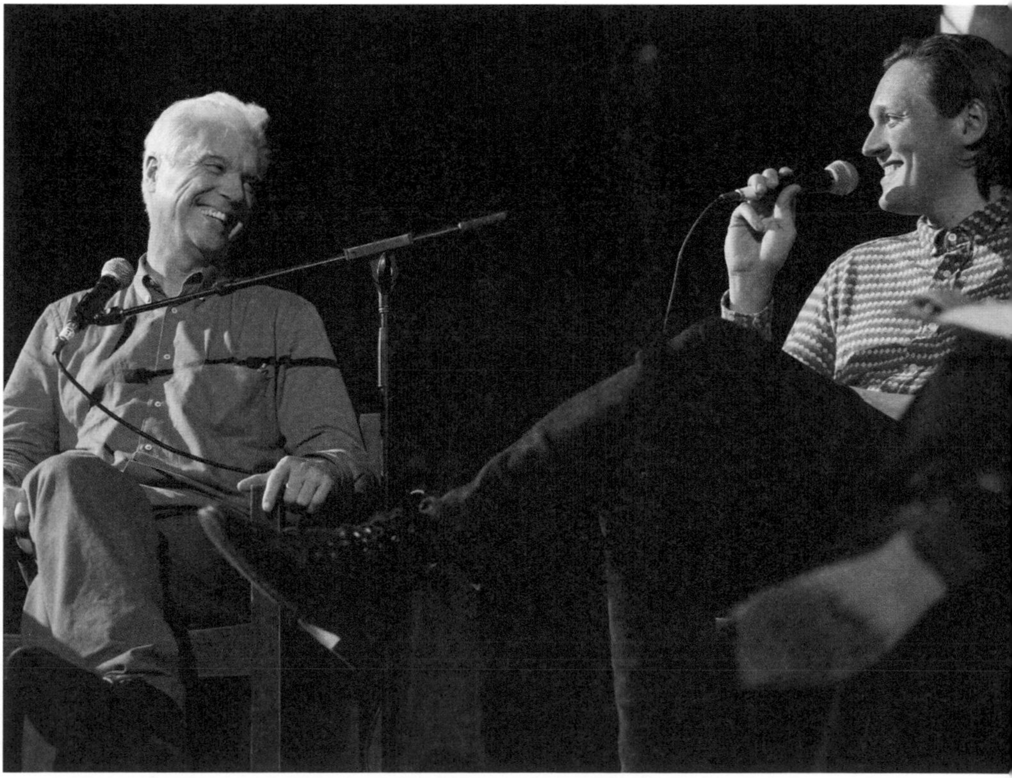

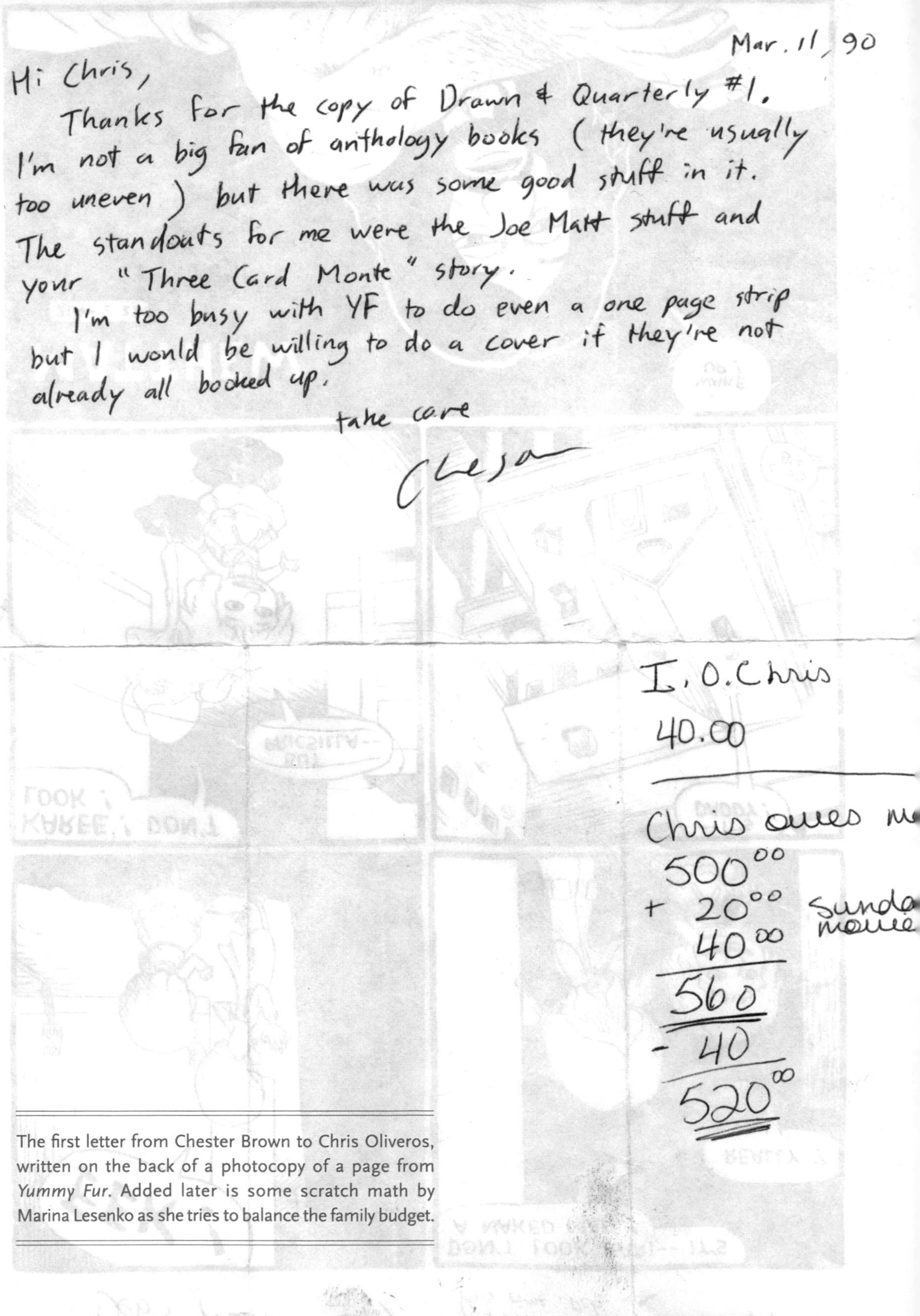

Mar. 11, 90

Hi Chris,

Thanks for the copy of Drawn & Quarterly #1. I'm not a big fan of anthology books (they're usually too uneven) but there was some good stuff in it. The standouts for me were the Joe Matt stuff and your "Three Card Monte" story.

I'm too busy with YF to do even a one page strip but I would be willing to do a cover if they're not already all booked up.

take care

Chester

I. O. Chris
40.00

Chris owes me
500.00
+ 20.00 Sunday movie
40.00
560
- 40
520.00

The first letter from Chester Brown to Chris Oliveros, written on the back of a photocopy of a page from *Yummy Fur*. Added later is some scratch math by Marina Lesenko as she tries to balance the family budget.

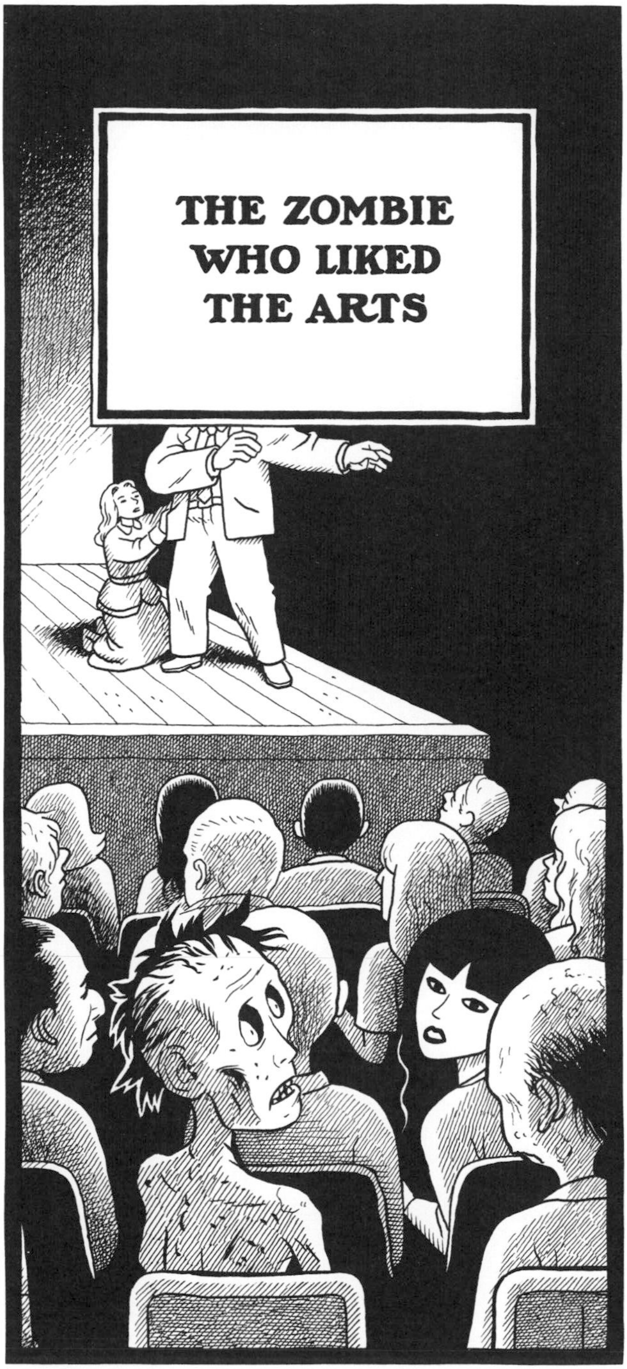
THE ZOMBIE WHO LIKED THE ARTS

"The Zombie Who Liked the Arts" appeared in *Now* magazine (October 4 to November 8, 2007). Chester Brown

ONE

LOOK! ZOMBIES!
OH NO! TORONTO IS BEING INVADED BY ZOMBIES!
Grrr...
Want... to... eat... people...
Eat... eat... people...
Hey look, there's a theatre.
Let's go eat some people in there.
I was thinking we could just watch whatever play is being performed in there.
Watch the play? But we're zombies. We're supposed to eat people.
It's been a while since I saw a good play. We can eat people later.
Oh, all right.

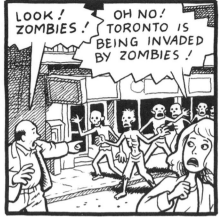

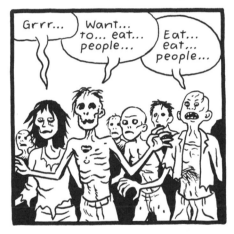

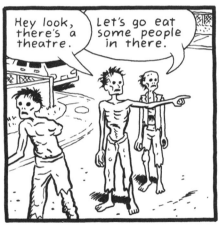

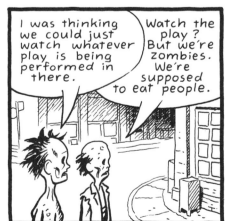

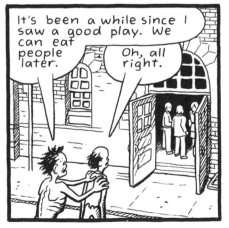

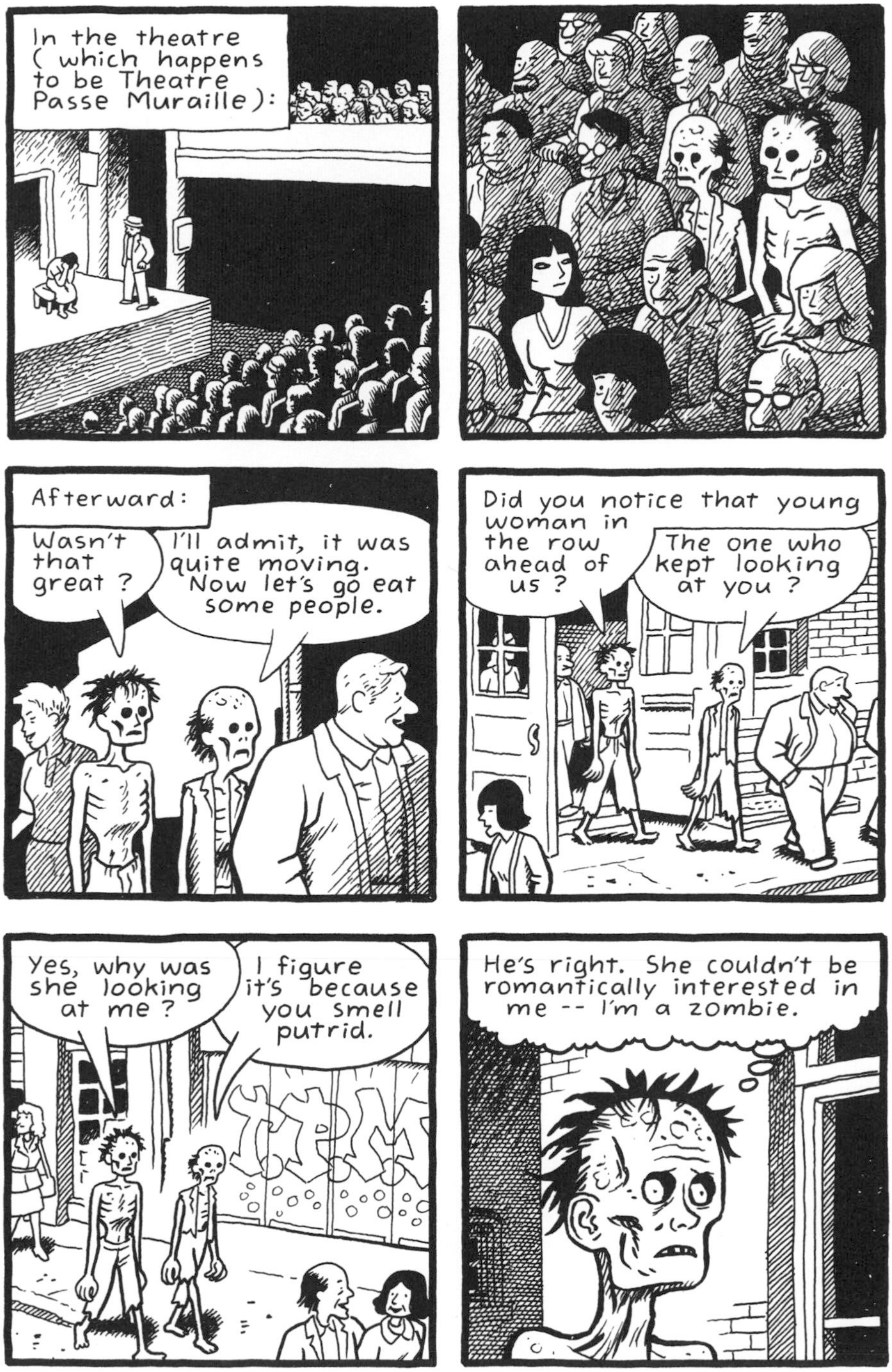
In the theatre (which happens to be Theatre Passe Muraille):
Afterward:
Wasn't that great ?
I'll admit, it was quite moving. Now let's go eat some people.
Did you notice that young woman in the row ahead of us ?
The one who kept looking at you ?
Yes, why was she looking at me ?
I figure it's because you smell putrid.
He's right. She couldn't be romantically interested in me -- I'm a zombie.

TWO

Let's go see that Toronto Dance Theatre performance tonight.

I don't know. Isn't it dangerous with all those zombies roaming the city?

There's not THAT much risk.

Maybe you're right. I went to Théâtre Passe Muraille last night, and there were two zombies in the audience watching the play.

I don't believe you.

It's true, I swear. One of them looked almost cute.

That night:

It's beautiful. They move so gracefully.

Look three rows back.

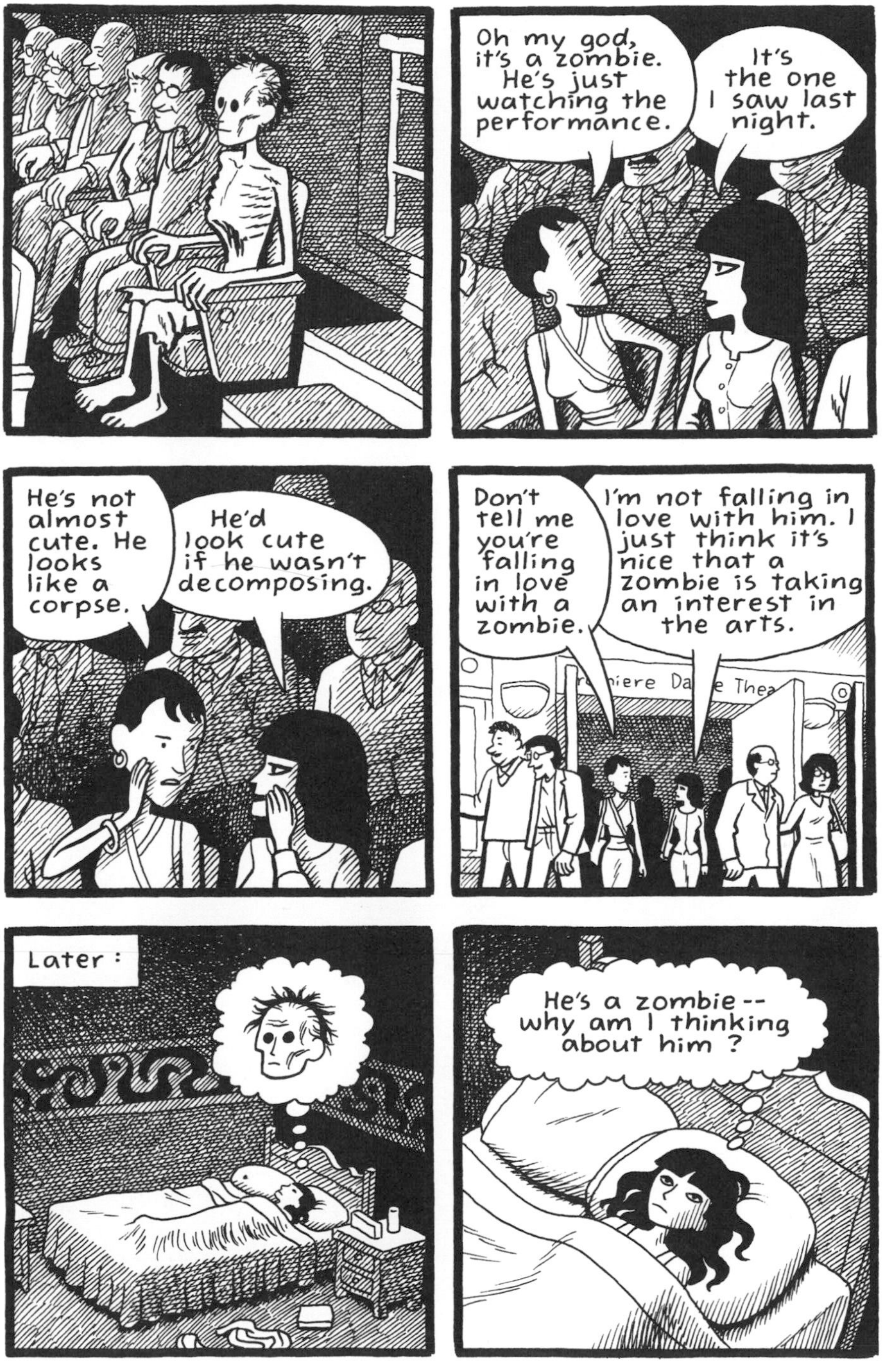
Oh my god, it's a zombie. He's just watching the performance.
It's the one I saw last night.
He's not almost cute. He looks like a corpse.
He'd look cute if he wasn't decomposing.
Don't tell me you're falling in love with a zombie.
I'm not falling in love with him. I just think it's nice that a zombie is taking an interest in the arts.
Later :
He's a zombie -- why am I thinking about him ?

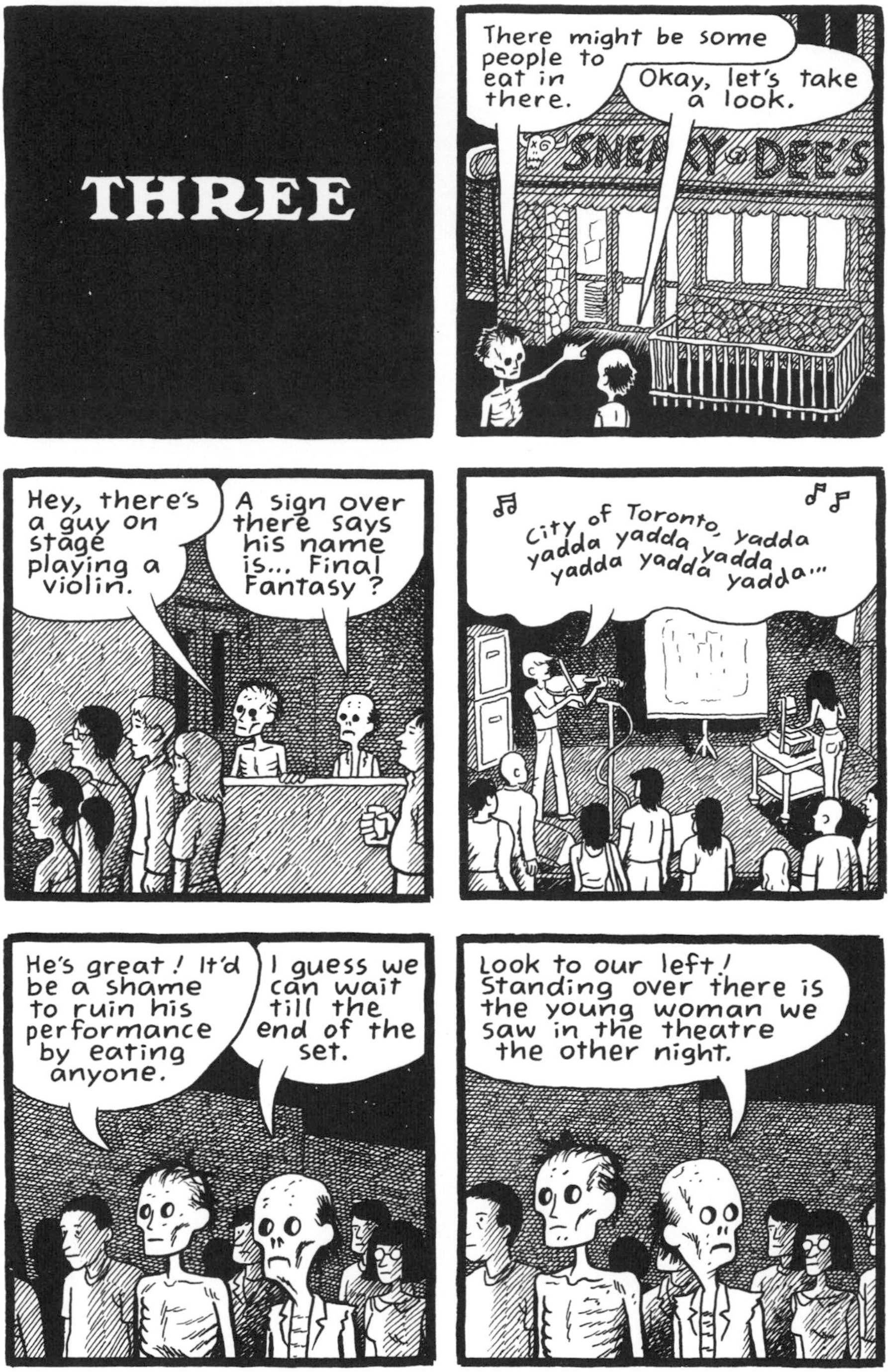
THREE
There might be some people to eat in there.
Okay, let's take a look.
SNEAKY DEE'S
Hey, there's a guy on stage playing a violin.
A sign over there says his name is... Final Fantasy?
City of Toronto, yadda yadda yadda yadda yadda yadda...
He's great! It'd be a shame to ruin his performance by eating anyone.
I guess we can wait till the end of the set.
Look to our left! Standing over there is the young woman we saw in the theatre the other night.

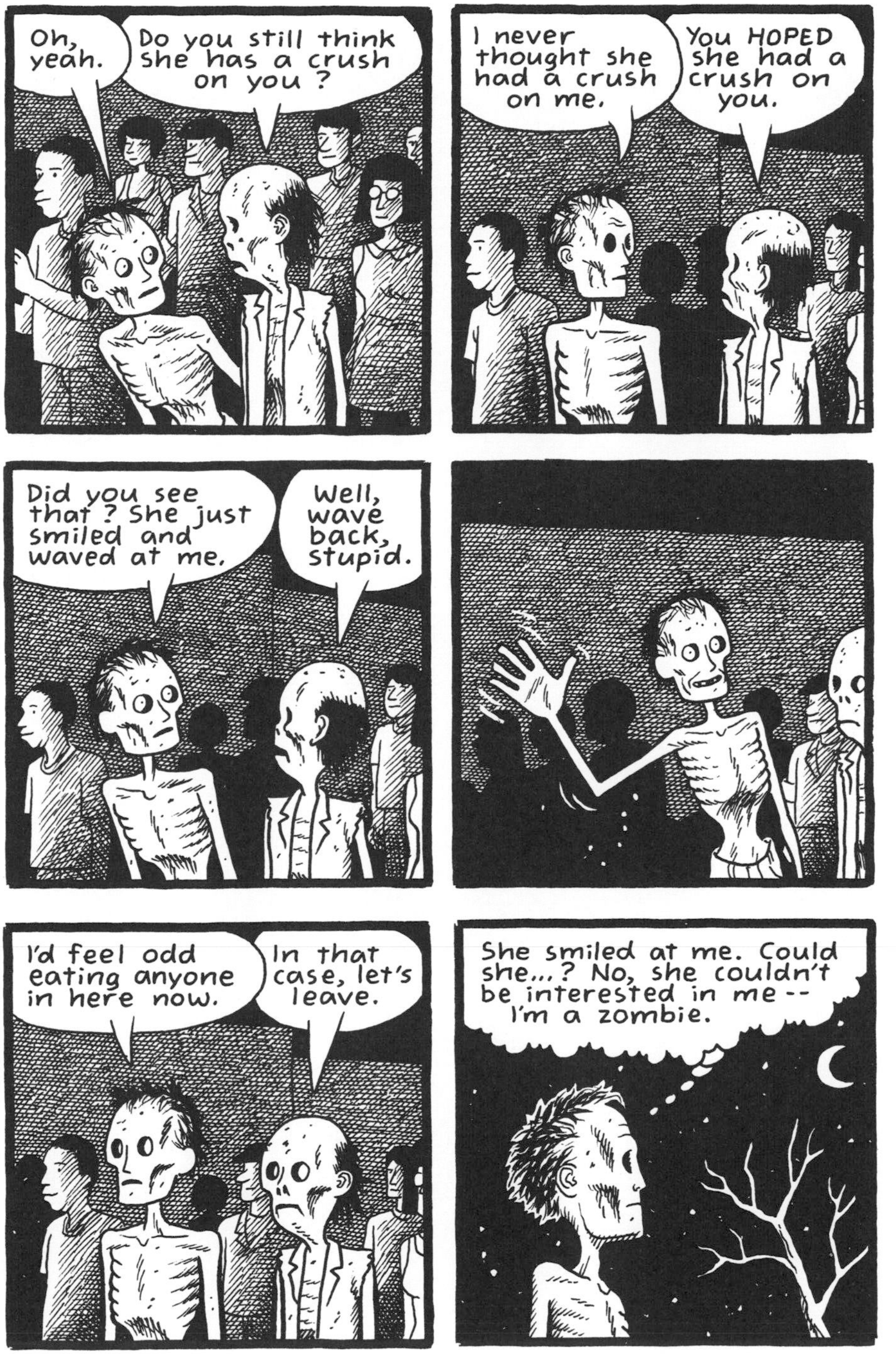
Oh, yeah.
Do you still think she has a crush on you ?
I never thought she had a crush on me.
You HOPED she had a crush on you.
Did you see that ? She just smiled and waved at me.
Well, wave back, stupid.
I'd feel odd eating anyone in here now.
In that case, let's leave.
She smiled at me. Could she...? No, she couldn't be interested in me -- I'm a zombie.

FOUR

MoCCA has a new show up. I should check it out.

I have time to take a quick look around before I have to be at the restaurant to meet Sharon.

museum of contemporary canadian art

Oh, there's that zombie again.

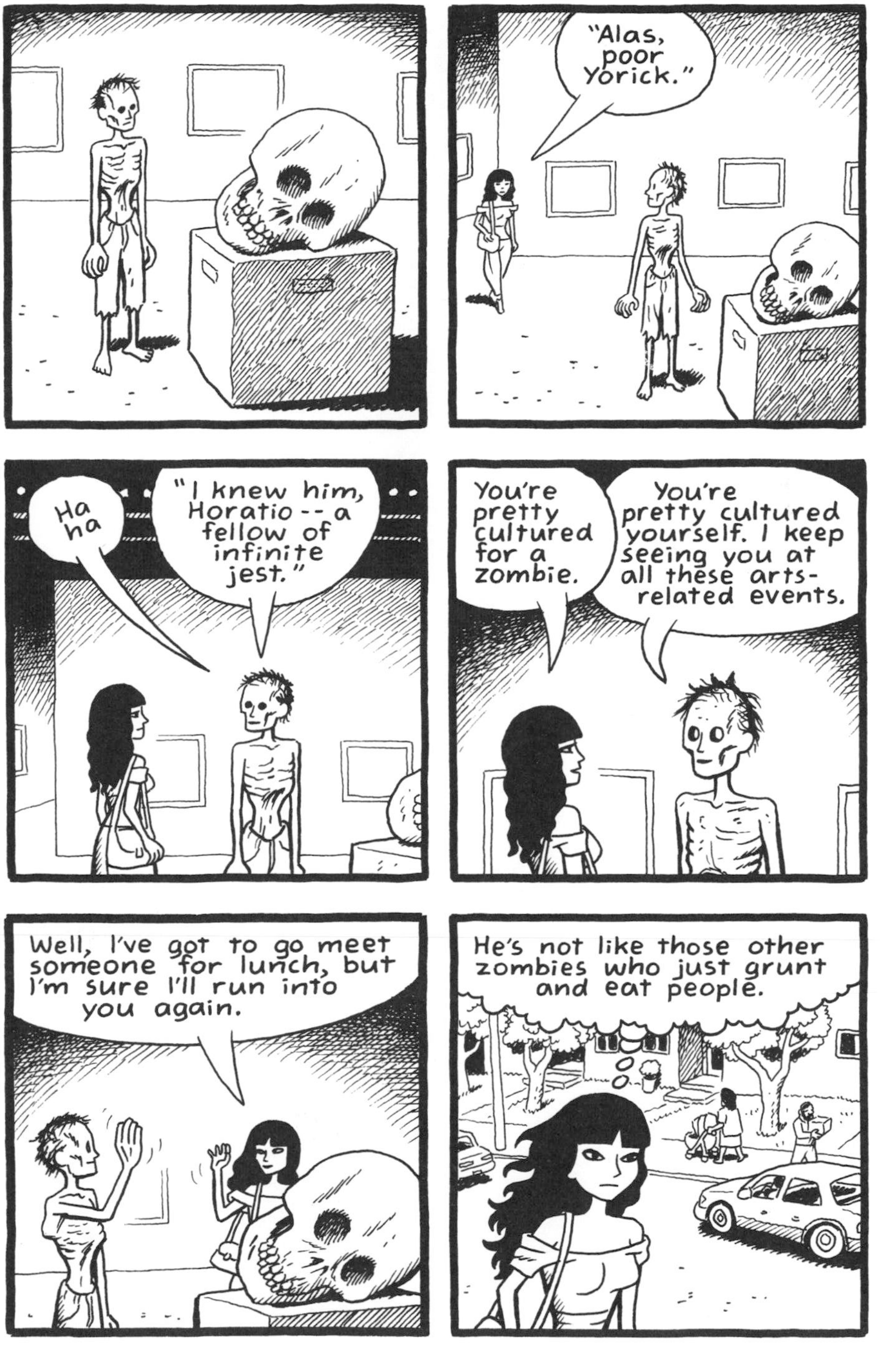
"Alas, poor Yorick."
Ha ha
"I knew him, Horatio -- a fellow of infinite jest."
You're pretty cultured for a zombie.
You're pretty cultured yourself. I keep seeing you at all these arts-related events.
Well, I've got to go meet someone for lunch, but I'm sure I'll run into you again.
He's not like those other zombies who just grunt and eat people.

FIVE
I wonder if I got that Shakespeare quote right the other day ?
Here's a bookstore -- This Ain't The Rosedale Library. I'll go in and check.
This ain't THE ROSEDALE LIBRARY
This ain't THE ROSEDALE LIBRARY
Where's the drama section ?
Oh! Look over there !
It's her ! And the cover on that book she's holding looks familiar.

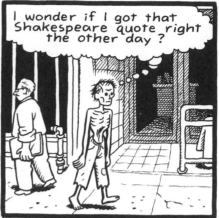

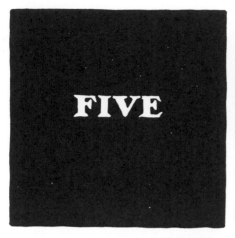

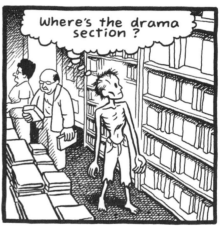

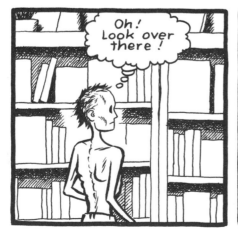

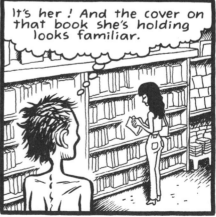

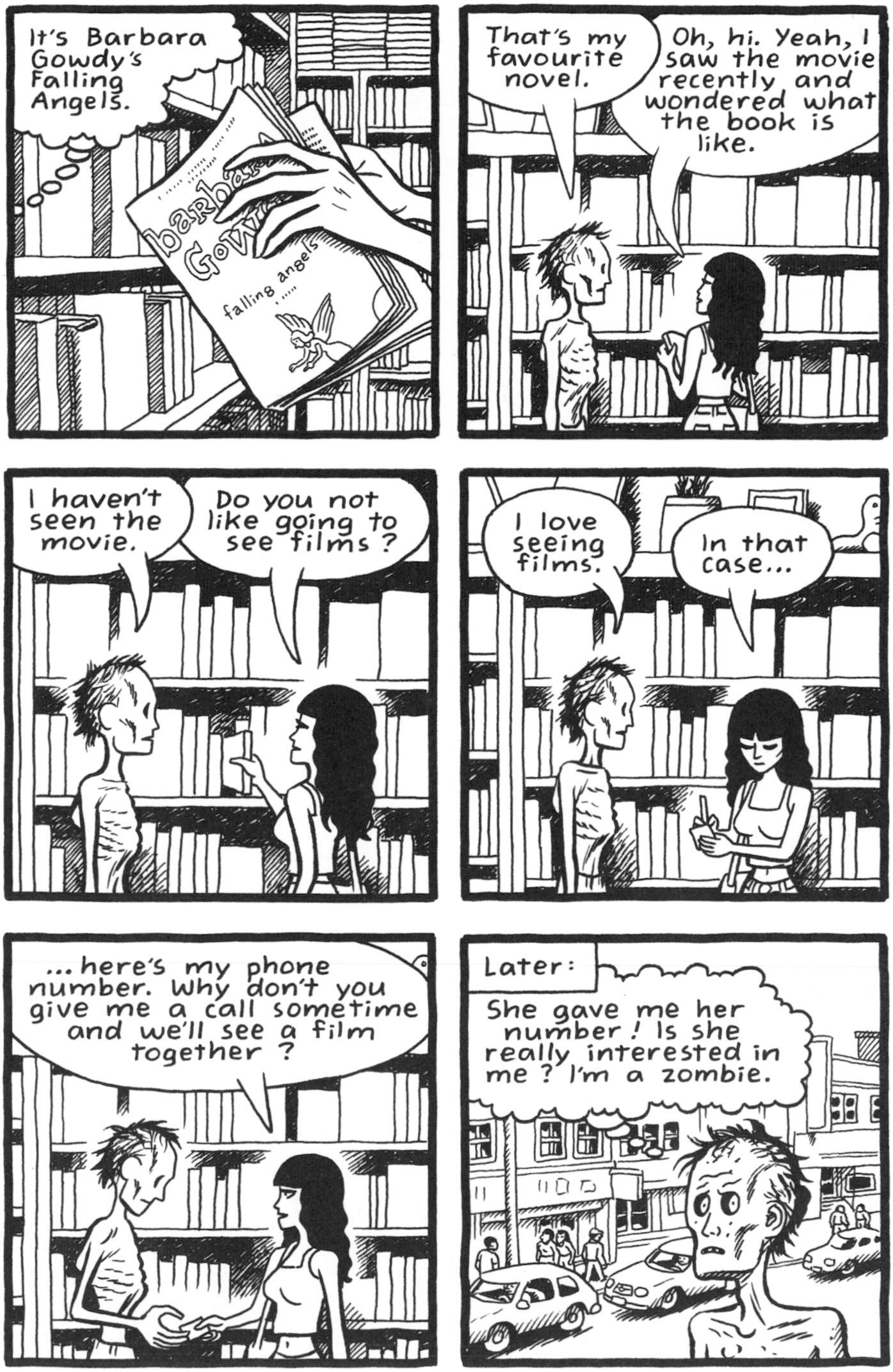
It's Barbara Gowdy's Falling Angels.
barbara Gow
falling angels
That's my favourite novel.
Oh, hi. Yeah, I saw the movie recently and wondered what the book is like.
I haven't seen the movie.
Do you not like going to see films?
I love seeing films.
In that case...
...here's my phone number. Why don't you give me a call sometime and we'll see a film together?
Later:
She gave me her number! Is she really interested in me? I'm a zombie.

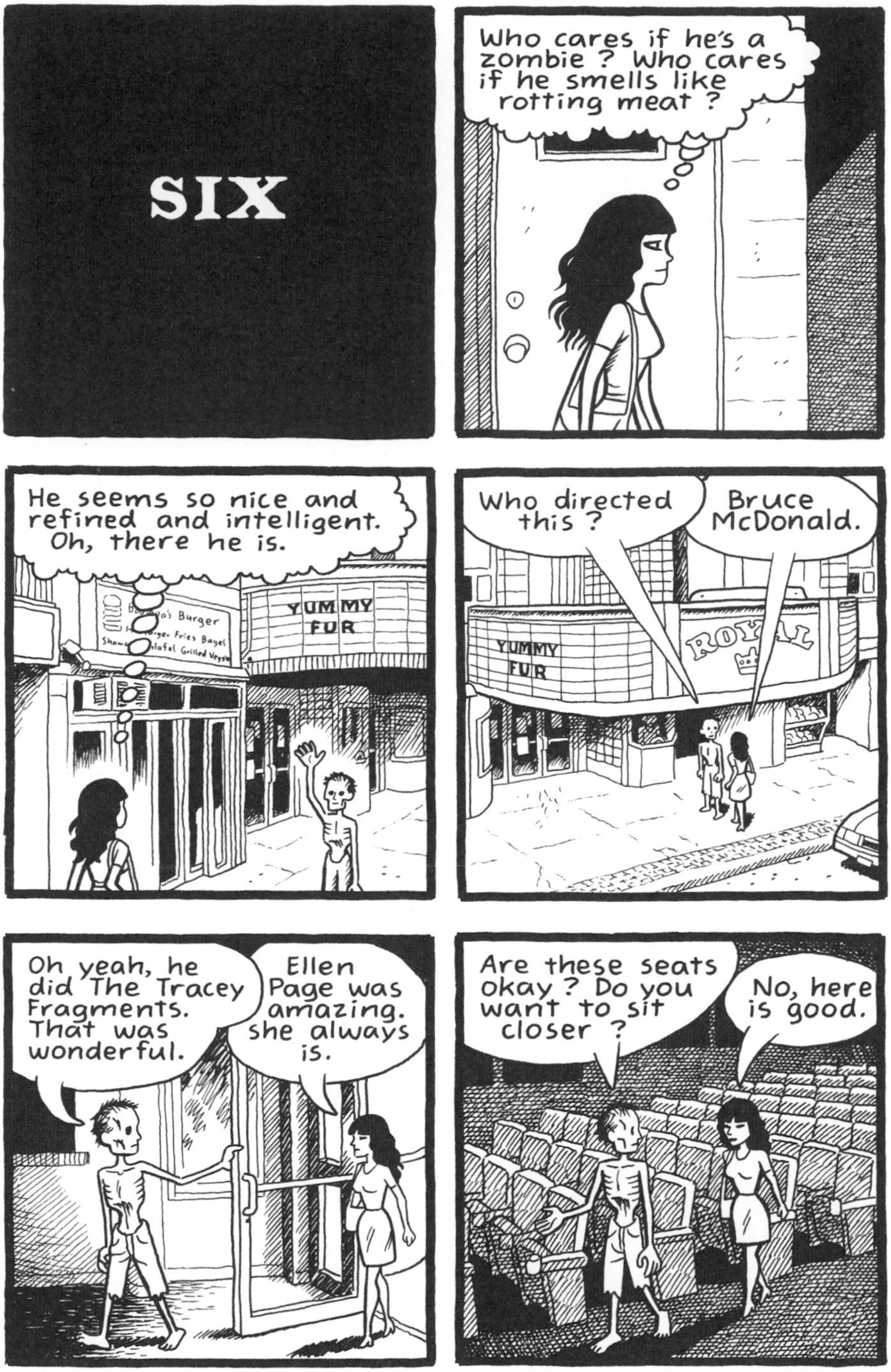
SIX
Who cares if he's a zombie ? Who cares if he smells like rotting meat ?
He seems so nice and refined and intelligent. Oh, there he is.
YUMMY FUR
Who directed this ?
Bruce McDonald.
YUMMY FUR
Oh yeah, he did The Tracey Fragments. That was wonderful.
Ellen Page was amazing. she always is.
Are these seats okay ? Do you want to sit closer ?
No, here is good.

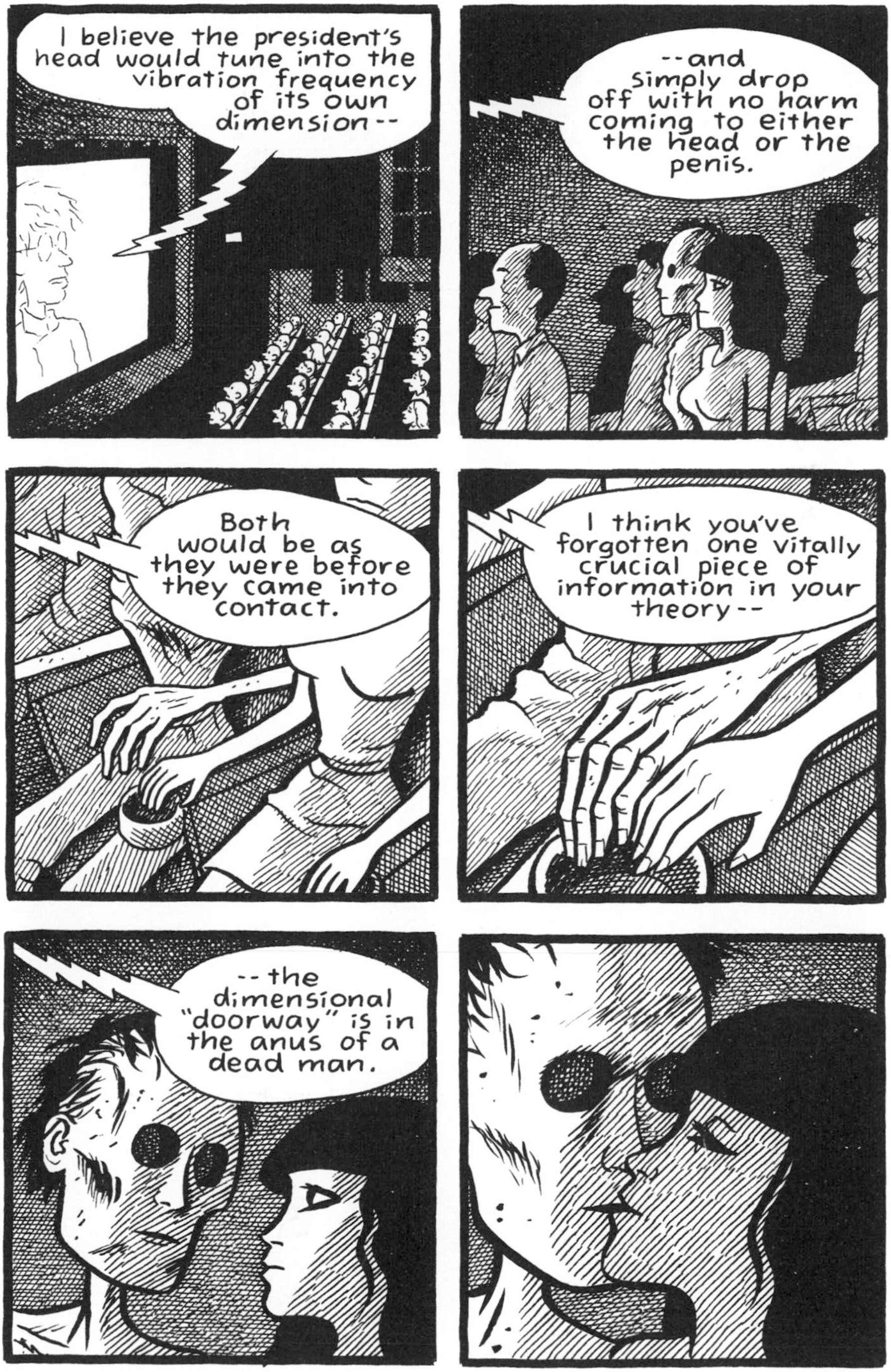
I believe the president's head would tune into the vibration frequency of its own dimension--
--and simply drop off with no harm coming to either the head or the penis.
Both would be as they were before they came into contact.
I think you've forgotten one vitally crucial piece of information in your theory--
--the dimensional "doorway" is in the anus of a dead man.

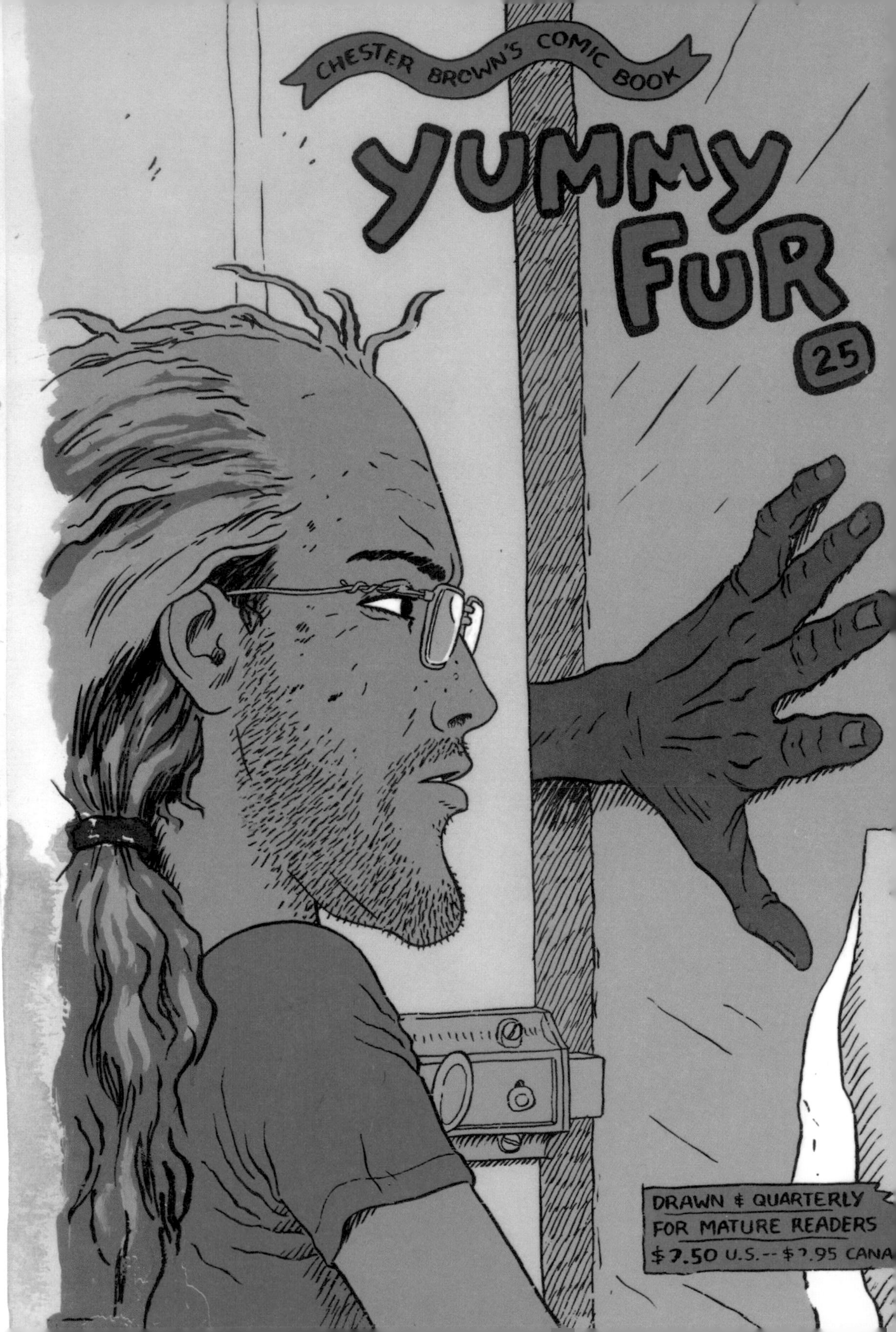
CHESTER BROWN'S COMIC BOOK
YUMMY FUR
25
DRAWN & QUARTERLY
FOR MATURE READERS
$2.50 U.S.-- $2.95 CANA

A FURTIVE EXCHANGE

an appreciation by Jonathan Lethem

Reading Chester Brown's *Paying for It,* I found myself unexpectedly recalling a trepidatious and exciting visit I once made, in 2000, to an anonymous-looking apartment in downtown Toronto. I went there looking to make a transaction, one in which I would exchange money for something I regard as beyond price, something from a realm outside that of transactions and money—but wait, before you leap to any conclusions, let me slow down and explain. Actually, before I explain, let me mention that I regard *Paying for It* as, simply, or not so simply, the most recent in a series of totally characteristic and totally unpredictable masterpieces by one of our greatest—one of our greatest ever—cartoonists, or comic-book artists, or graphic novelists, or whatever we're calling them. Note also how I avoided having to say "North American" by saying "our," which I prefer because, *Louis Riel* aside—and that's a big aside—Chester Brown seems to me both more iconoclastic and more universal than "Canadian" or "North American"; he's a citizen of the timeless nation of the dissident soul, as much as Dostoevsky's underground man. At the same time, he's also a citizen of a nation of one: Chesterbrownton, or Chesterbrownsylvania, a desolate but charged region he seems to have no choice but to inhabit, and of which I feel quite privileged to be a regular visitor.

So, what was I seeking at the anonymous-looking apartment in downtown Toronto in the year 2000?

I was seeking to commission Chester Brown to draw a cover for a small-press book I'd written, a novella, that I was designing myself. As it happens, I'd persuaded my publisher-collaborator that Brown was the ideal artist for the project—not difficult to do—and since, also as it happens, I was intermittently living in Toronto at the time, I made it a fair excuse to impress myself on the man. He was already at that point my favourite, and I wanted to describe the project to him in person. I had it in mind to propose a very particular two-part deal to him, as well: I wanted him to draw the cover image for the book, and I also wanted to own a Chester Brown original, and so I asked if I could arrange to purchase the drawing for the cover in advance.

What happened? Brown welcomed me in and listened to my wishes in a kind of attentively distant way, a kind of deadpan but not unfriendly way, one that was of course already somewhat familiar to me from his autobiographical comics and has subsequently become vastly more familiar—and then he agreed. Brown got the drift of what I wanted, and it was okay, he wasn't judgmental of my odd wishes, he could help me with this, yes.

Though this wasn't without its humorous aspects—neither the fiction I'd written that needed the illustration, nor the situation of my describing it to him: the novella concerned a slumbering army of soldiers living inside a gigantic body, and so the drawing I requested for the cover was of a commander and his lieutenant marching, lost, within an enormous human intestinal tract—the atmosphere between us was oddly furtive and clinical, somewhat clipped and efficient, though, as I said, not in any way unfriendly. The gist of it seemed to be that Brown was able to relieve me of my problem. I think he charged me eight hundred bucks. Or three hundred. Or five hundred. I can't remember.

Now, since I've never paid for sex (an assertion which, due to Brown's insinuating rhetorical powers in the footnotes to *Paying for It*—and because of the brilliantly pervasive aura of shame that infuses so much of Brown's work—I can practically verge on experiencing as an embarrassing

Original painted art for first D+Q issue of *Yummy Fur*. Photocopy of line art on acetate with cel-paint on back (1991).

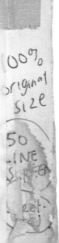

On *I Never Liked You* by Chester Brown, and all of *Yummy Fur*: "I was deeply moved and disturbed at the same time by the highly discomforting atmosphere of the book and the ill-being of the main character. By all of what is unsaid. Yet very impressed by Chester's very bare drawing style, which I LOVE."—***Julie Doucet***

confession: shouldn't I have done so at some point? But no, no, that's not right, I'm overidentifying with my subject right now), what this felt like, to me, was a visit to a drug dealer. I'd found the right address and been welcomed inside and told *Sure, I can hook you up.* And, *I'm not going to make you feel like a sick fuck for wanting what you want; some persons just need a drawing of army men lost inside an intestine from time to time. You've come to the right place.*

And I had. Though I ordinarily hate illustrational approaches to my writing and have fought like a cornered terrier repeatedly to get art directors from major publishers to revert to jacket designs that consist purely of metaphorical or abstract imagery, or of font, there's something about Brown's line that works for me entirely as a representation of what written language does. His lines, his compositions and forms, are both persuasively somatic—grotty, physical, homely, a testimony or confession of the body—and simultaneously a thing of the deep soul-ether; they fuse the actual and the metaphysical as their baseline operation. No matter how hard Brown may work to purge this spiritual, phantasmagorical element from his drawing and to ground us instead in a flensed and prosaic world (this is a supposition on my part; I have no idea whether he is attempting to do this), it is felt, under the skin. Of course, in describing this tension, I have the benefit of study of his progression of works, from *Ed the Happy Clown* to the Gospels, to the deeply problematic and awesomely hypnotic *Underwater* (a triad of monumental unfinished works, and how unusual is that, for Brown to begin his career with the habit of abandoning gigantic unwieldy canvases?), to the increasing focus on "actuality" in some of the great short works like "Helder" and "Showing Helder" and then of course in *I Never Liked You* (aka *Fuck*) and *Louis Riel* and *The Playboy* (a triad of finished works, and how odd for the serial abandoner of potential masterworks to become a consummate completer of them!). This progression helps us appreciate the quality of focus and restriction, the sublimely microscopic attentiveness of the style that subsequently evolved—but they also cue us to the atmosphere of the surreal and grotesque and the transcendent, those things that steadily hum just beneath the surface of Brown's contained panels, inside his silent passages, and in his metronomic silences and the dampened body language and facial expressions and blocking of his human figures, all of which are quivering in their containment and with their potential to erupt.

The first Drawn & Quarterly comic book I discovered informed every book I've written and drawn since. It was the last installment of Chester Brown's *Yummy Fur* (no. 32) with a cover of the prophet Jonah being hurled at a tempestuous sea into the gaping maw of a monstrous fish.

This was the summer of 1994. After barely graduating high school, I road-tripped with my best friend and her parents to Minneapolis and found myself rummaging through a record shop on Hennepin Avenue that had a small stash of indie comics crammed in a musty corner.

I still identified as a Christian, albeit a vegetarian, feminist Christian disillusioned with organized religion. Chester Brown's biblically themed cover arrested my attention, but what I found inside disturbed me—twenty-six pages adapting the Gospel of Matthew (chapters 11, 12, and 14) into comics form. I couldn't decipher if it was reverent or blasphemous of my personal saviour. Chester Brown's interpretation of Jesus was tough and imposing—a gutter-punk Jesus you could smell—with a mangy crypt-keeper haircut and a sharp beak of a face snapping at the Pharisees while breaking the laws of the Sabbath.

This vision helped shape how I came to imagine Jesus—a social revolutionary upturning the money changers' tables, refuting tradition, at odds with the conservative institutions and capitalism that now define American evangelicalism.

I was a product of the grunge generation—no plans for my future, no career ambitions, never considered college.

There's a panel in *I Never Liked You* that I feel captures my years of puberty. It shows Chester lying on his bed, looking up at the ceiling. You can sort of hear a Bowie record playing in the background or his mom asking him to go to the store. How many hours, days, did I spend in this state during those years? Lots, I tell ya. It's an autobiographical book that has a

So, what was it like to meet Chester Brown and to make that furtive exchange of cash for sublimity? What was it really like? (I should have probably mentioned up at the top of this piece that I am writing, helplessly, not as a critic but as a total fan.) I'm tempted to joke that the little man was not little, or that the happy clown did not seem particularly happy, but neither did he begin screaming and weeping and snapping his sticklike limbs but then it is the case that you know these things, because, in the tradition of R. Crumb and Daniel Clowes and Michel de Montaigne, Chester Brown has delivered himself to us, made himself knowable, despite the seeming impossibility of the human desire to be knowable and Brown's obvious ambivalence at even trying to do so. But what I want to say is this: though I've met many of my heroes, and many of them are writers, and many of them writers of great privacy and intensity and of powerful properties of both empathy and alienation, I think I'll never come as near as I did that day in Toronto in 2000 to being able to imagine what it would have been like to pay a call on Franz Kafka.

***Jonathan Lethem is the author of more than twenty works of fiction, non-fiction, and comics, including* The Fortress of Solitude, *which has been published in more than a dozen languages worldwide. He is a MacArthur Fellow and received the National Book Critics Circle Award for fiction for his novel* Motherless Brooklyn.**

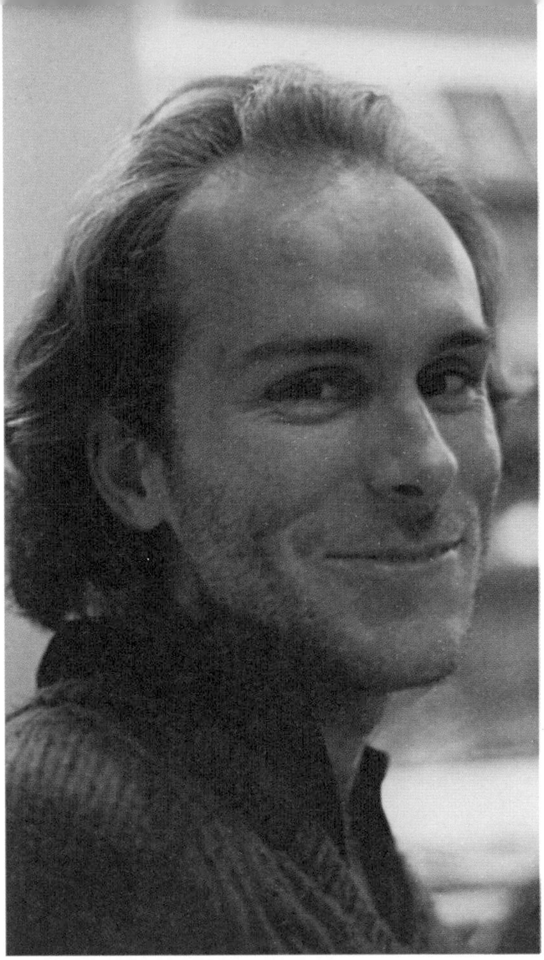

But by the end of the summer, I'd fallen in love with my best friend. She was beginning her senior year of high school, so I stuck around town, got a full-time job driving a delivery van, enrolled in some part-time classes at community college, and began a comic strip for the biweekly school newspaper.

Comics, once a medium I associated with the nerdy folly of my elementary days, now presented itself as a perfect DIY mode of expression (and, though I didn't yet dare to dream it, a potential career).

My first book, *Good-Bye, Chunky Rice*, directly referenced the story of Jonah in the whale. As does my current project, the kid-friendly, sci-fi comedy *Space Dumplins*. Chester Brown's powerful and menacing Christ inspired the swarthy Jesus present in the pages of *Blankets*; and Chester's exploration of sacred biblical themes in comics form gave permission for me to do the same in *Habibi*.

Back in 1994, my entire comic collection could be counted on one hand, so I memorized them like bible verses and puzzled over them like parables. That cover to *Yummy Fur* no. 32 still haunts me. It inverted the comic-book tradition of a hero hurling heavenward to face the enemy in bold lines and colours for a feeble prophet tumbling into a sea of muted watercolours, further subdued by a heavy grey frame—an artifact fished from the murky depths of adolescent uncertainty.

***—Craig Thompson, cartoonist of* Blankets**

perfect, unmessy ending, something that doesn't always happen with autobiography. You don't really need to know what happened after. And it's an ending that could break the heart of a stone. My book, *Hey, Wait*...never would have happened if I hadn't read *I Never Liked You*. It's a masterpiece.***—Jason, cartoonist of* Hey Wait...*and* Tell Me Something**

Chester Brown in Angoulême (1992).

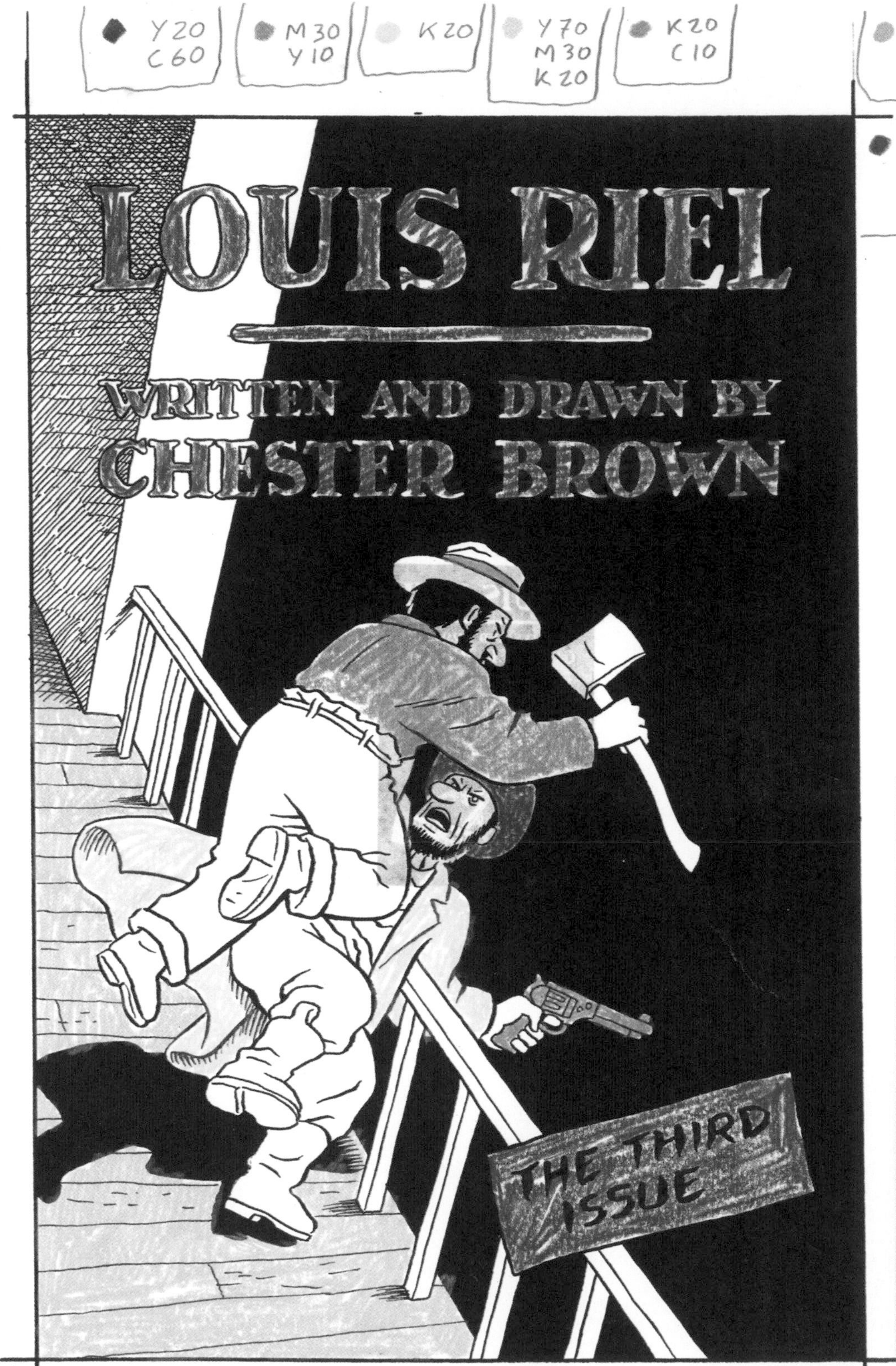
Y20 C60
M30 Y10
K20
Y70 M30 K20
K20 C10
M10 C20 Y20
K10 C10 M10
LOUIS RIEL
WRITTEN AND DRAWN BY
CHESTER BROWN
THE THIRD ISSUE

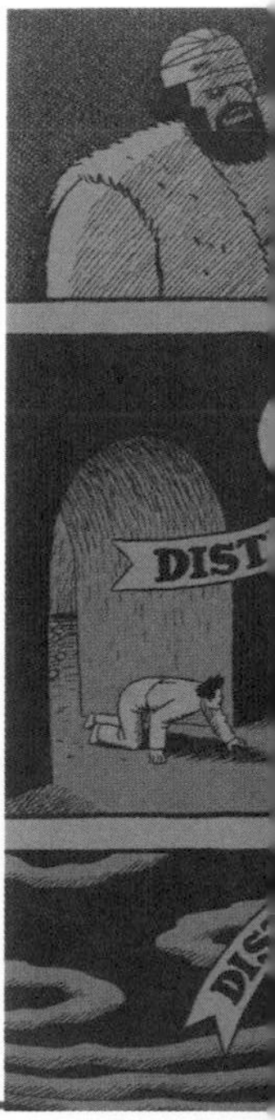

 Colour guide for *Louis Riel* no. 3 (1999). Chester still uses this method when submitting his covers.

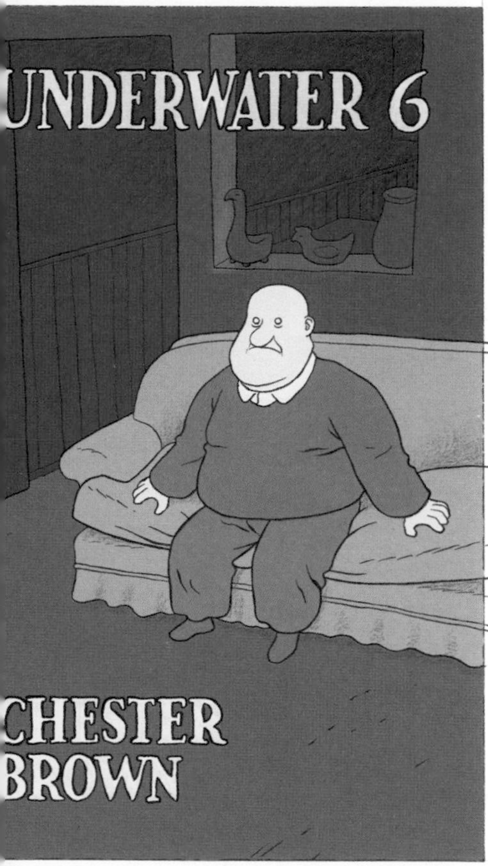
UNDERWATER 6
CHESTER
BROWN

When Chester Brown started *Louis Riel*, I realized that what I feared would happen had. *Underwater* was suspended (don't say "cancelled," please don't say it). I recall the letters columns (or maybe the fan press, or maybe the comic-store chatter) being consistently negative. And true enough, it didn't work well in comic-issue format, but I didn't care, it was Chester Brown. I'd read anything. The plan was for twenty issues initially, but that fell away and it would be as long as it took. Until Chester called it quits with issue 11. Years later, I met Chester Brown for the first time at San Diego Comic-Con. He was quiet and considered and I found him even more intimidating than I had imagined. I had met a good number of my comics idols by then but Chester terrified me. I wanted to ask about *Underwater* but the nerve wasn't there. A few years after that, I was in Toronto for an early TCAF and I was walking down the street with Chester and Seth and we were all chatting amiably and I thought "Now's my chance! I can ask him." I pounced. Really, it felt like a pounce. Or a blurt. I had to know. I couldn't help myself. "No, I'll never finish it. I didn't plan it very well. It would take thousands of pages to complete." I already knew this. We all knew it. But why did I have to ask?—***Tom Devlin***

(Left) Diamond solicitation cover for *Underwater* no. 6 (1996). Typically, because of tight timelines, fake covers like this one were created as placeholders and later replaced with final artwork.

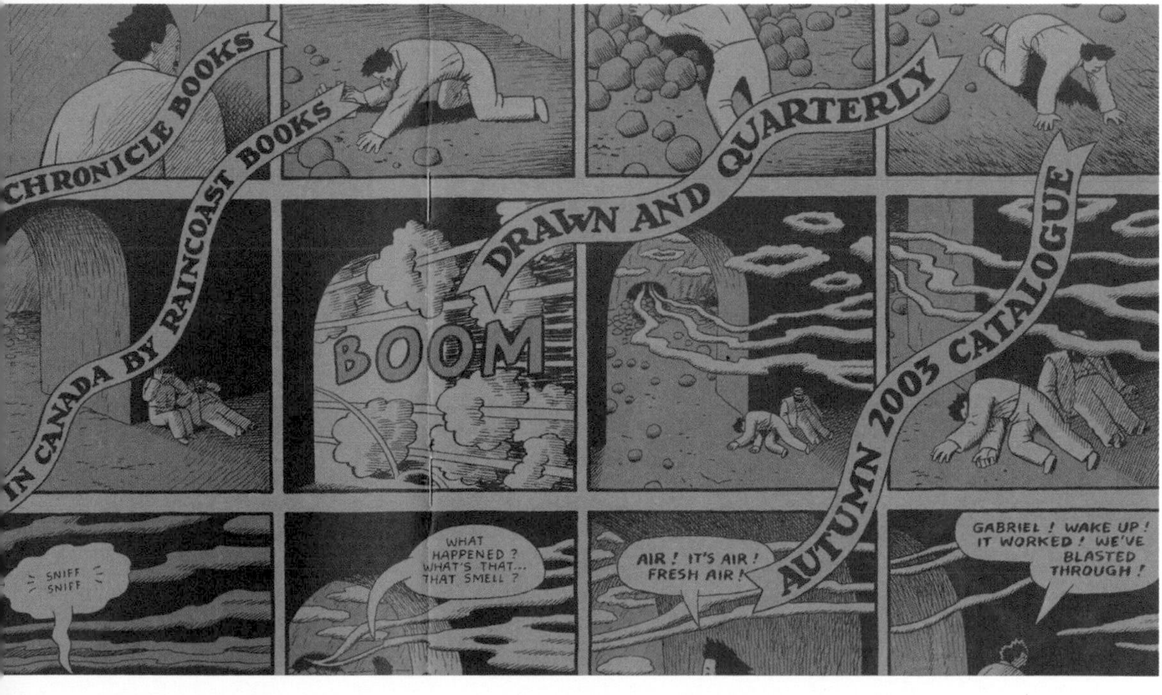
CHRONICLE BOOKS
IN CANADA BY RAINCOAST BOOKS
DRAWN AND QUARTERLY
AUTUMN 2003 CATALOGUE
BOOM
SNIFF
SNIFF
WHAT HAPPENED? WHAT'S THAT... THAT SMELL?
AIR! IT'S AIR! FRESH AIR!
GABRIEL! WAKE UP! IT WORKED! WE'VE BLASTED THROUGH!

(Bottom) Cover for the D+Q fall 2003 catalogue. *Louis Riel* was published in hardcover that year.

LOUIS RIEL

an appreciation by Candida Rifkind

U.S.$ 2.95
PUBLISHED BY D&Q
CAN.$ 4.25
LOUIS RIEL
THE SIXTH ISSUE
WRITTEN AND DRAWN BY CHESTER BROWN

 Diamond solicitation cover for *Louis Riel* no. 6 (2001).

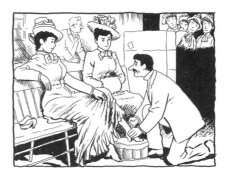

For a book that has become a powerhouse of Canadian publishing and a landmark of comics biography, Chester Brown's *Louis Riel* crept rather quietly onto the scene. Who would have guessed when the first serialized issues appeared in 1999 that fifteen years later *Louis Riel* would have sold over fifty thousand copies (in Canada a book is considered a bestseller when it sells five thousand copies) and paved the way in the media, bookstores, libraries, schools, and academia for other alternative comic books to be taken seriously? For that matter, how many fans of Brown's earlier surreal, taboo-breaking comics could have predicted that this edgy cartoonist would become celebrated for his meticulous rendering of a very difficult period in Canadian history to "get right"?

The comicscenti had already identified Brown's peculiar brilliance, but *Louis Riel* took him and alternative comics mainstream. Perhaps Canadian readers and history buffs were waiting all along for someone with Brown's attention to detail and sense of the absurd to give us a new take on Louis Riel's life story.[1] And perhaps the complex interplay of words and images that makes up comics is the best way to show that biography has always been a contested form, that even the driest histories and most ponderous prose rely on caricature in their representation of a complex person.

Louis Riel is a difficult book to encapsulate. It uses a spare, minimal style to convey messy, chaotic events that remain hotly debated today. The first three parts, which cover Riel's political ascendance in the Red River Settlement to his final surrender to the Canadian government in 1885, are action filled. Yet Brown draws this individual and collective drama as though watched from above or at a distance, often placing his characters against empty backgrounds that convey the endless snowy landscapes of the Canadian prairies. The dialogue is casual and contemporary, as if the major players are everyday folk we might know. Part 4, Riel's treason trial, at the end of which he was hanged, shows the characters in court against a jet-black background. They become actors on a darkened stage and we see how politics manipulates people like puppets. Then, after 241 pages of the comics biography, we get nearly 30 pages of densely hand-lettered endnotes. If the comics narrative is a bracingly offhanded take on Riel's biography, the endnotes are where Brown reveals his artistic, political, and personal passions. We see how he weighed the many versions of this life narrative to arrive at his own depiction, and we learn that his impetus was not political but personal: his mother's schizophrenia drew him to a character whose sanity remains in question today.

There is little doubt about Brown's take on Riel: he portrays the man as a reluctant hero who favours reason and the political process over violence, but whose fate is shaped by Ottawa's corruption, greed, and racism. *Louis Riel* straddles the biographical tradition of "great men's" stories and alterna-

---

1 *The success of* Louis Riel *is registered on many fronts. It was the first comic book to receive a grant for its completion from the Canada Council for the Arts and the first graphic narrative to make it onto the* Globe and Mail *bestseller list. It swept the major comics awards in 2004 by winning or being nominated for numerous Harvey, Ignatz, and Eisner prizes, has been translated into French, Italian, and Spanish, and has received notice or recognition in all the major magazines and newspapers, from* Maclean's *to* Time. *It is also the subject of several scholarly articles and academic theses, and in 2013 the Art Gallery of Ontario exhibited the original drawings in a show titled Chester Brown and Louis Riel.*

tive comics' love of outsiders and eccentrics. In 2000, when the project was still only partially complete, Douglas Wolk wrote in the *Village Voice* that Brown "has invented a biographical form unique to his medium." Many of these innovations are apparent in the wake of graphic biographies that have followed. Brown exploits comics' unique grammar of panels and gutters to pace Riel's story in ways that insert the reader back into history, combining dynamic battles with meditative silent sequences. He develops pictorial icons to mark when characters are speaking French and Cree and he x's out Scott's profanities so that we see he is swearing, but that the cartoonist wants to place these offensive words under erasure.

The work of the cartoonist is also visible in the endnotes, which both reference Brown's sources and tell us what he has invented or imagined. And these creative interventions extend beyond the narrative level of events and dialogue: throughout, Brown's drawings are influenced by the minimalism of Harold Gray and the visuals of classic cinema, from German expressionism to French new wave.[II] This is a (mostly) historically accurate life narrative of a real man, yet the form of comics itself tells us that what we think of as "the truth" is always mediated by the storyteller and the form in which he or she works. An aesthetically, philosophically, and psychologically complex portrayal of an elusive and controversial figure in Canadian history, Brown's *Louis Riel* has become a landmark of contemporary graphic narrative that has changed the publishing and literary landscapes around it. Just as Art Spiegelman's use of an animal comic to tell his family's Holocaust story in *Maus* might seem at best surprising and at worst reckless, Chester Brown took a risk entering the political fray that still surrounds Louis Riel, especially as a cartoonist. But it is only in comics that this cloudy history and complex individual could emerge in such clear lines, could seem so human and yet so extraordinary. Books about Canadian political history are a hard sell for even the most patriotic of readers. The ongoing success of *Louis Riel* proves that a new approach to the subject, even if it may seem crazy or impossible, can help us to see familiar figures with fresh eyes.

***Dr. Candida Rifkind is an associate professor at the University of Winnipeg, where her areas of study are comic books and Canadian literature. She is the author of* Comrades and Critics: Women, Literature, and the Left in 1930s Canada.**

II For a detailed discussion of these visual references, see Sean Rogers's untitled essay in the tenth-anniversary edition of Louis Riel *published by D+Q in 2013.*

1999 CATALOGUE

DRAWN AND QUARTERLY

MONTREAL -- THE HOME OF DRAWN AND QUARTERLY

The above drawing by Chester Brown is based on another drawing that appeared on the front page of "The Canadian Illustrated News" (April 25th, 1870); reprinted from Frank Rasky's "The Taming of The Canadian West" (1967). The scene depicted shows the coup-de-grace shot being fired by one of Louis Riel's followers at the execution of Thomas Scott in 1870.

Louis Riel
by Chester Brown

In true virtuoso fashion, **Chester Brown** is about to embark on an entirely new series, focusing on a subject matter as far removed from anything he has done before as one can imagine. **Brown** is using his formidable talents to write and draw a 250 page biography on the rather unlikely subject of **Louis Riel**, a 19th century figure who led two so-called "rebellions" against the Canadian government. Riel was known as the articulate and controversial leader of the French-speaking Métis people in central Canada and in 1869 he led the Métis in their first rebellion against the federal government. During their resistance to Canadian armed forces, Riel tried Thomas Scott for disobedience (under Métis law, refusing to obey leaders was a crime punishable by death). Scott was found guilty and executed by a firing squad in 1870, as depicted in the drawing above. Riel was forced into exile in the U.S. because of the outrage generated from this event, and when he returned 15 years later for his second rebellion he was a changed, and some would say, megalomanical man, likening himself to Jesus Christ. The story will be serialized in approximately ten 24-page issues.

Louis Riel # 1: $ 3.25 U.S./ $ 3.95 Cdn. (Please note: # 1 will be out in June 1999)

Cover for Drawn & Quarterly's 1999 catalogue.

the hymn of the pearl
a comic-strip adaptation of an ancient narrative poem
IN THE PALACE OF AN EASTERN KINGDOM, A KING AND QUEEN TALK TO THEIR SON:
Son, you're still a child, but we have to send you on an important quest.

 Originally created as a Christmas card for friends and family (2009).

You have to leave this palace and go west to Egypt where a dragon is guarding a pearl.
You must get the pearl and bring it back to us.
You won't be able to get close to the dragon if people know who you are --
-- so to disguise yourself you must take off your royal vestments and put on the dirty clothing that the Egyptians wear.
And remember, do not eat their food.
Good-bye, son.
We love you.

Egypt.
The dragon's lair.
Look, it's the prince from the eastern kingdom.
We must stop him.
Excuse me, we see that you're a poor stranger in our land. You must be hungry.
Here, have some of our bread.
I AM hungry. And it WOULD be rude to refuse. Surely it can't hurt to eat a LITTLE of their food.
Thank you.

Who are you ?
Who am I ? I can't remember.
You're a slave.
We'll bring you to meet our king.
Bow down to him.
This boy will be a slave in my household.

BACK IN THE EAST:
We have received reports that the prince has eaten the food of the Egyptians.
Oh no.
He's forgotten who he is and has become a slave to their king.
My son a slave?
Don't worry, darling, we'll write him a letter.
LATER, IN EGYPT:
I'm so tired.

?
Someone's left a piece of paper on my bed.
From your father, The King Of Kings, and your mother, The Mistress Of The East: Greetings to our son in Egypt.
Awake from your sleep. You are not a slave. Remember the pearl. Remember your name in the book of life.
I remember.

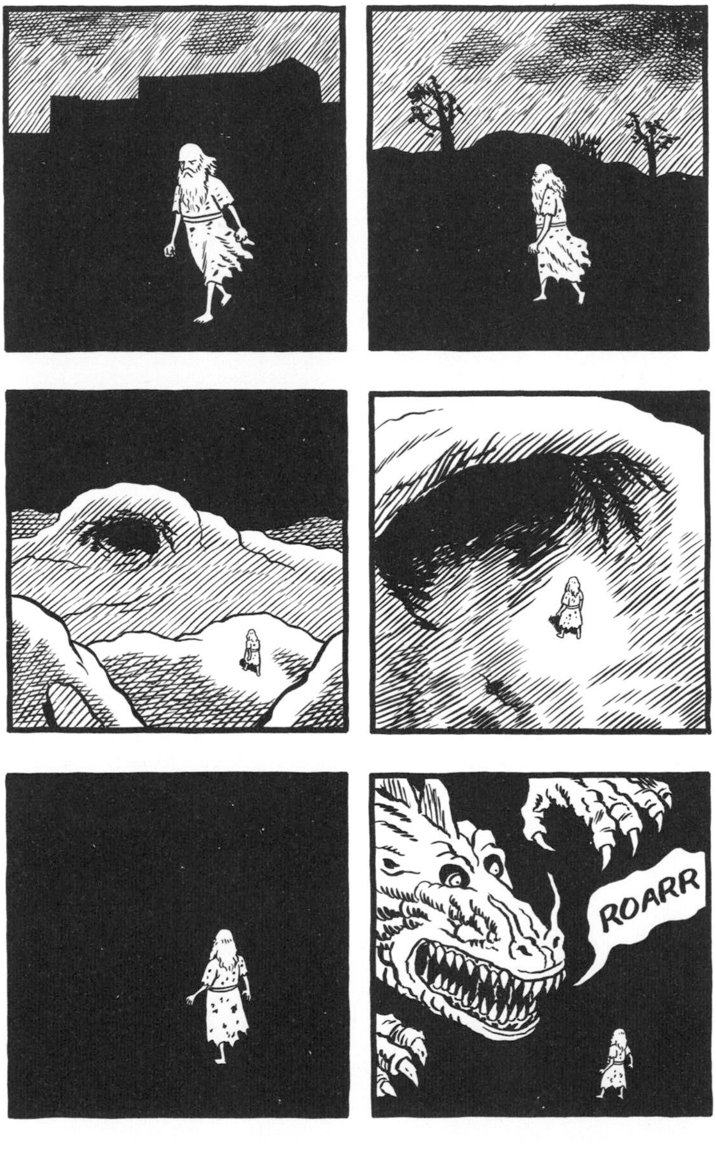
ROARR

Recently, Chester and I and writer Adam Litovitz have been attempting to adapt *Paying for It* into a live-action movie screenplay. It has been challenging to say the least because my best friend Chester is the most difficult person I have ever worked with. He is so particular and stubborn. I tell him that a comic is not a movie, and the hard part is incorpo-

IN THE NAME OF MY FATHER, THE KING OF KINGS, I ORDER YOU BACK!

There's the pearl.

THE PRINCE RETURNS TO THE EAST:

My dear parents, I've returned with the pearl.

rating his copious index notes on the decriminalization of prostitution into a dramatic comedy about people. I tell him that in movies, flawed characters undergo transformations, but he maintains that he has no flaws. We spar quite a bit. It's opening up a whole new intensity to our friendship.—*Sook-Yin Lee, broadcaster, musician, filmmaker, and actor*

NOTES FROM CHESTER ON *THE ZOMBIE WHO LIKED THE ARTS*

In early 2007, a fellow named Gregory Nixon phoned me up. He told me that he worked in Toronto's City Hall in a department that promotes the arts in the city. He wanted me to be part of a campaign they were running at the time called TO Live With Culture. The result was this strip about an art-loving zombie. It ran in six installments in *Now*, which is Toronto's significant "alternative" weekly newspaper. I'm not someone who believes that it's the role of government to promote art, but the job paid well—ten thousand dollars for the six installments—so I took the gig. I suggested several story ideas—one was about an art-loving zombie, another was about a couple falling in love. (I made other suggestions, but I can't remember them.) Gregory liked the zombie idea and the romance one but couldn't decide which he preferred, so I suggested we combine them. Of course, the main purpose of the strip was to feature as many references to Toronto cultural institutions and creators as possible (most were suggested by Gregory) so there wasn't a lot of room for narrative development.

In the third chapter, the musician is Owen Pallett—at that time he was performing under the name Final Fantasy.

The fifth chapter meant the most to me. The bookstore mentioned, This Ain't The Rosedale Library, is unfortunately no longer in business. I had a lot of affection for that place because they sold my self-published minicomics when I started my career as a cartoonist back in the 1980s. Plus, the guys who ran the place, Charlie Huisken and Danny Bazuin, are both really nice. And I just love any and all bookstores. Actually, I would have preferred it if the whole series had been devoted to promoting Toronto bookstores.

The last chapter features a non-existent film. For over twenty years, Bruce McDonald has been trying to make an adaptation of my graphic novel *Ed the Happy Clown* (which he wants to title *Yummy Fur*, the name of the comic book I serialized *Ed* in). So we thought it would be cute to pretend that the movie had finally been made. I say "we" because I think that might have been Gregory's idea. The film dialogue on the last page comes from *Ed*, and, not surprisingly, Gregory thought it was a bit much for the readers of *Now*, so he asked me to alter it. I switched in some less "offensive" lines from my book. So the "offensive" version is being published here for the first time.

The story originally ran from October 4 to November 8, 2007.

NOTES FROM CHESTER ON *THE HYMN OF THE PEARL*

The zombie strip was a commercial job done for the money; I'd had no particular desire to create a story about the walking dead when Gregory Nixon first contacted me. Most of my work reflects more personal interests, and that's the case for *The Hymn of the Pearl*.

Shortly after it was published in 1984, I picked up a copy of *The Other Bible*, edited by Willis Barnstone. In 1986 I created a short adaptation of one of the book's pieces—it was about Jesus, as a child, uniting with a spiritual twin. (That strip can now be found under the title "The Twin" in my book *The Little Man*.) But the work that really caught my attention in *The Other Bible* was a poem called "The Hymn of the Pearl." I loved it and wanted to turn it into a comic strip. Many times in the coming years I tried to figure out how to adapt it. Finally, in 2009, I decided to strip it down to its simplest story elements, making it almost a fairy tale. I'm reasonably pleased with the results, but my version doesn't convey the phantasmagorical power of the original.

"The Hymn of the Pearl" is part of a non-Biblical Christian work, *The Acts of Thomas*, that was probably written around 200 CE. But the hymn may predate *The Acts* and may even be pre-Christian.

Of course, in creating my version, I referred to Willis Barnstone's translation, but I also used Bentley Layton's in his book *The Gnostic Scriptures* (1987).

I printed the strip as a self-published minicomic for friends and family, so it hasn't been widely seen before now.

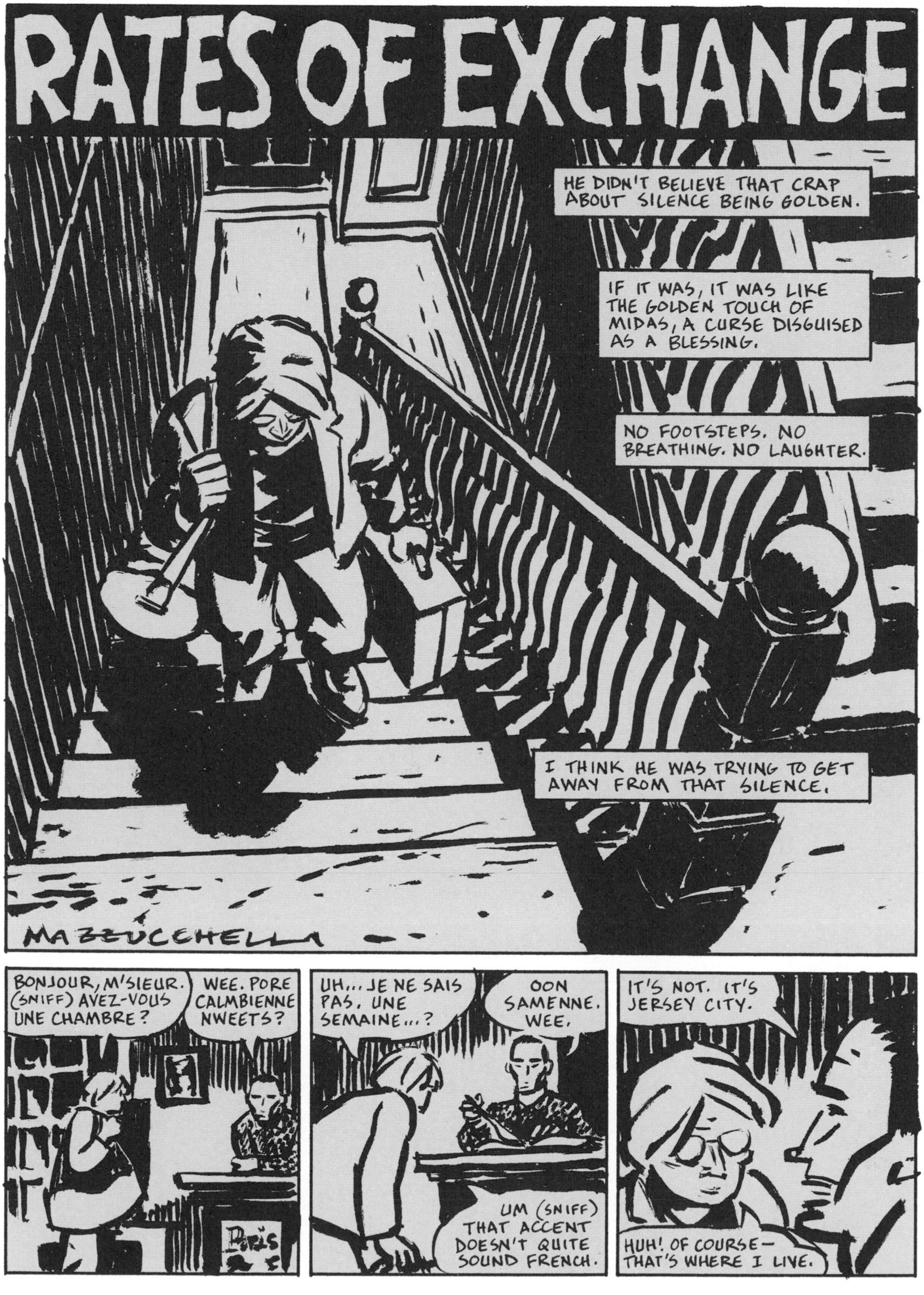
RATES OF EXCHANGE
HE DIDN'T BELIEVE THAT CRAP ABOUT SILENCE BEING GOLDEN.
IF IT WAS, IT WAS LIKE THE GOLDEN TOUCH OF MIDAS, A CURSE DISGUISED AS A BLESSING.
NO FOOTSTEPS. NO BREATHING. NO LAUGHTER.
I THINK HE WAS TRYING TO GET AWAY FROM THAT SILENCE.
MAZZUCCHELLI
BONJOUR, M'SIEUR. (SNIFF) AVEZ-VOUS UNE CHAMBRE?
WEE. PORE CALMBIENNE NWEETS?
PARIS
UH... JE NE SAIS PAS. UNE SEMAINE...?
OON SAMENNE. WEE.
UM (SNIFF) THAT ACCENT DOESN'T QUITE SOUND FRENCH.
IT'S NOT. IT'S JERSEY CITY.
HUH! OF COURSE— THAT'S WHERE I LIVE.

"Rates of Exchange" first appeared in vol. 2, no. 2 of *Drawn & Quarterly* (1994). David Mazzucchelli

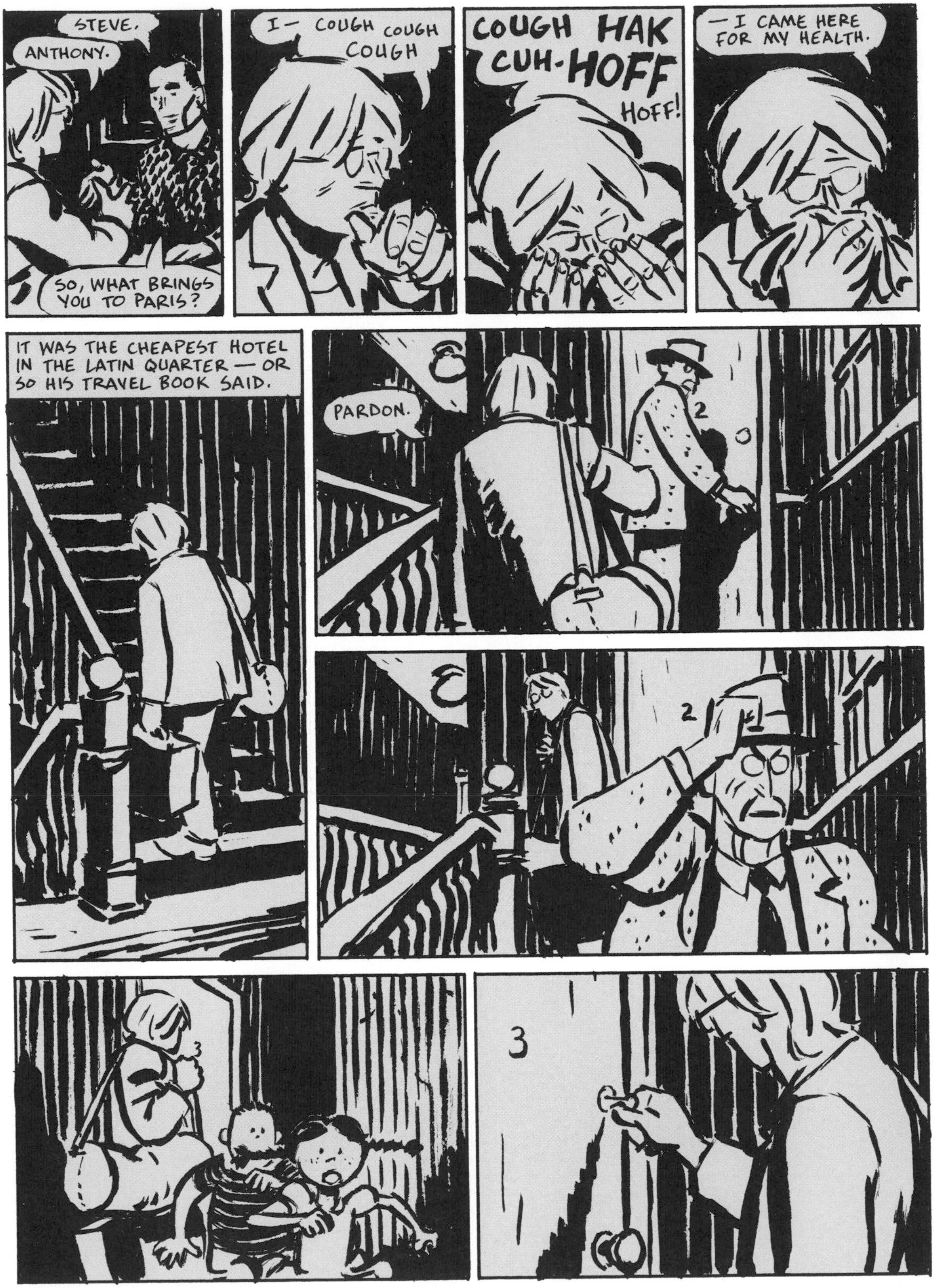
STEVE.
ANTHONY.
SO, WHAT BRINGS YOU TO PARIS?
I— COUGH COUGH COUGH
COUGH HAK CUH-HOFF HOFF!
—I CAME HERE FOR MY HEALTH.
IT WAS THE CHEAPEST HOTEL IN THE LATIN QUARTER — OR SO HIS TRAVEL BOOK SAID.
PARDON.
2
2
3
3

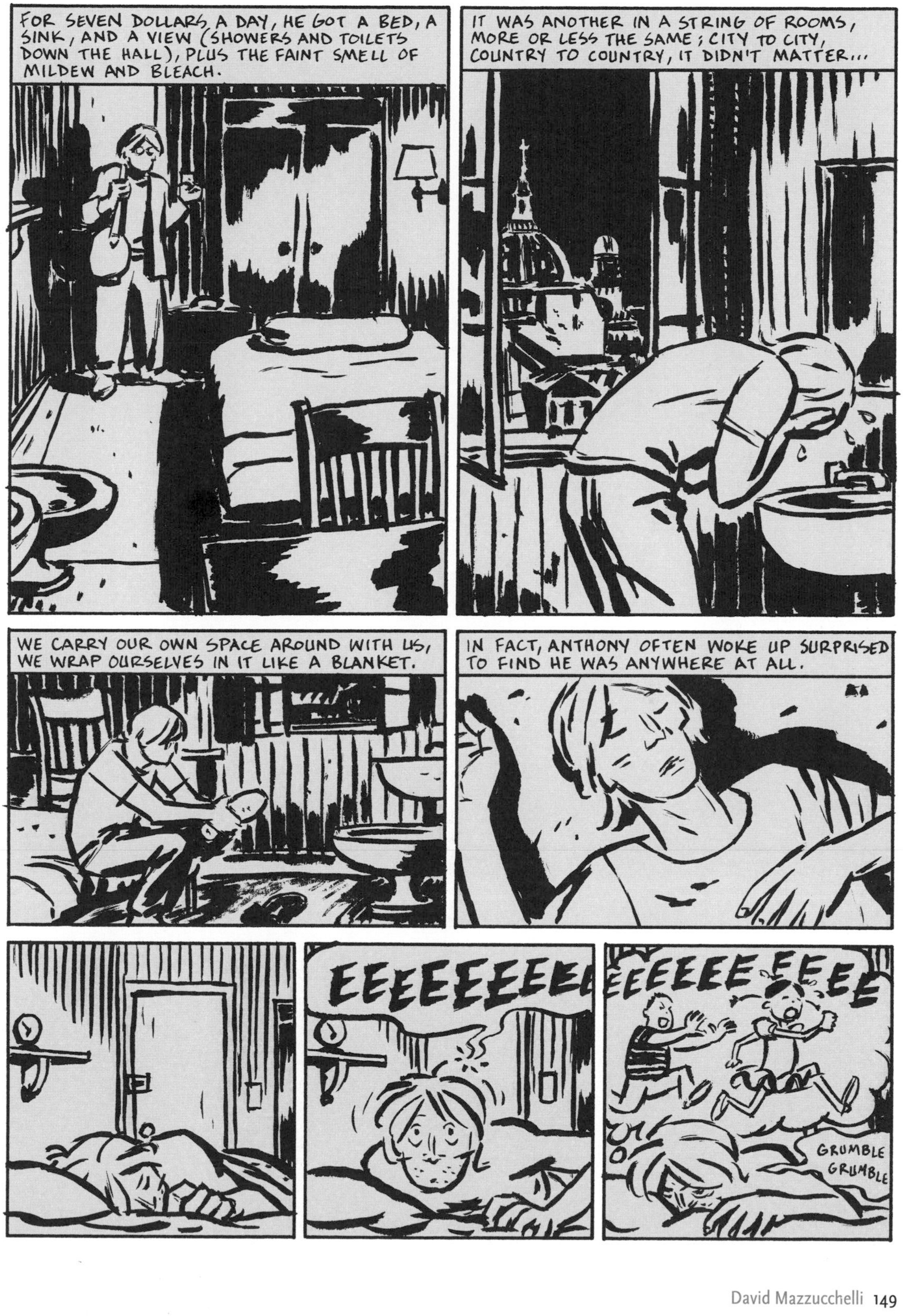
FOR SEVEN DOLLARS A DAY, HE GOT A BED, A SINK, AND A VIEW (SHOWERS AND TOILETS DOWN THE HALL), PLUS THE FAINT SMELL OF MILDEW AND BLEACH.
IT WAS ANOTHER IN A STRING OF ROOMS, MORE OR LESS THE SAME; CITY TO CITY, COUNTRY TO COUNTRY, IT DIDN'T MATTER...
WE CARRY OUR OWN SPACE AROUND WITH US, WE WRAP OURSELVES IN IT LIKE A BLANKET.
IN FACT, ANTHONY OFTEN WOKE UP SURPRISED TO FIND HE WAS ANYWHERE AT ALL.
EEEEEEEEEEEEEEEE EEEE
GRUMBLE
GRUMBLE

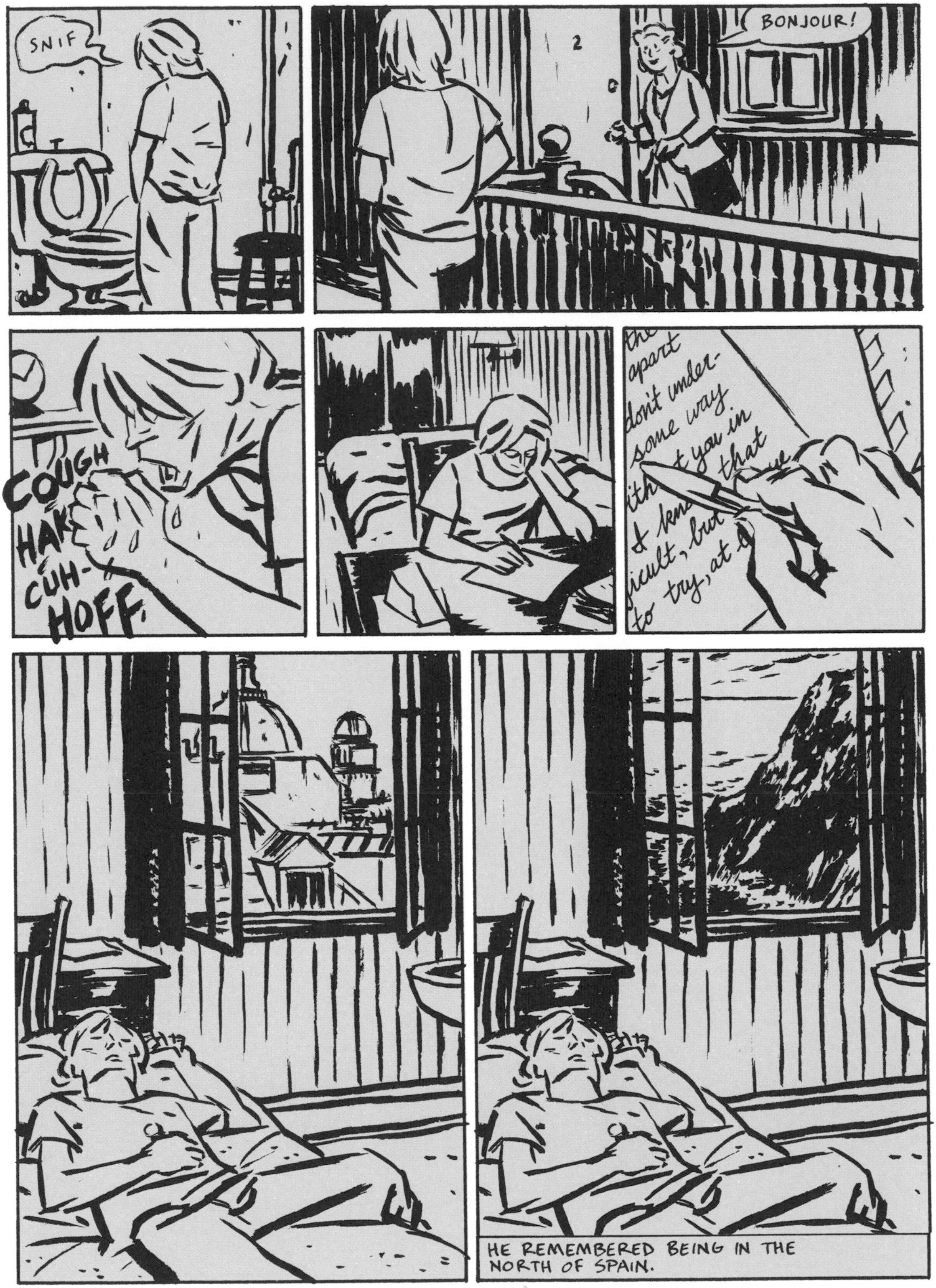
SNIF
BONJOUR!
COUGH
HAK
CUH-
HOFF.
apart
don't under-
some way
that
to try, at
HE REMEMBERED BEING IN THE NORTH OF SPAIN.

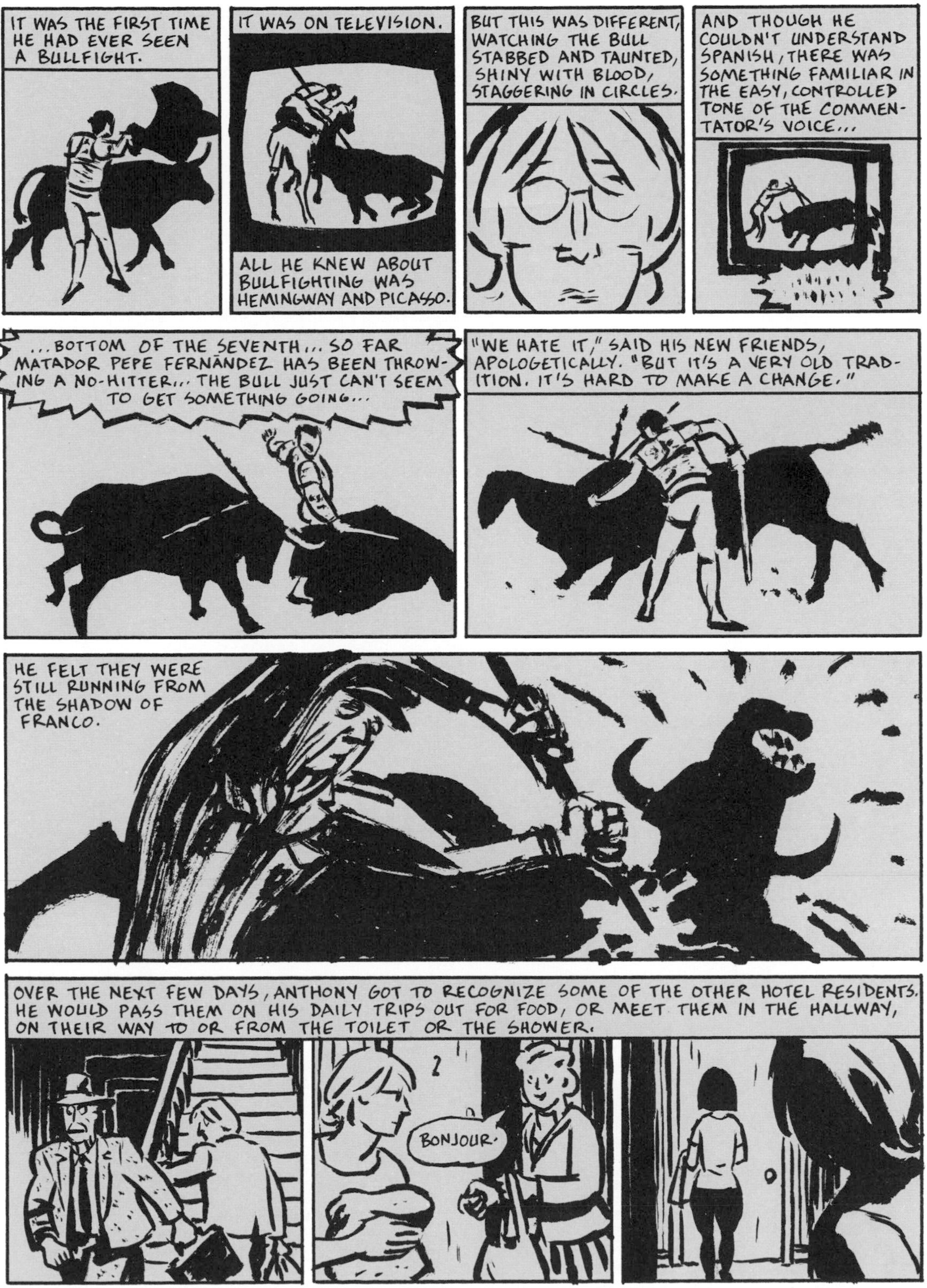
IT WAS THE FIRST TIME HE HAD EVER SEEN A BULLFIGHT.
IT WAS ON TELEVISION.
ALL HE KNEW ABOUT BULLFIGHTING WAS HEMINGWAY AND PICASSO.
BUT THIS WAS DIFFERENT, WATCHING THE BULL STABBED AND TAUNTED, SHINY WITH BLOOD, STAGGERING IN CIRCLES.
AND THOUGH HE COULDN'T UNDERSTAND SPANISH, THERE WAS SOMETHING FAMILIAR IN THE EASY, CONTROLLED TONE OF THE COMMENTATOR'S VOICE...
...BOTTOM OF THE SEVENTH... SO FAR MATADOR PEPE FERNÁNDEZ HAS BEEN THROWING A NO-HITTER... THE BULL JUST CAN'T SEEM TO GET SOMETHING GOING...
"WE HATE IT," SAID HIS NEW FRIENDS, APOLOGETICALLY. "BUT IT'S A VERY OLD TRADITION. IT'S HARD TO MAKE A CHANGE."
HE FELT THEY WERE STILL RUNNING FROM THE SHADOW OF FRANCO.
OVER THE NEXT FEW DAYS, ANTHONY GOT TO RECOGNIZE SOME OF THE OTHER HOTEL RESIDENTS. HE WOULD PASS THEM ON HIS DAILY TRIPS OUT FOR FOOD, OR MEET THEM IN THE HALLWAY, ON THEIR WAY TO OR FROM THE TOILET OR THE SHOWER.
?
BONJOUR.

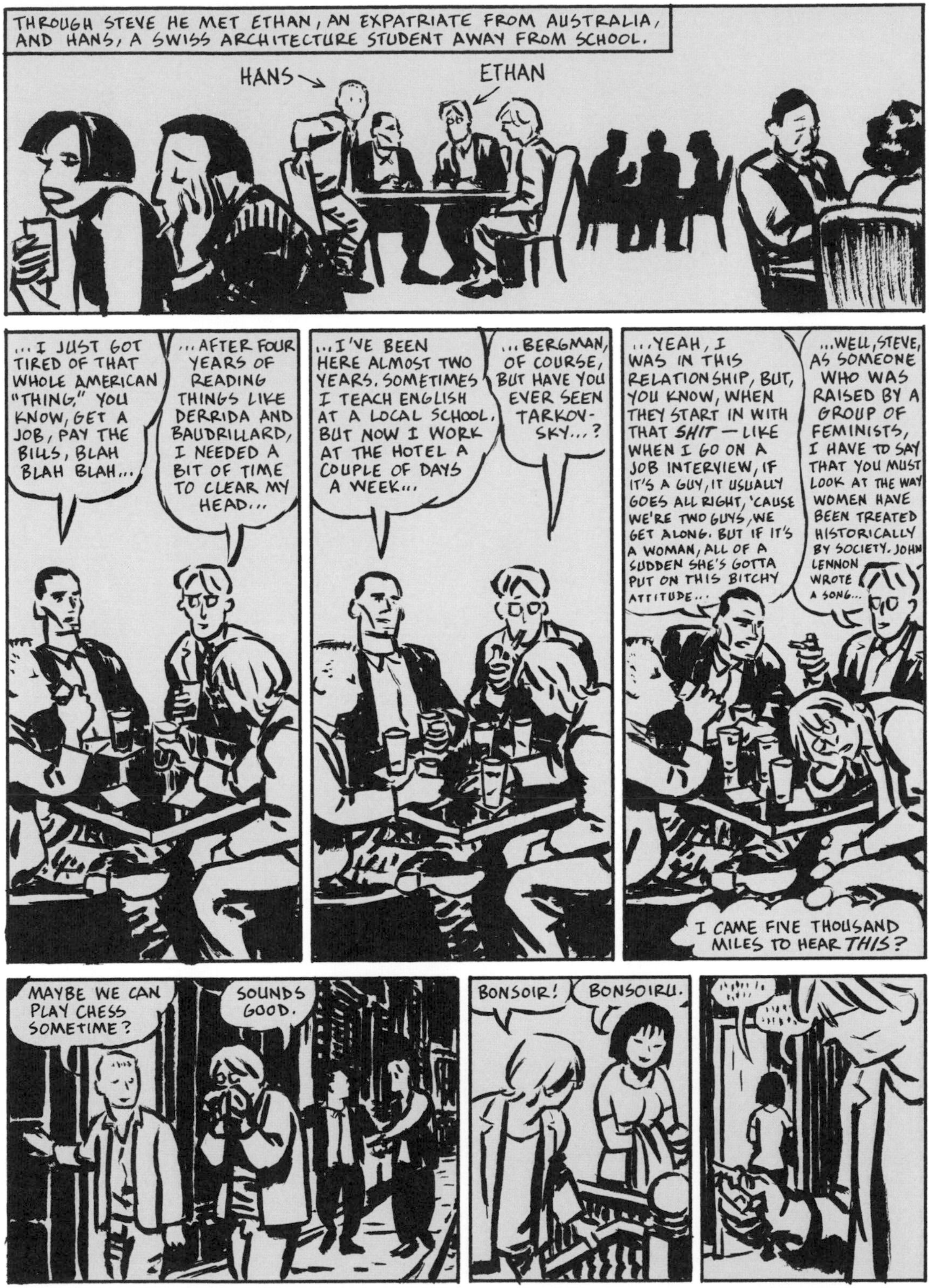
THROUGH STEVE HE MET ETHAN, AN EXPATRIATE FROM AUSTRALIA, AND HANS, A SWISS ARCHITECTURE STUDENT AWAY FROM SCHOOL.
HANS
ETHAN
...I JUST GOT TIRED OF THAT WHOLE AMERICAN "THING," YOU KNOW, GET A JOB, PAY THE BILLS, BLAH BLAH BLAH...
...AFTER FOUR YEARS OF READING THINGS LIKE DERRIDA AND BAUDRILLARD, I NEEDED A BIT OF TIME TO CLEAR MY HEAD...
...I'VE BEEN HERE ALMOST TWO YEARS. SOMETIMES I TEACH ENGLISH AT A LOCAL SCHOOL. BUT NOW I WORK AT THE HOTEL A COUPLE OF DAYS A WEEK...
...BERGMAN, OF COURSE, BUT HAVE YOU EVER SEEN TARKOVSKY...?
...YEAH, I WAS IN THIS RELATIONSHIP, BUT, YOU KNOW, WHEN THEY START IN WITH THAT SHIT — LIKE WHEN I GO ON A JOB INTERVIEW, IF IT'S A GUY, IT USUALLY GOES ALL RIGHT, 'CAUSE WE'RE TWO GUYS, WE GET ALONG. BUT IF IT'S A WOMAN, ALL OF A SUDDEN SHE'S GOTTA PUT ON THIS BITCHY ATTITUDE...
...WELL, STEVE, AS SOMEONE WHO WAS RAISED BY A GROUP OF FEMINISTS, I HAVE TO SAY THAT YOU MUST LOOK AT THE WAY WOMEN HAVE BEEN TREATED HISTORICALLY BY SOCIETY. JOHN LENNON WROTE A SONG...
I CAME FIVE THOUSAND MILES TO HEAR THIS?
MAYBE WE CAN PLAY CHESS SOMETIME?
SOUNDS GOOD.
BONSOIR!
BONSOIRU.

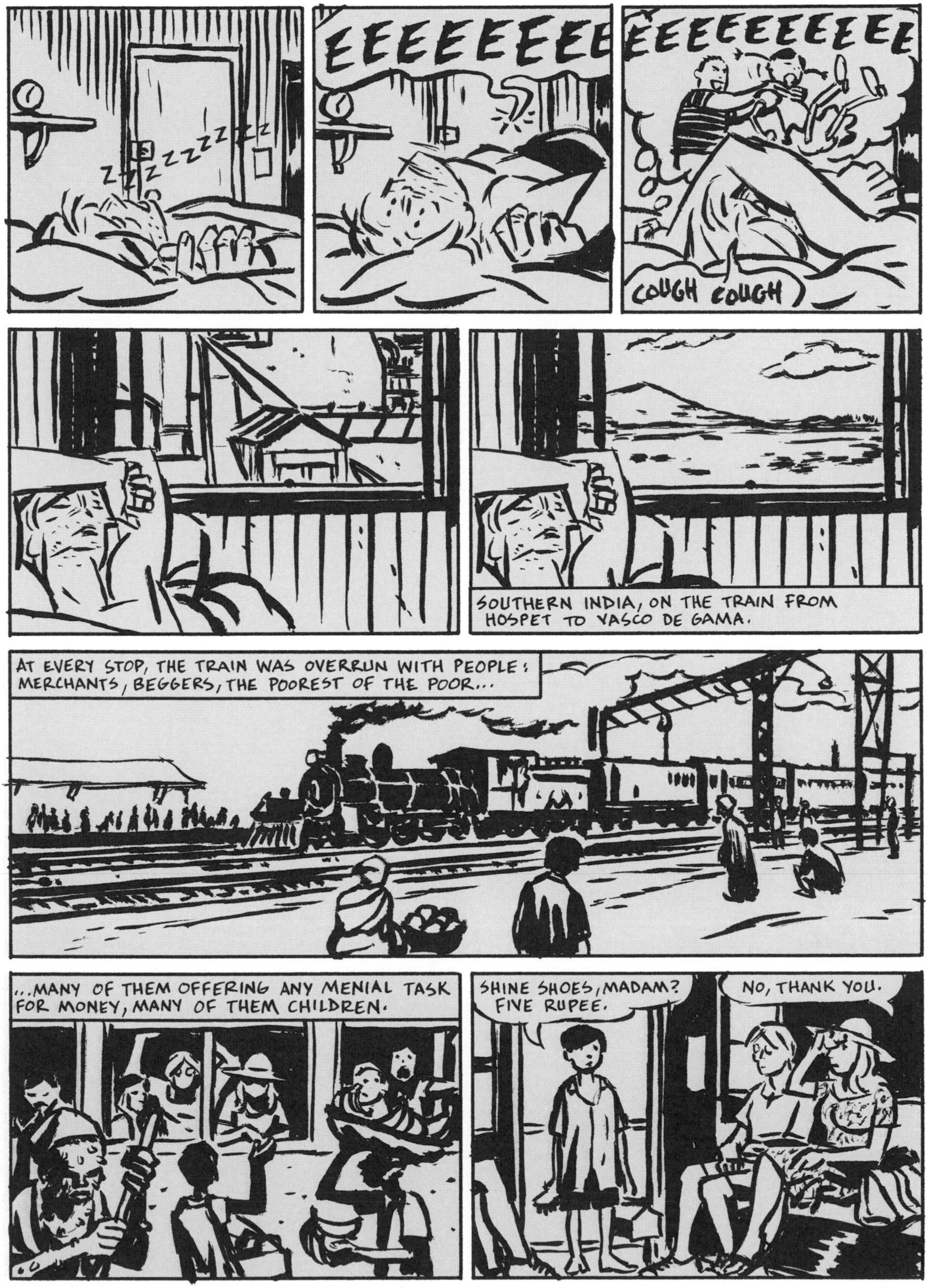
Z Z Z Z Z Z Z Z Z
EEEEEEEEE
EEEEEEEEEEE
COUGH COUGH
SOUTHERN INDIA, ON THE TRAIN FROM HOSPET TO VASCO DE GAMA.
AT EVERY STOP, THE TRAIN WAS OVERRUN WITH PEOPLE: MERCHANTS, BEGGERS, THE POOREST OF THE POOR...
...MANY OF THEM OFFERING ANY MENIAL TASK FOR MONEY, MANY OF THEM CHILDREN.
SHINE SHOES, MADAM? FIVE RUPEE.
NO, THANK YOU.

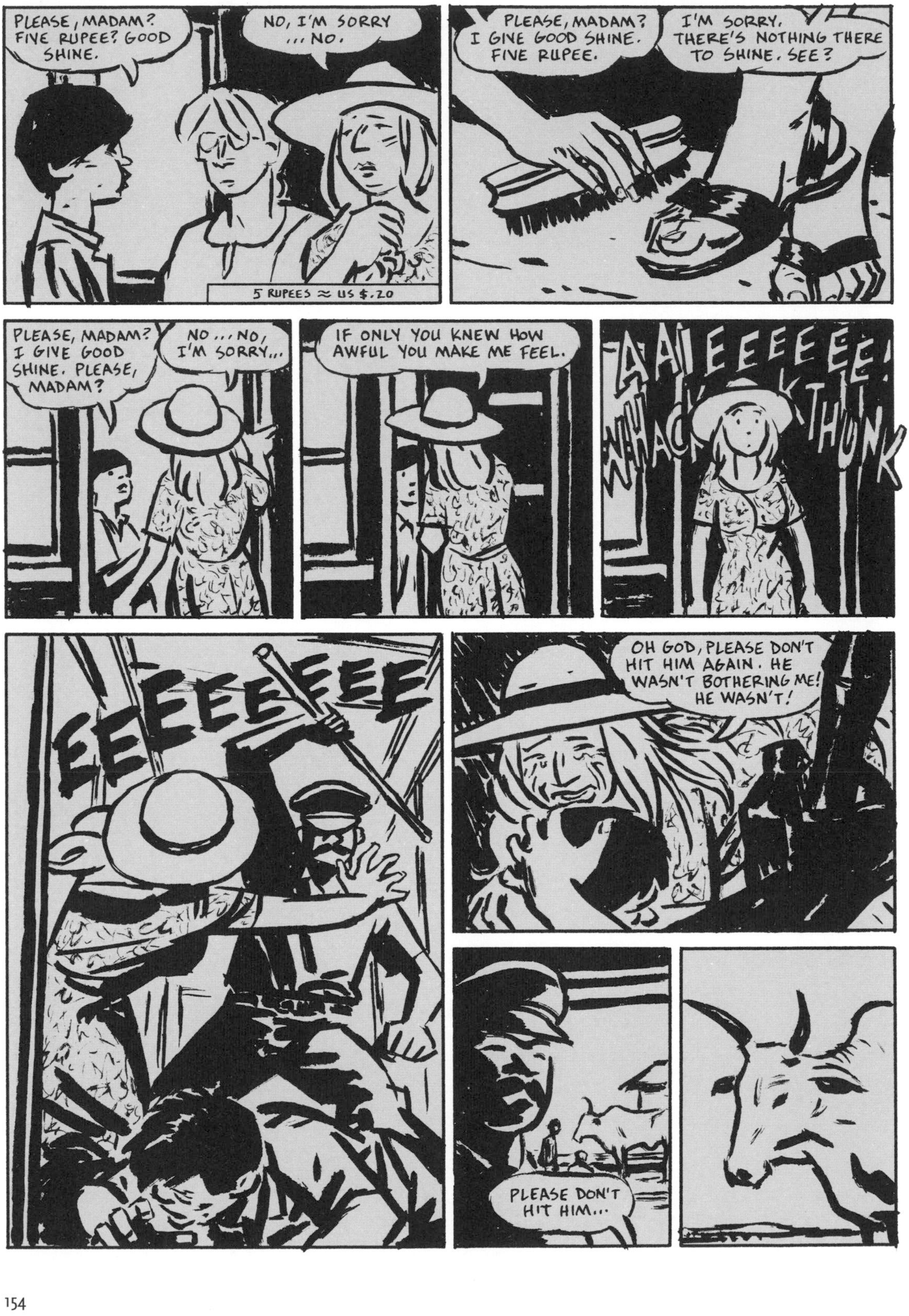
PLEASE, MADAM? FIVE RUPEE? GOOD SHINE.
NO, I'M SORRY ... NO.
5 RUPEES ≈ US $.20
PLEASE, MADAM? I GIVE GOOD SHINE. FIVE RUPEE.
I'M SORRY. THERE'S NOTHING THERE TO SHINE. SEE?
PLEASE, MADAM? I GIVE GOOD SHINE. PLEASE, MADAM?
NO ... NO, I'M SORRY...
IF ONLY YOU KNEW HOW AWFUL YOU MAKE ME FEEL.
AAIEEEEEE
WHACK
THUNK
EEEEEEEEE
OH GOD, PLEASE DON'T HIT HIM AGAIN. HE WASN'T BOTHERING ME! HE WASN'T!
PLEASE DON'T HIT HIM...

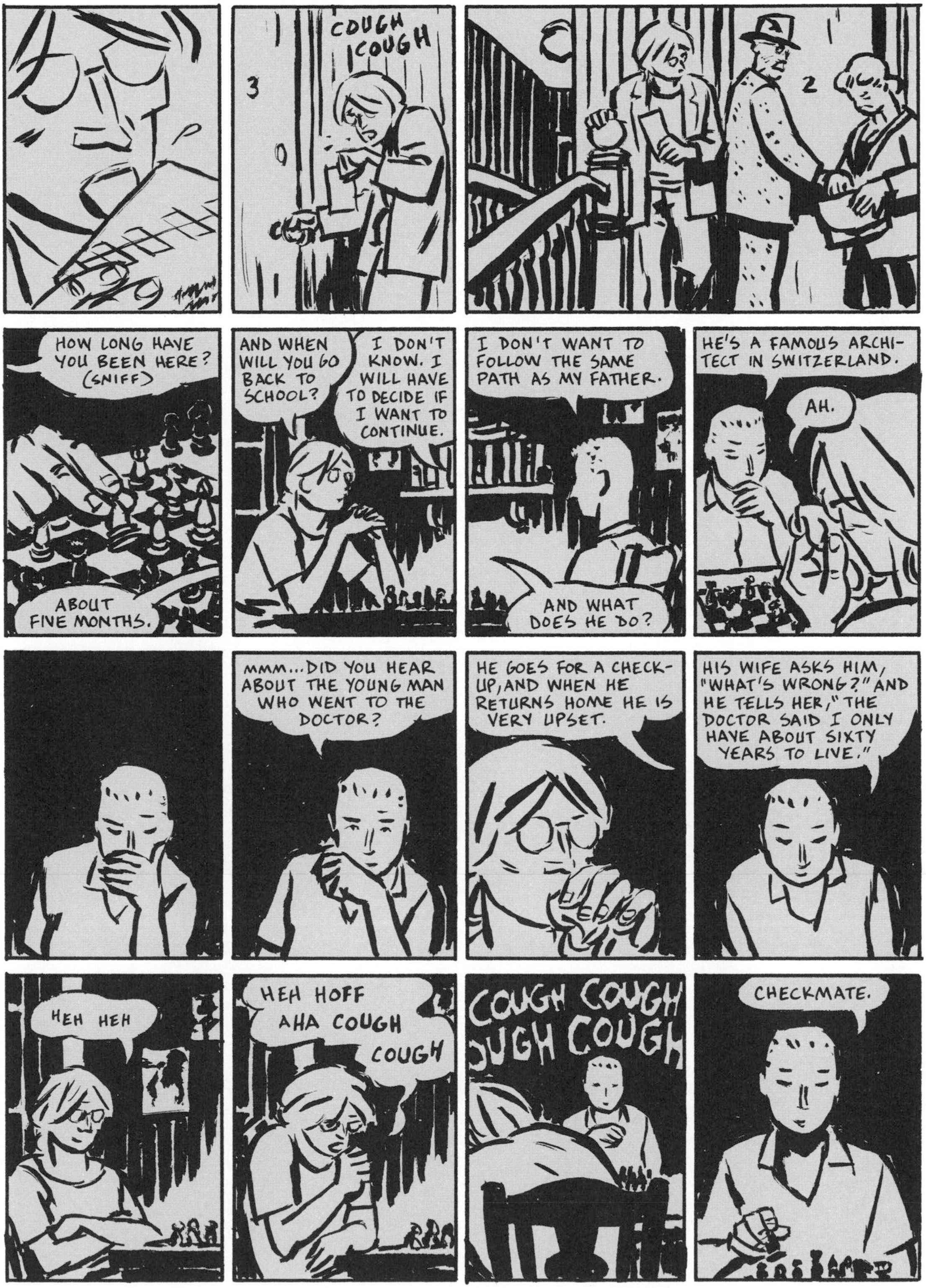
COUGH COUGH
3
2
HOW LONG HAVE YOU BEEN HERE? (SNIFF)
ABOUT FIVE MONTHS.
AND WHEN WILL YOU GO BACK TO SCHOOL?
I DON'T KNOW. I WILL HAVE TO DECIDE IF I WANT TO CONTINUE.
I DON'T WANT TO FOLLOW THE SAME PATH AS MY FATHER.
AND WHAT DOES HE DO?
HE'S A FAMOUS ARCHITECT IN SWITZERLAND.
AH.
MMM...DID YOU HEAR ABOUT THE YOUNG MAN WHO WENT TO THE DOCTOR?
HE GOES FOR A CHECK-UP, AND WHEN HE RETURNS HOME HE IS VERY UPSET.
HIS WIFE ASKS HIM, "WHAT'S WRONG?" AND HE TELLS HER, "THE DOCTOR SAID I ONLY HAVE ABOUT SIXTY YEARS TO LIVE."
HEH HEH
HEH HOFF AHA COUGH COUGH
COUGH COUGH OUGH COUGH
CHECKMATE.

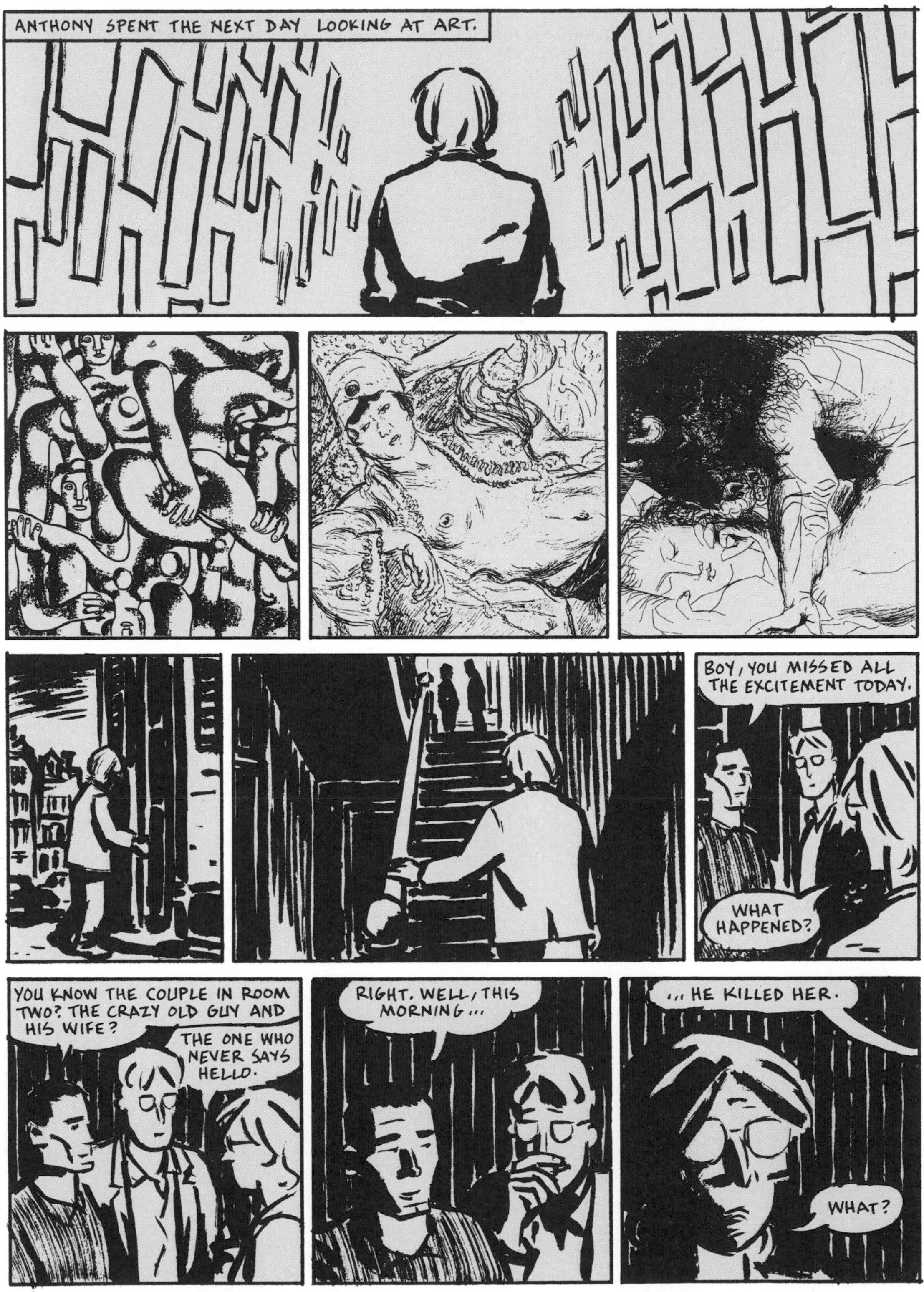

ANTHONY SPENT THE NEXT DAY LOOKING AT ART.
BOY, YOU MISSED ALL THE EXCITEMENT TODAY.
WHAT HAPPENED?
YOU KNOW THE COUPLE IN ROOM TWO? THE CRAZY OLD GUY AND HIS WIFE?
THE ONE WHO NEVER SAYS HELLO.
RIGHT. WELL, THIS MORNING...
... HE KILLED HER.
WHAT?

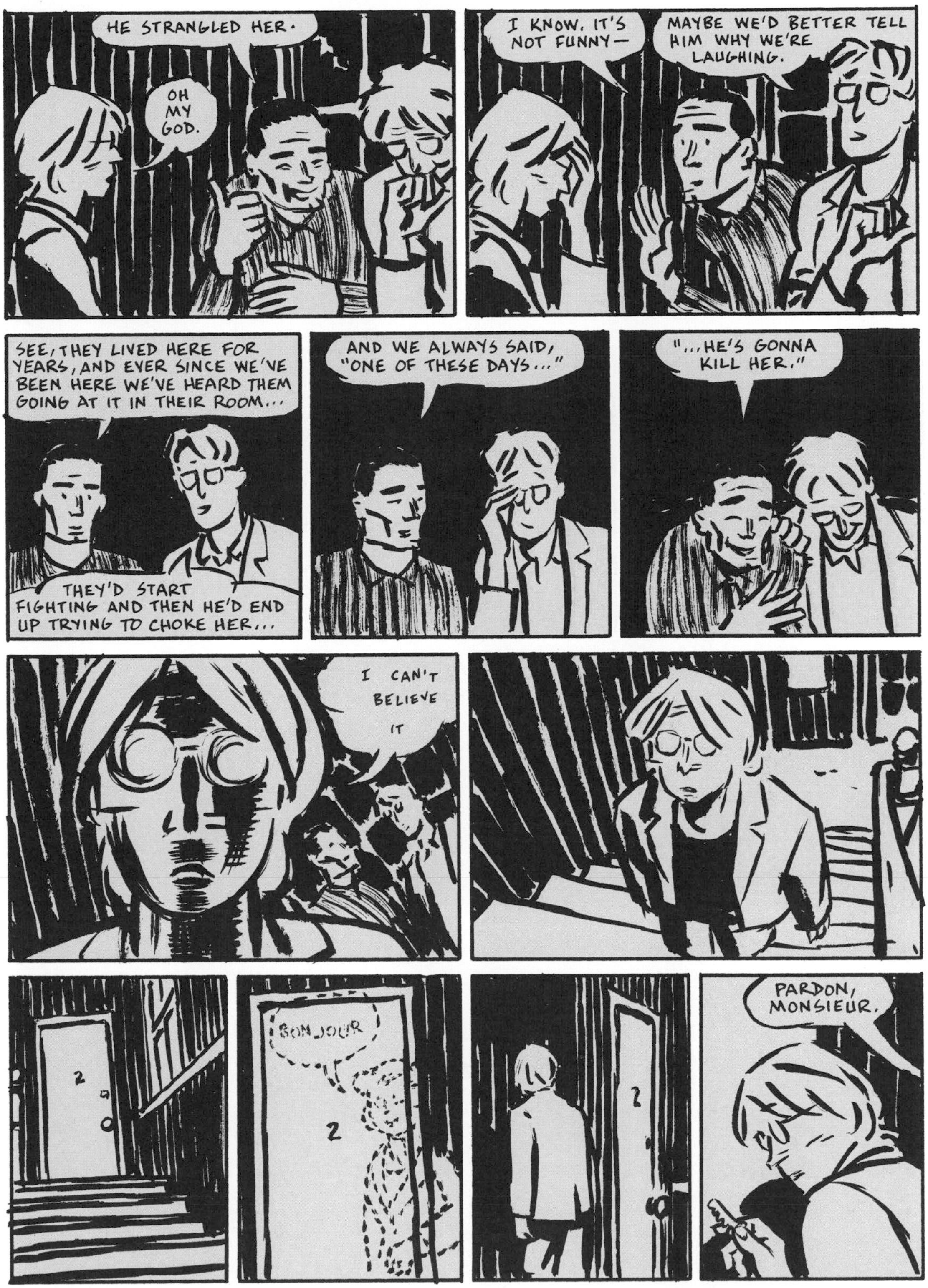
HE STRANGLED HER.
OH MY GOD.
I KNOW. IT'S NOT FUNNY—
MAYBE WE'D BETTER TELL HIM WHY WE'RE LAUGHING.
SEE, THEY LIVED HERE FOR YEARS, AND EVER SINCE WE'VE BEEN HERE WE'VE HEARD THEM GOING AT IT IN THEIR ROOM...
THEY'D START FIGHTING AND THEN HE'D END UP TRYING TO CHOKE HER...
AND WE ALWAYS SAID, "ONE OF THESE DAYS..."
"...HE'S GONNA KILL HER."
I CAN'T BELIEVE IT
2
BONJOUR
2
2
PARDON, MONSIEUR.

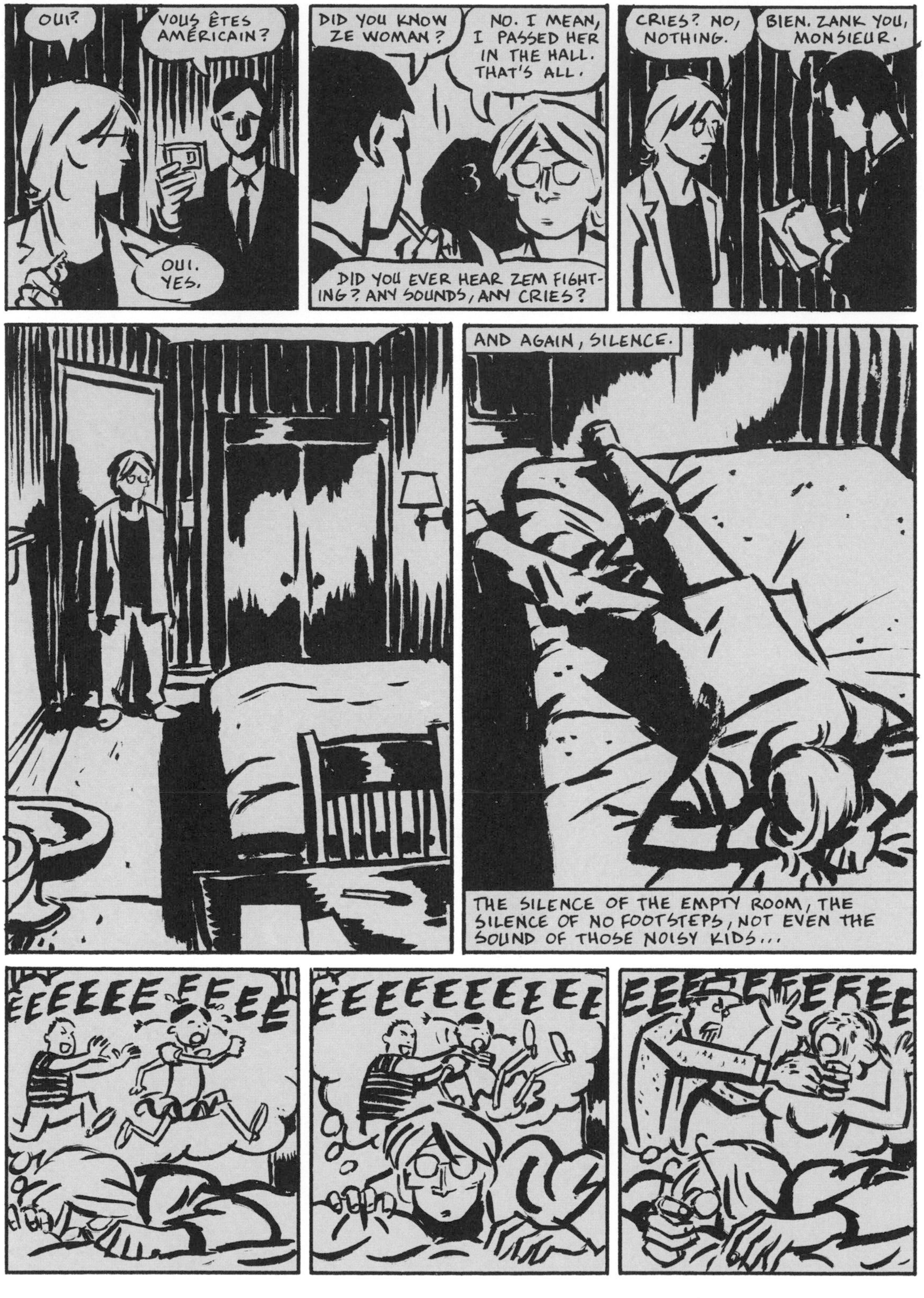

OUI?
VOUS ÊTES AMÉRICAIN?
OUI. YES.
DID YOU KNOW ZE WOMAN?
NO. I MEAN, I PASSED HER IN THE HALL. THAT'S ALL.
DID YOU EVER HEAR ZEM FIGHTING? ANY SOUNDS, ANY CRIES?
CRIES? NO, NOTHING.
BIEN. ZANK YOU, MONSIEUR.
AND AGAIN, SILENCE.
THE SILENCE OF THE EMPTY ROOM, THE SILENCE OF NO FOOTSTEPS, NOT EVEN THE SOUND OF THOSE NOISY KIDS...
EEEEEE EEEE
EEEEEEEEEEE
EEEEEEEEEE

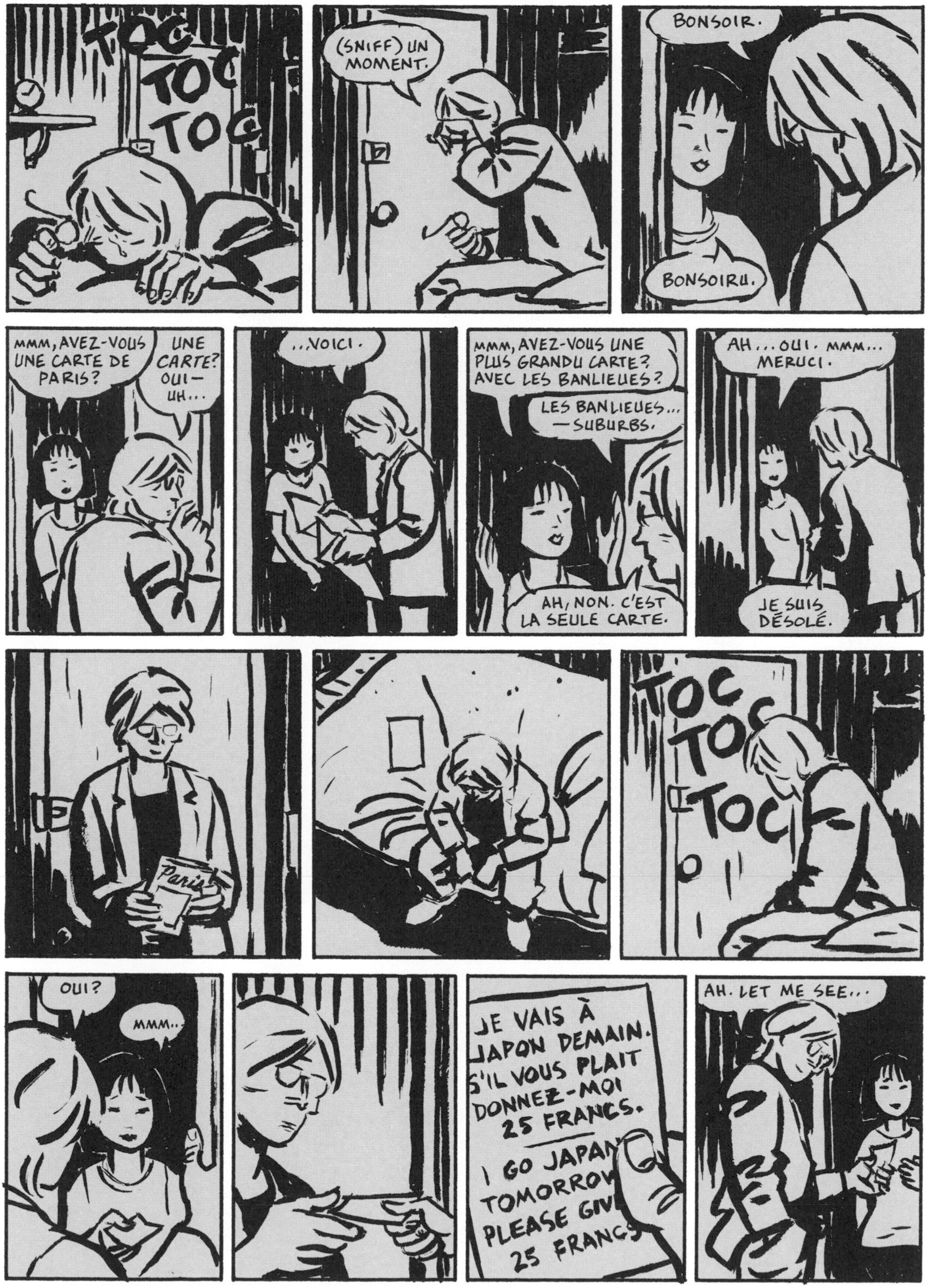
TOC
TOC
TOC
(SNIFF) UN MOMENT.
BONSOIR.
BONSOIRU.
MMM, AVEZ-VOUS UNE CARTE DE PARIS?
UNE CARTE? OUI— UH...
..VOICI.
MMM, AVEZ-VOUS UNE PLUS GRANDU CARTE? AVEC LES BANLIEUES?
LES BANLIEUES... —SUBURBS.
AH, NON. C'EST LA SEULE CARTE.
AH... OUI. MMM... MERUCI.
JE SUIS DÉSOLÉ.
Paris
TOC
TOC
TOC
OUI?
MMM...
JE VAIS À JAPON DEMAIN. S'IL VOUS PLAIT DONNEZ-MOI 25 FRANCS.
AH. LET ME SEE...

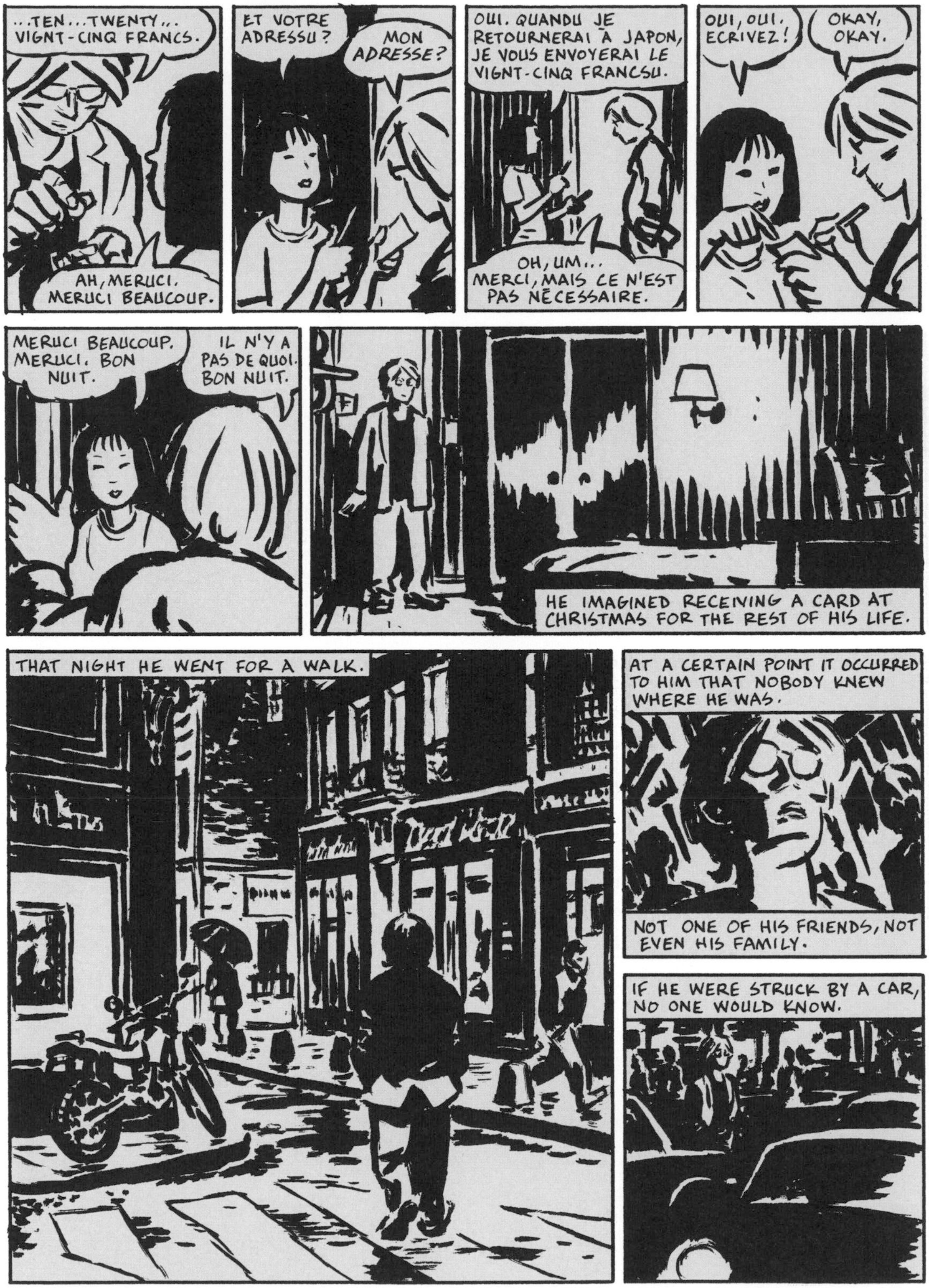
...TEN... TWENTY... VIGNT-CINQ FRANCS.
AH, MERUCI. MERUCI BEAUCOUP.
ET VOTRE ADRESSU?
MON ADRESSE?
OUI. QUANDU JE RETOURNERAI A JAPON, JE VOUS ENVOYERAI LE VIGNT-CINQ FRANCSU.
OH, UM... MERCI, MAIS CE N'EST PAS NÉCESSAIRE.
OUI, OUI. ECRIVEZ!
OKAY, OKAY.
MERUCI BEAUCOUP. MERUCI. BON NUIT.
IL N'Y A PAS DE QUOI. BON NUIT.
HE IMAGINED RECEIVING A CARD AT CHRISTMAS FOR THE REST OF HIS LIFE.
THAT NIGHT HE WENT FOR A WALK.
AT A CERTAIN POINT IT OCCURRED TO HIM THAT NOBODY KNEW WHERE HE WAS.
NOT ONE OF HIS FRIENDS, NOT EVEN HIS FAMILY.
IF HE WERE STRUCK BY A CAR, NO ONE WOULD KNOW.

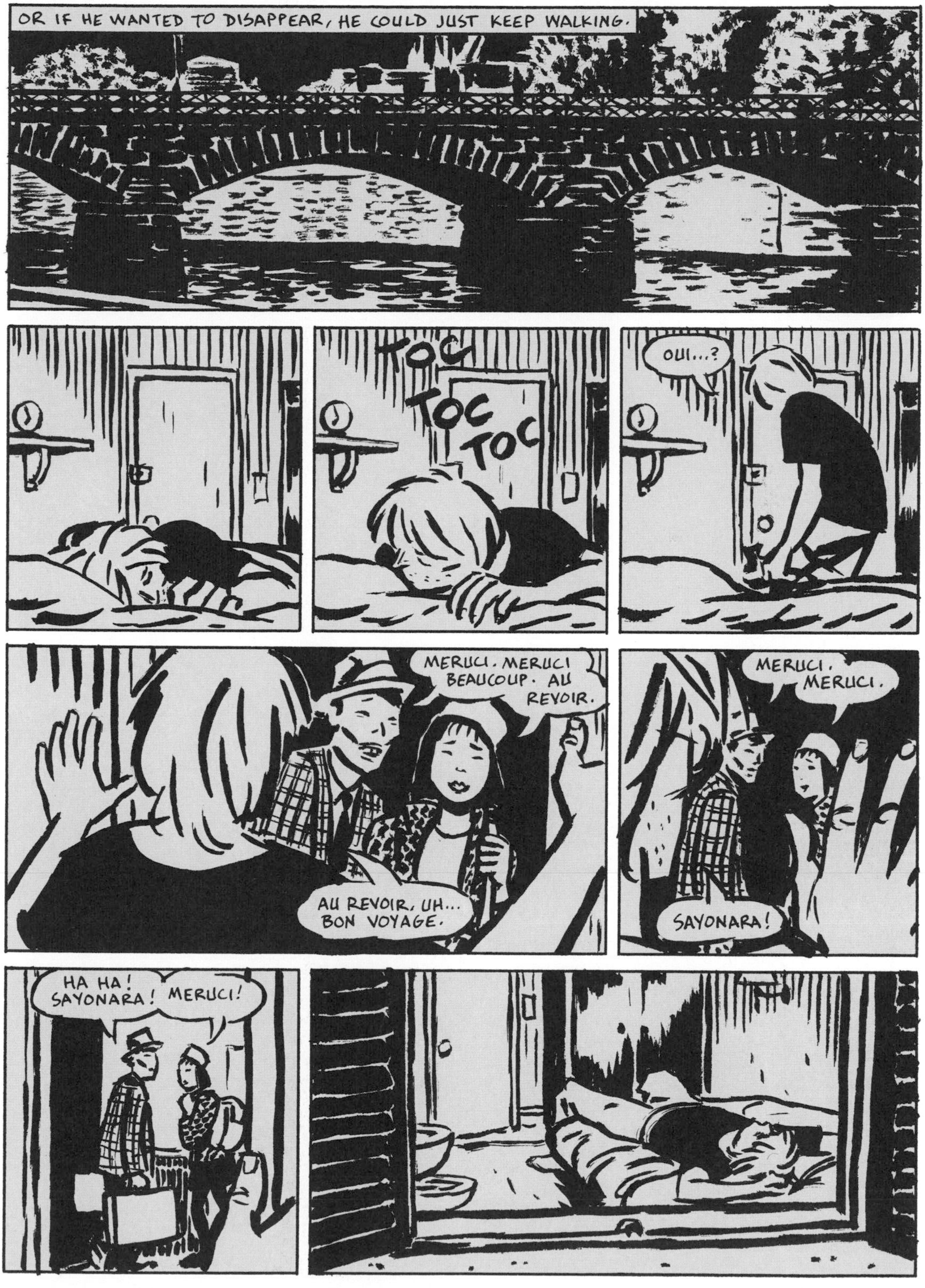
OR IF HE WANTED TO DISAPPEAR, HE COULD JUST KEEP WALKING.
TOC
TOC
TOC
OUI...?
MERUCI. MERUCI BEAUCOUP. AU REVOIR.
AU REVOIR, UH... BON VOYAGE.
MERUCI. MERUCI.
SAYONARA!
HA HA! SAYONARA!
MERUCI!

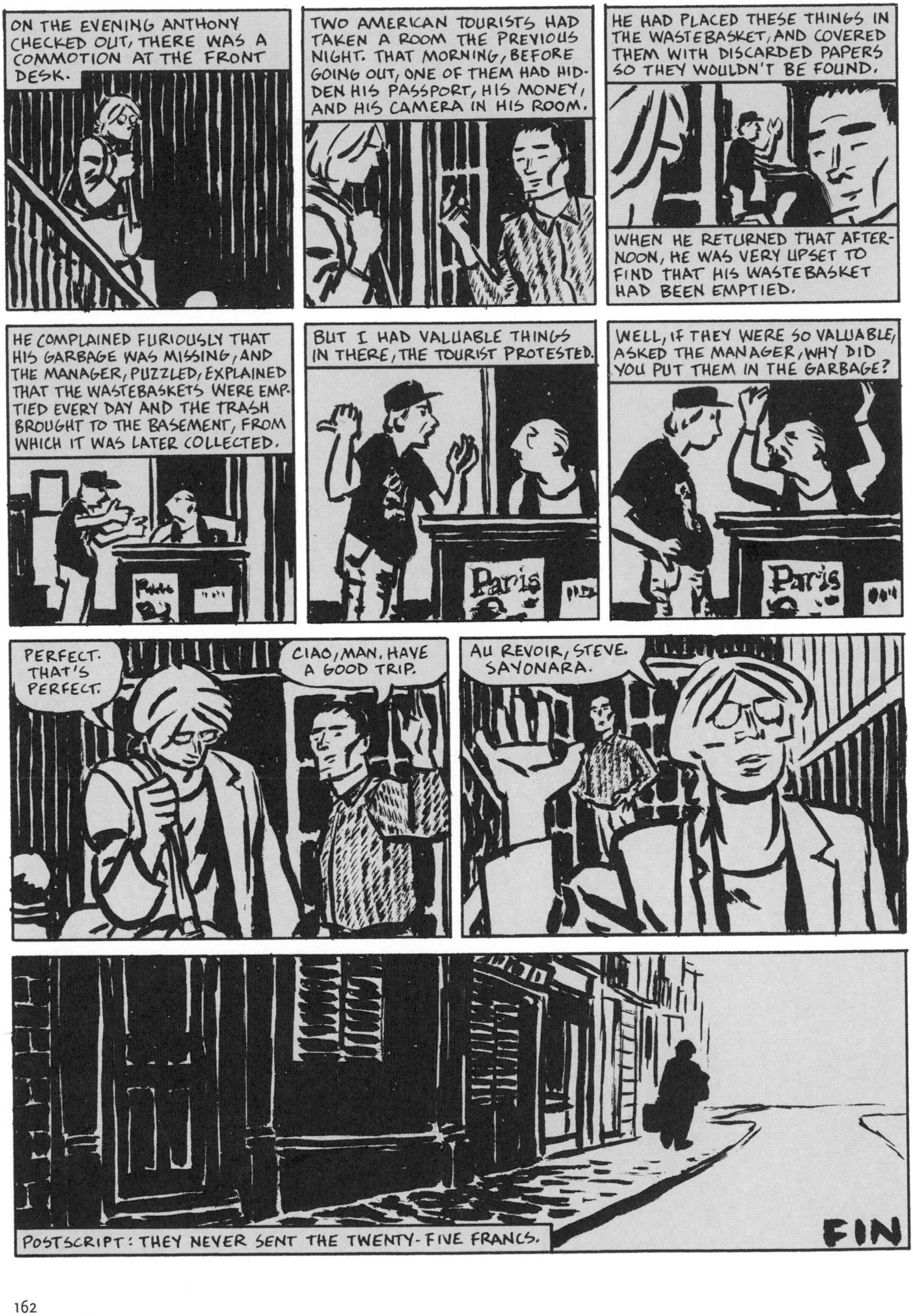
ON THE EVENING ANTHONY CHECKED OUT, THERE WAS A COMMOTION AT THE FRONT DESK.
TWO AMERICAN TOURISTS HAD TAKEN A ROOM THE PREVIOUS NIGHT. THAT MORNING, BEFORE GOING OUT, ONE OF THEM HAD HIDDEN HIS PASSPORT, HIS MONEY, AND HIS CAMERA IN HIS ROOM.
HE HAD PLACED THESE THINGS IN THE WASTEBASKET, AND COVERED THEM WITH DISCARDED PAPERS SO THEY WOULDN'T BE FOUND.
WHEN HE RETURNED THAT AFTERNOON, HE WAS VERY UPSET TO FIND THAT HIS WASTEBASKET HAD BEEN EMPTIED.
HE COMPLAINED FURIOUSLY THAT HIS GARBAGE WAS MISSING, AND THE MANAGER, PUZZLED, EXPLAINED THAT THE WASTEBASKETS WERE EMPTIED EVERY DAY AND THE TRASH BROUGHT TO THE BASEMENT, FROM WHICH IT WAS LATER COLLECTED.
BUT I HAD VALUABLE THINGS IN THERE, THE TOURIST PROTESTED.
Paris
WELL, IF THEY WERE SO VALUABLE, ASKED THE MANAGER, WHY DID YOU PUT THEM IN THE GARBAGE?
Paris
PERFECT. THAT'S PERFECT.
CIAO, MAN. HAVE A GOOD TRIP.
AU REVOIR, STEVE. SAYONARA.
POSTSCRIPT: THEY NEVER SENT THE TWENTY-FIVE FRANCS.
FIN

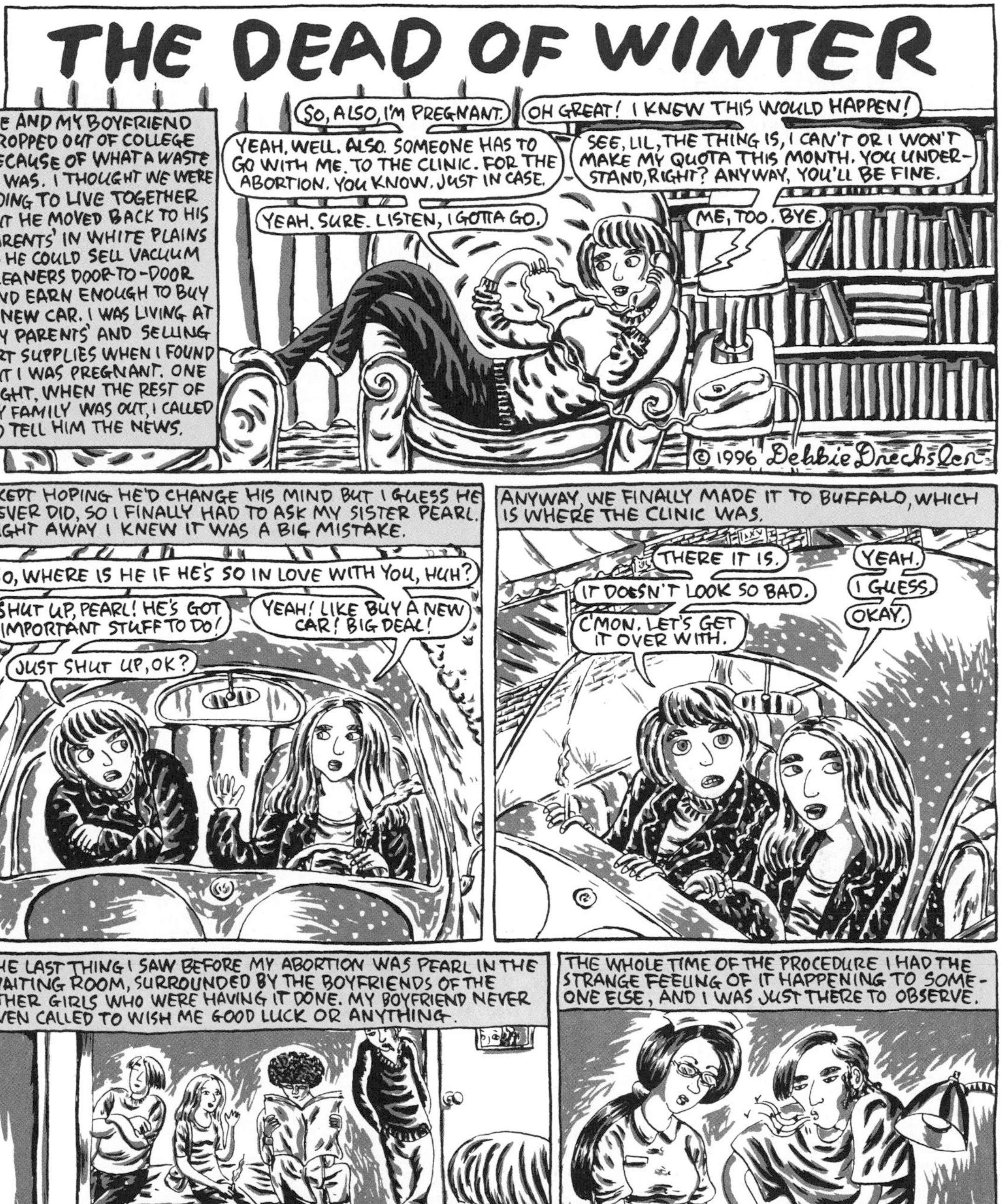
THE DEAD OF WINTER
ME AND MY BOYFRIEND DROPPED OUT OF COLLEGE BECAUSE OF WHAT A WASTE IT WAS. I THOUGHT WE WERE GOING TO LIVE TOGETHER BUT HE MOVED BACK TO HIS PARENTS' IN WHITE PLAINS SO HE COULD SELL VACUUM CLEANERS DOOR-TO-DOOR AND EARN ENOUGH TO BUY A NEW CAR. I WAS LIVING AT MY PARENTS' AND SELLING ART SUPPLIES WHEN I FOUND OUT I WAS PREGNANT. ONE NIGHT, WHEN THE REST OF MY FAMILY WAS OUT, I CALLED TO TELL HIM THE NEWS.
SO, ALSO, I'M PREGNANT.
OH GREAT! I KNEW THIS WOULD HAPPEN!
YEAH, WELL. ALSO. SOMEONE HAS TO GO WITH ME. TO THE CLINIC. FOR THE ABORTION. YOU KNOW. JUST IN CASE.
SEE, LIL, THE THING IS, I CAN'T OR I WON'T MAKE MY QUOTA THIS MONTH. YOU UNDERSTAND, RIGHT? ANYWAY, YOU'LL BE FINE.
YEAH. SURE. LISTEN, I GOTTA GO.
ME, TOO. BYE.
© 1996 Debbie Drechsler
I KEPT HOPING HE'D CHANGE HIS MIND BUT I GUESS HE NEVER DID, SO I FINALLY HAD TO ASK MY SISTER PEARL. RIGHT AWAY I KNEW IT WAS A BIG MISTAKE.
SO, WHERE IS HE IF HE'S SO IN LOVE WITH YOU, HUH?
SHUT UP, PEARL! HE'S GOT IMPORTANT STUFF TO DO!
YEAH! LIKE BUY A NEW CAR! BIG DEAL!
JUST SHUT UP, OK?
ANYWAY, WE FINALLY MADE IT TO BUFFALO, WHICH IS WHERE THE CLINIC WAS.
THERE IT IS.
IT DOESN'T LOOK SO BAD.
C'MON. LET'S GET IT OVER WITH.
YEAH. I GUESS. OKAY.
THE LAST THING I SAW BEFORE MY ABORTION WAS PEARL IN THE WAITING ROOM, SURROUNDED BY THE BOYFRIENDS OF THE OTHER GIRLS WHO WERE HAVING IT DONE. MY BOYFRIEND NEVER EVEN CALLED TO WISH ME GOOD LUCK OR ANYTHING.
THE WHOLE TIME OF THE PROCEDURE I HAD THE STRANGE FEELING OF IT HAPPENING TO SOMEONE ELSE, AND I WAS JUST THERE TO OBSERVE.

"The Dead of Winter" first appeared in vol. 2, no. 5 of *Drawn & Quarterly* (1996).

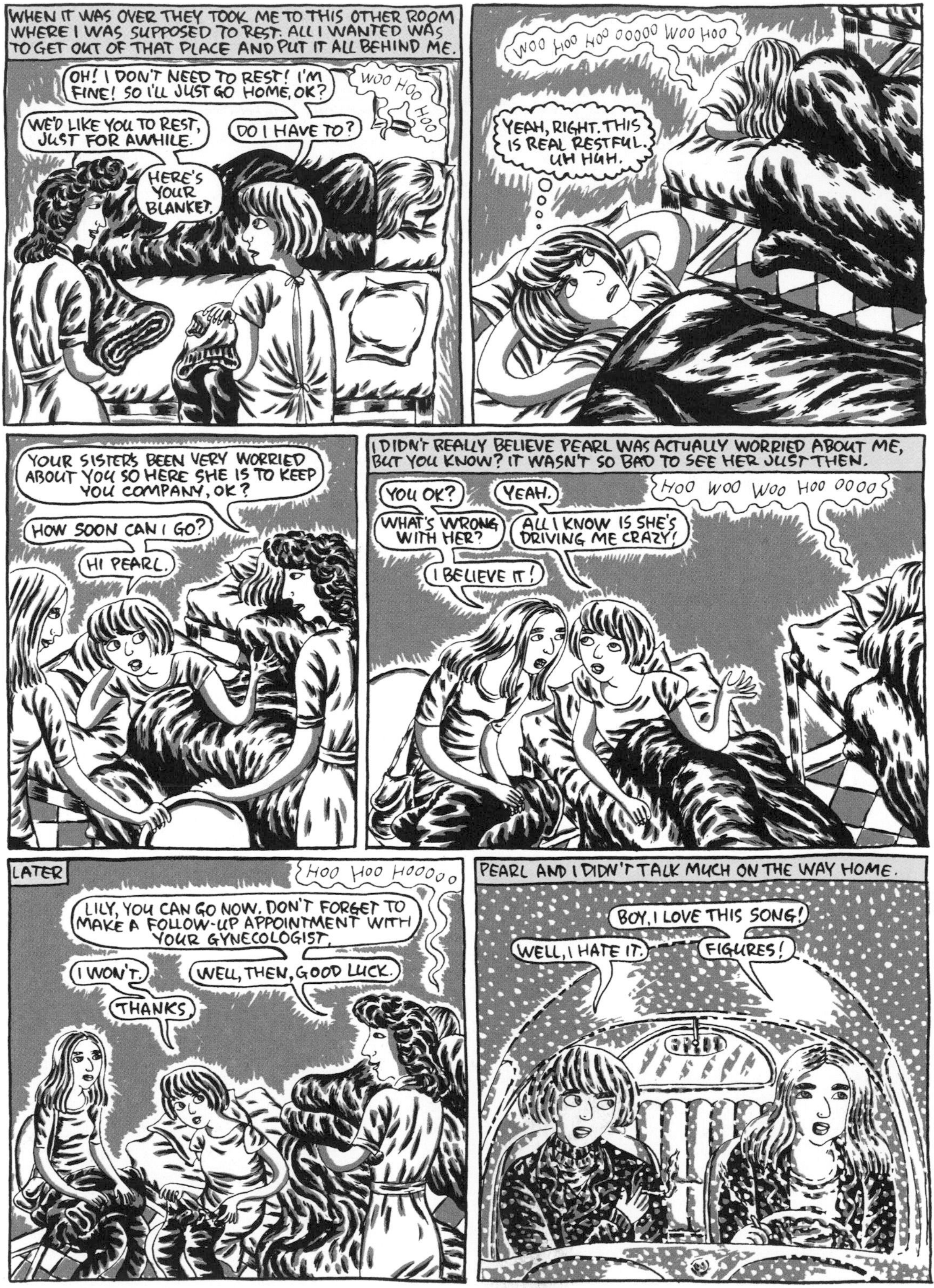
WHEN IT WAS OVER THEY TOOK ME TO THIS OTHER ROOM WHERE I WAS SUPPOSED TO REST. ALL I WANTED WAS TO GET OUT OF THAT PLACE AND PUT IT ALL BEHIND ME.
OH! I DON'T NEED TO REST! I'M FINE! SO I'LL JUST GO HOME, OK?
WOO HOO HOO
WE'D LIKE YOU TO REST, JUST FOR AWHILE.
DO I HAVE TO?
HERE'S YOUR BLANKET.
WOO HOO HOO OOOOO WOO HOO
YEAH, RIGHT. THIS IS REAL RESTFUL. UH HUH.
YOUR SISTER'S BEEN VERY WORRIED ABOUT YOU SO HERE SHE IS TO KEEP YOU COMPANY, OK?
HOW SOON CAN I GO?
HI PEARL.
I DIDN'T REALLY BELIEVE PEARL WAS ACTUALLY WORRIED ABOUT ME, BUT YOU KNOW? IT WASN'T SO BAD TO SEE HER JUST THEN.
YOU OK?
YEAH.
HOO WOO WOO HOO OOOO
WHAT'S WRONG WITH HER?
ALL I KNOW IS SHE'S DRIVING ME CRAZY!
I BELIEVE IT!
LATER
HOO HOO HOOOOOO
LILY, YOU CAN GO NOW. DON'T FORGET TO MAKE A FOLLOW-UP APPOINTMENT WITH YOUR GYNECOLOGIST.
I WON'T.
WELL, THEN, GOOD LUCK.
THANKS.
PEARL AND I DIDN'T TALK MUCH ON THE WAY HOME.
BOY, I LOVE THIS SONG!
WELL, I HATE IT.
FIGURES!

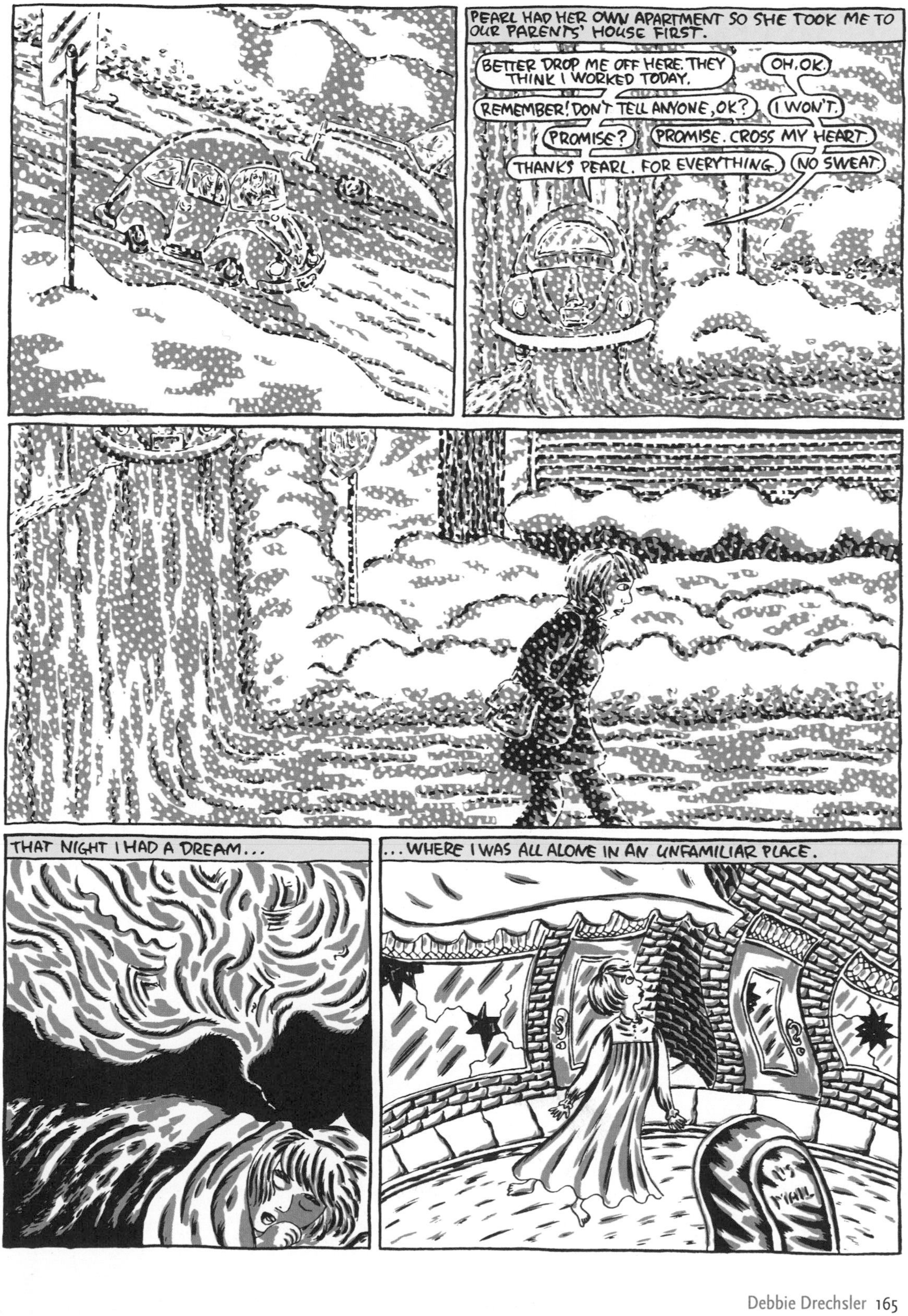
PEARL HAD HER OWN APARTMENT SO SHE TOOK ME TO OUR PARENTS' HOUSE FIRST.
BETTER DROP ME OFF HERE. THEY THINK I WORKED TODAY.
OH, OK.
REMEMBER! DON'T TELL ANYONE, OK?
I WON'T.
PROMISE?
PROMISE. CROSS MY HEART.
THANKS PEARL. FOR EVERYTHING.
NO SWEAT.
THAT NIGHT I HAD A DREAM...
...WHERE I WAS ALL ALONE IN AN UNFAMILIAR PLACE.

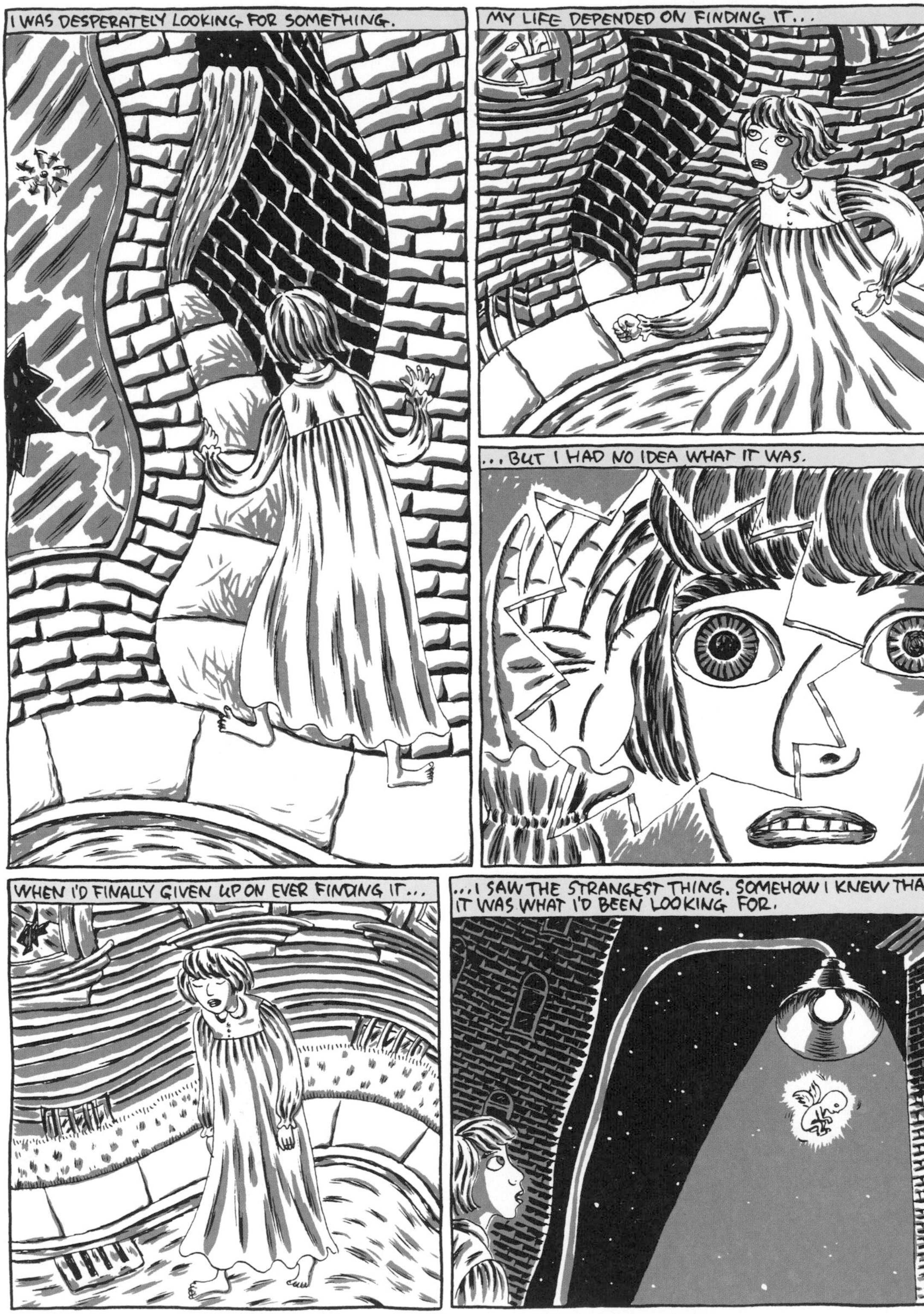
I WAS DESPERATELY LOOKING FOR SOMETHING.
MY LIFE DEPENDED ON FINDING IT...
...BUT I HAD NO IDEA WHAT IT WAS.
WHEN I'D FINALLY GIVEN UP ON EVER FINDING IT...
...I SAW THE STRANGEST THING. SOMEHOW I KNEW THAT IT WAS WHAT I'D BEEN LOOKING FOR.

I WAS REALLY HAPPY AND HORRIBLY SAD ALL AT ONCE. I WANTED SO BADLY TO TOUCH IT OR HOLD IT. OR SOMETHING.

BUT I GUESS I SCARED IT...

...AND THEN I COULDN'T FIND IT AT ALL, BECAUSE THERE WERE A MILLION STARS AND IT COULD'VE BEEN ANY ONE OF THEM.

WHEN I WOKE UP, I WAS CRYING HARDER THAN I EVER HAD SINCE I WAS A LITTLE KID. I CRIED AND CRIED AND CRIED...

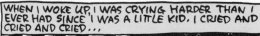

...AND THEN IT STOPPED. JUST LIKE THAT. BUT NO WAY COULD I GET BACK TO SLEEP.

I GOT THIS CRAZY URGE TO GO OUTSIDE.

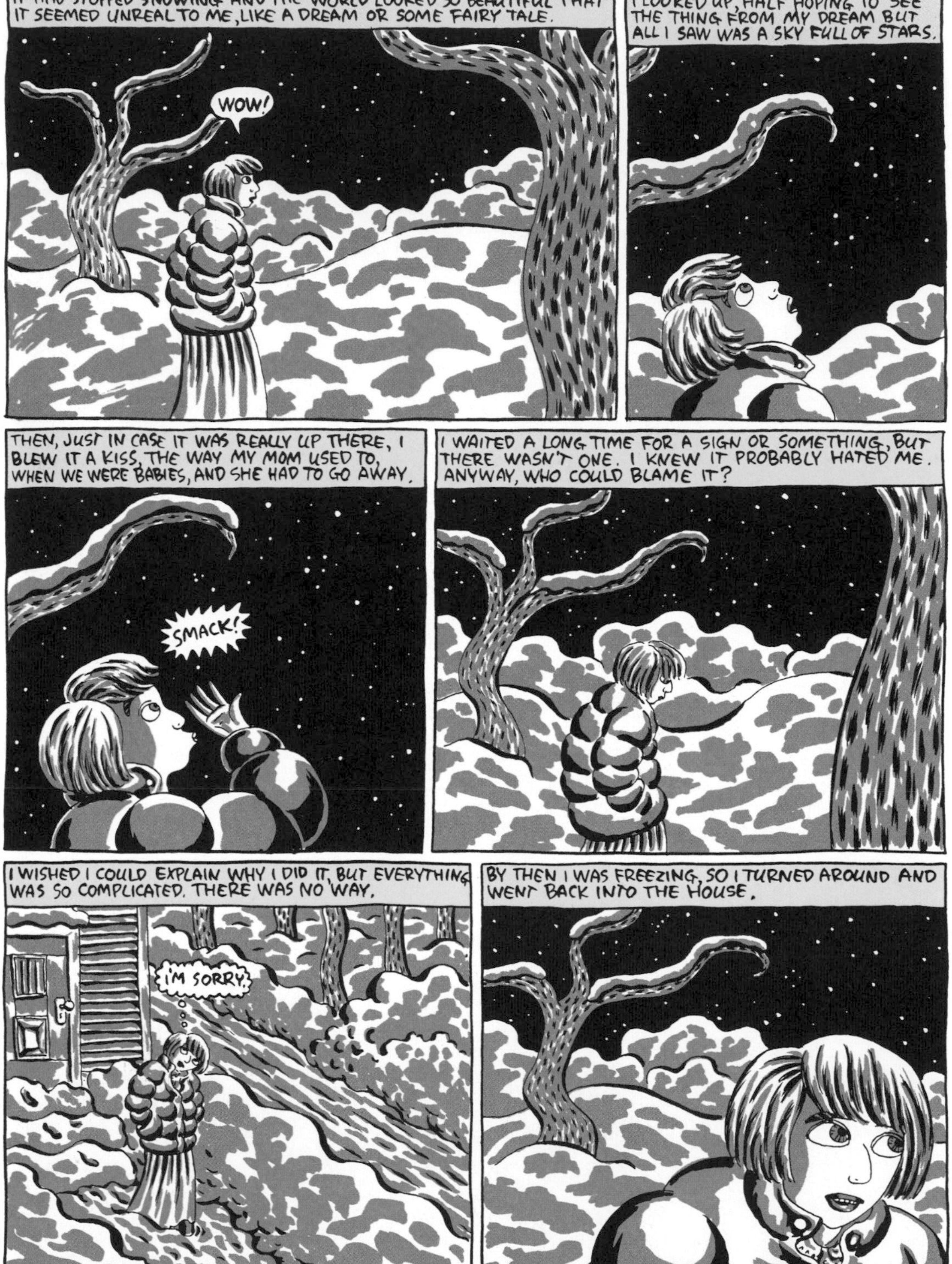
IT HAD STOPPED SNOWING AND THE WORLD LOOKED SO BEAUTIFUL THAT IT SEEMED UNREAL TO ME, LIKE A DREAM OR SOME FAIRY TALE.
WOW!
I LOOKED UP, HALF HOPING TO SEE THE THING FROM MY DREAM BUT ALL I SAW WAS A SKY FULL OF STARS.
THEN, JUST IN CASE IT WAS REALLY UP THERE, I BLEW IT A KISS, THE WAY MY MOM USED TO, WHEN WE WERE BABIES, AND SHE HAD TO GO AWAY.
SMACK!
I WAITED A LONG TIME FOR A SIGN OR SOMETHING, BUT THERE WASN'T ONE. I KNEW IT PROBABLY HATED ME. ANYWAY, WHO COULD BLAME IT?
I WISHED I COULD EXPLAIN WHY I DID IT, BUT EVERYTHING WAS SO COMPLICATED. THERE WAS NO WAY.
I'M SORRY.
BY THEN I WAS FREEZING, SO I TURNED AROUND AND WENT BACK INTO THE HOUSE.
END

IT HAS BEEN CALLED THE MOST DANGEROUS CONFLICT IN OUR SOCIETY; WORSE THAN DIVISIONS OF GENDER, RACE, OR CLASS! SO VAST IS THE CHASM-THIS "NEW GENERATION GAP"-THAT IF YOU'RE IN THE MIDDLE, YOU CAN GET A GREAT...
VIEW FROM THE BRIDGE!
-COLLIER
MAN, IT'S BEEN A LONG TIME -A LONG TIME!
THE BEGUILING
MIRVISH VILLAGE
THE BEGUILIN
TORONTO, WINTER 1995
STEVE YOU OLE SON-OF-A-BITCH! HOW THE HELL ARE YOU?!
NO HERO
WOMP!
HEY, I DIDN'T RECOGNIZE YOU--HOW TH' FUCK ARE YOU?!
IT'S THE PASSAGE OF TIME--IT'LL DO THAT--HEH-HEH, I'M DOING ALRITE FOR A MAN MY AGE!
'COURSE WHEN YOU GET UP TO BE OUR AGE, YOU CAN'T BLAME YOUR ACTIONS ON YOUTHFUL FOLLY ANY MORE--STILL, IT'S BETTER THAN THE SITUATION FACING THE POOR YOUNG PEOPLE NOWADAYS!
WHAT- YOU TALKING ABOUT THE KIDS TODAY?!
WHAM!
KISS ME I'M IRISH
KA-CHUNG!
$ $
THEY'VE GOT EVERY GODDAMN THING HANDED TO THEM!
BIG GULP
ALL THE BEST COMICS

"View From The Bridge" first appeared in *Just The Facts* (1998). David Collier

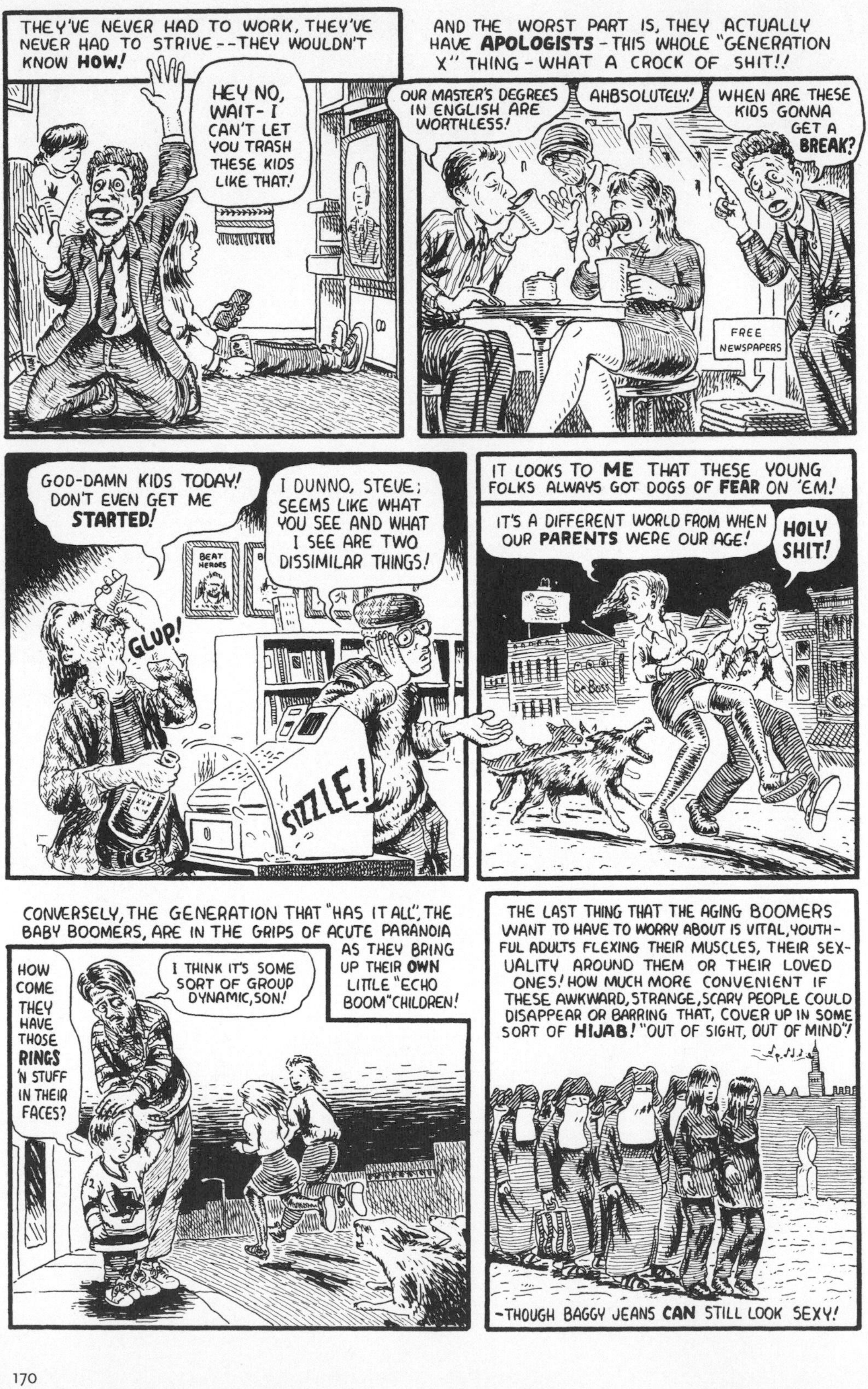
THEY'VE NEVER HAD TO WORK, THEY'VE NEVER HAD TO STRIVE--THEY WOULDN'T KNOW **HOW**!
HEY NO, WAIT- I CAN'T LET YOU TRASH THESE KIDS LIKE THAT!
AND THE WORST PART IS, THEY ACTUALLY HAVE **APOLOGISTS** - THIS WHOLE "GENERATION X" THING - WHAT A CROCK OF SHIT!!
OUR MASTER'S DEGREES IN ENGLISH ARE WORTHLESS!
AHBSOLUTELY!
WHEN ARE THESE KIDS GONNA GET A **BREAK?**
FREE NEWSPAPERS
GOD-DAMN KIDS TODAY! DON'T EVEN GET ME **STARTED**!
I DUNNO, STEVE; SEEMS LIKE WHAT YOU SEE AND WHAT I SEE ARE TWO DISSIMILAR THINGS!
BEAT HEROES
GLUP!
SIZZLE!
IT LOOKS TO **ME** THAT THESE YOUNG FOLKS ALWAYS GOT DOGS OF **FEAR** ON 'EM!
IT'S A DIFFERENT WORLD FROM WHEN OUR **PARENTS** WERE OUR AGE!
HOLY SHIT!
CONVERSELY, THE GENERATION THAT "HAS IT ALL", THE BABY BOOMERS, ARE IN THE GRIPS OF ACUTE PARANOIA AS THEY BRING UP THEIR **OWN** LITTLE "ECHO BOOM" CHILDREN!
HOW COME THEY HAVE THOSE **RINGS** 'N STUFF IN THEIR FACES?
I THINK IT'S SOME SORT OF GROUP DYNAMIC, SON!
THE LAST THING THAT THE AGING BOOMERS WANT TO HAVE TO WORRY ABOUT IS VITAL, YOUTHFUL ADULTS FLEXING THEIR MUSCLES, THEIR SEXUALITY AROUND THEM OR THEIR LOVED ONES! HOW MUCH MORE CONVENIENT IF THESE AWKWARD, STRANGE, SCARY PEOPLE COULD DISAPPEAR OR BARRING THAT, COVER UP IN SOME SORT OF **HIJAB**! "OUT OF SIGHT, OUT OF MIND"!
-THOUGH BAGGY JEANS **CAN** STILL LOOK SEXY!

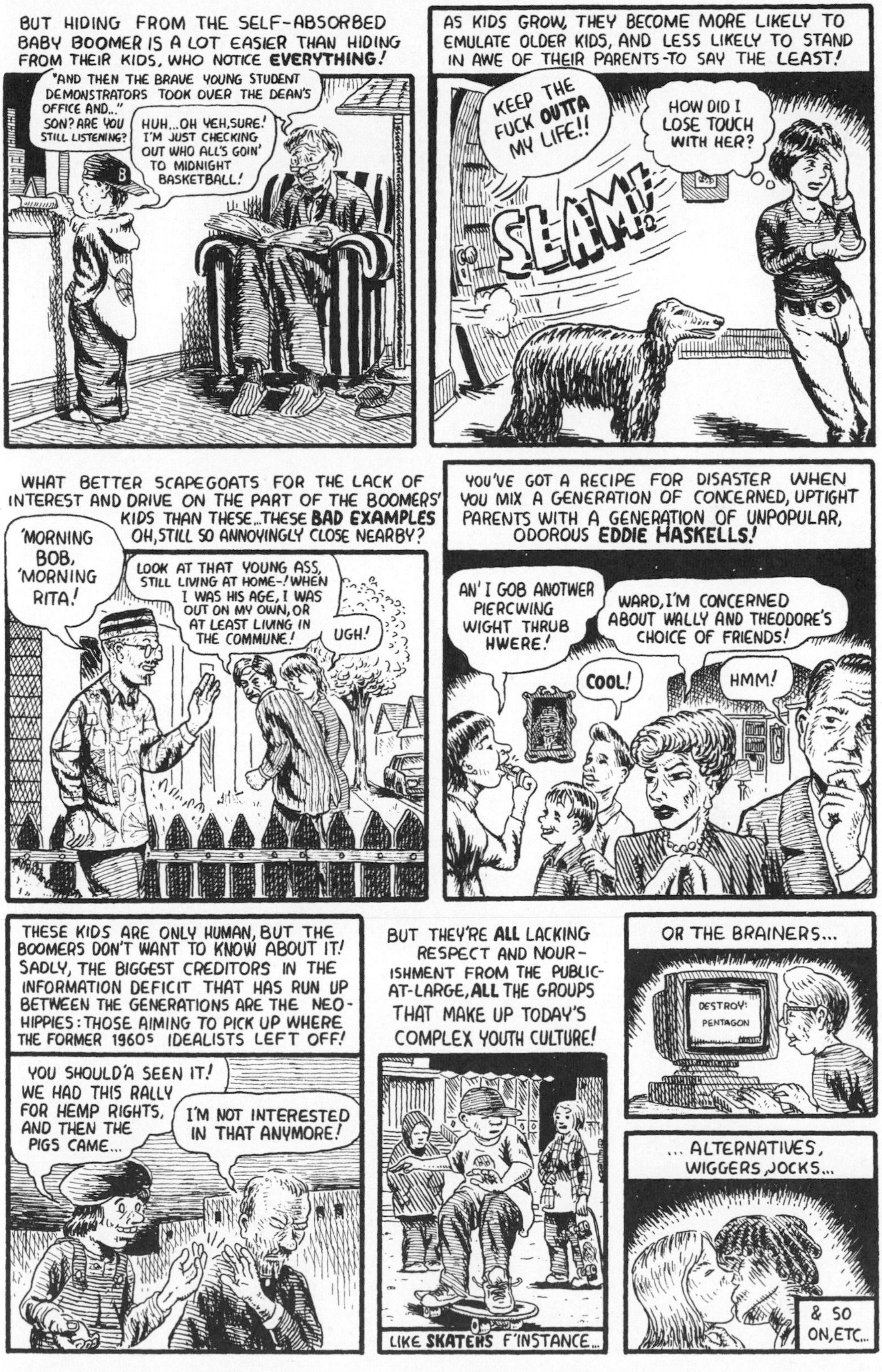
BUT HIDING FROM THE SELF-ABSORBED BABY BOOMER IS A LOT EASIER THAN HIDING FROM THEIR KIDS, WHO NOTICE EVERYTHING!
"AND THEN THE BRAVE YOUNG STUDENT DEMONSTRATORS TOOK OVER THE DEAN'S OFFICE AND..." SON? ARE YOU STILL LISTENING?
HUH...OH YEH, SURE! I'M JUST CHECKING OUT WHO ALL'S GOIN' TO MIDNIGHT BASKETBALL!
AS KIDS GROW, THEY BECOME MORE LIKELY TO EMULATE OLDER KIDS, AND LESS LIKELY TO STAND IN AWE OF THEIR PARENTS-TO SAY THE LEAST!
KEEP THE FUCK OUTTA MY LIFE!!
SLAM!
HOW DID I LOSE TOUCH WITH HER?
WHAT BETTER SCAPEGOATS FOR THE LACK OF INTEREST AND DRIVE ON THE PART OF THE BOOMERS' KIDS THAN THESE...THESE BAD EXAMPLES OH, STILL SO ANNOYINGLY CLOSE NEARBY?
'MORNING BOB, 'MORNING RITA!
LOOK AT THAT YOUNG ASS, STILL LIVING AT HOME-! WHEN I WAS HIS AGE, I WAS OUT ON MY OWN, OR AT LEAST LIVING IN THE COMMUNE!
UGH!
YOU'VE GOT A RECIPE FOR DISASTER WHEN YOU MIX A GENERATION OF CONCERNED, UPTIGHT PARENTS WITH A GENERATION OF UNPOPULAR, ODOROUS EDDIE HASKELLS!
AN' I GOB ANOTWER PIERCWING WIGHT THRUB HWERE!
WARD, I'M CONCERNED ABOUT WALLY AND THEODORE'S CHOICE OF FRIENDS!
COOL!
HMM!
THESE KIDS ARE ONLY HUMAN, BUT THE BOOMERS DON'T WANT TO KNOW ABOUT IT! SADLY, THE BIGGEST CREDITORS IN THE INFORMATION DEFICIT THAT HAS RUN UP BETWEEN THE GENERATIONS ARE THE NEO-HIPPIES: THOSE AIMING TO PICK UP WHERE THE FORMER 1960S IDEALISTS LEFT OFF!
YOU SHOULD'A SEEN IT! WE HAD THIS RALLY FOR HEMP RIGHTS, AND THEN THE PIGS CAME...
I'M NOT INTERESTED IN THAT ANYMORE!
BUT THEY'RE ALL LACKING RESPECT AND NOURISHMENT FROM THE PUBLIC-AT-LARGE, ALL THE GROUPS THAT MAKE UP TODAY'S COMPLEX YOUTH CULTURE!
LIKE SKATERS F'INSTANCE...
OR THE BRAINERS...
DESTROY: PENTAGON
... ALTERNATIVES, WIGGERS, JOCKS...
& SO ON, ETC...

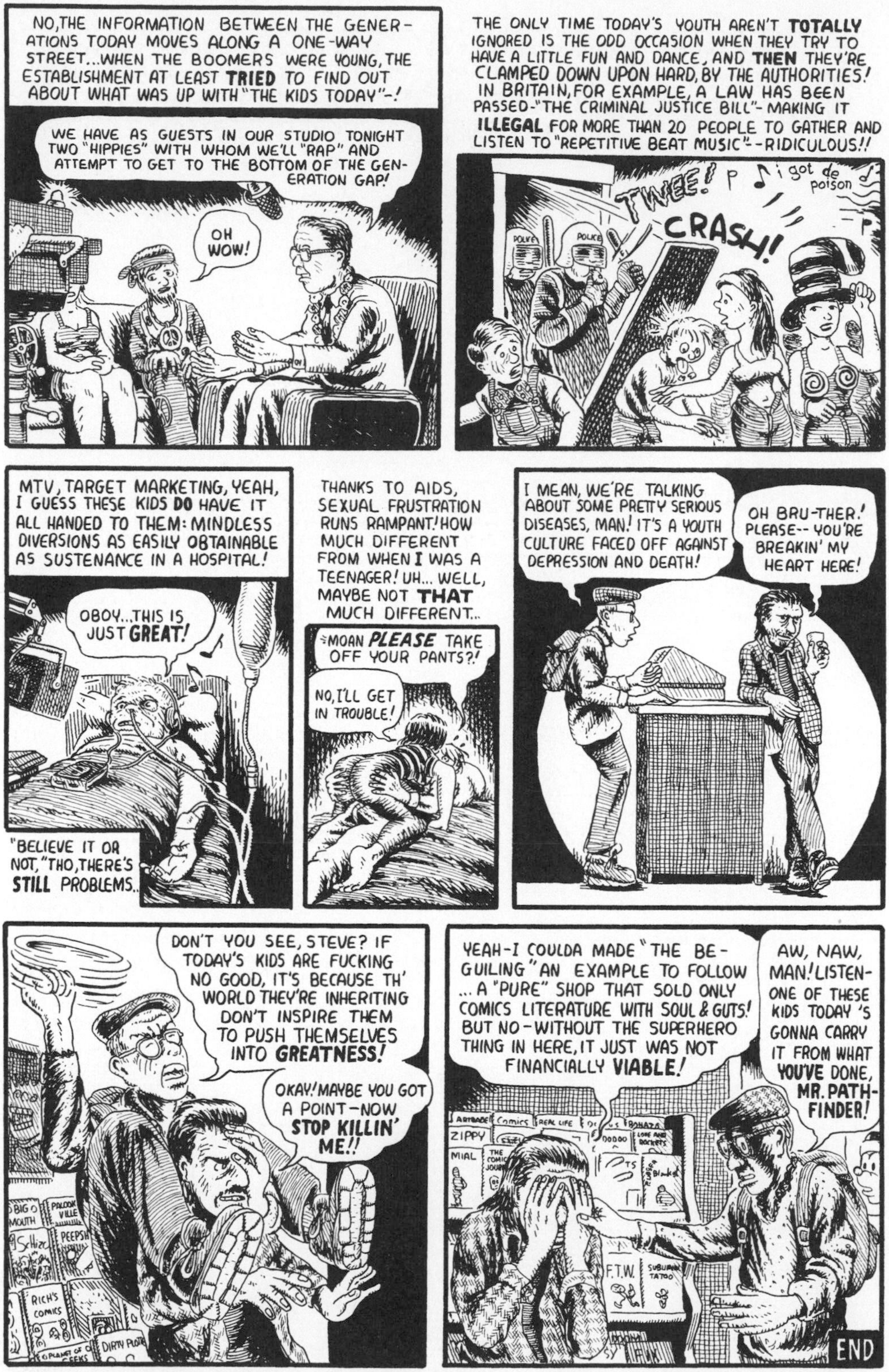
NO, THE INFORMATION BETWEEN THE GENERATIONS TODAY MOVES ALONG A ONE-WAY STREET...WHEN THE BOOMERS WERE YOUNG, THE ESTABLISHMENT AT LEAST TRIED TO FIND OUT ABOUT WHAT WAS UP WITH "THE KIDS TODAY"-!
WE HAVE AS GUESTS IN OUR STUDIO TONIGHT TWO "HIPPIES" WITH WHOM WE'LL "RAP" AND ATTEMPT TO GET TO THE BOTTOM OF THE GENERATION GAP!
OH WOW!
THE ONLY TIME TODAY'S YOUTH AREN'T TOTALLY IGNORED IS THE ODD OCCASION WHEN THEY TRY TO HAVE A LITTLE FUN AND DANCE, AND THEN THEY'RE CLAMPED DOWN UPON HARD, BY THE AUTHORITIES! IN BRITAIN, FOR EXAMPLE, A LAW HAS BEEN PASSED-"THE CRIMINAL JUSTICE BILL"- MAKING IT ILLEGAL FOR MORE THAN 20 PEOPLE TO GATHER AND LISTEN TO "REPETITIVE BEAT MUSIC"--RIDICULOUS!!
TWEE!
i got de poison
CRASH!
POLICE
POLICE
MTV, TARGET MARKETING, YEAH, I GUESS THESE KIDS DO HAVE IT ALL HANDED TO THEM: MINDLESS DIVERSIONS AS EASILY OBTAINABLE AS SUSTENANCE IN A HOSPITAL!
OBOY...THIS IS JUST GREAT!
"BELIEVE IT OR NOT," THO, THERE'S STILL PROBLEMS...
THANKS TO AIDS, SEXUAL FRUSTRATION RUNS RAMPANT! HOW MUCH DIFFERENT FROM WHEN I WAS A TEENAGER! UH... WELL, MAYBE NOT THAT MUCH DIFFERENT...
MOAN PLEASE TAKE OFF YOUR PANTS?!
NO, I'LL GET IN TROUBLE!
I MEAN, WE'RE TALKING ABOUT SOME PRETTY SERIOUS DISEASES, MAN! IT'S A YOUTH CULTURE FACED OFF AGAINST DEPRESSION AND DEATH!
OH BRU-THER! PLEASE-- YOU'RE BREAKIN' MY HEART HERE!
DON'T YOU SEE, STEVE? IF TODAY'S KIDS ARE FUCKING NO GOOD, IT'S BECAUSE TH' WORLD THEY'RE INHERITING DON'T INSPIRE THEM TO PUSH THEMSELVES INTO GREATNESS!
OKAY! MAYBE YOU GOT A POINT-NOW STOP KILLIN' ME!!
BIG MOUTH
PALOOKAVILLE
PEEPSH
RICH'S COMICS
DIRTY PLOTTE
YEAH-I COULDA MADE "THE BEGUILING" AN EXAMPLE TO FOLLOW ... A "PURE" SHOP THAT SOLD ONLY COMICS LITERATURE WITH SOUL & GUTS! BUT NO-WITHOUT THE SUPERHERO THING IN HERE, IT JUST WAS NOT FINANCIALLY VIABLE!
AW, NAW, MAN! LISTEN-ONE OF THESE KIDS TODAY'S GONNA CARRY IT FROM WHAT YOU'VE DONE, MR. PATHFINDER!
ZIPPY
THE COMICS JOURNAL
LOVE AND ROCKETS
F.T.W.
SUBURBAN TATOO
END

FIRST ISSUE

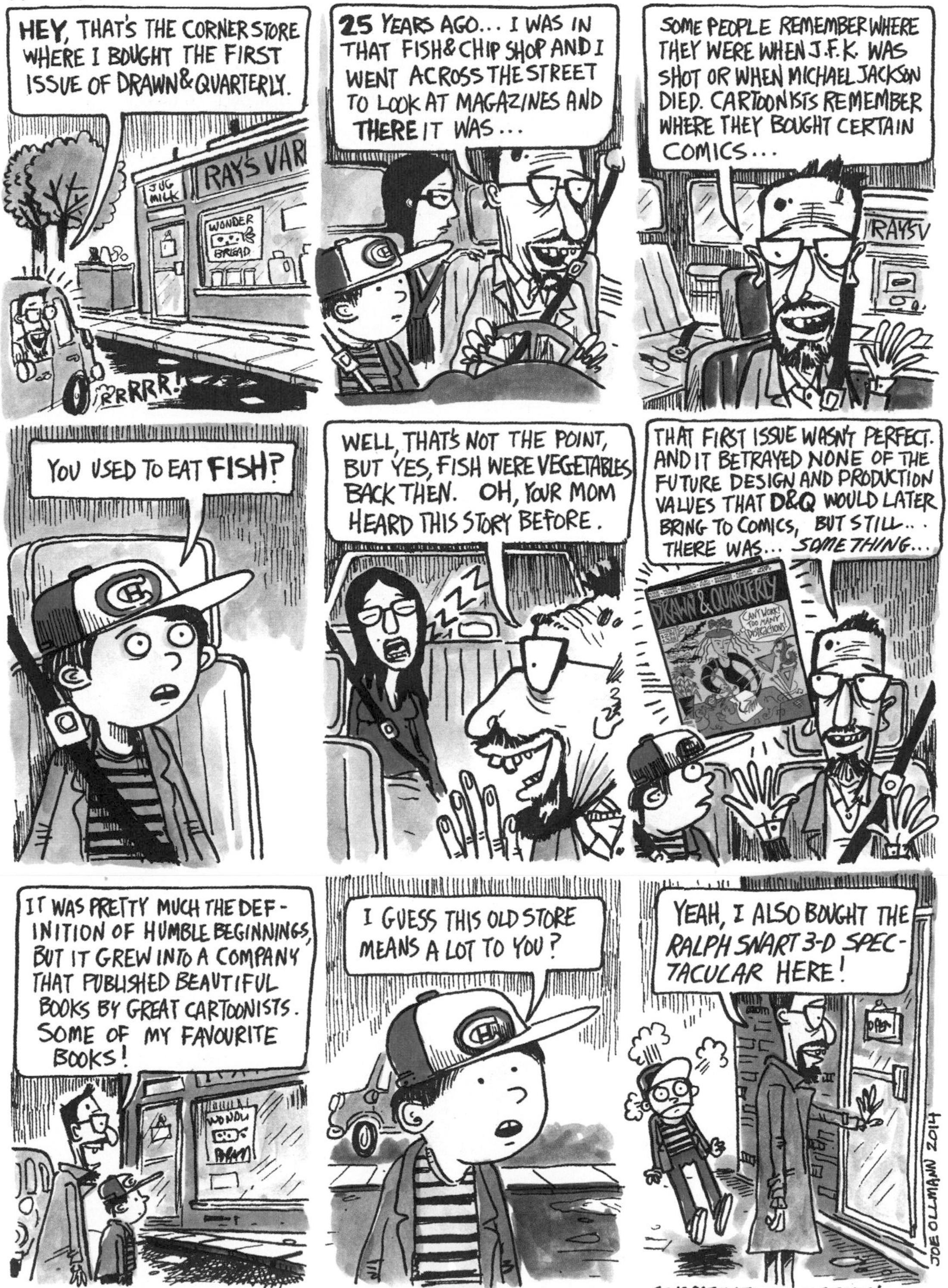
HEY, THAT'S THE CORNER STORE WHERE I BOUGHT THE FIRST ISSUE OF DRAWN & QUARTERLY.
JUG MILK
RAY'S VAR
WONDER BREAD
RRRRR!
25 YEARS AGO... I WAS IN THAT FISH & CHIP SHOP AND I WENT ACROSS THE STREET TO LOOK AT MAGAZINES AND THERE IT WAS...
SOME PEOPLE REMEMBER WHERE THEY WERE WHEN J.F.K. WAS SHOT OR WHEN MICHAEL JACKSON DIED. CARTOONISTS REMEMBER WHERE THEY BOUGHT CERTAIN COMICS...
RAYS V
YOU USED TO EAT FISH?
WELL, THAT'S NOT THE POINT, BUT YES, FISH WERE VEGETABLES BACK THEN. OH, YOUR MOM HEARD THIS STORY BEFORE.
ZZZ
THAT FIRST ISSUE WASN'T PERFECT. AND IT BETRAYED NONE OF THE FUTURE DESIGN AND PRODUCTION VALUES THAT D&Q WOULD LATER BRING TO COMICS, BUT STILL... THERE WAS... SOMETHING...
DRAWN & QUARTERLY
CAN'T WORK! TOO MANY DISTRACTIONS!
IT WAS PRETTY MUCH THE DEFINITION OF HUMBLE BEGINNINGS, BUT IT GREW INTO A COMPANY THAT PUBLISHED BEAUTIFUL BOOKS BY GREAT CARTOONISTS. SOME OF MY FAVOURITE BOOKS!
I GUESS THIS OLD STORE MEANS A LOT TO YOU?
YEAH, I ALSO BOUGHT THE RALPH SNART 3-D SPECTACULAR HERE!
OPEN
JOE OLLMANN 2014
CONGRATULATIONS ON 25 YRS!

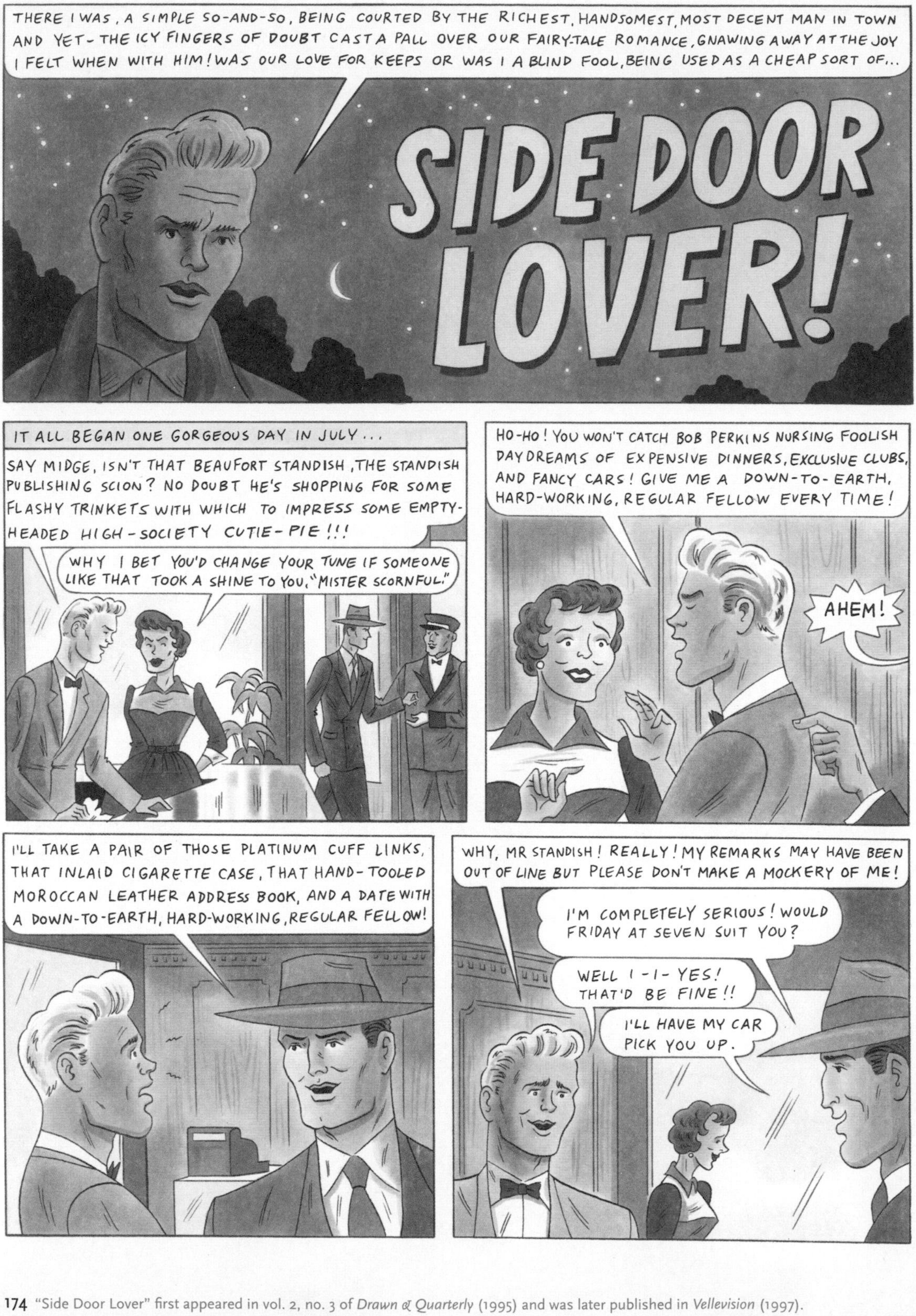
THERE I WAS, A SIMPLE SO-AND-SO, BEING COURTED BY THE RICHEST, HANDSOMEST, MOST DECENT MAN IN TOWN AND YET - THE ICY FINGERS OF DOUBT CAST A PALL OVER OUR FAIRY-TALE ROMANCE, GNAWING AWAY AT THE JOY I FELT WHEN WITH HIM! WAS OUR LOVE FOR KEEPS OR WAS I A BLIND FOOL, BEING USED AS A CHEAP SORT OF...
SIDE DOOR LOVER!
IT ALL BEGAN ONE GORGEOUS DAY IN JULY...
SAY MIDGE, ISN'T THAT BEAUFORT STANDISH, THE STANDISH PUBLISHING SCION? NO DOUBT HE'S SHOPPING FOR SOME FLASHY TRINKETS WITH WHICH TO IMPRESS SOME EMPTY-HEADED HIGH-SOCIETY CUTIE-PIE!!!
WHY I BET YOU'D CHANGE YOUR TUNE IF SOMEONE LIKE THAT TOOK A SHINE TO YOU, "MISTER SCORNFUL."
HO-HO! YOU WON'T CATCH BOB PERKINS NURSING FOOLISH DAYDREAMS OF EXPENSIVE DINNERS, EXCLUSIVE CLUBS, AND FANCY CARS! GIVE ME A DOWN-TO-EARTH, HARD-WORKING, REGULAR FELLOW EVERY TIME!
AHEM!
I'LL TAKE A PAIR OF THOSE PLATINUM CUFF LINKS, THAT INLAID CIGARETTE CASE, THAT HAND-TOOLED MOROCCAN LEATHER ADDRESS BOOK, AND A DATE WITH A DOWN-TO-EARTH, HARD-WORKING, REGULAR FELLOW!
WHY, MR STANDISH! REALLY! MY REMARKS MAY HAVE BEEN OUT OF LINE BUT PLEASE DON'T MAKE A MOCKERY OF ME!
I'M COMPLETELY SERIOUS! WOULD FRIDAY AT SEVEN SUIT YOU?
WELL I-I- YES! THAT'D BE FINE!!
I'LL HAVE MY CAR PICK YOU UP.

 "Side Door Lover" first appeared in vol. 2, no. 3 of *Drawn & Quarterly* (1995) and was later published in *Vellevision* (1997).

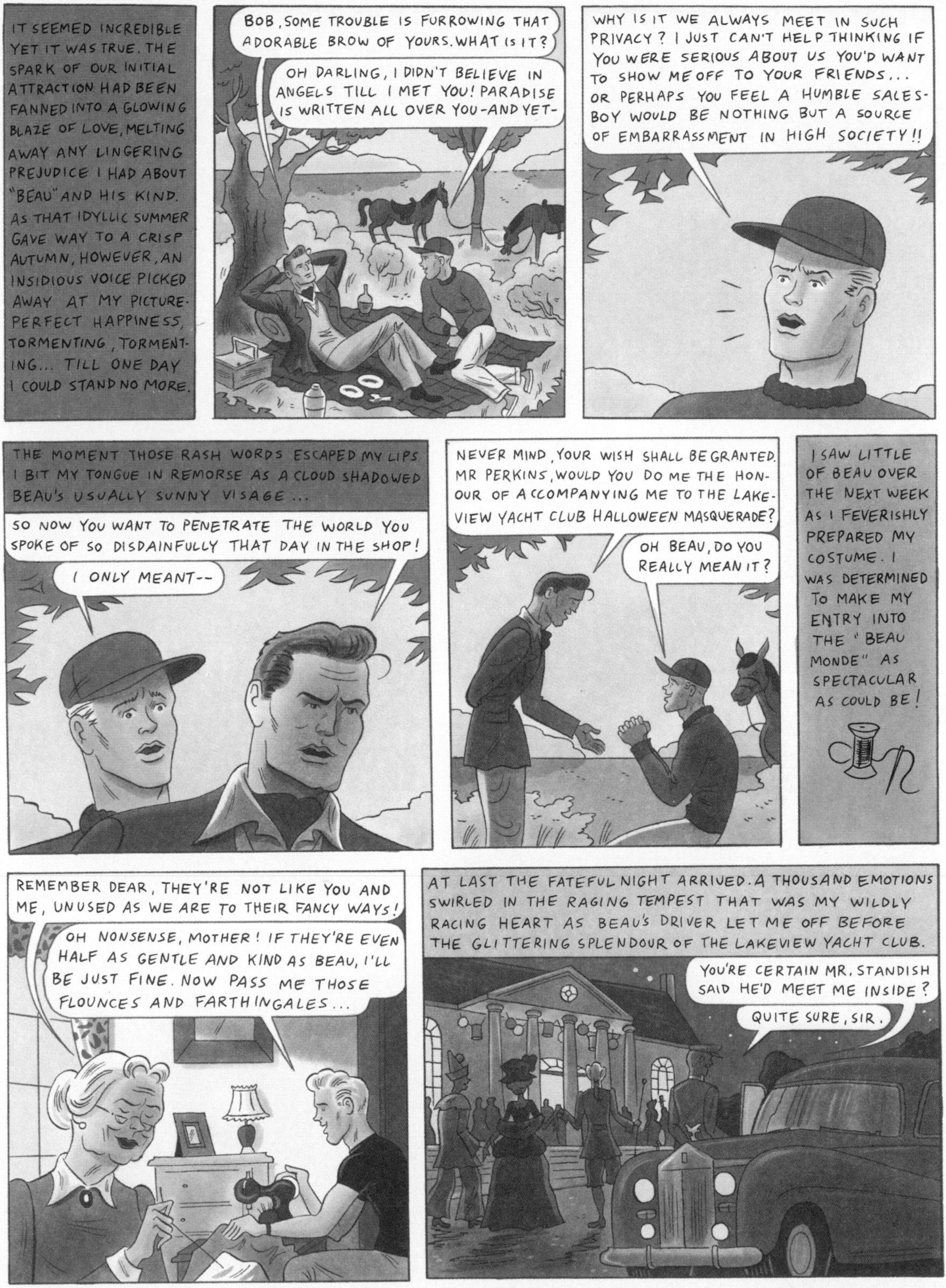
IT SEEMED INCREDIBLE YET IT WAS TRUE. THE SPARK OF OUR INITIAL ATTRACTION HAD BEEN FANNED INTO A GLOWING BLAZE OF LOVE, MELTING AWAY ANY LINGERING PREJUDICE I HAD ABOUT "BEAU" AND HIS KIND. AS THAT IDYLLIC SUMMER GAVE WAY TO A CRISP AUTUMN, HOWEVER, AN INSIDIOUS VOICE PICKED AWAY AT MY PICTURE-PERFECT HAPPINESS, TORMENTING, TORMENTING... TILL ONE DAY I COULD STAND NO MORE.
BOB, SOME TROUBLE IS FURROWING THAT ADORABLE BROW OF YOURS. WHAT IS IT?
OH DARLING, I DIDN'T BELIEVE IN ANGELS TILL I MET YOU! PARADISE IS WRITTEN ALL OVER YOU-AND YET-
WHY IS IT WE ALWAYS MEET IN SUCH PRIVACY? I JUST CAN'T HELP THINKING IF YOU WERE SERIOUS ABOUT US YOU'D WANT TO SHOW ME OFF TO YOUR FRIENDS... OR PERHAPS YOU FEEL A HUMBLE SALES-BOY WOULD BE NOTHING BUT A SOURCE OF EMBARRASSMENT IN HIGH SOCIETY!!
THE MOMENT THOSE RASH WORDS ESCAPED MY LIPS I BIT MY TONGUE IN REMORSE AS A CLOUD SHADOWED BEAU'S USUALLY SUNNY VISAGE...
SO NOW YOU WANT TO PENETRATE THE WORLD YOU SPOKE OF SO DISDAINFULLY THAT DAY IN THE SHOP!
I ONLY MEANT--
NEVER MIND, YOUR WISH SHALL BE GRANTED. MR PERKINS, WOULD YOU DO ME THE HON-OUR OF ACCOMPANYING ME TO THE LAKE-VIEW YACHT CLUB HALLOWEEN MASQUERADE?
OH BEAU, DO YOU REALLY MEAN IT?
I SAW LITTLE OF BEAU OVER THE NEXT WEEK AS I FEVERISHLY PREPARED MY COSTUME. I WAS DETERMINED TO MAKE MY ENTRY INTO THE "BEAU MONDE" AS SPECTACULAR AS COULD BE!
REMEMBER DEAR, THEY'RE NOT LIKE YOU AND ME, UNUSED AS WE ARE TO THEIR FANCY WAYS!
OH NONSENSE, MOTHER! IF THEY'RE EVEN HALF AS GENTLE AND KIND AS BEAU, I'LL BE JUST FINE. NOW PASS ME THOSE FLOUNCES AND FARTHINGALES...
AT LAST THE FATEFUL NIGHT ARRIVED. A THOUSAND EMOTIONS SWIRLED IN THE RAGING TEMPEST THAT WAS MY WILDLY RACING HEART AS BEAU'S DRIVER LET ME OFF BEFORE THE GLITTERING SPLENDOUR OF THE LAKEVIEW YACHT CLUB.
YOU'RE CERTAIN MR. STANDISH SAID HE'D MEET ME INSIDE?
QUITE SURE, SIR.

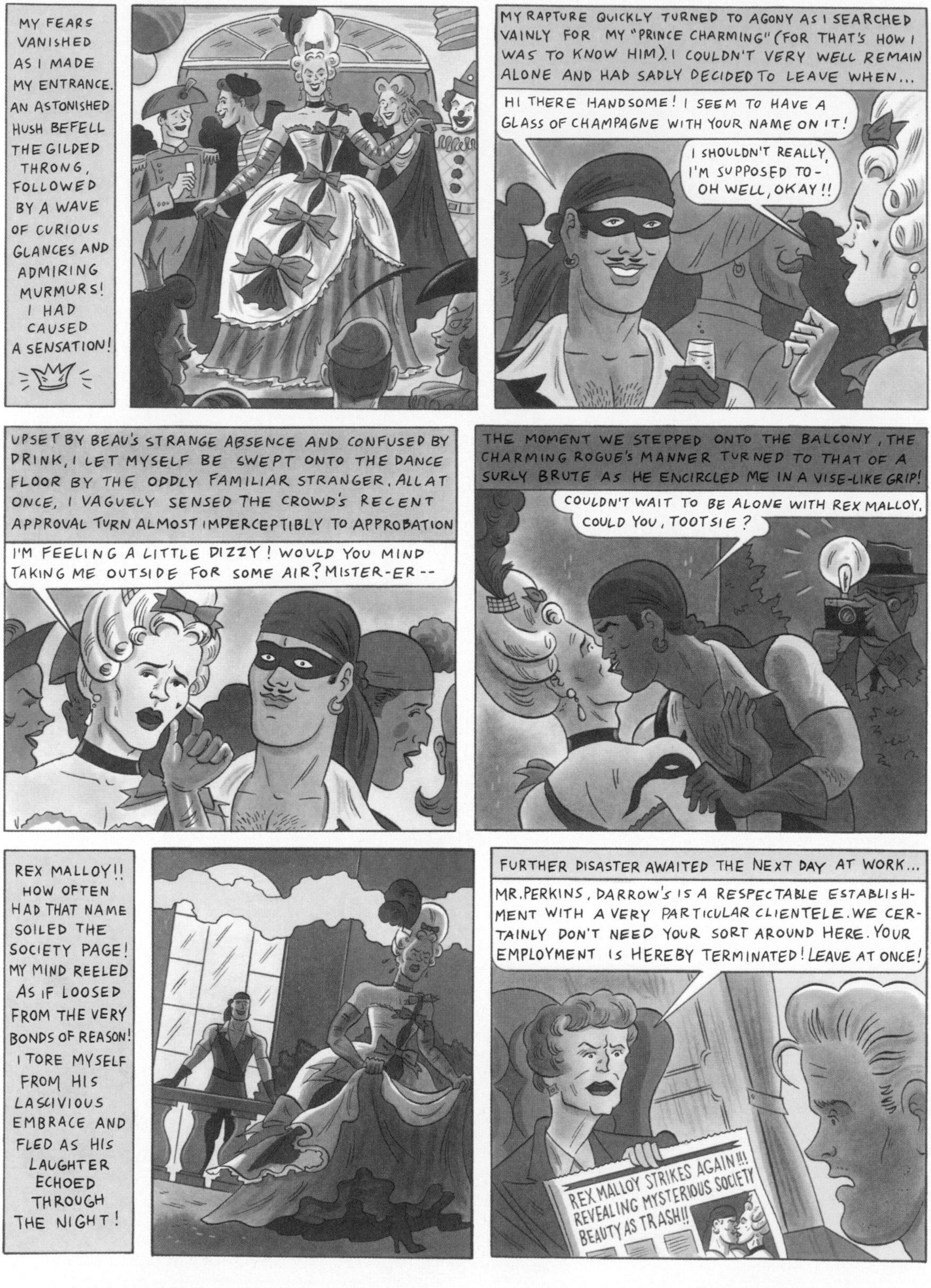

MY FEARS VANISHED AS I MADE MY ENTRANCE. AN ASTONISHED HUSH BEFELL THE GILDED THRONG, FOLLOWED BY A WAVE OF CURIOUS GLANCES AND ADMIRING MURMURS! I HAD CAUSED A SENSATION!
MY RAPTURE QUICKLY TURNED TO AGONY AS I SEARCHED VAINLY FOR MY "PRINCE CHARMING" (FOR THAT'S HOW I WAS TO KNOW HIM). I COULDN'T VERY WELL REMAIN ALONE AND HAD SADLY DECIDED TO LEAVE WHEN...
HI THERE HANDSOME! I SEEM TO HAVE A GLASS OF CHAMPAGNE WITH YOUR NAME ON IT!
I SHOULDN'T REALLY, I'M SUPPOSED TO- OH WELL, OKAY!!
UPSET BY BEAU'S STRANGE ABSENCE AND CONFUSED BY DRINK, I LET MYSELF BE SWEPT ONTO THE DANCE FLOOR BY THE ODDLY FAMILIAR STRANGER. ALL AT ONCE, I VAGUELY SENSED THE CROWD'S RECENT APPROVAL TURN ALMOST IMPERCEPTIBLY TO APPROBATION
I'M FEELING A LITTLE DIZZY! WOULD YOU MIND TAKING ME OUTSIDE FOR SOME AIR? MISTER-ER--
THE MOMENT WE STEPPED ONTO THE BALCONY, THE CHARMING ROGUE'S MANNER TURNED TO THAT OF A SURLY BRUTE AS HE ENCIRCLED ME IN A VISE-LIKE GRIP!
COULDN'T WAIT TO BE ALONE WITH REX MALLOY, COULD YOU, TOOTSIE?
REX MALLOY!! HOW OFTEN HAD THAT NAME SOILED THE SOCIETY PAGE! MY MIND REELED AS IF LOOSED FROM THE VERY BONDS OF REASON! I TORE MYSELF FROM HIS LASCIVIOUS EMBRACE AND FLED AS HIS LAUGHTER ECHOED THROUGH THE NIGHT!
FURTHER DISASTER AWAITED THE NEXT DAY AT WORK...
MR. PERKINS, DARROW'S IS A RESPECTABLE ESTABLISHMENT WITH A VERY PARTICULAR CLIENTELE. WE CERTAINLY DON'T NEED YOUR SORT AROUND HERE. YOUR EMPLOYMENT IS HEREBY TERMINATED! LEAVE AT ONCE!
REX MALLOY STRIKES AGAIN!!! REVEALING MYSTERIOUS SOCIETY BEAUTY AS TRASH!!

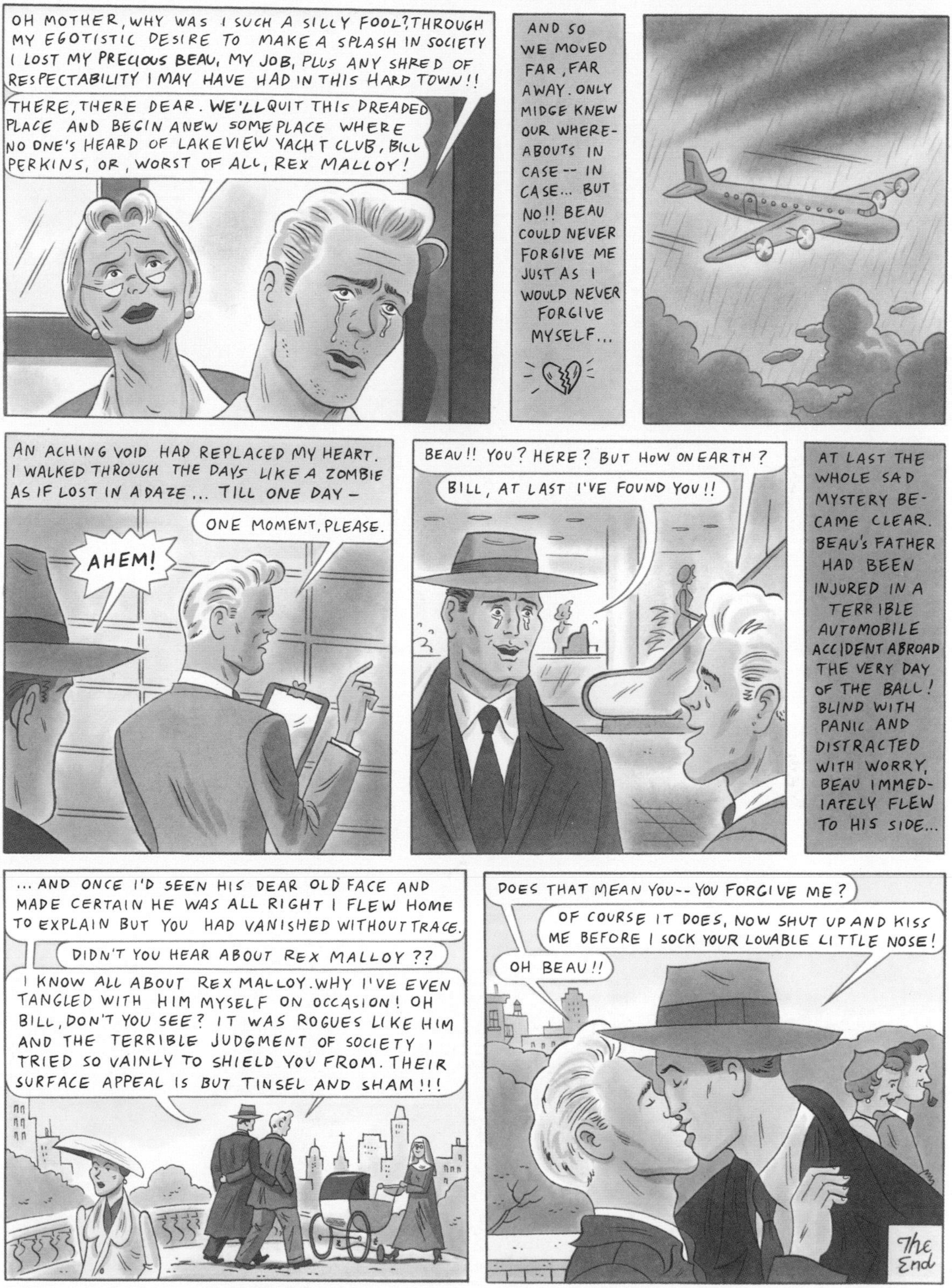
OH MOTHER, WHY WAS I SUCH A SILLY FOOL? THROUGH MY EGOTISTIC DESIRE TO MAKE A SPLASH IN SOCIETY I LOST MY PRECIOUS BEAU, MY JOB, PLUS ANY SHRED OF RESPECTABILITY I MAY HAVE HAD IN THIS HARD TOWN!!
THERE, THERE DEAR. WE'LL QUIT THIS DREADED PLACE AND BEGIN ANEW SOME PLACE WHERE NO ONE'S HEARD OF LAKEVIEW YACHT CLUB, BILL PERKINS, OR, WORST OF ALL, REX MALLOY!
AND SO WE MOVED FAR, FAR AWAY. ONLY MIDGE KNEW OUR WHEREABOUTS IN CASE -- IN CASE... BUT NO!! BEAU COULD NEVER FORGIVE ME JUST AS I WOULD NEVER FORGIVE MYSELF...
AN ACHING VOID HAD REPLACED MY HEART. I WALKED THROUGH THE DAYS LIKE A ZOMBIE AS IF LOST IN A DAZE... TILL ONE DAY –
ONE MOMENT, PLEASE.
AHEM!
BEAU!! YOU? HERE? BUT HOW ON EARTH?
BILL, AT LAST I'VE FOUND YOU!!
AT LAST THE WHOLE SAD MYSTERY BECAME CLEAR. BEAU'S FATHER HAD BEEN INJURED IN A TERRIBLE AUTOMOBILE ACCIDENT ABROAD THE VERY DAY OF THE BALL! BLIND WITH PANIC AND DISTRACTED WITH WORRY, BEAU IMMEDIATELY FLEW TO HIS SIDE...
...AND ONCE I'D SEEN HIS DEAR OLD FACE AND MADE CERTAIN HE WAS ALL RIGHT I FLEW HOME TO EXPLAIN BUT YOU HAD VANISHED WITHOUT TRACE.
DIDN'T YOU HEAR ABOUT REX MALLOY??
I KNOW ALL ABOUT REX MALLOY. WHY I'VE EVEN TANGLED WITH HIM MYSELF ON OCCASION! OH BILL, DON'T YOU SEE? IT WAS ROGUES LIKE HIM AND THE TERRIBLE JUDGMENT OF SOCIETY I TRIED SO VAINLY TO SHIELD YOU FROM. THEIR SURFACE APPEAL IS BUT TINSEL AND SHAM!!!
DOES THAT MEAN YOU-- YOU FORGIVE ME?
OF COURSE IT DOES, NOW SHUT UP AND KISS ME BEFORE I SOCK YOUR LOVABLE LITTLE NOSE!
OH BEAU!!
The End

JAMES STURM'S HARD, OLD WORLD

an appreciation by Noel Murray

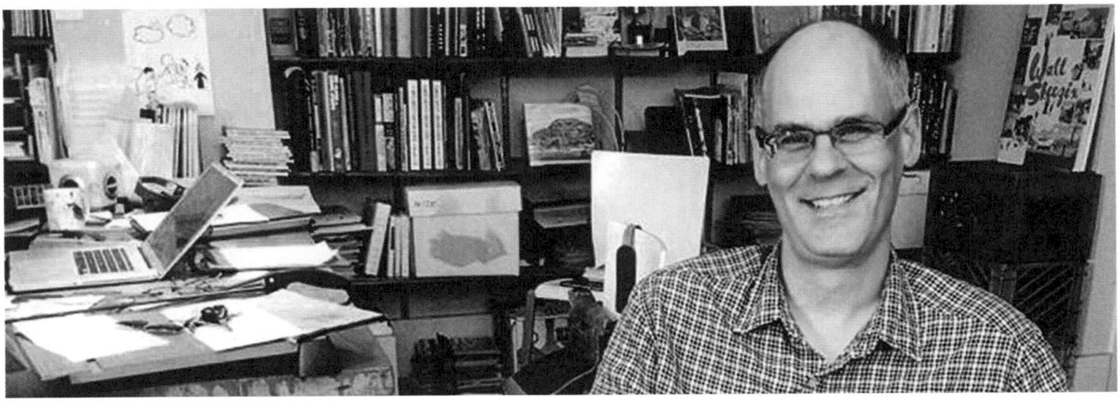

Open to any page in *Market Day*. Here's Mendleman, the weaver, counting his steps as he leads his horse and cart into town, comparing the rhythm of his feet to the reassuring this-follows-that of making a rug. Here's Mendleman regarding the first pink sliver of dawn and wondering if he could capture those colours and feelings in a textile. Here's Mendleman meeting up again with Rabbi Soyer and remembering their past conversation about the exact moment when the Sabbath begins. Here's Mendleman, dejected after a day of failing to sell his wares, thinking to himself, "I keep moving but to what end?" And here's James Sturm, the man behind *Market Day*, taking all of these threads of Mendleman's life and thoughts and stitching them together, one panel at a time, assembling a subdued, potent statement about the painstaking processes of making and selling art.

Sturm may not be the most prolific or the highest-profile cartoonist of his generation, but he's become one of the most influential. As the co-founder and director of the Center for Cartoon Studies, Sturm has stood up for the idea that comics are both a vital art form and a viable trade. The Sturm-written children's book series Adventures in Cartooning (drawn by CCS alums) has introduced countless kids to comics' creative possibilities. Sturm's Eisner-winning Marvel miniseries *Fantastic Four: Unstable Molecules* takes superhero mainstays and reframes them, making familiar characters seem more fragile and poignant. All of these projects are connected by their eagerness to teach, to inspire, and to reveal.

But it's in Sturm's major pieces—2010's *Market Day* and the three stories collected in 2007's *James Sturm's America: God, Gold, and Golems*—that he directly engages with what drives someone like Mendleman to get up and keep moving. Sturm considers what animates us, be it religious faith, or prejudice, or artistic inspiration. And Sturm does this while working in a style of illustration that looks convincingly archaic, akin to woodcut prints dug out of some forgotten archive. He's like the steward of lost knowledge.

Consider *The Revival*, the 1996 story that's part 1 of Sturm's *America* triptych. The comic follows a married couple in search of a miracle at a Kentucky religious camp meeting in 1801. Joseph and Sarah Bainbridge are travelling with the corpse of their daughter, Emma, recently bitten by a snake. Sturm withholds that grim little detail until the end, when Sarah presents Emma's body to evangelist/healer Elijah Young and asks him to bring her back. This is an older, alien America—drawn by Sturm so that characters look distorted and at times crazed—so for a moment, Sturm leaves open the possibility that Young is *not* a huckster, and that Emma might be resurrected. In one panel, Sturm even shows Emma's tiny hand moving up Sarah's arm. But the next panel is pitch black, shutting down the miracle. The morning after going to see Elijah, Joseph buries Emma, and he and Sarah make plans to press on to Missouri and start a new life.

 Photo: Charlotte Albright (2014).

This ends up being the real revival in *The Revival*: that the Bainbridges can let their daughter go and find hope in a new start. Sarah even expresses a Christian devotion to Joseph's assurances that they can do well in Missouri, using the words "I believe we can" as she adjusts her expectations. The final image of *The Revival* is fairly ambiguous, though. A tired Joseph and Sarah are boxed into a panel with the top of their cooking pot right below them like a dark hole that they could easily fall into, following Emma.

The third part of Sturm's *America* is also his best-known work, the 2001 graphic novella *The Golem's Mighty Swing*—another comic about the intersection of religious fervour and everyday life. Set in the early 1920s, *The Golem's Mighty Swing* is about a barnstorming Jewish baseball team, the Stars of David, who try to boost attendance by casting one of their players as a mythical giant and end up unleashing a small town's racist fury. Throughout the book, the players swap anecdotes and tall tales, which Sturm draws with darker shading and dynamic poses, making their stories look more like legends. Meanwhile, Sturm contrasts the ordinariness of the Stars—their petty concerns, their vulgar exchanges—with the way they try to make money by playing up the exoticism of their race. *The Golem's Mighty Swing* is a masterfully layered text, which can be read as a rollicking look back at early-twentieth-century baseball or as a carefully constructed argument against turning real people into cartoons.

But the trickiest book in *America* is the middle one, 1998's *Hundreds of Feet Below Daylight*. Because it's a study of greed and racism in an 1880s mining community, the comic is awash in deep, deep blacks and populated by craggy, unpleasant characters. Of all the pieces in *James Sturm's America*, *Hundreds of Feet Below Daylight* is the lightest on hope, and it's all but devoid of visual beauty. Like so many of Sturm's comics, *Hundreds Of Feet Below Daylight* establishes a straightforward realism early on in its artwork, which gives Sturm the power to jolt the reader with sequences that are more fantastical or emotional. But the effect of the plainness here is to normalize the violence and virulence of the past. The story's central metaphor is digging: the miners dig, and at one point a doctor searches deep within a sick man's mind. If Sturm means to dig into the roots of his country with this comic (the heart of his *America*), he unearths only ugliness and avarice.

Sturm doesn't write and draw what anyone would call "feel-good" comics. His heroes don't find what they're looking for, and the worlds Sturm builds on the page are hard edged to the point of being forbidding. Look again at *Market Day*. Sturm draws Mendleman as stooped, and the skies above him as cloudy. This is a book about gradual, inevitable transitions—be it day to night or success to failure. Mendleman's trip winds from home to town and back again, but the road really leads him to a conclusion he's been dreading: that he's going to have to quit his business.

And yet, formally, *Market Day* is so exciting that even at its bleakest it's a pleasure to read. Sturm sometimes illustrates Mendleman's interior monologues with moody, scene-setting landscape sketches, sometimes with vivid flashbacks, or with pure abstractions that speak to Mendleman's interest in turning life's fleeting moments into rugs. By the end of the book, Sturm is subdividing single pictures into multiple panels, literally tearing Mendleman apart—while simultaneously carrying forward *Market Day*'s motif of lines that separate one state of being from another. As Mendleman convinces himself that his time as an artist is done, Sturm makes the case with his own expressive, inventive art that creativity is its own reward.

Market Day is so precise about its situation, its characters, and its place that it's not hard to imagine it as a much longer novel that Sturm is merely excerpting. This is another of Sturm's hallmarks: this fullness that extends beyond the page. *The Revival*, for example, barely explores the revival meeting itself. Sturm's more interested in the Bainbridges and their distant relations, who each seem to be getting something different out of the experience. The kids are excited by all the hubbub, while the husbands fret over setting up tents and the women gush over their favourite evangelists (like teenyboppers at a rock 'n' roll show). The characters' reactions paint a larger picture.

Sturm's characters may lead stark lives, but his comics are far from austere. The thought and research that have gone into *The Golem's Mighty Swing* and *Hundreds of Feet Below Daylight* are evident in the wealth of tiny observations about how people once lived—and more importantly, how they felt. It's not hard to "get" James Sturm. Once again, open to any page in *Market Day*. Follow Mendleman's trains of thought. See his world through Sturm's eyes. And feel about these comics the way that Mendleman feels about the market: "First and foremost," he says, "I love the abundance."

Noel Murray is a contributing writer at the Dissolve and the A.V. Club who has written about film, television, music, and comics for a number of online and print publications, including Nashville Scene, the Hollywood Reporter, the Los Angeles Times, and Rolling Stone.

THE SPONSOR

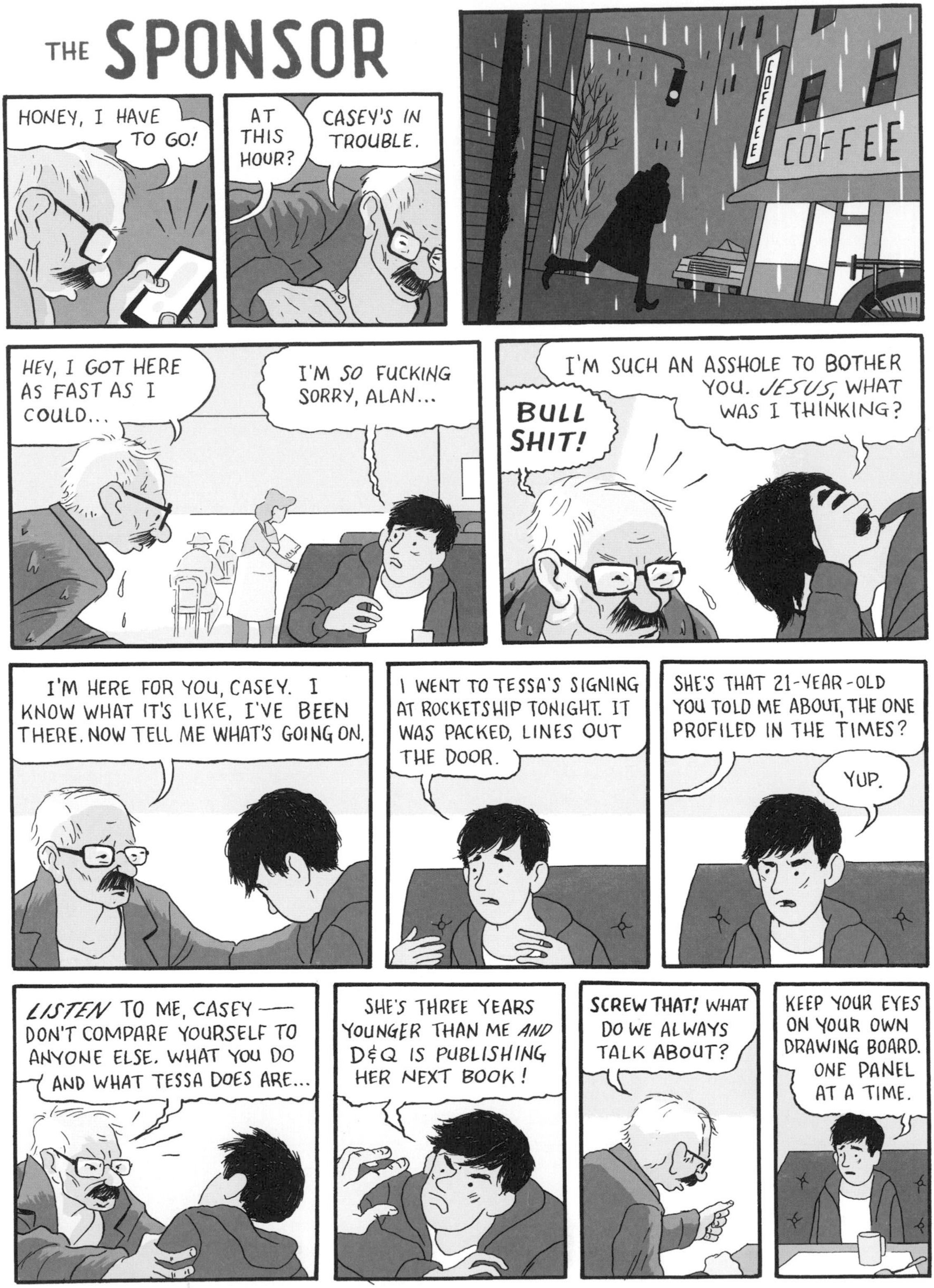

HONEY, I HAVE TO GO!
AT THIS HOUR?
CASEY'S IN TROUBLE.
COFFEE
COFFEE
HEY, I GOT HERE AS FAST AS I COULD...
I'M *SO* FUCKING SORRY, ALAN...
I'M SUCH AN ASSHOLE TO BOTHER YOU. *JESUS*, WHAT WAS I THINKING?
BULL SHIT!
I'M HERE FOR YOU, CASEY. I KNOW WHAT IT'S LIKE, I'VE BEEN THERE. NOW TELL ME WHAT'S GOING ON.
I WENT TO TESSA'S SIGNING AT ROCKETSHIP TONIGHT. IT WAS PACKED, LINES OUT THE DOOR.
SHE'S THAT 21-YEAR-OLD YOU TOLD ME ABOUT, THE ONE PROFILED IN THE TIMES?
YUP.
LISTEN TO ME, CASEY — DON'T COMPARE YOURSELF TO ANYONE ELSE. WHAT YOU DO AND WHAT TESSA DOES ARE...
SHE'S THREE YEARS YOUNGER THAN ME *AND* D&Q IS PUBLISHING HER NEXT BOOK!
SCREW THAT! WHAT DO WE ALWAYS TALK ABOUT?
KEEP YOUR EYES ON YOUR OWN DRAWING BOARD. ONE PANEL AT A TIME.

 An abridged version of this comic originally appeared on the *Nib* (2014).

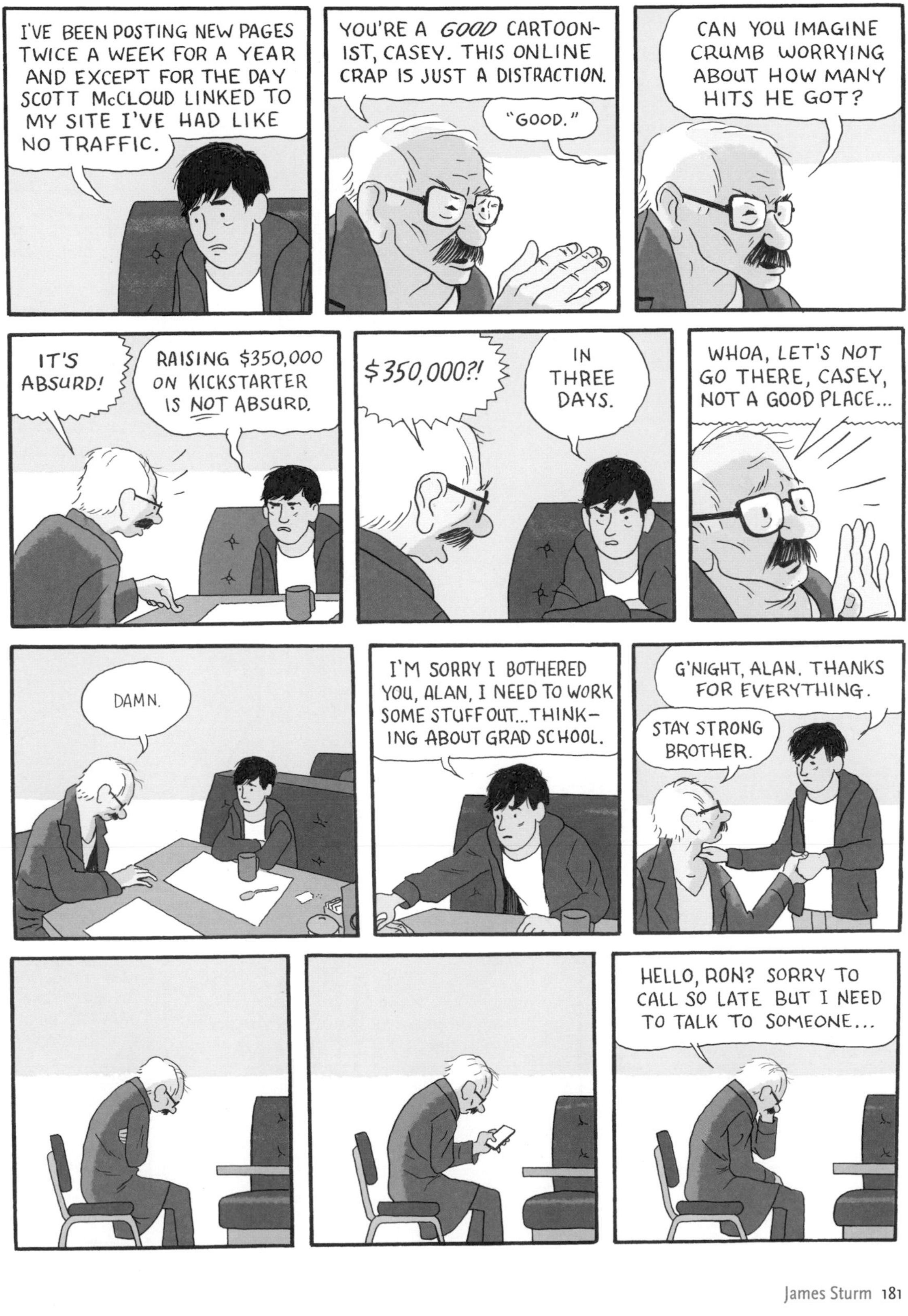
I'VE BEEN POSTING NEW PAGES TWICE A WEEK FOR A YEAR AND EXCEPT FOR THE DAY SCOTT McCLOUD LINKED TO MY SITE I'VE HAD LIKE NO TRAFFIC.
YOU'RE A *GOOD* CARTOON-IST, CASEY. THIS ONLINE CRAP IS JUST A DISTRACTION.
"GOOD."
CAN YOU IMAGINE CRUMB WORRYING ABOUT HOW MANY HITS HE GOT?
IT'S ABSURD!
RAISING $350,000 ON KICKSTARTER IS NOT ABSURD.
$350,000?!
IN THREE DAYS.
WHOA, LET'S NOT GO THERE, CASEY, NOT A GOOD PLACE...
DAMN.
I'M SORRY I BOTHERED YOU, ALAN, I NEED TO WORK SOME STUFF OUT...THINK-ING ABOUT GRAD SCHOOL.
G'NIGHT, ALAN. THANKS FOR EVERYTHING.
STAY STRONG BROTHER.
HELLO, RON? SORRY TO CALL SO LATE BUT I NEED TO TALK TO SOMEONE...

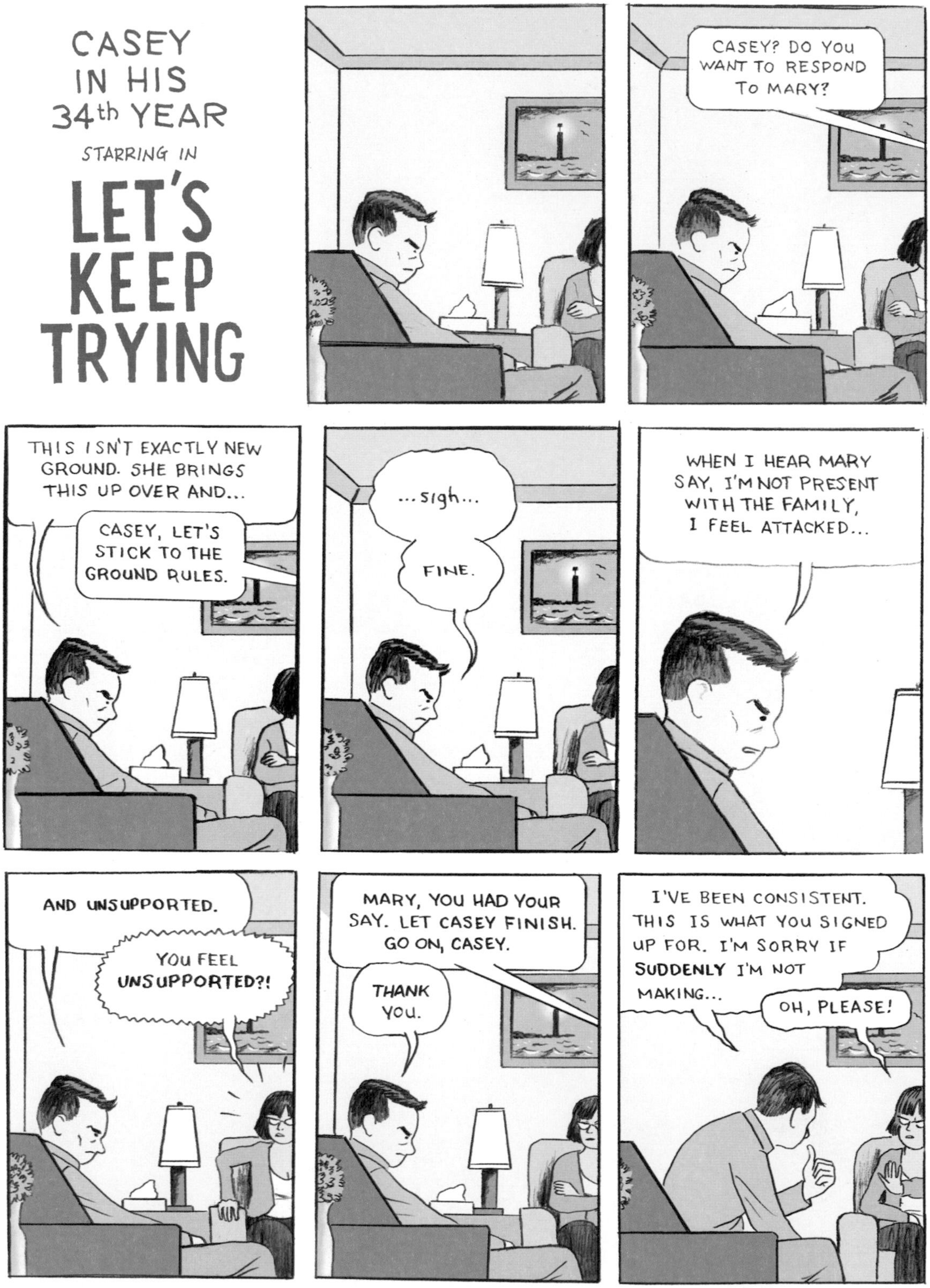
CASEY IN HIS 34th YEAR
STARRING IN
LET'S KEEP TRYING
CASEY? DO YOU WANT TO RESPOND TO MARY?
THIS ISN'T EXACTLY NEW GROUND. SHE BRINGS THIS UP OVER AND...
CASEY, LET'S STICK TO THE GROUND RULES.
...sigh...
FINE.
WHEN I HEAR MARY SAY, I'M NOT PRESENT WITH THE FAMILY, I FEEL ATTACKED...
AND UNSUPPORTED.
YOU FEEL UNSUPPORTED?!
MARY, YOU HAD YOUR SAY. LET CASEY FINISH. GO ON, CASEY.
THANK YOU.
I'VE BEEN CONSISTENT. THIS IS WHAT YOU SIGNED UP FOR. I'M SORRY IF SUDDENLY I'M NOT MAKING...
OH, PLEASE!

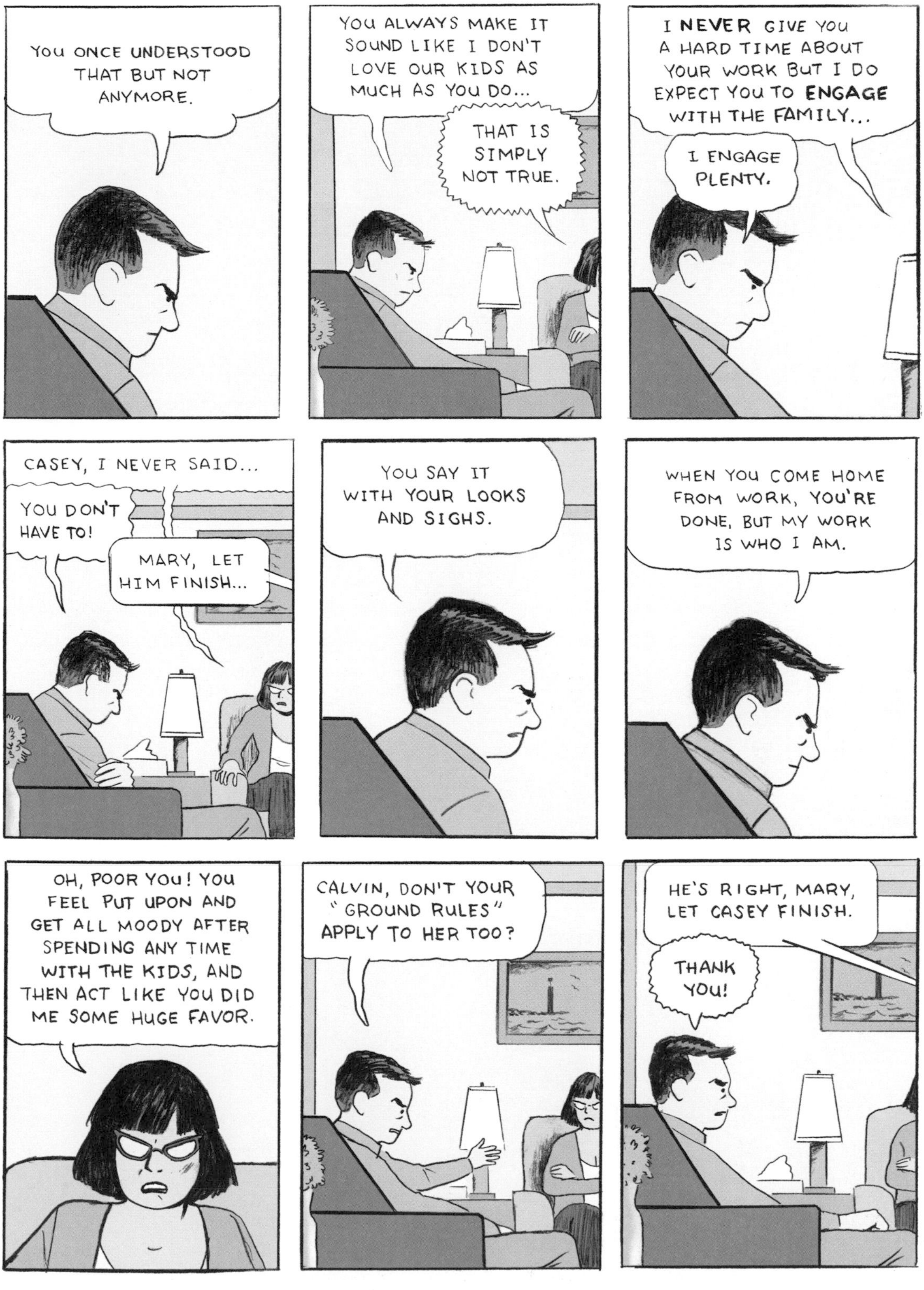
YOU ONCE UNDERSTOOD THAT BUT NOT ANYMORE.
YOU ALWAYS MAKE IT SOUND LIKE I DON'T LOVE OUR KIDS AS MUCH AS YOU DO...
THAT IS SIMPLY NOT TRUE.
I NEVER GIVE YOU A HARD TIME ABOUT YOUR WORK BUT I DO EXPECT YOU TO ENGAGE WITH THE FAMILY...
I ENGAGE PLENTY.
CASEY, I NEVER SAID...
YOU DON'T HAVE TO!
MARY, LET HIM FINISH...
YOU SAY IT WITH YOUR LOOKS AND SIGHS.
WHEN YOU COME HOME FROM WORK, YOU'RE DONE, BUT MY WORK IS WHO I AM.
OH, POOR YOU! YOU FEEL PUT UPON AND GET ALL MOODY AFTER SPENDING ANY TIME WITH THE KIDS, AND THEN ACT LIKE YOU DID ME SOME HUGE FAVOR.
CALVIN, DON'T YOUR "GROUND RULES" APPLY TO HER TOO?
HE'S RIGHT, MARY, LET CASEY FINISH.
THANK YOU!

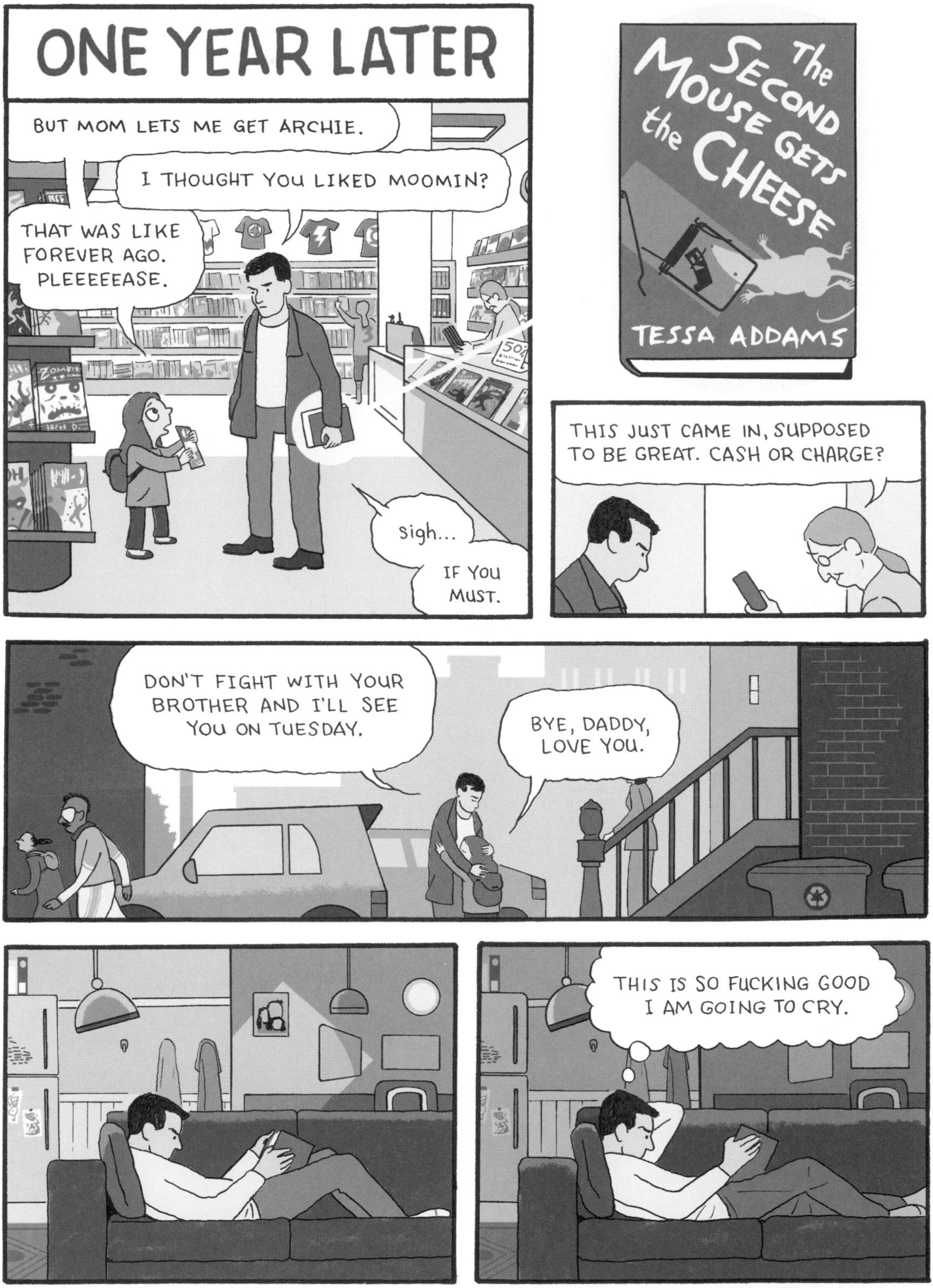
ONE YEAR LATER
BUT MOM LETS ME GET ARCHIE.
I THOUGHT YOU LIKED MOOMIN?
THAT WAS LIKE FOREVER AGO. PLEEEEEASE.
sigh...
IF YOU MUST.
The SECOND MOUSE GETS the CHEESE
TESSA ADDAMS
THIS JUST CAME IN, SUPPOSED TO BE GREAT. CASH OR CHARGE?
DON'T FIGHT WITH YOUR BROTHER AND I'LL SEE YOU ON TUESDAY.
BYE, DADDY, LOVE YOU.
THIS IS SO FUCKING GOOD I AM GOING TO CRY.

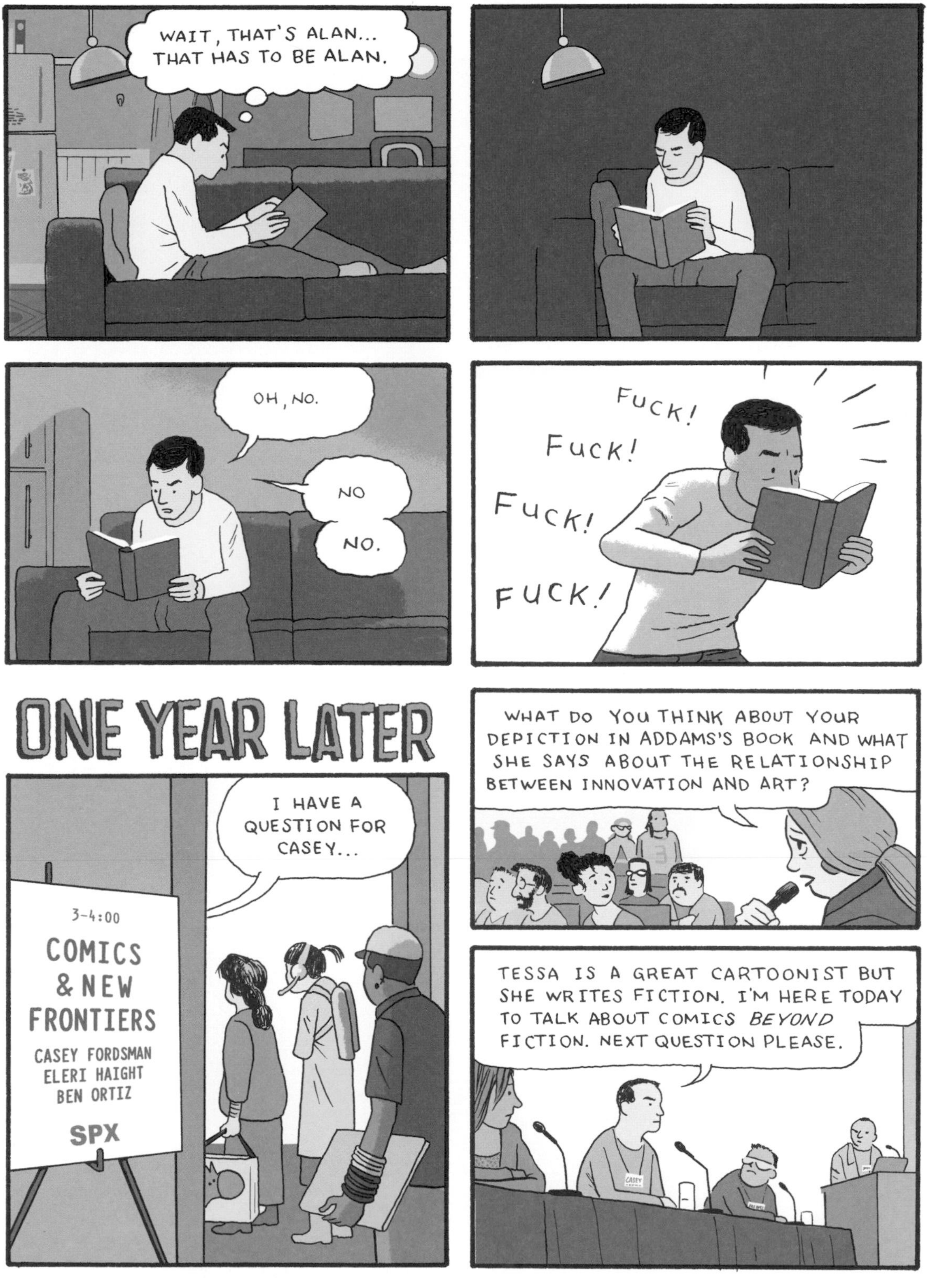
WAIT, THAT'S ALAN... THAT HAS TO BE ALAN.
OH, NO.
NO
NO.
FUCK!
Fuck!
Fuck!
FUCK!
ONE YEAR LATER
I HAVE A QUESTION FOR CASEY...
3-4:00
COMICS & NEW FRONTIERS
CASEY FORDSMAN
ELERI HAIGHT
BEN ORTIZ
SPX
WHAT DO YOU THINK ABOUT YOUR DEPICTION IN ADDAMS'S BOOK AND WHAT SHE SAYS ABOUT THE RELATIONSHIP BETWEEN INNOVATION AND ART?
TESSA IS A GREAT CARTOONIST BUT SHE WRITES FICTION. I'M HERE TODAY TO TALK ABOUT COMICS BEYOND FICTION. NEXT QUESTION PLEASE.

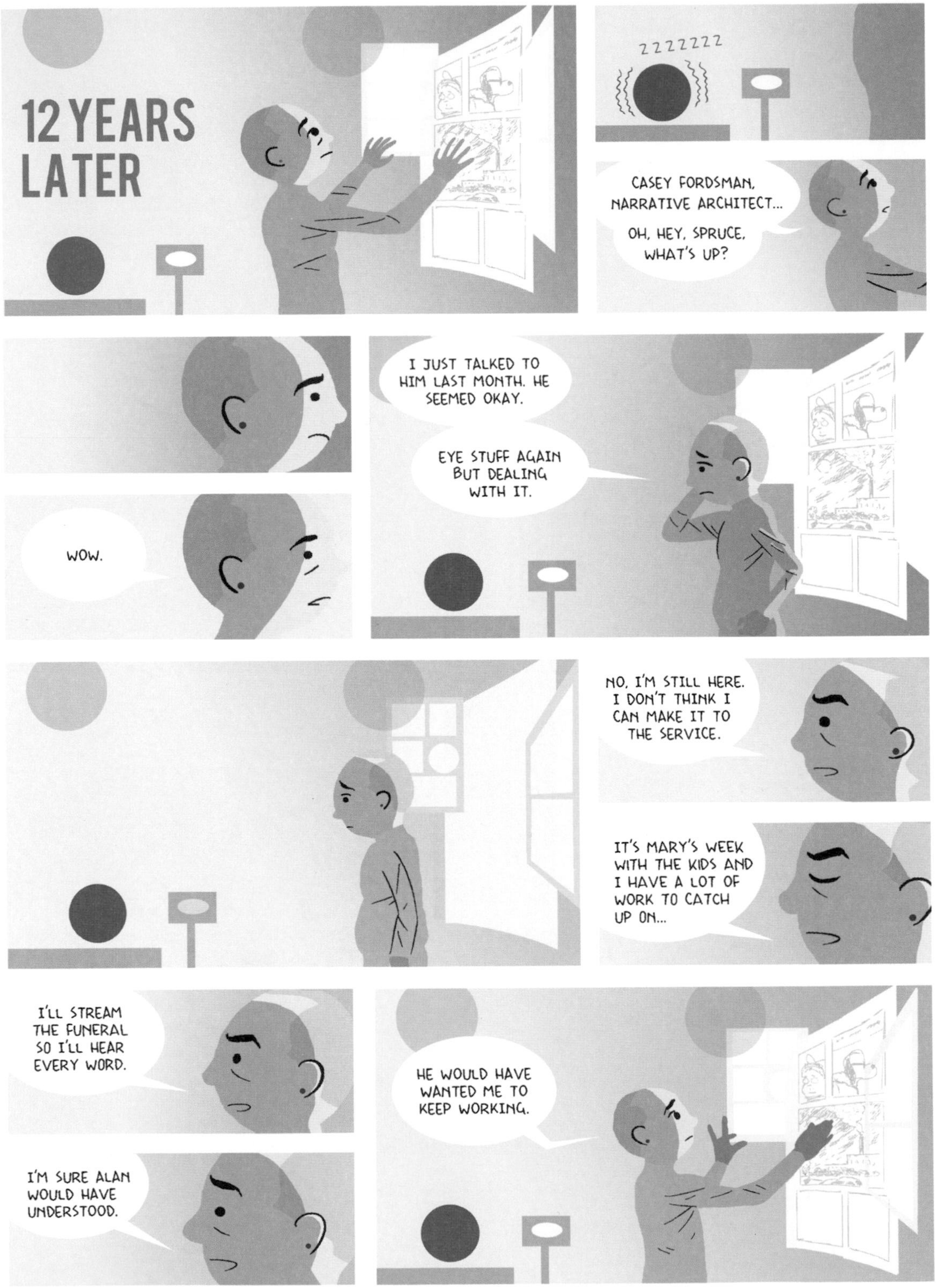

12 YEARS LATER
ZZZZZZZ
CASEY FORDSMAN, NARRATIVE ARCHITECT...
OH, HEY, SPRUCE, WHAT'S UP?
WOW.
I JUST TALKED TO HIM LAST MONTH. HE SEEMED OKAY.
EYE STUFF AGAIN BUT DEALING WITH IT.
NO, I'M STILL HERE. I DON'T THINK I CAN MAKE IT TO THE SERVICE.
IT'S MARY'S WEEK WITH THE KIDS AND I HAVE A LOT OF WORK TO CATCH UP ON...
I'LL STREAM THE FUNERAL SO I'LL HEAR EVERY WORD.
I'M SURE ALAN WOULD HAVE UNDERSTOOD.
HE WOULD HAVE WANTED ME TO KEEP WORKING.

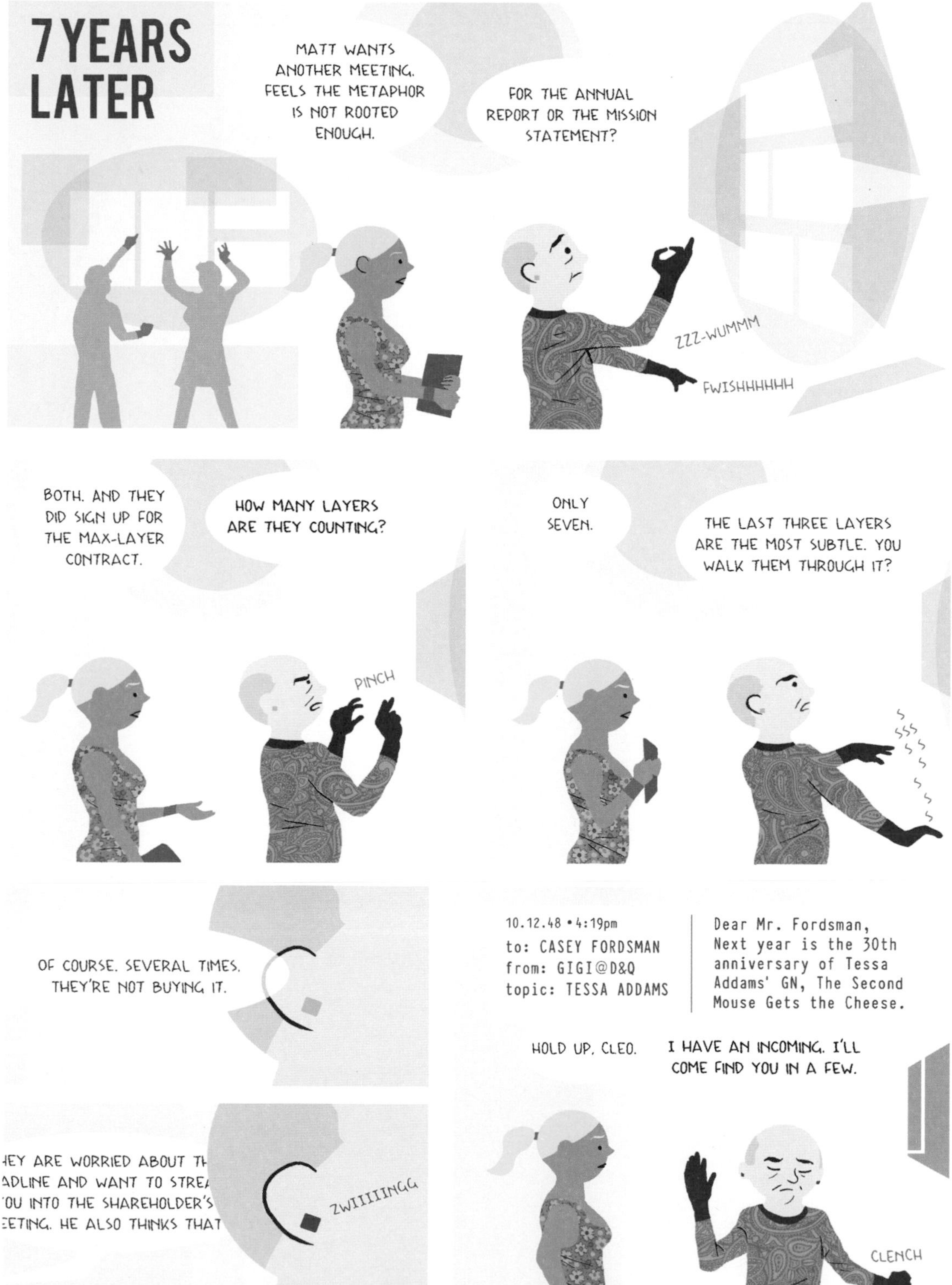
7 YEARS LATER
MATT WANTS ANOTHER MEETING. FEELS THE METAPHOR IS NOT ROOTED ENOUGH.
FOR THE ANNUAL REPORT OR THE MISSION STATEMENT?
ZZZ-WUMMM
FWISHHHHHH
BOTH. AND THEY DID SIGN UP FOR THE MAX-LAYER CONTRACT.
HOW MANY LAYERS ARE THEY COUNTING?
PINCH
ONLY SEVEN.
THE LAST THREE LAYERS ARE THE MOST SUBTLE. YOU WALK THEM THROUGH IT?
OF COURSE. SEVERAL TIMES. THEY'RE NOT BUYING IT.
HEY ARE WORRIED ABOUT TH
ADLINE AND WANT TO STREA
OU INTO THE SHAREHOLDER'S
EETING. HE ALSO THINKS THAT
ZWIIIIINGG
10.12.48 • 4:19pm
to: CASEY FORDSMAN
from: GIGI@D&Q
topic: TESSA ADDAMS
Dear Mr. Fordsman, Next year is the 30th anniversary of Tessa Addams' GN, The Second Mouse Gets the Cheese.
HOLD UP, CLEO.
I HAVE AN INCOMING. I'LL COME FIND YOU IN A FEW.
CLENCH

We are reaching out to cartoonists in hopes that they will contribute to an anthology to celebrate this enduring classic. As the cartoonist who inspired the character "Second Mouse," we would love to include your work in the book.

In Addition, all proceeds from the book will go towards Tessa's mounting medical expenses. Thanks for considering this request.

Please let me know if you have any questions or concerns. –GIGI

ZWAAAAH

JEEZ...

I'M FINALLY GOING TO BE PUBLISHED BY DRAWN AND QUARTERLY.

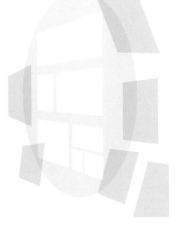

IT WILL GET DONE

an appreciation of Jason Lutes by Robert Boyd

Jason Lutes didn't expect a car to pull out of its hidden driveway as he sped downhill on his bike in Seattle in 1991. The next time I saw him was in the hospital, minus his spleen. I was visiting him with *Comics Journal* editor Frank Young. We had both become aware of him through his minicomics, and I got to know him better when he interned with Fantagraphics the previous summer. After the accident, he called up Fantagraphics co-owner Kim Thompson from his hospital bed to ask for work. "I'm pretty sure I guilt-tripped him into giving me a job," he said.

Lutes started publishing minicomics as an undergrad studying art at the Rhode Island School of Design. His Penny Dreadful Press put out nineteen minicomics in all. Many of the cartoonists whose work defined the art of comics in the nineties started out this way—Lutes, Adrian Tomine, Jessica Abel, James Kochalka, Matt Madden, etc. It was my desire to see this kind of work as soon as it was created that led me to start my column, Minimalism, in the *Comics Journal*. I felt lucky to have a nascent talent like Lutes in the office, but he was never totally happy there. After about a year, he quit. He had to have additional surgery for his spleen, and as he was recovering, James Sturm offered him part-time paste-up work at Seattle's new weekly paper, the *Stranger*, to help him get back on his feet. By this point, Lutes was burnt out on comics. The alternative comics subculture seemed provincial, embattled, and sexist. He was considering the possibilities of performance and multimedia art.

But it seems that Sturm—like me, like Frank Young, like his friend Ed Brubaker—recognized that Jason Lutes was a natural-born cartoonist. And Sturm was in an ideal position to do something about it. Sturm offered Lutes the

---

Jason Lutes was my first cartoonist friend. I know how to pick 'em, don't I? I found him quite haphazardly. I had graduated from college and was back in my hometown of Seattle trying to work a job, draw comics, and figure out my life. Although vaguely aware of Fantagraphics, I was oblivious to the teeming hordes of cartoonists in my city. I complained to my sister that I felt alone and that I would really like to meet another female cartoonist. A few months later, she told me that her friend's housemate's boss's girlfriend was a cartoonist, and perhaps through the housemate, I could meet the girlfriend. The housemate was Jason. The boss was Gary Groth and the girlfriend was Julie Doucet. Eventually I met them all, but Jason became my lifelong friend and mentor.

Looking back on it, Jason pretty much taught me how to draw comics. When I met him I was muddling along in self-imposed ignorance of the comics language. The building blocks of classic American cartooning—word balloons, sound effects, important words and phrases in all caps and bold—looked so cheesy to me. I was trying to draw comics without what I considered to be all that cheese, so I eschewed panel borders and word balloons altogether. You will not be surprised to hear my comics were a little confusing to read. Through his own gorgeous clear line work, Jason demonstrated many important lessons to me. First, that there is no need for a lot of complicated crosshatching or messing with grey tones: you can do everything you need to do with black and white. You don't have to letter in all caps. He showed me that you must figure out first what something really looks like before you can simplify it, and that the building blocks of the comics language needn't look cheesy. He taught me about silent panels, and those word balloons with no words but just an ellipsis that mean...who knows, exactly? A broken line can indicate that something is far away, or an edge that catches the light. He showed me how scattered dashes and dots can make things look old and worn out. He showed me Tintin.

Soon Jason and I were meeting regularly, sometimes to draw and sometimes to just hang out or go to comics events like signings and Fantagraphics parties. One afternoon he gave me a quick lesson on perspective, which I have never forgotten. He introduced me to other cartoonists: James Sturm, Jon Lewis,

(Next page) This is a string of thumbnails for *Berlin*. They are in fact pretty small but not this small.

opportunity to draw a weekly comic strip, giving him carte blanche on the content. And Lutes used this opportunity to tell the kind of story that answered some of his misgivings about the state of alternative comics—a story affirming that they could reach beyond the post-underground holding pen where they seemed stuck; that "comics-as-art" was a suitable goal; that there was an untapped readership out there if cartoonists were willing to reach out to it.

This strip was *Jar of Fools*, the story of Ernie Weiss, a young magician (of the stage type, not the Harry Potter type) whose brother has committed suicide and whose girlfriend has left him. At the time it was published, it wasn't so obvious, but now it seems clear that Lutes was thinking about stage magic as a metaphor for comics. He seemed to be wondering if it had reached its end as a viable art form. But even as it asked the question, *Jar of Fools* was its own answer. Comics had a right to exist and *Jar of Fools* proved it. In 1994, Lutes received a Xeric grant to publish the first half of *Jar of Fools* as a book. The second volume was published in 1995. It was unlike almost anything in comics at the time—a realistic,

novelistic, contemporary story not based on a set of ongoing characters. The world of comics as art had been moving in this direction for years, but the economic logic of comic-book serialization was still quite strong.

As Lutes was finishing *Jar of Fools*, he was already thinking about what he wanted to do next. "I wanted it to be big," he thought. "To have a thick spine…I wanted to get out of myself." While *Jar of Fools* had been fictional, Lutes had come to regard it as "semi-autobiographical navel-gazing." He saw an ad for *Bertolt Brecht's Berlin* (1993) in the *Nation*. He acquired a copy, which sparked his interest in Weimar-era Berlin. *Berlin* began as a comic-book series (a concept that now seems like a quaint anachronism for art comics). Initially published by Black Eye, it was picked up by Drawn & Quarterly after the former publisher shut its doors. The first collected edition, *City of Stones*, was published in 2000, followed by *City of Smoke* in 2008. The book is a kaleidoscope of the city with a huge number of characters and many distinct storylines. Lutes seemed determined not to have an alter ego for himself among the characters—there is no Ernie Weiss in *Berlin*.

David Lasky, Ed Brubaker, and eventually Tom Hart and Ellen Forney. He told me about the newly minted Xeric Foundation, which promised to award thousands of dollars to self-publishing cartoonists in order to help them make professional-looking books. By this time, Jennifer Daydreamer and Lin Lucas had joined our ranks; we had become a gang of cartoonist pals, almost all of us self-publishing Xeric grant recipients or applicants. We basically hung out all the time, mostly talking about comics and gathering periodically to share and critique each other's work. We also spent a lot of time just drinking beer and hanging out. If we hung out long and late enough, inevitably (to my dismay) the conversation would turn to Jack Kirby.

We few, we happy few, we band of Seattle cartoonists shared with each other everything we knew about self-publishing: distributors, how to prepare your book for the printers, how to conduct a mail-order operation, who the friendly retailers were. There was so much to know, and the only way to find out was to

have friends like Jason and the others who were connected to networks of cartoonists around the country. We pooled our resources to attend comics shows and shared tables, and then we started imagining an anthology. It would be a home for all of our work—short stories, or serialized episodes of longer works. I can't remember if Lasky or Lutes came up with the name *Story Ark*. With our combined talents we would conquer the world! Tom Hart had the ear of a poet and a talent for finding good cartoonists. Lasky had the best hatching technique and a knack for fostering collaboration. James Sturm was all bold, thick brushstrokes and Ellen Forney had the most excellent lettering. Both of them had talent for expanding opportunities for cartoonists and promoting comics to the wider world. Jon Lewis and Tom Hart were the funny ones. Jennifer, with the airy line, was the lyrical one. Lin saw political and educational potential for the kind of comics we did. I was really good at throwing parties. But let's face it, Jason was the best-known and

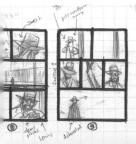      

Notably, many of the characters are women: Marthe Müller, the closest thing to a main character; her fellow art student Anna; the decadent Margarethe; the working-class girl Sylvia and her doomed mother; etc. Their stories weave in and out of one another, as well as the story of journalist Kurt Severing, who grows more disillusioned by the day as Weimar slowly comes unravelled.

Lutes wanted to understand the circumstances leading up to World War II and the Holocaust. "One overt goal from early on was to try to get into the mindset of the people of that time and place and imagine what their lives were like, to imagine that the future to them was unwritten and could go in any number of directions," he told me. The story takes place between 1928 and 1930 (so far), and the political and economic events that sent Germany in the direction of Nazism are the backdrop. Many historical figures from the time make cameo appearances, notably the Nazi "martyr" Horst Wessel. But mainly Lutes tells us about the lives, loves, and daily struggles of Marthe, Kurt, the Cocoa Kids jazz group, and many others.

Meanwhile, he followed James Sturm into teaching. He told me of how his interest in comics had been denigrated as a student at RISD. When Sturm founded the Center for Cartoon Studies in 2004, it seemed like a logical place for Lutes to go. "I love teaching comics. My approach has been to discard the negative approaches I witnessed at RISD, build on the positive ones, and combine them with my personal experiences as a working cartoonist." One result of his teaching was the collective creation of *Bingo Baby* by Donna Almendrala, Bill Bedard, Joseph Lambert, Amelia Onorato, and Denis St. John, all CCS students, under the direction of Lutes and using the role-playing game Fiasco to develop the narrative.

When I think of the young Jason I knew in Seattle, it seems perfect that he ended up a teacher. It's the ideal profession for him. At the same time, I've been waiting for the last volume of *Berlin* for years. I asked Lutes recently if he would finish it, and he wrote, "Yes. It will get done, goldurnit." I'm going to hold him to it.

Robert Boyd is an art critic and journalist who writes extensively about comics on his blog, the Great God Pan is Dead.

---

most commercially bankable cartoonist among us. His *Jar of Fools*, first serialized in the Seattle *Stranger*, then self-published as a graphic novel, was a sensation. He was the most technically proficient in terms of designing and producing books for print. The bottom line was that *Story Ark* would rest most heavily on Jason's shoulders. He had just begun imagining and drawing the first ideas for *Berlin* and, understandably, he quailed at the thought of taking on this huge anthology project in addition to supporting himself and trying to make his own comics.

I recall that we were at a *Story Ark* meeting at Ed's apartment when Jason told us he just couldn't do it. We were disappointed, but we couldn't argue with the truth that we all knew but nobody could bear to say out loud—that *Story Ark* would not happen without Jason guiding it. And so, reluctantly, we let the idea go. Tom moved to Morocco, then Austin. Jon moved to Gainesville. The gang loosened and expanded to include others in the ever-burgeoning Seattle com-

ics scene: Stefano Gaudiano, Brian Sendelbach, Greg Stump, Eric Reynolds, and for a while, Al Columbia. Time passed. We all got older, shouldered new responsibilities, and could no longer fleet the time carelessly, debating Jack Kirby. Making comics became less of a communal activity. Many of us from that group, including Jason, have gone on to be teachers of comics.

Truth be told, we all had our moments of rueful doubt about Jason committing himself to the gargantuan *Berlin* when he was so young. We would say incredulously to ourselves, "He won't finish *Berlin* until he's in his forties!!" which didn't even seem like a real thing. But now it is upon us; we are in our forties and Jason is tantalizingly close to finishing *Berlin*. It is a true masterwork. He is a born storyteller and teacher and his students and readers are lucky to have him.

P.S. If you're interested, you can find two decades' worth of back issues of *Story Ark* in the Hicksville Library.

—Megan Kelso, cartoonist of Artichoke Tales, The Squirrel Mother, and Queen of the Black Black

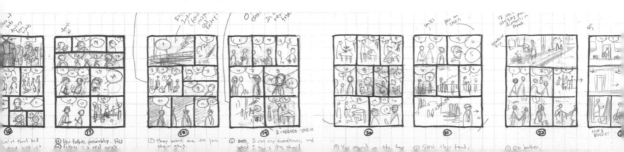

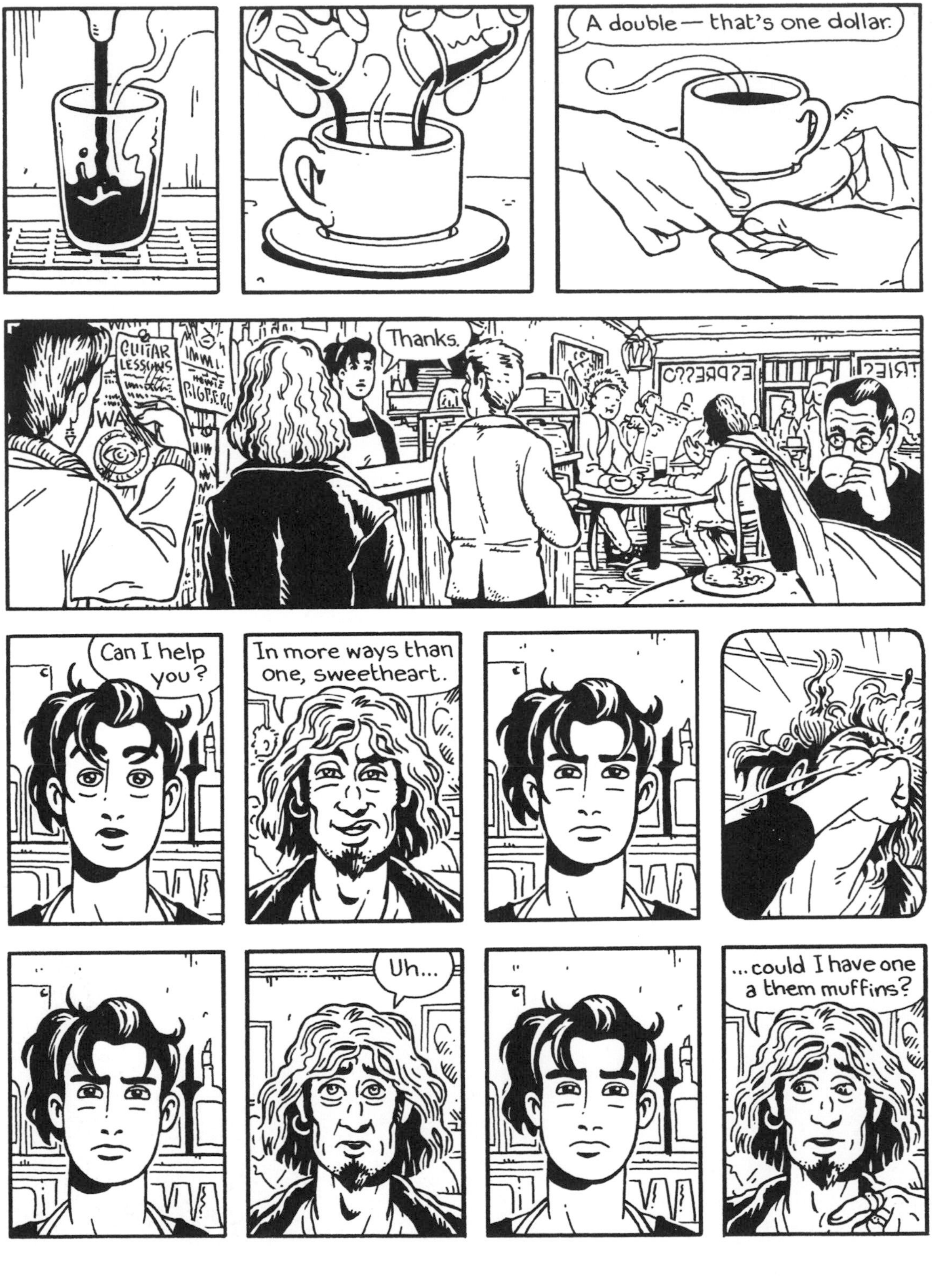
A double — that's one dollar.
Thanks.
Can I help you?
In more ways than one, sweetheart.
Uh...
...could I have one a them muffins?

 Jar of Fools was first serialized in the *Stranger* (1994). It was collected in book form in 1994 and later published as a D+Q edition (2001).

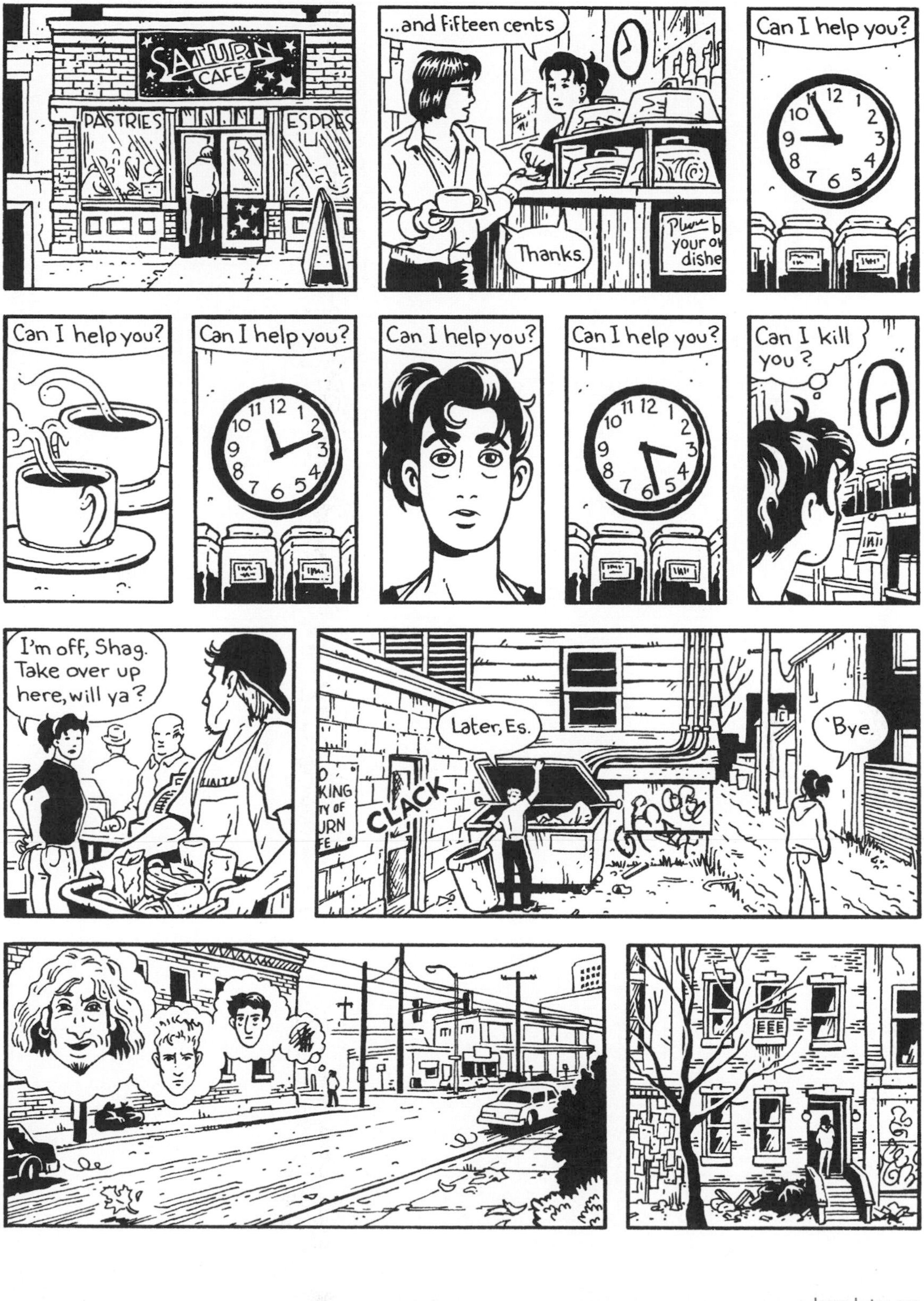
SATURN CAFÉ
PASTRIES
ESPRES
...and fifteen cents
Thanks.
Can I help you?
Can I help you?
Can I help you?
Can I help you?
Can I help you?
Can I kill you ?
I'm off, Shag. Take over up here, will ya ?
CLACK
Later, Es.
`Bye.

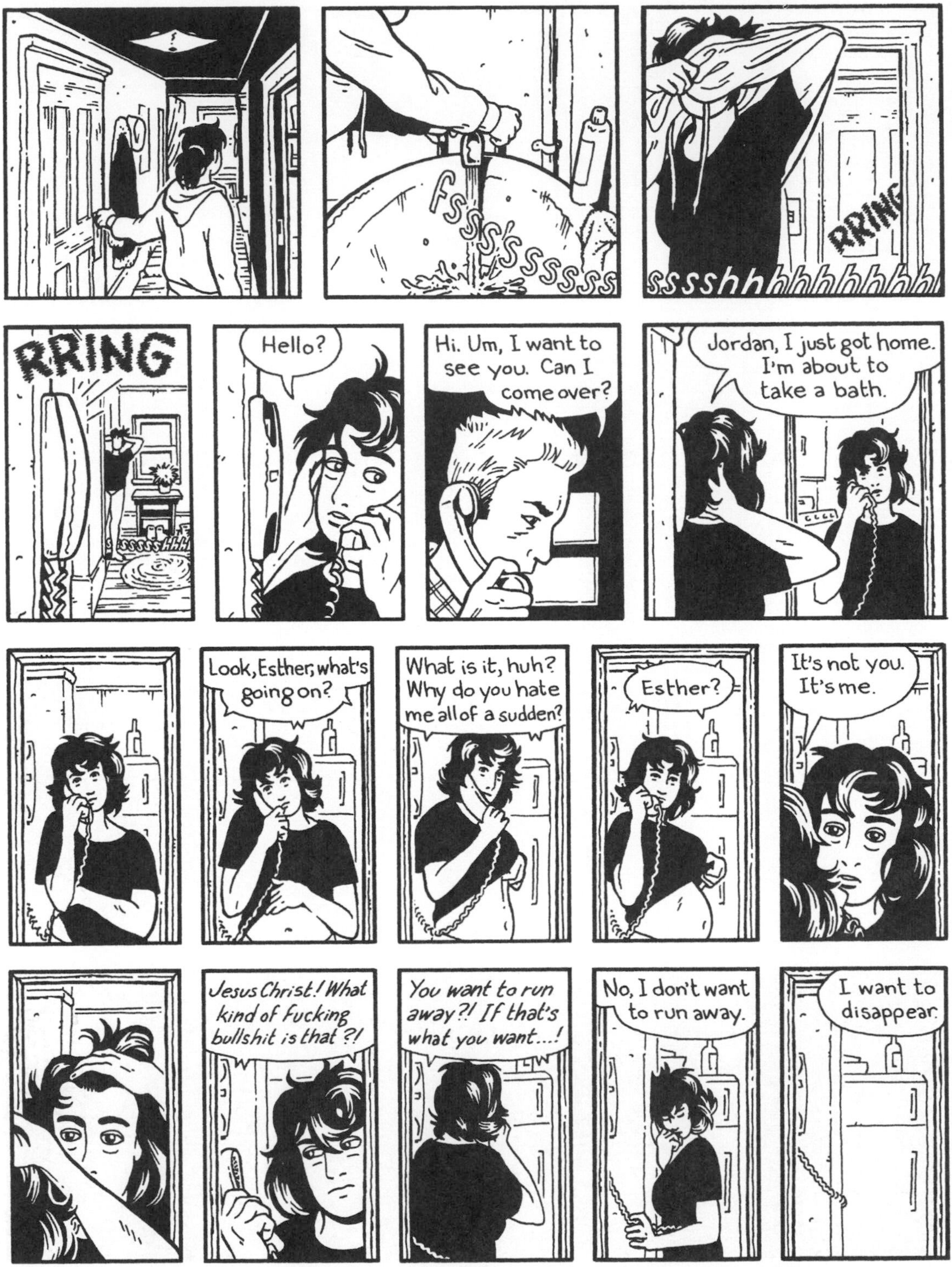
fssss'sssssss
RRING
ssssshhhhhhhhh
RRING
Hello?
Hi. Um, I want to see you. Can I come over?
Jordan, I just got home. I'm about to take a bath.
Look, Esther, what's going on?
What is it, huh? Why do you hate me all of a sudden?
Esther?
It's not you. It's me.
Jesus Christ! What kind of fucking bullshit is that?!
You want to run away?! If that's what you want...!
No, I don't want to run away.
I want to disappear.

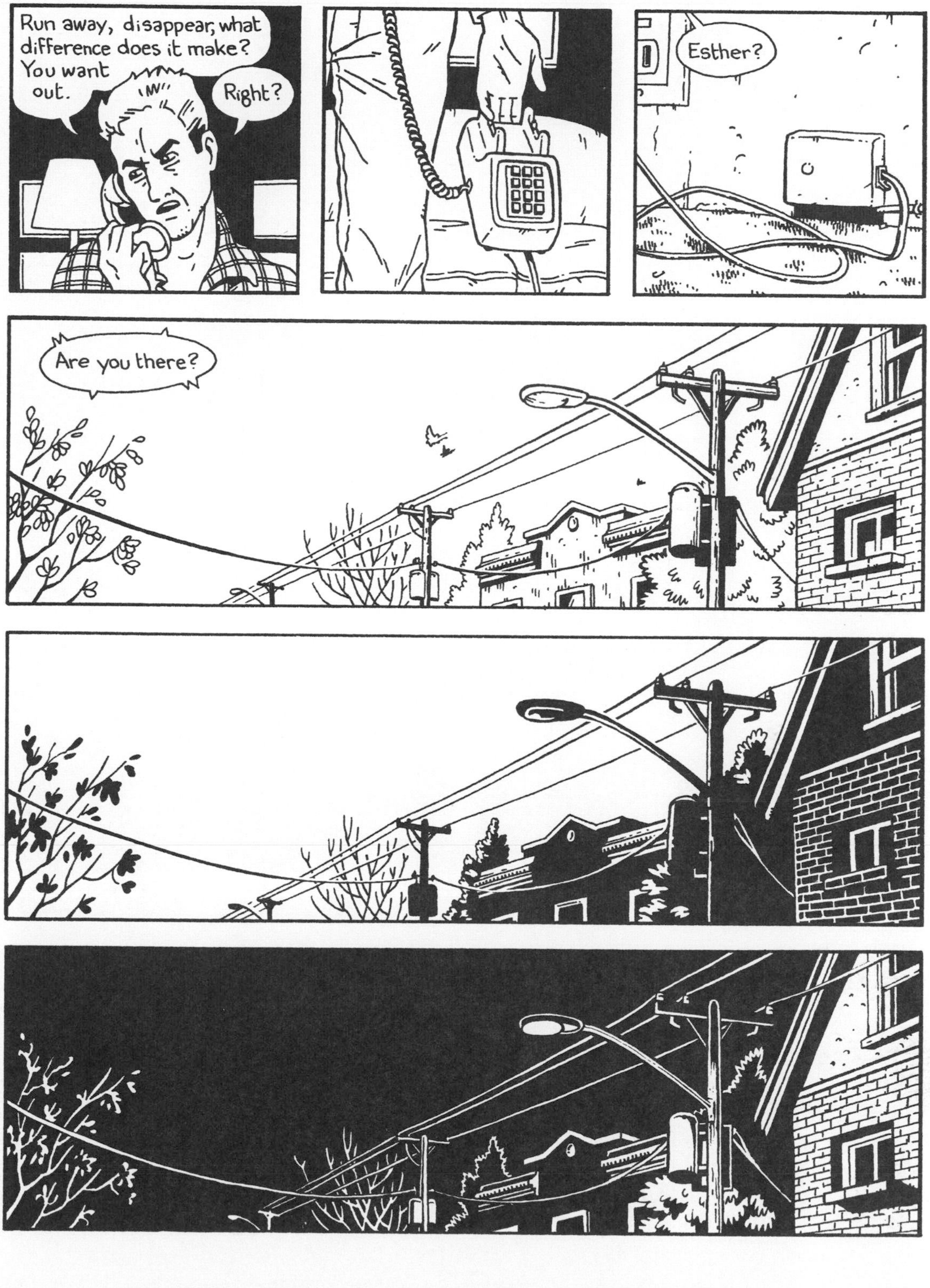
Run away, disappear, what difference does it make? You want out.
Right?
Esther?
Are you there?

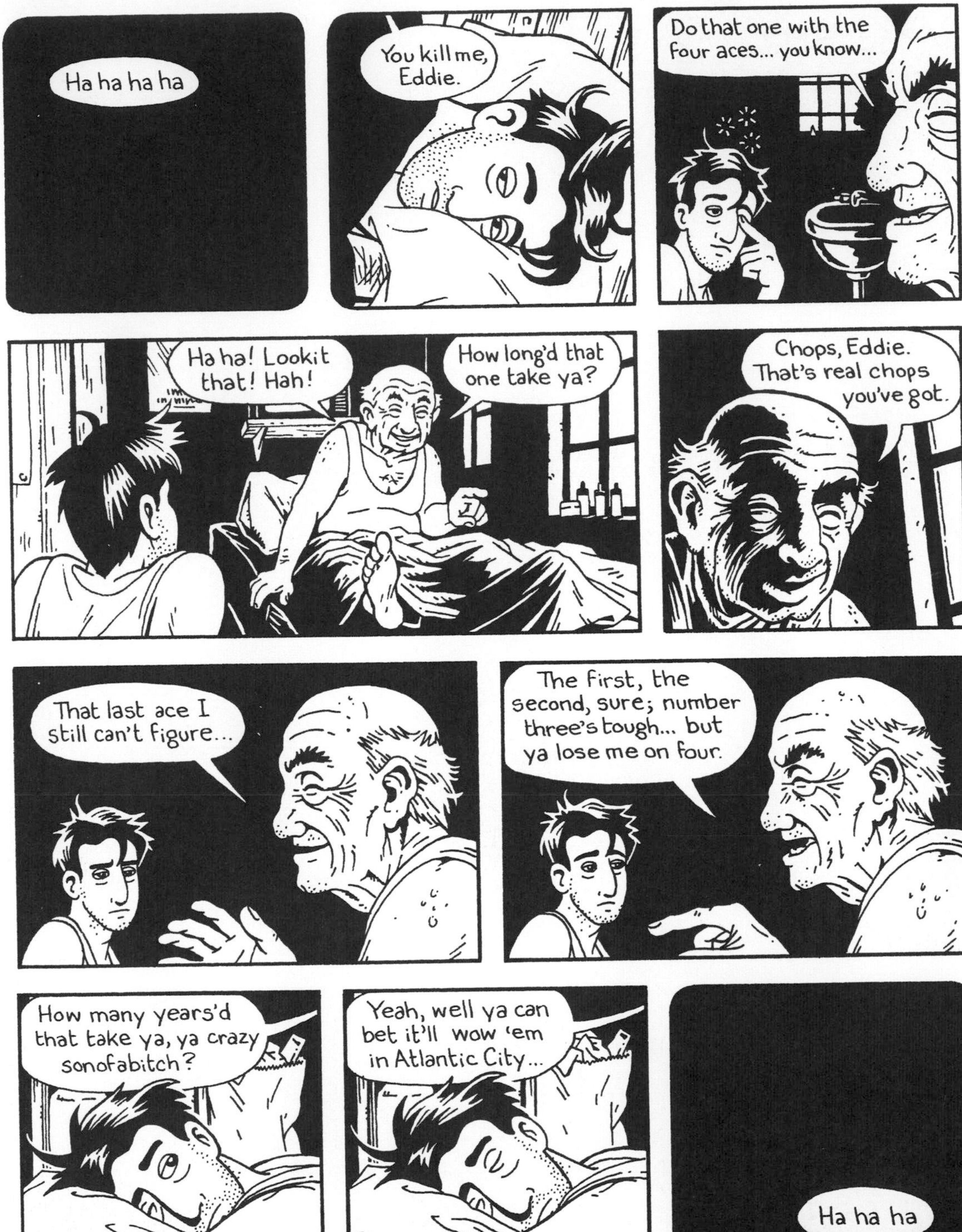
Ha ha ha ha
You kill me, Eddie.
Do that one with the four aces... you know...
Ha ha! Lookit that! Hah!
How long'd that one take ya?
Chops, Eddie. That's real chops you've got.
That last ace I still can't figure...
The first, the second, sure; number three's tough... but ya lose me on four.
How many years'd that take ya, ya crazy sonofabitch?
Yeah, well ya can bet it'll wow 'em in Atlantic City...
Ha ha ha

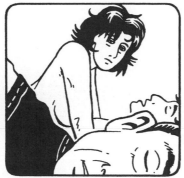

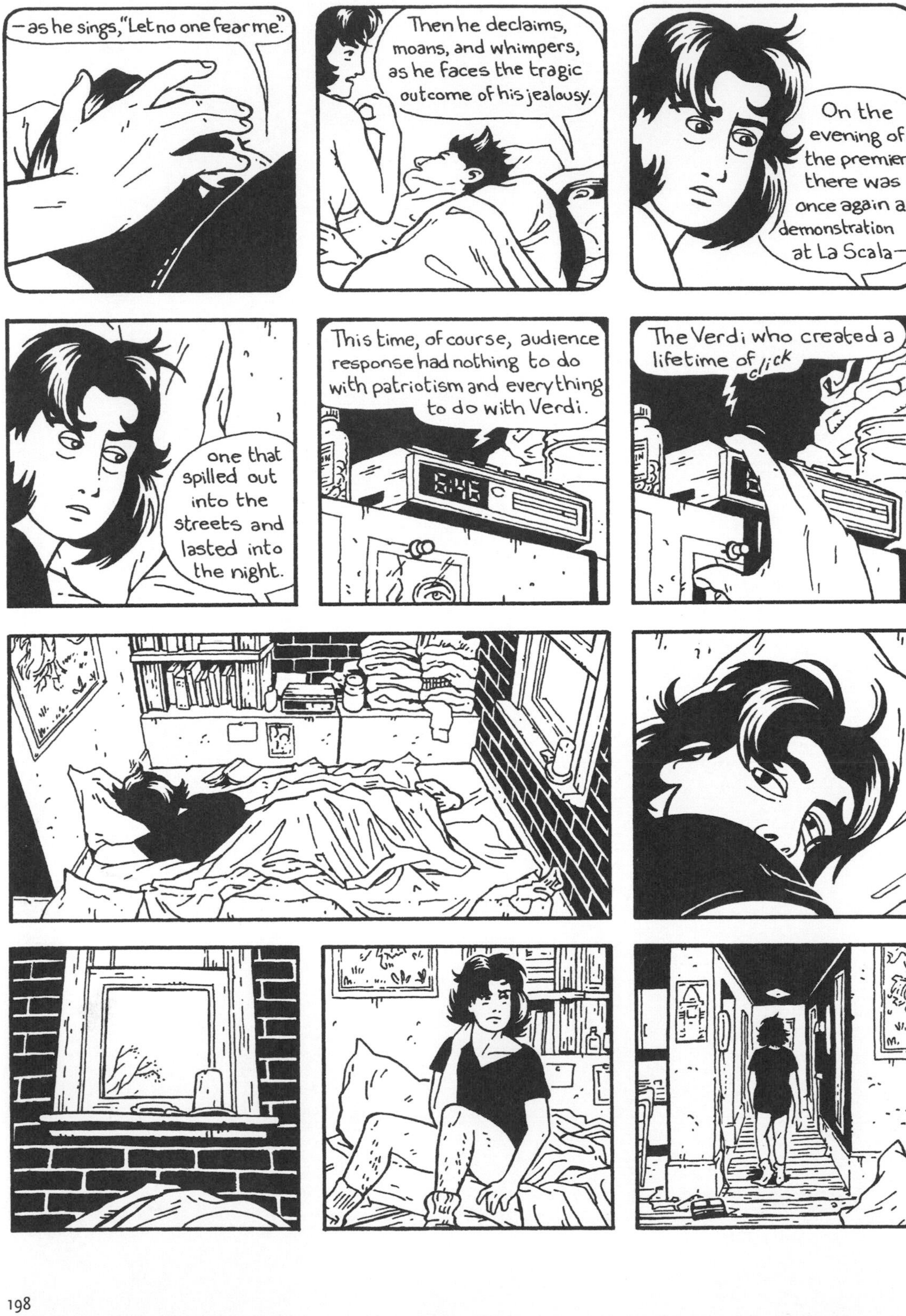
—as he sings, "Let no one fear me."
Then he declaims, moans, and whimpers, as he faces the tragic outcome of his jealousy.
On the evening of the premiere there was once again a demonstration at La Scala—
one that spilled out into the streets and lasted into the night.
This time, of course, audience response had nothing to do with patriotism and everything to do with Verdi.
The Verdi who created a lifetime of
click

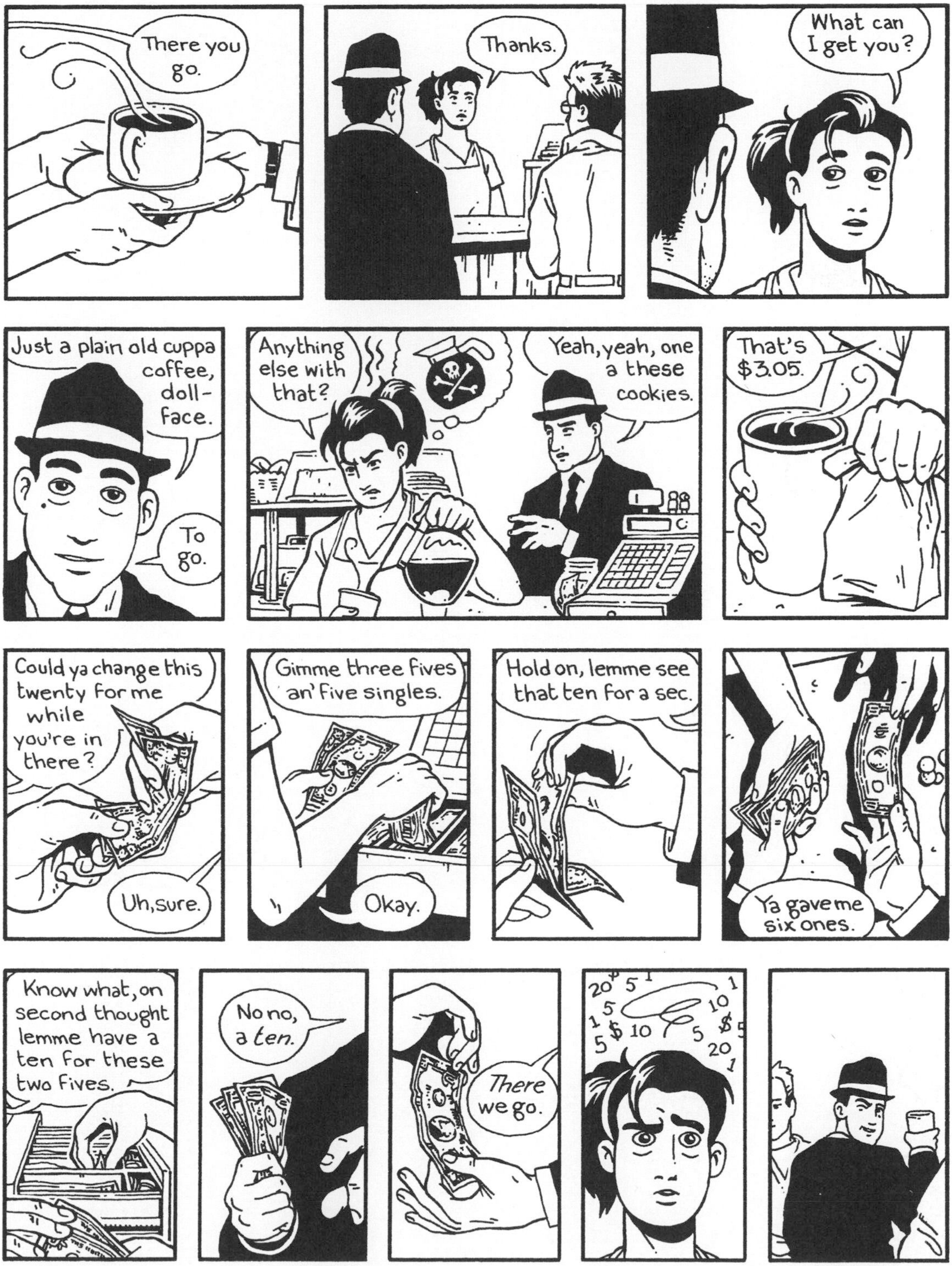
There you go.
Thanks.
What can I get you?
Just a plain old cuppa coffee, doll-face.
To go.
Anything else with that?
Yeah, yeah, one a these cookies.
That's $3.05.
Could ya change this twenty for me while you're in there?
Uh, sure.
Gimme three fives an' five singles.
Okay.
Hold on, lemme see that ten for a sec.
Ya gave me six ones.
Know what, on second thought lemme have a ten for these two fives.
No no, a *ten*.
There we go.
20 $ 5 1 1 5 10 1 $ 10 5 $ 5 5 20 1

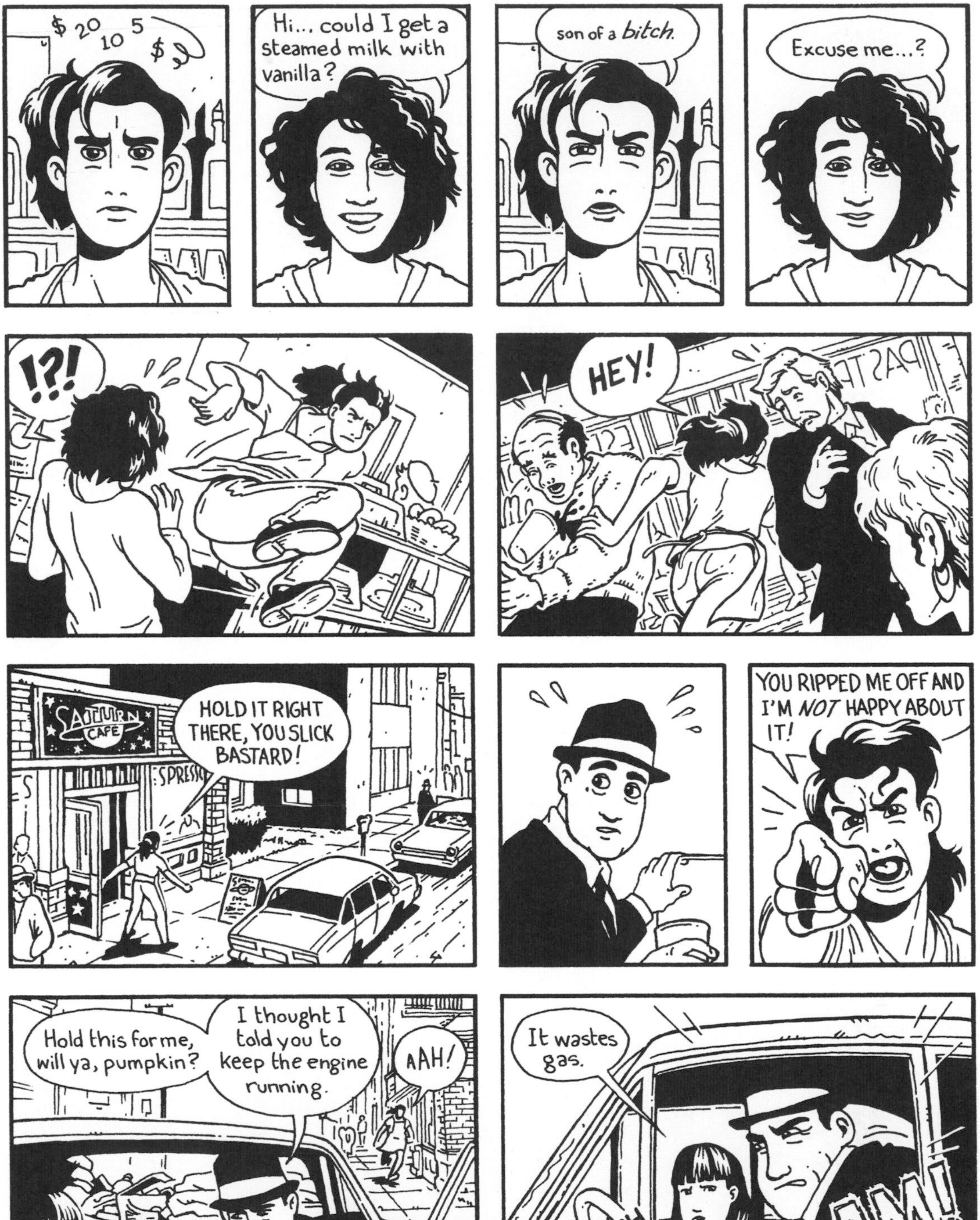
$ 20 10 5 $
Hi... could I get a steamed milk with vanilla?
son of a bitch.
Excuse me...?
!?!
HEY!
PASTE
SATURN CAFE
SPRESSO
HOLD IT RIGHT THERE, YOU SLICK BASTARD!
YOU RIPPED ME OFF AND I'M NOT HAPPY ABOUT IT!
Hold this for me, will ya, pumpkin?
I thought I told you to keep the engine running.
AAH!
It wastes gas.
K-CHUH K-CHUH
SLAM!

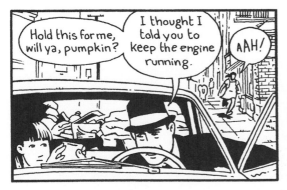

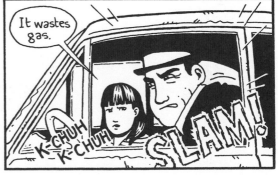

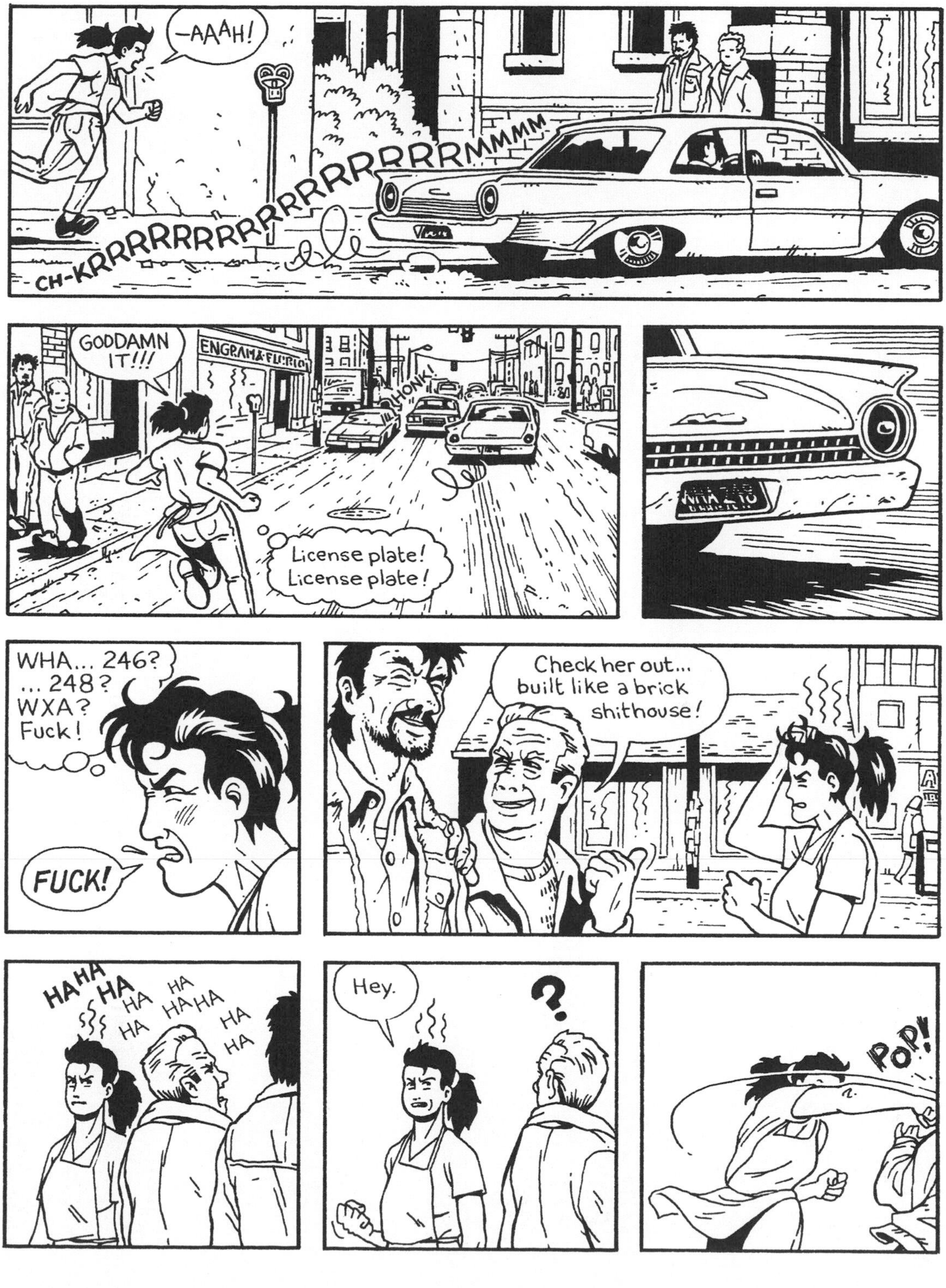
–AAAH!
CH-KRRRRRRRRRRRRRRRRRRRMMMM
GODDAMN IT!!!
ENGRAM & FLORIO
HONK!
License plate! License plate!
WHA... 246? ... 248? WXA? Fuck!
FUCK!
Check her out... built like a brick shithouse!
HA HA HA HA HA HA HA HA HA HA
Hey.
?
POP!

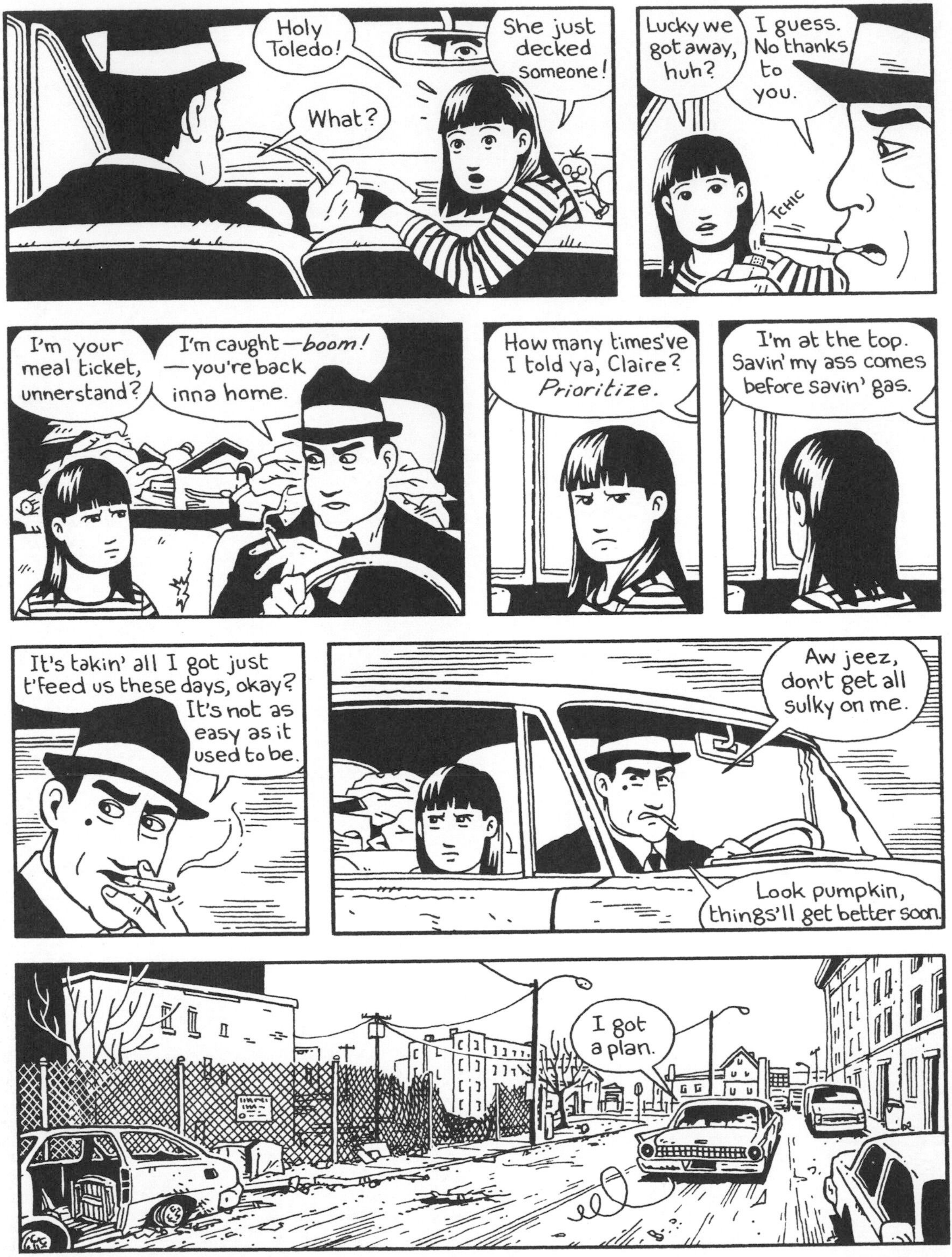

Holy Toledo!
She just decked someone!
What?
Lucky we got away, huh?
I guess. No thanks to you.
TCHIC
I'm your meal ticket, unnerstand?
I'm caught—*boom!* —you're back inna home.
How many times've I told ya, Claire? *Prioritize.*
I'm at the top. Savin' my ass comes before savin' gas.
It's takin' all I got just t'feed us these days, okay?
It's not as easy as it used to be.
Aw jeez, don't get all sulky on me.
Look pumpkin, things'll get better soon.
I got a plan.

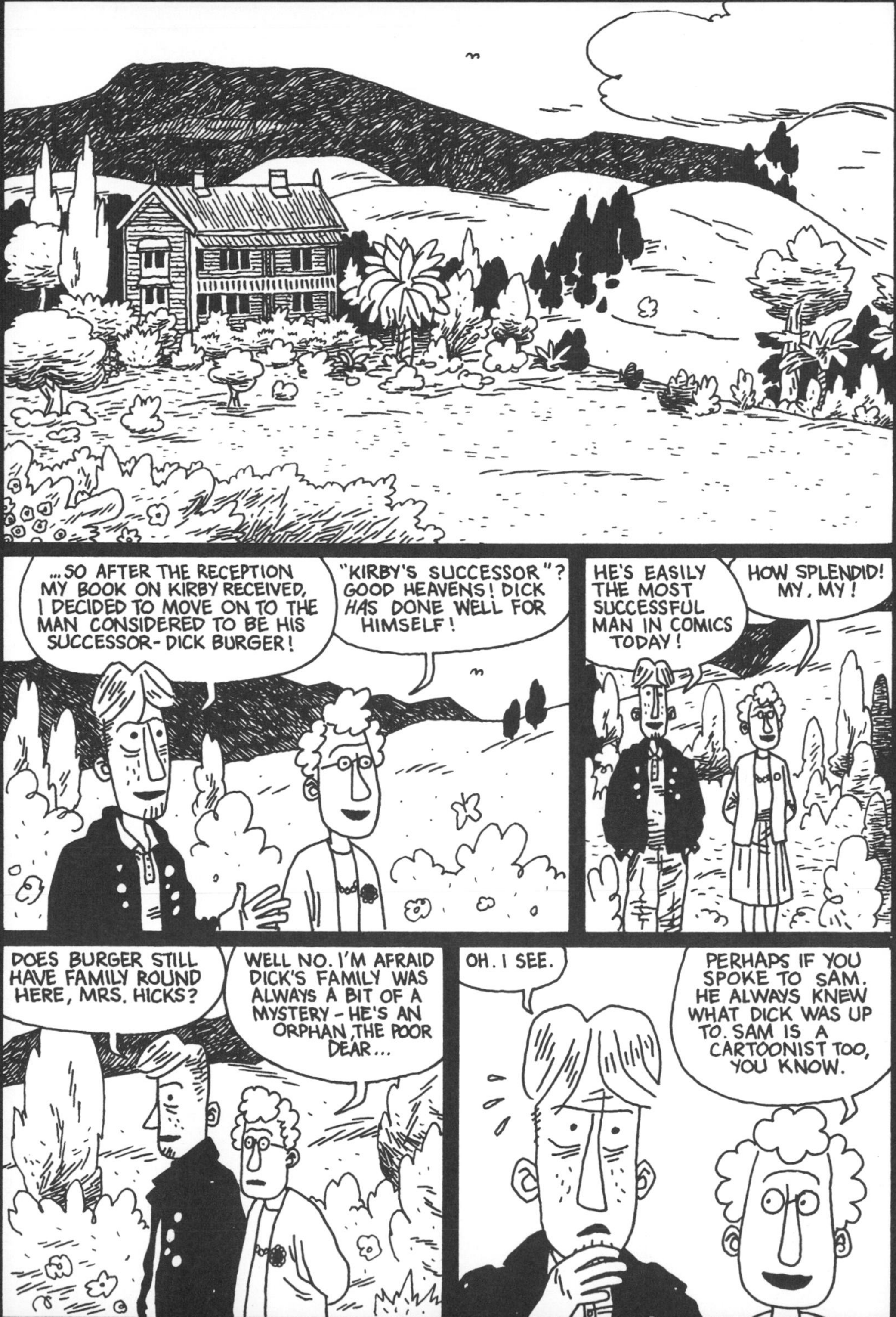

...SO AFTER THE RECEPTION MY BOOK ON KIRBY RECEIVED, I DECIDED TO MOVE ON TO THE MAN CONSIDERED TO BE HIS SUCCESSOR - DICK BURGER!
"KIRBY'S SUCCESSOR"? GOOD HEAVENS! DICK *HAS* DONE WELL FOR HIMSELF!
HE'S EASILY THE MOST SUCCESSFUL MAN IN COMICS TODAY!
HOW SPLENDID! MY, MY!
DOES BURGER STILL HAVE FAMILY ROUND HERE, MRS. HICKS?
WELL NO. I'M AFRAID DICK'S FAMILY WAS ALWAYS A BIT OF A MYSTERY - HE'S AN ORPHAN, THE POOR DEAR...
OH. I SEE.
PERHAPS IF YOU SPOKE TO SAM. HE ALWAYS KNEW WHAT DICK WAS UP TO. SAM IS A CARTOONIST TOO, YOU KNOW.

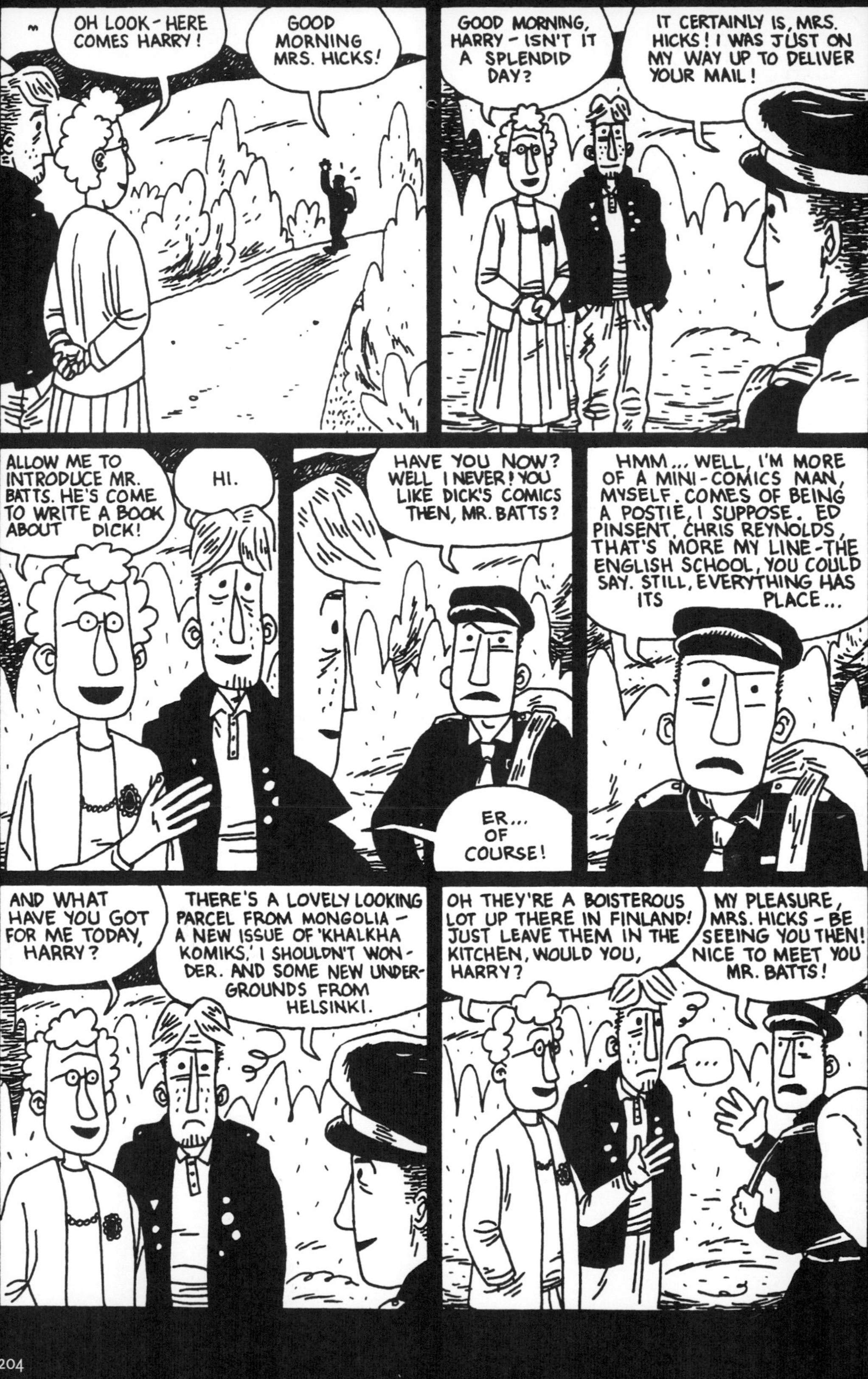
OH LOOK - HERE COMES HARRY!
GOOD MORNING MRS. HICKS!
GOOD MORNING, HARRY - ISN'T IT A SPLENDID DAY?
IT CERTAINLY IS, MRS. HICKS! I WAS JUST ON MY WAY UP TO DELIVER YOUR MAIL!
ALLOW ME TO INTRODUCE MR. BATTS. HE'S COME TO WRITE A BOOK ABOUT DICK!
HI.
HAVE YOU NOW? WELL I NEVER! YOU LIKE DICK'S COMICS THEN, MR. BATTS?
ER... OF COURSE!
HMM... WELL, I'M MORE OF A MINI-COMICS MAN, MYSELF. COMES OF BEING A POSTIE, I SUPPOSE. ED PINSENT, CHRIS REYNOLDS, THAT'S MORE MY LINE-THE ENGLISH SCHOOL, YOU COULD SAY. STILL, EVERYTHING HAS ITS PLACE...
AND WHAT HAVE YOU GOT FOR ME TODAY, HARRY?
THERE'S A LOVELY LOOKING PARCEL FROM MONGOLIA - A NEW ISSUE OF 'KHALKHA KOMIKS,' I SHOULDN'T WONDER. AND SOME NEW UNDERGROUNDS FROM HELSINKI.
OH THEY'RE A BOISTEROUS LOT UP THERE IN FINLAND! JUST LEAVE THEM IN THE KITCHEN, WOULD YOU, HARRY?
MY PLEASURE, MRS. HICKS - BE SEEING YOU THEN! NICE TO MEET YOU MR. BATTS!
....

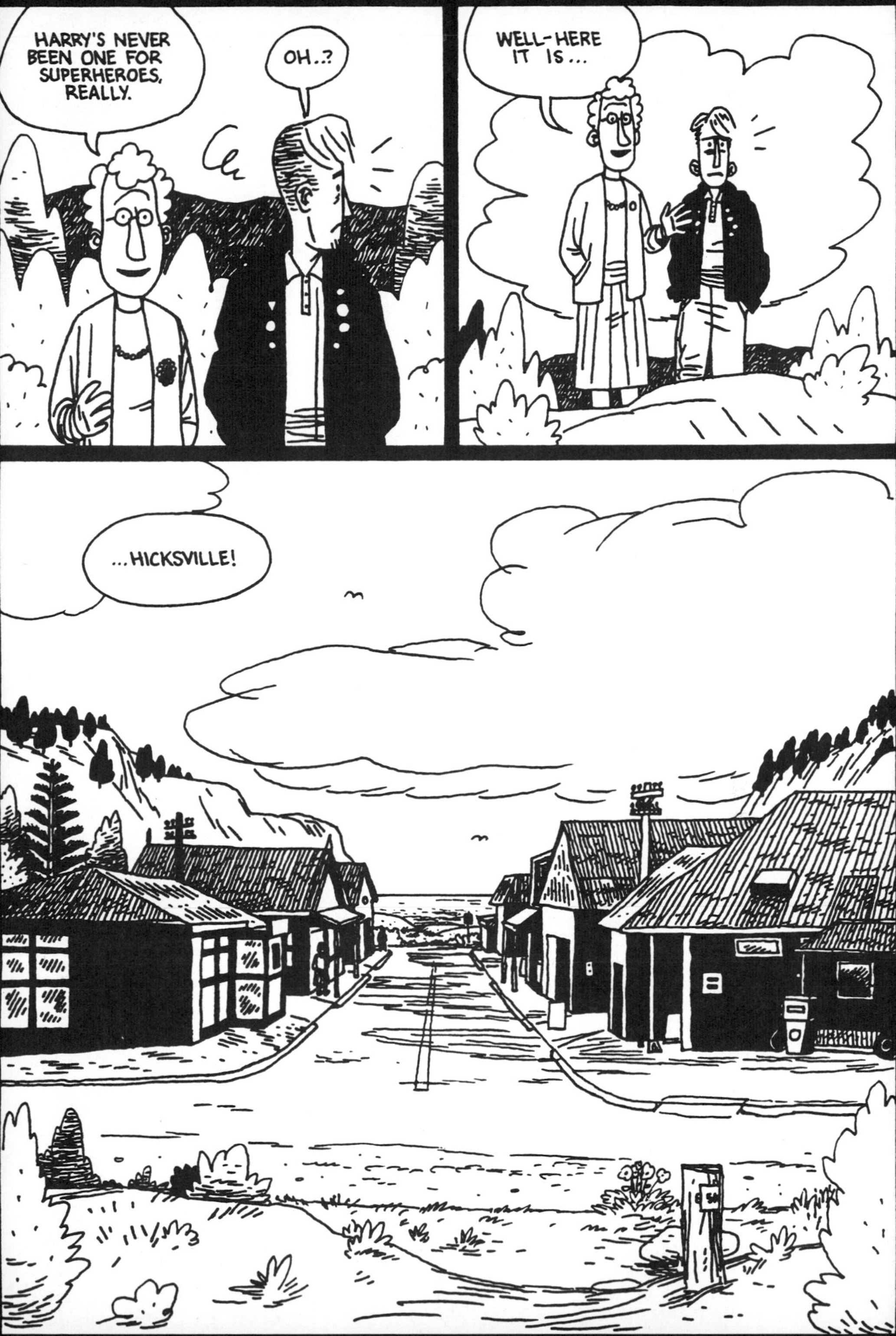
HARRY'S NEVER BEEN ONE FOR SUPERHEROES, REALLY.
OH..?
WELL-HERE IT IS...
...HICKSVILLE!

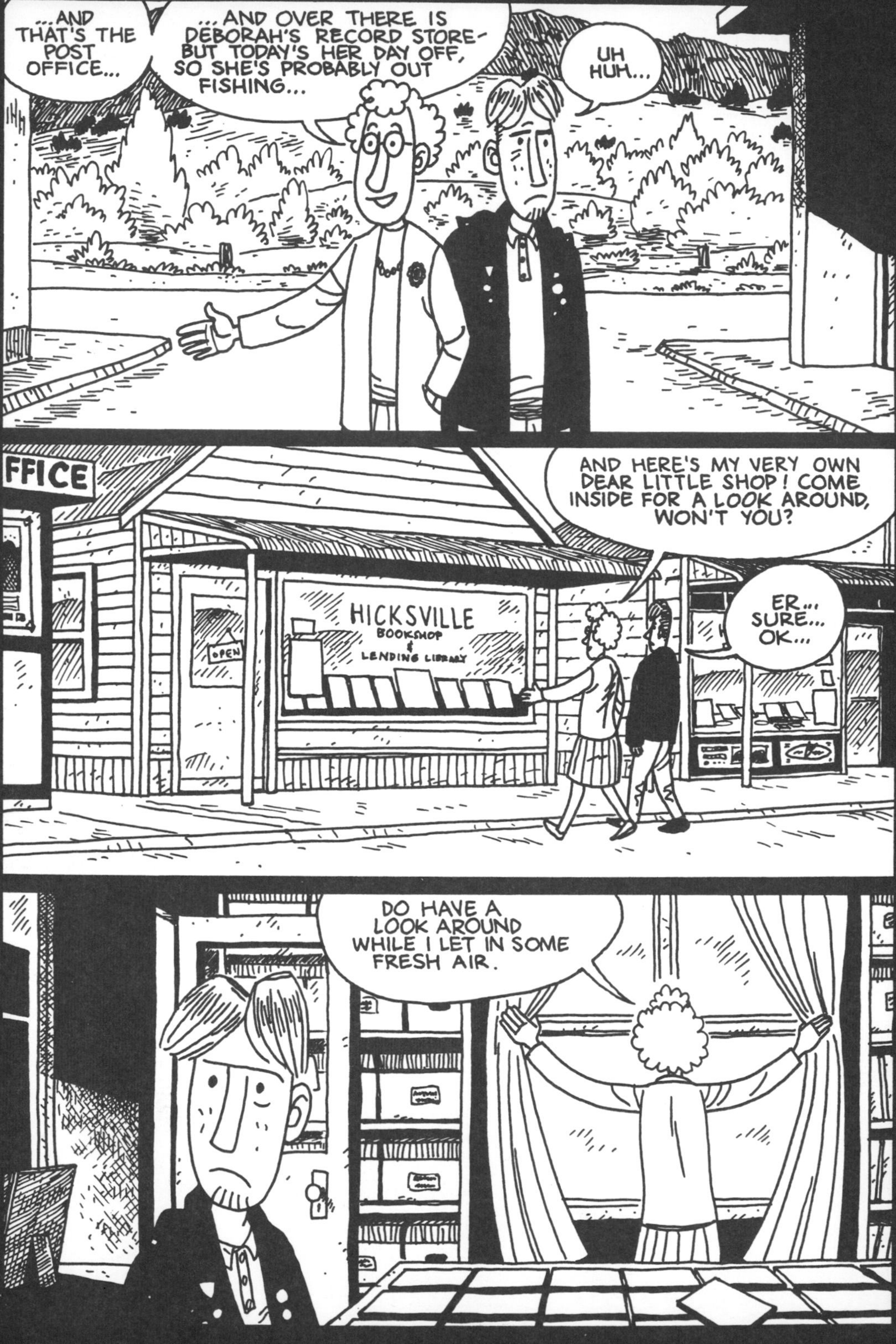
...AND THAT'S THE POST OFFICE...
...AND OVER THERE IS DEBORAH'S RECORD STORE- BUT TODAY'S HER DAY OFF, SO SHE'S PROBABLY OUT FISHING...
UH HUH...
FFICE
HICKSVILLE BOOKSHOP & LENDING LIBRARY
OPEN
AND HERE'S MY VERY OWN DEAR LITTLE SHOP! COME INSIDE FOR A LOOK AROUND, WON'T YOU?
ER... SURE... OK...
DO HAVE A LOOK AROUND WHILE I LET IN SOME FRESH AIR.

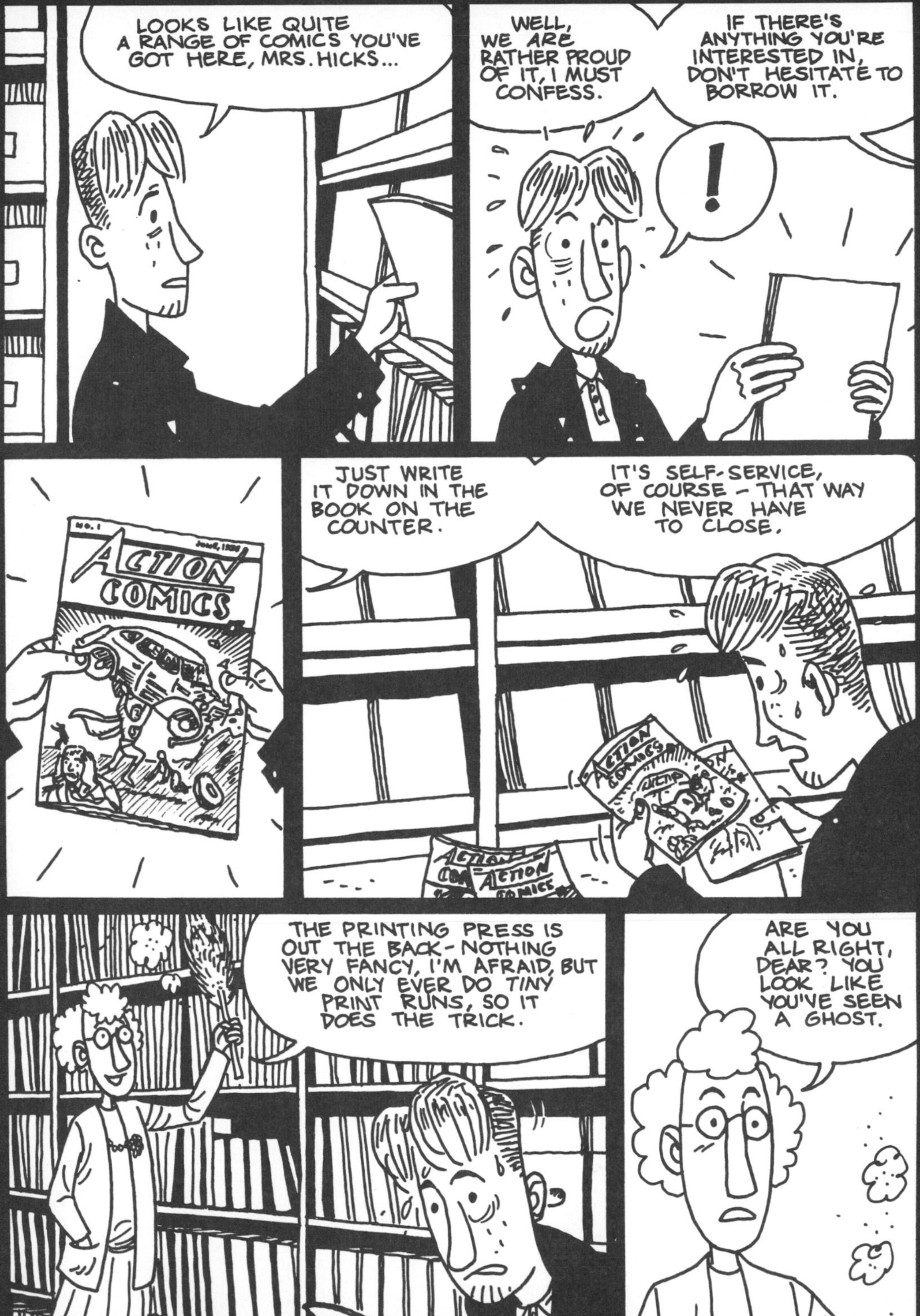
LOOKS LIKE QUITE A RANGE OF COMICS YOU'VE GOT HERE, MRS. HICKS...
WELL, WE *ARE* RATHER PROUD OF IT, I MUST CONFESS.
IF THERE'S ANYTHING YOU'RE INTERESTED IN, DON'T HESITATE TO BORROW IT.
!
NO. 1
ACTION COMICS
JUST WRITE IT DOWN IN THE BOOK ON THE COUNTER.
IT'S SELF-SERVICE, OF COURSE - THAT WAY WE NEVER HAVE TO CLOSE.
ACTION COMICS
THE PRINTING PRESS IS OUT THE BACK - NOTHING VERY FANCY, I'M AFRAID, BUT WE ONLY EVER DO *TINY* PRINT RUNS, SO IT DOES THE TRICK.
ARE YOU ALL RIGHT, DEAR? YOU LOOK LIKE YOU'VE SEEN A GHOST.

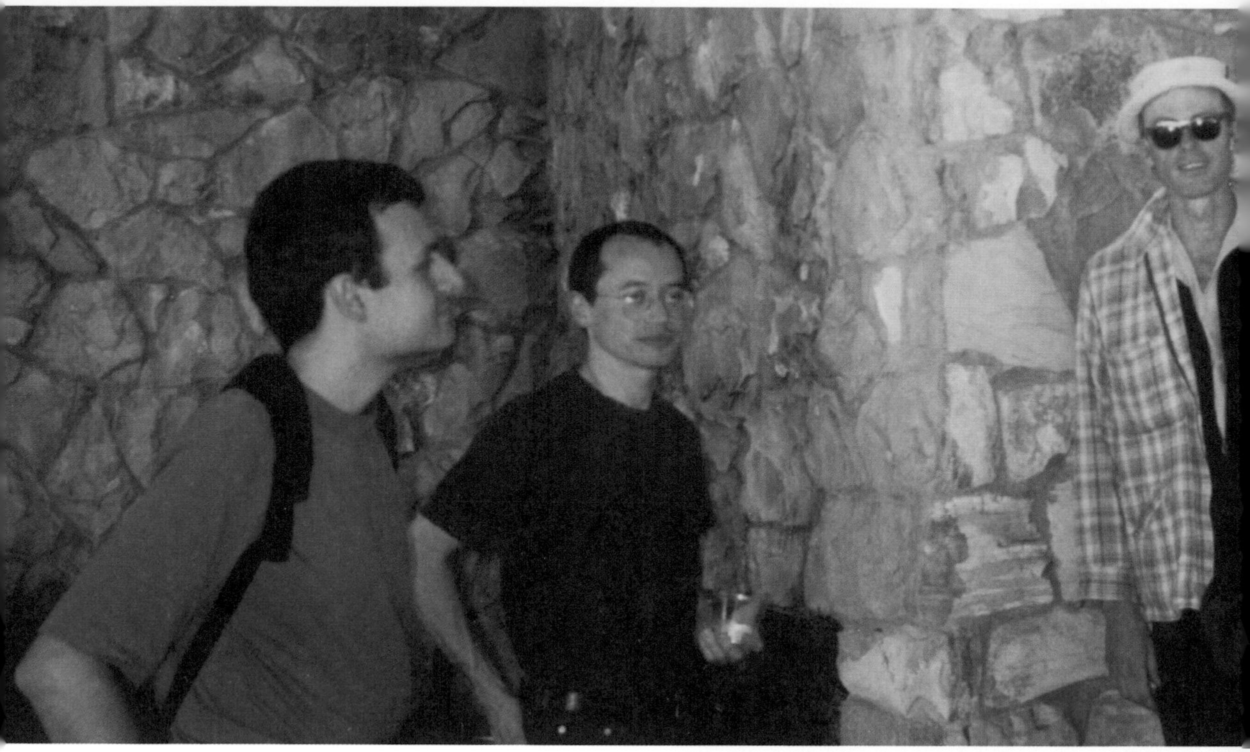

My first day working at DC Comics, Heidi MacDonald, unprompted, told me *Hicksville* was the best comic ever written. She was right. I'd picked it up at Hanley's, where my new gang went every Wednesday. Hanley's had a whole rack entirely devoted to D+Q. I made it my business to read everything on it.

There's no escaping *Hicksville*. It's my favourite. I've fallen in love with other comics since, but *Hicksville*'s gravity always brings me back home. The art evolves, from simple, even wonky, to complex to elegant, but it's the story that breaks my heart every time. There's a big reveal in *Hicksville*: the library contains comics from the world's greatest artists, including Picasso. Horrocks often quotes Picasso: "Art is a lie that tells the truth." I get why Dylan insists the last part of that quote is a lie. His book presents a fantasy, yes, but it raises a question that haunts me—why the fuck aren't there comics from Picasso? Following Leonard as he digs deeper into comics, to the most intimate work, to the work that should exist, had me wondering what comics would be if it weren't always at the margins. It's safer hiding, but it cripples the world's greatest medium.

—Leon Avelino, publisher, Secret Acres

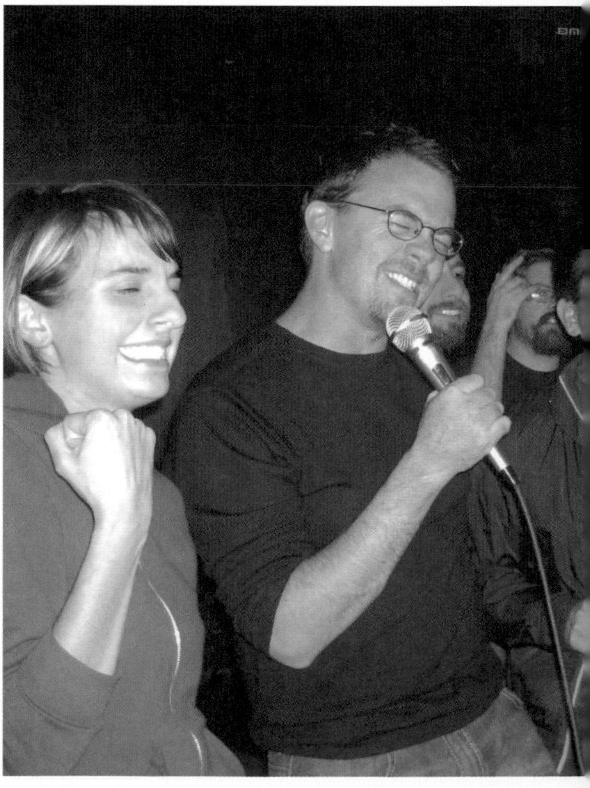

 (Top) Chris Oliveros, Joe Sacco, David Collier, Seth & Julie Doucet in LA (1998). (Bottom) Jason Lutes with CCS students Melissa Mendes, Alexis Frederick Fr

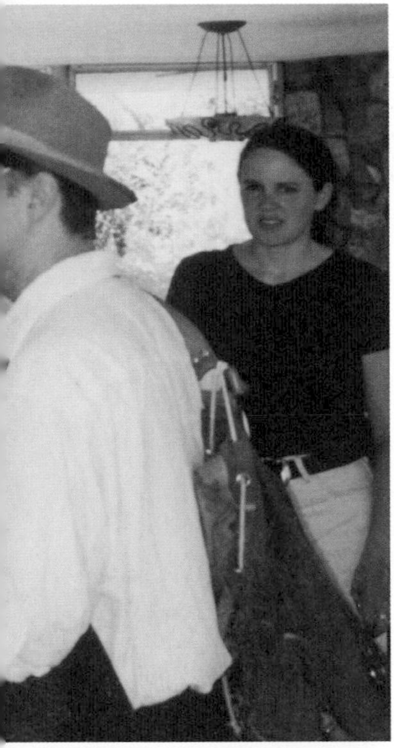

Too much has happened over my years with D+Q to pick a favourite moment. It could be Seth's wonderful wedding, which was followed by a panel discussion the next day that was a complete debacle; or swimming in the ocean with Julie Doucet during Comic-Con; or hanging out with Seth and Chester and feeling like I was Joe Matt's understudy. Or the time Rutu and I were at a literary festival in Toronto and Rutu revealed that all of her art was done digitally. When I expressed amazement that her lovely, expressive artwork could be—gasp!—drawn on a computer, Rutu, in her direct Israeli way, replied, "I tell the computer what to do, it doesn't tell me what to do!" Or being on tour with Seth the year *Golem* and *Vernacular Drawings* came out and during the first signing being in awe of the quick, wonderful drawings Seth would make in people's books. That evening I stayed up late practising several drawings I could rely on so I wouldn't embarrass myself as we travelled together. Or my first big event after the release of *Market Day*. I was so excited to be at the Strand (one of favourite bookstores) and there was a good crowd with many old friends present. I was nervous. When I started to speak I was incoherent. And the more I spoke the more self-conscious I became. But before I went down in flames, Peggy just sort of took over and my presentation became an interview and she saved the evening.

—James Sturm

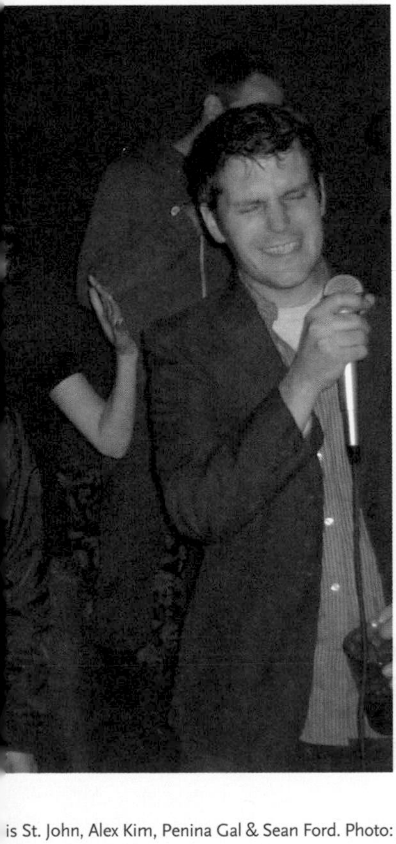

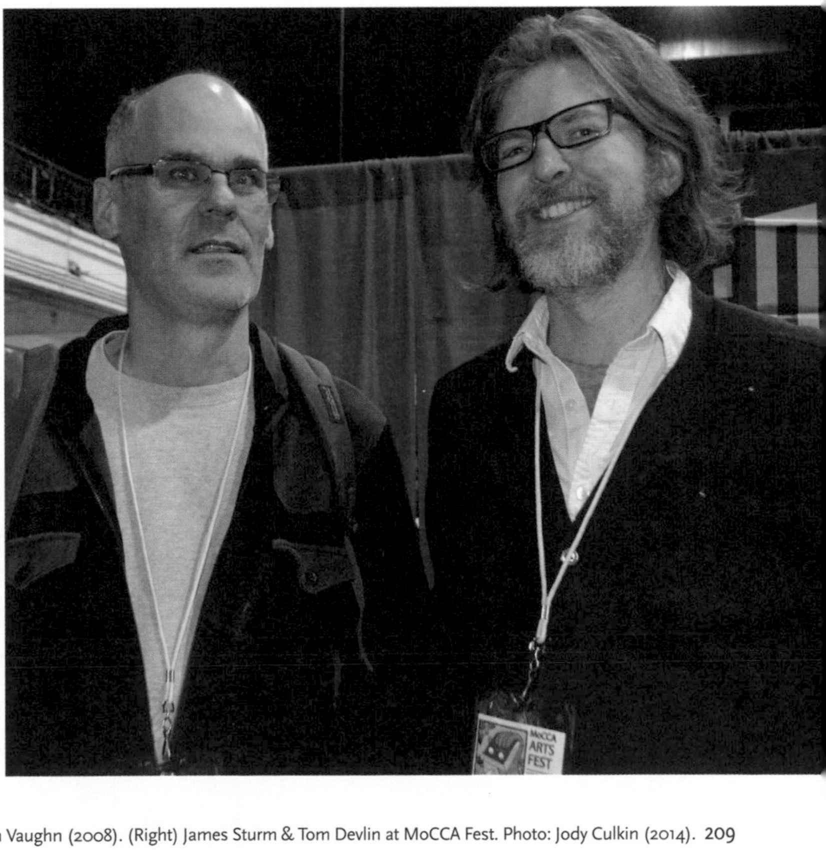

MoCCA
ARTS
FEST

is St. John, Alex Kim, Penina Gal & Sean Ford. Photo: Jen Vaughn (2008). (Right) James Sturm & Tom Devlin at MoCCA Fest. Photo: Jody Culkin (2014).

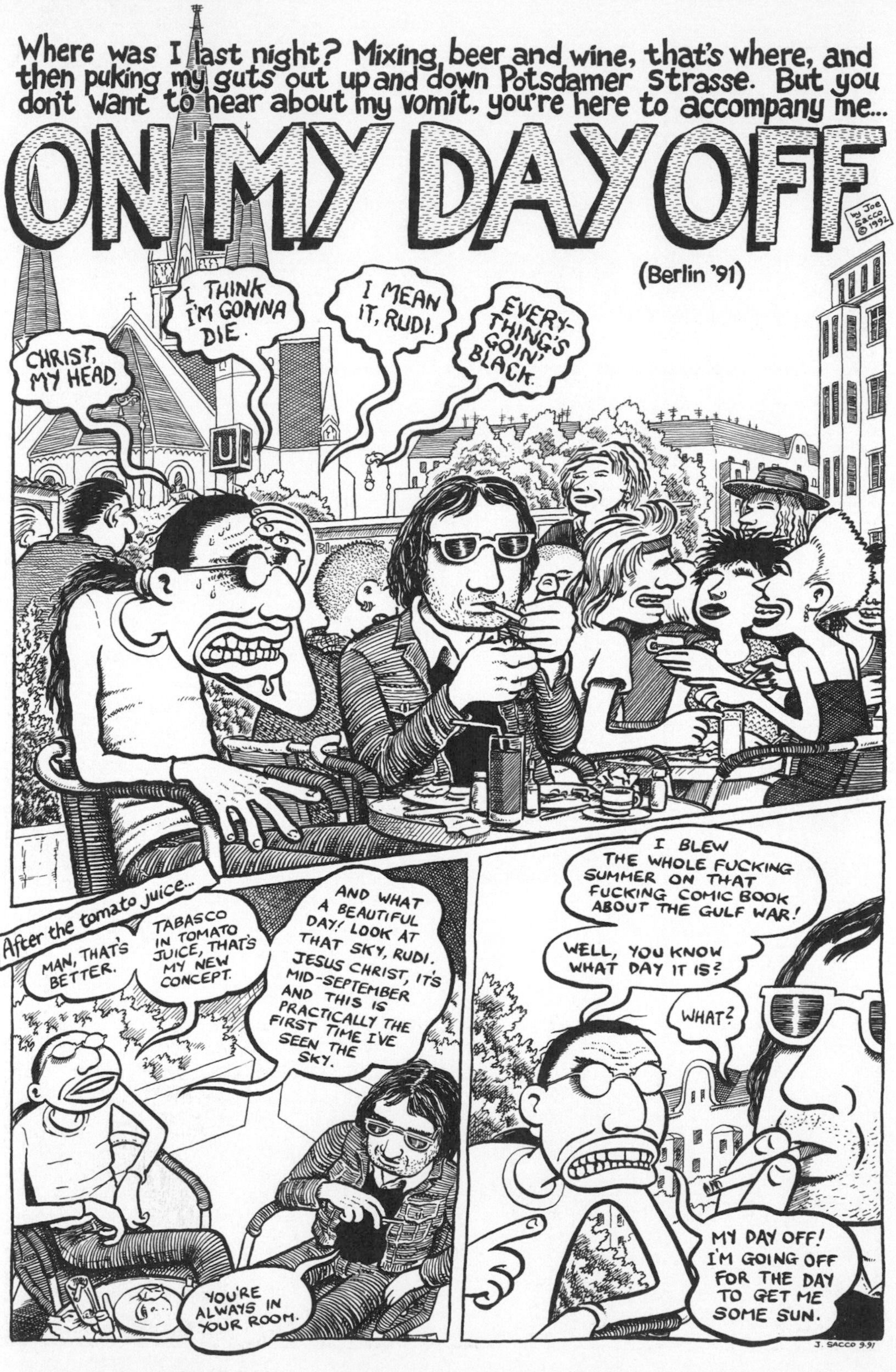
Where was I last night? Mixing beer and wine, that's where, and then puking my guts out up and down Potsdamer Strasse. But you don't want to hear about my vomit, you're here to accompany me...
ON MY DAY OFF
by Joe Sacco © 1992
(Berlin '91)
CHRIST, MY HEAD.
I THINK I'M GONNA DIE.
I MEAN IT, RUDI.
EVERY-THING'S GOIN' BLACK.
After the tomato juice...
MAN, THAT'S BETTER.
TABASCO IN TOMATO JUICE, THAT'S MY NEW CONCEPT.
AND WHAT A BEAUTIFUL DAY! LOOK AT THAT SKY, RUDI. JESUS CHRIST, IT'S MID-SEPTEMBER AND THIS IS PRACTICALLY THE FIRST TIME I'VE SEEN THE SKY.
YOU'RE ALWAYS IN YOUR ROOM.
I BLEW THE WHOLE FUCKING SUMMER ON THAT FUCKING COMIC BOOK ABOUT THE GULF WAR!
WELL, YOU KNOW WHAT DAY IT IS?
WHAT?
MY DAY OFF! I'M GOING OFF FOR THE DAY TO GET ME SOME SUN.
J. SACCO 9-91

 "On My Day Off" first appeared in vol. 1, no. 8 of *Drawn & Quarterly* (1992).

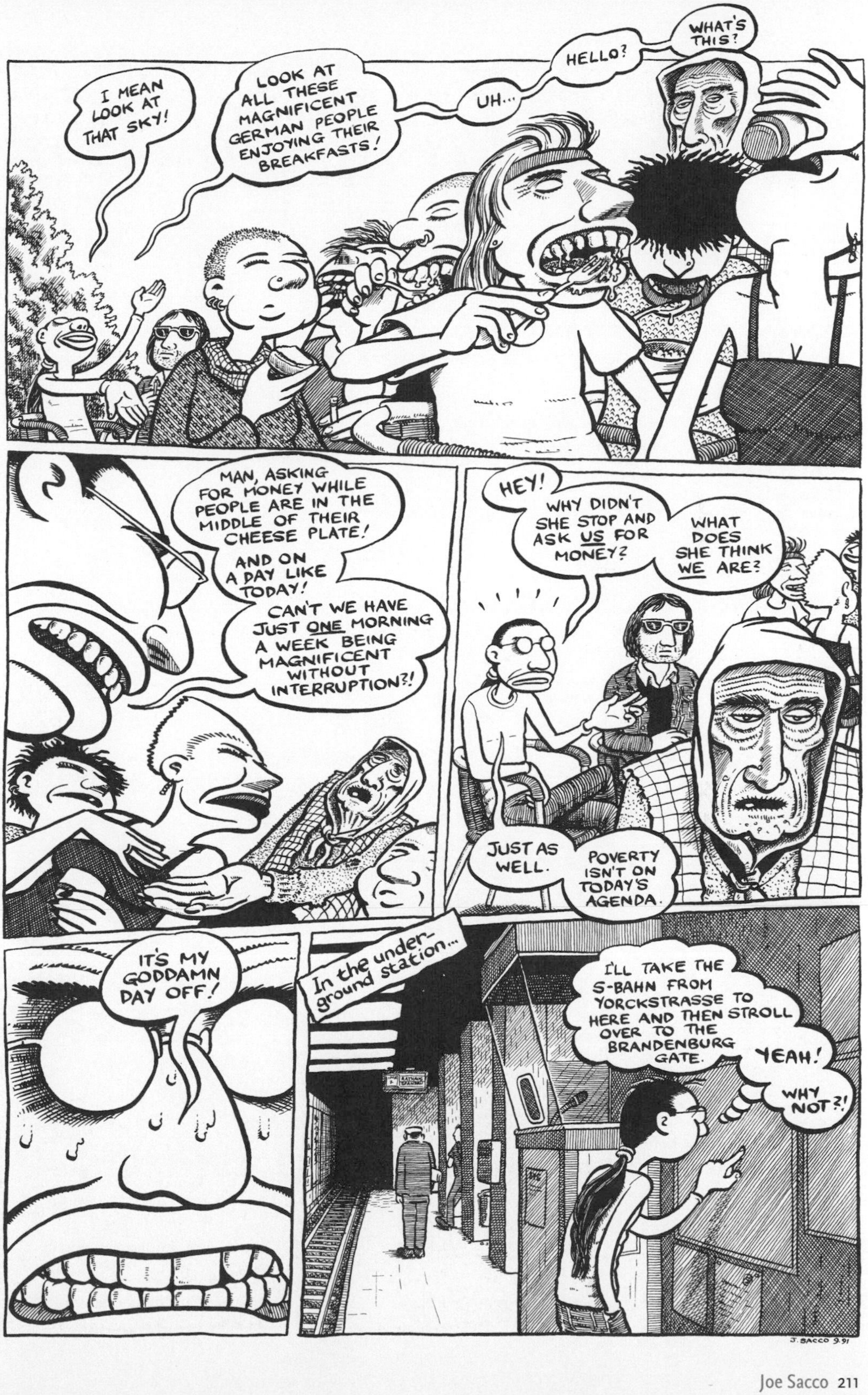
I MEAN LOOK AT THAT SKY!
LOOK AT ALL THESE MAGNIFICENT GERMAN PEOPLE ENJOYING THEIR BREAKFASTS!
UH...
HELLO?
WHAT'S THIS?
MAN, ASKING FOR MONEY WHILE PEOPLE ARE IN THE MIDDLE OF THEIR CHEESE PLATE!
AND ON A DAY LIKE TODAY!
CAN'T WE HAVE JUST ONE MORNING A WEEK BEING MAGNIFICENT WITHOUT INTERRUPTION?!
HEY!
WHY DIDN'T SHE STOP AND ASK US FOR MONEY?
WHAT DOES SHE THINK WE ARE?
JUST AS WELL.
POVERTY ISN'T ON TODAY'S AGENDA.
IT'S MY GODDAMN DAY OFF!
In the underground station...
I'LL TAKE THE S-BAHN FROM YORCKSTRASSE TO HERE AND THEN STROLL OVER TO THE BRANDENBURG GATE.
YEAH!
WHY NOT?!
J. SACCO 9.91

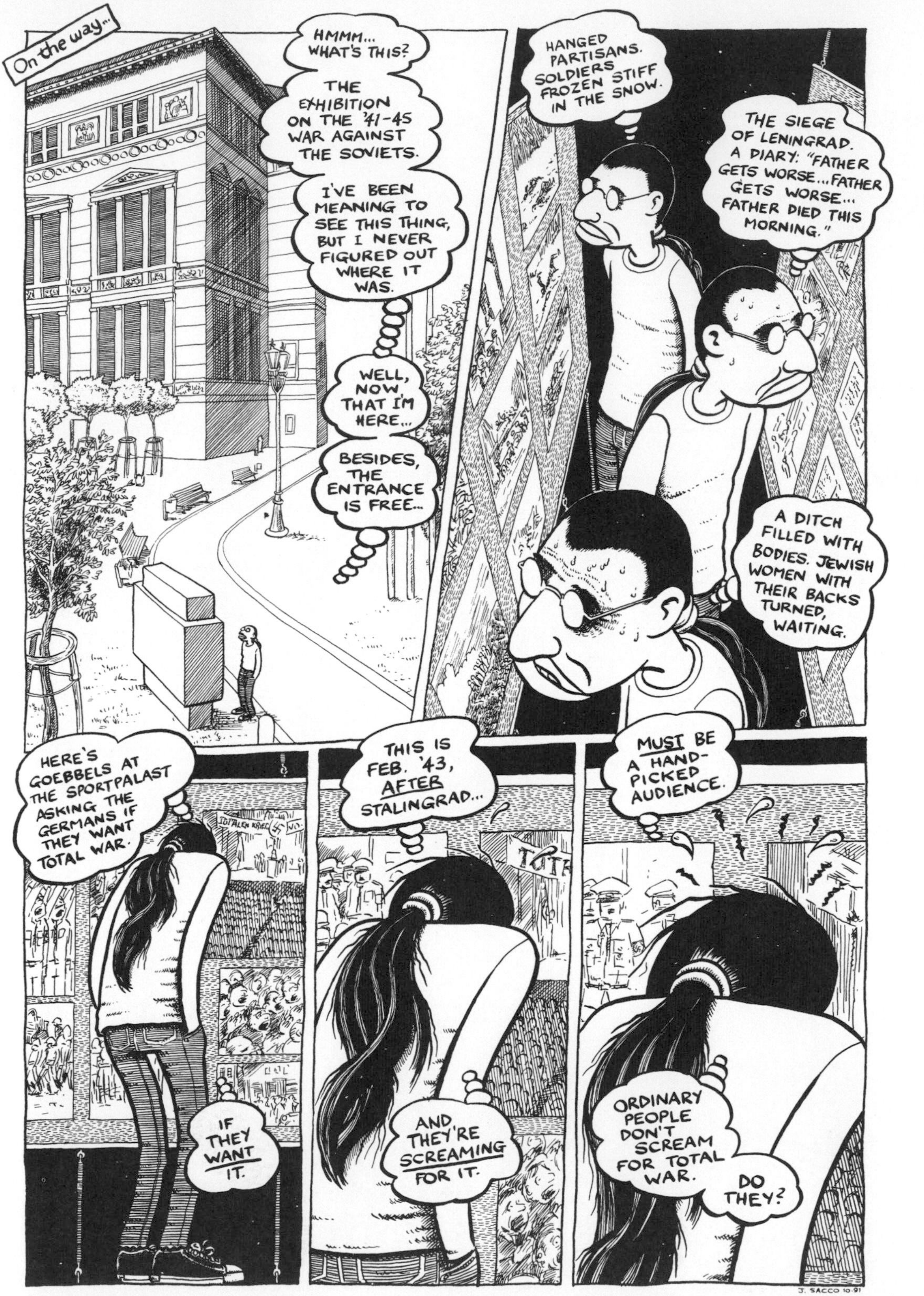
On the way...
HMMM... WHAT'S THIS?
THE EXHIBITION ON THE '41-45 WAR AGAINST THE SOVIETS.
I'VE BEEN MEANING TO SEE THIS THING, BUT I NEVER FIGURED OUT WHERE IT WAS.
WELL, NOW THAT I'M HERE...
BESIDES, THE ENTRANCE IS FREE...
HANGED PARTISANS. SOLDIERS FROZEN STIFF IN THE SNOW.
THE SIEGE OF LENINGRAD. A DIARY: "FATHER GETS WORSE... FATHER GETS WORSE... FATHER DIED THIS MORNING."
A DITCH FILLED WITH BODIES. JEWISH WOMEN WITH THEIR BACKS TURNED, WAITING.
HERE'S GOEBBELS AT THE SPORTPALAST ASKING THE GERMANS IF THEY WANT TOTAL WAR.
IF THEY WANT IT.
THIS IS FEB. '43, AFTER STALINGRAD...
AND THEY'RE SCREAMING FOR IT.
MUST BE A HAND-PICKED AUDIENCE.
ORDINARY PEOPLE DON'T SCREAM FOR TOTAL WAR.
DO THEY?
J. SACCO 10·91

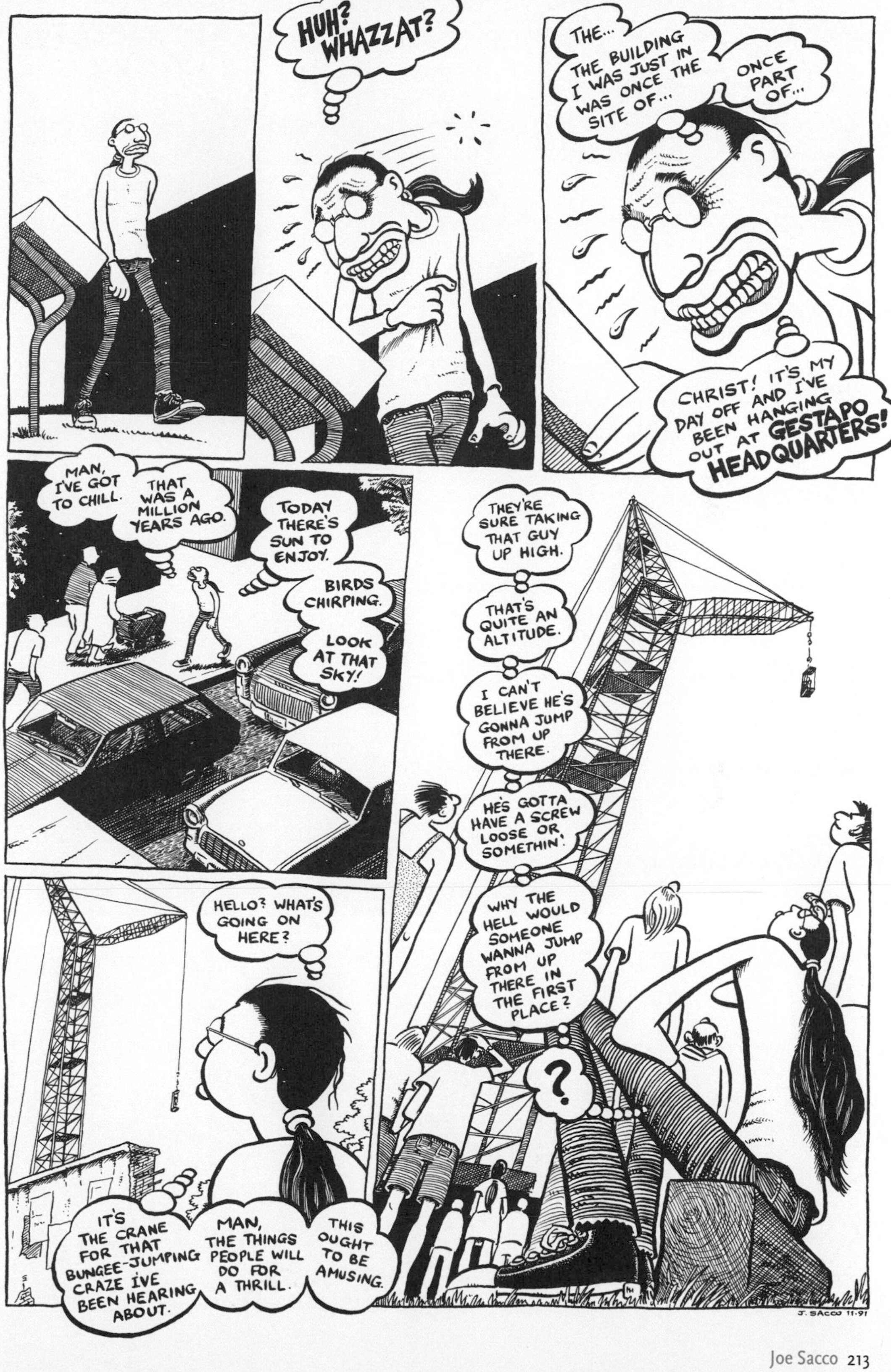
HUH? WHAZZAT?
THE... THE BUILDING I WAS JUST IN WAS ONCE THE SITE OF...
ONCE PART OF...
CHRIST! IT'S MY DAY OFF AND I'VE BEEN HANGING OUT AT GESTAPO HEADQUARTERS!
MAN, I'VE GOT TO CHILL.
THAT WAS A MILLION YEARS AGO.
TODAY THERE'S SUN TO ENJOY.
BIRDS CHIRPING.
LOOK AT THAT SKY!
HELLO? WHAT'S GOING ON HERE?
IT'S THE CRANE FOR THAT BUNGEE-JUMPING CRAZE I'VE BEEN HEARING ABOUT.
MAN, THE THINGS PEOPLE WILL DO FOR A THRILL.
THIS OUGHT TO BE AMUSING.
THEY'RE SURE TAKING THAT GUY UP HIGH.
THAT'S QUITE AN ALTITUDE.
I CAN'T BELIEVE HE'S GONNA JUMP FROM UP THERE.
HE'S GOTTA HAVE A SCREW LOOSE OR SOMETHIN'.
WHY THE HELL WOULD SOMEONE WANNA JUMP FROM UP THERE IN THE FIRST PLACE?
?
J. SACCO 11-91

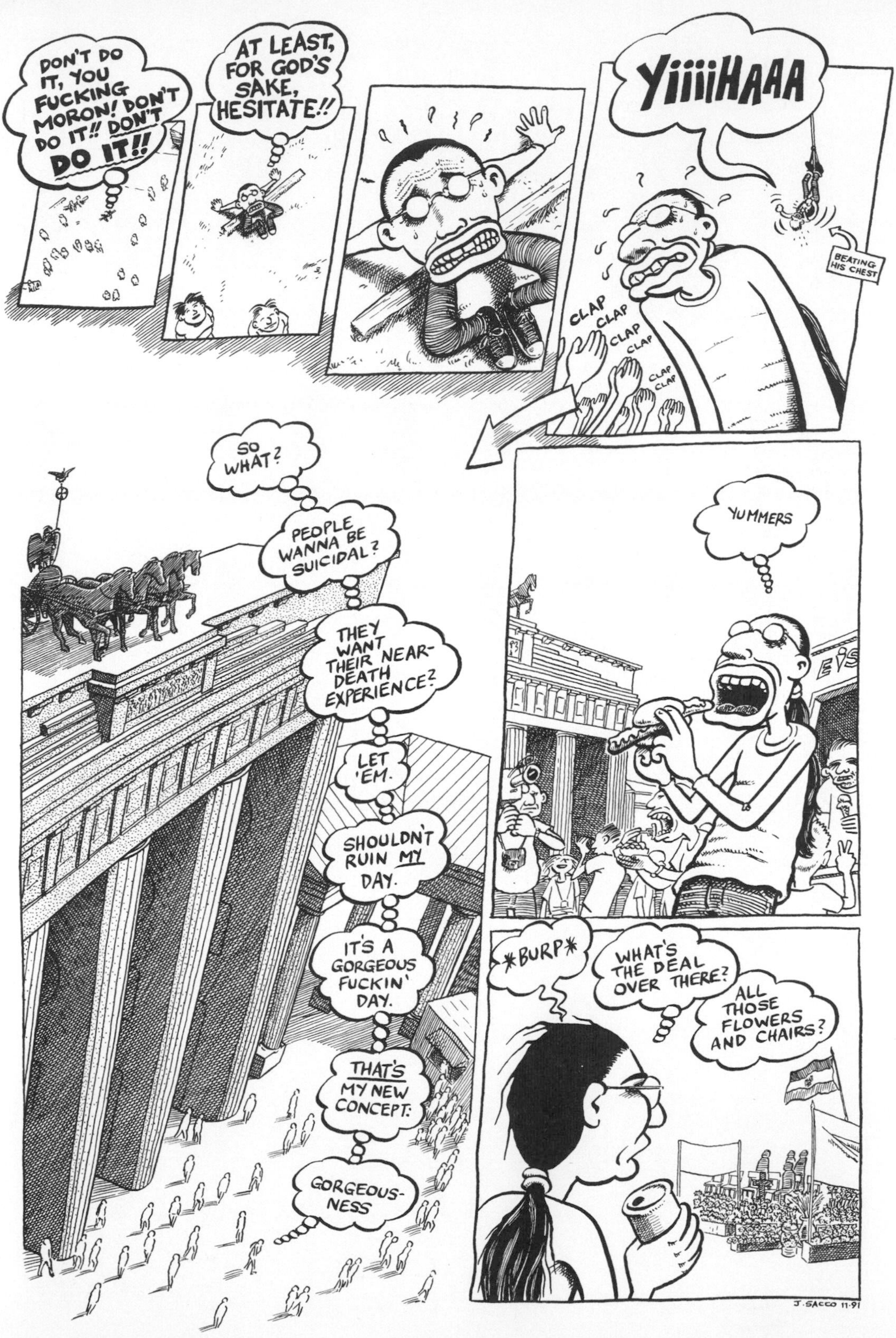
DON'T DO IT, YOU FUCKING MORON! DON'T DO IT!! DON'T DO IT!!
AT LEAST, FOR GOD'S SAKE, HESITATE!!
YiiiiHAAA
BEATING HIS CHEST
CLAP CLAP CLAP CLAP CLAP CLAP
SO WHAT?
PEOPLE WANNA BE SUICIDAL?
THEY WANT THEIR NEAR-DEATH EXPERIENCE?
LET 'EM.
SHOULDN'T RUIN MY DAY.
IT'S A GORGEOUS FUCKIN' DAY.
THAT'S MY NEW CONCEPT:
GORGEOUS-NESS
YUMMERS
BURP
WHAT'S THE DEAL OVER THERE?
ALL THOSE FLOWERS AND CHAIRS?
J. SACCO 11·91

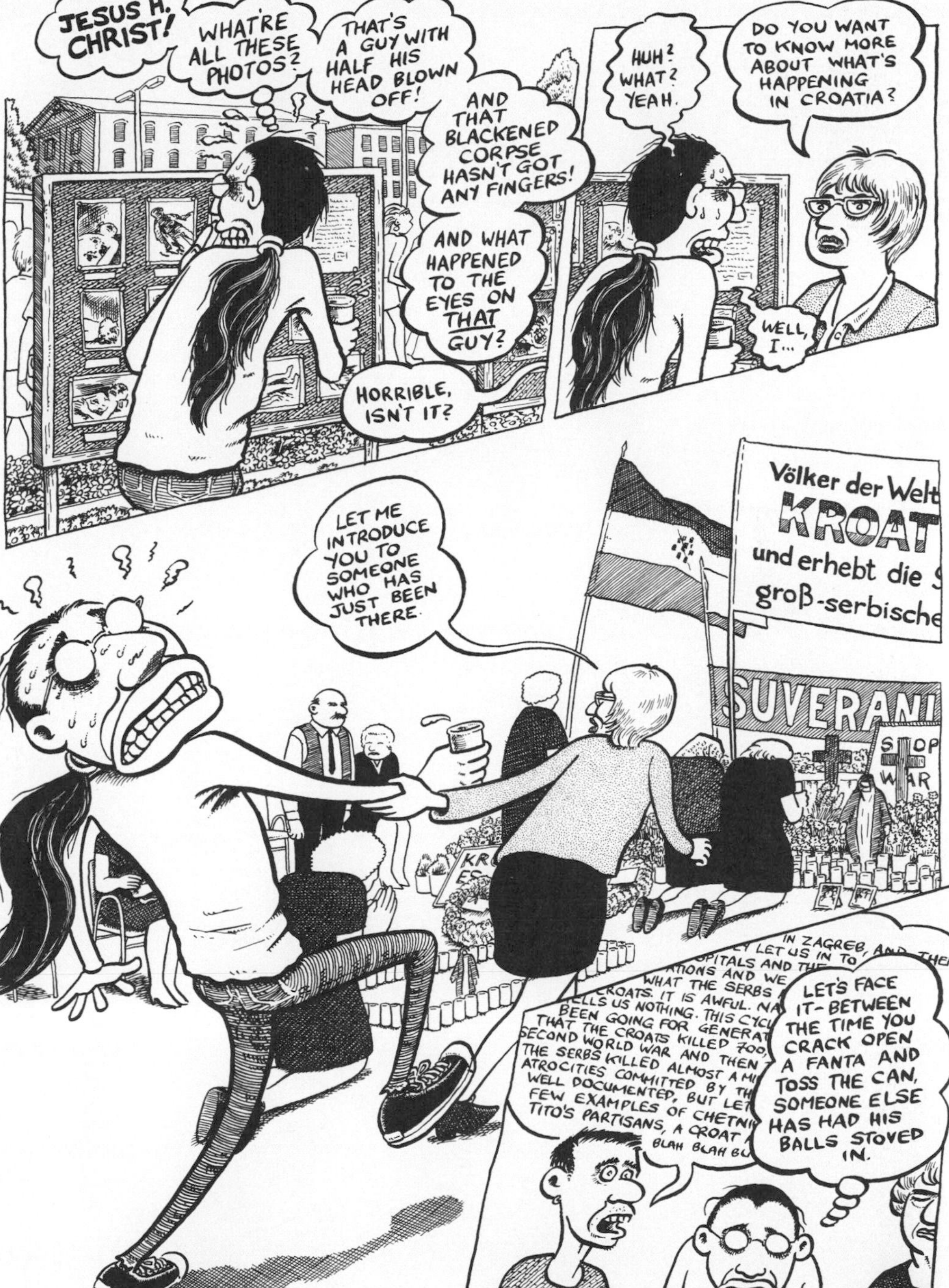
JESUS H. CHRIST!
WHAT'RE ALL THESE PHOTOS?
THAT'S A GUY WITH HALF HIS HEAD BLOWN OFF!
AND THAT BLACKENED CORPSE HASN'T GOT ANY FINGERS!
AND WHAT HAPPENED TO THE EYES ON THAT GUY?
HORRIBLE, ISN'T IT?
HUH? WHAT? YEAH.
DO YOU WANT TO KNOW MORE ABOUT WHAT'S HAPPENING IN CROATIA?
WELL, I...
LET ME INTRODUCE YOU TO SOMEONE WHO HAS JUST BEEN THERE.
Völker der Welt
KROAT
und erhebt die
groß-serbische
SUVERANI
STOP WAR
IN ZAGREB, AND THEN
LET US IN TO
AND WE
WHAT THE SERBS
IT IS AWFUL.
US NOTHING. THIS
BEEN GOING FOR
THAT THE CROATS KILLED
SECOND WORLD WAR AND THEN
THE SERBS KILLED ALMOST A
ATROCITIES COMMITTED BY
WELL DOCUMENTED, BUT
FEW EXAMPLES OF
TITO'S PARTISANS, A CROAT
BLAH BLAH
LET'S FACE IT - BETWEEN THE TIME YOU CRACK OPEN A FANTA AND TOSS THE CAN, SOMEONE ELSE HAS HAD HIS BALLS STOVED IN.
J. SACCO 11-91

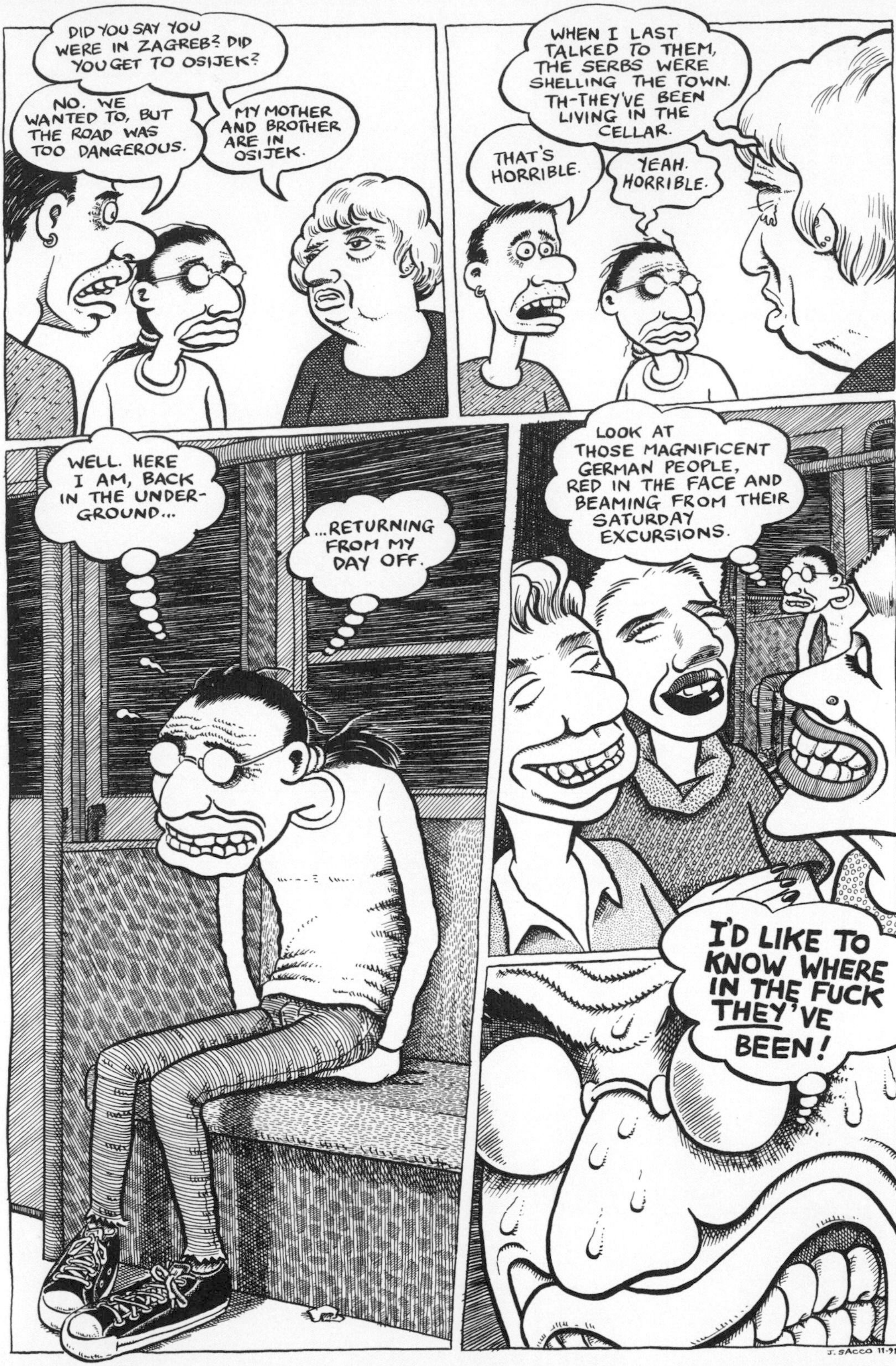
DID YOU SAY YOU WERE IN ZAGREB? DID YOU GET TO OSIJEK?
NO. WE WANTED TO, BUT THE ROAD WAS TOO DANGEROUS.
MY MOTHER AND BROTHER ARE IN OSIJEK.
WHEN I LAST TALKED TO THEM, THE SERBS WERE SHELLING THE TOWN. TH-THEY'VE BEEN LIVING IN THE CELLAR.
THAT'S HORRIBLE.
YEAH. HORRIBLE.
WELL. HERE I AM, BACK IN THE UNDER-GROUND...
...RETURNING FROM MY DAY OFF.
LOOK AT THOSE MAGNIFICENT GERMAN PEOPLE, RED IN THE FACE AND BEAMING FROM THEIR SATURDAY EXCURSIONS.
I'D LIKE TO KNOW WHERE IN THE FUCK THEY'VE BEEN!
J. SACCO 11-91

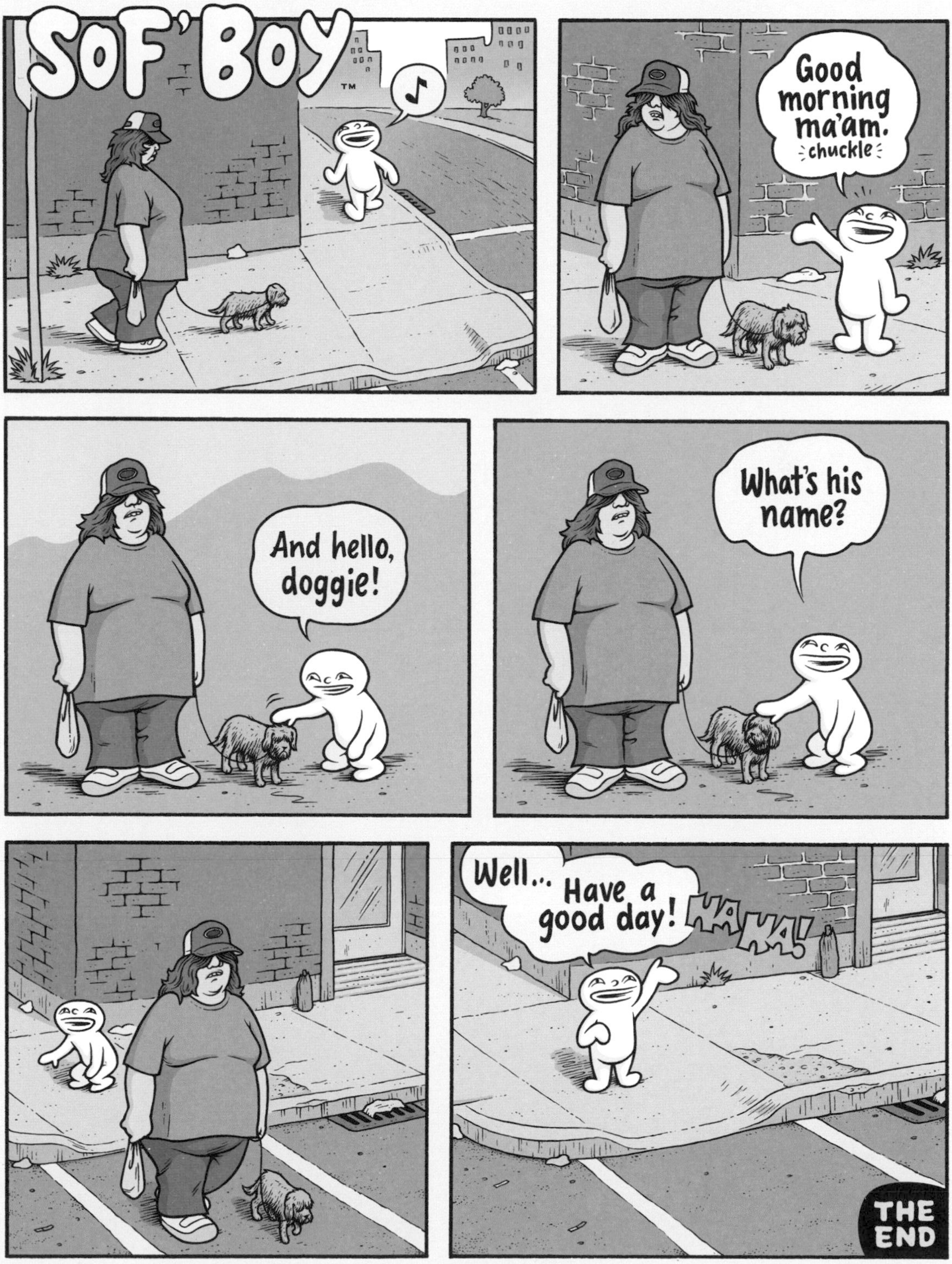
SOF' BOY
TM
♪
Good morning ma'am.
chuckle
And hello, doggie!
What's his name?
Well... Have a good day! HA HA!
THE END

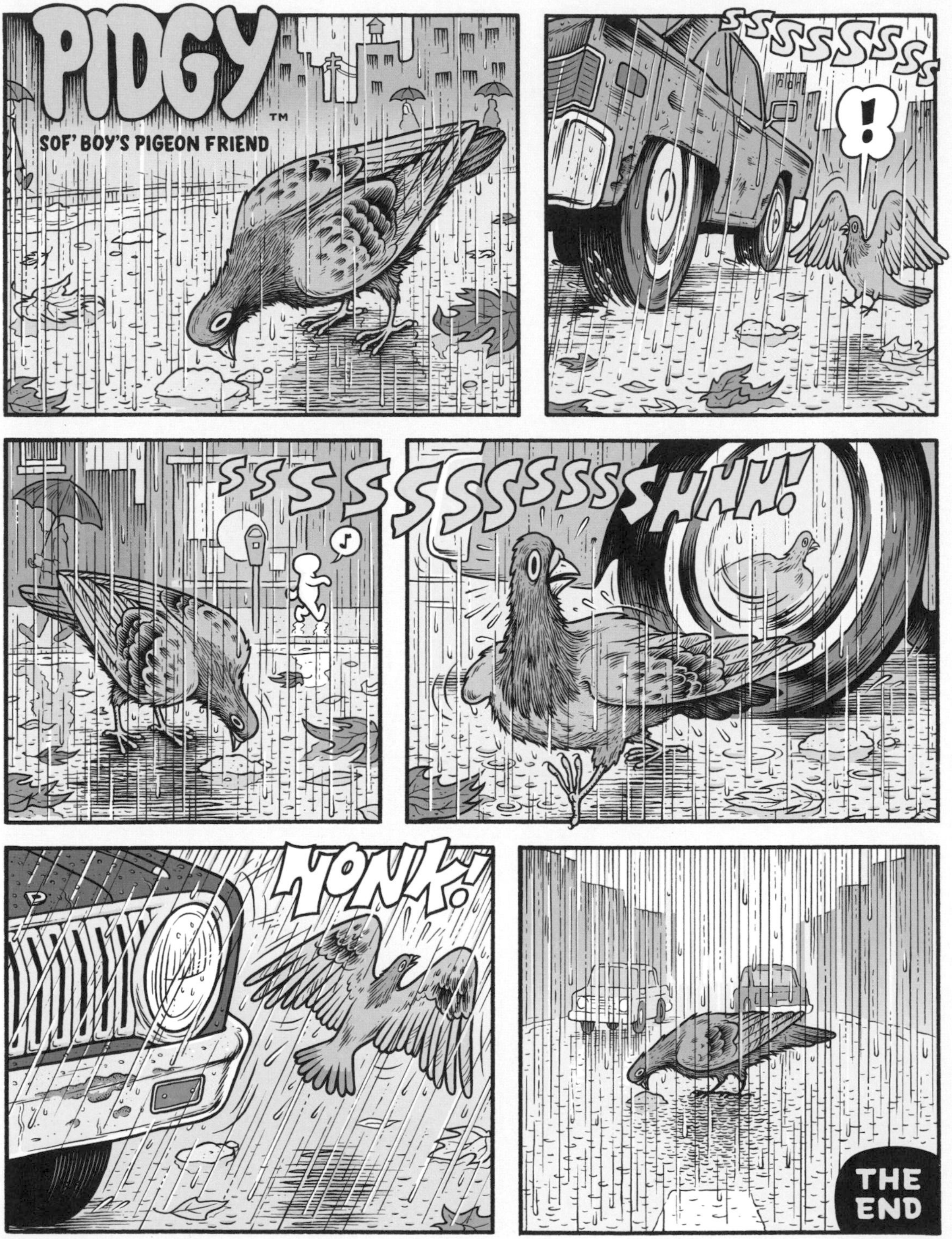
PIDGY™
SOF' BOY'S PIGEON FRIEND
SSSSSSSSS
!
SSSSSSSSSSHHH!
NONK!
THE END

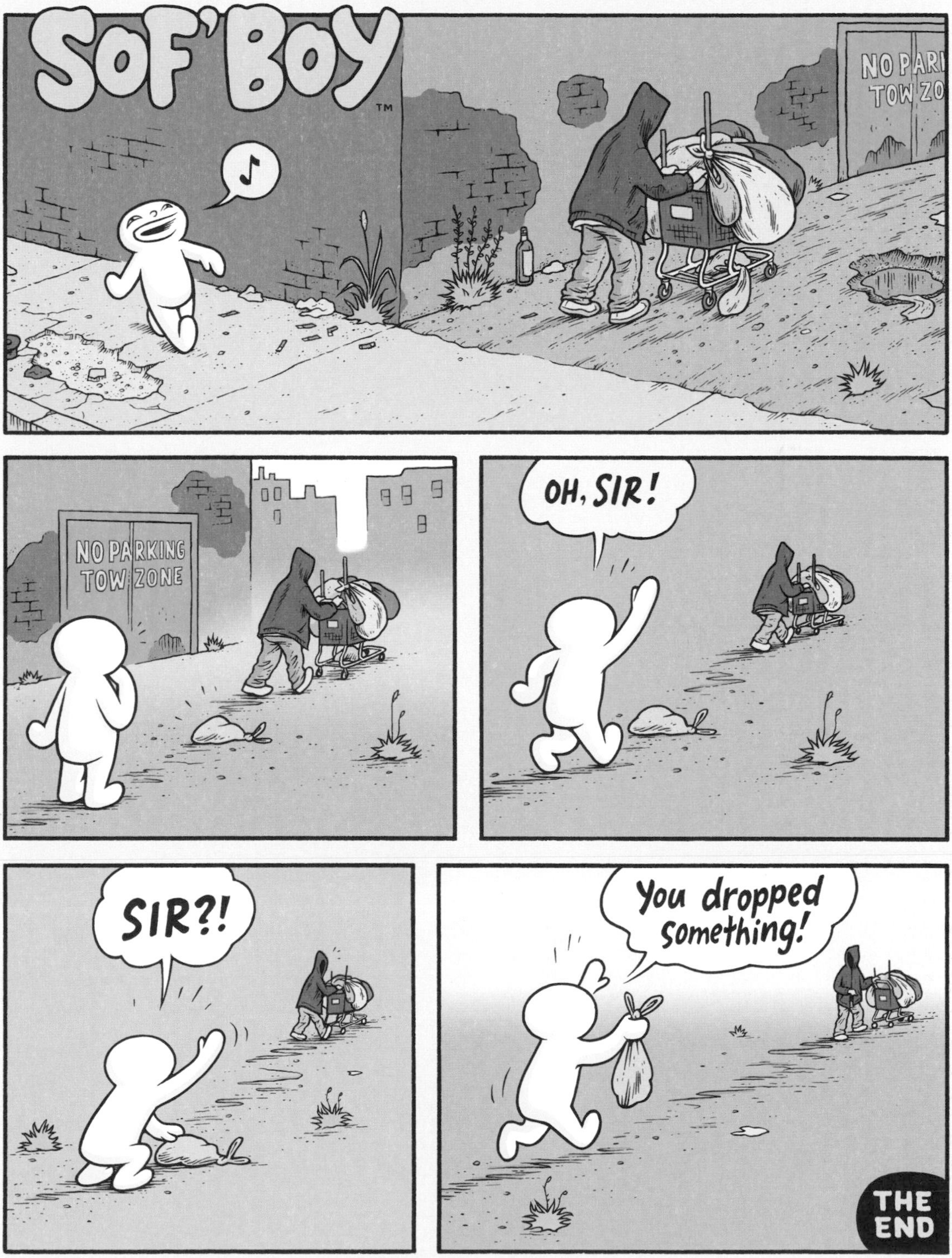
SOF'BOY
TM
♪
NO PARKI
TOW ZO
NO PARKING
TOW ZONE
OH, SIR!
SIR?!
You dropped something!
THE END

THE CLOWES INSIDE ME

an appreciation of Daniel Clowes by Naomi Fry

Dan Clowes makes me feel things very deeply, and I don't mean this metaphorically. When I think about my body and its reactions as my eye and mind are experiencing a Clowes page, I envision a slow, solid object making its way into my chest cavity, jostling my heart to and fro before moving downward to nudge at my intestines and turn my stomach. This is a clumsy, embarrassing way of explaining a sensation that's both ineffable and highly particularized, just like Clowes's comics themselves, with their use of hyperdistinct details to achieve a holistic, almost spiritual effect (although I'm not completely sure what I mean by that word, like the young protagonist in the Clowes strip "Immortal, Invisible" I'd still venture that "that's the word I want to use").

We can see this effect at work in almost any Clowes comic we can name, but let's take, for example, a brief chapter called "Andy's World" from 2011's *The Death-Ray*. Andy and his high school friend Louie are in gym class, where, in a series of tight minipanels, we first see Andy—who has not yet experienced the Hulk-like, cigarette-induced physical transformation on which the book hinges—do an embarrassingly negligible number of pull-ups ("I'll give you 4," says the coach); then Stoob, the alpha-male class bully, does twenty-seven; and finally Louie, a socially marginalized, rageful weakling, surprises his classmates by besting Stoob by one pull-up. ("Louie put on some muscle over the summer!") In the locker room, Louie tries to suggest to Stoob that he should "pace [himself] a little better, like coach Pasternak said," and in a cringingly awkward moment offers him his hand to shake, thanking him for "being such a good sport and everything"—an overture that Stoob refuses to reciprocate, staring expressionlessly at Louie's hand as it dangles, disembodied, at the panel's left. "What the fuck is that supposed to mean?" Louie fumes to Andy on the way home from school. "I don't give a shit if you like me, but you damn well better show some respect!"

There's so much here, and it's all rendered exactly right, completely physical and completely recognizable: Stoob's stiff, ginger hairdo, a tightly ringleted seventies whiteboy afro; Louie's wispy beginnings of a mustache and his transition glasses; the abstract-y public sculpture (yellow-ish, vaguely figure-eight-shaped) Louie and Andy pass by when walking home, the sort that resides dependably at the margins of our collective metropolitan consciousness just as it does at the far edge of the panel; even the name "Stoob" is spot-on, suggesting in its very denseness the character's opaque aggression. The drab colours the scene is washed in—chalk blue, asphalt grey, shit brown—have the quality of something that you wish you didn't remember but do anyway. And it's Louie's cry for respect that bears out the real truth of the matter: if you weren't consistently humiliated by life, you wouldn't recall every stupid moment of it in such intense detail.

In *The Death-Ray*, the corollary to Andy's cigarette-fueled violent encounters is the eponymous object itself, the fantastic gun that disappears anything that comes in its path, relegating it to a maw of nothingness. The overt brutality Andy inflicts on his victims feels somehow well deserved, even meaningful—his bloody revenge-taking on Stoob in Louie's name is reminiscent of the half-harrowing, half-celebratory scene in Paul Thomas Anderson's *Boogie Nights*, in which the beleaguered porn star Rollergirl attacks a bullying, rapey former classmate, kicking him with her roller skates as she hysterically shrieks, "You don't ever disrespect me, fucker!" The death-ray, in contradistinction, is not about making a satisfying, if pugnacious, body-to-body connection, but about a complete negation of connection—a sinister evacuation of memory and feeling. It also represents the flipside of Clowes's own creative project. In opposition to the death-ray's decimating actions, Clowes doesn't repress bad situations, instead rendering them scrupulously.

Wilson, published in 2010, is, too, a continuous series of weird hurts and embarrassments in the lives of its protagonist and his cohort, lives barely leavened by brief moments of relief—in fact, I'd argue that the book's famously shifting drawing style is Clowes's way of evoking characters so uncomfortable that they continuously try, and fail, to escape their own skins, as it were—but there is something real and, again, almost spiritual in that brutality. When the sorry Wilson throws his hands up toward the end of the

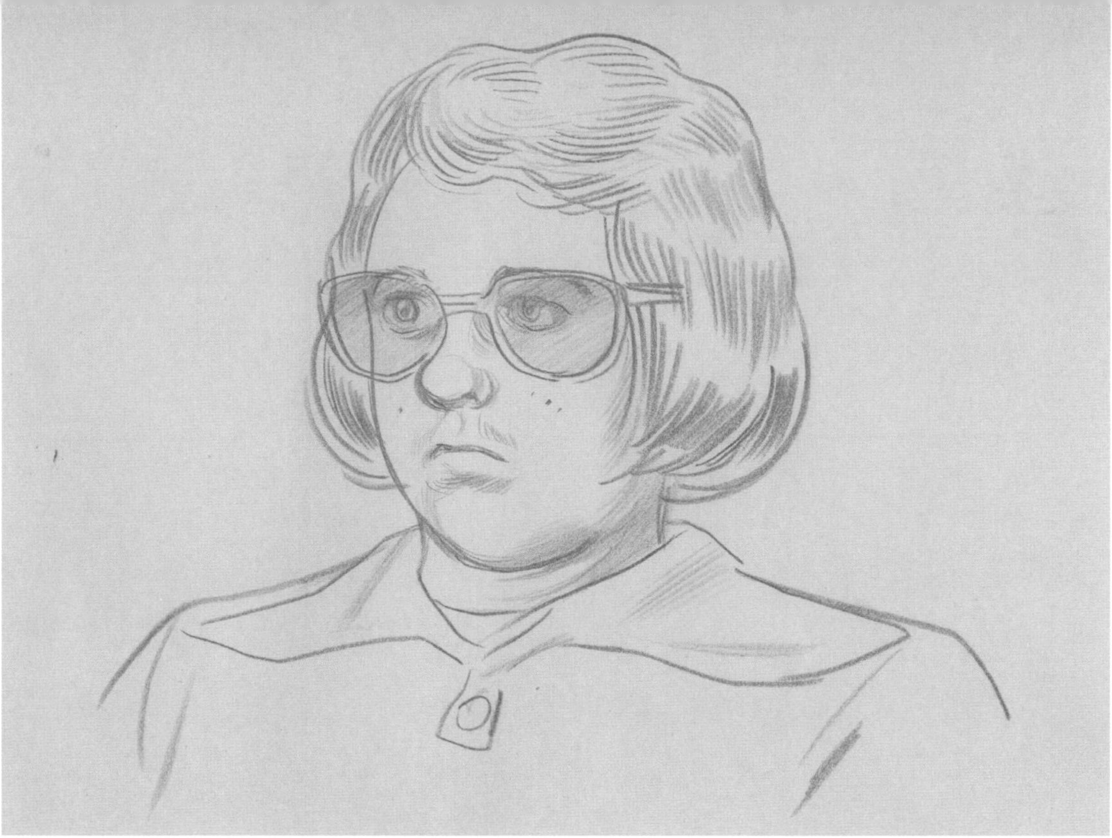

book and announces, "I am a beautiful creature! I'm a living monument to nature's genius! I'm alive and breathing and strong!" it's clearly a joke, but also not. The point in which authors represent people in their fully problematic, fully complicated, fully shameful personhoods is also the point in which we begin to feel things toward the books we read and, maybe, toward one another.

As I was starting to think about this piece, it came to me that the first time I tried to write something for publication, it was actually about Clowes. This was back in 1998, and I was twenty-two; a new, overdesigned, soon-to-be-defunct "youth culture" magazine in Tel Aviv, where I was living at the time, agreed to let me write a review of *Ghost World*, and I set about eking out some thoughts onto a page. I had a lot of feelings—it was my first encounter with that uncanny Clowesian ability to move around my insides—and finding the words to express them was difficult and took me a long time. When I was done, I walked over to the editor's apartment to deliver the piece. The editor, a very short guy with very long sideburns, sat me down and told me that the piece needed "major work." "What is this?" he said. "You handed *this* in?" Another editor weighed in over the phone and told me the piece was "boring." "You need to let me see the candy right away, up front!" she instructed harshly (but what did that mean?). When the piece was published, many months later, it was unrecognizable, and my name was misspelled in the byline.

This is a small, stupid, embarrassing story, and I have many stories just like it: the time I fell into a large hole in an unpaved road while walking to a party and two guys had to pull me out as multiple people watched; the time I farted nervously when a guy I liked was about to kiss me and when he asked me about it I denied it, the obvious lie hanging in the air like my fart (I could go on). One of the reasons Clowes is a genius is because he sketches out this sort of humiliation and self-loathing not to do away with it, but to make the act of expressing it a sort of revenge, even a triumph. It's as if to say: I hate myself and it's fine, I know and remember everything about it, here, let me draw it for you.

***Naomi Fry is a writer and editor. She has taught at the Rhode Island School of Design, New York University, and Johns Hopkins University and has written about art, literature, and culture for the* London Review of Books, *the* New York Times Book Review, n+1, *and* Frieze, *among other publications. She is also the copy chief at* T: The New York Times Style Magazine.**

Character sketch for *The Death-Ray* (2002).

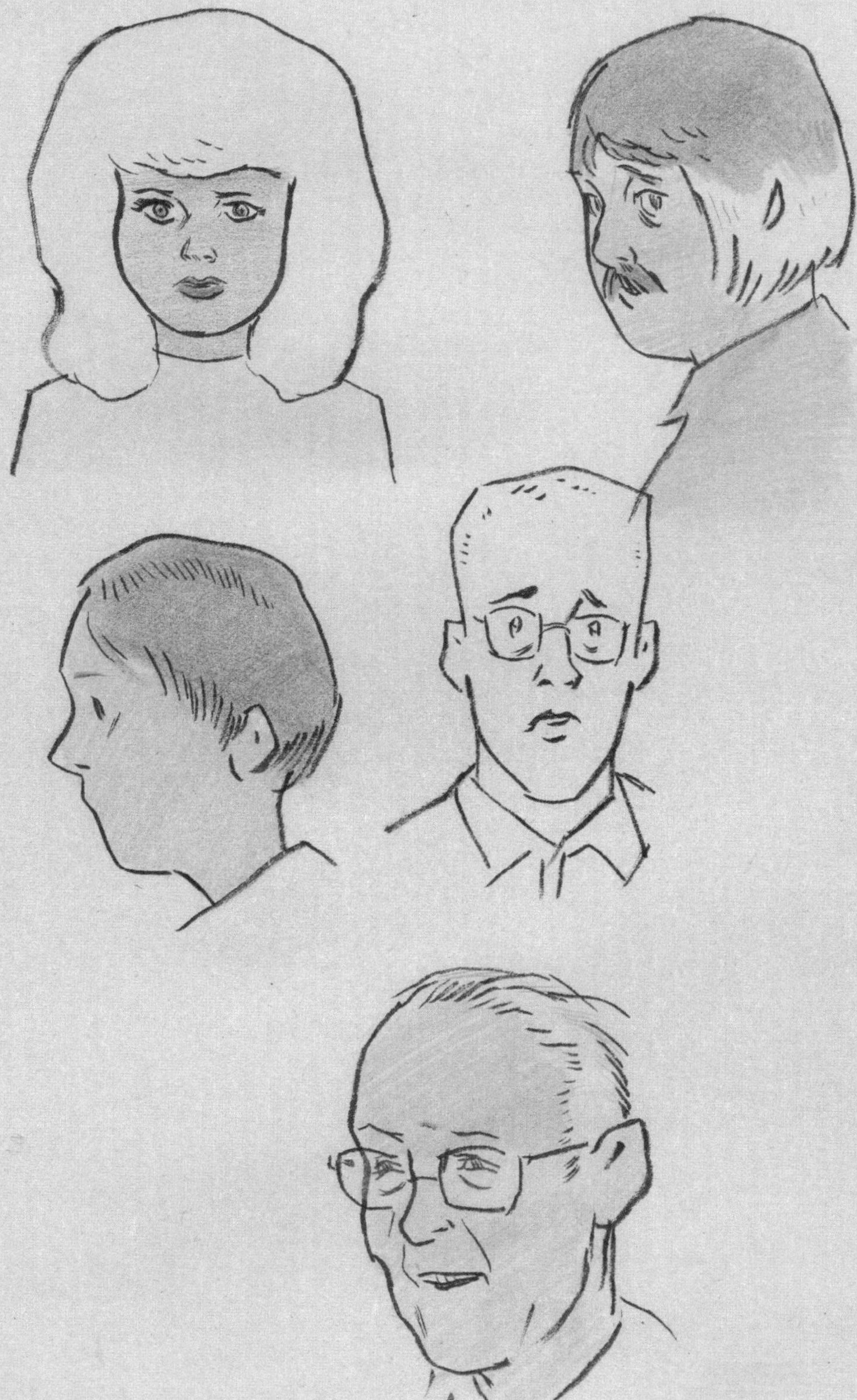

222 Character sketches for *The Death-Ray* (2002).

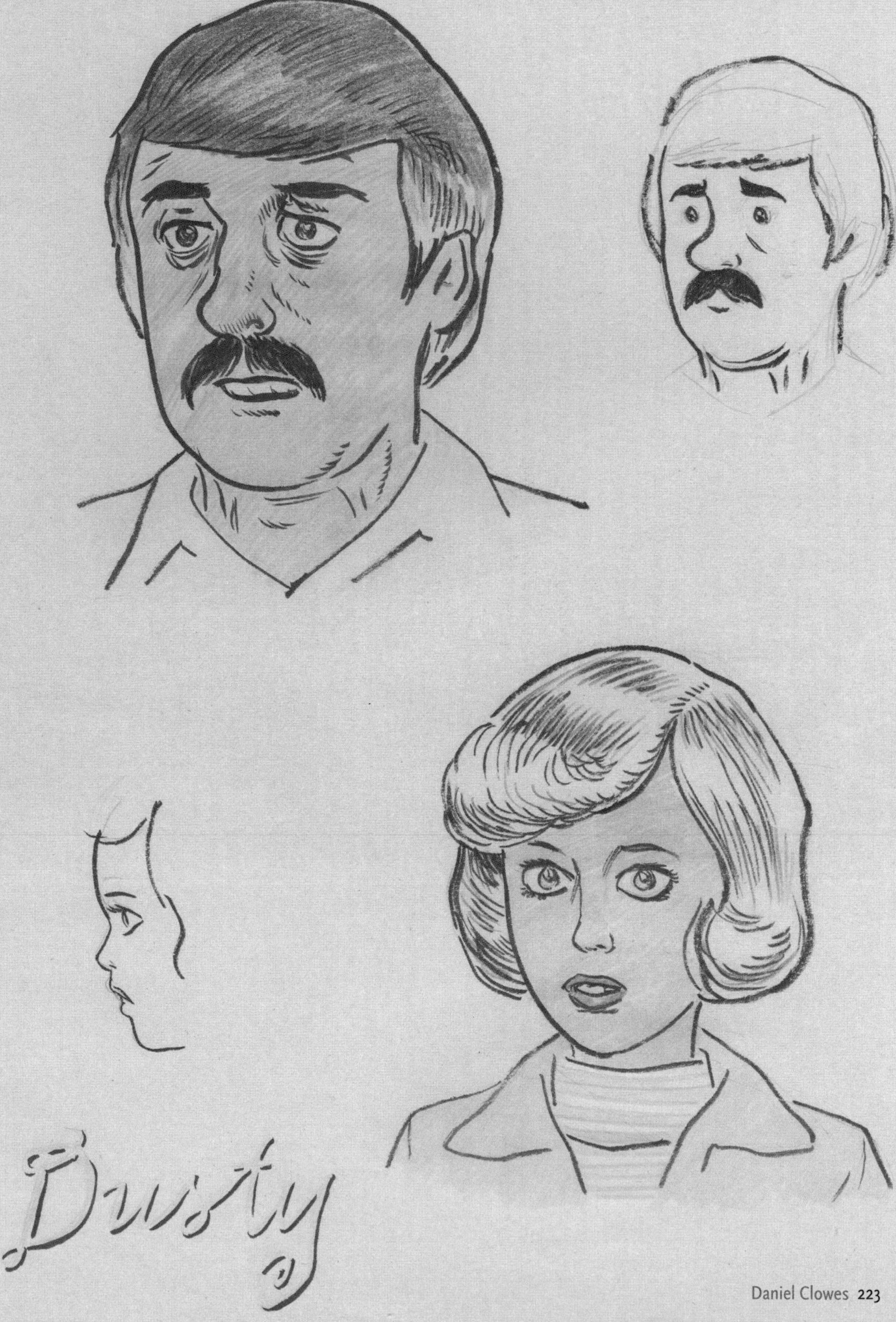
Dusty

Wilson IN DAY 16,412

BY DANIEL CLOWES

LOOK AT THIS— A FRONT-PAGE STORY ABOUT HOW BAD THINGS ARE IN THE NEWSPAPER BUSINESS!

TALK ABOUT SOLIPSISTIC! MY GOD, IT'S LIKE LISTENING TO SOME OLD LADY COMPLAIN ABOUT HER ARTHRITIS!

HELLO?

HEY! I'M TALKING TO YOU!

WHAT? I'M TRYING TO LISTEN TO SOMETHING...

GOSH! I'M SO SORRY!

PLEASE ACCEPT MY DEEPEST APOLOGIES FOR ATTEMPTING TO INITIATE A BRIEF MOMENT OF "HUMAN INTERACTION." IT SHAN'T HAPPEN AGAIN!

MY GOD! HERE WE ARE, STRANGE ORGANISMS, EVOLVED OVER THE MILLENNIA, ENDURING CENTURIES OF WAR AND TORTURE, TO FINALLY ARRIVE AT THE WONDERFUL DAY WHEN JOE GOOFBALL CAN LISTEN AT ANY GIVEN SECOND TO WHATEVER MUSICAL ATROCITY SUITS HIS WHIM!

HEY, DO YOU HAVE 30 SECONDS TO SAVE THE PLANET?

30 SECONDS? O.K. ....

GO!

WELL, DID YOU KNOW THE POLAR ICE CAPS ARE—

WAIT A MINUTE! ARE YOU ONE OF THOSE GLOBAL-WARMING GUYS?

CLIMATE CHANGE

HA! MANY—

GOOD LUCK WITH THAT, BUDDY! I'M FREEZING MY ASS OFF OUT HERE! IT'S SUPPOSED TO SNOW TOMORROW!

WELL, PART OF WHAT WE'RE TRYING TO DO IS EDUCATE THE PUBLIC A—

BZZZT! I'M SO SORRY, BUT YOUR TIME IS UP!

"Wilson in Day 16,412" first appeared in the *New Yorker* (March 15, 2010).

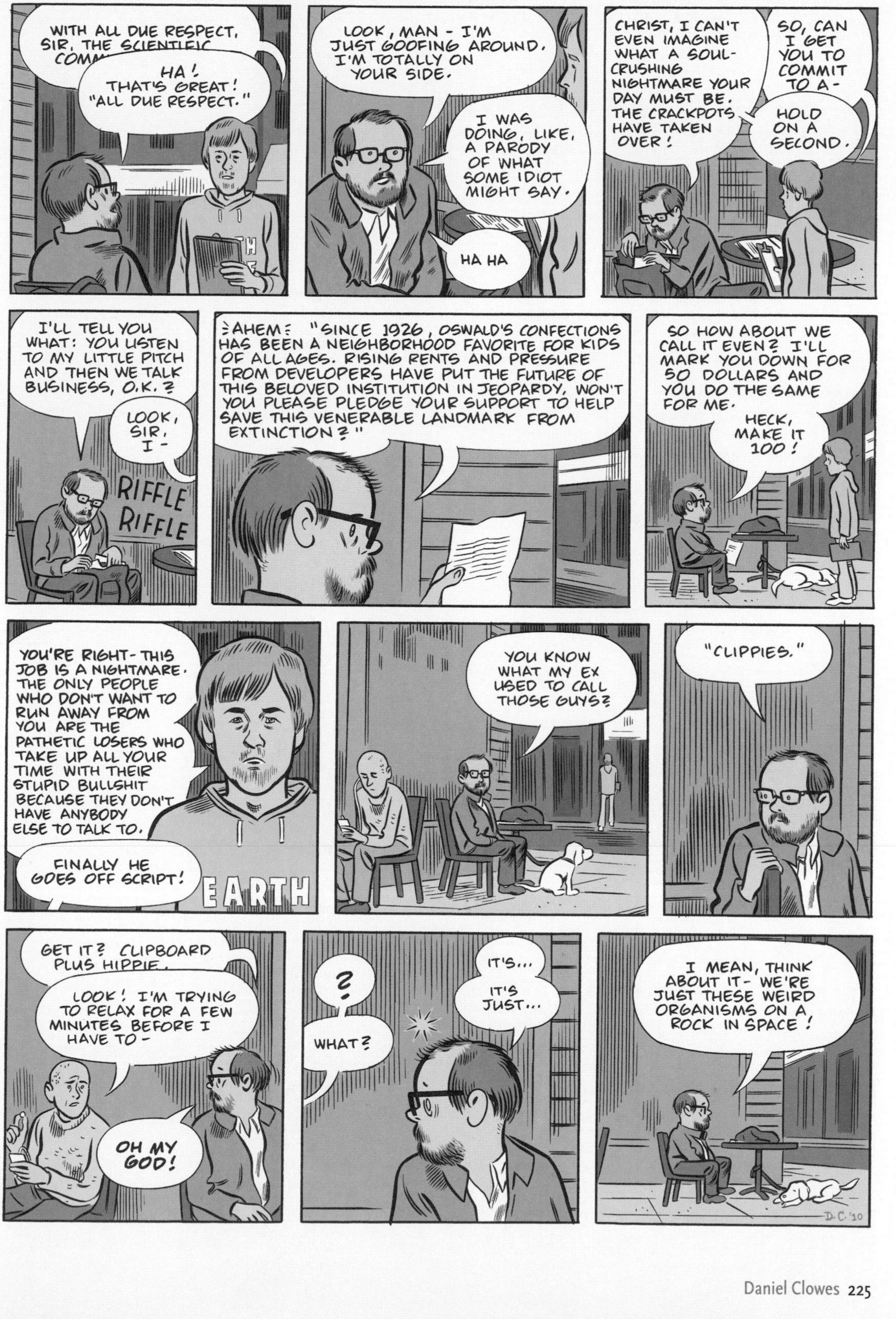
WITH ALL DUE RESPECT, SIR, THE SCIENTIFIC COMM
HA! THAT'S GREAT! "ALL DUE RESPECT."
LOOK, MAN - I'M JUST GOOFING AROUND. I'M TOTALLY ON YOUR SIDE.
I WAS DOING, LIKE, A PARODY OF WHAT SOME IDIOT MIGHT SAY.
HA HA
CHRIST, I CAN'T EVEN IMAGINE WHAT A SOUL-CRUSHING NIGHTMARE YOUR DAY MUST BE. THE CRACKPOTS HAVE TAKEN OVER!
SO, CAN I GET YOU TO COMMIT TO A -
HOLD ON A SECOND.
I'LL TELL YOU WHAT: YOU LISTEN TO MY LITTLE PITCH AND THEN WE TALK BUSINESS, O.K.?
LOOK, SIR. I -
RIFFLE RIFFLE
:AHEM: "SINCE 1926, OSWALD'S CONFECTIONS HAS BEEN A NEIGHBORHOOD FAVORITE FOR KIDS OF ALL AGES. RISING RENTS AND PRESSURE FROM DEVELOPERS HAVE PUT THE FUTURE OF THIS BELOVED INSTITUTION IN JEOPARDY. WON'T YOU PLEASE PLEDGE YOUR SUPPORT TO HELP SAVE THIS VENERABLE LANDMARK FROM EXTINCTION?"
SO HOW ABOUT WE CALL IT EVEN? I'LL MARK YOU DOWN FOR 50 DOLLARS AND YOU DO THE SAME FOR ME.
HECK, MAKE IT 100!
YOU'RE RIGHT- THIS JOB IS A NIGHTMARE. THE ONLY PEOPLE WHO DON'T WANT TO RUN AWAY FROM YOU ARE THE PATHETIC LOSERS WHO TAKE UP ALL YOUR TIME WITH THEIR STUPID BULLSHIT BECAUSE THEY DON'T HAVE ANYBODY ELSE TO TALK TO.
FINALLY HE GOES OFF SCRIPT!
EARTH
YOU KNOW WHAT MY EX USED TO CALL THOSE GUYS?
"CLIPPIES."
GET IT? CLIPBOARD PLUS HIPPIE.
LOOK! I'M TRYING TO RELAX FOR A FEW MINUTES BEFORE I HAVE TO -
OH MY GOD!
?
WHAT?
IT'S...
IT'S JUST...
I MEAN, THINK ABOUT IT- WE'RE JUST THESE WEIRD ORGANISMS ON A ROCK IN SPACE!
D.C. '10

AESTHETICS, ETHICS, AND TACOS

an appreciation of Chris Ware by Ivan Brunetti

It is a strange sensation, writing an essay about a friend's work, trying to balance affection and enthusiasm with a high-minded, objective detachment; I feel like a dead man writing the eulogy of a living person. I suppose Drawn & Quarterly could have commissioned any number of more qualified individuals (comics theorists, journalists, other cartoonists) to describe concisely Chris's formal mastery and expansion of the comics language, detail his central role in the current flowering of graphic novels as a viable art form, and articulate his command of and deep respect for his craft. While these are all worthy topics, I'm not sure what new insights I could contribute to the extensive body of books, articles, interviews, dissertations, and blog entries that already exists. Because I have been fortunate enough to know Chris as a confidant and consider him my closest friend—to paraphrase a characterization made by our mutual friend Dan Raeburn, Chris is the Frog to my Toad—I would like to offer something perhaps a little less analytical and instead a bit more personal.

Sometimes people ask me, "Wow, you know Chris Ware?" and I understand their incredulity. Long before I ever got to know Chris, I was in awe of him, having clipped out a sizable stack of his strips from the Chicago alternative newspaper *New City*. I thought this back then and still think it now, though Chris may cringe: "Thrilling Adventure Stories" in *RAW* vol. 2, no. 3, is one of the most important stories ever drawn in comics. In a mere six pages, the potential expressive power of the possible combinations of words, images, panel borders, balloons, sound effects, etc., infinitely expands. This was only the beginning, of course: the shapeshifting ACME Novelty Library series, the seminal *Jimmy Corrigan*, the underrated *Quimby the Mouse*, the essential *McSweeney's* no. 13, the exemplary *Walt & Skeezix* reprint project, the revealing *Datebooks*, the intertwined *New Yorker* covers, the groundbreaking *Building Stories*, and many other masterpieces still lay ahead (the above list is dizzying but incomplete, amazingly). He is truly a genius, *sui generis*, and I am still in awe of him, even as—incongruously—I sit across from him every Sunday evening for our traditional dinner at our favourite Mexican restaurant, making bad jokes, scarfing

down tortilla chips, and spilling at least one requisite gob of salsa onto my shirt.

The thing is, Chris would never in a million years make you feel that you should be in any way in awe of him. It's simply not in his nature. Here's another incomplete list: he is down to earth, incapable of pretension, un-snooty, humble, polite, attentive, deferential, kind, thoughtful, generous, and self-effacing to a fault, as sincere as the most sincere pumpkin patch. I fear that itemizing or isolating an example of Chris exhibiting any of the above qualities would serve only to trivialize the matter. But I *can* say that Chris has never once made me feel bad about anything (not even the time I watched his cats and managed to shatter an antique picture frame that I shouldn't have been messing with anyway when I dropped it behind the piano).

Despite possessing an abundance of admirable qualities, he is unsparingly hard on himself and racked with doubt, holding himself to a harsh and unforgiving standard. It is this self-critical faculty that undoubtedly drives him to labour long hours, forever push and challenge himself, immerse himself in every project (not only attending to every imaginable detail but also discovering new, previously unexplored ones along the way), and ultimately attain everincreasing, mind-boggling levels of complexity and quality with his work. As a friend, however, it can be painful to watch this self-imposed torture, especially knowing that Chris would never inflict such judgment on others, but rather go out of his way to offer mercy and encouragement.

I can certainly attest to his forgiving and tolerant nature: when we first became friends, I was almost feral, wounded, confused with misplaced anger (translation: going through a bad divorce), but through his example, concern, guidance, and sometimes cajoling (Frog and Toad again), I was eventually able to calm down, focus, and stabilize my life. When I was afraid to risk ever having my heart broken again, he pointed out that this was absurd, akin to never getting a pet because someday it will die. There's a whole philosophy of art-making and life-living embedded in that simple statement. It occurs to me that, likewise, he has contributed a great deal to the comics medium's maturation—in form, but

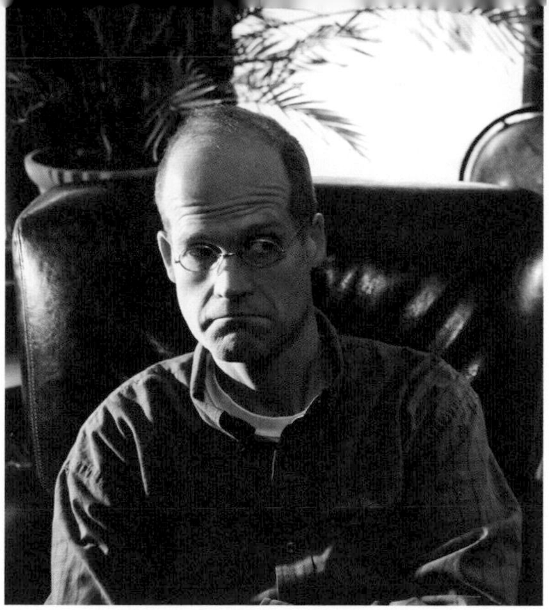

I love to look at cartoonists' sketchbooks. I think they are often as interesting as their comics (and sometimes more). I'm glad that D+Q published two volumes of sketchbooks by one of my favourite cartoonists, Chris Ware. Apart from the funny strips and glimpses into the life, work process, evolution, and doubts of Chris during those years, most importantly you can see a genuine love of drawing, which always gets to me. I always thought, as long as I am drawing, everything will be all right. When I look at the multiple observational drawings in these books, I have the feeling (and maybe I'm wrong) that Chris felt the same while he was doing them.—***Pascal Girard***

perhaps more importantly in ethics. It's certainly an overall much more humane and emotively evolved milieu than it once was, and Chris's work was a crucial part of that shift.

This all sounds so heavy, though. Did I mention that Chris is also devastatingly funny and has that rare ability to laugh at himself? The selection of sketches that follows will give the reader an inkling of what it's like to spend time with Chris and his impeccable perceptiveness, empathic sensitivity, and deep-rooted sense of humour. Our weekly dinner conversation usually winds through a free-associative tangle of topics—anything from speculations about the nature of consciousness to the vagaries of rapidographs to memories of the specific textures of 1970s television broadcasts. Sure, we constantly express dismay and worry over our teetering world's crumbling façade of civility, but, honestly, when I picture myself on my deathbed, I am remembering our conversations as pleasant ones, and I'm laughing at one of Chris's observations about, oh, the frenzied atmosphere of a Costco parking lot, or the dialogue-as-exposition style of most Hollywood movie scripts, or birds continually defecating on his sketchbook while he tries to draw a stretch of nondescript architecture.

Not surprisingly, Chris notices everything in his environment and is offended by anything ugly, shoddy, false, ill-thought, or in any way demeaning to human existence (by contrast, to me, "reality" is just a bunch of stuff to bump into, plus it's usually the wrong temperature, and anyhow I have no suggestions for improvement because I possess zero practical skills). He once confessed to me that he was compelled to remove a bright orange highlighter marker from the top of his wife's desk and place it at a particular angle into a cup, because otherwise it violated the immediate visual field, and that his wife remarked that he had a *problem, man*—which he admitted was true. But it's that very same problem that has blessed the rest of us with books that approach the delicately interlaced immensity of cathedrals.

One last thing I wanted to mention: Chris is genuinely interested in people, in both the observant and sympathetic sense; moreover, I believe this quality provides the undergirding that makes his characters come alive on the page. One of Chris's pet peeves, in novels, plays, films, and comics, is when characters do not behave in the way real people would actually behave in the depicted situation. While he himself often fears that he is going out on a limb, writing characters far removed from direct autobiography, he naturally possesses a deep reserve of Kieslowski-like compassion and has honed an exquisitely fine-tuned B.S. detector that, I believe, keeps him honest. His is a humanist endeavour, and to me this is evident in the care he takes to depict both the mundane and the cosmic (merging them, really), find the dignity inherent in life while acknowledging its folly, and explore the hearts and minds of characters that would otherwise be given short shrift or ignored entirely. As the commentator Aleksandr Voronsky said of Tolstoy (one of Chris's heroes), "It is as if he were reading the secret code inherent in things, people, and events."

Ivan Brunetti is the cartoonist behind the series* Schizo *and the books* Cartooning: Philosophy and Practice *and* Aesthetics: A Memoir. *His illustrations have appeared all over, including on the cover of the* New Yorker. *Brunetti teaches comics and editorial illustration at the University of Chicago and Columbia College Chicago.

Photo: Seth Kushner (2011).

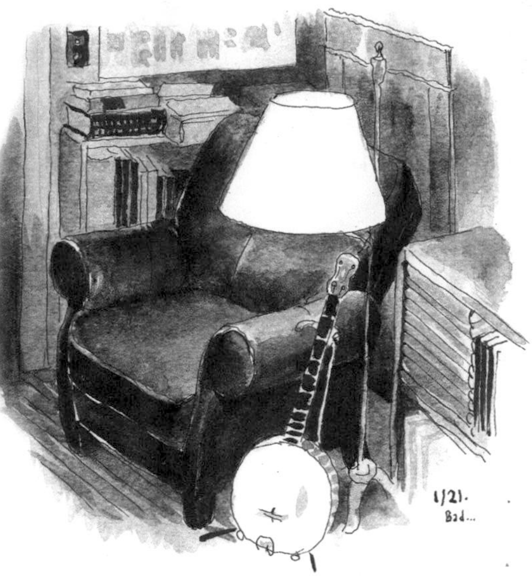
1/21.
Bad...

"BUT LAURA LAY AWAKE A LITTLE WHILE, LISTENING TO PA'S FIDDLE SOFTLY PLAYING AND TO THE LONELY SOUND OF THE WIND IN THE BIG WOODS. SHE LOOKED AT PA SITTING ON THE BENCH BY THE HEARTH, THE FIRELIGHT GLEAMING ON HIS BROWN HAIR AND BEARD AND GLISTENING ON THE HONEY-BROWN FIDDLE. SHE LOOKED AT MA, GENTLY ROCKING AND KNITTING.

SHE THOUGHT TO HERSELF, "THIS IS NOW."

SHE WAS GLAD THAT THE COSY HOUSE, AND PA AND MA AND THE FIRELIGHT AND THE MUSIC, WERE NOW. THEY COULD NOT BE FORGOTTEN, SHE THOUGHT, BECAUSE NOW IS NOW. IT CAN NEVER BE A LONG TIME AGO."

— "Little House in the Big Woods," 1930, last page.

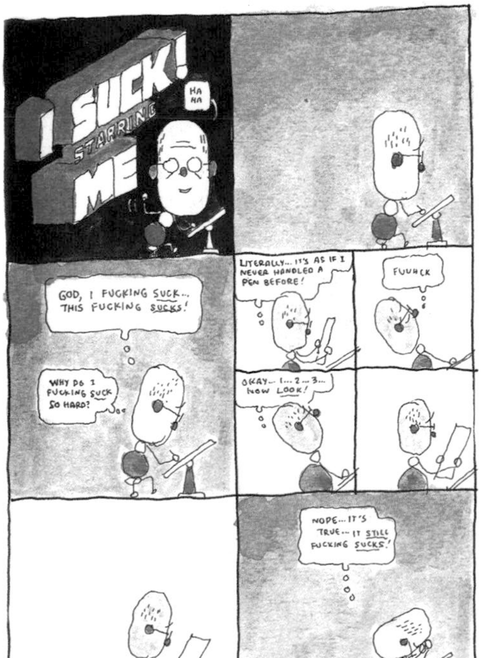
I SUCK!
STARRING
ME
HA HA
GOD, I FUCKING SUCK... THIS FUCKING SUCKS!
WHY DO I FUCKING SUCK SO HARD?
LITERALLY... IT'S AS IF I NEVER HANDLED A PEN BEFORE!
FUUUCK
OKAY... 1... 2... 3... NOW LOOK!
NOPE... IT'S TRUE... IT STILL FUCKING SUCKS!
FUCK!

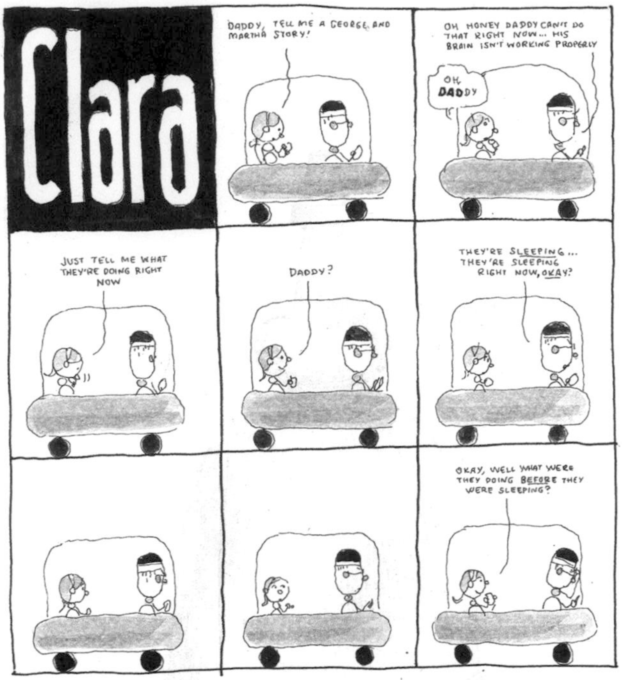
Clara
DADDY, TELL ME A GEORGE AND MARTHA STORY!
OH HONEY DADDY CAN'T DO THAT RIGHT NOW... HIS BRAIN ISN'T WORKING PROPERLY
OH, DADDY
JUST TELL ME WHAT THEY'RE DOING RIGHT NOW
DADDY?
THEY'RE SLEEPING... THEY'RE SLEEPING RIGHT NOW, OKAY?
OKAY, WELL WHAT WERE THEY DOING BEFORE THEY WERE SLEEPING?

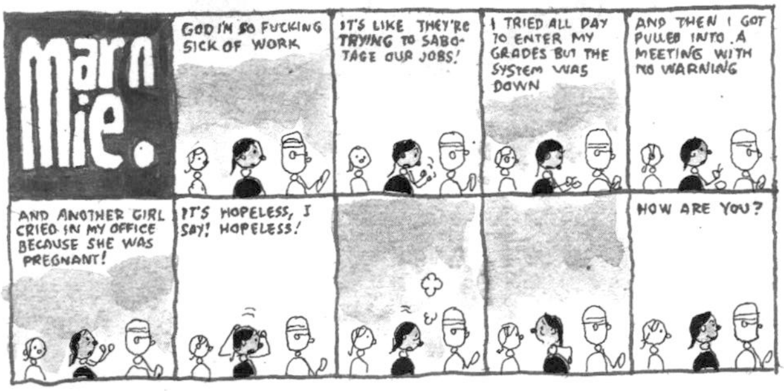
Marnie.
GOD I'M SO FUCKING SICK OF WORK
IT'S LIKE THEY'RE TRYING TO SABOTAGE OUR JOBS!
I TRIED ALL DAY TO ENTER MY GRADES BUT THE SYSTEM WAS DOWN
AND THEN I GOT PULLED INTO A MEETING WITH NO WARNING
AND ANOTHER GIRL CRIED IN MY OFFICE BECAUSE SHE WAS PREGNANT!
IT'S HOPELESS, I SAY! HOPELESS!
HOW ARE YOU?

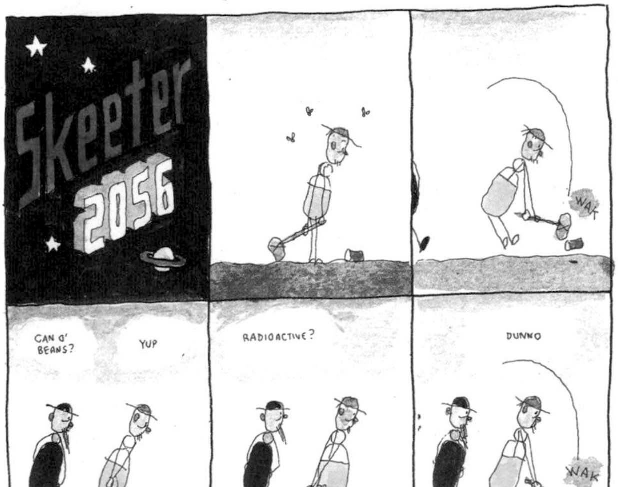
Skeeter
2056
WAK
CAN O' BEANS?
YUP
RADIOACTIVE?
DUNNO
WAK

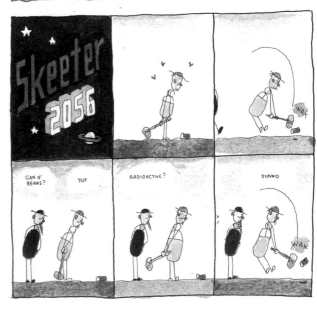

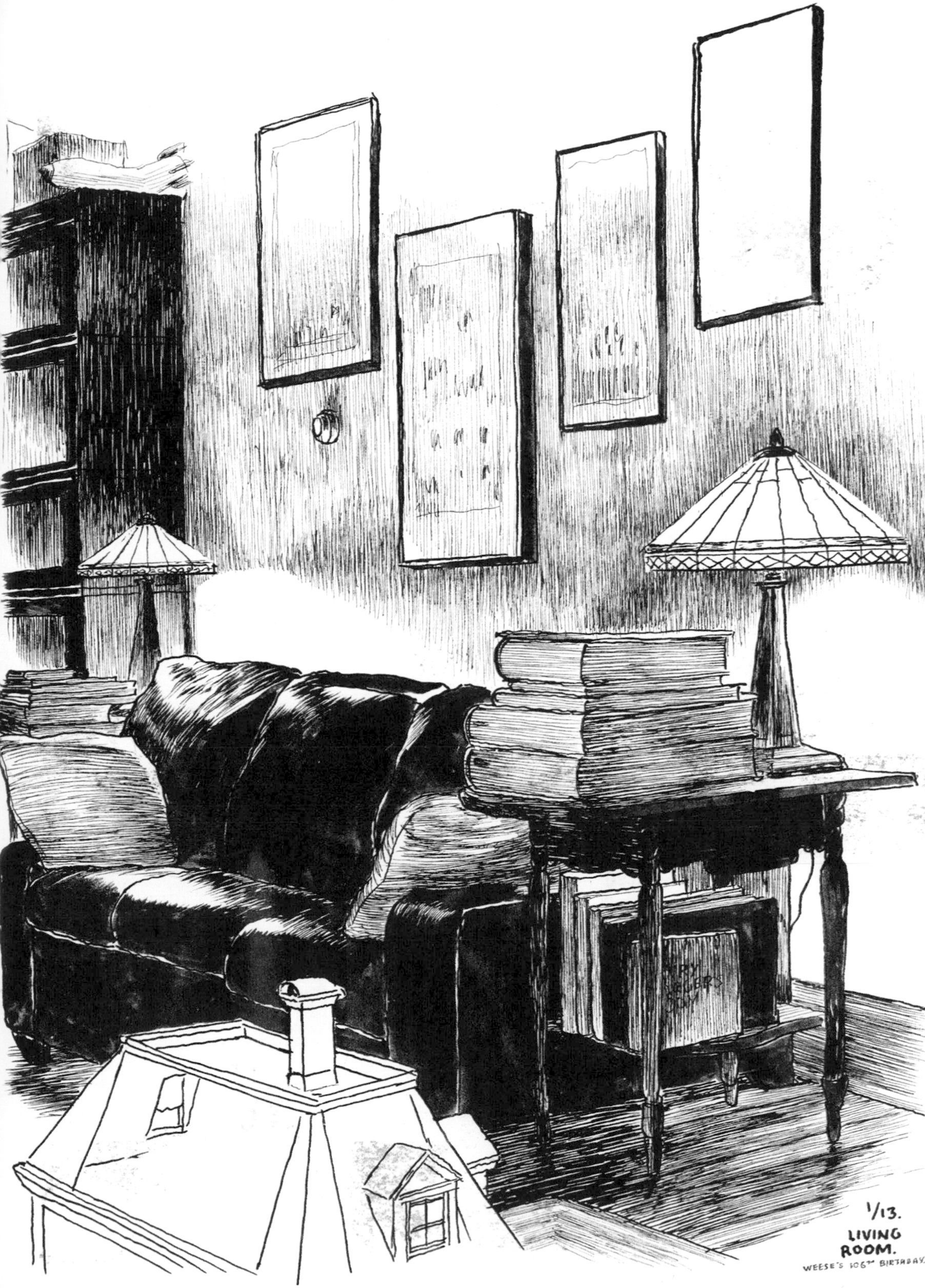
1/13.
LIVING
ROOM.
WEESE'S 106TH BIRTHDAY.

Sketchbook, 2011. Chris Ware

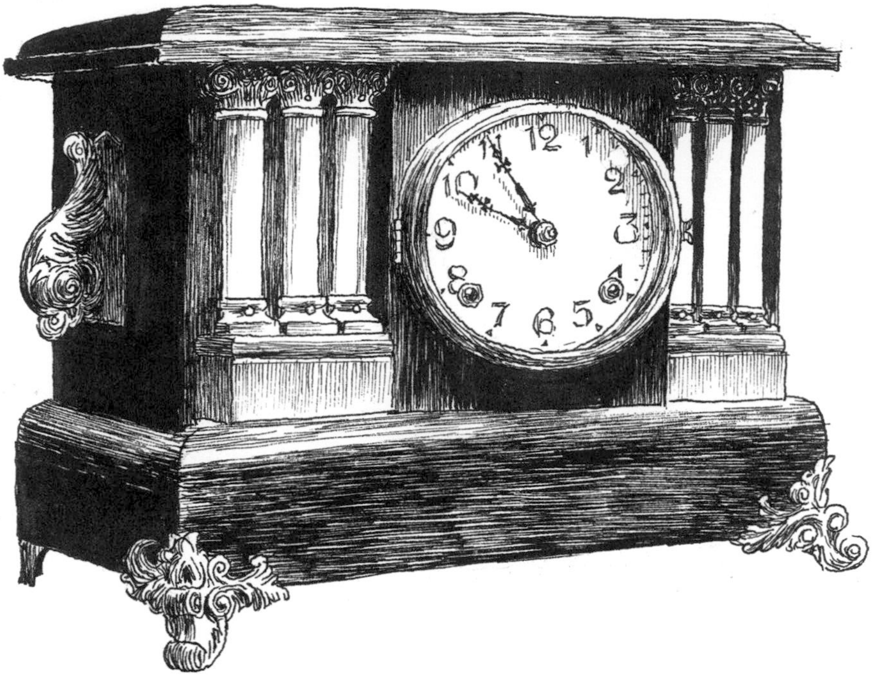

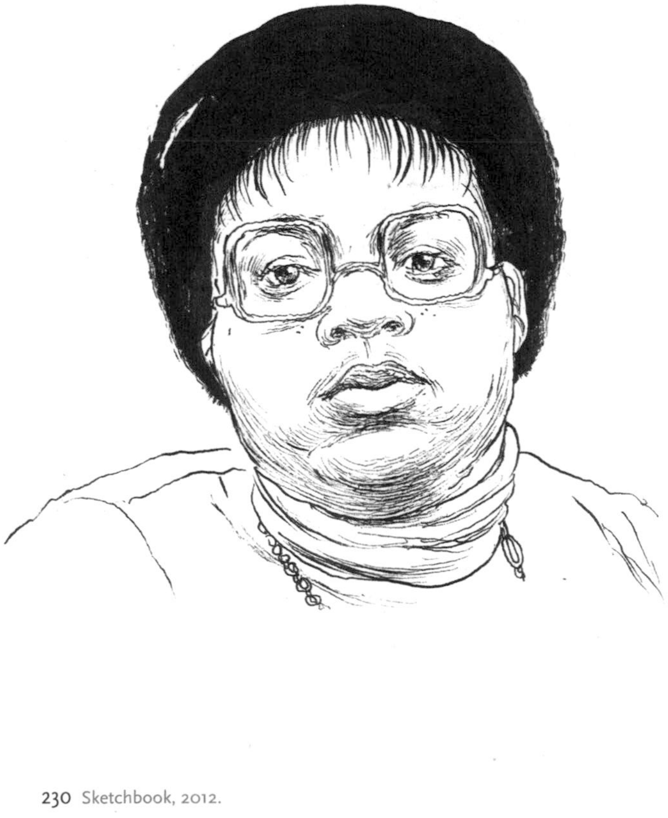

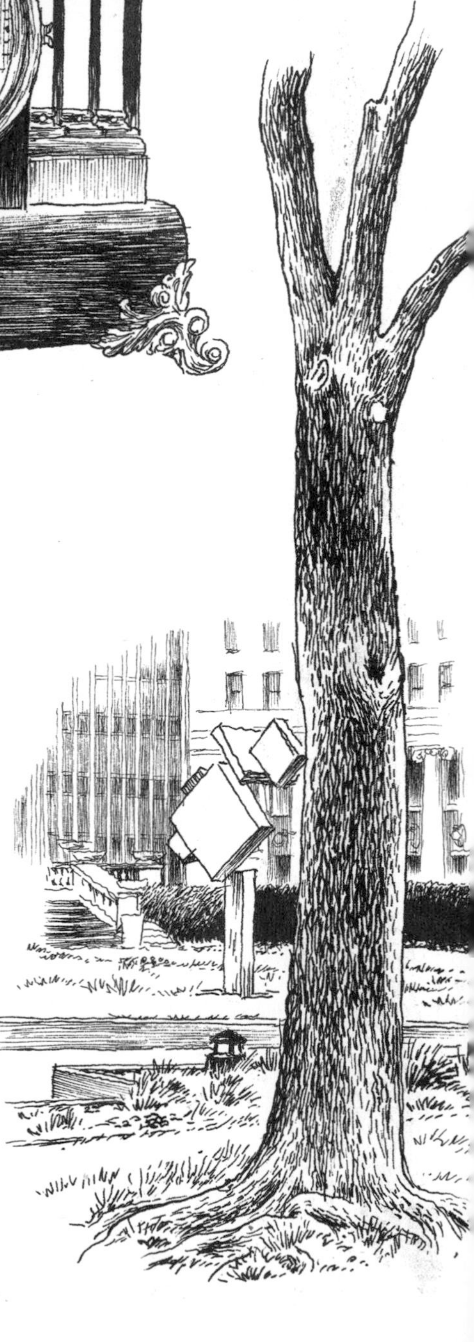

Sketchbook, 2012.

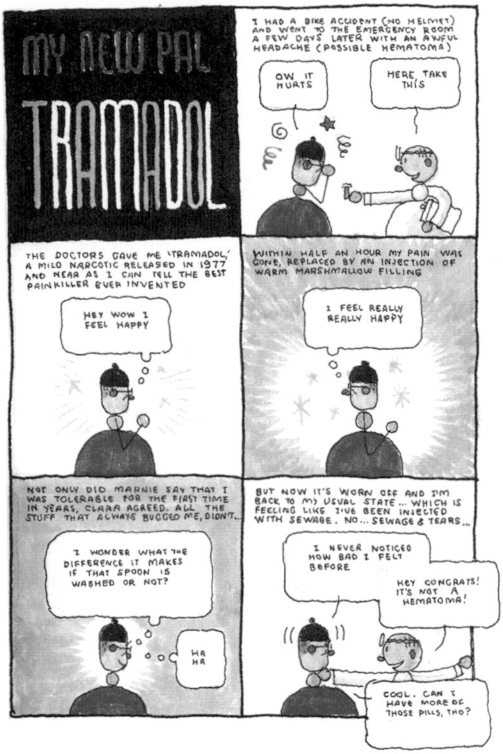
MY NEW PAL
TRAMADOL
I HAD A BIKE ACCIDENT (NO HELMET) AND WENT TO THE EMERGENCY ROOM A FEW DAYS LATER WITH AN AWFUL HEADACHE (POSSIBLE HEMATOMA)
OW IT HURTS
HERE, TAKE THIS
THE DOCTORS GAVE ME 'TRAMADOL,' A MILD NARCOTIC RELEASED IN 1977 AND NEAR AS I CAN TELL THE BEST PAINKILLER EVER INVENTED
HEY WOW I FEEL HAPPY
WITHIN HALF AN HOUR MY PAIN WAS GONE, REPLACED BY AN INJECTION OF WARM MARSHMALLOW FILLING
I FEEL REALLY REALLY HAPPY
NOT ONLY DID MARNIE SAY THAT I WAS TOLERABLE FOR THE FIRST TIME IN YEARS, CLARA AGREED. ALL THE STUFF THAT ALWAYS BUGGED ME, DIDN'T...
I WONDER WHAT THE DIFFERENCE IT MAKES IF THAT SPOON IS WASHED OR NOT?
HA HA
BUT NOW IT'S WORN OFF AND I'M BACK TO MY USUAL STATE... WHICH IS FEELING LIKE I'VE BEEN INJECTED WITH SEWAGE. NO... SEWAGE & TEARS...
I NEVER NOTICED HOW BAD I FELT BEFORE
HEY CONGRATS! IT'S NOT A HEMATOMA!
COOL. CAN I HAVE MORE OF THOSE PILLS, THO?

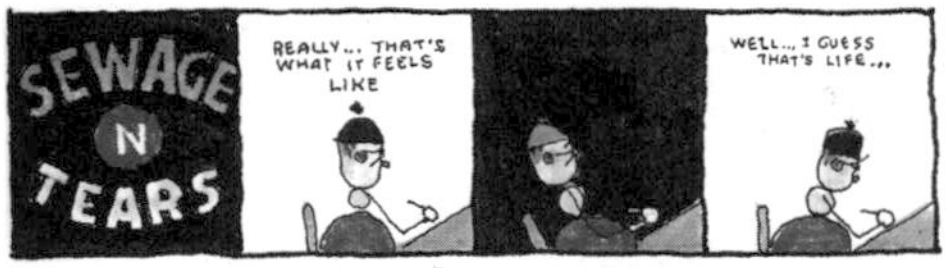
SEWAGE N TEARS
REALLY... THAT'S WHAT IT FEELS LIKE
WELL... I GUESS THAT'S LIFE...

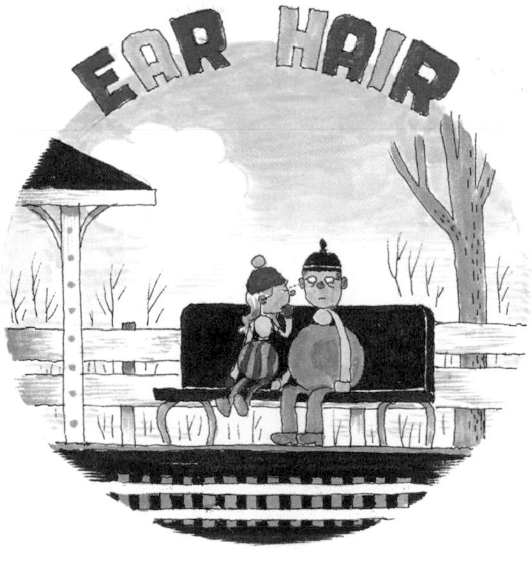
EAR HAIR

DADDY, DID MOMMY **KNOW** WHAT YOU LOOKED LIKE WHEN SHE MARRIED YOU?

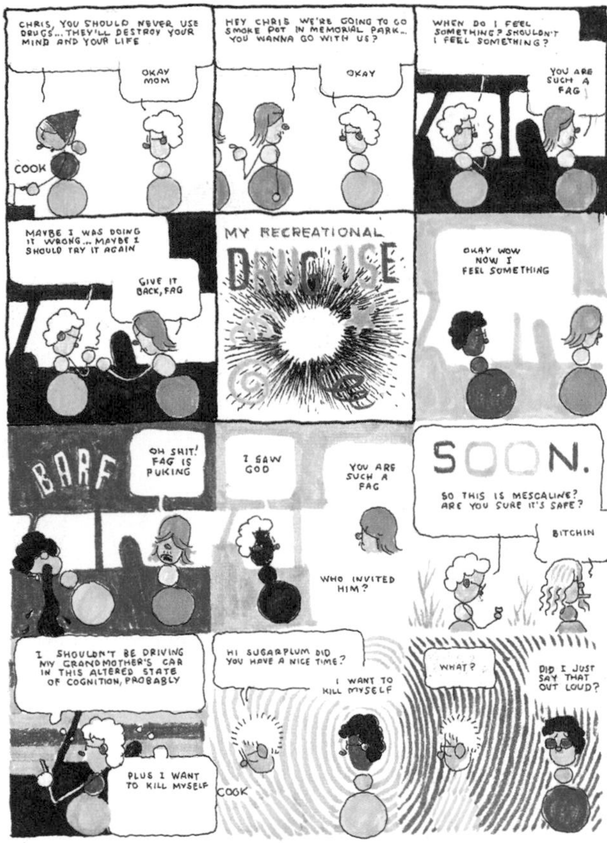
CHRIS, YOU SHOULD NEVER USE DRUGS... THEY'LL DESTROY YOUR MIND AND YOUR LIFE
OKAY MOM
COOK
HEY CHRIS WE'RE GOING TO GO SMOKE POT IN MEMORIAL PARK.. YOU WANNA GO WITH US?
OKAY
WHEN DO I FEEL SOMETHING? SHOULDN'T I FEEL SOMETHING?
YOU ARE SUCH A FAG
MAYBE I WAS DOING IT WRONG... MAYBE I SHOULD TRY IT AGAIN
GIVE IT BACK, FAG
MY RECREATIONAL DRUG USE
OKAY WOW NOW I FEEL SOMETHING
BARF
OH SHIT! FAG IS PUKING
I SAW GOD
YOU ARE SUCH A FAG
WHO INVITED HIM?
SOON.
SO THIS IS MESCALINE? ARE YOU SURE IT'S SAFE?
BITCHIN
I SHOULDN'T BE DRIVING MY GRANDMOTHER'S CAR IN THIS ALTERED STATE OF COGNITION, PROBABLY
PLUS I WANT TO KILL MYSELF
HI SUGARPLUM DID YOU HAVE A NICE TIME?
I WANT TO KILL MYSELF
COOK
WHAT?
DID I JUST SAY THAT OUT LOUD?

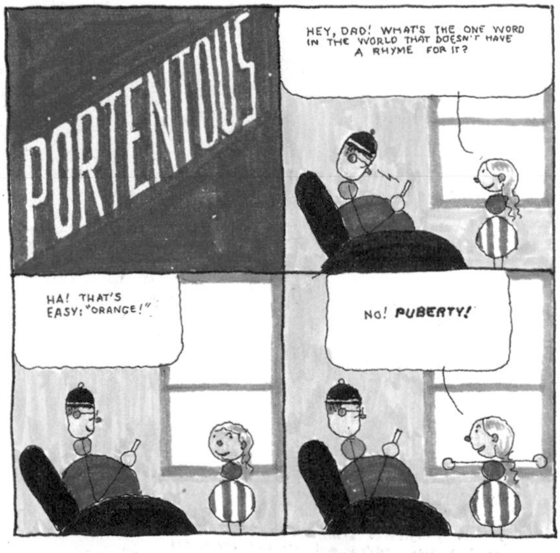
PORTENTOUS
HEY, DAD! WHAT'S THE ONE WORD IN THE WORLD THAT DOESN'T HAVE A RHYME FOR IT?
HA! THAT'S EASY: "ORANGE!"
NO! PUBERTY!

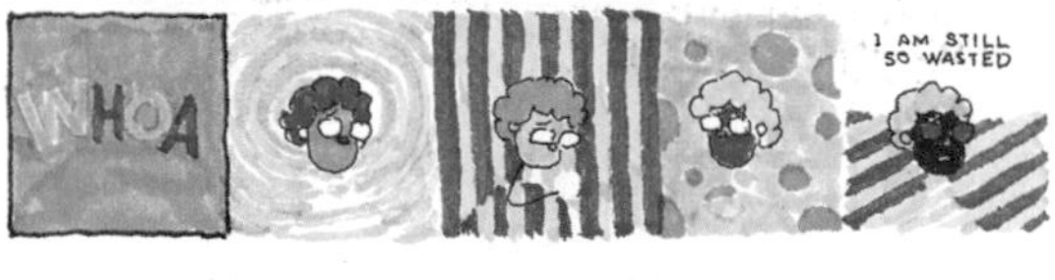
WHOA
I AM STILL SO WASTED

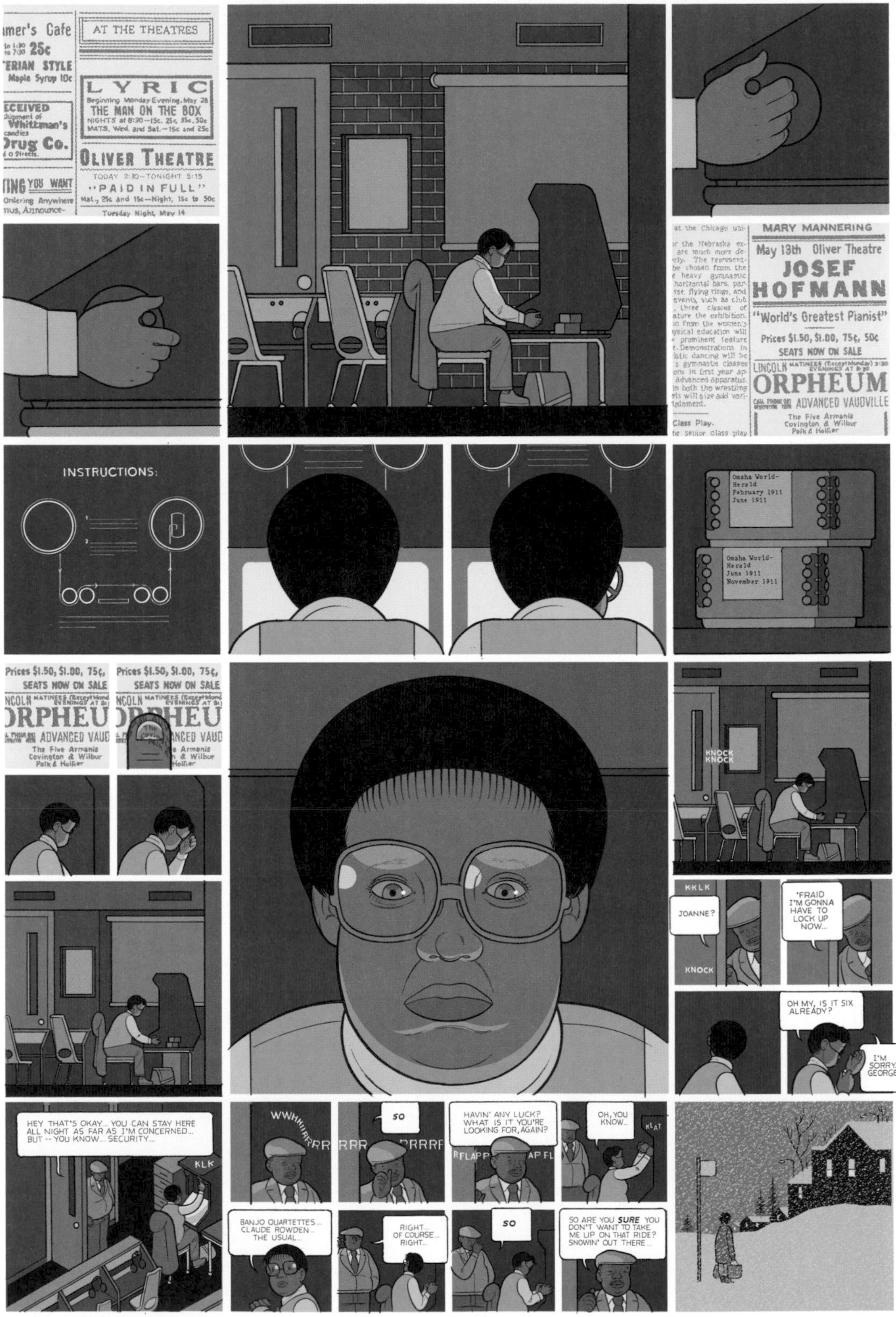

mer's Cafe
to 1:30 to 7:30 25c
TERIAN STYLE
Maple Syrup 10c
ECEIVED
shipment of
Whittman's
candies
Drug Co.
d O Streets.
TING YOU WANT
Ordering Anywhere
mus, Announce-
AT THE THEATRES
LYRIC
Beginning Monday Evening, May 28
THE MAN ON THE BOX
NIGHTS at 8:30—15c, 25c, 35c, 50c
MATS. Wed. and Sat.—15c and 25c
OLIVER THEATRE
TODAY 2:30—TONIGHT 5:15
"PAID IN FULL"
Mat. 25c and 15c—Night, 15c to 50c
Tuesday Night, May 14
MARY MANNERING
May 13th Oliver Theatre
JOSEF HOFMANN
"World's Greatest Pianist"
Prices $1.50, $1.00, 75¢, 50¢
SEATS NOW ON SALE
LINCOLN MATINEES (Except Monday) 2:30 EVENINGS AT 8:30
ORPHEUM
ADVANCED VAUDVILLE
The Five Armanis
Covington & Wilbur
Polk & Hollier
INSTRUCTIONS:
Omaha World-Herald February 1911 June 1911
Omaha World-Herald June 1911 November 1911
KNOCK KNOCK
KKLK
JOANNE?
KNOCK
'FRAID I'M GONNA HAVE TO LOCK UP NOW...
OH MY, IS IT SIX ALREADY?
I'M SORRY, GEORGE...
HEY THAT'S OKAY... YOU CAN STAY HERE ALL NIGHT AS FAR AS I'M CONCERNED... BUT -- YOU KNOW... SECURITY...
KLK
SO
HAVIN' ANY LUCK? WHAT IS IT YOU'RE LOOKING FOR, AGAIN?
OH, YOU KNOW...
KLAT
BANJO QUARTETTES... CLAUDE ROWDEN... THE USUAL...
RIGHT... OF COURSE... RIGHT...
SO
SO ARE YOU **SURE** YOU DON'T WANT TO TAKE ME UP ON THAT RIDE? SNOWIN' OUT THERE...

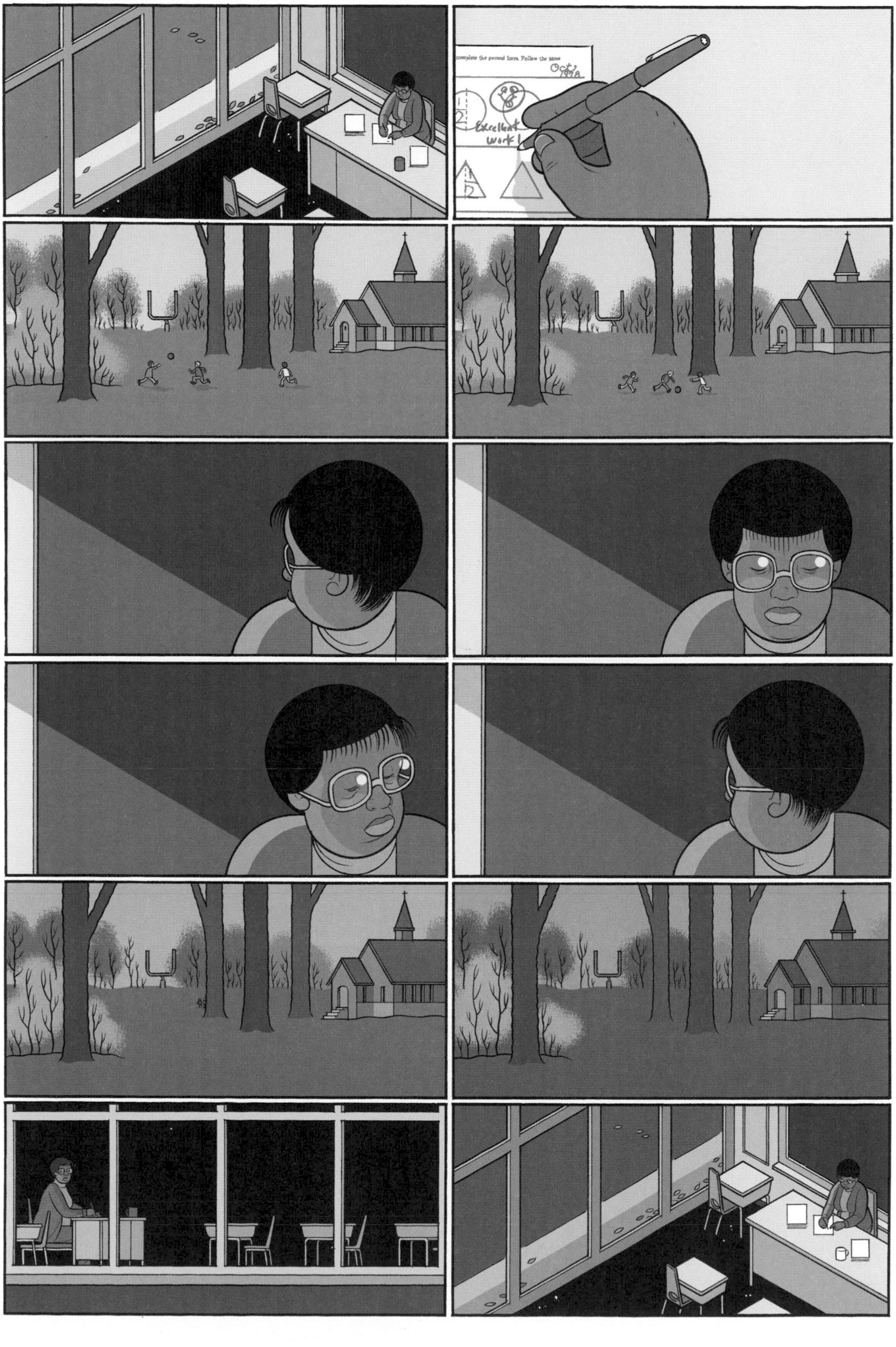
complete the second form. Follow the same
Excellent work!

the last SATURDAY

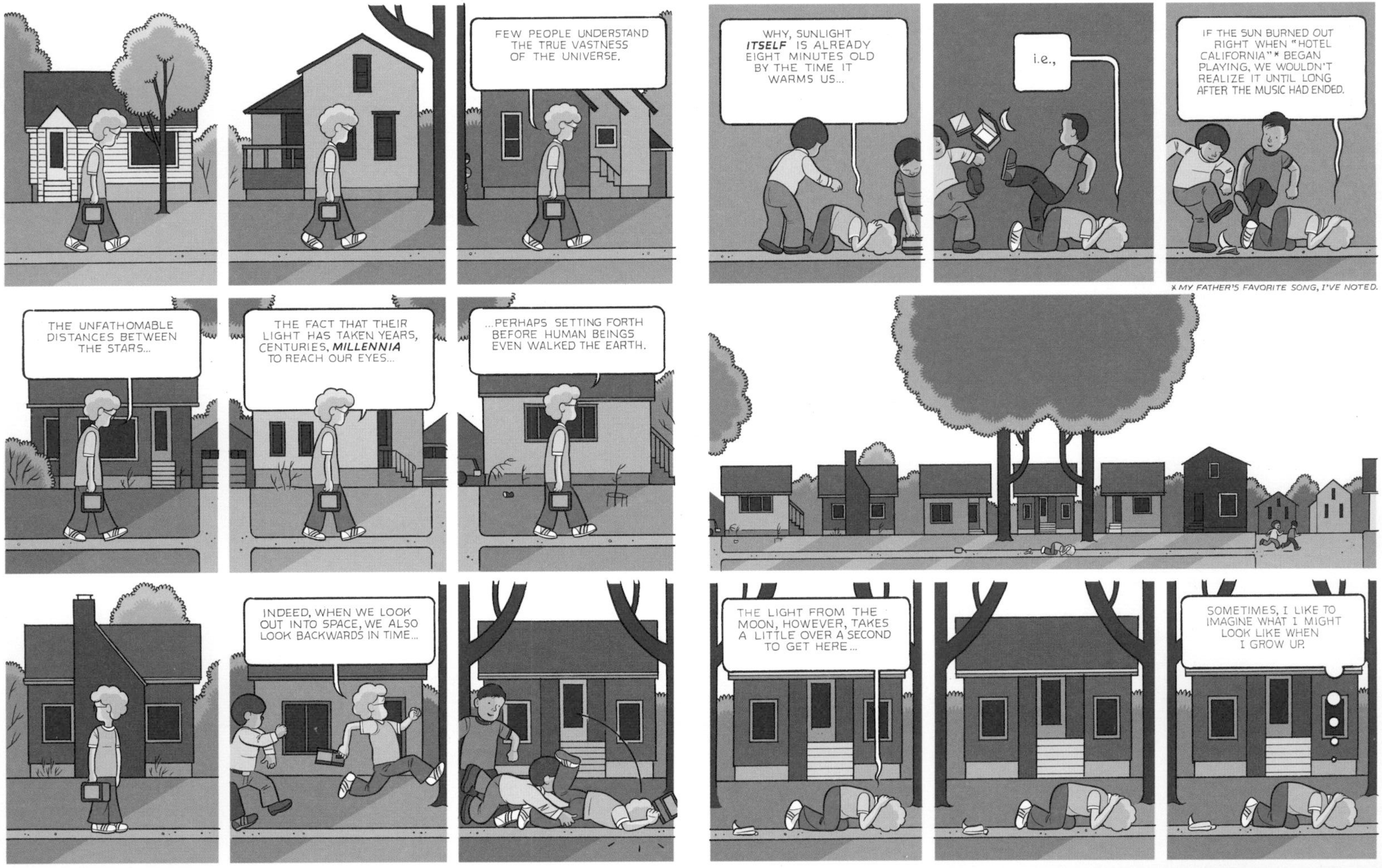
FEW PEOPLE UNDERSTAND THE TRUE VASTNESS OF THE UNIVERSE.
THE UNFATHOMABLE DISTANCES BETWEEN THE STARS...
THE FACT THAT THEIR LIGHT HAS TAKEN YEARS, CENTURIES, ***MILLENNIA*** TO REACH OUR EYES...
...PERHAPS SETTING FORTH BEFORE HUMAN BEINGS EVEN WALKED THE EARTH.
INDEED, WHEN WE LOOK OUT INTO SPACE, WE ALSO LOOK BACKWARDS IN TIME...
WHY, SUNLIGHT ***ITSELF*** IS ALREADY EIGHT MINUTES OLD BY THE TIME IT WARMS US...
i.e.,
IF THE SUN BURNED OUT RIGHT WHEN "HOTEL CALIFORNIA"* BEGAN PLAYING, WE WOULDN'T REALIZE IT UNTIL LONG AFTER THE MUSIC HAD ENDED.
*MY FATHER'S FAVORITE SONG, I'VE NOTED.
THE LIGHT FROM THE MOON, HOWEVER, TAKES A LITTLE OVER A SECOND TO GET HERE...
SOMETIMES, I LIKE TO IMAGINE WHAT I MIGHT LOOK LIKE WHEN I GROW UP.

 First appeared in the *Guardian* (2014).

the last SATURDAY

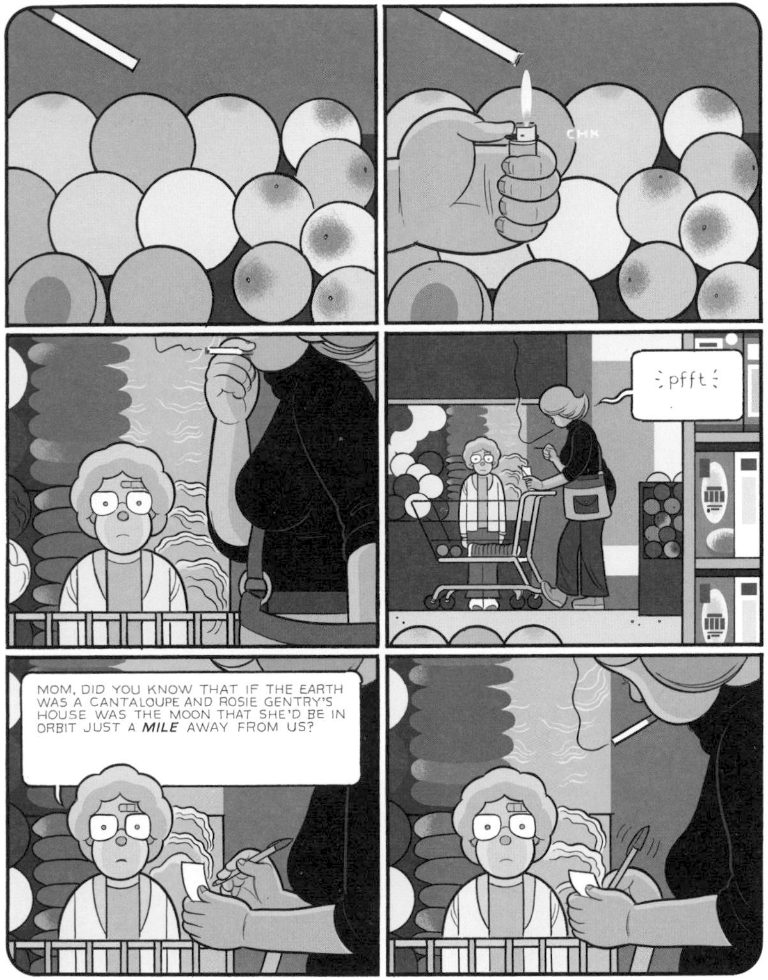
CHK
pfft
MOM, DID YOU KNOW THAT IF THE EARTH WAS A CANTALOUPE AND ROSIE GENTRY'S HOUSE WAS THE MOON THAT SHE'D BE IN ORBIT JUST A ***MILE*** AWAY FROM US?

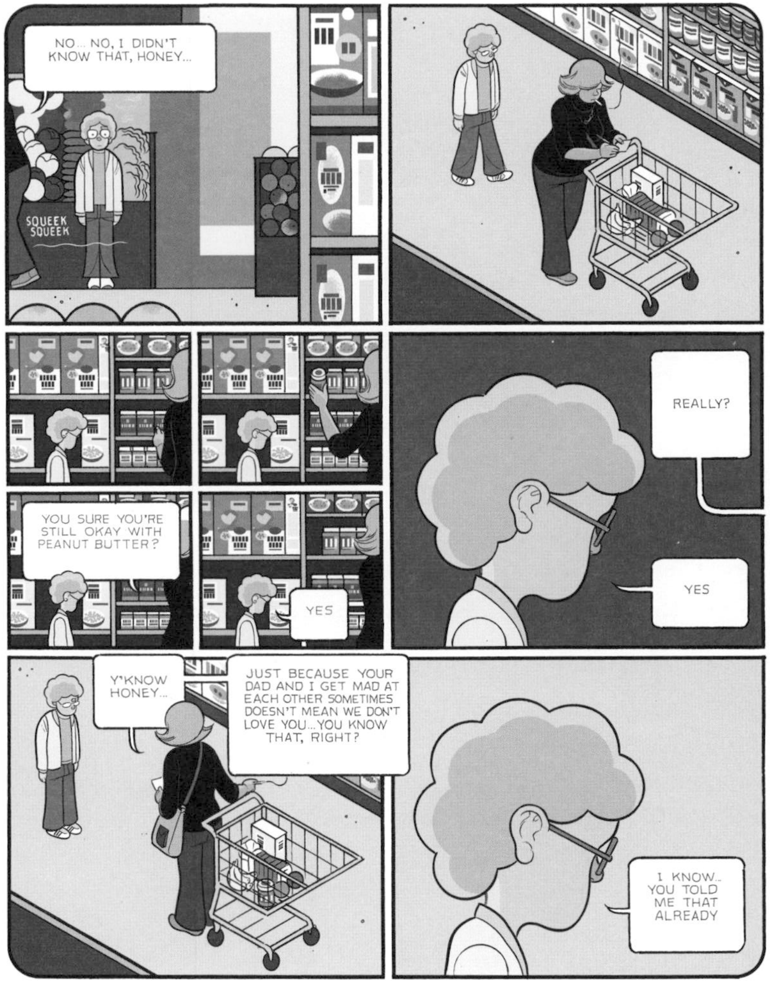
NO... NO, I DIDN'T KNOW THAT, HONEY...
SQUEEK SQUEEK
YOU SURE YOU'RE STILL OKAY WITH PEANUT BUTTER?
YES
REALLY?
YES
Y'KNOW HONEY...
JUST BECAUSE YOUR DAD AND I GET MAD AT EACH OTHER SOMETIMES DOESN'T MEAN WE DON'T LOVE YOU... YOU KNOW THAT, RIGHT?
I KNOW.. YOU TOLD ME THAT ALREADY

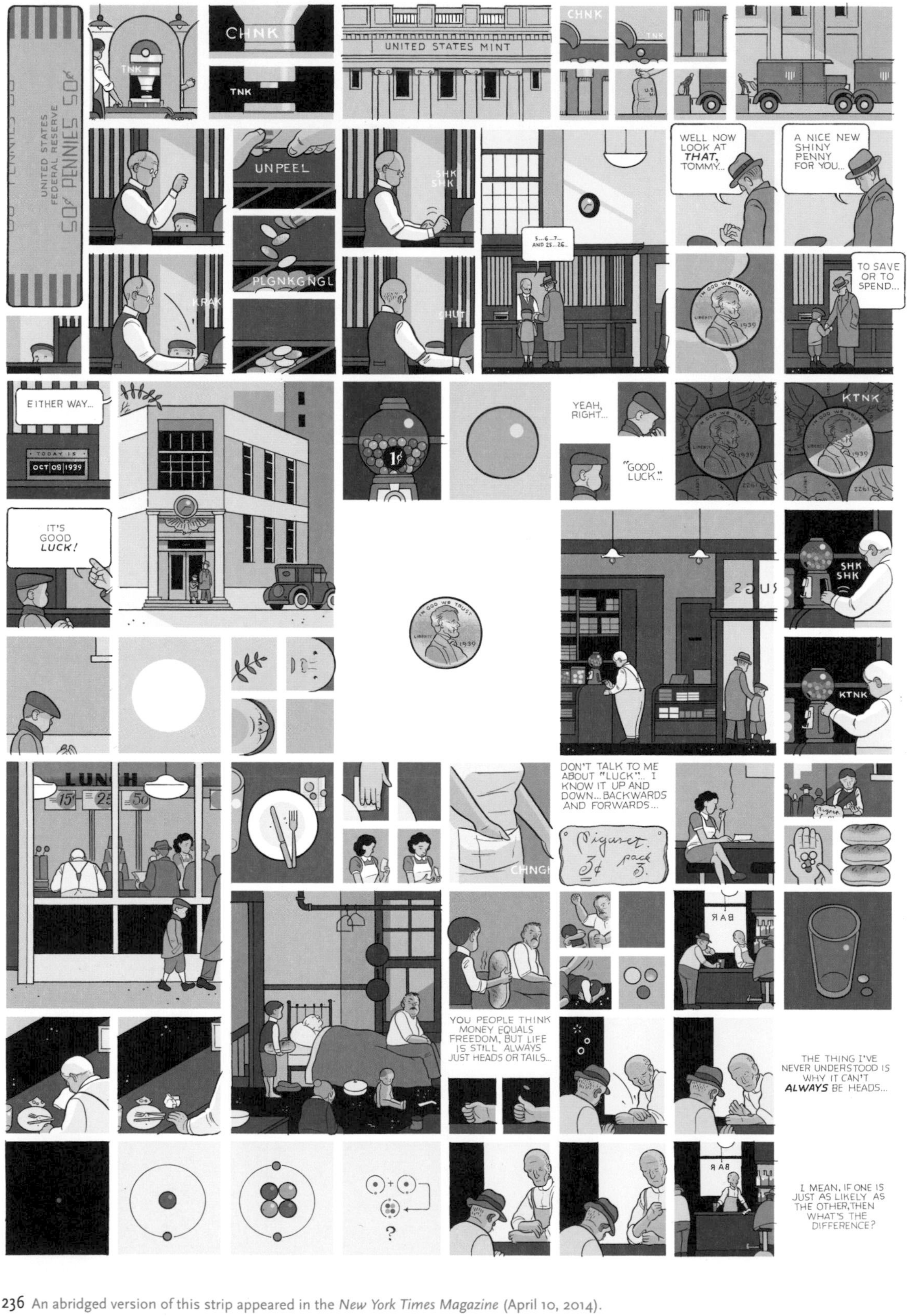
UNITED STATES FEDERAL RESERVE
50¢ PENNIES 50¢
TNK
CHNK
TNK
UNITED STATES MINT
CHNK
TNK
UNPEEL
SHK SHK
WELL NOW LOOK AT THAT, TOMMY...
A NICE NEW SHINY PENNY FOR YOU...
KRAK
PLGNKGNGL
5...6...7... AND 25...26...
IN GOD WE TRUST
LIBERTY
1939
TO SAVE OR TO SPEND...
EITHER WAY...
TODAY IS
OCT 08 1939
IT'S GOOD LUCK!
1¢
YEAH, RIGHT...
"GOOD LUCK."
KTNK
SHK SHK
KTNK
LUNCH
15¢
25
50
DON'T TALK TO ME ABOUT "LUCK"... I KNOW IT UP AND DOWN... BACKWARDS AND FORWARDS...
BAR
YOU PEOPLE THINK MONEY EQUALS FREEDOM, BUT LIFE IS STILL ALWAYS JUST HEADS OR TAILS...
THE THING I'VE NEVER UNDERSTOOD IS WHY IT CAN'T ALWAYS BE HEADS...
BAR
I MEAN, IF ONE IS JUST AS LIKELY AS THE OTHER, THEN WHAT'S THE DIFFERENCE?

 An abridged version of this strip appeared in the *New York Times Magazine* (April 10, 2014).

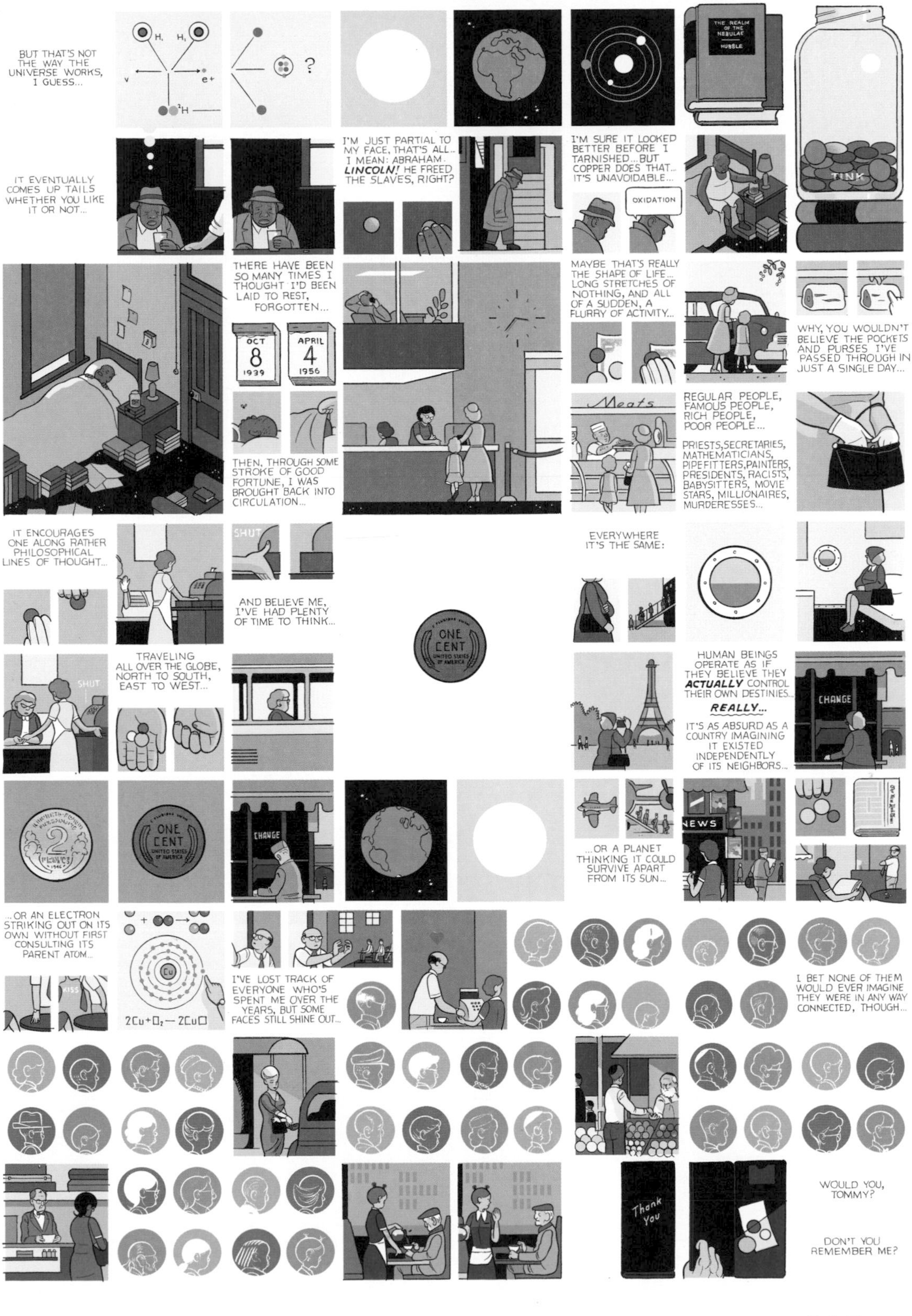
BUT THAT'S NOT THE WAY THE UNIVERSE WORKS, I GUESS...
THE REALM OF THE NEBULAE
HUBBLE
IT EVENTUALLY COMES UP TAILS WHETHER YOU LIKE IT OR NOT...
I'M JUST PARTIAL TO MY FACE, THAT'S ALL... I MEAN: ABRAHAM **LINCOLN!** HE FREED THE SLAVES, RIGHT?
I'M SURE IT LOOKED BETTER BEFORE I TARNISHED... BUT COPPER DOES THAT... IT'S UNAVOIDABLE...
OXIDATION
TINK
THERE HAVE BEEN SO MANY TIMES I THOUGHT I'D BEEN LAID TO REST, FORGOTTEN...
OCT 8 1939
APRIL 4 1956
THEN, THROUGH SOME STROKE OF GOOD FORTUNE, I WAS BROUGHT BACK INTO CIRCULATION...
MAYBE THAT'S REALLY THE SHAPE OF LIFE... LONG STRETCHES OF NOTHING, AND ALL OF A SUDDEN, A FLURRY OF ACTIVITY...
WHY, YOU WOULDN'T BELIEVE THE POCKETS AND PURSES I'VE PASSED THROUGH IN JUST A SINGLE DAY...
Meats
REGULAR PEOPLE, FAMOUS PEOPLE, RICH PEOPLE, POOR PEOPLE...
PRIESTS, SECRETARIES, MATHEMATICIANS, PIPEFITTERS, PAINTERS, PRESIDENTS, RACISTS, BABYSITTERS, MOVIE STARS, MILLIONAIRES, MURDERESSES...
IT ENCOURAGES ONE ALONG RATHER PHILOSOPHICAL LINES OF THOUGHT...
SHUT
AND BELIEVE ME, I'VE HAD PLENTY OF TIME TO THINK...
ONE CENT
UNITED STATES OF AMERICA
EVERYWHERE IT'S THE SAME:
SHUT
TRAVELING ALL OVER THE GLOBE, NORTH TO SOUTH, EAST TO WEST...
HUMAN BEINGS OPERATE AS IF THEY BELIEVE THEY **ACTUALLY** CONTROL THEIR OWN DESTINIES...
REALLY...
IT'S AS ABSURD AS A COUNTRY IMAGINING IT EXISTED INDEPENDENTLY OF ITS NEIGHBORS...
CHANGE
2
ONE CENT
UNITED STATES OF AMERICA
CHANGE
...OR A PLANET THINKING IT COULD SURVIVE APART FROM ITS SUN...
NEWS
...OR AN ELECTRON STRIKING OUT ON ITS OWN WITHOUT FIRST CONSULTING ITS PARENT ATOM...
Cu
2Cu+O2 — 2CuO
I'VE LOST TRACK OF EVERYONE WHO'S SPENT ME OVER THE YEARS, BUT SOME FACES STILL SHINE OUT...
I BET NONE OF THEM WOULD EVER IMAGINE THEY WERE IN ANY WAY CONNECTED, THOUGH...
Thank You
WOULD YOU, TOMMY?
DON'T YOU REMEMBER ME?

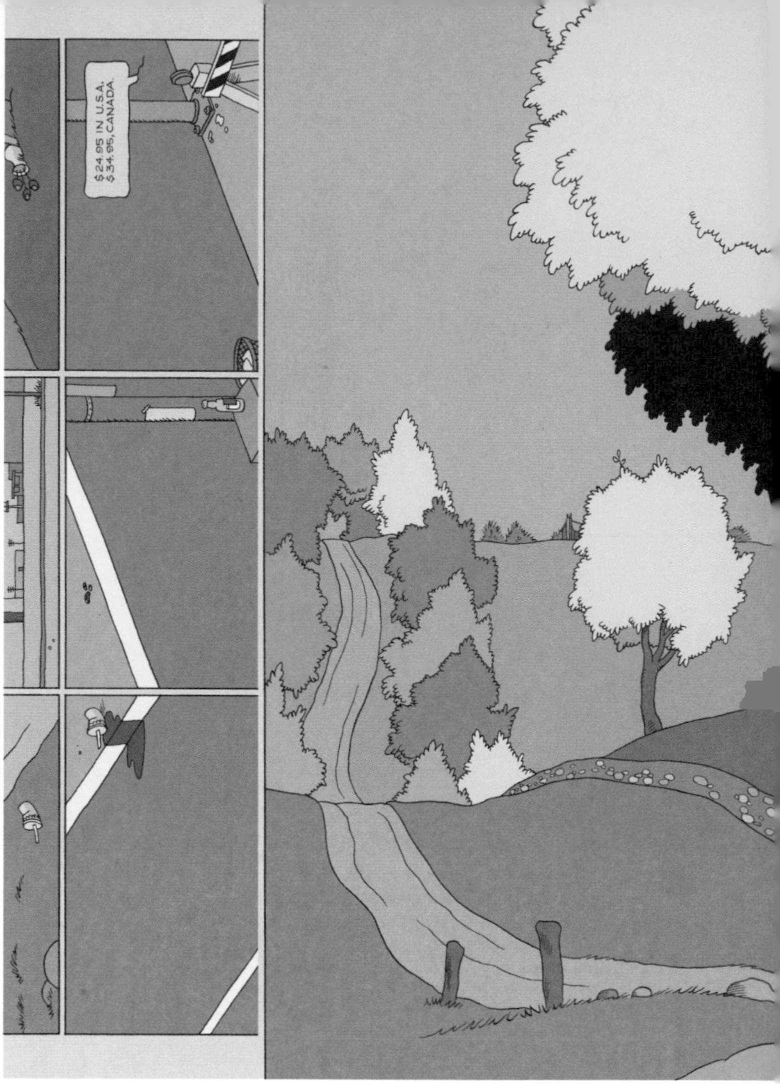
$24.95 IN U.S.A.
$34.95, CANADA

I can't remember when I first met Chris Oliveros, but his anthology periodical, *Drawn & Quarterly*, was well known to me as a young cartoonist, and I admired it greatly. Conspicuously Canadian for its gentle editorial tone, the magazine seemed to point toward a new disposition from which to cartoon, offering a kind and congenial challenge to the sometimes sneery adolescence of American alternative comics of the late 1980s and early 1990s. Chester Brown, Maurice Vellekoop, and Seth (and yes, even you, Joe Matt) all seemed to be getting at something generous, uncertain, and awkwardly human in their work, something that some American cartoonists such as myself were also hoping to approach—while at the same time fearing being made fun of for attempting. I think I even once heard the magazine described as "fey." But "literary," I think, is the word.

Because cartoonists are deviously suspicious people, we all got to know each other pretty quickly, and, after sizing up Chris Oliveros while visiting Montreal on a couple of press checks for my regular comic-book series, The ACME Novelty Library (trips on which Fantagraphics' publisher, Kim Thompson, had very generously sent me), I invited him to stay with me and my girlfriend, Marnie, when he was visiting Chicago for some reason or another in the mid-1990s. I'm a pretty quiet guy, but Chris is so faultlessly polite and seemingly embarrassed to have to even open his mouth to sound words, I felt by contrast like a sweaty football player; even the most casual comment from me felt like a loud guffaw, an American slap on the back of good-old-boy cartooning. It must have been exhausting for him. One night—so probably as to not inconvenience us—he quietly took a train and then a bus south to the University of Chicago to see some experimental foreign film, passing through what was then (and remains) one of the most crime-ridden, poverty-stricken parts of Chicago, if not the whole country. When the next morning I expressed absolute astonishment at his guilelessness, he offered, in a subdued reserve, "Yes, some of the people around there did seem quite hostile." (It was only a year or so

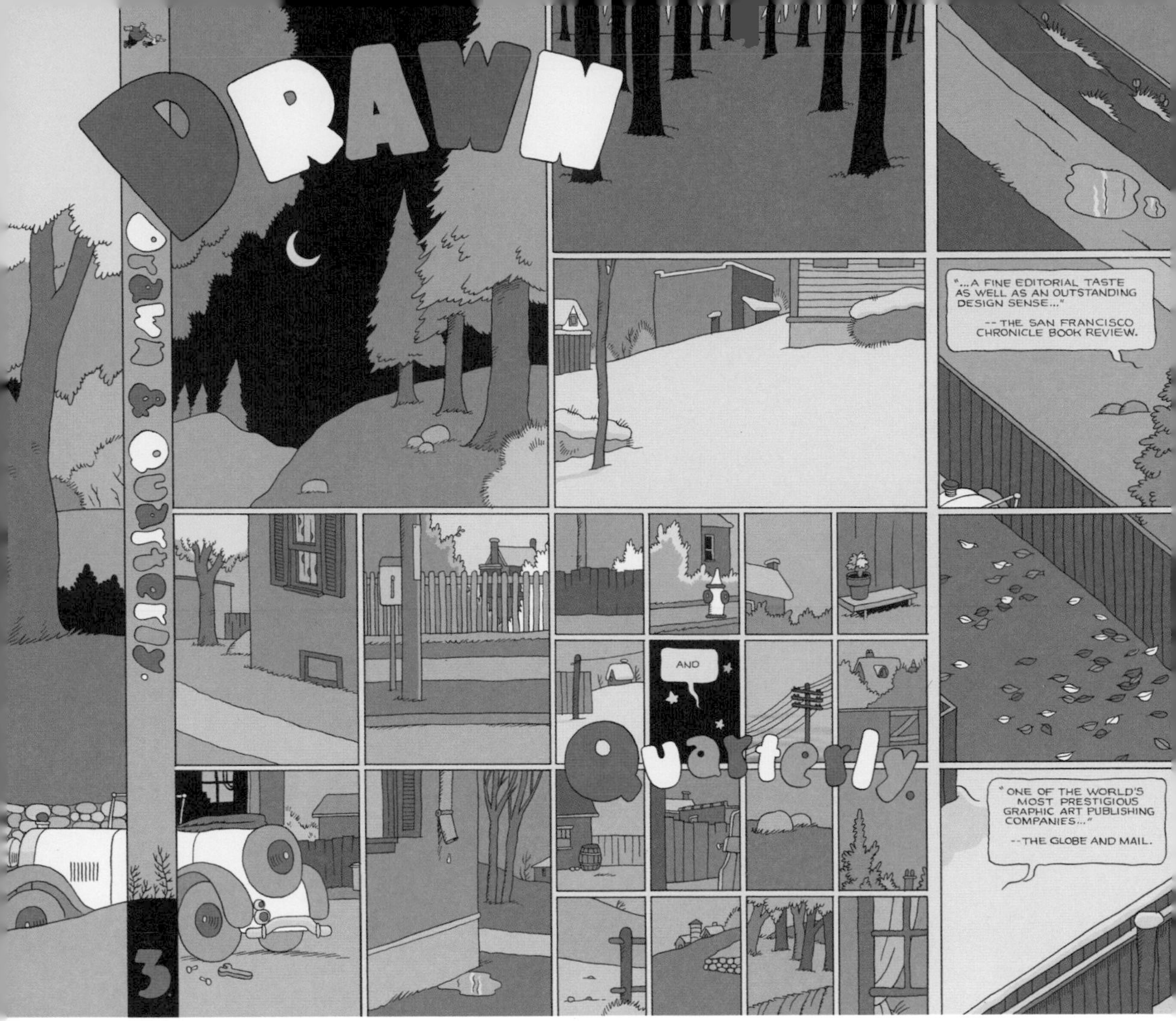
DRAWN
Drawn & Quarterly
3
"...A FINE EDITORIAL TASTE AS WELL AS AN OUTSTANDING DESIGN SENSE..."
-- THE SAN FRANCISCO CHRONICLE BOOK REVIEW.
AND
Quarterly.
"ONE OF THE WORLD'S MOST PRESTIGIOUS GRAPHIC ART PUBLISHING COMPANIES..."
--THE GLOBE AND MAIL.

later that a Danish tourist was murdered at the same train stop at which he had arrived.) To me, though, this anecdote sort of sums up Chris's character: a generous trust in what he is sure is the best in people, heedless of any possible endangerment, peril, or ruin to himself. Drawn & Quarterly, by extension, offers this same generosity and trust to its artists, and, of course, to its readers. The previous pages dribble out samples of stories/sketchbooks on which I've been recently working, but the first publishing venture I took up with Chris was in 1999, designing the cover of his rethought anthology and the issue in which he first published Frank King's *Gasoline Alley*, a strip for which we both (and yes, even you, Joe Matt) shared an affection. I based the design directly on King's work and around a biographical strip I'd done a couple of years before (and which appears on the next page). As one of the only American cartoonists of his generation to demonstrate the same gentleness of spirit that Chris embodied, King seemed an appropriate subject.

I won't embarrass Drawn & Quarterly by detailing the unbelievably equitable terms they offer all their artists and writers, or the notoriously chaste accommodations Chris and crew always assume at festivals to allow for the comfort of their artists. I will, however, point the reader toward noting that "literary" comics are now, by and large, the standard, and that younger cartoonists are overall friendlier and more compassionate in both their work and selves than the older generation ever was. So thanks for setting such a good example, Chris. You showed us all how to grow up.

—***Chris Ware***

Cover by Chris Ware first appeared in vol. 3, no. 1 of *Drawn & Quarterly* (2000).

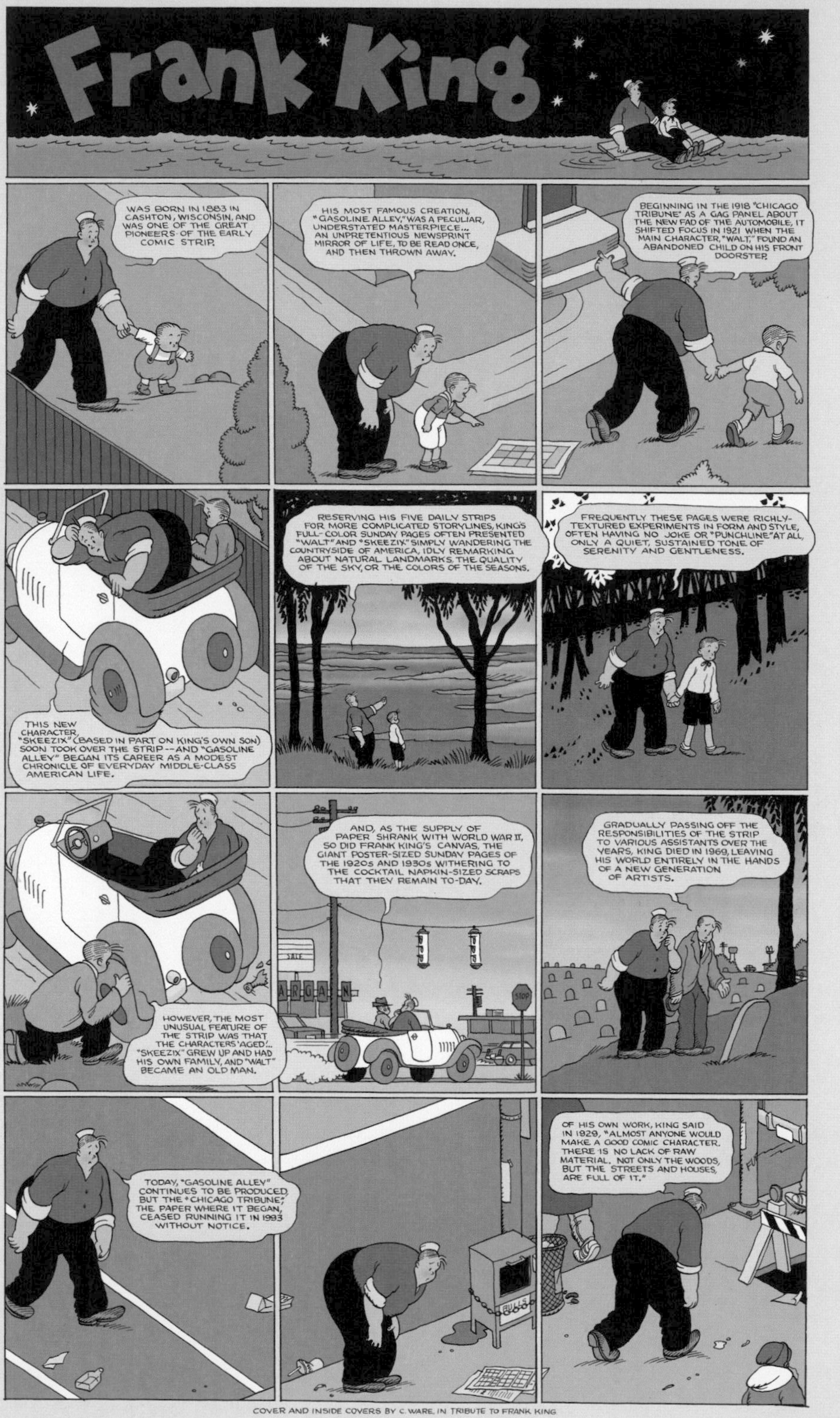
Frank King
WAS BORN IN 1883 IN CASHTON, WISCONSIN, AND WAS ONE OF THE GREAT PIONEERS OF THE EARLY COMIC STRIP.
HIS MOST FAMOUS CREATION, "GASOLINE ALLEY," WAS A PECULIAR, UNDERSTATED MASTERPIECE... AN UNPRETENTIOUS NEWSPRINT MIRROR OF LIFE, TO BE READ ONCE, AND THEN THROWN AWAY.
BEGINNING IN THE 1918 "CHICAGO TRIBUNE" AS A GAG PANEL ABOUT THE NEW FAD OF THE AUTOMOBILE, IT SHIFTED FOCUS IN 1921 WHEN THE MAIN CHARACTER, "WALT," FOUND AN ABANDONED CHILD ON HIS FRONT DOORSTEP.
THIS NEW CHARACTER, "SKEEZIX" (BASED IN PART ON KING'S OWN SON) SOON TOOK OVER THE STRIP--AND "GASOLINE ALLEY" BEGAN ITS CAREER AS A MODEST CHRONICLE OF EVERYDAY MIDDLE-CLASS AMERICAN LIFE.
RESERVING HIS FIVE DAILY STRIPS FOR MORE COMPLICATED STORYLINES, KING'S FULL-COLOR SUNDAY PAGES OFTEN PRESENTED "WALT" AND "SKEEZIX" SIMPLY WANDERING THE COUNTRYSIDE OF AMERICA, IDLY REMARKING ABOUT NATURAL LANDMARKS, THE QUALITY OF THE SKY, OR THE COLORS OF THE SEASONS.
FREQUENTLY THESE PAGES WERE RICHLY-TEXTURED EXPERIMENTS IN FORM AND STYLE, OFTEN HAVING NO JOKE OR "PUNCHLINE" AT ALL, ONLY A QUIET, SUSTAINED TONE OF SERENITY AND GENTLENESS.
HOWEVER, THE MOST UNUSUAL FEATURE OF THE STRIP WAS THAT THE CHARACTERS 'AGED'... "SKEEZIX" GREW UP AND HAD HIS OWN FAMILY, AND "WALT" BECAME AN OLD MAN.
AND, AS THE SUPPLY OF PAPER SHRANK WITH WORLD WAR II, SO DID FRANK KING'S CANVAS, THE GIANT POSTER-SIZED SUNDAY PAGES OF THE 1920s AND 1930s WITHERING TO THE COCKTAIL NAPKIN-SIZED SCRAPS THAT THEY REMAIN TO-DAY.
SALE
STOP
GRADUALLY PASSING OFF THE RESPONSIBILITIES OF THE STRIP TO VARIOUS ASSISTANTS OVER THE YEARS, KING DIED IN 1969, LEAVING HIS WORLD ENTIRELY IN THE HANDS OF A NEW GENERATION OF ARTISTS.
TODAY, "GASOLINE ALLEY" CONTINUES TO BE PRODUCED, BUT THE "CHICAGO TRIBUNE," THE PAPER WHERE IT BEGAN, CEASED RUNNING IT IN 1993 WITHOUT NOTICE.
OF HIS OWN WORK, KING SAID IN 1929, "ALMOST ANYONE WOULD MAKE A GOOD COMIC CHARACTER. THERE IS NO LACK OF RAW MATERIAL. NOT ONLY THE WOODS, BUT THE STREETS AND HOUSES, ARE FULL OF IT."
COVER AND INSIDE COVERS BY C. WARE, IN TRIBUTE TO FRANK KING

"Frank King" by Chris Ware first appeared in vol. 3, no. 1 of *Drawn & Quarterly* (2000).

FRANK KING

an appreciation by Chris Ware

I've written more about Frank King than about any other cartoonist, and that's no accident; when I was a young artist trying to find my way into making emotional, hopefully moving comics using the blunt tools of a form grounded in graphic bludgeoning, it was his art that most compelled me, even though it took years to find out who he was and how he did it.

Born Frank Oscar King in Cashton, Wisconsin, in 1883, King arrived at his life's work relatively late, having run through a series of relatively unremarkable and occasionally derivative strips for a series of midwestern newspapers in Minnesota and Illinois, ending up at the *Chicago Tribune* before, pushing forty, he stumbled into *Gasoline Alley*. Not

that King's work until then wasn't good; he was revered, known, and respected, but it was with this feature, a single panel about the new fad of the automobile, that his work quietly grew into something new, warm, and human. Weekly it peered down into a South Side Chicago alley, a semifictional setting that King began to populate with characters derived from his own family: first Walt Wallet, based on his brother-in-law and childhood friend Walter Drew, and then Bill, Drew's friend William Gannon, with whom he roomed. But it was the appearance of a foundling orphan on Walt Wallet's doorstep that changed the strip, and comics, forever. Already well versed in the doings of kid strips with the pretty successful feature *Bobby Make-Believe*

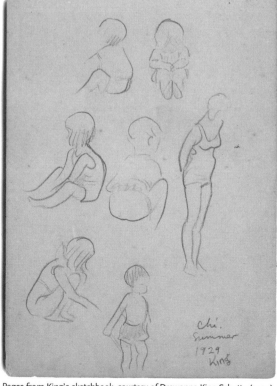

Pages from King's sketchbook, courtesy of Drewanna King Schutte (1929).

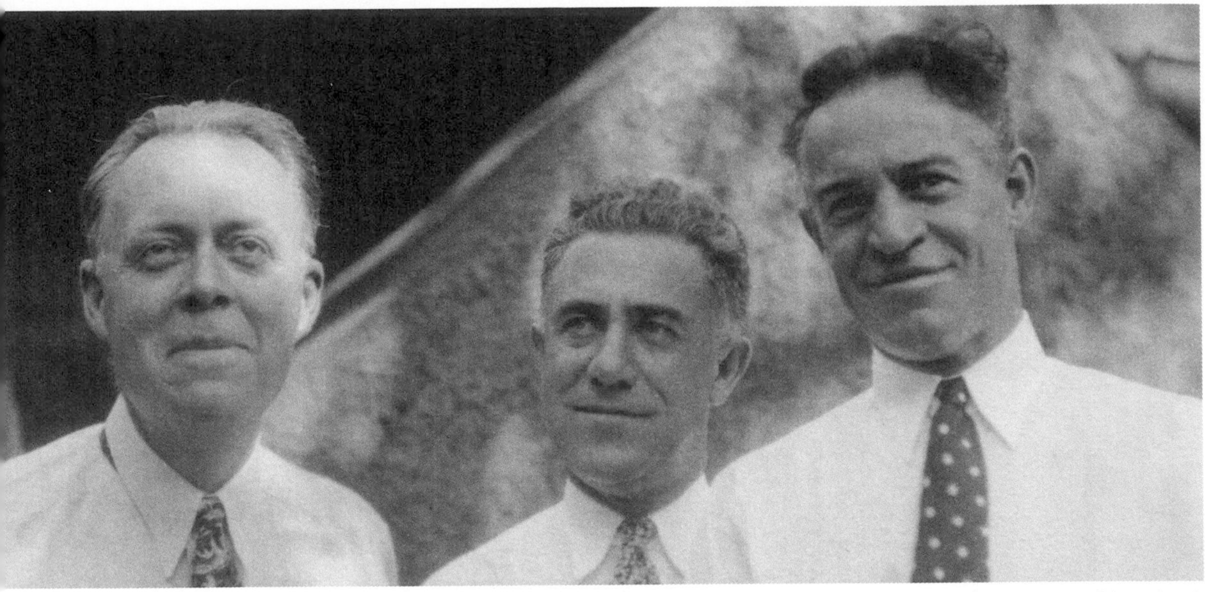

(Left to right) Walter Drew, King's brother-in-law and inspiration for Walt Wallet; Frank King; Bill Gannon, King's friend. Courtesy of Drewanna King Schutte (1930).

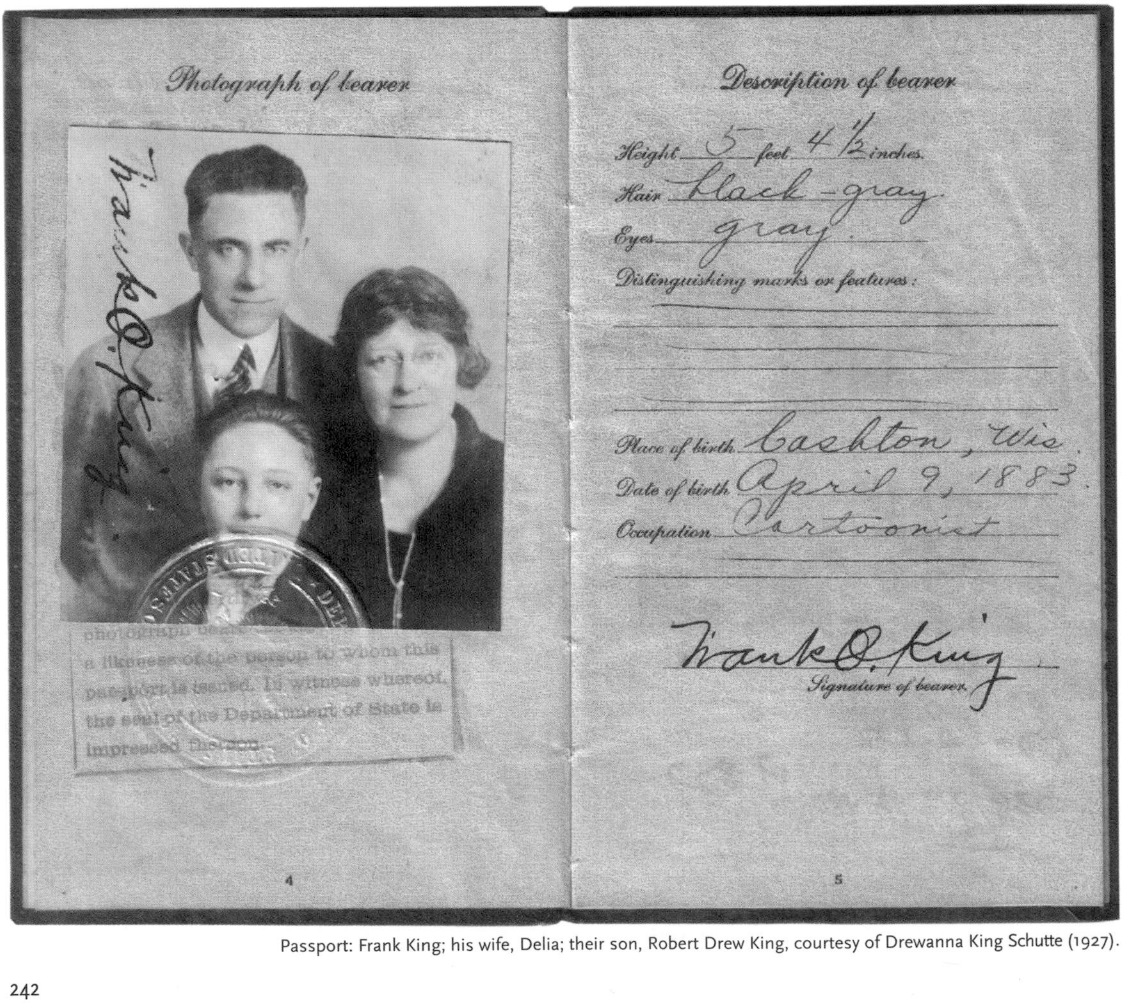
Photograph of bearer
Frank O. King
a likeness of the person to whom this
passport is issued. In witness whereof,
the seal of the Department of State is
impressed thereon.
4
Description of bearer
Height 5 feet 4 1/2 inches.
Hair black-gray
Eyes gray
Distinguishing marks or features:
Place of birth Cashton, Wis.
Date of birth April 9, 1883.
Occupation Cartoonist
Frank O. King
Signature of bearer.
5

Passport: Frank King; his wife, Delia; their son, Robert Drew King, courtesy of Drewanna King Schutte (1927).

(something of a Little Nemo derivative), King had also started his own family in 1916, his wife, Delia, giving birth to a boy, Robert Drew (note the congruencies of the name). Delia, however, also had suffered a painful miscarriage years before, highlighting the fragility and uncertainty of Bobby's life once he was born (and under harrowing circumstances: the birth almost killed Delia). The foundling, nicknamed "Skeezix," first and now famously appeared in the strip on Valentine's Day 1921, and the strip almost immediately shifted focus from automobiles to, well, life.

But that wasn't King's genius. The comic strip, being an ephemeral, throwaway art form still in its early adolescence, also provided King with his sculptural base: by allowing Skeezix to grow up literally one day at a time—the same rate at which time passed for the readers of the newspaper—the strip became an ever-stacking paper mirror of life itself, progressing inevitably and inexorably forward, yellowing, fading, and forgetting. In the course of its approximately thirty-year run under King's gentle hand, Skeezix grew from a toddler to a boy to an adolescent to a man. He joined the army, married, and had children of his own. In real life, King's own son followed a similar path but, at the apparent urging of King's wife, was sent away at a relatively young age to a military academy, which made the strip all the more personal for King, as it became something of a fictional account of a father and a child based on the child who was no longer there.

As a young cartoonist who wanted to write about life, I'd only seen a handful of examples of *Gasoline Alley* in my generation's bible of cartooning, Bill Blackbeard and Martin Sheridan's *The Smithsonian Book of Newspaper Comics*, and the colourful ache that it created on the page made me want to find more. But, incredibly, while most strips of King's day had been reprinted, *Gasoline Alley* had not, excepting an inadequate and misguided 1920s volume editorially centring on cars. So in those pre-eBay days, I spent weekends with my cartoonist pal John Keen driving around rural Texas, stopping at every junk store and flea market we could find in search of any example of the strip, especially the Sunday pages for their occasional haiku-like lack of resolve, sometimes openly eschewing a punchline in favour of a quiet observation or poignant moment—the aesthetic equivalent in the 1930s of Ozu or Bergman when largely everything else in the funny pages was still the Three Stooges.

But who was this cartoonist, Frank King? The histories of the comic strip up to that time gave scant details and only a muddy halftone photo or two. So when Chris Oliveros mentioned to me that he was interested in reprinting the *Gasoline Alley* daily strip, I jumped at the chance to work on the book, not only for the opportunity to design it in as dignified a manner as I could muster, but also because the project presented the opportunity of meeting King's surviving family, Drewanna King Schutte and her husband, John Schutte, who opened up Drewanna's inherited archive of King's art, thousands of family photographs, sketchbooks, diaries—and, incredibly, even films. Suddenly a cartoonist who had been all but forgotten came into extraordinary focus and, under the sharp mind and pen of my collaborator, Jeet Heer, the subject of an ongoing illustrated biography agglomerating with each successive volume of the strip. Needless to say, none of this would have been possible without the largesse and munificence of Drewanna and her husband, to whom Jeet and I are enduringly grateful. There were some surprises along the way, most notably the revelation of the degree to which King drew from the details of his own life, the revelation of Delia's miscarriage, and, personally for me, the discovery of two letters to King from my grandfather, the managing editor of the *Omaha World-Herald* and devoted booster of the strip.

Frank King's genius at seeing the advantage of a story told in a time-centred medium that faded like time itself led to what was essentially America's first serious long-form literary comic strip (or, in contemporary parlance, "graphic novel"). And long-form it certainly is: King's assistant Bill Perry directly helped with the work of creating *Gasoline Alley* beginning in the mid-1920s, so he was well acquainted with both the tone and the form of the strip when he assumed the helm in 1951. Dick Moores (who began as Perry's assistant in 1956 and took over entirely in the late 1960s) introduced characters and complications that imbued the strip with a more contemporary direction and feel, but without ever losing sight of its origins. Jim Scancarelli, who began as Moores's assistant and has exclusively lent the strip his mind and firm hand since 1986, has announced he will end the continuity with his own retirement in 2015, nearly a century after its first appearance.

Of course, this end awaits every one of us, as grim as it is to say; we have our memories, but retold and reworked, those recollections become part of a story we write and rewrite about ourselves, until, eventually, that story is all that remains. But rather than take his story with him, King left behind one for us all to relive, and especially, to feel, in a medium that perfectly suited it. He turned his life into art, and his art into life.

YOU KIDS ARE GRAND CLIMBERS AREN'T YOU!
SURE!
I'LL BET YOU CAN'T CLIMB ONTO MY GARAGE.
SURE WE COULD.
IF WE WANTED TO
HE WANTS US TO FIX HIS AERIAL, SKEEZIX.
I CAN'T UNDERSTAND HOW THEY CAN DO SO MUCH AND NOT ACCIDENTALLY DO SOMETHING USEFUL SOMETIME.
THERE'S SOME MORE ENERGY GOING TO WASTE AVERY. HOW'S YOUR SCHEME TO UTILIZE IT COMING ALONG?
I'M ALL WASHED UP, WALT. IT DIDN'T WORK.
NO, INSTEAD I'M GOING TO HARNESS THE POWER OF THE TIDES, OR UTILIZE THE HEAT OF THE EARTH'S INTERIOR.
EXTRACT POWER FROM SUNSHINE OR CRACK THE ATOM. THEY'RE ALL CHILD'S PLAY BESIDES PUTTING THOSE KIDS TO WORK.
GEE, FELLAS, I'VE GOT A JOB FOR ALL OF US—TEN CENTS A HEAD.
SWELL—WHAT DOIN'?
I'LL BET THERE'S WORK TO IT.
HERE Y'ARE EACH OF YOU TAKE A STREET AN' PUT A HANDBILL AT EVERY FRONT DOOR.
GEE. THAT MEANS A LOT OF HOUSES.
NOT IF YOU'RE WISE IT DOESN'T. I CAN BEAT THIS GAME.
ONE AT EVERY HOUSE. THAT'S GOIN' TO TAKE HALF THE MORNIN'.
FOR YOU MAYBE—NOT FOR ME!
CLARENCE HOW DID YOU GET THROUGH SO SOON?
YOU COULDN'T HAVE!
I BELIEVE IN USIN' MY HEAD AN' SAVIN' OF MY FEET.
THERE'S YOUR MONEY FOR DISTRIBUTING HANDBILLS.
THANKS, MR. QUAD.
WHERE'S MINE?
YOURS? I CHECKED UP ON YOU, CLARENCE, AND FOUND A BUNDLE OF BILLS THE FIRST PLACE I LOOKED—STUFFED INTO THE END OF A DRAIN PIPE.
BUT—I DIDN'T—
THAT'S JUST THE TROUBLE. NOW CLEAR OUT OF HERE BEFORE I BOOST YOU OUT

 January 20–24, 1934 (All comic strips courtesy of Joe Matt).

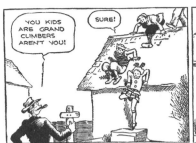

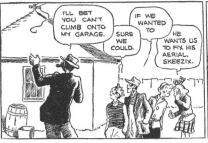

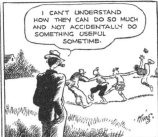

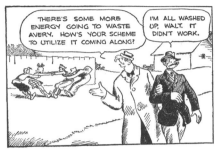

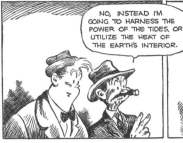

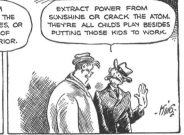

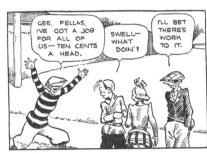

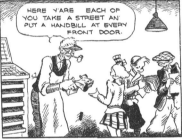

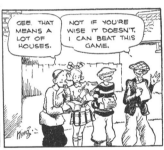

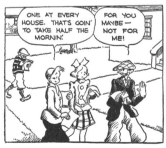

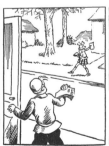

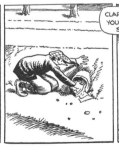

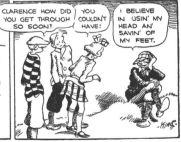

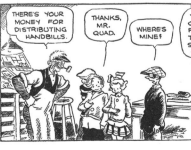

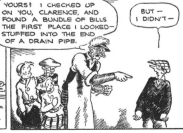

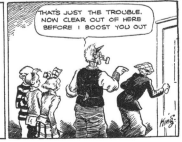

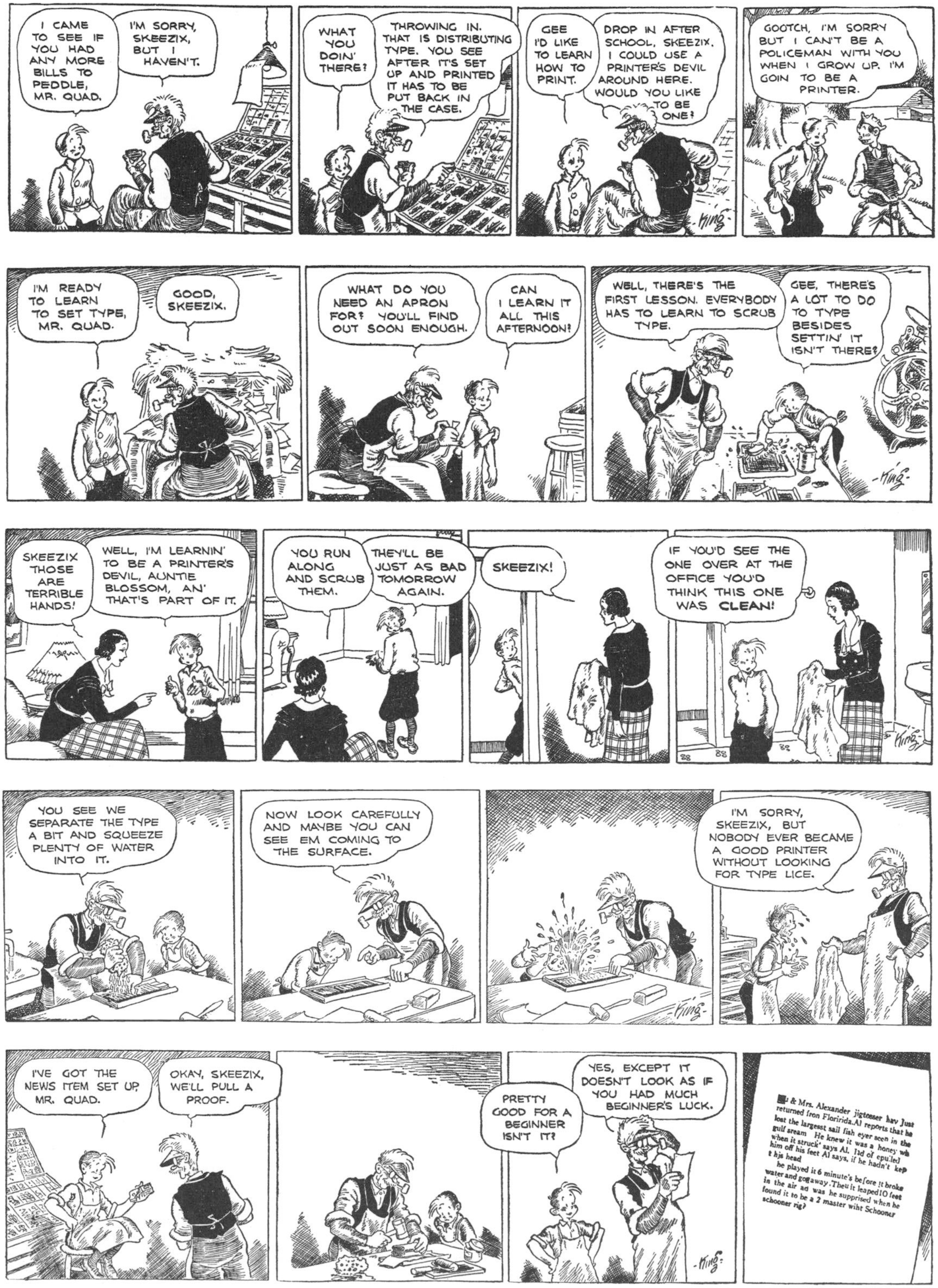
I CAME TO SEE IF YOU HAD ANY MORE BILLS TO PEDDLE, MR. QUAD.
I'M SORRY, SKEEZIX, BUT I HAVEN'T.
WHAT YOU DOIN' THERE?
THROWING IN. THAT IS DISTRIBUTING TYPE. YOU SEE AFTER IT'S SET UP AND PRINTED IT HAS TO BE PUT BACK IN THE CASE.
GEE I'D LIKE TO LEARN HOW TO PRINT.
DROP IN AFTER SCHOOL, SKEEZIX. I COULD USE A PRINTER'S DEVIL AROUND HERE. WOULD YOU LIKE TO BE ONE?
-KING-
GOOTCH, I'M SORRY BUT I CAN'T BE A POLICEMAN WITH YOU WHEN I GROW UP. I'M GOIN TO BE A PRINTER.
I'M READY TO LEARN TO SET TYPE, MR. QUAD.
GOOD, SKEEZIX.
WHAT DO YOU NEED AN APRON FOR? YOU'LL FIND OUT SOON ENOUGH.
CAN I LEARN IT ALL THIS AFTERNOON?
WELL, THERE'S THE FIRST LESSON. EVERYBODY HAS TO LEARN TO SCRUB TYPE.
GEE, THERE'S A LOT TO DO TO TYPE BESIDES SETTIN' IT ISN'T THERE?
-KING-
SKEEZIX THOSE ARE TERRIBLE HANDS!
WELL, I'M LEARNIN' TO BE A PRINTER'S DEVIL, AUNTIE BLOSSOM, AN' THAT'S PART OF IT.
YOU RUN ALONG AND SCRUB THEM.
THEY'LL BE JUST AS BAD TOMORROW AGAIN.
SKEEZIX!
IF YOU'D SEE THE ONE OVER AT THE OFFICE YOU'D THINK THIS ONE WAS CLEAN!
-KING-
YOU SEE WE SEPARATE THE TYPE A BIT AND SQUEEZE PLENTY OF WATER INTO IT.
NOW LOOK CAREFULLY AND MAYBE YOU CAN SEE EM COMING TO THE SURFACE.
-KING-
I'M SORRY, SKEEZIX, BUT NOBODY EVER BECAME A GOOD PRINTER WITHOUT LOOKING FOR TYPE LICE.
I'VE GOT THE NEWS ITEM SET UP, MR. QUAD.
OKAY, SKEEZIX, WE'LL PULL A PROOF.
PRETTY GOOD FOR A BEGINNER ISN'T IT?
YES, EXCEPT IT DOESN'T LOOK AS IF YOU HAD MUCH BEGINNER'S LUCK.
-KING-
u & Mrs. Alexander jigtosser hav Just returned fron Floririda.Al reports that he lost the largesst sail fish eyer seen in the gulf sream He knew it was a honey wh when it struck' says Al. I1d of epu:led him off his feet Al says, if he hadn't kep t hjs head
he played it 6 minute's before !t broke water and gogaway.Theu it leaped1O feet in the air an was he supprised when he found it to be a 2 master wiht Schooner schooner rig?

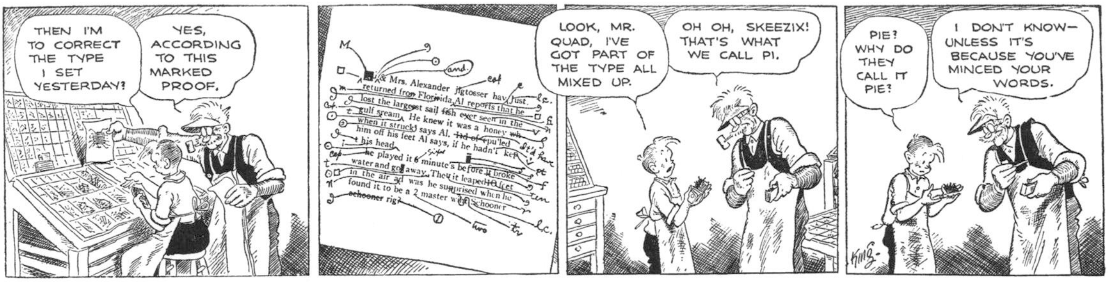

THEN I'M TO CORRECT THE TYPE I SET YESTERDAY?
YES, ACCORDING TO THIS MARKED PROOF.
& Mrs. Alexander jigtosser hav just
returned from Floriida Al reports that he
lost the largest sail fish ever seen in the
gulf sream. He knew it was a honey wh
when it struck says Al. lid of pu'led
him off his feet Al says, if he hadn't kep
his head
he played it 6 minute's before it broke
water and got away. Then it leaped 10 feet
in the air ad was he surprised when he
found it to be a 2 master with Schooner
schooner rig?
LOOK, MR. QUAD, I'VE GOT PART OF THE TYPE ALL MIXED UP.
OH OH, SKEEZIX! THAT'S WHAT WE CALL PI.
PIE? WHY DO THEY CALL IT PIE?
I DON'T KNOW— UNLESS IT'S BECAUSE YOU'VE MINCED YOUR WORDS.
KING

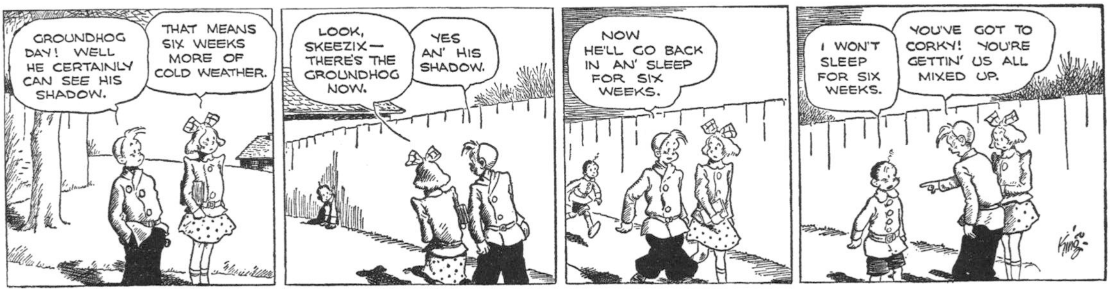

GROUNDHOG DAY! WELL HE CERTAINLY CAN SEE HIS SHADOW.
THAT MEANS SIX WEEKS MORE OF COLD WEATHER.
LOOK, SKEEZIX— THERE'S THE GROUNDHOG NOW.
YES AN' HIS SHADOW.
NOW HE'LL GO BACK IN AN' SLEEP FOR SIX WEEKS.
I WON'T SLEEP FOR SIX WEEKS.
YOU'VE GOT TO CORKY! YOU'RE GETTIN' US ALL MIXED UP.
KING

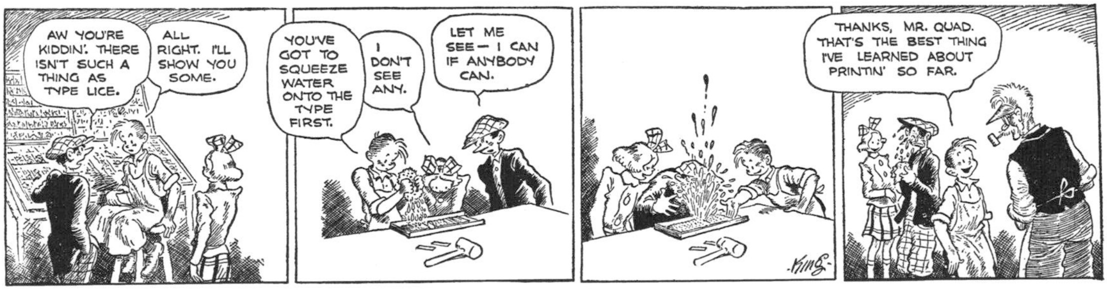

AW YOU'RE KIDDIN'. THERE ISN'T SUCH A THING AS TYPE LICE.
ALL RIGHT. I'LL SHOW YOU SOME.
YOU'VE GOT TO SQUEEZE WATER ONTO THE TYPE FIRST.
I DON'T SEE ANY.
LET ME SEE— I CAN IF ANYBODY CAN.
THANKS, MR. QUAD. THAT'S THE BEST THING I'VE LEARNED ABOUT PRINTIN' SO FAR.
KING

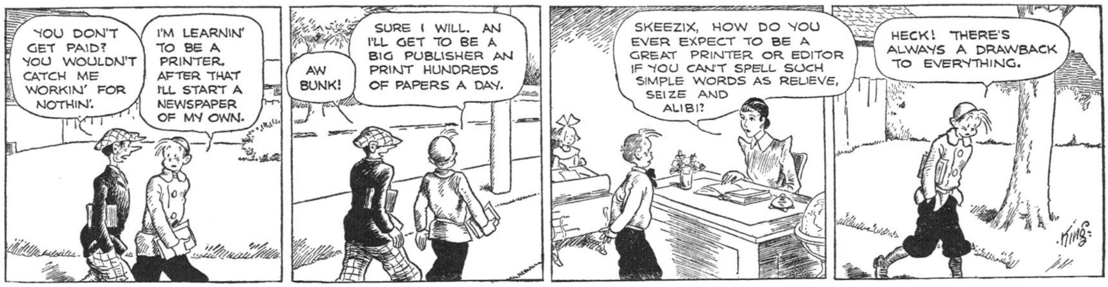

YOU DON'T GET PAID? YOU WOULDN'T CATCH ME WORKIN' FOR NOTHIN'.
I'M LEARNIN' TO BE A PRINTER. AFTER THAT I'LL START A NEWSPAPER OF MY OWN.
AW BUNK!
SURE I WILL. AN I'LL GET TO BE A BIG PUBLISHER AN PRINT HUNDREDS OF PAPERS A DAY.
SKEEZIX, HOW DO YOU EVER EXPECT TO BE A GREAT PRINTER OR EDITOR IF YOU CAN'T SPELL SUCH SIMPLE WORDS AS RELIEVE, SEIZE AND ALIBI?
HECK! THERE'S ALWAYS A DRAWBACK TO EVERYTHING.
KING

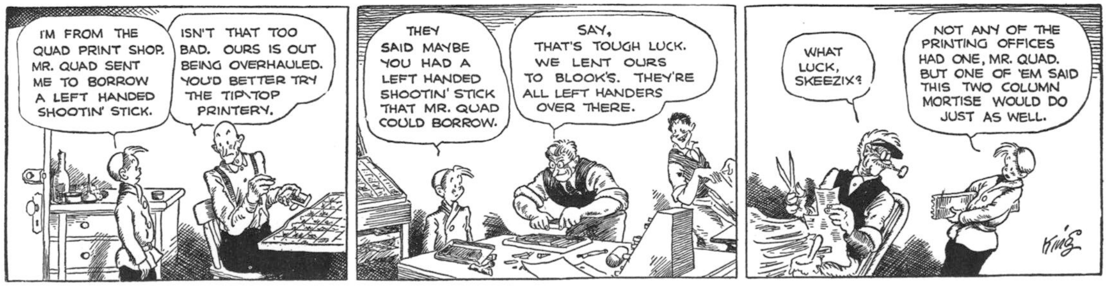

I'M FROM THE QUAD PRINT SHOP. MR. QUAD SENT ME TO BORROW A LEFT HANDED SHOOTIN' STICK.
ISN'T THAT TOO BAD. OURS IS OUT BEING OVERHAULED. YOU'D BETTER TRY THE TIP-TOP PRINTERY.
THEY SAID MAYBE YOU HAD A LEFT HANDED SHOOTIN' STICK THAT MR. QUAD COULD BORROW.
SAY, THAT'S TOUGH LUCK. WE LENT OURS TO BLOOK'S. THEY'RE ALL LEFT HANDERS OVER THERE.
WHAT LUCK, SKEEZIX?
NOT ANY OF THE PRINTING OFFICES HAD ONE, MR. QUAD. BUT ONE OF 'EM SAID THIS TWO COLUMN MORTISE WOULD DO JUST AS WELL.
KING

 January 31–February 1 & 3–5, 1934.

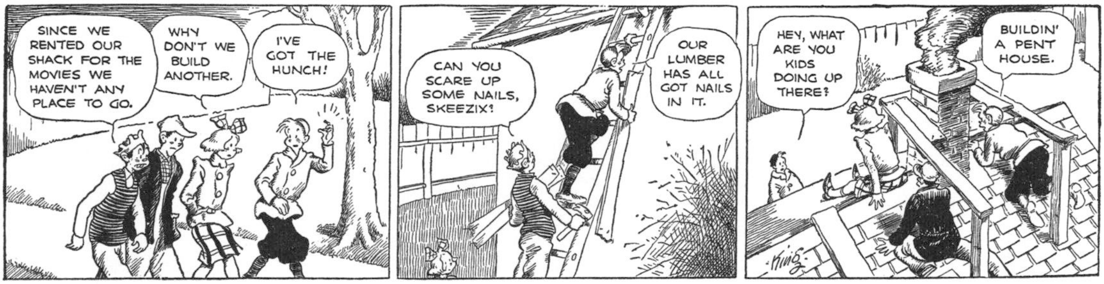
SINCE WE RENTED OUR SHACK FOR THE MOVIES WE HAVEN'T ANY PLACE TO GO.
WHY DON'T WE BUILD ANOTHER.
I'VE GOT THE HUNCH!
CAN YOU SCARE UP SOME NAILS, SKEEZIX?
OUR LUMBER HAS ALL GOT NAILS IN IT.
HEY, WHAT ARE YOU KIDS DOING UP THERE?
BUILDIN' A PENT HOUSE.
KING

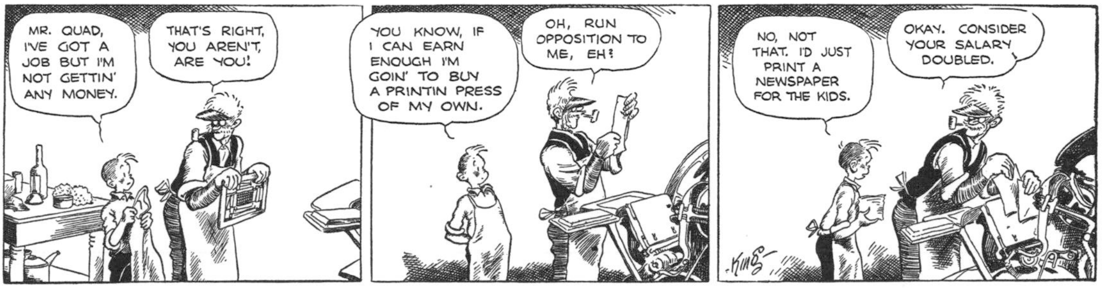
MR. QUAD, I'VE GOT A JOB BUT I'M NOT GETTIN' ANY MONEY.
THAT'S RIGHT, YOU AREN'T, ARE YOU!
YOU KNOW, IF I CAN EARN ENOUGH I'M GOIN' TO BUY A PRINTIN PRESS OF MY OWN.
OH, RUN OPPOSITION TO ME, EH?
NO, NOT THAT. I'D JUST PRINT A NEWSPAPER FOR THE KIDS.
OKAY. CONSIDER YOUR SALARY DOUBLED.
KING

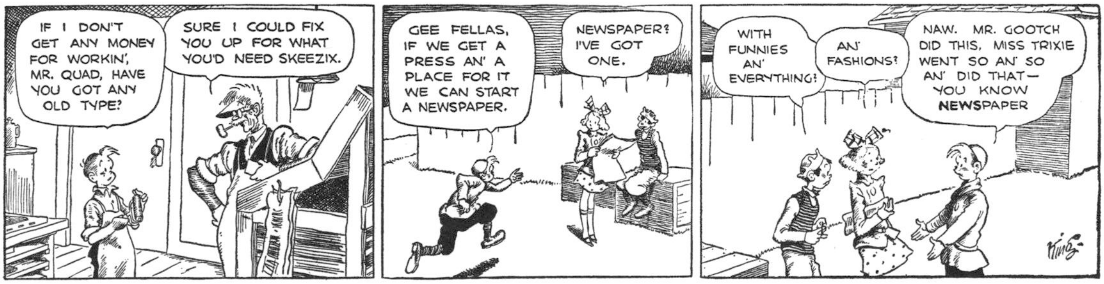
IF I DON'T GET ANY MONEY FOR WORKIN', MR. QUAD, HAVE YOU GOT ANY OLD TYPE?
SURE I COULD FIX YOU UP FOR WHAT YOU'D NEED SKEEZIX.
GEE FELLAS, IF WE GET A PRESS AN' A PLACE FOR IT WE CAN START A NEWSPAPER.
NEWSPAPER? I'VE GOT ONE.
WITH FUNNIES AN' EVERYTHING?
AN' FASHIONS?
NAW. MR. GOOTCH DID THIS, MISS TRIXIE WENT SO AN' SO AN' DID THAT— YOU KNOW NEWSPAPER
KING

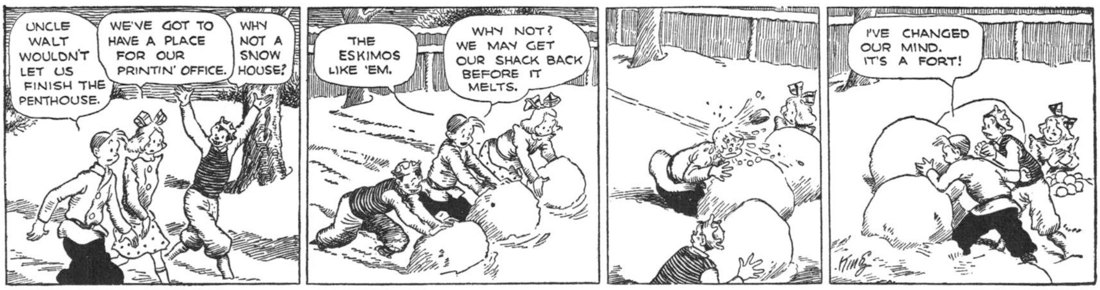
UNCLE WALT WOULDN'T LET US FINISH THE PENTHOUSE.
WE'VE GOT TO HAVE A PLACE FOR OUR PRINTIN' OFFICE.
WHY NOT A SNOW HOUSE?
THE ESKIMOS LIKE 'EM.
WHY NOT? WE MAY GET OUR SHACK BACK BEFORE IT MELTS.
I'VE CHANGED OUR MIND. IT'S A FORT!
KING

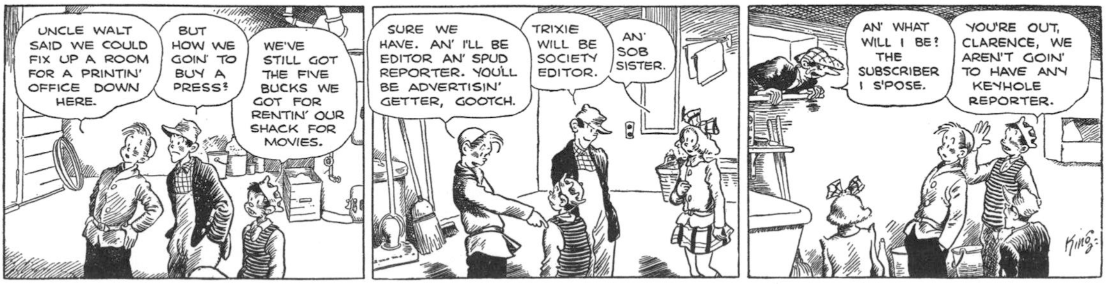
UNCLE WALT SAID WE COULD FIX UP A ROOM FOR A PRINTIN' OFFICE DOWN HERE.
BUT HOW WE GOIN' TO BUY A PRESS?
WE'VE STILL GOT THE FIVE BUCKS WE GOT FOR RENTIN' OUR SHACK FOR MOVIES.
SURE WE HAVE. AN' I'LL BE EDITOR AN' SPUD REPORTER. YOU'LL BE ADVERTISIN' GETTER, GOOTCH.
TRIXIE WILL BE SOCIETY EDITOR.
AN' SOB SISTER.
AN' WHAT WILL I BE? THE SUBSCRIBER I S'POSE.
YOU'RE OUT, CLARENCE, WE AREN'T GOIN' TO HAVE ANY KEYHOLE REPORTER.
KING

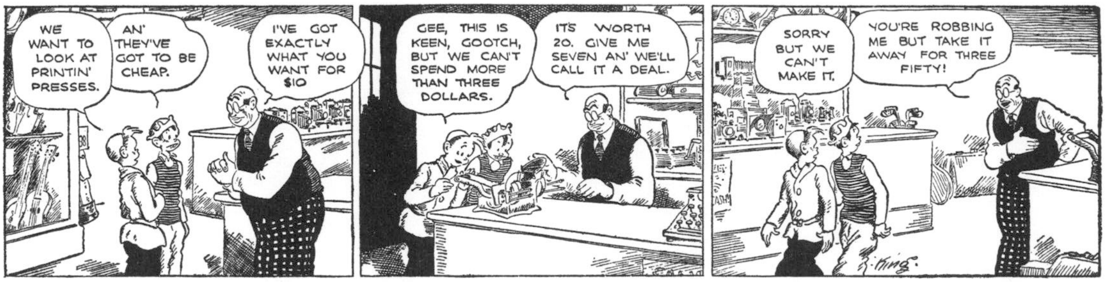
WE WANT TO LOOK AT PRINTIN' PRESSES.
AN' THEY'VE GOT TO BE CHEAP.
I'VE GOT EXACTLY WHAT YOU WANT FOR $10
GEE, THIS IS KEEN, GOOTCH, BUT WE CAN'T SPEND MORE THAN THREE DOLLARS.
IT'S WORTH 20. GIVE ME SEVEN AN' WE'LL CALL IT A DEAL.
SORRY BUT WE CAN'T MAKE IT.
YOU'RE ROBBING ME BUT TAKE IT AWAY FOR THREE FIFTY!
King

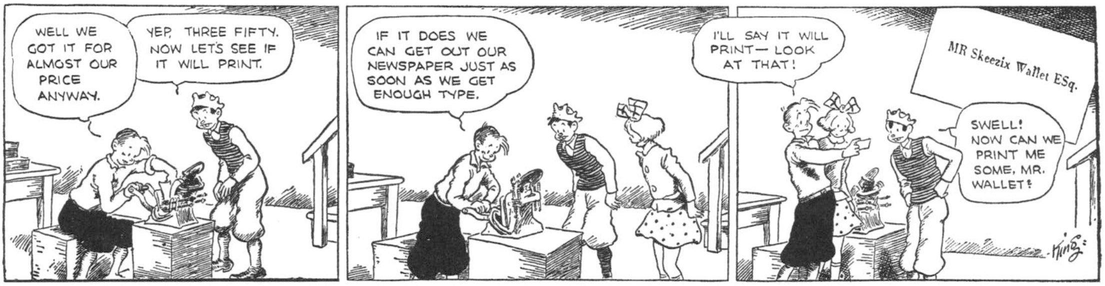
WELL WE GOT IT FOR ALMOST OUR PRICE ANYWAY.
YEP, THREE FIFTY. NOW LET'S SEE IF IT WILL PRINT.
IF IT DOES WE CAN GET OUT OUR NEWSPAPER JUST AS SOON AS WE GET ENOUGH TYPE.
I'LL SAY IT WILL PRINT— LOOK AT THAT!
MR Skeezix Wallet ESq.
SWELL! NOW CAN WE PRINT ME SOME, MR. WALLET?
King

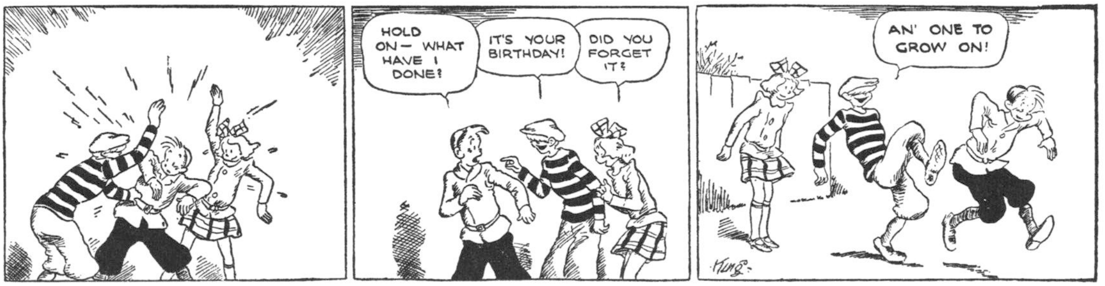
HOLD ON— WHAT HAVE I DONE?
IT'S YOUR BIRTHDAY!
DID YOU FORGET IT?
AN' ONE TO GROW ON!
King

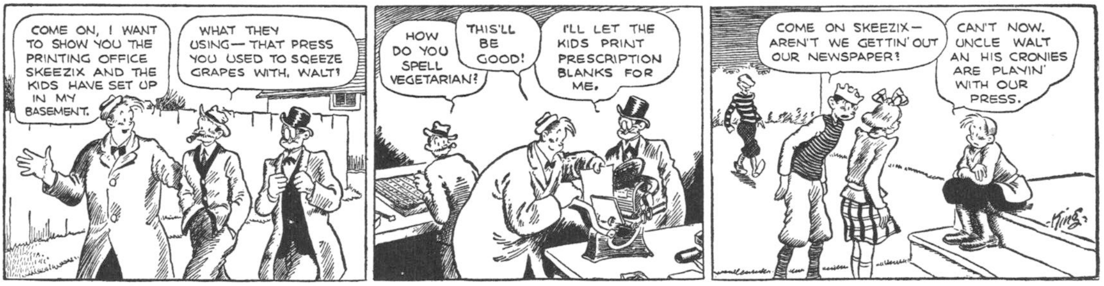
COME ON, I WANT TO SHOW YOU THE PRINTING OFFICE SKEEZIX AND THE KIDS HAVE SET UP IN MY BASEMENT.
WHAT THEY USING— THAT PRESS YOU USED TO SQEEZE GRAPES WITH, WALT?
HOW DO YOU SPELL VEGETARIAN?
THIS'LL BE GOOD!
I'LL LET THE KIDS PRINT PRESCRIPTION BLANKS FOR ME.
COME ON SKEEZIX— AREN'T WE GETTIN' OUT OUR NEWSPAPER?
CAN'T NOW. UNCLE WALT AN HIS CRONIES ARE PLAYIN' WITH OUR PRESS.
King

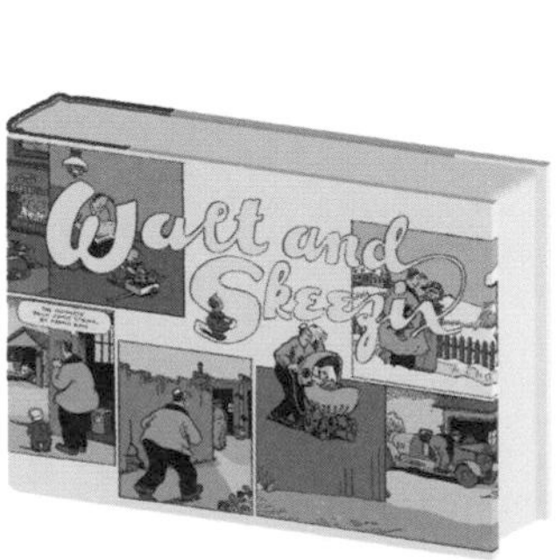
Walt and Skeezix

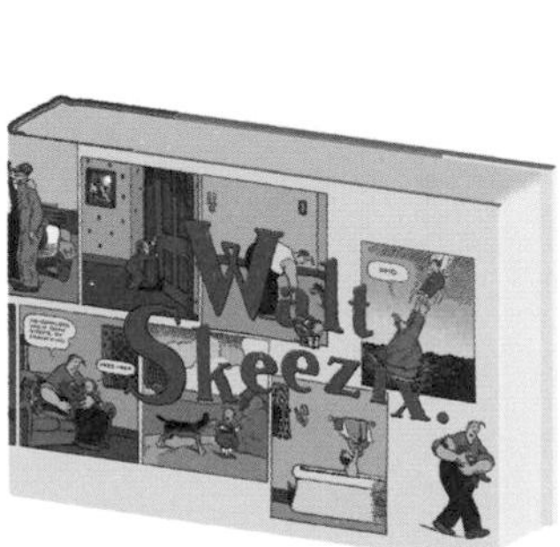
Walt Skeezix.

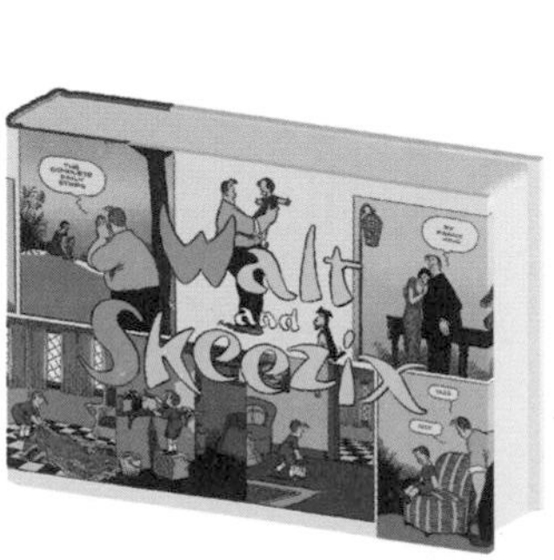
Walt and Skeezix

 February 12–15, 1934.

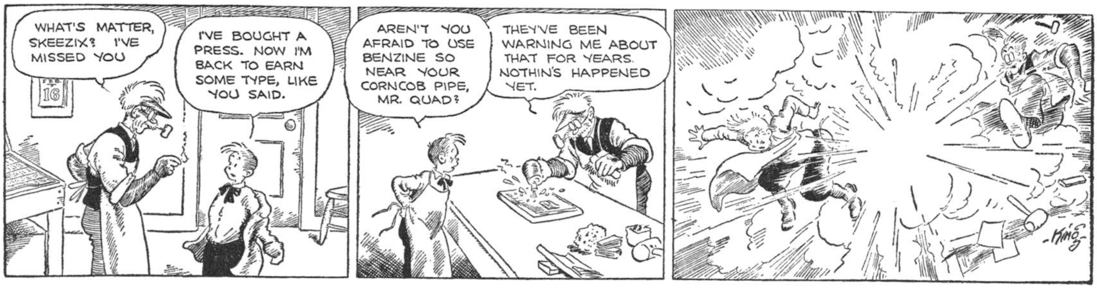
WHAT'S MATTER, SKEEZIX? I'VE MISSED YOU
I'VE BOUGHT A PRESS. NOW I'M BACK TO EARN SOME TYPE, LIKE YOU SAID.
AREN'T YOU AFRAID TO USE BENZINE SO NEAR YOUR CORNCOB PIPE, MR. QUAD?
THEY'VE BEEN WARNING ME ABOUT THAT FOR YEARS. NOTHIN'S HAPPENED YET.
King

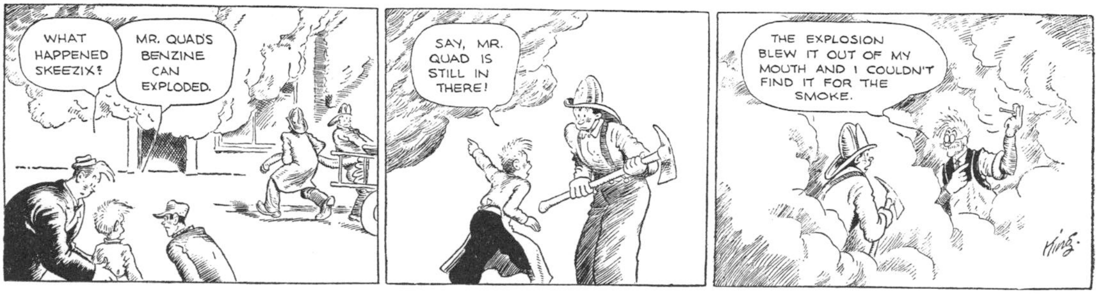
WHAT HAPPENED SKEEZIX?
MR. QUAD'S BENZINE CAN EXPLODED.
SAY, MR. QUAD IS STILL IN THERE!
THE EXPLOSION BLEW IT OUT OF MY MOUTH AND I COULDN'T FIND IT FOR THE SMOKE.
King

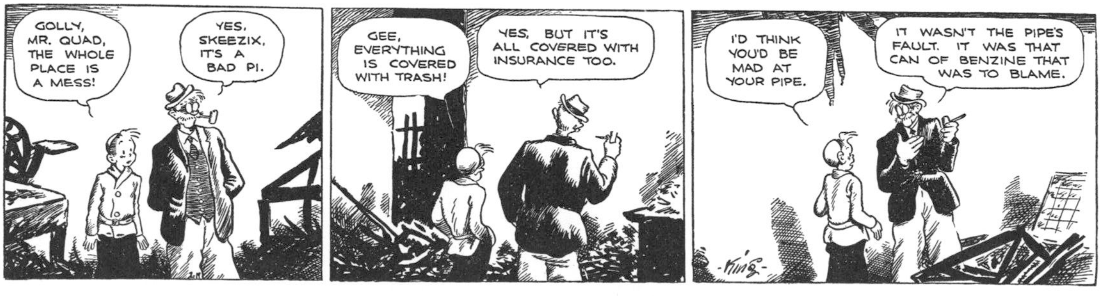
GOLLY, MR. QUAD, THE WHOLE PLACE IS A MESS!
YES, SKEEZIX, IT'S A BAD PI.
GEE, EVERYTHING IS COVERED WITH TRASH!
YES, BUT IT'S ALL COVERED WITH INSURANCE TOO.
I'D THINK YOU'D BE MAD AT YOUR PIPE.
IT WASN'T THE PIPE'S FAULT. IT WAS THAT CAN OF BENZINE THAT WAS TO BLAME.
King

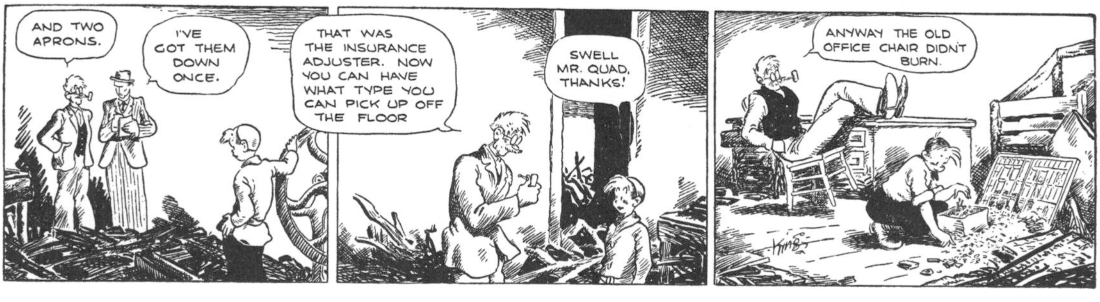
AND TWO APRONS.
I'VE GOT THEM DOWN ONCE.
THAT WAS THE INSURANCE ADJUSTER. NOW YOU CAN HAVE WHAT TYPE YOU CAN PICK UP OFF THE FLOOR
SWELL MR. QUAD, THANKS!
ANYWAY THE OLD OFFICE CHAIR DIDN'T BURN.
King

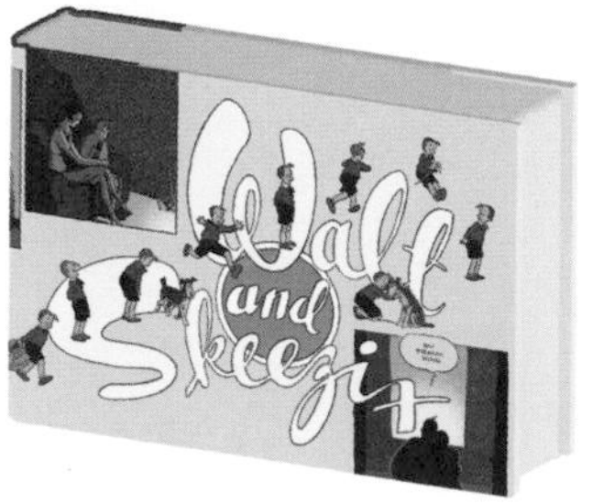
Walt and Skeezix

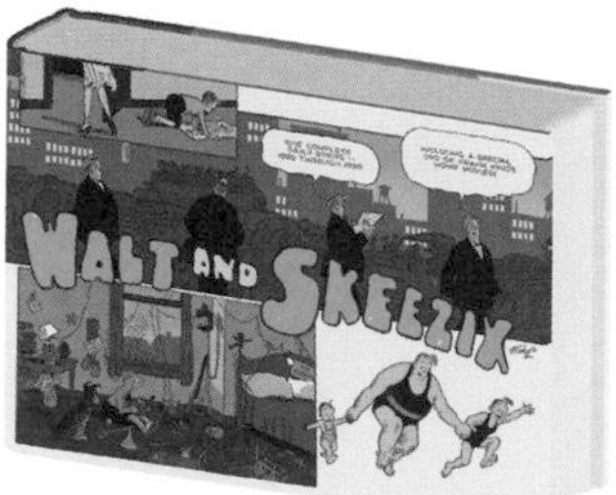
WALT AND SKEEZIX

In the "hindsight is 20/20" department, to the left are revised jackets for the first five *Walt & Skeezix* volumes, reinterpreted in identifiable synchrony with the distinctive colours of the bindings themselves. While none will likely ever be reprinted, it adds to my sense of self-laceration to at least pretend.—***Chris Ware***

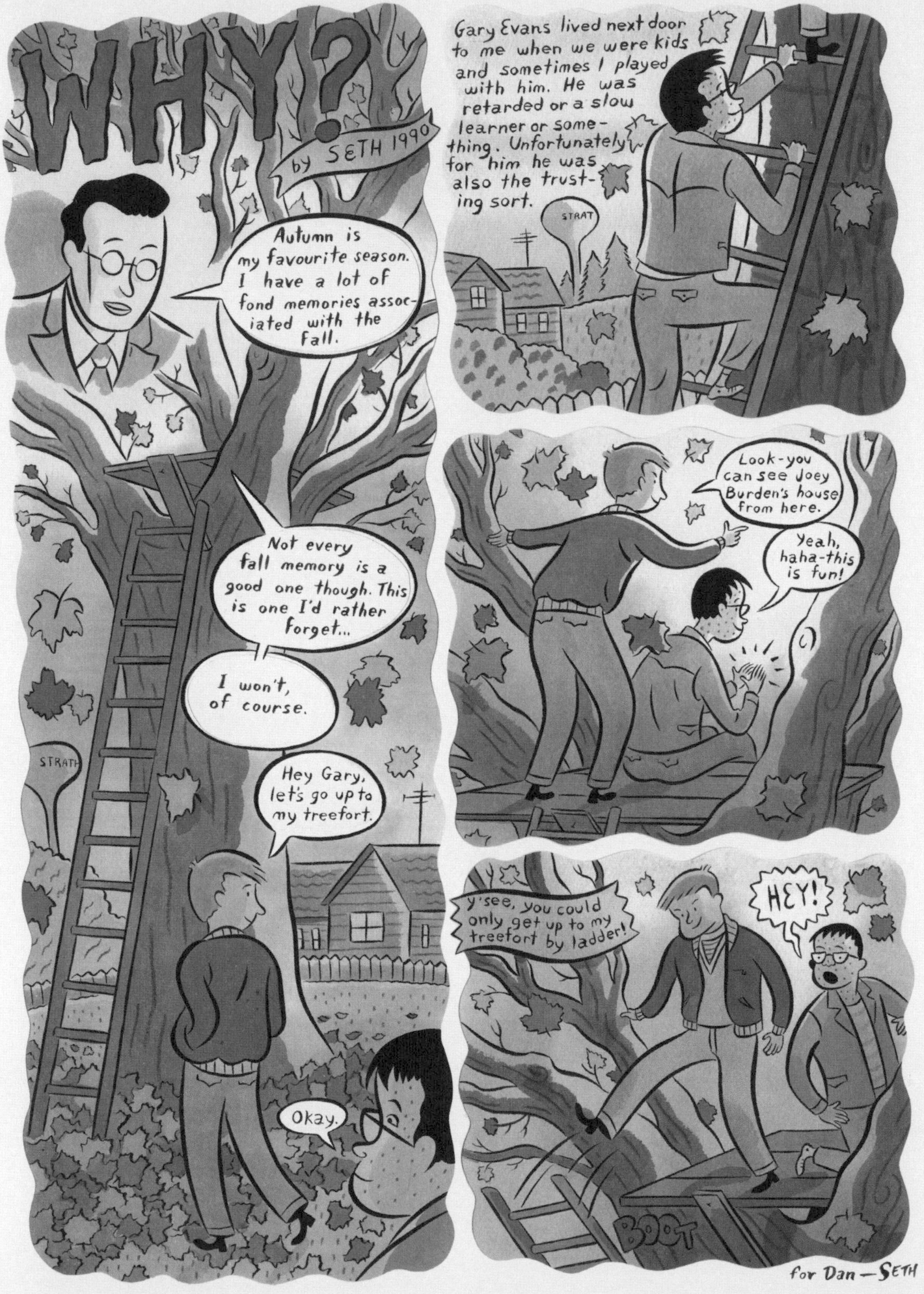
WHY?
by SETH 1990
Autumn is my favourite season. I have a lot of fond memories associated with the fall.
Not every fall memory is a good one though. This is one I'd rather forget...
I won't, of course.
STRATH
Hey Gary, let's go up to my treefort.
Okay.
Gary Evans lived next door to me when we were kids and sometimes I played with him. He was retarded or a slow learner or something. Unfortunately for him he was also the trusting sort.
STRAT
Look-you can see Joey Burden's house from here.
Yeah, haha-this is fun!
y'see, you could only get up to my treefort by ladder!
HEY!
BOOT
for Dan — SETH

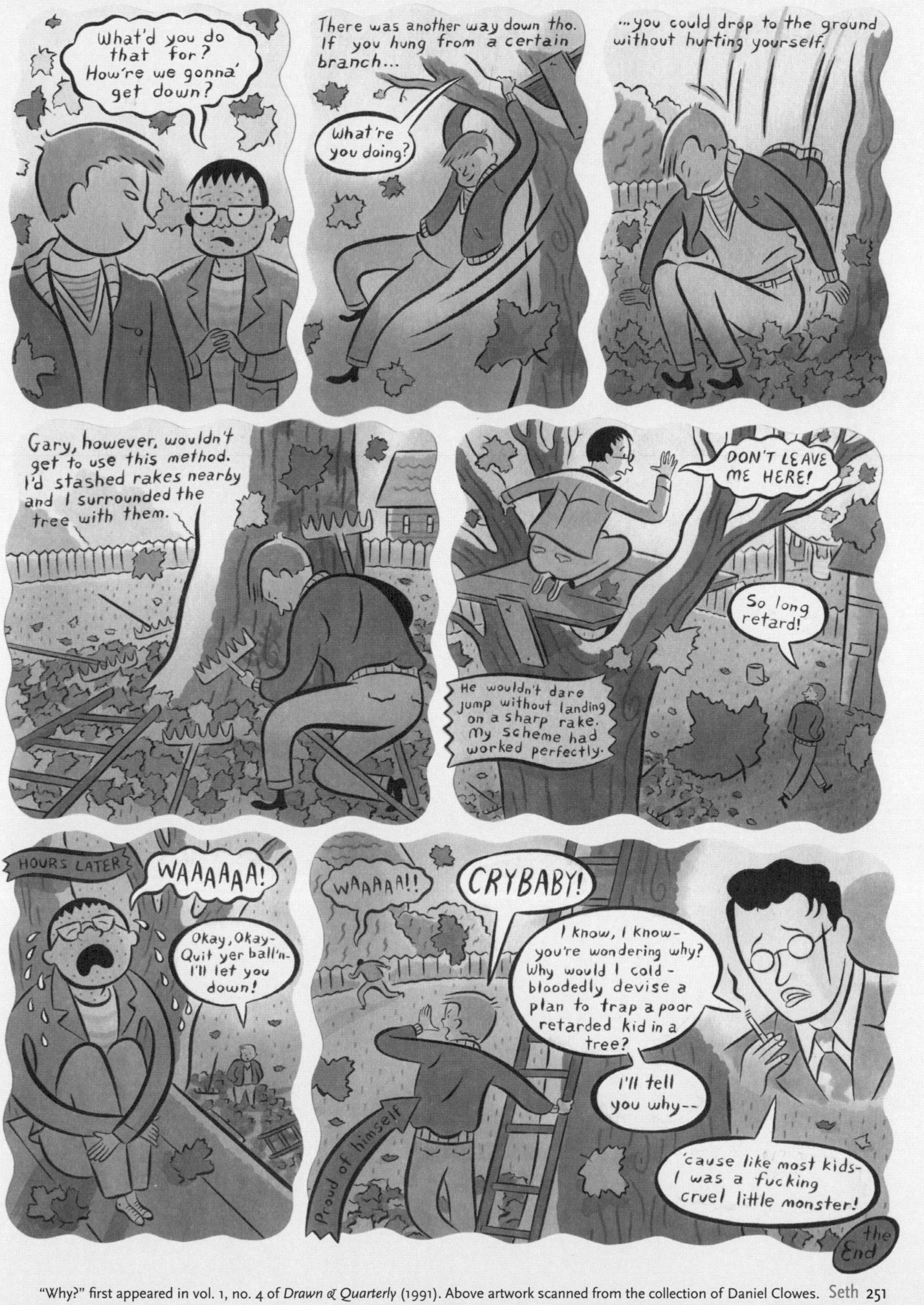
What'd you do that for? How're we gonna' get down?
There was another way down tho. If you hung from a certain branch...
What're you doing?
...you could drop to the ground without hurting yourself.
Gary, however, wouldn't get to use this method. I'd stashed rakes nearby and I surrounded the tree with them.
DON'T LEAVE ME HERE!
So long retard!
He wouldn't dare jump without landing on a sharp rake. My scheme had worked perfectly.
HOURS LATER
WAAAAAA!
Okay, Okay- Quit yer ball'n- I'll let you down!
WAAAAA!!
CRYBABY!
Proud of himself
I know, I know- you're wondering why? Why would I cold-bloodedly devise a plan to trap a poor retarded kid in a tree?
I'll tell you why--
'cause like most kids- I was a fucking cruel little monster!
the End

"Why?" first appeared in vol. 1, no. 4 of *Drawn & Quarterly* (1991). Above artwork scanned from the collection of Daniel Clowes.

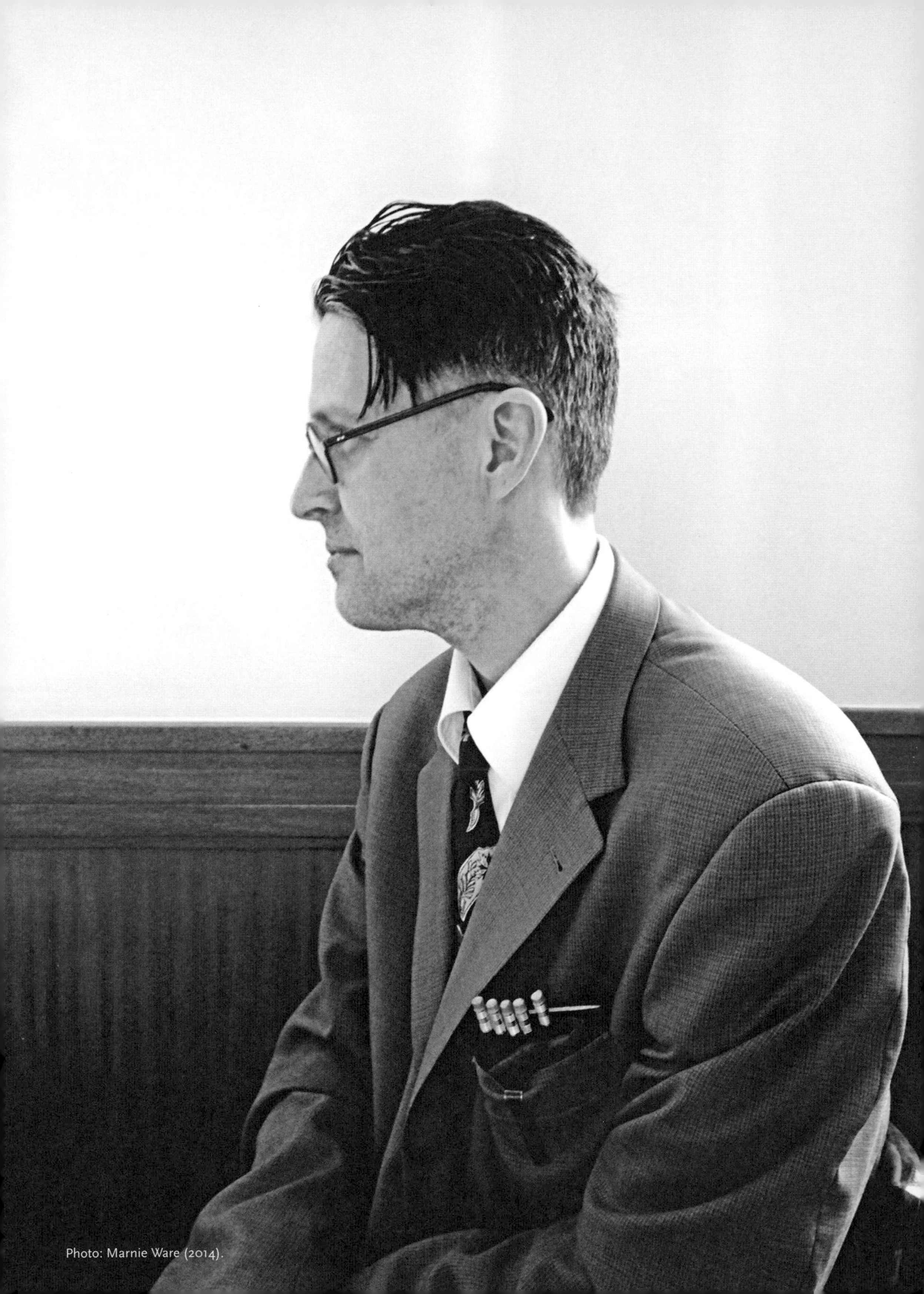

Photo: Marnie Ware (2014).

SETH: A DOSSIER

an appreciation by Lemony Snicket

I first encountered the work of Seth on a cold day in a grey town, or perhaps vice versa, when I happened upon his first book, *It's a Good Life, If You Don't Weaken*, in a shop window. I was on a broody walk, a common activity at this difficult time in my life—I had written a collection of pessimistic essays and light verse entitled *It's a Terrible Life, Particularly If You Possess No Strength Whatsoever*, which was in the process of being rejected for publication throughout North America and most of Eastern Europe. An elderly editor, particularly bored with my offerings, had mentioned that my unwieldy title mirrored that of a Canadian artist whose work he also did not admire, and just a few days later, with the sleet season approaching, there the book was, staring at me from the window. After a short, confusing interlude—it turns out the window was not a shop window after all, and the woman at home was not at all interested in selling the possessions that happened to be visible from the street—I had the book in my hands. Over a cup of Earl Grey in a tea shop, I read the book from beginning to end, my heart racing and my eyes wide and grateful, not only for the exacting peculiarity and startling empathy of Seth's work, but for having escaped from an angry and surprisingly lithe woman who lived in a house with a broken window. I soon had to leave. It turns out the tea shop was also a private home. As I said, this was a difficult time.

Some years later, Seth would find it in his packed schedule and psyche to illustrate some of my work, and our collaboration is its own tale of rack and ruin that need not be printed here. Likewise, summations, appreciations, and criticism of his work can be easily found in libraries and archives, or by simply questioning lonely-looking Canadians, who will have much to say about how his clean and exacting lines contrast with the intangible, slippery truths found in his characters and their thwarted, achy journeys. But I do have some additional materials that may be of interest to Sethusiasts such as myself. Over the years, I have kept close tabs on Seth, a phrase which here means "acquired his books and read them, and compiled a dossier of biographical ephemera." Now that Seth and I are associates, it would cause no small amount of embarrassment if he stumbled upon this dossier while visiting me for refreshment or consultation, so I offer highlights of it here, so that I may destroy the originals.

Peruse these items, Sethusiast. Perhaps these small details can shine a flashlight, alongside the spotlight Seth so richly deserves.

With all due respect,

Lemony Snicket

George Sprott 1894–1975 by Seth. In 2015, we might take Seth's stylistic approach for granted and forget just what an odd choice it was back in the '80s when *RAW* and *Weirdo* were both built on either a Crumbish scuzzy technical virtuosity or a more abstracted, angular formalism. Seth's smooth, brushy curves really stuck out as a throwback to the early- to mid-twentieth-century deadline-making *New Yorker* illustrator and certainly he was trying to affect that entire persona. As great as *It's a Good Life, If You Don't Weaken* and the still ongoing *Clyde Fans* are, *George Sprott* has the heat of a work produced under extreme pressure and the artist rising to the occasion. In many ways, it's impossible to separate any single one of Seth's works out from the performance of his artistic life but this book is a tour-de-force of all Seth's concerns and tics and strengths. The format is large, probably too large for any bookstore, and lavishly produced with cover debossing and removable back band and multiple foldouts and spreads. The entire book would have been printed in pantones had cooler heads not prevailed. The story focuses on a deluded blowhard TV-show host who lives through history and remakes it in his own image. His version is skewed and thus all the more interesting. Seth is fascinated with these types—people who build empires and wreck them or misuse them or sully them for those who come later—failed business people, failed people, forgotten. This book is large and on the cover we see a man's name and the years he lived and died. It's an actual tombstone or what a tombstone hopes to be.

—***Tom Devlin***

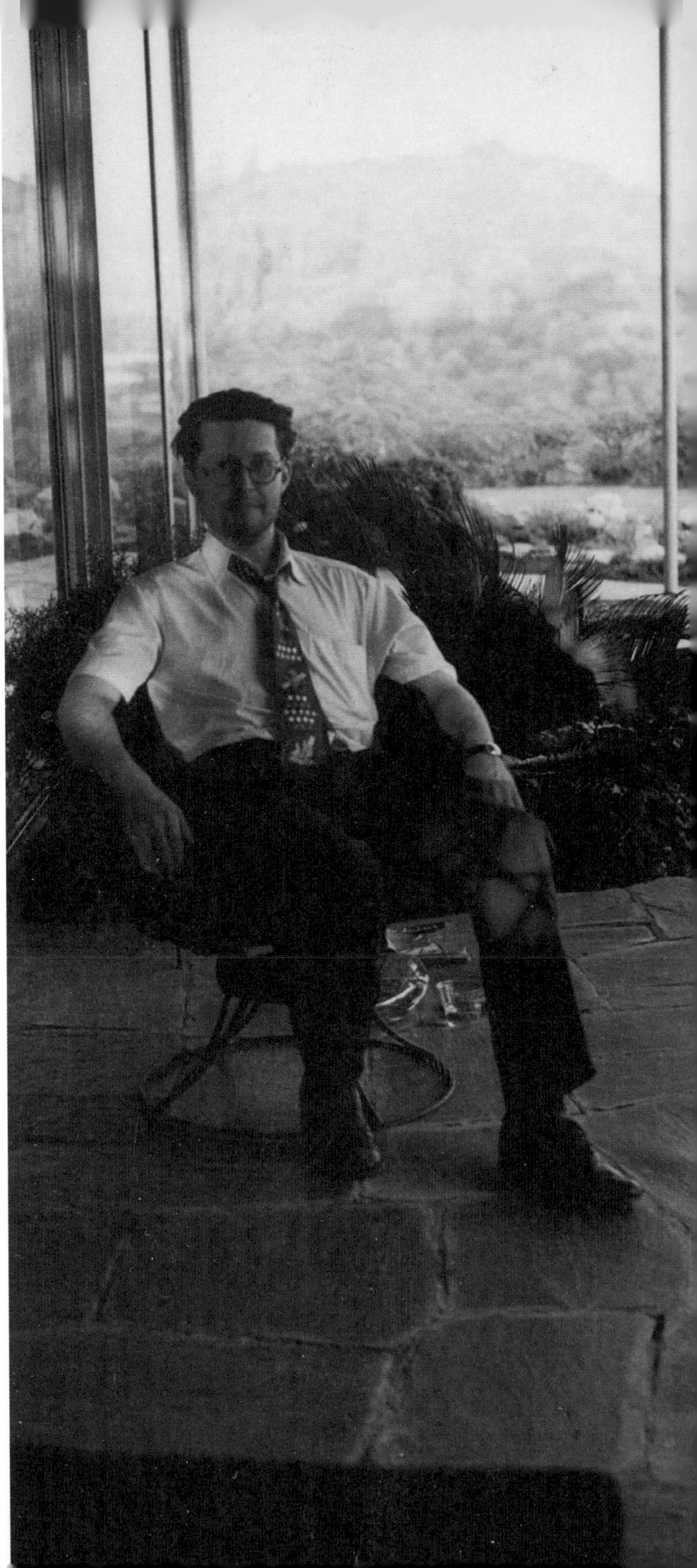

 Seth in Los Angeles (1998).

from report of private investigator engaged in surveillance of Seth, late September through mid-February, 20   :

Dear Client,

On February 5, subject slept late and took late-morning constitutional or perhaps simply an aimless walk. Dined per usual and returned to home/office for duration. Silhouette seen in window at 6:30 PM, 9 PM, 11:30. Subject has performed same ritual for previous 155 days save Christmas, when silhouette was seen at different intervals. Given diminishing funds of client, the sustainability and applicableness of surveillance continues to be a question had by this investigator.

*

diary of unknown woman, possibly from Topeka or Tokyo (several mentions of noodles in downtown "T"), April 19, unknown year:

Another Wednesday. The sky is the colour of slate. Out my window the blackbirds are either sick or bored. I'm out of the good kind of coffee. *Palookaville* offers respite, but also additional ennui.

*

extract from dissertation for PhD in sociology, "I'm Sad Too: Similarities in Cultural Exposure and Consumption among North American Depressives:"

...more than 62 percent reported interest in "graphic novels," the work of Seth among the most prominent amongst readers who felt between "great reluctance" and "sheer impossibility" of leaving bed before 10 AM. The team could offer no solid reason for this, only sympathies.

*

least funny jokes from *The Pen Is Mightier Than the Chortle?!? Jokes and Riddles about North America's Greatest Cartoonists* (Malarkey Press, Victoria Island, 1923 [?!]), chapter 7: "Seth!"

How many Seths does it take to install an industrial fan?
Two full-length volumes, so far.

What's the difference between George Sprott and Seth?
Sprott's book on Seth is way less organized.

Why did Seth cross the road?
He always does, every late afternoon, so as to have a cup of coffee in the same old place.

Seth walks into a bar and asks if the volume of the music could possibly be lowered.
"Why should I turn the volume down for you?" the barman says.
"Never mind," Seth says.

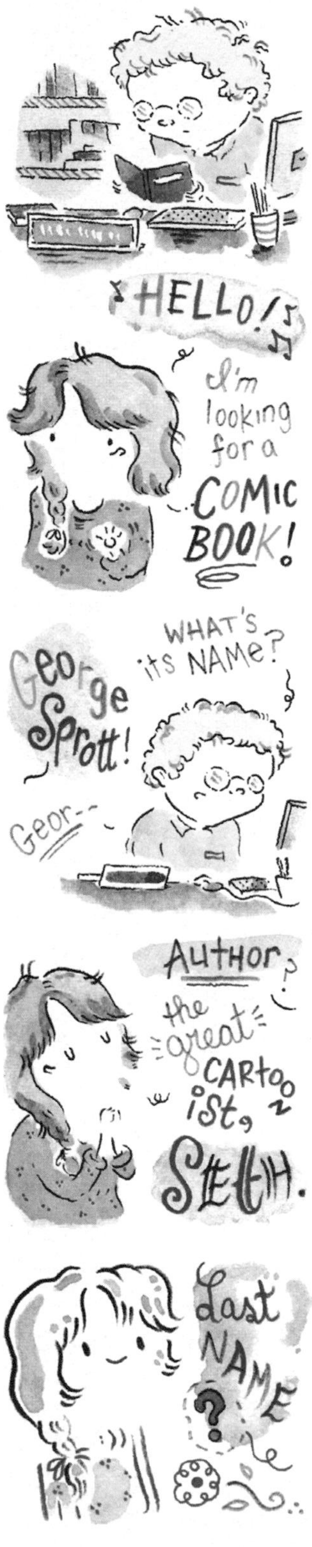
HELLO!
I'm looking for a COMIC BOOK!
WHAT'S its NAME?
George Sprott!
Geor--
Author?
the great cartoonist, SETH.
Last NAME?

Comic by Leslie Stein (2014).

I remember opening *Wimbledon Green* and seeing a splash page of two hobos walking down a road with stick bags dangling and patchwork laced all over their mismatched, tattered clothing. I was curious about what these characters did on a daily basis. I wanted to see a story about them. "Why doesn't Seth make a story about these two Laurel and Hardy bozos?" I'd think to myself. I wanted more!

Looking at this drawing a decade later, it still strikes me in the same way. I realize the curiosity it spun inside me greatly influences the type of mood and story I've grown into creating myself.

—Keith Jones

There are too many great D+Q books to call one my favourite but I do, however, have a soft spot for Seth's *Vernacular Drawings* sketchbook. It was published in 2001, the same year as *The Golem's Mighty Swing* and the same year I moved to Vermont. Seth and I were on a book-signing tour together and I got to spend a lot of time with him and a lot of time with that book as well.

In 2002 my second daughter was born and I had to find a place to work outside my small (and loud) rural Vermont home. I rented a studio space in the small railroad village of White River Junction. The village felt like it was ripped from the pages of *Vernacular Drawings*. When I decided to go ahead and start a cartooning school I couldn't imagine another cartoonist to work with in creating the Center for Cartoon Studies' first brochure. In this way, D+Q's DNA is part of the Center for Cartoon Studies.

—James Sturm

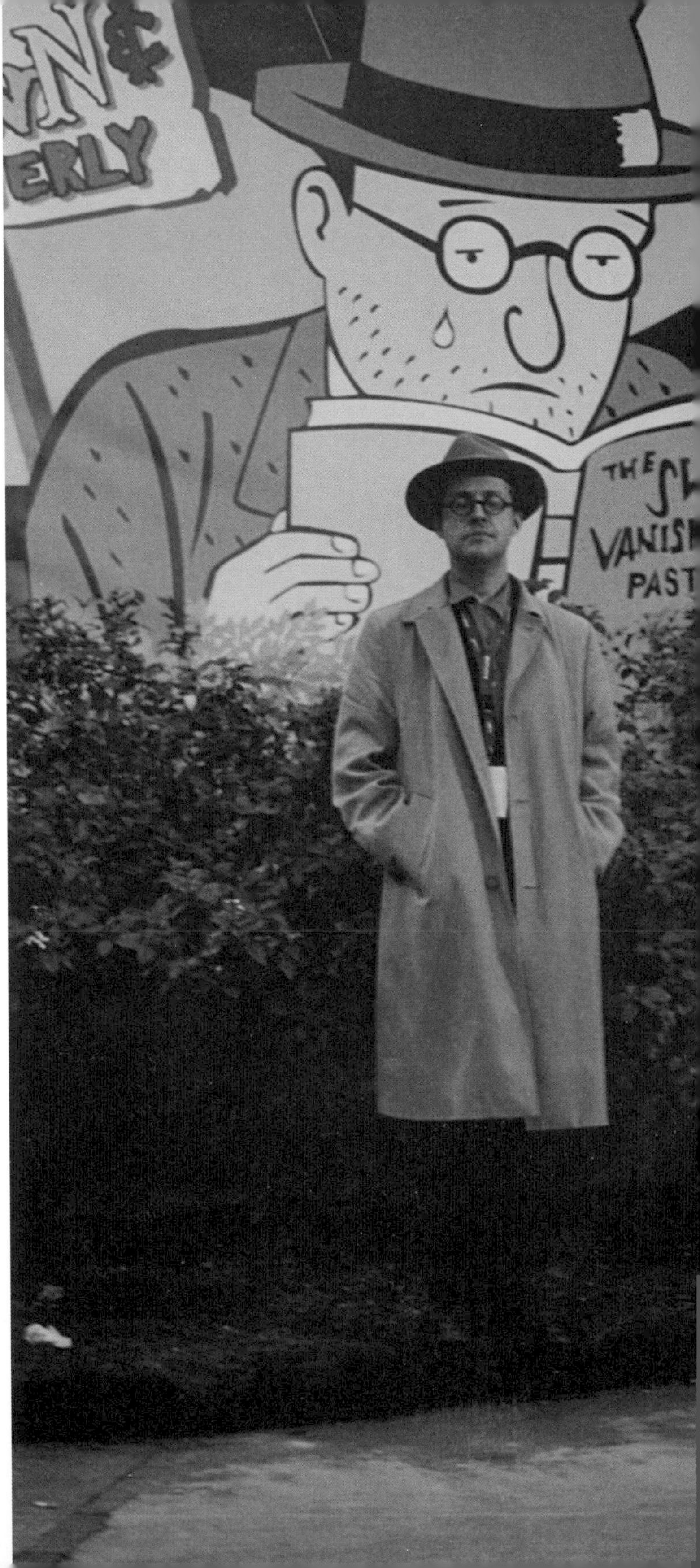

 Seth in Italy (2003).

from *Just for Kidz: Games and Riddles to Aid in the Appreciation of Seth* (Drawn & Quarterly promotional pamphlet, severely limited edition, 2010):

This is a fun one! Read all the short bits of prose below and mark each one with an S, if you think the phrase comes from volume 20 of Seth's *Palookaville* comic, or with a B, if you think the phrase comes from the travel diary of Bashō, famed seventeenth-century haiku poet. Be careful! Maybe one tricky phrase needs to be marked "BS!"

1. I remember.
2. Departing spring.
3. He was hidden by the door.
4. Perhaps—
5. Thank you very much.
6. That is common knowledge.
7. I don't think so.
8. What with swollen waters, boat ran risks.
9. Elizabeth Trudeau.
10. Where was I that day?
11. With unanticipated pleasure talked day and night, his brother Tosui coming over faithfully morning and night, had us to his place and then, at their insistence, to relatives of his, and days passed: one in strolling about the outskirts, inspecting the site of the Inuomono, another in wandering around the Nasu reed-brakes to see Tamamo-no-Mae's old tomb.

*

"Seth" verse of hardly used geographical anthem/rhyming game for the Great Northern Brotherhood of Canadian Cartoonists, as depicted in Seth's *The Great Northern Brotherhood of Canadian Cartoonists*:

S is for Saskatoon, quite isolated
E is for Edmonton, so often berated
T is Toronto, too big and too smarmy
H is for Halifax, comparatively balmy

*

partial transcription of accidentally recorded phone call between L. Snicket and Seth, re: artwork for Mr. Snicket's four-volume account *All The Wrong Questions*:

S: ...impossible deadlines, poor pay, and an overall shoddy experience.
LS: Sorry, I missed the last of that. We seem to have a poor connection. Is there any possibility your line is being tapped?
S: My line *what?*
LS: Never mind, never mind. Well, to the business at hand. I must compliment you absolutely on the townscapes I received. I admit I had some hesitations that you would be able to capture the sad and fading essence of the town of Stain'd-by-the-Sea just from my descriptions and notes, but your artwork here is splendid, splendid. However did you manage to show so completely the town's intractable greyness, its quiet unhappiness, its dilapidated quasi-squalor?
S:

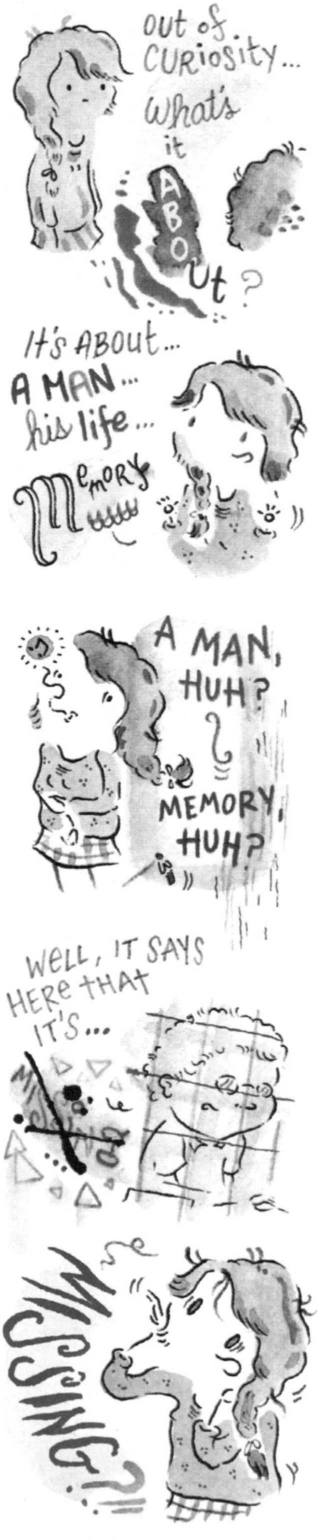
OUT OF CURIOSITY... WHAT'S IT ABOUT?
IT'S ABOUT... A MAN... HIS LIFE... MEMORY
A MAN, HUH?
MEMORY, HUH?
WELL, IT SAYS HERE THAT IT'S...
MISSING?

For as long as I can remember I've been trying to convince Chester and Seth to allow us to publish some of their early, out-of-print work. With Chester every couple of years I ask about publishing his adaptations of the Gospels. Each time he politely but firmly declines. Seth has been equally adamant about the first three issues of *Palookaville*. Oh sure, there are small victories along the way: in 2001 I managed to convince Seth to allow us to reprint the first issue for its tenth anniversary that year. But when it came to "Beaches," the short graphic novel serialized in the second and third issues, the "no" from Seth was more adamant and unbending. Sure, I can sympathize with the fact that many artists dislike their formative work to the point where they prefer to disown it. But in my opinion Seth is being too hard on himself in dismissing this, and I still contend that "Beaches" is an important work. Perhaps of greater significance, it's a book that solidly stands on its own and it's a rare example of Seth's evolution as a cartoonist. Here's a short quiz to prove my point: What was Seth working on just a couple of years before this? Something called *Mr. X*—he may not forgive me for even mentioning that here. And what was his next project immediately following the "Beaches" storyline? That book was *It's a Good Life, If You Don't Weaken*, widely regarded as one of the great graphic novels. Seth may not be able to bear looking at this, but without the trial and error of these early works he could not have become the masterful cartoonist that he is today. I can't believe that I finally managed to trick Seth into publishing this (see page 261). Okay, at eleven pages this represents less than a quarter of the finished book, but it's one more small victory that I'll take.—**Chris Oliveros**

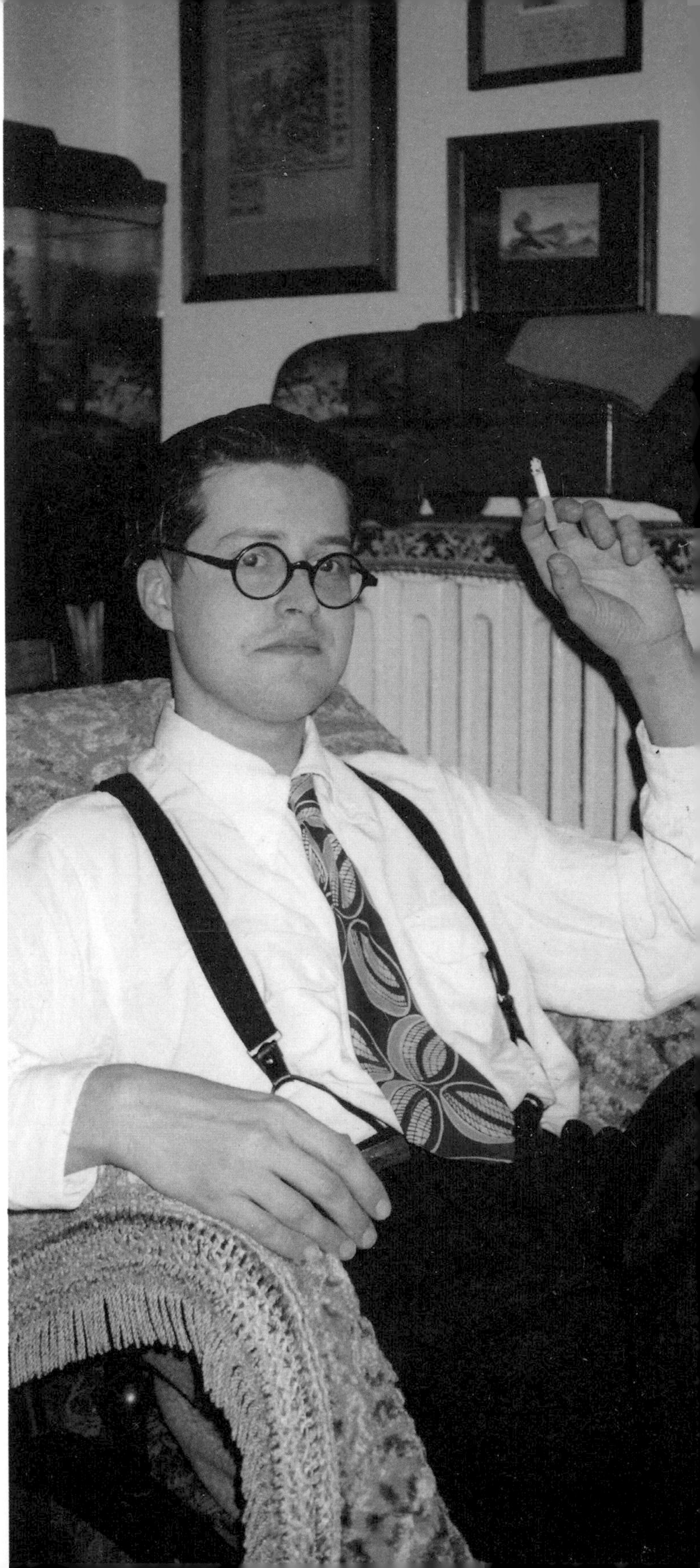

 Seth at home (1989).

LS: Hello?
S:
LS: Hello? Are you—
S: Mr. Snicket, have you ever been to Guelph?
LS: Right, I see what you mean. Now, if we might turn our attention to the small figure in the lower left-hand corner, which requires some minute adjustments the better to match my memory of the man in question.
S: [redacted], you mean.
LS: Yes, [redacted].
S: A terrible name.
LS: Well, he was a terrible person. [redacted] haunts me to this day. I have found no way to redact his name from my life. Do you think there's a way to render him even more bone-chilling, even at such a great distance?
S: Bone-chilling, you say?
LS: Yes, did you not hear me?
S: Not hear—?
LS: What?
S: What?

*

CBC studio notes from the cancelled development of *Clyde Fans* as a situation comedy:

Since we first acquired the adaptation rights to *Clyde Fans*, we have been thrilled to tackle the material and to see how Seth's artful, desolate landscaping and careful depictions, both inked and literary, of humdrum life might be transformed into some zippy, fast-paced episodic television show that might run for years at the rate of many giggles per minute. Sadly, by "we," we mean "several executives who quit in despair, leaving us a pilot episode to oversee despite very little knowledge of or enthusiasm for Seth's work." In any case, please find our notes below.

From a budget standpoint, the use of a small number of sets is appreciated. Limiting locations in *Clyde Fans* to the titular establishment, a single shabby apartment, and two city streets will certainly keep set decorating funds low. Most of us here feel that's a positive.

On the negative side, there's the lack of narrative momentum, the frequent narration, absence of suspense, and a complete and utter dearth of anything that could pass for a "laugh."

Eugene Levy has passed. Tentative interest from Neve Campbell.

*

LS: There is a school of thought that art exists to create beauty, to lure us out of our ugly everyday world and show us something shimmery and new. And there is a school of thought that art exists to capture the beauty we may otherwise miss around us. But you seem to believe that the everyday, the banality of—
S: Wait, who did you say this is?
LS: Seth?
S[?]: No. Snicket?
LS[?]: No.
[?]: Then who—
[?]: Hello?
[?]

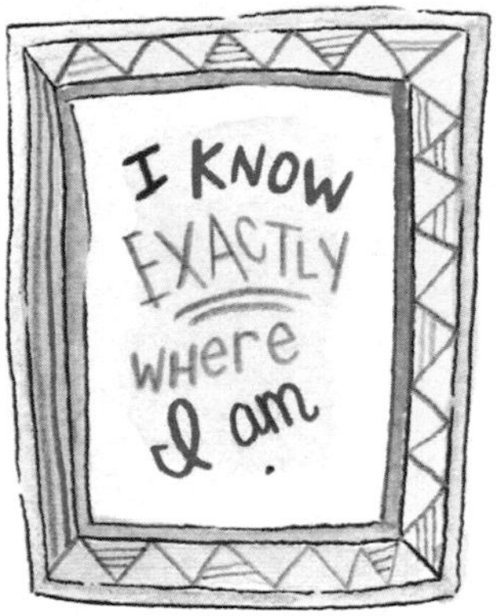
I KNOW EXACTLY WHERE I am.

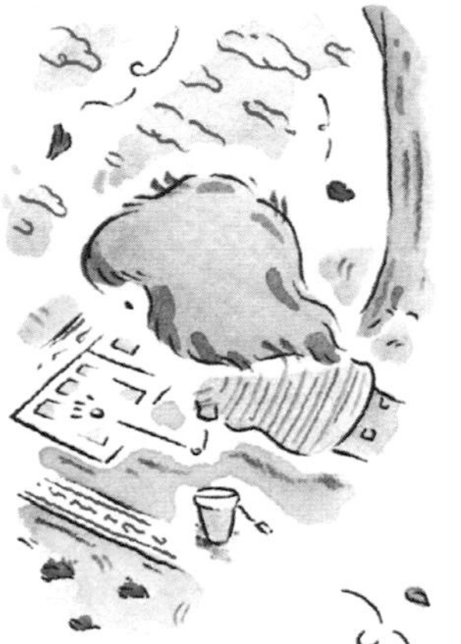

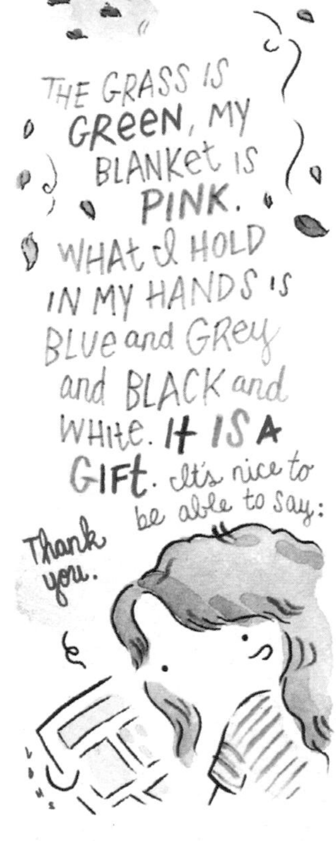
THE GRASS IS GREEN, MY BLANKET IS PINK. WHAT I HOLD IN MY HANDS IS BLUE and GREY and BLACK and WHITE. IT IS A GIFT. It's nice to be able to say:
Thank you.

I pretty much despise the first three issues of *Palookaville*. Maybe all artists hate their early work. I certainly do. Can't bear to even look at it. The drawing is feeble and my understanding of comic storytelling is rudimentary. I'm not using tones very well. I could live with that. What makes me uncomfortable is the writing. It feels so very flat to me. Forced. I don't recognize the "voice." I guess we all have to start somewhere though.—***Seth***

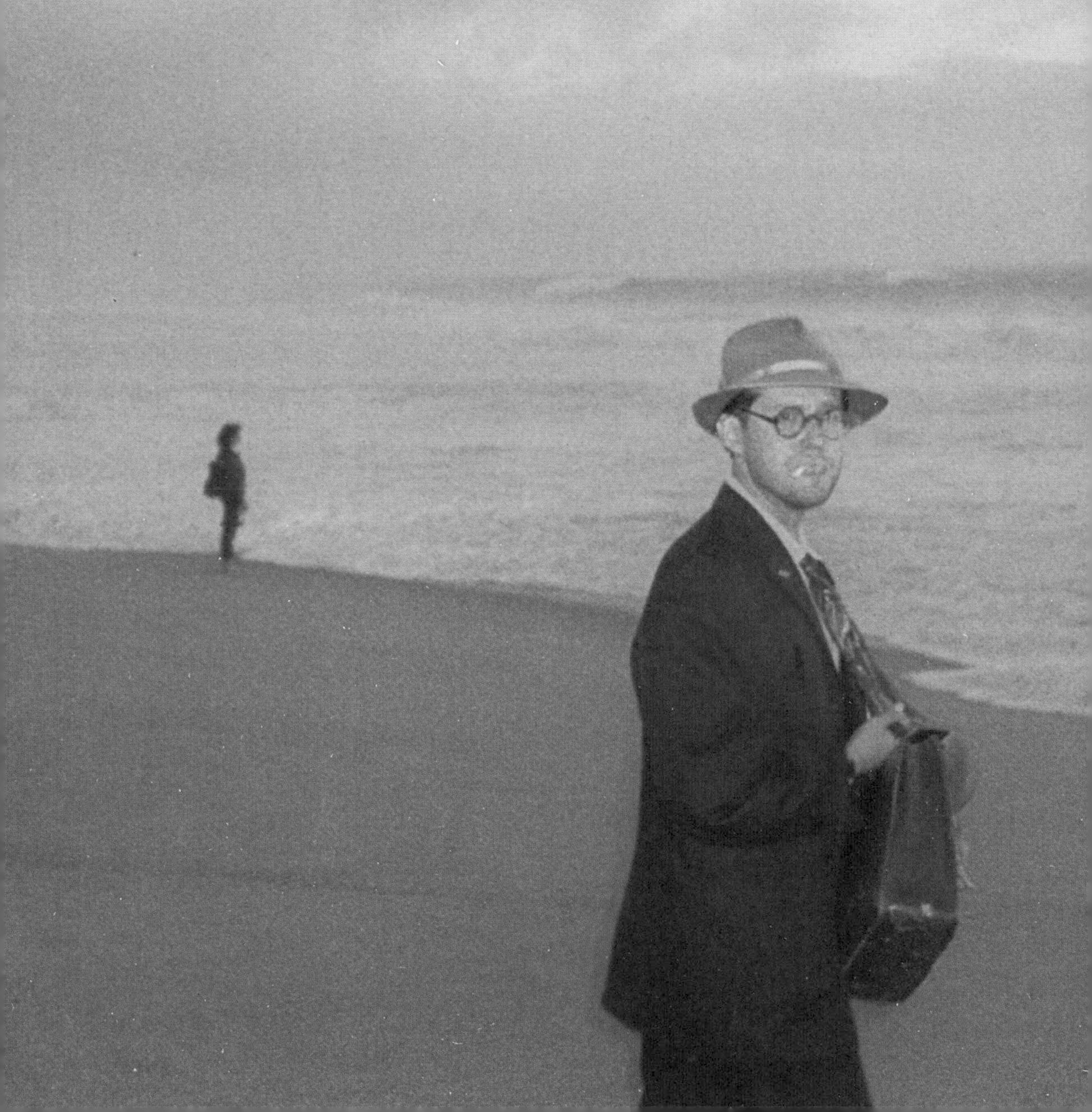

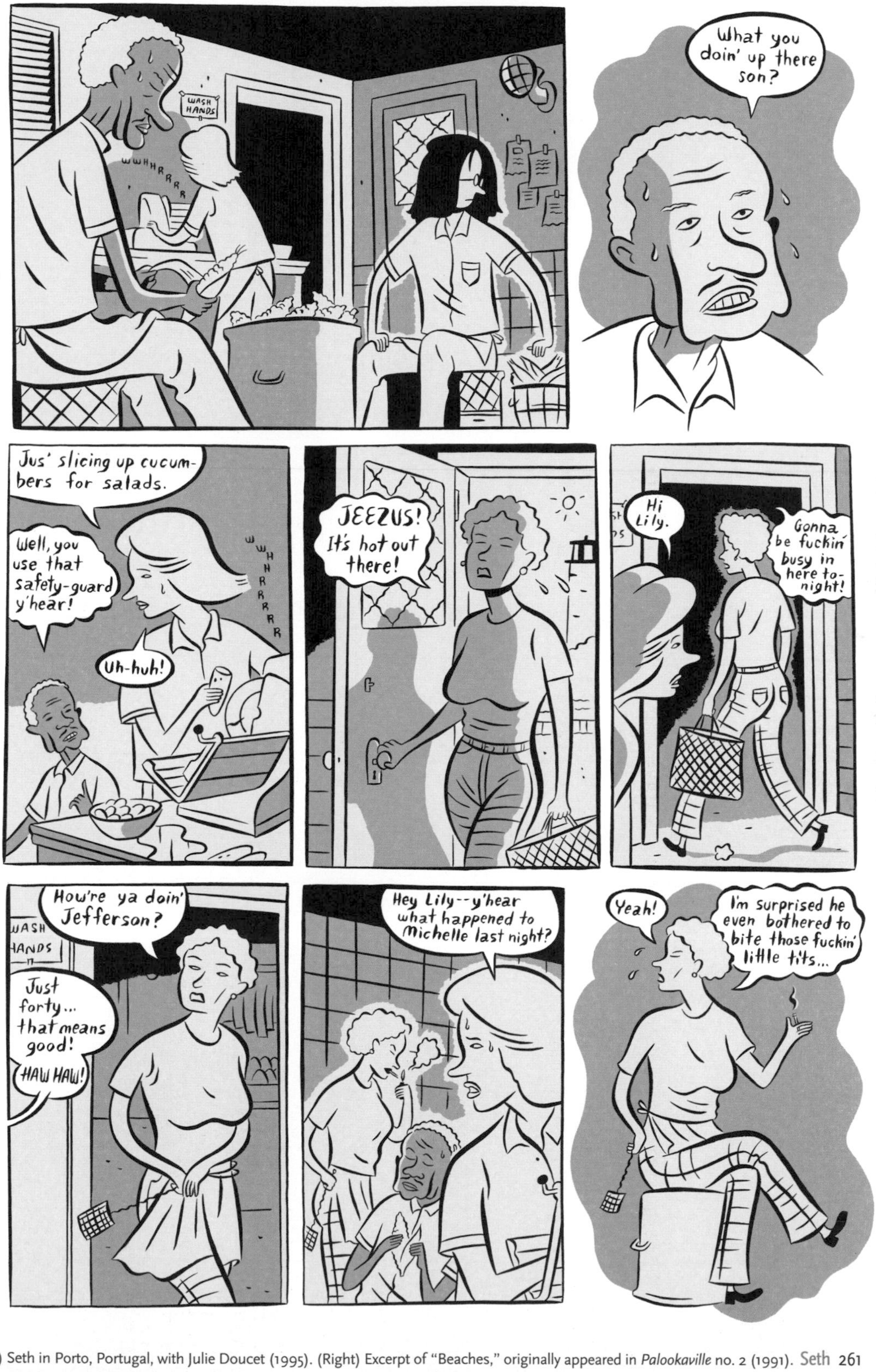
WASH HANDS
WWHHRRRR
What you doin' up there son?
Jus' slicing up cucumbers for salads.
Well, you use that safety-guard y'hear!
WWHHRRRRR
Uh-huh!
JEEZUS! It's hot out there!
Hi Lily.
Gonna be fuckin' busy in here to-night!
How're ya doin' Jefferson?
WASH HANDS
Just forty... that means good!
HAW HAW!
Hey Lily--y'hear what happened to Michelle last night?
Yeah!
I'm surprised he even bothered to bite those fuckin' little tits...

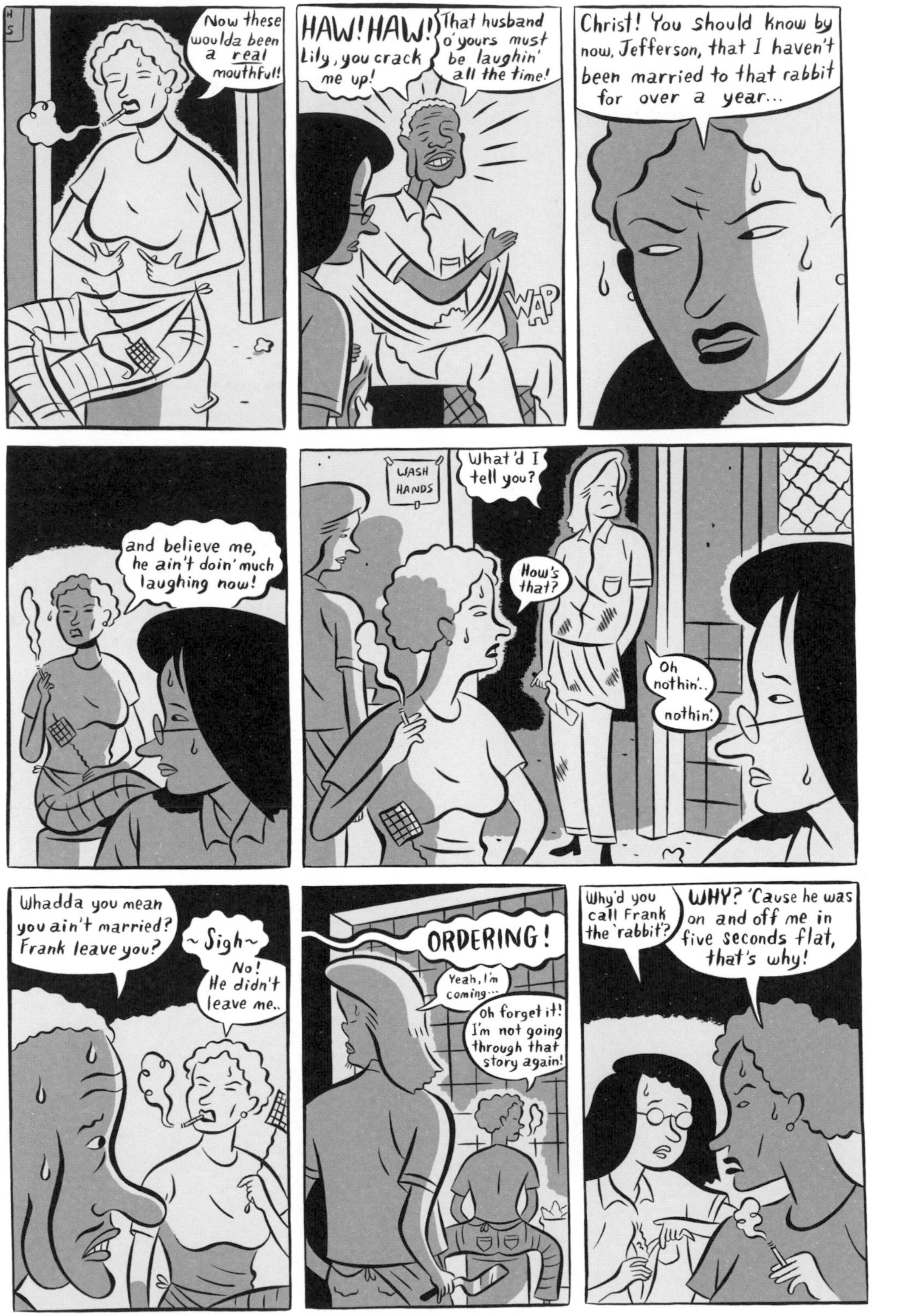
H S
Now these woulda been a real mouthful!
HAW! HAW! Lily, you crack me up!
That husband o'yours must be laughin' all the time!
WAP
Christ! You should know by now, Jefferson, that I haven't been married to that rabbit for over a year...
and believe me, he ain't doin' much laughing now!
WASH HANDS
What'd I tell you?
How's that?
Oh nothin'..
nothin'.
Whadda you mean you ain't married? Frank leave you?
~Sigh~
No! He didn't leave me..
ORDERING!
Yeah, I'm coming...
Oh forget it! I'm not going through that story again!
Why'd you call Frank the 'rabbit'?
WHY? 'Cause he was on and off me in five seconds flat, that's why!

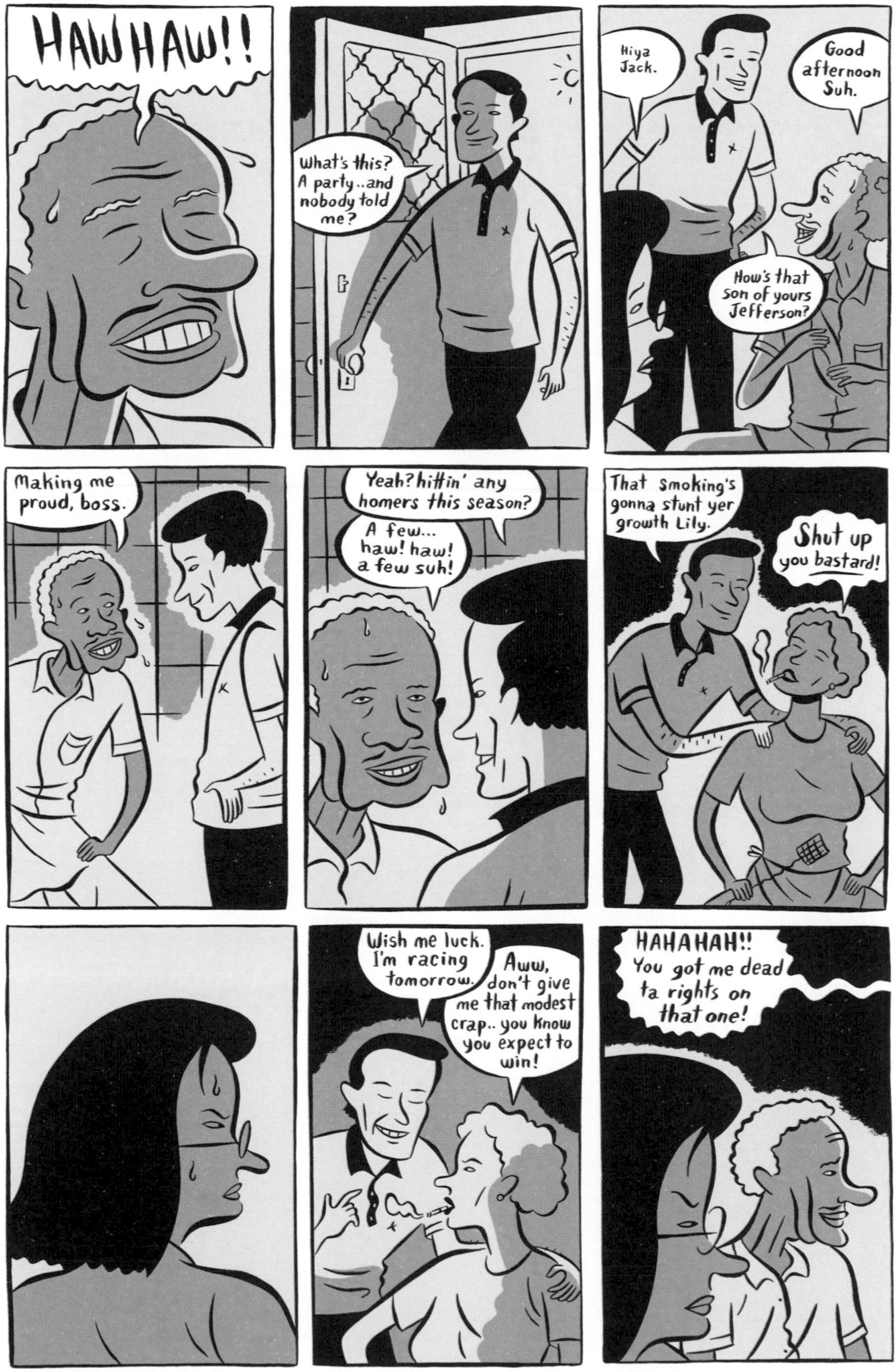
HAWHAW!!
What's this? A party..and nobody told me?
Hiya Jack.
Good afternoon Suh.
How's that son of yours Jefferson?
Making me proud, boss.
Yeah? hittin' any homers this season?
A few... haw! haw! a few suh!
That smoking's gonna stunt yer growth Lily.
Shut up you bastard!
Wish me luck. I'm racing tomorrow.
Aww, don't give me that modest crap.. you know you expect to win!
HAHAHAH!! You got me dead ta rights on that one!

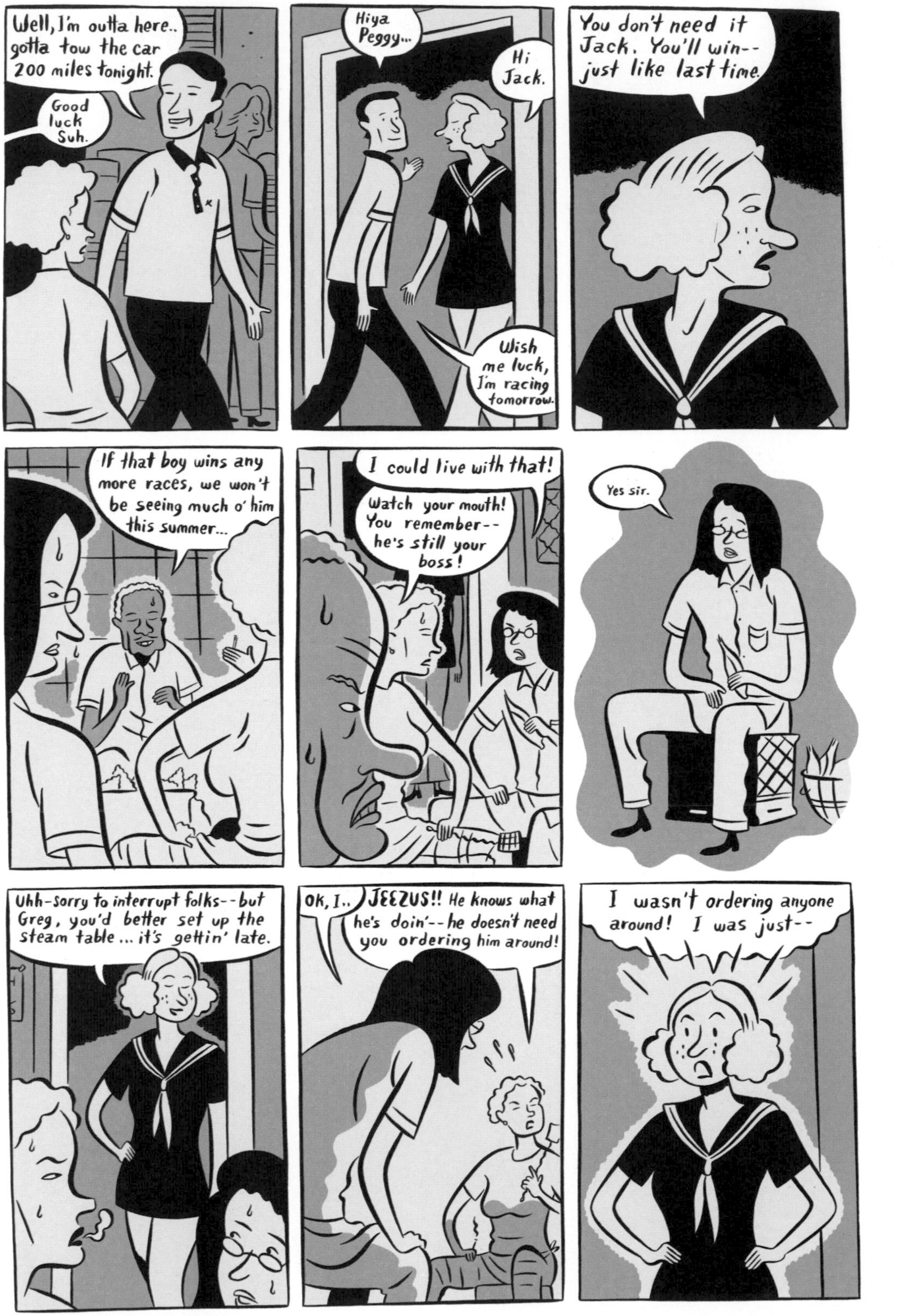
Well, I'm outta here.. gotta tow the car 200 miles tonight.
Good luck Suh.
Hiya Peggy...
Hi Jack.
Wish me luck, I'm racing tomorrow.
You don't need it Jack. You'll win-- just like last time.
If that boy wins any more races, we won't be seeing much o' him this summer...
I could live with that!
Watch your mouth! You remember-- he's still your boss!
Yes sir.
Uhh-sorry to interrupt folks--but Greg, you'd better set up the steam table ... it's gettin' late.
OK, I..
JEEZUS!! He knows what he's doin'--he doesn't need you ordering him around!
I wasn't ordering anyone around! I was just--

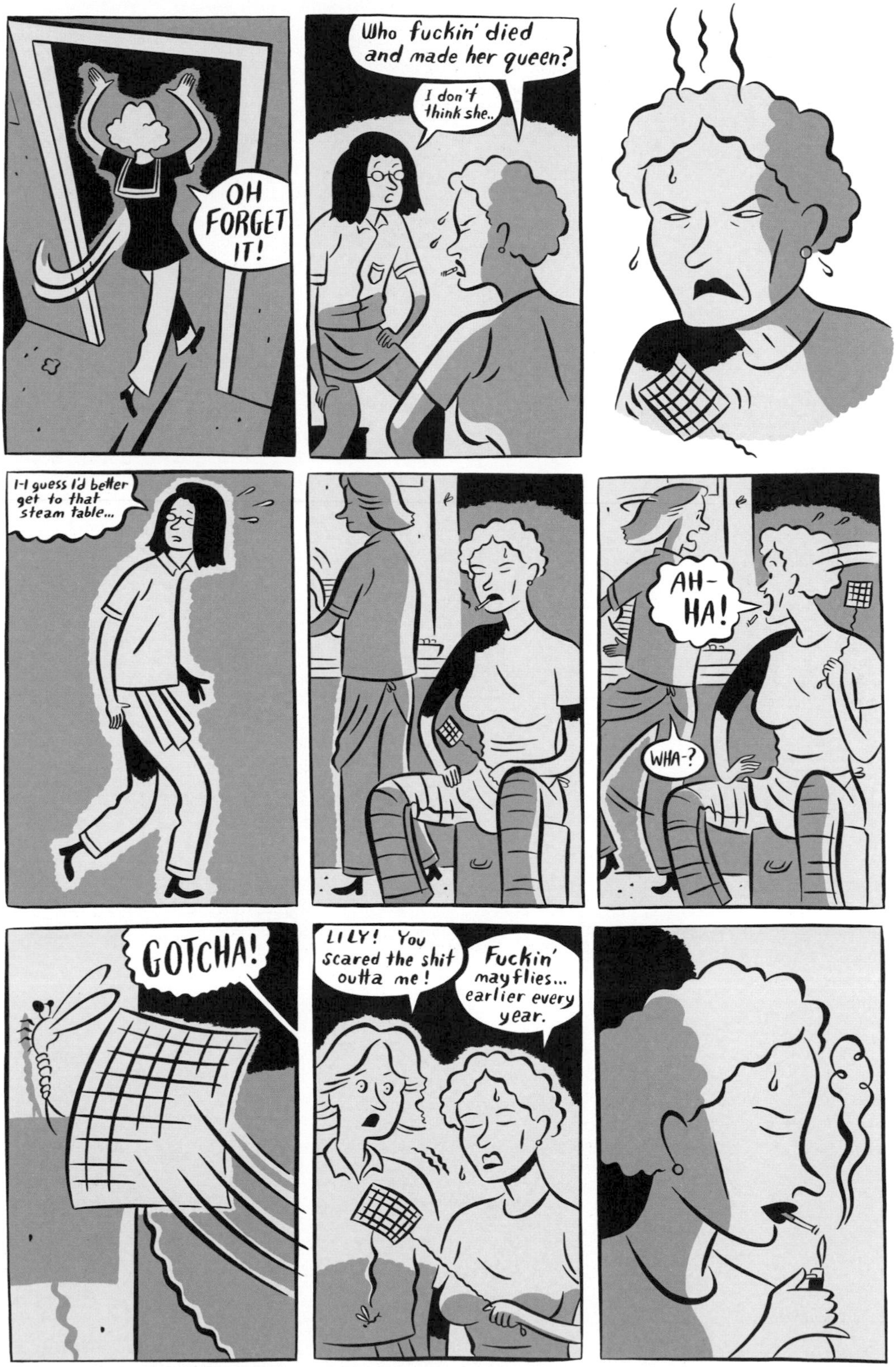
OH FORGET IT!
Who fuckin' died and made her queen?
I don't think she..
I-I guess I'd better get to that steam table...
AH-HA!
WHA-?
GOTCHA!
LILY! You scared the shit outta me!
Fuckin' mayflies... earlier every year.

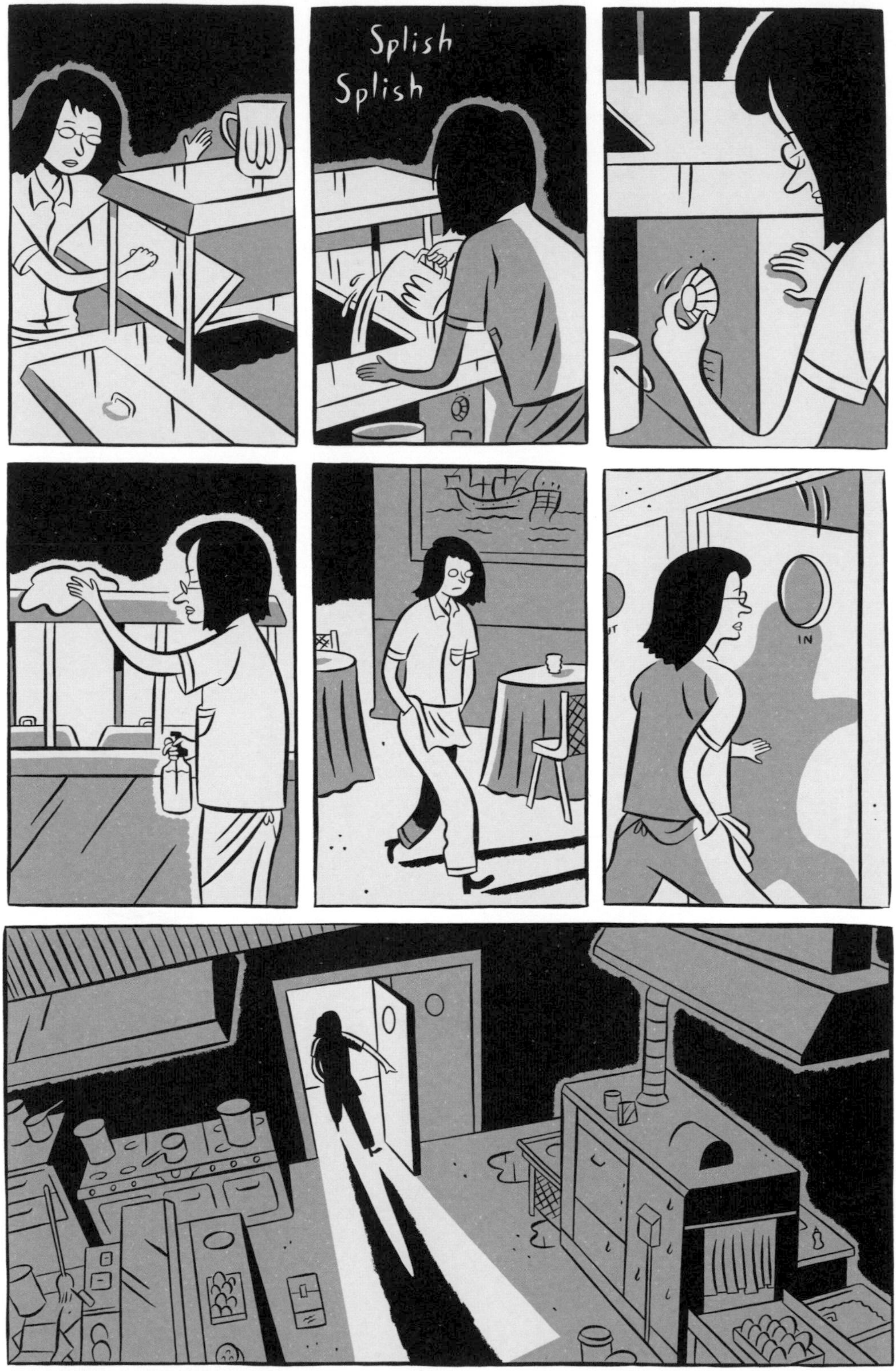
Splish
Splish
IN

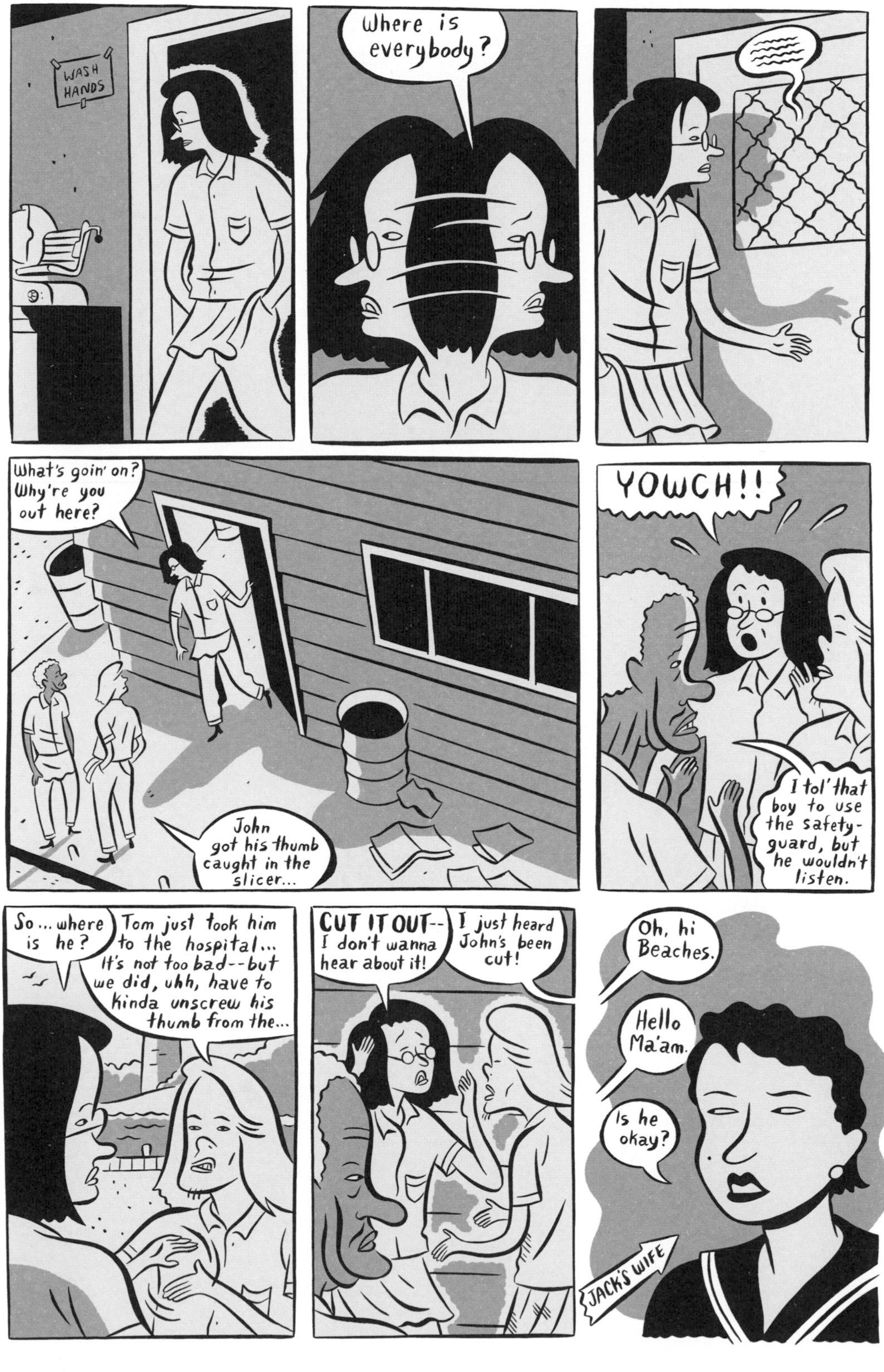
WASH HANDS
Where is everybody?
What's goin' on? Why're you out here?
John got his thumb caught in the slicer...
YOWCH!!
I tol' that boy to use the safety-guard, but he wouldn't listen.
So... where is he?
Tom just took him to the hospital... It's not too bad--but we did, uhh, have to kinda unscrew his thumb from the...
CUT IT OUT-- I don't wanna hear about it!
I just heard John's been cut!
Oh, hi Beaches.
Hello Ma'am.
Is he okay?
JACK'S WIFE

It's nothin' Ma'am. Yeah, he's okay. Prob'ly just a coupla stitches.

How you doin' little Jack? You gonna be a racer like yer daddy?

You figure Mr. Baker's gonna win again Ma'am?

Oh sure -- I s'pose.

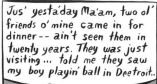

Jus' yesta'day Ma'am, two ol' friends o' mine came in for dinner -- ain't seen them in twenty years. They was just visiting ... told me they saw my boy playin' ball in Deetroit..

This ain't getting me nowhere... I'm headin' back in.

Yeah? Catch ya later.

So - ha hah -- how're those melons growing?

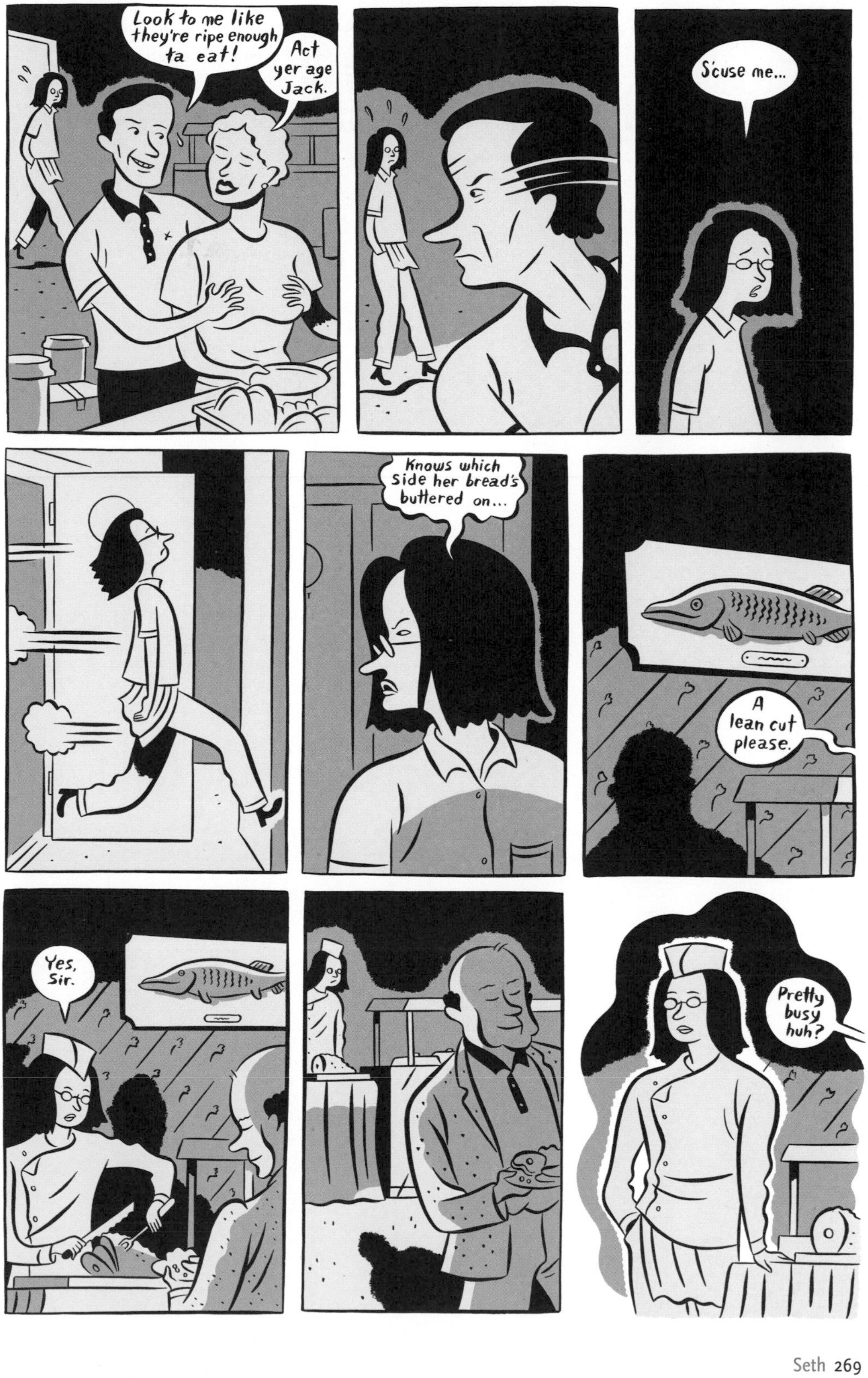
Look to me like they're ripe enough ta eat!
Act yer age Jack.
S'cuse me...
Knows which side her bread's buttered on...
A lean cut please.
Yes, Sir.
Pretty busy huh?

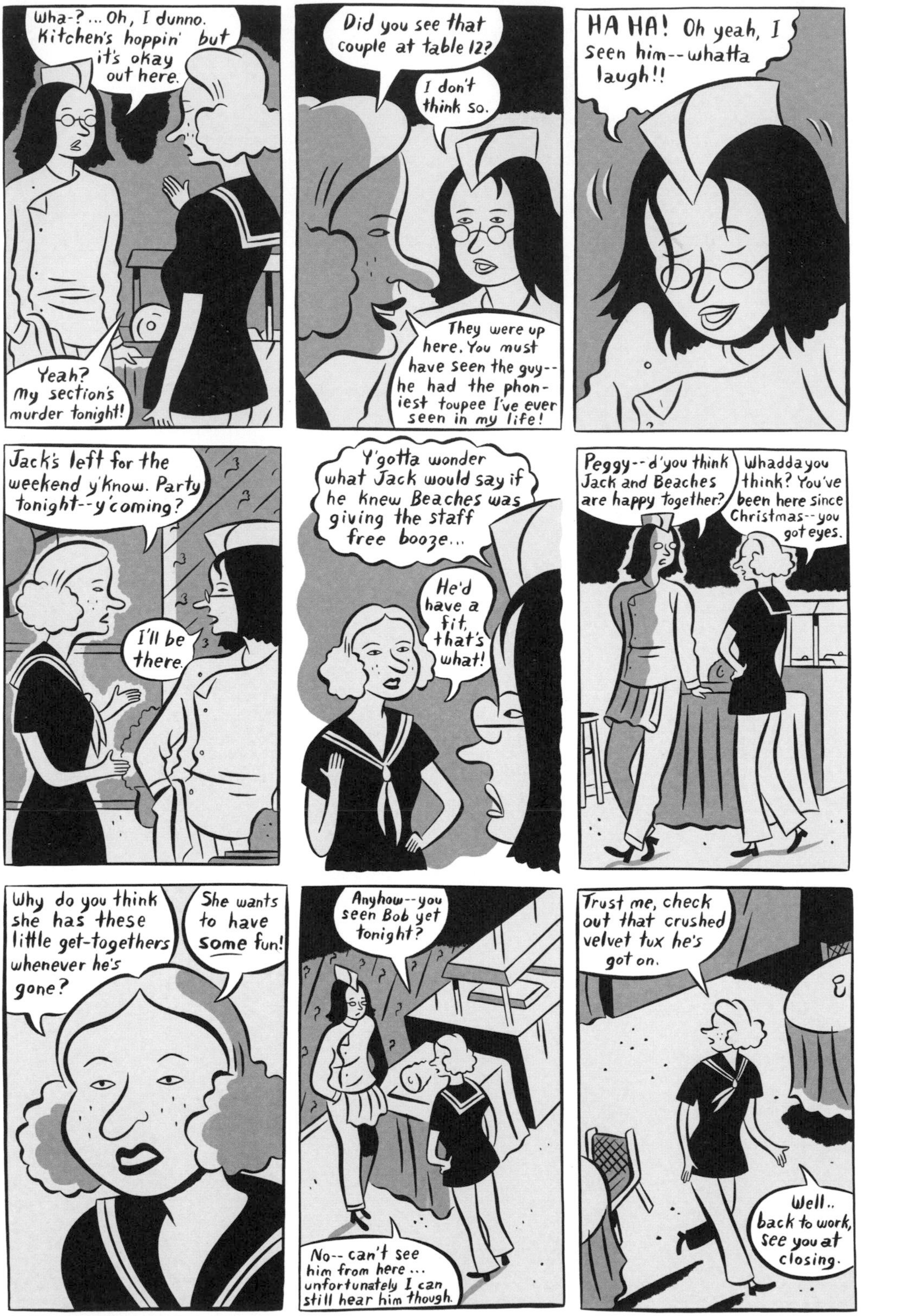

Wha-? ... Oh, I dunno. Kitchen's hoppin' but it's okay out here.
Yeah? My section's murder tonight!
Did you see that couple at table 12?
I don't think so.
They were up here. You must have seen the guy-- he had the phoniest toupee I've ever seen in my life!
HA HA! Oh yeah, I seen him--whatta laugh!!
Jack's left for the weekend y'know. Party tonight--y'coming?
I'll be there.
Y'gotta wonder what Jack would say if he knew Beaches was giving the staff free booze...
He'd have a fit, that's what!
Peggy--d'you think Jack and Beaches are happy together?
Whadda you think? You've been here since Christmas--you got eyes.
Why do you think she has these little get-togethers whenever he's gone?
She wants to have some fun!
Anyhow--you seen Bob yet tonight?
No--can't see him from here ... unfortunately I can still hear him though.
Trust me, check out that crushed velvet tux he's got on.
Well.. back to work, see you at closing.

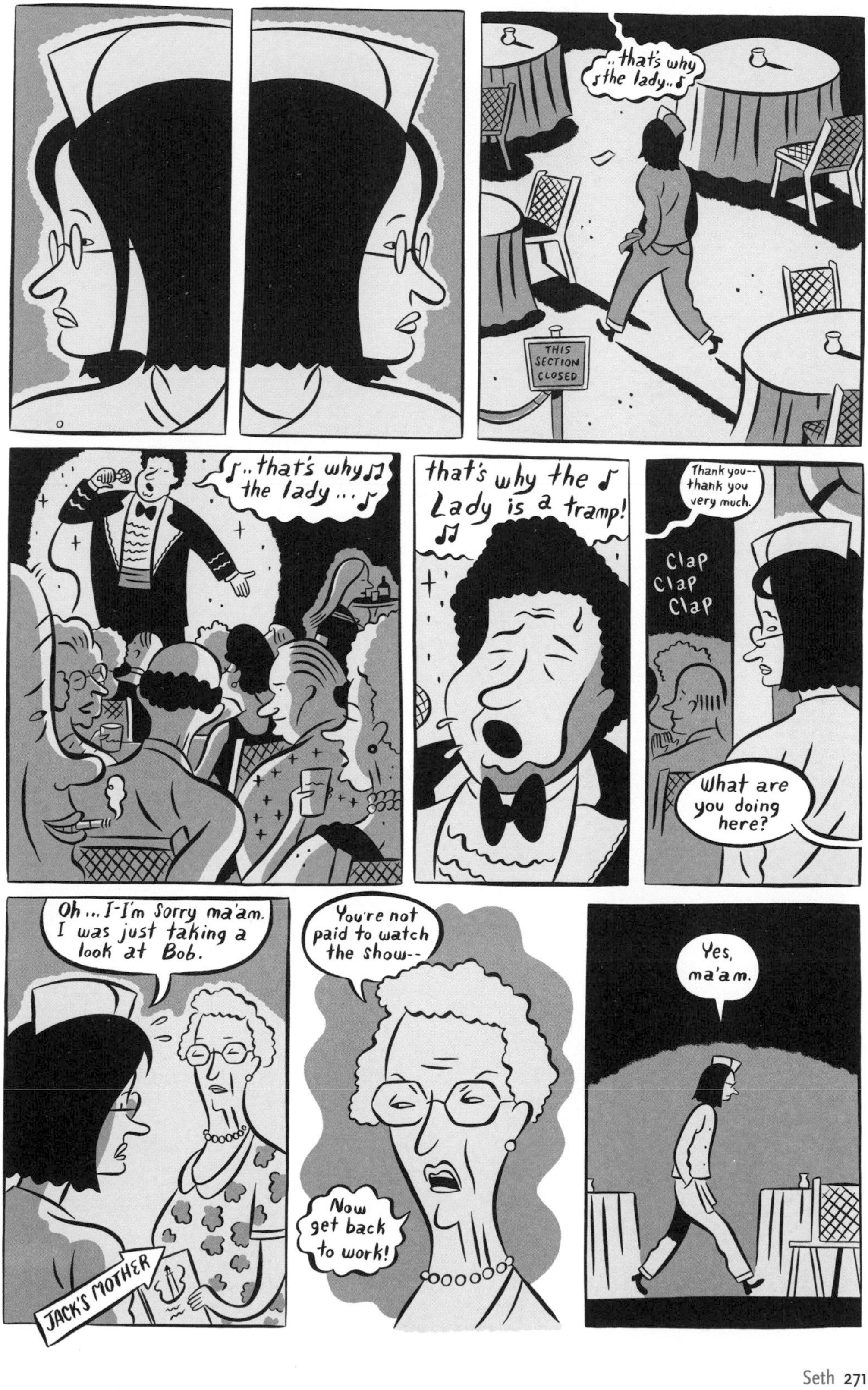
..that's why the lady..
THIS SECTION CLOSED
..that's why the lady...
that's why the Lady is a tramp!
Thank you-- thank you very much.
Clap Clap Clap
What are you doing here?
Oh... I-I'm sorry ma'am. I was just taking a look at Bob.
JACK'S MOTHER
You're not paid to watch the show--
Now get back to work!
Yes, ma'am.

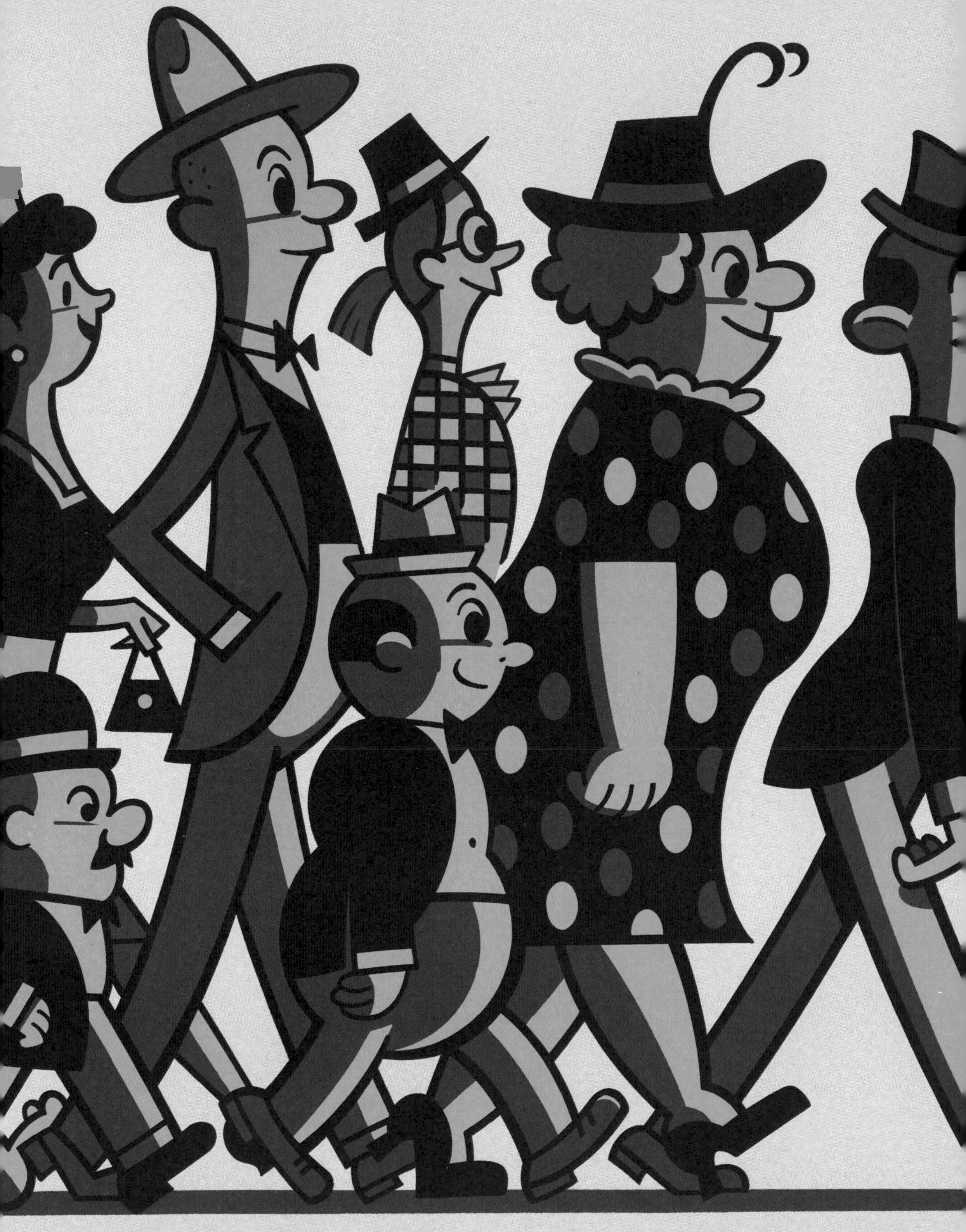

I think one of the key moments that marks when I became an adult was the day—in my early twenties—that I walked into the Silver Snail comic shop and traded my battered copies of *X-Men* for a hardcover set of *Little Lulu* comics by John Stanley. It's not like I was still a fan of those *X-Men* comics, but they were something of a symbol for my childhood (or teenhood, I suppose) and the *Lulu* comics represented where I was going as a "grown-up" artist.

I had only recently read, for the first time, the *Little Lulu* stories reprinted in *A Smithsonian Book of Comic-Book Comics* and had fallen head over heels in love with them. I enthused about them endlessly to my new friend Chester Brown. I scoured the city for any *Lulu* comics I could find. I had the zeal of a convert. Over the next few years I came to know Stanley's other comics work and eventually found my favourite—*Thirteen Going on Eighteen*. Again, I read and reread. I studied. I learned. When one day Tom Devlin finally called me and told me about his ambitious plan to create the John Stanley Library and have me design it, I couldn't have been more pleased.

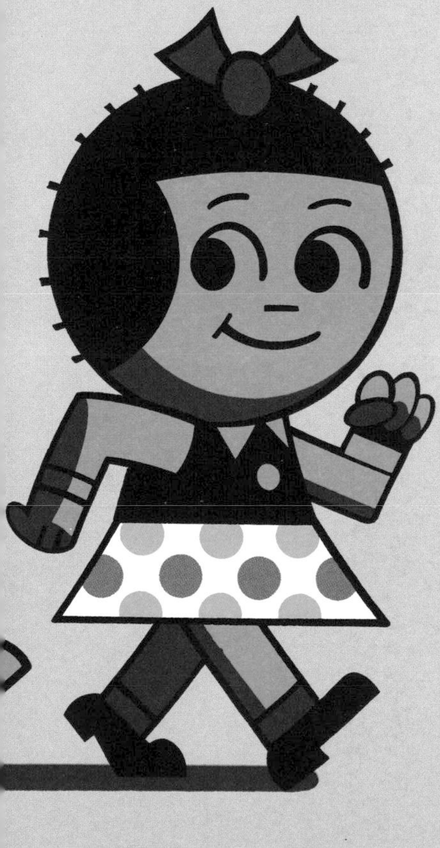

Though, later, I wasn't all that pleased when they rejected my initial plans for how I wanted the series to look. In fact, I got quite snippy about it. Emails were hastily sent. Pride was swallowed. New designs were offered...and kindly accepted. I sometimes wonder if Chris, Peggy, and Tom really did like the eventual design or if they just decided not to reject me twice (and bruise my fragile ego again)!

Personally, I thought the final design for the John Stanley Library was *somewhat* clever. I tried to make the books resemble those old children's library series that I recalled seeing when I was a child—books published in the 1940s and '50s (and still lingering around for my childhood in the '60s). Nicely institutional books with their fancy bindings, yet also brightly coloured and pleasingly big to hold in a child's hands. I even made a medal-style seal to go on the back that I hoped would bring forth associations with those classic libraries. In the end, now, I wonder if the books were too "classy" for today's children's market. Maybe I should have gone more "pop culture." Maybe pandered a bit more to the perceived tastes of today. I don't know. I'm the last person to guess what today's child is attracted by.

I will say this: as with the *Complete Peanuts* series (which I also design), I'm very proud to have been associated somehow with Mr. Stanley's work. I'm gratified we got so much Stanley into print again. My only regret is that the *Thirteen* series stalled. If there were a fire in my house, while rushing out the window, I'd grab those *Thirteen* comic books right after my wife and the cats.

Unlike Charles Schulz, Stanley wasn't a childhood influence. As I said above, he came later. And yet, his influence on me has been quite profound. People probably wouldn't recognize it much in my work, though. So, let me point out a spot where I stole right from him. In the first chapter of *Clyde Fans* I recall trying to figure out how to have my main character's inner dialogue represented in the comic. Thought balloons seemed very awkward to me then, and narration boxes just felt too distant. Only when I remembered how much Tubby and Lulu spoke aloud to themselves (when they were alone) in Stanley's comics did it occur to me to simply have Abe Matchcard talk to himself for eighty pages. If it was good enough for Tubby, it was good enough for me.

—Seth, John Stanley Library series designer

(Left) Artwork created by Seth for *Nancy* vol. 2 (2009).

I JUST HOPED FOR THE BEST: THE DEEPLY HUMAN LEGACY OF JOHN STANLEY

an appreciation by Frank M. Young

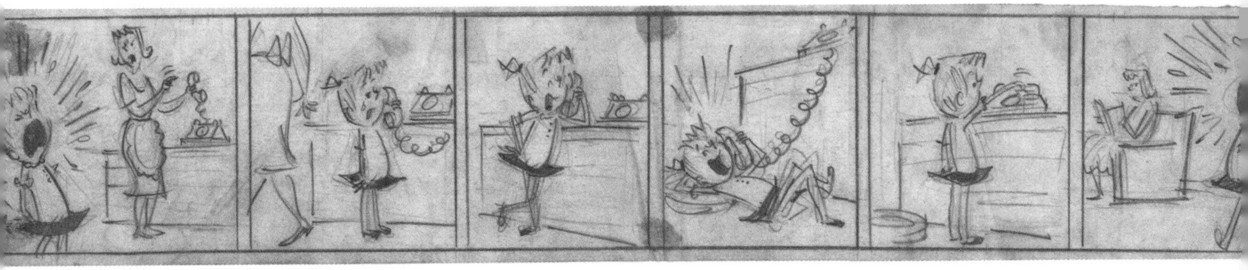

Pencil sketches for a proposed Brigitte newspaper strip that may have never left John Stanley's archive (late 1960s). Provided by James Stanley.

Had John Stanley written prose fiction, he would be known to a much larger audience. At his best, Stanley merits comparison to celebrated American authors Philip Roth, Saul Bellow, Bruce Jay Friedman, and Joseph Heller. His writing is blunt yet adroit. Every word counts; each thought has clarity and concision. Wordplay, alliteration, and the occasional dreadful pun are the fabric of his style. In its heyday, John Stanley's work was widely read and enjoyed by all ages and appeared in some of America's bestselling magazines. But Stanley's medium was comics—unfortunate for his legacy. Even worse, those comics belonged to the subcategory of children's comics. Two strikes against him in mainstream American culture. Thus, many people who might be amused, moved, or otherwise affected by the human comedy of John Stanley have never—and, likely, will never—read his work.

Doomed to transience by its publication in poorly printed ten-cent comic magazines, Stanley's was a work-for-hire career. He began in comics in 1943, at age twenty-nine, and continued until 1970. At his career peak, he was the sole writer and mastermind of one of America's most popular monthly comics, *Marge's Little Lulu*. Read and enjoyed by children and savvy adults, *Lulu* was cited, in 1954, as "...one of the 25 largest selling magazines on newsstands."[I]

Why was this great twentieth-century writer left so far behind? Corporate anonymity may be to blame. With the exception of *Peterkin Pottle* and *Jigg and Mooch*, two short-lived late-1940s series, a large part of John Stanley's career was based on licensed properties: newspaper comic strips, animated cartoons, and magazine gag panels. He was given credit once, in a 1952 issue of *Little Lulu*. That credit did not even acknowledge him as the series' writer.

Stanley was not a methodical writer. His scripts, drawn in loose, striking cartoons on typing paper, were improvised. In a 1976 interview, Stanley revealed his work process:

> I made no synopsis. I started from the very first panel on the page without the faintest notion of how it would turn out. And I just hoped for the best, that's all...I never gave too much thought to anything in stories. I just wrote the stories. That's it.[II]

The grind of monthly deadlines, the use of licensed properties, and the sheer volume of Stanley's work—at least 7,300 pages of *Little Lulu* and *Tubby* material—would seem a recipe for hackwork. *Lulu*, like George Herriman's celebrated *Krazy Kat*, became a series of bulletproof variations on a theme. *Little Lulu*, at its best, expresses the frustrations, malfunctions, digressions, and the utter human-ness of life in our culture. Even at its darkest, the impulse to keep

---

I Testimony of Helen C. Meyer and Matthew Murphy, United States Senate Subcommittee to Investigate Juvenile Delinquency, Juvenile Delinquency (Comic Books), 83rd Cong., 2nd session, New York, NY, June 4, 1954 (www.thecomicbooks.com/meyermurphy.html).

II "Interview: Carl Barks and John Stanley," the Comics Journal *no. 250 (February 2003): 159.*

 (Right) This strip appeared on the last page of *Melvin Monster* no. 9, the very last issue in the series (1967).

going—to survive humiliations and to redress failures—vibrates from Stanley's panels and pages.

Consequences and aftermaths drive Stanley's comics. His characters make colossally good—or colossally bad—decisions. Each move raises the narrative stakes. Their schemes snowball, invert, mutate, and sometimes, against all odds, succeed. They are forever riders on a wheel of comedic karma. We can relate to his characters' byzantine flaws and virtues. This keen sense of dark and light—of tangible, viable triumph and failure—signifies Stanley's work much more strongly than a byline.

Stanley's work has a strong undertow of despair, vulnerability, and gloom. His protagonists are often losers or eccentrics who work from the wrong end of the telescope. They pursue a myopic, selfish agenda—one that impacts their community and world. Tubby Tompkins, from *Lulu*, is the quintessential John Stanley character. His mulish determination, blended with rose-coloured high self-regard, gives him licence to fearlessly step into scenarios of personal humiliation, anti-social behavior, and belittlement. Tubby's (usually flawed) assumption that he's unerringly right, despite overwhelming evidence to the contrary, makes his occasional victories bittersweet but meaningful. Tubby's self-titled comic, started in 1952, gave John Stanley a welcome outlet to further elaborate on this rich character. At first a series of book-length dramedies—several illustrated by Stanley—the title offers a POV of the *Lulu* world, sans Lulu. Stanley seemed to have enjoyed writing (and cartooning) from this stubborn, sweetly blemished male perspective.

All of this was achieved in regular installments, with deadlines and publishing schedules to meet. The success of *Marge's Little Lulu* depended on John Stanley—and he delivered the goods.

Stanley and *Little Lulu* parted ways in 1959. Still in kid-mode, the writer stepped sideways to inhabit the world of Ernie Bushmiller's iconic *Nancy and Sluggo*. The *Nancy* stories gave Stanley some breathing room from the rules and regulations of *Lulu*. As with *Lulu*, he created several new characters—the eerie, inexplicable Oona Goosepimple and her unearthly kin, and Bunion "Bunny" McOnion, hulking bipolar neighbor of Sluggo. The often-tense showdowns between Sluggo and McOnion, and Nancy's mind-fudge misadventures inside Oona's nightmarish house, showed a new side to Stanley's wit and sensibilities. At its best, Stanley's *Nancy* is a bracing, unpredictable slice of space-age sitcomics, its hard-edged humour unlike anything seen in Lulu and Tubby's world.

In 1961 and 1962, Stanley's career was reborn. Western Printing and Lithographing Co., the packager and editorial for Dell's comics line, parted ways with the publisher to form Gold Key Comics. Stanley did not tag along. He was accorded carte blanche by panic-stricken Dell, now shorn of all its long-standing series.

Just before this break, Stanley had created a bundle of fresh original titles: horror comics (*Tales from the Tomb* and *Ghost Stories*), soap operas (*Linda Lark, Student Nurse*), and a trifecta of comedic series that are his career apogee—*Around the Block with Dunc and Loo, Thirteen Going on Eighteen, Melvin Monster. Around The Block with Dunc and Loo*, in collaboration with cartoonist Bill Williams, debuted in late 1961. Williams and Stanley's other co-mix, the brilliant beatnik comedy *Kookie*, expired after two issues. Both series recall Max Shulman's hit TV show *Dobie Gillis* with their quick wit, big characters, and broad situations. They teem with urban atmosphere and achieve a striking democratic comedy.

At this same time, *Thirteen Going on Eighteen* quietly began. At first dully drawn by staff artist Tony Tallarico, *Thirteen*, from its third issue, restored John Stanley's cartooning to mass circulation. For its next twenty-two issues, Stanley the writer-cartoonist fearlessly explored the human comedy and revelled in the flaws and joys of a credible cast of cruel, inept, and indelicate characters. *Thirteen* is the anti-*Archie*. It lays bare the fears, desires, and shortcomings of puberty in space-age America. The reader cringes at the missteps of its twin protagonists, Val and Judy. Val's raw, reckless, and highly emotional journey through life, paved with stumbling blocks, is a strong ancestor of the misery-comedy of Larry David and Ricky Gervais. *Thirteen* is almost entirely about the teenage experience. We never see Val's parents. Other adult figures are fleeting, harmless stock types. Stanley is an omniscient observer, but we never feel he disdains Val, Judy, or the series' other regulars. This tacit compassion, filtered through hard-edged comedy, is unique to American comics.

Tucked in the back pages of *Thirteen* is the existential battleground of "Judy Junior." Imagine *Peanuts* directed by horror filmmaker Herschell Gordon Lewis and you've got the basic idea. Its bleak theatre of cruelty, in which vulnerable, sensitive Jimmy Fuzzi is tormented, outwitted, and second-guessed by Judy's (apparent) younger sister, makes the sufferings of Val seem like comic relief.

Thirteen's quarterly publishing schedule allowed Stanley to get back up to speed on the company dime. Aside from the loose cover illustrations for the monthly *Little Lulu*, Stanley had abandoned print cartooning after 1956. This showed, painfully, in *Thirteen*'s first few issues. That said, his scripts were highly regarded by his peers. Said longtime *Lulu* artist Irving Tripp: "…you could almost reproduce Stanley's [scripts as is], they were so well done."[III] By 1963, his simple, evocative brush lines, sparse but effective backgrounds, and expressive human figures had a lived-in, rumpled, and convincing feel. Every brush stroke counts, in accord with Stanley's plots and dialogue. Though couched in situation comedy, *Thirteen Going on Eighteen* gets to the heart of the American adolescent experience. In prose form, these stories might have eclipsed Judy Blume's in popularity. As the title lasted twenty-seven issues, it must have sold consistently well. Its low berth on the cultural food chain guaranteed a marginal status.

In 1965, Stanley began another original series. *Melvin Monster* was *au courant* with the trend of the macabre TV hits *The Addams Family* and *The Munsters*. Those programs lacked the slightest trace of the gravitas that looms over Stanley's series. *Melvin* is the darkest of Stanley's worlds, trumping the Roald Dahl–flavoured *Peterkin Pottle*, a 1949 series about an ostracized daydreamer lost in violent genre fantasies. Melvin is a sensitive, gentle soul in a dark, misshapen world. Cruelty, violence, and death are common currency in the town of Monsterville. Melvin's loud, brutal "Baddy" and passive "Mummy" are nightmare inversions of our expectations of parents. Melvin's life is in constant danger—from the assaults of the family pet, the ravenous alligator Cleopatra, to those of Mrs. McGargoyle, homicidal head of the "little black schoolhouse" he struggles to attend. Melvin's darkness may have proved too much for its demographic. After nine issues, it was dropped, and its intriguing, still-developing world ended.

Stanley's final page for the series—reproduced herein—is a heartbreaking meditation on self-image and belonging. It was the last of Stanley's hundreds of pantomime one-page strips, and an appropriately wistful note for the second-act curtain of his comics career.

Stanley made a brief return to comics in 1969—this time for Western Printing's Gold Key line. His final comics creation, *O. G. Whiz*, loaded with familiar Stanley characters, themes, and witty verbal comedy à la underground comix legend Gilbert Shelton, appeared in 1970.

III Bruce Hamilton, "A Tripp Down Memory Lane," published in set VI of The Little Lulu Library, *Another Rainbow Publications*, 1984.

At age fifty-seven, John Stanley shifted careers. Stanley worked for Fairgate Rule, a small company in Cold Spring, New York, that manufactured high-end rulers, into the 1980s. The hands-on craftsman work seemed to be a balm for the ex-cartoonist.

If Stanley was bitter, he never let it show at work. Fellow Fairgate employee Tim Lahey remembers him as a smart, dry-humoured man who took refuge in the exacting craft of screen printing. Stanley drove a VW Bug, read Tom Wolfe and the *New York Times*, was interested in current affairs, and spoke affectionately of his wife and children. Stanley spoke of comics as "a young man's game" and chose to focus on the daily tasks at hand.

Lahey remembers one of Stanley's on-the-job bons mots. Faced with the task of moving large pallets of aluminum sheets—a dreary chore by anyone's standards—Stanley quipped, "With any luck I will be dead before we have to do this again."[IV]

Lahey's memories of Stanley as co-worker and mentor are positive. His summation of Stanley: "In spite of any faults he may have had, he was almost a hero to me, an example who proved that I didn't have to grow up to be a stodgy adult."[V] This message can be had in Stanley's comics, in their brightest moments. It might be more interesting to be an adult Tubby, after all.

Stanley continued to read comics but shunned their fandom. After one appearance at the 1976 Newcon in Boston, Stanley retreated into his private and work life. By the time he was coaxed out again by persistent fans in the late 1980s, it was too late to claim any of the turf won by Carl Barks, by then comics' official loveable elder statesman.

John Stanley died in 1993, his work out of mass circulation and remembered by a handful of devoted collectors. As one of the great American authors of the twentieth century, Stanley's return to print, over the last decade, is welcome and significant. His deep understanding of the tangled, illogical, needy things we human beings are remains vital, droll, and poignant.

Frank M. Young is a writer and editor who has contributed to newspapers and magazines across the country. He is the co-creator of the Eisner Award–winning The Carter Family: Don't Forget This Song *with cartoonist David Lasky and a former editor of the* Comics Journal. *He maintains stanleystories.blogspot.com, an in-depth analytical look at the entire comics work of John Stanley.*

IV *Author's correspondence with Tim Lahey, January 8, 2014.*
V *Ibid.*

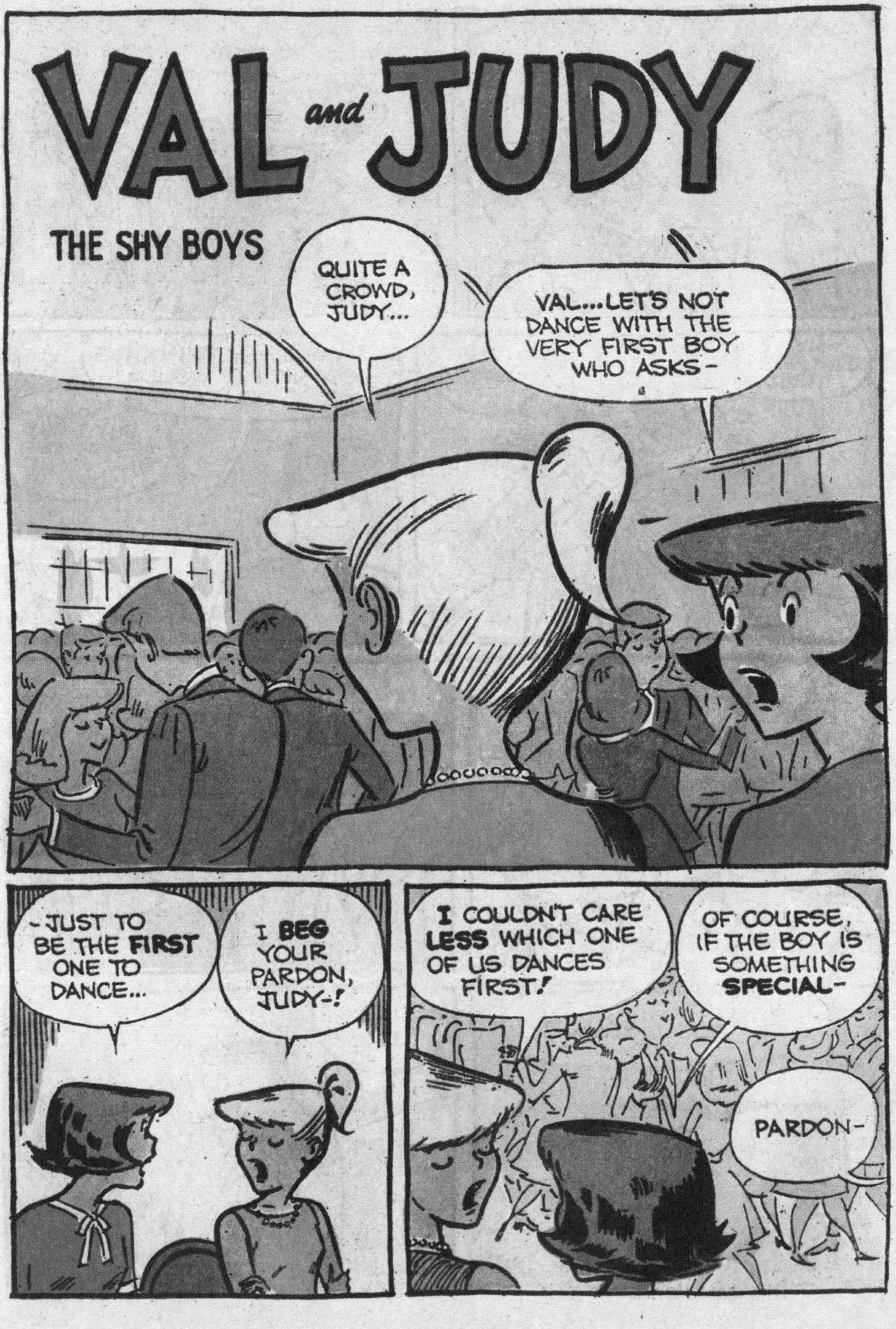
VAL and JUDY
THE SHY BOYS
QUITE A CROWD, JUDY...
VAL...LET'S NOT DANCE WITH THE VERY FIRST BOY WHO ASKS-
-JUST TO BE THE FIRST ONE TO DANCE...
I BEG YOUR PARDON, JUDY-!
I COULDN'T CARE LESS WHICH ONE OF US DANCES FIRST!
OF COURSE, IF THE BOY IS SOMETHING SPECIAL-
PARDON-

278 Val and Judy in "The Shy Boys" is from *Thirteen Going on Eighteen* no. 18 (1965).

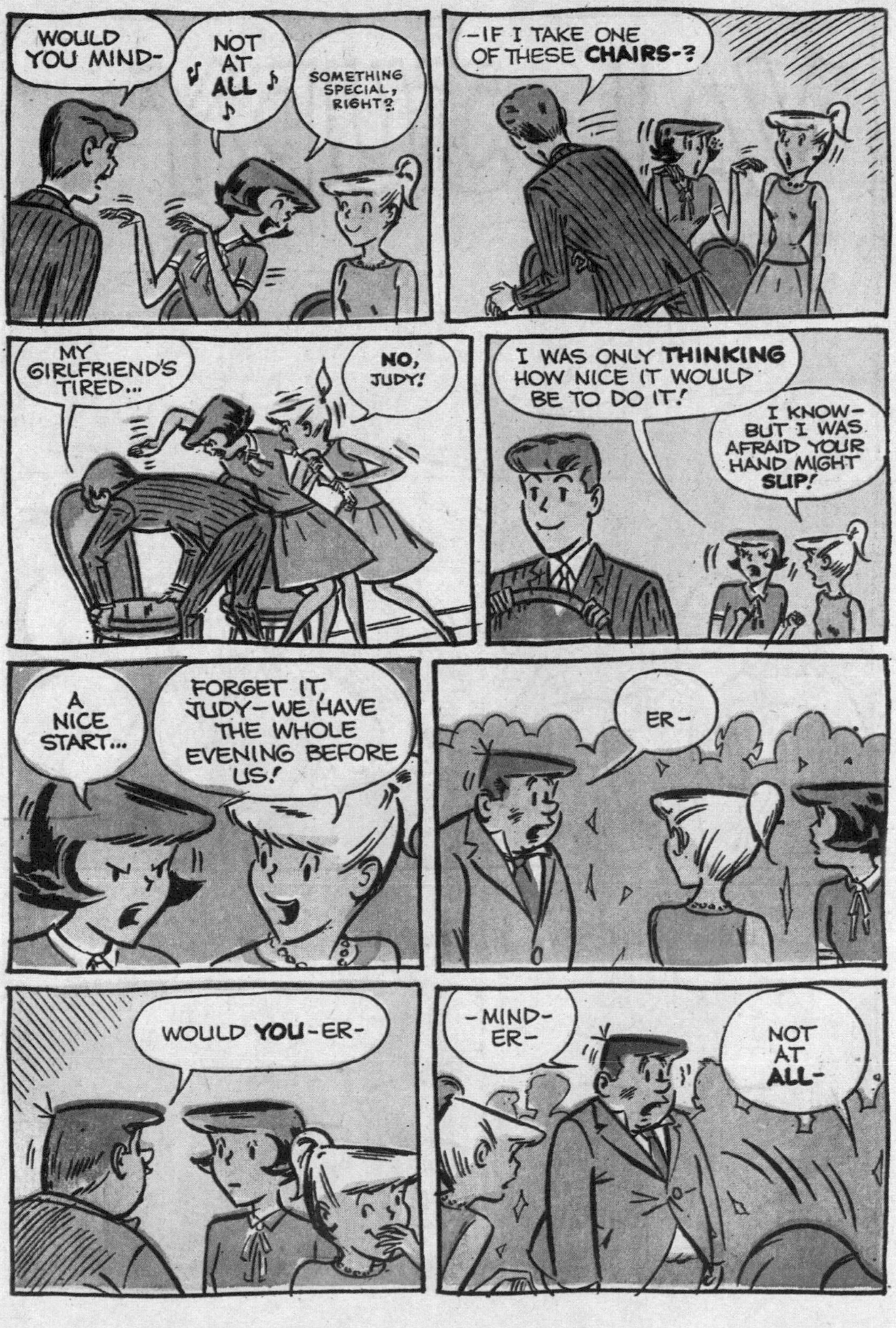
WOULD YOU MIND-
NOT AT ALL
SOMETHING SPECIAL, RIGHT?
-IF I TAKE ONE OF THESE CHAIRS-?
MY GIRLFRIEND'S TIRED...
NO, JUDY!
I WAS ONLY THINKING HOW NICE IT WOULD BE TO DO IT!
I KNOW- BUT I WAS AFRAID YOUR HAND MIGHT SLIP!
A NICE START...
FORGET IT, JUDY-WE HAVE THE WHOLE EVENING BEFORE US!
ER-
WOULD YOU-ER-
-MIND- ER-
NOT AT ALL-

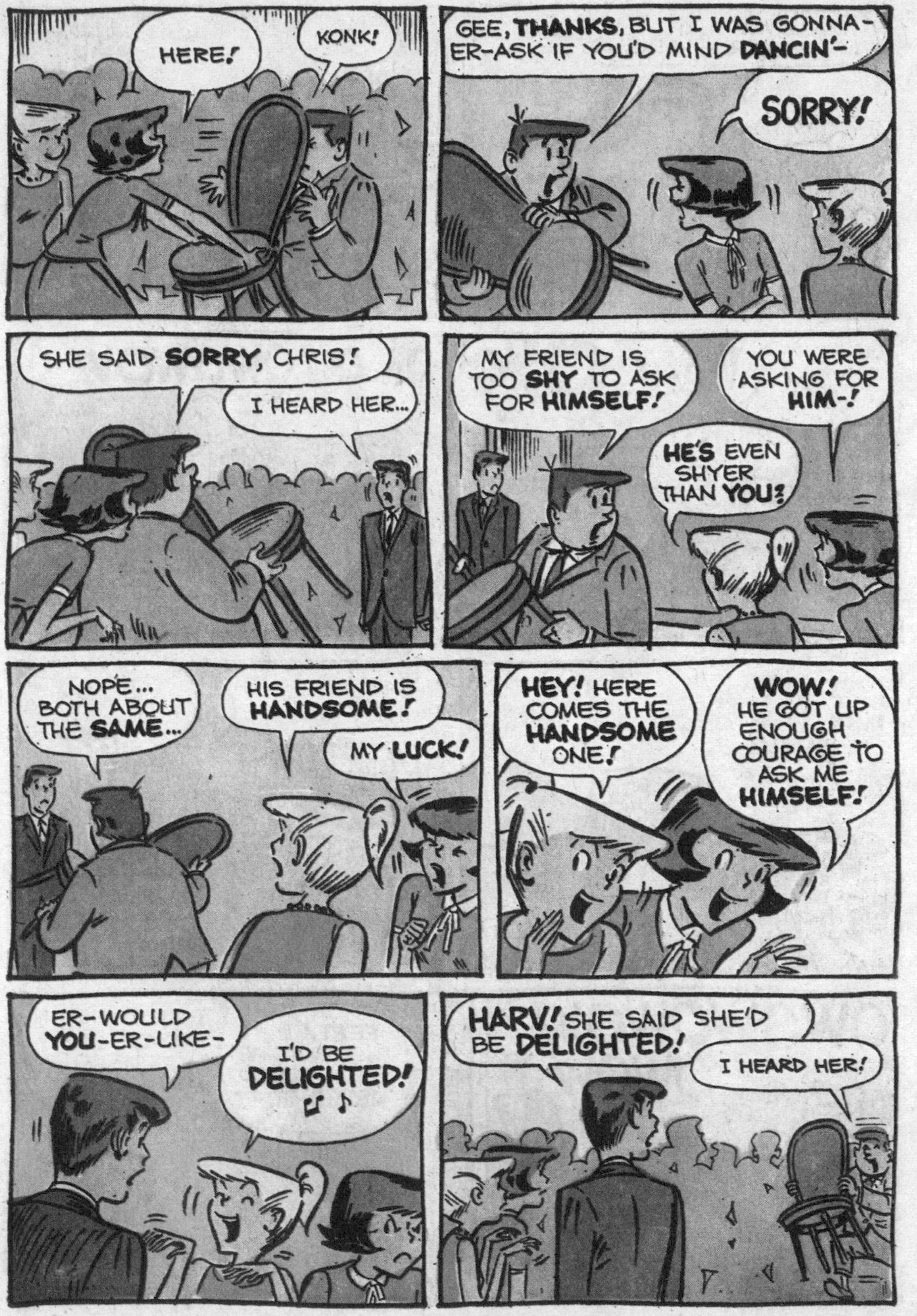
HERE!
KONK!
GEE, THANKS, BUT I WAS GONNA-ER-ASK IF YOU'D MIND DANCIN'-
SORRY!
SHE SAID SORRY, CHRIS!
I HEARD HER...
MY FRIEND IS TOO SHY TO ASK FOR HIMSELF!
YOU WERE ASKING FOR HIM-!
HE'S EVEN SHYER THAN YOU?
NOPE... BOTH ABOUT THE SAME...
HIS FRIEND IS HANDSOME!
MY LUCK!
HEY! HERE COMES THE HANDSOME ONE!
WOW! HE GOT UP ENOUGH COURAGE TO ASK ME HIMSELF!
ER-WOULD YOU-ER-LIKE-
I'D BE DELIGHTED!
HARV! SHE SAID SHE'D BE DELIGHTED!
I HEARD HER!

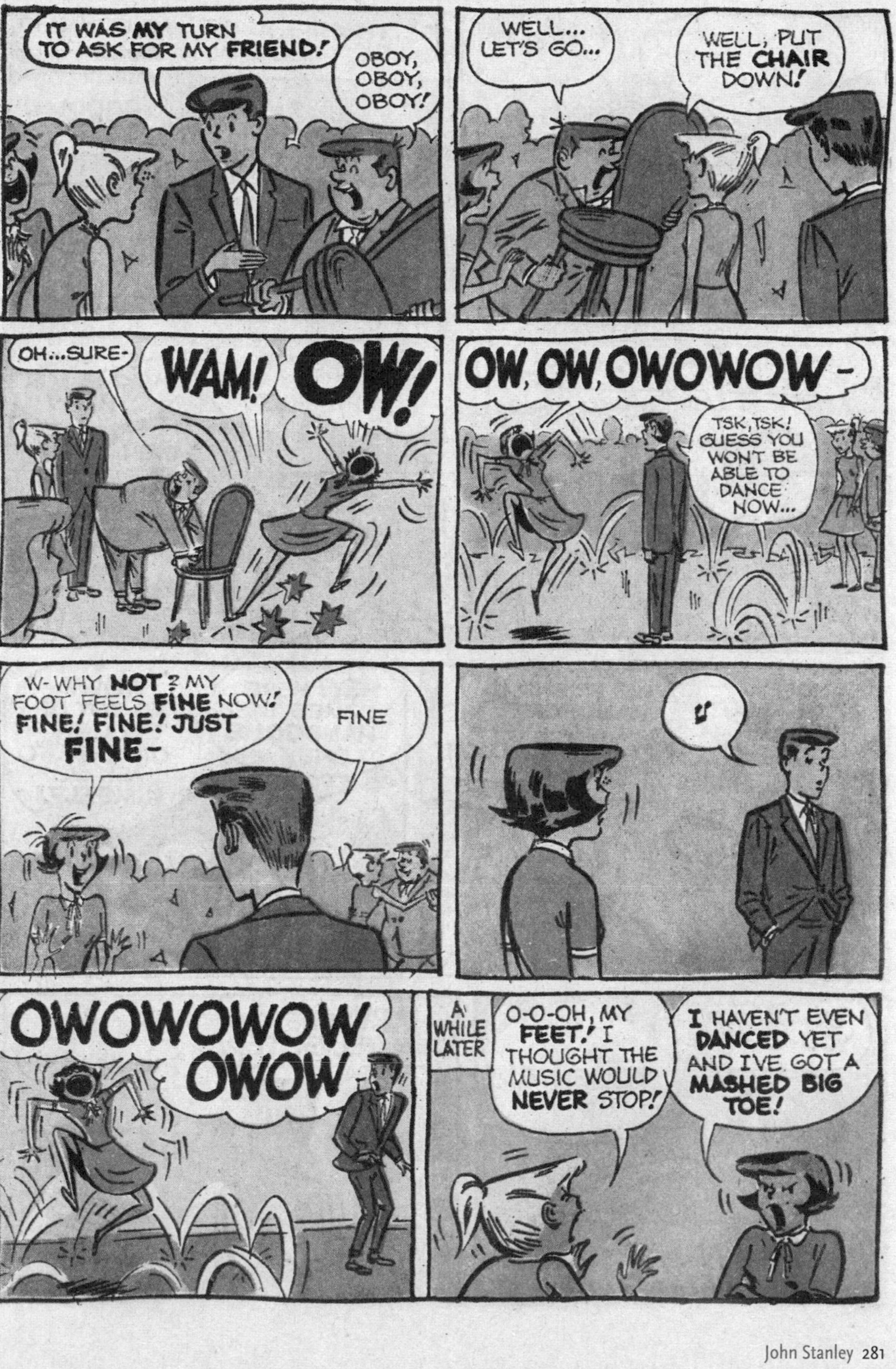
IT WAS MY TURN TO ASK FOR MY FRIEND!
OBOY, OBOY, OBOY!
WELL... LET'S GO...
WELL, PUT THE CHAIR DOWN!
OH...SURE-
WAM!
OW!
OW, OW, OWOWOW-
TSK, TSK! GUESS YOU WON'T BE ABLE TO DANCE NOW...
W-WHY NOT? MY FOOT FEELS FINE NOW! FINE! FINE! JUST FINE-
FINE
OWOWOWOW OWOW
A WHILE LATER
O-O-OH, MY FEET! I THOUGHT THE MUSIC WOULD NEVER STOP!
I HAVEN'T EVEN DANCED YET AND I'VE GOT A MASHED BIG TOE!

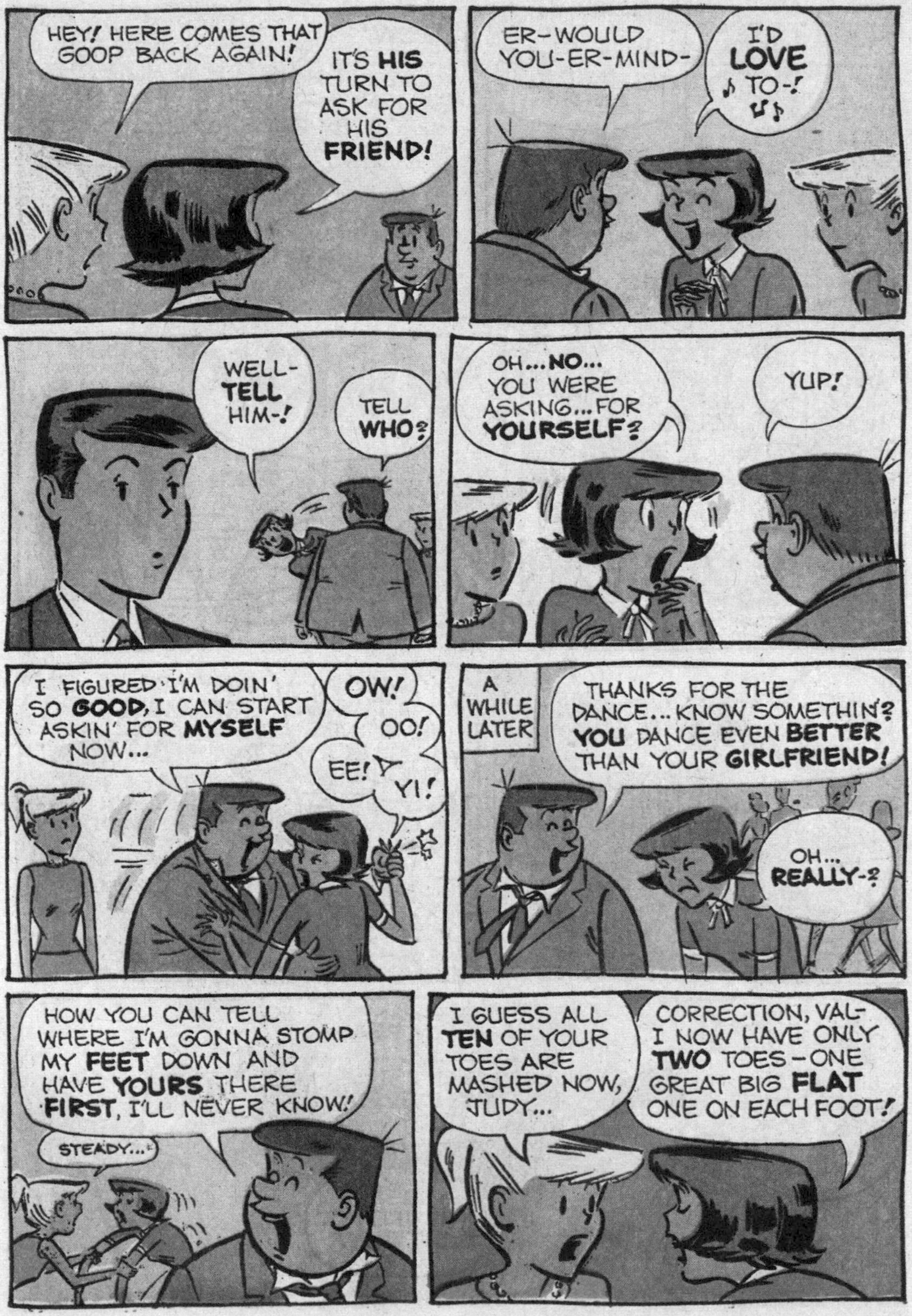
HEY! HERE COMES THAT GOOP BACK AGAIN!
IT'S HIS TURN TO ASK FOR HIS FRIEND!
ER-WOULD YOU-ER-MIND-
I'D LOVE TO-!
WELL- TELL HIM-!
TELL WHO?
OH... NO... YOU WERE ASKING... FOR YOURSELF?
YUP!
I FIGURED I'M DOIN' SO GOOD, I CAN START ASKIN' FOR MYSELF NOW...
OW!
OO!
EE!
YI!
A WHILE LATER
THANKS FOR THE DANCE... KNOW SOMETHIN'? YOU DANCE EVEN BETTER THAN YOUR GIRLFRIEND!
OH... REALLY-?
HOW YOU CAN TELL WHERE I'M GONNA STOMP MY FEET DOWN AND HAVE YOURS THERE FIRST, I'LL NEVER KNOW!
STEADY...!
I GUESS ALL TEN OF YOUR TOES ARE MASHED NOW, JUDY...
CORRECTION, VAL- I NOW HAVE ONLY TWO TOES-ONE GREAT BIG FLAT ONE ON EACH FOOT!

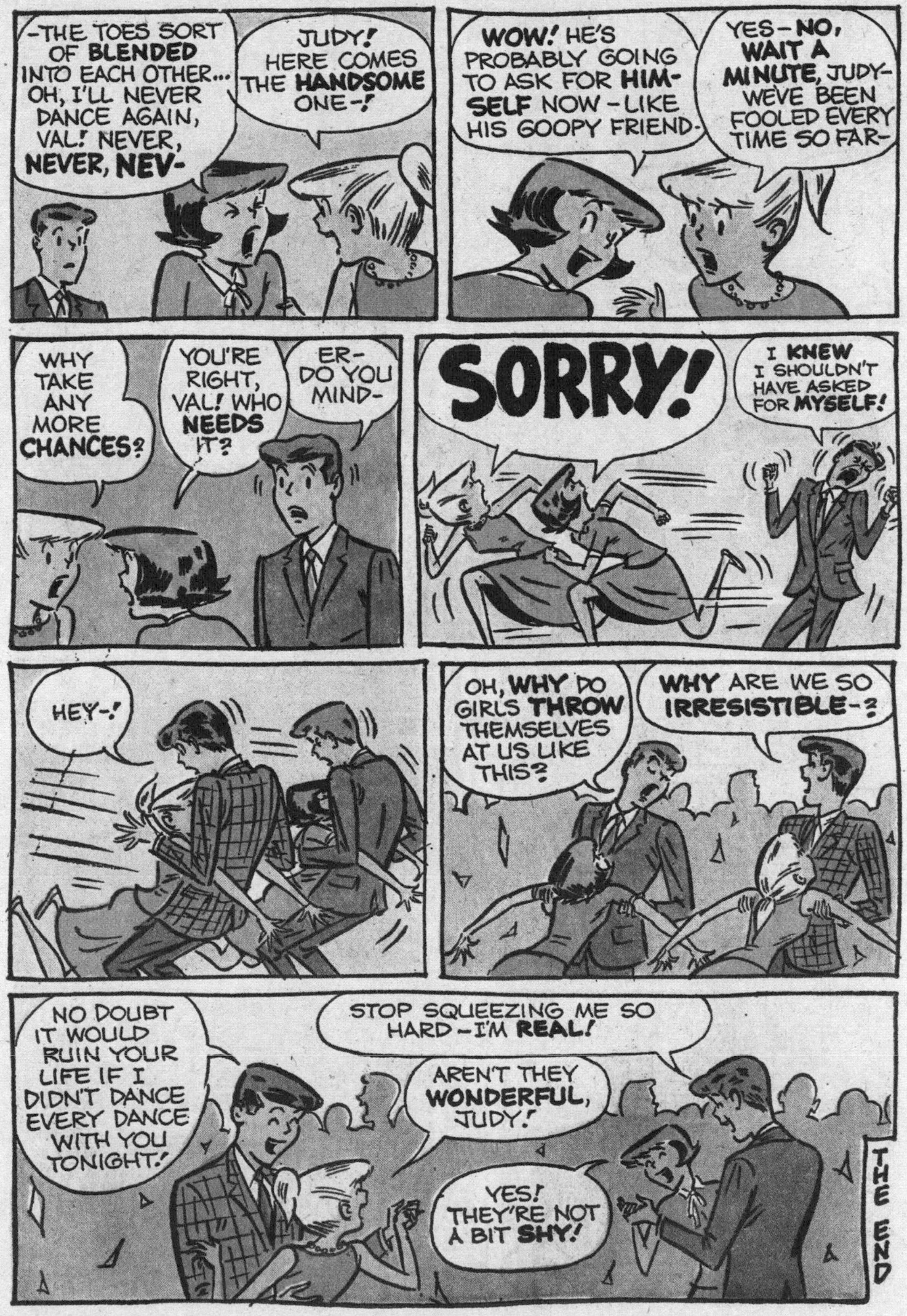
-THE TOES SORT OF BLENDED INTO EACH OTHER... OH, I'LL NEVER DANCE AGAIN, VAL! NEVER, NEVER, NEV-
JUDY! HERE COMES THE HANDSOME ONE-!
WOW! HE'S PROBABLY GOING TO ASK FOR HIM-SELF NOW-LIKE HIS GOOPY FRIEND-
YES-NO, WAIT A MINUTE, JUDY-WE'VE BEEN FOOLED EVERY TIME SO FAR-
WHY TAKE ANY MORE CHANCES?
YOU'RE RIGHT, VAL! WHO NEEDS IT?
ER-DO YOU MIND-
SORRY!
I KNEW I SHOULDN'T HAVE ASKED FOR MYSELF!
HEY-!
OH, WHY DO GIRLS THROW THEMSELVES AT US LIKE THIS?
WHY ARE WE SO IRRESISTIBLE-?
NO DOUBT IT WOULD RUIN YOUR LIFE IF I DIDN'T DANCE EVERY DANCE WITH YOU TONIGHT!
STOP SQUEEZING ME SO HARD-I'M REAL!
AREN'T THEY WONDERFUL, JUDY!
YES! THEY'RE NOT A BIT SHY!
THE END

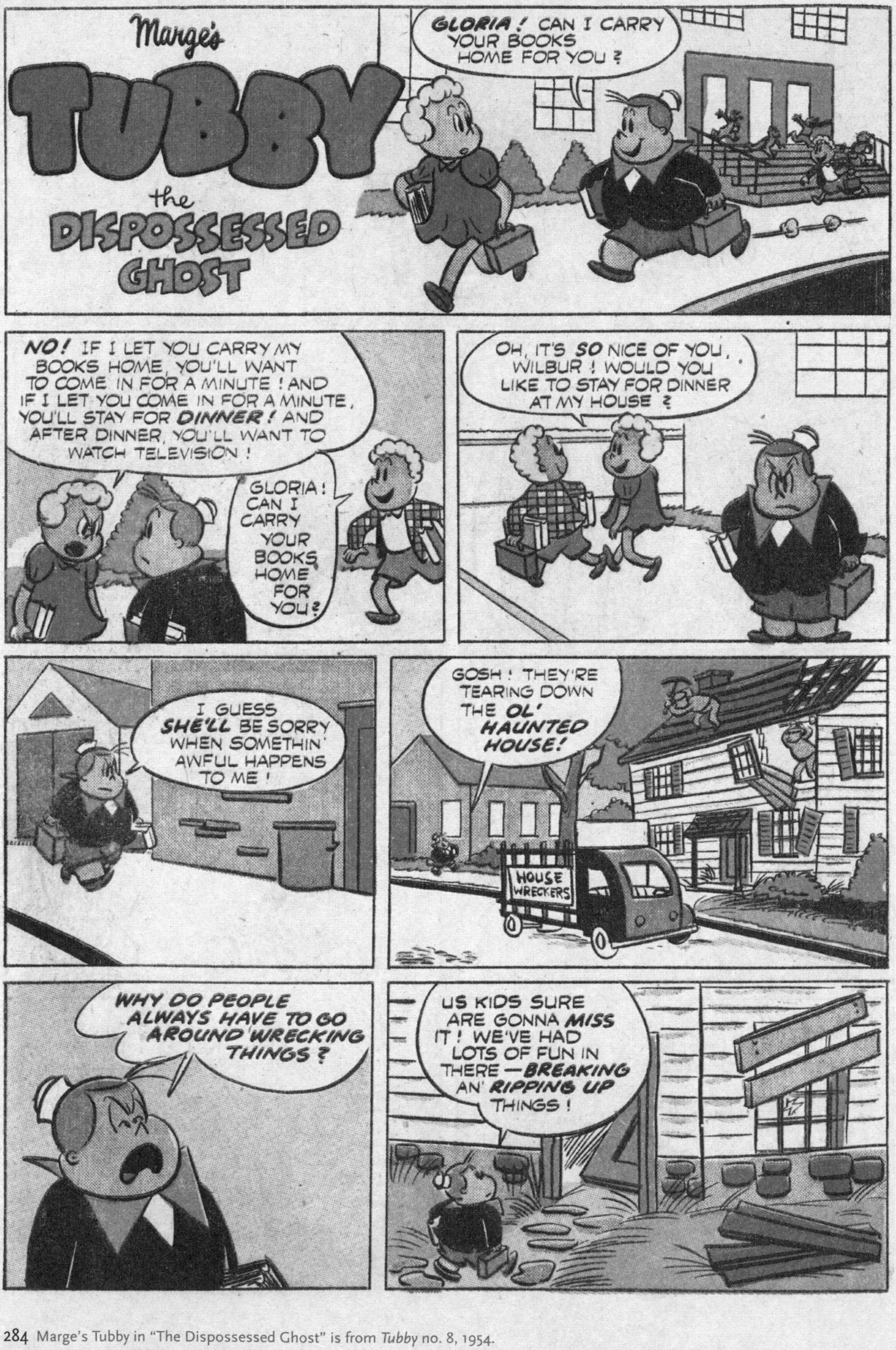
Marge's
TUBBY
the DISPOSSESSED GHOST
GLORIA! CAN I CARRY YOUR BOOKS HOME FOR YOU?
NO! IF I LET YOU CARRY MY BOOKS HOME, YOU'LL WANT TO COME IN FOR A MINUTE! AND IF I LET YOU COME IN FOR A MINUTE, YOU'LL STAY FOR DINNER! AND AFTER DINNER, YOU'LL WANT TO WATCH TELEVISION!
GLORIA! CAN I CARRY YOUR BOOKS HOME FOR YOU?
OH, IT'S SO NICE OF YOU, WILBUR! WOULD YOU LIKE TO STAY FOR DINNER AT MY HOUSE?
I GUESS SHE'LL BE SORRY WHEN SOMETHIN' AWFUL HAPPENS TO ME!
GOSH! THEY'RE TEARING DOWN THE OL' HAUNTED HOUSE!
HOUSE WRECKERS
WHY DO PEOPLE ALWAYS HAVE TO GO AROUND WRECKING THINGS?
US KIDS SURE ARE GONNA MISS IT! WE'VE HAD LOTS OF FUN IN THERE—BREAKING AN' RIPPING UP THINGS!

 Marge's Tubby in "The Dispossessed Ghost" is from *Tubby* no. 8, 1954.

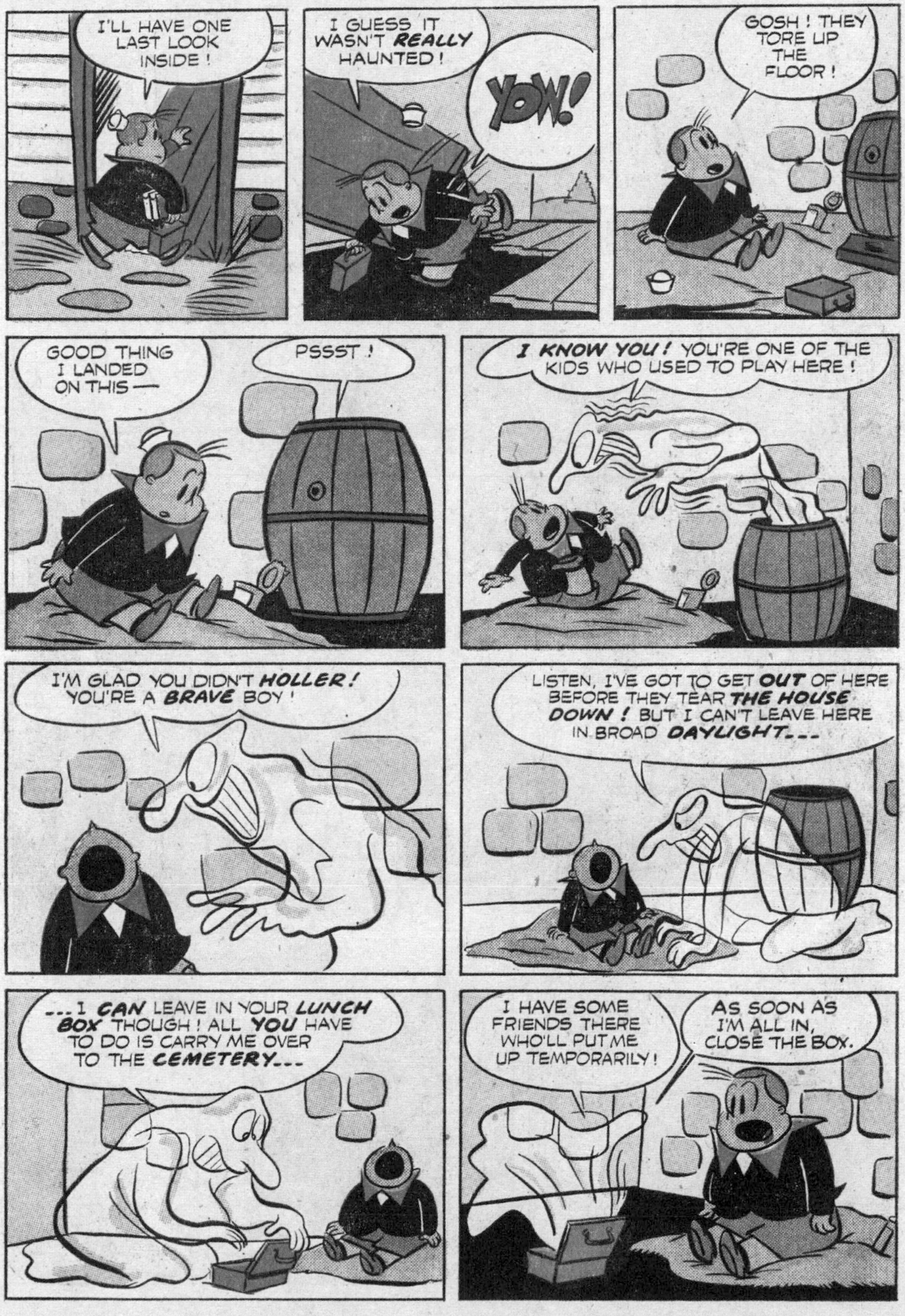
I'LL HAVE ONE LAST LOOK INSIDE !
I GUESS IT WASN'T REALLY HAUNTED !
YOW!
GOSH ! THEY TORE UP THE FLOOR !
GOOD THING I LANDED ON THIS—
PSSST !
I KNOW YOU ! YOU'RE ONE OF THE KIDS WHO USED TO PLAY HERE !
I'M GLAD YOU DIDN'T HOLLER ! YOU'RE A BRAVE BOY !
LISTEN, I'VE GOT TO GET OUT OF HERE BEFORE THEY TEAR THE HOUSE DOWN ! BUT I CAN'T LEAVE HERE IN BROAD DAYLIGHT...
...I CAN LEAVE IN YOUR LUNCH BOX THOUGH ! ALL YOU HAVE TO DO IS CARRY ME OVER TO THE CEMETERY...
I HAVE SOME FRIENDS THERE WHO'LL PUT ME UP TEMPORARILY !
AS SOON AS I'M ALL IN, CLOSE THE BOX.

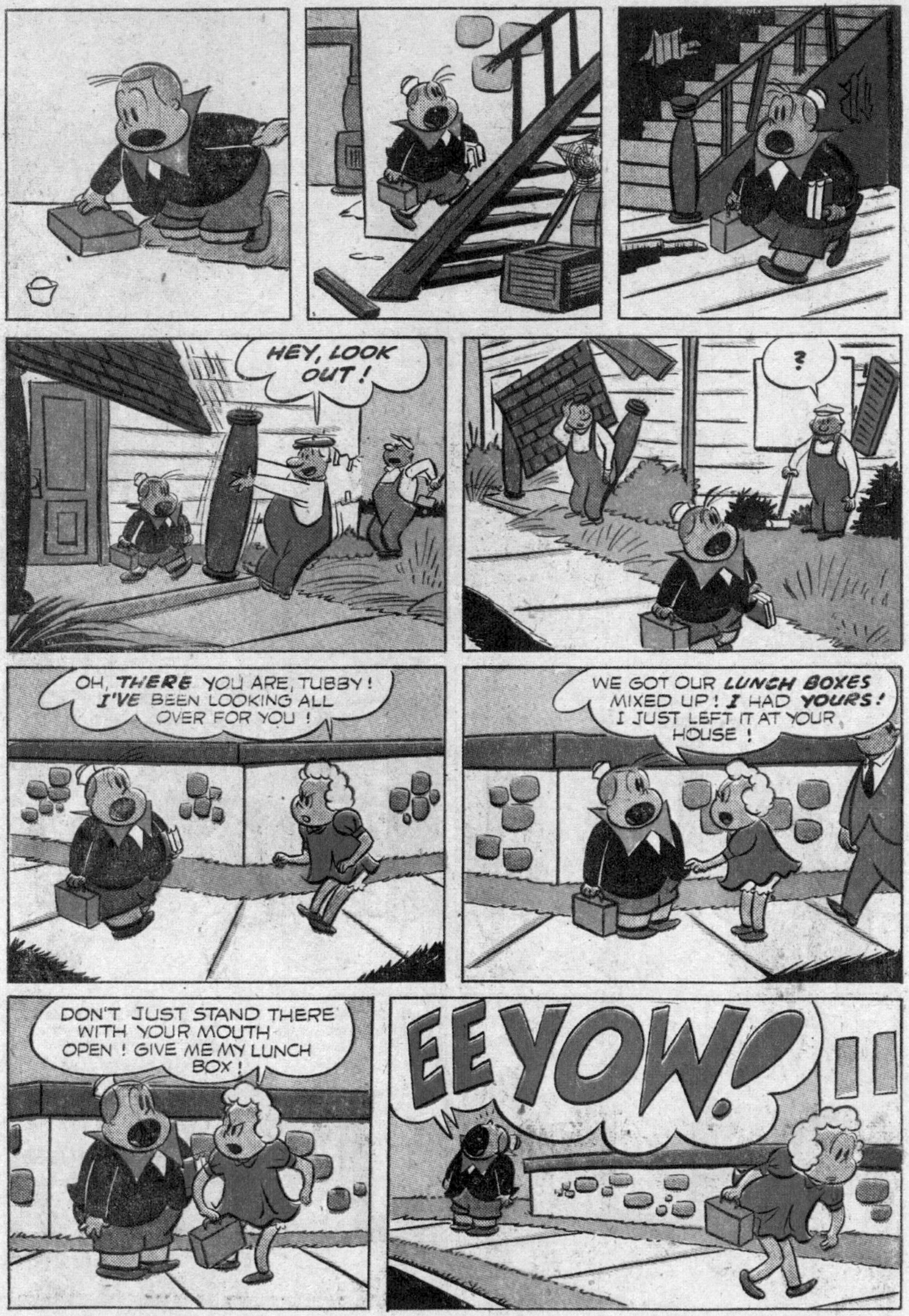
HEY, LOOK OUT!
?
OH, THERE YOU ARE, TUBBY! I'VE BEEN LOOKING ALL OVER FOR YOU!
WE GOT OUR LUNCH BOXES MIXED UP! I HAD YOURS! I JUST LEFT IT AT YOUR HOUSE!
DON'T JUST STAND THERE WITH YOUR MOUTH OPEN! GIVE ME MY LUNCH BOX!
EEYOW!!

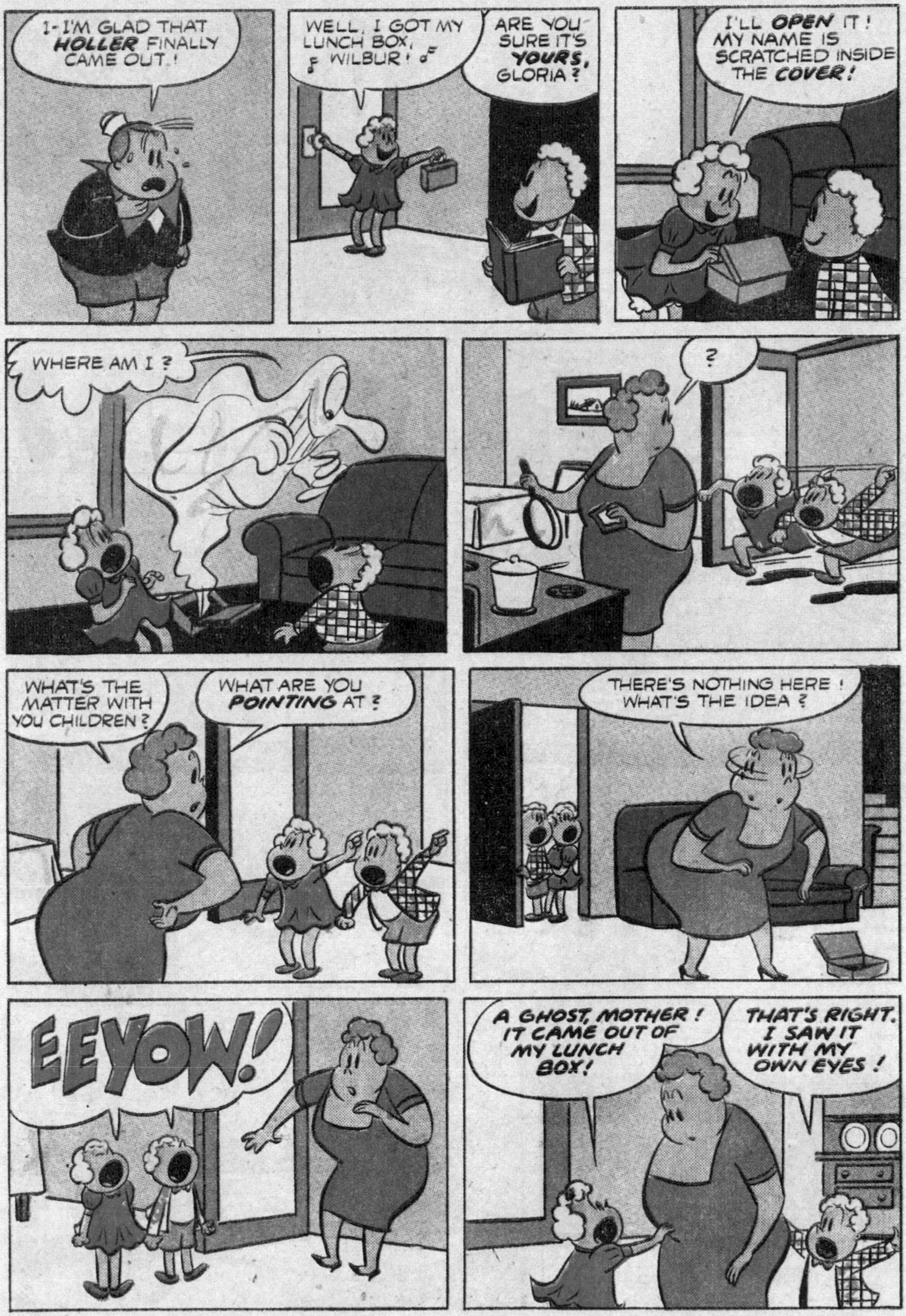
I-I'M GLAD THAT HOLLER FINALLY CAME OUT...!
WELL, I GOT MY LUNCH BOX, WILBUR!
ARE YOU SURE IT'S YOURS, GLORIA?
I'LL OPEN IT! MY NAME IS SCRATCHED INSIDE THE COVER!
WHERE AM I?
?
WHAT'S THE MATTER WITH YOU CHILDREN?
WHAT ARE YOU POINTING AT?
THERE'S NOTHING HERE! WHAT'S THE IDEA?
EEYOW!
A GHOST, MOTHER! IT CAME OUT OF MY LUNCH BOX!
THAT'S RIGHT. I SAW IT WITH MY OWN EYES!

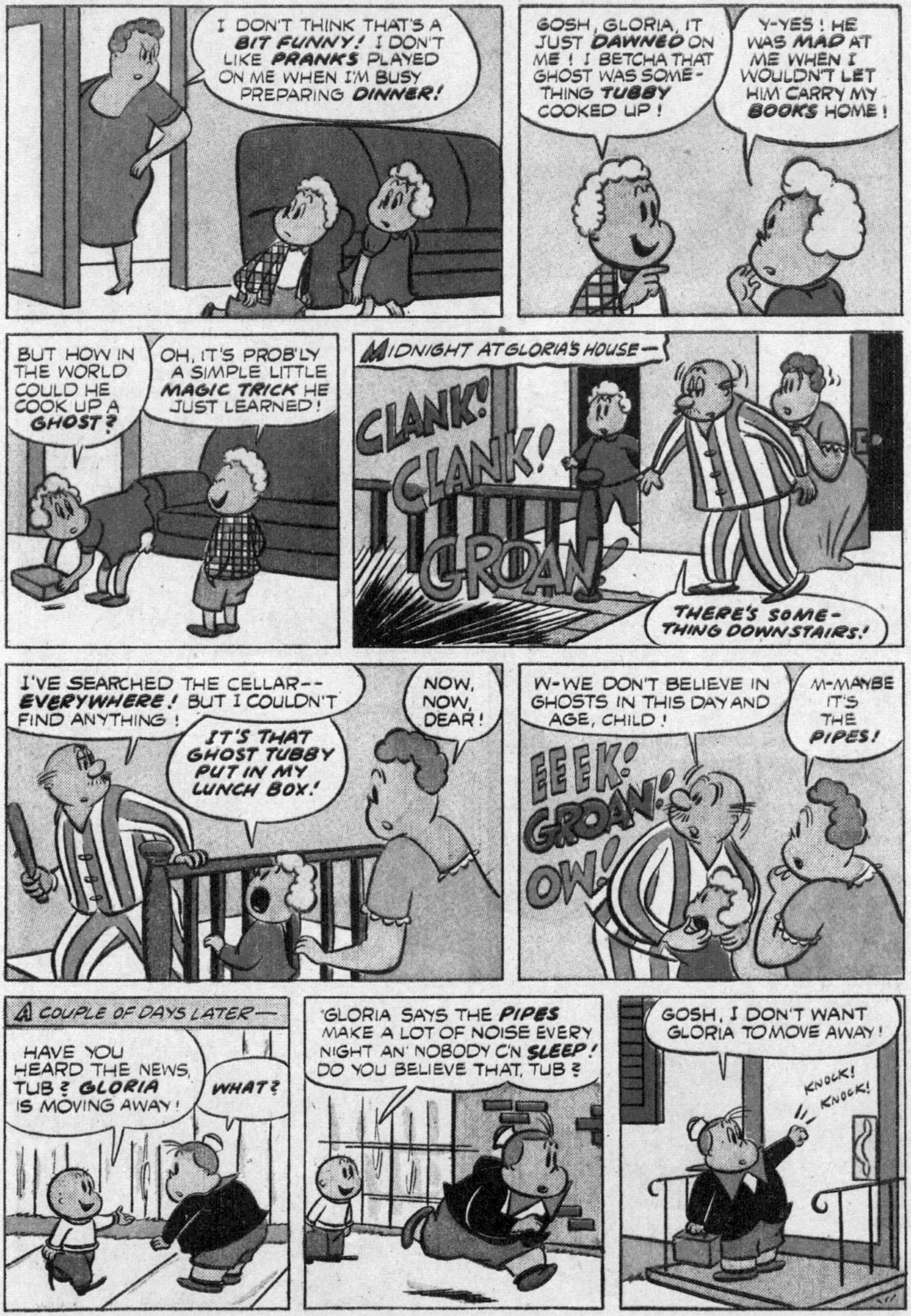
I DON'T THINK THAT'S A BIT FUNNY! I DON'T LIKE PRANKS PLAYED ON ME WHEN I'M BUSY PREPARING DINNER!
GOSH, GLORIA, IT JUST DAWNED ON ME! I BETCHA THAT GHOST WAS SOME-THING TUBBY COOKED UP!
Y-YES! HE WAS MAD AT ME WHEN I WOULDN'T LET HIM CARRY MY BOOKS HOME!
BUT HOW IN THE WORLD COULD HE COOK UP A GHOST?
OH, IT'S PROB'LY A SIMPLE LITTLE MAGIC TRICK HE JUST LEARNED!
MIDNIGHT AT GLORIA'S HOUSE—
CLANK! CLANK! GROAN
THERE'S SOME-THING DOWNSTAIRS!
I'VE SEARCHED THE CELLAR-- EVERYWHERE! BUT I COULDN'T FIND ANYTHING!
IT'S THAT GHOST TUBBY PUT IN MY LUNCH BOX!
NOW, NOW, DEAR!
W-WE DON'T BELIEVE IN GHOSTS IN THIS DAY AND AGE, CHILD!
M-MAYBE IT'S THE PIPES!
EEEK! GROAN! OW!
A COUPLE OF DAYS LATER—
HAVE YOU HEARD THE NEWS, TUB? GLORIA IS MOVING AWAY!
WHAT?
GLORIA SAYS THE PIPES MAKE A LOT OF NOISE EVERY NIGHT AN' NOBODY C'N SLEEP! DO YOU BELIEVE THAT, TUB?
GOSH, I DON'T WANT GLORIA TO MOVE AWAY!
KNOCK! KNOCK!

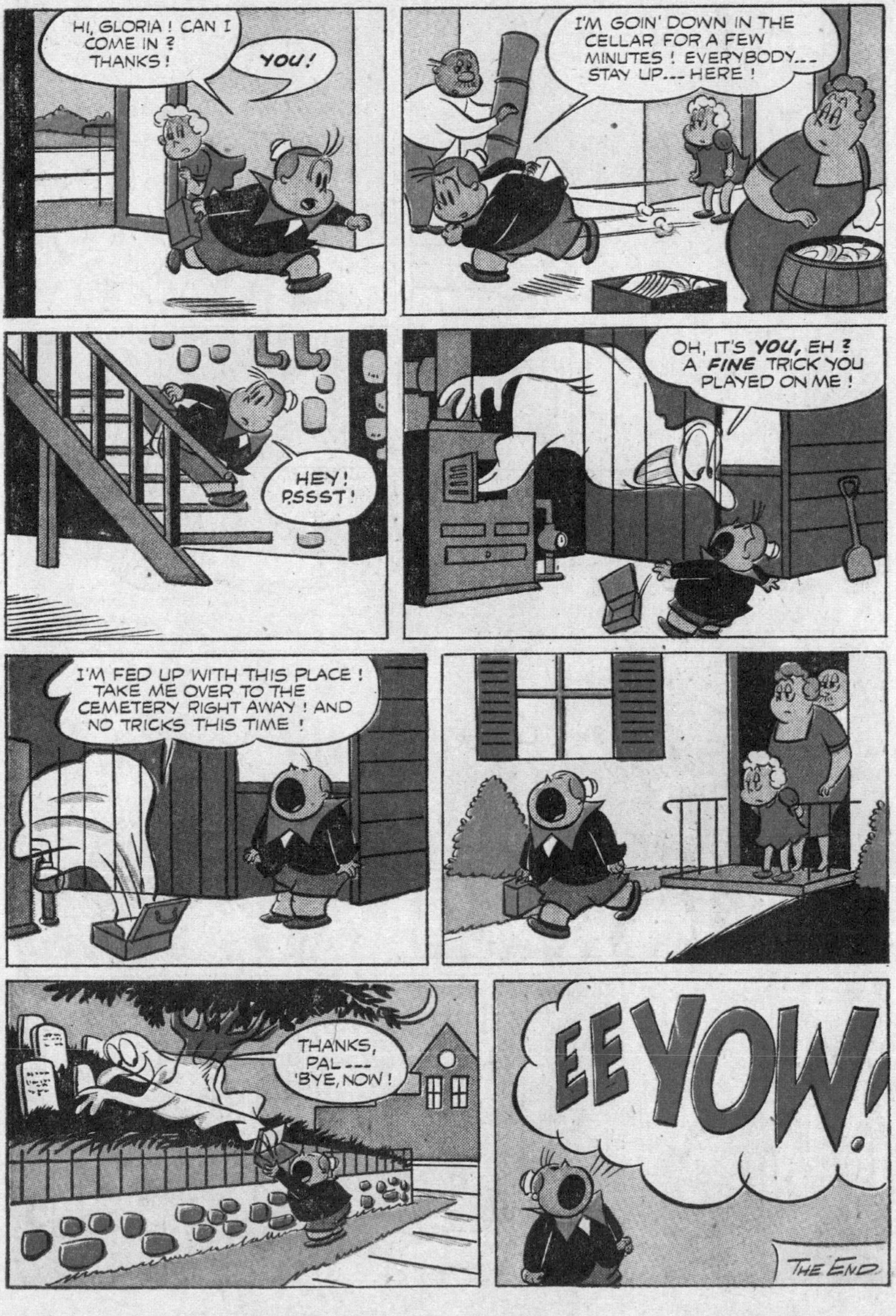

HI, GLORIA ! CAN I COME IN ? THANKS !
YOU!
I'M GOIN' DOWN IN THE CELLAR FOR A FEW MINUTES ! EVERYBODY... STAY UP... HERE !
HEY! PSSST!
OH, IT'S YOU, EH ? A FINE TRICK YOU PLAYED ON ME !
I'M FED UP WITH THIS PLACE ! TAKE ME OVER TO THE CEMETERY RIGHT AWAY ! AND NO TRICKS THIS TIME !
THANKS, PAL--- 'BYE, NOW !
EEYOW!
THE END

DRAWING FROM REAL LIFE

an appreciation of Doug Wright by Brad Mackay

Like all of us, Doug Wright played a number of roles in his life: loving husband, harried father, gifted draftsman, disgruntled taxpayer, devoted car-racing fan, maniacal model builder, and proud World War II veteran. But I think Wright would agree when I say that two words best sum up his time on earth: working cartoonist.

There can be little doubt that he harboured a strong work ethic. From the moment he took over the popular *Birdseye Center* strip in June 1948 following the death of its creator, Jimmy Frise, to the day in 1980 when a massive stroke cut short his own career, Wright was singularly dedicated to his craft.

Much like Charles Schulz, to whom he was often compared, Wright thrived on routine. After rising every day at around 8:00 AM, he ate a spare breakfast of toast and jam, drank a cup of tea, then climbed the stairs to his home studio on Rankin Drive in Burlington, Ontario, where he spent the next ten hours or so drawing one of his many comic-strip features, which totalled seven at the peak of his career. This was in addition to his freelance illustration gigs, which he worked on after he downed his five o'clock rye and water and had dinner with his wife and three kids.

And while all of his strips held their appeal, we probably would not be discussing Wright today if it weren't for *Doug Wright's Family*, which ran weekly in newspapers and magazines from 1949 to 1980. First appearing on March 12, 1949, in the back pages of the *Montreal Standard*, the untitled black-and-white strip about a mayhem magnet of a toddler was an instant hit with readers. The paper quickly responded with a contest to name the suddenly popular brat. There were dozens of entries, but "Nipper" won out (like Schulz with *Peanuts*, Wright hated the title) and the strip would use it as its title for the next eighteen years. That is until Wright moved the strip to a new paper and copyright issues forced him to change it to the more literal *Doug Wright's Family*. He chafed at that name too, but it couldn't have been more perfect.

By the 1960s the strip was a literal reflection of Wright's growing family life. When he started the strip he was a bachelor, with zero insight into kids. By 1960 he was married (to Phyllis Wright) and had three boys, aged one, four, and seven. The strip, once a simplistic gag-a-week, had grown along with him. The mom and dad were dead ringers for Phyllis and Doug, and the strip added a second boy shortly after their second son was born.

Without realizing it, Wright had created a comic-strip simulacrum of 1960s family life. The strips that weren't based on his own experiences were usually based on another family he knew, which rooted the strip in a recognizable domestic reality—one complete with agitated moms in hair curlers and fuming, frazzled dads beset by kids who could switch from engines of bedlam one minute to refuges of pure joy the next. This was—and is—family life for most of us, and people came to appreciate Wright's unsanitized domestic snapshots.

For all of the comparisons to Charles Schulz's enormously popular *Peanuts* (which Wright privately bristled at), it's not fair to compare the two. As a child of the 1970s I loved *Peanuts*, but even I didn't think of Charlie Brown and the rest of his gang as actual kids. To me Schulz's universe was a stage for complex anxieties played out by children understudying their adult counterparts. *Peanuts* is an undeniable masterpiece, but its children were funny paper orphans. They tormented the hell out of each other but never had a mom or dad to go to when they got hurt.

That's why even though as a reader I loved *Peanuts*, as a kid I identified with *Doug Wright's Family*. And I wasn't alone. Wright's work inspired at least two generations of cartoonists including Lynn Johnston (who credits Wright as one of the two reasons she became an artist), Chester Brown (whose first published work at the age of eleven was a *Doug Wright's Family* rip-off), and Seth, whose reverence for Wright has been channelled into four books and an annual comics awards show named in his honour.

It's not a stretch to say that Wright was unconsciously creating a form of comic-strip vérité. Wright's bald-headed boys acted like kids—not adults—and they had parents who loved them and were there for them. Like hundreds of other Canadians of my generation, I saw myself in *Doug Wright's Family*, and now that I have three kids of my own, I still do.

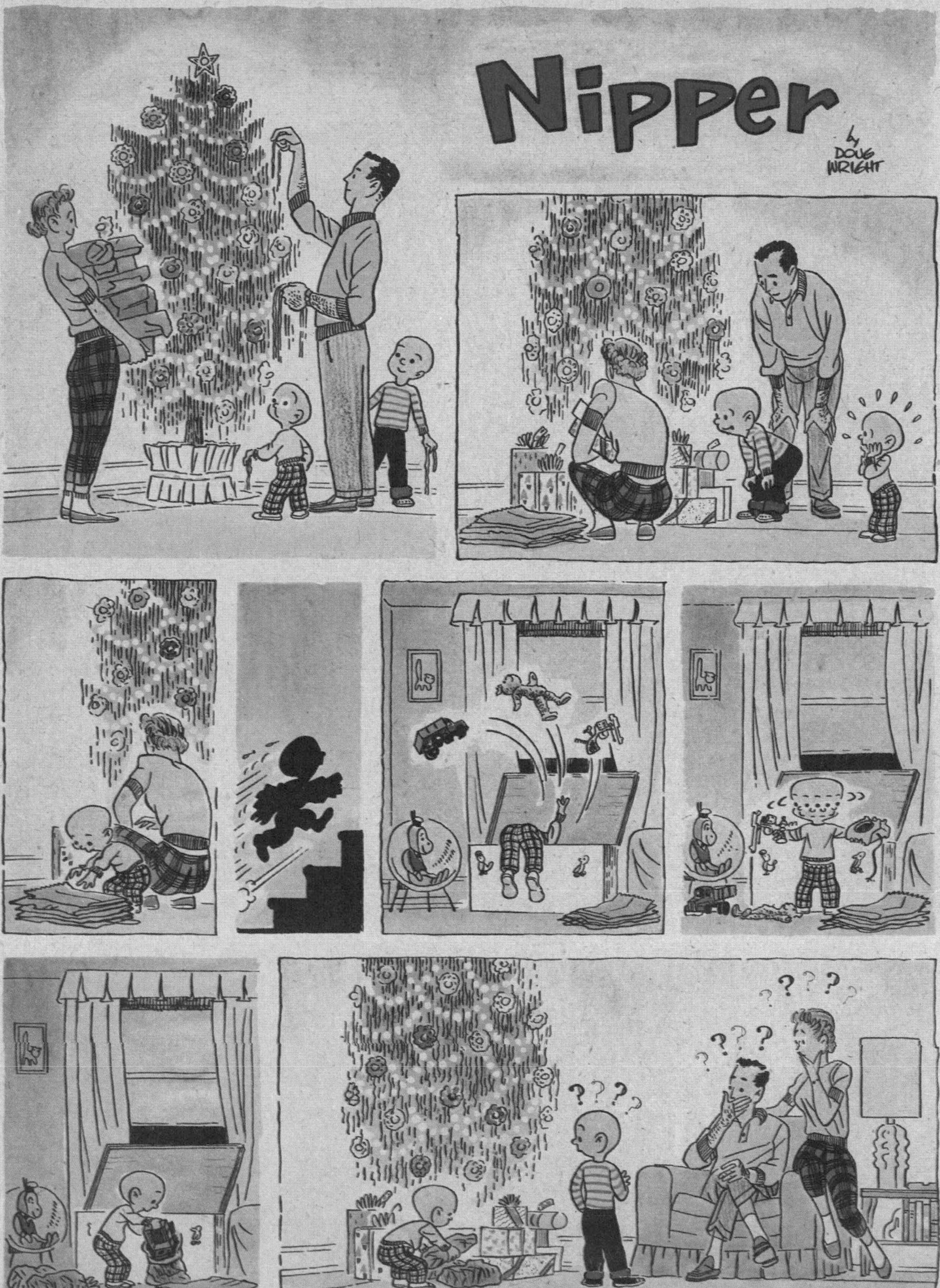
Nipper
by DOUG WRIGHT

I have known Doug Wright's work as long as I've known Charles Schulz's. Which means, as long as I can remember. I encountered them both so early that I have no first memories of either of them. I've simply always known them. Or more accurately, I've always known *their cartooning*. They were both primary influences on me. Both very much involved in my choice to become a cartoonist. It's remarkable to me that I would end up designing career book collections for both of them.

I loved both these cartoonists deeply in childhood and, strangely, abandoned both during my teen years.

Well, maybe not so strangely, really. In my teen years, my cartooning passions turned to Marvel superheroes and *Heavy Metal* magazine. Power and sex fantasies. Utterly appropriate to that dreadful period of life. In my twenties, thank goodness, I returned to my senses and re-embraced Schulz and Wright.

It was rather easy to revisit the work of Charles Schulz. There was a tremendous number of his book collections floating around in every thrift shop or used bookstore. Not so with Doug Wright. It was almost impossible to find his cartoons. Wright only had two reprint books during his life, and they were

rare enough that it took me years to uncover them. Sadly, this isn't because they were much-sought-after, expensive volumes. No, these were just cheap paperbacks. They were probably hard to find because no one bothered to keep them or pass them along to the used book trade. I think I found them both in junk stores. Probably paid a buck each. On top of this frustration, these two books were tiny and poorly reproduced and missing his signature red spot colour. No way to appreciate such a great cartoonist's work.

So, early on, I understood I would have no choice but to go out and find and hand-collect the hundreds of original magazines (*Weekend* and *Canadian* magazines) where Doug Wright's work appeared. In those magazines his work was printed large and clear and in colour. I didn't know it then, but Wright had died just a few years earlier...and already his work was rapidly fading from the Canadian consciousness and was very hard to locate.

I won't bore you with the details of that arduous collecting task. Let's just jump many years ahead to the day when I first showed Wright's work to Chris Oliveros and made a convert of him. If memory serves, the Chief

DOUG WRIGHT
WINDING ROAD 21 MI.
600
REST ROOMS
DO NOT PASS

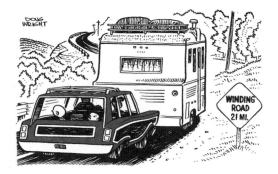

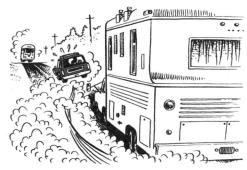

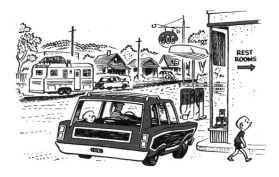

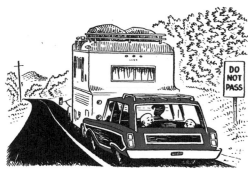

was visiting and I was proudly showing off a hodgepodge of old Canadian cartooning that I had gathered up over the years. I expected the Chief to warm up to Jimmy Frise or Peter Whalley most of all, so I was a bit surprised when he so sharply focused in on Wright as his clear favourite. Probably I underestimated the power Wright's work has for fathers. Whatever the case, the Chief became a strong advocate for Wright in the years that followed. And thank goodness, too—without his enthusiasm, there wouldn't be a small shelf of Wright's brilliant cartooning back in print today.

I had a similar afternoon visit back then with writer Brad Mackay, with much the same results: another Wright convert (or more likely, a lapsed Wright enthusiast, since Brad already knew the work from childhood). I had invited Brad over to my house specifically to interest him in those same old Canadian cartoonists in hopes of drafting him onto a book project I was considering on the subject. However, like the Chief, he was most enthusiastic about Doug Wright out of the bunch. That book on Canadian cartooning never happened. Instead the three of us got together for *The Collected Doug Wright*, a book I could never have imagined existing back when I started digging around for those old Wright comics.

As I mentioned in the John Stanley section, I have been designing *The Complete Peanuts* for over a decade. Having anything to do with that great man's work has been very gratifying to me. However, being involved in the resurrection of Wright's work and reputation might be even dearer to my heart. Schulz is firmly set in the cartooning canon. No one is likely to overlook his huge contribution. Wright was just the opposite. It's hard not to root harder for the underdog (and let's face it, it's hard not to root harder for the Canadian!).

I feel a personal connection to Wright's cartooning. I've said it many times—his drawings bring back the world of my Ontario childhood more vividly than just about anything. More than any photos or old films or even the actual places themselves. Wright captured, with great specificity, the texture of those times. And he did so through work that was focused on quiet, tiny little moments. The work has an oddness to it that marks it as REAL art—the oddness of real experience and genuine expression.

—Seth, Doug Wright series designer

August 2, 1969.

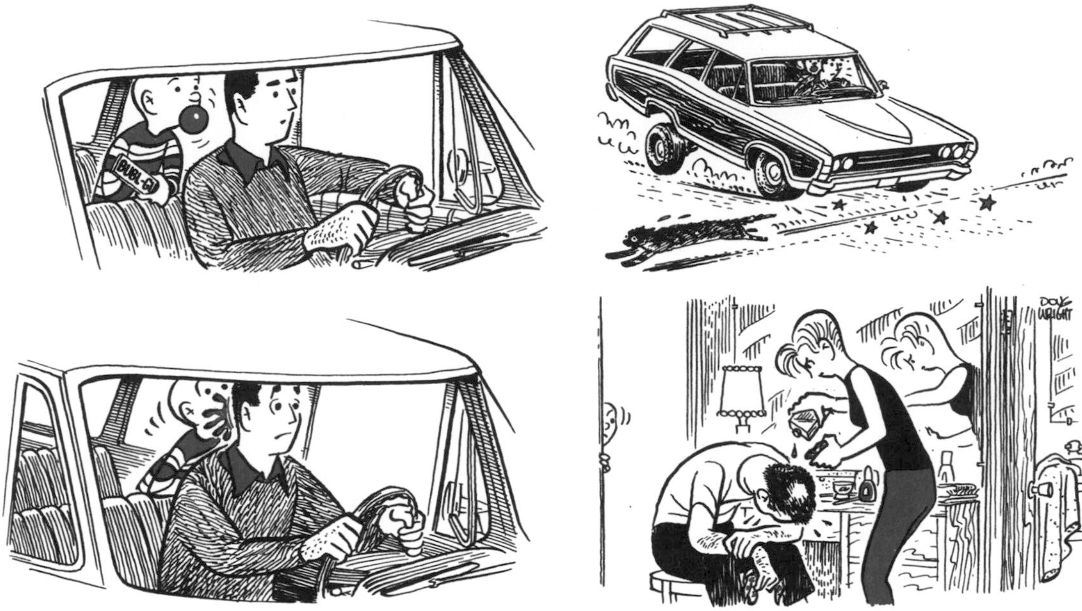

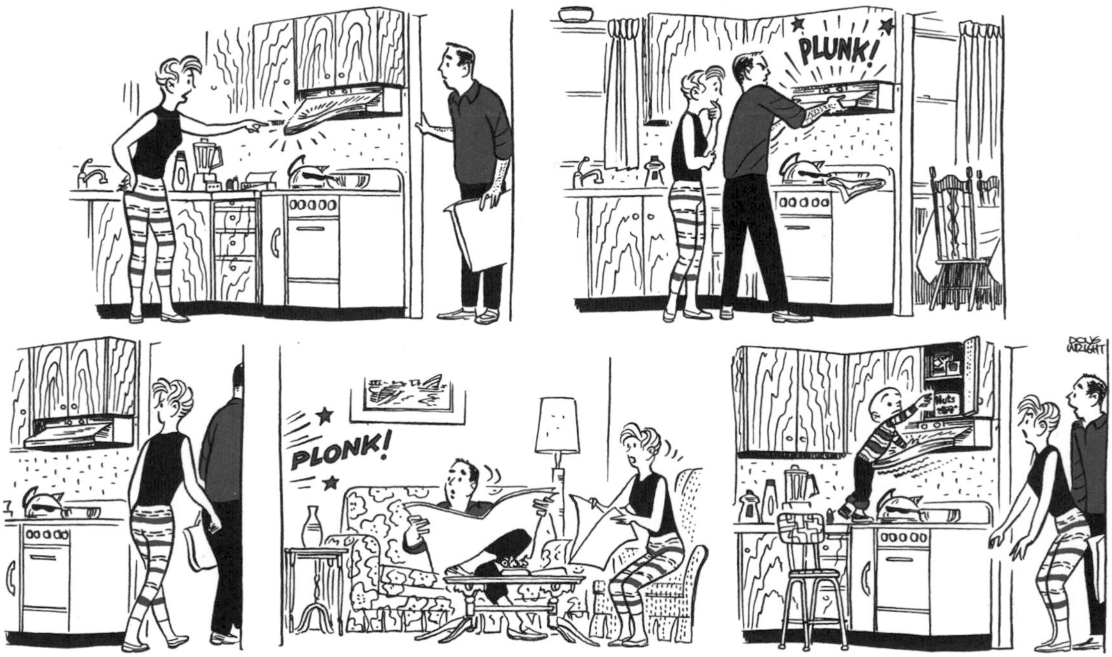
PLUNK!
PLONK!

 September 6 & 20, 1969.

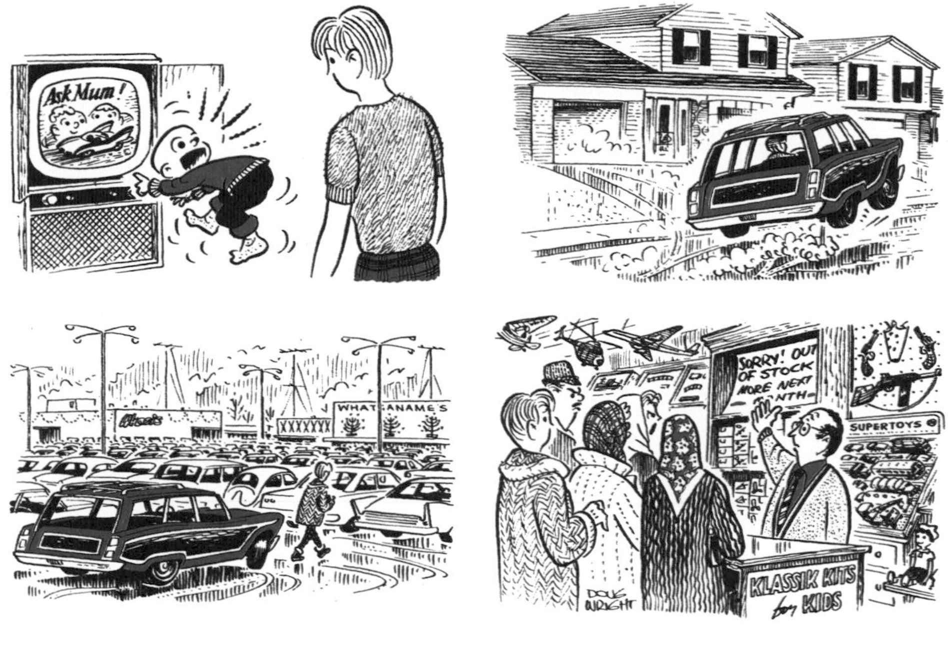
Ask Mum!
WHATSANAMES
XXXXXXX
SORRY! OUT OF STOCK MORE NEXT
SUPERTOYS
KLASSIK KITS
KIDS
DOUG WRIGHT

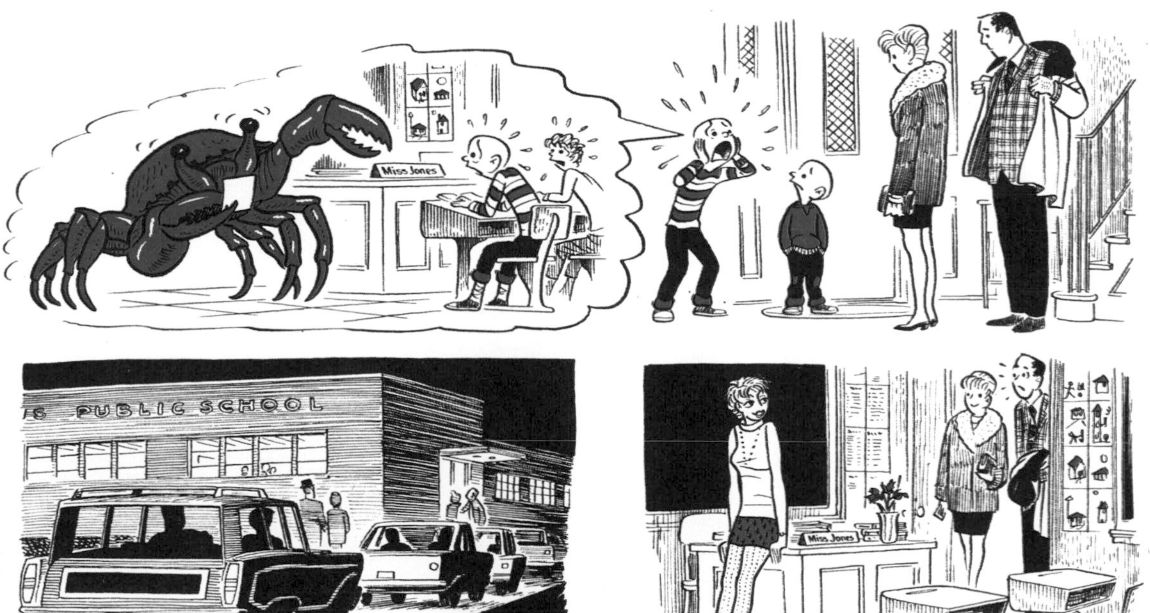
Miss Jones
PUBLIC SCHOOL
Miss Jones
DOUG WRIGHT

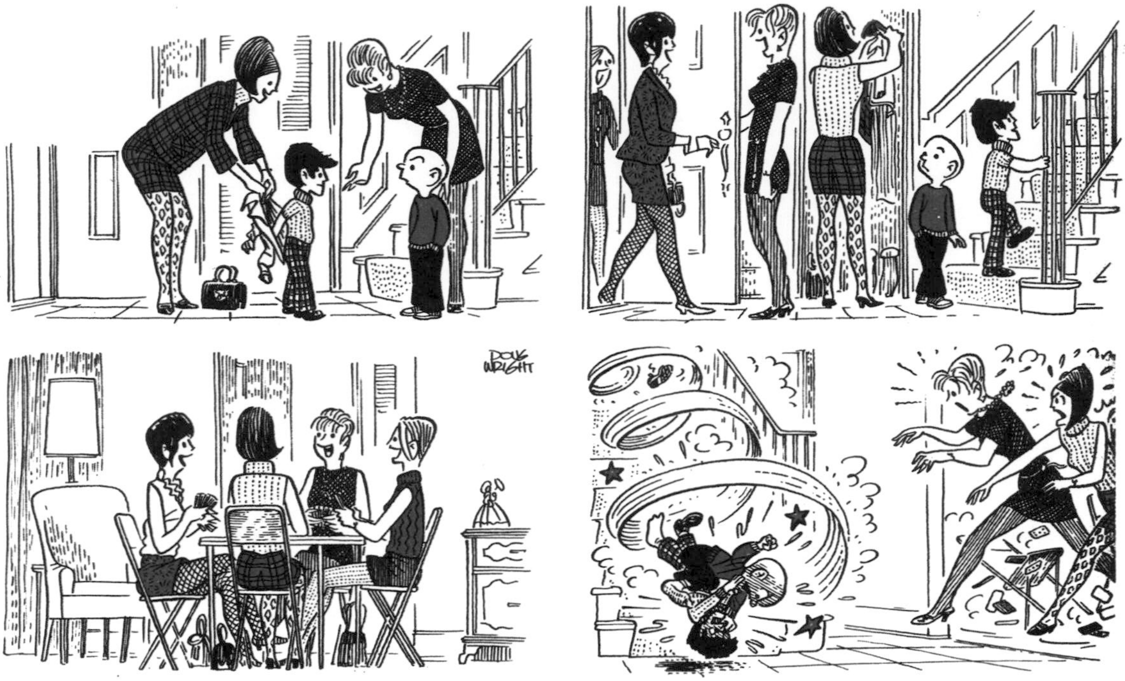
DOUG WRIGHT

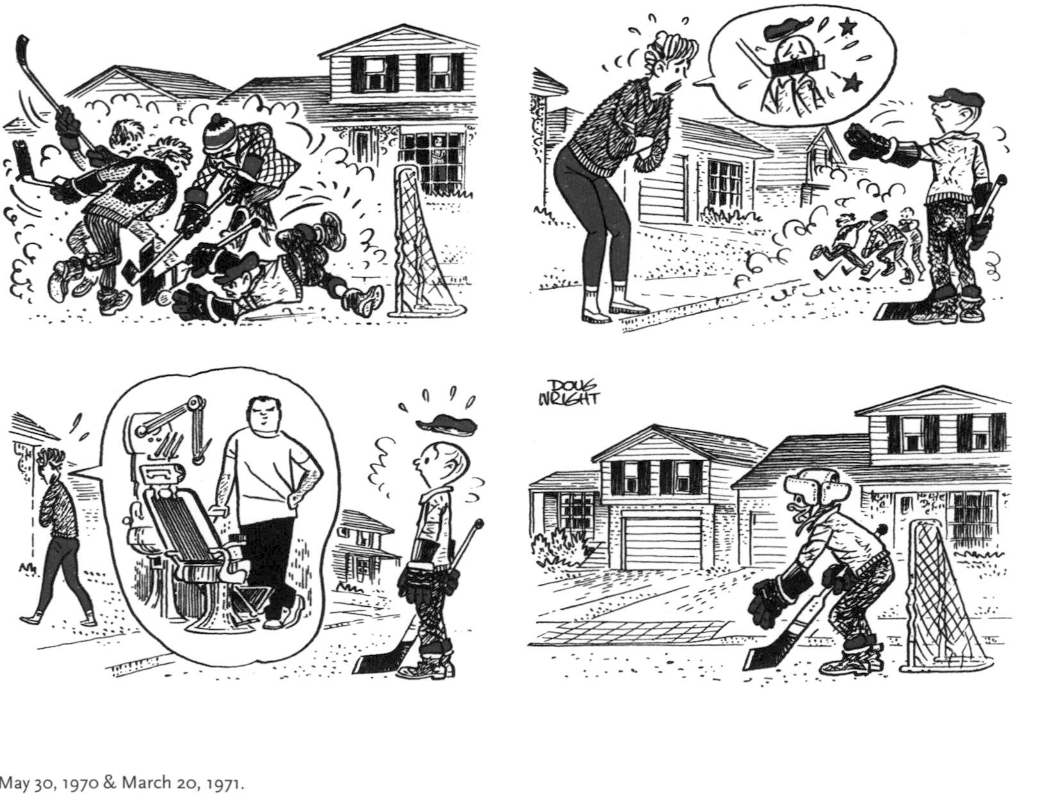
DOUG WRIGHT

 May 30, 1970 & March 20, 1971.

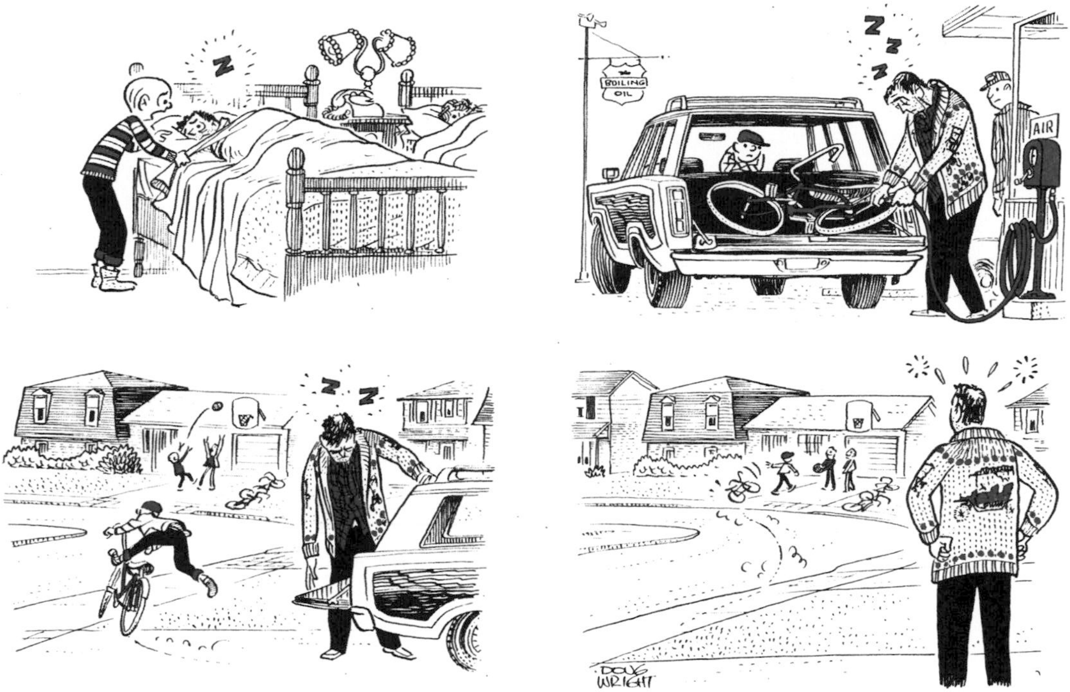
Z
Z Z Z
BOILING OIL
AIR
Z Z
DOUG WRIGHT

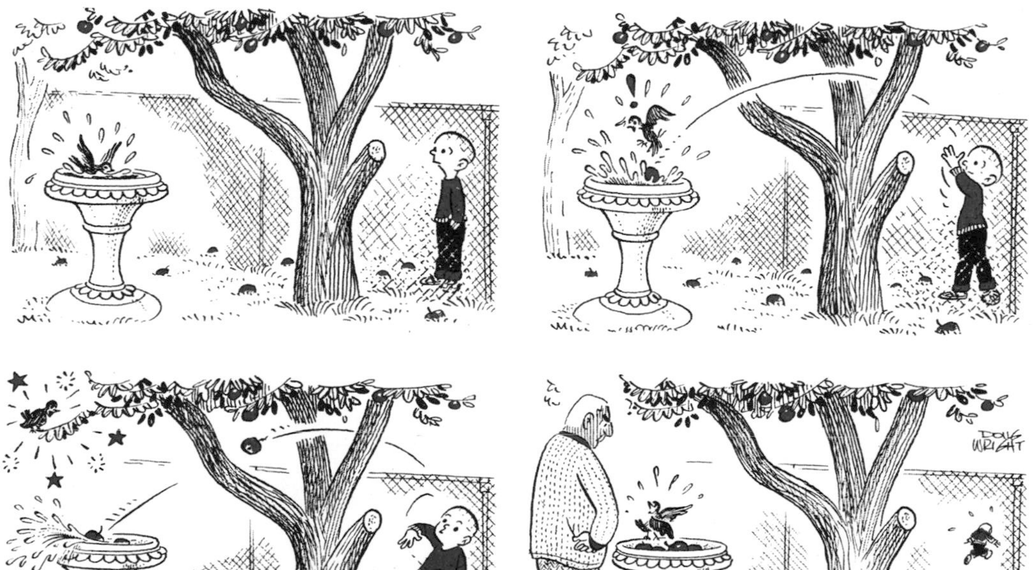
DOUG WRIGHT

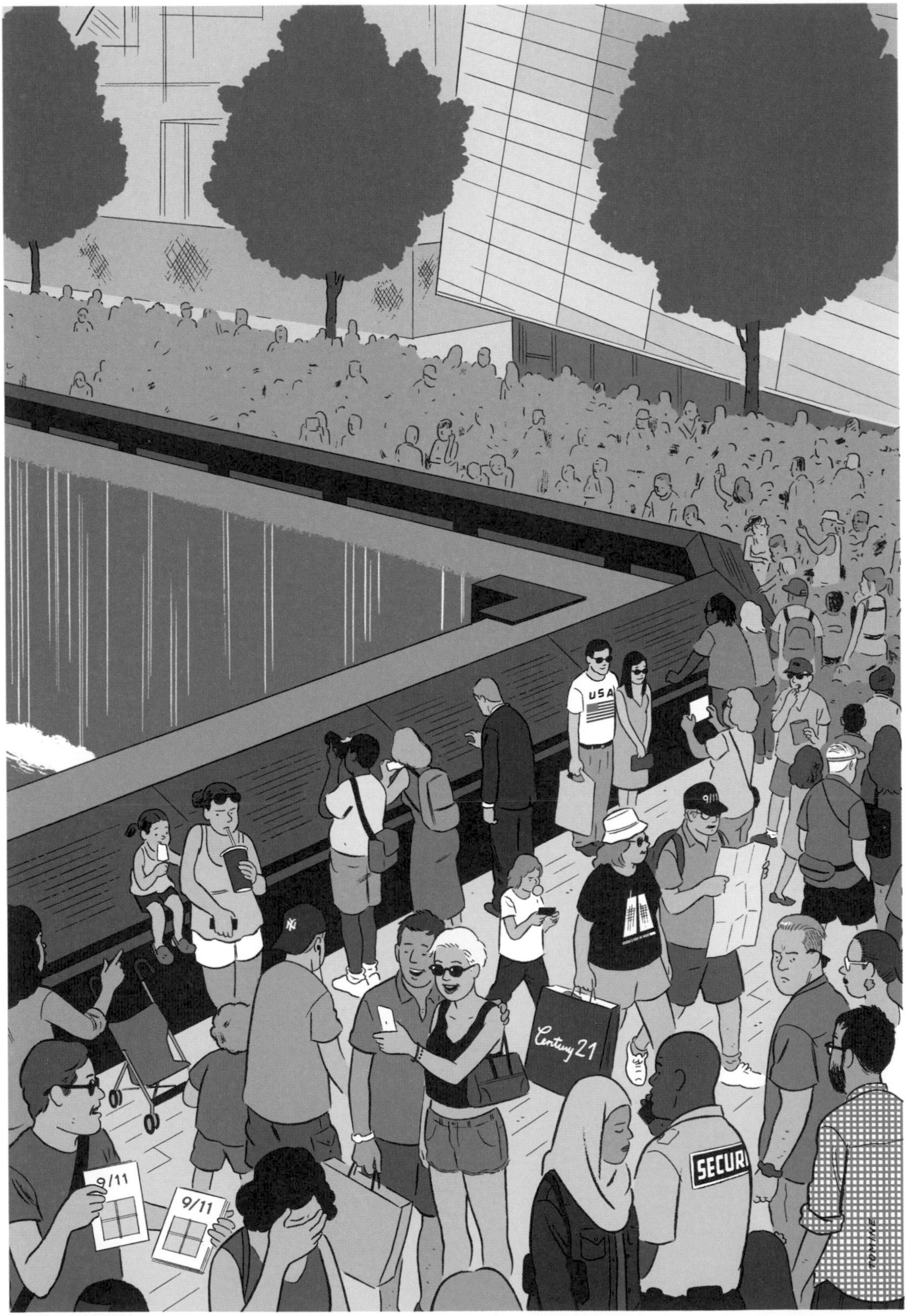
USA
9/11
Century 21
SECURI
9/11
9/11
TOMINE

 "Memorial Plaza" first appeared as the cover of the *New Yorker* (July 7, 2014).

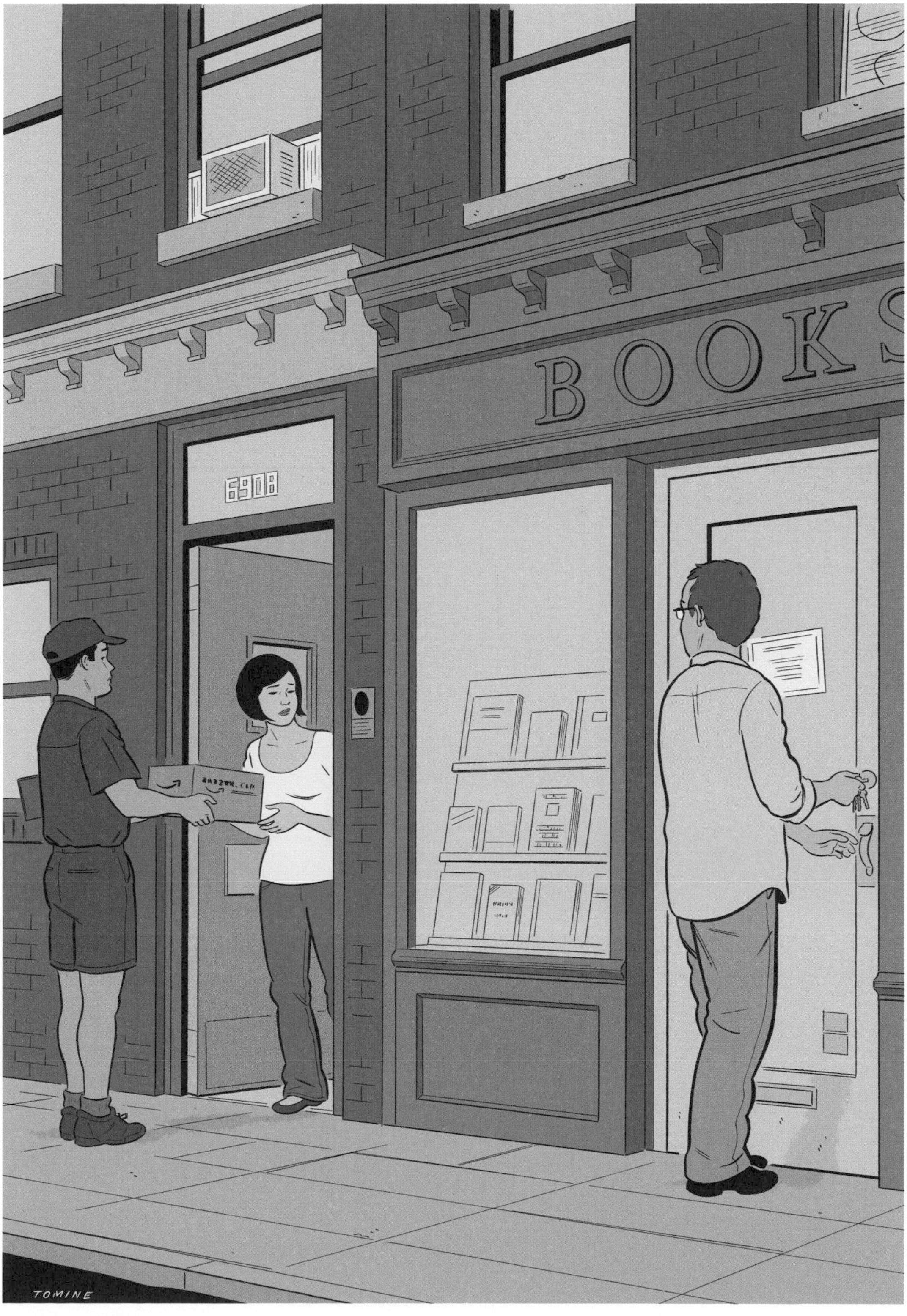
BOOKS
6908
TOMINE

"Read-Handed" appeared first as the cover of the *New Yorker* (June 9 & 16, 2008) and later in *New York Drawings* (2012). Adrian Tomine

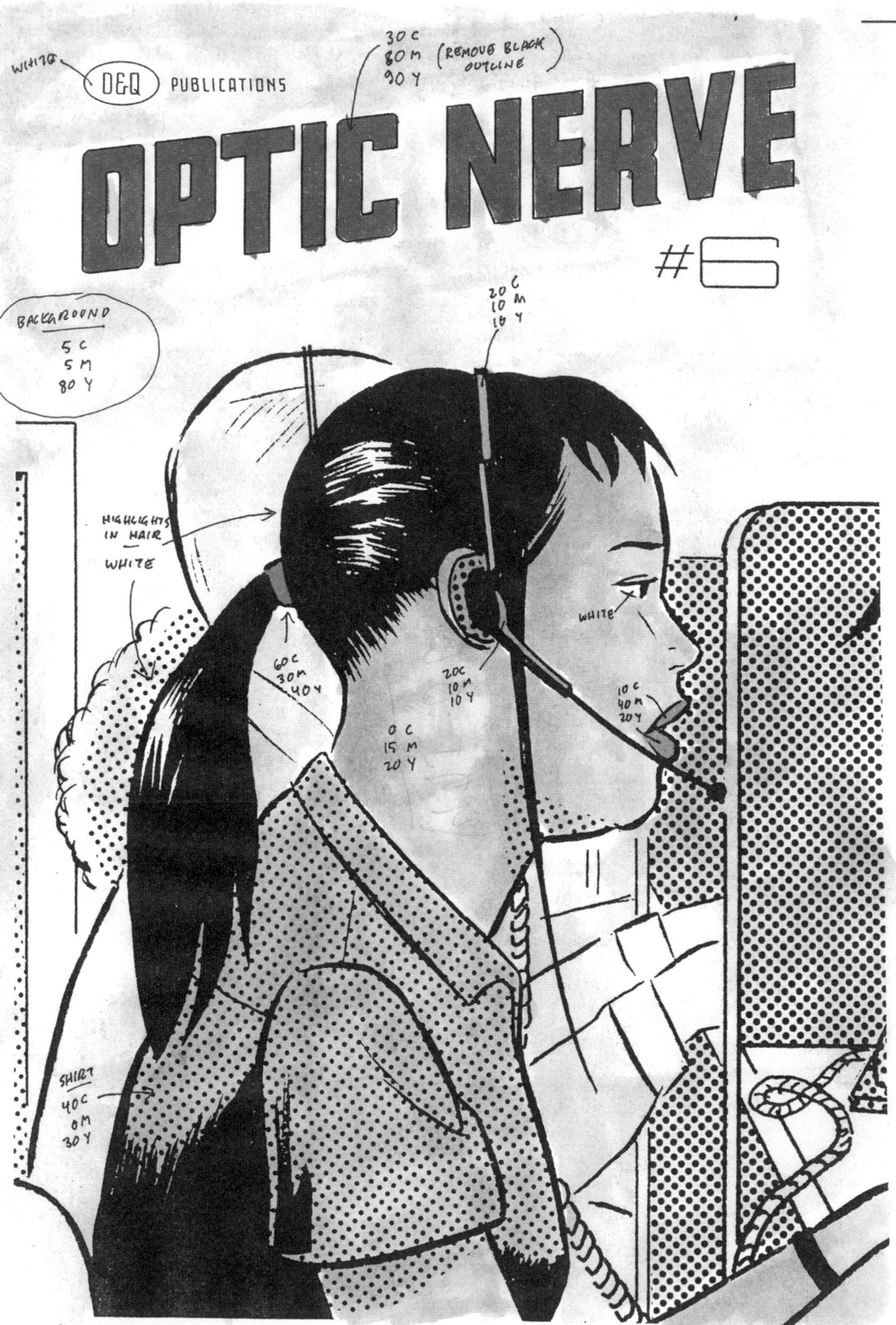
WHITE
D&Q PUBLICATIONS
30 C
80 M
90 Y
(REMOVE BLACK OUTLINE)
OPTIC NERVE
#6
20 C
10 M
10 Y
BACKGROUND
5 C
5 M
80 Y
HIGHLIGHTS IN HAIR
WHITE
WHITE
60 C
30 M
40 Y
20 C
10 M
10 Y
10 C
40 M
20 Y
0 C
15 M
20 Y
SHIRT
40 C
0 M
30 Y

A WIDE-EYED, KEEN OBSERVER

an appreciation of Adrian Tomine by Françoise Mouly

"I guess that's the last time I walk past this wall," Adrian Tomine said wistfully as we exited the Condé Nast cafeteria in Times Square. I had just finished saying how much I would miss this corridor of curving and distorting mirrors, which I see as architect Frank Gehry's joke on the gorgeous creatures of the *Vogue* world. We, everyone at the *New Yorker*, everyone at Condé Nast, were in the midst of preparing for our upcoming move to the Freedom Tower downtown. This would be my last Times Square meal with Adrian. He's one of my local artists, one of the very few I can easily invite for lunch at the *New Yorker* offices.

"When I started as an illustrator at the *New Yorker* in the early 2000s," Adrian reminisced, "I used to sit in the cartoonists' lounge, opposite Bob Mankoff's office." Mankoff is in charge of the gag cartoons, but since we have always had terribly few spaces for our artists on deadline, illustrators are also occasionally assigned to the cartoonists' lounge. "Mankoff left his door open as he harangued the petitioning cartoonists about humour," continued Tomine. "I'm glad I never had to deal with that. That would have discouraged artists like Chris Ware, or me, the delicate flowers, from *ever* submitting our work." But while I know that Adrian is sensitive, and nearly as forthcoming with the self-deprecating humour—both in his work and in person—as his contemporaries, I actually find him better adapted, less neurotic, and less alienated than many of the artists I know.

Like his pictures, Tomine the person is very composed. The delicate flower may be somewhat reserved, yet he's far from timid. He appears even-tempered and socially at ease. As a matter of fact, from the start I noticed that my young assistants and interns, who recognize themselves in his drawings and strips, often see Adrian as the ideal sensitive male.

I was first exposed to Tomine's work through his comic book, *Optic Nerve*, which he had begun while in high school in Sacramento in the late nineties. Tomine draws in the European *ligne claire* style, with the clear line of Hergé's Tintin, yet it fits perfectly with the *New Yorker*'s aesthetics while modernizing and updating them. His work as an illustrator—meeting deadlines and reliably coming up with interesting and pleasing images—made me think he would be a great fit for our covers. I knew that neither of his college professor parents (his dad, an artistically inclined engineer who painted in his spare time, and his mom, a licensed family therapist) had had a *New Yorker* subscription when

---

I became aware of Drawn & Quarterly when I found out that Adrian Tomine was no longer self-publishing his comic *Optic Nerve*. When I asked about any new work, he uttered "D+Q" under his breath and fell silent. I felt like I was more excited about his work than he was! I think we first met at Comic-Con in 1993 (or 1994?). I knew nothing about D+Q at the time—D+Q was only about Adrian Tomine for me—but I quickly realized that this was a comic publisher like no other (I pretty much only knew Marvel and DC at that time). These comics were art. These comics had a style that made me wonder what else was out there. Those aisles in my local comic shop that I never went near suddenly became the most important aisles to me. It was a new world. What was it that drew me to Adrian's comics in the first place? Adrian Tomine took the indie-rock world of cute short-haired women—who never gave me the time of day—and the undeserving guys around them and made stories that hit home. There was a sense of unease and open endings that made me want more. As the long-time publisher of the Asian culture magazine *Giant Robot*, I enjoyed how Adrian slowly established his own Asian-American roots with his graphic novel *Shortcomings*. It was nice to see him dig into that part of his identity and add to the rich culture of Asian storytelling. One of my favourite memories of being a magazine editor is working with Adrian on his one-page comic "The Donger and Me," his epic takedown of that crappy *Sixteen Candles* character that was the bane of every Japanese-American boy's existence for decades.

—*Eric Nakamura, publisher,* Giant Robot

(Left) Diamond *Previews* solicitation cover for *Optic Nerve* no. 6 (1999).

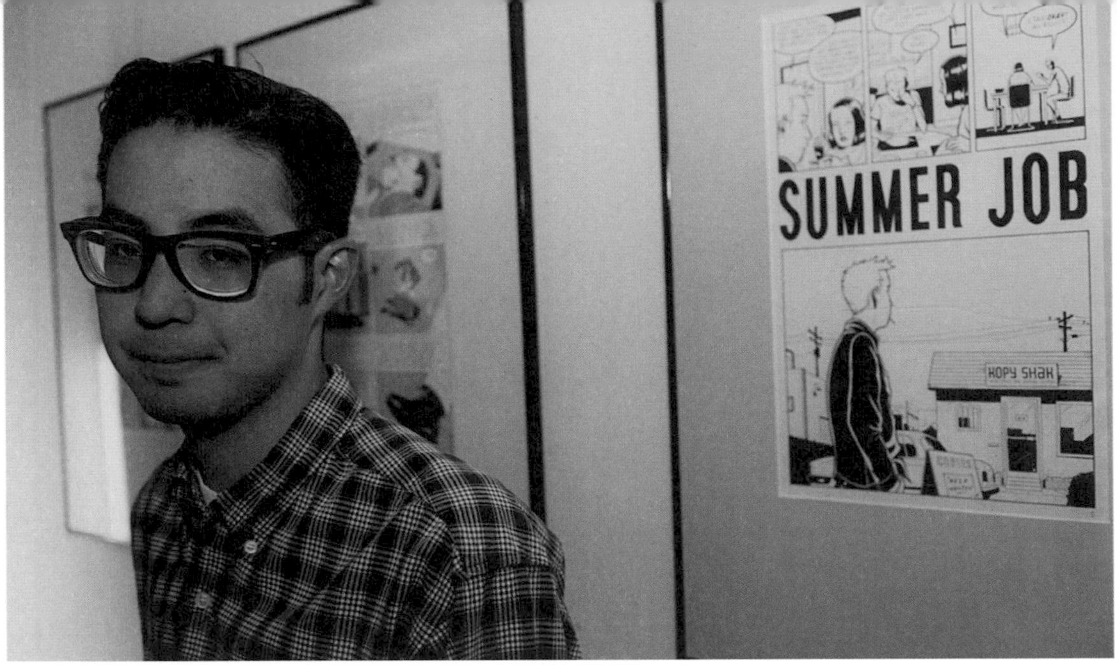
SUMMER JOB

he was growing up. His parents divorced when he was two, and young Adrian travelled around with his mom before settling in Sacramento for high school, so he was late in discovering the *New Yorker*. But he had pored over the big books of covers and spent time looking at the great storytelling covers of the thirties and forties by the likes of Peter Arno, Mary Petty, Helen Hokinson, and Charles Addams.

Still, even after I had asked him specifically for cover sketches, I didn't hear back for a year. I was somewhat frustrated—artists commonly respond by flooding me with ideas. Not sure what the hang-up was, I eventually called him to say I was counting on him for the cover of an upcoming special books issue and provided him with the deadline. He later told me that the thought of doing a cover had left him terrified, "for reasons probably best explained by a psychologist," but when I made it a concrete assignment, I jump-started his creative process. We were off and running. That first image by Adrian has become one of our most classic modern covers. It hasn't aged in ten years. In it, like-minded sophisticates let their eyes meet through the glass panes of passing subway trains.

In the years since, Tomine has become one of my go-to artists for New York–centric scenes. His handsome, stripped-down aesthetics form a paean to the poignancy of daily life in the big city. He finds the humanity of a small town within this big one. His pictures show the quirky, intimate, tender moments that would otherwise be so easily lost in the hustle and bustle. I was delighted that after his first child, Nora, was born, he spent a lot of time exploring the neighbourhoods of Brooklyn from the perspective of a stroller-pushing dad. I also value that despite his years here (he moved in 2003), he's never lost the perspective of an out-of-towner. He's a wide-eyed, keen observer who continues to see what many of us long-time city-dwellers end up relegating to our peripheral vision.

Among the things I appreciate most about Tomine's work is his ability to convey far more than static images sometimes do. His pictures tell stories; they unfold into a before and an after. In this sense, he's a natural cartoonist. Although he shows us only one telling moment, each of his covers contains a whole narrative that can play itself out in our imagination.

Even if most of Adrian's covers show outdoor scenes—architecture is a common theme—the precision of the details he chooses emphasizes the human dimension of his work. In another of his covers, from spring 2008, which has also only become sharper with the passing of time, we see a UPS delivery guy bringing a box to a woman who lives right next to a bookstore. I like it when artists tackle budding trends: at the time, the ordering of books on Amazon had just begun to affect the economics of the book business. Interestingly, this is the only one of his book-themed covers that doesn't show someone reading a book. Other artists may have tried to tackle the issue by showing a woman in her apartment, surrounded by books, placing an order on a computer screen—that is to say by showing the action itself rather than its human consequences. What Tomine gave us is a moment, a moment

 Adrian Tomine at Lambiek in Amsterdam. Photo: Rob Becker (1996).

fraught with tension and ambivalence. He could have shown us the bookseller's face so that we could see his disapproval, empathize with the aggrieved, and pat ourselves on the back for this simple indictment of online ordering. But instead, he chose to focus our attention on the woman receiving the package. Her expression telegraphs to us both what's in the box and the intensity of her discomfort. Tomine's goal is not so much to indict one of the actors in a drama but to bring to light the tension between his characters. His images often hinge on the electricity generated by people looking at each other.

Tomine's covers seem pleasingly realistic, and yet on closer inspection, every detail is simultaneously specific and abstracted. We can't recognize the books in the store window or identify which street this is. Yet we recognize the brownstones with old-fashioned air conditioners in the upper-floor windows as those lining the streets of a familiar middle-class residential neighbourhood: this isn't Fifth Avenue. So much is said with so little: because of the store's scale, the man's old-fashioned keys, his frumpy clothes, and his posture, we can assume the man opening the door is the owner of this small shop rather than some alienated employee. Adrian and I debated whether to keep the telltale arrow on the box, but the phenomenon wasn't yet universally recognizable in 2008 and we decided to leave the logo in its abstracted, almost subliminal form.

What makes Tomine's work so striking isn't only apparent in his *New Yorker* covers, of course. He's just as perceptive in his strips. *Scenes from an Impending Marriage*, in which he takes us through the trepidations that he and Sarah, his bride-to-be, experience, is a must to give to any couple who's considering tying the knot. What Tomine consistently achieves in everything he does is to create images of New York or scenes from his own life that are both well-observed, specific snapshots of our time and timeless works in the best *New Yorker* tradition.

Françoise Mouly is the publisher of TOON Books and art editor at the New Yorker, where she has been responsible for more than a thousand covers since 1993. Mouly is the co-creator of the pioneering 1980s comics anthology RAW, the author of Blown Covers, and the editor of Houghton Mifflin's 2012 Best American Comics. Among the many honours she has received are an honorary doctorate from Pratt Institute, gold and silver medals as well as the Richard Gangel Art Director Award from the Society of Illustrators, and France's highest honour, the Legion of Honour.

Shortcomings features one of my favourite characters of all time: Ben Tanaka's best friend, Alice Kim. I love her loyalty to Ben, whose one redeeming quality may be that Alice is his best friend. Alice's friends hate Ben, and she understands why. He says horrible things and makes bad jokes, but the bottom line is that they are friends. As the story unfolds, you can see why Alice is friends with Ben: she sees a little of herself in him. A proud lesbian who has Ben pose as her boyfriend for her parents, she bullies Ben into putting the moves on the woman he is seeing. She is jealous when Ben scores with the "fence-sitter" slash "dabbler." She relentlessly teases him about size. She's flawed, judgmental, just not as bitter. Alice sees that Ben may be unlikeable, but he is in no way unlovable. You can see just how much he wants to engage with the world, how he longs to be carefree and spontaneous, but he just can't. In the end, when he sees his friends changing and growing, he knows he has to figure out how to move on as well. He couldn't do that without Alice.—***Peggy Burns***

In the spring of 1996, I moved to Austin, Texas. Near my apartment was all the great stuff—punk-rock record store, fantastic coffee shop, crummy bar, and a little boutique that sold the kind of tchotchke stuff you buy when you're in your twenties and into "independent" culture. Sort of sci-fi/fifties greaser culture–inspired stuff, just generally dripping with irony and ennui.

In the back they had a little shelf for comics and books. As I recall, there were maybe five or ten, not too many. Tucked in there was a copy of *Optic Nerve* no. 2. The cover jumped out at me: this sad lady just walking down the street. It was the only item in there that wasn't screaming, "*Notice me! Give me attention!*" Since it looked so intriguing and was $2.95, I picked it up. And it was incredible.

Those four stories *still* knock me out. That may be my favourite single issue of a comic ever. "Layover," "Pink Frosting," "Summer Job," and "The Connecting Thread." *Amazing.* And I'll never forget the texture of the cover stock. Before then, most of what I read was slapped together and put out on whatever materials were the cheapest. But this was different; I fell in love with it completely. From there on out, I bought every issue of *Optic Nerve* as they came out, and anytime I found the Drawn & Quarterly logo on a comic, I bought it.

—*Dan Stafford, co-owner of Kilgore Books and Comics and director of Root Hog or Die*

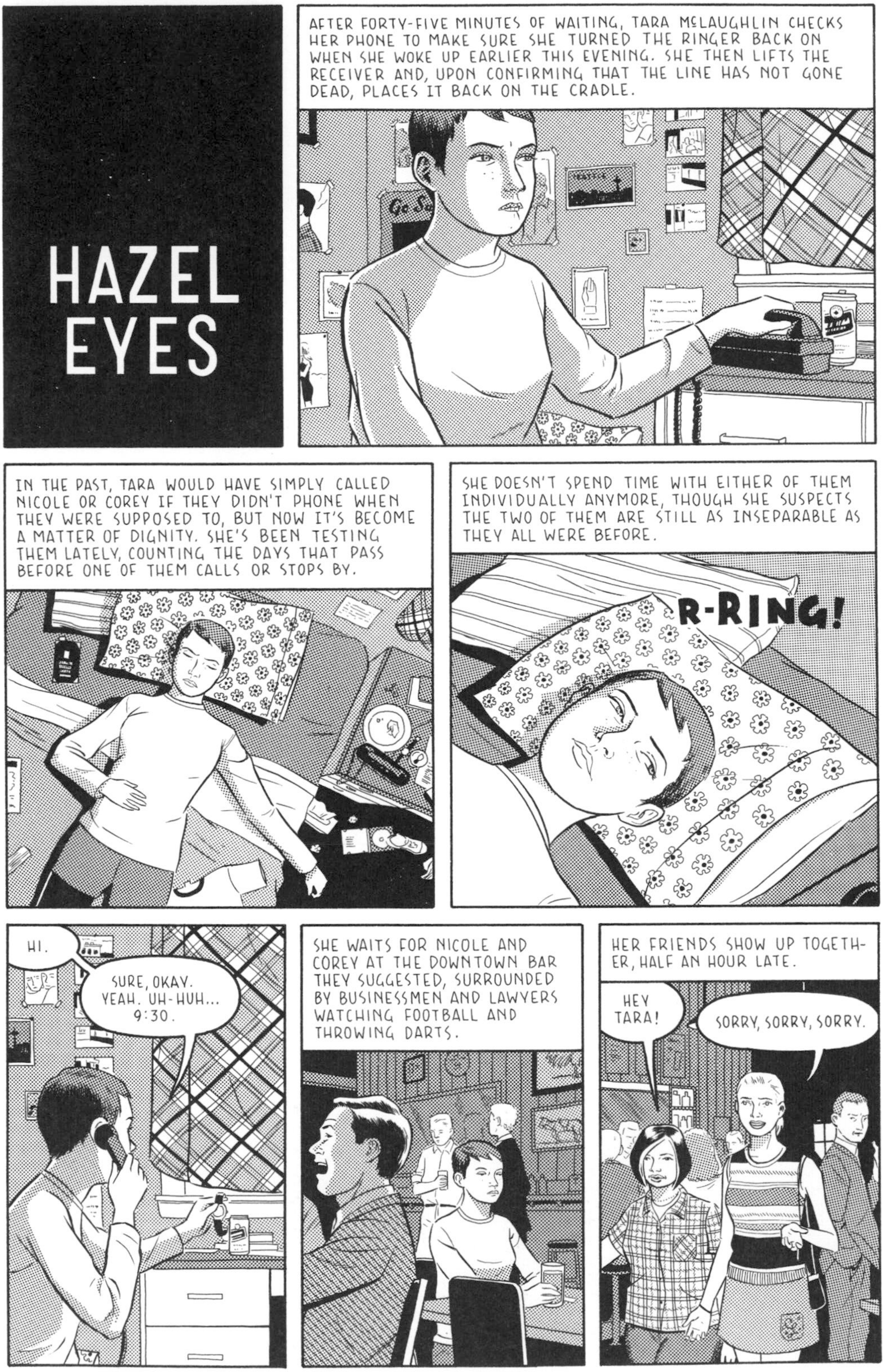
HAZEL EYES
AFTER FORTY-FIVE MINUTES OF WAITING, TARA McLAUGHLIN CHECKS HER PHONE TO MAKE SURE SHE TURNED THE RINGER BACK ON WHEN SHE WOKE UP EARLIER THIS EVENING. SHE THEN LIFTS THE RECEIVER AND, UPON CONFIRMING THAT THE LINE HAS NOT GONE DEAD, PLACES IT BACK ON THE CRADLE.
IN THE PAST, TARA WOULD HAVE SIMPLY CALLED NICOLE OR COREY IF THEY DIDN'T PHONE WHEN THEY WERE SUPPOSED TO, BUT NOW IT'S BECOME A MATTER OF DIGNITY. SHE'S BEEN TESTING THEM LATELY, COUNTING THE DAYS THAT PASS BEFORE ONE OF THEM CALLS OR STOPS BY.
SHE DOESN'T SPEND TIME WITH EITHER OF THEM INDIVIDUALLY ANYMORE, THOUGH SHE SUSPECTS THE TWO OF THEM ARE STILL AS INSEPARABLE AS THEY ALL WERE BEFORE.
R-RING!
HI.
SURE, OKAY. YEAH. UH-HUH... 9:30.
SHE WAITS FOR NICOLE AND COREY AT THE DOWNTOWN BAR THEY SUGGESTED, SURROUNDED BY BUSINESSMEN AND LAWYERS WATCHING FOOTBALL AND THROWING DARTS.
HER FRIENDS SHOW UP TOGETH-ER, HALF AN HOUR LATE.
HEY TARA!
SORRY, SORRY, SORRY.

 "Hazel Eyes" first appeared in *Optic Nerve* no. 4 (1997) and was later published in *Sleepwalk and Other Stories* (1997).

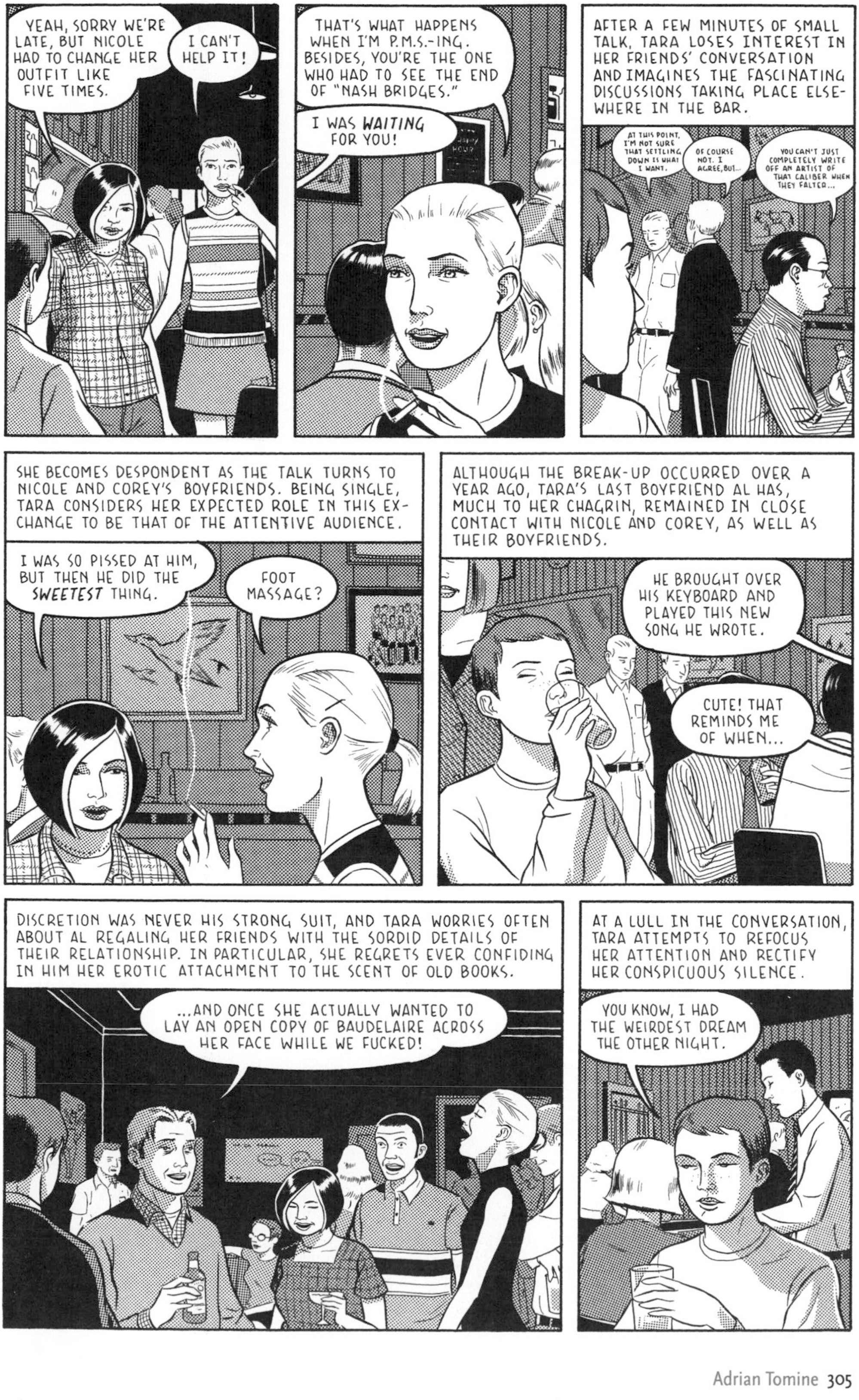
YEAH, SORRY WE'RE LATE, BUT NICOLE HAD TO CHANGE HER OUTFIT LIKE FIVE TIMES.
I CAN'T HELP IT!
THAT'S WHAT HAPPENS WHEN I'M P.M.S.-ING. BESIDES, YOU'RE THE ONE WHO HAD TO SEE THE END OF "NASH BRIDGES."
I WAS *WAITING* FOR YOU!
AFTER A FEW MINUTES OF SMALL TALK, TARA LOSES INTEREST IN HER FRIENDS' CONVERSATION AND IMAGINES THE FASCINATING DISCUSSIONS TAKING PLACE ELSEWHERE IN THE BAR.
AT THIS POINT, I'M NOT SURE THAT SETTLING DOWN IS WHAT I WANT.
OF COURSE NOT. I AGREE, BUT...
YOU CAN'T JUST COMPLETELY WRITE OFF AN ARTIST OF THAT CALIBER WHEN THEY FALTER...
SHE BECOMES DESPONDENT AS THE TALK TURNS TO NICOLE AND COREY'S BOYFRIENDS. BEING SINGLE, TARA CONSIDERS HER EXPECTED ROLE IN THIS EXCHANGE TO BE THAT OF THE ATTENTIVE AUDIENCE.
I WAS SO PISSED AT HIM, BUT THEN HE DID THE *SWEETEST* THING.
FOOT MASSAGE?
ALTHOUGH THE BREAK-UP OCCURRED OVER A YEAR AGO, TARA'S LAST BOYFRIEND AL HAS, MUCH TO HER CHAGRIN, REMAINED IN CLOSE CONTACT WITH NICOLE AND COREY, AS WELL AS THEIR BOYFRIENDS.
HE BROUGHT OVER HIS KEYBOARD AND PLAYED THIS NEW SONG HE WROTE.
CUTE! THAT REMINDS ME OF WHEN...
DISCRETION WAS NEVER HIS STRONG SUIT, AND TARA WORRIES OFTEN ABOUT AL REGALING HER FRIENDS WITH THE SORDID DETAILS OF THEIR RELATIONSHIP. IN PARTICULAR, SHE REGRETS EVER CONFIDING IN HIM HER EROTIC ATTACHMENT TO THE SCENT OF OLD BOOKS.
...AND ONCE SHE ACTUALLY WANTED TO LAY AN OPEN COPY OF BAUDELAIRE ACROSS HER FACE WHILE WE FUCKED!
AT A LULL IN THE CONVERSATION, TARA ATTEMPTS TO REFOCUS HER ATTENTION AND RECTIFY HER CONSPICUOUS SILENCE.
YOU KNOW, I HAD THE WEIRDEST DREAM THE OTHER NIGHT.

"IT WAS ABOUT AL. HE'D COMMITTED SOME CRIME AND WAS BEING SENT AWAY TO LIVE ON A DESERTED ISLAND SOMEWHERE. WE HAD JUST A FEW MINUTES TO TALK BEFORE THE COPS WERE GONNA HAUL HIM AWAY."

"HE TOLD ME THE THING HE WAS GONNA MISS THE MOST WAS LOOKING AT MY HAZEL EYES. I TOLD HIM THE THING I WAS GONNA MISS THE MOST WAS FEELING HIS SMOOTH SKIN."

"SO WE AGREED TO TRADE. HE STUCK HIS FINGERS INTO MY LEFT SOCKET AND PULLED OUT THE EYEBALL."

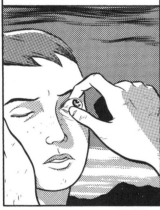

"THEN I DUG MY NAILS INTO HIS ARM AND PEELED OFF A CHUNK OF SKIN. THERE WASN'T ANY BLOOD OR ANYTHING..."

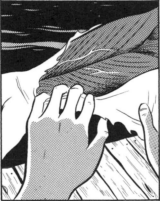

TARA'S VOICE TRAILS OFF AS SHE NOTICES NICOLE AND COREY EXCHANGE BRIEF, KNOWING GLANCES.

WHAT?

WHAT WAS THAT LOOK FOR?

NOTHING! IT'S JUST... YOU'RE ALWAYS HAVING THESE *FREAKY* DREAMS. THEY'RE SO...*VIVID.*

YEAH, I HARDLY *EVER* HAVE DREAMS LIKE THAT. IT'S ALMOST LIKE A MOVIE OR SOMETHING.

TARA FEELS A SWELL OF DEFENSIVENESS, BUT MAKES A CONCERTED EFFORT TO REMAIN AGREEABLE.

WELL, I TOLD YOU IT WAS PRETTY WEIRD.

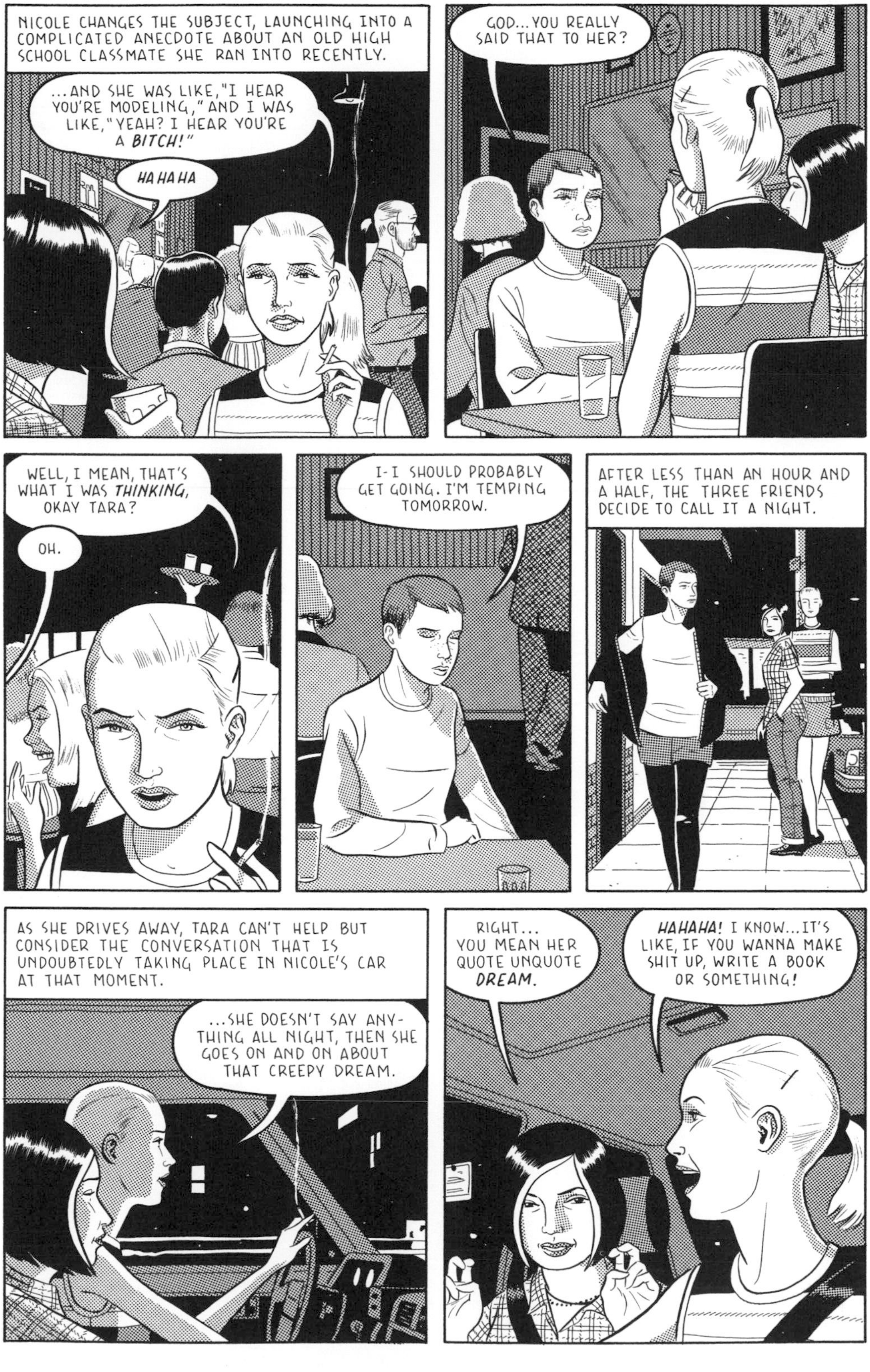

NICOLE CHANGES THE SUBJECT, LAUNCHING INTO A COMPLICATED ANECDOTE ABOUT AN OLD HIGH SCHOOL CLASSMATE SHE RAN INTO RECENTLY.
...AND SHE WAS LIKE, "I HEAR YOU'RE MODELING," AND I WAS LIKE, "YEAH? I HEAR YOU'RE A *BITCH!*"
HAHAHA
GOD... YOU REALLY SAID THAT TO HER?
WELL, I MEAN, THAT'S WHAT I WAS *THINKING*, OKAY TARA?
OH.
I-I SHOULD PROBABLY GET GOING. I'M TEMPING TOMORROW.
AFTER LESS THAN AN HOUR AND A HALF, THE THREE FRIENDS DECIDE TO CALL IT A NIGHT.
AS SHE DRIVES AWAY, TARA CAN'T HELP BUT CONSIDER THE CONVERSATION THAT IS UNDOUBTEDLY TAKING PLACE IN NICOLE'S CAR AT THAT MOMENT.
...SHE DOESN'T SAY ANYTHING ALL NIGHT, THEN SHE GOES ON AND ON ABOUT THAT CREEPY DREAM.
RIGHT... YOU MEAN HER QUOTE UNQUOTE *DREAM*.
HAHAHA! I KNOW... IT'S LIKE, IF YOU WANNA MAKE SHIT UP, WRITE A BOOK OR SOMETHING!

"AND PLUS, QUIT PATHETICALLY TALKING ABOUT A GUY WHO *DUMPED* YOU!"
"YEAH...LIKE TWO YEARS AGO!"

...FUCKING *HATE* YOU...

TARA DRIVES TO AN OLDER, EMPTIER BAR ON THE OUTSKIRTS OF TOWN AND EMBARKS ON A SERIES OF DRINKS, ALTERNATING VODKA GIMLETS AND BEER.

...BUT I MEAN, BACK IN SCHOOL, ME AND THIS GIRL AMBER WERE *CLOSE*. THAT'S WHY IT PISSED ME OFF SO MUCH.

MM-HMN?

SO ANYWAY, LAST WEEK I'M OVER AT LUCKY'S, AND GUESS WHO I BUMP INTO? IT'S AMBER, AND SHE JUST MOVED BACK FROM BOSTON.

SO SHE STARTS TALK-ING TO ME AND SHE'S LIKE, "I HEAR YOU'RE MODELING," AND I'M LIKE, "YEAH? I HEAR YOU'RE A *BITCH*!"

HMM.

HEY, LOOK AT MY EYES. SOMEBODY TOLD ME ONCE, "I CAN OVERLOOK ALL YOUR SHIT BECAUSE OF THEM."

HA HA

EXIT

YOU EVER HAVE THAT? WHERE JUST ONE GOOD THING ABOUT SOMEONE IS ENOUGH?

I DON'T KNOW... I GUESS...

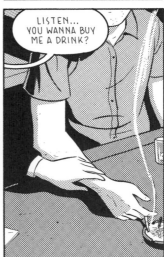

LISTEN... YOU WANNA BUY ME A DRINK?

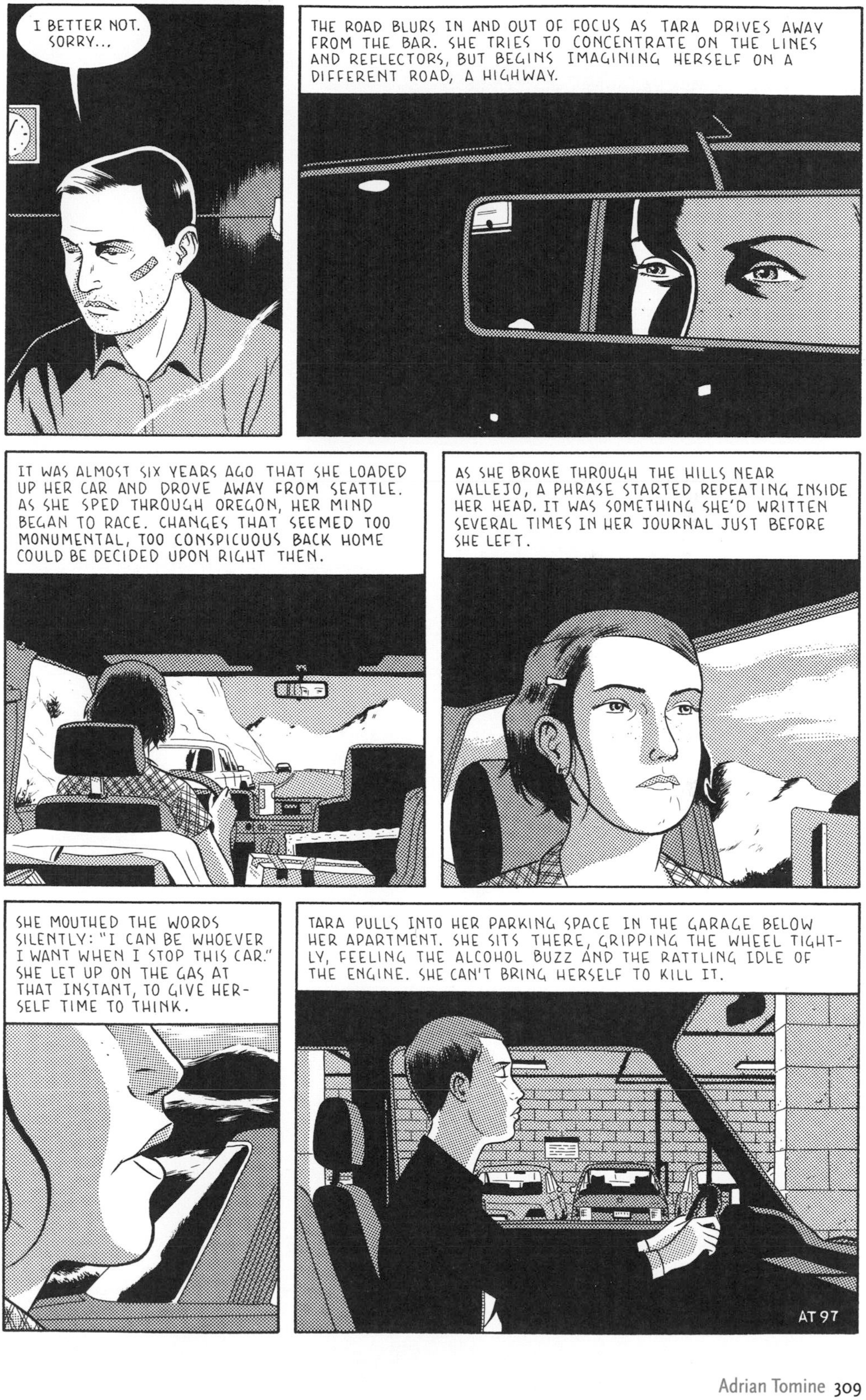
I BETTER NOT. SORRY...
THE ROAD BLURS IN AND OUT OF FOCUS AS TARA DRIVES AWAY FROM THE BAR. SHE TRIES TO CONCENTRATE ON THE LINES AND REFLECTORS, BUT BEGINS IMAGINING HERSELF ON A DIFFERENT ROAD, A HIGHWAY.
IT WAS ALMOST SIX YEARS AGO THAT SHE LOADED UP HER CAR AND DROVE AWAY FROM SEATTLE. AS SHE SPED THROUGH OREGON, HER MIND BEGAN TO RACE. CHANGES THAT SEEMED TOO MONUMENTAL, TOO CONSPICUOUS BACK HOME COULD BE DECIDED UPON RIGHT THEN.
AS SHE BROKE THROUGH THE HILLS NEAR VALLEJO, A PHRASE STARTED REPEATING INSIDE HER HEAD. IT WAS SOMETHING SHE'D WRITTEN SEVERAL TIMES IN HER JOURNAL JUST BEFORE SHE LEFT.
SHE MOUTHED THE WORDS SILENTLY: "I CAN BE WHOEVER I WANT WHEN I STOP THIS CAR." SHE LET UP ON THE GAS AT THAT INSTANT, TO GIVE HER-SELF TIME TO THINK.
TARA PULLS INTO HER PARKING SPACE IN THE GARAGE BELOW HER APARTMENT. SHE SITS THERE, GRIPPING THE WHEEL TIGHT-LY, FEELING THE ALCOHOL BUZZ AND THE RATTLING IDLE OF THE ENGINE. SHE CAN'T BRING HERSELF TO KILL IT.
AT 97

Pink Frosting

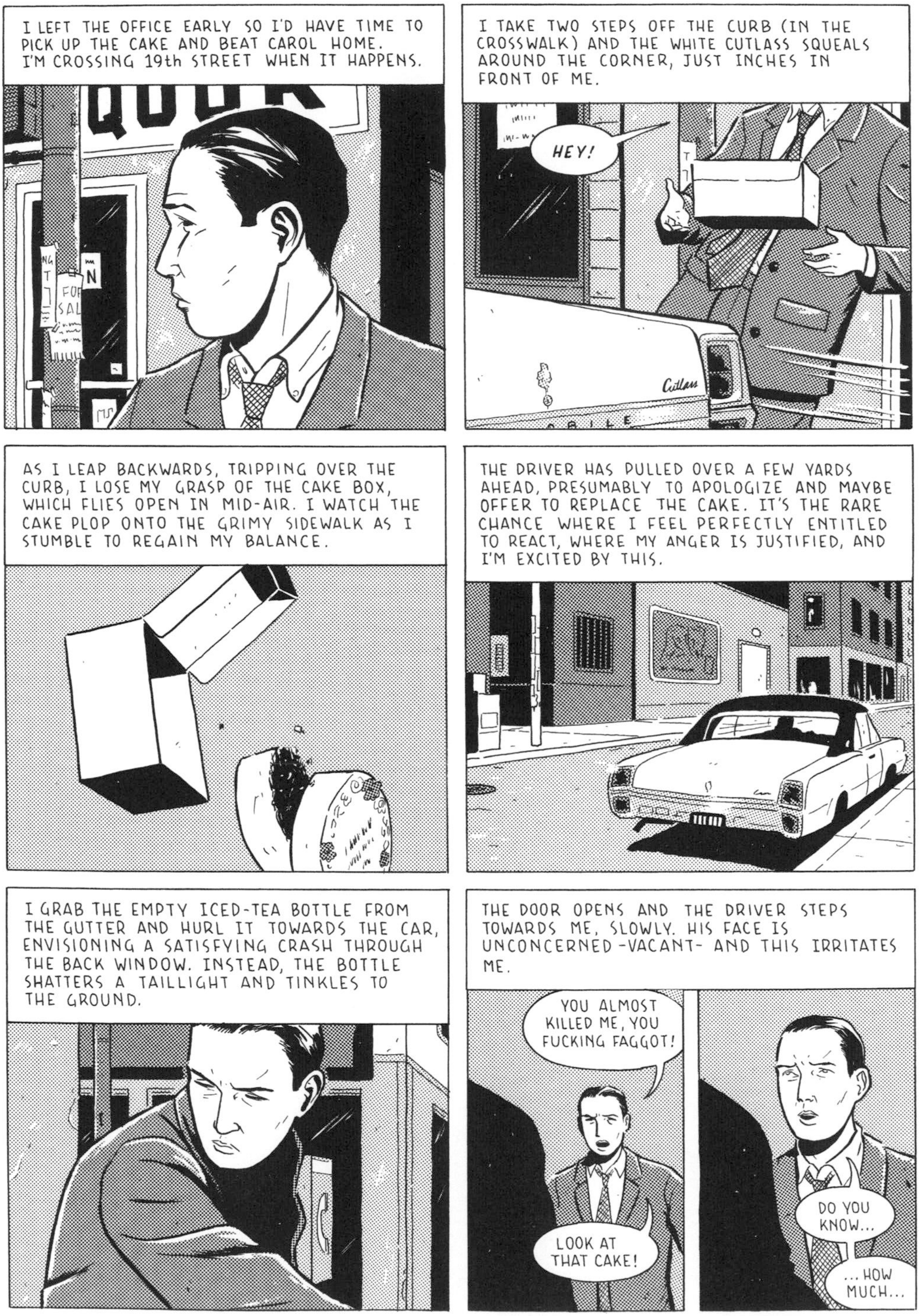
I LEFT THE OFFICE EARLY SO I'D HAVE TIME TO PICK UP THE CAKE AND BEAT CAROL HOME. I'M CROSSING 19th STREET WHEN IT HAPPENS.
I TAKE TWO STEPS OFF THE CURB (IN THE CROSSWALK) AND THE WHITE CUTLASS SQUEALS AROUND THE CORNER, JUST INCHES IN FRONT OF ME.
HEY!
Cutlass
AS I LEAP BACKWARDS, TRIPPING OVER THE CURB, I LOSE MY GRASP OF THE CAKE BOX, WHICH FLIES OPEN IN MID-AIR. I WATCH THE CAKE PLOP ONTO THE GRIMY SIDEWALK AS I STUMBLE TO REGAIN MY BALANCE.
THE DRIVER HAS PULLED OVER A FEW YARDS AHEAD, PRESUMABLY TO APOLOGIZE AND MAYBE OFFER TO REPLACE THE CAKE. IT'S THE RARE CHANCE WHERE I FEEL PERFECTLY ENTITLED TO REACT, WHERE MY ANGER IS JUSTIFIED, AND I'M EXCITED BY THIS.
I GRAB THE EMPTY ICED-TEA BOTTLE FROM THE GUTTER AND HURL IT TOWARDS THE CAR, ENVISIONING A SATISFYING CRASH THROUGH THE BACK WINDOW. INSTEAD, THE BOTTLE SHATTERS A TAILLIGHT AND TINKLES TO THE GROUND.
THE DOOR OPENS AND THE DRIVER STEPS TOWARDS ME, SLOWLY. HIS FACE IS UNCONCERNED -VACANT- AND THIS IRRITATES ME.
YOU ALMOST KILLED ME, YOU FUCKING FAGGOT!
LOOK AT THAT CAKE!
DO YOU KNOW...
...HOW MUCH...

 “Pink Frosting” first appeared in *Optic Nerve* no. 2 (1995) and was later published in *Sleepwalk and Other Stories* (1997).

IT ISN'T UNTIL A SPLIT SECOND AFTERWARDS THAT I REALIZE I'VE BEEN HIT. MY NOSE EXPLODES AND I DROP TO THE PAVEMENT. IT OCCURS TO ME THAT IT'S THE FIRST TIME I'VE EVER REALLY BEEN PUNCHED.

I KNOW I SHOULD GET UP AND PUNCH BACK OR RUN OR SAY SOMETHING, BUT PAIN AND DISBELIEF GRIP ME AND I JUST LIE THERE, SILENT. I CAN'T EVEN RESIST WHEN THE DRIVER DRAGS ME OFF THE SIDEWALK, INTO THE GUTTER.

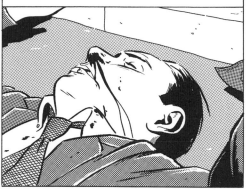

HE SAYS SOMETHING THAT I DON'T QUITE UNDERSTAND, AND THEN SAYS IT AGAIN WHEN I DON'T RESPOND.

BITE THE CURB.

I LOOK UP AT HIS FACE AS HE REPEATS HIMSELF, THIS TIME MUCH LOUDER. I MAKE A SUDDEN MOVE TO GET UP AND HE KICKS ME HARD IN THE SIDE AND I WONDER WHY NO ONE IS DOING ANYTHING TO STOP THIS.

DO IT!

I GET UP ON MY HANDS AND KNEES AND CRAWL FORWARD, UNCERTAIN OF HIS INTENT. THE CURB IS SMEARED WITH PINK FROSTING FROM THE CAKE, AND I TASTE THE COMFORTING SWEETNESS AS MY TEETH SETTLE AGAINST THE CEMENT.

HE LIFTS ONE FOOT, RAISING IT BEHIND MY HEAD. RIGHT NOW, CAROL IS WALKING THROUGH THE FRONT DOOR. SHE LOOKS AROUND AT THE CREPE PAPER AND BALLOONS, AND FOR A MOMENT, WAITS FOR ME TO LEAP OUT AND YELL "SURPRISE!"

WINTER, 2012

GOD DAMN FUCKING PIECE OF--

HI DAD!

OH, HI GUYS! I DIDN'T HEAR YOU COME IN!

WHAT'S WRONG?

WELL, YOU KNOW THAT GIANT STACK OF PAPER I BOUGHT? IT'S A TOTAL DISASTER!

I SPENT THREE DAYS PENCILING THIS PAGE, AND WHEN I TRIED TO INK IT, THE LINES BLED LIKE I WAS DRAWING ON TOILET PAPER!

I'VE BEEN USING THIS BRAND FOR TWENTY YEARS AND NOW IT'S GARBAGE!

SEE?

AND IT'S NOT JUST THE PAPER! THESE NEW ▬▬▬▬ PENS ARE HORRIBLE! WHY DOES EVERY-THING IN THE WORLD KEEP GETTING WORSE?!

HOW WAS BALLET CLASS?

LATER...

I'VE BEEN HAVING TROUBLE WITH ▬▬▬▬ BRISTOL BOARD LATELY. CAN YOU RECOMMEND A BRAND THAT DOESN'T BLEED?

HAVE YOU TRIED USING A CINTIQ? THERE'S A BIT OF A LEARNING CURVE, BUT IT'S REALLY QUITE AMAZING.

WHY WOULD YOU SAY THAT? I CAME TO YOUR "BRICK AND MORTAR" ART STORE TO BUY PAPER, AND YOU'RE PROSELYTIZ-ING ABOUT COMPUTER GADGETS?

HEY, I'M JUST TALK-ING TO YOU AS A FELLOW ARTIST! YOU'RE THE ONE COMPLAINING ABOUT PAPER, AND I'M TRYING TO HELP!

THERE WAS PROB-ABLY A TIME WHEN BRISTOL BOARD WAS A SCARY INNOVA-TION TO PEOPLE LIKE YOU!

IDIOT!

BUT SOON...

MAYBE HE HAS A POINT. AM I JUST A STODGY COWARD? IS IT TIME TO "EVOLVE OR DIE"?

BOOKS

HI...I'M LOOKING FOR A BOOK...IT'S A BIO-GRAPHY OF CROCKETT JOHNSON AND RUTH KRAUSS...?

IF IT'S NOT ON THE SHELF, WE DON'T HAVE IT. I COULD ORDER IT FOR YOU, BUT IT'S PROBABLY CHEAPER TO JUST GET IT FROM AMAZON.

UNBELIEVABLE! IS THAT WHAT IT'S COME TO? AT VERY LEAST, WOULDN'T YOU WANT TO GO DOWN SWINGING?

:SIGH:

MIGHT AS WELL CHECK MY P.O. BOX WHILE I'M OUT.

WELL, THE VOLUME HAS CERTAINLY DWINDLED IN RECENT YEARS, BUT THERE'S ALWAYS AT LEAST A LITTLE BIT OF MAIL HERE TO LIFT MY SPIRITS.

IT'S HARD TO BE TOO CYNICAL WHEN THERE ARE STILL READERS OUT THERE WHO TAKE THE TIME TO SEND ME THOUGHT-FUL, HAND-WRITTEN NOTES THROUGH THE MAIL.

FPP

tomine don't be an asshole put your shit on ipad / kindle get on fb and twitter print email address check out my tumblr

"Winter 2012" first appeared in *Optic Nerve* no. 13 (2013).

OPTIC NERVE

WHAT ARE YOU DOING?
OH, NO... ARE YOU LOOKING AT THOSE STUPID **MESSAGE BOARDS** AGAIN?
LISTEN TO THIS: "IMHO, OPTIC NERVE WILL ALWAYS BE THE POOR MAN'S MR. VISION. HE SHOULD'VE STAYED A SIDE-KICK."
WHEN ARE YOU GOING TO REALIZE THAT THE PEOPLE WHO FEEL THE NEED TO BROADCAST THEIR OPINIONS LIKE THAT ARE JUST LONELY IDIOTS?
IF IT WAS JUST ONE NUT-JOB, THAT WOULD BE FINE. BUT YOU SCROLL DOWN, AND PEOPLE MOSTLY AGREE!
YOU CAN'T JUST DISMISS THAT KIND OF CONSENSUS!

"Optic Nerve" first appeared in no. 33 of *McSweeney's: The San Francisco Panorama* (2010).

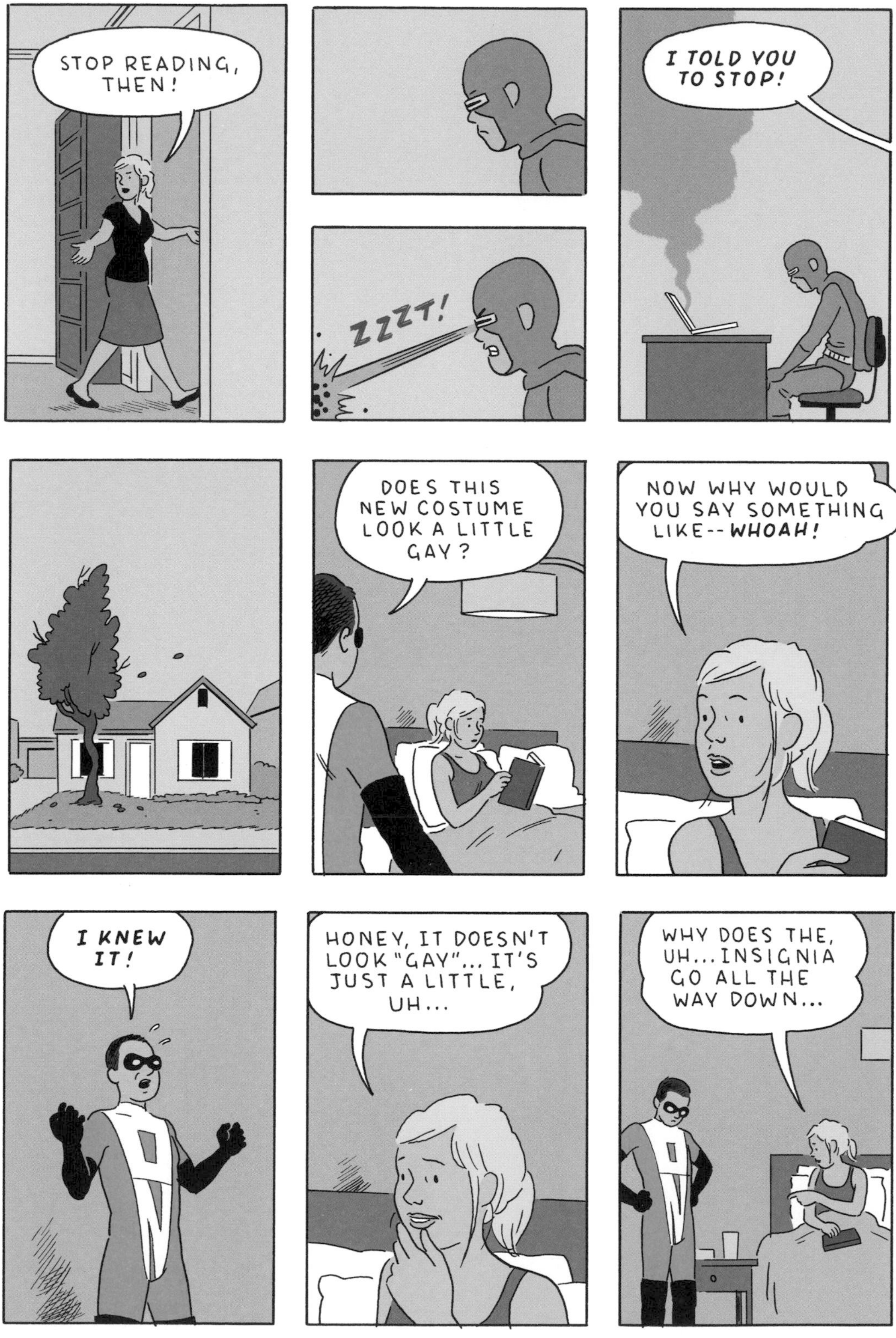
STOP READING, THEN!
ZZZT!
I TOLD YOU TO STOP!
DOES THIS NEW COSTUME LOOK A LITTLE GAY?
NOW WHY WOULD YOU SAY SOMETHING LIKE--WHOAH!
I KNEW IT!
HONEY, IT DOESN'T LOOK "GAY"... IT'S JUST A LITTLE, UH...
WHY DOES THE, UH... INSIGNIA GO ALL THE WAY DOWN...

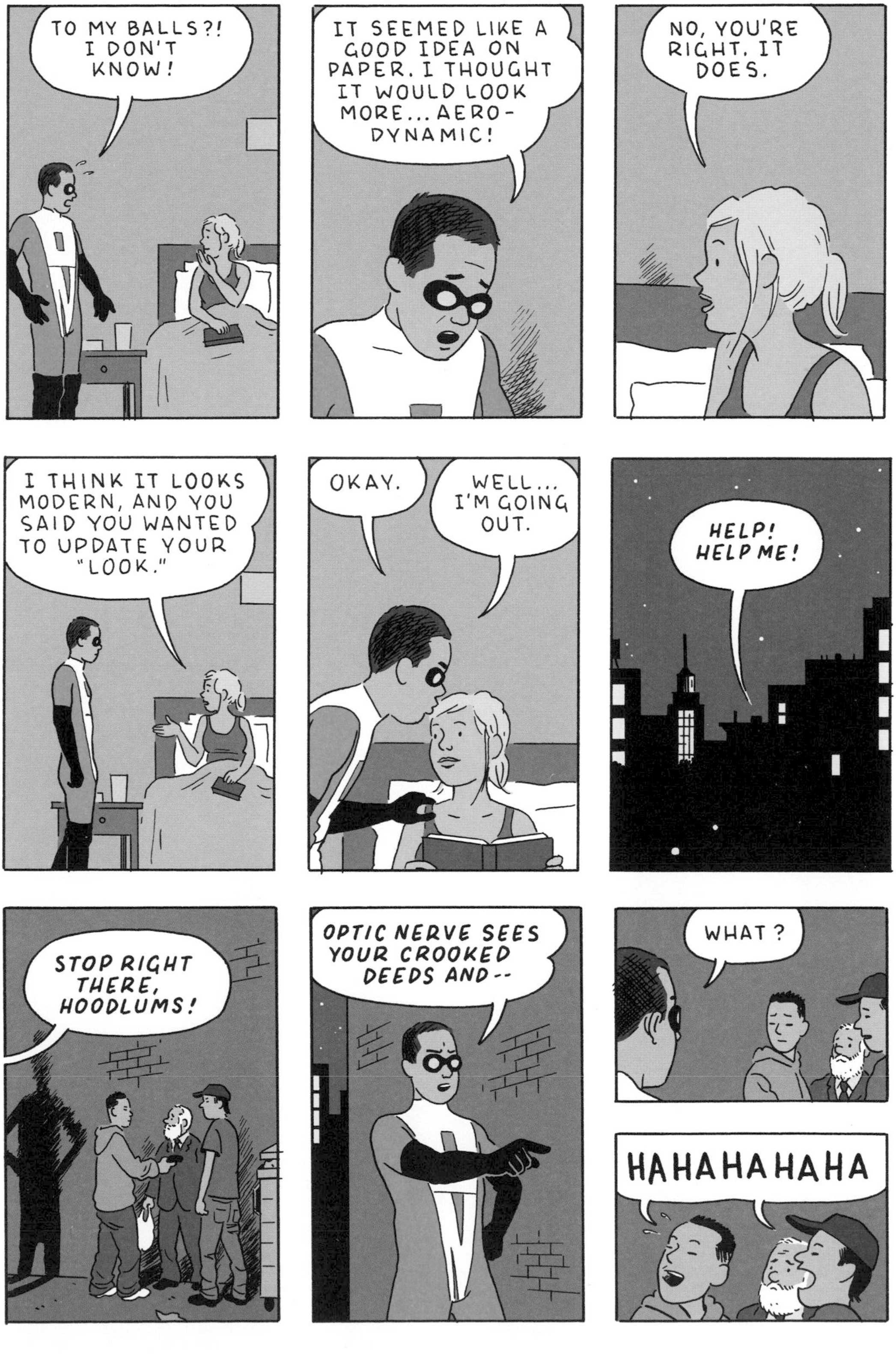
TO MY BALLS?! I DON'T KNOW!
IT SEEMED LIKE A GOOD IDEA ON PAPER. I THOUGHT IT WOULD LOOK MORE... AERO-DYNAMIC!
NO, YOU'RE RIGHT. IT DOES.
I THINK IT LOOKS MODERN, AND YOU SAID YOU WANTED TO UPDATE YOUR "LOOK."
OKAY.
WELL... I'M GOING OUT.
HELP! HELP ME!
STOP RIGHT THERE, HOODLUMS!
OPTIC NERVE SEES YOUR CROOKED DEEDS AND --
WHAT?
HAHAHAHAHA

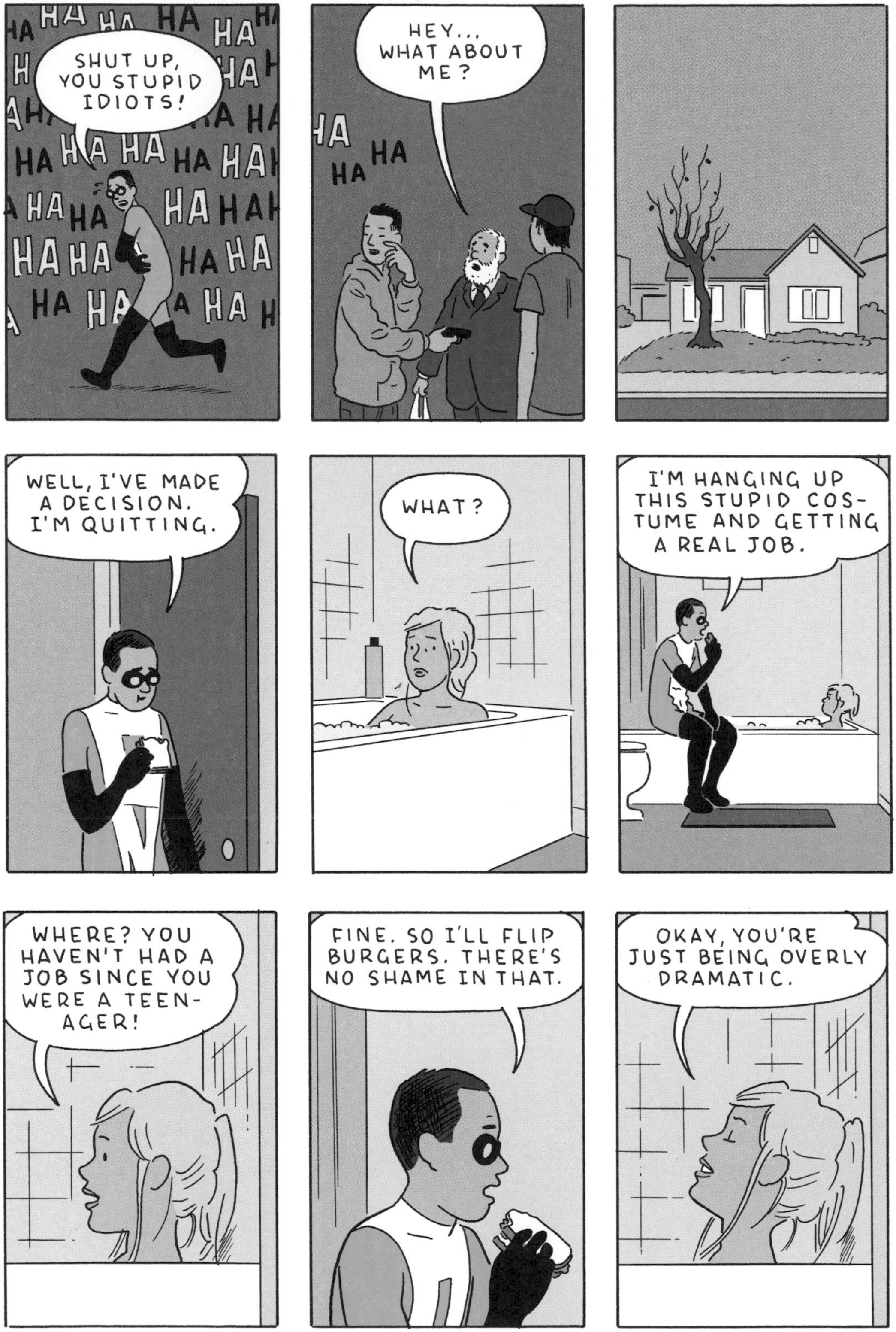

HA HA HA HA HA HA
SHUT UP, YOU STUPID IDIOTS!
HA HA HA HA HA HA HA HA HA HA HA HA HA HA HA HA HA HA HA HA
HA HA HA
HEY... WHAT ABOUT ME?
WELL, I'VE MADE A DECISION. I'M QUITTING.
WHAT?
I'M HANGING UP THIS STUPID COS-TUME AND GETTING A REAL JOB.
WHERE? YOU HAVEN'T HAD A JOB SINCE YOU WERE A TEEN-AGER!
FINE. SO I'LL FLIP BURGERS. THERE'S NO SHAME IN THAT.
OKAY, YOU'RE JUST BEING OVERLY DRAMATIC.

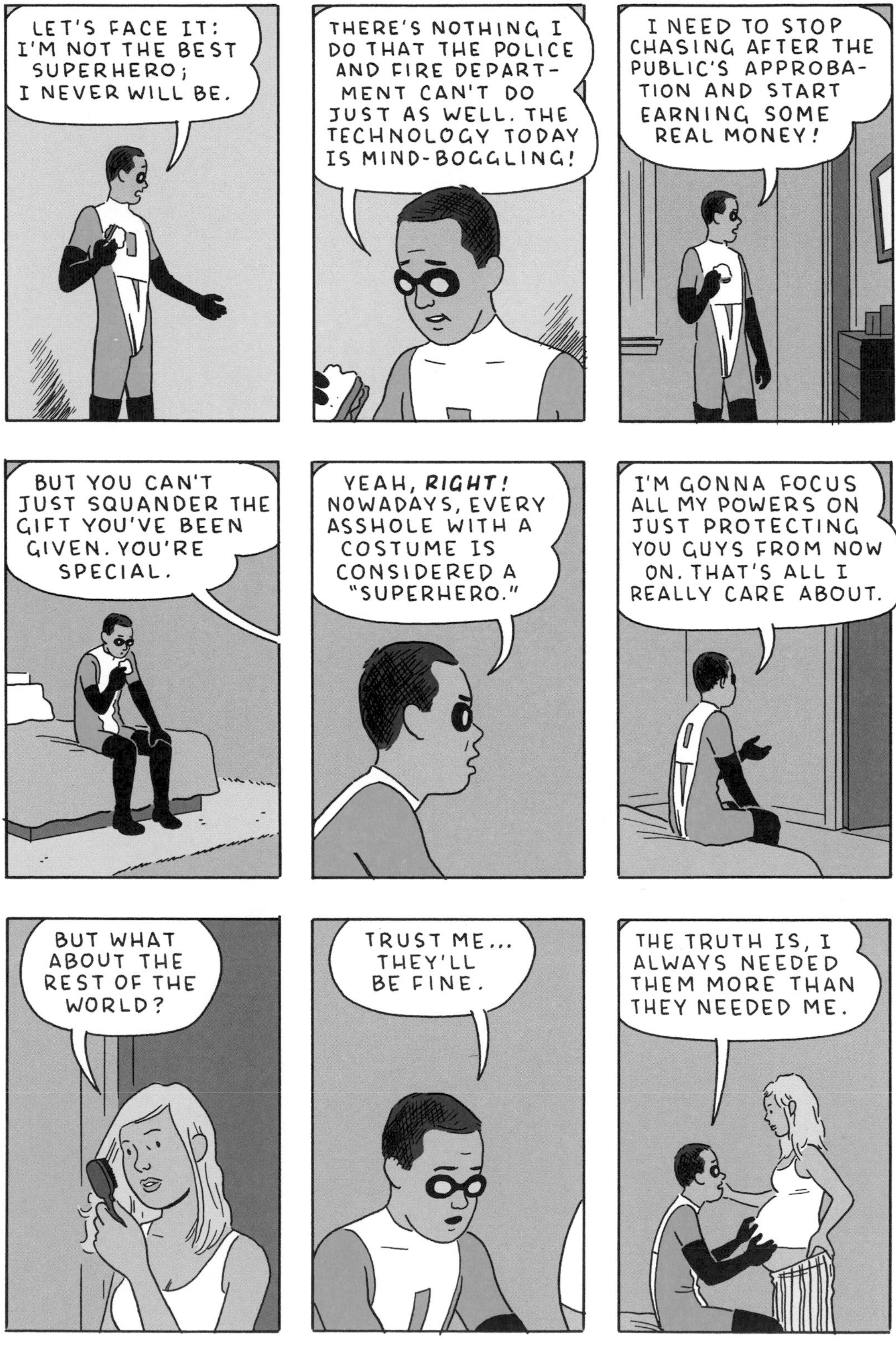
LET'S FACE IT: I'M NOT THE BEST SUPERHERO; I NEVER WILL BE.
THERE'S NOTHING I DO THAT THE POLICE AND FIRE DEPARTMENT CAN'T DO JUST AS WELL. THE TECHNOLOGY TODAY IS MIND-BOGGLING!
I NEED TO STOP CHASING AFTER THE PUBLIC'S APPROBATION AND START EARNING SOME REAL MONEY!
BUT YOU CAN'T JUST SQUANDER THE GIFT YOU'VE BEEN GIVEN. YOU'RE SPECIAL.
YEAH, **RIGHT!** NOWADAYS, EVERY ASSHOLE WITH A COSTUME IS CONSIDERED A "SUPERHERO."
I'M GONNA FOCUS ALL MY POWERS ON JUST PROTECTING YOU GUYS FROM NOW ON. THAT'S ALL I REALLY CARE ABOUT.
BUT WHAT ABOUT THE REST OF THE WORLD?
TRUST ME... THEY'LL BE FINE.
THE TRUTH IS, I ALWAYS NEEDED THEM MORE THAN THEY NEEDED ME.

Yoshihiro Tatsumi was a name I'd heard only in passing, in the footnotes of articles online, or next to a small thumbnail cover in a few paragraphs in Fred Schodt's pioneering tome on Japanese comics, *Manga! Manga!* Growing up in the very first generation of junior high school students raised on the availability of translated manga, my obsession with mainstream adventure and science fiction comics took a turn to the obscure, dark, and literary during college and the years after graduation. Even during trips to Japan in the mid-2000s spent hunting for weird horror and experimental manga, I never encountered the works of Tatsumi—he remained simply a name I saw referenced in the history of manga, always in the context of his relationship to Osamu Tezuka, someone that Fred and my friend Anne Ishii told me was key to understanding the development of manga during a potent and tumultuous period of Japanese theatre, music, and culture in the early 1970s.

The Push Man and Other Stories was a real breakthrough piece of literature for me, one that connected all these wild threads and styles and interconnected drama through the development of manga and gekiga. The individual short stories in the three collections of Yoshihiro Tatsumi work published by Drawn & Quarterly captivated me entirely—his subtle comics shook me up in their depravity and banality, and with how unforeign they seemed after I'd wanted to find and read them for so many years. Meeting Tatsumi in person in 2009 at Toronto Comic Arts Festival remains one of my fondest memories as a reader of books, and it is gratifying to see Yoshihiro Tatsumi now thoroughly enshrined in the canon of comics for readers worldwide.

—Ryan Sands, publisher, Youth in Decline

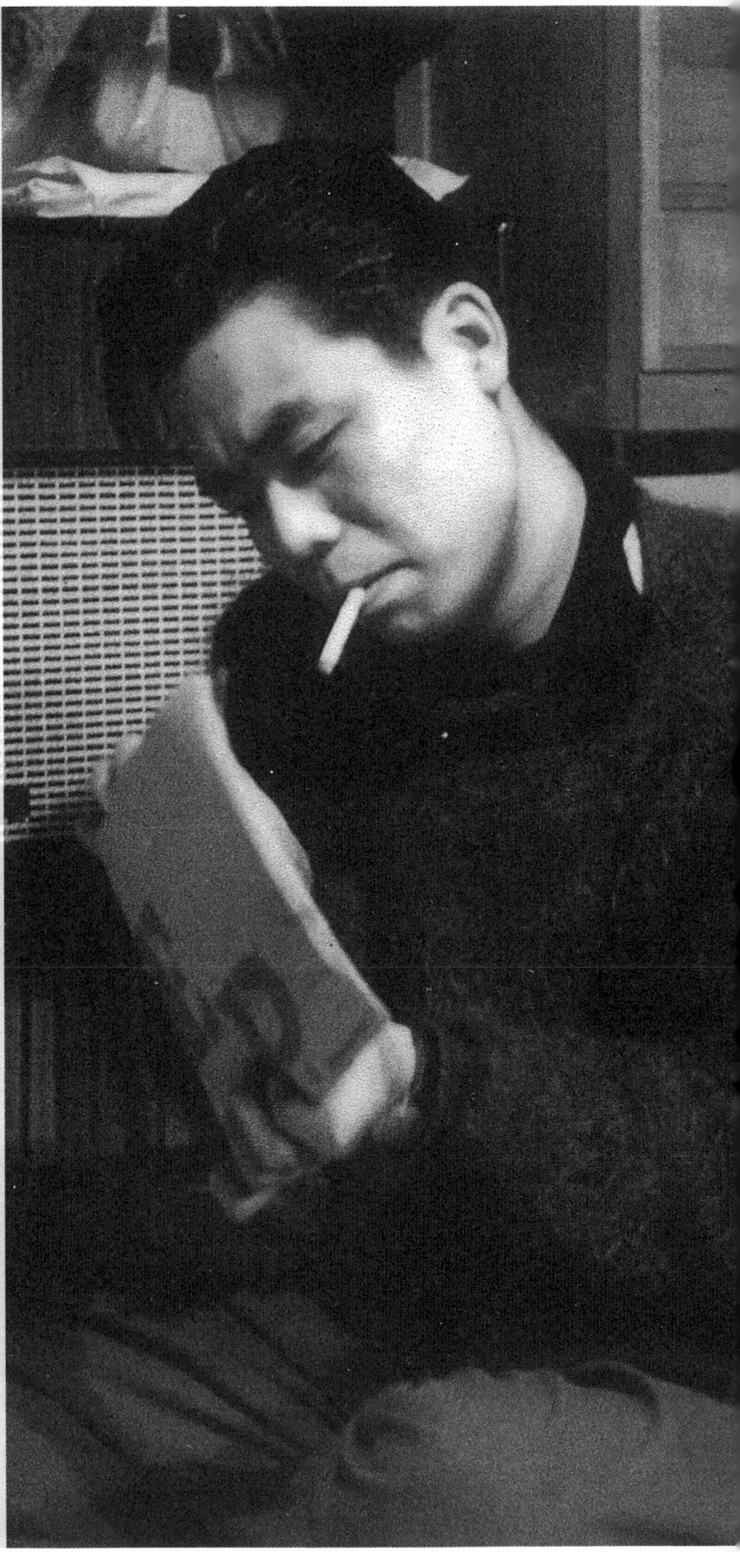

YOSHIHIRO TATSUMI

an appreciation by Adrian Tomine, Yoshihiro Tatsumi's English-language editor*

In 1988, at the age of fourteen, I experienced a crisis of faith. Except, instead of doubting longheld religious beliefs, I was suddenly questioning my lifelong love of comic books. I found myself ritualistically purchasing the latest issue of, say, *Web of Spider-Man*, filing it away in protective Mylar and acid-free cardboard, but increasingly skipping the step of actually reading the thing. I became depressed by the possibility that comics were yet another childhood hobby, like skateboards or action figures, that I'd suddenly outgrown. In a last-ditch effort to resuscitate my interest and justify my weekly trips to the comic store, I began a process of wild experimentation, giving almost anything that seemed unusual or "alternative" a try. For every five (or ten) disappointments, there was usually one gem, and one such find was *Good-Bye* by Yoshihiro Tatsumi. This book (along with others such as *Love and Rockets*, *Weirdo*, and *RAW*) not only reignited my passion for comics, but it made very clear to me the now-commonplace fact that comics were simply a medium, just as capable of expressing personal, artistic stories for adults as they were of indulging childhood fantasy.

At the time, Tatsumi's work seemed to me like a refreshing, eye-opening rebellion against everything I'd come to expect from comics. Unlike the garish, full-colour, action-packed comic art I'd grown up with, Tatsumi's visuals were restrained, minimal, and stylized in a manner that seemed appealingly foreign. The potentially discordant placement of slightly cartoon-y characters within realistic backgrounds worked beautifully, communicating a sense of place and emotion that more photorealistic comics couldn't approach. Instead of epic, ever-continuing storylines, Tatsumi's work comprised compact, elliptical short stories which, like the best modern prose fiction, were simultaneously satisfying and open-ended. The stories' focus alternated between stretches of mundane daily life and moments of surprising violence and sexuality, and both extremes were equally refreshing and unsettling to me. In place of one-dimensional heroes and villains, there were real people: faces in a crowd, seemingly plucked at random and then examined down to their darkest, most private moments. Characters didn't recur from story to story, but the depiction of an overwhelming, alienating modern world remained constant. I had seen some Japanese comics, or manga, before, but none of it had appealed to me in the way that Tatsumi's did.

In the years since that discovery, I've managed to become a cartoonist myself; examining Tatsumi's work now, I'm pleased to find that it holds up just as well as it did upon my first exposure to it. But instead of viewing it in relation to the subpar comics I was attempting to replace at the time, I see it simply as a significant work of modern cartooning. Like all my favourite comics, from *Peanuts* to *Yummy Fur* to *Eightball*, it reads like the direct expression of a personality that is keenly observant, deeply self-critical, and constantly torn between sympathy and misanthropy.

Critics have always been eager to identify the various influences that are so apparent in my comics, and I've never denied my great debt to American artists such as the Hernandez brothers and Daniel Clowes. In revisiting the work of Tatsumi, it's now apparent to me how much his comics also impacted me, and I'm sure that elements of his style continue to influence my work to this day.

In November 2012 I met Yoshihiro Tatsumi while on a business trip to Japan. We were at a restaurant in Tokyo when he arrived carrying a box that seemed a little too large and unwieldy for a man who was then seventy-seven. He opened the box and pulled out approximately two hundred pages of original artwork, all early pencil drafts for the upcoming second volume of his memoir, *A Drifting Life*. The first volume, a *New York Times* bestseller when it was first published in English in 2009, covered the formative years of his life as a *manga-ka* in 1950s Japan. With this follow-up book, Tatsumi takes us through a much broader timeframe, from his days as a *Garo* artist mainstay right through to the early 2000s and his first meeting with his English-language editor, Adrian Tomine. An excerpt from this new volume is presented on the following pages.
—*Chris Oliveros*

---

*An unabridged version of this essay originally appeared in The Push Man and Other Stories by Yoshihiro Tatsumi (2005).

A DRIFTING LIFE PART TWO (SELECTION)

TRANSLATED BY ZACK DAVISSON

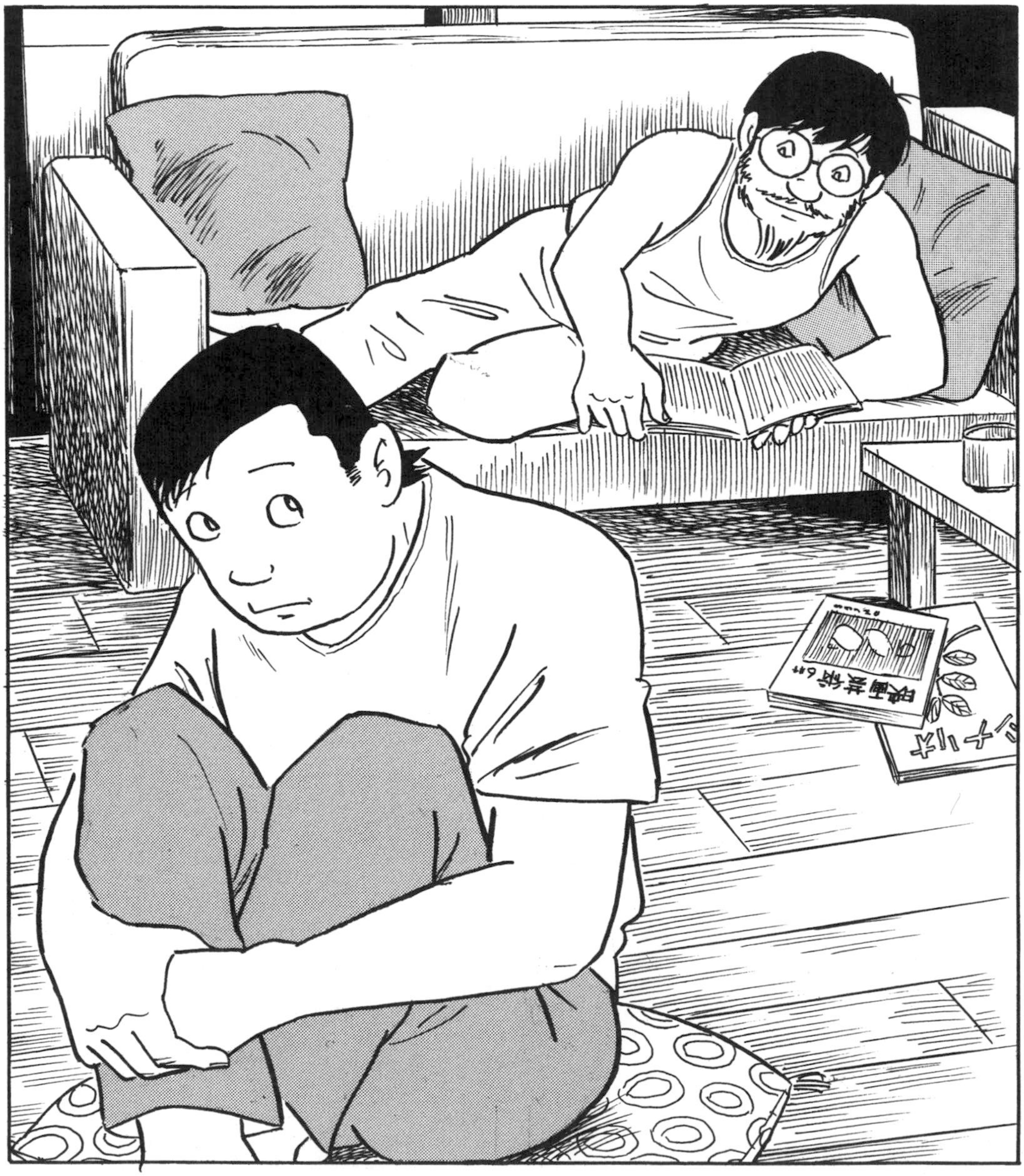

VROOOOMMM

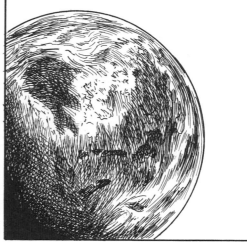

AUGUST 19, 1960
SOVIET RUSSIA
SUCESSFULLY LAUNCHES
ANOTHER SPUTNIK, WITH A
PAIR OF LAIKAS ON BOARD.

BOTH DOGS HAVE
BEEN RETURNED TO
EARTH SAFELY.

NOTE: THIS WAS THE KORABL—SPUTNIK 2 SPACECRAFT, OFTEN MISTAKENLY REFERRED TO AS SPUTNIK.

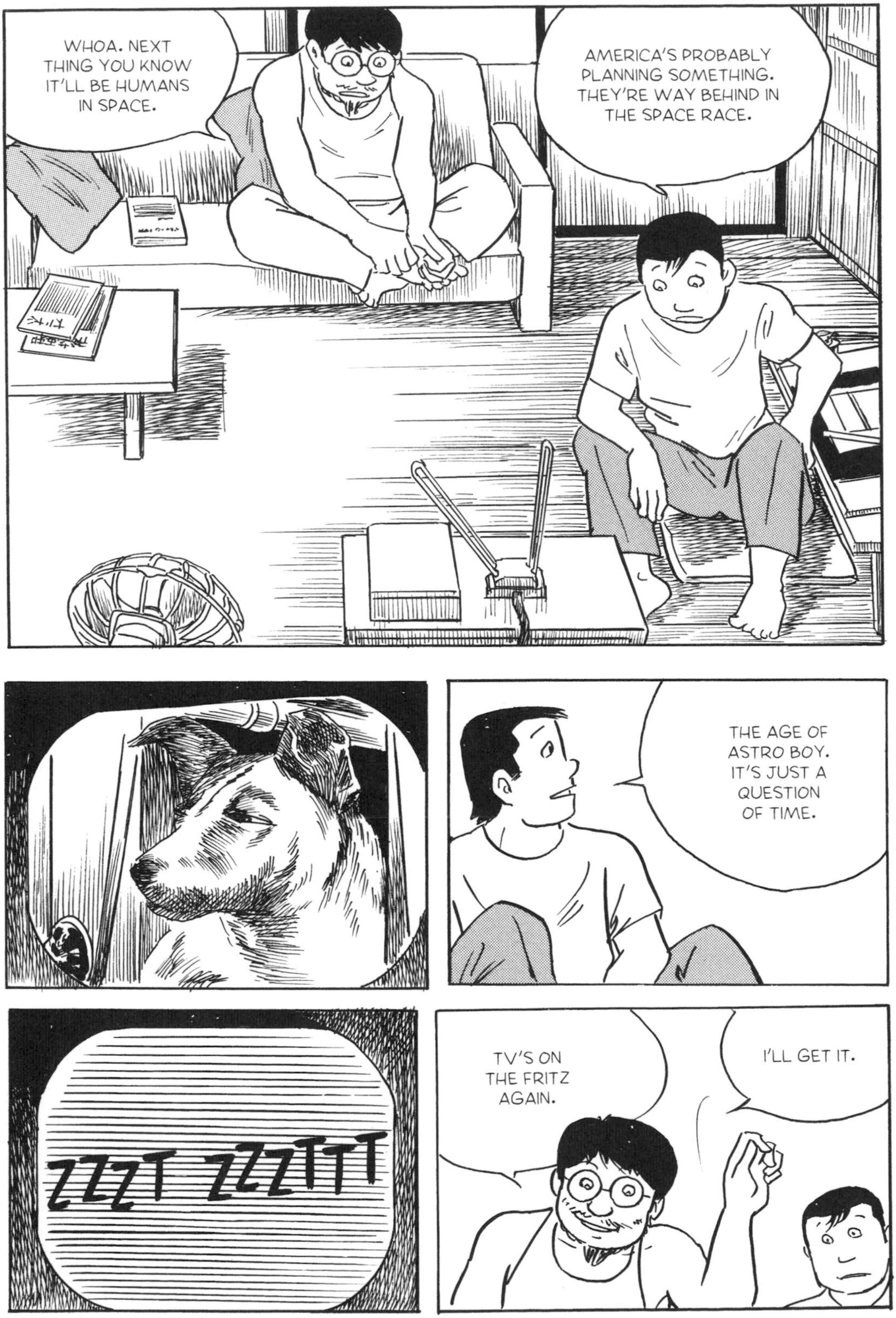
WHOA. NEXT THING YOU KNOW IT'LL BE HUMANS IN SPACE.
AMERICA'S PROBABLY PLANNING SOMETHING. THEY'RE WAY BEHIND IN THE SPACE RACE.
THE AGE OF ASTRO BOY. IT'S JUST A QUESTION OF TIME.
ZZZT ZZZTTT
TV'S ON THE FRITZ AGAIN.
I'LL GET IT.

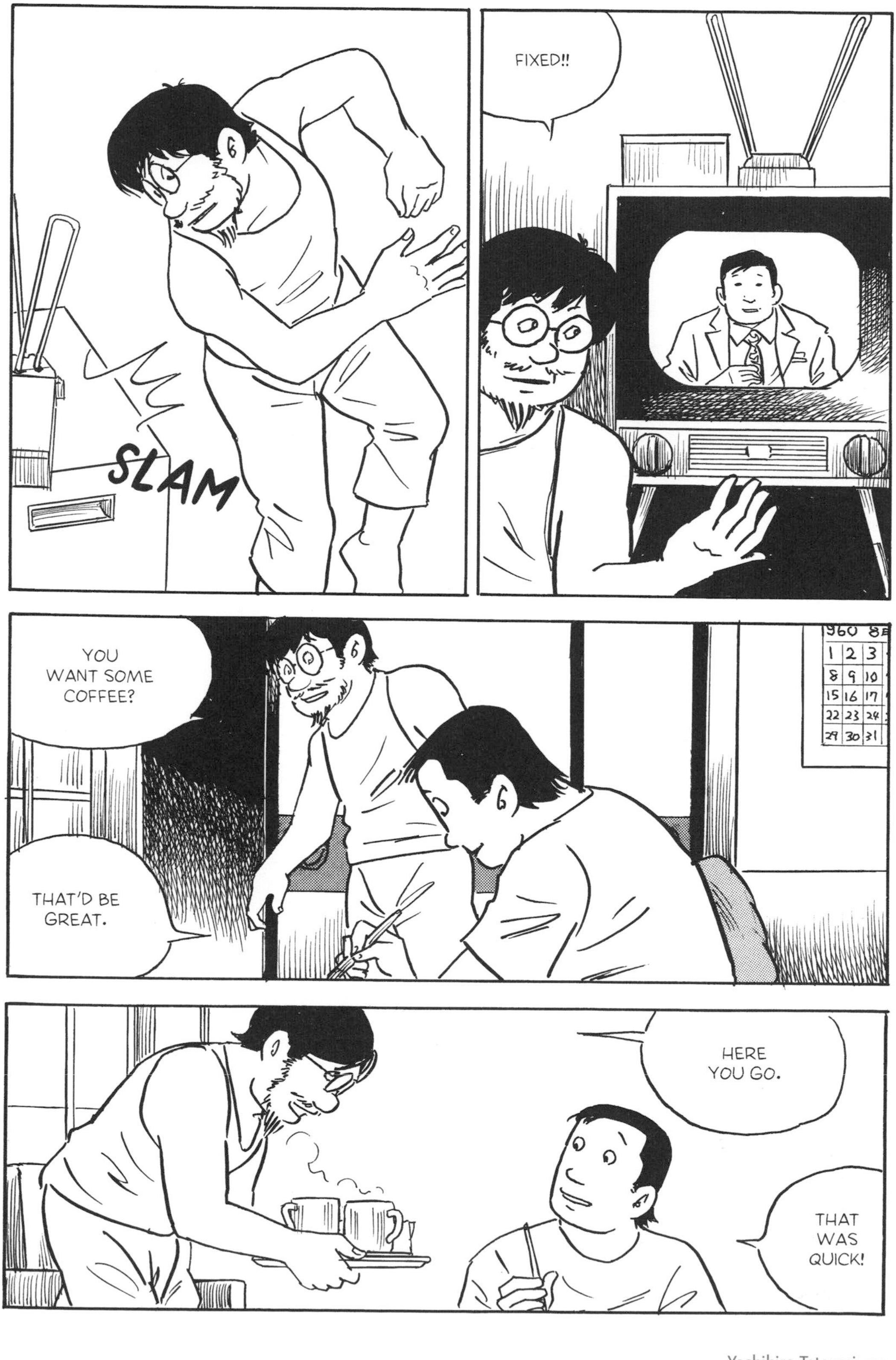
SLAM
FIXED!!
YOU WANT SOME COFFEE?
THAT'D BE GREAT.
HERE YOU GO.
THAT WAS QUICK!

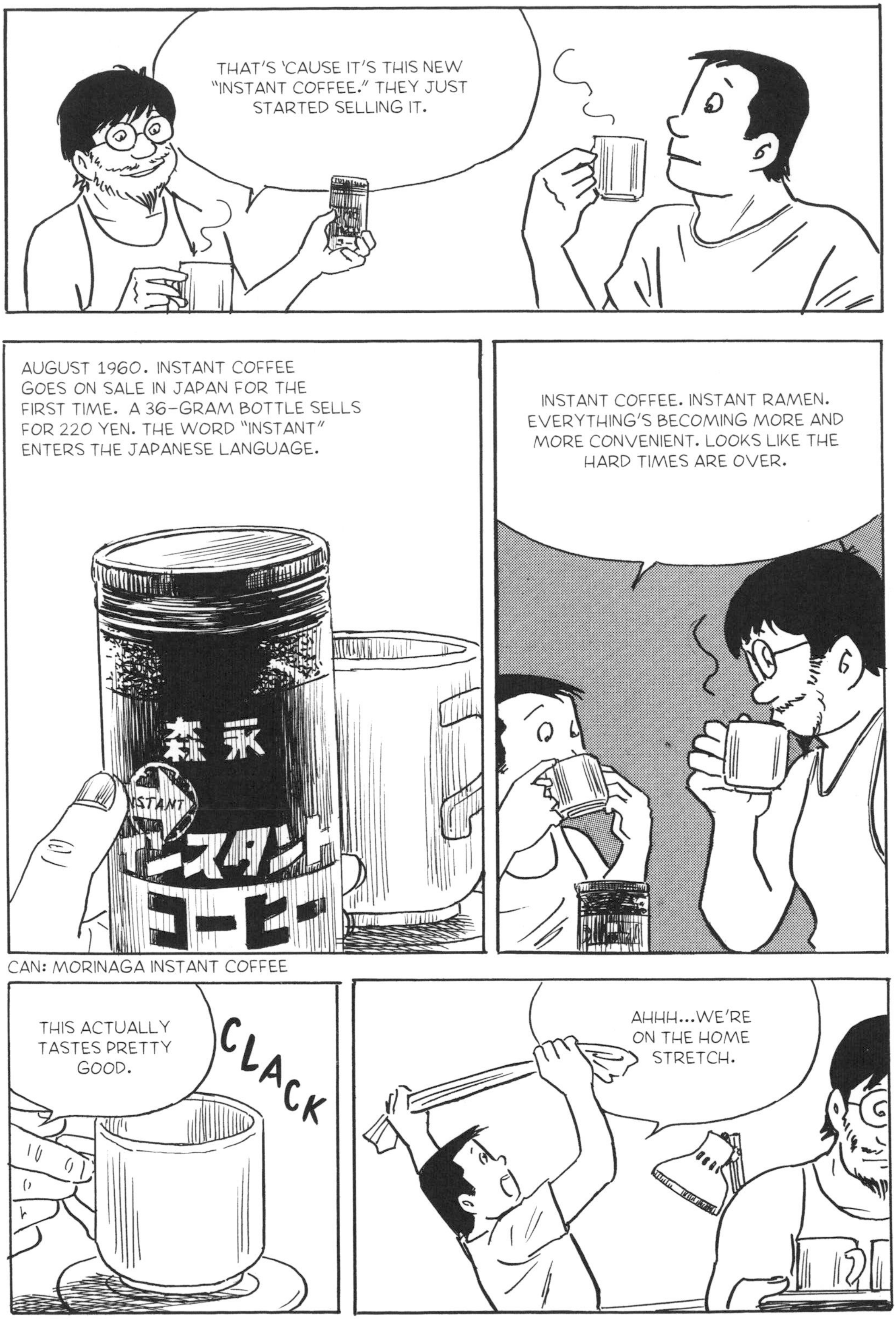
THAT'S 'CAUSE IT'S THIS NEW "INSTANT COFFEE." THEY JUST STARTED SELLING IT.
AUGUST 1960. INSTANT COFFEE GOES ON SALE IN JAPAN FOR THE FIRST TIME. A 36-GRAM BOTTLE SELLS FOR 220 YEN. THE WORD "INSTANT" ENTERS THE JAPANESE LANGUAGE.
森永
INSTANT
コーヒー
INSTANT COFFEE. INSTANT RAMEN. EVERYTHING'S BECOMING MORE AND MORE CONVENIENT. LOOKS LIKE THE HARD TIMES ARE OVER.
CAN: MORINAGA INSTANT COFFEE
THIS ACTUALLY TASTES PRETTY GOOD.
CLACK
AHHH...WE'RE ON THE HOME STRETCH.

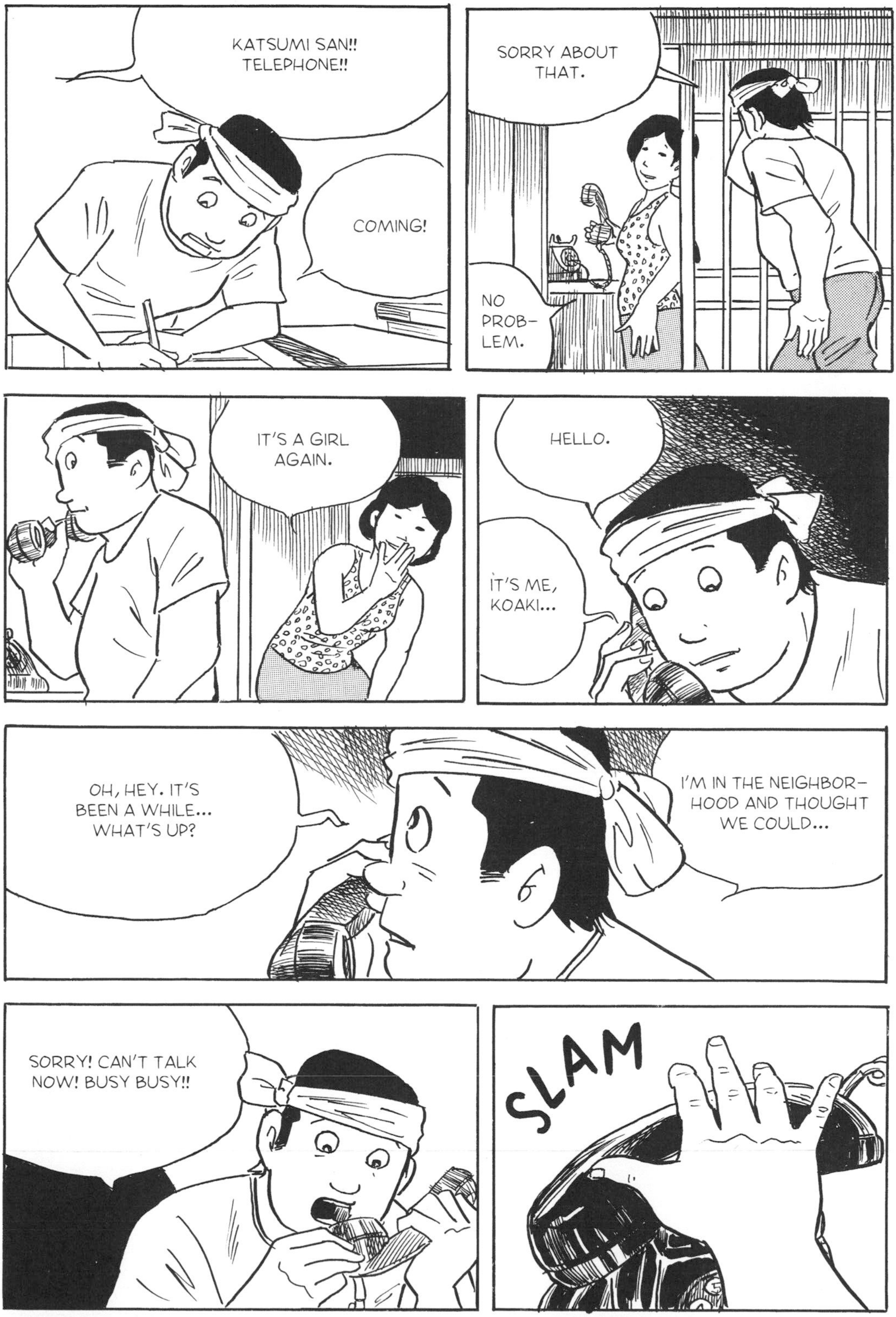
KATSUMI SAN!! TELEPHONE!!
COMING!
SORRY ABOUT THAT.
NO PROB-LEM.
IT'S A GIRL AGAIN.
HELLO.
IT'S ME, KOAKI...
OH, HEY. IT'S BEEN A WHILE... WHAT'S UP?
I'M IN THE NEIGHBOR-HOOD AND THOUGHT WE COULD...
SORRY! CAN'T TALK NOW! BUSY BUSY!!
SLAM

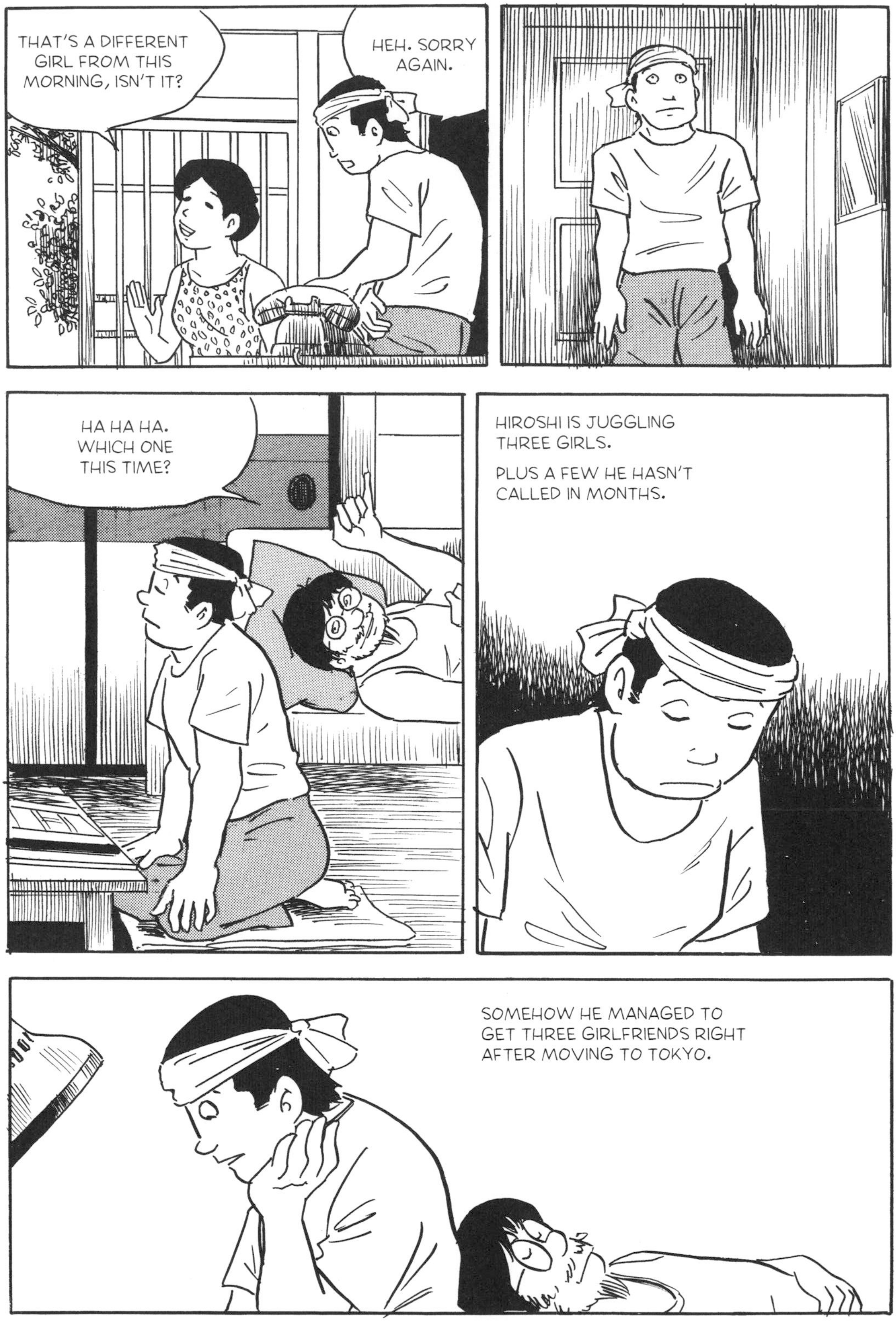
THAT'S A DIFFERENT GIRL FROM THIS MORNING, ISN'T IT?
HEH. SORRY AGAIN.
HA HA HA. WHICH ONE THIS TIME?
HIROSHI IS JUGGLING THREE GIRLS.
PLUS A FEW HE HASN'T CALLED IN MONTHS.
SOMEHOW HE MANAGED TO GET THREE GIRLFRIENDS RIGHT AFTER MOVING TO TOKYO.

HIGH SCHOOL
STUDENT KEIKO

OFFICE WORKER
KOAKI

EIKO THE
WAITRESS

YOU REALLY SHOULD JUST PICK ONE, YOU KNOW. THEY'RE GETTING NOISY.

KATSUMI HIROSHI LIVES IN THE RENTAL MANGA WORLD. HE SPENDS EVERY DAY DRAWING. HIS ROOMMATE IS AMEMIYA SABURO, WHO WRITES FOR THE MOVIE MAGAZINE *SCENARIO*.

THEY ARE TWENTY-FIVE YEARS OLD.

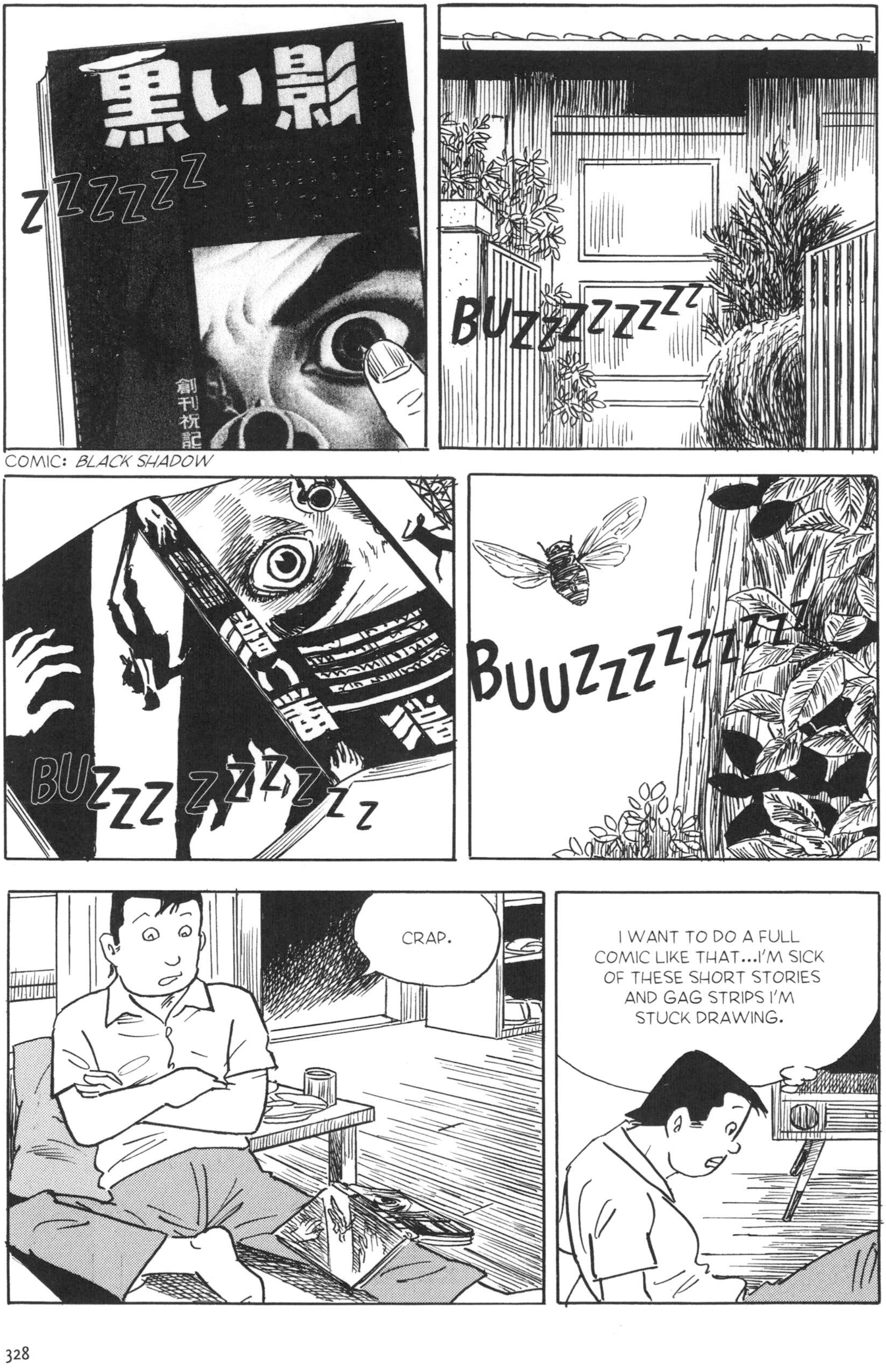
黒い影
ZZZZZZZ
BUZZZZZZZZZ
COMIC: *BLACK SHADOW*
BUZZZ ZZZZZZZ
BUUZZZZZZZZZZ
CRAP.
I WANT TO DO A FULL COMIC LIKE THAT...I'M SICK OF THESE SHORT STORIES AND GAG STRIPS I'M STUCK DRAWING.

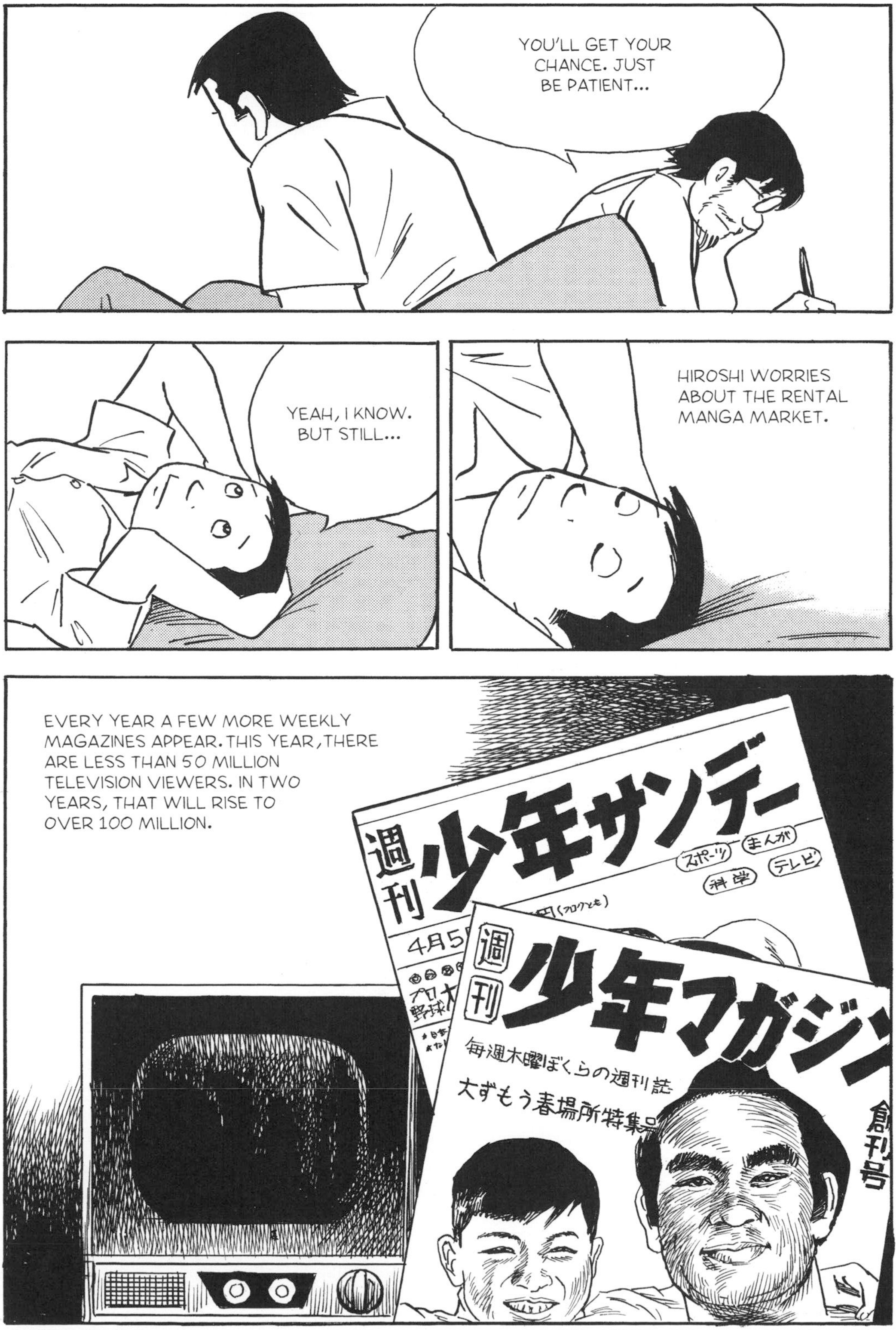
YOU'LL GET YOUR CHANCE. JUST BE PATIENT...
YEAH, I KNOW. BUT STILL...
HIROSHI WORRIES ABOUT THE RENTAL MANGA MARKET.
EVERY YEAR A FEW MORE WEEKLY MAGAZINES APPEAR. THIS YEAR, THERE ARE LESS THAN 50 MILLION TELEVISION VIEWERS. IN TWO YEARS, THAT WILL RISE TO OVER 100 MILLION.
週刊
少年サンデー
スポーツ
まんが
科学
テレビ
週刊
少年マガジ
毎週木曜ぼくらの週刊誌
大ずもう春場所特集号
創刊号

BOY'S MAGAZINE; YOUR EVERY THURSDAY WEEKLY MAGAZINE; SPECIAL BIG SUMO SPRING EDITION

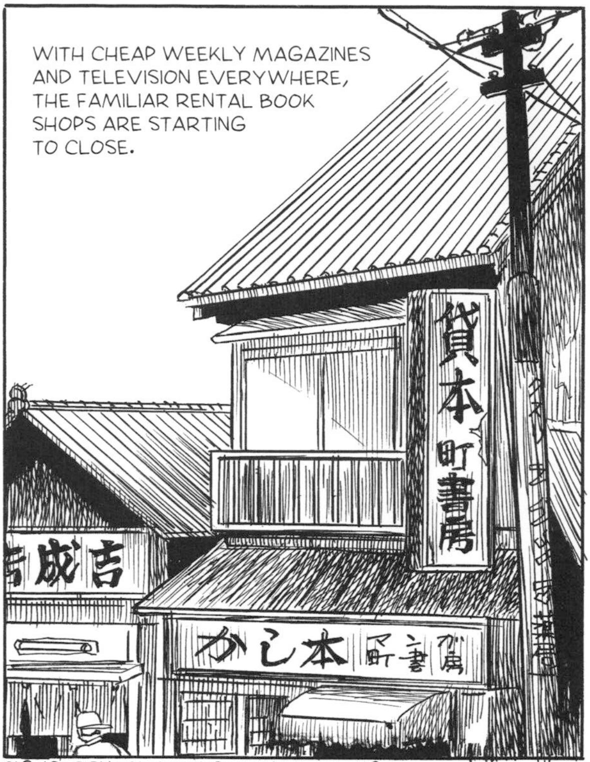
WITH CHEAP WEEKLY MAGAZINES AND TELEVISION EVERYWHERE, THE FAMILIAR RENTAL BOOK SHOPS ARE STARTING TO CLOSE.
貸本町書房
かし本

SIGNS: RENTAL BOOKS; RENTAL MANGA

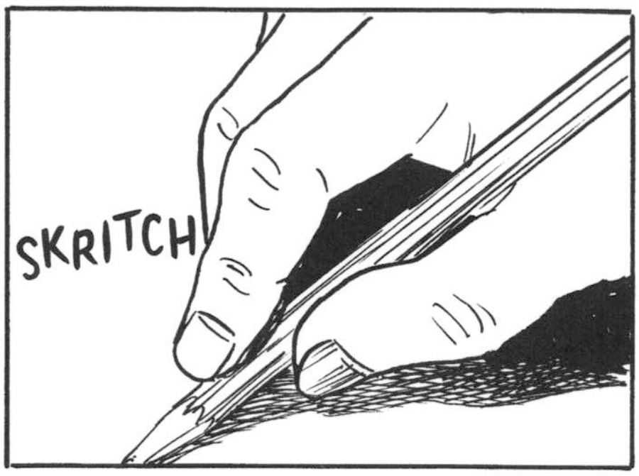
SKRITCH

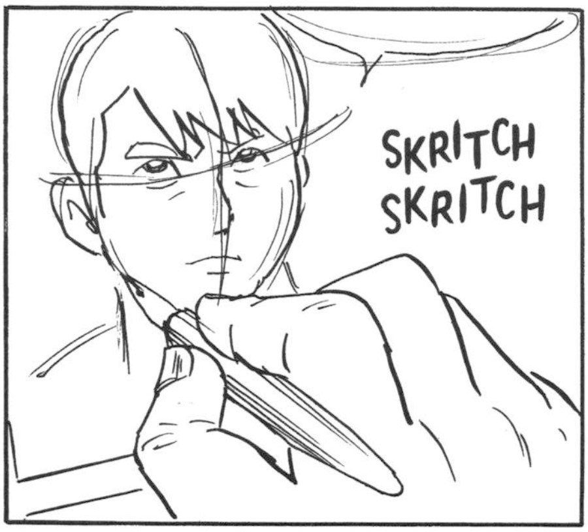
SKRITCH SKRITCH

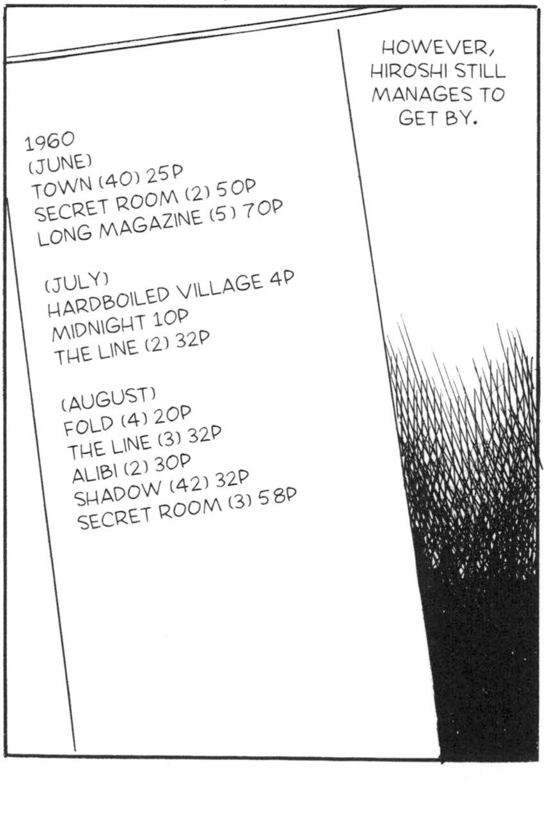
HOWEVER, HIROSHI STILL MANAGES TO GET BY.
1960
(JUNE)
TOWN (40) 25P
SECRET ROOM (2) 50P
LONG MAGAZINE (5) 70P
(JULY)
HARDBOILED VILLAGE 4P
MIDNIGHT 10P
THE LINE (2) 32P
(AUGUST)
FOLD (4) 20P
THE LINE (3) 32P
ALIBI (2) 30P
SHADOW (42) 32P
SECRET ROOM (3) 58P

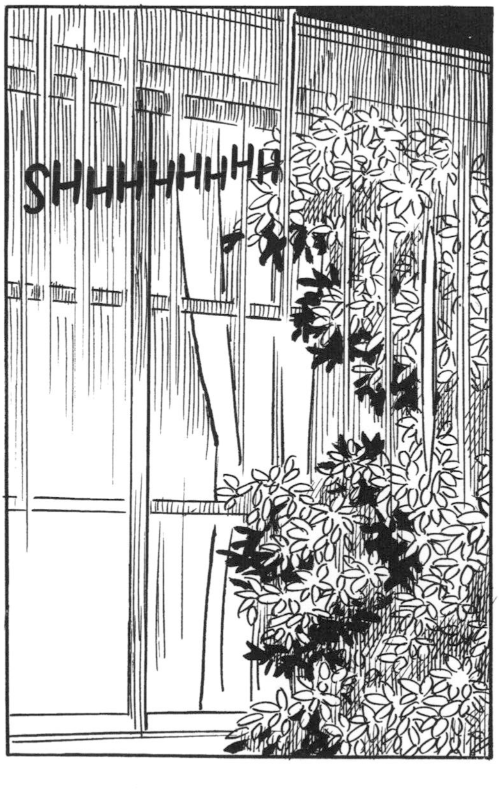
SHHHHHHHH

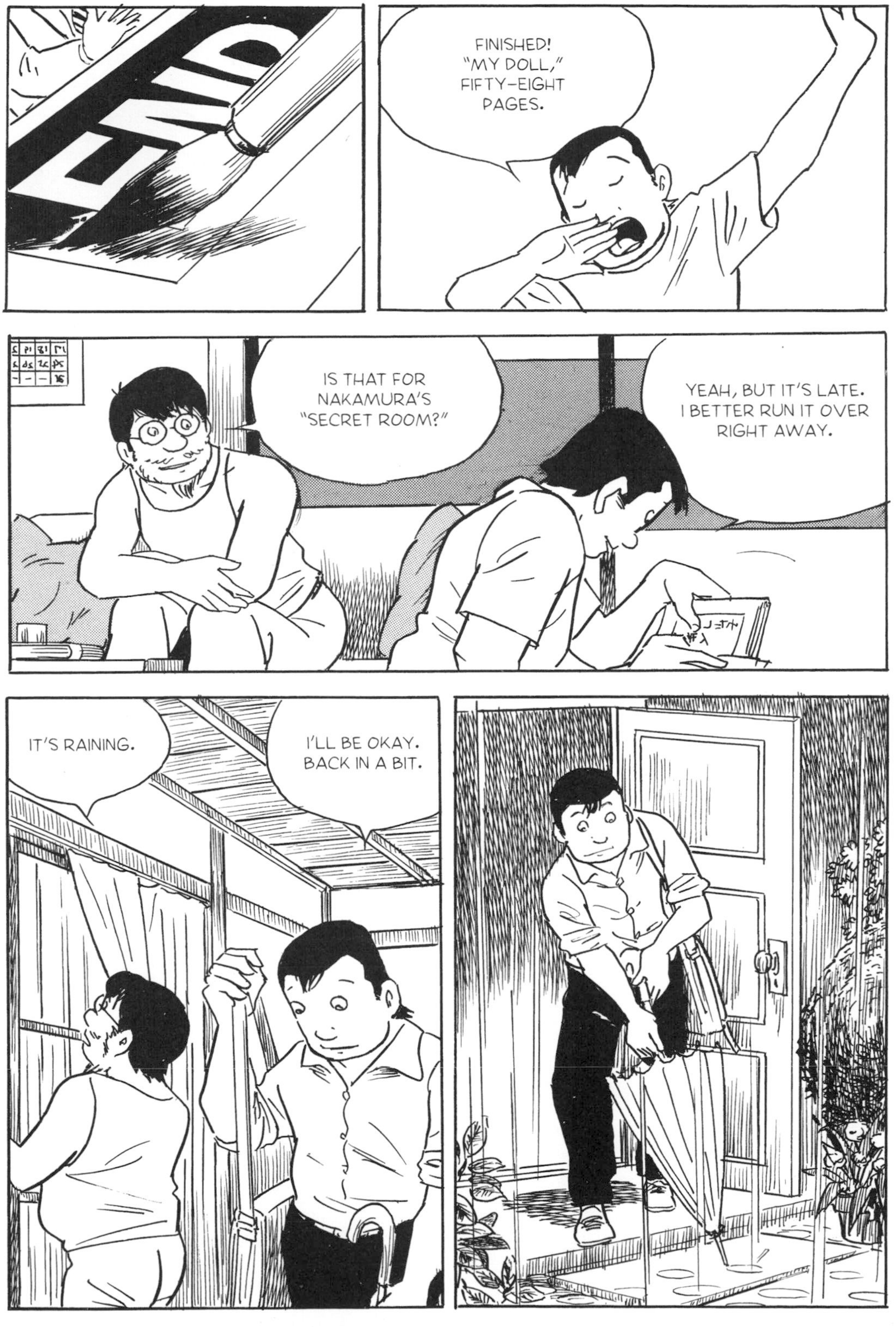
END
FINISHED! "MY DOLL," FIFTY-EIGHT PAGES.
IS THAT FOR NAKAMURA'S "SECRET ROOM?"
YEAH, BUT IT'S LATE. I BETTER RUN IT OVER RIGHT AWAY.
IT'S RAINING.
I'LL BE OKAY. BACK IN A BIT.

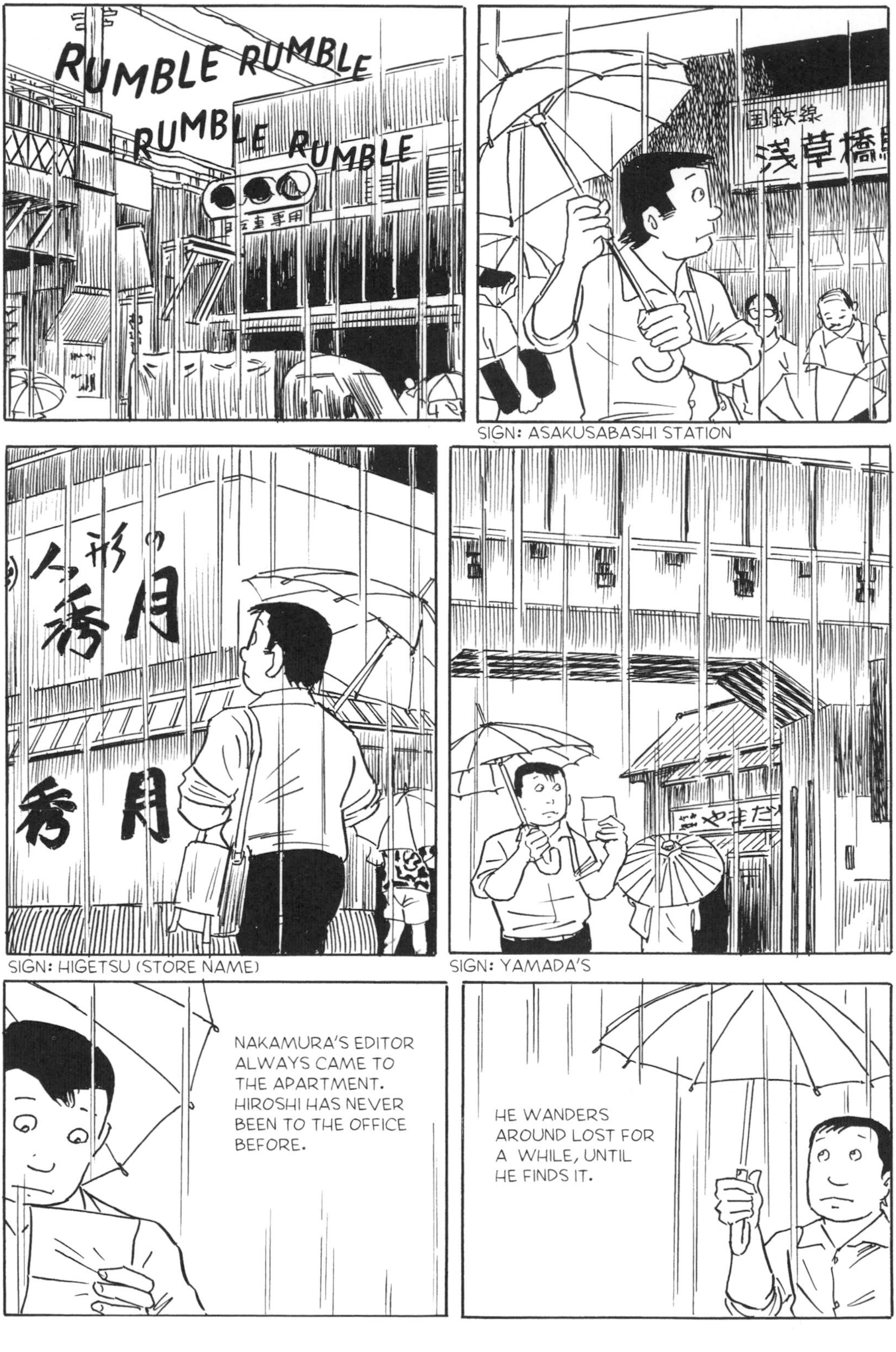
RUMBLE RUMBLE
RUMBLE RUMBLE RUMBLE
国鉄線
浅草橋
SIGN: ASAKUSABASHI STATION
人形の
秀月
秀月
SIGN: HIGETSU (STORE NAME)
やまだ
SIGN: YAMADA'S
NAKAMURA'S EDITOR ALWAYS CAME TO THE APARTMENT. HIROSHI HAS NEVER BEEN TO THE OFFICE BEFORE.
HE WANDERS AROUND LOST FOR A WHILE, UNTIL HE FINDS IT.

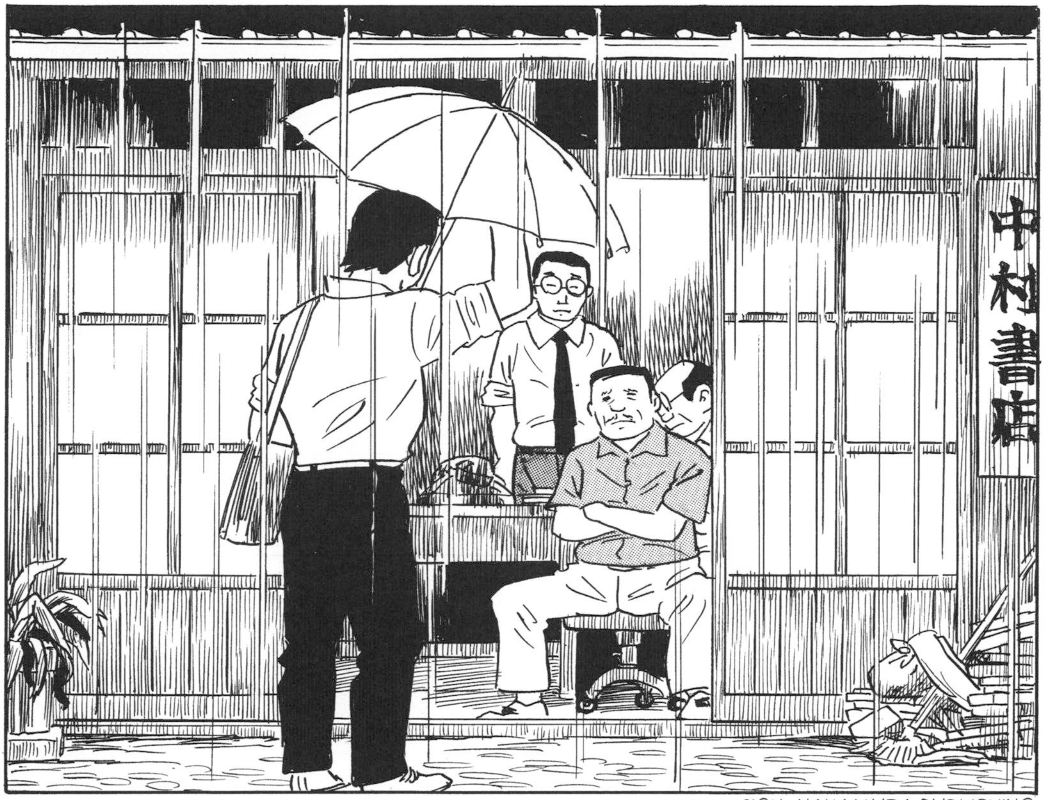
中村書店

SIGN: NAKAMURA PUBLISHING

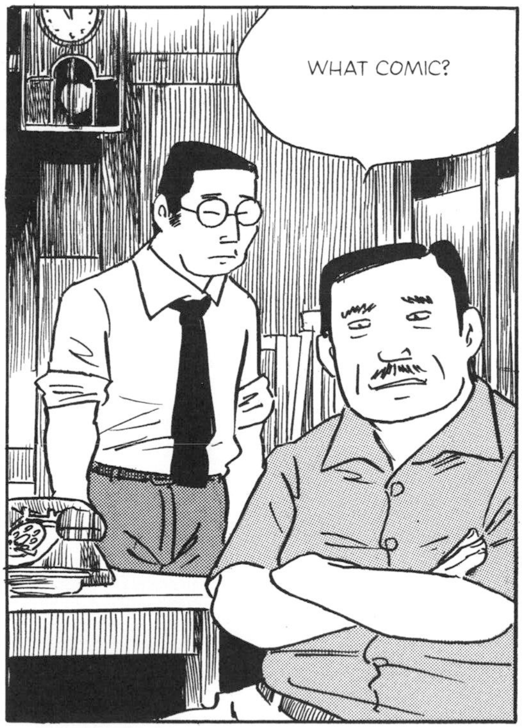
WHAT COMIC?

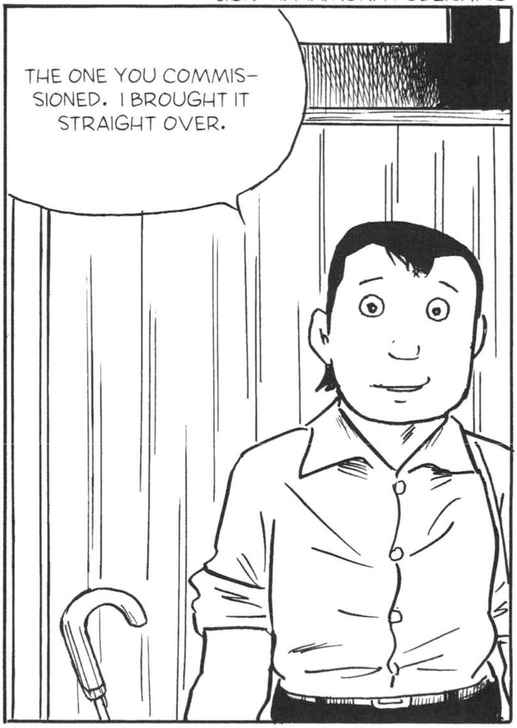
THE ONE YOU COMMISSIONED. I BROUGHT IT STRAIGHT OVER.

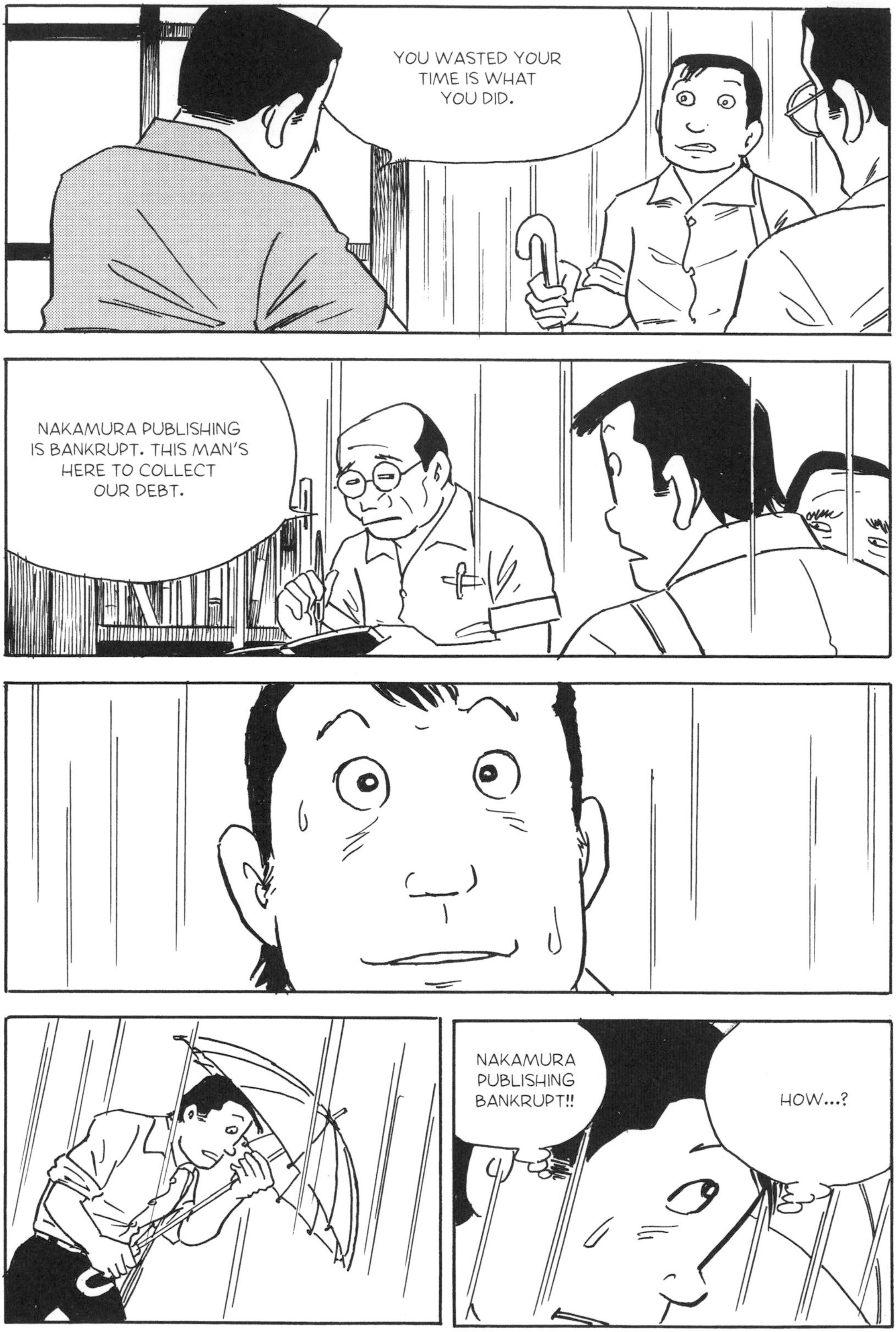
YOU WASTED YOUR TIME IS WHAT YOU DID.
NAKAMURA PUBLISHING IS BANKRUPT. THIS MAN'S HERE TO COLLECT OUR DEBT.
NAKAMURA PUBLISHING BANKRUPT!!
HOW...?

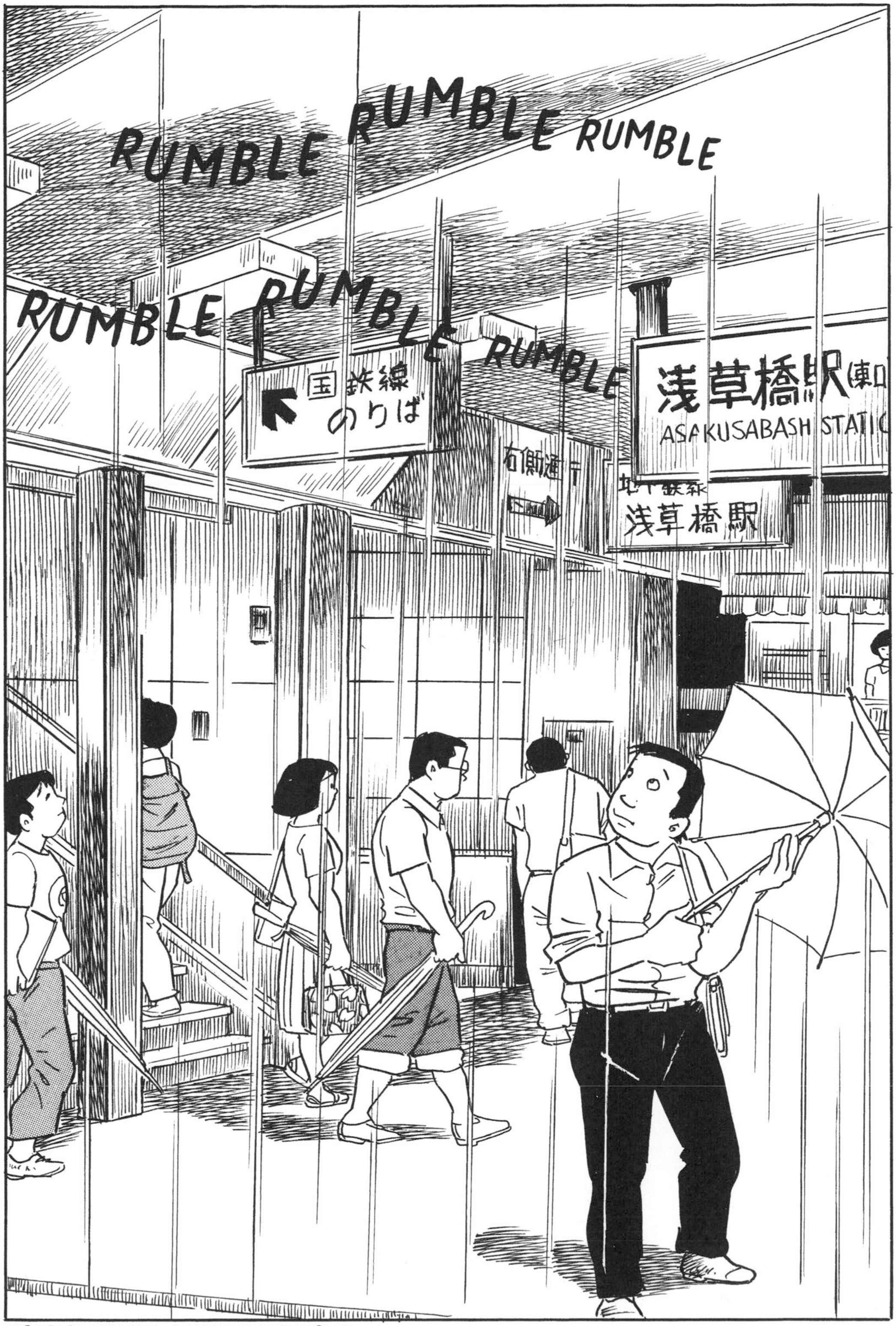
RUMBLE RUMBLE RUMBLE
RUMBLE RUMBLE RUMBLE
国鉄線
のりば
浅草橋駅
ASAKUSABASH
浅草橋駅

SIGNS: PLATFORM; WALK TO THE RIGHT

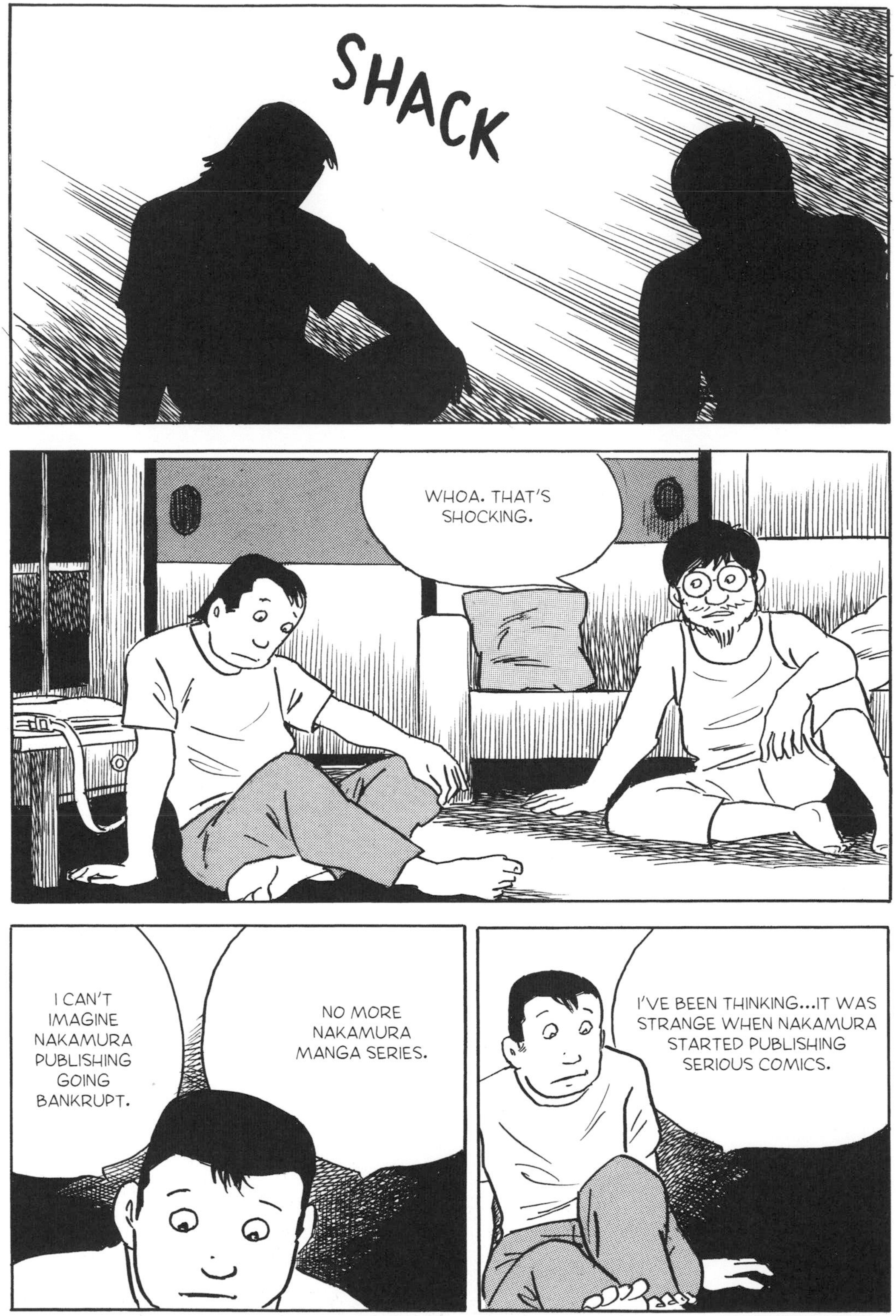
SHACK
WHOA. THAT'S SHOCKING.
I CAN'T IMAGINE NAKAMURA PUBLISHING GOING BANKRUPT.
NO MORE NAKAMURA MANGA SERIES.
I'VE BEEN THINKING...IT WAS STRANGE WHEN NAKAMURA STARTED PUBLISHING SERIOUS COMICS.

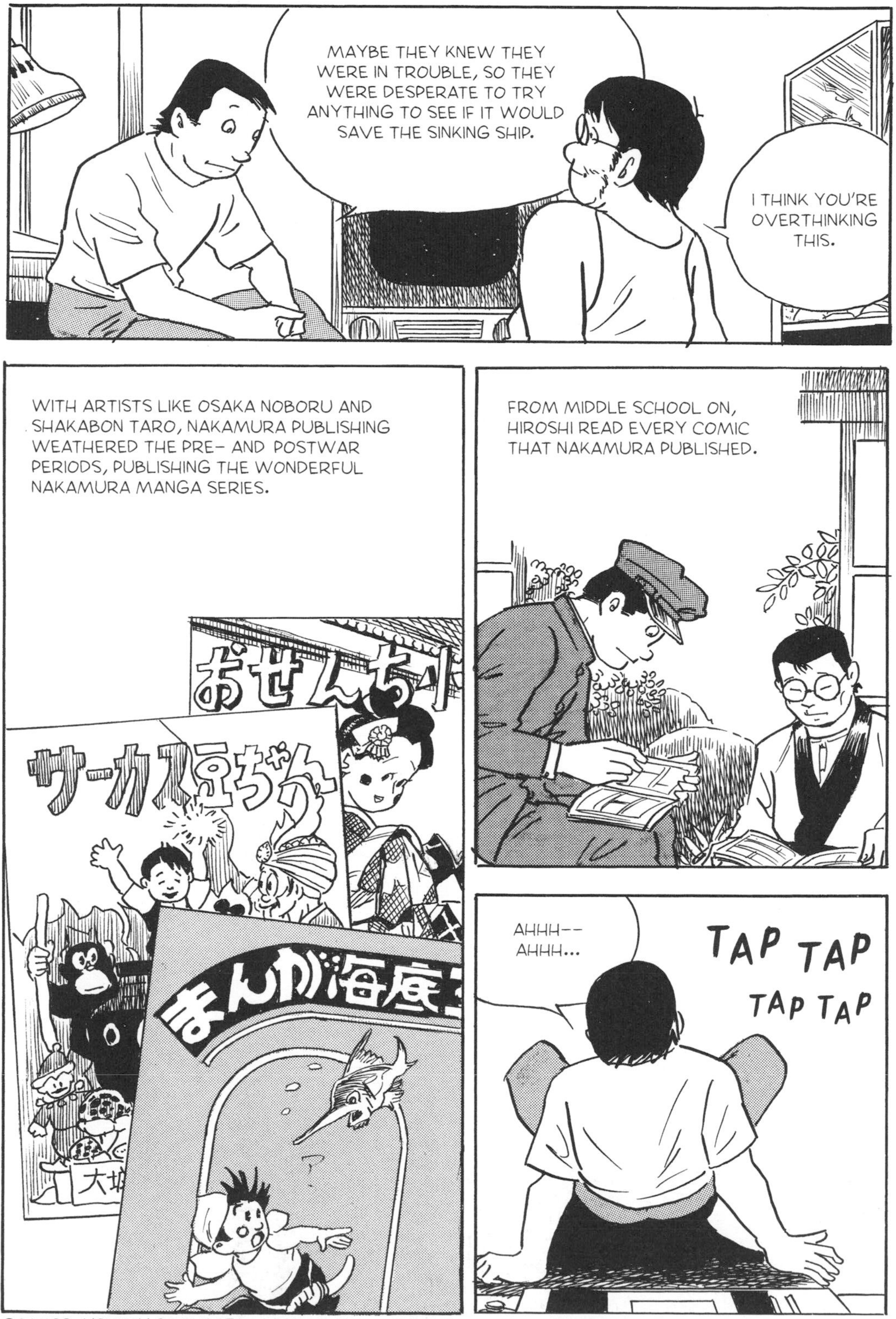
MAYBE THEY KNEW THEY WERE IN TROUBLE, SO THEY WERE DESPERATE TO TRY ANYTHING TO SEE IF IT WOULD SAVE THE SINKING SHIP.
I THINK YOU'RE OVERTHINKING THIS.
WITH ARTISTS LIKE OSAKA NOBORU AND SHAKABON TARO, NAKAMURA PUBLISHING WEATHERED THE PRE- AND POSTWAR PERIODS, PUBLISHING THE WONDERFUL NAKAMURA MANGA SERIES.
おせんち
サーカス豆ちゃん
まんが海底
FROM MIDDLE SCHOOL ON, HIROSHI READ EVERY COMIC THAT NAKAMURA PUBLISHED.
AHHH-- AHHH...
TAP TAP
TAP TAP

COMICS: USHIMU SOJI (1951) *OSEN-CHIKO*; OSAKA NOBORU (1945) *CIRCUS MAME-CHAN*; SHAKABON TARO (1950) *UNDERSEA MANGA*

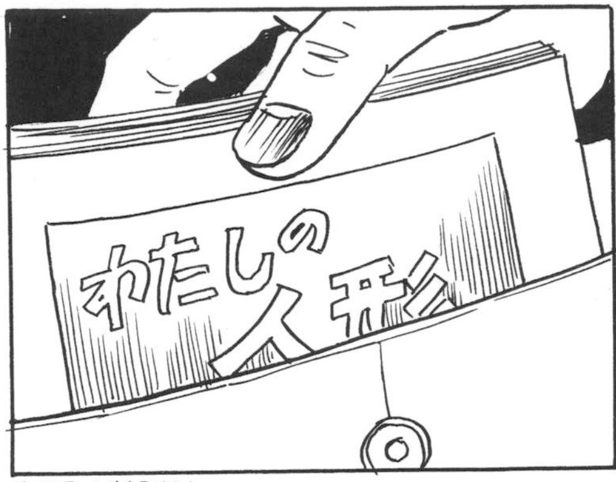
わたしの人形

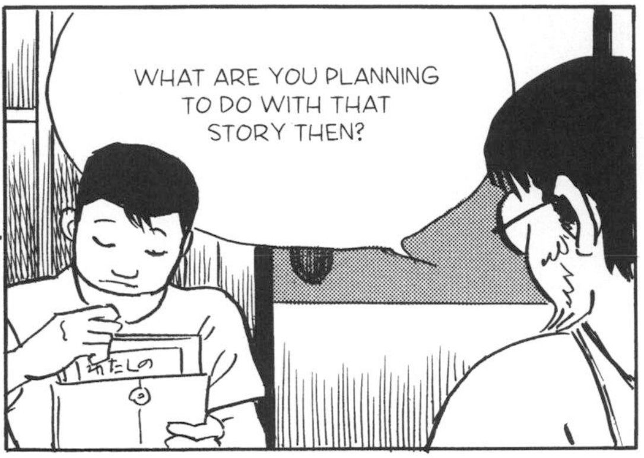
WHAT ARE YOU PLANNING TO DO WITH THAT STORY THEN?

TEXT: MY DOLL

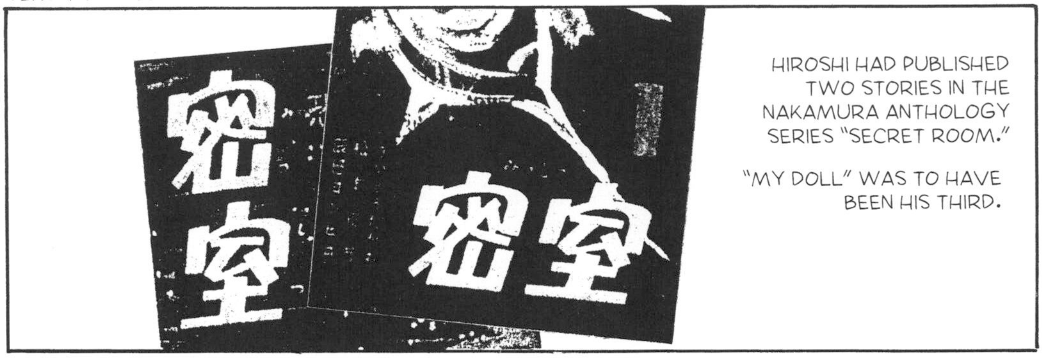
密室
密室
HIROSHI HAD PUBLISHED TWO STORIES IN THE NAKAMURA ANTHOLOGY SERIES "SECRET ROOM."
"MY DOLL" WAS TO HAVE BEEN HIS THIRD.

COMIC: *SECRET ROOM*

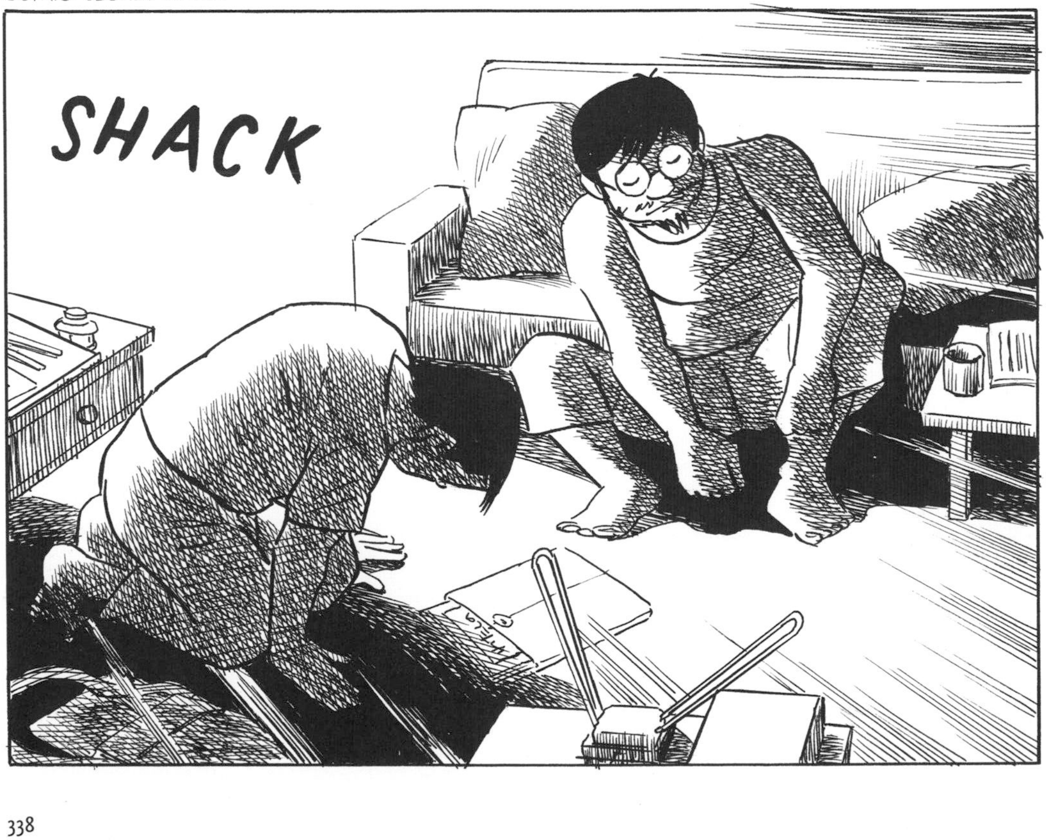
SHACK

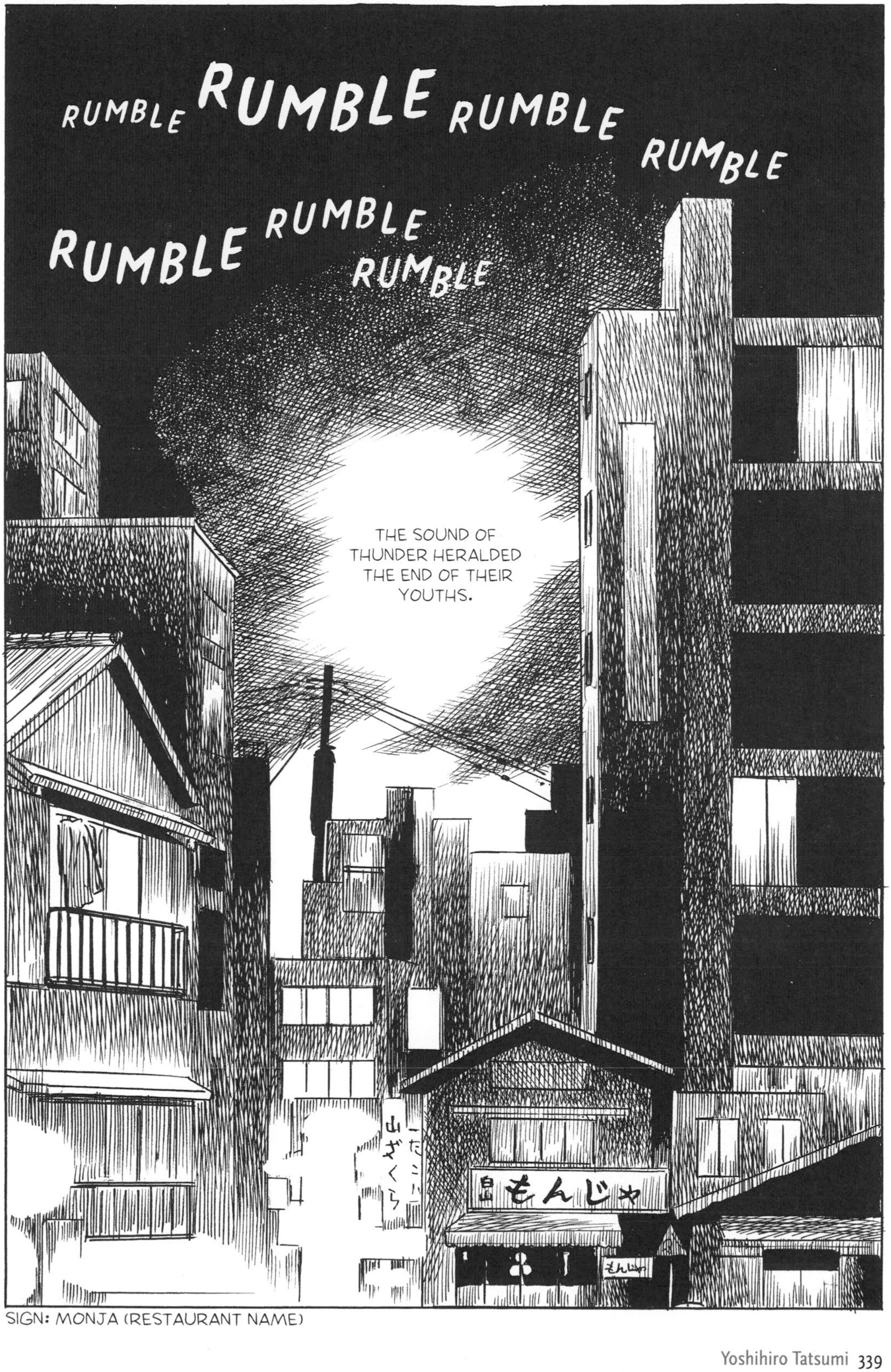
RUMBLE RUMBLE RUMBLE RUMBLE
RUMBLE RUMBLE RUMBLE
THE SOUND OF THUNDER HERALDED THE END OF THEIR YOUTHS.
もんじゃ
もんじゃ
SIGN: MONJA (RESTAURANT NAME)

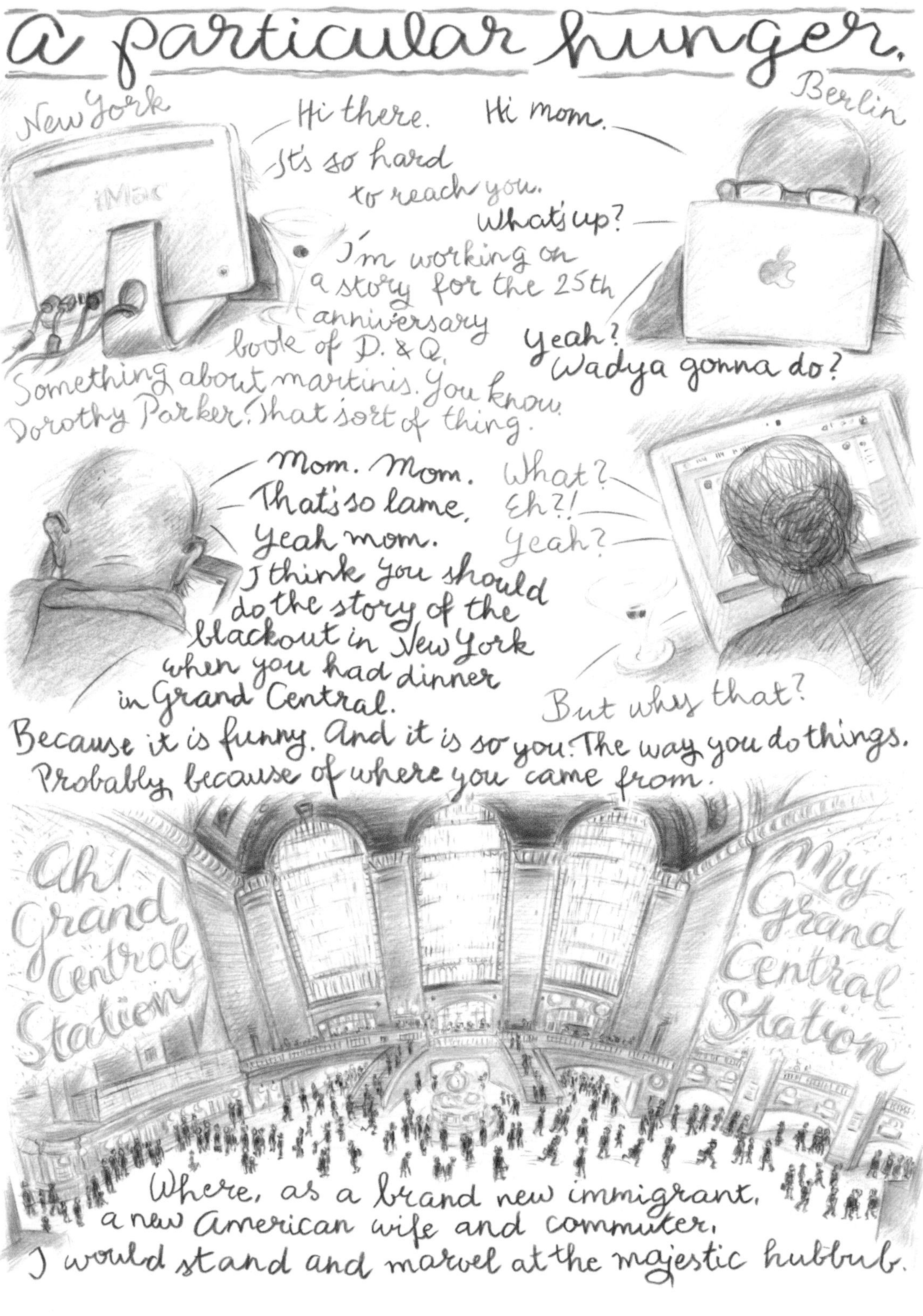
a particular hunger.
New York
Berlin
Hi there.
Hi mom.
It's so hard to reach you.
What's up?
I'm working on a story for the 25th anniversary book of D. & Q.
Yeah? Wadya gonna do?
Something about martinis. You know. Dorothy Parker. That sort of thing.
Mom. Mom. That's so lame. Yeah mom. I think you should do the story of the blackout in New York when you had dinner in Grand Central.
What? Eh?! Yeah?
But why that?
Because it is funny. And it is so you. The way you do things. Probably because of where you came from.
Ah! Grand Central Station
My Grand Central Station
Where, as a brand new immigrant, a new American wife and commuter, I would stand and marvel at the majestic hubbub.

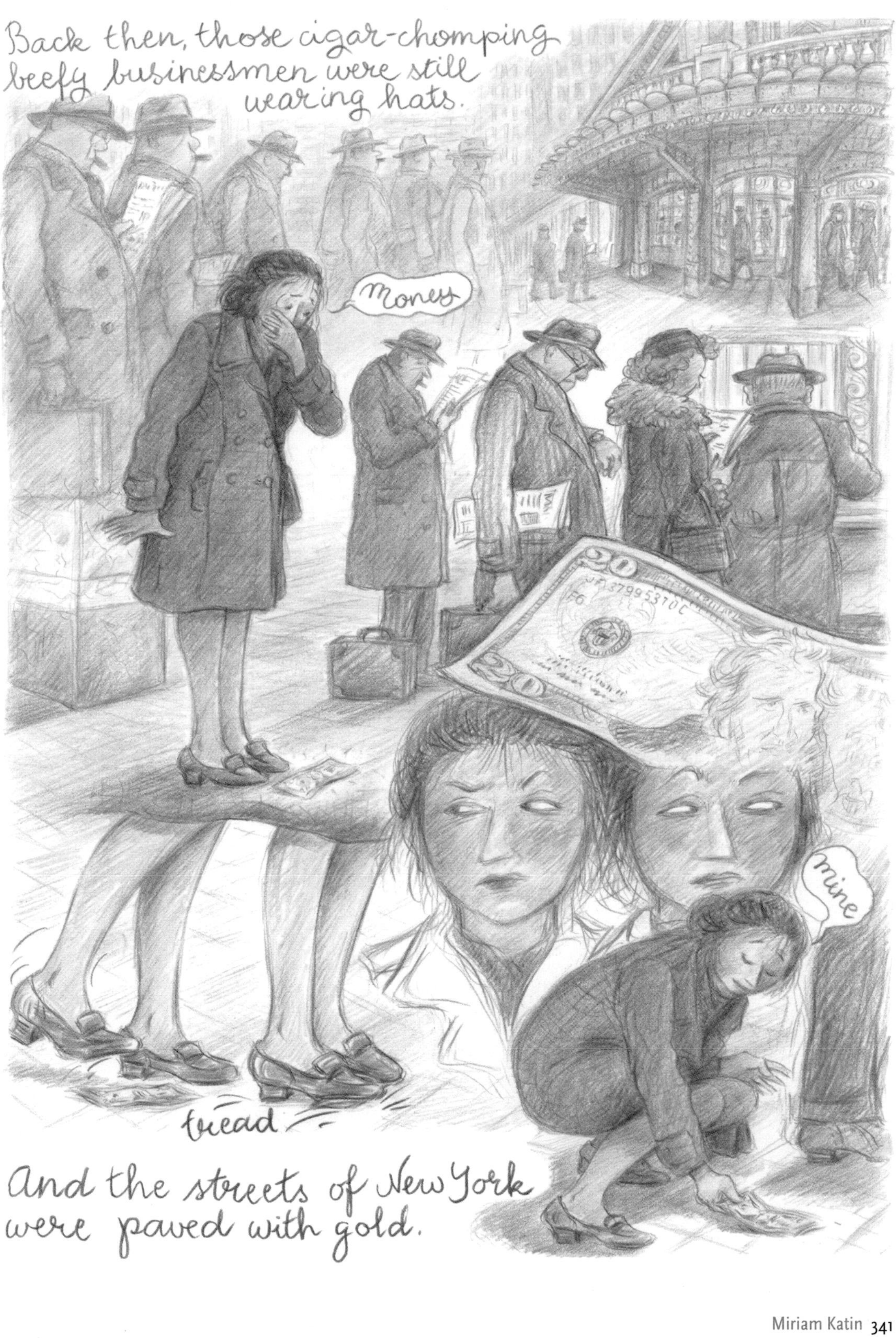
Back then, those cigar-chomping beefy businessmen were still wearing hats.
Money
mine
tread
And the streets of New York were paved with gold.

November 9th, 1965. 5th Avenue and 38th Street.
5:57 pm and 59 seconds. Then, 5:28 pm.

Those towels are much too expensive.

Holy, shit!

What the hell?!

What exactly happened,

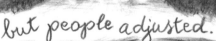

nobody knew yet,

but people adjusted.

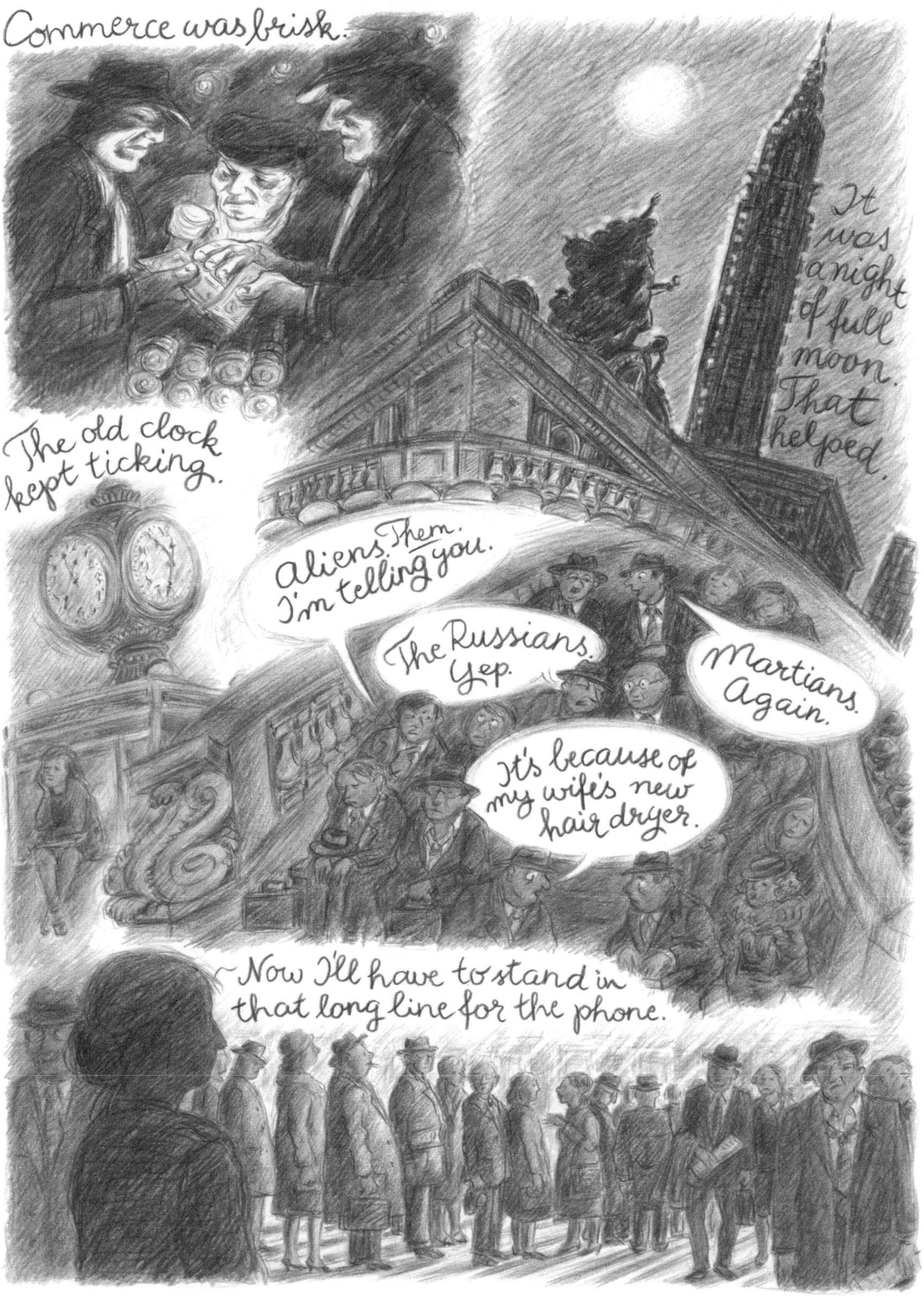
Commerce was brisk.
It was a night of full moon. That helped.
The old clock kept ticking.
Aliens. Them. I'm telling you.
The Russians. Yep.
Martians. Again.
It's because of my wife's new hair dryer.
Now I'll have to stand in that long line for the phone.

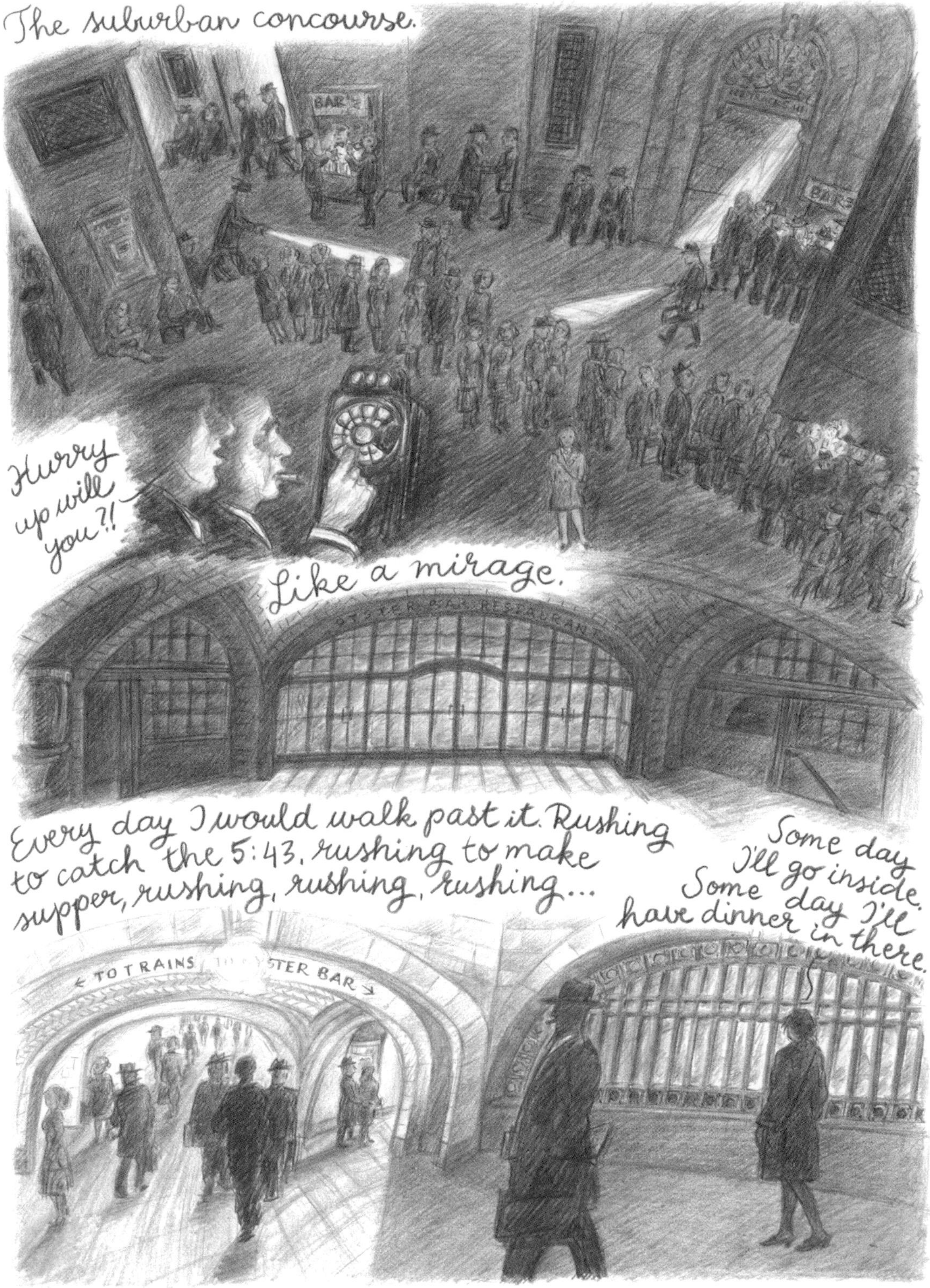
The suburban concourse.
BAR
BAR
Hurry up will you?!
Like a mirage.
Every day I would walk past it. Rushing to catch the 5:43, rushing to make supper, rushing, rushing, rushing...
Some day I'll go inside. Some day I'll have dinner in there.
← TO TRAINS

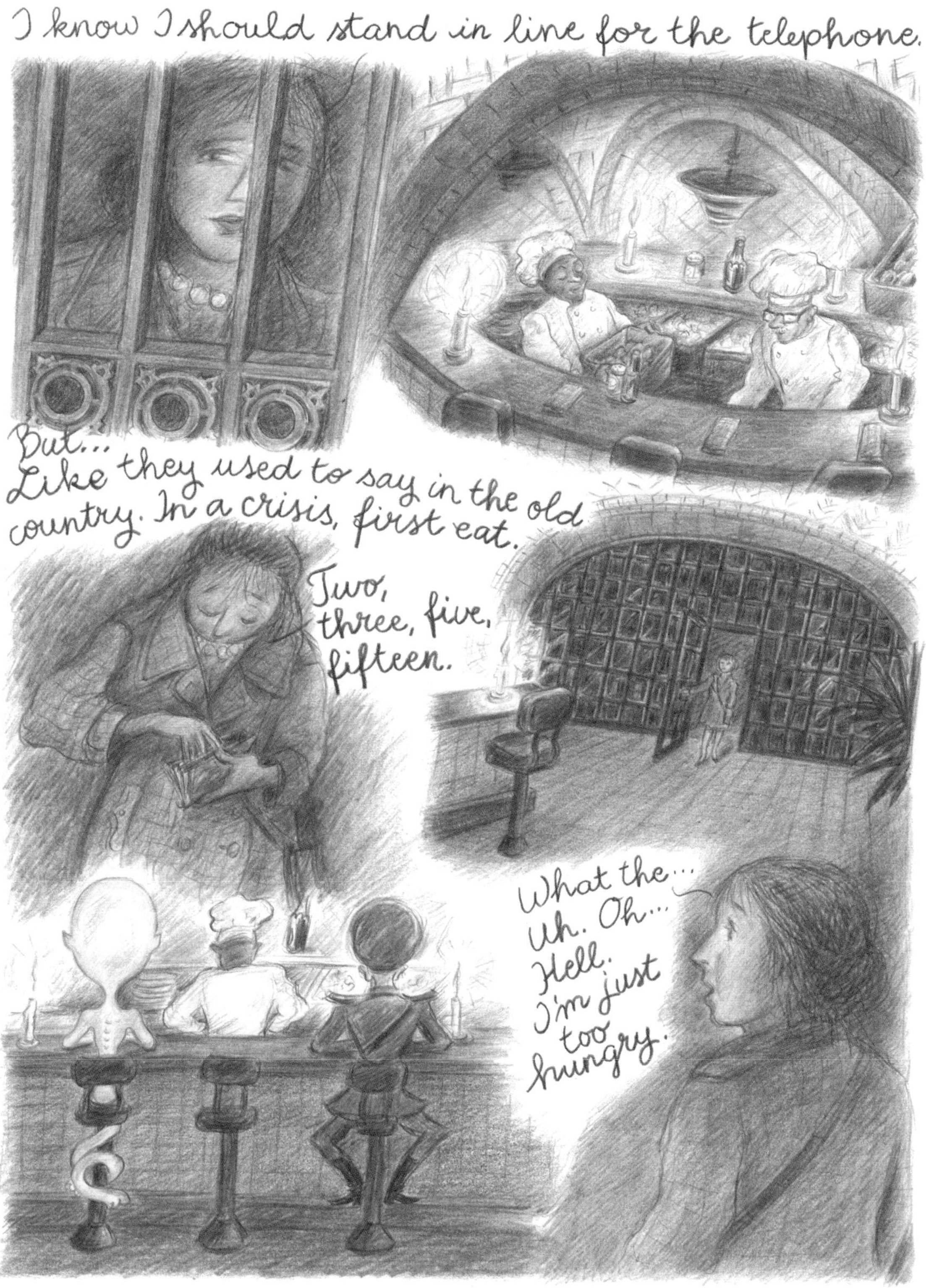
I know I should stand in line for the telephone.
But...
Like they used to say in the old country. In a crisis, first eat.
Two, three, five, fifteen.
What the...
Uh. Oh...
Hell.
I'm just too hungry.

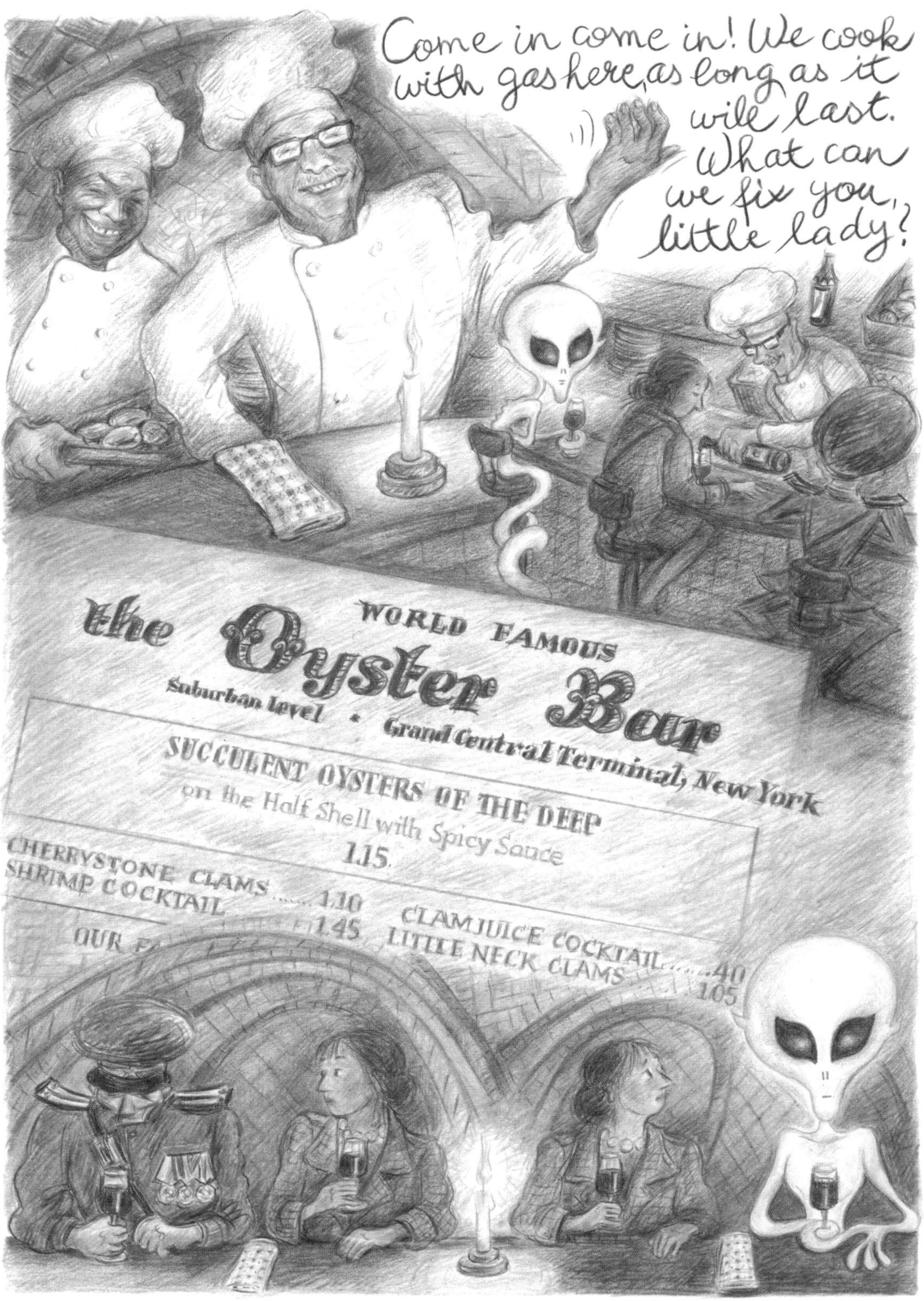
Come in come in! We cook with gas here, as long as it will last. What can we fix you, little lady?
WORLD FAMOUS
the Oyster Bar
Suburban level • Grand Central Terminal, New York
SUCCULENT OYSTERS OF THE DEEP
on the Half Shell with Spicy Sauce
1.15
CHERRYSTONE CLAMS 1.10
SHRIMP COCKTAIL 1.45
CLAMJUICE COCKTAIL........40
LITTLE NECK CLAMS 1.05

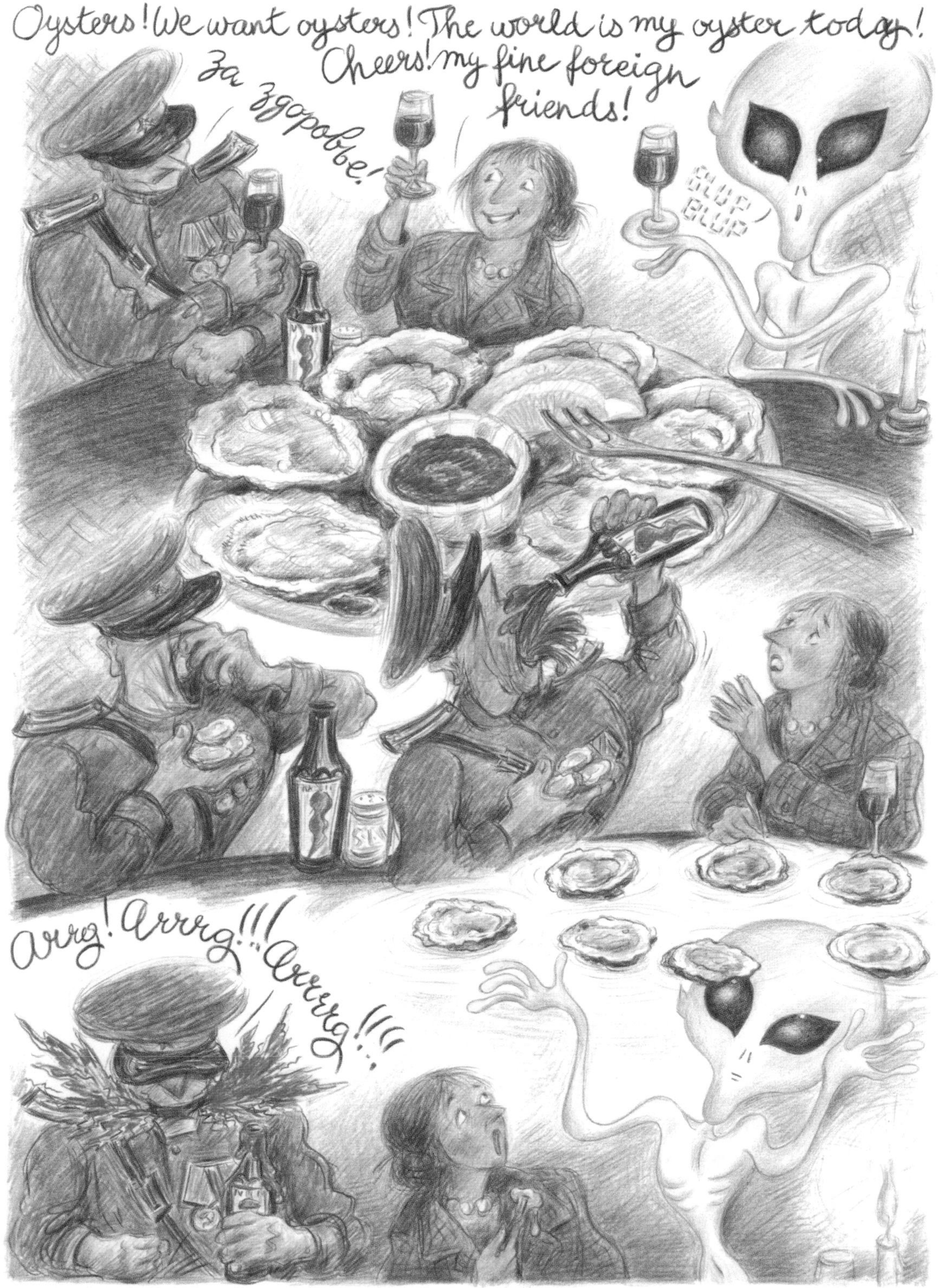
Oysters! We want oysters! The world is my oyster today!
За Здоровье!
Cheers! my fine foreign friends!
SLUP BLUP
Arrg! Arrrg!!! Arrrg!!!

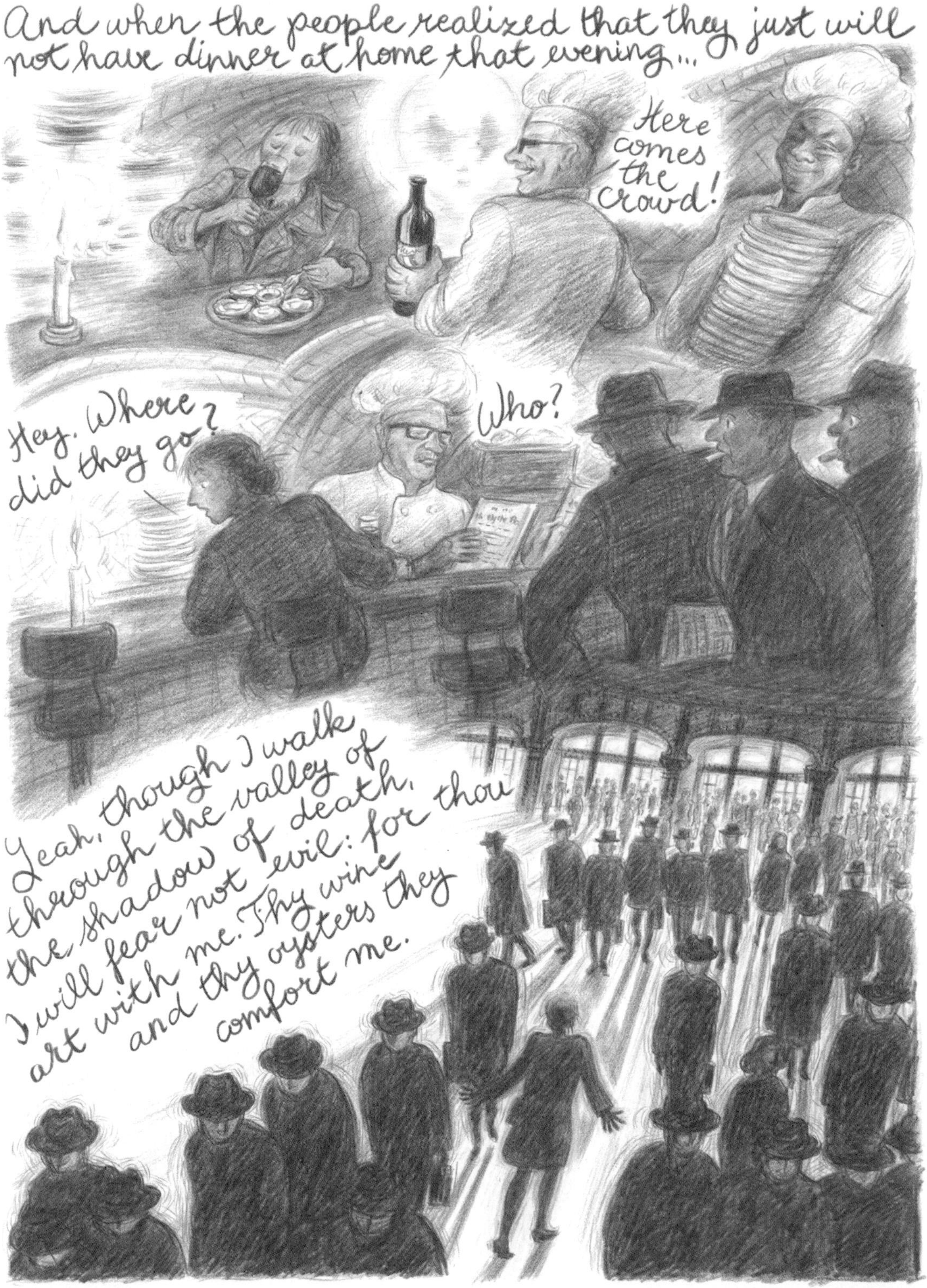
And when the people realized that they just will not have dinner at home that evening...
Here comes the crowd!
Hey. Where did they go?
Who?
Yeah, though I walk through the valley of the shadow of death, I will fear not evil: for thou art with me. Thy wine and thy oysters they comfort me.

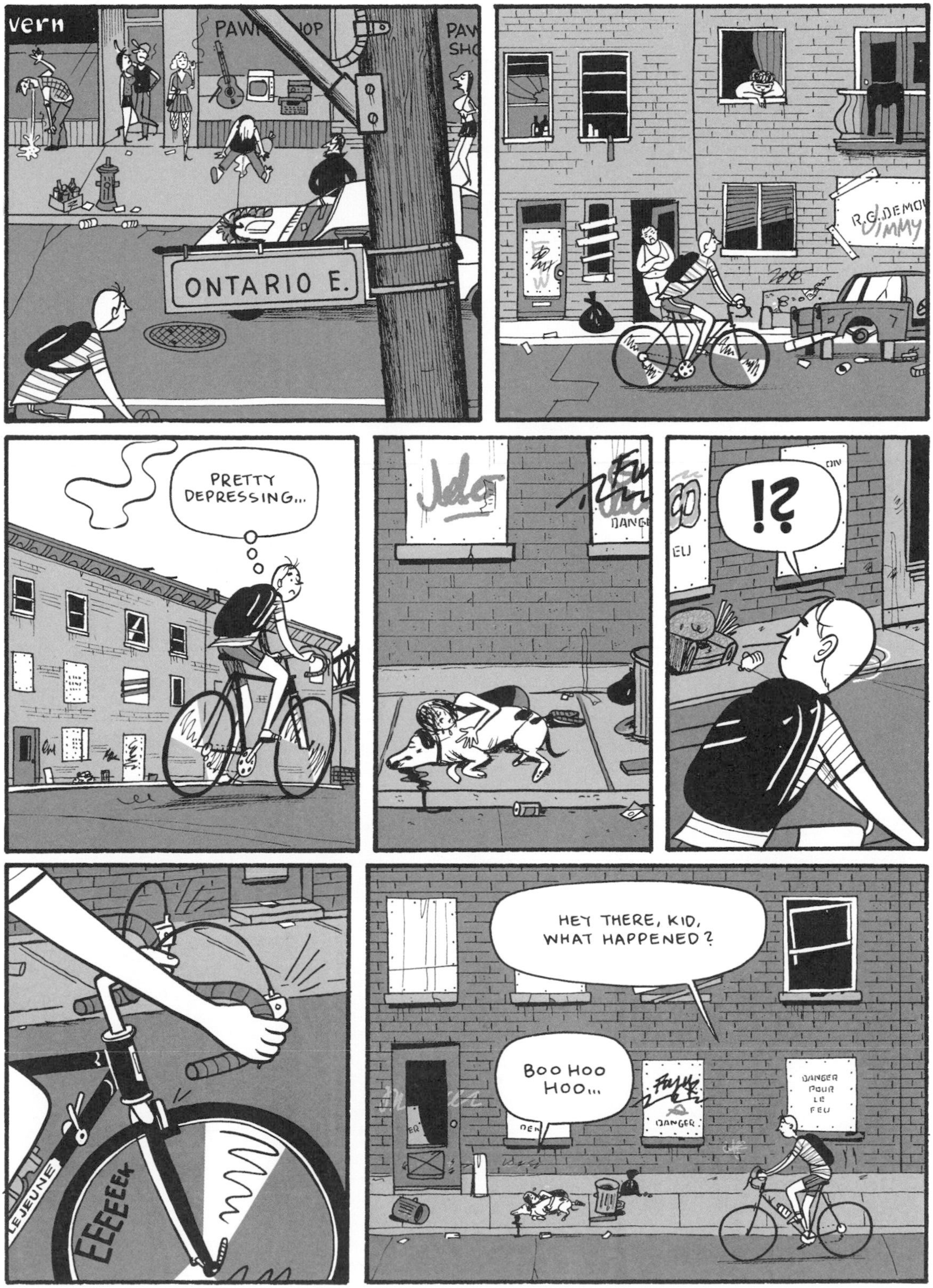
vern
ONTARIO E.
R.G. DEMO
JIMMY
PRETTY DEPRESSING...
!?
EEEEEEK
LEJEUNE
HEY THERE, KID, WHAT HAPPENED?
BOO HOO HOO...
DANGER
DANGER POUR LE FEU

Excerpt from *Paul Goes Fishing* (2008). Michel Rabagliati with translation by Helge Dascher

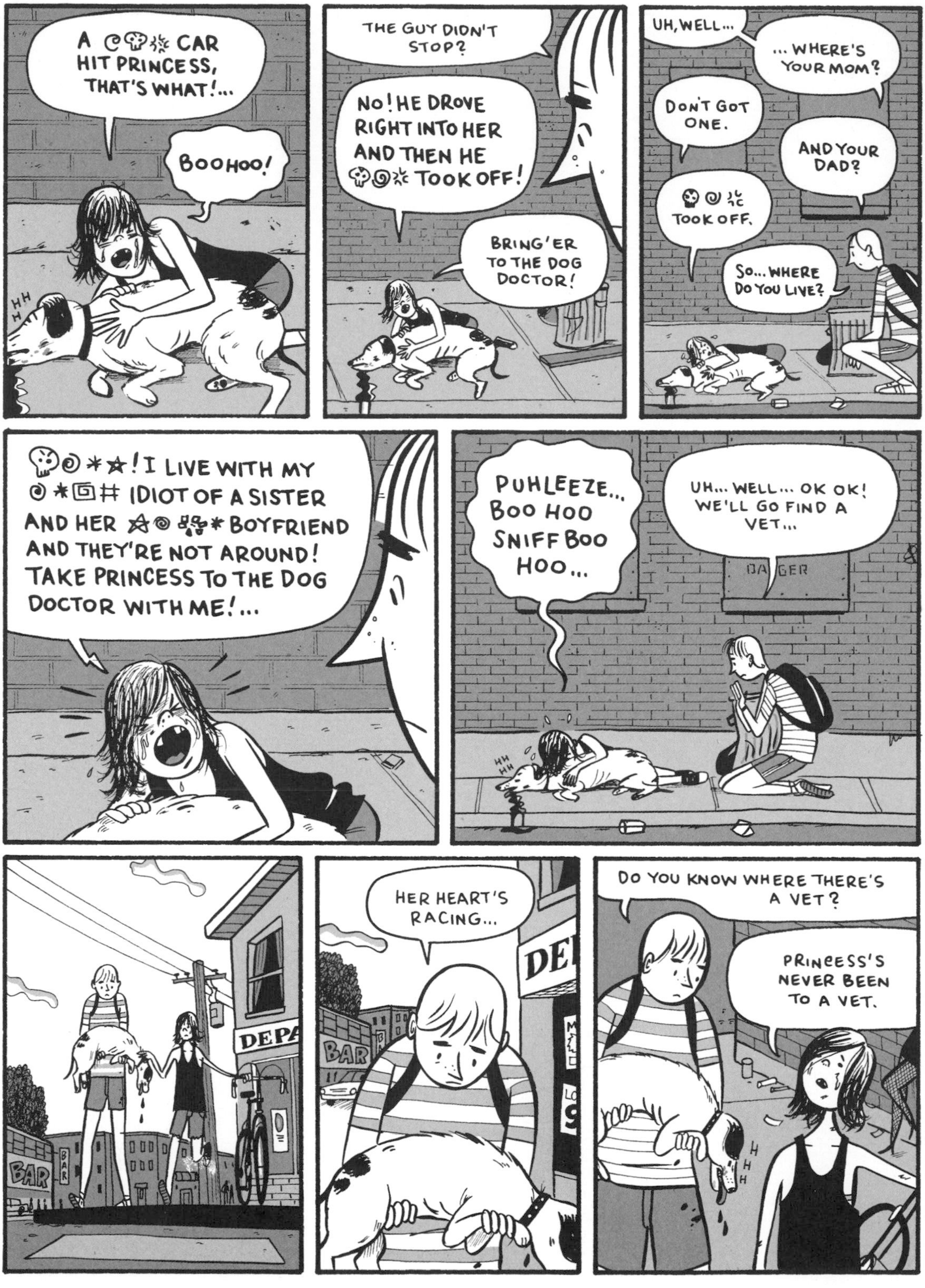
A @💀※ CAR HIT PRINCESS, THAT'S WHAT!...
BOOHOO!
HH H
THE GUY DIDN'T STOP?
NO! HE DROVE RIGHT INTO HER AND THEN HE 💀@※ TOOK OFF!
BRING'ER TO THE DOG DOCTOR!
UH, WELL...
... WHERE'S YOUR MOM?
DON'T GOT ONE.
AND YOUR DAD?
💀@※ TOOK OFF.
SO... WHERE DO YOU LIVE?
💀@*★! I LIVE WITH MY @*回# IDIOT OF A SISTER AND HER ★@※* BOYFRIEND AND THEY'RE NOT AROUND! TAKE PRINCESS TO THE DOG DOCTOR WITH ME!...
PUHLEEZE... BOO HOO SNIFF BOO HOO...
UH... WELL... OK OK! WE'LL GO FIND A VET...
HH HH
BAR
BAR
DEPA
HER HEART'S RACING...
DE
BAR
DO YOU KNOW WHERE THERE'S A VET?
PRINCESS'S NEVER BEEN TO A VET.
H H H

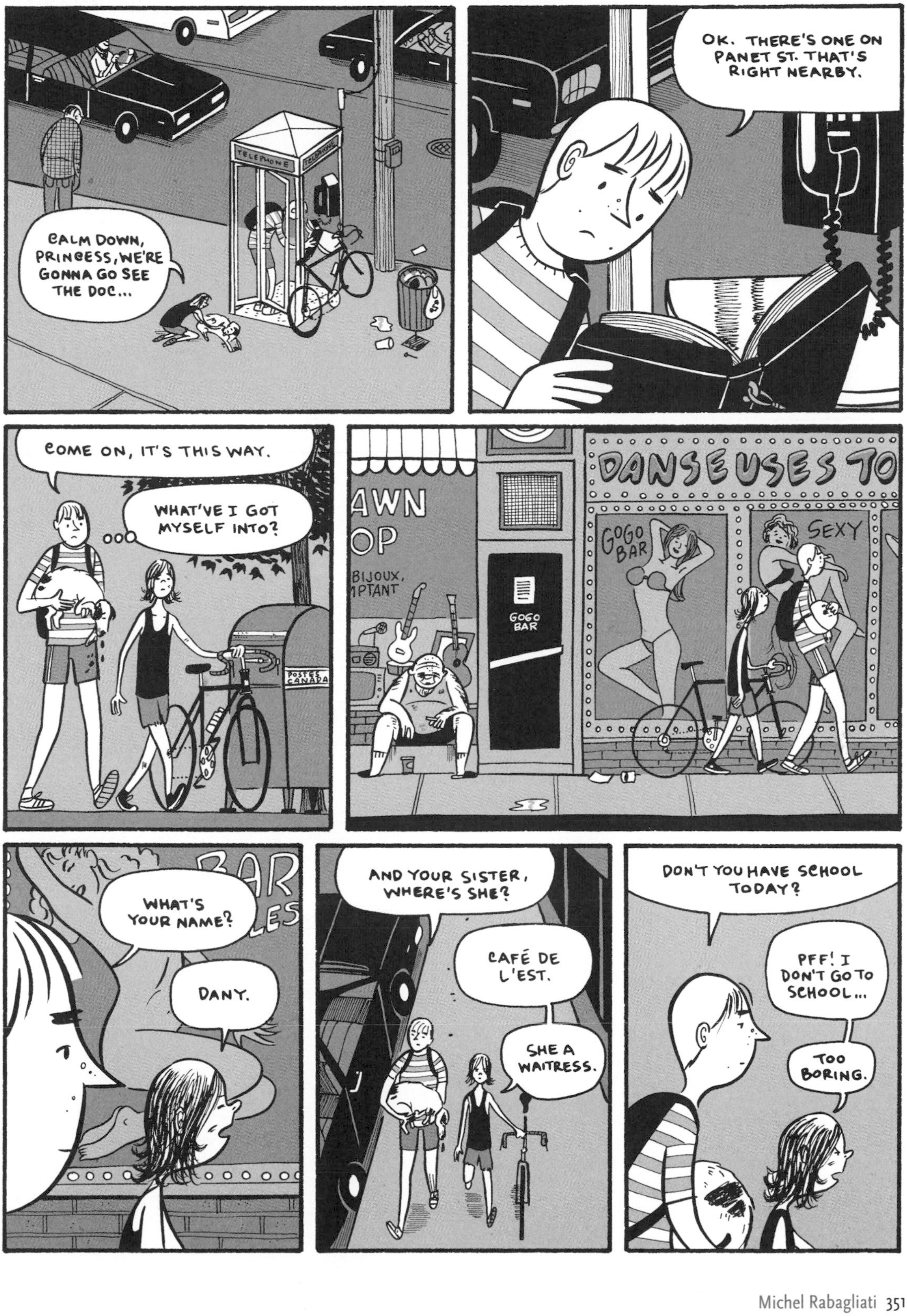
TELEPHONE
TÉLÉPHONE
CALM DOWN, PRINCESS, WE'RE GONNA GO SEE THE DOC...
OK. THERE'S ONE ON PANET ST. THAT'S RIGHT NEARBY.
COME ON, IT'S THIS WAY.
WHAT'VE I GOT MYSELF INTO?
POSTES CANADA
DANSEUSES TO
AWN
OP
BIJOUX,
MPTANT
GOGO BAR
GOGO BAR
SEXY
BAR
LES
WHAT'S YOUR NAME?
DANY.
AND YOUR SISTER, WHERE'S SHE?
CAFÉ DE L'EST.
SHE A WAITRESS.
DON'T YOU HAVE SCHOOL TODAY?
PFF! I DON'T GO TO SCHOOL...
TOO BORING.

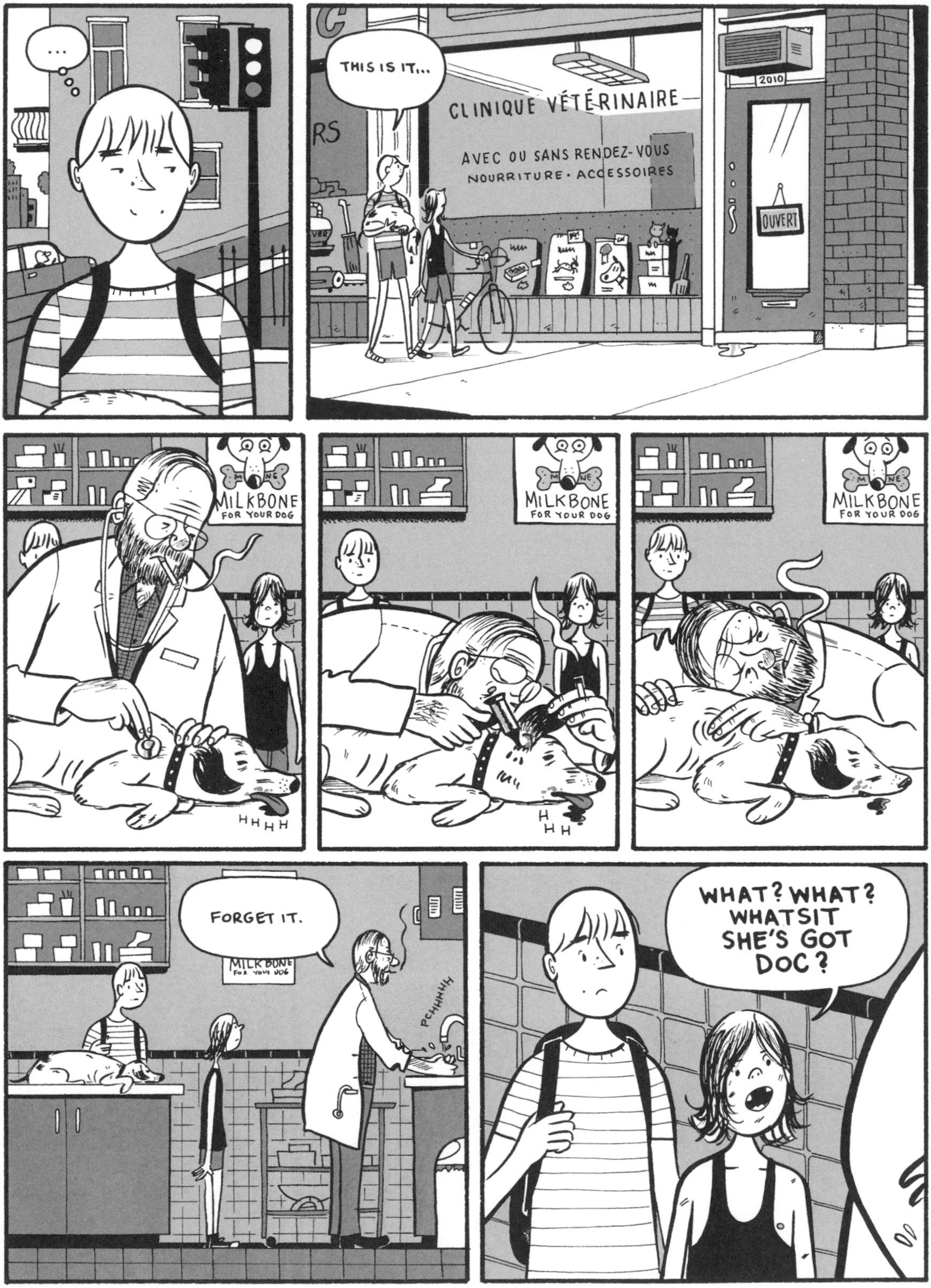
...
THIS IS IT...
CLINIQUE VÉTÉRINAIRE
AVEC OU SANS RENDEZ-VOUS
NOURRITURE • ACCESSOIRES
2010
OUVERT
MILKBONE
FOR YOUR DOG
HHHH
MILKBONE
FOR YOUR DOG
H
HH
MILKBONE
FOR YOUR DOG
FORGET IT.
MILKBONE
FOR YOUR DOG
PCHHHHH
WHAT? WHAT? WHATSIT SHE'S GOT DOC?

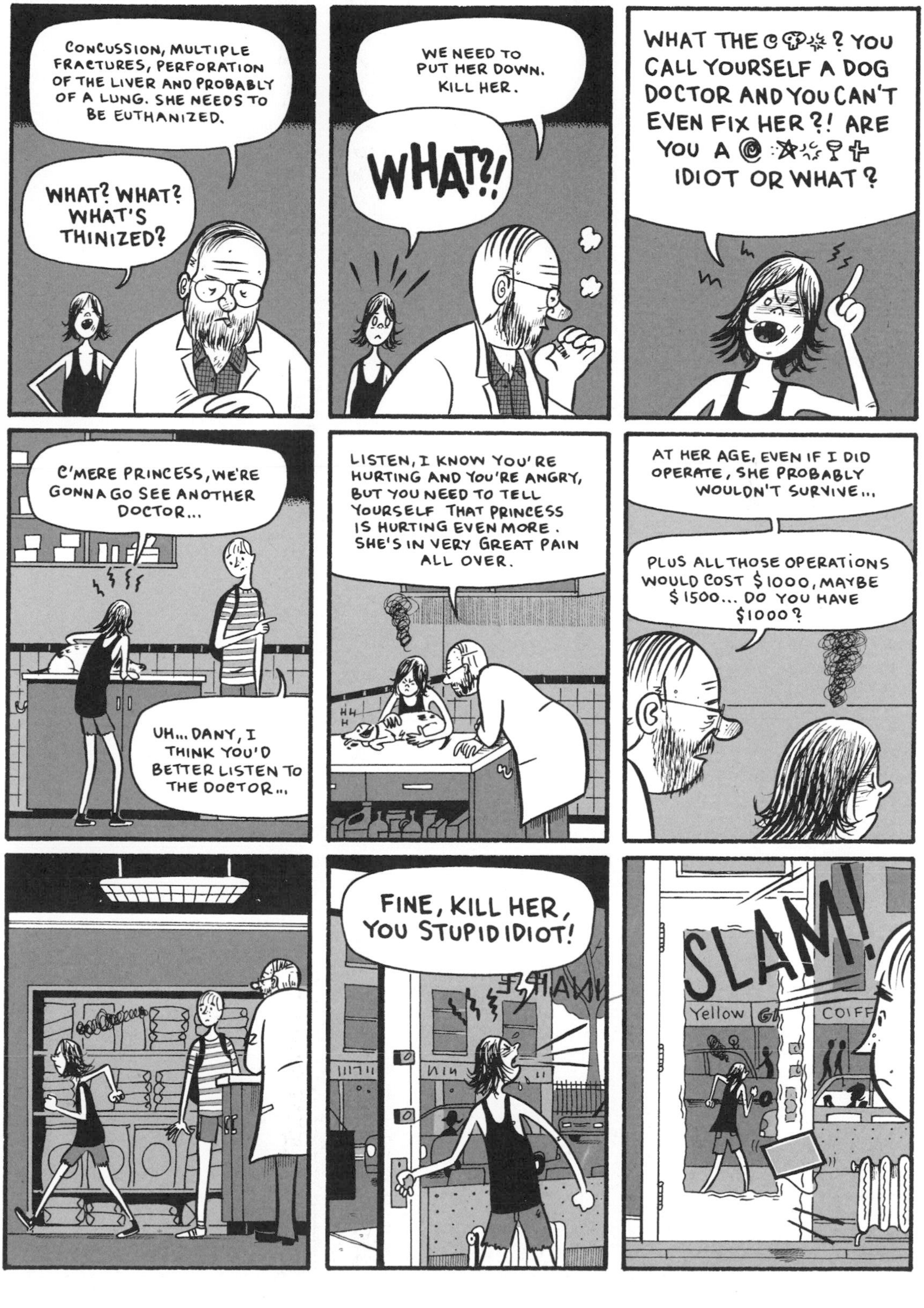
CONCUSSION, MULTIPLE FRACTURES, PERFORATION OF THE LIVER AND PROBABLY OF A LUNG. SHE NEEDS TO BE EUTHANIZED.
WHAT? WHAT? WHAT'S THINIZED?
WE NEED TO PUT HER DOWN. KILL HER.
WHAT?!
WHAT THE @ ? YOU CALL YOURSELF A DOG DOCTOR AND YOU CAN'T EVEN FIX HER?! ARE YOU A @ IDIOT OR WHAT?
C'MERE PRINCESS, WE'RE GONNA GO SEE ANOTHER DOCTOR...
UH... DANY, I THINK YOU'D BETTER LISTEN TO THE DOCTOR...
LISTEN, I KNOW YOU'RE HURTING AND YOU'RE ANGRY, BUT YOU NEED TO TELL YOURSELF THAT PRINCESS IS HURTING EVEN MORE. SHE'S IN VERY GREAT PAIN ALL OVER.
AT HER AGE, EVEN IF I DID OPERATE, SHE PROBABLY WOULDN'T SURVIVE...
PLUS ALL THOSE OPERATIONS WOULD COST $1000, MAYBE $1500... DO YOU HAVE $1000?
FINE, KILL HER, YOU STUPID IDIOT!
SLAM!
Yellow

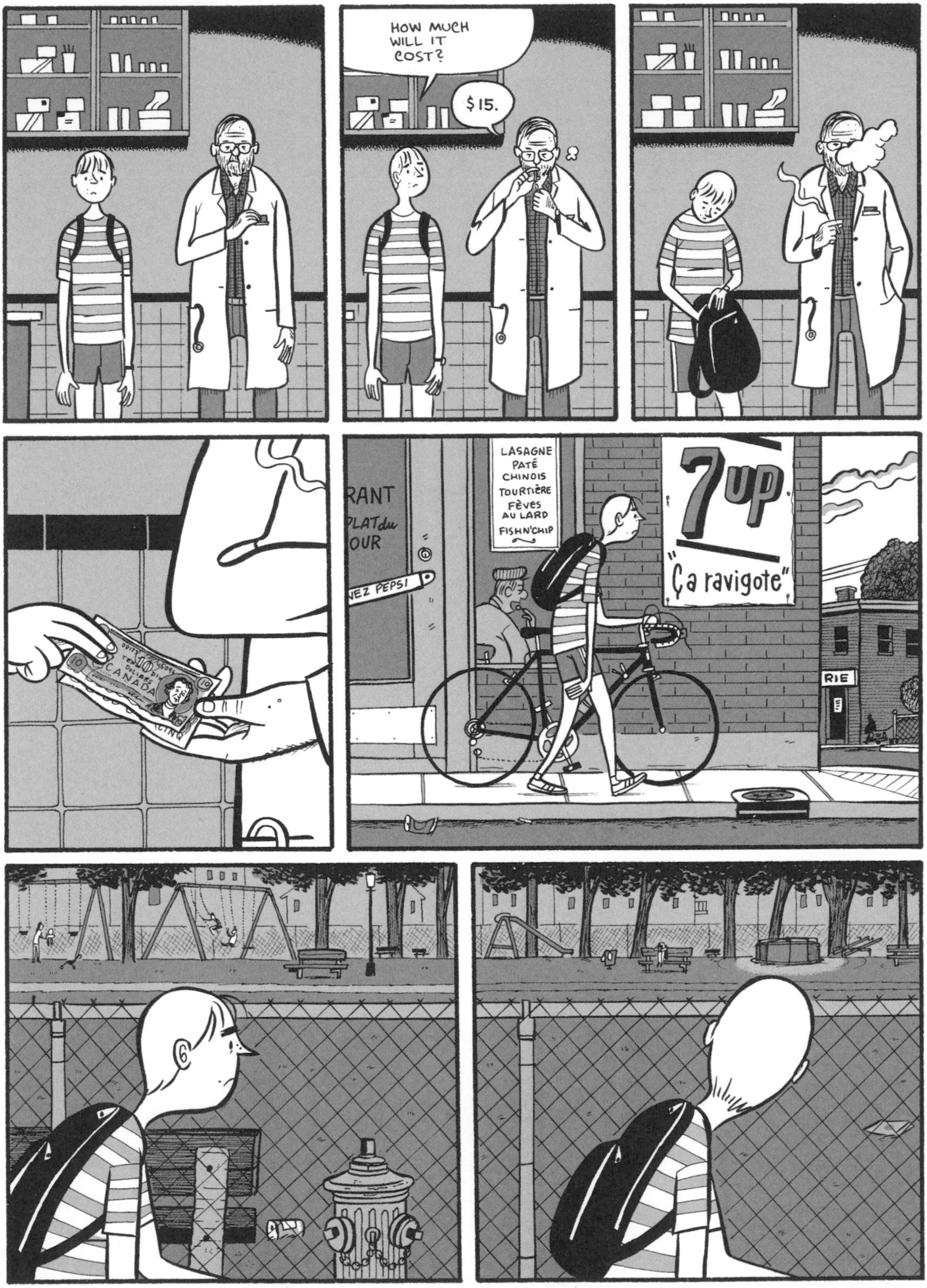

HOW MUCH WILL IT COST?
$15.
CANADA
LASAGNE
PATÉ CHINOIS
TOURTIÈRE
FÈVES AU LARD
FISHN'CHIP
RANT
PLAT du
OUR
NEZ PEPSI
7up
"Ça ravigote"
RIE

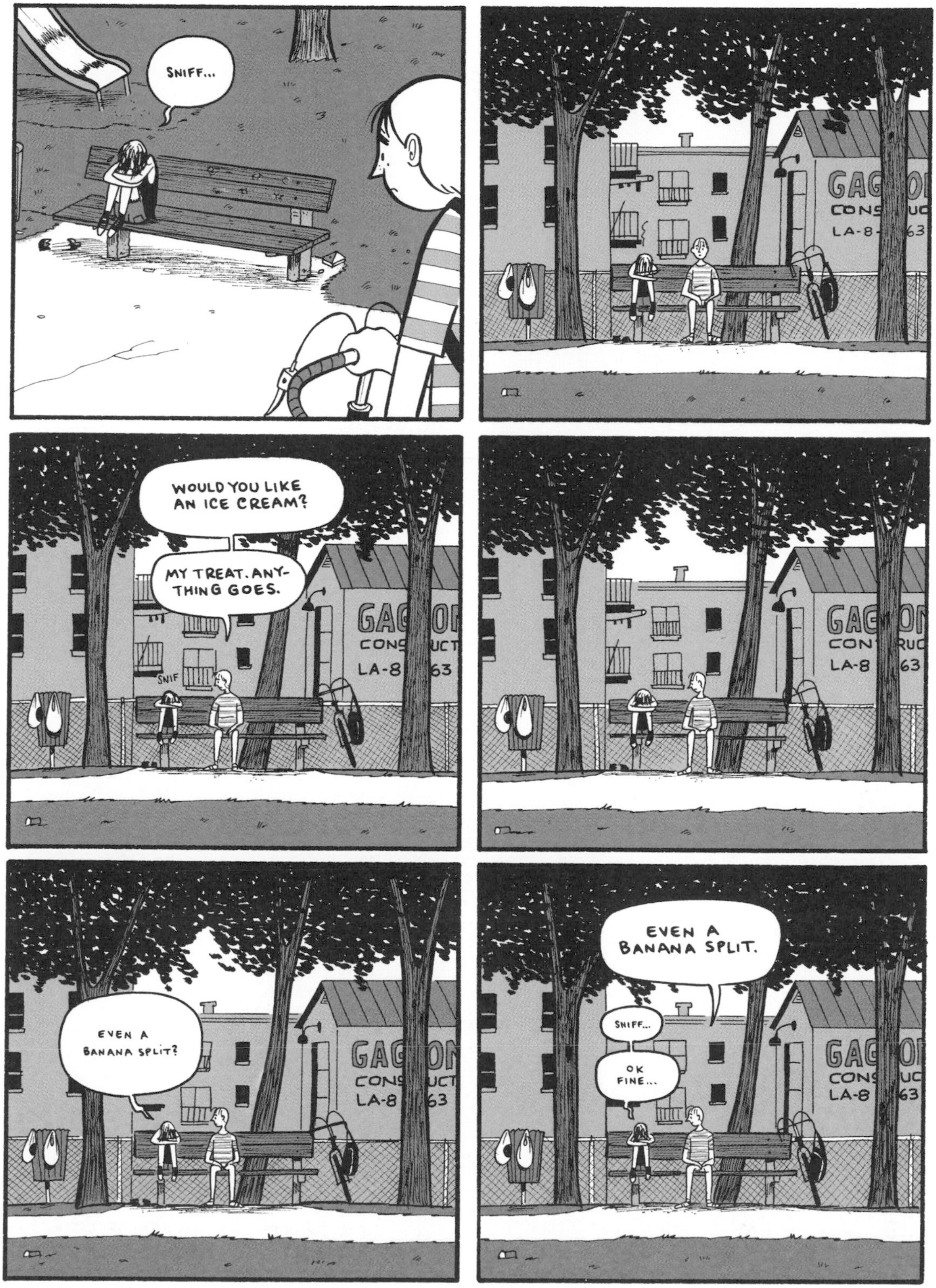
SNIFF...
GAGNON
CONSTRUC
LA-8 63
WOULD YOU LIKE AN ICE CREAM?
MY TREAT. ANY-THING GOES.
SNIF
EVEN A BANANA SPLIT?
EVEN A BANANA SPLIT.
SNIFF...
OK FINE...

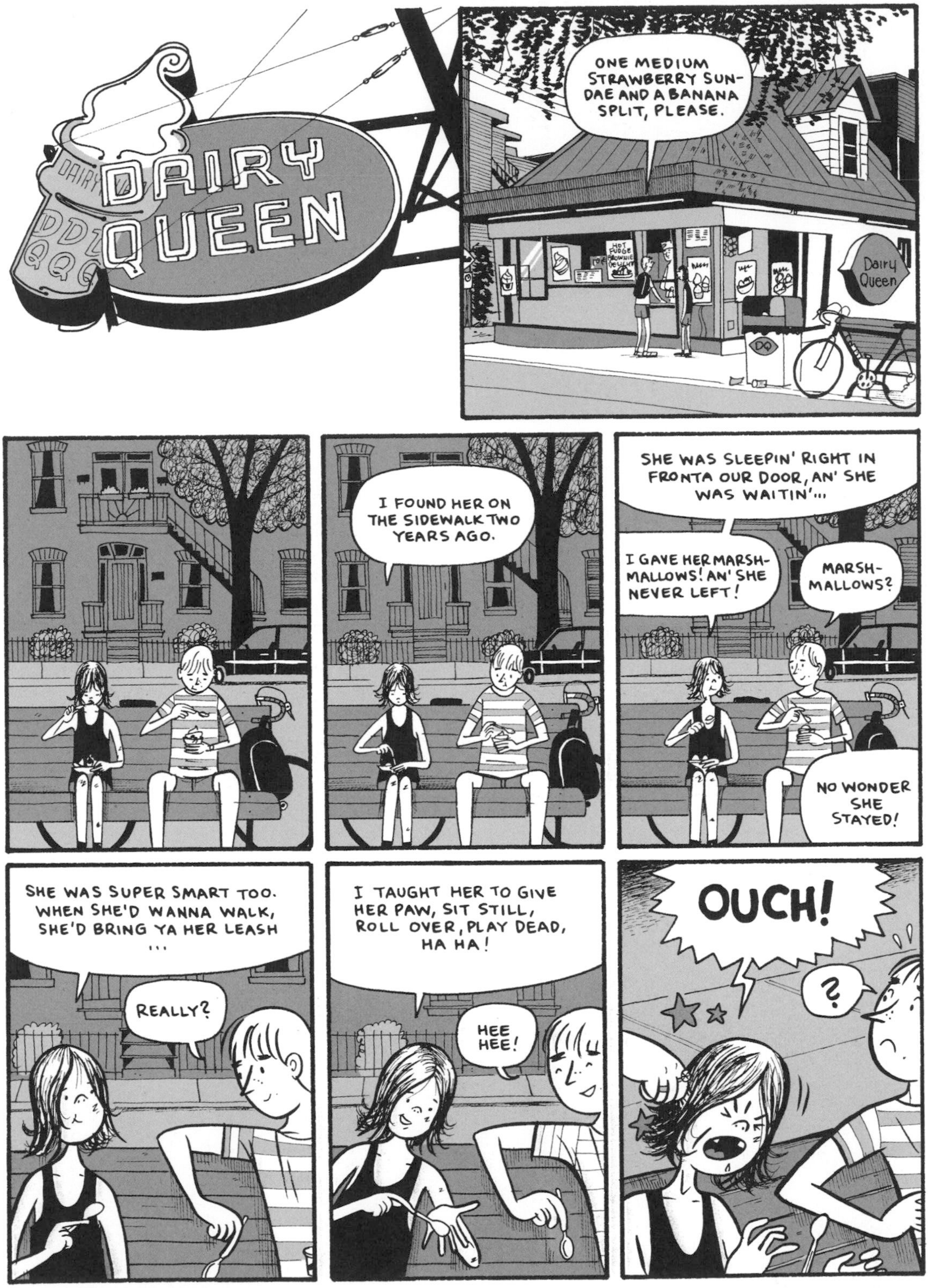
DAIRY QUEEN
ONE MEDIUM STRAWBERRY SUNDAE AND A BANANA SPLIT, PLEASE.
Dairy Queen
I FOUND HER ON THE SIDEWALK TWO YEARS AGO.
SHE WAS SLEEPIN' RIGHT IN FRONTA OUR DOOR, AN' SHE WAS WAITIN'...
I GAVE HER MARSHMALLOWS! AN' SHE NEVER LEFT!
MARSHMALLOWS?
NO WONDER SHE STAYED!
SHE WAS SUPER SMART TOO. WHEN SHE'D WANNA WALK, SHE'D BRING YA HER LEASH ...
REALLY?
I TAUGHT HER TO GIVE HER PAW, SIT STILL, ROLL OVER, PLAY DEAD, HA HA!
HEE HEE!
OUCH!
?

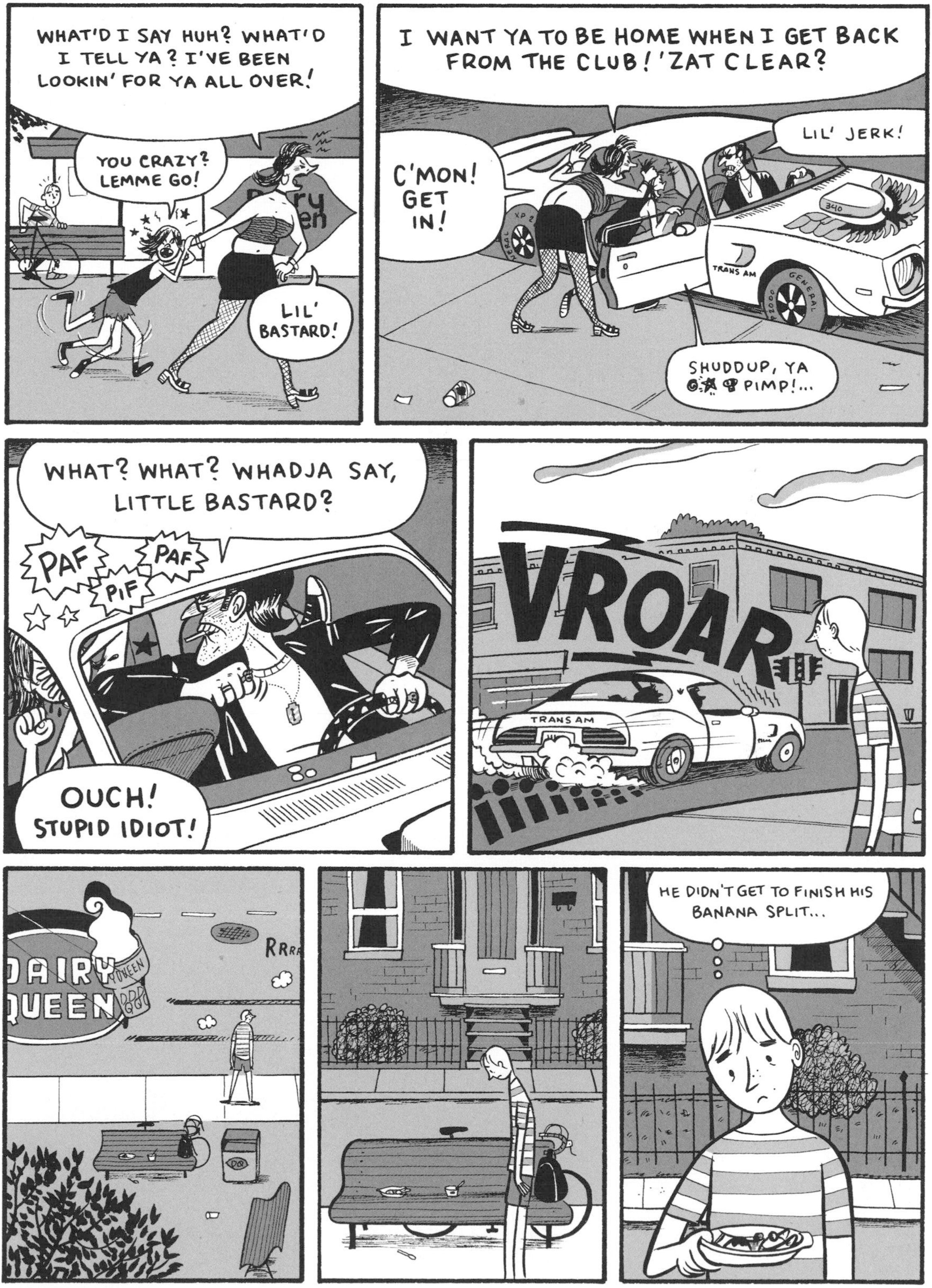
WHAT'D I SAY HUH? WHAT'D I TELL YA? I'VE BEEN LOOKIN' FOR YA ALL OVER!
YOU CRAZY? LEMME GO!
LIL' BASTARD!
I WANT YA TO BE HOME WHEN I GET BACK FROM THE CLUB! 'ZAT CLEAR?
C'MON! GET IN!
LIL' JERK!
TRANS AM
SHUDDUP, YA @*¶ PIMP!...
WHAT? WHAT? WHADJA SAY, LITTLE BASTARD?
PAF
PIF
PAF
OUCH! STUPID IDIOT!
VROAR
TRANS AM
DAIRY QUEEN
RRRR
HE DIDN'T GET TO FINISH HIS BANANA SPLIT...

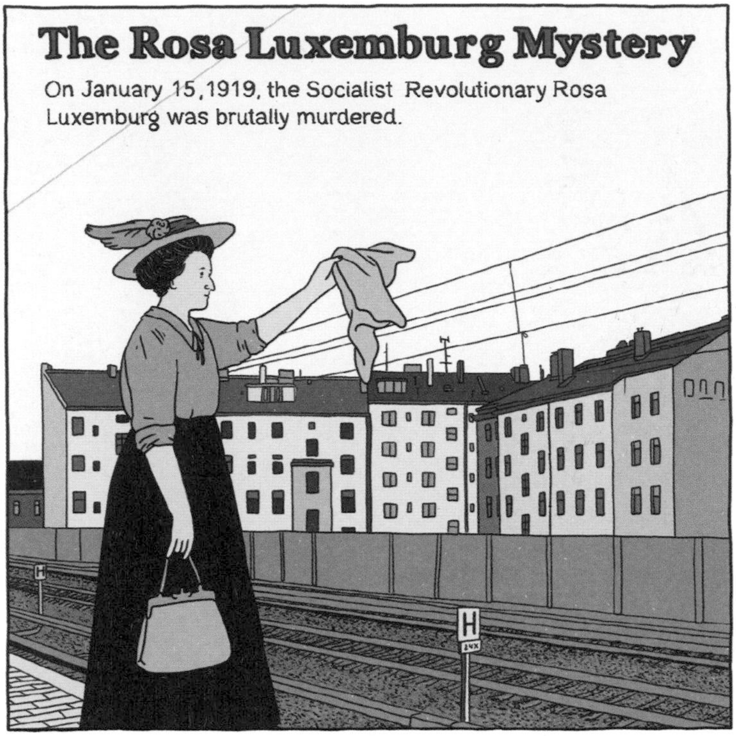
The Rosa Luxemburg Mystery
On January 15, 1919, the Socialist Revolutionary Rosa Luxemburg was brutally murdered.
H

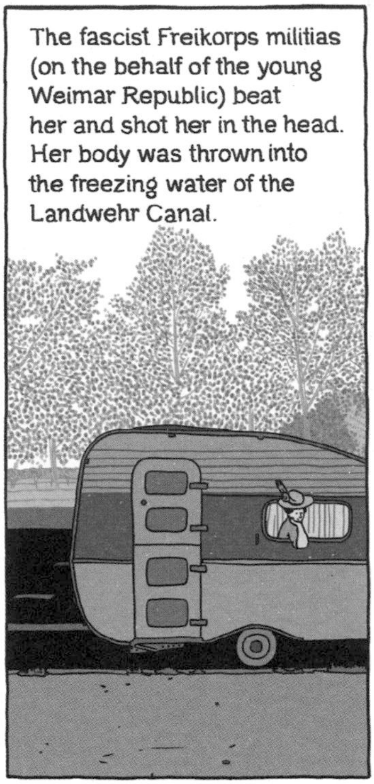
The fascist Freikorps militias (on the behalf of the young Weimar Republic) beat her and shot her in the head. Her body was thrown into the freezing water of the Landwehr Canal.

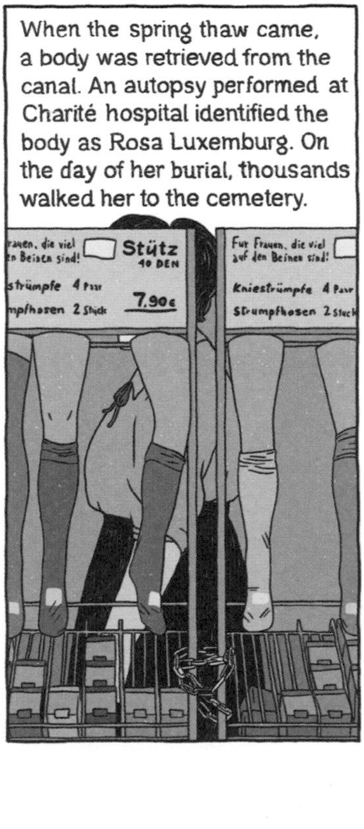
When the spring thaw came, a body was retrieved from the canal. An autopsy performed at Charité hospital identified the body as Rosa Luxemburg. On the day of her burial, thousands walked her to the cemetery.
Stütz
40 DEN
7.90€
Fur Frauen, die viel auf den Beinen sind!
Kniestrümpfe
Strumpfhosen 2 Stück

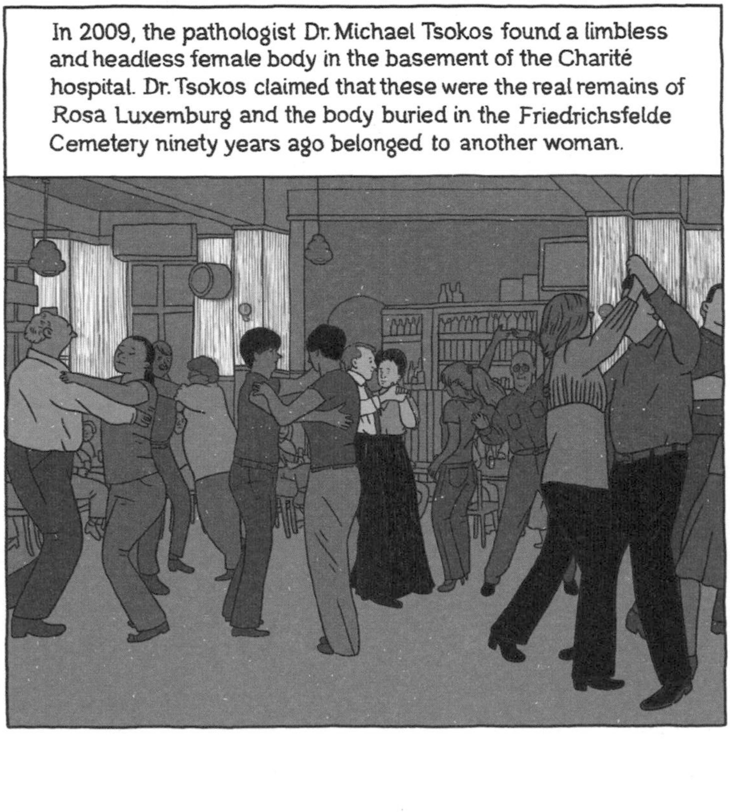
In 2009, the pathologist Dr. Michael Tsokos found a limbless and headless female body in the basement of the Charité hospital. Dr. Tsokos claimed that these were the real remains of Rosa Luxemburg and the body buried in the Friedrichsfelde Cemetery ninety years ago belonged to another woman.

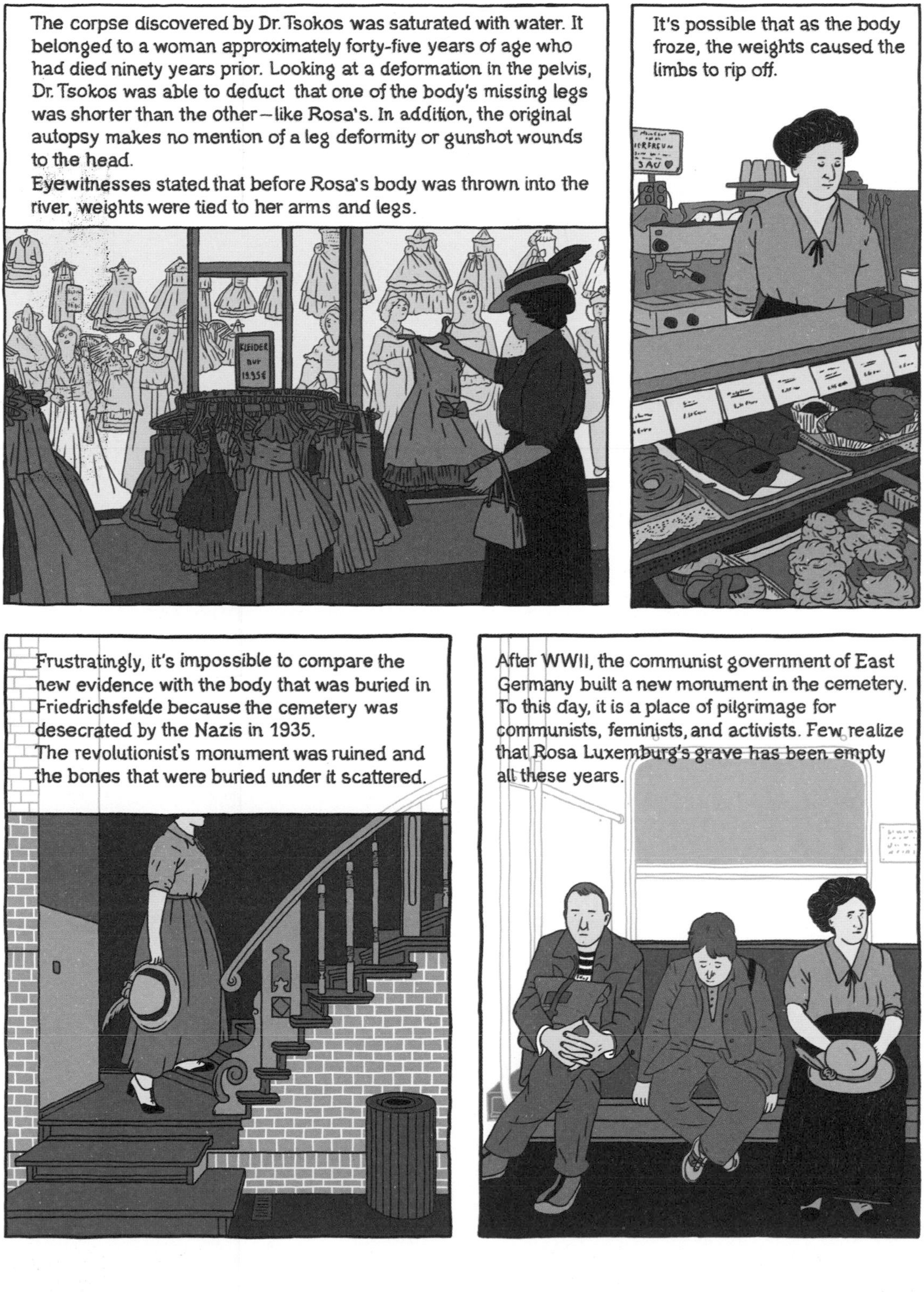
The corpse discovered by Dr. Tsokos was saturated with water. It belonged to a woman approximately forty-five years of age who had died ninety years prior. Looking at a deformation in the pelvis, Dr. Tsokos was able to deduct that one of the body's missing legs was shorter than the other—like Rosa's. In addition, the original autopsy makes no mention of a leg deformity or gunshot wounds to the head.
Eyewitnesses stated that before Rosa's body was thrown into the river, weights were tied to her arms and legs.
KLEIDER nur 19,95€
It's possible that as the body froze, the weights caused the limbs to rip off.
Frustratingly, it's impossible to compare the new evidence with the body that was buried in Friedrichsfelde because the cemetery was desecrated by the Nazis in 1935.
The revolutionist's monument was ruined and the bones that were buried under it scattered.
After WWII, the communist government of East Germany built a new monument in the cemetery. To this day, it is a place of pilgrimage for communists, feminists, and activists. Few realize that Rosa Luxemburg's grave has been empty all these years.

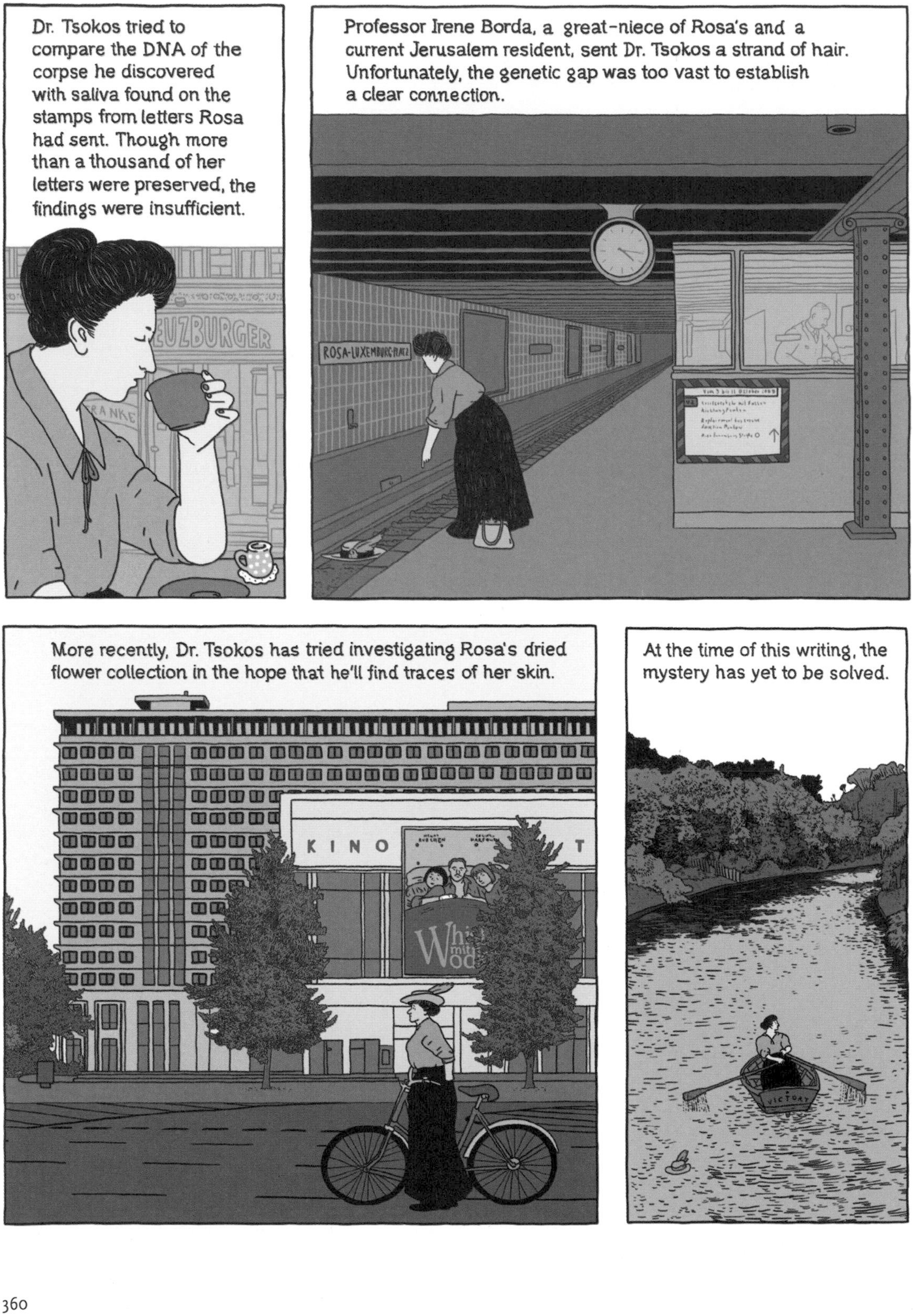
Dr. Tsokos tried to compare the DNA of the corpse he discovered with saliva found on the stamps from letters Rosa had sent. Though more than a thousand of her letters were preserved, the findings were insufficient.
Professor Irene Borda, a great-niece of Rosa's and a current Jerusalem resident, sent Dr. Tsokos a strand of hair. Unfortunately, the genetic gap was too vast to establish a clear connection.
ROSA-LUXEMBURG-PLATZ
More recently, Dr. Tsokos has tried investigating Rosa's dried flower collection in the hope that he'll find traces of her skin.
KINO
At the time of this writing, the mystery has yet to be solved.
VICTORY

SAVING FICTIONS: A HISTORY OF LOVE

an appreciation of Rutu Modan by Ariel Kahn

Rutu Modan has created an inspirational body of comics, ranging from the autobiographical column Mixed Emotions and the fictional strip *Murder of the Terminal Patient*, both for the *New York Times*, to *Jamilti*, an anthology of short stories. Her two full-length graphic novels, *Exit Wounds* and *The Property*, both Eisner Award winners, are amongst my all-time favourite books.

Her work gives a vivid sense of dialogue with the comics tradition, incorporating the legacies of both European and American artists. She has adopted the *ligne claire* style associated with Hergé and made it her own, subverting the ossified moral binaries usually associated with it. Into her cocktail shaker she adds a dash of the visionary colouring of Winsor McKay's *Little Nemo*. Colour becomes almost another character in her work, taking on the rhythmic and emotional power of visual music. Different chapters of *Exit Wounds*, for example, have their own palettes. Shifts in colour often suggest the emotional realizations of her protagonists and, potentially, of her readers. Their delicacy supports the lightness and playfulness of her humour, which touches every subject and every character, stripping away delusion with surprising gentleness.

The possibility of love, its challenges, and the dangerous vulnerability it requires form a leitmotif in her work, from her early collaborations with Israeli short story writer Etgar Keret to the experimental, innovative productions of the Actus comics collective, which she set up in Tel Aviv together with Yirmi Pinkus, essentially founding the comics tradition in Israel. Her work is both visually and conceptually sophisticated, mediating between competing versions of the past and present and suggesting the possibility of a more nuanced and complex future. As befits an initially "outsider" medium, her work evinces a sensitivity to outsiders, to marginalized figures and voices.

The fact that our sense of reality is often composed of helpfully self-serving fictions, and what happens when these unravel, is a key thematic preoccupation. *Exit Wounds* provides a vivid picture of a country in crisis, repressing trauma and loss. The tentative and touching relationships that unfold in her work do so against this potent backdrop, which enhances the sense of their fragility and preciousness. Modan explores the impact of this public denial on private lives with a warmth and humour that usefully complicate our response to both the country and her characters.

Photo: Ephrat Beloosesky (2014). 361

Both *Exit Wounds* and the title story of her collection *Jamilti* take real historical events as their starting point, in both cases centring on an unidentified body. The stories focus on the meanings those bodies might have for those who seek to confront or avoid them. A minor figure in *Exit Wounds* identifies his dead father by a video recording of his ear. Our experiences of both love and loss are too mediated, Modan argues, and through her characters' journeys, we are led to confront our own secret histories. Her work allows the reader to confront reality in all its indeterminacy and ambiguity.

Rutu challenges her readers and protagonists to connect—to the past, to others, and to themselves. To do this, she suggests, we must engage with the palpable presence of absence, from the habitually missing father in *Exit Wounds* to Regina's dead son in *The Property*. Both absences propel her protagonists on transformative journeys, and we travel along with them. The roots of this preoccupation are evident in her short stories, from the suicide bomber whom she allows us to see as a person in the title story of *Jamilti* to the mother who proves not to be quite as dead as her daughter imagined in "Bygone" and the missing son who may or may not be the pilot of a crashed plane in "Homecoming," depending on the personal agendas of those at the scene. Modan highlights the ways in which holding on to the past can prevent us from moving forward and leaping into the unknown, as her protagonist Koby does at the end of *Exit Wounds*.

The Property depicts the complex dialectic between Israel and its European past, contrasting public and private narrative histories. These are played out in the parallel relationships of grandmother Regina Segal and her granddaughter Mica with the men in their lives, culminating in a masterpiece of tragicomic staging at a graveyard during Zaduszki, the Polish day of the dead. With deft assurance, Rutu conveys a strong sense of the multiple voices and meanings that "make" history, in so doing subverting received ideologies and truths. Israel emerges as a kind of cultural palimpsest, built on what it has sought to efface. Rutu empowers us to mediate between competing visions and versions through her bravura use of silent pages or panels, which amplify the emotional subtext of the narrative. She makes a potent argument for the mimetic power of the medium in the way that gestures and words are always open to misinterpretation and need to be experienced together. It is fitting that this layered work was a collaborative production: actors staged the tableaux, and the comic-within-a-comic of the Warsaw Ghetto uprising drawn by Mica's Polish love interest, Tomasz, was produced by fellow Israeli artist Asaf Hanuka.

As might be expected in work of such subtlety, her characterization is consistently complex and surprising. In addition to romantic entanglements, she is brilliant at depicting familial relationships, especially between women, and she has done much to expand the visual vocabulary of gender representation, without the ideological heaviness that this might suggest. Numi, the lover of both Koby and his father in *Exit Wounds*, is a delightfully unconventional woman, yet she struggles with how she looks and the way she is treated as a result. The realization of parallels and connections between genders is a powerful tool for empathy in Modan's work. Koby, the "hero" of *Exit Wounds*, has a moment of such insight while sitting in the kitchen of another woman his father has abandoned. He realises that loss is not his own private domain, but a shared thread of feeling that has as much power to unite and transform as love does. Perhaps for this reason, as Rutu once commented, the word "love" is never mentioned in *Exit Wounds*; it must be discovered rather than spoken. As a result, her panels vibrate with the energy of suppressed feelings.

I've had the pleasure of meeting Rutu at several points in her recent comics career, which has seemed to map the changing relationship between comics and mainstream literary culture in the UK, from a coffee at Tate Britain when she and her family moved to England for her partner's post-doc in Sheffield to her recent quick stopover in London en route to the Edinburgh Festival. She generously welcomed me to her studio in Tel Aviv when she was working away on one of her glorious, anarchic picture books for children, *Maya Makes a Mess*.

In person, she's a fantastic listener, quick and perceptive in her comments and insights. You can see where her pitch-perfect ear for dialogue comes from. She hit it off with my wife, who is also Israeli, and produced a beautiful one-off portrait for her. This is not a conventional representation, but a symbolic portrait which I feel is simultaneously a portrait of the artist. In it, a boat sails through the sky, kept aloft by the willpower of the young girl in the sailor's cap at the helm, who aims a telescope toward some vista only she can see, while the boat's funnels pour out flowers behind her. The image shrewdly combines whimsy and toughness, its lush colour conveying a sense of curiosity and delight at the unfolding possibilities of a journey into the unknown. Now a professor at Bezalel, the Jerusalem art school where she first studied, Rutu is engaging the next generation of Israeli comics artists and illustrators as fellow travellers, to explore the extraordinary possibilities of the medium she has made her own.

Dr. Ariel Kahn is a senior lecturer in creative writing at Roehampton University, where he teaches comics and graphic novels as part of the creative writing degree. He has written widely on comics in academic journals and the national and international press.

Some jerk meets a broad, she falls for him, it goes to his head and he walks out on his wife, leaves her with two little girls. They don't hear a word from him for fifteen years.

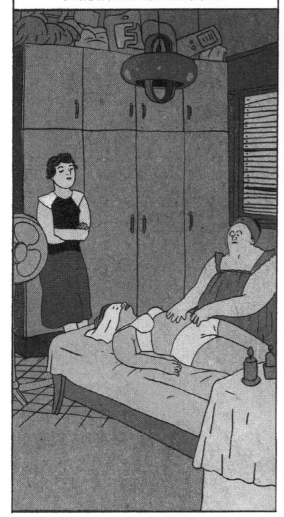

The wife swallows some pills and almost croaks.

Do you feel the current?

Yes... Oh yes!

Almost? She croaks, all right. Brain dead, then comes back to life. But it all worked out for the best.

That means she's located the problematic area with her energies...

Because while she was lying there dead, she had a vision. She saw the light, encountered spectral beings from the beyond, and woke up with healing powers. Electricity in her hands that can cure any sickness.

You can get up now. The session is over.

The first English edition of "Energy Blockage" appeared in *Jamilti and Other Stories* (2008). Rutu Modan with translation by Noah Stollman 363

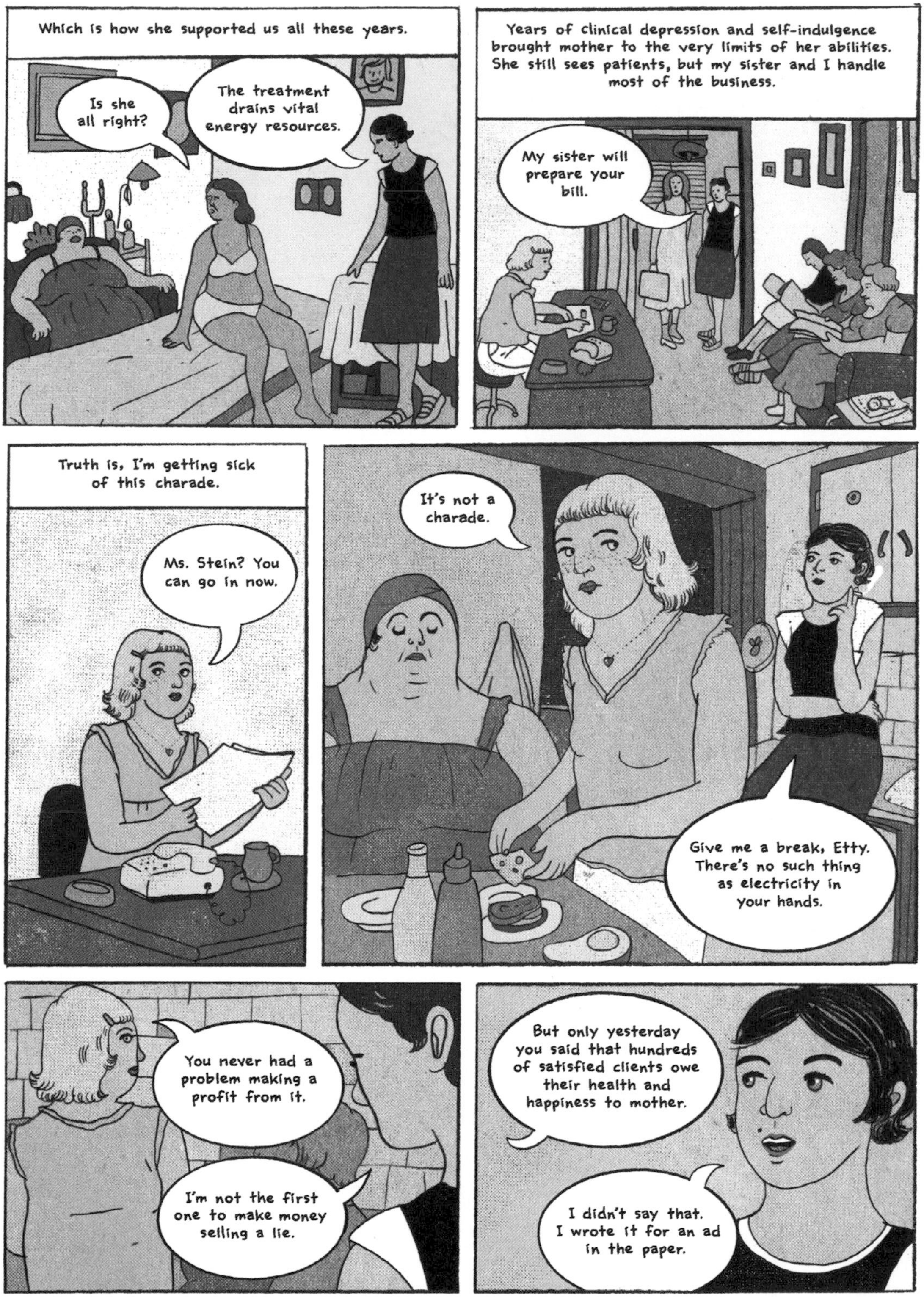
Which is how she supported us all these years.
Is she all right?
The treatment drains vital energy resources.
Years of clinical depression and self-indulgence brought mother to the very limits of her abilities. She still sees patients, but my sister and I handle most of the business.
My sister will prepare your bill.
Truth is, I'm getting sick of this charade.
Ms. Stein? You can go in now.
It's not a charade.
Give me a break, Etty. There's no such thing as electricity in your hands.
You never had a problem making a profit from it.
I'm not the first one to make money selling a lie.
But only yesterday you said that hundreds of satisfied clients owe their health and happiness to mother.
I didn't say that. I wrote it for an ad in the paper.

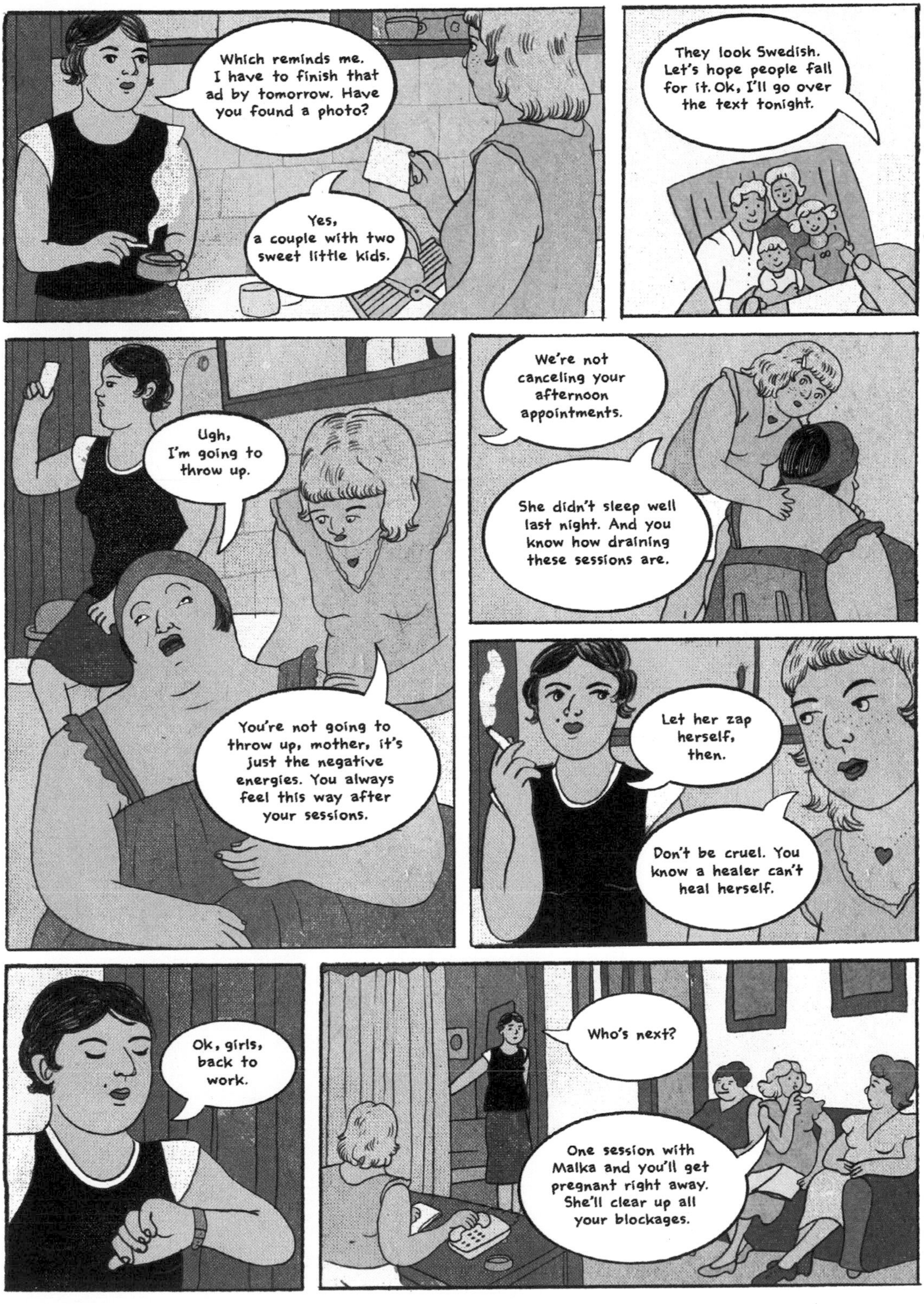

Which reminds me. I have to finish that ad by tomorrow. Have you found a photo?
Yes, a couple with two sweet little kids.
They look Swedish. Let's hope people fall for it. Ok, I'll go over the text tonight.
Ugh, I'm going to throw up.
You're not going to throw up, mother, it's just the negative energies. You always feel this way after your sessions.
We're not canceling your afternoon appointments.
She didn't sleep well last night. And you know how draining these sessions are.
Let her zap herself, then.
Don't be cruel. You know a healer can't heal herself.
Ok, girls, back to work.
Who's next?
One session with Malka and you'll get pregnant right away. She'll clear up all your blockages.

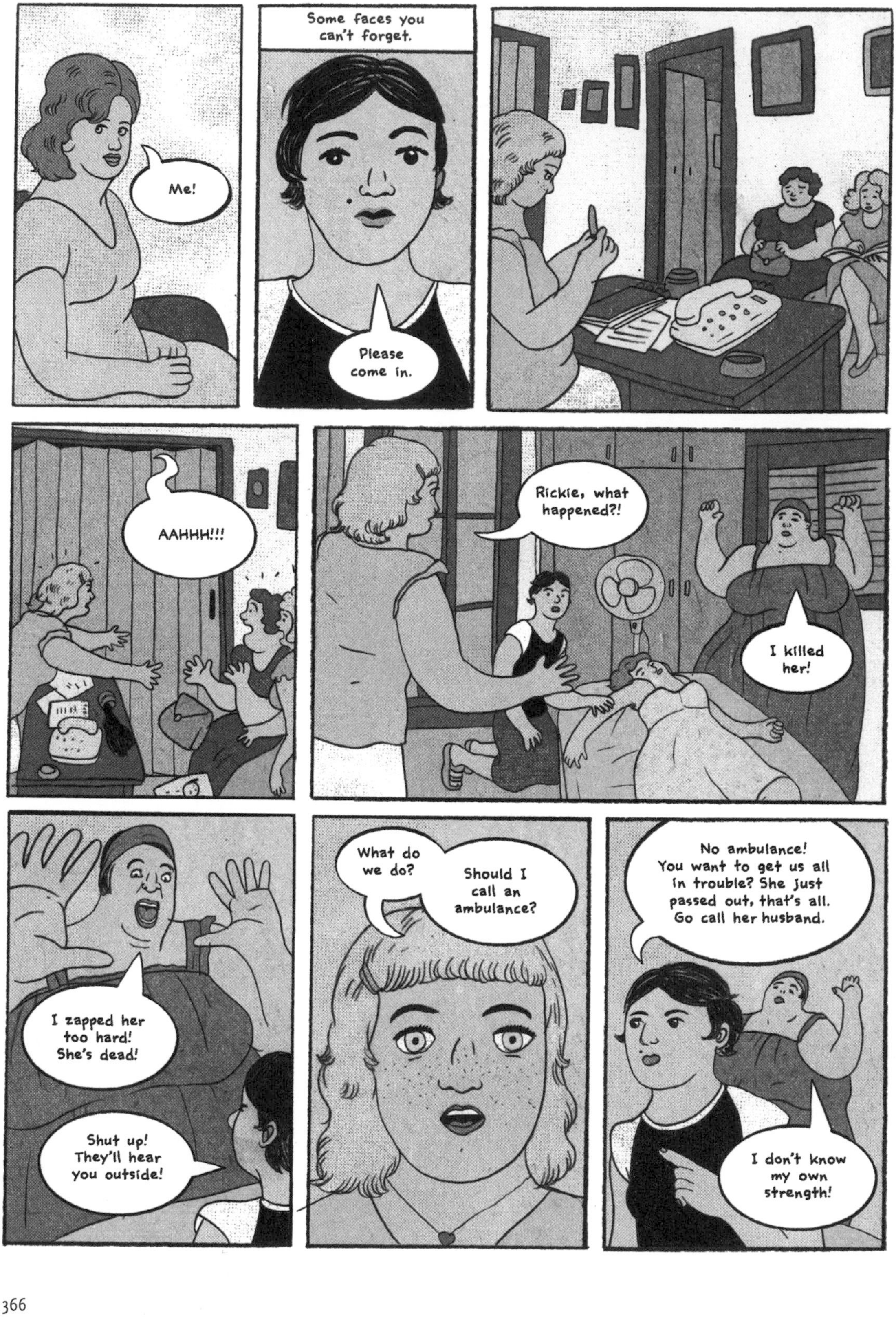
Me!
Some faces you can't forget.
Please come in.
AAHHH!!!
Rickie, what happened?!
I killed her!
I zapped her too hard! She's dead!
Shut up! They'll hear you outside!
What do we do?
Should I call an ambulance?
No ambulance! You want to get us all in trouble? She just passed out, that's all. Go call her husband.
I don't know my own strength!

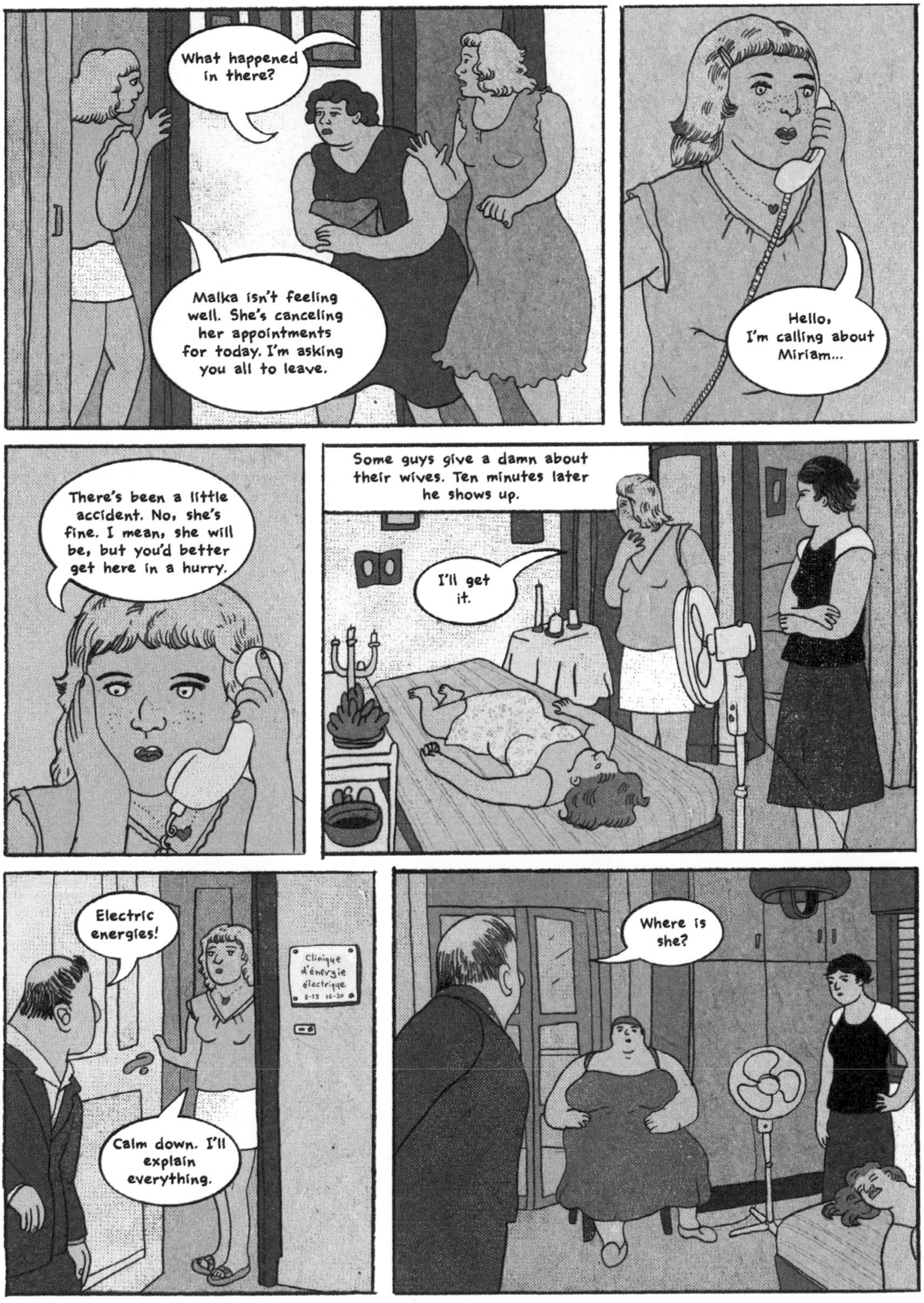
What happened in there?
Malka isn't feeling well. She's canceling her appointments for today. I'm asking you all to leave.
Hello, I'm calling about Miriam...
There's been a little accident. No, she's fine. I mean, she will be, but you'd better get here in a hurry.
Some guys give a damn about their wives. Ten minutes later he shows up.
I'll get it.
Electric energies!
Clinique d'énergie électrique 8-13 16-20
Calm down. I'll explain everything.
Where is she?

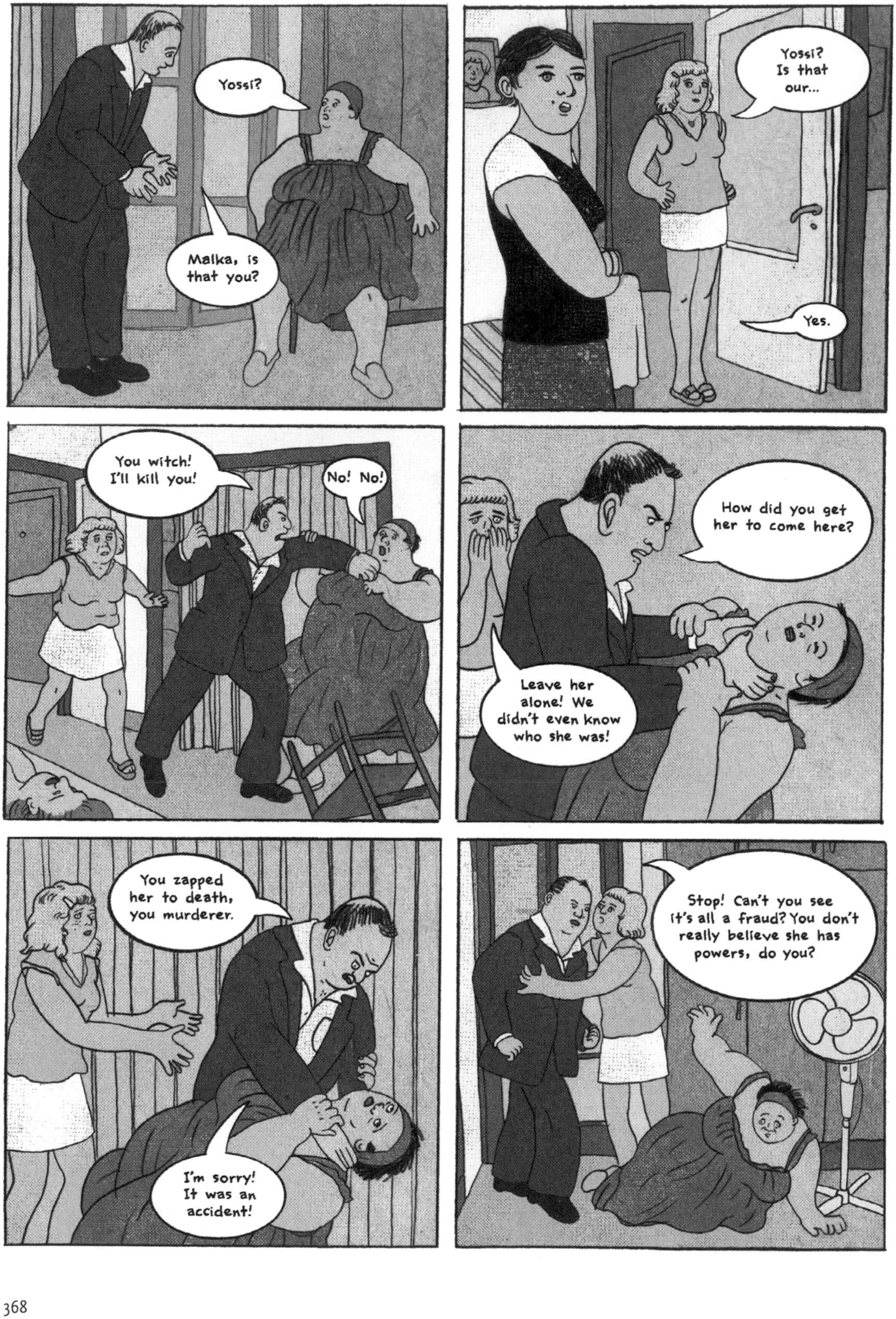
Yossi?
Malka, is that you?
Yossi? Is that our...
Yes.
You witch! I'll kill you!
No! No!
How did you get her to come here?
Leave her alone! We didn't even know who she was!
You zapped her to death, you murderer.
I'm sorry! It was an accident!
Stop! Can't you see it's all a fraud? You don't really believe she has powers, do you?

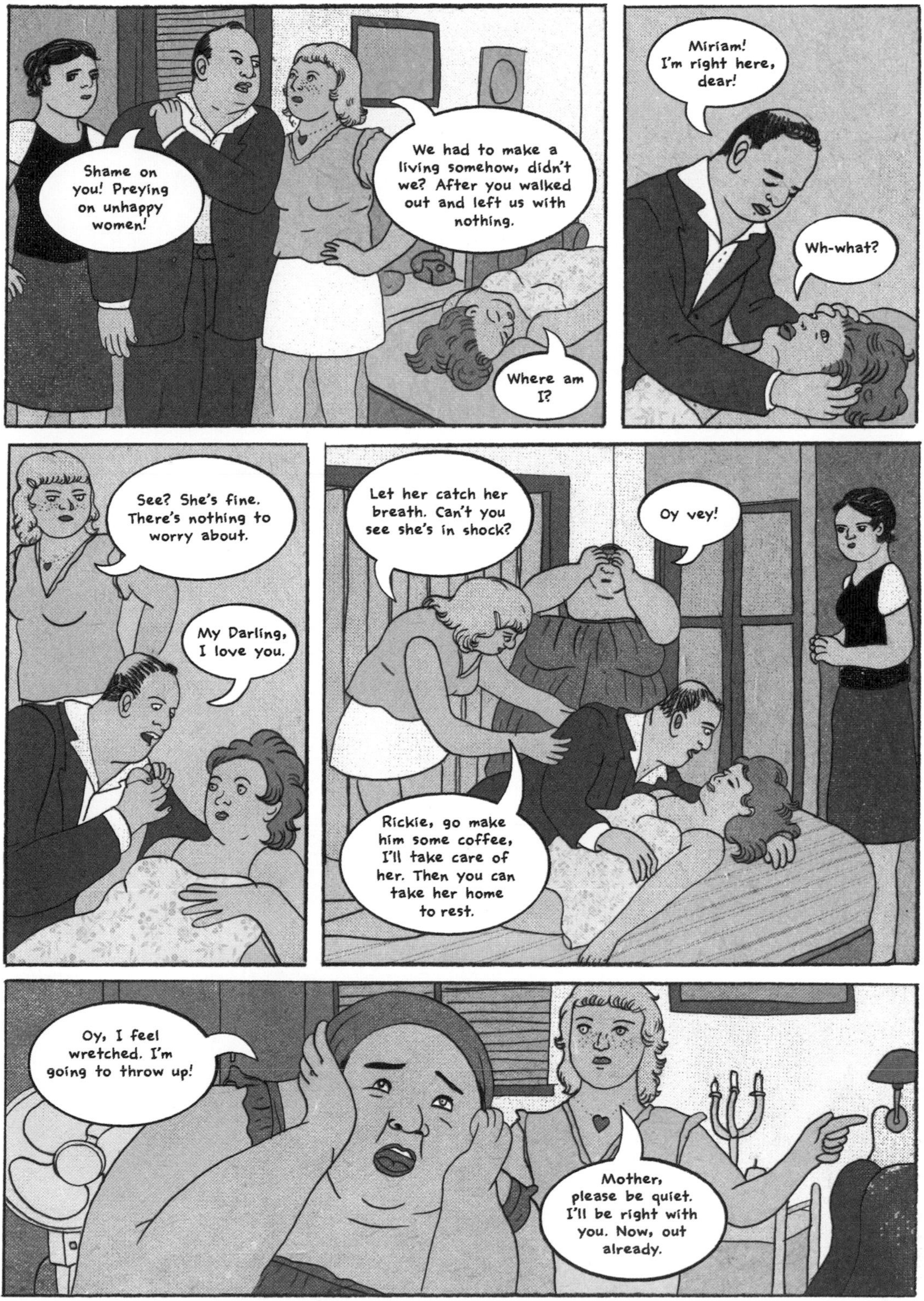
Shame on you! Preying on unhappy women!
We had to make a living somehow, didn't we? After you walked out and left us with nothing.
Where am I?
Miriam! I'm right here, dear!
Wh-what?
See? She's fine. There's nothing to worry about.
My Darling, I love you.
Let her catch her breath. Can't you see she's in shock?
Oy vey!
Rickie, go make him some coffee, I'll take care of her. Then you can take her home to rest.
Oy, I feel wretched. I'm going to throw up!
Mother, please be quiet. I'll be right with you. Now, out already.

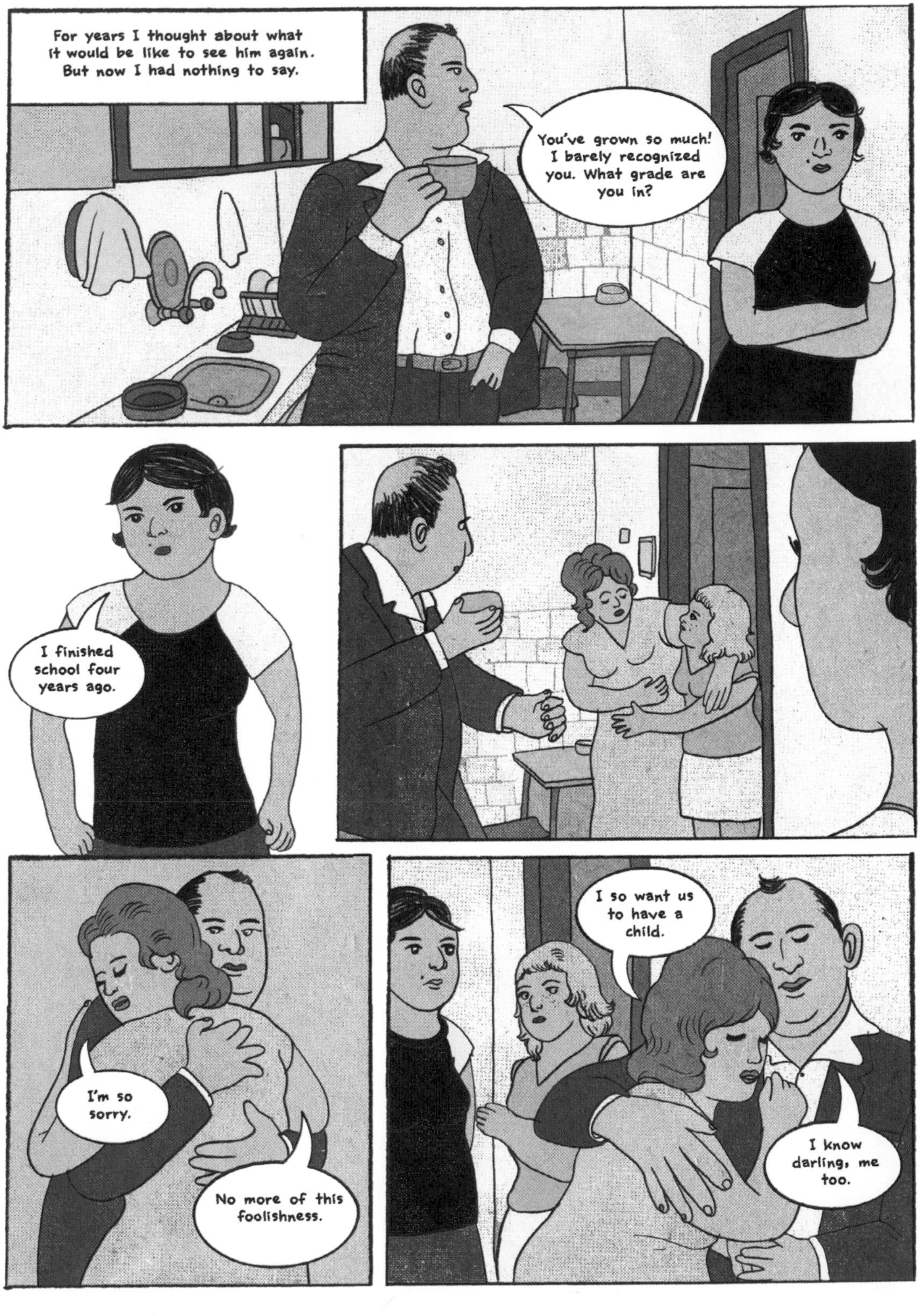
For years I thought about what it would be like to see him again. But now I had nothing to say.
You've grown so much! I barely recognized you. What grade are you in?
I finished school four years ago.
I'm so sorry.
No more of this foolishness.
I so want us to have a child.
I know darling, me too.

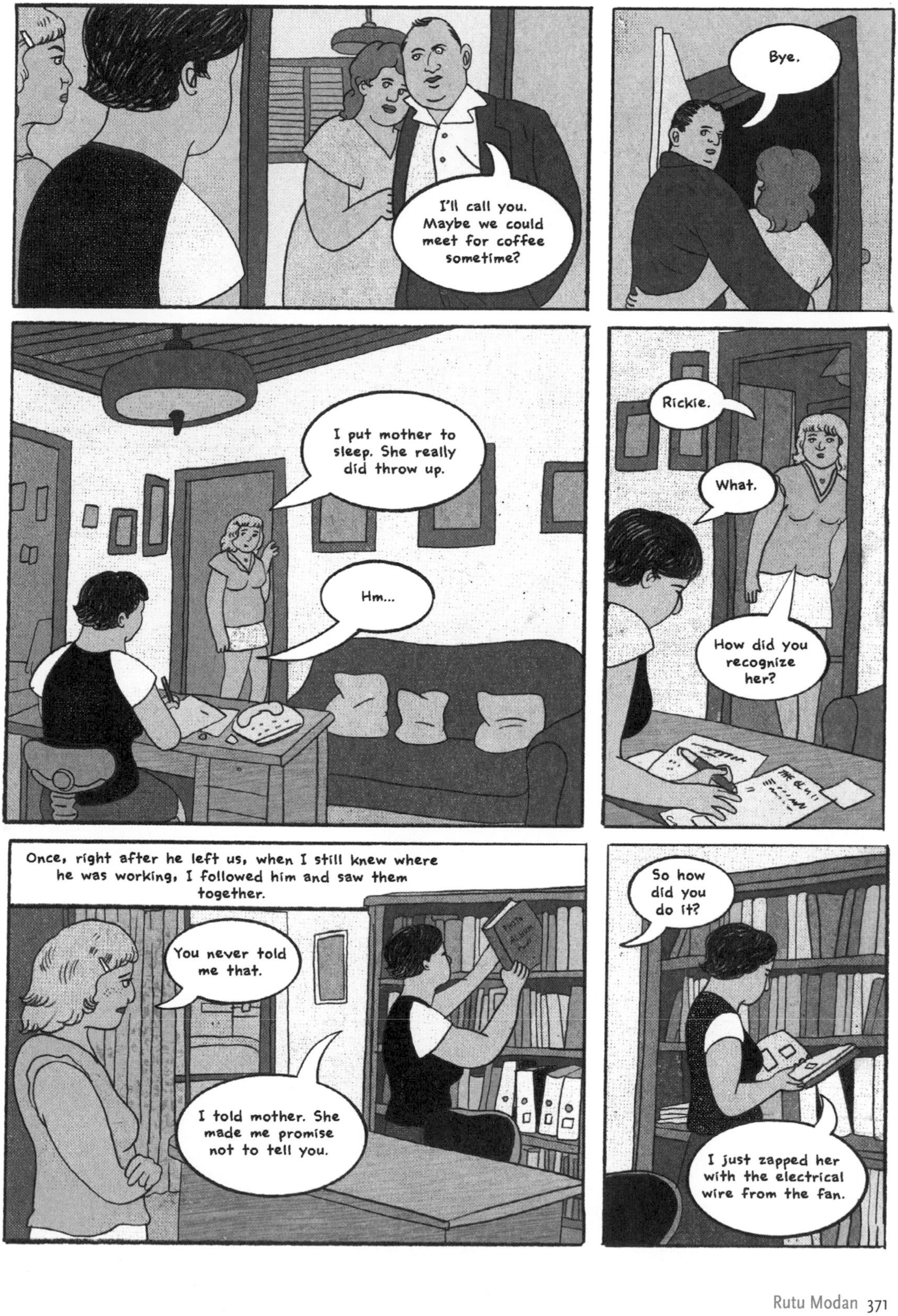
I'll call you. Maybe we could meet for coffee sometime?
Bye.
I put mother to sleep. She really did throw up.
Hm...
Rickie.
What.
How did you recognize her?
Once, right after he left us, when I still knew where he was working, I followed him and saw them together.
You never told me that.
I told mother. She made me promise not to tell you.
So how did you do it?
I just zapped her with the electrical wire from the fan.

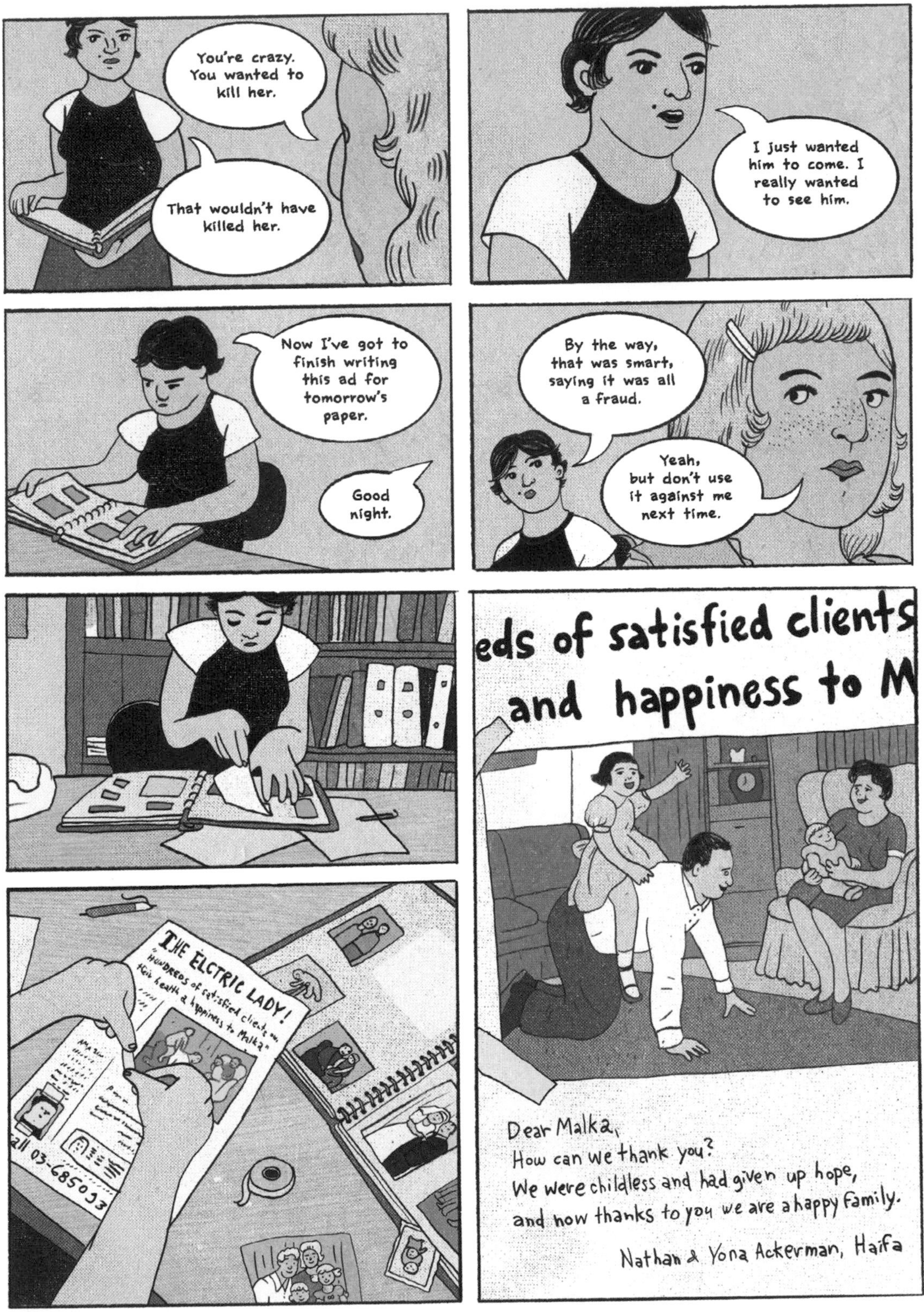
You're crazy. You wanted to kill her.
That wouldn't have killed her.
I just wanted him to come. I really wanted to see him.
Now I've got to finish writing this ad for tomorrow's paper.
Good night.
By the way, that was smart, saying it was all a fraud.
Yeah, but don't use it against me next time.
THE ELCTRIC LADY!
"HUNDREDS of satisfied clients ... their health & happiness to Malka"
all 03-685033
eds of satisfied clients
and happiness to M
Dear Malka,
How can we thank you?
We were childless and had given up hope,
and now thanks to you we are a happy family.
Nathan & Yona Ackerman, Haifa

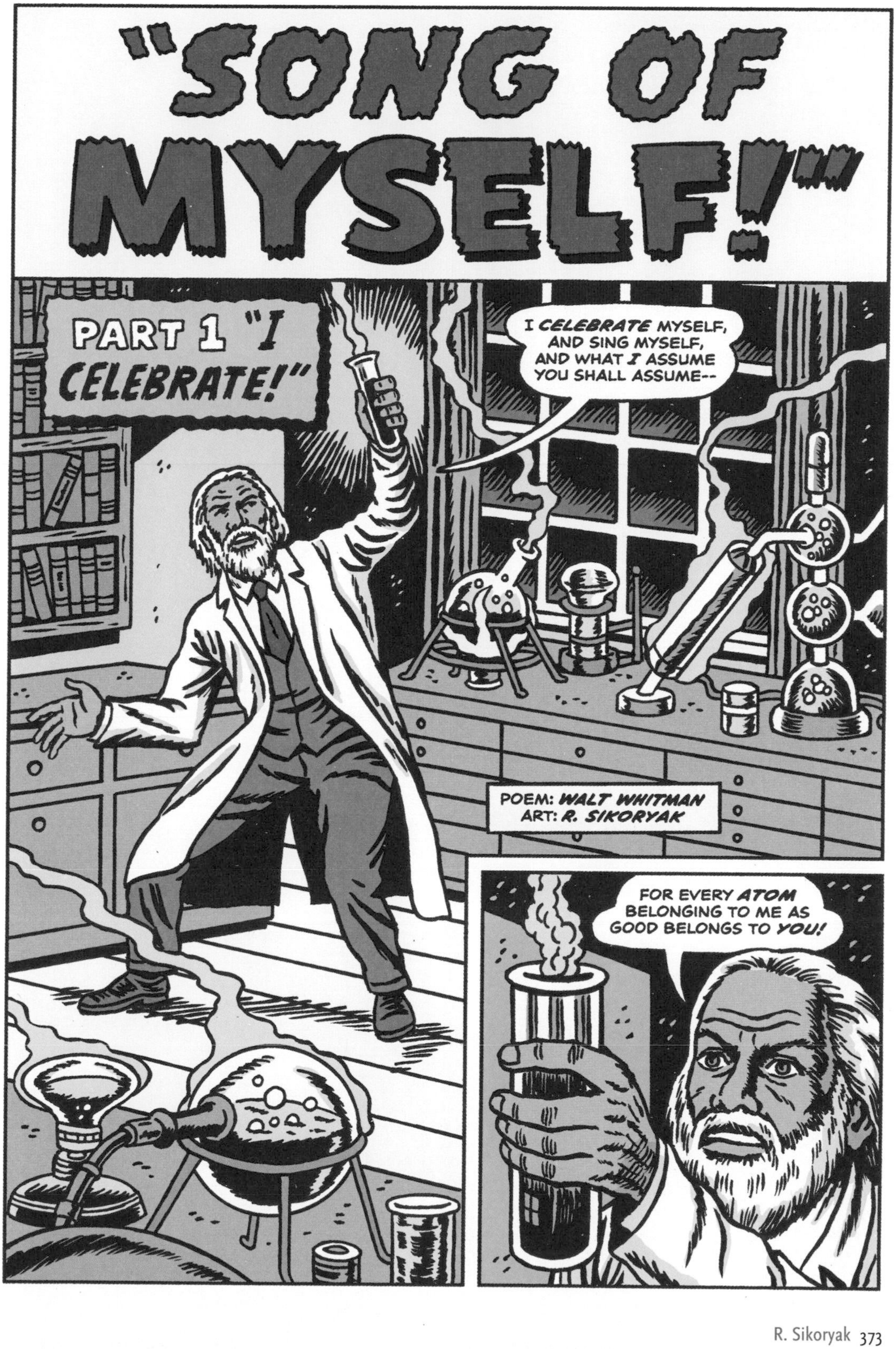
"SONG OF MYSELF!"
PART 1 "I CELEBRATE!"
I CELEBRATE MYSELF, AND SING MYSELF, AND WHAT I ASSUME YOU SHALL ASSUME--
POEM: WALT WHITMAN
ART: R. SIKORYAK
FOR EVERY ATOM BELONGING TO ME AS GOOD BELONGS TO YOU!

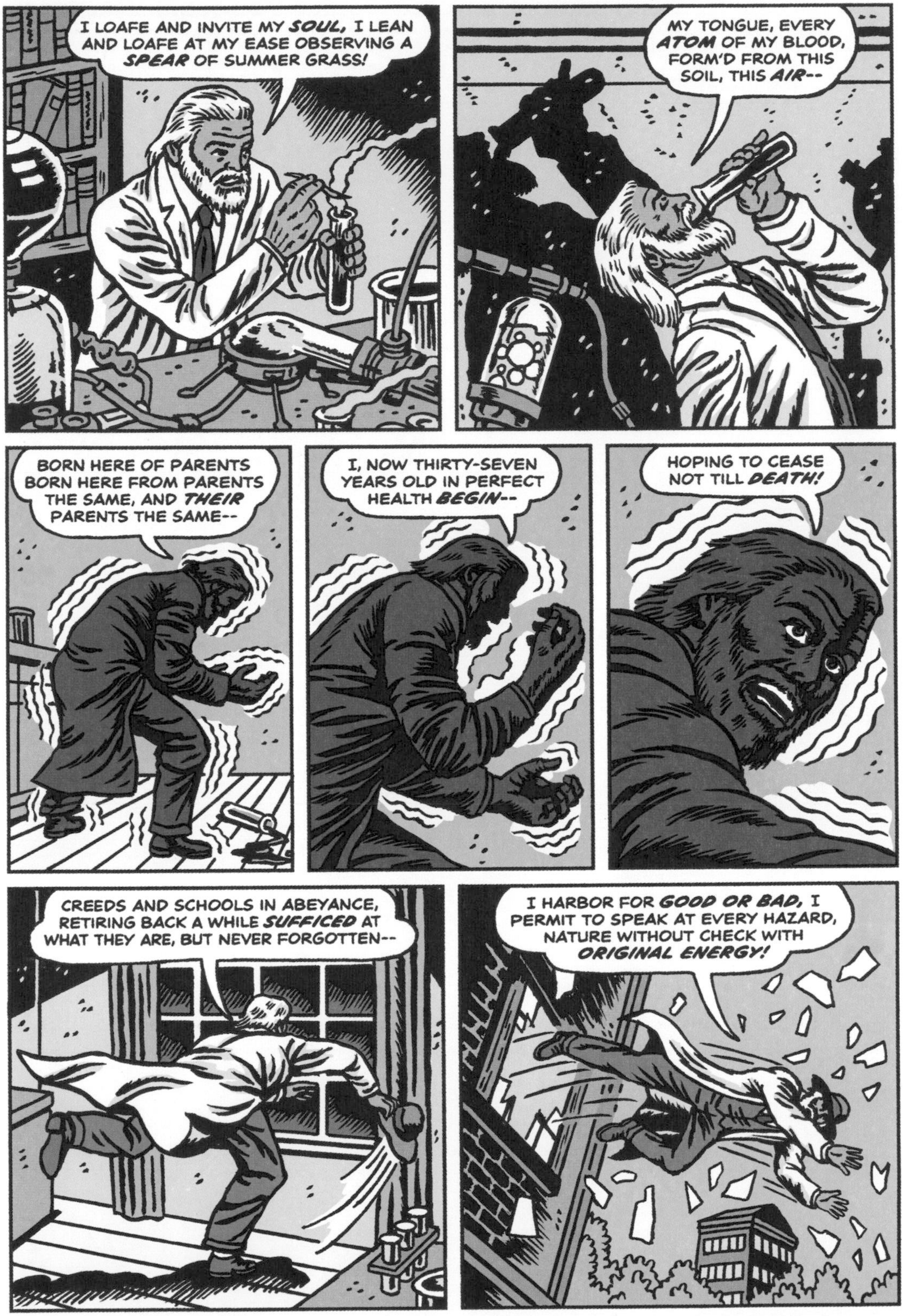
I LOAFE AND INVITE MY SOUL, I LEAN AND LOAFE AT MY EASE OBSERVING A SPEAR OF SUMMER GRASS!
MY TONGUE, EVERY ATOM OF MY BLOOD, FORM'D FROM THIS SOIL, THIS AIR--
BORN HERE OF PARENTS BORN HERE FROM PARENTS THE SAME, AND THEIR PARENTS THE SAME--
I, NOW THIRTY-SEVEN YEARS OLD IN PERFECT HEALTH BEGIN--
HOPING TO CEASE NOT TILL DEATH!
CREEDS AND SCHOOLS IN ABEYANCE, RETIRING BACK A WHILE SUFFICED AT WHAT THEY ARE, BUT NEVER FORGOTTEN--
I HARBOR FOR GOOD OR BAD, I PERMIT TO SPEAK AT EVERY HAZARD, NATURE WITHOUT CHECK WITH ORIGINAL ENERGY!

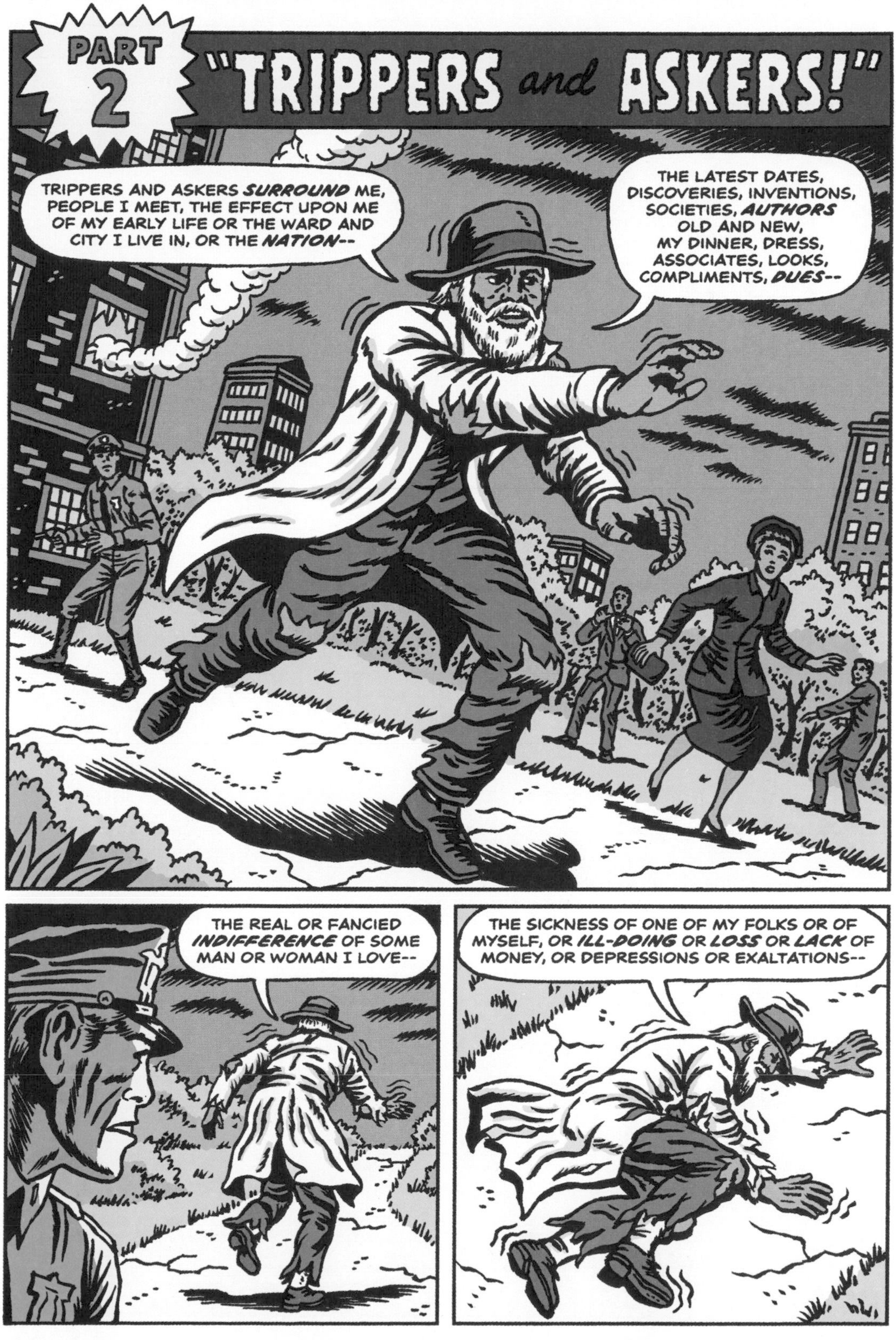
PART 2
"TRIPPERS and ASKERS!"
TRIPPERS AND ASKERS SURROUND ME, PEOPLE I MEET, THE EFFECT UPON ME OF MY EARLY LIFE OR THE WARD AND CITY I LIVE IN, OR THE NATION--
THE LATEST DATES, DISCOVERIES, INVENTIONS, SOCIETIES, AUTHORS OLD AND NEW, MY DINNER, DRESS, ASSOCIATES, LOOKS, COMPLIMENTS, DUES--
THE REAL OR FANCIED INDIFFERENCE OF SOME MAN OR WOMAN I LOVE--
THE SICKNESS OF ONE OF MY FOLKS OR OF MYSELF, OR ILL-DOING OR LOSS OR LACK OF MONEY, OR DEPRESSIONS OR EXALTATIONS--

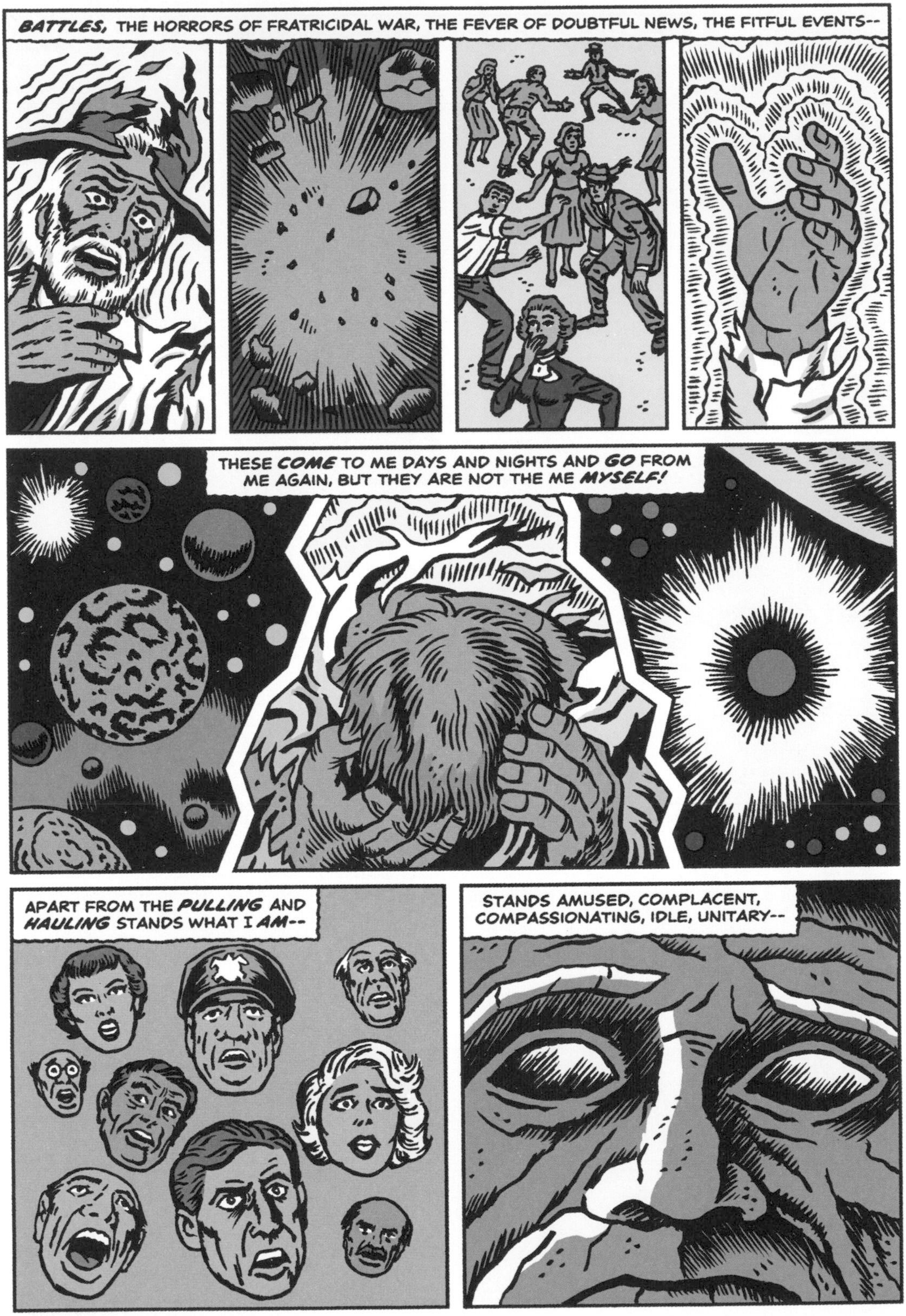
BATTLES, THE HORRORS OF FRATRICIDAL WAR, THE FEVER OF DOUBTFUL NEWS, THE FITFUL EVENTS--
THESE COME TO ME DAYS AND NIGHTS AND GO FROM ME AGAIN, BUT THEY ARE NOT THE ME MYSELF!
APART FROM THE PULLING AND HAULING STANDS WHAT I AM--
STANDS AMUSED, COMPLACENT, COMPASSIONATING, IDLE, UNITARY--

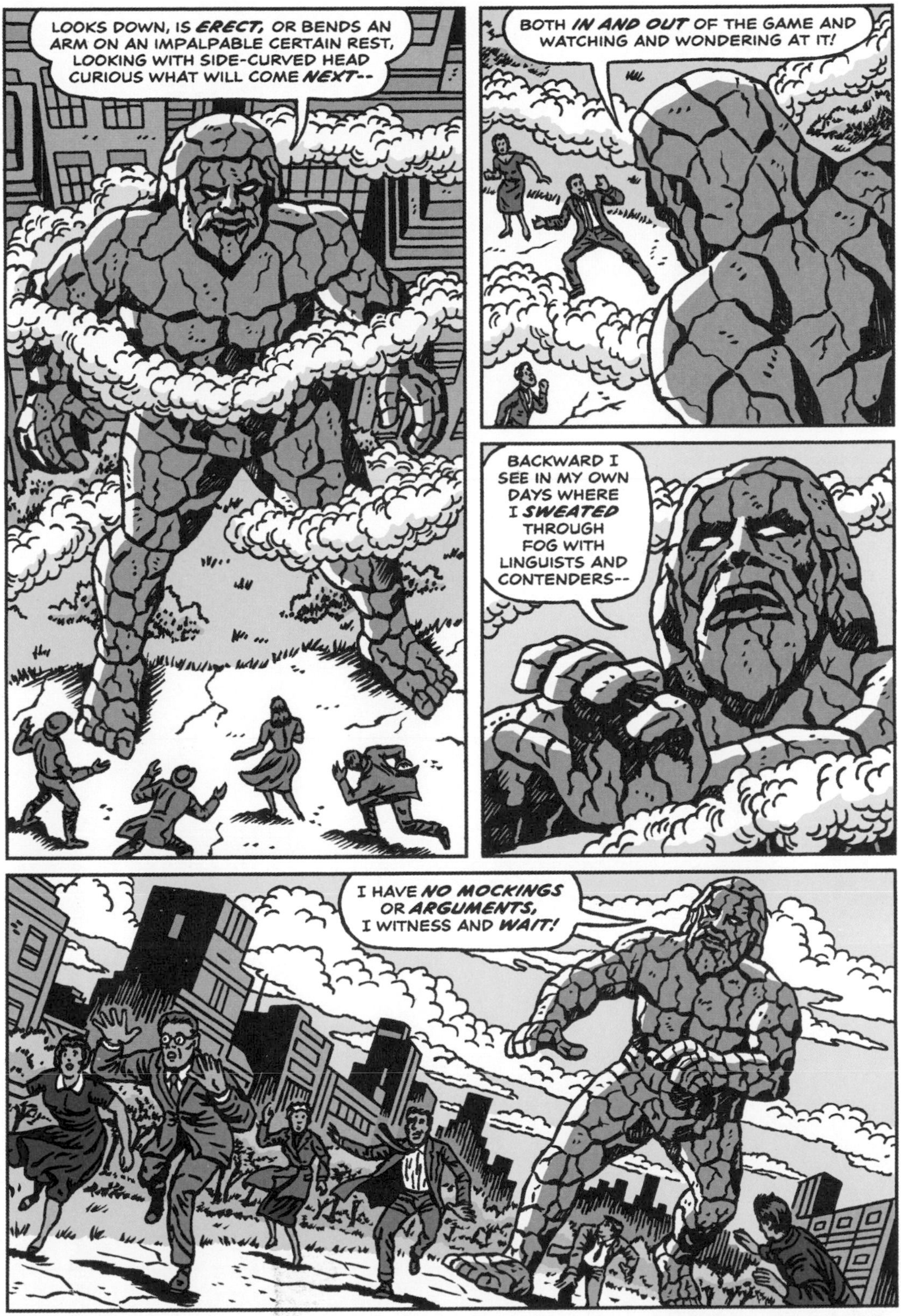
LOOKS DOWN, IS ERECT, OR BENDS AN ARM ON AN IMPALPABLE CERTAIN REST, LOOKING WITH SIDE-CURVED HEAD CURIOUS WHAT WILL COME NEXT--
BOTH IN AND OUT OF THE GAME AND WATCHING AND WONDERING AT IT!
BACKWARD I SEE IN MY OWN DAYS WHERE I SWEATED THROUGH FOG WITH LINGUISTS AND CONTENDERS--
I HAVE NO MOCKINGS OR ARGUMENTS, I WITNESS AND WAIT!

CONTINUED NEXT ISSUE...

I met Bob Sikoryak fifteen years ago and he invited me to do one of his Carousel shows, where a cartoonist reads slides of their work in front of an audience. I was intimidated and flattered that someone whose work I'd admired in *RAW* would take a chance on me. But Bob is one of the kindest, most ego-less human beings I've ever met, letting others have the spotlight for years in his shows and always taking chances in debuting new talent. He is a great teacher, never telling anyone how to present their work, but giving the right, detailed advice when asked. I don't think I've ever really seen him stress out despite any technical trouble we might have before a show. Audiences are always won over by Bob, who subtly times each slide, pristinely frames each image, and gets amazing actors like James Urbaniak and Julie Klausner to do the voices of his *Masterpiece Comics*. Maybe it is this same tendency that allows him to slip so seamlessly into different styles for his mash-ups of Kafka and *Peanuts* or *Tales from the Crypt* and *Wuthering Heights*. He humbles himself to both the drawing style and the text and painstakingly emulates the style of John Stanley or Charles Schulz, paring down text until it becomes something completely his own.—***Lauren Weinstein, cartoonist of* The Goddess of War**

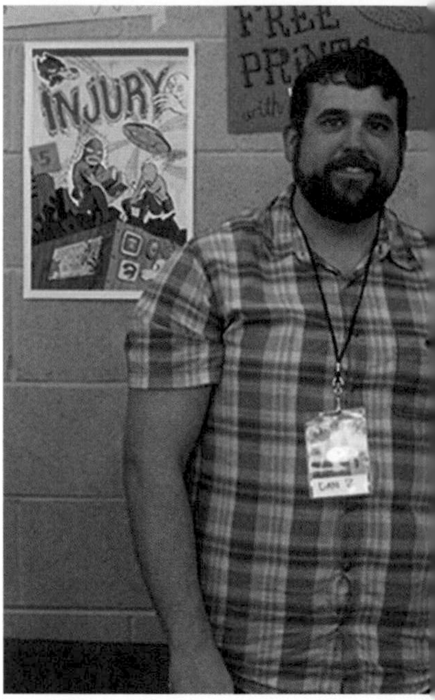
INJURY

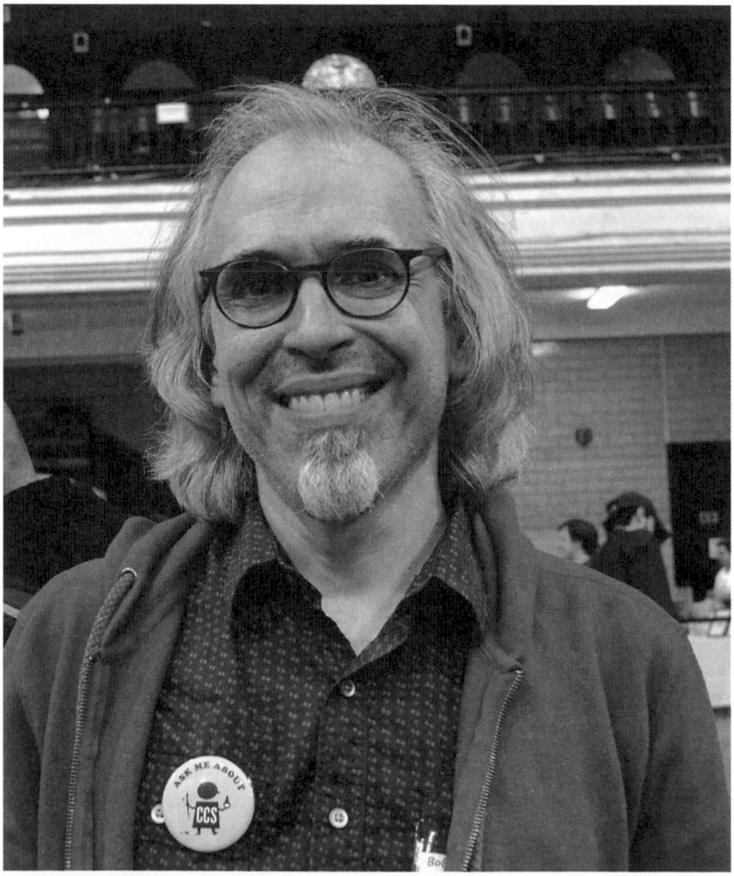
ASK ME ABOUT
CCS

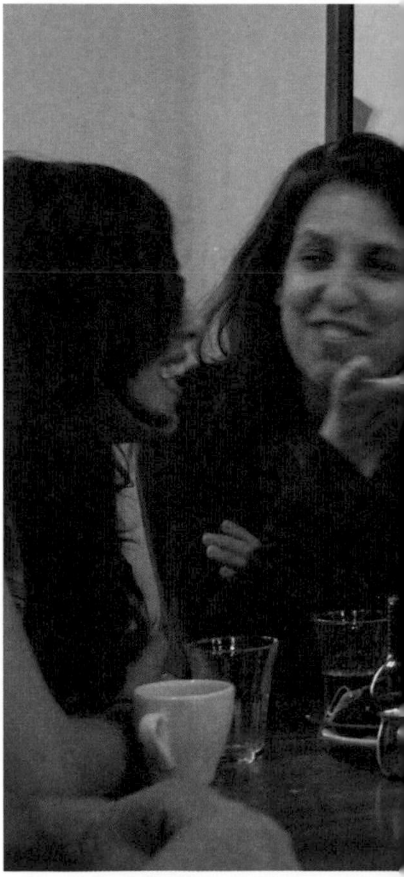

 (Clockwise): Dan Zettwoch & Kevin Huizenga at CAKE (2013). Zak Sally, Julie Doucet, John Porcellino & Mr. Mike in Seattle (1994). Miriam Katin & Mimi Pond in Miria

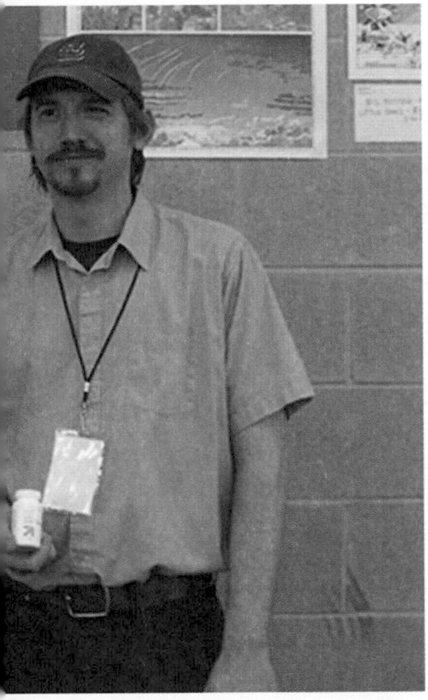

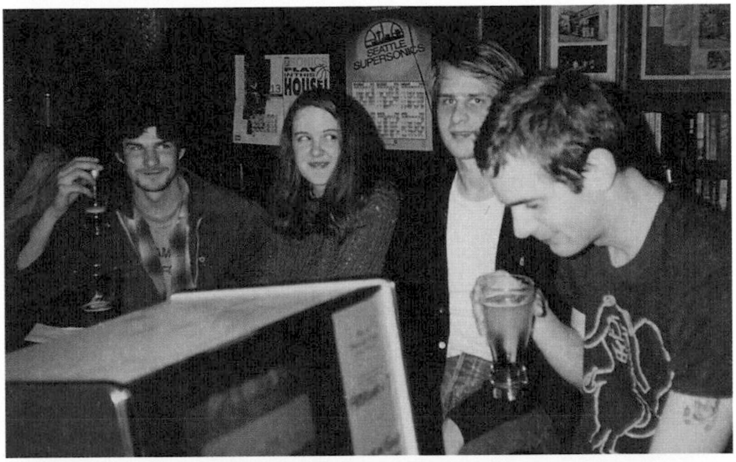
SEATTLE SUPERSONICS

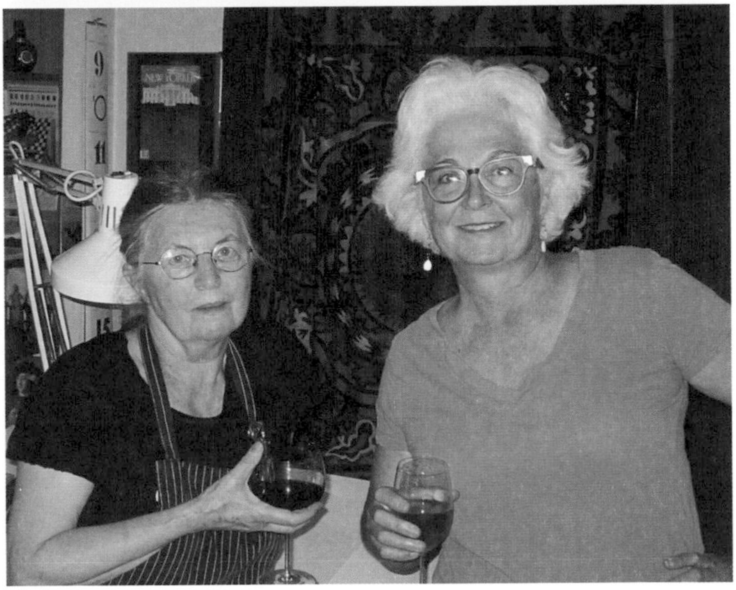

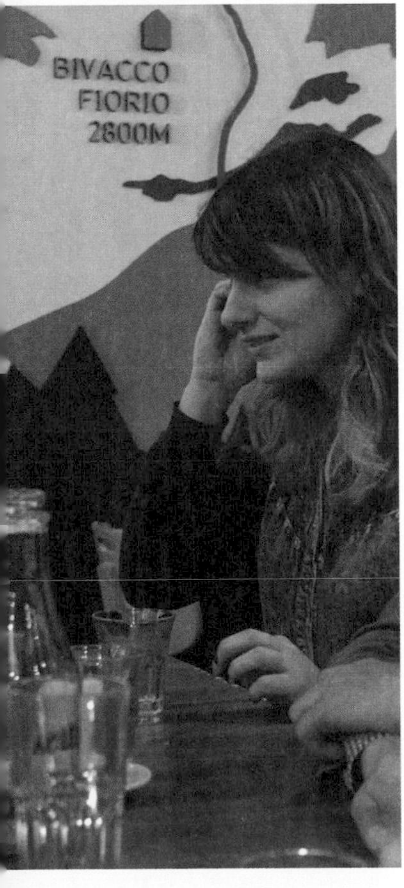
BIVACCO
FIORIO
2800M

On the final page of Dan Zettwoch's *Birdseye Bristoe* our title character and his niece and nephew walk across a rotting horizontal billboard. Patches of paper are torn off in numerous places, displaying several different eras of advertising. The characters are *in* history, not just living it but standing on several manifestations of the past at once. At the outset of the book we see Birdseye walking through the rubble of a fallen cell phone tower. There is nothing here but debris—bent metal and screws, no history, nothing to read. This is the crux of Dan's story. He's damning our modern world for its lack of history and its lack of story and no feeling for the hand-made. In lesser hands this would be an over-the-top angry screed, but Dan knows the score. He wants to show us the beauty in the things that human hands have made.—***Tom Devlin***

dio. Photo: Geoffrey Katin (2014). Julia Pohl-Miranda, Rutu Modan & Lisa Hanawalt at TCAF (2013). Bob Sikoryak at MoCCA Fest. Photo: Jody Culkin (2013).

I WAS SAVED...FROM MY OWN LIFE!

an appreciation of Kevin Huizenga by Joe McCulloch

This was what we hate—
the same forces that converge on minds and
cultures like they do farmland and forest...
I have seen it with my own eyes:
everything gets covered with asphalt.
but I noticed at this job we all had nature
pictures on our computer desktops.
　　　—captions, *Or Else* no. 3 (2005), pp. 35–36

Years ago, when I was in Catholic school, we had an auxiliary bishop come in to deliver a lecture on perception—one of several identical talks to be shared with captive bodies across the diocese. Nobody understood a single blessed word of it, but from what I can gather in retrospect, it was intended as an introductory challenge to the relativistic bases of postmodernism: a longstanding bugbear of Church philosophy. "Believe your eyes!" the steeple-hatted man cried. "Trust! Trust what God has shown you!"

All of us sat bored and impatient, if essentially polite; at least he'd gotten us out of class. A subsequent talk several boroughs away met with a less charitable reception, as one student elected to make the case for materialism by whipping a penny as hard as he could at His Excellency's face. The school cancelled its senior prom in punishment, inspiring a local corporate-owned nü-metal/hard-rawk meathead radio station to make the private funding of a replacement prom the centrepiece of its spring advertising campaign, until parents complained, at which point it stopped.

This all reminds me a lot of Kevin Huizenga.

I was twenty-two years old in 2003 when the first volume of *Drawn & Quarterly Showcase* arrived in stores. Huizenga had contributed forty pages of new comics to the anthology: the largest outlay of his work yet seen beyond the small circles of self-publishing, though I knew nothing about that. I'd attended no zine or comics shows, no festivals at any point in my life; I corresponded with nobody involved in writing, publishing, or art. But with this cartoonist, I felt a connection. Viscerally, he communicated the world I saw every day, my eyes never failing to deliver the truths of God's benediction

that all meat and green be given unto us: Best Buys and Borders, Taco Bell and Panera Bread, stretching again and again in the same way, forever, into the horizon. I may have bought that book at a Borders; I cannot recall.

Huizenga's were the first comics I'd found that represented these experiences. Glenn Ganges, his hero, is on a mission to aid the fertility of Wendy, his wife. This requires an item quest, and a set of favours done for townsfolk, inhabitants of a long, linear highway of corporate retailers: "28th Street." Huizenga is of the generation that understands the psychological pull of video games, so I suspect he knows that what gaming quests and retail consumerism have in common is that their play fields are orderly and predictable enough that all elements can be realistically catalogued, and thus, from understanding everything, you might feel for a moment that you are genuinely in charge of reality. As I would later discover, Huizenga was also doing a rendition of Italo Calvino's restatement of an Italian folk tale: an older narrative tradition of forthright moral calculus, though his graphics were exceedingly modern, his canopy of store logos, stripped of actionable specificity, made relatable in the manner of a cartoon face distilled to dot eyes and a nose that's just a capital C.

This was the landscape of "28th Street": the work of an artist bent on depicting business not as a plague, but rather a zoological usurper, bade after its conquest to administer the ecosystem. The main story is framed by two smaller stories, both of them metaphorically concerning the interaction of business and nature. In the first, a cleaning service distributes postcards with technologically aged photos of missing children as well as valuable coupons, "like sowing seed," Glenn muses; this outlay is contrasted with the activities of Sudanese refugees, "missing" orphans absorbed into retail jobs in the developed United States. The other short, coming after the main action, depicts the introduction of starlings to North America at the behest of a naturalist bent on acclimating all of the birds mentioned by Shakespeare into the domestic system; their population soon exploded, seizing nests and darkening skies.

Starlings, in Huizenga's scheme, are the elusive form of the Feathered Ogre, which dwells inside the retail sprawl like a final boss. Still, it holds the keys to good living—the very secrets of human reproduction—and to deal with its noise is to live here in the world, to exist under its curse, and hear, forever, its noise.

Drawn & Quarterly collected the triptych among other stories, three years after it was first published, under the title of *Curses*. I confess that I never bought it; by that time I'd gathered all of its constituent parts on my own buying missions.

In popular comic books, the tendency has long been to encourage hyperconsumption; to connect storylines across dozens of issues, making it incumbent upon the reader to buy as much as possible so as to maintain an unimpeded view of their window into a virtual reality, if not simply stoking the completist impulse by releasing flocks of titles with related characters, or putting different covers on the same comic. If you are making comic books, you too must adapt to this environment; biblically, it is a flood, but instead of spying the dove's return there's only more starlings cawing overhead, inedible, and the question then is how to find a means of ballasting atop the flow of content.

For Huizenga, for Drawn & Quarterly, the means was distinctly retrospective. *Or Else* was a solo comic-book series released from 2004 to 2008, consisting mainly of revised or reprinted stories from Huizenga's self-published minicomics. I was not the only one who'd seen very few of those, it seems, and I liked them all very much. Issue no. 1 (2004) contains some of Huizenga's most offhandedly lovely art, as Glenn and Wendy bicycle along windy streets, ink lines swirling around into abstract curls of motion. Elsewhere, Huizenga presents landscape illustrations in the style of Chinese ink wash paintings, juxtaposed against found text concerning a young child's birth to parents of disadvantaged economic circumstance, who give him up for adoption—the trees and cliffs calling to a cultural dream of eternity. By issue no. 5 (2008), the dream had faded, and Huizenga was presenting an entirely new Italian literary adaptation (Giorgio Manganelli, *Centuria: One Hundred Ouroboric Novels*), planting Glenn in the midst of a chaotic landscape wracked by religious war.

"It's insane," I thought, frequently, "to run a comic-book series like this right now." Consumers are coerced into mobilization so often these days that arch-consumers like me have a habit of thinking themselves business experts, but it didn't take very much observation to see that almost all of Huizenga's peers were releasing work as thicker, sturdier "graphic novels" or, increasingly, online. Still, Huizenga and his publisher seemed to favour this process, for a while, and I confess that I too loved the succinctness of these small

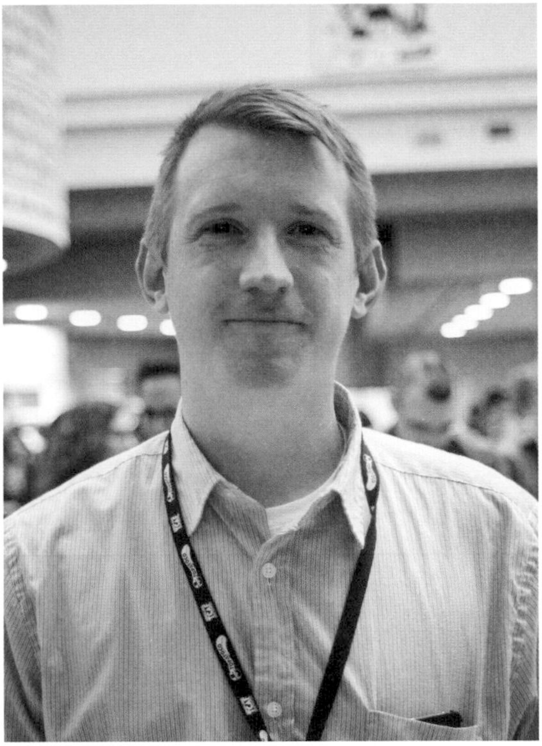

packages: how they turned small, similar stories into expressions of their artist's thought processes.

Issue no. 3 (2005) strikes me as the most explicitly autobiographical issue: a narrator, visiting parents, talks with neighbours and ultimately finds himself trapped by a philosophical struggle in considering whether or not to lay down some incredibly stupid ad copy on a promotional flyer at his day job: "FASHIONABLY ZEN." Of course it was another expression of business uneasily mingling with nature, but what fascinated me was how by that point in the comic the typical pleasantries of autobio-styled work has begun to break up, so that Huizenga wasn't just matching captions or word bubbles with pictures, but dialogue trees were being laid out on the page, all possible options visible. A full-page splash consists of ad copy transitioning into the protagonist's mental impressions. Jesus Christ makes a special guest appearance as a floating head.

These weren't just collections of stories, I realized, but stumblings toward a means of addressing reality.

Huizenga is not simply concerned with scenes and tales, but with ascertainment, perception. In this way, he is successor to that doyen of literary comics, Chris Ware, and his schema of visual language as a combination of memory and

Kevin Huizenga at Toronto Comic Arts Festival. Photo: Chris Anthony Diaz & Graham Willcox (2014).

experience. Huizenga's work can be read as similarly paired: an interaction of the conscious and subconscious.

His two best works are the easiest to obtain at the moment. *Or Else* no. 2 (2005) and *Or Else* no. 4 (2006) were both revised and/or expanded from millennial minicomics, as mentioned before, but they were also subsequently reformatted by Drawn & Quarterly into stand-alone books: *Gloriana* (2012) and *The Wild Kingdom* (2010). Perhaps this makes it a little easier to keep them available, or maybe it's just useful to get Huizenga out of the comic-book environment and in front of "graphic novel" readers. Probably you need to constantly evolve—not to remain relevant, but merely visible. Fittingly, both of these books threaten an evolution of how comics should be read.

Gloriana, like *Drawn & Quarterly Showcase*, is built mainly from three stories, but here the associations between the component parts are not just literary, but formal and perceptual. A conversation between Glenn and his wife, again concerning pregnancy, sees its panels shift without warning from action to imagination, the chronology of this very basic story skipping ahead by days and years, frame by frame. The second story is magnificent: sheer perceptual blur, as Glenn attempts to explain something to someone on the telephone, except what we see is not what he intends to explain, but a massively fragmented recollection of his day at the library, scenes and captions looping and backtracking, characters switching positions, and ultimately the comic itself *erupting* into a foldout image of close to one hundred panels as Glenn's eye catches the glare of the sun, images seared from this lapse in vision, rolling and smearing until the third story begins mid-page, at which point there is lots and lots of text as Glenn actually gets to the point of his telephone conversation, which is that he explained another ocular (now lunar) phenomenon to his neighbours in severely rational detail.

It is a canard in comics criticism that the comics page, if good, will strike a careful balance between text and image to prioritize readability. It's both exquisitely arrogant and incorrect, in the way critics reliably are. Over-read, thirty-three years old, I respect Huizenga for making this comic the *wrong* way, for "wasting" so much space and then *choking* his pages with text to convey the intensity of personal communication versus the fancy of personal recollection; to set the material, yes, against the divine, as the communion of his labour. Believe your eyes! Trust! Trust!

And as with all Christian tales, apocalypse waits at the end.

"And surely your blood of your lives will I require; at the hand of every beast will I require it, and at the hand of man; at the hand *of every man's brother will I require the life of man."* I have never dealt well with mortality, though I can recall a preadolescence when playing in the woods and finding living and dead things was still an option. So too do I recall the lorazepamian focus that would flood my senses from the practice of visiting one big-box consumer retailer, and—hungry for an out-of-stock item—rushing just a few miles away to find another location, with all the same departments arranged in a slightly different order. This too reminds me of Kevin Huizenga.

The Wild Kingdom draws together all of Huizenga's concerns in the most elegant and deranged manner. I love *Gloriana* the most, but this I've found to be his most passionate expression of life in the world. There is very little text in the first half of the book. Mostly we see animals interacting with the flotsam of industry, from a squirrel subsiding on a rotten apple thrown by Glenn Ganges into his yard to a bird swooning after eating a discarded french fry and getting crushed under a car's tire. Yet then a larger bird seizes the carcass, and nature, as observed, adapts to man's intervention with logic.

Suddenly, the book distends—in the 2010 edition, it also explodes into full colour, like Dorothy entering Oz. You have no idea exactly what is happening, save that the idea of selling things has become perceptually one with reality. Snatches of normal interaction become commercials, matching incorrect words to pictures. Hype men cough up bromides—"I was saved…from my own life!" We have all been drafted into consumptive effort; we are all salesmen. Hell, I'm doing it now. Huizenga, for his part, struggles to compensate. The veil between the fictive and instructive frays, as the book begins explaining uncomplicated images from earlier in the comic, pasting down lengthy, philosophically weird naturist texts along with criticisms thereof, unable to settle on any firm reality. There is no truth in science; there is no settled philosophy; this is the end of success, and efforts can only be made to catalogue, to chart, to record what is observed.

Then, there is calm.

A bird strikes a power line.

Its corpse starts a brush fire.

The smoke causes a highway pileup.

Further and further—planes crashing, cities exploding! It is the Last Day. It is the final adaptation. It is the only way, it seems, to be saved from seeing things forever.

Joe McCulloch is a columnist for the Comics Journal *and the recipient of numerous awards for his powerful muscles.*

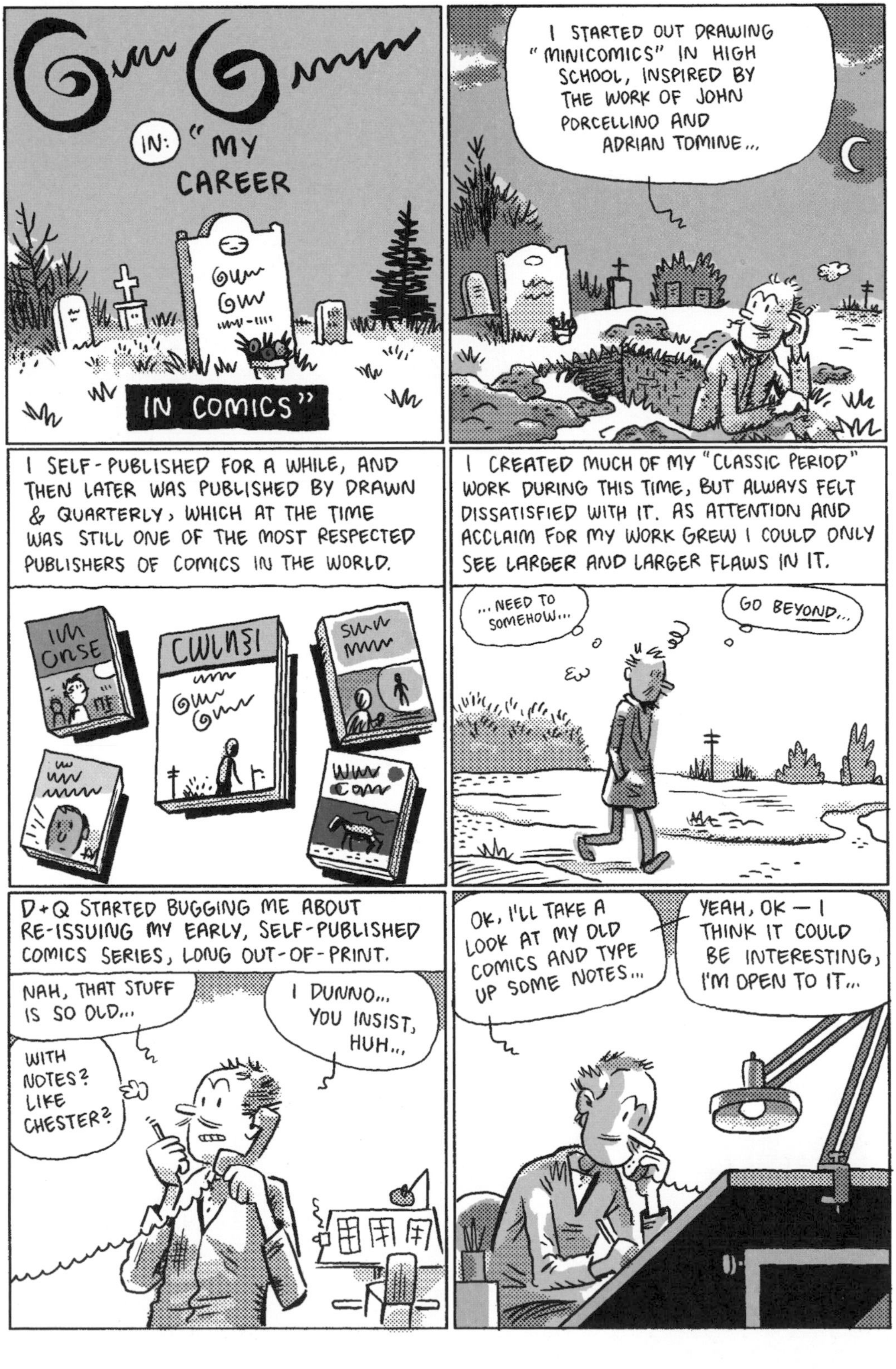
IN: "MY CAREER IN COMICS"
I STARTED OUT DRAWING "MINICOMICS" IN HIGH SCHOOL, INSPIRED BY THE WORK OF JOHN PORCELLINO AND ADRIAN TOMINE...
I SELF-PUBLISHED FOR A WHILE, AND THEN LATER WAS PUBLISHED BY DRAWN & QUARTERLY, WHICH AT THE TIME WAS STILL ONE OF THE MOST RESPECTED PUBLISHERS OF COMICS IN THE WORLD.
I CREATED MUCH OF MY "CLASSIC PERIOD" WORK DURING THIS TIME, BUT ALWAYS FELT DISSATISFIED WITH IT. AS ATTENTION AND ACCLAIM FOR MY WORK GREW I COULD ONLY SEE LARGER AND LARGER FLAWS IN IT.
...NEED TO SOMEHOW...
GO BEYOND...
D+Q STARTED BUGGING ME ABOUT RE-ISSUING MY EARLY, SELF-PUBLISHED COMICS SERIES, LONG OUT-OF-PRINT.
NAH, THAT STUFF IS SO OLD...
I DUNNO... YOU INSIST, HUH...
WITH NOTES? LIKE CHESTER?
OK, I'LL TAKE A LOOK AT MY OLD COMICS AND TYPE UP SOME NOTES...
YEAH, OK — I THINK IT COULD BE INTERESTING, I'M OPEN TO IT...

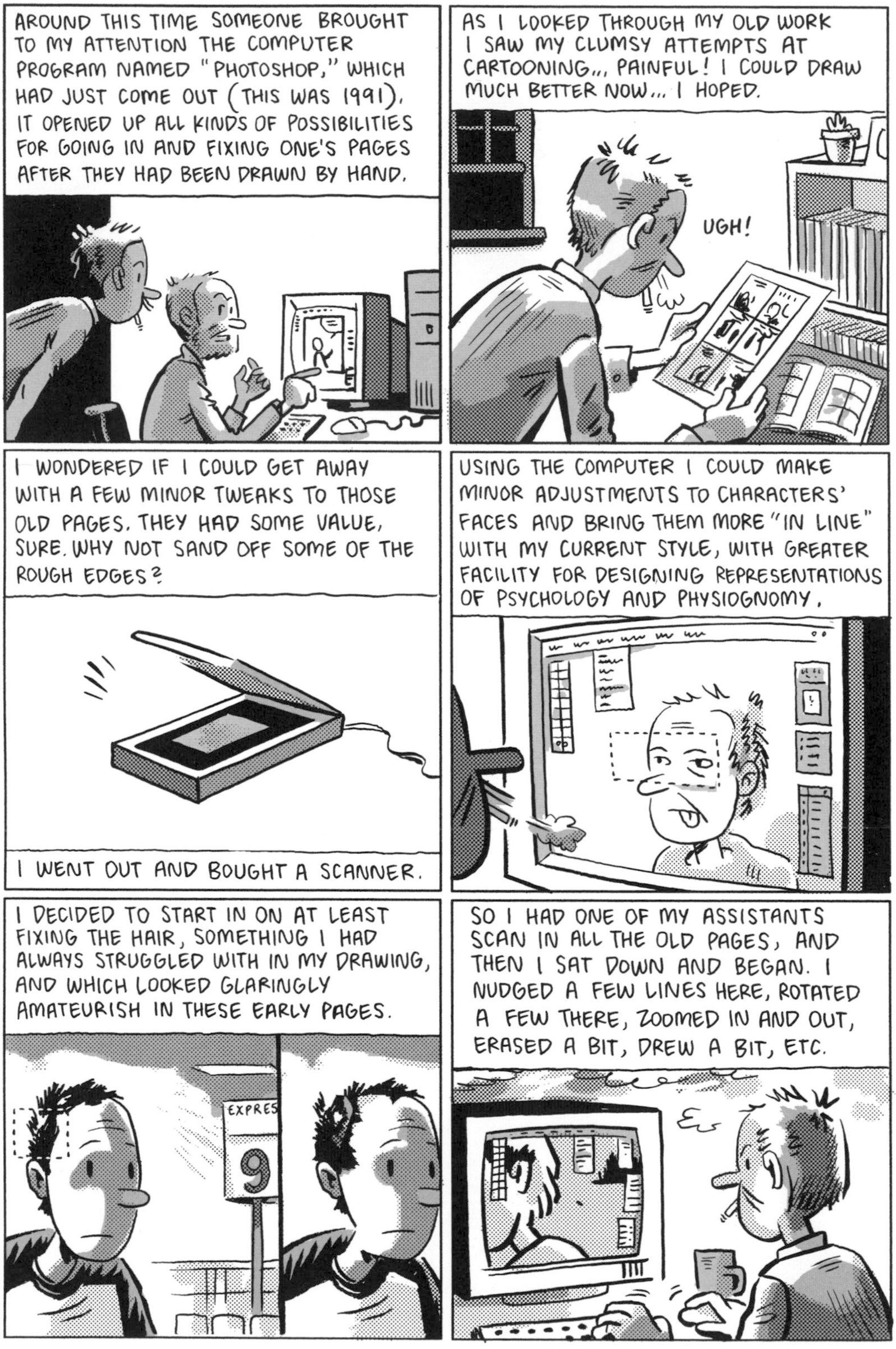
AROUND THIS TIME SOMEONE BROUGHT TO MY ATTENTION THE COMPUTER PROGRAM NAMED "PHOTOSHOP," WHICH HAD JUST COME OUT (THIS WAS 1991). IT OPENED UP ALL KINDS OF POSSIBILITIES FOR GOING IN AND FIXING ONE'S PAGES AFTER THEY HAD BEEN DRAWN BY HAND.
AS I LOOKED THROUGH MY OLD WORK I SAW MY CLUMSY ATTEMPTS AT CARTOONING... PAINFUL! I COULD DRAW MUCH BETTER NOW... I HOPED.
UGH!
I WONDERED IF I COULD GET AWAY WITH A FEW MINOR TWEAKS TO THOSE OLD PAGES. THEY HAD SOME VALUE, SURE. WHY NOT SAND OFF SOME OF THE ROUGH EDGES?
I WENT OUT AND BOUGHT A SCANNER.
USING THE COMPUTER I COULD MAKE MINOR ADJUSTMENTS TO CHARACTERS' FACES AND BRING THEM MORE "IN LINE" WITH MY CURRENT STYLE, WITH GREATER FACILITY FOR DESIGNING REPRESENTATIONS OF PSYCHOLOGY AND PHYSIOGNOMY.
I DECIDED TO START IN ON AT LEAST FIXING THE HAIR, SOMETHING I HAD ALWAYS STRUGGLED WITH IN MY DRAWING, AND WHICH LOOKED GLARINGLY AMATEURISH IN THESE EARLY PAGES.
EXPRES
9
SO I HAD ONE OF MY ASSISTANTS SCAN IN ALL THE OLD PAGES, AND THEN I SAT DOWN AND BEGAN. I NUDGED A FEW LINES HERE, ROTATED A FEW THERE, ZOOMED IN AND OUT, ERASED A BIT, DREW A BIT, ETC.

OVER THE COMING WEEKS, AS I LEARNED MORE AND MORE ABOUT THE POSSIBILITIES PHOTOSHOP OPENED UP FOR ME I BEGAN TO SEE MORE AND MORE LEVELS OF COMPLEXITY IN THE CARTOONING OF HAIR.

I FANTASIZED:

WHAT IF THE RESOLUTION WERE SO FINE THAT I COULD ZOOM IN AND "MAGIC LASSO" AND ADJUST EACH INDIVIDUAL HAIR?! IMAGINE THAT!

CUT!

UNDO!

PASTE!

ROTATE

ZOOM

RGB

THRESHOLD!

ADJUST LEVELS!

THOUGH I WAS ENJOYING FIXING OLD PAGES, I ALSO BEGAN TO SEE EXCITING POSSIBILITIES FOR FUTURE STORIES AND HOW I WOULD DO THE CHARACTERS' HAIR, HOW IT WOULD CHANGE...

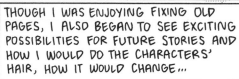

AND THEN HE

Ha Ha Ha

"... SO I SAID TO HIM, "LOOK HERE—

Ha Ha

I HAD SEEN—REALLY SEEN—HOW TO CARTOON HAIR. THIS IS WHEN EVERYTHING CHANGED FOR ME.

I COULD ALMOST PHYSICALLY SENSE IT, AS IF IN THREE DIMENSIONS. NOT JUST THE COLOR, THE SHINE, BUT ALSO FEEL ITS TEXTURE, ITS BODY...

MY SKETCHBOOK FILLED WITH COMBINATIONS OF HEAD TYPES AND HAIR TYPES GENERATING ENDLESS IDEAS FOR CHARACTERS AND STORIES.

I CHALLENGED MYSELF, TRYING DIFFICULT ANGLES AND EXOTIC CUTS, DIFFERENT BRUSHES AND PEN TECHNIQUES, ALWAYS PUSHING MYSELF.

AND WOMEN'S HAIR... DON'T GET ME STARTED! THE STYLES! THE WAY THEY TURN THEIR HEADS OR TILT THEIR NECKS, SHOULDERS...

COLORS OF HAIR, OF LIGHT... INDOOR LIGHT, OUTDOOR LIGHT... TIMES OF DAY...

THE EFFECT THE AIR HAS ON HAIR — A THING TO CONSIDER. WIND, HUMIDITY, AND BAROMETRIC PRESSURE — ALL CAN AFFECT THE ATMOSPHERE AND DRAMATIC ENERGY OF A SEQUENCE.

THE END.

THERE'S CHILDREN'S HAIR...

RICH HAIR, POOR HAIR: CLASS AND HAIR CONSCIOUSNESS.

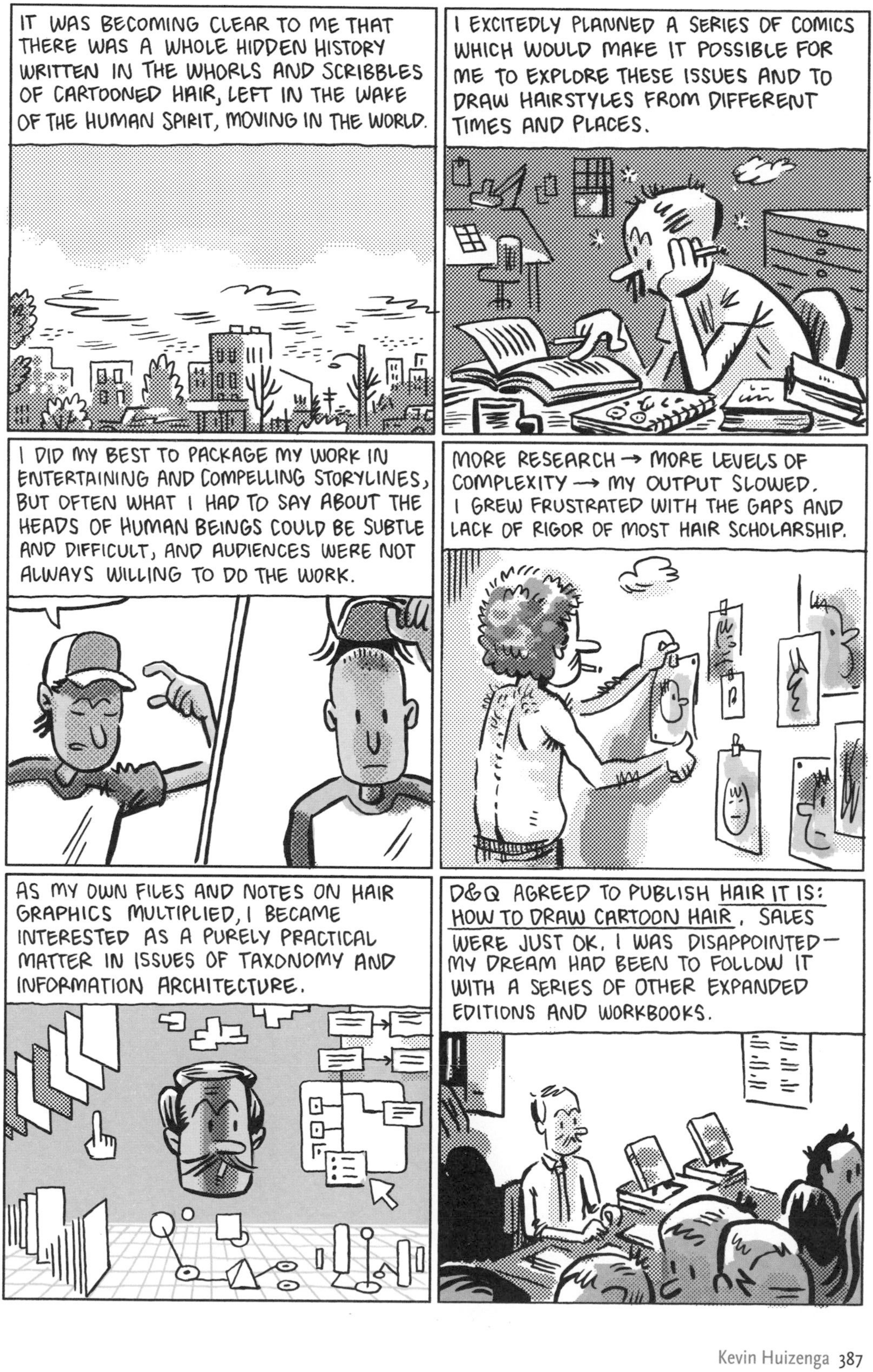
IT WAS BECOMING CLEAR TO ME THAT THERE WAS A WHOLE HIDDEN HISTORY WRITTEN IN THE WHORLS AND SCRIBBLES OF CARTOONED HAIR, LEFT IN THE WAKE OF THE HUMAN SPIRIT, MOVING IN THE WORLD.
I EXCITEDLY PLANNED A SERIES OF COMICS WHICH WOULD MAKE IT POSSIBLE FOR ME TO EXPLORE THESE ISSUES AND TO DRAW HAIRSTYLES FROM DIFFERENT TIMES AND PLACES.
I DID MY BEST TO PACKAGE MY WORK IN ENTERTAINING AND COMPELLING STORYLINES, BUT OFTEN WHAT I HAD TO SAY ABOUT THE HEADS OF HUMAN BEINGS COULD BE SUBTLE AND DIFFICULT, AND AUDIENCES WERE NOT ALWAYS WILLING TO DO THE WORK.
MORE RESEARCH → MORE LEVELS OF COMPLEXITY → MY OUTPUT SLOWED. I GREW FRUSTRATED WITH THE GAPS AND LACK OF RIGOR OF MOST HAIR SCHOLARSHIP.
AS MY OWN FILES AND NOTES ON HAIR GRAPHICS MULTIPLIED, I BECAME INTERESTED AS A PURELY PRACTICAL MATTER IN ISSUES OF TAXONOMY AND INFORMATION ARCHITECTURE.
D&Q AGREED TO PUBLISH HAIR IT IS: HOW TO DRAW CARTOON HAIR. SALES WERE JUST OK. I WAS DISAPPOINTED— MY DREAM HAD BEEN TO FOLLOW IT WITH A SERIES OF OTHER EXPANDED EDITIONS AND WORKBOOKS.

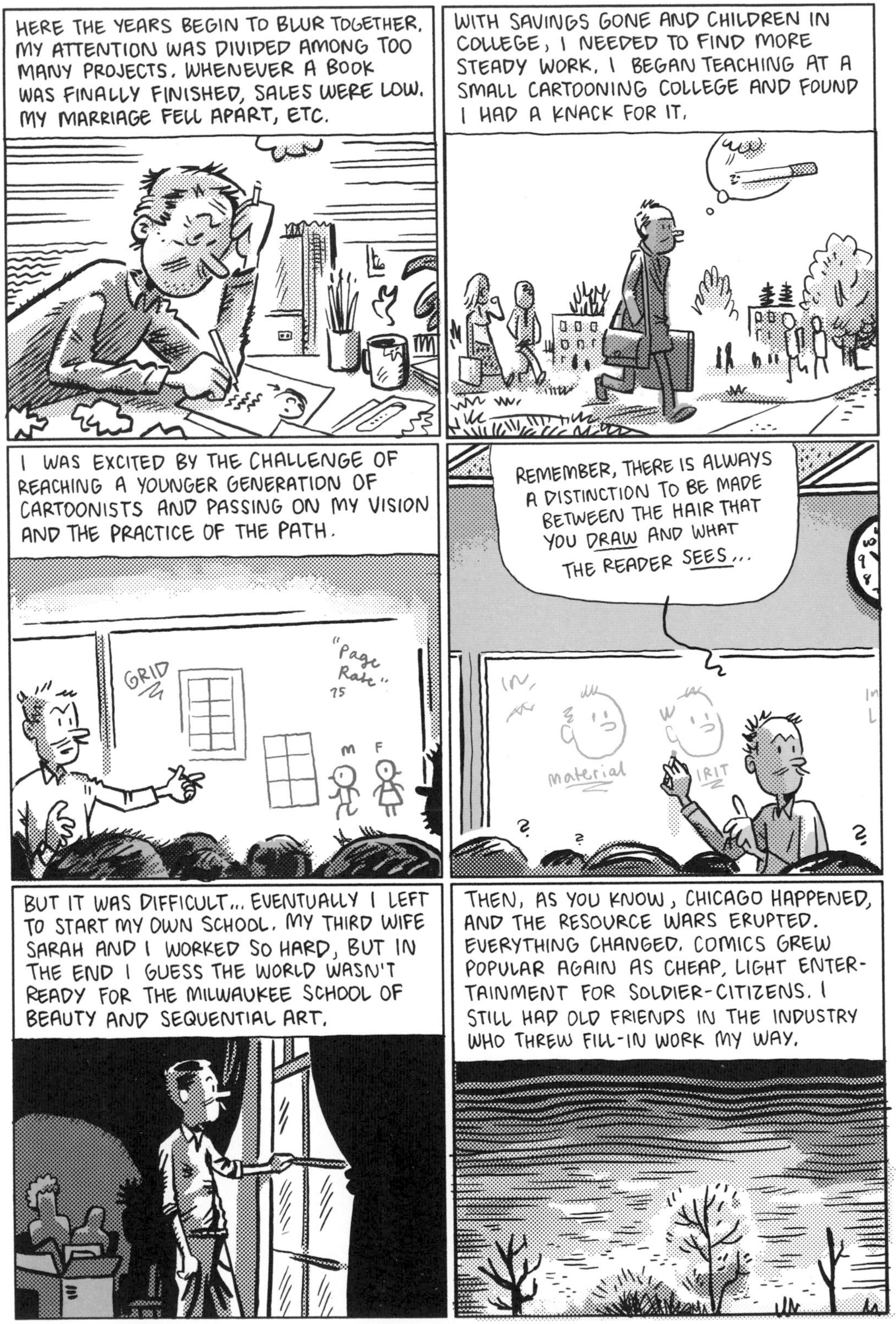
HERE THE YEARS BEGIN TO BLUR TOGETHER. MY ATTENTION WAS DIVIDED AMONG TOO MANY PROJECTS. WHENEVER A BOOK WAS FINALLY FINISHED, SALES WERE LOW. MY MARRIAGE FELL APART, ETC.
WITH SAVINGS GONE AND CHILDREN IN COLLEGE, I NEEDED TO FIND MORE STEADY WORK. I BEGAN TEACHING AT A SMALL CARTOONING COLLEGE AND FOUND I HAD A KNACK FOR IT.
I WAS EXCITED BY THE CHALLENGE OF REACHING A YOUNGER GENERATION OF CARTOONISTS AND PASSING ON MY VISION AND THE PRACTICE OF THE PATH.
GRID
"Page Rate"
M
F
REMEMBER, THERE IS ALWAYS A DISTINCTION TO BE MADE BETWEEN THE HAIR THAT YOU DRAW AND WHAT THE READER SEES...
material
BUT IT WAS DIFFICULT... EVENTUALLY I LEFT TO START MY OWN SCHOOL. MY THIRD WIFE SARAH AND I WORKED SO HARD, BUT IN THE END I GUESS THE WORLD WASN'T READY FOR THE MILWAUKEE SCHOOL OF BEAUTY AND SEQUENTIAL ART.
THEN, AS YOU KNOW, CHICAGO HAPPENED, AND THE RESOURCE WARS ERUPTED. EVERYTHING CHANGED. COMICS GREW POPULAR AGAIN AS CHEAP, LIGHT ENTERTAINMENT FOR SOLDIER-CITIZENS. I STILL HAD OLD FRIENDS IN THE INDUSTRY WHO THREW FILL-IN WORK MY WAY.

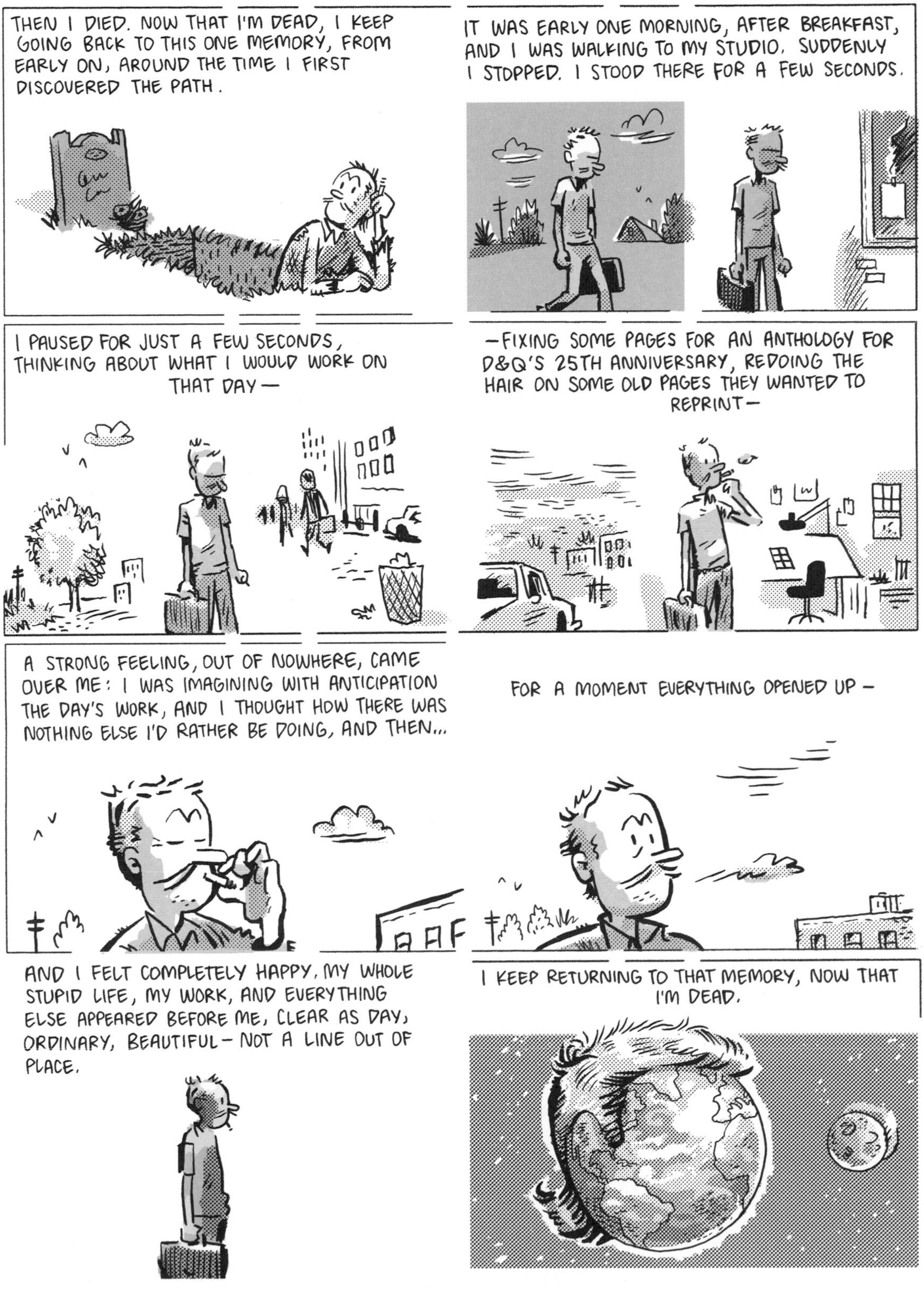

THEN I DIED. NOW THAT I'M DEAD, I KEEP GOING BACK TO THIS ONE MEMORY, FROM EARLY ON, AROUND THE TIME I FIRST DISCOVERED THE PATH.
IT WAS EARLY ONE MORNING, AFTER BREAKFAST, AND I WAS WALKING TO MY STUDIO. SUDDENLY I STOPPED. I STOOD THERE FOR A FEW SECONDS.
I PAUSED FOR JUST A FEW SECONDS, THINKING ABOUT WHAT I WOULD WORK ON THAT DAY—
—FIXING SOME PAGES FOR AN ANTHOLOGY FOR D&Q'S 25TH ANNIVERSARY, REDOING THE HAIR ON SOME OLD PAGES THEY WANTED TO REPRINT—
A STRONG FEELING, OUT OF NOWHERE, CAME OVER ME: I WAS IMAGINING WITH ANTICIPATION THE DAY'S WORK, AND I THOUGHT HOW THERE WAS NOTHING ELSE I'D RATHER BE DOING, AND THEN...
FOR A MOMENT EVERYTHING OPENED UP—
AND I FELT COMPLETELY HAPPY. MY WHOLE STUPID LIFE, MY WORK, AND EVERYTHING ELSE APPEARED BEFORE ME, CLEAR AS DAY, ORDINARY, BEAUTIFUL— NOT A LINE OUT OF PLACE.
I KEEP RETURNING TO THAT MEMORY, NOW THAT I'M DEAD.

On February 14, 2003, I was working as a line cook running a special Valentine's Day prix fixe dinner at Lula Cafe in Chicago. In the lull between the six and nine o'clock seatings, I went downstairs to the office to take a short break and check my email. There I found a message from Chris Oliveros asking me to do a story for a new anthology he was doing called the *D+Q Showcase*. I felt like I'd just won the lottery. I didn't mention it to anyone as service started again upstairs—no one there would have known what I was talking about. But I was floating on air.

I'd been self-publishing in earnest for a couple of years and none of my cartoonist friends were working with actual publishers of any kind yet. There was no publisher I wanted to work with more than D+Q. I agreed in an email the next day and soon had two near-simultaneous thoughts: 1) whatever I make for them has to be the best thing I've ever done, and 2) starting a project with that kind of internal pressure is the worst-possible creative poison. That conundrum was borne out over the following months. From an old sketchbook I took a small strip that seemed to have some potential and proceeded to make a huge mess of it. As I flailed, the story grew, soon outpacing the thirty to forty pages Chris had asked for. Finally finishing the story—I thought—at around seventy-two pages, I burned it all onto a CD and sent it to Montreal.

Time passed. Eventually I got an email saying that, regrettably, the story was so long now that including it would mean losing money selling the book at the price at which it had already been solicited to stores. My story had to be cut from the book. The proper response would have been relief. The piece was a disaster, narratively speaking. I was being saved from my incompetence being put on display. Still, I felt like I'd been given the chance of a lifetime and utterly blown it. I was devastated. To this day I'm not sure why, but after a few months, Chris wrote to ask if I would want to turn the story into a book of its own. By then I'd come to terms with the fact that the story was no good and said I would need six months or so to try to salvage it. After some time away I was able to see the story clearly again—what parts actually worked, what parts didn't, and what it actually wanted to be about. I threw away twenty-five pages, drew about forty new ones, and rearranged much else. The result was *Dogs and Water*, my first published book. Even after the revision, though, I clearly remember what I was thinking when I handed in the final files: "The best possible outcome here is that the book will disappear. No one will notice it, no one will read it, it will be forgotten." It still felt like a failure. It ended up being received much better than I could have hoped; it has in some ways taken on a life of its own and, apparently, connected with people.

In the intervening years my harsh appraisal has softened. I look at the book now with fondness and thank the delicate economics of small-press publishing that it didn't go out the door in its original form. The experience helped me put the artistic self-loathing that afflicts so many cartoonists into perspective. I seem to be better able to see it coming, now, and step out of its way. The experience also put in perspective for me the concern that my work impress people. I tried that once and it was a mess. Work always seems to come out better when I'm just trying to honour the ideas that come into my head, be honest and rigorous, and, maybe most of all, keep myself entertained.

—*Anders Nilsen*

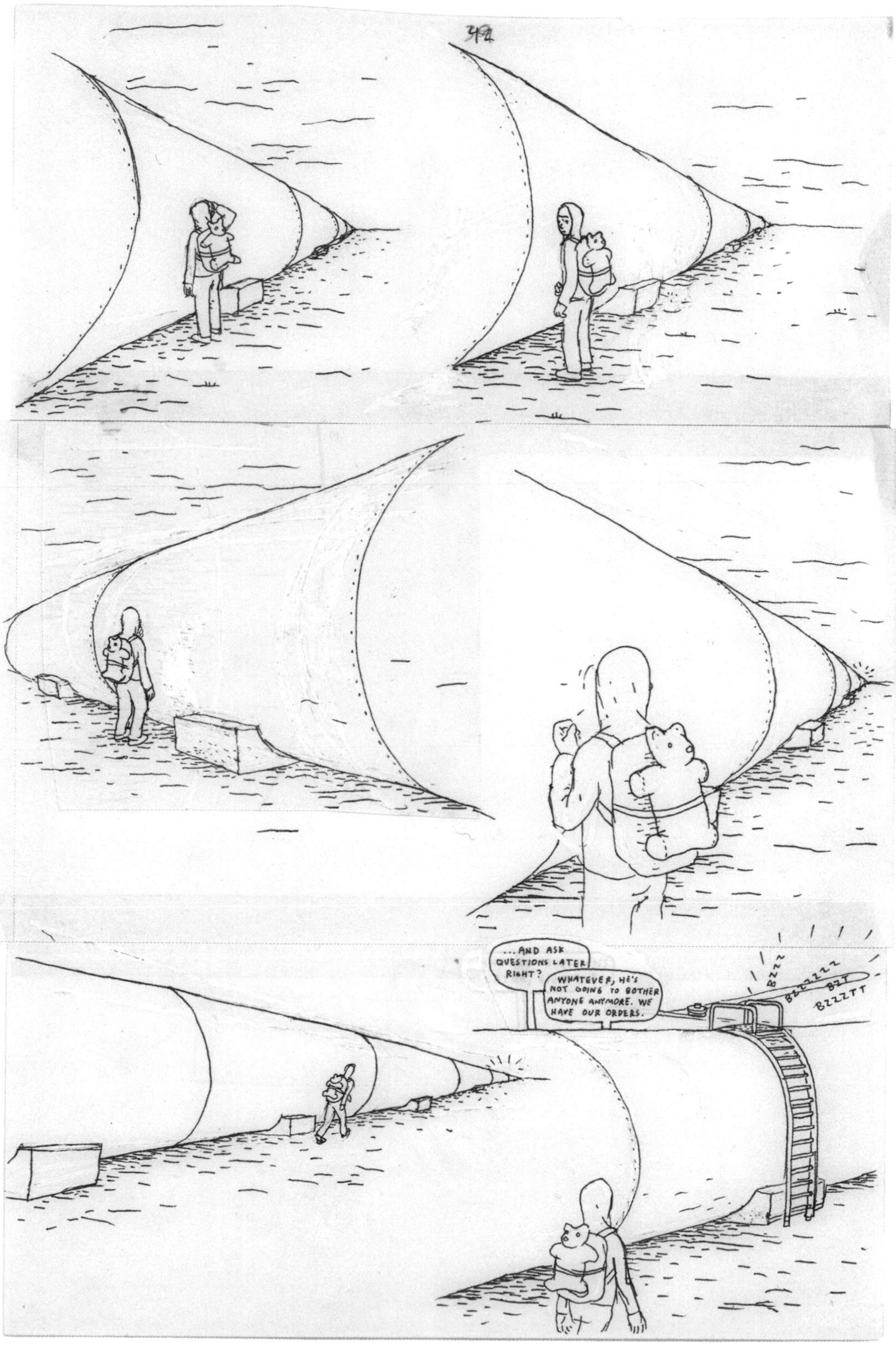
...AND ASK QUESTIONS LATER RIGHT?
WHATEVER, HE'S NOT GOING TO BOTHER ANYONE ANYMORE. WE HAVE OUR ORDERS.
BZZZ
BZZZZZZ
BZT
BZZZTT

Scratch pages from *Dogs and Water* (2004).

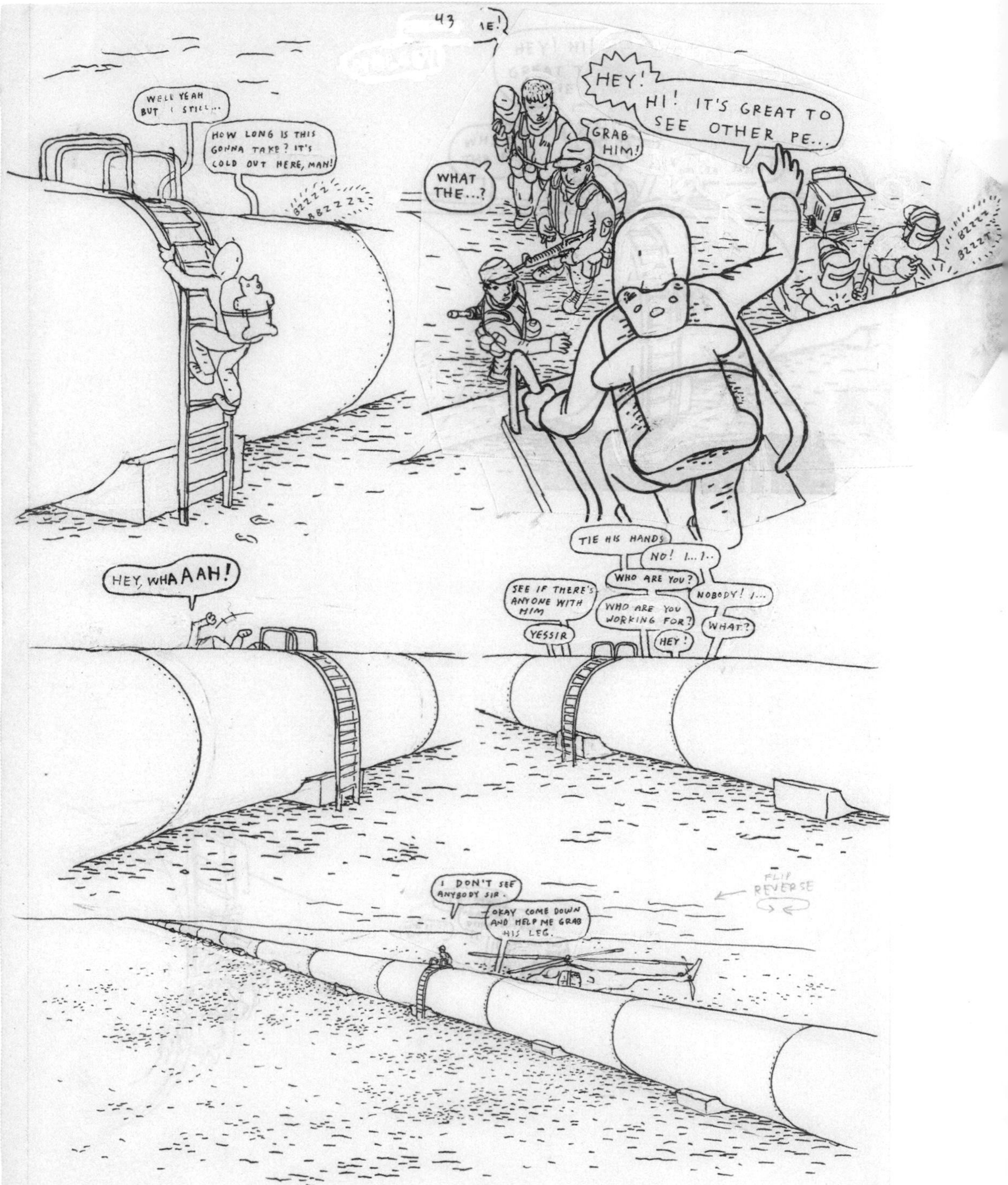
43
WELL YEAH BUT I STILL...
HOW LONG IS THIS GONNA TAKE? IT'S COLD OUT HERE, MAN!
BZZZZZ BZZZZZ
WHAT THE...?
GRAB HIM!
HEY!
HI! IT'S GREAT TO SEE OTHER PE...
BZZZZ BZZZT
HEY, WHAAAH!
TIE HIS HANDS
NO! I...I..
WHO ARE YOU?
SEE IF THERE'S ANYONE WITH HIM
YESSIR
WHO ARE YOU WORKING FOR?
NOBODY! I...
HEY!
WHAT?
I DON'T SEE ANYBODY SIR.
OKAY COME DOWN AND HELP ME GRAB HIS LEG.
FLIP REVERSE

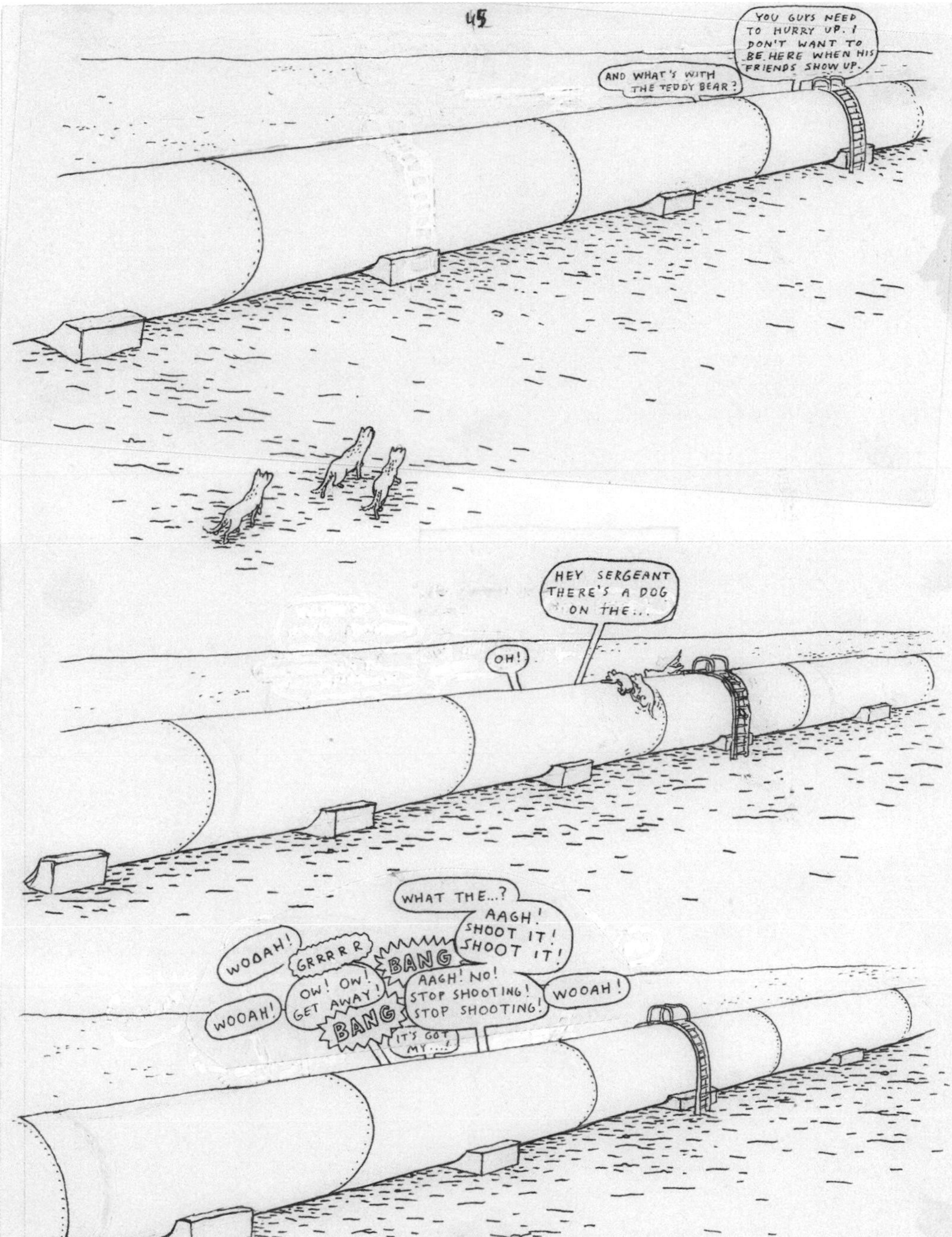
45
AND WHAT'S WITH THE TEDDY BEAR?
YOU GUYS NEED TO HURRY UP. I DON'T WANT TO BE HERE WHEN HIS FRIENDS SHOW UP.
HEY SERGEANT THERE'S A DOG ON THE...
OH!
WHAT THE...?
AAGH! SHOOT IT! SHOOT IT!
WOOAH!
GRRRRR
BANG
WOOAH!
OW! OW! GET AWAY!
BANG
AAGH! NO! STOP SHOOTING! STOP SHOOTING!
WOOAH!
IT'S GOT MY...!

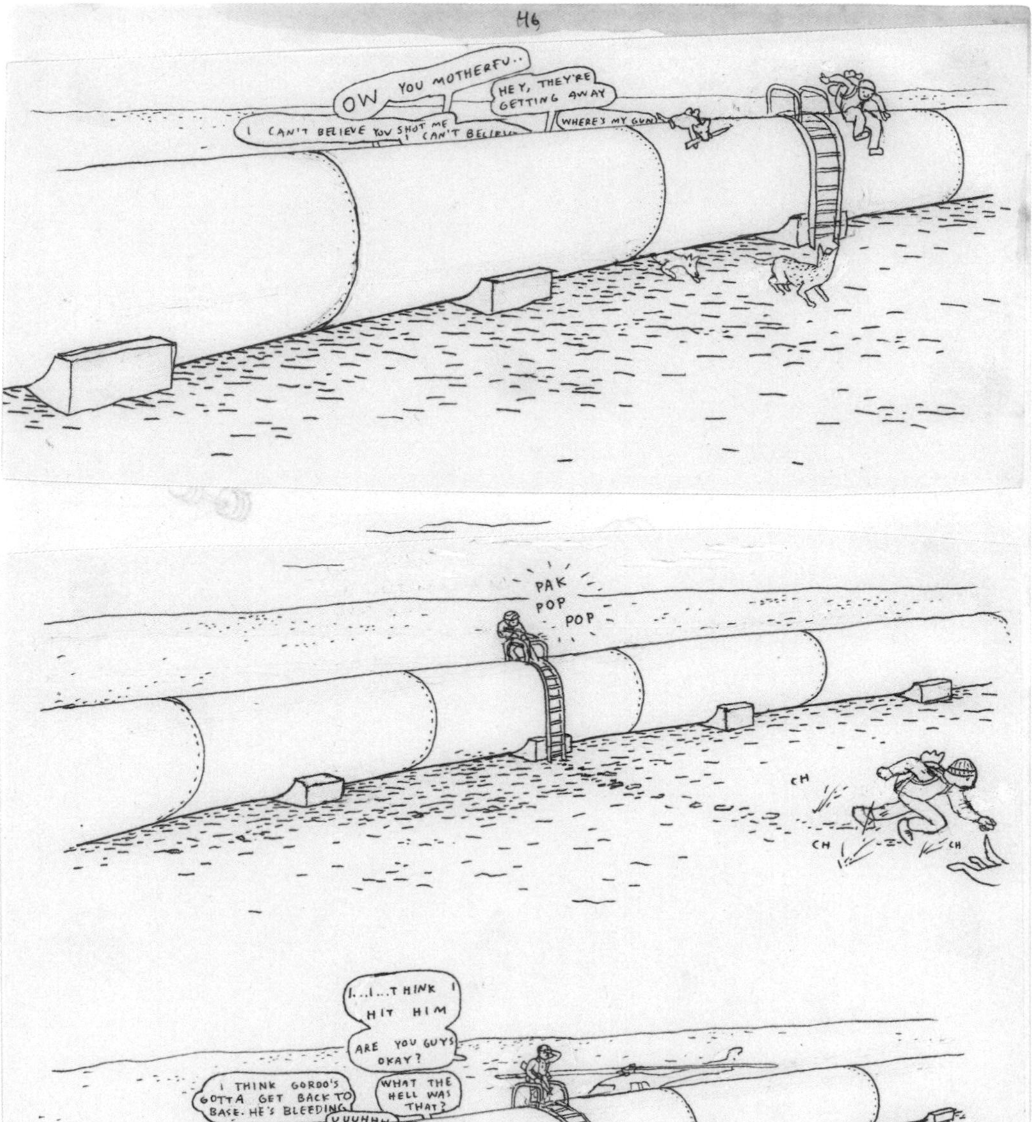
46
OW YOU MOTHERFU..
HEY, THEY'RE GETTING AWAY
I CAN'T BELIEVE YOU SHOT ME I CAN'T BELIEV
WHERE'S MY GUN
PAK POP POP
CH
CH
CH
I...I...THINK I HIT HIM
ARE YOU GUYS OKAY?
I THINK GORDO'S GOTTA GET BACK TO BASE. HE'S BLEEDING
WHAT THE HELL WAS THAT?
UUUHH

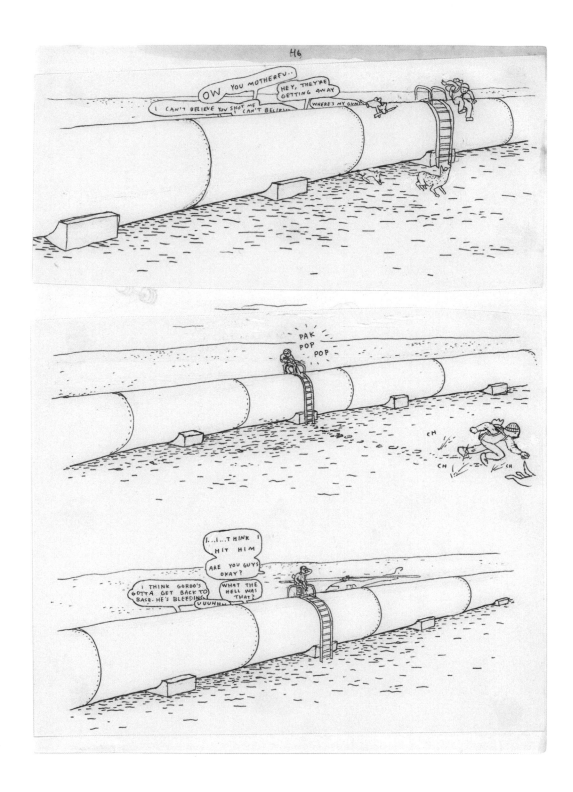

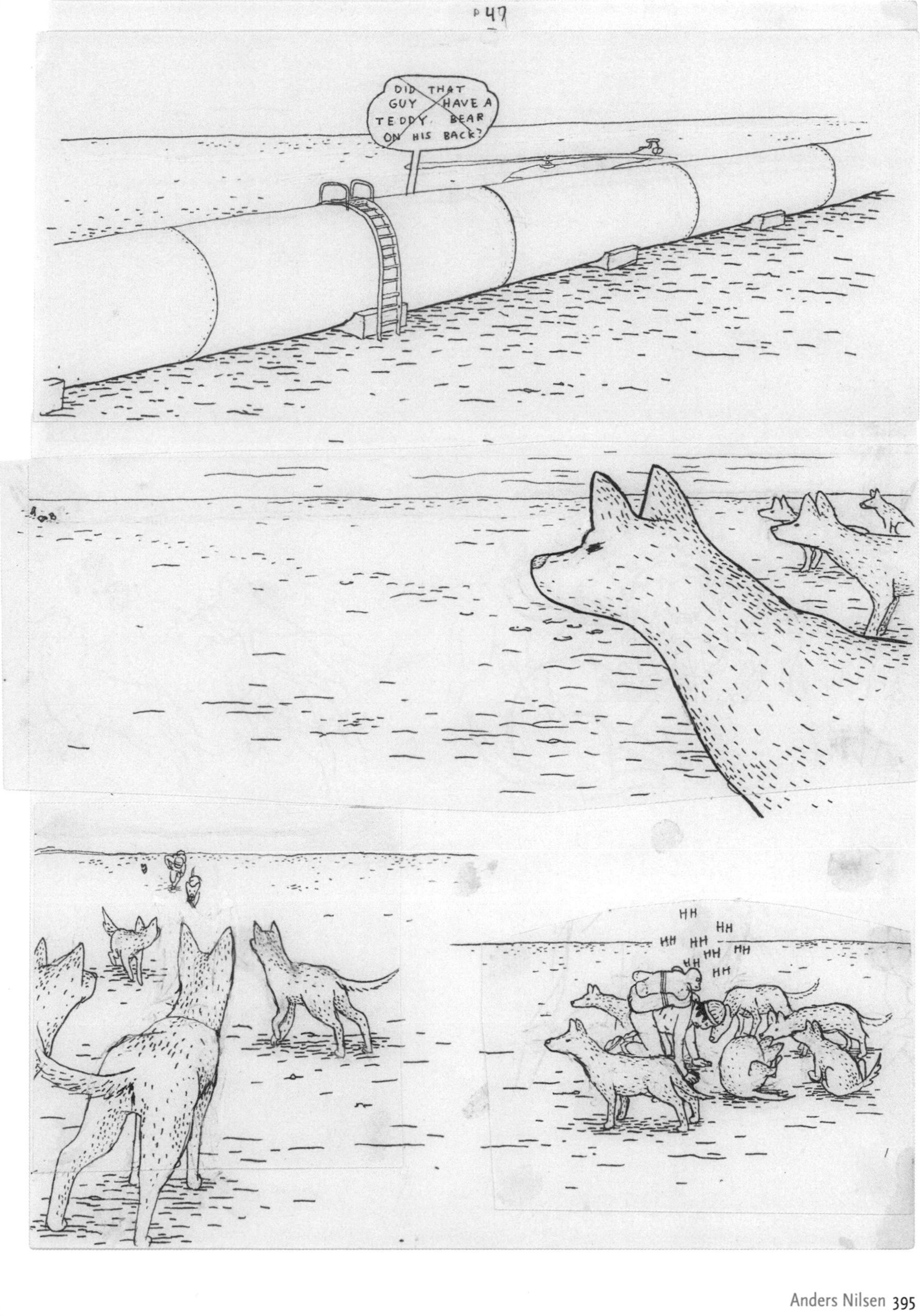
p47
DID THAT GUY HAVE A TEDDY BEAR ON HIS BACK?
HH HH HH HH HH HH HH HH

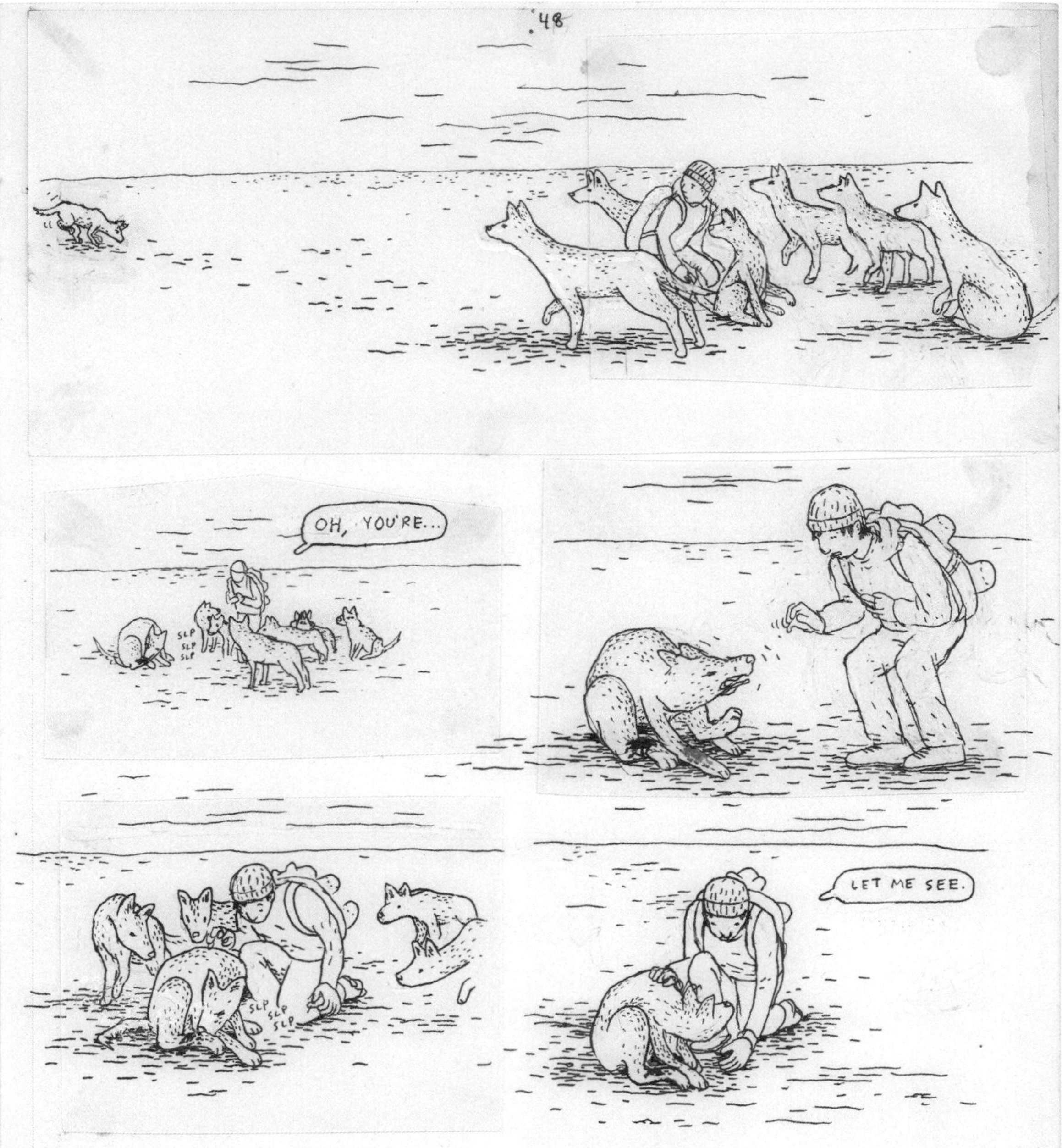
48
OH, YOU'RE...
SLP
SLP
SLP
SLP
SLP
SLP
LET ME SEE.
move these two bottom panels to next page etc, through next 4 pages

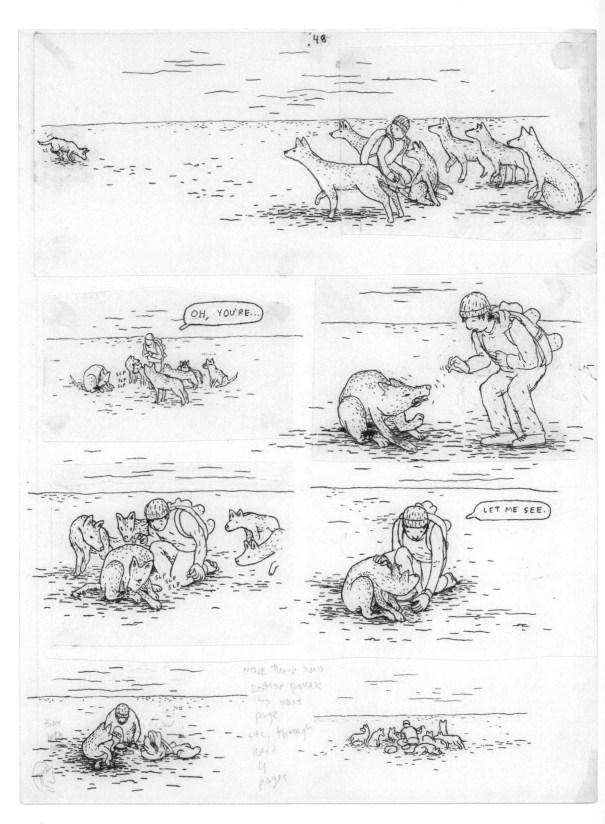

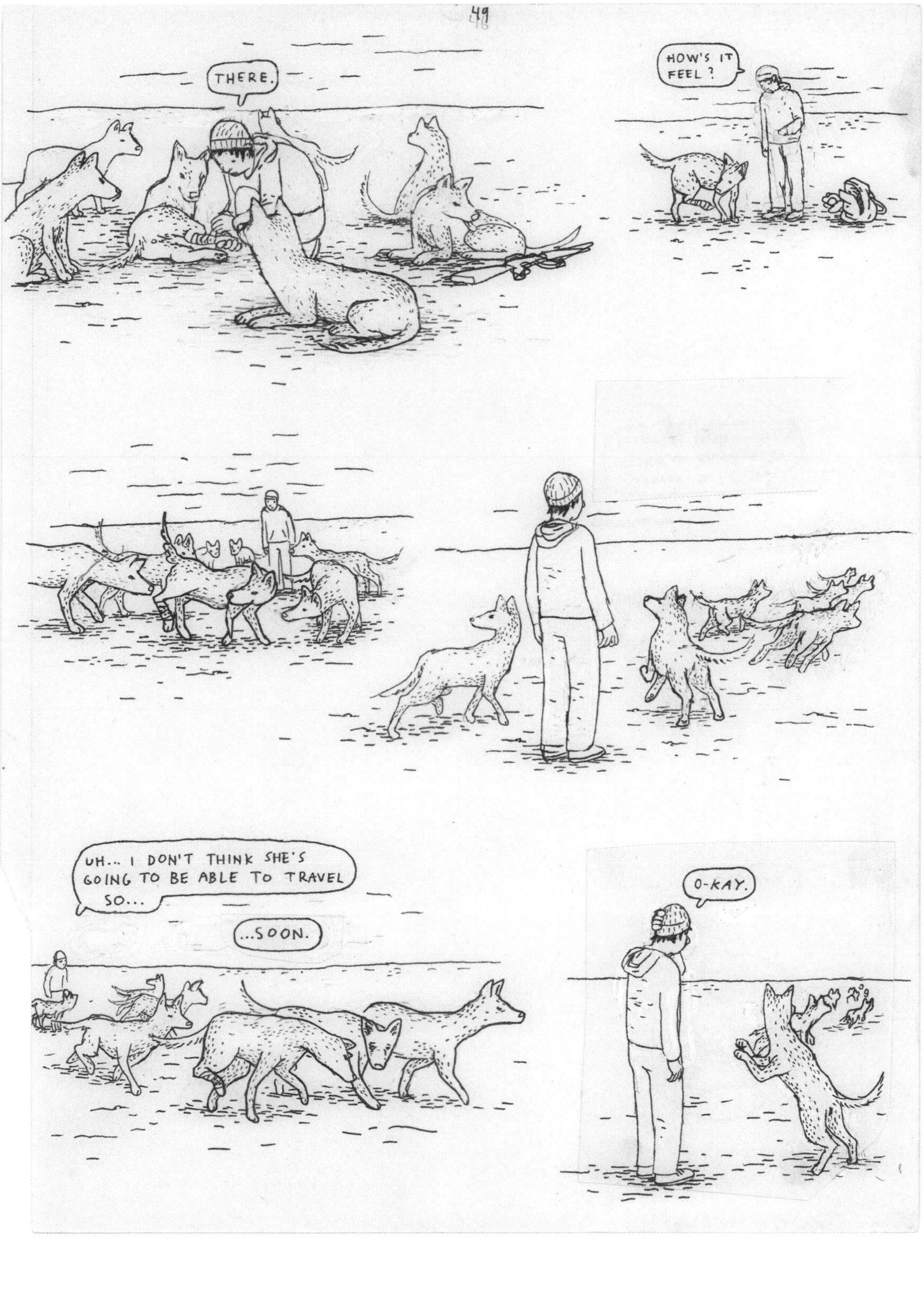
49
THERE.
HOW'S IT FEEL?
UH... I DON'T THINK SHE'S GOING TO BE ABLE TO TRAVEL SO...
...SOON.
O-KAY.

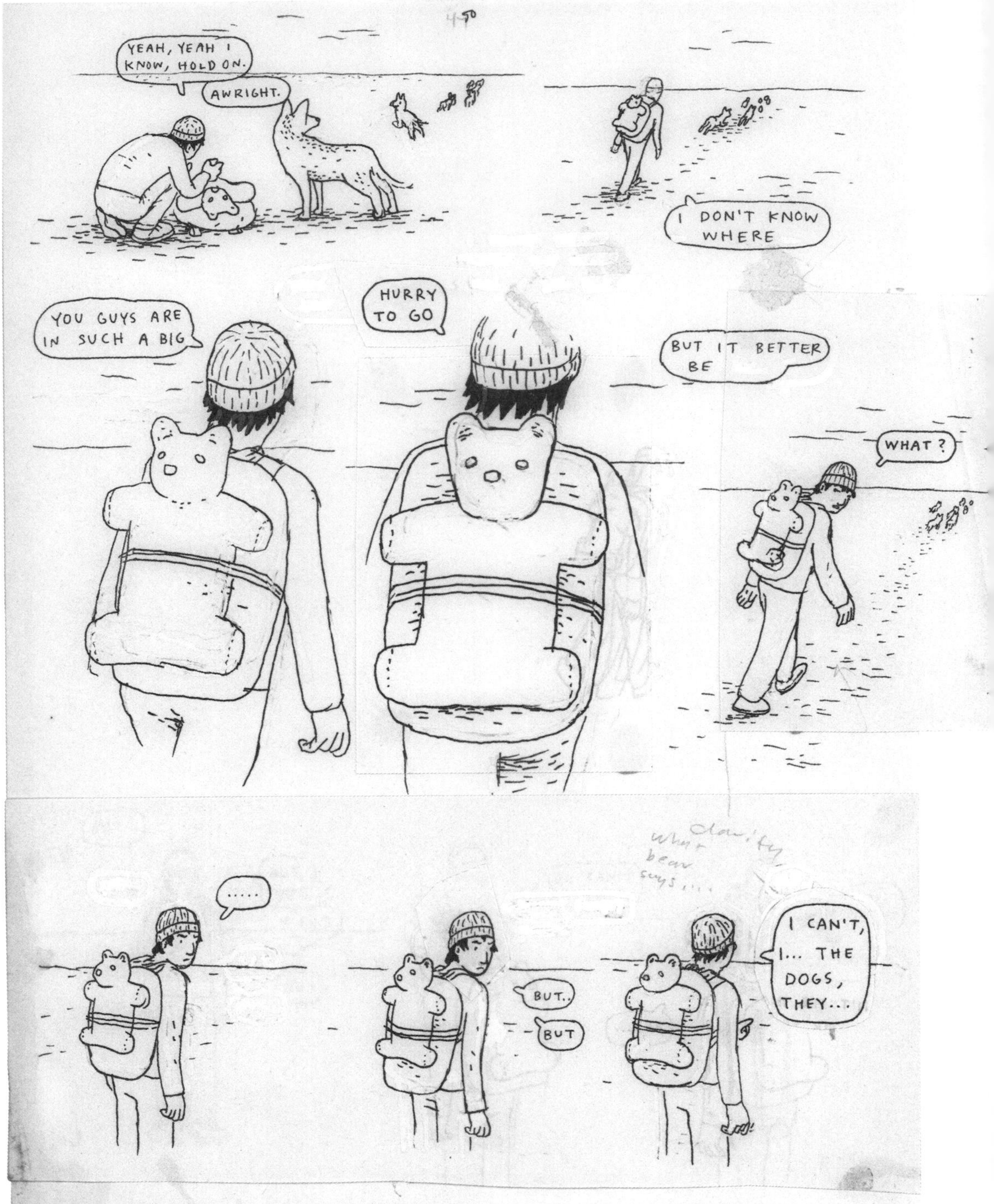
YEAH, YEAH I KNOW, HOLD ON.
AWRIGHT.
I DON'T KNOW WHERE
YOU GUYS ARE IN SUCH A BIG
HURRY TO GO
BUT IT BETTER BE
WHAT?
.....
BUT..
BUT
I CAN'T, I... THE DOGS, THEY...

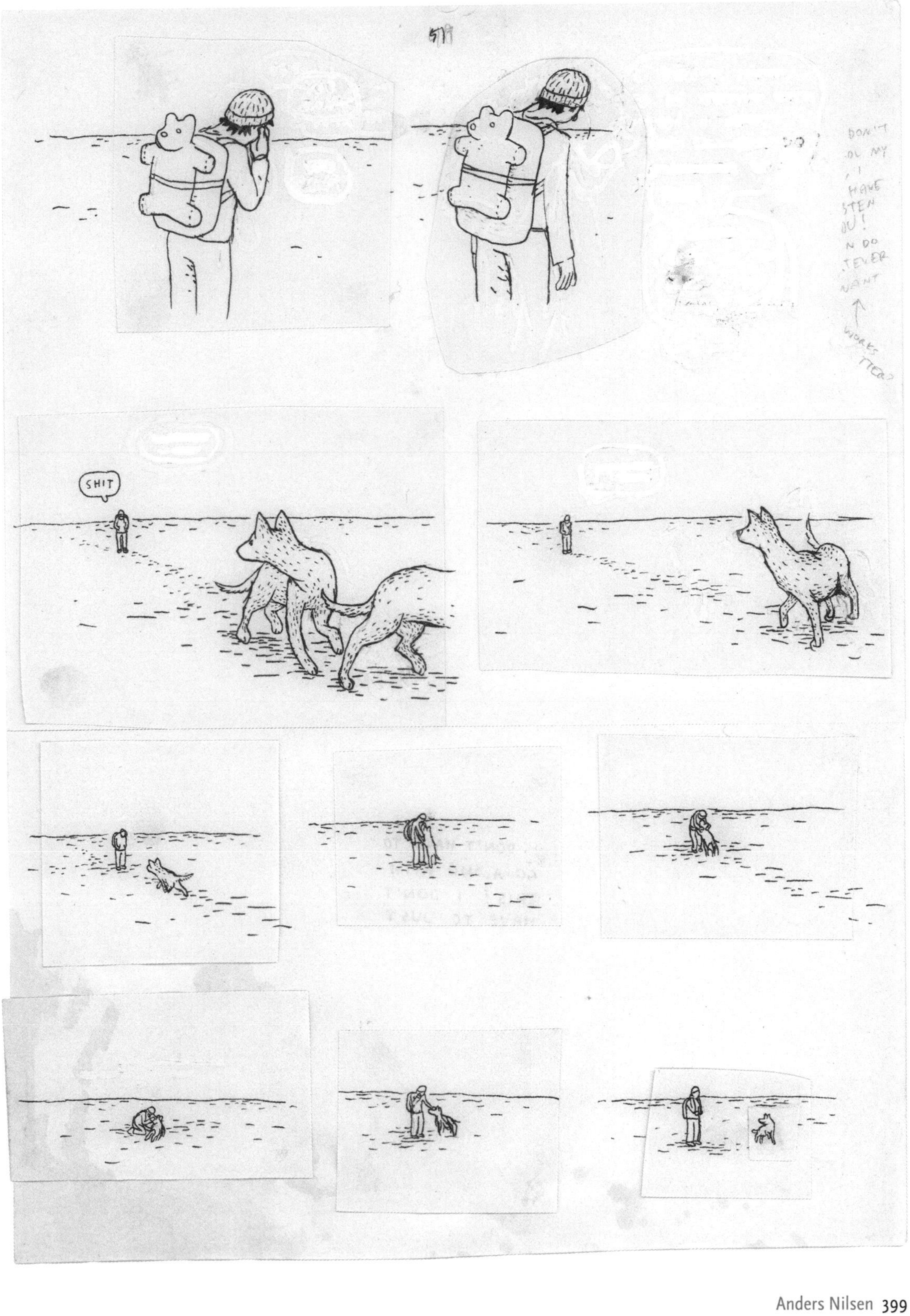
SHIT

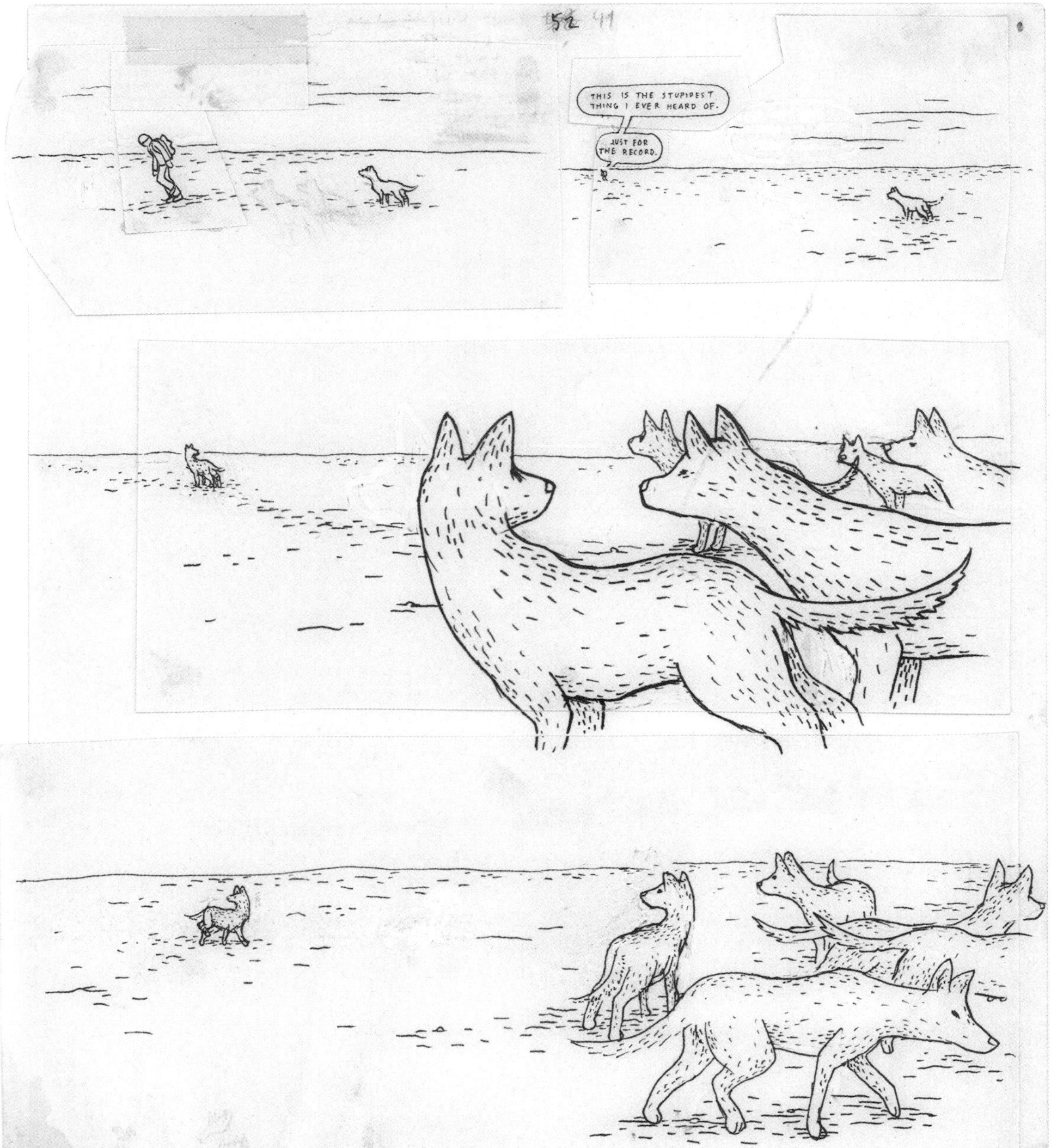
THIS IS THE STUPIDEST THING I EVER HEARD OF.
JUST FOR THE RECORD.

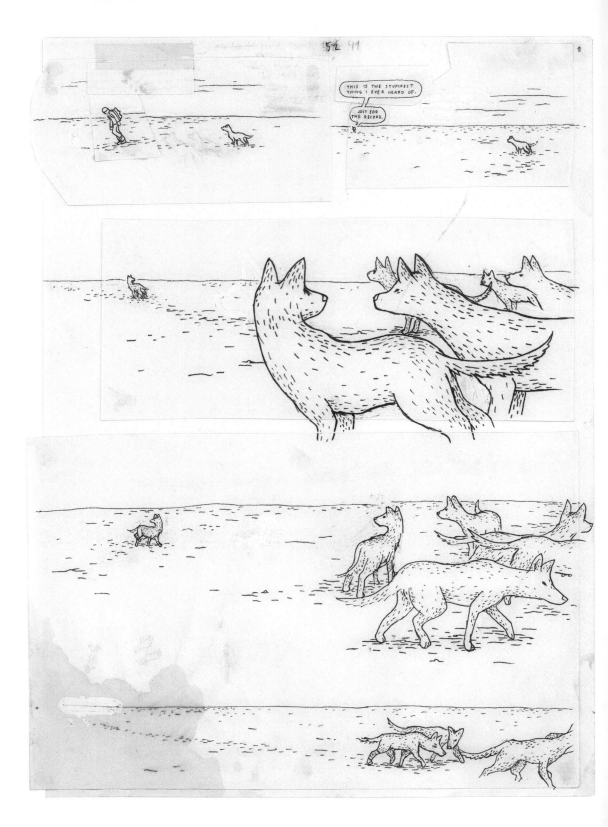

A TERRIBLY HUMAN, DOODLING, HONEST HAND

an appreciation of Anders Nilsen by Fiona Duncan

I stack Anders Nilsen's books in two piles, separating fiction from non. I do this thinking the material divide may inspire some order in mind. On my right, there's fiction: *Big Questions*, *Dogs and Water*, and *Rage of Poseidon*. On my left, the rest: *Don't Go Where I Can't Follow* and *The End*. This is all the Anders I own. I lift each stack, guess at its mass. The fiction far outweighs the other two: *Don't Go* and *The End* are volumes so slim, I forget them in bed with me.

Big Questions, on the other hand, became my nightstand. When my bed was a mattress on the floor. Okay, it's still that now, but it feels less so. Now I've got a proper nightstand: a brown cardboard box. Now *Big Questions* is no longer a prop. It made an attractive table, minimally ornate and handcrafted, like an art nouveau repro you find at a flea market and paint all white. My point is *Big Questions* is big: six hundred pages, thick stock. The spine's too broad for my bite. You can hardly take it anywhere, but that's chill because, like ice cream, this book is best consumed in private, in bed.

I started *Big Questions* not in bed, but in a nearby park; I carried the weight in a cloth sack, alternating shoulders. In the grass, under trees, I remember, I opened to the front matter. There, an alternative title was writ small. Beneath *Big Questions*, Nilsen had penned, *Or, Asomatognosia: Whose Hand Is It Anyway?* That multisyllabic diagnostic means, I learned in search, *a lack of awareness of the condition of all or part of one's body.*

Whose hand? His style is unmistakable. I'd recognize it from across a convention hall. Now, though, after having come to create daily myself, I think I get the remove: in making, sometimes, often, when it's good, you don't feel as though you are there, in body. You become medium, pneuma, higher planed; ideas pass through you, materialize on the page.

I sense such creative grace in *Big Questions*. The tome started with gag strips, one- or two-page "funny animal" cartoons starring a set of existential finches. From these birds, Nilsen zoomed out, manifesting a world around them. He introduced anthropomorphic owls, snakes, and squirrels, and a few animalistic humans (quite base). The work streams so seamlessly, it doesn't look like work—it looks like a mind wandering between work, like a hand

channelling another cosmos. Automatic drawing, doodles.

I can't figure an easy way into writing about Anders Nilsen's art. I see his oeuvre as a lavish garden, hedge heavy, into which I must carve an entry. I see his books as him, a man I've met. I see in them a true tragedy I'm afraid to represent. I think it's his hand that haunts me, his terribly human, doodling, honest hand. The hand of a man who as a kid—I'd bet—was always the best in art class. The hand of someone who creates for himself.

I stack Anders Nilsen's books in two piles, separating fiction from non. I do this thinking the material divide may inspire some order in mind. His books of fiction far outweigh the non. And yet, *Don't Go Where I Can't Follow* and *The End* are the ones that weigh on me. They document a personal tragedy. Nilsen lost his partner, artist Cheryl Weaver, to cancer in 2005. She was thirty-seven, he five years younger. They'd been engaged a year, were together for six.

Don't Go is as raw as stories come. Nilsen and Weaver's relationship, or some of its middle and end, is told through a selected archive of letters, postcards, photographs, sketches, and journal entries. The immediacy of these documents heaves their gravity upon me. *The End* is heavy, too. But it's less material, more philosophical. Nilsen projects his grief onto a universal plane. The book's led by a masculine "I" outline, who floats in space and asks big questions of his lost love's ghost; she responds never knowing more than that she is a projection of his mind.

To write of personal tragedy is questionable, as any non-fiction is. In non-fiction, we are confronted with our subjectivity, the nature of reality, which may be in our head. Of experience, one wonders: what's singularly mine, what's shared? What did or didn't I sense? Non-fiction is always, no matter how verifiable the facts, a sharing of perception, not absolute truth.

Cheryl Weaver is no longer around to tell her story. Nilsen is, but his stories, even those about her, are his (as mine are mine). Storytelling in comics makes this clear. There's no forgetting the artist's hand. Nilsen's may as well be on the page; its image is summoned in thin black strokes, started and stopped, by words written and crossed out.

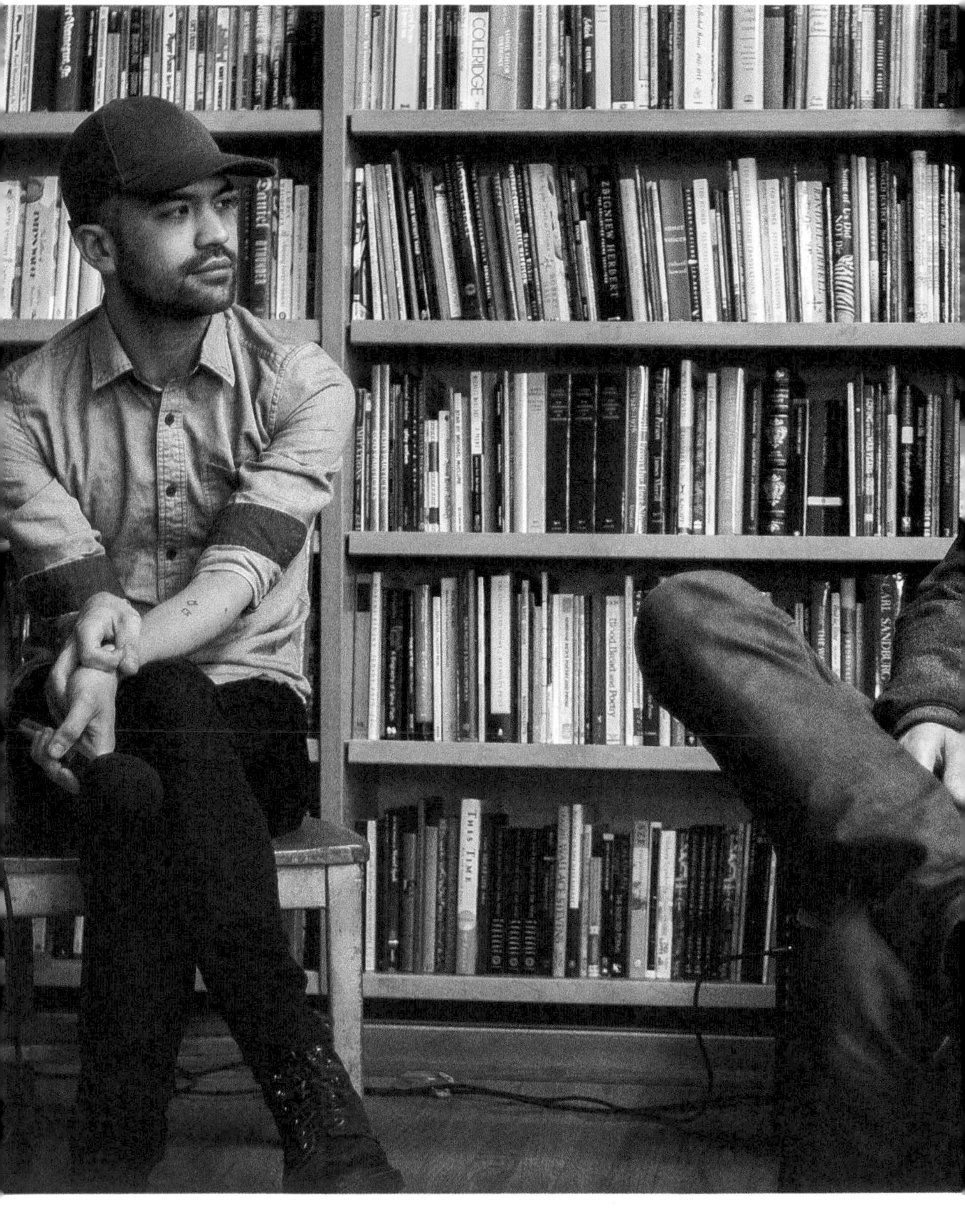
COLERIDGE
ZBIGNIEW HERBERT
THIS TIME

 Michael DeForge & Anders Nilsen at their joint book launch at Pegasus Books. Photo: Chris Anthony Diaz & Graham Willcox (2014).

The writer's version of the doodle is perhaps the note. Mine on Anders stream metres. For seven weeks now I've reread his texts, knowing I'd have to compose a response. I reflected on them between reads, at work, on walks, in the shower; struck by inspiration, I noted it. These notes have been tried as tools: I thought one would function to carve an entry into his garden. Instead, they seeded more growth. Can't see the books for the trees.

Here, a small plot of notes on the work of Anders Nilsen:

Big Questions *befits the existential insomniac, afternoon leisure readers, lucid day-dreamers, anyone with the time to forget about time—the work is lived, it unfolds, over time—*Rage of Poseidon *unfolds too, literally, the pages accordion*

Anders's pointillism—feels like if you zoomed in even his lines would be made of these little dots, as in atoms—his work represents the micro & macro—earthworm & bird & man & Gods (Gods like in Rage of Poseidon, *which is not dotted, like the earthy* Big Questions*—us humans, animals, composites—but filled, full, solid, like Gods)*

Big Q. jokes echo like ba-Dum-CH!

Is this all there is? *is a question Anders Nilsen repeats in* The End. *It is the Big One*

After/during his loss, her sickness, he repeats "too much," as in, "it's too much to bear," which means maybe rather, "it's not enough"

So, he's existential

Artists give permission: allowance to experience, to access, matters the everyday often denies

There's a default levity to comics; silly, these abstract forms. Whereas writing, esp. the printed word, assumes gravity—it's for the record, "canonized" (the root of which, btw, is "rule," as in decree)

To separate fiction from nonfiction is a false divide, I've come to believe. All communication is storytelling. Even in *Don't Go Where I Can't Follow*, a story is told in archive. Anders Nilsen has chosen what to share, what to put where.

Perception is storytelling. The mind assembles patterns through the senses, makes sense of the infinite information before us at any given moment. If Anders Nilsen's books—all, fiction and non—do one thing for me, one common thing, that is this: they scramble my senses, my me-centred gaze, the assumptions of order I've accumulated in education and experience. Whether that's seeing the assembly of life on earth through a bird's eye or a God's eye or a grief-striking eye, I am shaken. I am awakened anew to familiar material—to my hand, to how clouds are cartooned, to the heft of certain books.

Fiona Duncan is a freelance journalist and bookseller who regularly writes for Adult, Bullett, New Inquiry, New York *magazine,* Vice, *and more. Her crowning journalistic achievement is popularizing the term "normcore."*

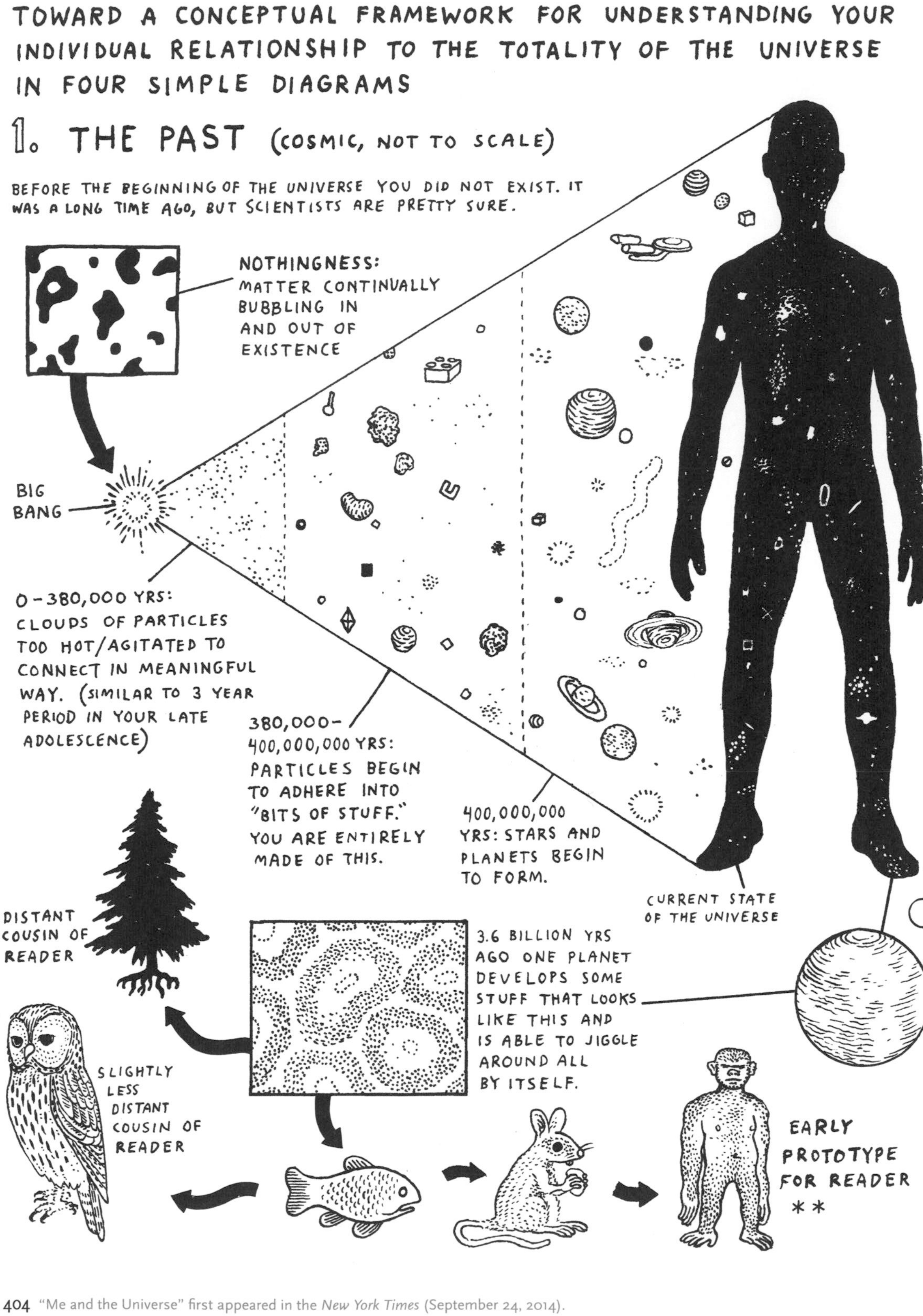
TOWARD A CONCEPTUAL FRAMEWORK FOR UNDERSTANDING YOUR INDIVIDUAL RELATIONSHIP TO THE TOTALITY OF THE UNIVERSE IN FOUR SIMPLE DIAGRAMS
1. THE PAST (COSMIC, NOT TO SCALE)
BEFORE THE BEGINNING OF THE UNIVERSE YOU DID NOT EXIST. IT WAS A LONG TIME AGO, BUT SCIENTISTS ARE PRETTY SURE.
NOTHINGNESS: MATTER CONTINUALLY BUBBLING IN AND OUT OF EXISTENCE
BIG BANG
0-380,000 YRS: CLOUDS OF PARTICLES TOO HOT/AGITATED TO CONNECT IN MEANINGFUL WAY. (SIMILAR TO 3 YEAR PERIOD IN YOUR LATE ADOLESCENCE)
380,000-400,000,000 YRS: PARTICLES BEGIN TO ADHERE INTO "BITS OF STUFF." YOU ARE ENTIRELY MADE OF THIS.
400,000,000 YRS: STARS AND PLANETS BEGIN TO FORM.
CURRENT STATE OF THE UNIVERSE
3.6 BILLION YRS AGO ONE PLANET DEVELOPS SOME STUFF THAT LOOKS LIKE THIS AND IS ABLE TO JIGGLE AROUND ALL BY ITSELF.
DISTANT COUSIN OF READER
SLIGHTLY LESS DISTANT COUSIN OF READER
EARLY PROTOTYPE FOR READER **

 "Me and the Universe" first appeared in the *New York Times* (September 24, 2014).

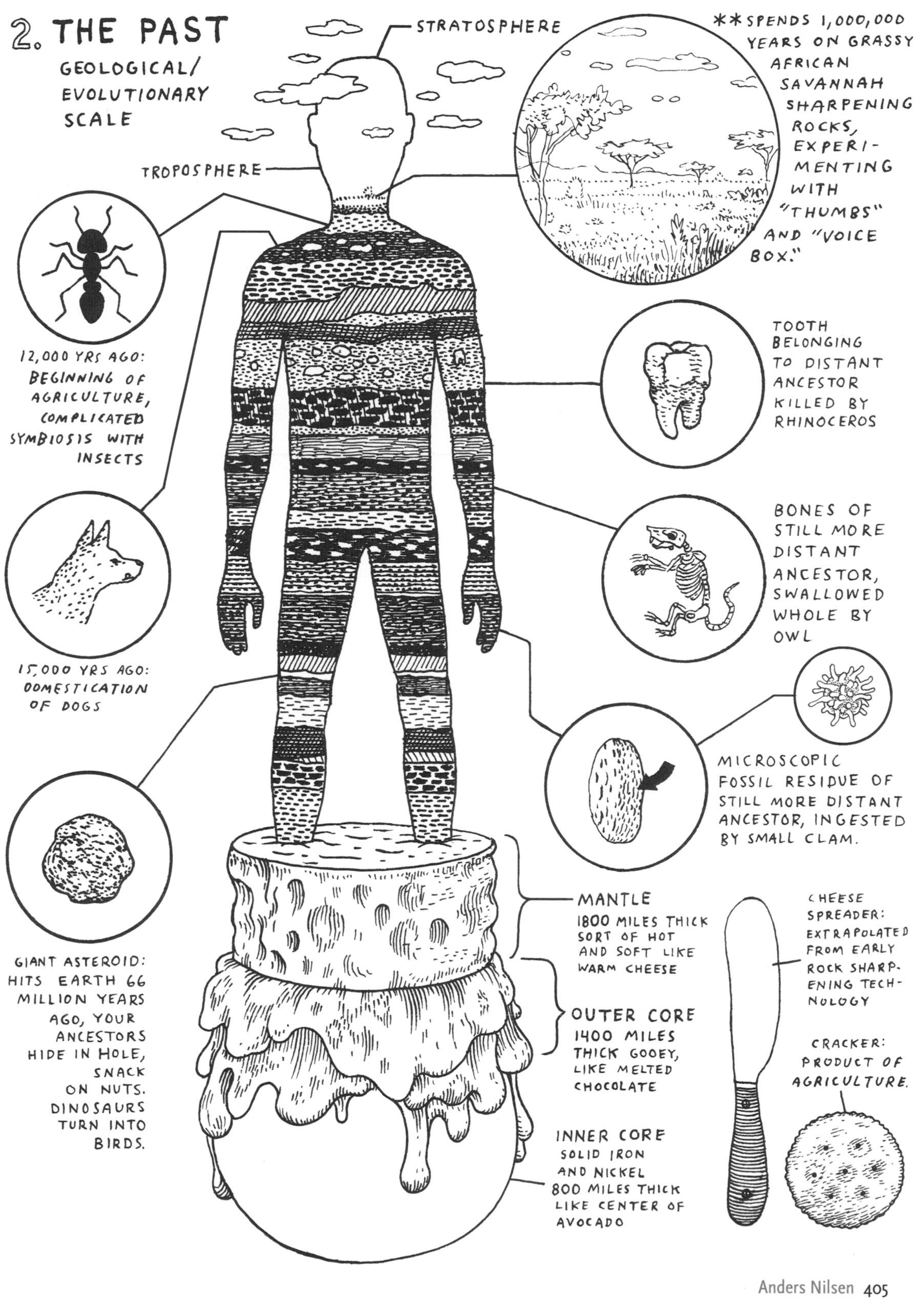

2. THE PAST
GEOLOGICAL/ EVOLUTIONARY SCALE
STRATOSPHERE
**SPENDS 1,000,000 YEARS ON GRASSY AFRICAN SAVANNAH SHARPENING ROCKS, EXPERIMENTING WITH "THUMBS" AND "VOICE BOX."
TROPOSPHERE
12,000 YRS AGO: BEGINNING OF AGRICULTURE, COMPLICATED SYMBIOSIS WITH INSECTS
TOOTH BELONGING TO DISTANT ANCESTOR KILLED BY RHINOCEROS
BONES OF STILL MORE DISTANT ANCESTOR, SWALLOWED WHOLE BY OWL
15,000 YRS AGO: DOMESTICATION OF DOGS
MICROSCOPIC FOSSIL RESIDUE OF STILL MORE DISTANT ANCESTOR, INGESTED BY SMALL CLAM.
MANTLE
1800 MILES THICK SORT OF HOT AND SOFT LIKE WARM CHEESE
CHEESE SPREADER: EXTRAPOLATED FROM EARLY ROCK SHARPENING TECHNOLOGY
GIANT ASTEROID: HITS EARTH 66 MILLION YEARS AGO, YOUR ANCESTORS HIDE IN HOLE, SNACK ON NUTS. DINOSAURS TURN INTO BIRDS.
OUTER CORE
1400 MILES THICK GOOEY, LIKE MELTED CHOCOLATE
CRACKER: PRODUCT OF AGRICULTURE.
INNER CORE
SOLID IRON AND NICKEL 800 MILES THICK LIKE CENTER OF AVOCADO

3. THE PRESENT (MORE OR LESS)

1903 - ANNA BREKHUS, AGE 16, RECEIVES LETTER IN NORWAY FROM AMERICAN COUSIN: "MY HUSBAND HAS A BROTHER."

BECOMES YOUR GREAT-GRANDMOTHER.

1906 - ANNA NILSEN EXPELLED FROM CANADA FOR ASSAULTING POLICE OFFICER DURING STRIKE.

BECOMES YOUR OTHER GREAT-GRANDMOTHER.

1972 - EN ROUTE FROM SAN FRANCISCO TO ERIE, PENNSYLVANIA YOUR MOTHER TO YOUR FATHER: "I DON'T WANT TO BE IN THE COMMUNE ANYMORE."

1973 - YOU ARE CONCEIVED ON LONG, COLD WINTER NIGHT DURING SNOW STORM. CELLS BEGIN DIVIDING ACCORDING TO ANCIENT PATTERN.

1973 • YOU ARE BORN.

U.S. PULLS OUT OF VIETNAM.

1977-1979 • YOU GRADUALLY BECOME SELF-AWARE.

PUNK ROCK INVENTED.

GENOCIDE IN CAMBODIA.

1981 • YOU PRACTICE DRAWING SPACESHIPS, DINOSAURS, GIANT DIAGRAMMATIC BATTLE SCENES.

RONALD REAGAN SHOT.

1983 • YOU ARE CAUGHT SHOPLIFTING LEGOS AT TARGET.

1984 • CLASSMATE PUNCHES YOU IN STOMACH FOLLOWING COMMENT RE: HIS MOTHER.

YOU GO THROUGH BRIEF CRIMINAL PHASE:

1986 • STEAL FIRST HOOD ORNAMENT.

1987 • STEAL SUNGLASSES, CANDY, CASSETTE TAPES, UMBRELLA. ALMOST CAUGHT STEALING EXPENSIVE CHOCOLATE, GIVE FALSE NAME TO MALL SECURITY WHERE-UPON CRIMINAL PHASE MOSTLY ABATES UNTIL 2010 WHEN YOU FAIL TO FILE STATE INCOME TAX.

1987 • YOU EXPERIENCE MUTABILITY OF BRAIN CHEMISTRY VIA COMBUSTION/ INHALATION OF THC: STARE AT DOORKNOB FOR 138 MINUTES.

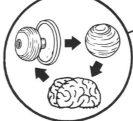

1990 • YOU HAVE SEX FOR THE FIRST TIME AFTER WATCHING MOVIE: *THE ADVENTURES OF BARON MUNCHAUSEN*.

SOVIET UNION COLLAPSES, COLD WAR ENDS.

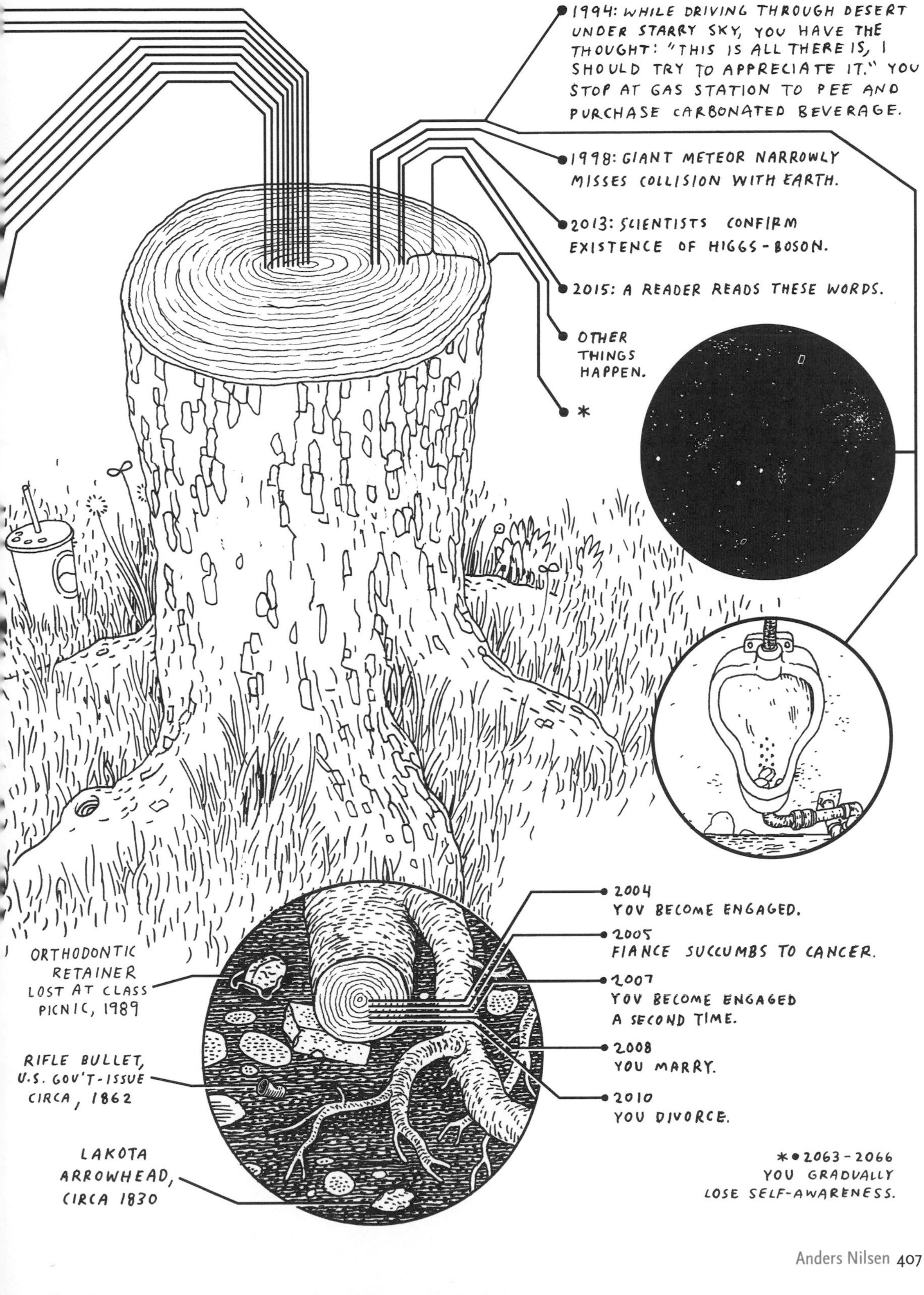
1994: WHILE DRIVING THROUGH DESERT UNDER STARRY SKY, YOU HAVE THE THOUGHT: "THIS IS ALL THERE IS, I SHOULD TRY TO APPRECIATE IT." YOU STOP AT GAS STATION TO PEE AND PURCHASE CARBONATED BEVERAGE.
1998: GIANT METEOR NARROWLY MISSES COLLISION WITH EARTH.
2013: SCIENTISTS CONFIRM EXISTENCE OF HIGGS-BOSON.
2015: A READER READS THESE WORDS.
OTHER THINGS HAPPEN.
*
ORTHODONTIC RETAINER LOST AT CLASS PICNIC, 1989
RIFLE BULLET, U.S. GOV'T-ISSUE CIRCA, 1862
LAKOTA ARROWHEAD, CIRCA 1830
2004 YOU BECOME ENGAGED.
2005 FIANCE SUCCUMBS TO CANCER.
2007 YOU BECOME ENGAGED A SECOND TIME.
2008 YOU MARRY.
2010 YOU DIVORCE.
*2063-2066 YOU GRADUALLY LOSE SELF-AWARENESS.

3. THE FUTURE (NOT TO SCALE)

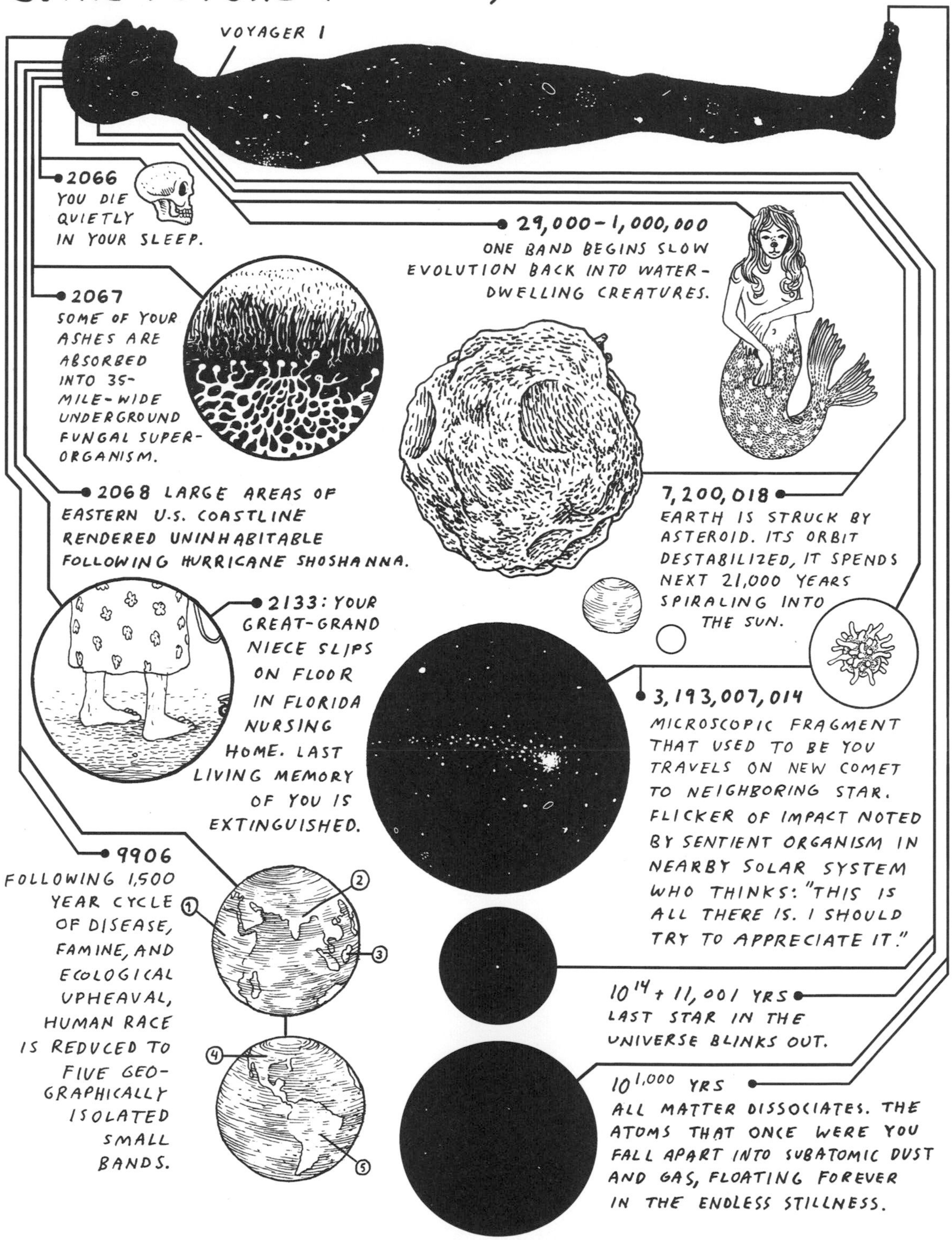
VOYAGER I
2066 YOU DIE QUIETLY IN YOUR SLEEP.
29,000–1,000,000 ONE BAND BEGINS SLOW EVOLUTION BACK INTO WATER-DWELLING CREATURES.
2067 SOME OF YOUR ASHES ARE ABSORBED INTO 35-MILE-WIDE UNDERGROUND FUNGAL SUPER-ORGANISM.
2068 LARGE AREAS OF EASTERN U.S. COASTLINE RENDERED UNINHABITABLE FOLLOWING HURRICANE SHOSHANNA.
7,200,018 EARTH IS STRUCK BY ASTEROID. ITS ORBIT DESTABILIZED, IT SPENDS NEXT 21,000 YEARS SPIRALING INTO THE SUN.
2133: YOUR GREAT-GRAND NIECE SLIPS ON FLOOR IN FLORIDA NURSING HOME. LAST LIVING MEMORY OF YOU IS EXTINGUISHED.
3,193,007,014 MICROSCOPIC FRAGMENT THAT USED TO BE YOU TRAVELS ON NEW COMET TO NEIGHBORING STAR. FLICKER OF IMPACT NOTED BY SENTIENT ORGANISM IN NEARBY SOLAR SYSTEM WHO THINKS: "THIS IS ALL THERE IS. I SHOULD TRY TO APPRECIATE IT."
9906 FOLLOWING 1,500 YEAR CYCLE OF DISEASE, FAMINE, AND ECOLOGICAL UPHEAVAL, HUMAN RACE IS REDUCED TO FIVE GEOGRAPHICALLY ISOLATED SMALL BANDS.
1
2
3
4
5
10^{14} + 11,001 YRS LAST STAR IN THE UNIVERSE BLINKS OUT.
$10^{1,000}$ YRS ALL MATTER DISSOCIATES. THE ATOMS THAT ONCE WERE YOU FALL APART INTO SUBATOMIC DUST AND GAS, FLOATING FOREVER IN THE ENDLESS STILLNESS.

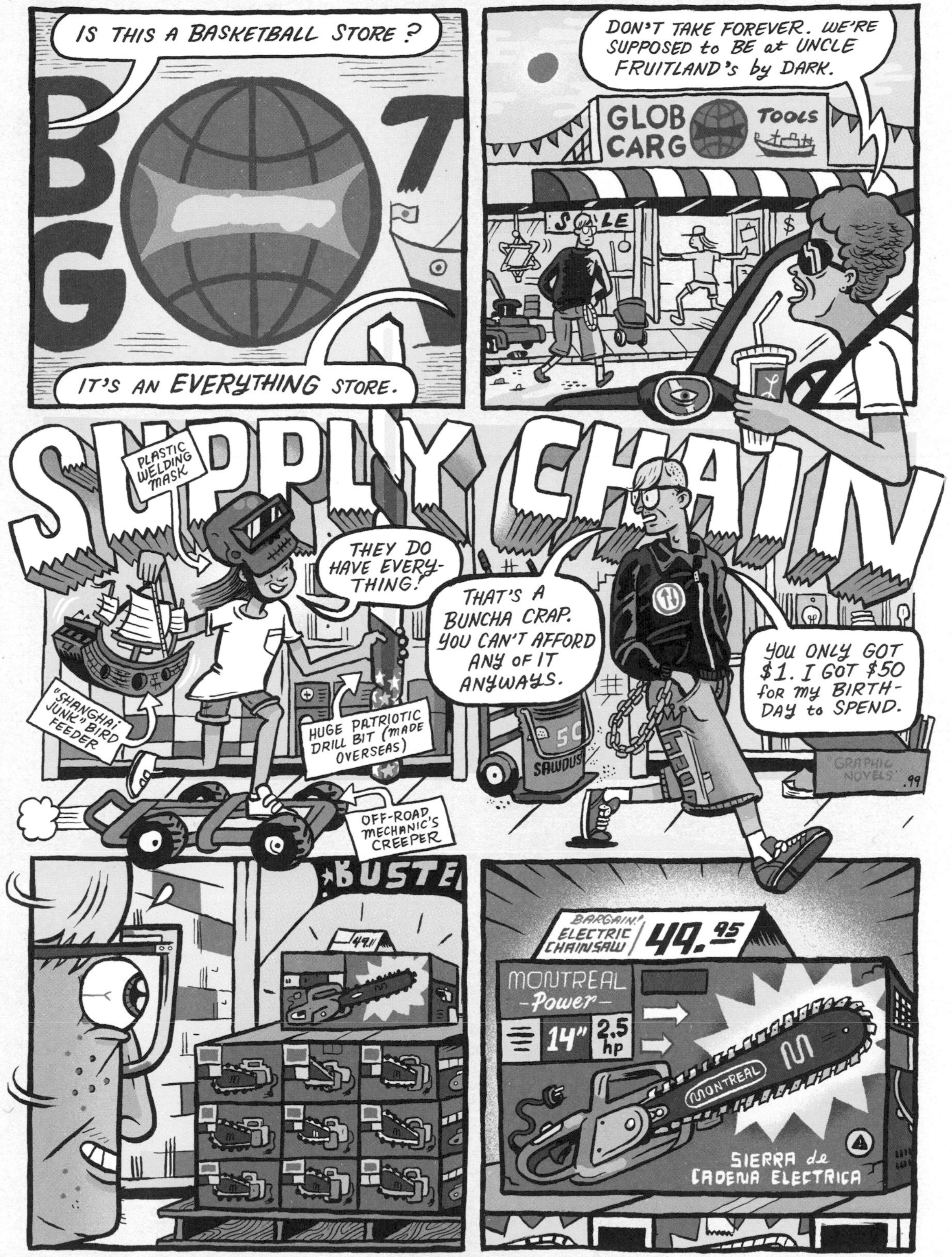
IS THIS A BASKETBALL STORE ?
IT'S AN EVERYTHING STORE.
DON'T TAKE FOREVER. WE'RE SUPPOSED to BE at UNCLE FRUITLAND'S by DARK.
GLOB CARG
TOOLS
SALE
SUPPLY CHAIN
PLASTIC WELDING MASK
THEY DO HAVE EVERY-THING!
THAT'S A BUNCHA CRAP. YOU CAN'T AFFORD ANY OF IT ANYWAYS.
YOU ONLY GOT $1. I GOT $50 for MY BIRTH-DAY to SPEND.
"SHANGHAI JUNK" BIRD FEEDER
HUGE PATRIOTIC DRILL BIT (MADE OVERSEAS)
OFF-ROAD MECHANIC'S CREEPER
SAWDUST
"GRAPHIC NOVELS" .99
BUSTE
BARGAIN! ELECTRIC CHAINSAW 49.95
MONTREAL -Power-
14"
2.5 hp
MONTREAL
SIERRA de CADENA ELECTRICA

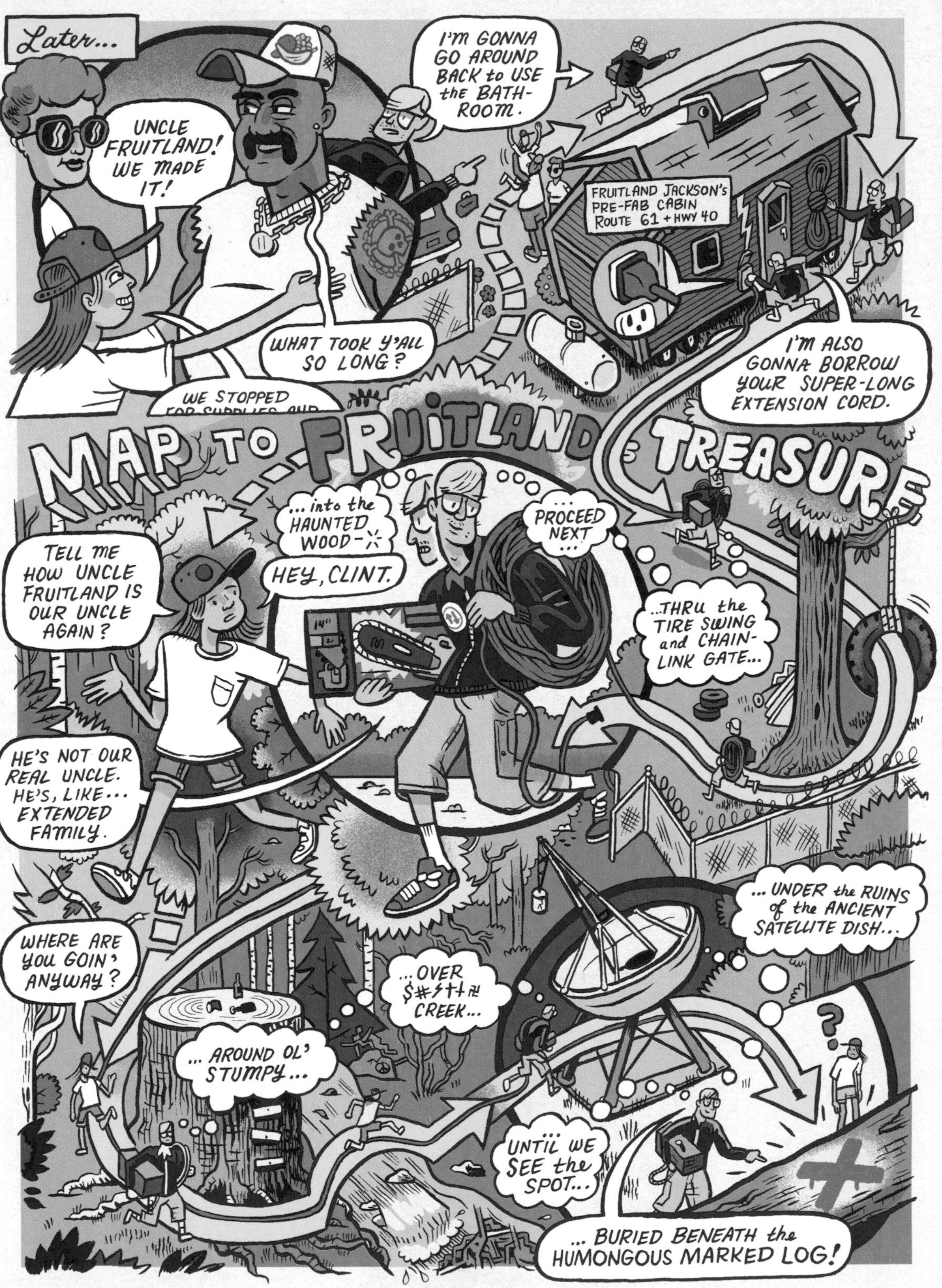
Later...
UNCLE FRUITLAND! WE MADE IT!
I'M GONNA GO AROUND BACK to USE the BATH-ROOM.
FRUITLAND JACKSON'S PRE-FAB CABIN ROUTE 61 + HWY 40
WHAT TOOK Y'ALL SO LONG?
WE STOPPED
I'M ALSO GONNA BORROW YOUR SUPER-LONG EXTENSION CORD.
MAP TO FRUITLAND TREASURE
TELL ME HOW UNCLE FRUITLAND IS OUR UNCLE AGAIN?
...into the HAUNTED WOOD-
HEY, CLINT.
...PROCEED NEXT...
...THRU the TIRE SWING and CHAIN-LINK GATE...
HE'S NOT OUR REAL UNCLE. HE'S, LIKE... EXTENDED FAMILY.
...UNDER the RUINS of the ANCIENT SATELLITE DISH...
WHERE ARE YOU GOIN' ANYWAY?
...OVER $#$†‡ CREEK...
...AROUND OL' STUMPY...
UNTIL WE SEE the SPOT...
...BURIED BENEATH the HUMONGOUS MARKED LOG!

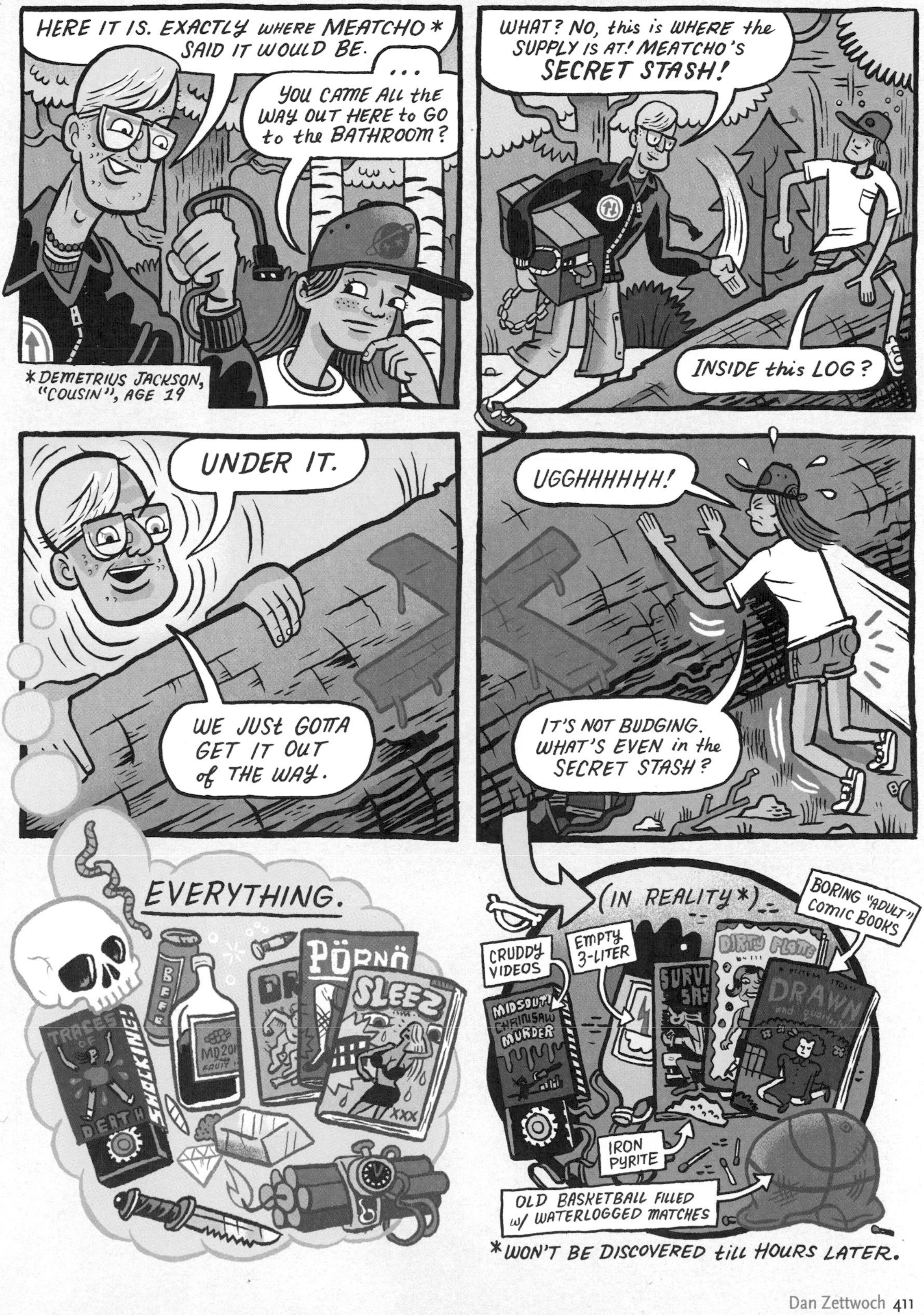
HERE IT IS. EXACTLY WHERE MEATCHO * SAID IT WOULD BE.
...
YOU CAME ALL the WAY OUT HERE to GO to the BATHROOM?
* DEMETRIUS JACKSON, "COUSIN", AGE 19
WHAT? NO, this is WHERE the SUPPLY is AT! MEATCHO's SECRET STASH!
INSIDE this LOG?
UNDER IT.
WE JUST GOTTA GET IT OUT of THE WAY.
UGGHHHHHH!
IT'S NOT BUDGING. WHAT'S EVEN in the SECRET STASH?
EVERYTHING.
BEER
PÖRNO
SLEEZ
XXX
TRACES OF DEATH
SHOCKING!
(IN REALITY*)
BORING "ADULT" COMIC BOOKS
CRUDDY VIDEOS
Empty 3-LITER
DRAWN and quarterly
IRON PYRITE
OLD BASKETBALL FILLED w/ WATERLOGGED MATCHES
*WON'T BE DISCOVERED till HOURS LATER.

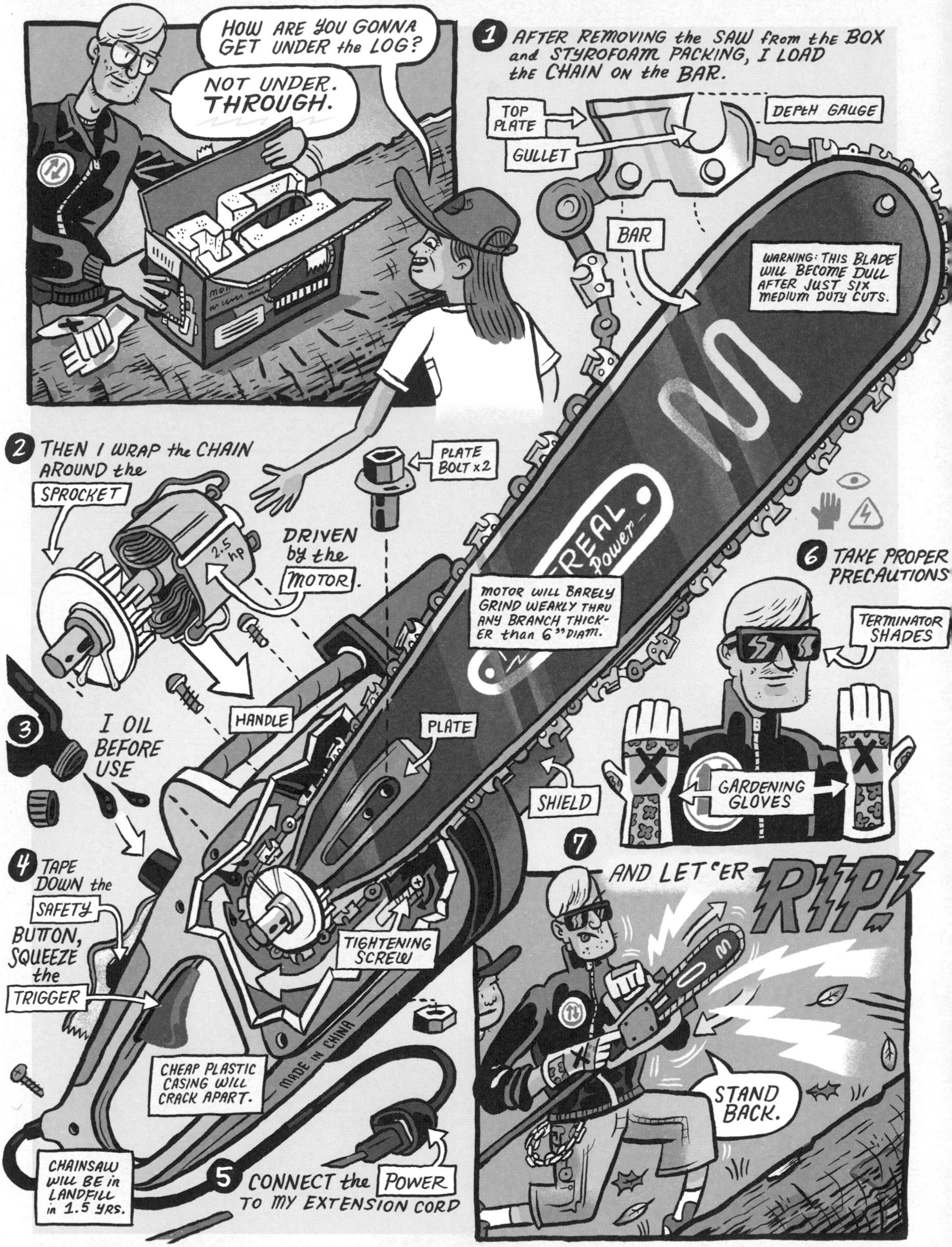
HOW ARE YOU GONNA GET UNDER the LOG?
NOT UNDER. THROUGH.
1 AFTER REMOVING the SAW from the BOX and STYROFOAM PACKING, I LOAD the CHAIN ON the BAR.
TOP PLATE
GULLET
DEPTH GAUGE
BAR
WARNING: THIS BLADE WILL BECOME DULL AFTER JUST SIX MEDIUM DUTY CUTS.
2 THEN I WRAP the CHAIN AROUND the SPROCKET
DRIVEN by the MOTOR.
2.5 hp
PLATE BOLT x2
REAL power
MOTOR WILL BARELY GRIND WEAKLY THRU ANY BRANCH THICKER than 6" DIAM.
6 TAKE PROPER PRECAUTIONS
TERMINATOR SHADES
GARDENING GLOVES
3 I OIL BEFORE USE
HANDLE
PLATE
SHIELD
4 TAPE DOWN the SAFETY BUTTON, SQUEEZE the TRIGGER
TIGHTENING SCREW
MADE IN CHINA
CHEAP PLASTIC CASING WILL CRACK APART.
CHAINSAW WILL BE in LANDFILL in 1.5 YRS.
5 CONNECT the POWER TO MY EXTENSION CORD
7 AND LET'ER RIP!
STAND BACK.

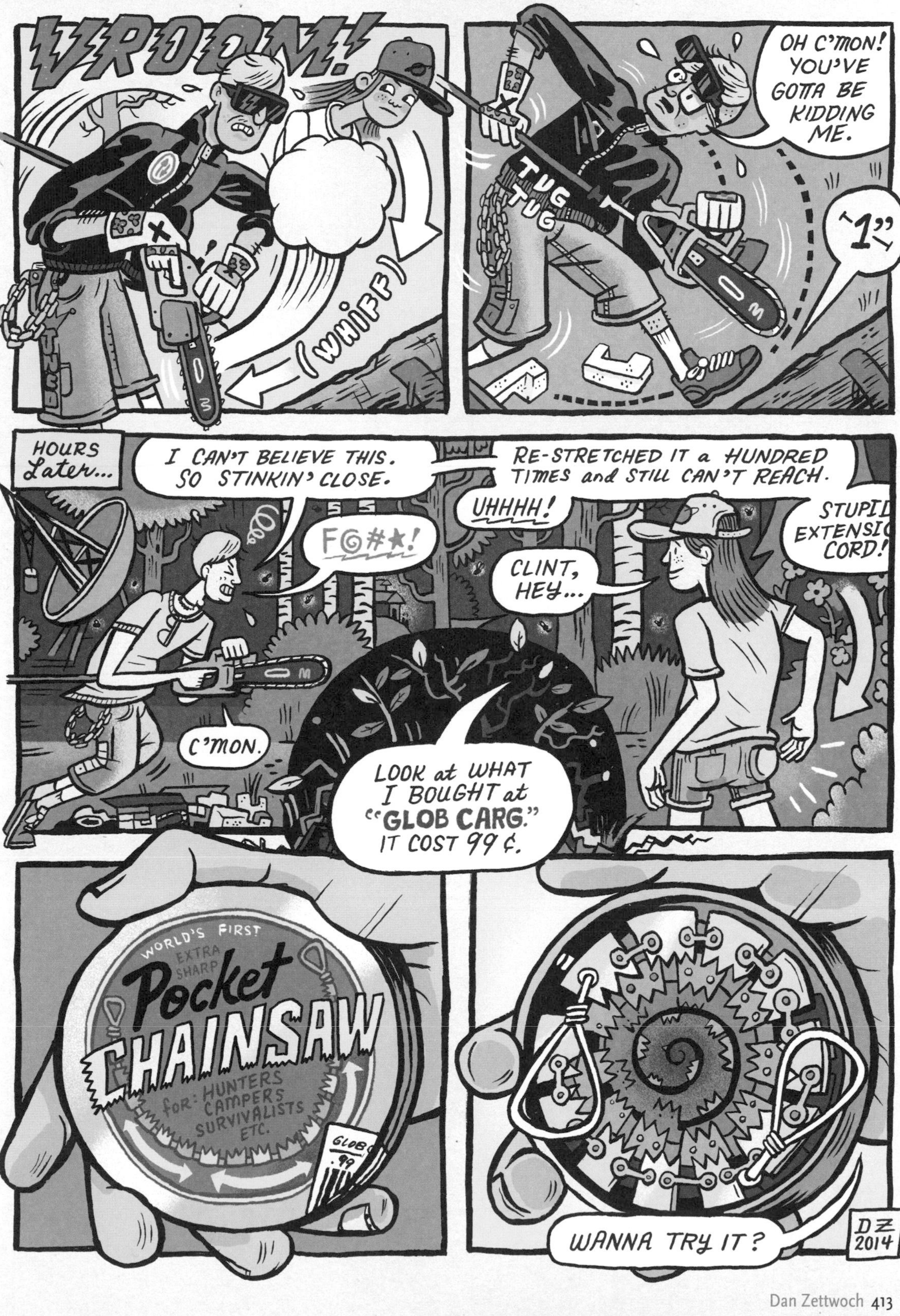
VROOM!
(WHIFF)
OH C'MON! YOU'VE GOTTA BE KIDDING ME.
TUG TUG
"1"
HOURS Later...
I CAN'T BELIEVE THIS. SO STINKIN' CLOSE.
RE-STRETCHED IT a HUNDRED TIMES and STILL CAN'T REACH.
UHHHH!
STUPID EXTENSIO CORD!
F@#★!
CLINT, HEY...
C'MON.
LOOK at WHAT I BOUGHT at "GLOB CARG." IT COST 99¢.
WORLD'S FIRST EXTRA SHARP Pocket CHAINSAW for: HUNTERS CAMPERS SURVIVALISTS ETC.
GLOB .99
WANNA TRY IT?
DZ 2014

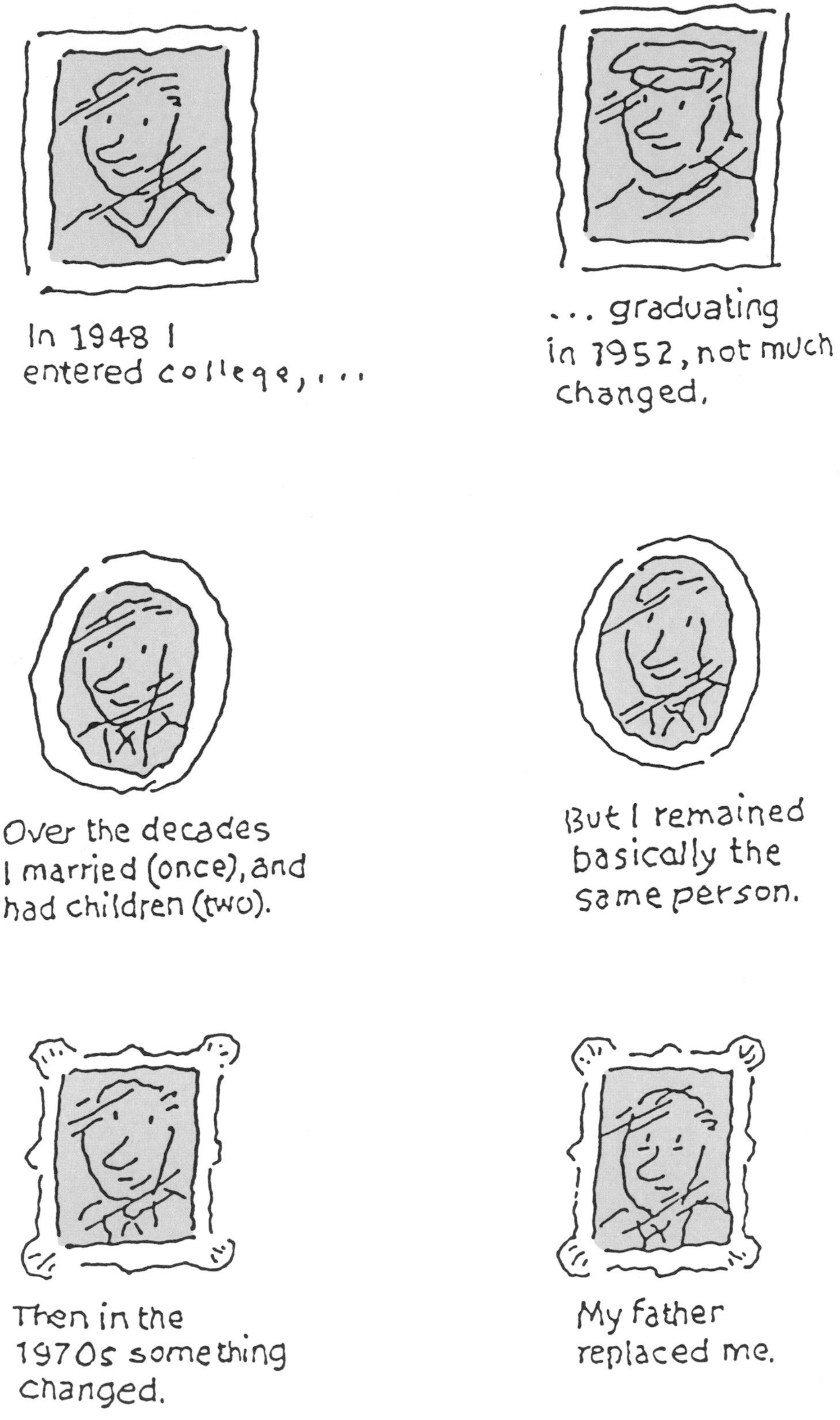
In 1948 I entered college, . . .
. . . graduating in 1952, not much changed.
Over the decades I married (once), and had children (two).
But I remained basically the same person.
Then in the 1970s something changed.
My father replaced me.

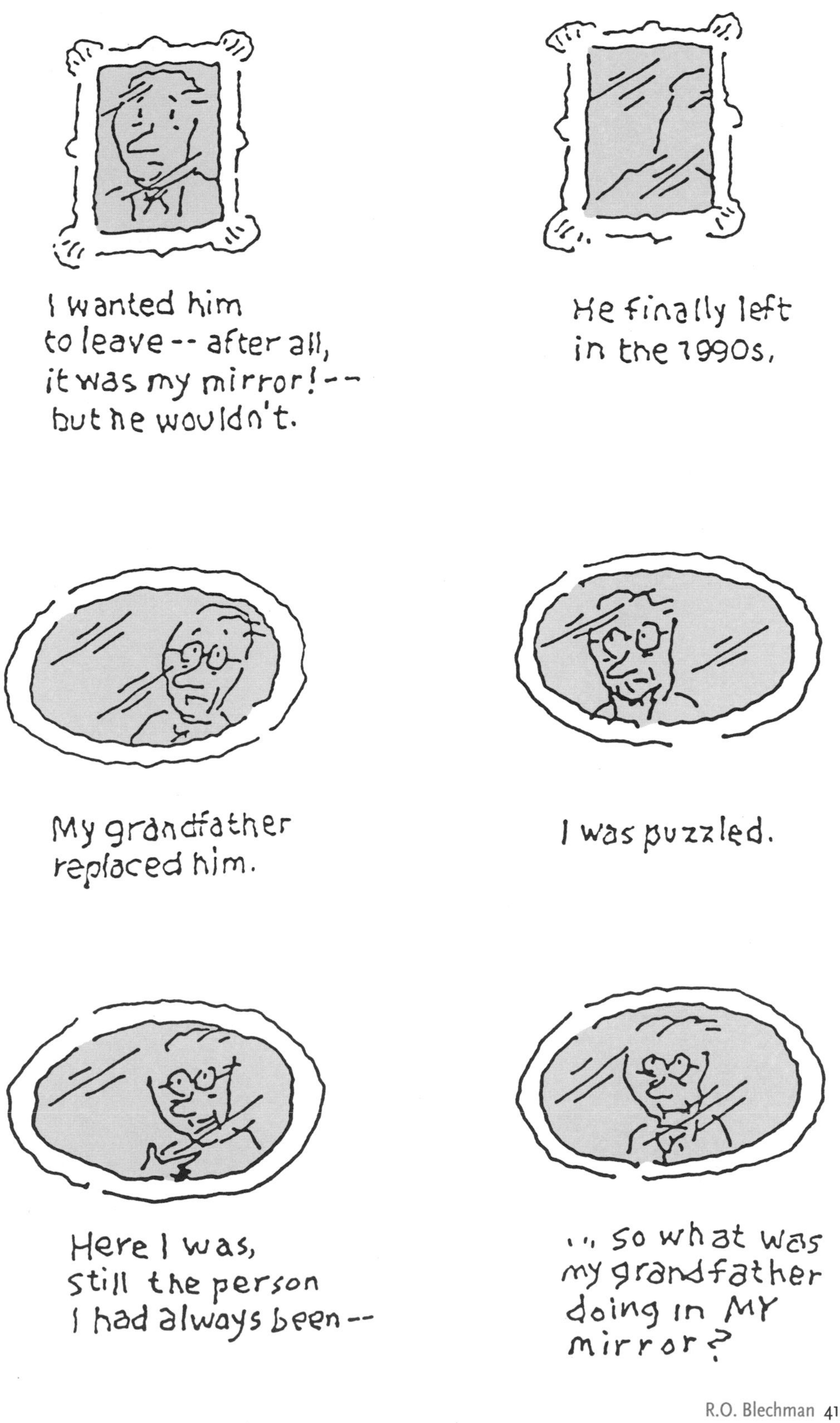
I wanted him to leave -- after all, it was my mirror! -- but he wouldn't.
He finally left in the 1990s.
My grandfather replaced him.
I was puzzled.
Here I was, still the person I had always been --
... so what was my grandfather doing in MY mirror?

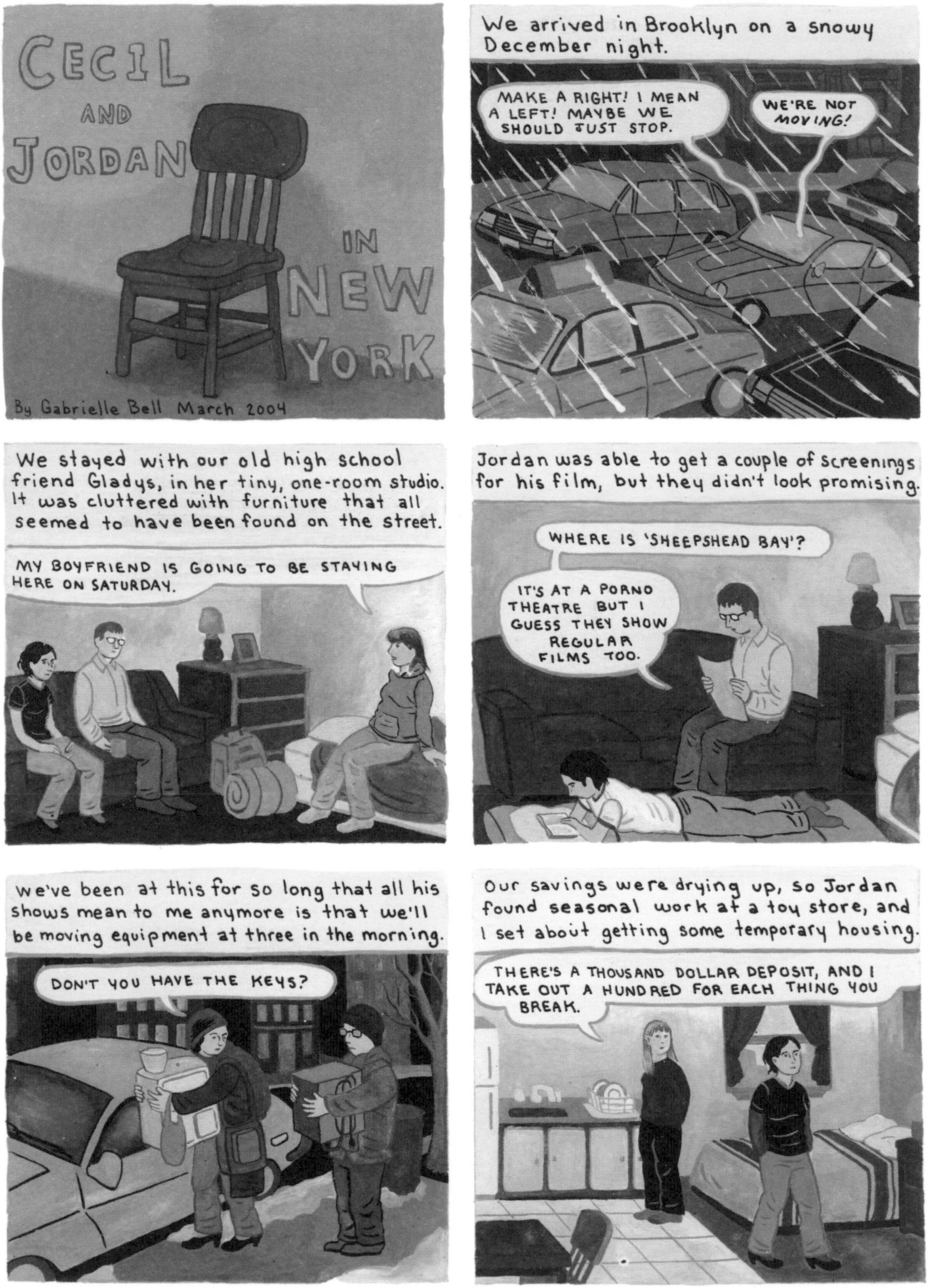
CECIL AND JORDAN IN NEW YORK
By Gabrielle Bell March 2004
We arrived in Brooklyn on a snowy December night.
MAKE A RIGHT! I MEAN A LEFT! MAYBE WE SHOULD JUST STOP.
WE'RE NOT MOVING!
We stayed with our old high school friend Gladys, in her tiny, one-room studio. It was cluttered with furniture that all seemed to have been found on the street.
MY BOYFRIEND IS GOING TO BE STAYING HERE ON SATURDAY.
Jordan was able to get a couple of screenings for his film, but they didn't look promising.
WHERE IS 'SHEEPSHEAD BAY'?
IT'S AT A PORNO THEATRE BUT I GUESS THEY SHOW REGULAR FILMS TOO.
We've been at this for so long that all his shows mean to me anymore is that we'll be moving equipment at three in the morning.
DON'T YOU HAVE THE KEYS?
Our savings were drying up, so Jordan found seasonal work at a toy store, and I set about getting some temporary housing.
THERE'S A THOUSAND DOLLAR DEPOSIT, AND I TAKE OUT A HUNDRED FOR EACH THING YOU BREAK.

 "Cecil and Jordan in New York" was first published in 2005 and later collected by D+Q in *Cecil and Jordan in New York* (2009).

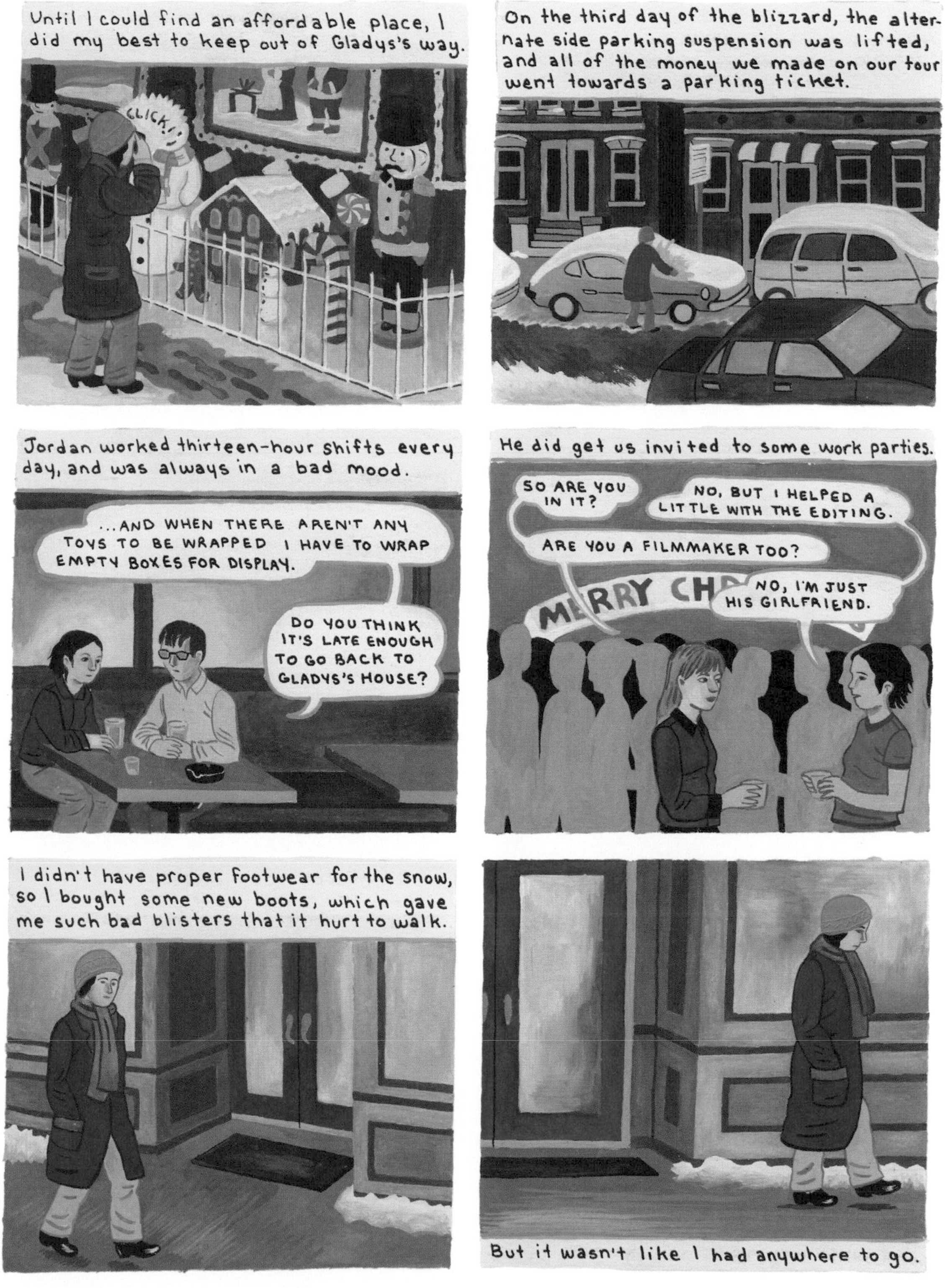
Until I could find an affordable place, I did my best to keep out of Gladys's way.
CLICK!
On the third day of the blizzard, the alternate side parking suspension was lifted, and all of the money we made on our tour went towards a parking ticket.
Jordan worked thirteen-hour shifts every day, and was always in a bad mood.
...AND WHEN THERE AREN'T ANY TOYS TO BE WRAPPED I HAVE TO WRAP EMPTY BOXES FOR DISPLAY.
DO YOU THINK IT'S LATE ENOUGH TO GO BACK TO GLADYS'S HOUSE?
He did get us invited to some work parties.
SO ARE YOU IN IT?
NO, BUT I HELPED A LITTLE WITH THE EDITING.
ARE YOU A FILMMAKER TOO?
MERRY CH
NO, I'M JUST HIS GIRLFRIEND.
I didn't have proper footwear for the snow, so I bought some new boots, which gave me such bad blisters that it hurt to walk.
But it wasn't like I had anywhere to go.

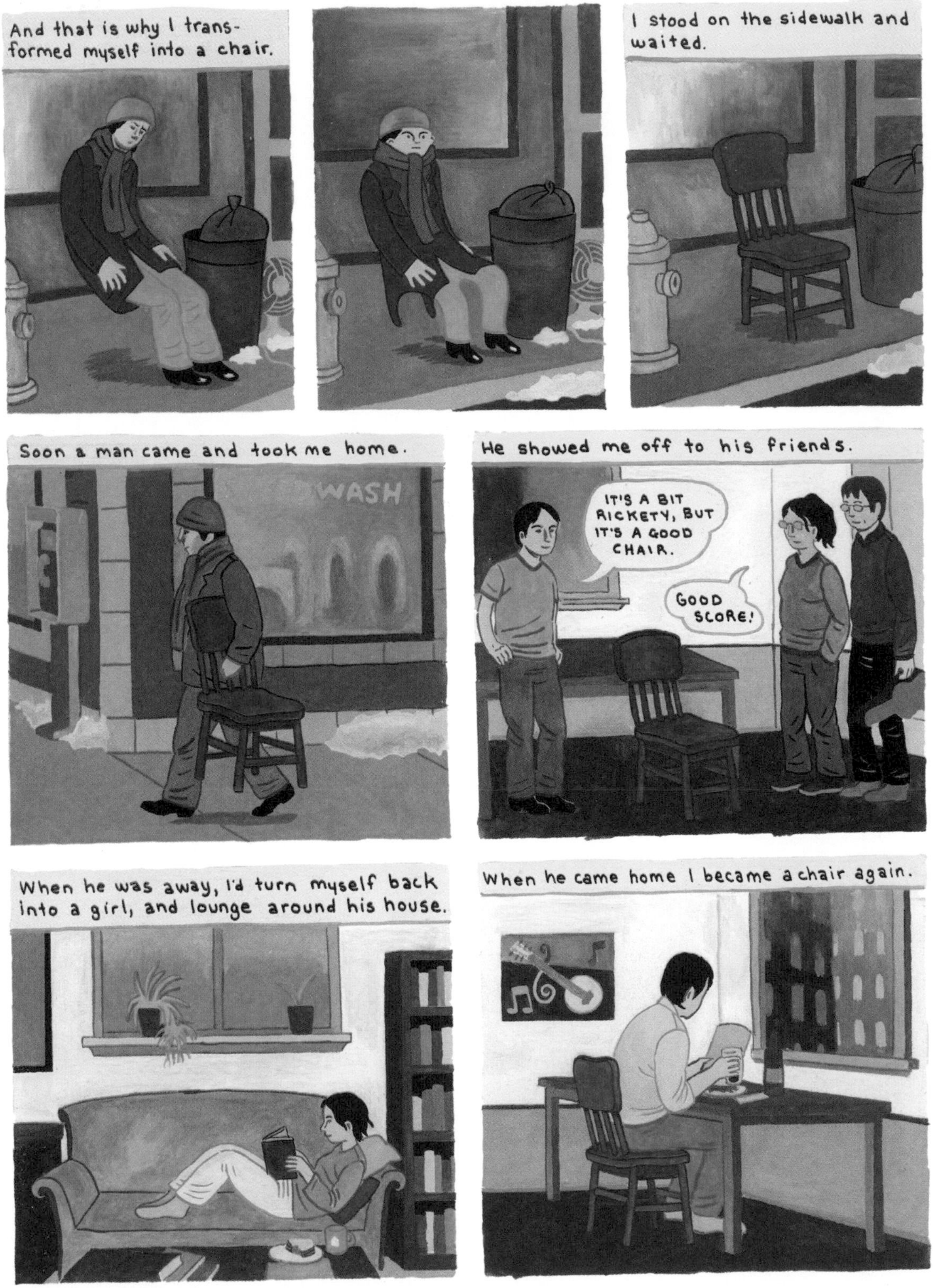
And that is why I transformed myself into a chair.
I stood on the sidewalk and waited.
Soon a man came and took me home.
WASH
He showed me off to his friends.
IT'S A BIT RICKETY, BUT IT'S A GOOD CHAIR.
GOOD SCORE!
When he was away, I'd turn myself back into a girl, and lounge around his house.
When he came home I became a chair again.

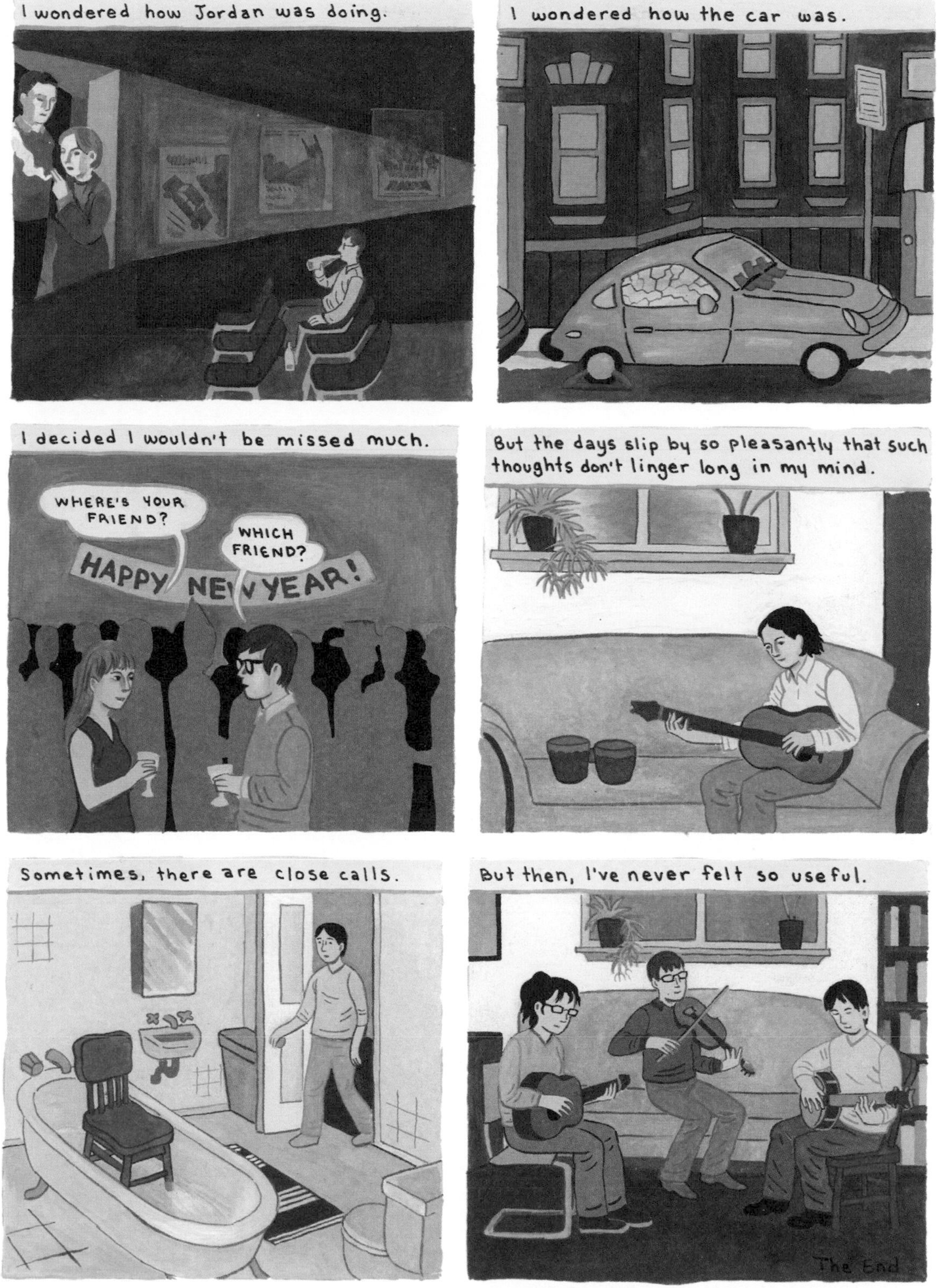
I wondered how Jordan was doing.
I wondered how the car was.
I decided I wouldn't be missed much.
WHERE'S YOUR FRIEND?
WHICH FRIEND?
HAPPY NEW YEAR!
But the days slip by so pleasantly that such thoughts don't linger long in my mind.
Sometimes, there are close calls.
But then, I've never felt so useful.
The End

SO, IS IT TRUE THAT YOU DID ALL THE BAD PARENTING BOOKS WITH YOUR LEFT HAND?
YES. I HAD TENDONITIS IN MY RIGHT ARM... I COULDN'T DRAW ANYMORE.
IS THAT WHY YOU COPY AND PASTED ALL THOSE PANELS?
YEAH... DAMN ARM WAS OUT FOR ALMOST TWO YEARS... EVER SINCE THAT TRIP TO QUEBEC CITY.
WHAT DID YOU DO?... CHOP TOO MUCH WOOD?
NO... I SIGNED FOR MORE THAN FIVE HOURS AT A FESTIVAL.
OH WOW...
YOU SAID IT...
WHAT ABOUT YOUR PAGE FOR DRAWN & QUATERLY'S 25TH ANNIVERSARY? YOU GOT TENDONITIS TOO?
NAH. SLACKERITIS...
LEWIS TRONDHEIM

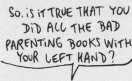

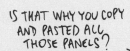

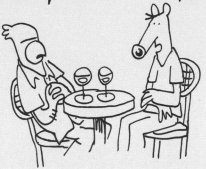

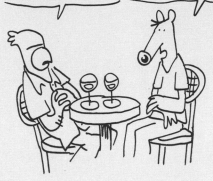

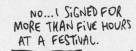

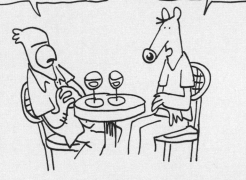

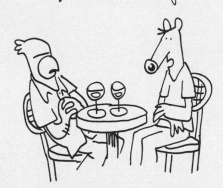

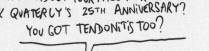

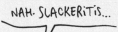

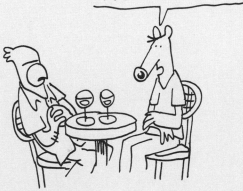

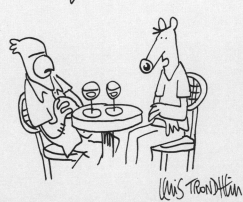

 Comic by Lewis Trondheim with translation by Helge Dascher (2014).

THE SEEING HAND

an appreciation of Guy Delisle by Helge Dascher

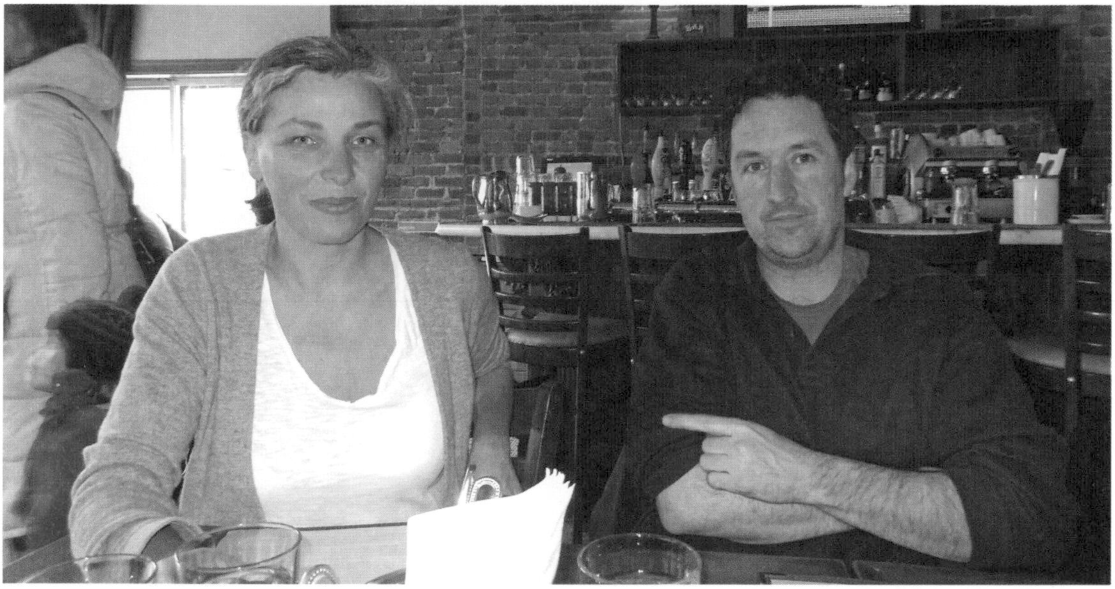

Drawn & Quarterly's history with Guy Delisle goes back to 2004, when Chris acquired the English rights to *Pyongyang*. An autobiographical account of two months spent in the North Korean capital, it came out in English in 2005. It couldn't have been more timely. In February 2005, North Korea announced it had nuclear weapons, then withdrew from security talks. In May, on the eve of a Non-Proliferation Treaty meeting, it fired a short-range missile into the Sea of Japan. The hermit nation was suddenly in the news.

I had translated *Pyongyang*, so I knew from my research how little had been written about North Korea and how much Guy's account covered. The book filled a real gap. What's more, readers who turned to it for information also came away with exposure to a masterful graphic novel. It quickly became not only a reference for understanding a little-known country, but also one of a handful of crossover books that put independent comics on the literature shelves of bookstores and brought a whole new readership to the medium.

Pyongyang was Guy's second travelogue. D+Q followed up in 2006 with an English edition of the first, *Shenzhen*, and in 2008 with *Burma Chronicles*, another report from a hardship destination (this time in the company of his wife, an administrator for Doctors Without Borders). *Shenzhen* started out as a ten-page story based on a sketchbook diary, and those origins established the point of view for all the travelogues that followed. The books never show more than what the observing eye registers. It's the perspective of a travelling Westerner who is a caricature of Guy: more complacent and naive, and a bit slow to grasp the corrosiveness of the constraints he encounters. As he gradually steps outside himself, his assumptions dissolve: things become more complex, but more human, too.

Of the authors I've worked with, Guy has been the most involved in the translation process. Accuracy, timing, and tone are the things we end up talking about. He might be looking for something "stronger" or "more tender"; I've got a note about needing to replace "slurp" with something "smaller and more relaxed." Guy worked in animation for ten years, and rhythm is a constant concern, with his own writing becoming progressively more straightforward over the course of his books—a cleaner match for his lean drawing style.

Helge Dascher & Guy Delisle in Montreal (2012).

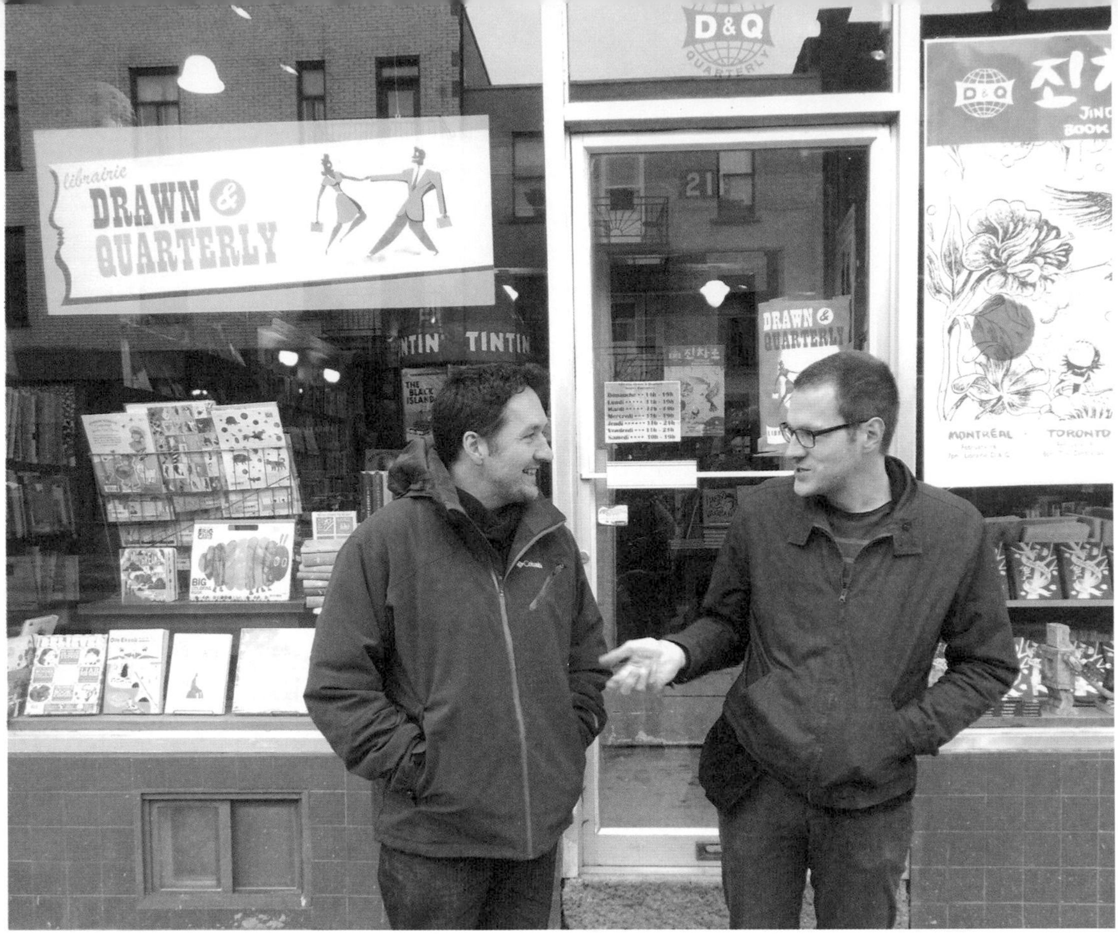
D&Q
QUARTERLY
librairie
DRAWN & QUARTERLY
TINTIN TINTIN
DRAWN & QUARTERLY
MONTRÉAL
TORONTO
Guy Delisle & Pascal Girard in Montreal (2012).

When I first heard about the *Jerusalem* project, I was fascinated. Up to that point, Guy had always leveraged a kind of exclusiveness: privileged access to areas that are poorly known. *Jerusalem* would be a whole other challenge—an addition to a vast body of writing about a highly contentious region. That challenge may have created the book: Guy was feeling pigeonholed as a "travel writer," but I think the daunting context convinced him to send his alter ego into the field one more time.

Just like the sketching hand documents more than it understands, Guy's panels often give more information than the storyline engages. In *Jerusalem,* a garbage truck could be a Palestinian decoy equipped to fire missiles, but Guy doesn't say. His aim isn't to be an investigative journalist. Every detail of daily experience carries a trace of the larger issues that mark life in Jerusalem, and the accretion of those details makes the book the powerful reading experience it is. Translated into thirteen languages, it earned Guy a Fauve d'Or, the award for best comic at Angoulême.

Guy's career has spanned massive changes in the fields he has worked in. It has seen the outsourcing of animation, with the closure of many established studios. And it has also witnessed—and been instrumental in—an explosion of interest in graphic novels. Today Guy lives in the south of France. He no longer does animation, working only on graphic novels now. D+Q will soon be releasing his third "bad dad" book—a series of how-to books on ineffectual parenting that grew out of a few anecdotes in *Burma Chronicles*. Currently, Guy is working on a book that has its roots in an evocative three-panel page in *Shenzhen* that starts with the dog Laïka drifting through space and ends with a man caught in the high beams of an oncoming car. The page ponders the question of freedom through the stories of those held captive. What's "the best way out," it wonders. He's a hundred pages in, with at least two hundred pages to go.

Helge Dascher has translated for Drawn & Quarterly for twenty years. She has translated the works of Guy Delisle, Dupuy & Berbérian, Pascal Girard, Michel Rabagliati, Aisha Franz, Marguerite Abouet, Diane Obomsawin, and many more.

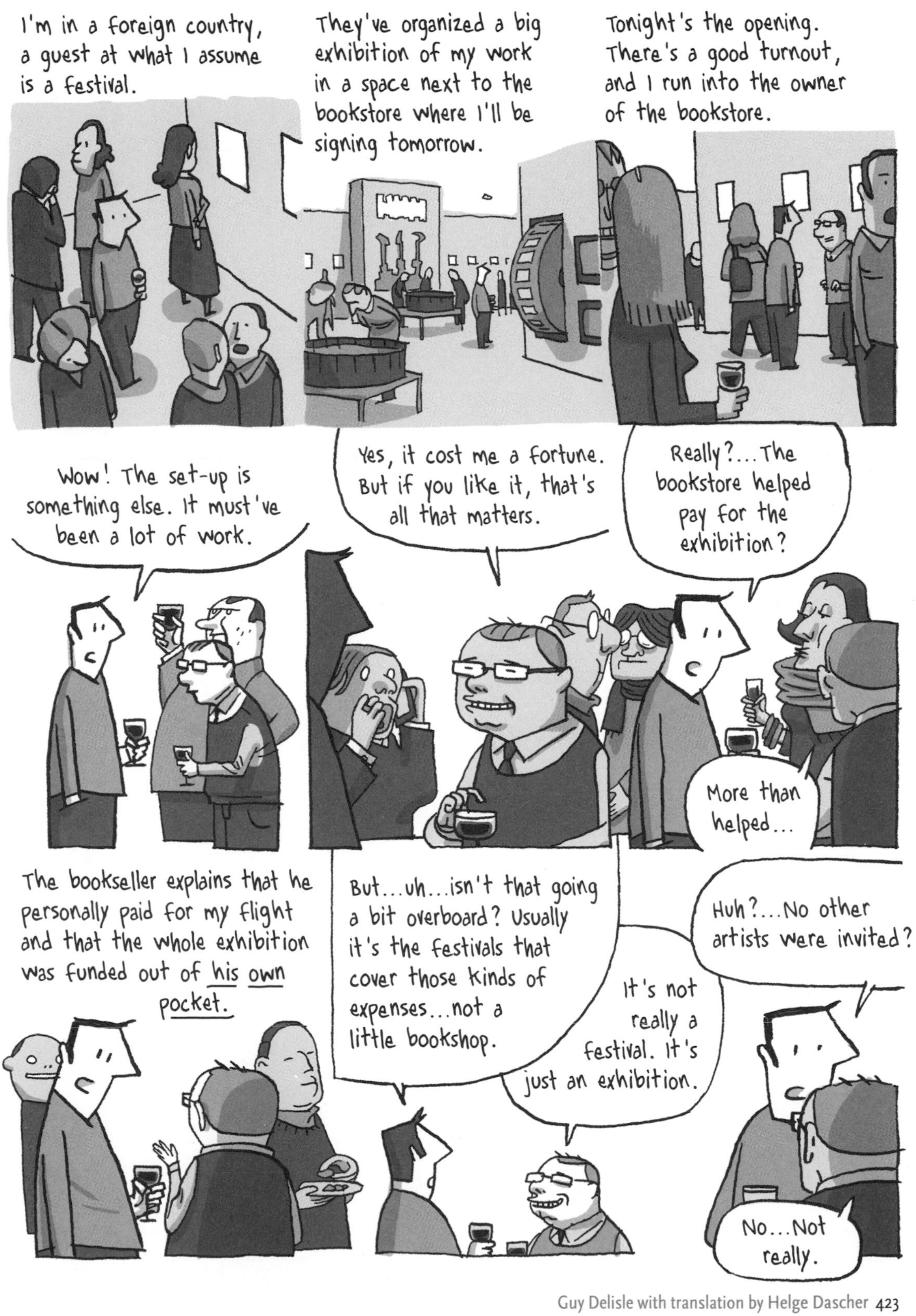
I'm in a foreign country, a guest at what I assume is a festival.
They've organized a big exhibition of my work in a space next to the bookstore where I'll be signing tomorrow.
Tonight's the opening. There's a good turnout, and I run into the owner of the bookstore.
Wow! The set-up is something else. It must've been a lot of work.
Yes, it cost me a fortune. But if you like it, that's all that matters.
Really?... The bookstore helped pay for the exhibition?
More than helped...
The bookseller explains that he personally paid for my flight and that the whole exhibition was funded out of his own pocket.
But...uh...isn't that going a bit overboard? Usually it's the festivals that cover those kinds of expenses...not a little bookshop.
It's not really a festival. It's just an exhibition.
Huh?...No other artists were invited?
No...Not really.

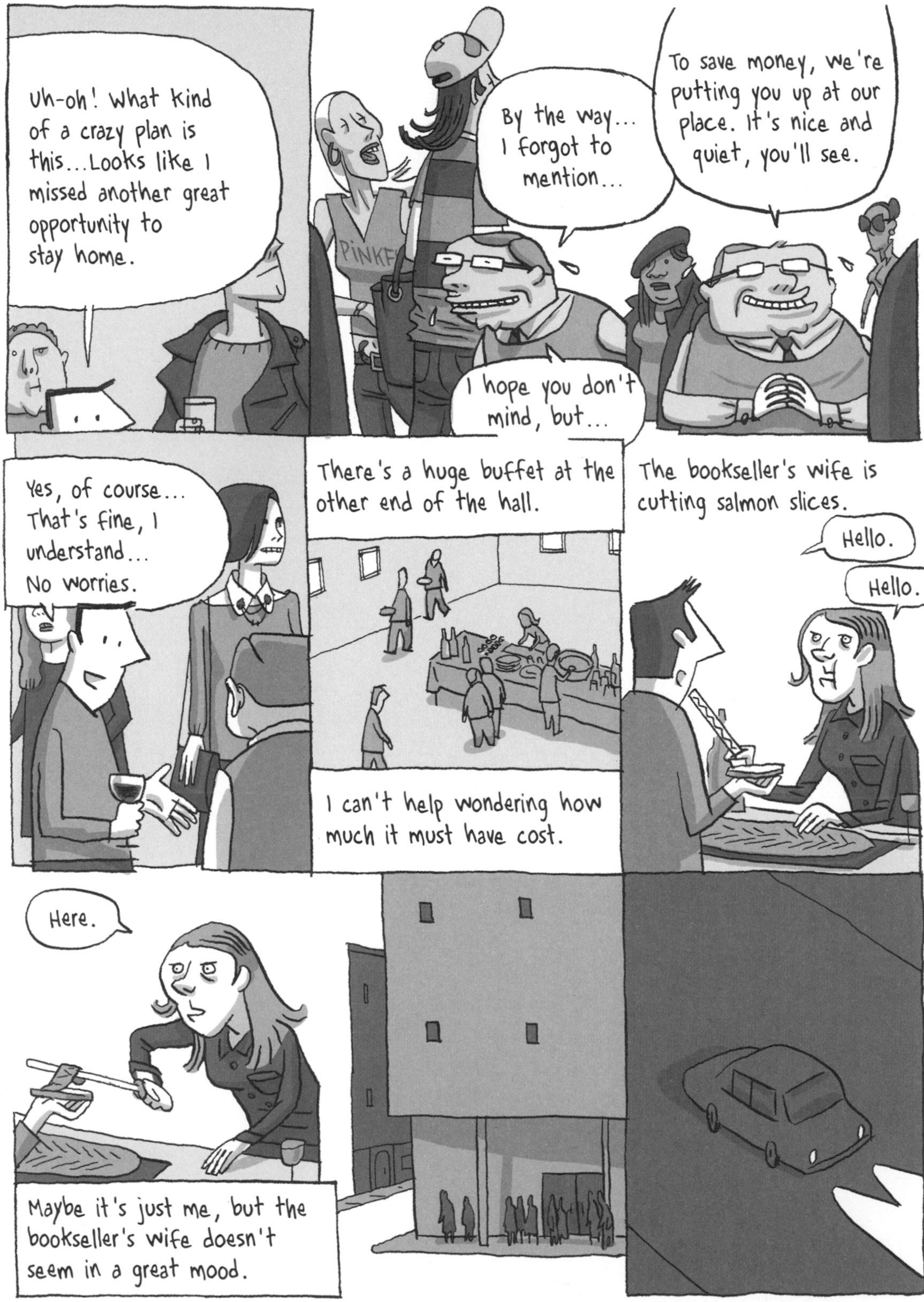
Uh-oh! What kind of a crazy plan is this...Looks like I missed another great opportunity to stay home.
By the way... I forgot to mention...
I hope you don't mind, but...
To save money, we're putting you up at our place. It's nice and quiet, you'll see.
Yes, of course... That's fine, I understand... No worries.
There's a huge buffet at the other end of the hall.
I can't help wondering how much it must have cost.
The bookseller's wife is cutting salmon slices.
Hello.
Hello.
Here.
Maybe it's just me, but the bookseller's wife doesn't seem in a great mood.

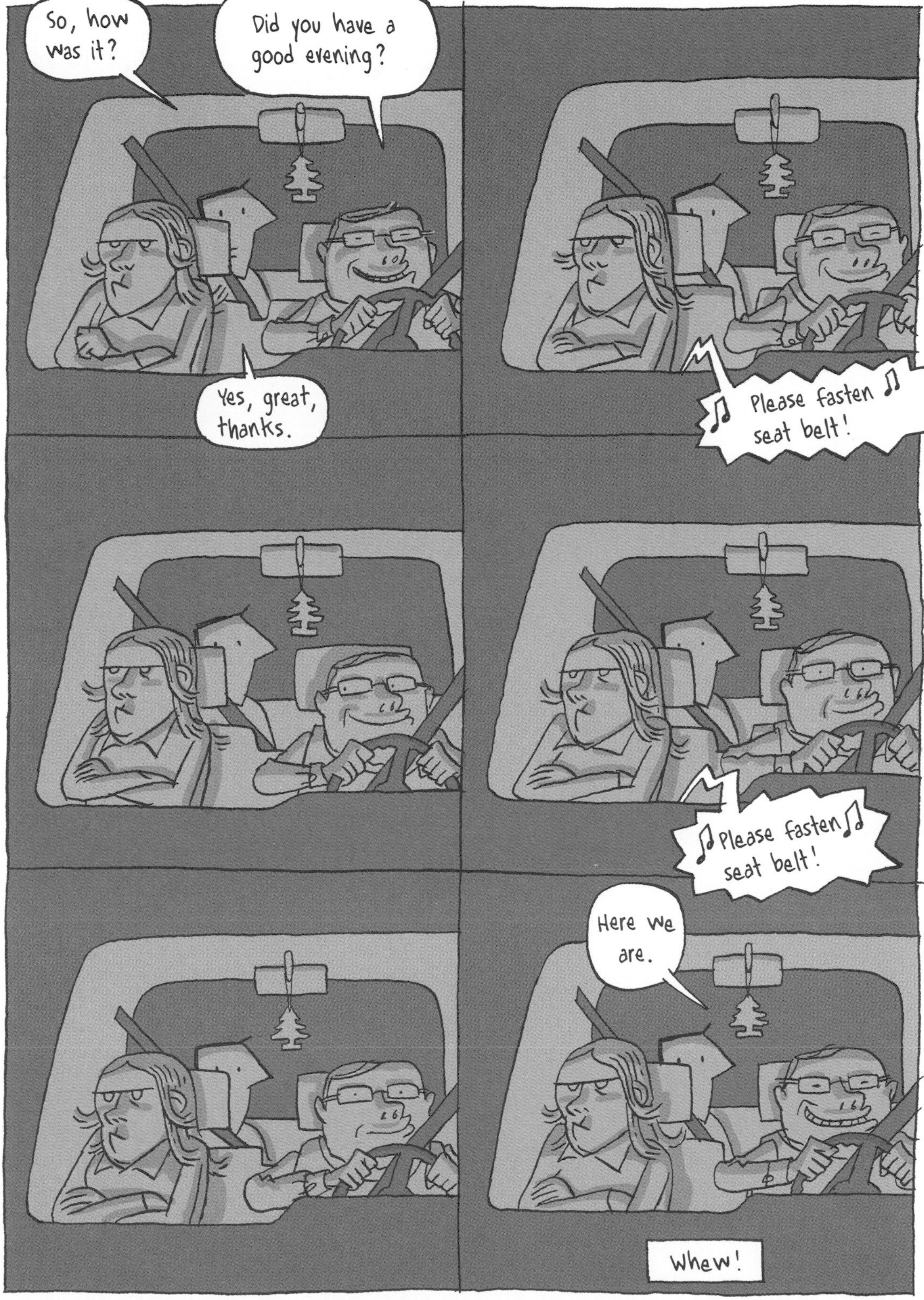
So, how was it?
Did you have a good evening?
Yes, great, thanks.
♫ Please fasten seat belt! ♫
♫ Please fasten ♫ seat belt!
Here we are.
Whew!

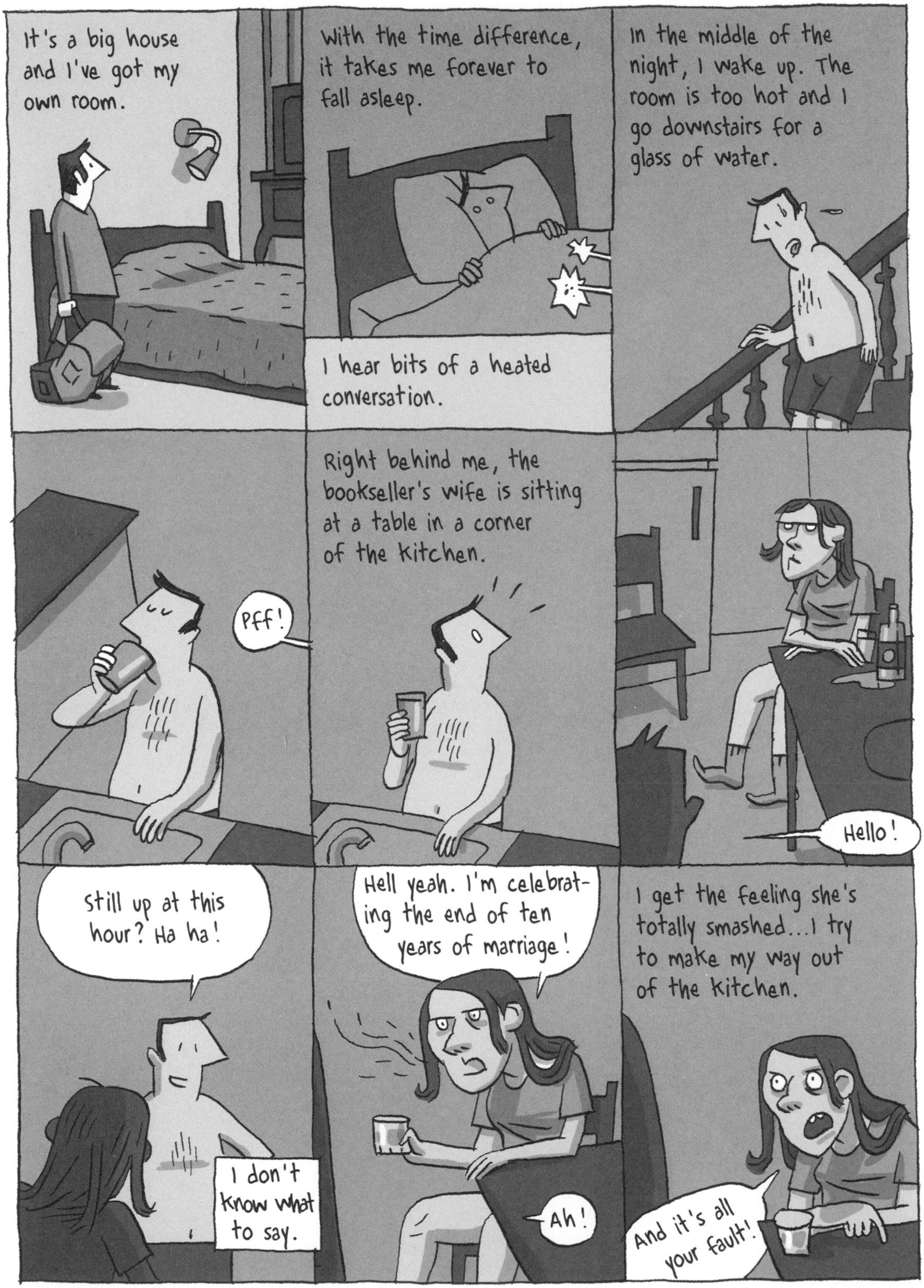
It's a big house and I've got my own room.
With the time difference, it takes me forever to fall asleep.
I hear bits of a heated conversation.
In the middle of the night, I wake up. The room is too hot and I go downstairs for a glass of water.
Pff!
Right behind me, the bookseller's wife is sitting at a table in a corner of the kitchen.
Hello!
Still up at this hour? Ha ha!
I don't know what to say.
Hell yeah. I'm celebrating the end of ten years of marriage!
Ah!
I get the feeling she's totally smashed... I try to make my way out of the kitchen.
And it's all your fault!

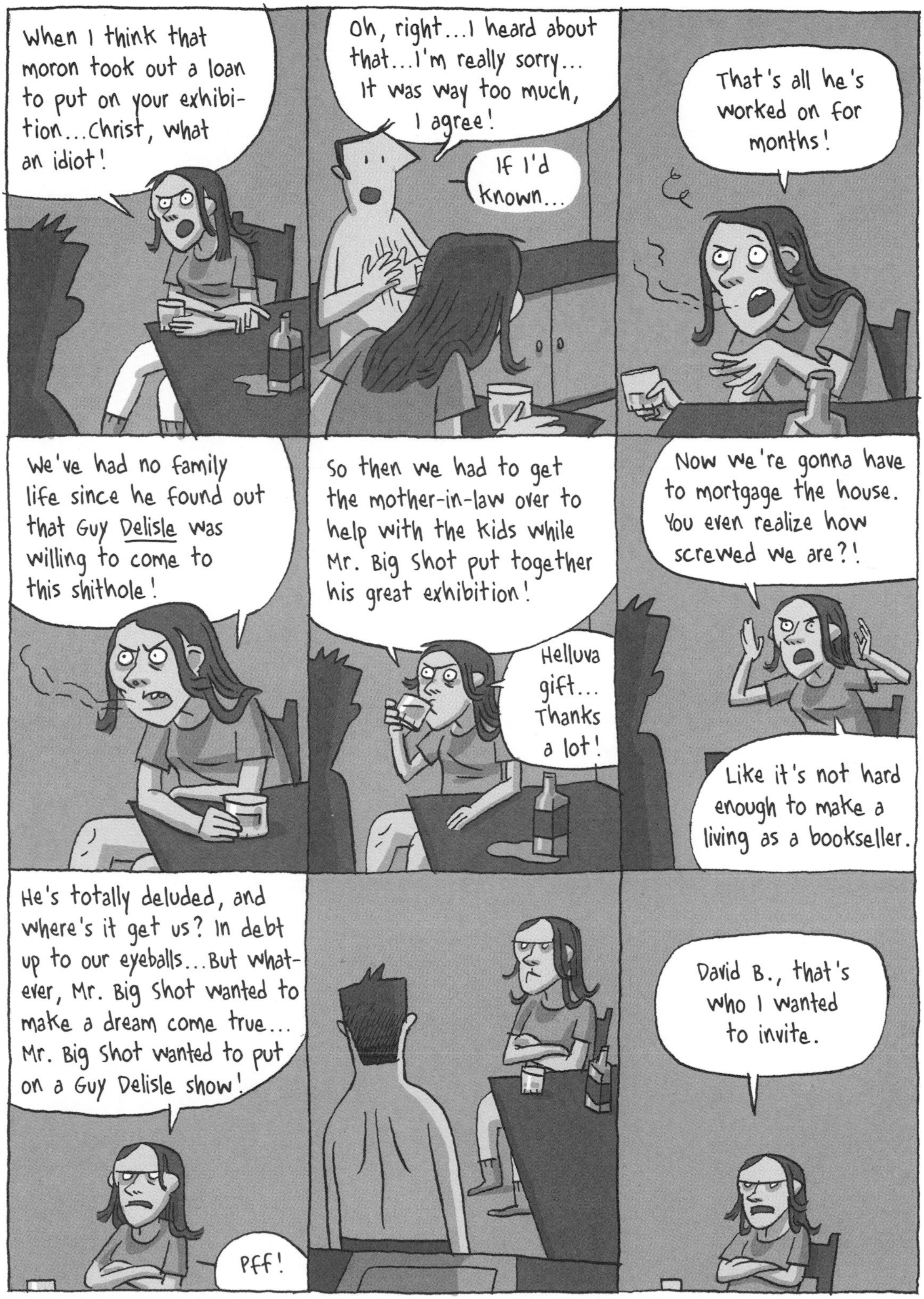
When I think that moron took out a loan to put on your exhibition...Christ, what an idiot!
Oh, right...I heard about that...I'm really sorry... It was way too much, I agree!
If I'd known...
That's all he's worked on for months!
We've had no family life since he found out that Guy Delisle was willing to come to this shithole!
So then we had to get the mother-in-law over to help with the kids while Mr. Big Shot put together his great exhibition!
Helluva gift... Thanks a lot!
Now we're gonna have to mortgage the house. You even realize how screwed we are?!
Like it's not hard enough to make a living as a bookseller.
He's totally deluded, and where's it get us? In debt up to our eyeballs...But whatever, Mr. Big Shot wanted to make a dream come true... Mr. Big Shot wanted to put on a Guy Delisle show!
Pff!
David B., that's who I wanted to invite.

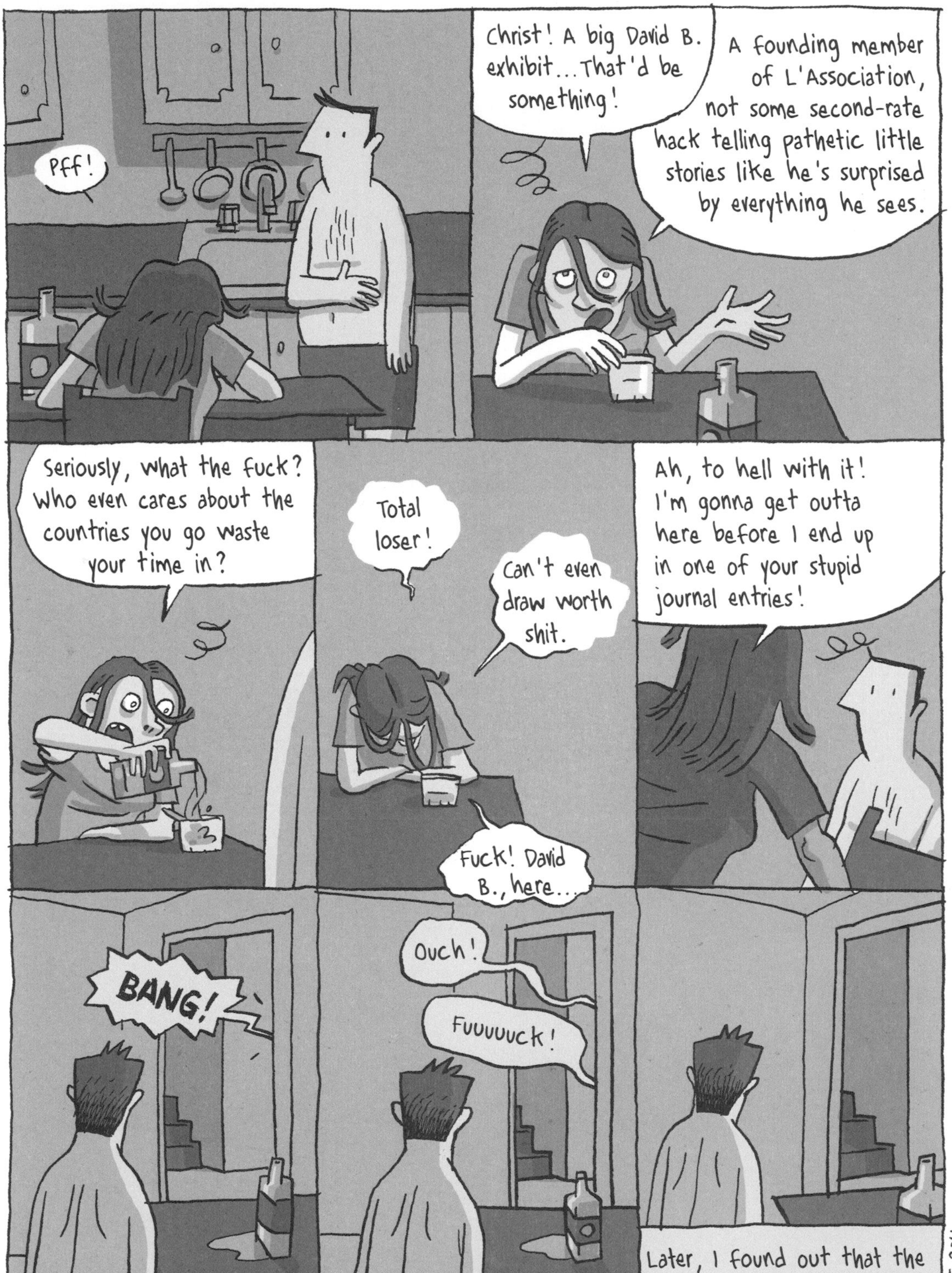
Pff!
Christ! A big David B. exhibit... That'd be something!
A founding member of L'Association, not some second-rate hack telling pathetic little stories like he's surprised by everything he sees.
Seriously, what the fuck? Who even cares about the countries you go waste your time in?
Total loser!
Can't even draw worth shit.
Fuck! David B., here...
Ah, to hell with it! I'm gonna get outta here before I end up in one of your stupid journal entries!
BANG!
Ouch!
Fuuuuuck!
Later, I found out that the bookshop had changed hands.
DELISLE 2011

Chantal

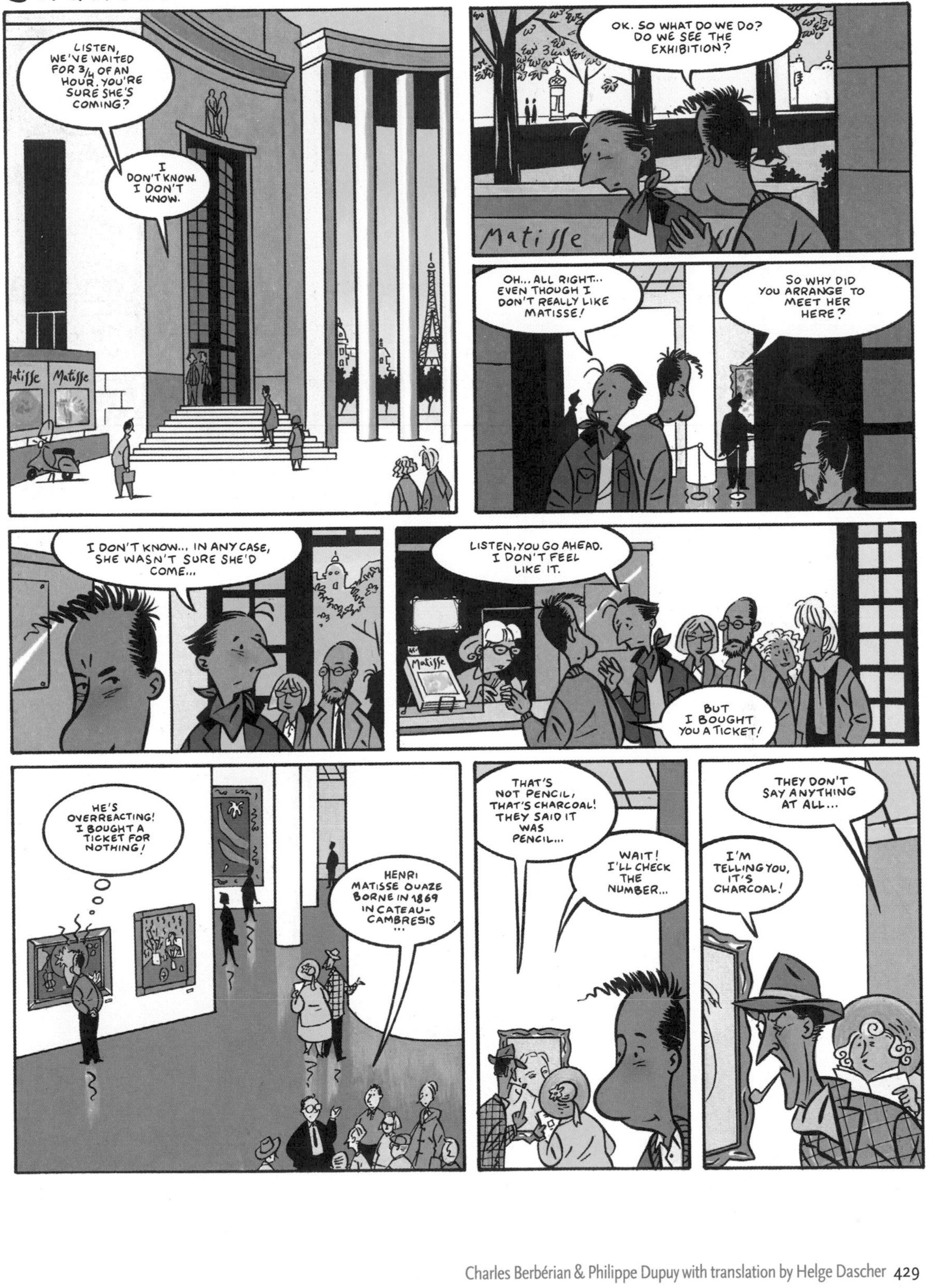
LISTEN, WE'VE WAITED FOR 3/4 OF AN HOUR. YOU'RE SURE SHE'S COMING?
I DON'T KNOW. I DON'T KNOW.
Matisse
Matisse
OK. SO WHAT DO WE DO? DO WE SEE THE EXHIBITION?
Matisse
OH... ALL RIGHT... EVEN THOUGH I DON'T REALLY LIKE MATISSE!
SO WHY DID YOU ARRANGE TO MEET HER HERE?
I DON'T KNOW... IN ANY CASE, SHE WASN'T SURE SHE'D COME...
LISTEN, YOU GO AHEAD. I DON'T FEEL LIKE IT.
Matisse
BUT I BOUGHT YOU A TICKET!
HE'S OVERREACTING! I BOUGHT A TICKET FOR NOTHING!
HENRI MATISSE OUAZE BORNE IN 1869 IN CATEAU-CAMBRESIS ...
THAT'S NOT PENCIL, THAT'S CHARCOAL! THEY SAID IT WAS PENCIL...
WAIT! I'LL CHECK THE NUMBER...
THEY DON'T SAY ANYTHING AT ALL...
I'M TELLING YOU, IT'S CHARCOAL!

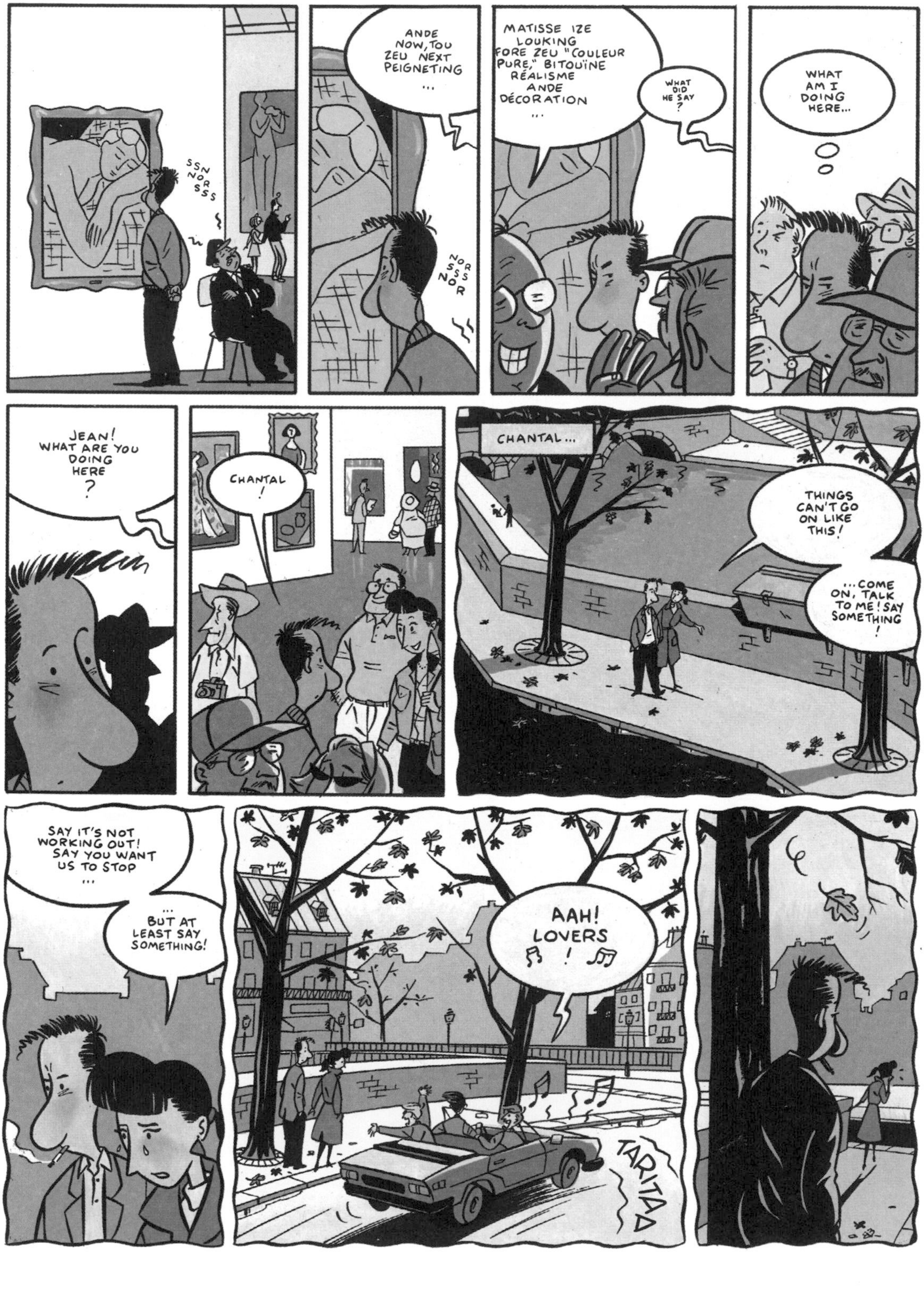
SSN NOR SSS
ANDE NOW, TOU ZEU NEXT PEIGNETING ...
NOR SSS NOR
MATISSE IZE LOUKING FORE ZEU "COULEUR PURE," BITOUÏNE RÉALISME ANDE DÉCORATION ...
WHAT DID HE SAY ?
WHAT AM I DOING HERE...
JEAN! WHAT ARE YOU DOING HERE ?
CHANTAL !
CHANTAL...
THINGS CAN'T GO ON LIKE THIS!
...COME ON, TALK TO ME! SAY SOMETHING !
SAY IT'S NOT WORKING OUT! SAY YOU WANT US TO STOP ...
... BUT AT LEAST SAY SOMETHING!
AAH! LOVERS !
TARITAA

 "Chantal" first appeared in vol. 2, no. 4 of *Drawn & Quarterly* (1995) and was later published in *Get A Life* (2006).

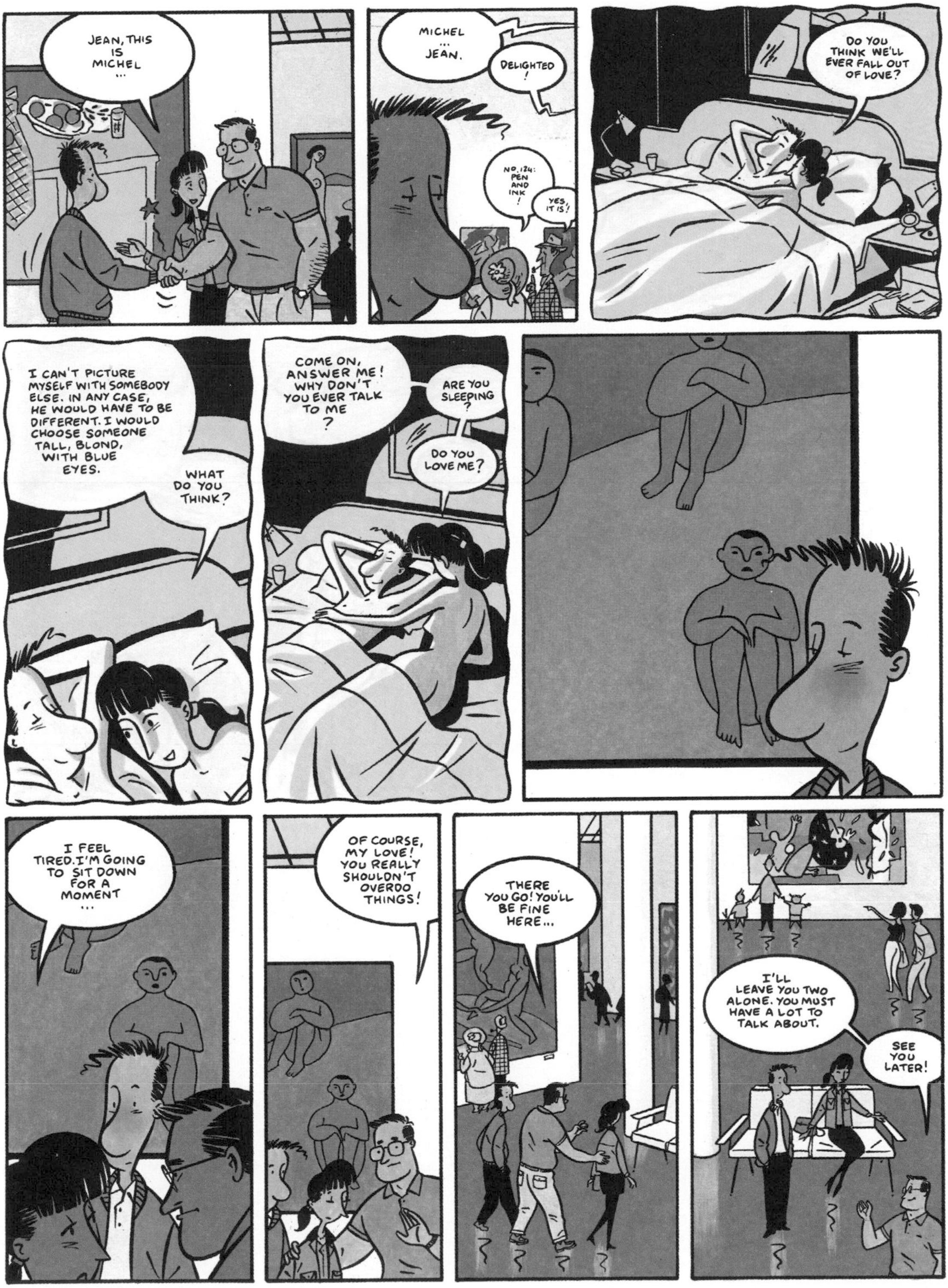
JEAN, THIS IS MICHEL ...
MICHEL ... JEAN.
DELIGHTED!
NO. 124: PEN AND INK!
YES, IT IS!
DO YOU THINK WE'LL EVER FALL OUT OF LOVE?
I CAN'T PICTURE MYSELF WITH SOMEBODY ELSE. IN ANY CASE, HE WOULD HAVE TO BE DIFFERENT. I WOULD CHOOSE SOMEONE TALL, BLOND, WITH BLUE EYES.
WHAT DO YOU THINK?
COME ON, ANSWER ME! WHY DON'T YOU EVER TALK TO ME?
ARE YOU SLEEPING?
DO YOU LOVE ME?
I FEEL TIRED. I'M GOING TO SIT DOWN FOR A MOMENT ...
OF COURSE, MY LOVE! YOU REALLY SHOULDN'T OVERDO THINGS!
THERE YOU GO! YOU'LL BE FINE HERE...
I'LL LEAVE YOU TWO ALONE. YOU MUST HAVE A LOT TO TALK ABOUT.
SEE YOU LATER!

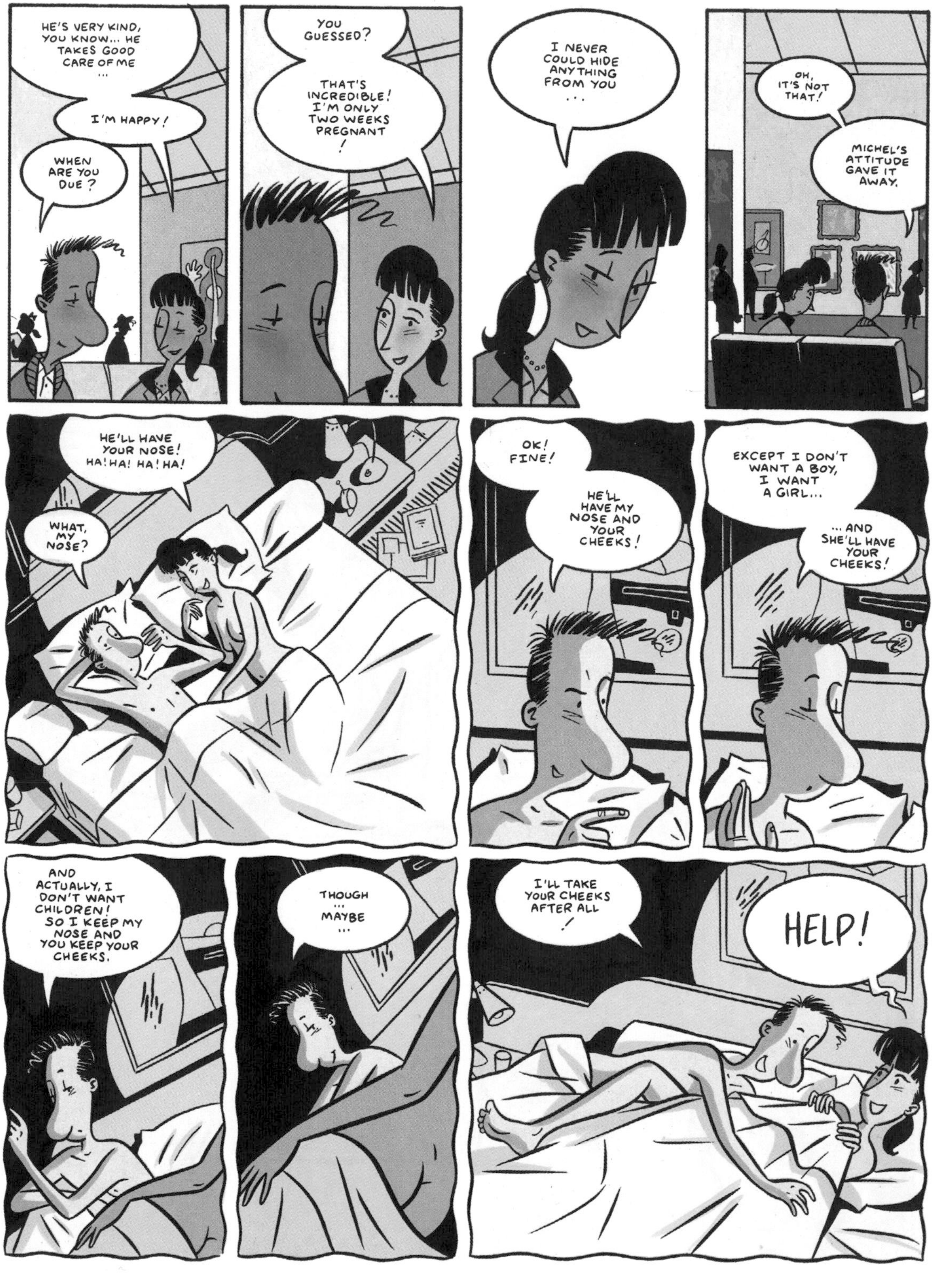
HE'S VERY KIND, YOU KNOW... HE TAKES GOOD CARE OF ME ...
I'M HAPPY!
WHEN ARE YOU DUE?
YOU GUESSED?
THAT'S INCREDIBLE! I'M ONLY TWO WEEKS PREGNANT!
I NEVER COULD HIDE ANYTHING FROM YOU ...
OH, IT'S NOT THAT!
MICHEL'S ATTITUDE GAVE IT AWAY.
HE'LL HAVE YOUR NOSE! HA! HA! HA! HA!
WHAT, MY NOSE?
OK! FINE!
HE'LL HAVE MY NOSE AND YOUR CHEEKS!
EXCEPT I DON'T WANT A BOY, I WANT A GIRL...
... AND SHE'LL HAVE YOUR CHEEKS!
AND ACTUALLY, I DON'T WANT CHILDREN! SO I KEEP MY NOSE AND YOU KEEP YOUR CHEEKS.
THOUGH ... MAYBE ...
I'LL TAKE YOUR CHEEKS AFTER ALL!
HELP!

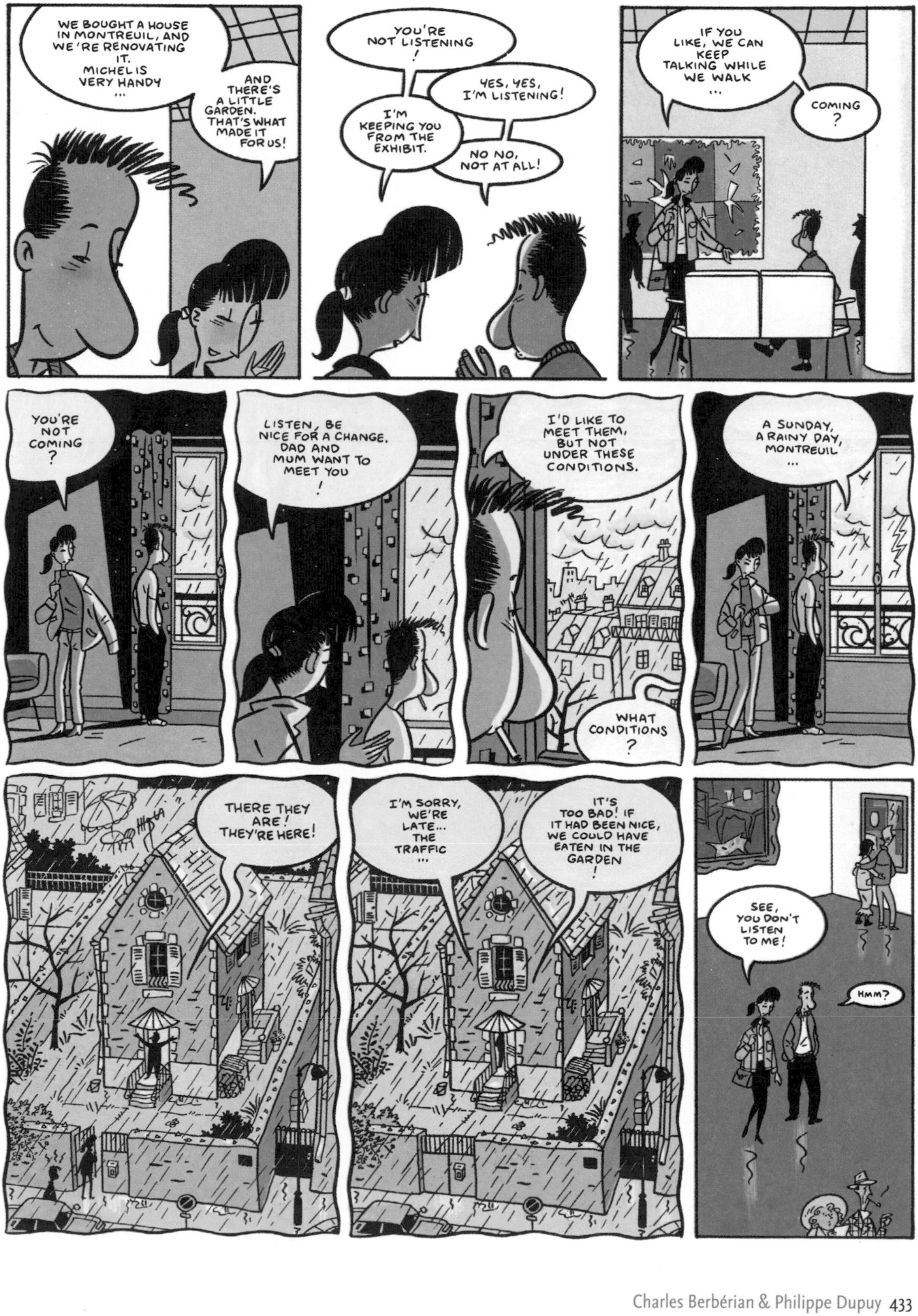
WE BOUGHT A HOUSE IN MONTREUIL, AND WE'RE RENOVATING IT. MICHEL IS VERY HANDY ...
AND THERE'S A LITTLE GARDEN. THAT'S WHAT MADE IT FOR US!
YOU'RE NOT LISTENING !
I'M KEEPING YOU FROM THE EXHIBIT.
YES, YES, I'M LISTENING!
NO NO, NOT AT ALL!
IF YOU LIKE, WE CAN KEEP TALKING WHILE WE WALK ...
COMING ?
YOU'RE NOT COMING ?
LISTEN, BE NICE FOR A CHANGE. DAD AND MUM WANT TO MEET YOU !
I'D LIKE TO MEET THEM, BUT NOT UNDER THESE CONDITIONS.
WHAT CONDITIONS ?
A SUNDAY, A RAINY DAY, MONTREUIL ...
THERE THEY ARE! THEY'RE HERE!
I'M SORRY, WE'RE LATE... THE TRAFFIC ...
IT'S TOO BAD! IF IT HAD BEEN NICE, WE COULD HAVE EATEN IN THE GARDEN !
SEE, YOU DON'T LISTEN TO ME!
HMM?

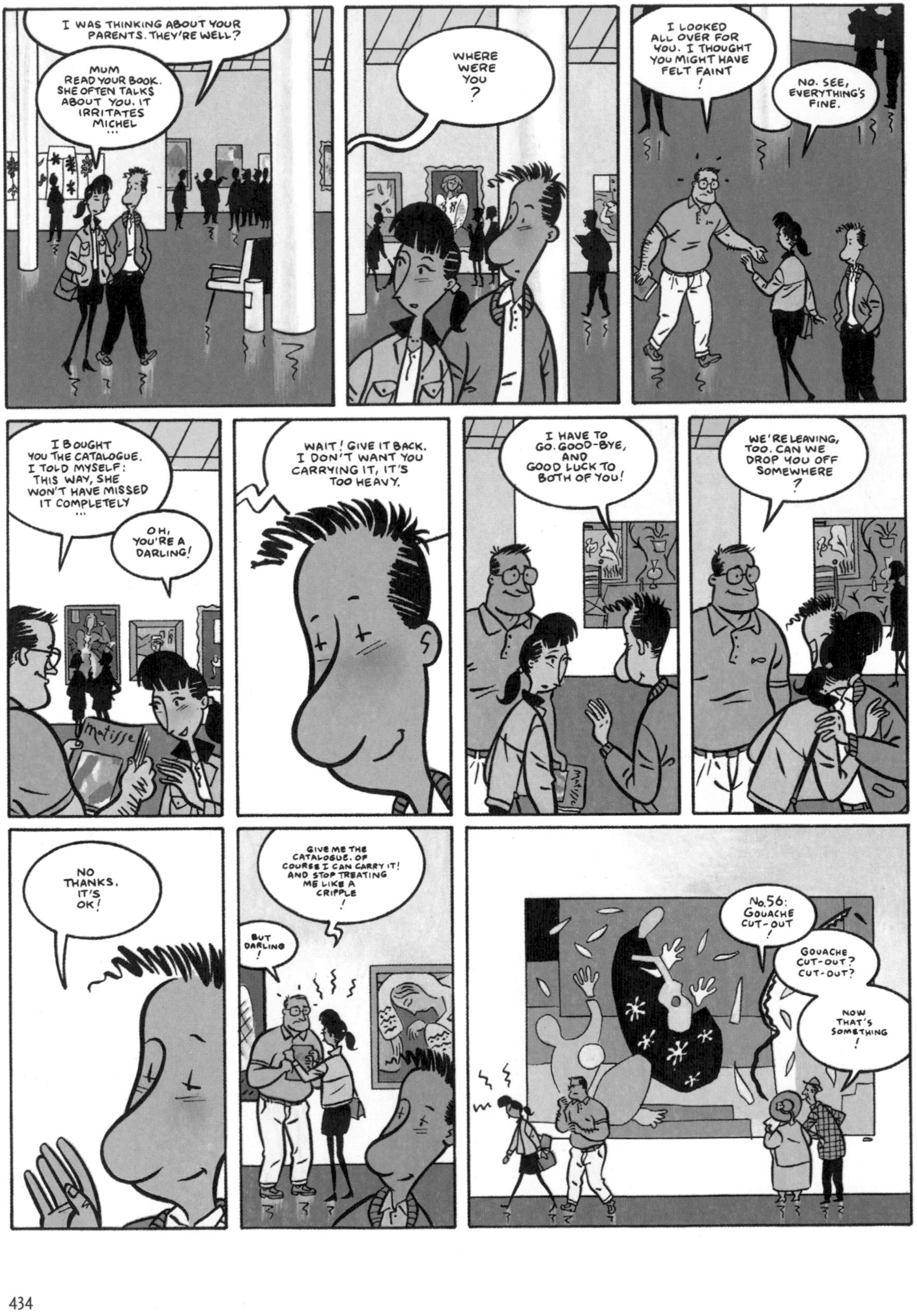
I WAS THINKING ABOUT YOUR PARENTS. THEY'RE WELL?
MUM READ YOUR BOOK. SHE OFTEN TALKS ABOUT YOU. IT IRRITATES MICHEL ...
WHERE WERE YOU ?
I LOOKED ALL OVER FOR YOU. I THOUGHT YOU MIGHT HAVE FELT FAINT !
NO. SEE, EVERYTHING'S FINE.
I BOUGHT YOU THE CATALOGUE. I TOLD MYSELF: THIS WAY, SHE WON'T HAVE MISSED IT COMPLETELY ...
OH, YOU'RE A DARLING!
matisse
WAIT! GIVE IT BACK. I DON'T WANT YOU CARRYING IT, IT'S TOO HEAVY.
I HAVE TO GO. GOOD-BYE, AND GOOD LUCK TO BOTH OF YOU!
WE'RE LEAVING, TOO. CAN WE DROP YOU OFF SOMEWHERE ?
NO THANKS. IT'S OK!
GIVE ME THE CATALOGUE. OF COURSE I CAN CARRY IT! AND STOP TREATING ME LIKE A CRIPPLE !
BUT DARLING !
No.56: GOUACHE CUT-OUT !
GOUACHE CUT-OUT? CUT-OUT?
NOW THAT'S SOMETHING !

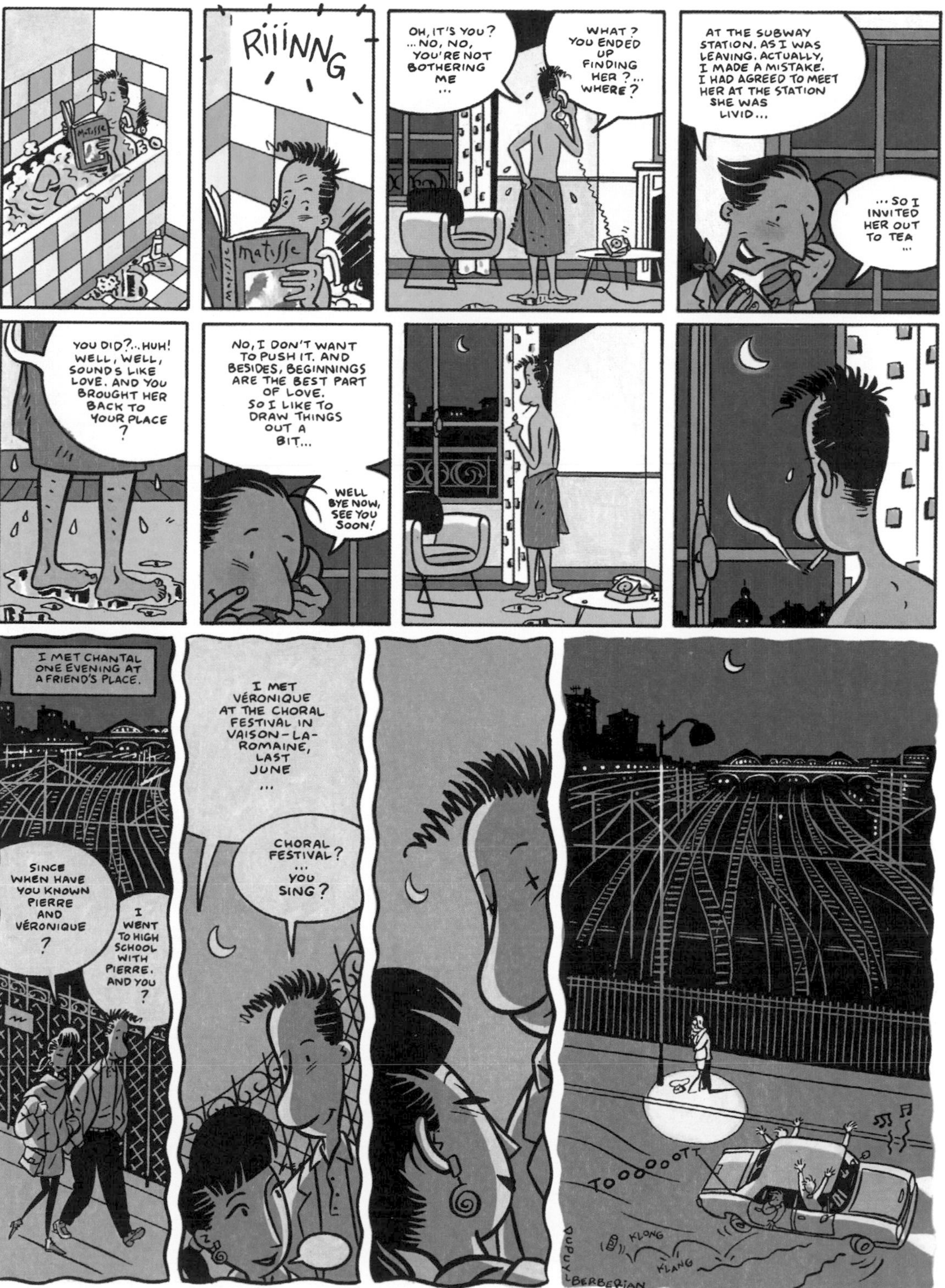
RIIINNG
OH, IT'S YOU? ...NO, NO, YOU'RE NOT BOTHERING ME ...
WHAT? YOU ENDED UP FINDING HER?... WHERE?
AT THE SUBWAY STATION. AS I WAS LEAVING. ACTUALLY, I MADE A MISTAKE. I HAD AGREED TO MEET HER AT THE STATION SHE WAS LIVID...
...SO I INVITED HER OUT TO TEA ...
YOU DID?...HUH! WELL, WELL, SOUNDS LIKE LOVE. AND YOU BROUGHT HER BACK TO YOUR PLACE ?
NO, I DON'T WANT TO PUSH IT. AND BESIDES, BEGINNINGS ARE THE BEST PART OF LOVE. SO I LIKE TO DRAW THINGS OUT A BIT...
WELL BYE NOW, SEE YOU SOON!
I MET CHANTAL ONE EVENING AT A FRIEND'S PLACE.
SINCE WHEN HAVE YOU KNOWN PIERRE AND VÉRONIQUE ?
I WENT TO HIGH SCHOOL WITH PIERRE. AND YOU ?
I MET VÉRONIQUE AT THE CHORAL FESTIVAL IN VAISON-LA-ROMAINE, LAST JUNE ...
CHORAL FESTIVAL? ... YOU SING?
TOOOOOOTT
KLONG
KLANG
DUPUY BERBERIAN

NEGATIVE SPACE

an appreciation of John Porcellino by Aaron Cometbus

I had a picnic in the park with a well-known sculptor whose new show had just opened. The centrepiece was a stunning tower rising sixty feet in the air.

She herself was rather stunning, sitting on the grass under a cloudless sky, so what she said next came as a surprise:

"I'm sure everyone who walks into that room says, 'Wow, a sixty-foot tower. The girl who made it must really think she's a piece of shit.'"

The confidence and joy she radiated was apparently for outside consumption only. It reminded me of a similar admission by John Porcellino that completely changed the way I saw his work. It was at a fanzine expo in Chicago. An audience member asked, "Were your parents supportive of your creativity, growing up?"

"As a matter of fact, no," he said. "They've always been ashamed of what I do—of my comics, which are my life's work. That's been a real struggle, one I'll probably never get over: needing their approval, and knowing that it's never going to come."

The whole audience was KO'd, stunned from the blow and the honesty with which it was delivered. We were reeling in our seats, but the next panellist didn't take the cue. "My parents were *totally* supportive," she beamed. "Even now, they read every single page and send cute little notes that say..."

I tuned her out. After that knockout punch, anyone with a happy childhood and loving family seemed moronic, boring, not fully formed. Who cared what they had to say, much less write or draw? Art was a response to unhappiness and death—at least the art that I liked best. It made me want to joyfully blow up a few buildings or drive off a cliff.

Porcellino's own art hadn't always slain me, though. I dug it, but it didn't always sink in that deep. Coming home from the expo, I returned to my copies of *King Cat* to see if there was something I had missed. Indeed, the sentimental stories and stripped-down line work seemed quite different the second time around. The serenity and simplicity now felt unnatural and forced. That made me appreciate them all the more.

It was like a coping mechanism or a Buddhist exercise: simply block out everything you hate, everything in the world that makes you sick. Now focus on what remains.

For Porcellino, a couple of cats and a walk in the woods were all that was left. The spareness of his line work was a result of the same approach. It was the negative space: the only thing remaining when all the darkness and shadows had been removed.

The shadows of what, though? That was harder to figure out. *King Cat* celebrated the everyday and mundane. Yet there was a rippling tension just below the surface. The chirping birds and rising sun weren't there to prove that cartoonists' lives are incredibly dull. They felt like roadblocks, or perhaps a list: What Kept Me From Killing Myself Today, So Far.

Every beautiful sunrise seemed to signify a storm gathering just off the page. The optimism and Buddhism could be a little glaring at times, but a deeper sense of Catholic guilt provided the shade. Big black clouds of anger and fear kept *King Cat* cool. Even the optimism was a kind of rage—against expectations, wasted potential, and broken promises. Adulthood, in other words.

Many pages were spent pining for the author's lost youth: a combination of innocence, nature, and mystery. Yet it was all as temporary, and probably as illusory, as the suburbia in which it was spent. When the blackberry bushes got paved over, the gig was up, not just for Porcellino, but for millions of North American kids. Condos and subdivisions took their place. It was a rip-off, and not what they were equipped to face. Literally, in his case: he was diagnosed with an autoimmune disease that made urban living all but impossible.

Yet as he grew older and odder, the suburbs became increasingly inhospitable as well. He relocated again and again, trying to find some in between: an idyllic town that wasn't hostile or filled with strip malls. It was as elusive as the American Dream.

The promise of the suburbs was a cynical one, so it's no surprise that cynicism was the result. *King Cat* is Porcellino's attempt to hold on to idealism instead—the idealism of youth, and of the childhood-extending miracle drug that he found next: punk rock. In *King Cat*, the child's wide-eyed wonder and attention to detail is hitched to the fierce self-discipline of Black Flag and their record label. Self-loathing

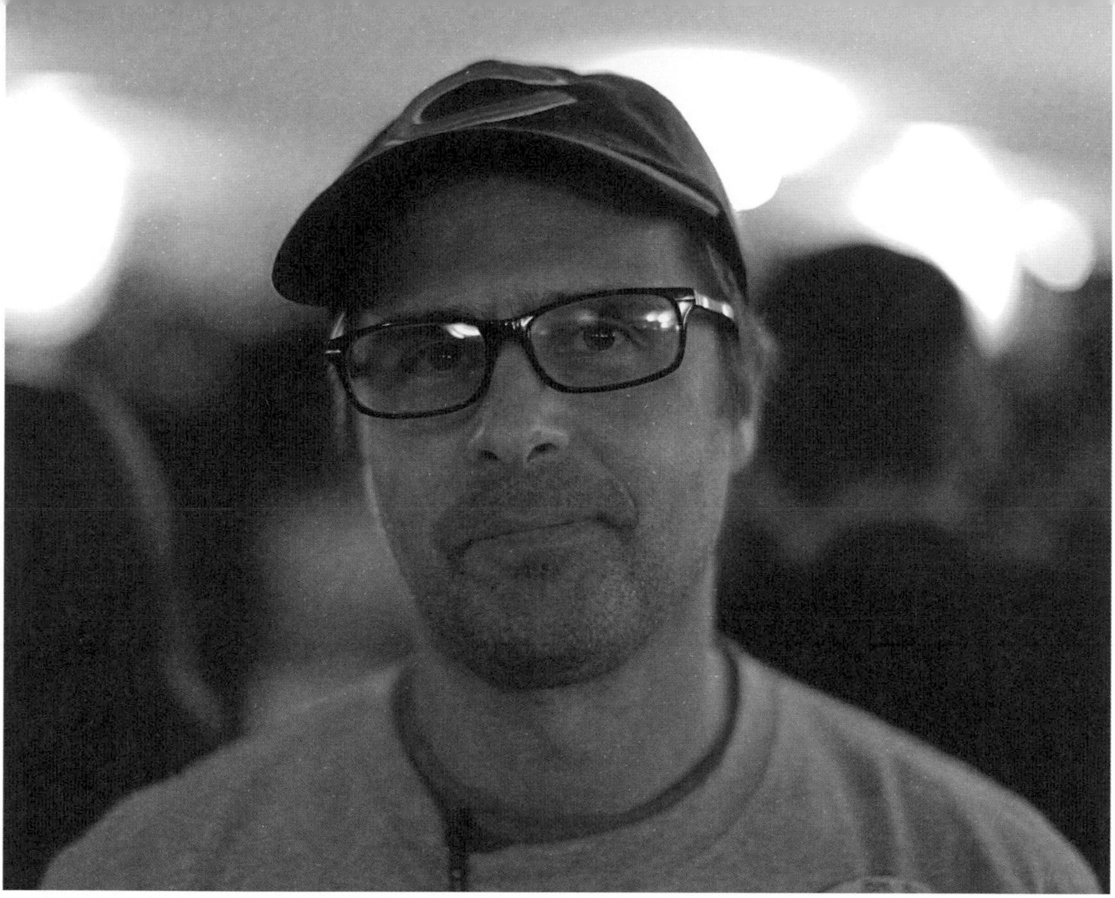

is something childhood and punk both share, so where he picked that up isn't clear.

He's a naturalist, yet his own existence seems unnatural; that's the ongoing conflict. Just being alive seems a struggle, and a conscious decision. It's that choice, and that choice alone—not to die—that allows for the possibility of happiness. That's what his comics seem to say, repeatedly, in different ways.

Like my sculptor friend's, Porcellino's work is a beautiful monument made not out of joy but out of spite—an attempt to prove the intrinsic value of life, which leaves no one but its creator in doubt.

The creator and his parents, too, who still aren't impressed. They stand on the sidelines casting disapproving looks, which is what they do best.

It's a tragic state of affairs, but an effective one, because it keeps the creative folks hard at work. For Porcellino, that means not only writing and drawing, but all the behind-the-scenes drudgery of putting *King Cat* out: pleading with printers, invoicing stores, and going to the post office as routinely as other people go to the bar.

He's an anomaly in the comics world for sticking with self-publishing for so long. His DIY ethics and ethos are, I suspect, why I was chosen to write about him, for I am a self-publisher, too. But what's there for fish to say about water? It's getting a little shallow in here—that's all.

Reading the collected *King Cat* can be eerie, though; you see the author's phobias and illnesses develop, while his circle of friends and romantic possibilities shrinks. He reveals himself as he discovers himself, working out his problems on paper. We watch him grow up, issue by issue, one disclosure or revelation at a time.

The idealism remains and even gathers steam, but so do the bad moods, the love of nature, and the ties to his folks. The suburbs fade away, the crowds, the scenes, the noise.

How much can you lose and still be you? In fact, how much do you have to shed before you can find the core? That's the *King Cat* process of less-is-more. We watch Porcellino's world recede, yet see him inch closer toward finding a sense of peace and discovering what was most important all along.

Aaron Cometbus has been a mainstay of independent publishing since 1981. Besides editing* Cometbus *magazine, he is a songwriter and the author of several novels.

John Porcellino in Seattle at Short Run on his tour for *The Hospital Suite*. Photo: Alex Stonehill (2014).

OUTSIDER

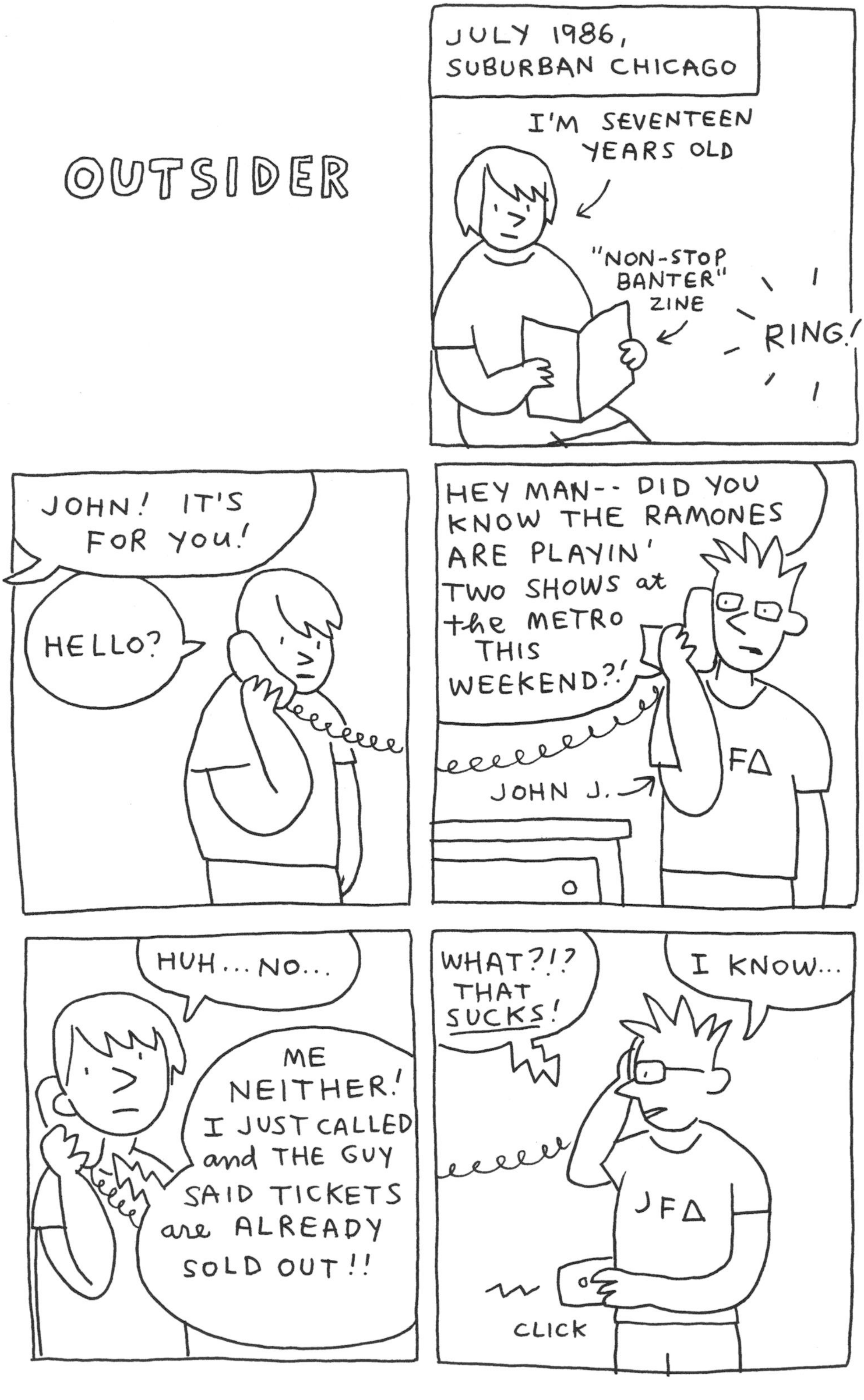
JULY 1986, SUBURBAN CHICAGO
I'M SEVENTEEN YEARS OLD
"NON-STOP BANTER" ZINE
RING!
JOHN! IT'S FOR YOU!
HELLO?
HEY MAN-- DID YOU KNOW THE RAMONES ARE PLAYIN' TWO SHOWS at the METRO THIS WEEKEND?!
JOHN J.
FΔ
HUH... NO...
ME NEITHER! I JUST CALLED and THE GUY SAID TICKETS are ALREADY SOLD OUT!!
WHAT?!? THAT SUCKS!
I KNOW...
JFΔ
CLICK

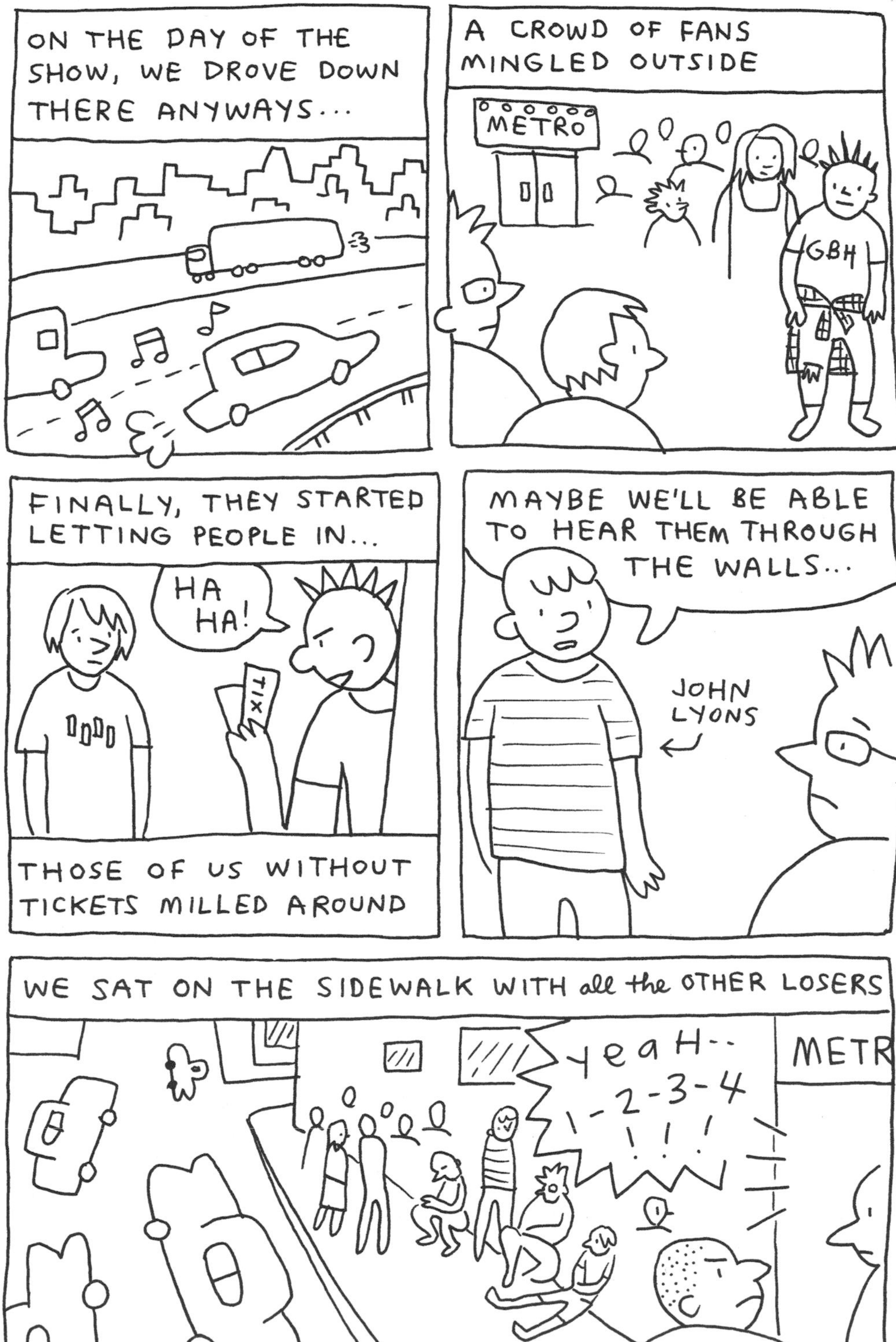
ON THE DAY OF THE SHOW, WE DROVE DOWN THERE ANYWAYS...
A CROWD OF FANS MINGLED OUTSIDE
METRO
GBH
FINALLY, THEY STARTED LETTING PEOPLE IN...
HA HA!
TIX
THOSE OF US WITHOUT TICKETS MILLED AROUND
MAYBE WE'LL BE ABLE TO HEAR THEM THROUGH THE WALLS...
JOHN LYONS
WE SAT ON THE SIDEWALK WITH all the OTHER LOSERS
METR
yeaH-- 1-2-3-4 !!!

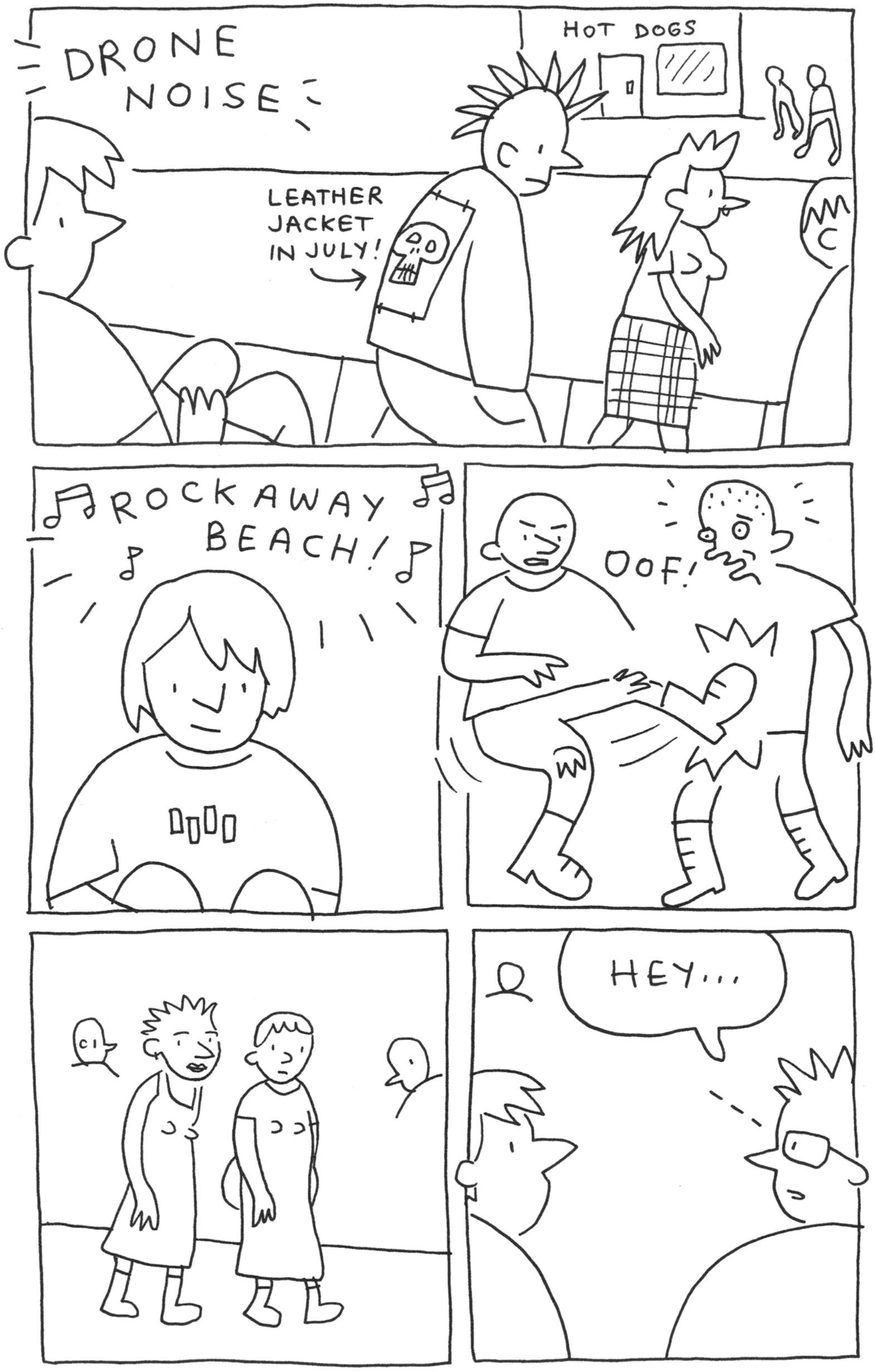
DRONE NOISE
HOT DOGS
LEATHER JACKET IN JULY!
ROCKAWAY BEACH!
OOF!
HEY...

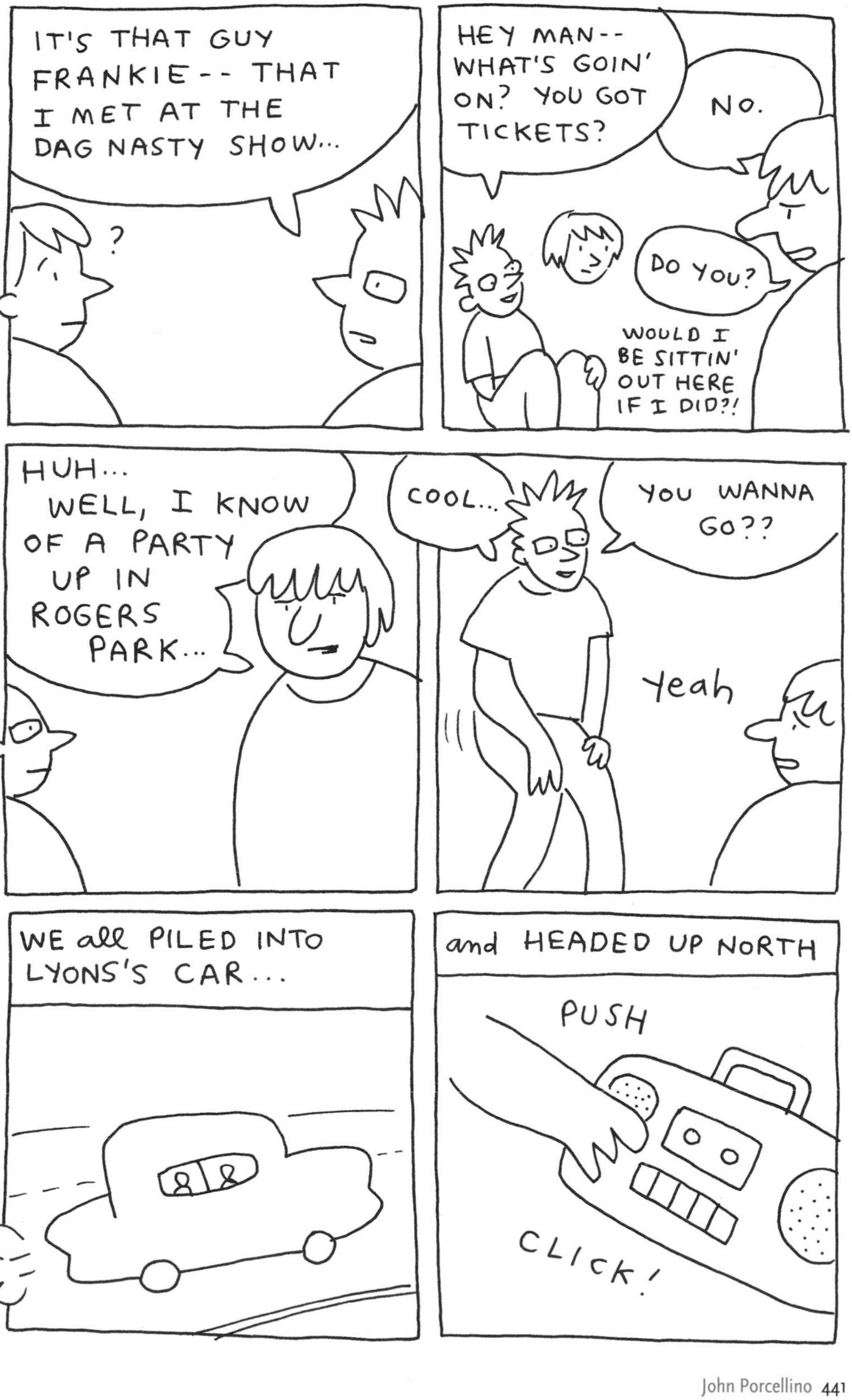
IT'S THAT GUY FRANKIE-- THAT I MET AT THE DAG NASTY SHOW...
?
HEY MAN-- WHAT'S GOIN' ON? YOU GOT TICKETS?
NO.
DO YOU?
WOULD I BE SITTIN' OUT HERE IF I DID?!
HUH... WELL, I KNOW OF A PARTY UP IN ROGERS PARK...
COOL...
YOU WANNA GO??
Yeah
WE all PILED INTO LYONS'S CAR...
and HEADED UP NORTH
PUSH
CLICK!

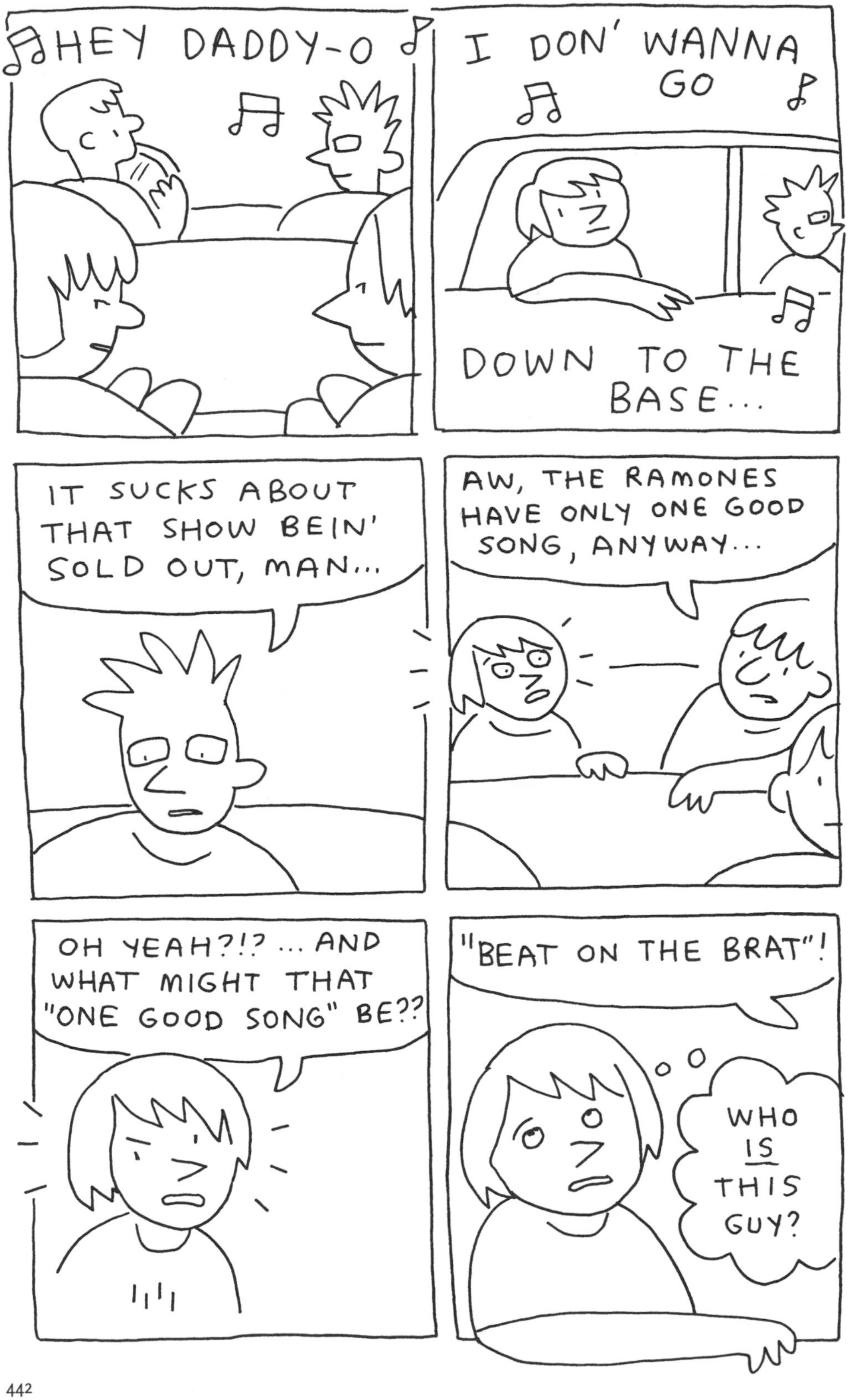
HEY DADDY-O
I DON' WANNA GO
DOWN TO THE BASE...
IT SUCKS ABOUT THAT SHOW BEIN' SOLD OUT, MAN...
AW, THE RAMONES HAVE ONLY ONE GOOD SONG, ANYWAY...
OH YEAH?!? ... AND WHAT MIGHT THAT "ONE GOOD SONG" BE??
"BEAT ON THE BRAT"!
WHO IS THIS GUY?

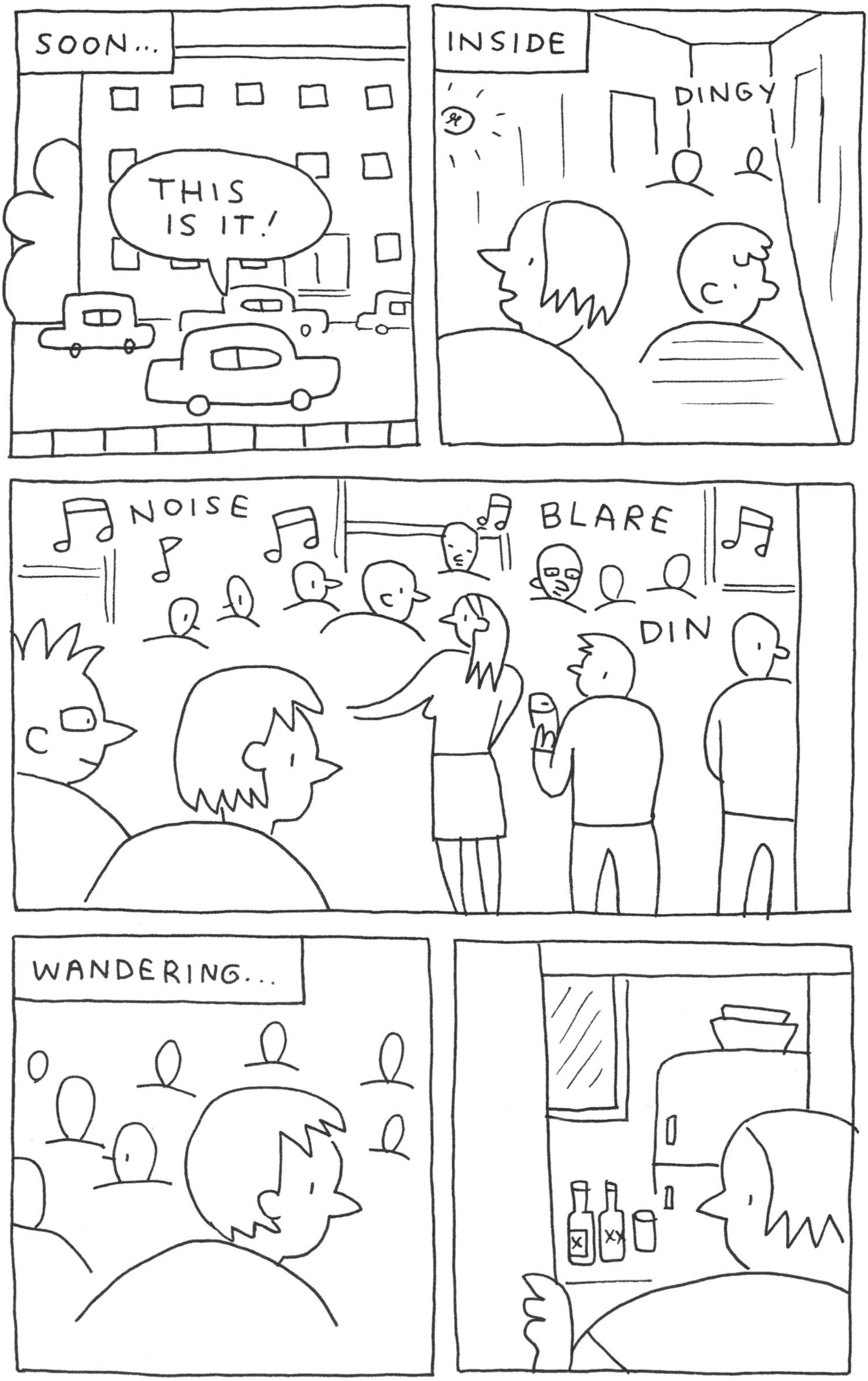
SOON...
THIS IS IT!
INSIDE
DINGY
NOISE
BLARE
DIN
WANDERING...

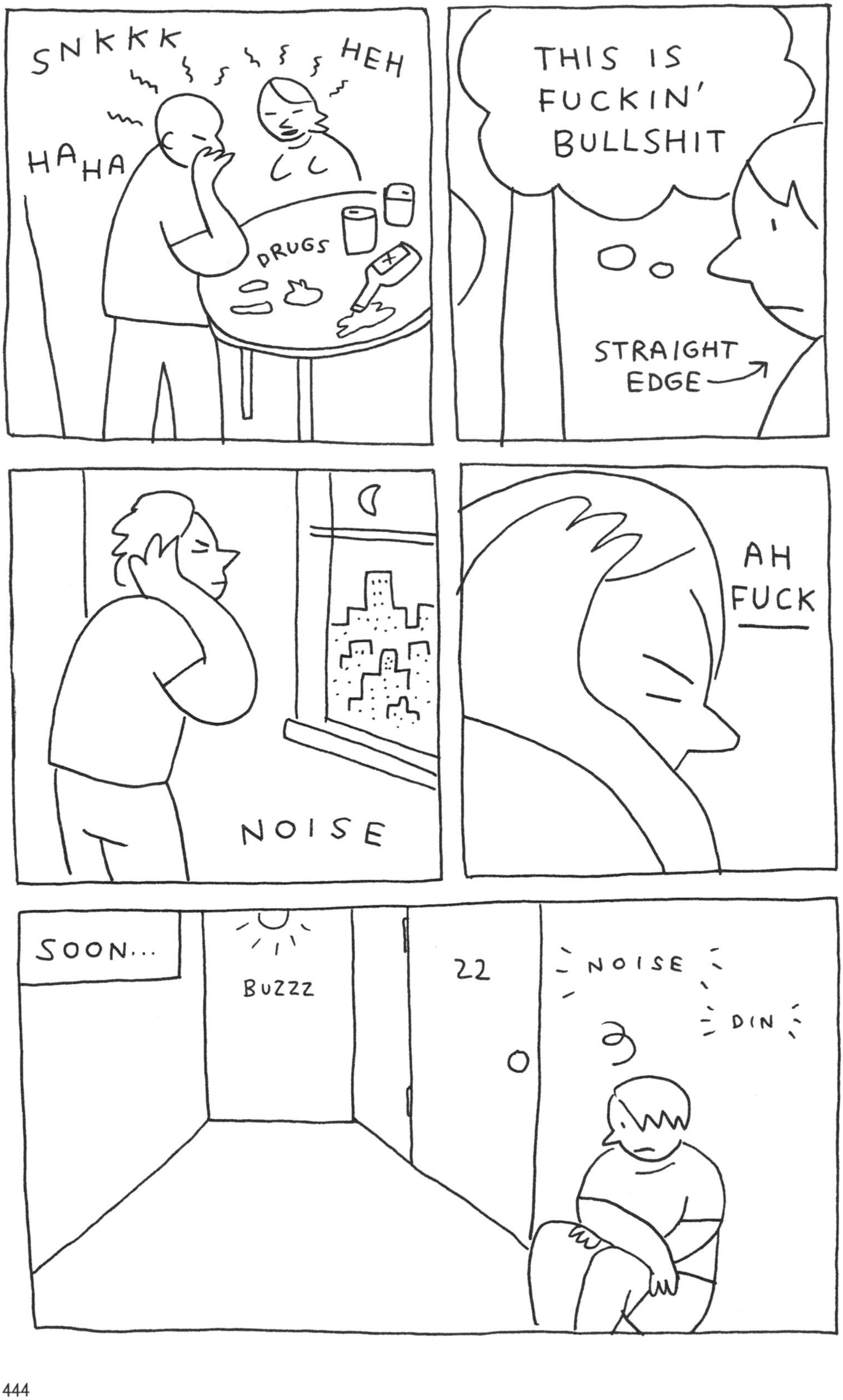
SNKKK
HEH
HAHA
DRUGS
THIS IS FUCKIN' BULLSHIT
STRAIGHT EDGE
NOISE
AH FUCK
SOON...
BUZZZ
22
NOISE
DIN

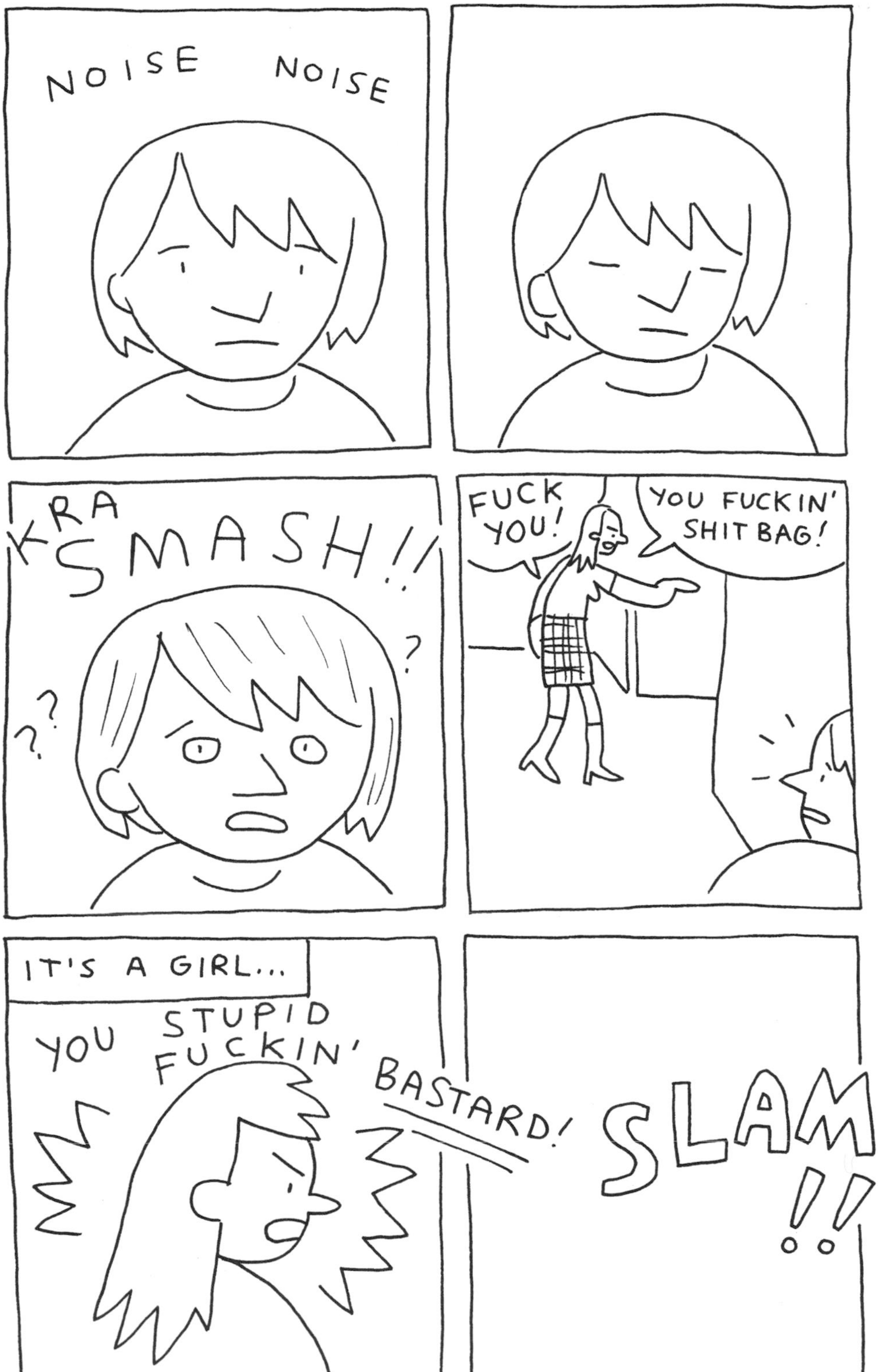

NOISE NOISE
KRA SMASH!!
??
?
FUCK YOU!
YOU FUCKIN' SHIT BAG!
IT'S A GIRL...
YOU STUPID FUCKIN' BASTARD!
SLAM!!

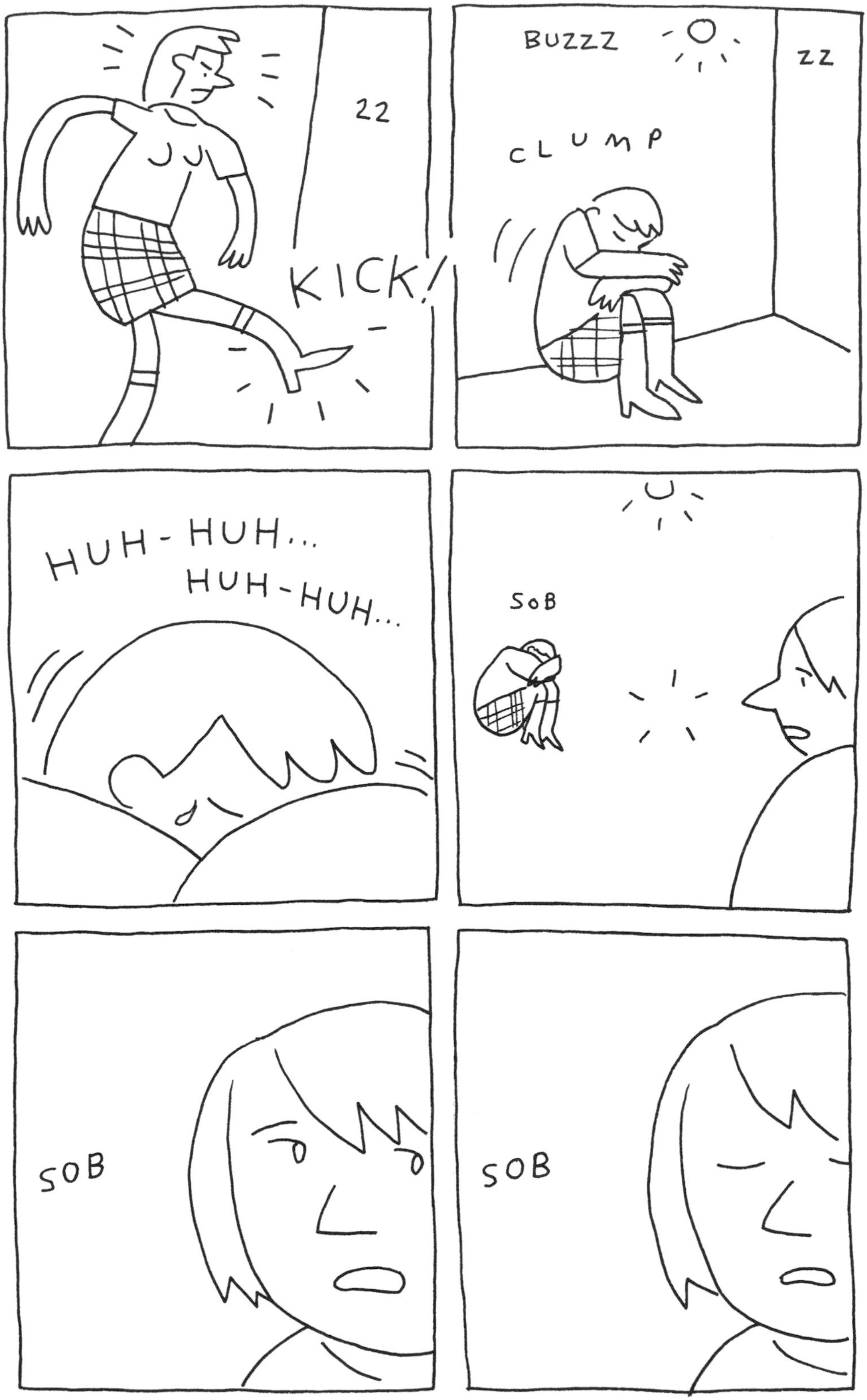
22
KICK!
BUZZZ
ZZ
CLUMP
HUH-HUH...
HUH-HUH...
SOB
SOB
SOB

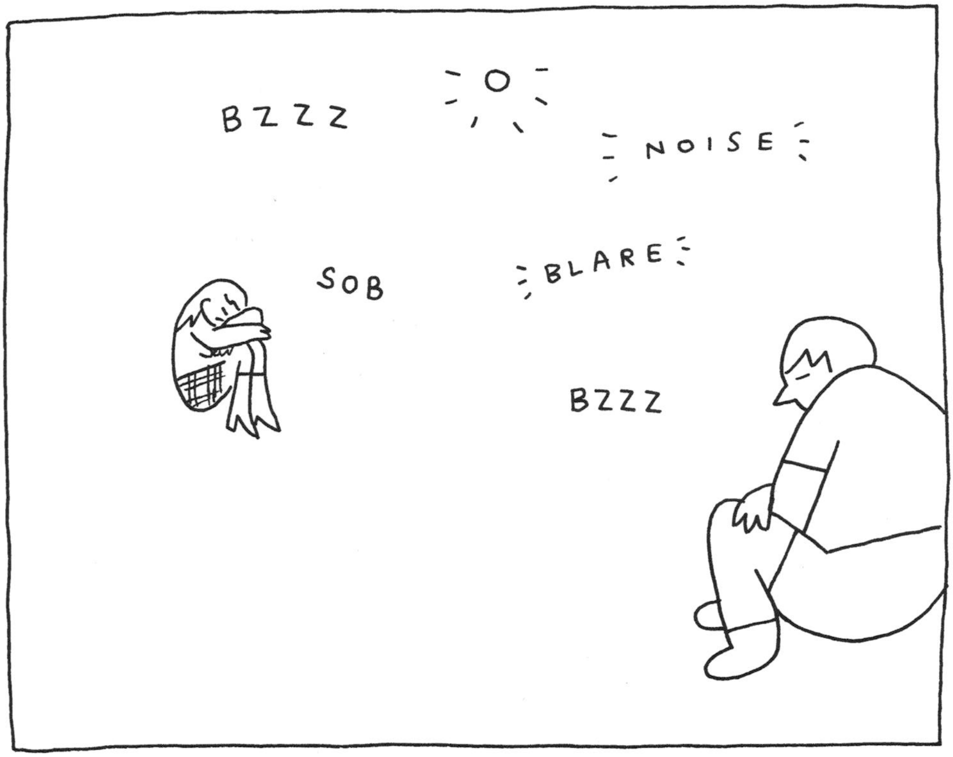
BZZZ
NOISE
SOB
BLARE
BZZZ

John Porcellino
JULY 2009

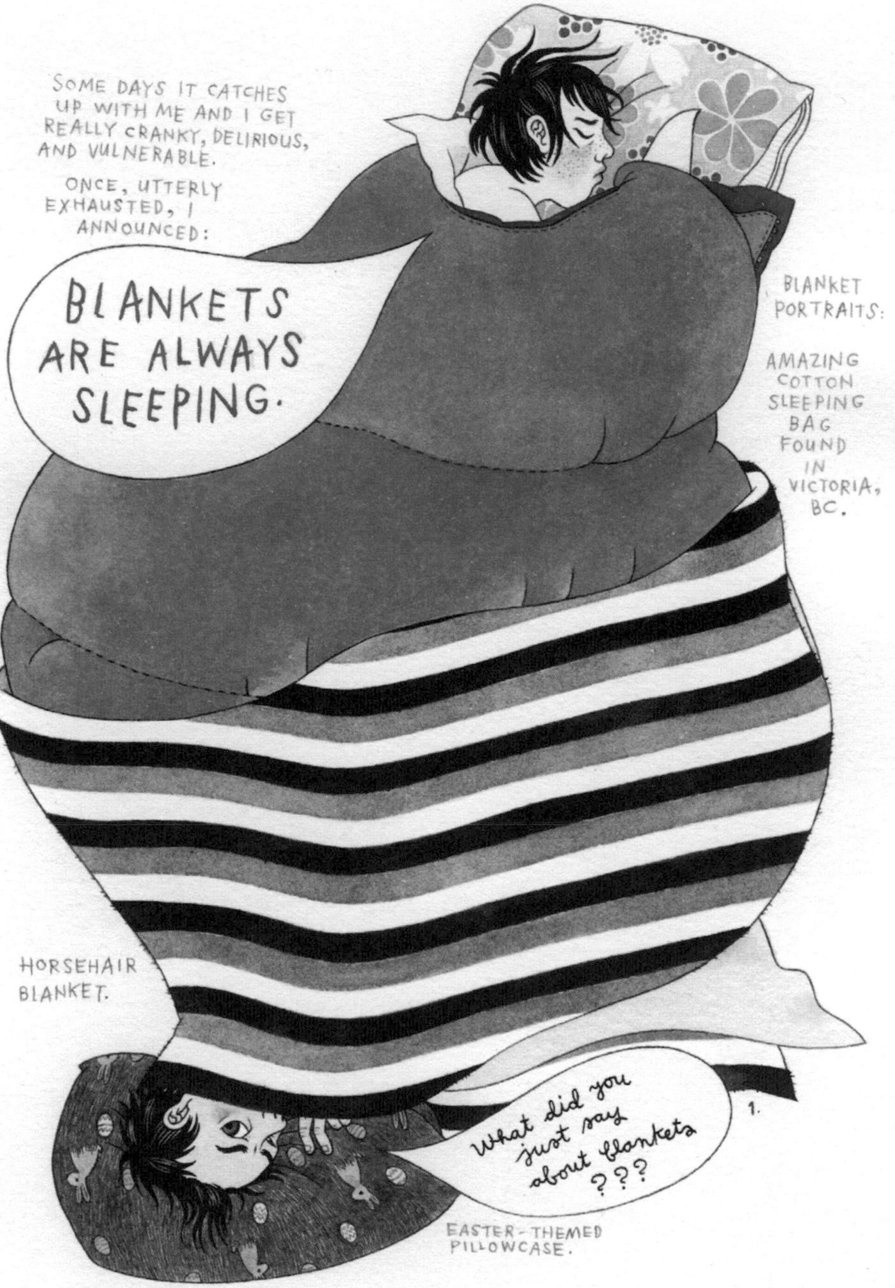

SOME DAYS IT CATCHES UP WITH ME AND I GET REALLY CRANKY, DELIRIOUS, AND VULNERABLE.
ONCE, UTTERLY EXHAUSTED, I ANNOUNCED:
BLANKETS ARE ALWAYS SLEEPING.
BLANKET PORTRAITS:
AMAZING COTTON SLEEPING BAG FOUND IN VICTORIA, BC.
HORSEHAIR BLANKET.
What did you just say about blankets ???
1.
EASTER-THEMED PILLOWCASE.

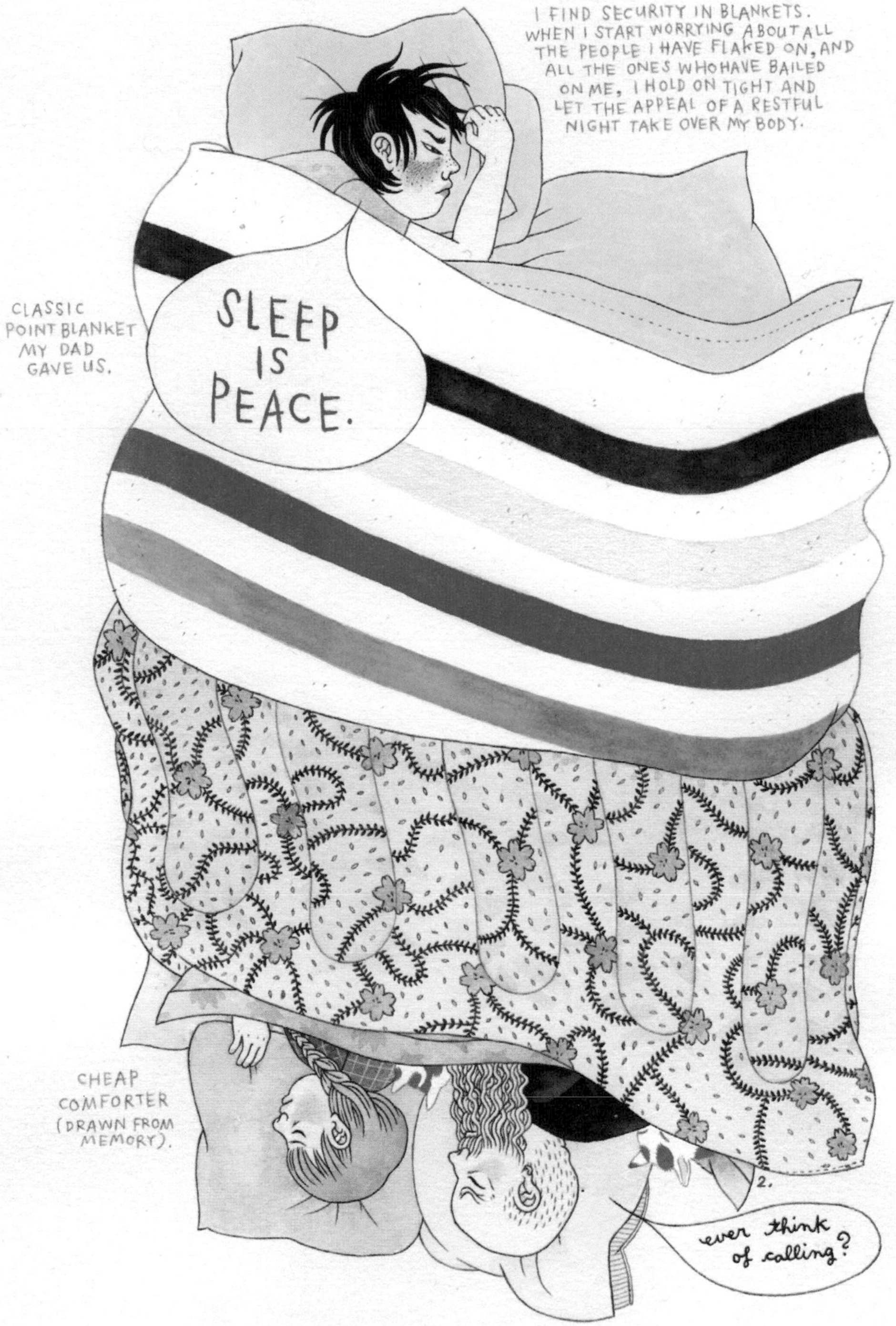
I FIND SECURITY IN BLANKETS. WHEN I START WORRYING ABOUT ALL THE PEOPLE I HAVE FLAKED ON, AND ALL THE ONES WHO HAVE BAILED ON ME, I HOLD ON TIGHT AND LET THE APPEAL OF A RESTFUL NIGHT TAKE OVER MY BODY.
CLASSIC POINT BLANKET MY DAD GAVE US.
SLEEP IS PEACE.
CHEAP COMFORTER (DRAWN FROM MEMORY).
2.
ever think of calling?

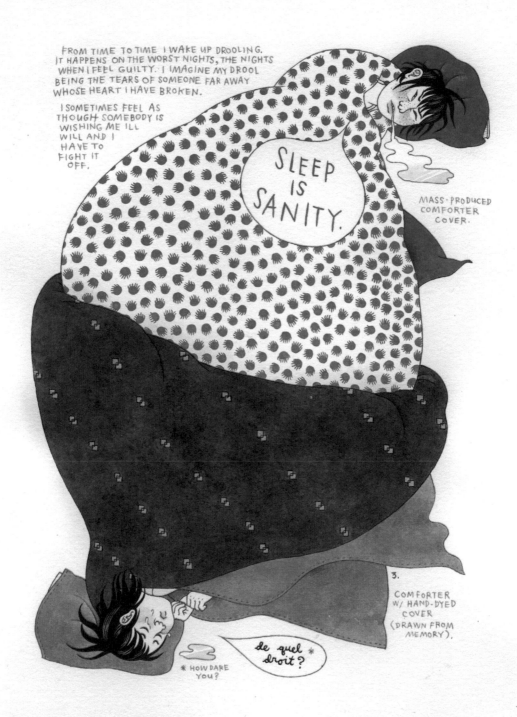

FROM TIME TO TIME I WAKE UP DROOLING.
IT HAPPENS ON THE WORST NIGHTS, THE NIGHTS
WHEN I FEEL GUILTY. I IMAGINE MY DROOL
BEING THE TEARS OF SOMEONE FAR AWAY
WHOSE HEART I HAVE BROKEN.

I SOMETIMES FEEL AS
THOUGH SOMEBODY IS
WISHING ME ILL
WILL AND I
HAVE TO
FIGHT IT
OFF.

SLEEP
IS
SANITY.

MASS-PRODUCED
COMFORTER
COVER.

3.
COMFORTER
W/ HAND-DYED
COVER
(DRAWN FROM
MEMORY).

* HOW DARE
YOU?

de quel
droit? *

450

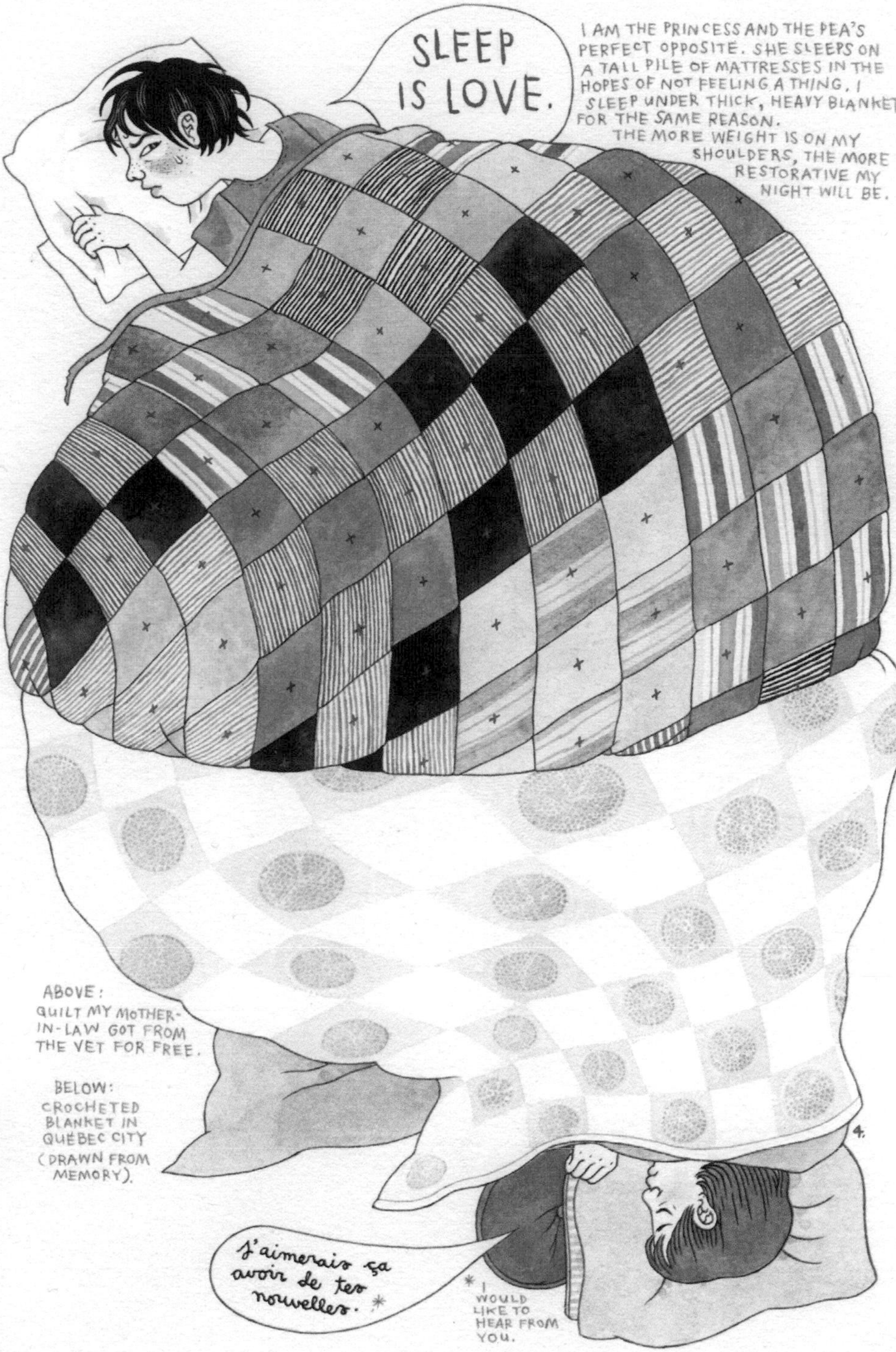
SLEEP IS LOVE.
I AM THE PRINCESS AND THE PEA'S PERFECT OPPOSITE. SHE SLEEPS ON A TALL PILE OF MATTRESSES IN THE HOPES OF NOT FEELING A THING. I SLEEP UNDER THICK, HEAVY BLANKETS FOR THE SAME REASON.
THE MORE WEIGHT IS ON MY SHOULDERS, THE MORE RESTORATIVE MY NIGHT WILL BE.
ABOVE: QUILT MY MOTHER-IN-LAW GOT FROM THE VET FOR FREE.
BELOW: CROCHETED BLANKET IN QUÉBEC CITY (DRAWN FROM MEMORY).
4.
J'aimerais ça avoir de tes nouvelles.*
* I WOULD LIKE TO HEAR FROM YOU.

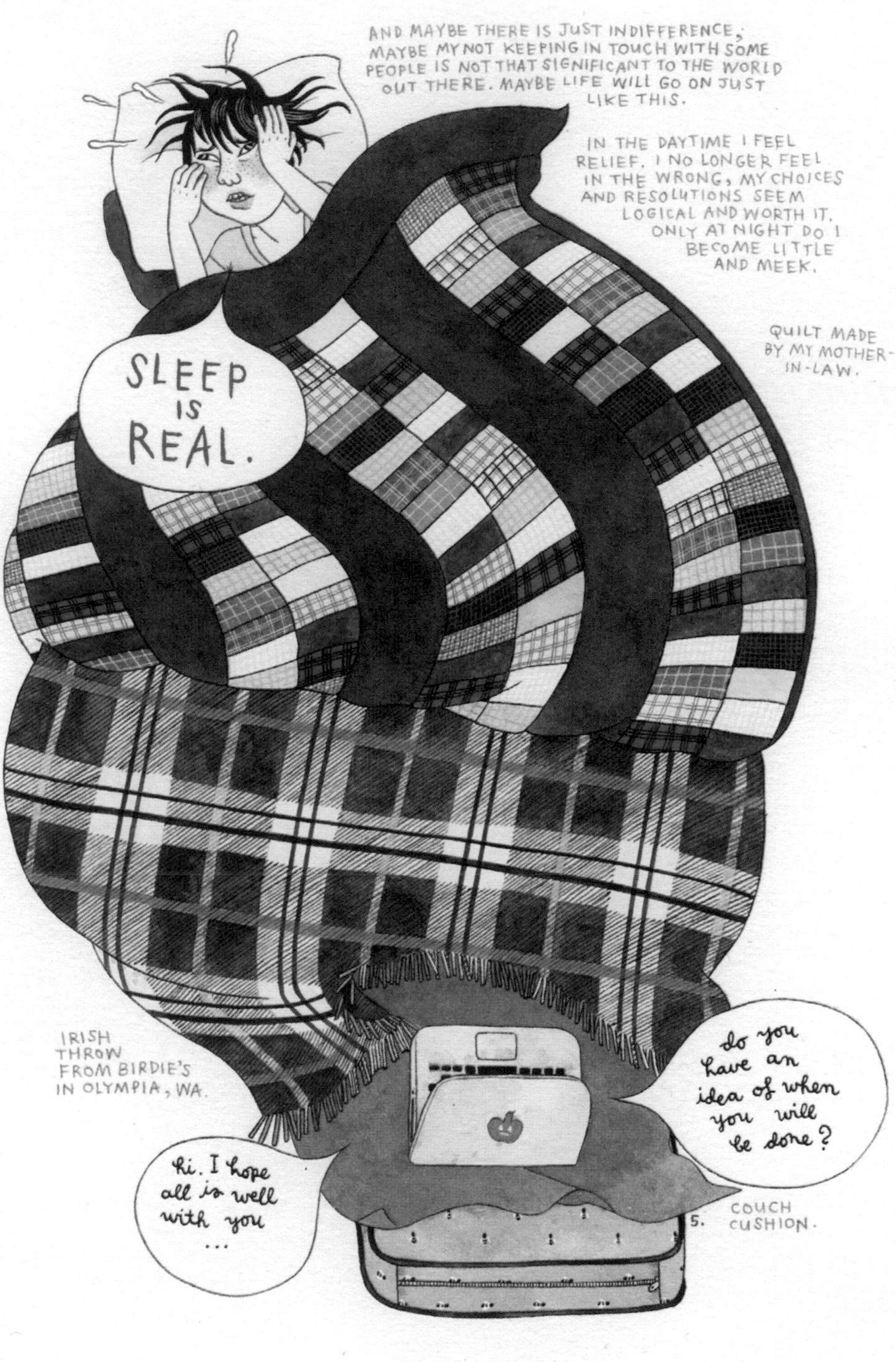
AND MAYBE THERE IS JUST INDIFFERENCE; MAYBE MY NOT KEEPING IN TOUCH WITH SOME PEOPLE IS NOT THAT SIGNIFICANT TO THE WORLD OUT THERE. MAYBE LIFE WILL GO ON JUST LIKE THIS.
IN THE DAYTIME I FEEL RELIEF. I NO LONGER FEEL IN THE WRONG, MY CHOICES AND RESOLUTIONS SEEM LOGICAL AND WORTH IT. ONLY AT NIGHT DO I BECOME LITTLE AND MEEK.
SLEEP IS REAL.
QUILT MADE BY MY MOTHER-IN-LAW.
IRISH THROW FROM BIRDIE'S IN OLYMPIA, WA.
do you have an idea of when you will be done?
hi. I hope all is well with you ...
5. COUCH CUSHION.

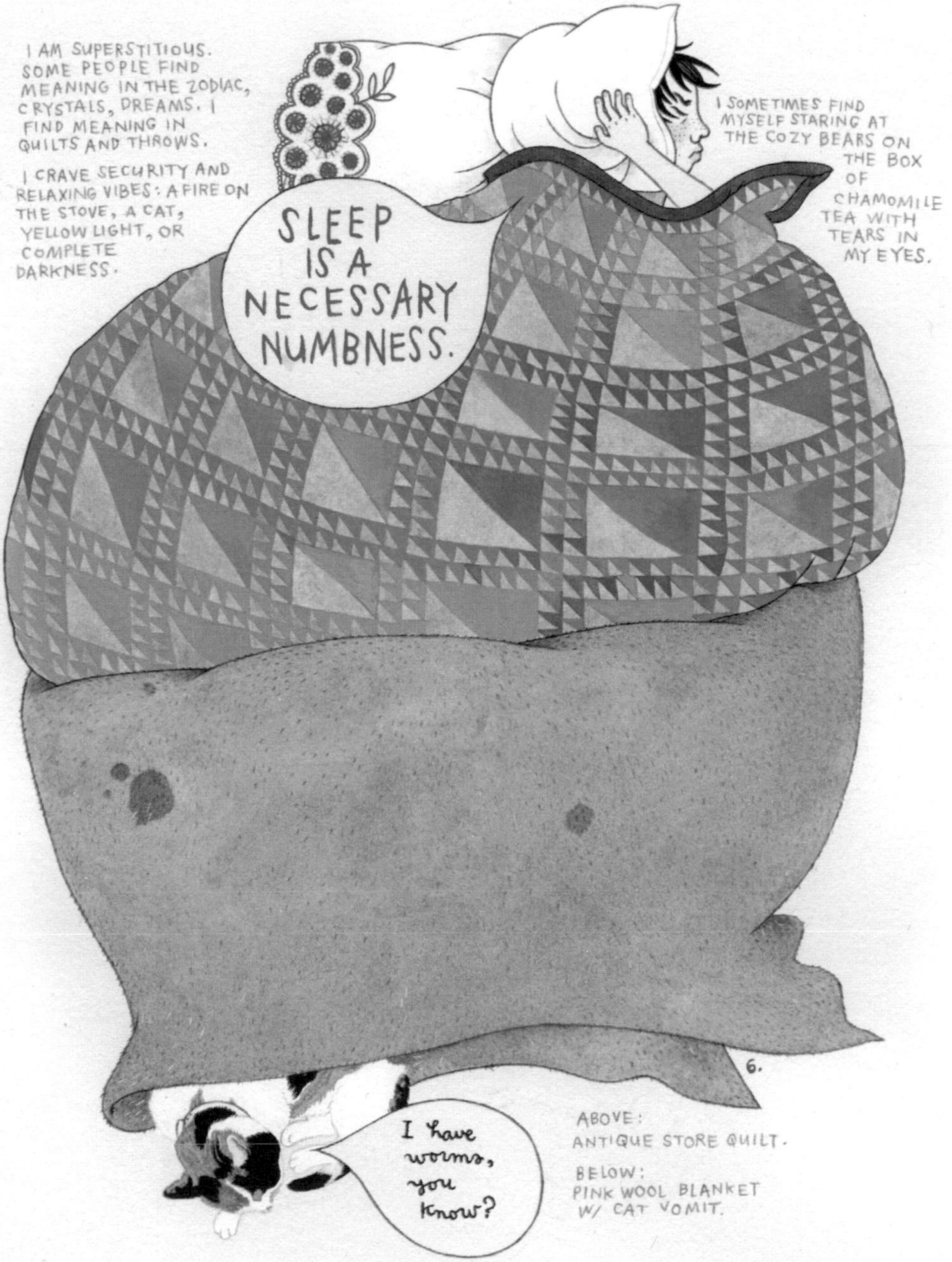
I AM SUPERSTITIOUS. SOME PEOPLE FIND MEANING IN THE ZODIAC, CRYSTALS, DREAMS. I FIND MEANING IN QUILTS AND THROWS.
I CRAVE SECURITY AND RELAXING VIBES: A FIRE ON THE STOVE, A CAT, YELLOW LIGHT, OR COMPLETE DARKNESS.
SLEEP IS A NECESSARY NUMBNESS.
I SOMETIMES FIND MYSELF STARING AT THE COZY BEARS ON THE BOX OF CHAMOMILE TEA WITH TEARS IN MY EYES.
6.
I have worms, you know?
ABOVE: ANTIQUE STORE QUILT.
BELOW: PINK WOOL BLANKET W/ CAT VOMIT.

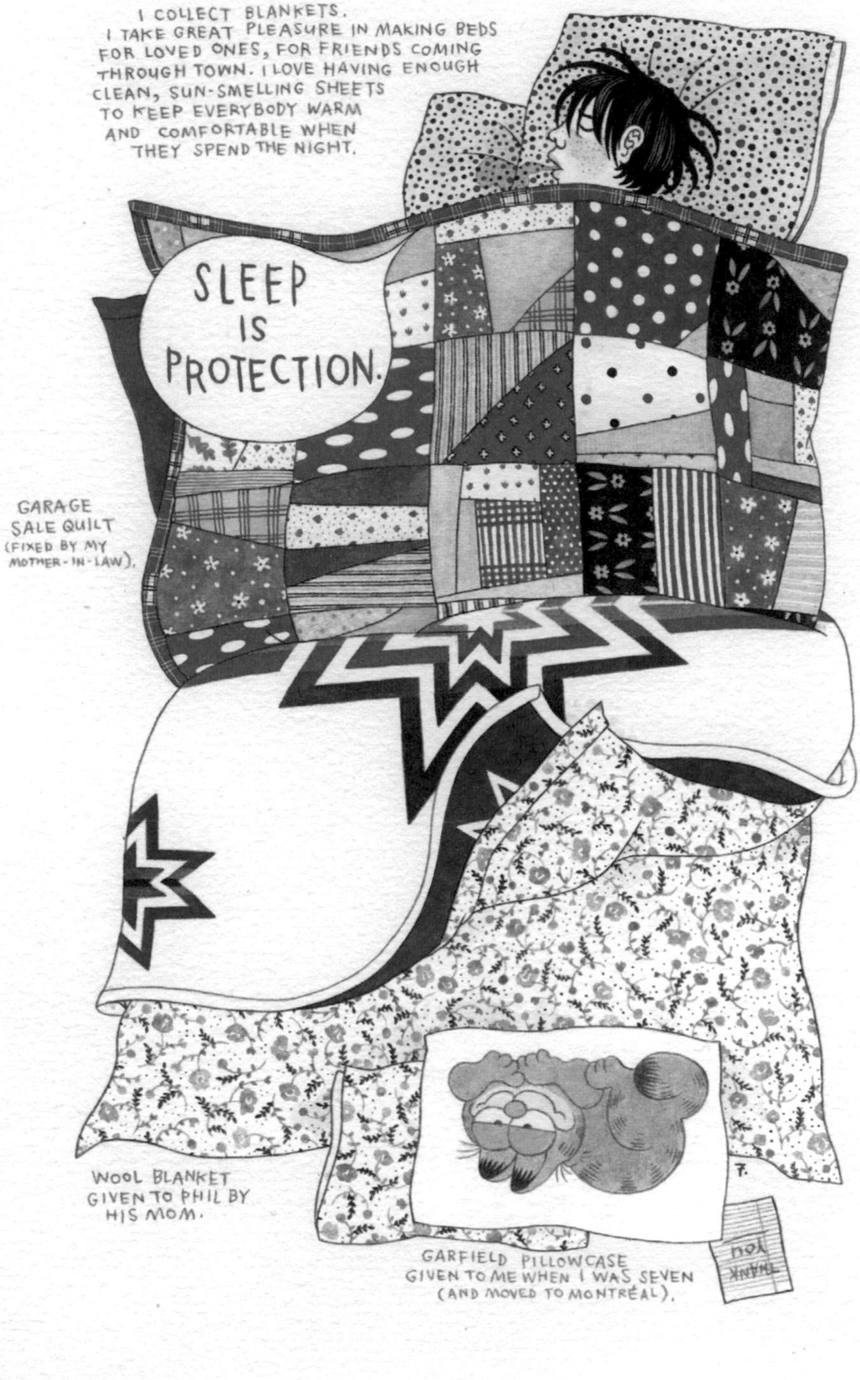
I COLLECT BLANKETS.
I TAKE GREAT PLEASURE IN MAKING BEDS FOR LOVED ONES, FOR FRIENDS COMING THROUGH TOWN. I LOVE HAVING ENOUGH CLEAN, SUN-SMELLING SHEETS TO KEEP EVERYBODY WARM AND COMFORTABLE WHEN THEY SPEND THE NIGHT.
SLEEP IS PROTECTION.
GARAGE SALE QUILT (FIXED BY MY MOTHER-IN-LAW).
WOOL BLANKET GIVEN TO PHIL BY HIS MOM.
7.
GARFIELD PILLOWCASE GIVEN TO ME WHEN I WAS SEVEN (AND MOVED TO MONTRÉAL).
THANK YOU

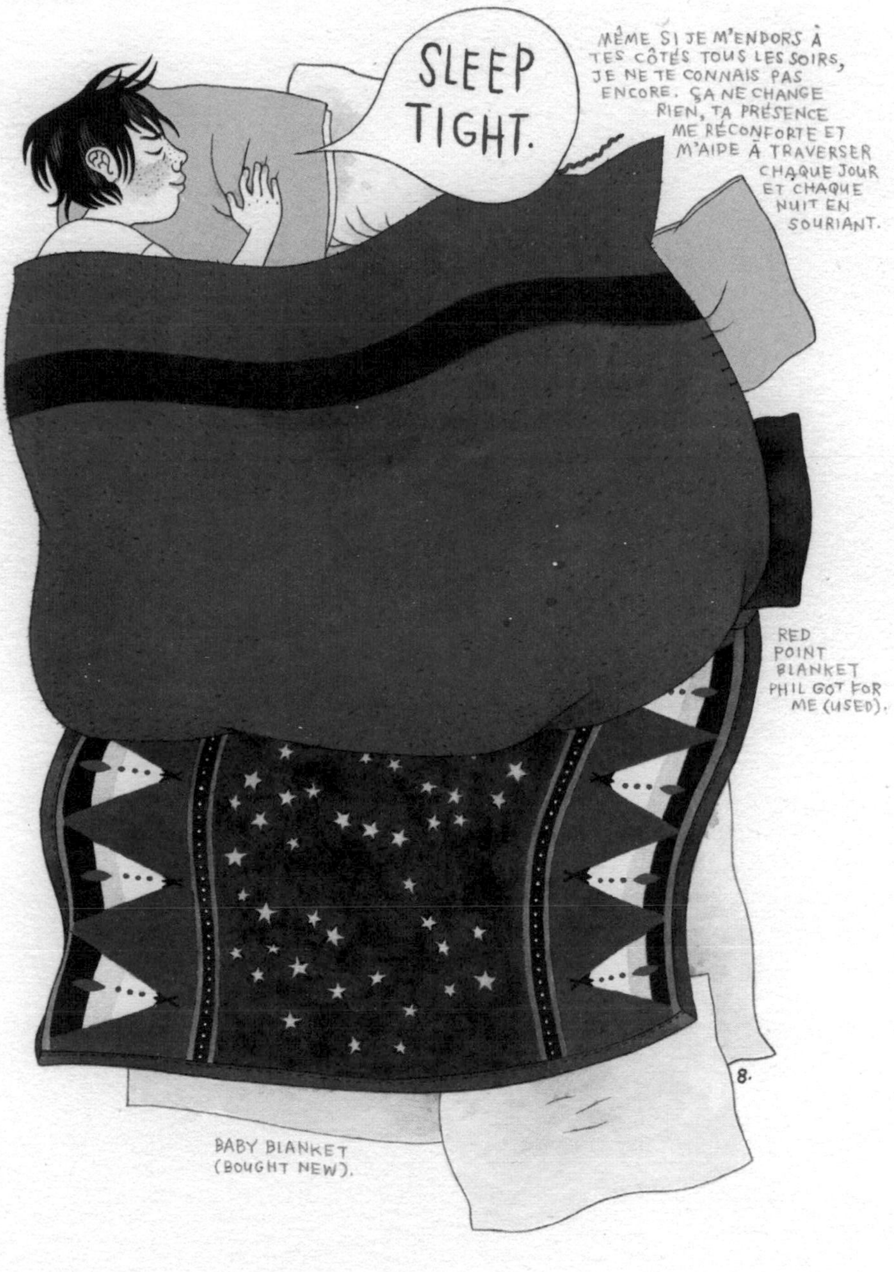
SLEEP TIGHT.
MÊME SI JE M'ENDORS À TES CÔTÉS TOUS LES SOIRS, JE NE TE CONNAIS PAS ENCORE. ÇA NE CHANGE RIEN, TA PRÉSENCE ME RÉCONFORTE ET M'AIDE À TRAVERSER CHAQUE JOUR ET CHAQUE NUIT EN SOURIANT.
RED POINT BLANKET PHIL GOT FOR ME (USED).
8.
BABY BLANKET (BOUGHT NEW).

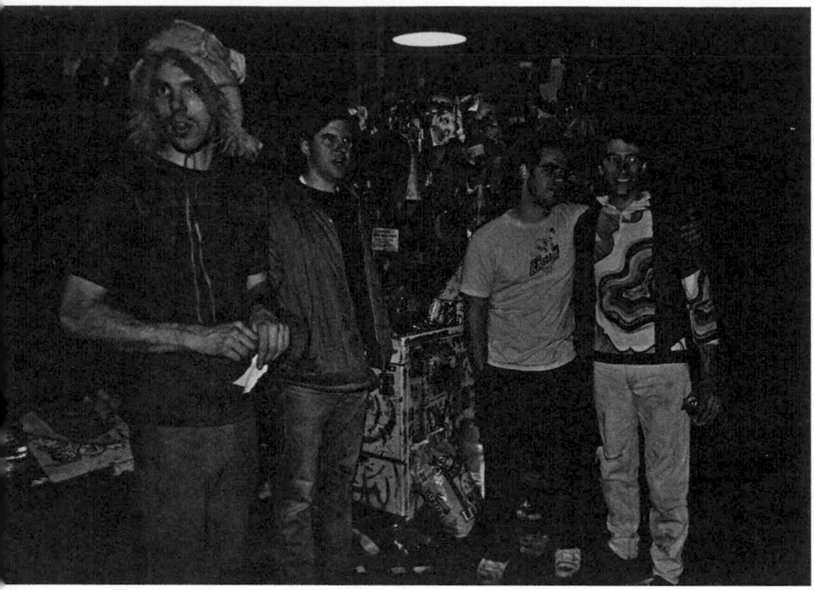

Hanging at Fort Thunder: Brian Chippendale, Tom Devlin, Brian Ralph & Leif Goldberg (1996).

Brian sent me a pile of his comics and a letter when I was a new editor at *Nickelodeon* magazine in the late nineties. The letter ended with "aliens, robots, monsters—I can do it all." Even though his sample pages from *Cave~In* (his great wordless comic about a little moleman guy exploring underground caverns) were not quite right for *Nick* mag, I liked that closing statement: it was smart but also goofy. Whoever wrote that sentence clearly had a love for the stuff kids love mixed with enough irony to be able to step back from it—and love it even *more* from that vantage. (I made a lot of assumptions from that one sentence...) Plus he really *could* draw all that cool stuff. His art was like a great black light poster but with a real story.

A little while later, I started calling up Brian to do comics for *Nickelodeon* magazine—and other editors did too. For a while we only got in touch with Brian if the story had a cave or starred a weird little dude. He took this pigeonholing in stride. But pretty soon he ended up on my mental list of cartoonists who are just fun to work with and who can be depended on to come up with a comic with the right mix of cool visuals and funny gags. My favourite Brian Ralph character created for *Nick* mag was Twiggy Stumps—an outdoorsman with feeble wits and a snarky skunk pal named Juniper. Brian still owns the rights to Twiggy and I'm hoping to see more of him someday!

Humour might seem like an afterthought to Brian Ralph's comics—the visuals are so strong it's easy to let the gags slide by. But to me it's the perfect mix. Even when the situation is deadly serious, like with his zombie comic *Daybreak*, every panel seems to be a carefully considered mix of cool stuff to look at, forward-moving plot points, and humour. He really can do it all!

***—Chris Duffy, former comics editor at* Nickelodeon *magazine, current editor of* SpongeBob Comics**

While the rest of us were stapling garbage to the roof or shoving microphones into speakers, Ralph was busy drawing and making comics. Sitting in his room, sitting by the window, standing at the photocopy shop, always sharpening his craft. He was, and is, truly a comic-book artist. Focused on the form.

—Brian Chippendale, cartoonist, drummer in Lightning Bolt, founding member of Fort Thunder

Lynda Barry, Chester Brown, Daniel Clowes, Gilbert Hernandez, Anders Nilsen, and Adrian Tomine are all master cartoonists who would receive genius grants in a perfect world. But the artist who will always be closest to me is Brian Ralph, specifically for *Reggie-12*. Personally digging up the files for those comics that ran in the back of *Giant Robot* for years and getting to hang out with Brian when he went on a West Coast book tour made me realize that we both started as punks stapling our zines/minicomics together and now we're dads. It was cool looking back at the entire indie publishing arc that we traveled in parallel paths. Sometimes I think that the history of *Giant Robot* may vanish like a fart in the wind but I'm gratified to know that at least Brian's brilliant strips have been collected for posterity.

—Martin Wong, co-founder and editor of* Giant Robot*, talking about the collected* Reggie-12 *(2013)

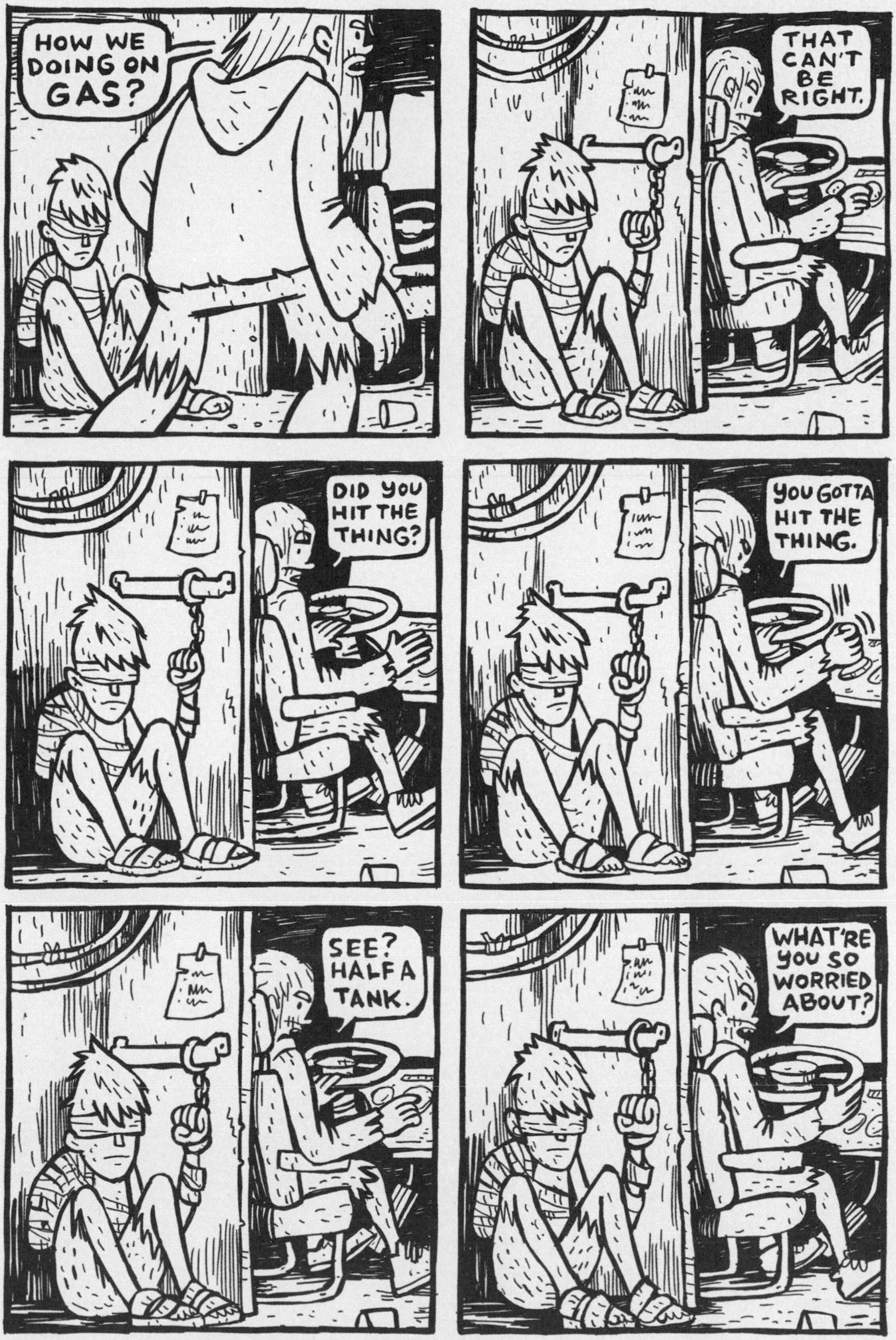
HOW WE DOING ON GAS?
THAT CAN'T BE RIGHT.
DID YOU HIT THE THING?
YOU GOTTA HIT THE THING.
SEE? HALF A TANK.
WHAT'RE YOU SO WORRIED ABOUT?

Daybreak first appeared as a three-issue miniseries (2006–2008) and was later collected by D+Q (2011).

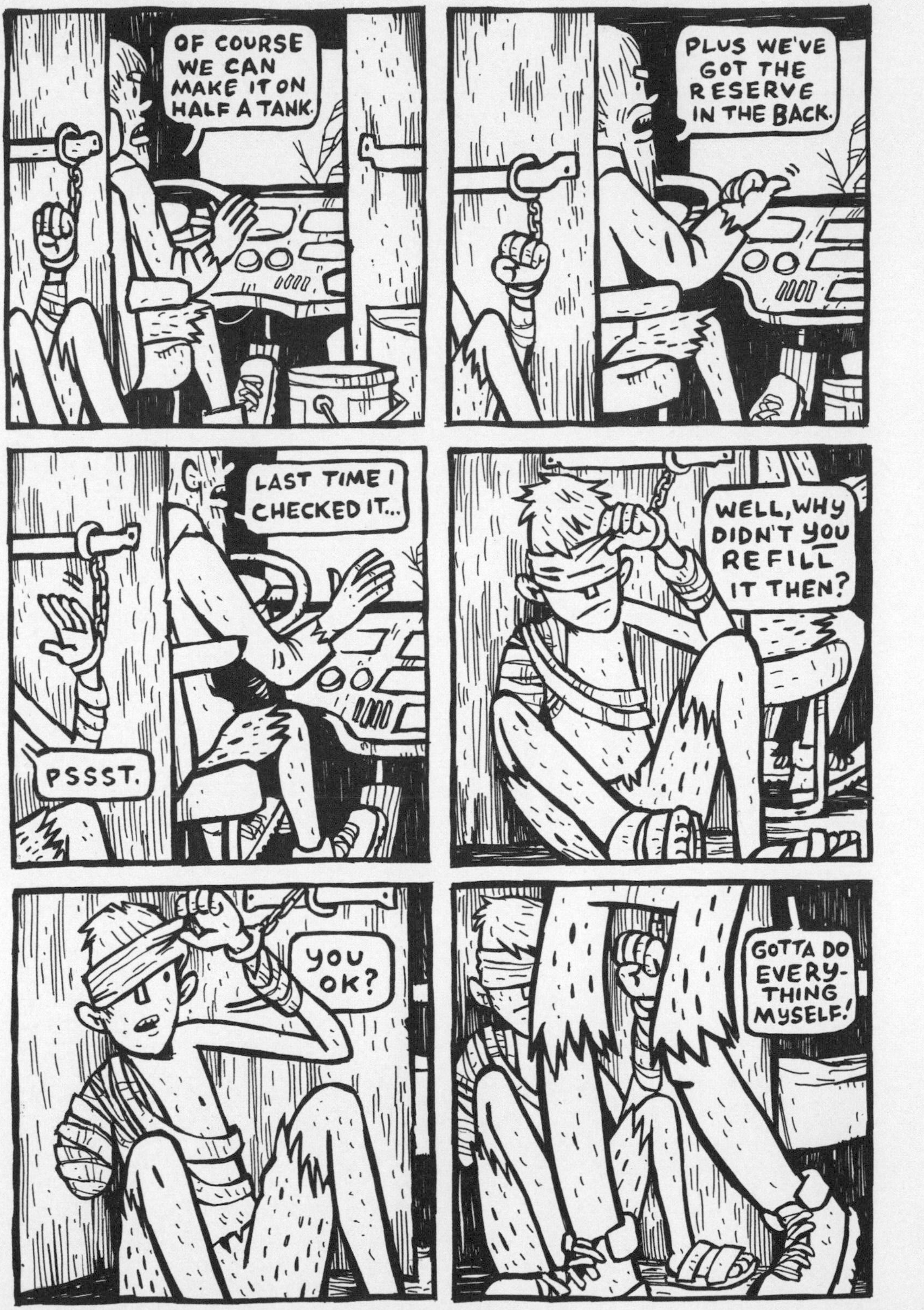
OF COURSE WE CAN MAKE IT ON HALF A TANK.
PLUS WE'VE GOT THE RESERVE IN THE BACK.
LAST TIME I CHECKED IT...
PSSST.
WELL, WHY DIDN'T YOU REFILL IT THEN?
YOU OK?
GOTTA DO EVERY-THING MYSELF!

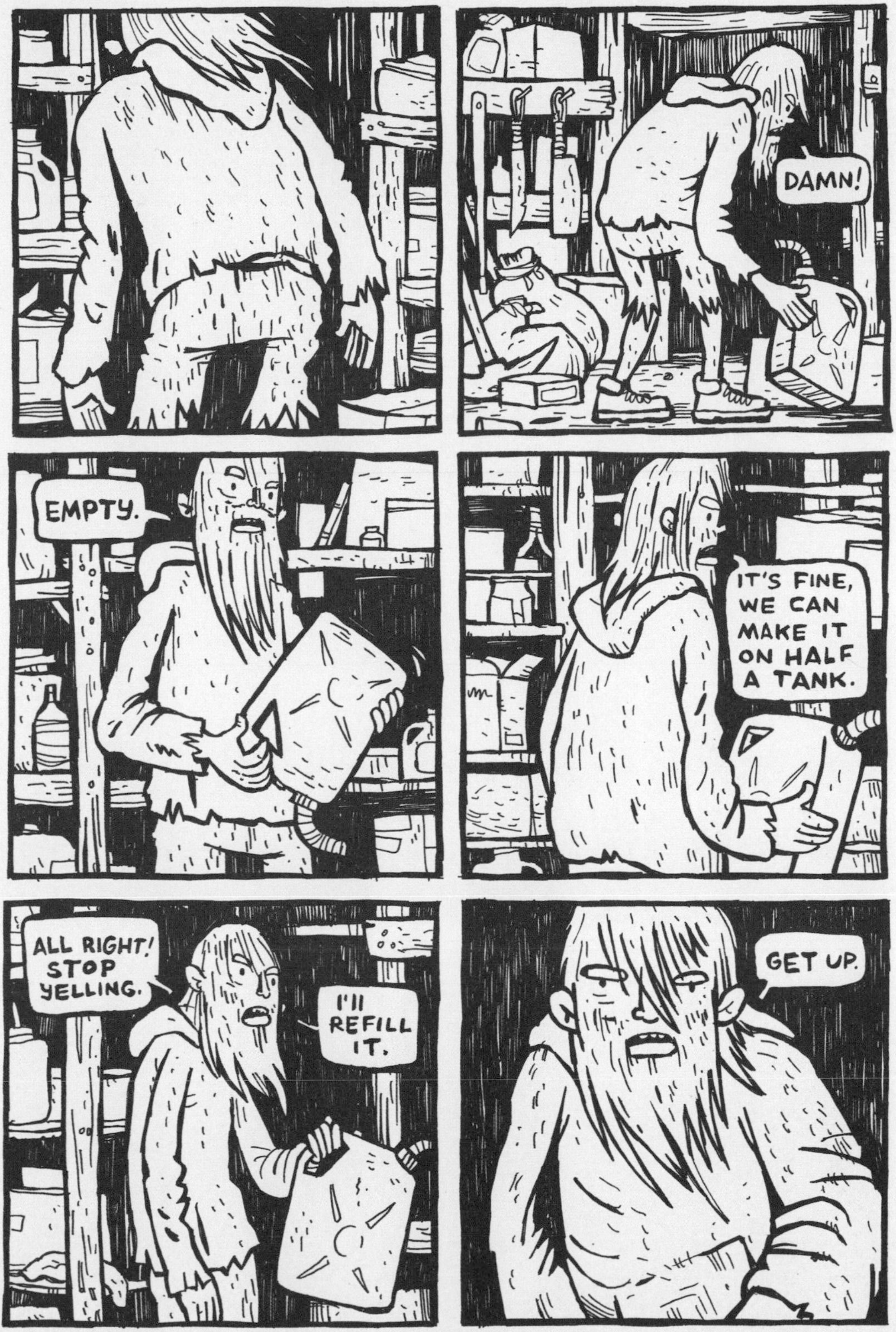
DAMN!
EMPTY.
IT'S FINE, WE CAN MAKE IT ON HALF A TANK.
ALL RIGHT! STOP YELLING.
I'll REFILL IT.
GET UP.

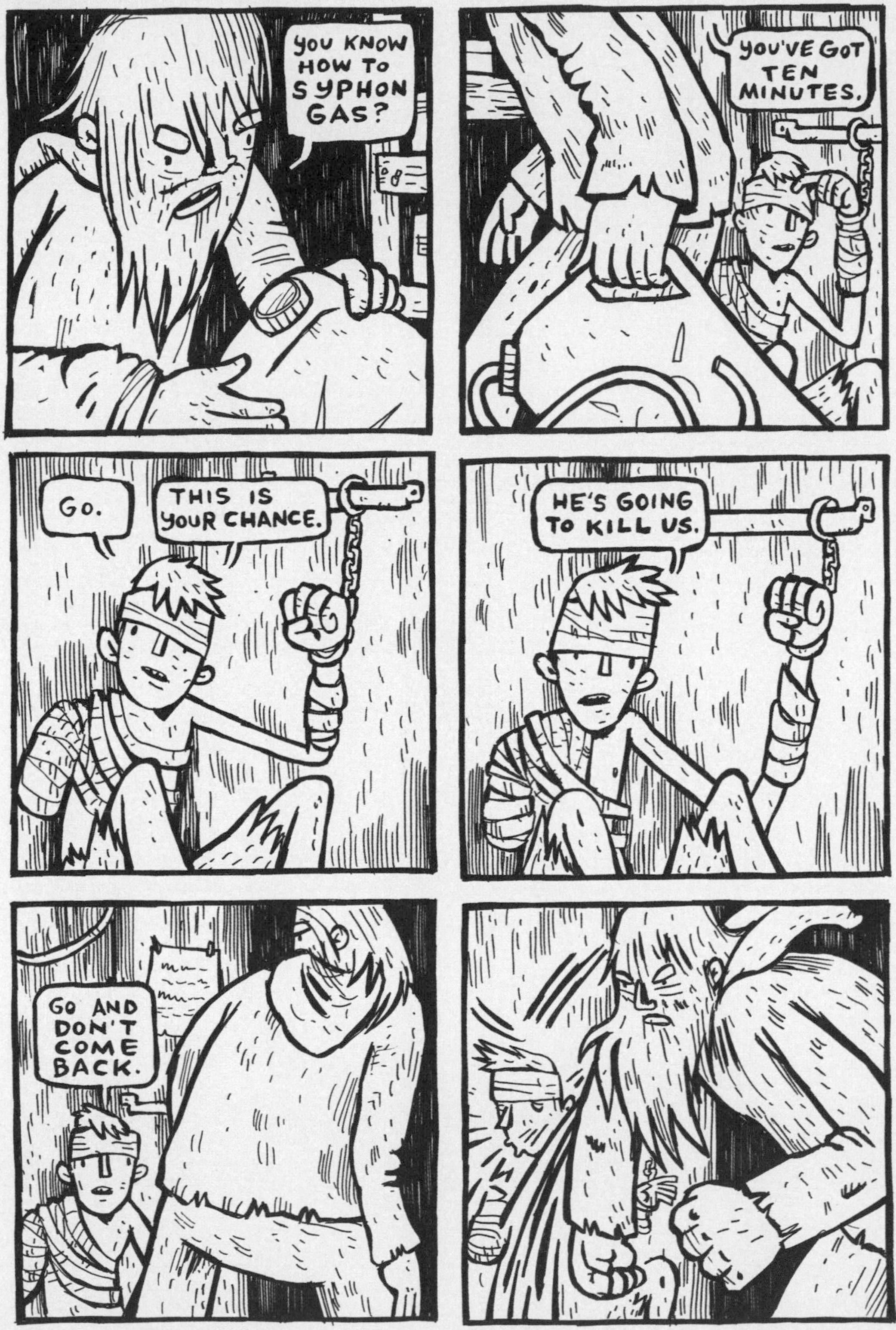
YOU KNOW HOW TO SYPHON GAS?
YOU'VE GOT TEN MINUTES.
GO.
THIS IS YOUR CHANCE.
HE'S GOING TO KILL US.
GO AND DON'T COME BACK.

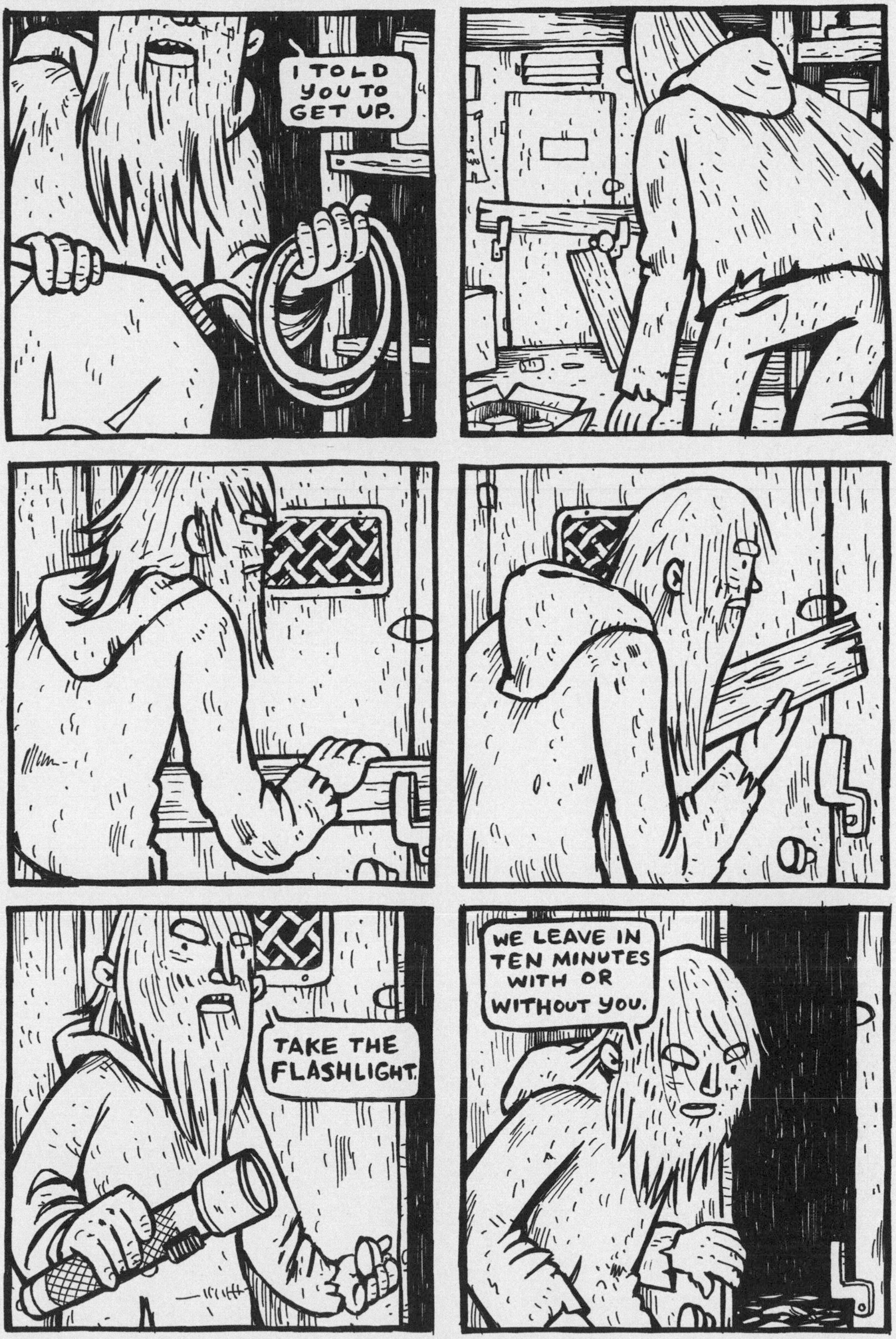
I TOLD YOU TO GET UP.
TAKE THE FLASHLIGHT.
WE LEAVE IN TEN MINUTES WITH OR WITHOUT YOU.

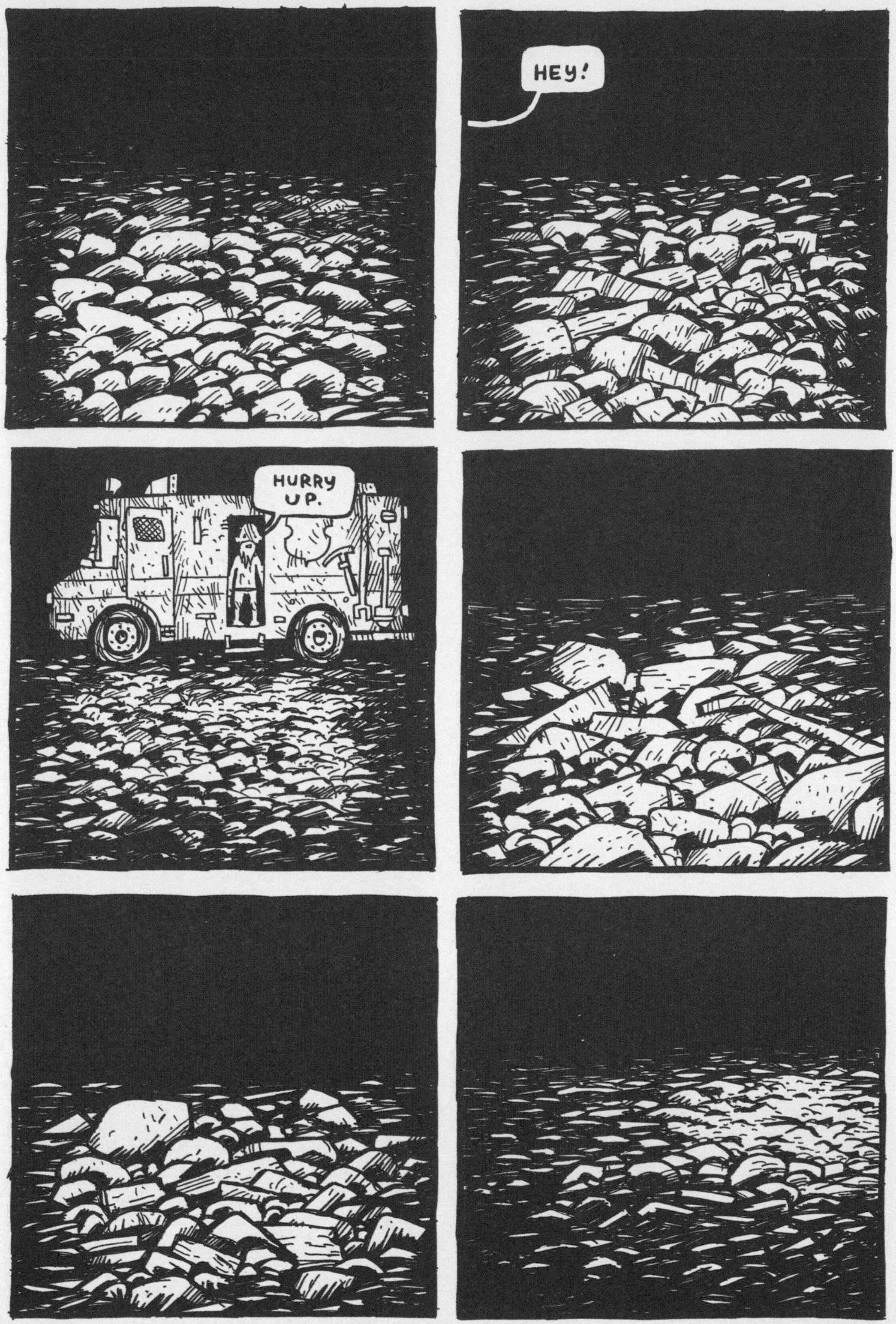
HEY!
HURRY UP.

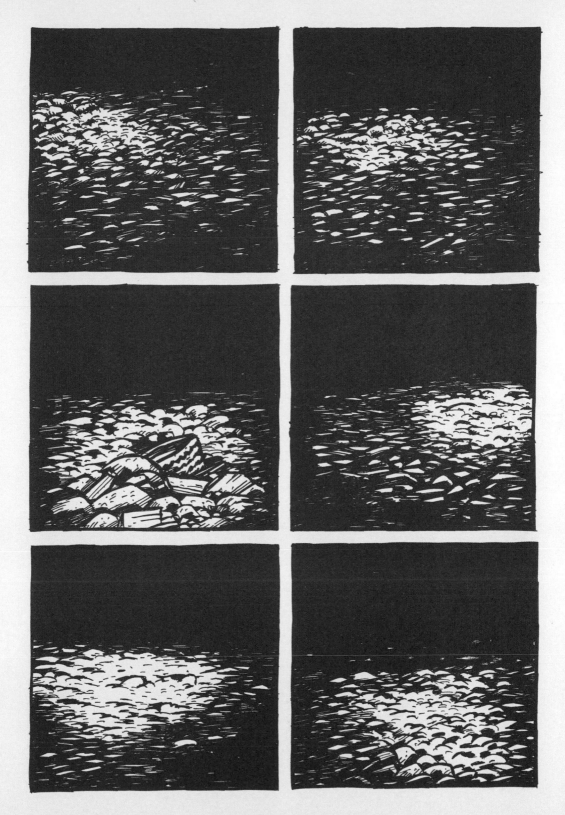

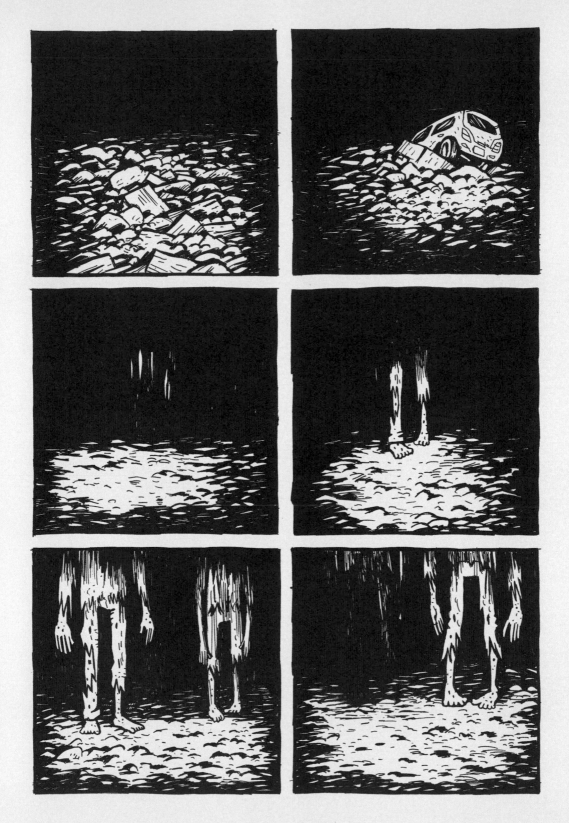

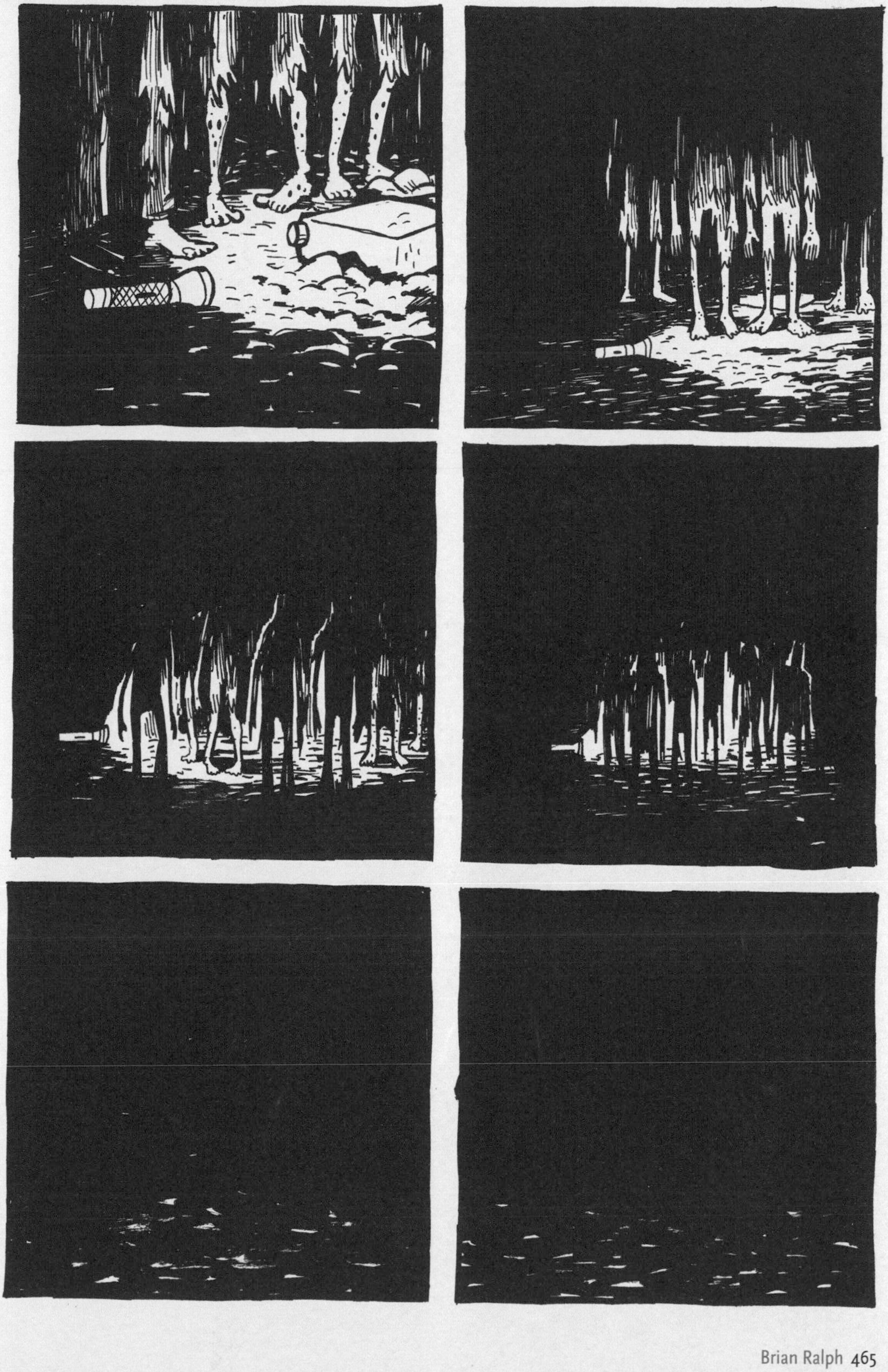

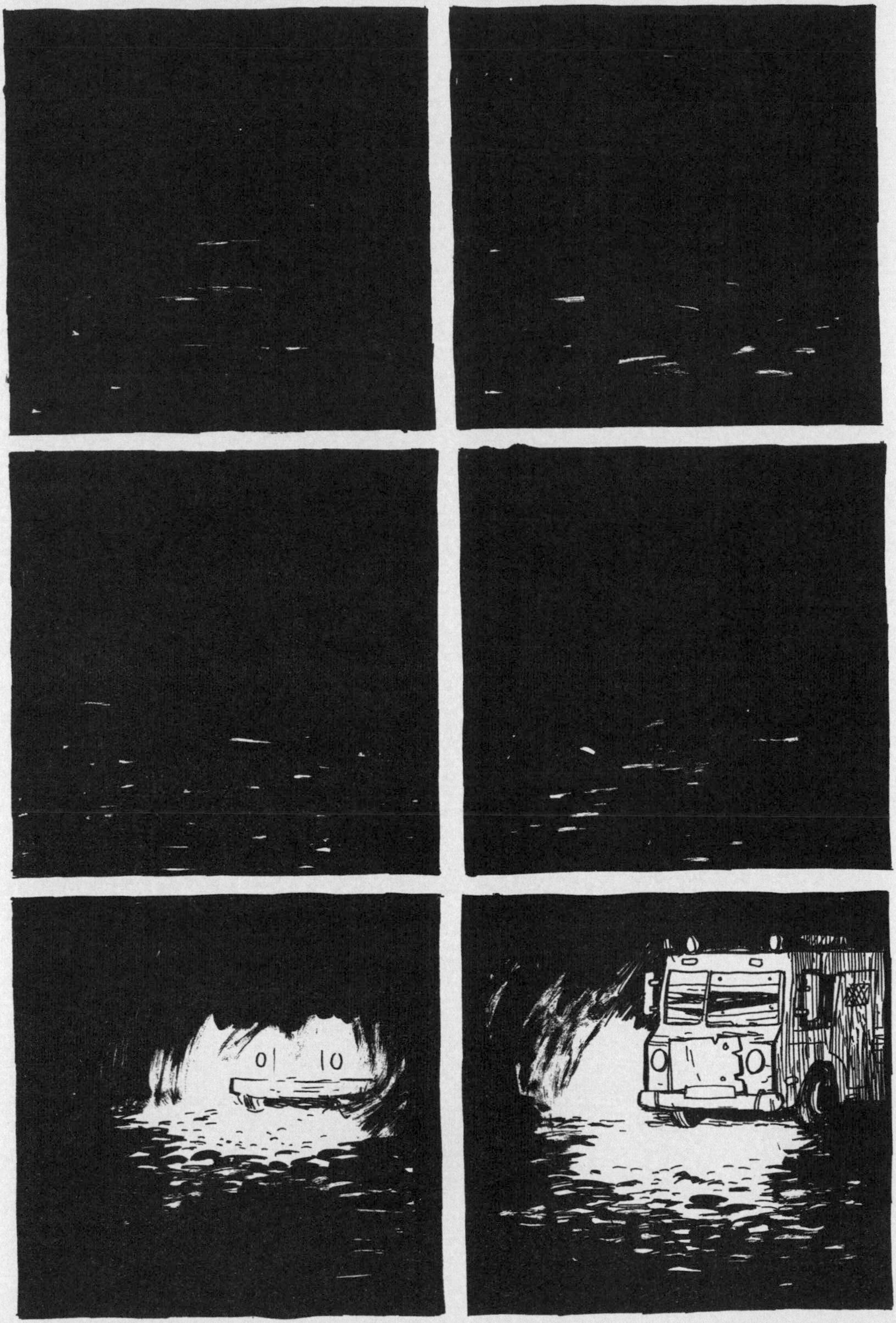

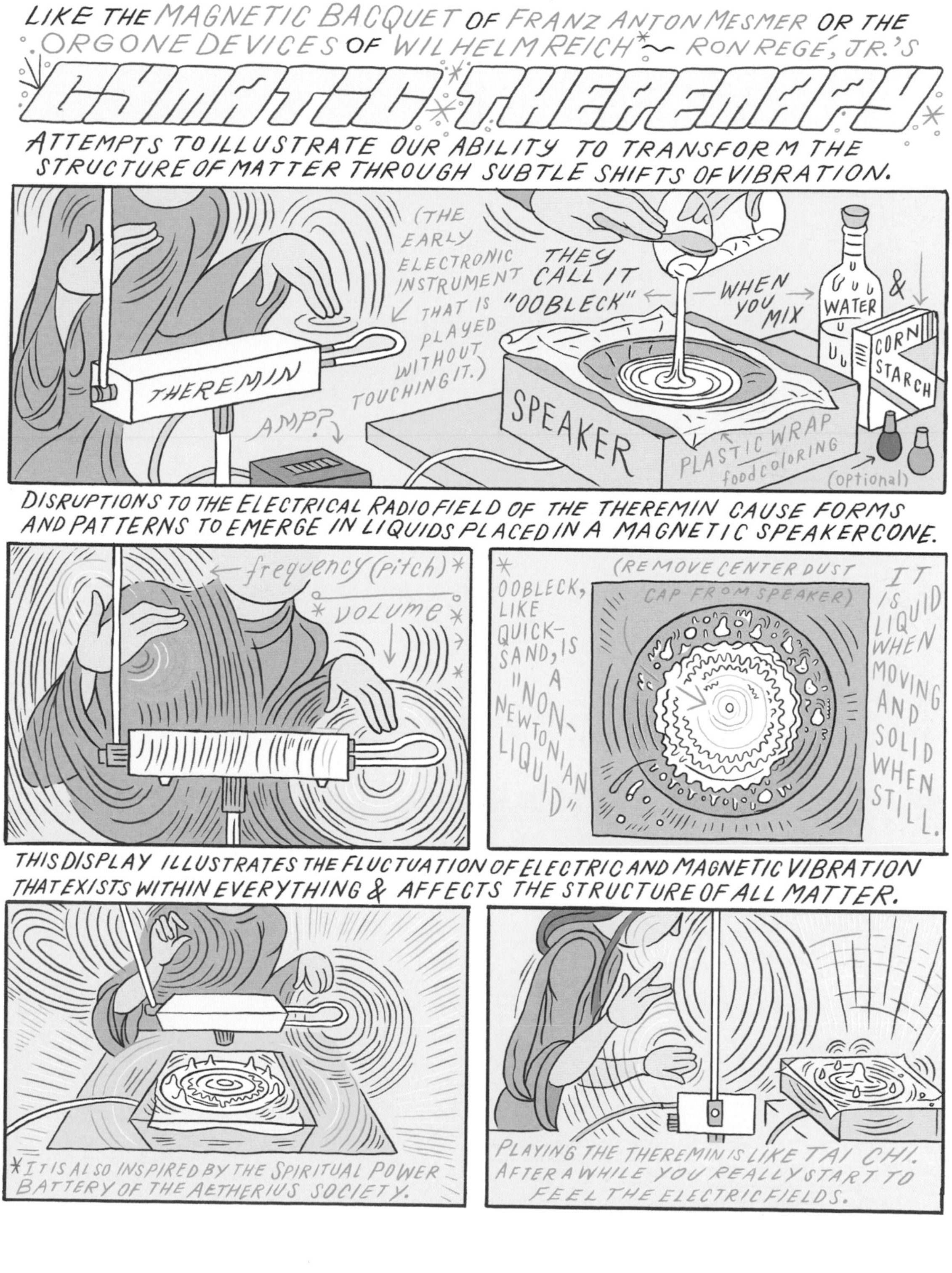
LIKE THE MAGNETIC BACQUET OF FRANZ ANTON MESMER OR THE ORGONE DEVICES OF WILHELM REICH* ~ RON REGÉ, JR.'S
CYMATIC THEREMAPY
ATTEMPTS TO ILLUSTRATE OUR ABILITY TO TRANSFORM THE STRUCTURE OF MATTER THROUGH SUBTLE SHIFTS OF VIBRATION.
(THE EARLY ELECTRONIC INSTRUMENT THAT IS PLAYED WITHOUT TOUCHING IT.)
THEREMIN
AMP?
THEY CALL IT "OOBLECK" WHEN YOU MIX
WATER
&
CORN STARCH
SPEAKER
PLASTIC WRAP
food coloring
(optional)
DISRUPTIONS TO THE ELECTRICAL RADIO FIELD OF THE THEREMIN CAUSE FORMS AND PATTERNS TO EMERGE IN LIQUIDS PLACED IN A MAGNETIC SPEAKER CONE.
frequency (pitch)
volume
OOBLECK, LIKE QUICK-SAND, IS A "NON-NEWTONIAN LIQUID"
(REMOVE CENTER DUST CAP FROM SPEAKER)
IT IS LIQUID WHEN MOVING AND SOLID WHEN STILL.
THIS DISPLAY ILLUSTRATES THE FLUCTUATION OF ELECTRIC AND MAGNETIC VIBRATION THAT EXISTS WITHIN EVERYTHING & AFFECTS THE STRUCTURE OF ALL MATTER.
*IT IS ALSO INSPIRED BY THE SPIRITUAL POWER BATTERY OF THE AETHERIUS SOCIETY.
PLAYING THE THEREMIN IS LIKE TAI CHI. AFTER A WHILE YOU REALLY START TO FEEL THE ELECTRIC FIELDS.

"Cymatic Theremapy" first appeared in *Pitchfork Review* no. 3 (summer 2014). Ron Regé, Jr.

THE MYSTERIOUS CONTENTS OF OUR OWN THOUGHTS & EMOTIONS OPERATE ON THESE SAME PRINCIPLES OF FLUCTUATING VIBRATION.

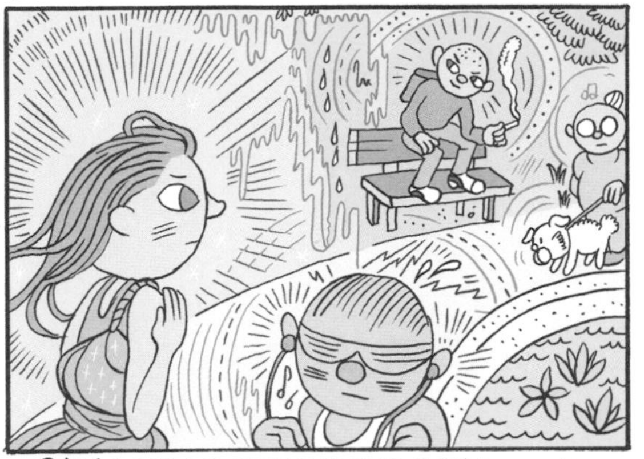

LIKE THE SHIFTING CYMATIC PATTERNS IN A DROP OF WATER, OUR MINDS BOTH CREATE & ARE AFFECTED BY THE VIBRATIONS SURROUNDING US.

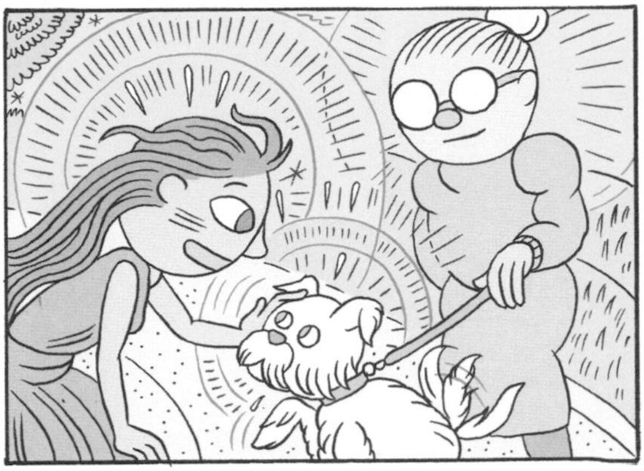

CYMATIC THEREMAPY IS A VISUAL REMINDER THAT OUR EXISTENCE IS NOT LIKE A SHIP CAST OUT ON A SEA OF STATIC. OUR MINDS POSSESS THE ABILITY TO CREATE AND TRANSFORM INFINITE VARIATIONS OF VIBRATING FORMS.

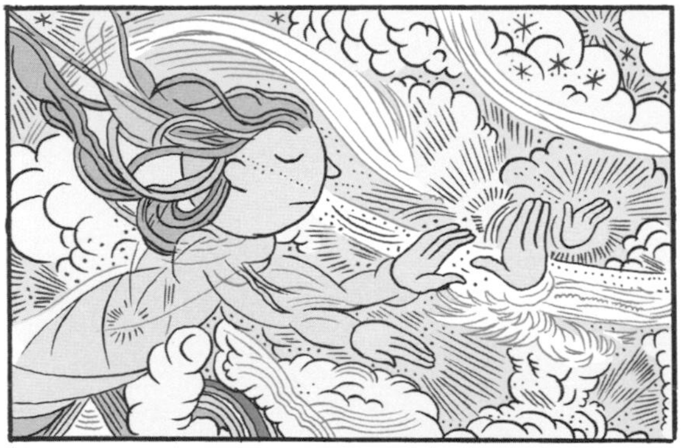

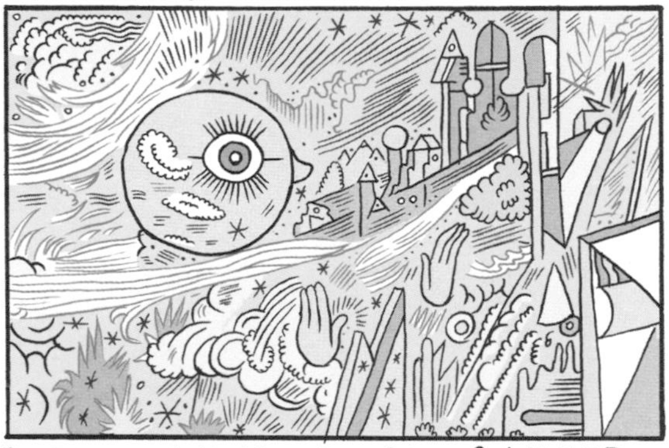

THE STRUCTURE OF ALL MATTER ON EARTH, OUR FLOATING SPECK OF DUST & WATER, CAN BE TRANSFORMED INSTANTLY BY THE SLIGHTEST SHIFT OF VIBRATION.

~ ALL CONSCIOUSNESS IS UNIFIED IN THIS CREATION ~

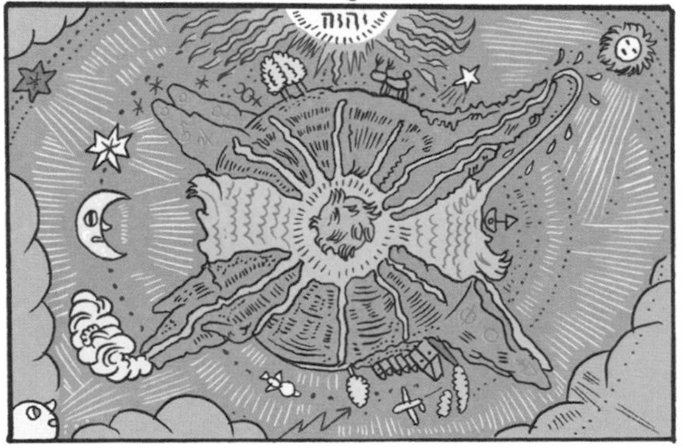

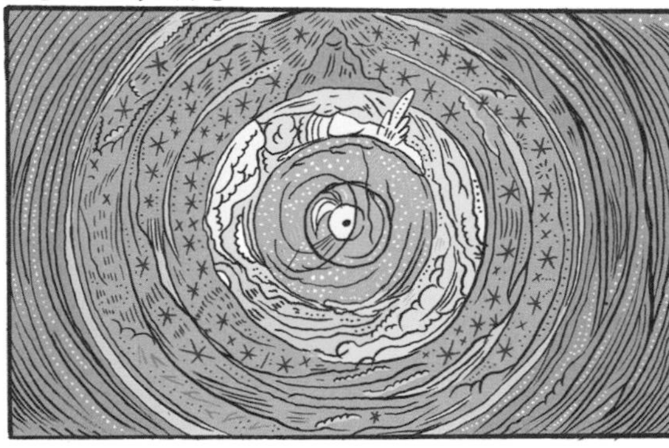

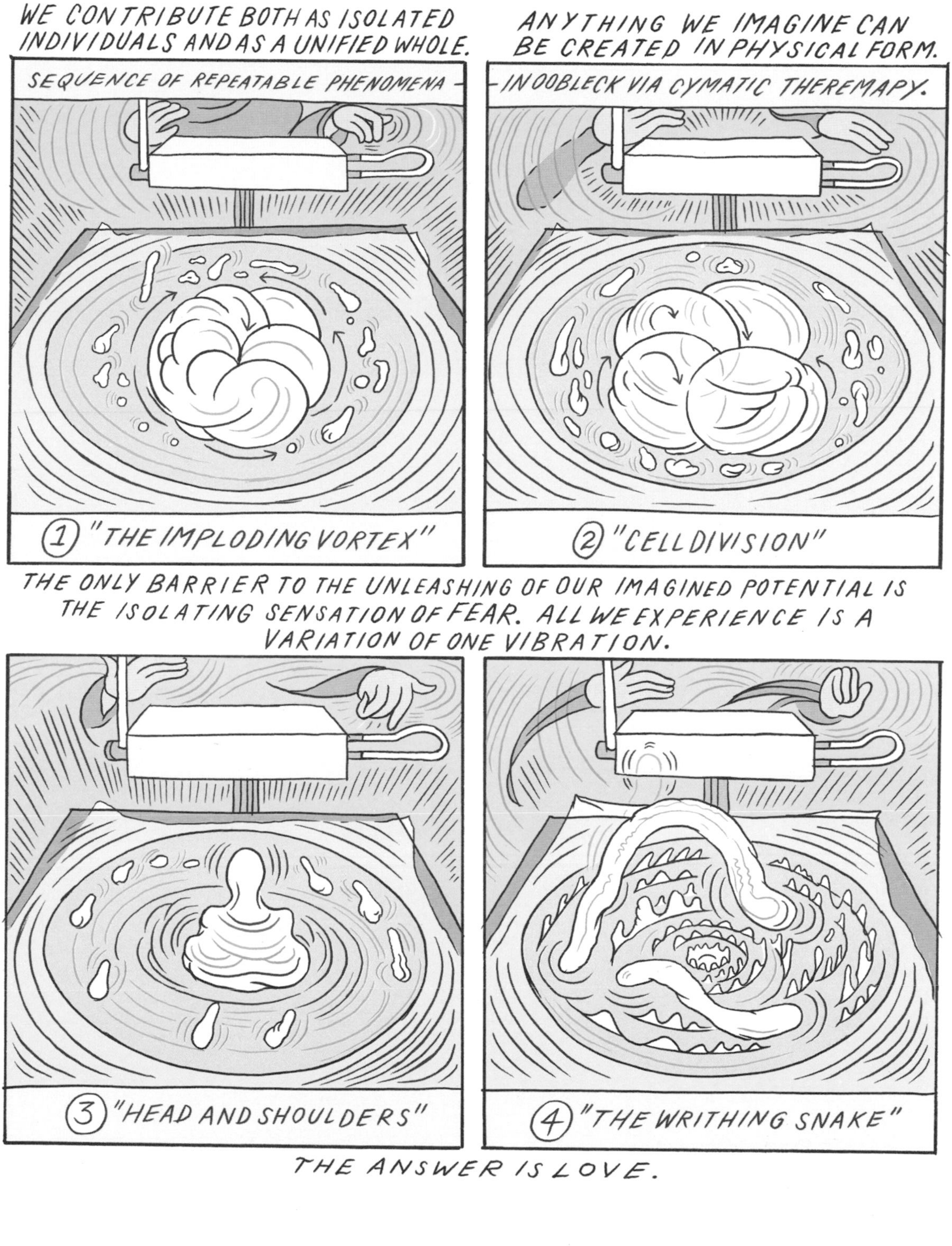
WE CONTRIBUTE BOTH AS ISOLATED INDIVIDUALS AND AS A UNIFIED WHOLE.
SEQUENCE OF REPEATABLE PHENOMENA -
① "THE IMPLODING VORTEX"
ANYTHING WE IMAGINE CAN BE CREATED IN PHYSICAL FORM.
- IN OOBLECK VIA CYMATIC THEREMAPY.
② "CELL DIVISION"
THE ONLY BARRIER TO THE UNLEASHING OF OUR IMAGINED POTENTIAL IS THE ISOLATING SENSATION OF FEAR. ALL WE EXPERIENCE IS A VARIATION OF ONE VIBRATION.
③ "HEAD AND SHOULDERS"
④ "THE WRITHING SNAKE"
THE ANSWER IS LOVE.

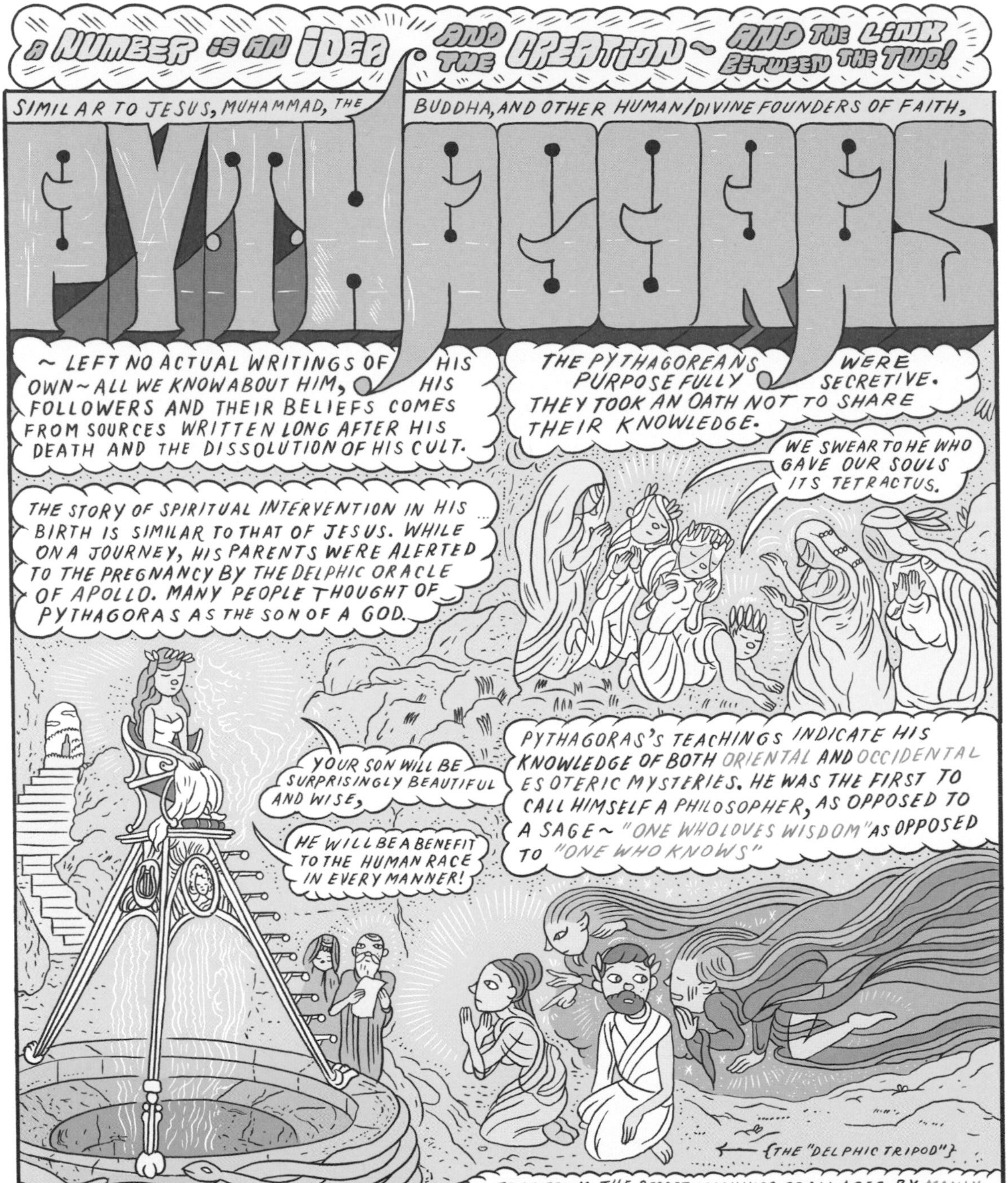
A NUMBER IS AN IDEA AND THE CREATION ~ AND THE LINK BETWEEN THE TWO!
SIMILAR TO JESUS, MUHAMMAD, THE BUDDHA, AND OTHER HUMAN/DIVINE FOUNDERS OF FAITH,
PYTHAGORAS
~ LEFT NO ACTUAL WRITINGS OF HIS OWN ~ ALL WE KNOW ABOUT HIM, HIS FOLLOWERS AND THEIR BELIEFS COMES FROM SOURCES WRITTEN LONG AFTER HIS DEATH AND THE DISSOLUTION OF HIS CULT.
THE PYTHAGOREANS WERE PURPOSEFULLY SECRETIVE. THEY TOOK AN OATH NOT TO SHARE THEIR KNOWLEDGE.
WE SWEAR TO HE WHO GAVE OUR SOULS ITS TETRACTUS.
THE STORY OF SPIRITUAL INTERVENTION IN HIS BIRTH IS SIMILAR TO THAT OF JESUS. WHILE ON A JOURNEY, HIS PARENTS WERE ALERTED TO THE PREGNANCY BY THE DELPHIC ORACLE OF APOLLO. MANY PEOPLE THOUGHT OF PYTHAGORAS AS THE SON OF A GOD.
YOUR SON WILL BE SURPRISINGLY BEAUTIFUL AND WISE,
HE WILL BE A BENEFIT TO THE HUMAN RACE IN EVERY MANNER!
PYTHAGORAS'S TEACHINGS INDICATE HIS KNOWLEDGE OF BOTH ORIENTAL AND OCCIDENTAL ESOTERIC MYSTERIES. HE WAS THE FIRST TO CALL HIMSELF A PHILOSOPHER, AS OPPOSED TO A SAGE ~ "ONE WHO LOVES WISDOM" AS OPPOSED TO "ONE WHO KNOWS"
← {THE "DELPHIC TRIPOD"}
TEXT FROM THE SECRET TEACHINGS OF ALL AGES BY MANLY P. HALL & THE MUSIC OF PYTHAGORAS BY KITTY FERGUSON. DRAWN BY RON REGÉ, JR. IN ECHO PARK 4 - OCTOBER 2013

 "Pythagoras" first appeared in *Pitchfork Review* no. 1 (winter 2014).

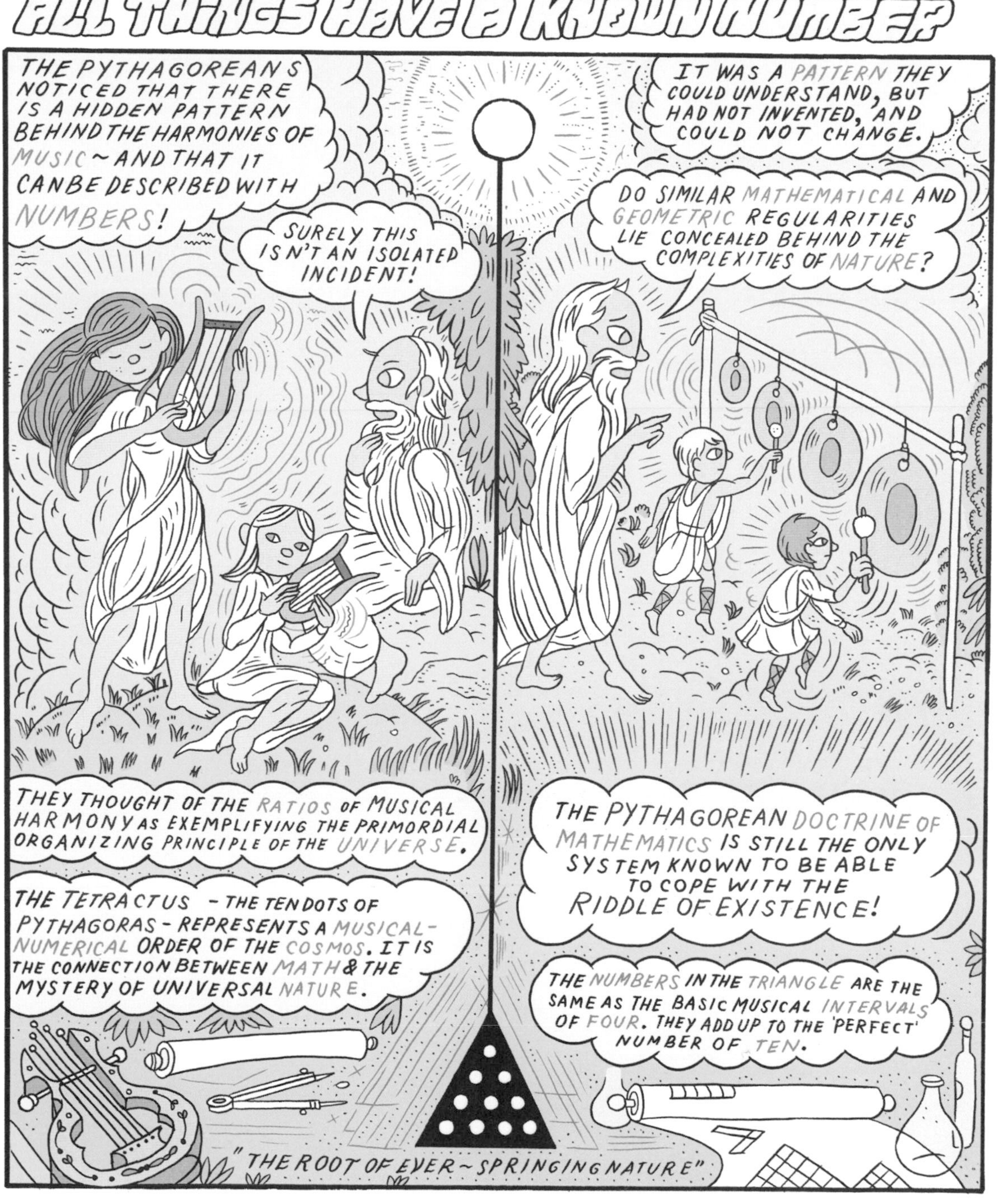
ALL THINGS HAVE A KNOWN NUMBER
THE PYTHAGOREANS NOTICED THAT THERE IS A HIDDEN PATTERN BEHIND THE HARMONIES OF MUSIC ~ AND THAT IT CANBE DESCRIBED WITH NUMBERS!
SURELY THIS ISN'T AN ISOLATED INCIDENT!
IT WAS A PATTERN THEY COULD UNDERSTAND, BUT HAD NOT INVENTED, AND COULD NOT CHANGE.
DO SIMILAR MATHEMATICAL AND GEOMETRIC REGULARITIES LIE CONCEALED BEHIND THE COMPLEXITIES OF NATURE?
THEY THOUGHT OF THE RATIOS OF MUSICAL HARMONY AS EXEMPLIFYING THE PRIMORDIAL ORGANIZING PRINCIPLE OF THE UNIVERSE.
THE TETRACTUS - THE TEN DOTS OF PYTHAGORAS - REPRESENTS A MUSICAL-NUMERICAL ORDER OF THE COSMOS. IT IS THE CONNECTION BETWEEN MATH & THE MYSTERY OF UNIVERSAL NATURE.
THE PYTHAGOREAN DOCTRINE OF MATHEMATICS IS STILL THE ONLY SYSTEM KNOWN TO BE ABLE TO COPE WITH THE RIDDLE OF EXISTENCE!
THE NUMBERS IN THE TRIANGLE ARE THE SAME AS THE BASIC MUSICAL INTERVALS OF FOUR. THEY ADD UP TO THE 'PERFECT' NUMBER OF TEN.
"THE ROOT OF EVER ~ SPRINGING NATURE"

THE MUNDANE MONOCHORD

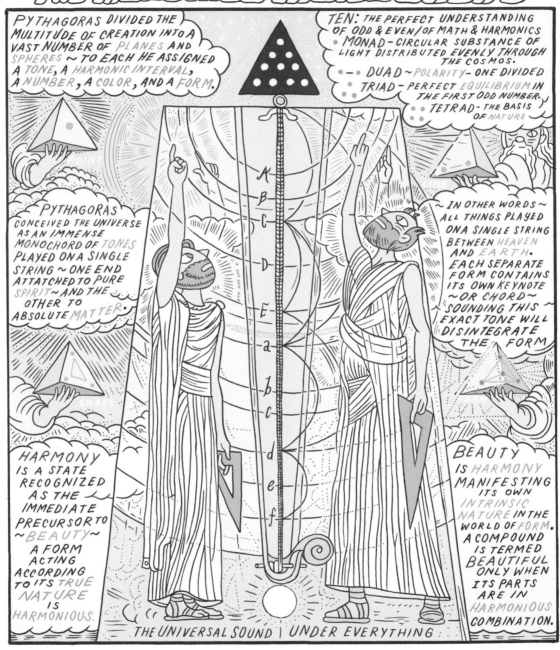

PYTHAGORAS DIVIDED THE MULTITUDE OF CREATION INTO A VAST NUMBER OF *PLANES* AND *SPHERES* ~ TO EACH HE ASSIGNED A TONE, A *HARMONIC INTERVAL*, A *NUMBER*, A *COLOR*, AND A *FORM*.

TEN: THE PERFECT UNDERSTANDING OF ODD & EVEN / OF MATH & HARMONICS
MONAD — CIRCULAR SUBSTANCE OF LIGHT DISTRIBUTED EVENLY THROUGH THE COSMOS.
DUAD ~ *POLARITY* — ONE DIVIDED
TRIAD — PERFECT *EQUILIBRIUM* IN THE FIRST ODD NUMBER.
TETRAD — THE BASIS OF *NATURE*

POINT

LINE

PYTHAGORAS CONCEIVED THE UNIVERSE AS AN IMMENSE MONOCHORD OF *TONES* PLAYED ON A SINGLE STRING ~ ONE END ATTACHED TO PURE *SPIRIT* ~ AND THE OTHER TO ABSOLUTE *MATTER*.

~ IN OTHER WORDS ~ ALL THINGS PLAYED ON A SINGLE STRING BETWEEN *HEAVEN* AND *EARTH*. EACH SEPARATE FORM CONTAINS ITS OWN KEYNOTE ~ OR CHORD ~ SOUNDING THIS EXACT TONE WILL DISINTEGRATE THE FORM

SHAPE

FORM

A
B
C
D
E
a
b
c
d
e
f

HARMONY IS A STATE RECOGNIZED AS THE IMMEDIATE PRECURSOR TO ~ *BEAUTY* ~ A FORM ACTING ACCORDING TO ITS TRUE *NATURE* IS *HARMONIOUS*.

BEAUTY IS *HARMONY* MANIFESTING ITS OWN *INTRINSIC NATURE* IN THE WORLD OF *FORM*. A COMPOUND IS TERMED BEAUTIFUL ONLY WHEN ITS PARTS ARE IN *HARMONIOUS* COMBINATION.

THE UNIVERSAL SOUND | UNDER EVERYTHING

SO FAR OUT, YOU CAN'T EVEN SEE HOW HE GOT THERE

an appreciation of Marc Bell by Lee Henderson

Marc Bell's work has problems. For one, he is Canada's preeminent experimental comics artist, and for two, his twenty-five-year career in comics is notable for a commitment to drawing at the farthest reaches of cartoon potentiality. Bell toils in weird oceans of doodle and goes deep below the surface of the mainstream understanding of *comics*. Another problem: the paradox of seeking out and depicting obscurities. Few artists have swum farther out or for as long as Marc Bell has into these treacherous waters of pure cartooning. He's a deep-sea diver with an eye for the uncategorizable, and the result is that his works are peerless. That's a problem. For as much as artists like Chris Ware helped raise indie comics up into the mainstream in the nineties, Marc Bell seemed determined to rally for the continuation of the eternal ghettoization of comix—to exaggerate the differences between comix and literature, or contemporary art for that matter. Bell is all for comix's scuzzy underground appeal and not so much into this brand of wholesome literary oomph.

Bell was self-schooled in the laissez-faire anarchism of Fleischer Studios cartoons and the underground comix of the 1960s and '70s, and his ambitious efforts to set new horizons beyond these groundbreaking works has meant, as a result, there is something *sui generis* about his style. Despite all their embedded knowledge, his comics remind us there have never been limits to the form, and there shouldn't need to be any constraints. His approach might be dazzling, but he makes it look so tempting to try to explore these ultrathin dimensions between the personal subconscious and the encyclopedic pastiche. Well, if not tempting, at least accessible. Proper exploration of this zone takes years—some artists never dare to go, and some artists never come home. Bell's most straightforward comics are his most infrequent. He takes shore leaves back to realism and autobiography but for the most part sticks it out in the choppy seas of bottomless absurdity. His free-associative masterpieces tear up the maps of traditional comics and do something entirely uncharted.

Although his subject matter almost never gets as taboo as things got in the sixties and seventies, Bell's anything-goes style takes its earliest cues from the most far-out references. The gonzo imagery in *Illusztraijuns For Brain Police* and *Pure Pajamas* takes the freewheeling comics Robert Crumb printed in *Zap* and the illustrations Saul Steinberg made for the *New Yorker* and mixes them with frequent references to fine art stuff like the existential reductions of cartoon self-portraits in Philip Guston's late paintings. There was never a traditional Marc Bell—his comic style began like this in the 1990s. He never hesitates to introduce an animated inanimate object, a walking hot dog or talking shoes, like those teapots that rollick in old Disney skits. Bell renders it all with the scuzzy downtown noise of a heavy cross-hatcher like Julie Doucet. His book *The Stacks* compiles many of his paintings alongside some of his most poignant and strange short comics. There's a touch of George Dunning in there; Kaz, Kim Deitch, and Spain Rodriguez, too.

Marc Bell's stories seem to be the result of hours and hours of improvisational doodling that he's slowly and meticulously trying to make coherent for the rest of us. It's not a bad thing that most cartoonists stick to the calmer shores of style and are content to make sandcastles with the basic bric-a-brac of storytelling. Many great books are made this way. Not Marc Bell's, though. He's way out, so far out sometimes you can't even see how he got there. This is what's exciting about his books and it's what has made his work relevant for over two decades. He's constantly stretching our conception of comics.

Born in 1971, Bell started to publish comics in the early 1990s. Before the internet forever changed the access cartoonists had to their audience and peers, before widespread email, Bell was sharing minicomics through the mail with Jason McLean, John Porcellino, the Royal Art Lodge, Mark Connery, Peter Thompson, and other artists. During the nineties, Bell bounced around Canada from one coast to the other, living on the cheap in London, Vancouver, Montreal, Sackville, and elsewhere as he self-published books; showed single pieces of art; made gig posters and album covers for real bands and for his own non-existent rock trio, the All-Star Schnauzer Band (with McLean and Thompson); and provided regular contribu-

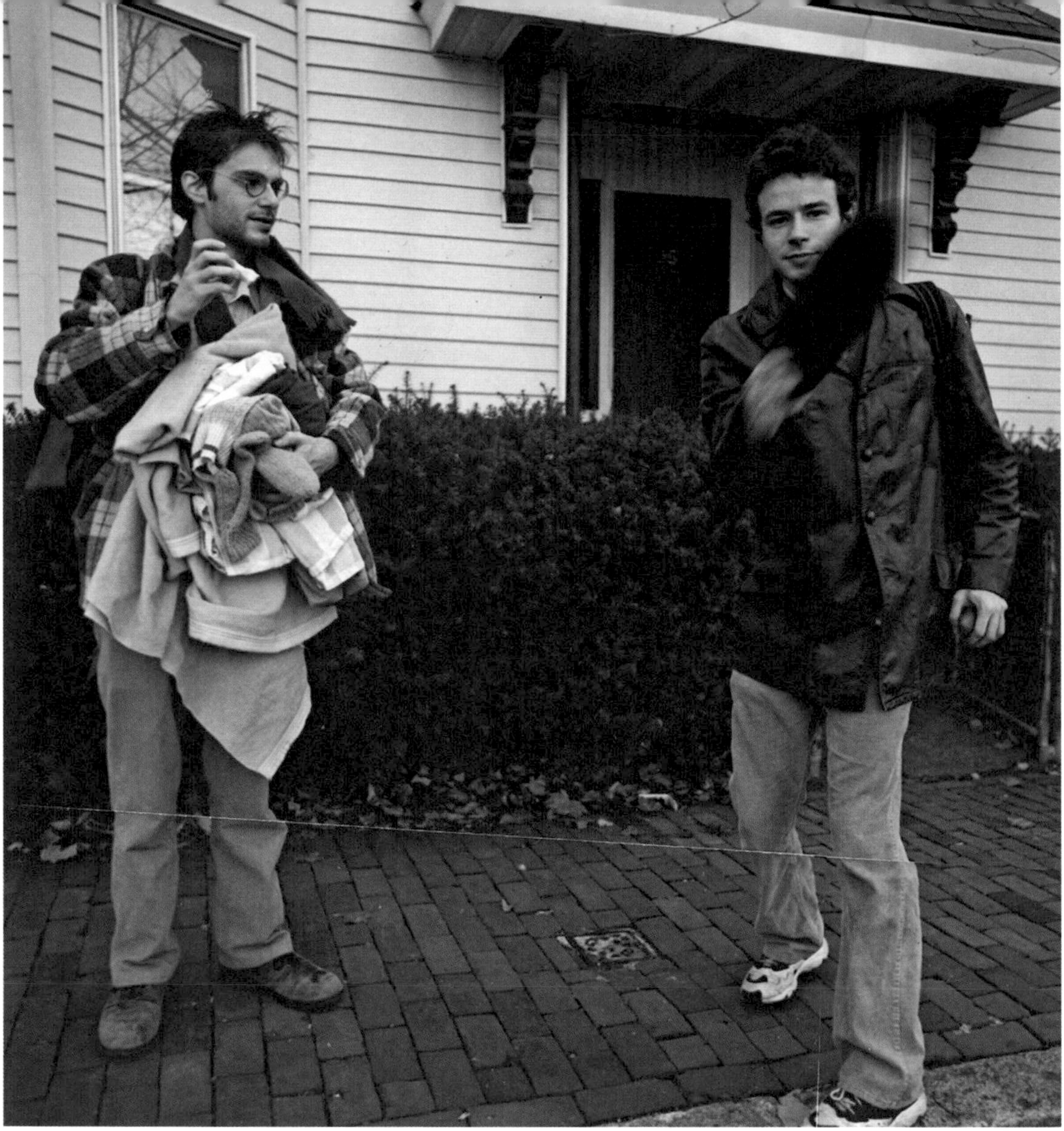

tions to the comic pages of the free newspapers *Terminal City* and *Exclaim!* Some of his most iconic work appeared in the earliest issues of *Vice* magazine.

Bell's characters Shrimpy and Paul first showed up in these periodicals. Paul is a what? He's a hot-dog-shaped man with highly visible nipples, more like rubber pacifier nipples than those of a man or woman. Shrimpy is his best friend, or accidental adversary, always dressed in a onesie like a baby. They live in a world *not* like our own, a world more like Toontown from *Who Framed Roger Rabbit*—overpopulated with rascally animated inanimate objects like talking tables, teeth, and baloney. Someone *lives* inside Paul's nipples. No matter how tweaked the world of Belltropolis is, though, Shrimpy and Paul are instantly familiar as a classic comedy duo. In the grand old tradition of vaudeville skits, of Don Quixote and Sancho Panza and of Rosencrantz and Guildenstern, Shrimpy and Paul act as foils for each other's frolicsome hijinks and provide some anchor in this antigravity Dr. Seuss-y universe.

In the nineties, Bell made hundreds of drawings and comics in which recurring motifs included strips of bacon, hobnail shoes, Pac-Man eyes, perky nipples, lots of waffles, everyone in kid gloves, and a brick snake with the Canada Council for the Arts logo for a face. He dedicated himself not to cool conceptual objects for galleries but to cheap zines for friends and humour comix for the alternative newspapers.

 Marc Bell & Ron Regé, Jr., in front of Ron's apartment in Cambridge, MA, on Marc's birthday. Photo: Neil Rough (1997).

And he frequently collaborated with other artists like Jason McLean, Shayne Ehman, and Peter Thompson. Out of this period came such an abundance of unclassifiable work that Bell was convinced to edit an anthology of the art from this era. The anthology, called *Nog a Dod*, a nonsense word combination that McLean made up, contains examples of Bell's comics as well as many of his early forays into the kind of abstract work seen in *Hot Potatoe*. There's Amy Lockhart paintings and formative drawings by Jeff Ladouceur in there along with many, many others. *Nog a Dod* is analog to a book like *Ask the Dust* by the Royal Art Lodge or to an issue of *Kramers Ergot* full of Fort Thunder artwork—there's inspiring art, and evidence of a highly productive time for a group of like minds. By the time Bell's work began to appear in the now-famous avant-comix anthologies *Ganzfeld* and *Kramers Ergot*, his panels were entirely replaced by rivers of white space between doodle structures of startling detail and complexity. These delicate and impressive drawings signalled a shift that was happening in Bell's work in the 2000s away from the sequential, into a series of stand-alone works that connected to a new alternative comix scene that defenestrated coherence and pathos and bum-rushed art gallery walls with noisy cartoon abstractions.

Bell is one of those artists whose creative independence has given them funny accents, and he tells his stories using an eccentric form of English. It takes foreigners to Bellville a few pages to get used to his way with the language. And rather than simply helping to move the story along, Bell's language seeps into and influences the imagery—the words bend and recast the reality around them. Silly wordplay, subliminal combinations of puns, and a thematic subtext run through his work. Krazy Kat–like misspellings abound; oblique homages are frequent; sentence fragments appear here and there, as do semi-slogans, aphorisms, bits of poetry. One is not subservient to the other—each part of his comic exerts its own will, image, and text. Word games impact the content. It is as if the definitions got all mixed up in Marc Bell's mental dictionary so they no longer match the words. His pages are filled with an entirely different universe of signs and symbols that are all familiar, but not in this context. His language games pick up where George Herriman and E.C. Segar left off. A kinship might also be found in the stories of Gertrude Stein and Ben Marcus, whose preference in prose is to distort and deform the world at the mercy of language. Bell might rather base a landscape on a pun than a place. No logic, no censor, no idea what's next, just letting his hand wander across the page to follow patterns that come and go in the mind's eye, then polishing that doodle until it's flawless.

That's the look of the work collected in *Hot Potatoe*, a book of the dazzling artwork Bell made in the 2000s that will scramble the eggs of your mind.

Looking at Bell's assemblage pieces, I think as readily of Golden Age comics and underground comix as I do the fine arts from the same periods, of Joan Miró and Kurt Schwitters, of Braque, Picasso, Hannah Höch, and, from later on in the century, the work of Ray Johnson and Richard Tuttle. I'm thinking of the uncompromising music and creative ethos of Miles Davis and John Coltrane, the music and aesthetic of the Silver Jews, Pavement, John Zorn, and Yamatsuka Eye. Not only are there all these deeply embedded references to the history of comics in his pictures, but cultural references of all kinds abound; they come out intuitively and seemingly without effort thanks to Bell's lifetime of studies in esoterica. Can a sculpture be a comic? Yes, for Marc Bell has made it so. His art tackles problems like this, how to turn a comic into something else, and something else into a comic.

By design there is a lot of noise in Bell's art: line work and words cover the page so densely sometimes, the eye can't contain it all in one gulp. Even the stand-alone artworks require a slow read like his sequential comics. But it's not a quiet immersion. The experience is more like plunging into *Finnegans Wake* or the Nihilist Spasm Band at full volume—you just have to let yourself be numbed to the beautiful squall.

Today abstraction in comics is a busier pool, and no longer is Bell so alone in taking these absurdist non sequitur leaps of faith into the deep. His style is almost popular, almost mainstream. His commitment to a style on the very outer edges, far margins, and distant peripheries of the norm is ironic, too, because his drawings are always so rich with a history of the form. His drawings come from the interzones and the out-of-bounds, and he has helped make it safer to explore these depths and find an audience for it. He's helped open up twenty-first-century readers to new concepts for comics. When Dan Nadel interviewed Marc Bell for the *Comics Journal*, he asked, "Are you still interested in characters in your comics?" And Bell answered, "I don't know. See, I am still confused. Just like in the '90s. I do sort of appreciate things that are confused. I usually like work that has some problems."

Lee Henderson has published three books—the story collection The Broken Record Technique *and the novels* The Man Game *and* The Road Narrows As You Go. *His fiction and art writing regularly appears in the* Walrus *and* Border Crossings. *He is an associate professor at the University of Victoria writing department.*

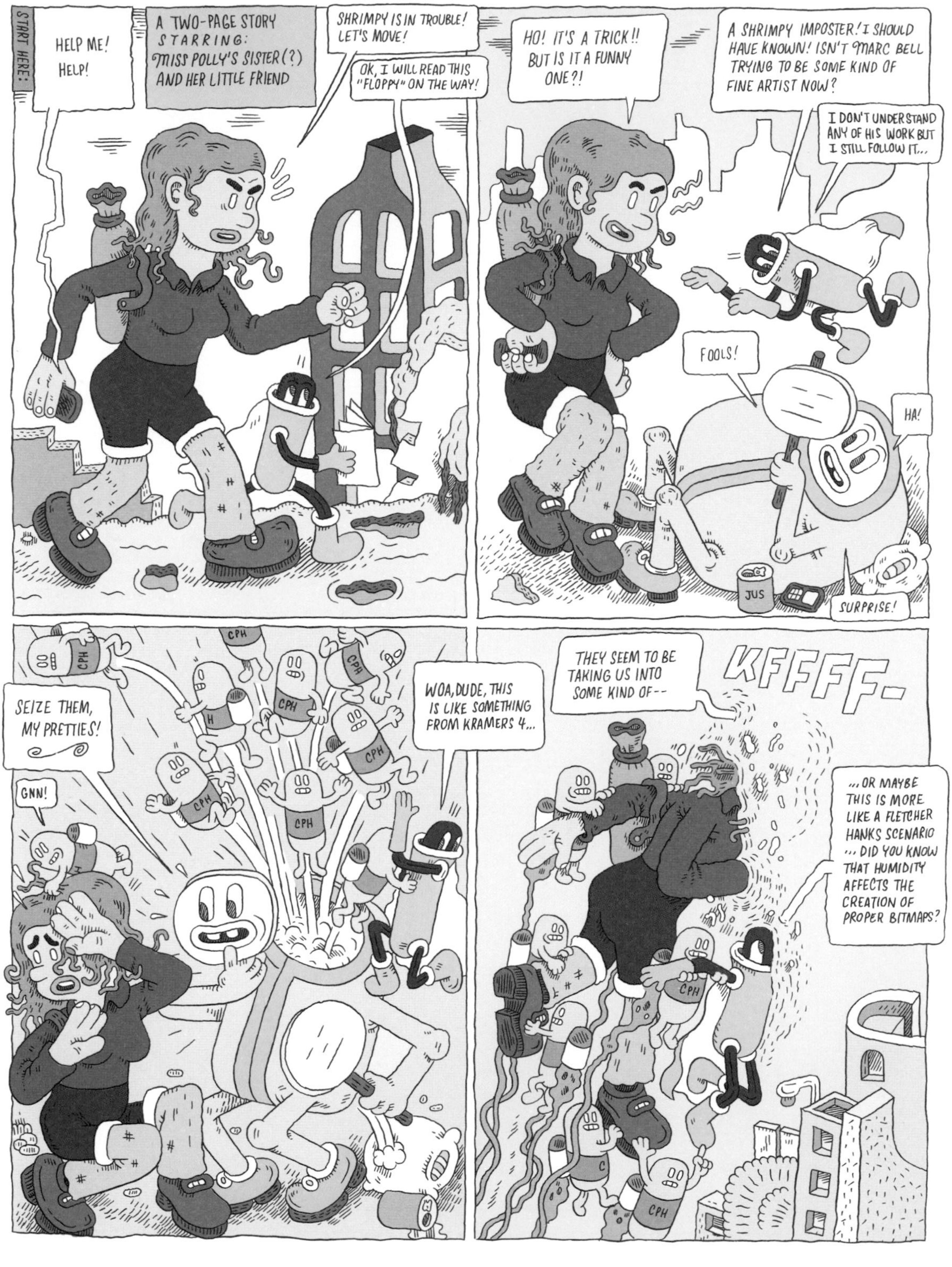
START HERE:
HELP ME! HELP!
A TWO-PAGE STORY STARRING: MISS POLLY'S SISTER (?) AND HER LITTLE FRIEND
SHRIMPY IS IN TROUBLE! LET'S MOVE!
OK, I WILL READ THIS "FLOPPY" ON THE WAY!
HO! IT'S A TRICK!! BUT IS IT A FUNNY ONE?!
A SHRIMPY IMPOSTER! I SHOULD HAVE KNOWN! ISN'T MARC BELL TRYING TO BE SOME KIND OF FINE ARTIST NOW?
I DON'T UNDERSTAND ANY OF HIS WORK BUT I STILL FOLLOW IT...
FOOLS!
HA!
JUS
SURPRISE!
SEIZE THEM, MY PRETTIES!
GNN!
WOA, DUDE, THIS IS LIKE SOMETHING FROM KRAMERS 4...
THEY SEEM TO BE TAKING US INTO SOME KIND OF--
KFFFFF-
...OR MAYBE THIS IS MORE LIKE A FLETCHER HANKS SCENARIO ... DID YOU KNOW THAT HUMIDITY AFFECTS THE CREATION OF PROPER BITMAPS?

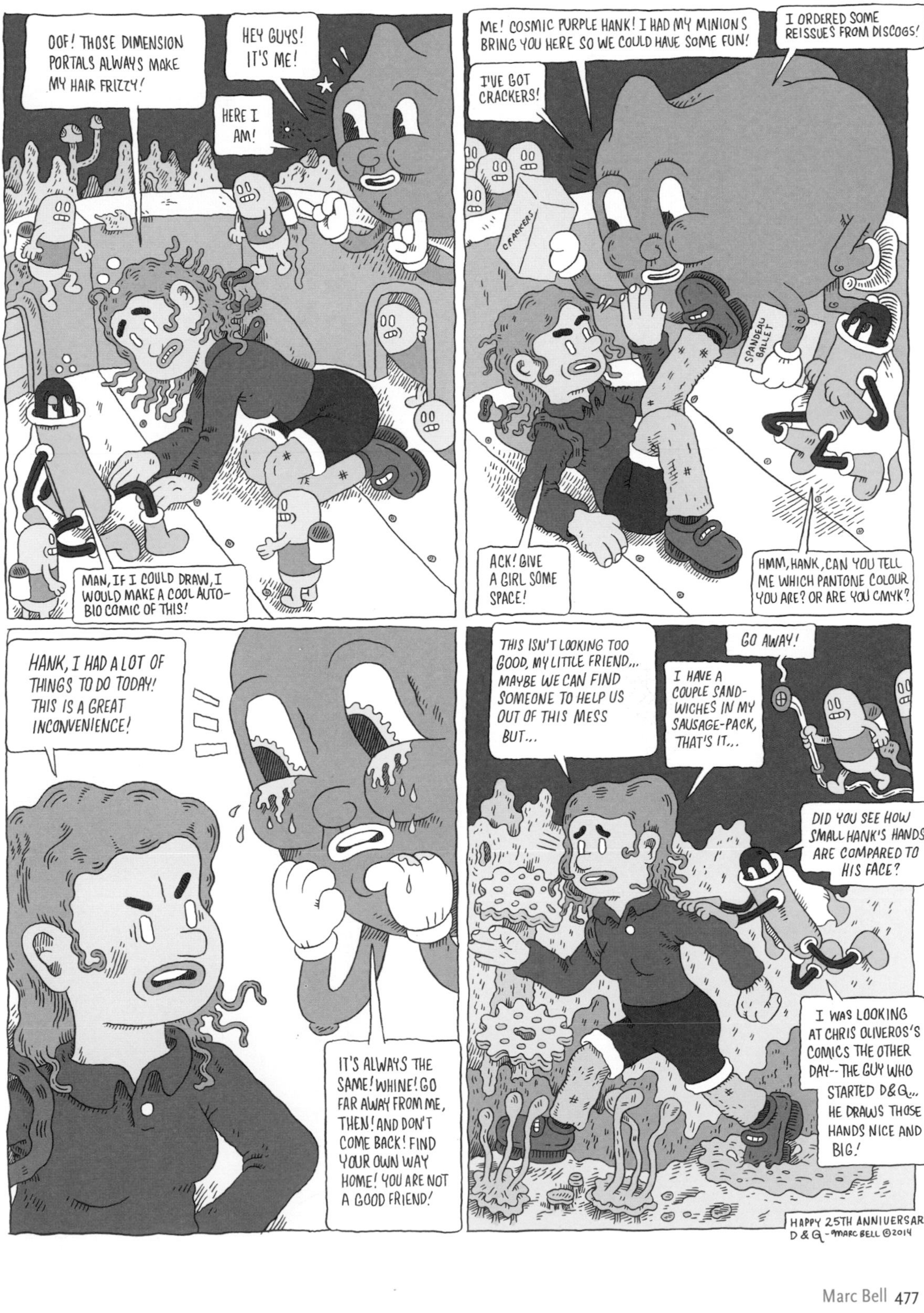
OOF! THOSE DIMENSION PORTALS ALWAYS MAKE MY HAIR FRIZZY!
HEY GUYS! IT'S ME!
HERE I AM!
MAN, IF I COULD DRAW, I WOULD MAKE A COOL AUTO-BIO COMIC OF THIS!
ME! COSMIC PURPLE HANK! I HAD MY MINIONS BRING YOU HERE SO WE COULD HAVE SOME FUN!
I ORDERED SOME REISSUES FROM DISCOGS!
I'VE GOT CRACKERS!
CRACKERS
SPANDEAU BALLET
ACK! GIVE A GIRL SOME SPACE!
HMM, HANK, CAN YOU TELL ME WHICH PANTONE COLOUR YOU ARE? OR ARE YOU CMYK?
HANK, I HAD A LOT OF THINGS TO DO TODAY! THIS IS A GREAT INCONVENIENCE!
IT'S ALWAYS THE SAME! WHINE! GO FAR AWAY FROM ME, THEN! AND DON'T COME BACK! FIND YOUR OWN WAY HOME! YOU ARE NOT A GOOD FRIEND!
THIS ISN'T LOOKING TOO GOOD, MY LITTLE FRIEND... MAYBE WE CAN FIND SOMEONE TO HELP US OUT OF THIS MESS BUT...
GO AWAY!
I HAVE A COUPLE SAND-WICHES IN MY SAUSAGE-PACK, THAT'S IT...
DID YOU SEE HOW SMALL HANK'S HANDS ARE COMPARED TO HIS FACE?
I WAS LOOKING AT CHRIS OLIVEROS'S COMICS THE OTHER DAY--THE GUY WHO STARTED D&Q... HE DRAWS THOSE HANDS NICE AND BIG!
HAPPY 25TH ANNIVERSARY D&Q - MARC BELL ©2014

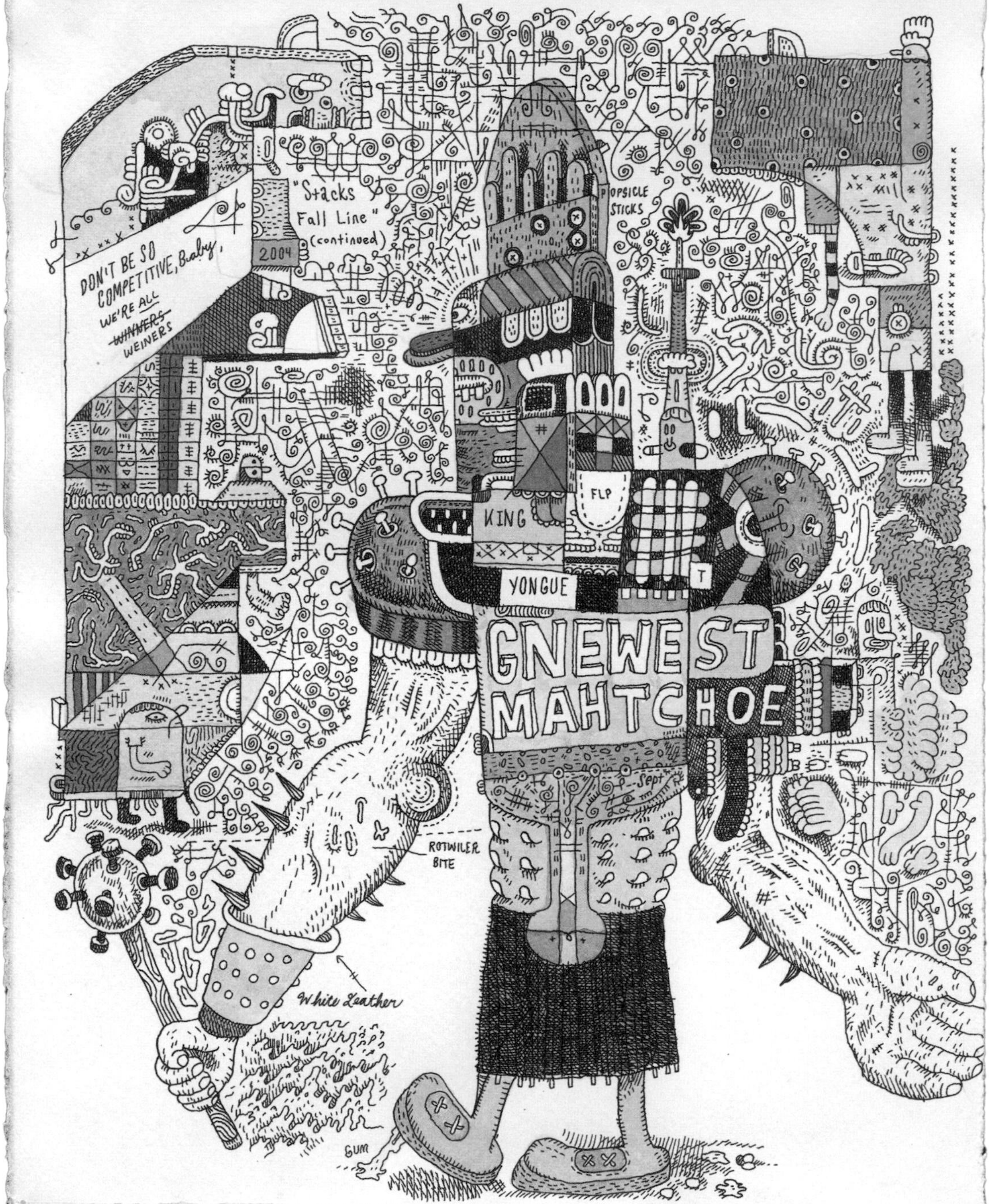
"Stacks
Fall Line"
(continued)
2004
DON'T BE SO
COMPETITIVE, Baby,
WE'RE ALL
WINNERS
WEINERS
POPSICLE
STICKS
KING
FLP
YONGUE
T
GNEWEST
MAHTCHOE
Sept
ROTWILER
BITE
White Leather
GUM

 "Gnewest Matchoe," 2004, first appeared in *Hot Potatoe* (2009).

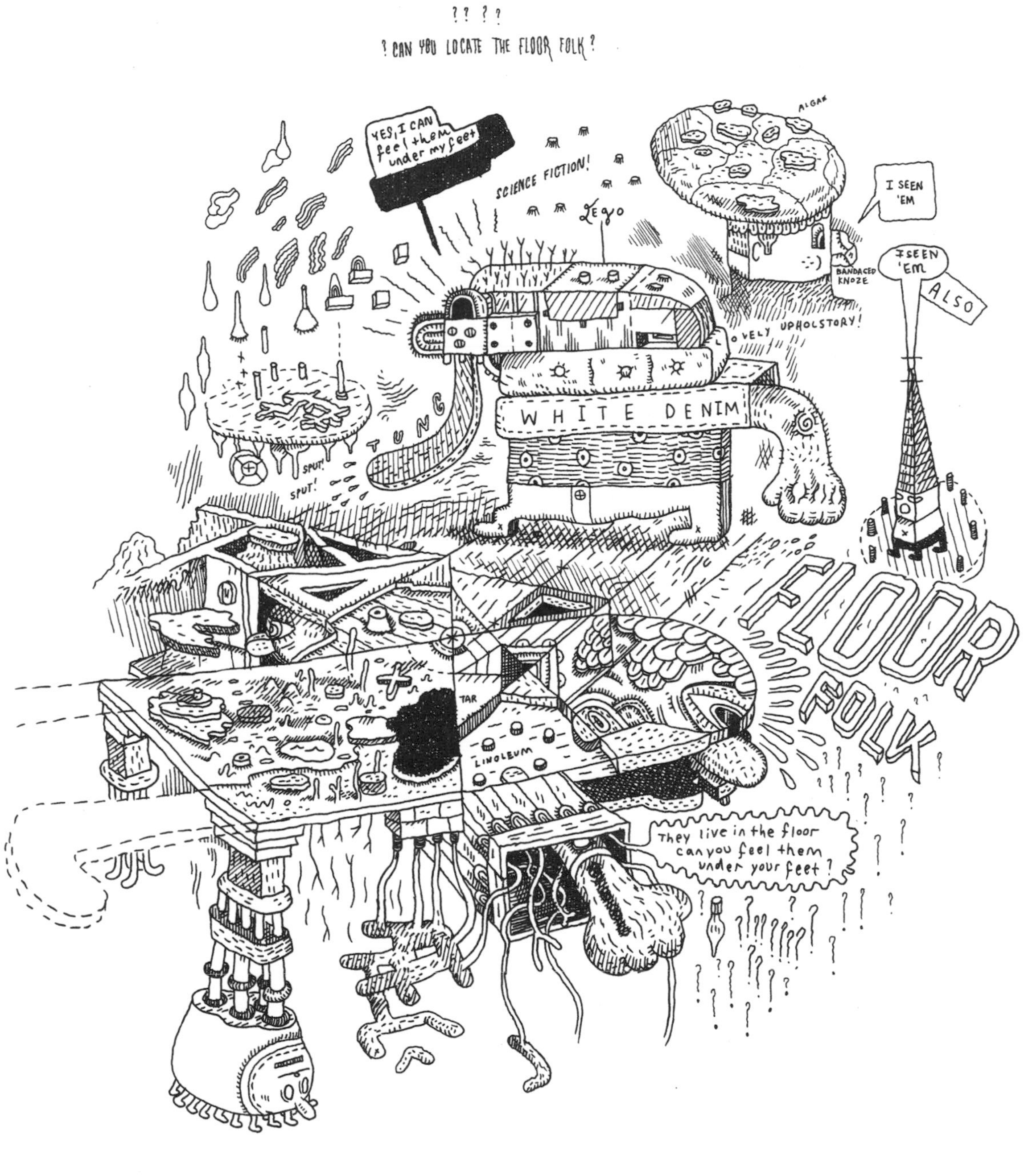
A QUESTION:
? ? ? ?
? CAN YOU LOCATE THE FLOOR FOLK ?
YES, I CAN feel them under my feet
SCIENCE FICTION!
Lego
ALGAE
I SEEN 'EM
BANDAGED KNOZE
I SEEN 'EM
ALSO
LOVELY UPHOLSTORY!
WHITE DENIM
TUNG
SPUT!
SPUT!
FLOOR FOLK
TAR
LINOLEUM
They live in the floor can you feel them under your feet ?

First appeared in *Illusztraijuns* (2009).

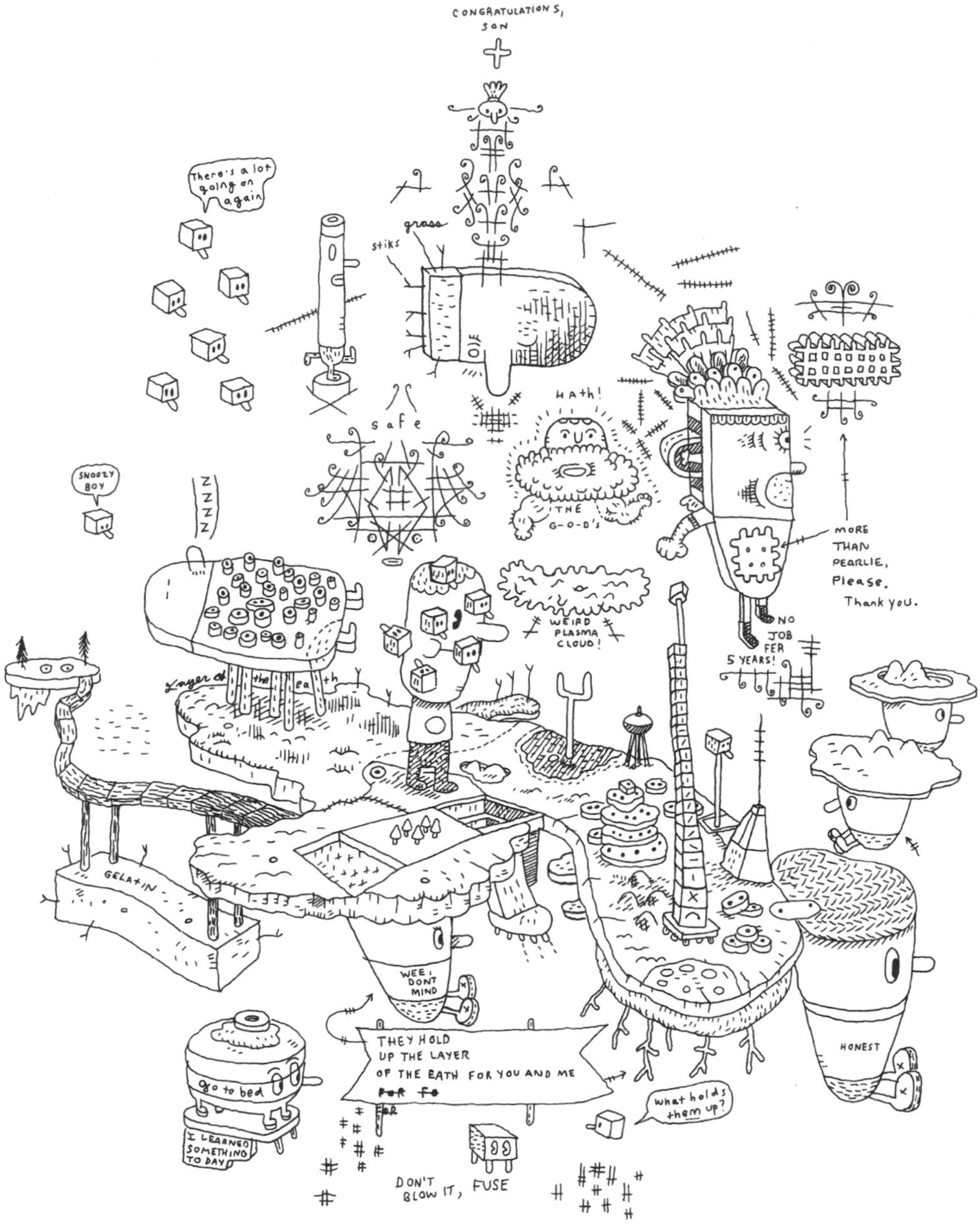
CONGRATULATIONS, SON
There's a lot going on again
stiks
grass
safe
HATH!
THE G-O-D's
SNOOZY BOY
WEIRD PLASMA CLOUD!
MORE THAN PEARLIE, Please. Thank you.
NO JOB FER 5 YEARS!
GELATIN
WEE, DONT MIND
HONEST
THEY HOLD UP THE LAYER OF THE EATH FOR YOU AND ME
go to bed
I LEARNED SOMETHING TO DAY
what holds them up?
DON'T BLOW IT, FUSE

I went to Mount Allison University from 2001 to 2005, and that's where I really began cartooning. I wanted to be in the comics section of the student newspaper as soon as I found out there was one. Over time I became pretty well known for the humour column and comics I made, so eventually, I was the editor of that section. The submissions I'd get were a real mixed bag, and I looked to the archives for ideas on how to run things. All the past years looked generally similar—same jokes about house parties, same bad anime-style drawing, not much to see—until I got to the mid-1990s, I think it was papers from 1996. That's when Marc Bell was working the comics section. And his work burst off the page. The lines were bold, the ink was spattered, and he drew circles around everyone else. He was trying things out. If there was empty space, he

 Both images first appeared in *Illusztraijuns* (2009).

WHUT A DAY
3 PRONGED APPROACH
krispy kremes
SEPT
03
DUH!
This Famed cartoonist had WOODEN TEETH
time to get Stupid-er
PLAYER OF THE WEEK
PHILLY
ICE ICE BEBE
GREEDY

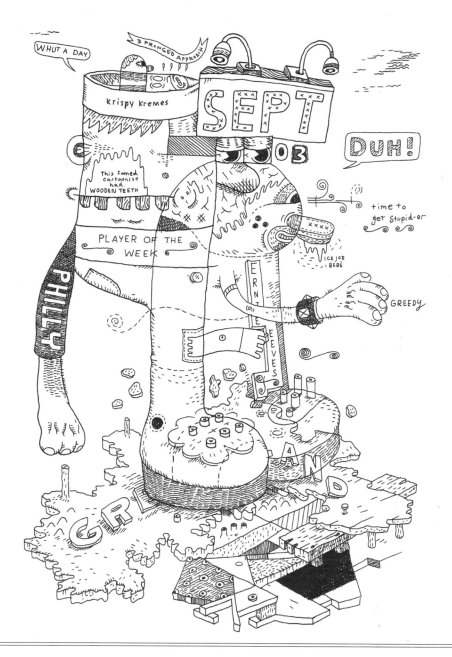

filled it. I had never seen anything like it, and I remember thinking, "This is what talent looks like. This is what good comics look like." Eventually I saw that his comics were in the Halifax alt-weekly at that time, the *Coast*. So I thought, you know, wow, he's still doing it. But I had never really seen many indie comics before then. There were no comic stores where I grew up, there was no intro to it, there was no internet. I was in my last year of university, and I hadn't really thought about what you could do with comics once there was no more student paper to put them in. I found out the university library had a small section of graphic novels, one shelf. I ran my finger along the book spines and pulled out one with an interesting title. I sat on the floor in the library aisle and read it cover to cover. It was Chester Brown's *I Never Liked You*.—***Kate Beaton***

LITERARY SUPPLEMENT: A BRIEF AND INCOMPLETE ATLAS OF D+Q'S PETITS LIVRES

an appreciation by Gabrielle Moser

Over the last five years of his life, German art historian Aby Warburg attempted to write a history of art without using words. The *Mnemosyne Atlas* (1924–29), his final project, was a cartography of images: sixty-three thematic panels that arranged photographs, drawings, and newspaper illustrations into a map of visual forms as they moved between cultures and time periods. For Warburg, certain images—such as the serpent or the rising sun—had life forces of their own, appearing and reappearing in cultures in ways that traditional art historical methods could not explain. By grouping images intuitively, Warburg wanted to draw out non-rational connections between forms.

Like the *Mnemosyne Atlas*, the books that make up Drawn & Quarterly's Petits Livres imprint are composed almost entirely of images that, taken together, create another kind of atlas of mark-making. Different from the graphic novels that Drawn & Quarterly typically publishes, the Petits Livres are monographs that are dedicated to the work of a single visual artist, or that operate as an experimental annex for authors whose main output usually takes the form of more traditional novels and cartoons. Books without (very many) words, the collection includes works by artists who usually exhibit in galleries and film screenings (Amy Lockhart, Adrian Norvid, Seth Scriver, Michael Dumontier, and Neil Farber), image-focused projects by cartoonists and graphic novelists (Charles Burns, Marc Bell, Keith Jones, Jillian Tamaki, and Julie Doucet) and loose narrative series by illustrators (Julie Morstad, Leanne Shapton, and Sonja Ahlers). Instead of surveying each author's career, the Petits Livres imprint is a space where the ephemera around artists' practices, whether as visual artists or as graphic novelists, briefly settle into a publication. It records the marginalia to the more "official" histories of images told by gallery exhibitions, catalogues, and novels, emphasizing sketches (both literal and comedic), prototypes, and experiments over finished works. This glimpse of these artists' working methods is only possible because of Drawn & Quarterly's unique role as an arts institution that acts as a publisher rather than an exhibition-maker. If essays, books, and artists' statements are usually supplementary texts to the "main event" of the exhibition, the Petits Livres series reverses this relationship, treating publications as public spaces. Turned over to these individual artists, the books are visual atlases that chart the emergence of forms in their works.

To leaf through the series' pages is to follow the trajectory of these artists' working methods. As a fellow wanderer with both Warburg and the Petits Livres, I find myself returning again and again to the uncanny way that certain figures seem to embed themselves into the minds of readers and viewers. I begin to recognize—or think that I recognize—a particular strip mall in London, Ontario, or the familiar shape of a Hudson's Bay Company blanket draped over a swing set: banal forms that would normally be overlooked in the grand narratives of the history of art, but which punctuate the series with the regularity and force of Warburg's ascending sun.

These formal connections are not accidental. Nearly every artist in the Petits Livres series is Canadian, a conscious decision on the part of the publisher that underscores the circulation of images and texts between artistic centres in Vancouver, Winnipeg, London, Toronto, Montreal, and Halifax (to name just a few). Artists appear in one another's works, contributing illustrations, ideas, and forms to books by other authors. Marc Bell's doodles appear in Seth Scriver's *Stooge Pile* (2010), for instance, while Jason McLean's Canada Council "brick snakes" (a composite of the Canada Council logo stuck to the face of one of Ray Johnson's brick snakes) slither through the pages of Bell's *The Stacks* (2004). Bell is credited as an editor and designer of Amy Lockhart's *Dirty Dishes* (2009), and Sonja Ahlers thanks fellow author Julie Morstad for her contributions to *The Selves* (2010). This collaborative impulse builds another kind of atlas of artistic production, one that charts the persistence of certain images across a generation of Canadian artists. Turning the pages of the Petits Livres volumes, I am often reminded of the Surrealists' drawing games, such as the exquisite corpse, which relied on the unconscious associations of two or more artists to create bizarre composite figures. Or of Michael Morris and Vincent Trasov's Image Bank, which in 1969 invited artists to mail postcards, texts, and other visual ephemera to one another to build a cross-country catalogue of research imagezvvvrons.

Perhaps most importantly, the Petits Livres format permits a level of self-reflection on the part of its artists that is both hilarious and illuminating. Notes at the end of many of the books, for instance, explain the genealogy of certain scenes or images. Others, such as Bell's *The Stacks*, include hand-drawn checklists, itemizing the contents of the book and providing a provenance for the images, including lists of exhibitions and publications where they have appeared in the past. In some cases, it is impossible to imagine these images taking shape in any other format, such as in Michael Dumontier and Neil Farber's genre-bending *Animals with Sharpies* (2013), a hysterically funny montage of different animals in the midst of writing out messages—using their mouths to manipulate Sharpies—on blank walls. ("Reasons to Live," writes one tortoise: "1. my children; 2. work to be done; 3. flowers; 4. love; 5. transcendence." "Dear cat asshole," composes a field mouse on the preceding page, "How would you like it if I ate your husband?") These works borrow from the humour and collaborative drawing practices of the Royal Art Lodge, the Winnipeg-based collective Dumontier and Farber helped found in 1996, but they follow an absurd logic of their own, one that makes perfect sense in the pages of a single book.

For other artists, there is an educational function to the Petits Livres, as there is in Sonja Ahlers's combinations of found images and texts about iconic women like Marilyn Monroe and Gloria Steinem, alongside her own drawings and writing, in *The Selves*. Seth Scriver includes an explicit do-it-yourself section in *Stooge Pile*, instructing the reader on how to make Dadaist sculptures out of materials in her home (including fish sauce, toilet plungers, and cat hair), while Leanne Shapton's index of leaves in *The Native Trees of Canada* (2010) is the self-taught naturist's guide to indigenous plant life (a reproduction of a pamphlet the artist found at a rare bookstore in Toronto).

"Petit Livre," the title of the imprint, is borrowed from the French term for booklet or pamphlet, and it serves as a reminder of the tradition of carrying tomes on our person: a kind of literary supplement to the body. Like Warburg's panels of images, these small books are intended to move, building new associations between images and artistic practices as they exchange hands, pockets, bookshelves, and bedside tables. It is tempting to imagine that their printed form is not the end point for these atlases of images, but only the beginning.

***Gabrielle Moser is a writer and independent curator. She regularly contributes to artforum.com, and her writing has appeared in venues including* ARTnews, Canadian Art, Fillip, n paradoxa, *and* Photography & Culture.**

GUSTON
MOLECULE
ARMS

"Blueberry Juice Molecule (Guston)," 2003, first appeared in Marc Bell's *Hot Potatoe* (2009).

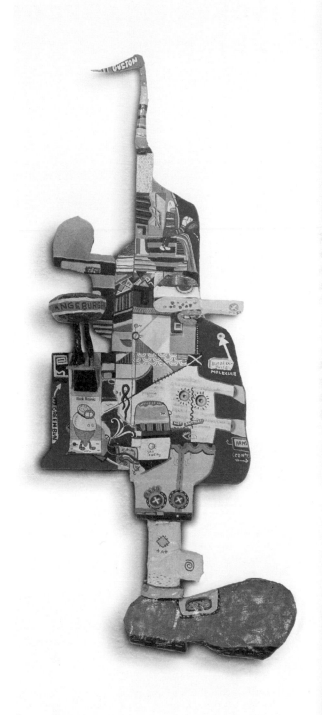

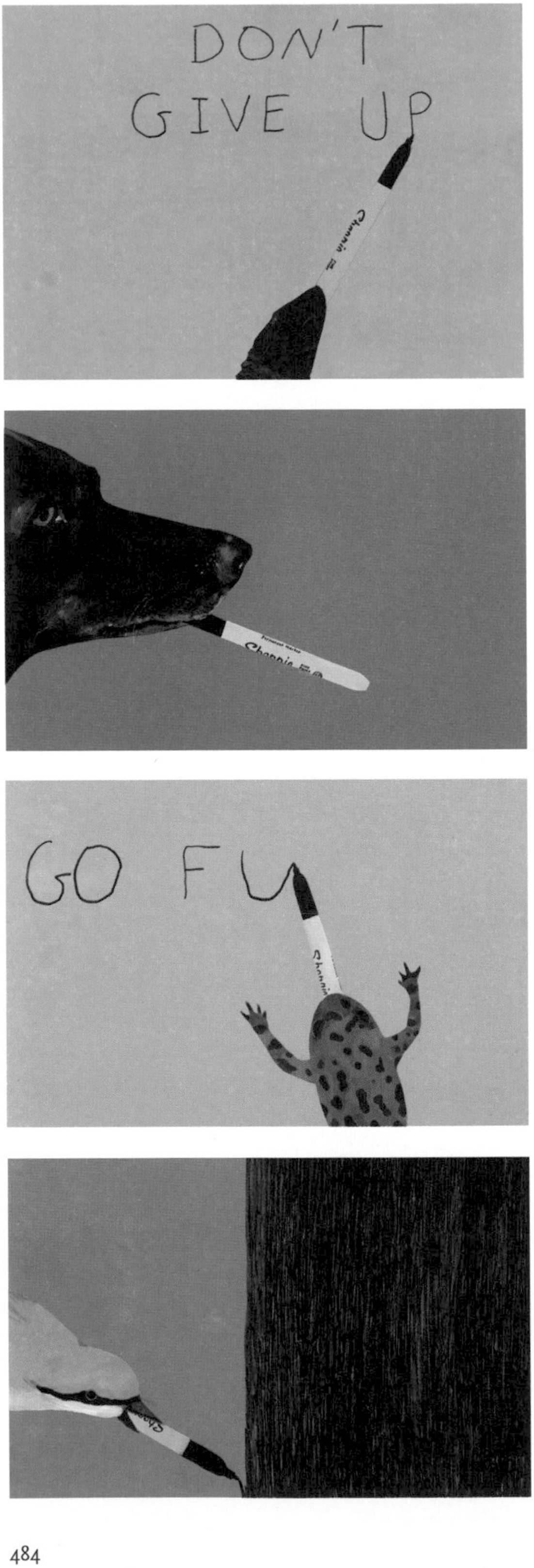
DON'T
GIVE UP
GO FU
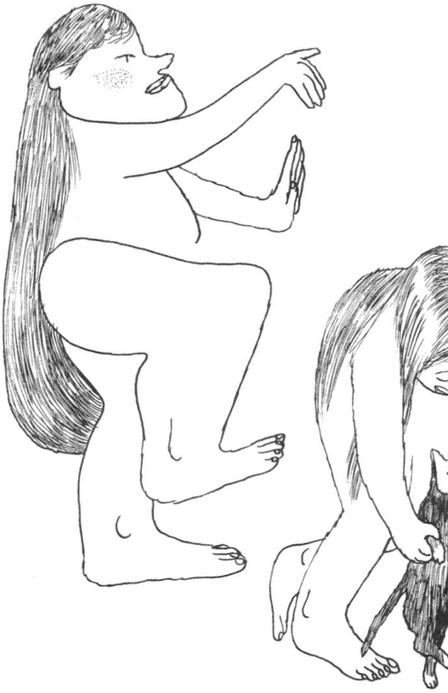
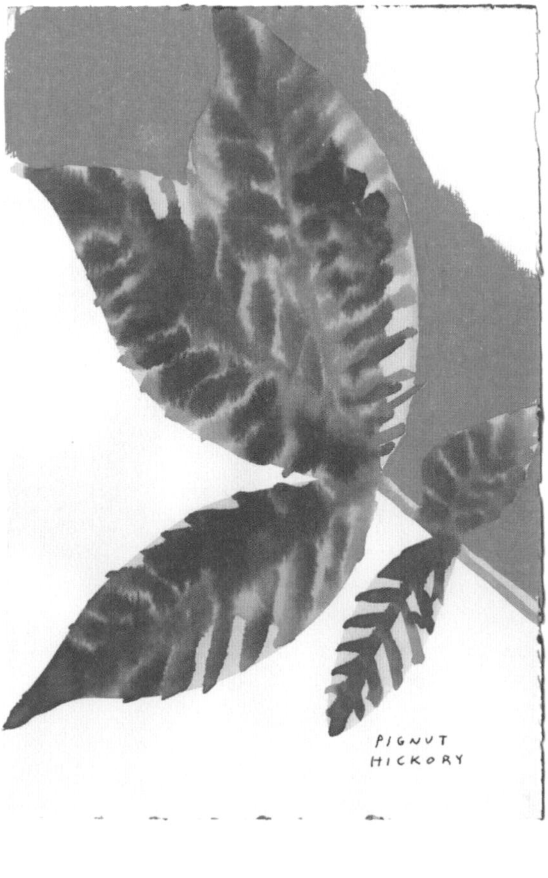
PIGNUT
HICKORY

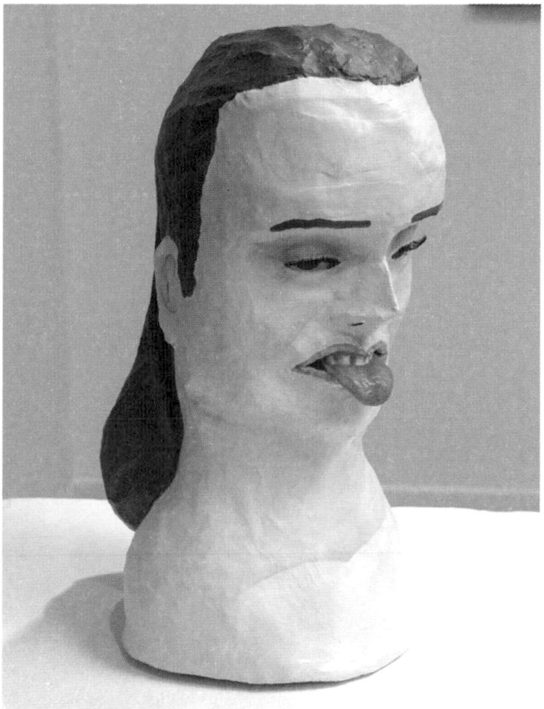

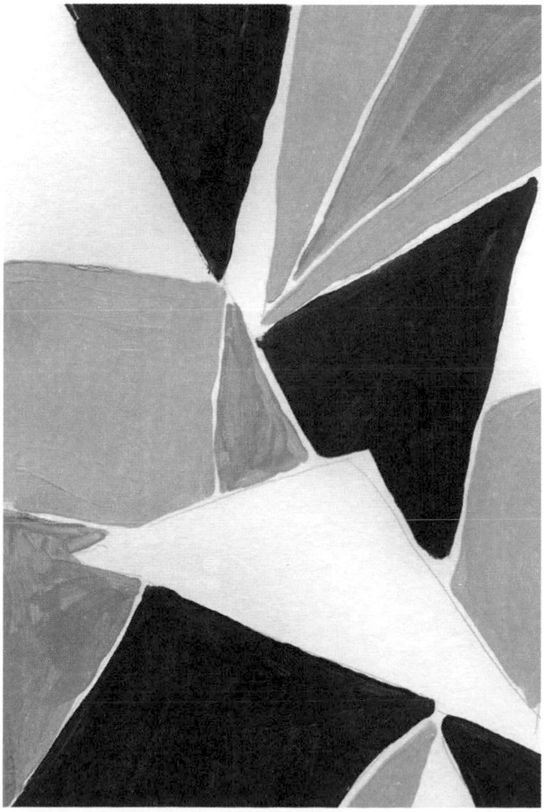

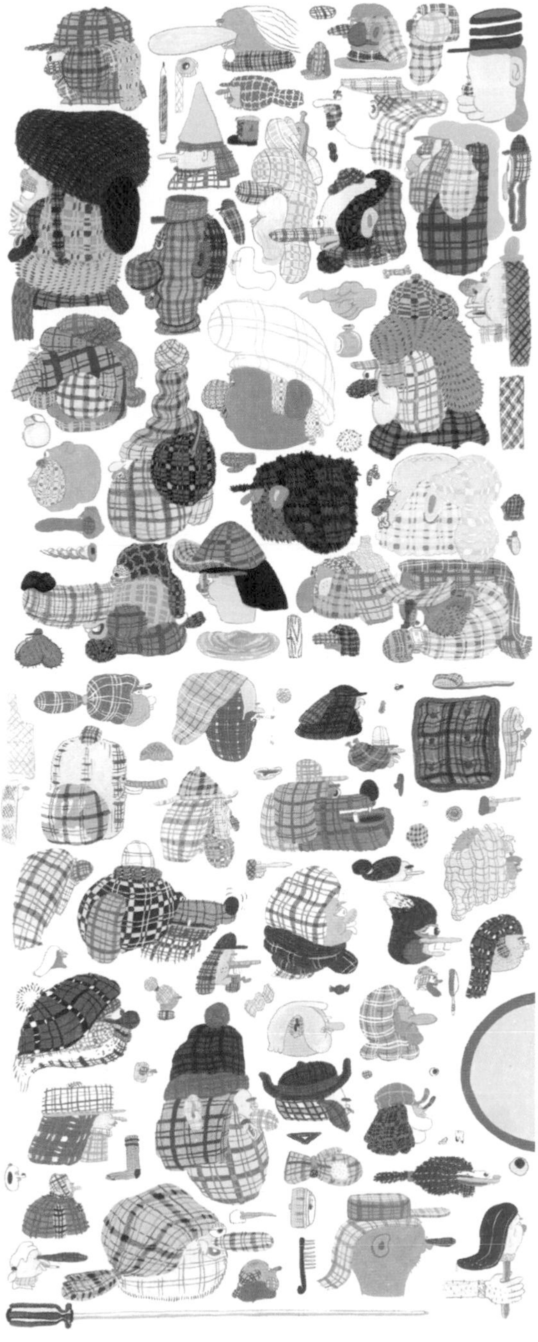

Left page: (Left) Michael Dumontier & Neil Farber's *Animals with Sharpies* (2013). (Top right) Jillian Tamaki's *Indoor Voice* (2010). (Bottom right) Leanne Shapton's *Native Trees of Canada* (2010). This page: (Top left) Amy Lockhart's *Dirty Dishes* (2010). (Bottom left) Leanne Shapton, unpublished. (Right) Seth Scriver's *Stooge Pile* (2010).

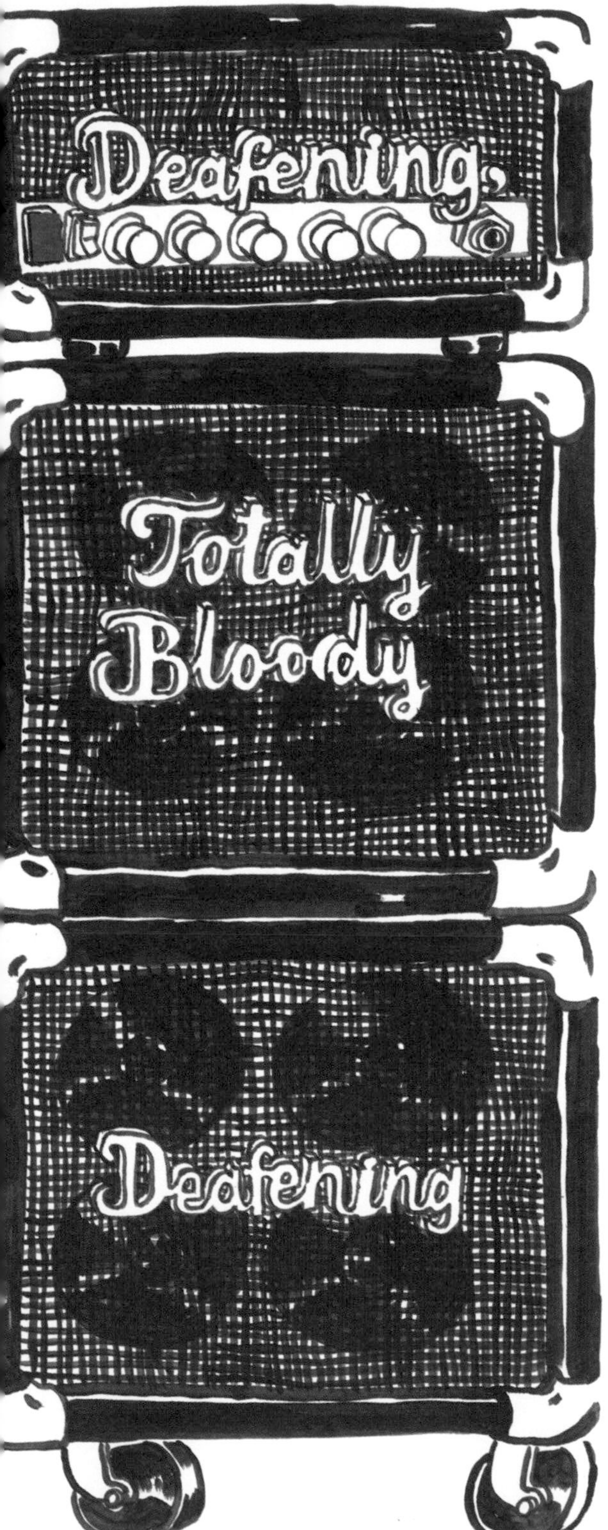
Deafening,
Totally
Bloody
Deafening

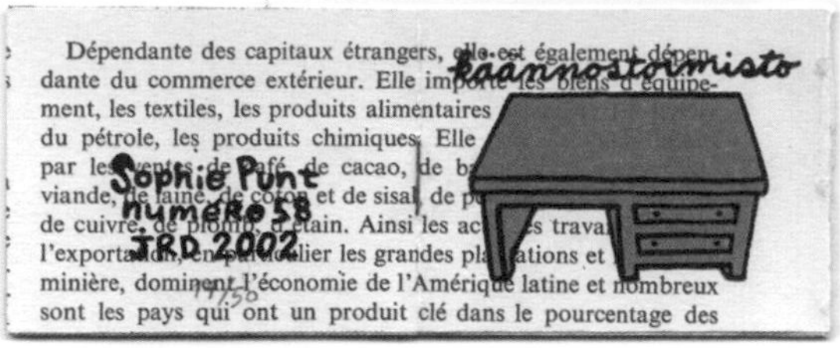
käännostoimisto
Dépendante des capitaux étrangers, elle est également dépendante du commerce extérieur. Elle importe les biens d'équipe-
ment, les textiles, les produits alimentaires
du pétrole, les produits chimiques. Elle
par les ventes de café, de cacao, de ba
viande, de laine, de coton et de sisal, de p
de cuivre, de plomb, d'étain. Ainsi les ac es travai
l'exportation, en particulier les grandes plantations et
minière, dominent l'économie de l'Amérique latine et nombreux
sont les pays qui ont un produit clé dans le pourcentage des
Sophie Punt
numéro 58
JRD 2002

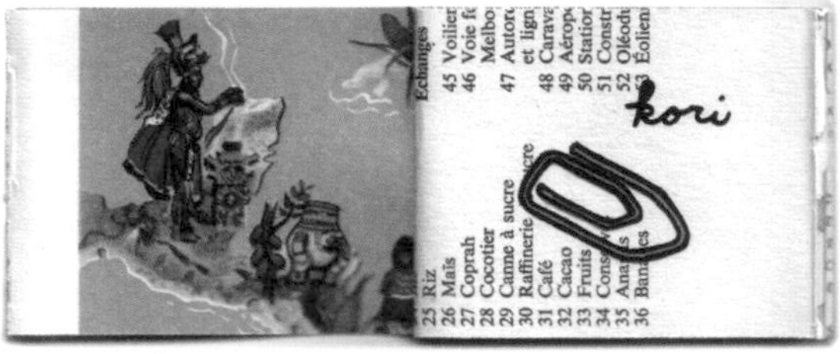
kori

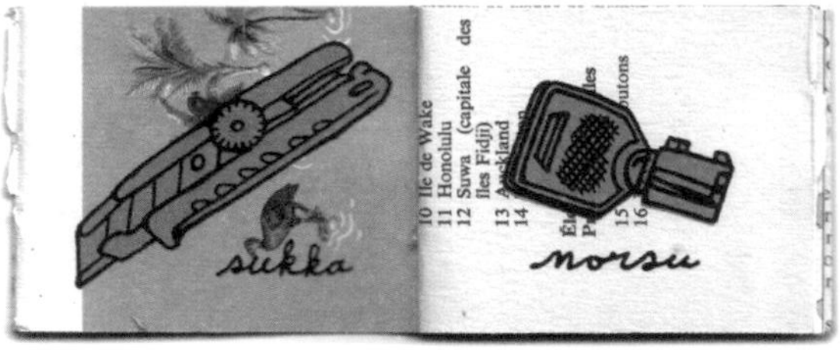
sukka
norsu

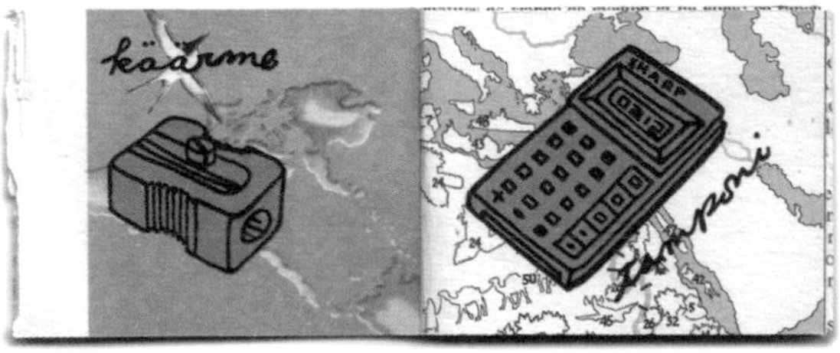
käärme

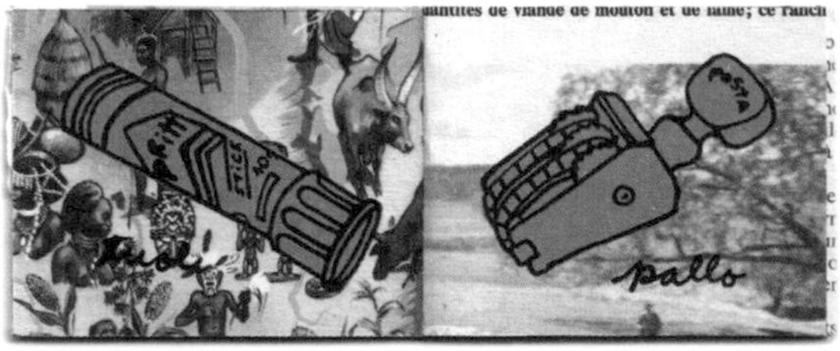
pallo

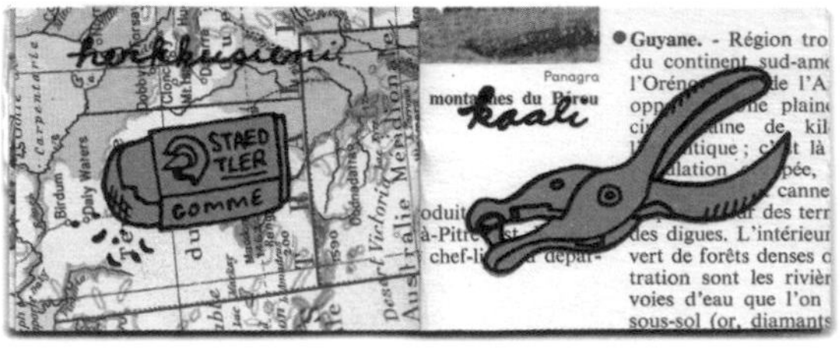
herkkusieni
kaali
STAEDTLER
GOMME

MARKS-A-LOT
korppu
LIQUID PAPER
perhonen
HUNT
pöyta
ATLANTIQUE
parsakaali
taivas
pitkät housut
OFREX 105
pusero

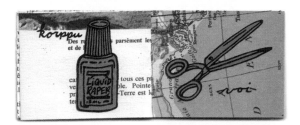

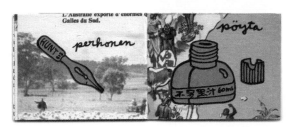

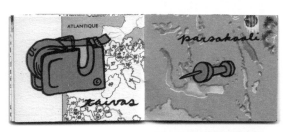

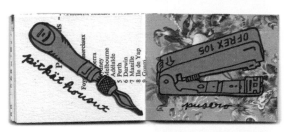

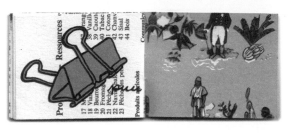

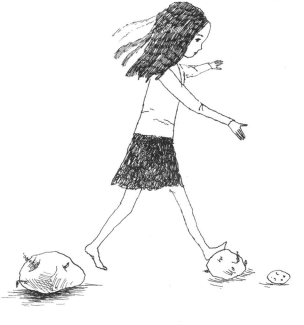

(Left) Adrian Norvid's *Nogoodniks* (2011); (Centre) Julie Doucet's *Sophie Punt*, photographed by Jamie Quail for *Lady Pep* (2004); (Right) Julie Morstad's *The Wayside* (2012).

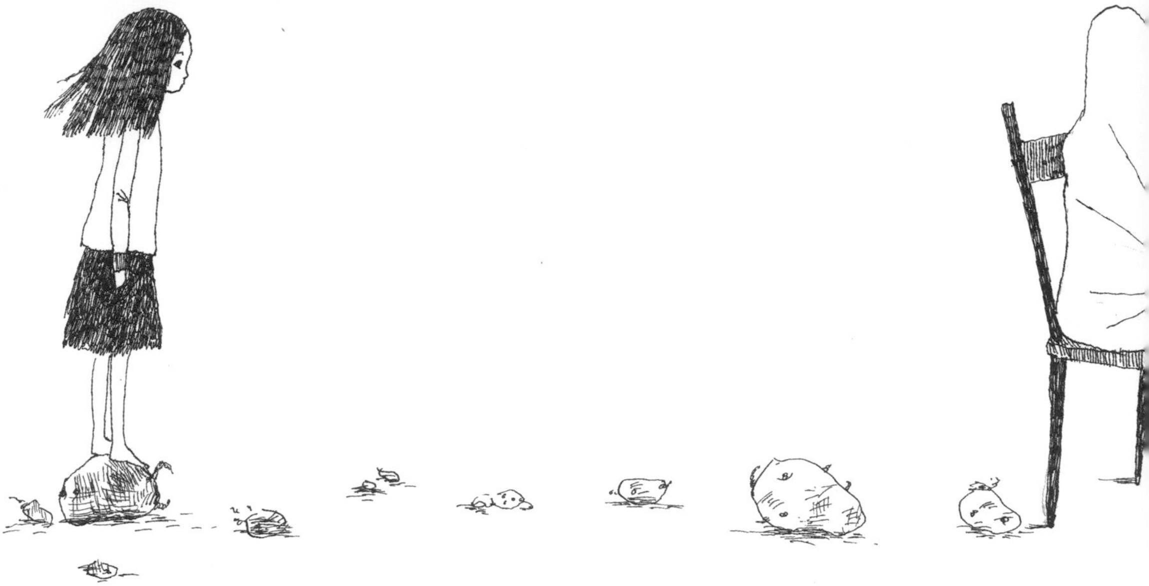

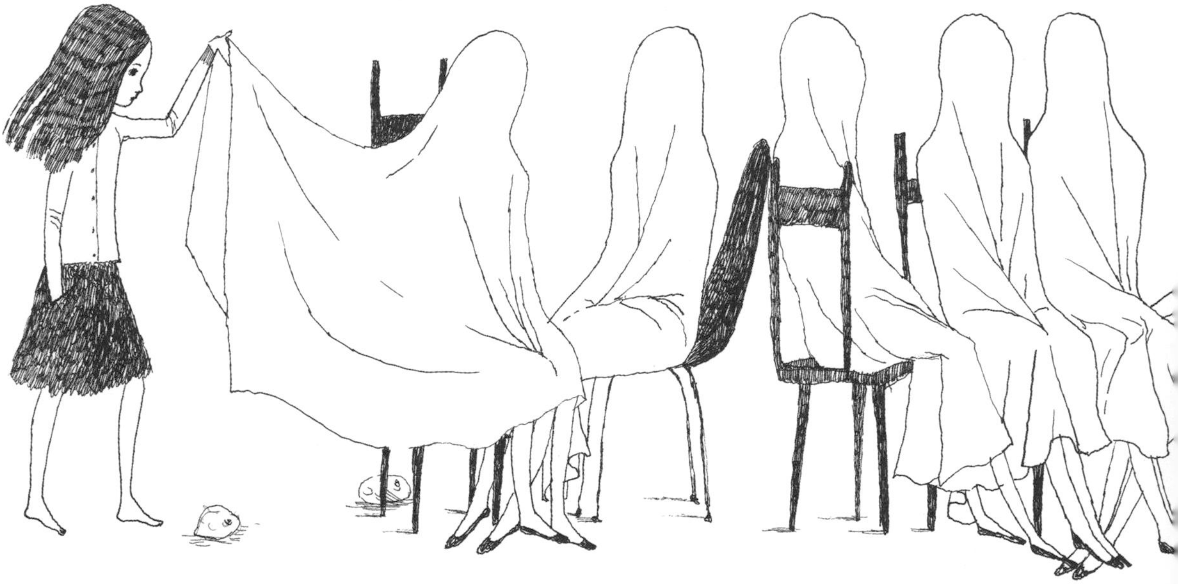

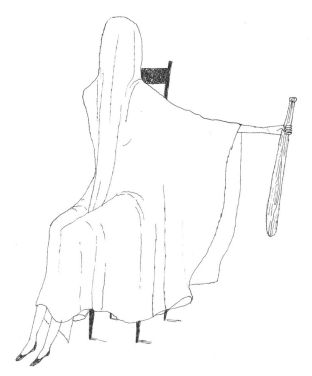

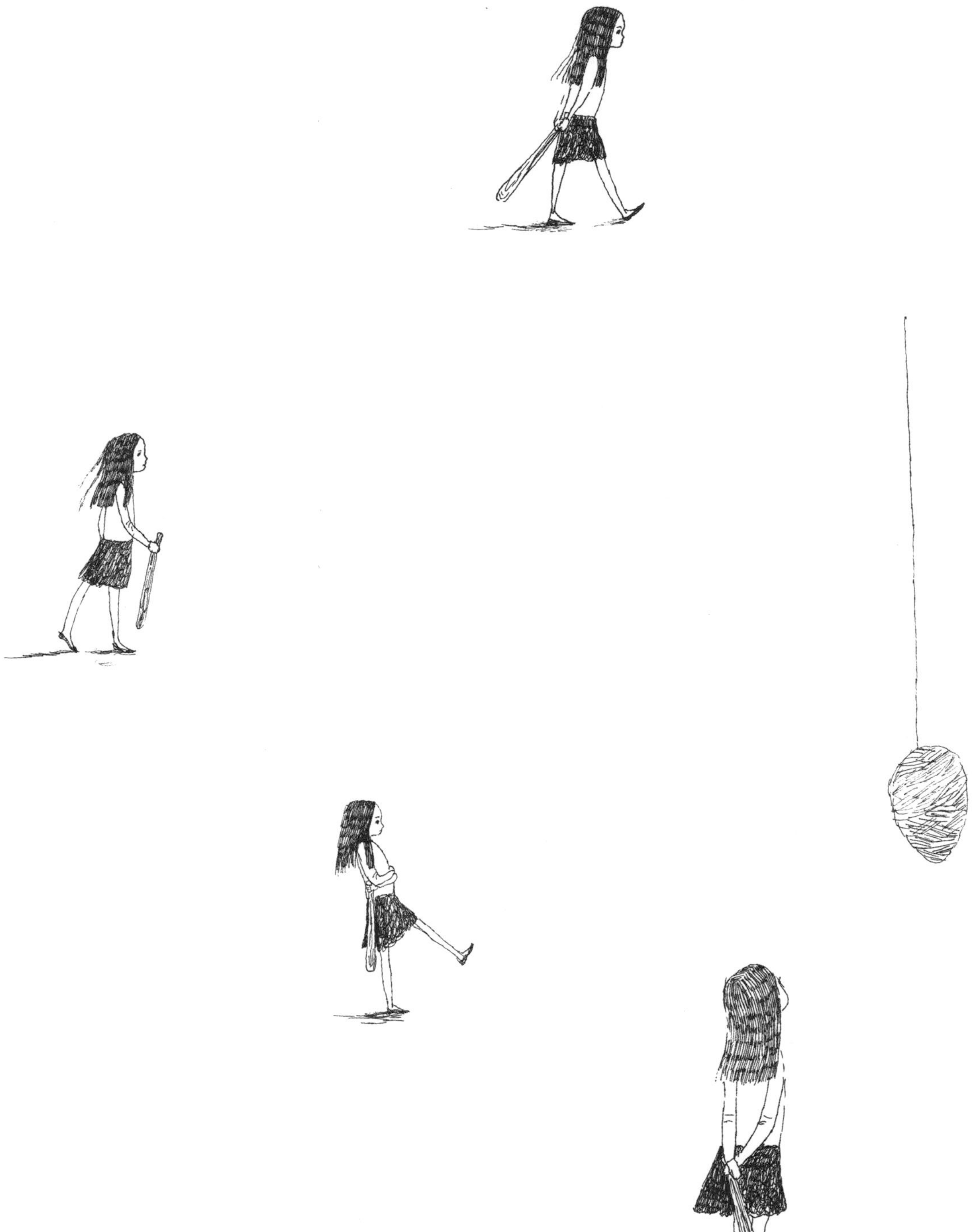

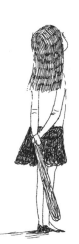

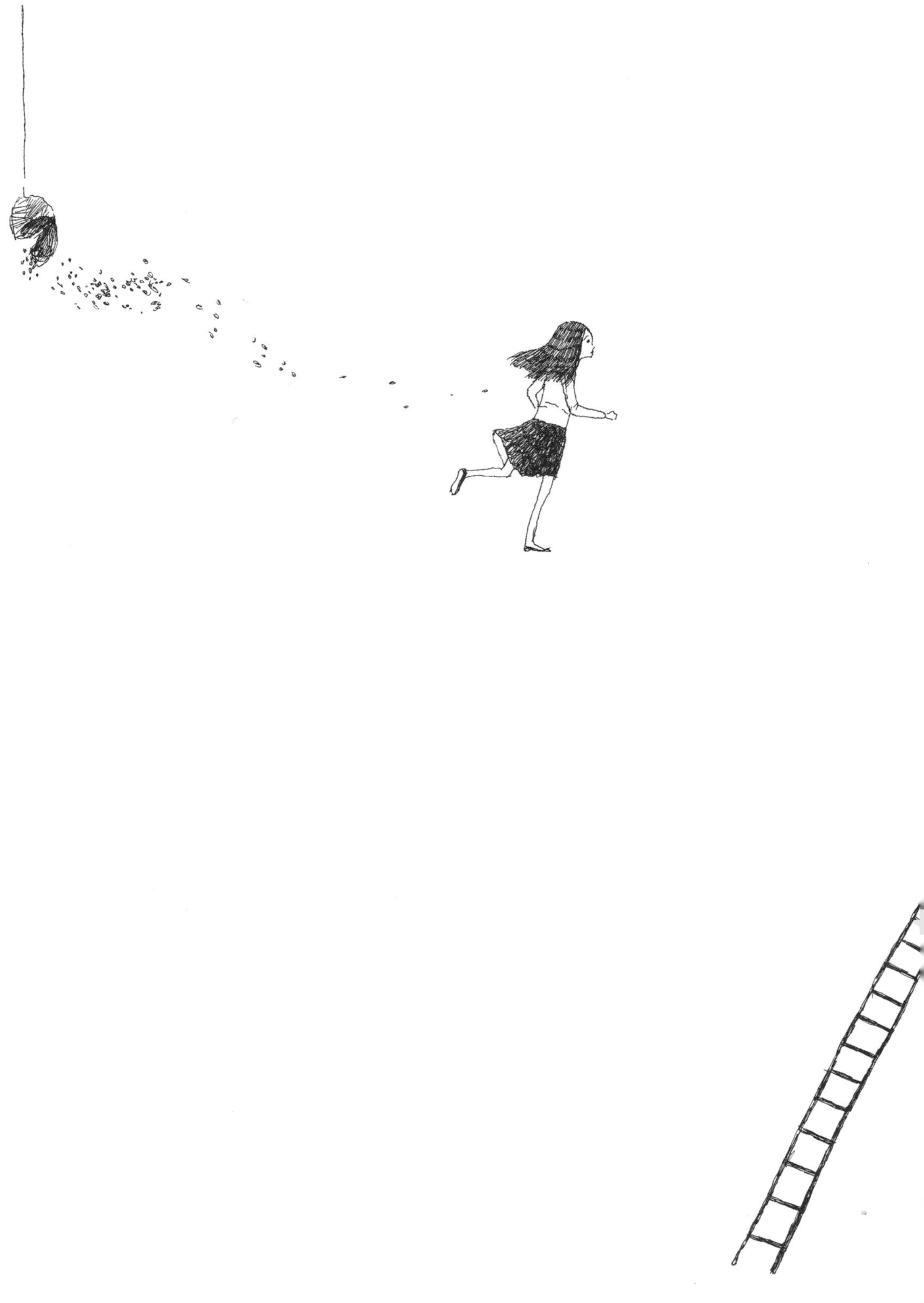

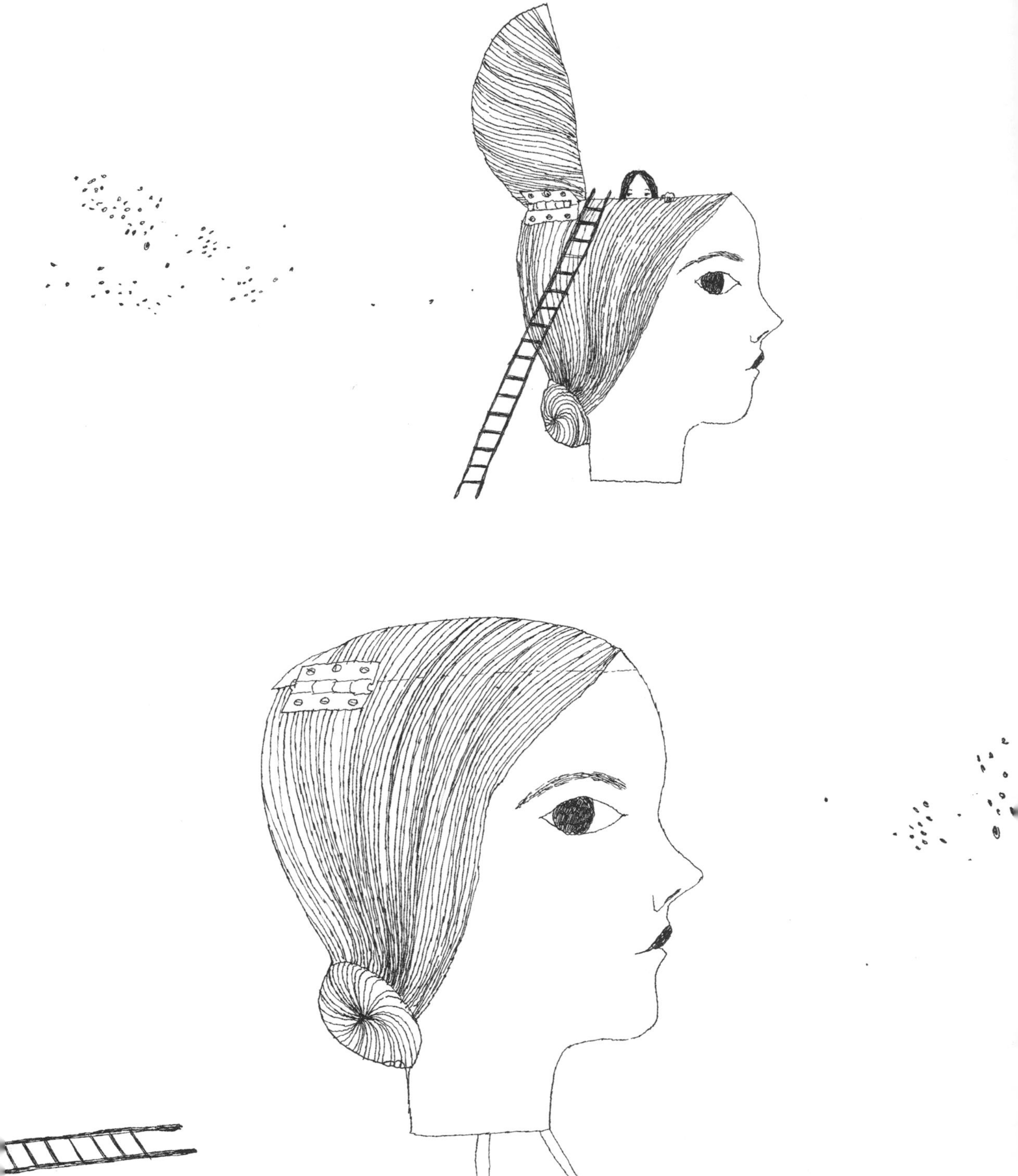

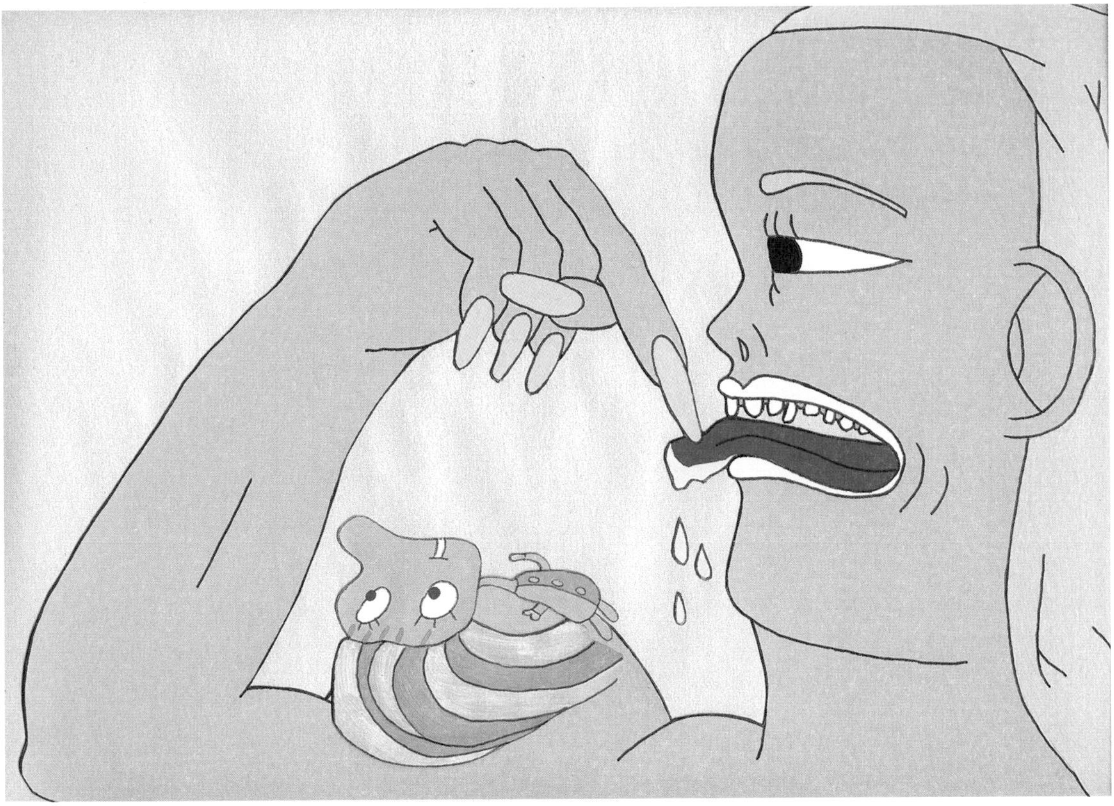

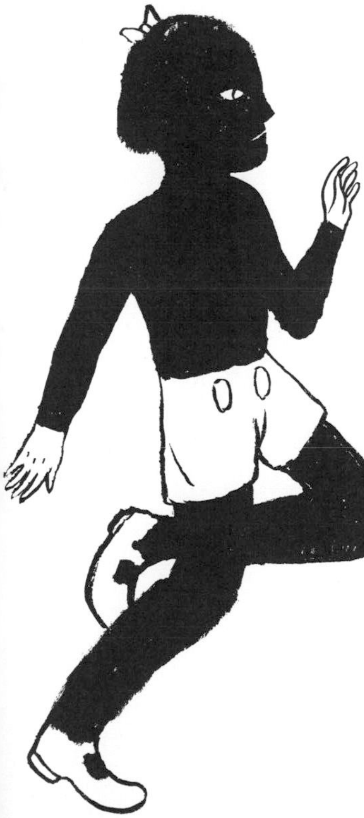

Back when D+Q started as a publisher, there were very few "art" books in the comic-book market. If you happened to be looking for anything in this milieu, you probably would have been directed to the section stocked with Frank Frazetta books, usually recognizable by their covers of sexy ladies riding bare naked on the backs of fearsome-looking dragons. I'm happy to report that the door to a wider range of material has opened up, if only slightly. I can't say exactly how or when the change came about, but I'm grateful that a certain market evolution has made it possible for us to publish the Petits Livres imprint, a series of quirky, beautiful little books that could not possibly have existed at an earlier time. We started off with Marc Bell's *The Stacks* and Julie Doucet's *Lady Pep*, both visually stunning, non-narrative books, each a perfect embodiment of its respective artist's singular talents. *Indoor Voice* was a compendium of Jillian Tamaki's drawings and short comics, and when it first came out I found myself looking through its pages over and over again, entranced by her virtuosity as an artist. And there's so much more: Julie Morstad's achingly delicate line work in *Milk Teeth* and *The Wayside*; Leanne Shapton's lush *Native Trees of Canada*. How can we even begin to classify Adrian Norvid's *Nogoodniks* or Michael Dumontier and Neil Farber's *Animals with Sharpies*, other than to say that both are among the funniest books ever published by D+Q?

—***Chris Oliveros***

(Left) Jillian Tamaki's *Indoor Voice* (2010). (Right) Amy Lockhart's *Dirty Dishes* (2010).

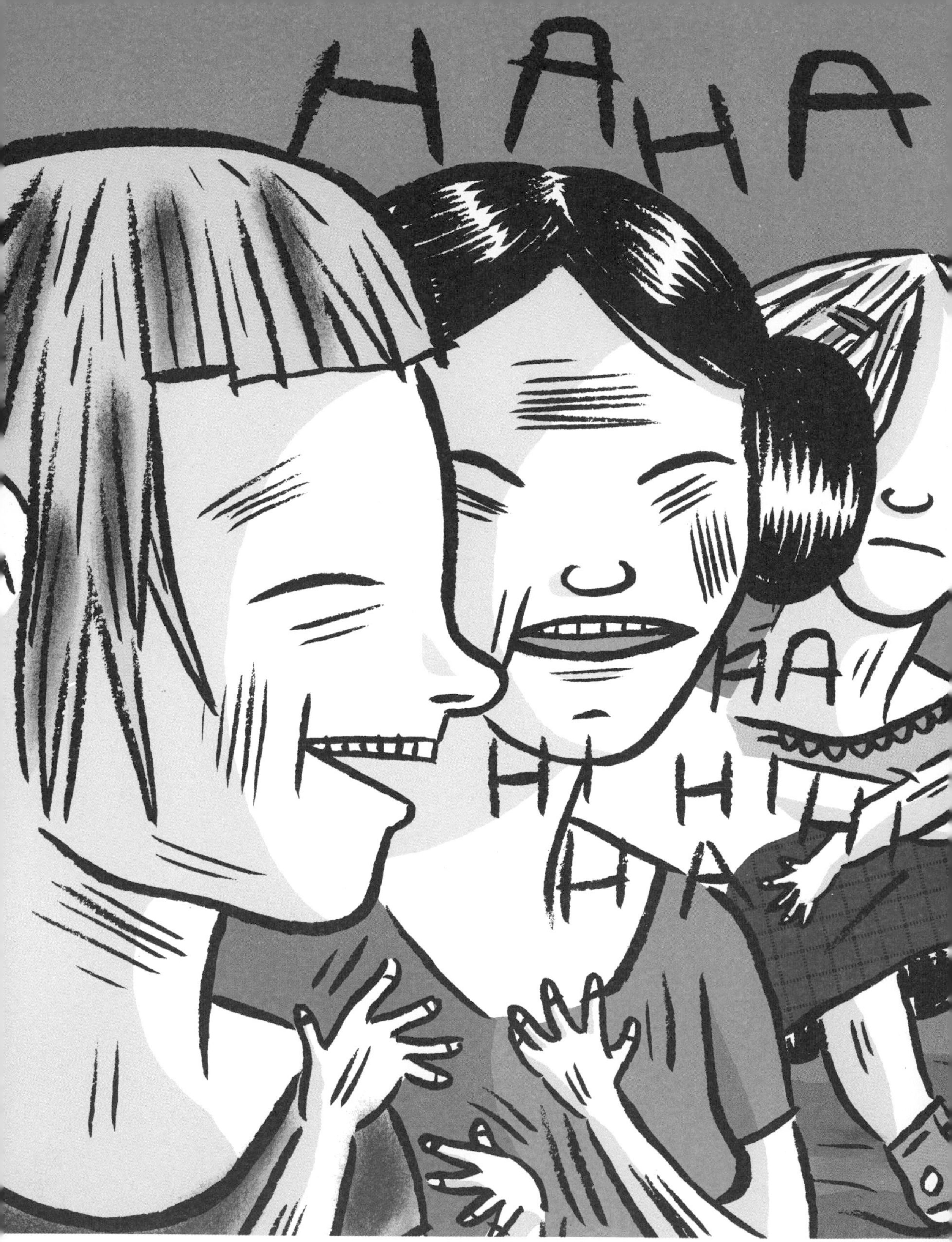
HAHAHA
HA
HI
HI
HAHA

494 Nicolas Robel Originally appeared in *Fallen Angel* (2006).

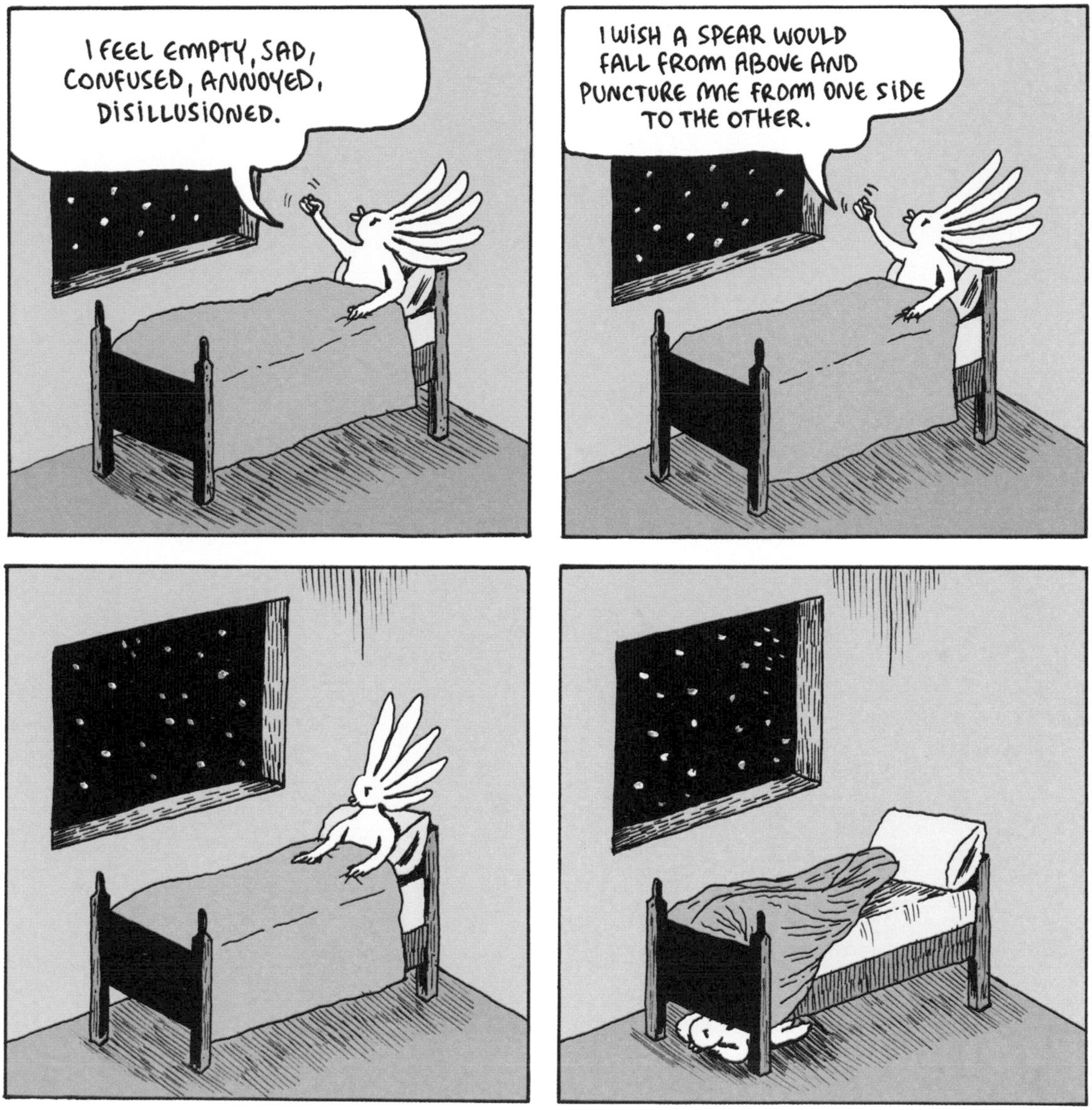
I FEEL EMPTY, SAD, CONFUSED, ANNOYED, DISILLUSIONED.
I WISH A SPEAR WOULD FALL FROM ABOVE AND PUNCTURE ME FROM ONE SIDE TO THE OTHER.

I keep *Eden* by Pablo Holmberg next to my bed. I pull it out whenever I need some comfort, some reassurance that everything is okay and that there's still beauty in the world. When my grandpa died a few months ago, I opened the book to the page where a character is saying goodbye to her grandfather, who is a big lumpy looking guy (kind of like my grandpa). It summed up my grief perfectly, and expressed something I was having trouble communicating on my own.

I brought *Eden* with me when I traveled to the Adirondacks for my grandpa's memorial. It's like a friend I carry around and save for whenever I'm feeling emotionally overwhelmed. Just knowing it's there is enough to make me feel better. *Eden* is humble, honest, and heartfelt—three things I strive for in my own life and work. I'm so glad it exists.

***—Melissa Mendes, cartoonist of* Freddy Stories, Lou, *and* The Weight**

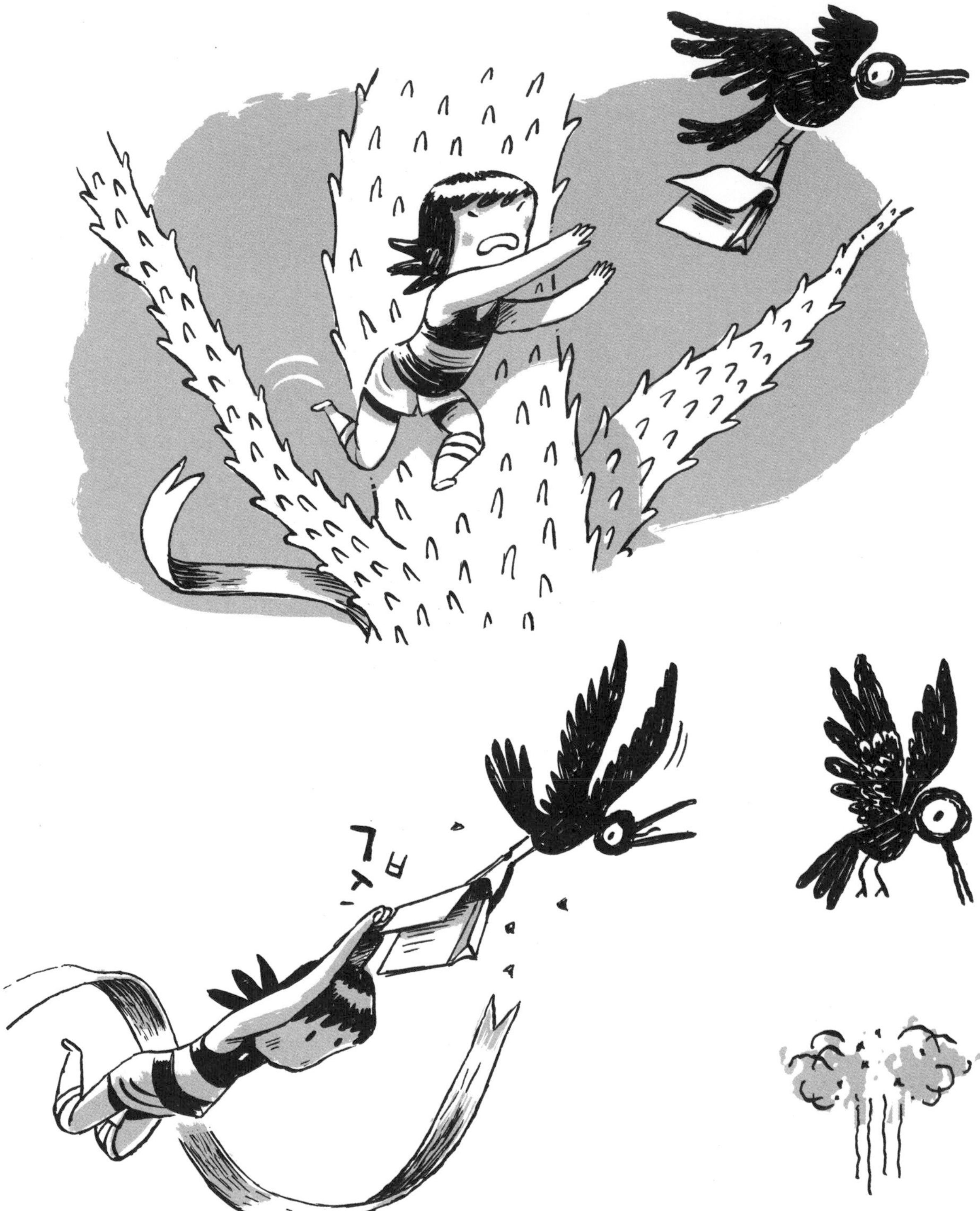

 Matt Forsythe Originally appeared in *Jinchalo* (2012).

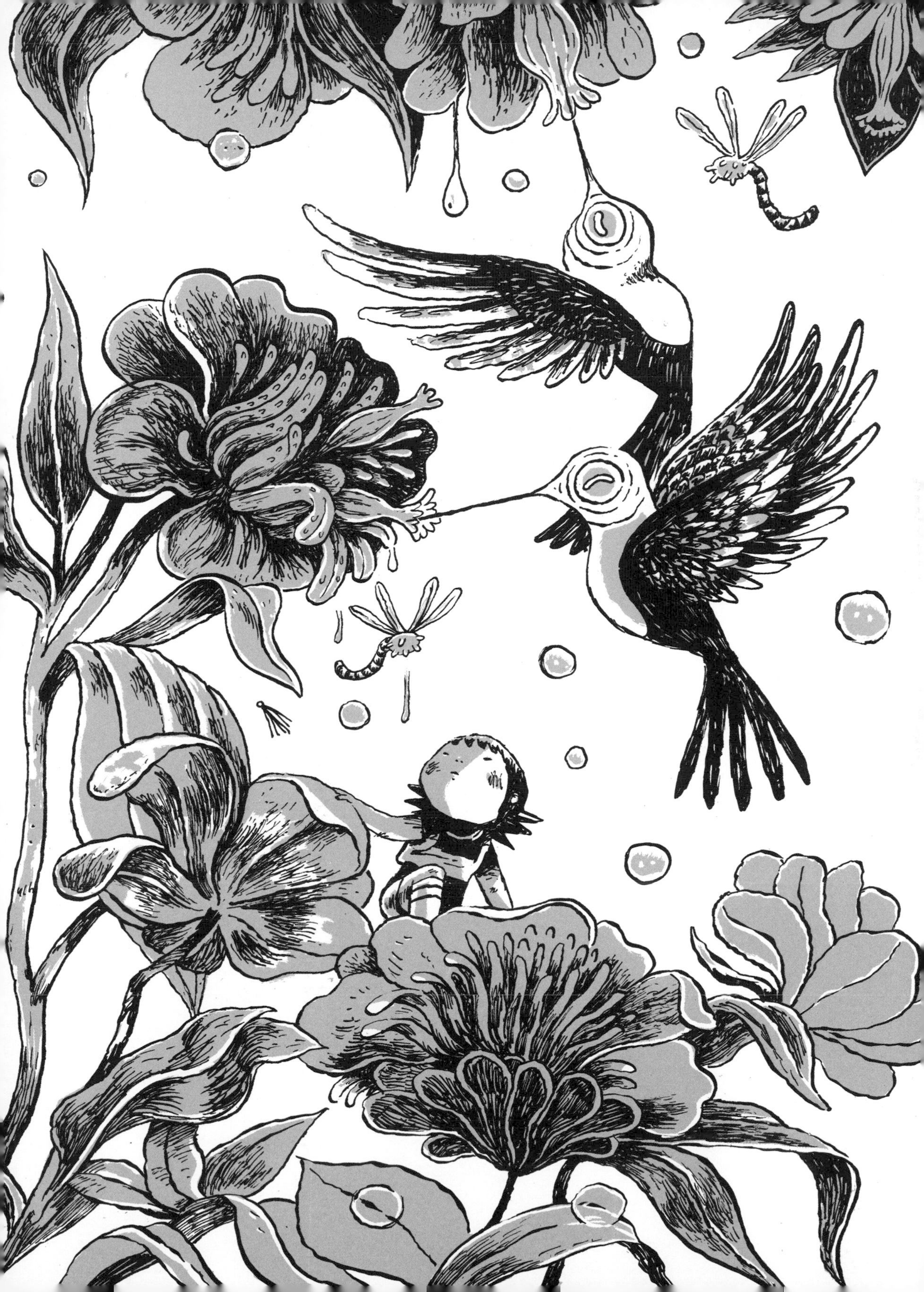

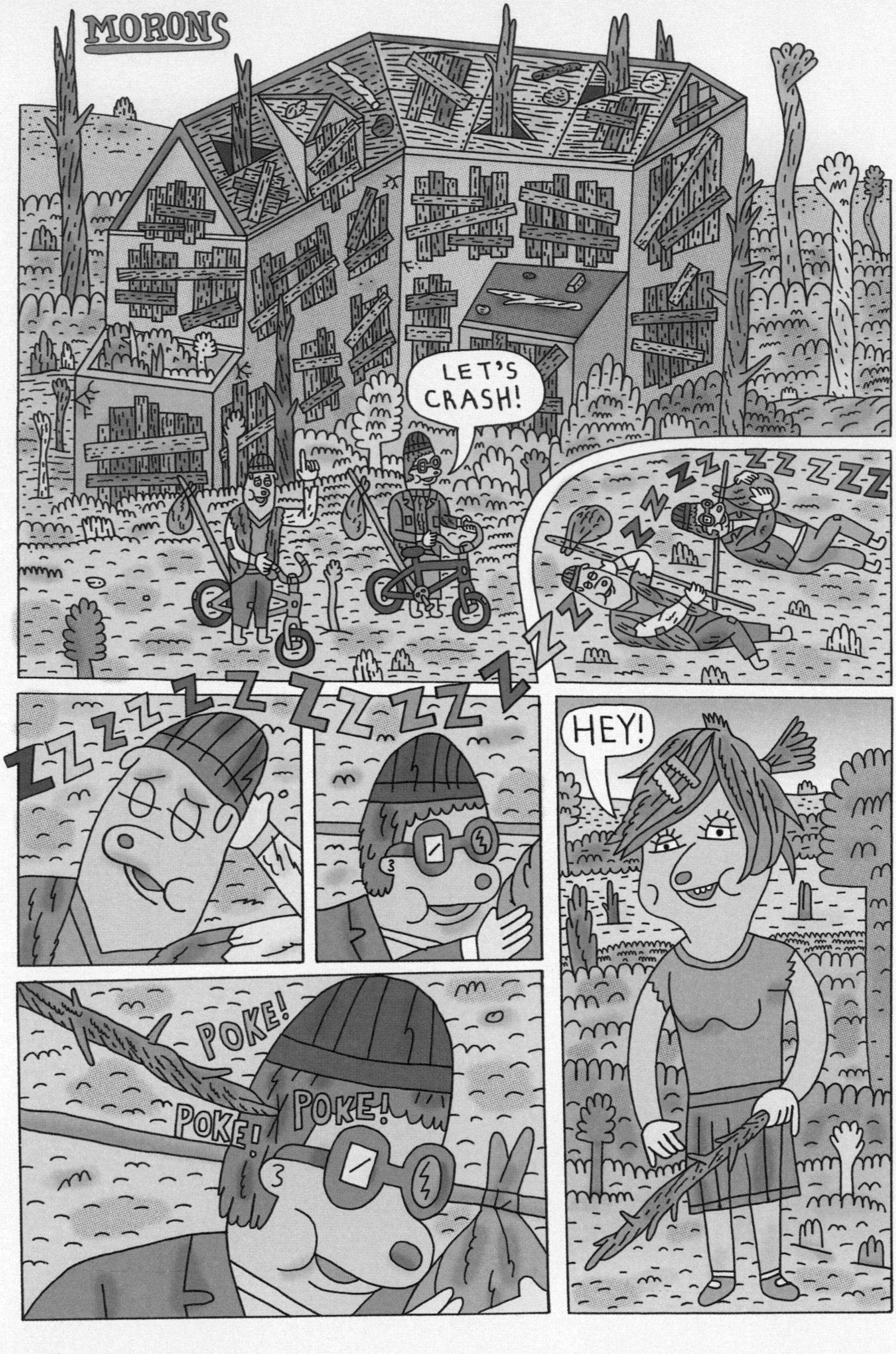
MORONS
LET'S CRASH!
HEY!
POKE!
POKE!
POKE!

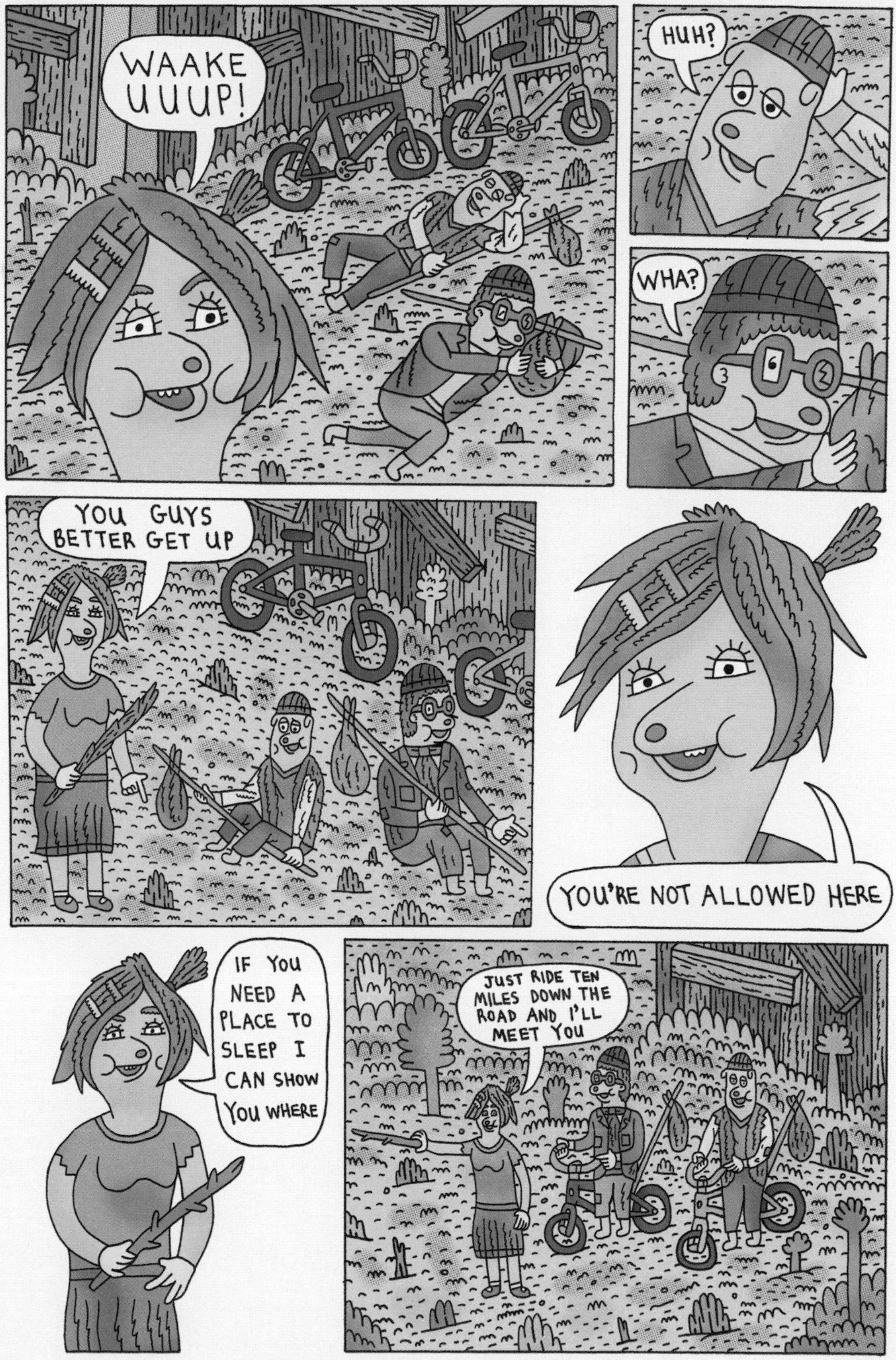
WAAKE UUUP!
HUH?
WHA?
YOU GUYS BETTER GET UP
YOU'RE NOT ALLOWED HERE
IF YOU NEED A PLACE TO SLEEP I CAN SHOW YOU WHERE
JUST RIDE TEN MILES DOWN THE ROAD AND I'LL MEET YOU

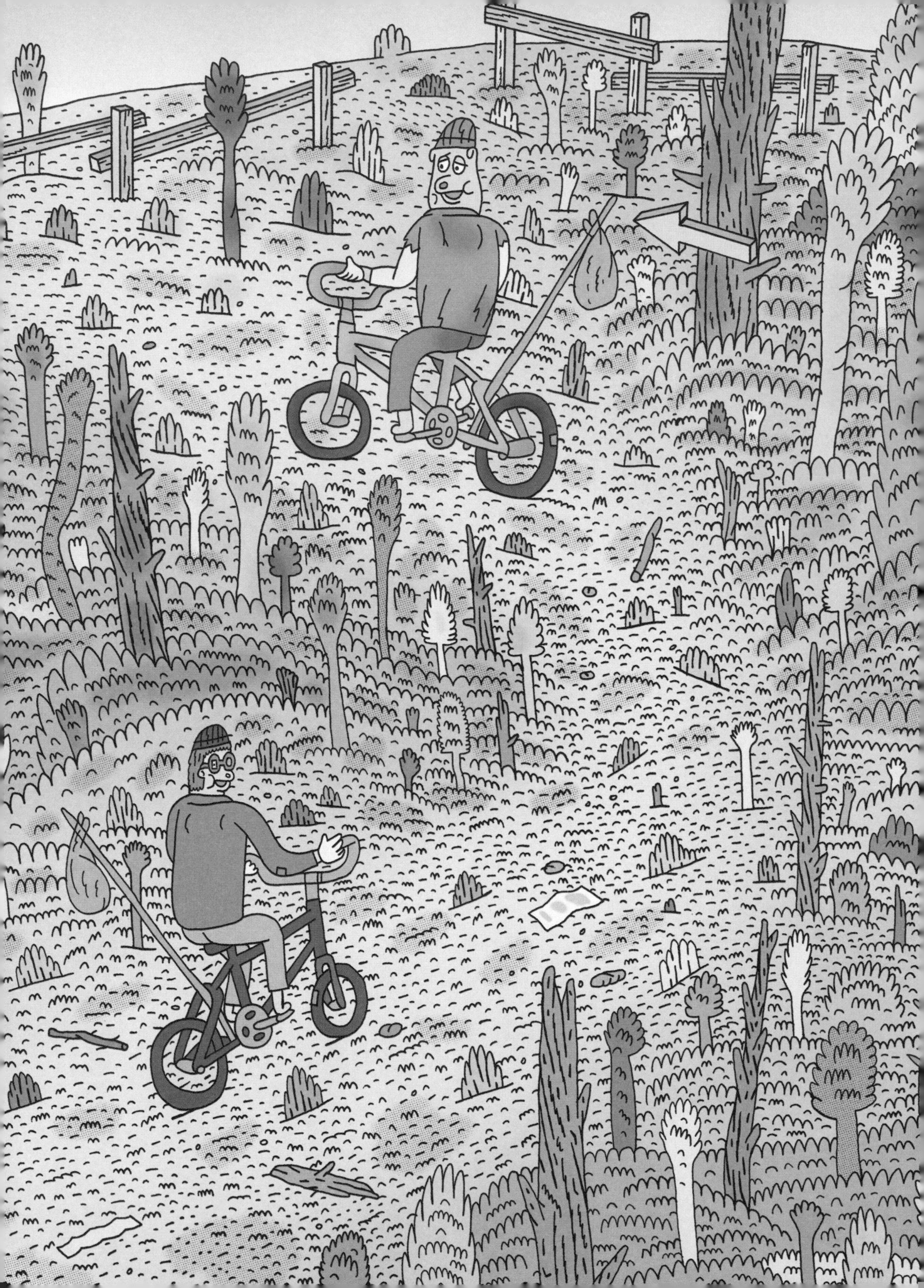

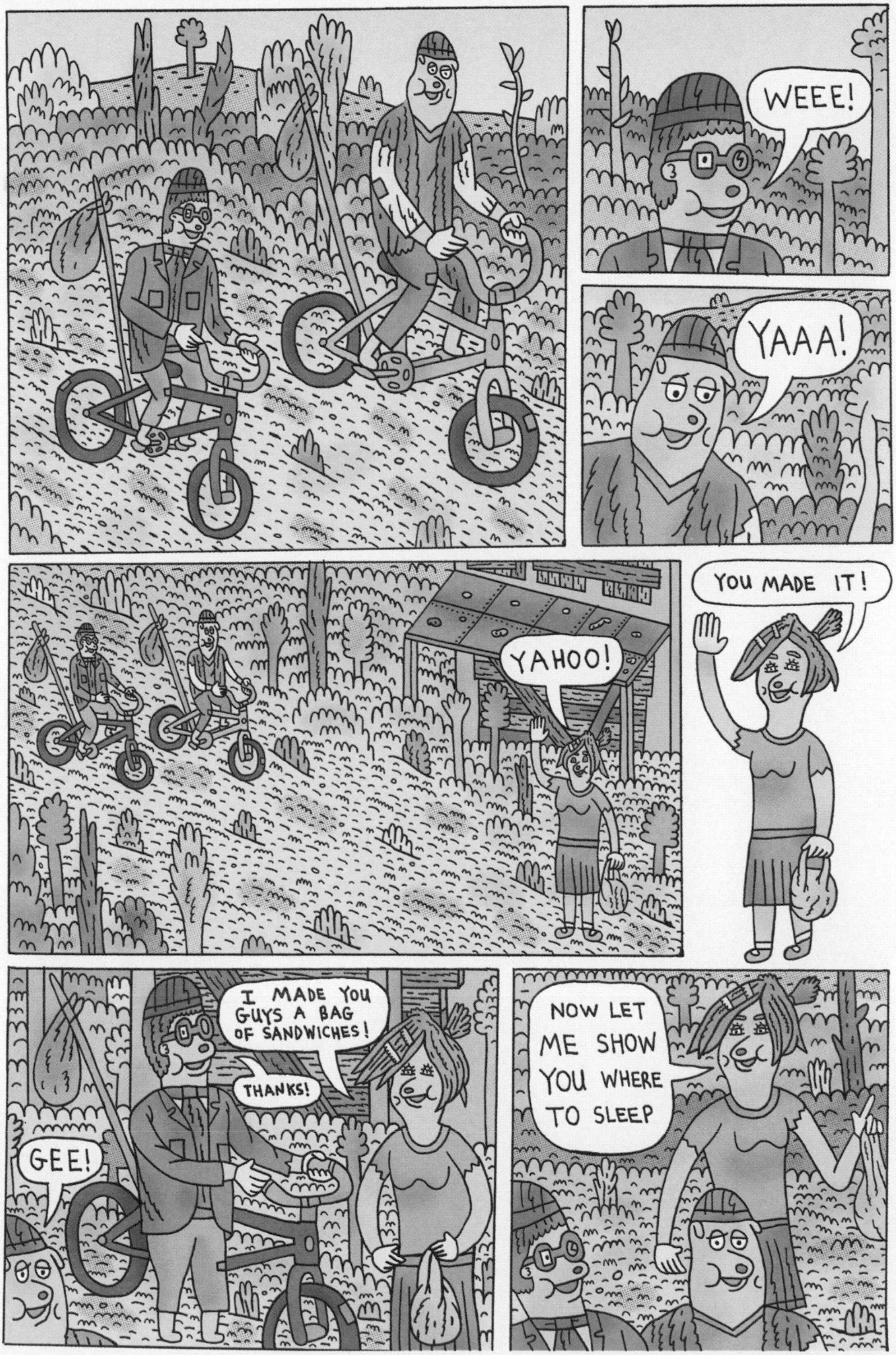
WEEE!
YAAA!
YAHOO!
YOU MADE IT!
I MADE YOU GUYS A BAG OF SANDWICHES!
THANKS!
GEE!
NOW LET ME SHOW YOU WHERE TO SLEEP

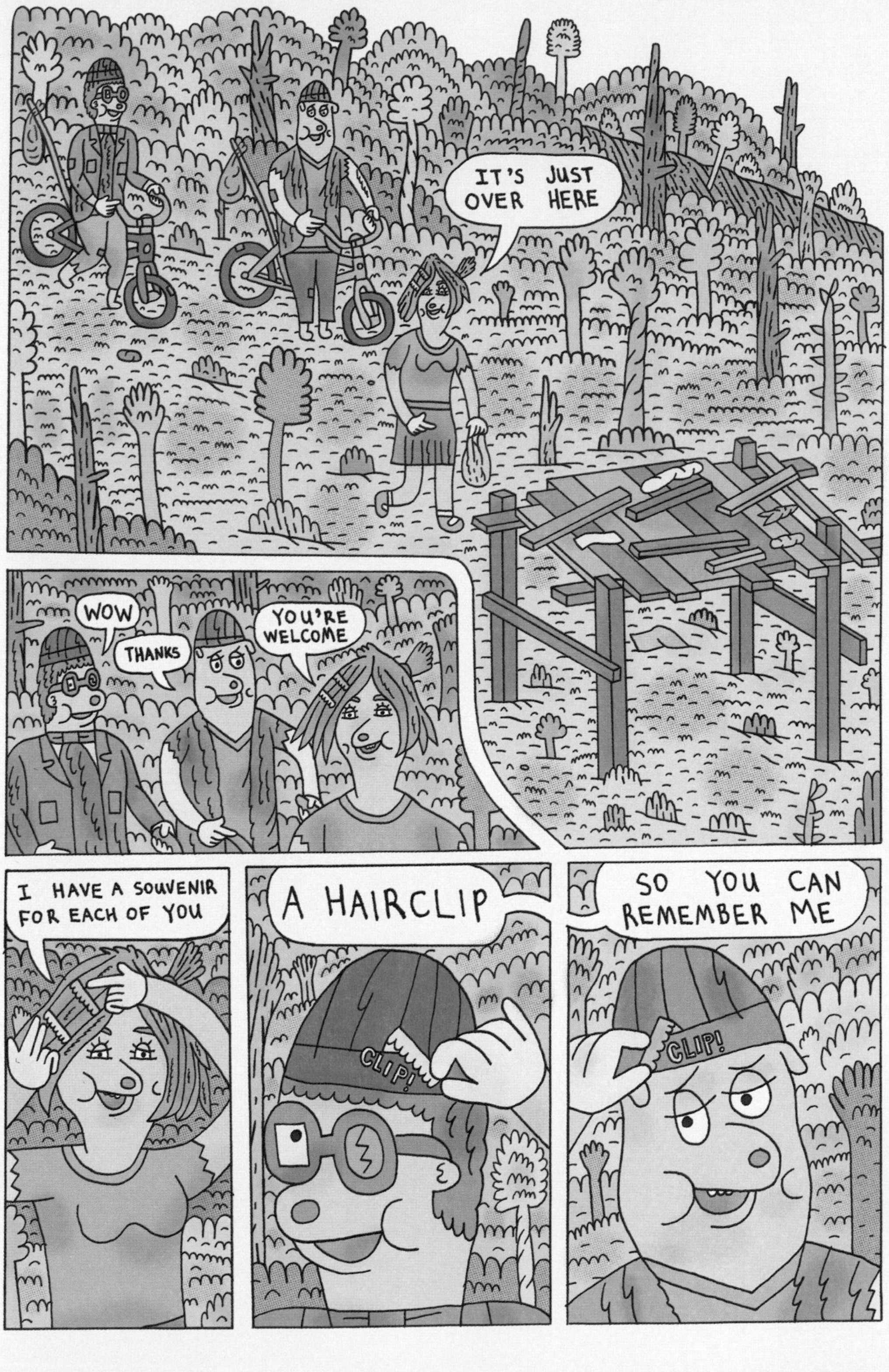
IT'S JUST OVER HERE
WOW
THANKS
YOU'RE WELCOME
I HAVE A SOUVENIR FOR EACH OF YOU
A HAIRCLIP
CLIP!
SO YOU CAN REMEMBER ME
CLIP!

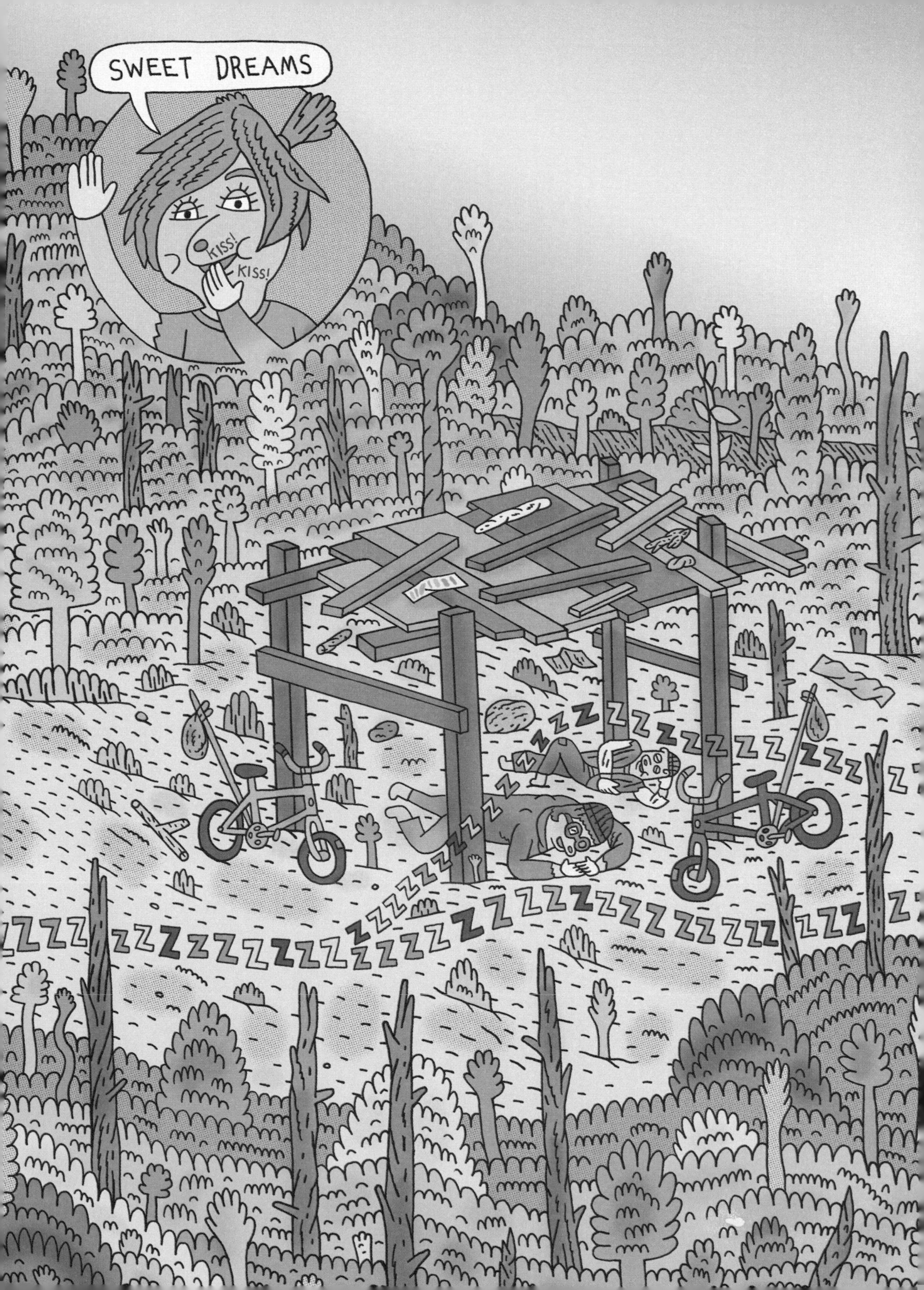
SWEET DREAMS
KISS!
KISS!
ZZZZZZZZZZZZZZZZZZZZZZZZZZZZZZZZ

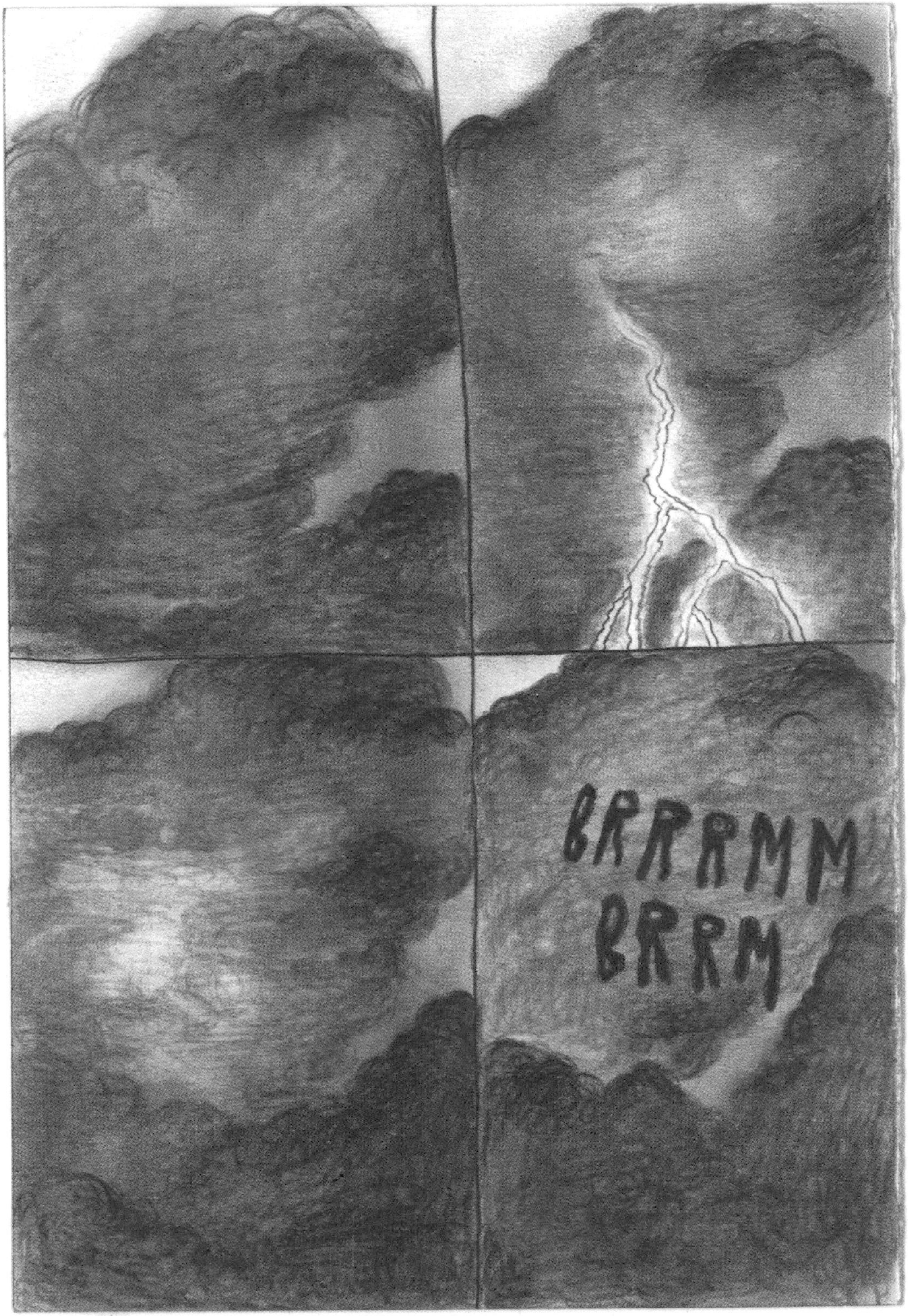
BRRRMM
BRRM

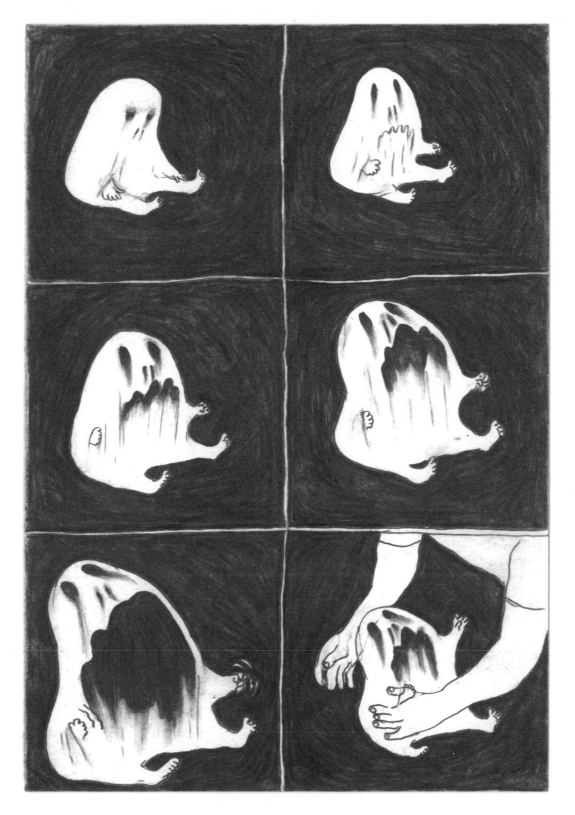

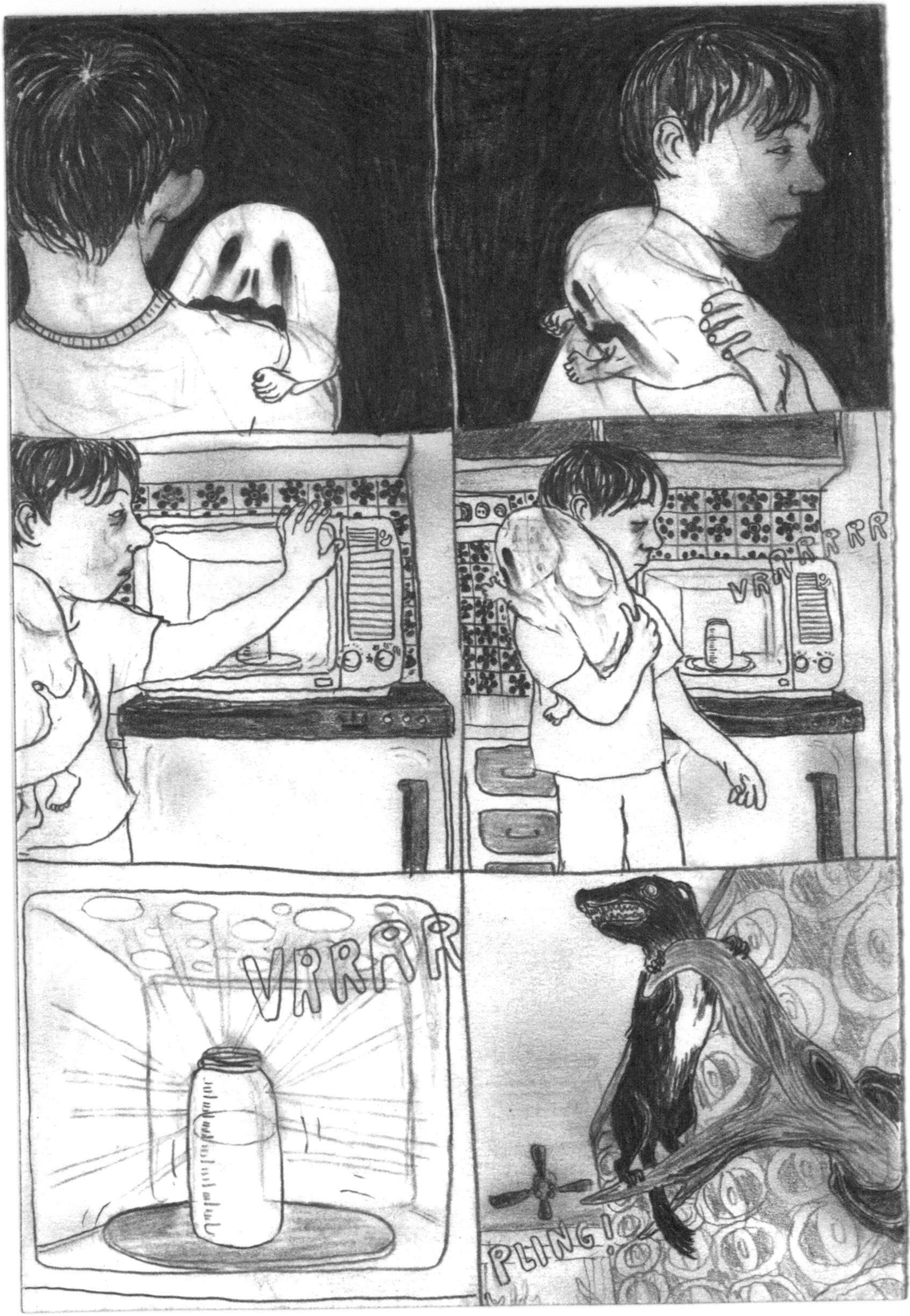
VRRRRRRR
VRRRR
PLING!

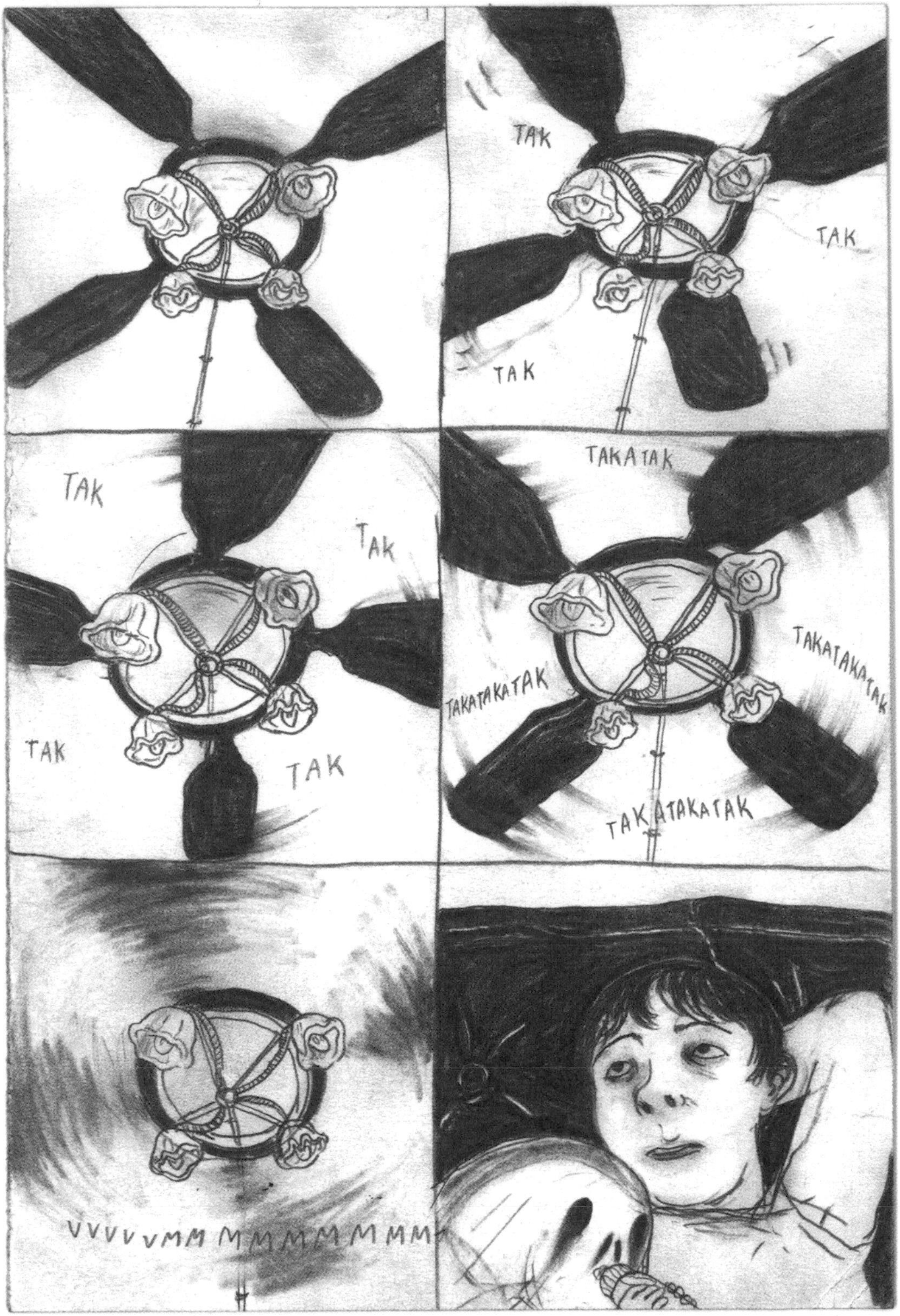
TAK
TAK
TAK
TAK
TAK
TAK
TAK
TAKATAK
TAKATAKATAK
TAKATAKATAK
TAKATAKATAK
VVVVVMM MMMMMMMM

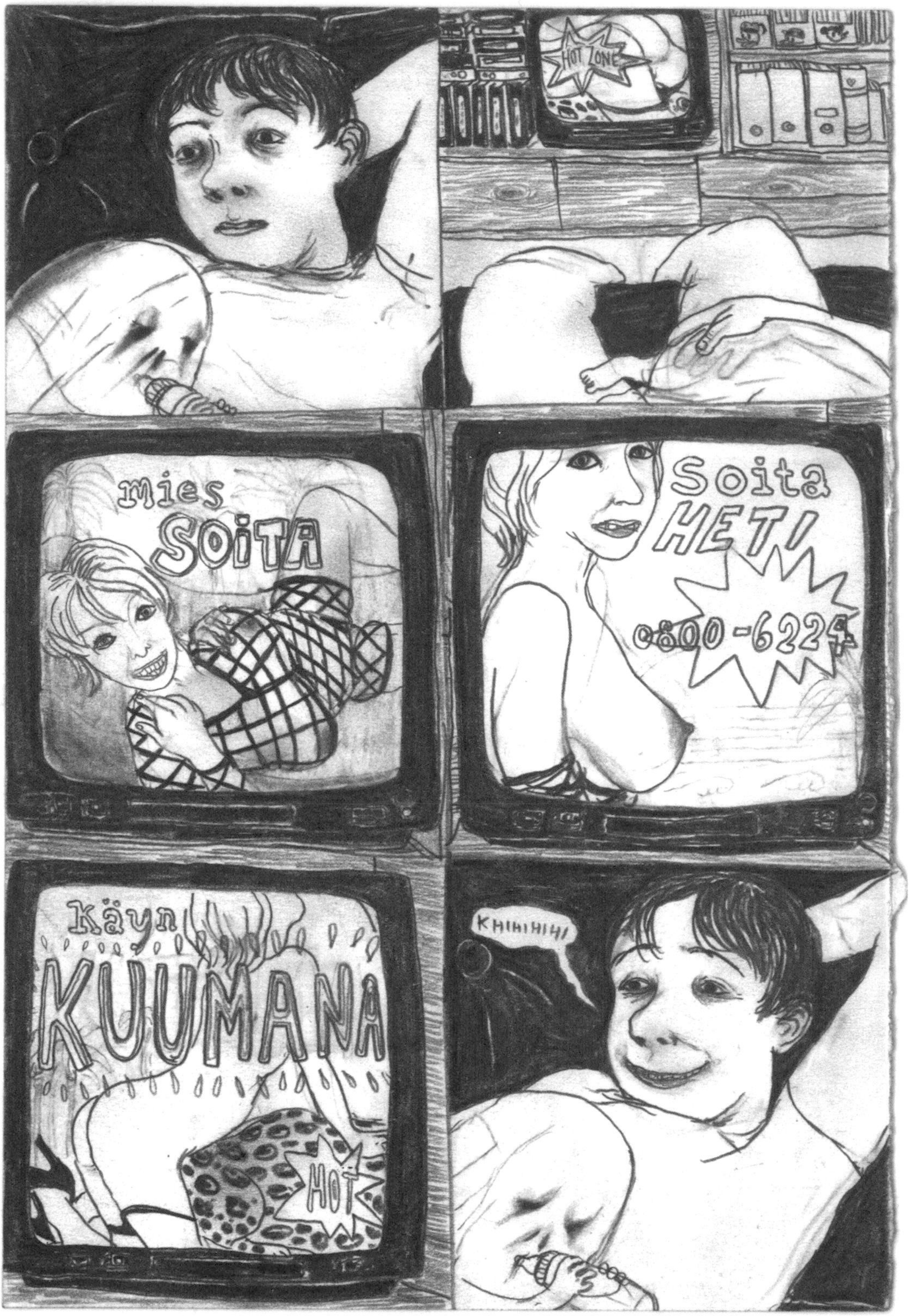
HOT ZONE
mies
SOITA
Soita
HETI
0800-6224
Käyn
KUUMANA
HOT
KHIHIHIHI

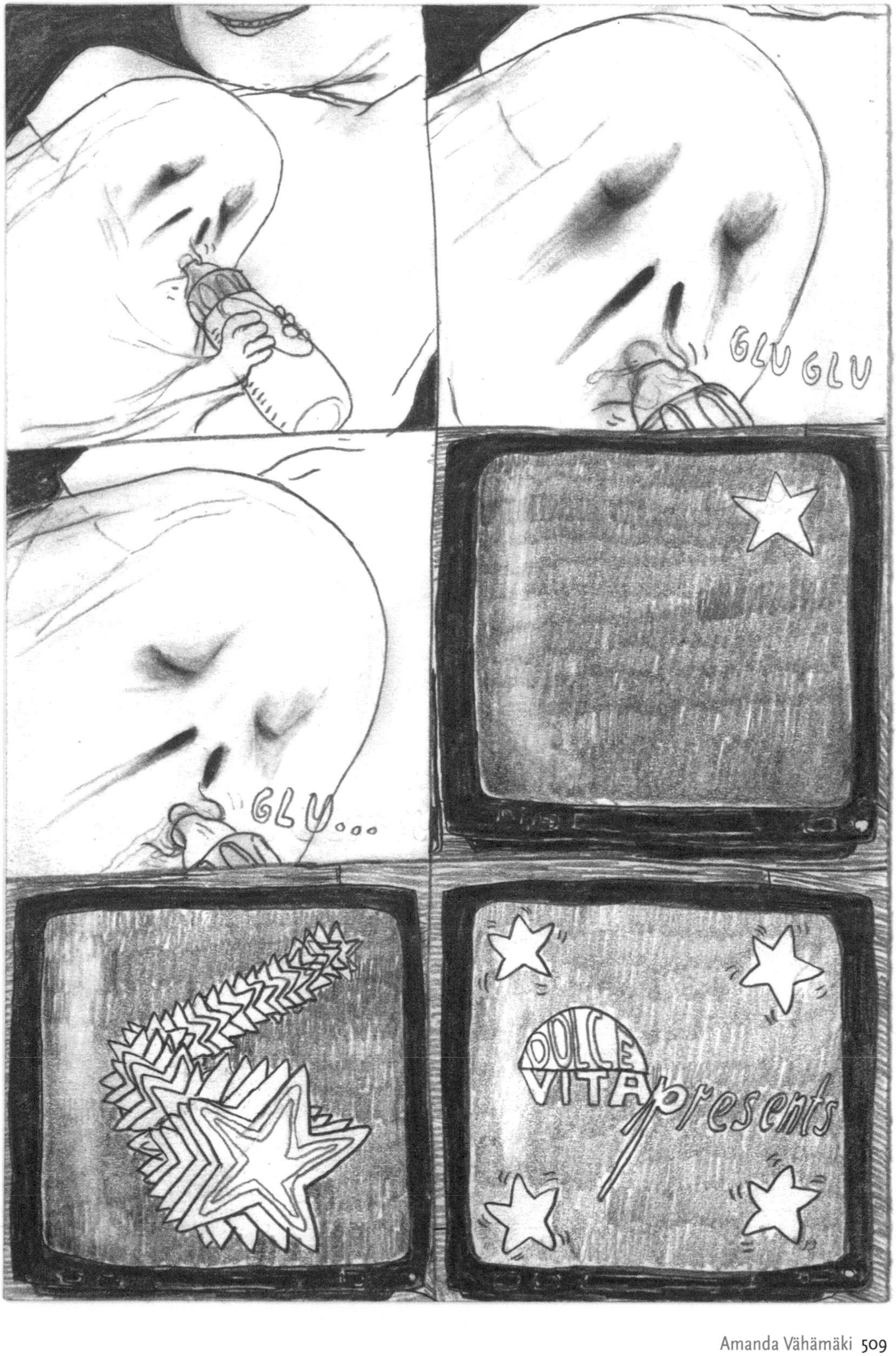
GLU GLU
GLU...
DOLCE
VITA presents

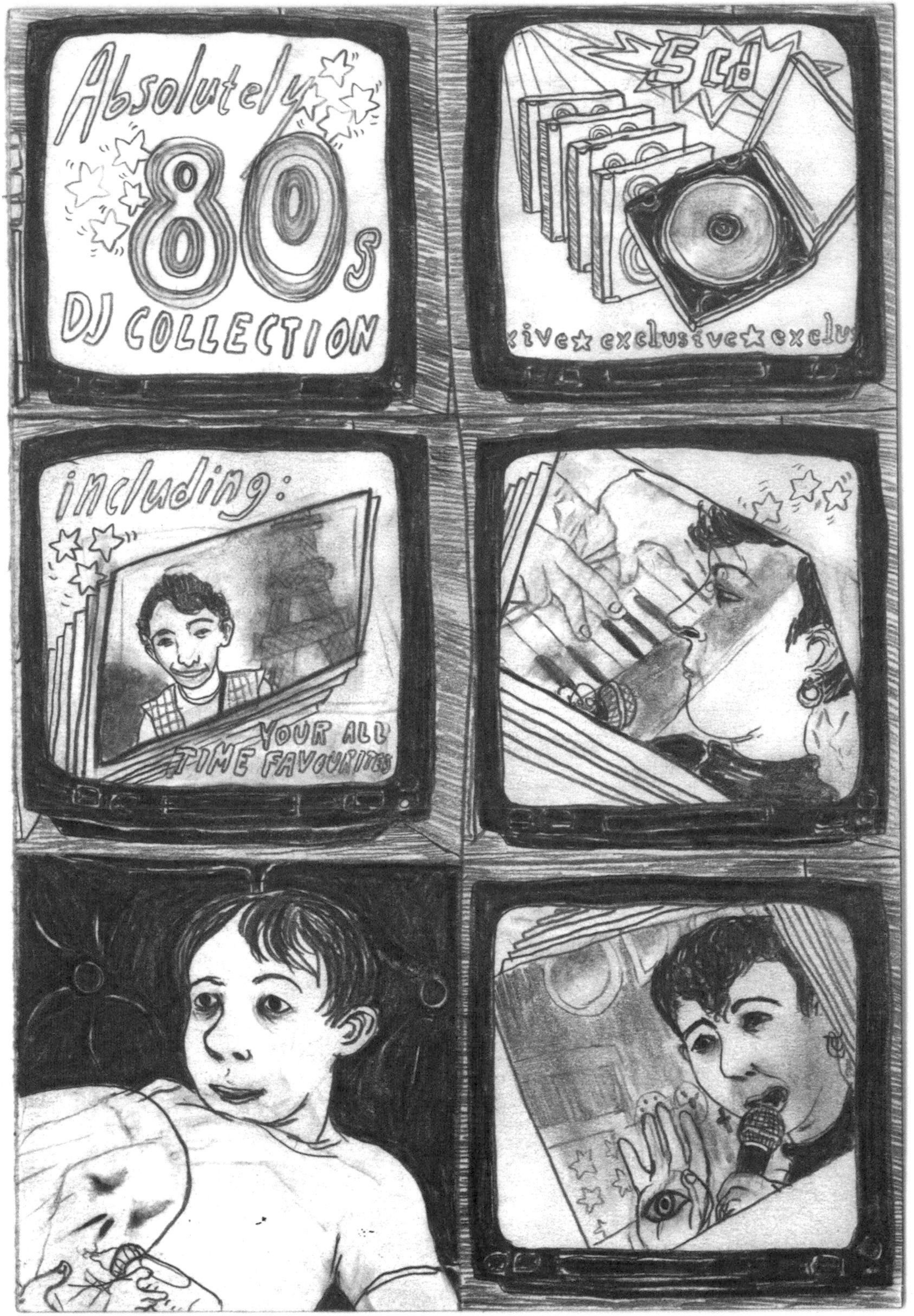
Absolutely
80s
DJ COLLECTION
5CD
xive★exclusive★exclu
including:
YOUR ALL TIME FAVOURITES

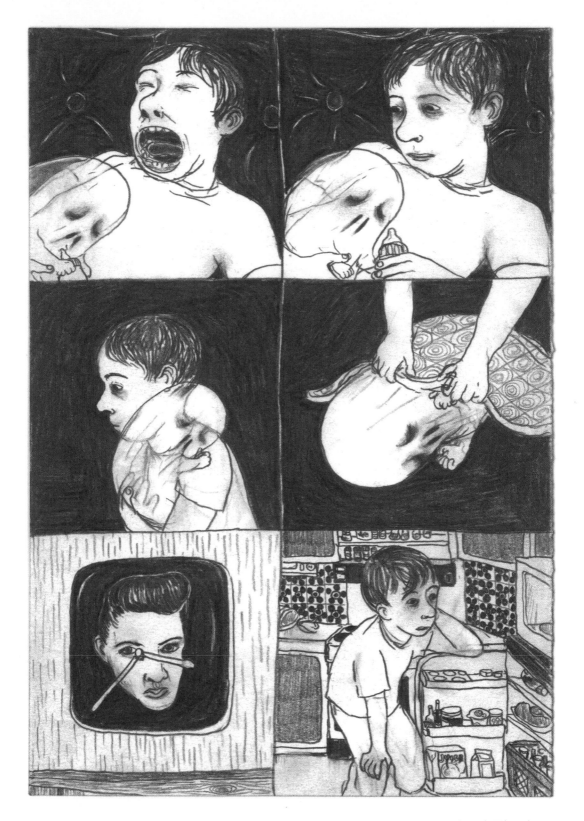

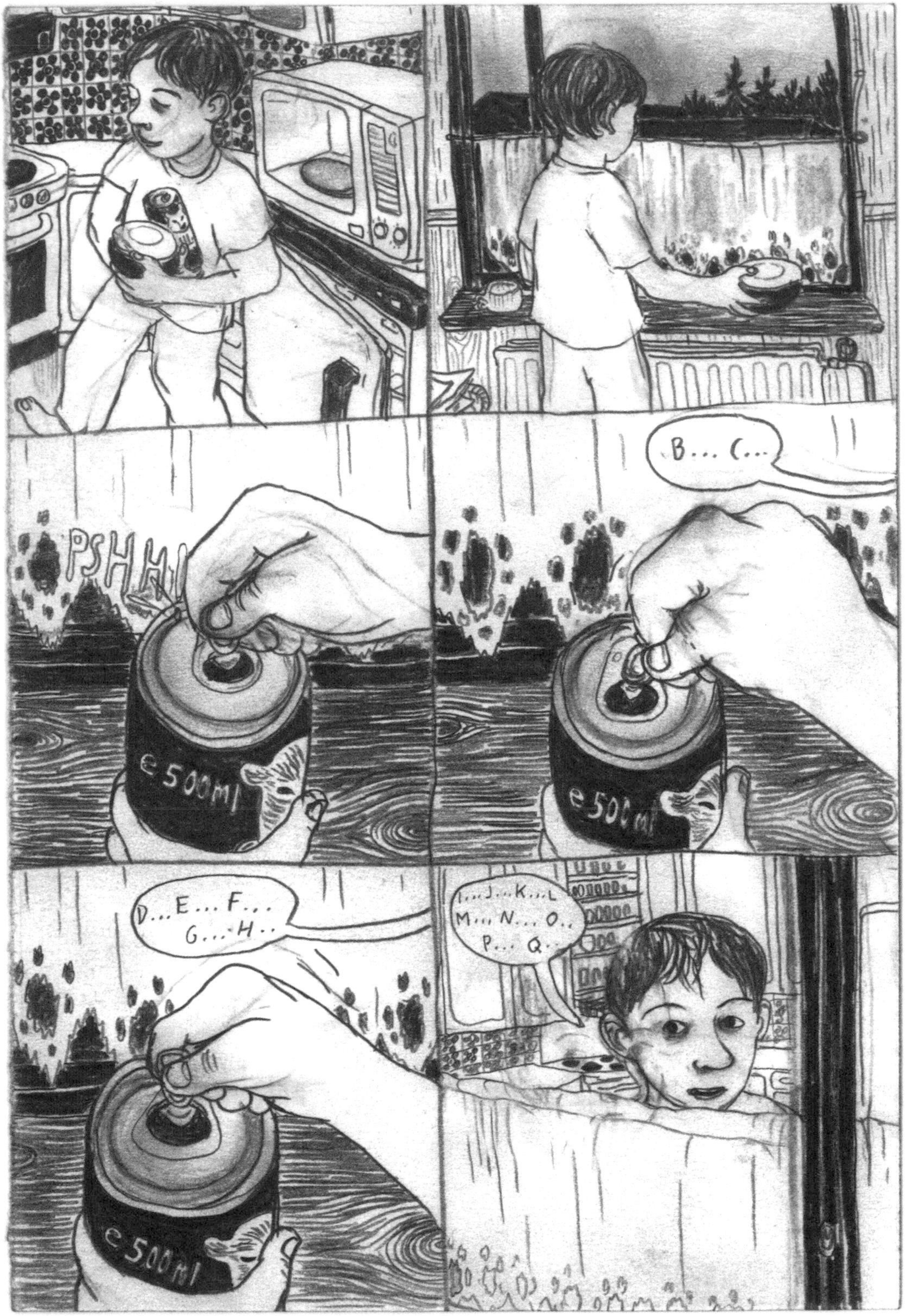
PSHHH
B... C...
D... E... F...
G... H...
I... J... K... L
M... N... O...
P... Q...

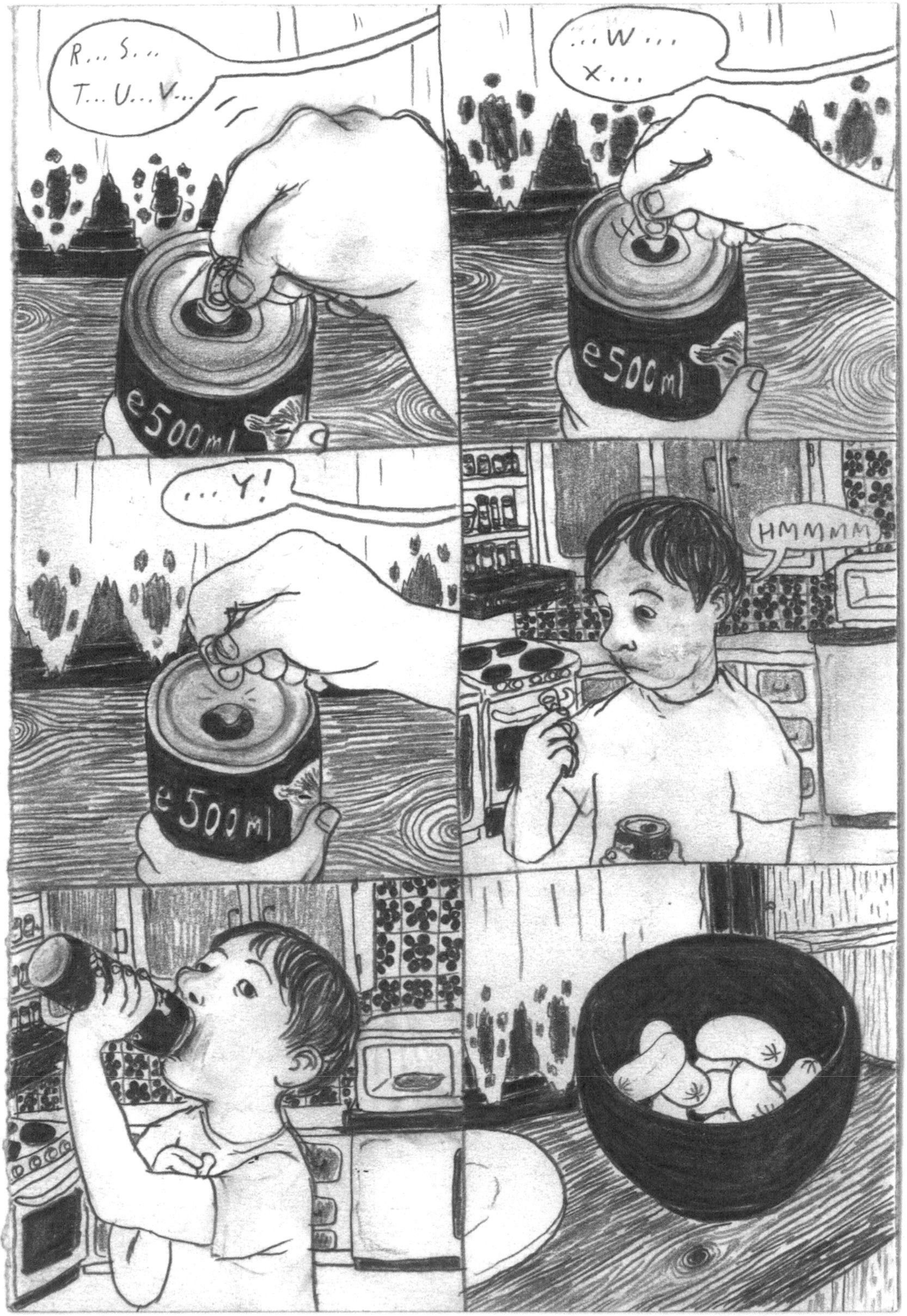
R... S...
T... U... V...
e500ml
...W...
X...
e500ml
...Y!
e500ml
HMMMM

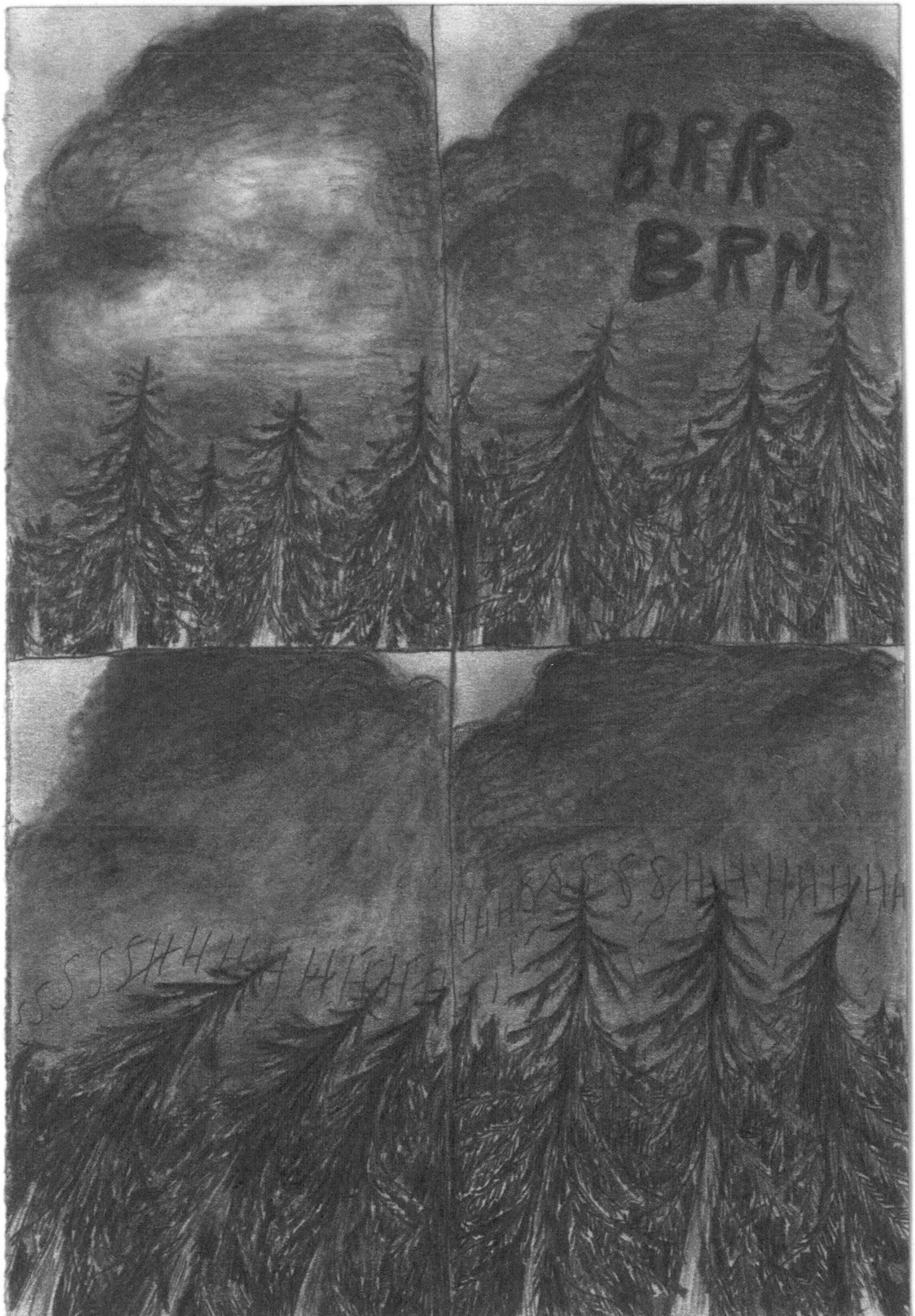
BRR
BRM

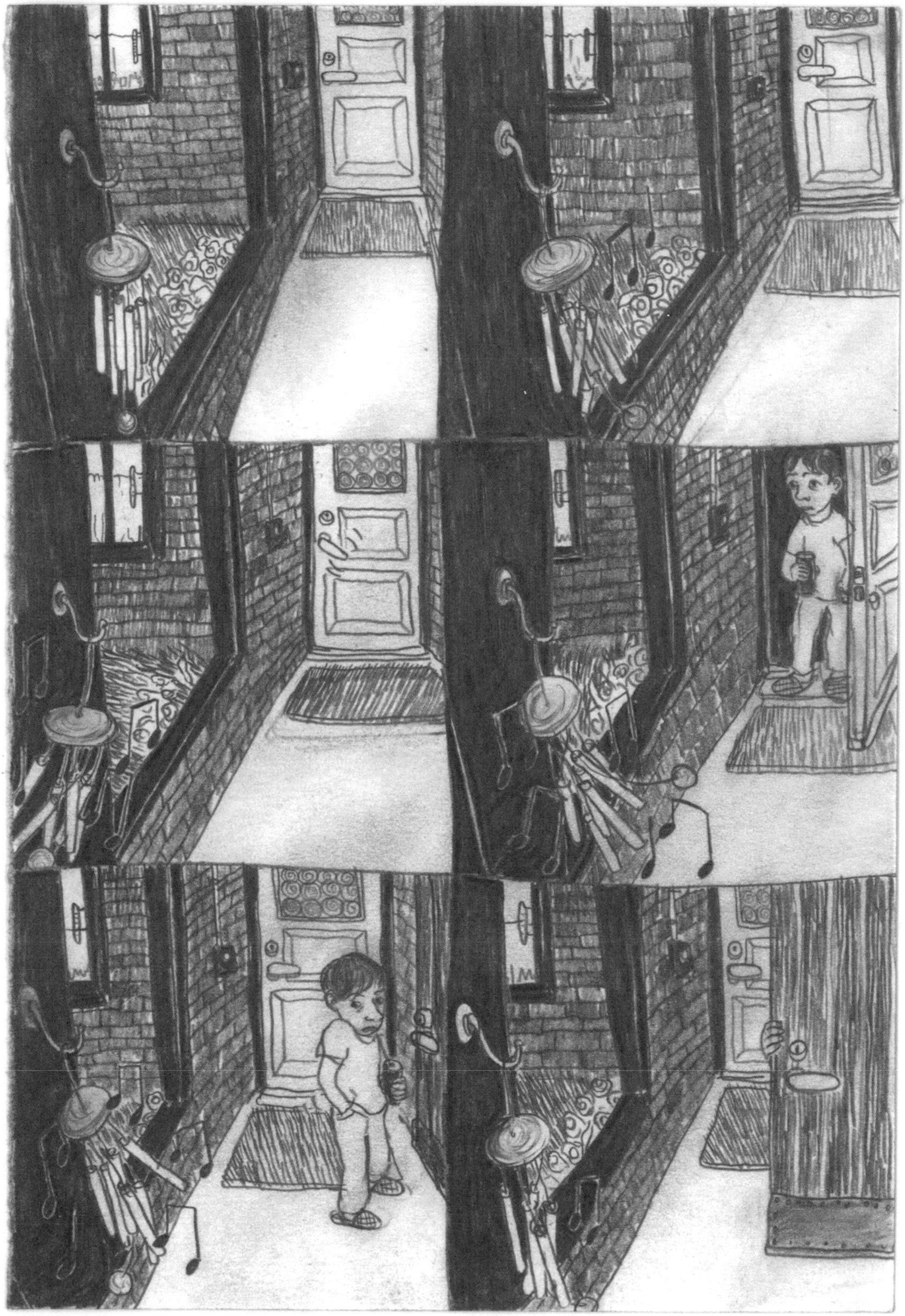

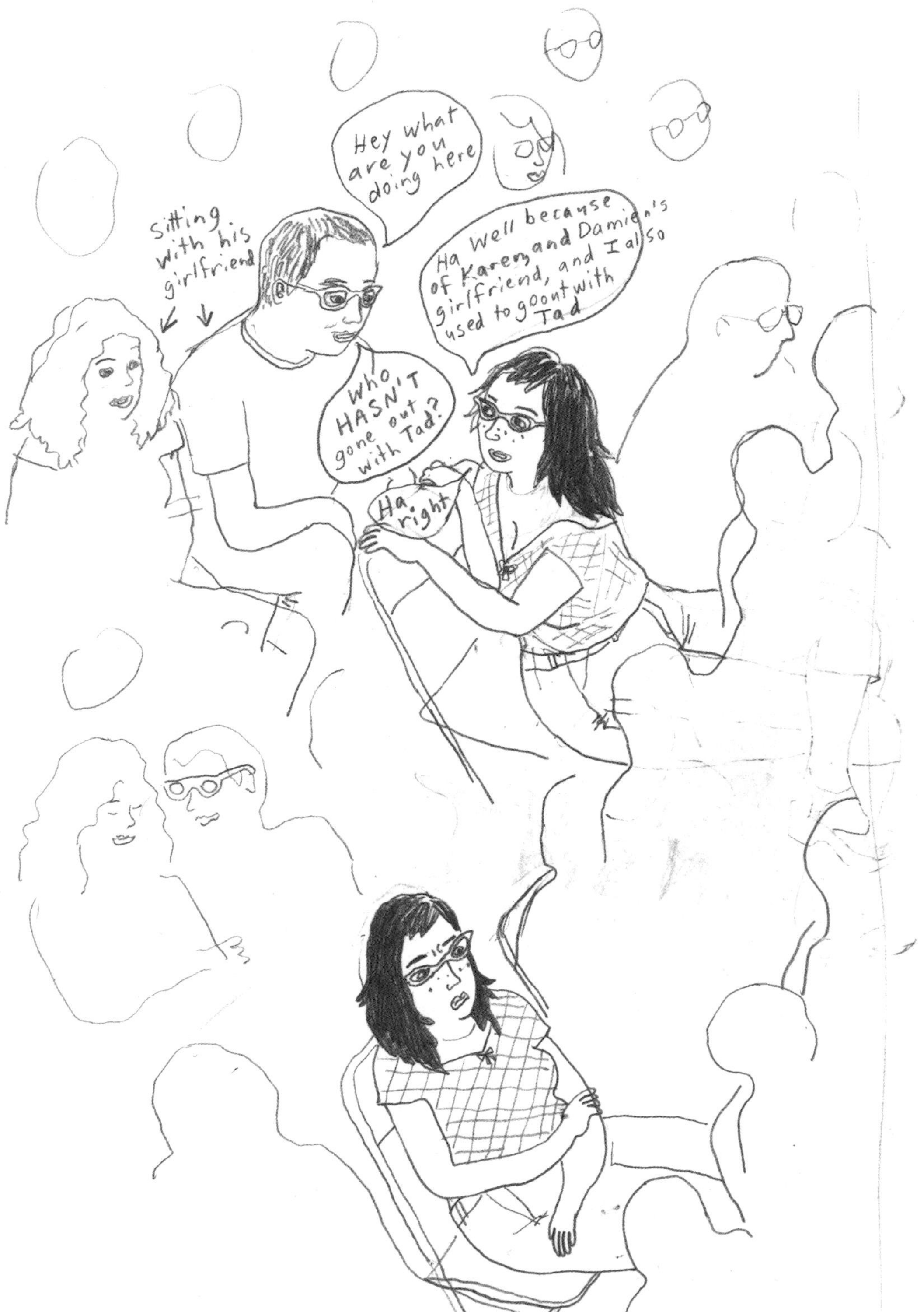
Hey what are you doing here
Sitting with his girlfriend
Ha well because of Karen and Damien's girlfriend, and I also used to go out with Tad
Who HASN'T gone out with Tad?
Ha right

 Comic first appeared in Vanessa Davis's *Make Me a Woman* (2010).

MY FRIEND VANESSA DAVIS

an appreciation by Mimi Pond

I became aware of D+Q when it was still a magazine. But in the 2000s, I noticed with wild jealousy that stories by D+Q artists Chris Ware, Seth, and Rutu Modan were being published in the *New York Times Magazine*. The books D+Q was putting out blew my mind. I began to follow them while also juggling raising children and trying desperately to revive my own (at one time flourishing) cartooning career, which had suffered from parenthood/the internet/publishing mayhem.

As the 2000s progressed, I also discovered the work of Vanessa Davis. Even though she was in Santa Rosa and I was in LA, we began to talk and really hit it off. I had finally found someone who shared my sensibilities! We both love drawing, we both strive to express the absurdity of real-life situations in our comics, we're both kind of unapologetically middle-class women cartoonists. In a world of weirdo bohemian cartoonists, we're the ones talking about recipes and home décor—*who still nonetheless dig comics!* Since I'd moved to LA from New York, I hadn't had any cartoonist friends. Instead, I was sucked up in a maelstrom of socializing with the parents of my children's friends. I told Vanessa that I was trying to find a publisher for my graphic novel, and since of course she was already doing a book with D+Q, without hesitation she told me to get in touch with Tom Devlin. I did, and eventually D+Q published *Over Easy*. Thank you, Vanessa!

The first time I met Vanessa in person, in LA in 2010, she came over with her wonderful boyfriend (now fiancé), Trevor Alixopulos. They met our kids, we played badminton in our backyard, ate dinner, and guzzled rosé, and everyone looked at everyone's artwork. It was love all around. The second time she came to town, for her event for her D+Q book, *Make Me a Woman*, it was her birthday, so of course I had to bake her a pink lady cake. Anyone who has made a book like *Make Me a Woman* deserves way more than a girly dessert made with strawberries. IT WAS THE LEAST I COULD DO!

I can't browse through *Make Me a Woman* without finding something to marvel over, again and again. Of course I revel in the idea that someone else besides me enjoys making observational cartoon asides. Example: the fact that the boy mauling her while dancing with her at a bar mitzvah had the last name "Boner." I am dazzled by her skills as a cartoonist, by her

ability to capture great expressions like looks of total revulsion for both herself and others. Her draftsmanship and her poetic ease with the human form blow my mind. Do you know how hard it is to make a drawing of yourself, having fainted, both comic and expertly executed, even though it's from a low perspective? Her sly and subtle drawings of herself in awkward situations—everything from chemical depilatory lip rash to having her wisdom teeth removed—make the inelegant elegant. They make us fall in love with her.

Mimi's made a lot of comics, about so many things. LA, teenagers, Richard Simmons, the seventies, art school, sex. But so particularly, so idiosyncratically, about these things. She loves DETAILS! And who doesn't? But I really love details. Her panel in *Over Easy* where she's peeling a suction-cupped industrial restaurant kitchen mat up in order to hose it off filled me with recognition and gratitude. Page 215 is completely devoted to the knick-knacks one might find on a "paint-flaked windowsill" in an artsy young person's apartment in Oakland in 1979. They're the exact same ones you'd find today—it's almost embarrassing. The "broken miniature figurine with its head knocked off, waiting to be re-glued, some day...no time soon...because the years, we know, stretch on and on, we have plenty of time." Mimi!—***Vanessa Davis***

And I have. Vanessa is a bridge friend. We are very good friends, but she also has become good friends with both my children—especially my daughter, Lulu, who was fourteen when they first met. During her emotional teens, Lulu would surprise both Vanessa and me with a sudden tearful confession about her hopes and fears. Vanessa's advice for her at the time worked better than mine. And that's okay! We all have so much in common. Vanessa toggles well between the generations. I think this is true because of her essential objectivity, very evident in her work. She examines all sides—and then usually takes the funniest and most oblique point of view. She'll make you think she's just this adorable pixie, then she leads you down the garden path to some wicked and weirdly funny place that leaves you with your mind blown.

Bring Your Daughter to Work by Vid

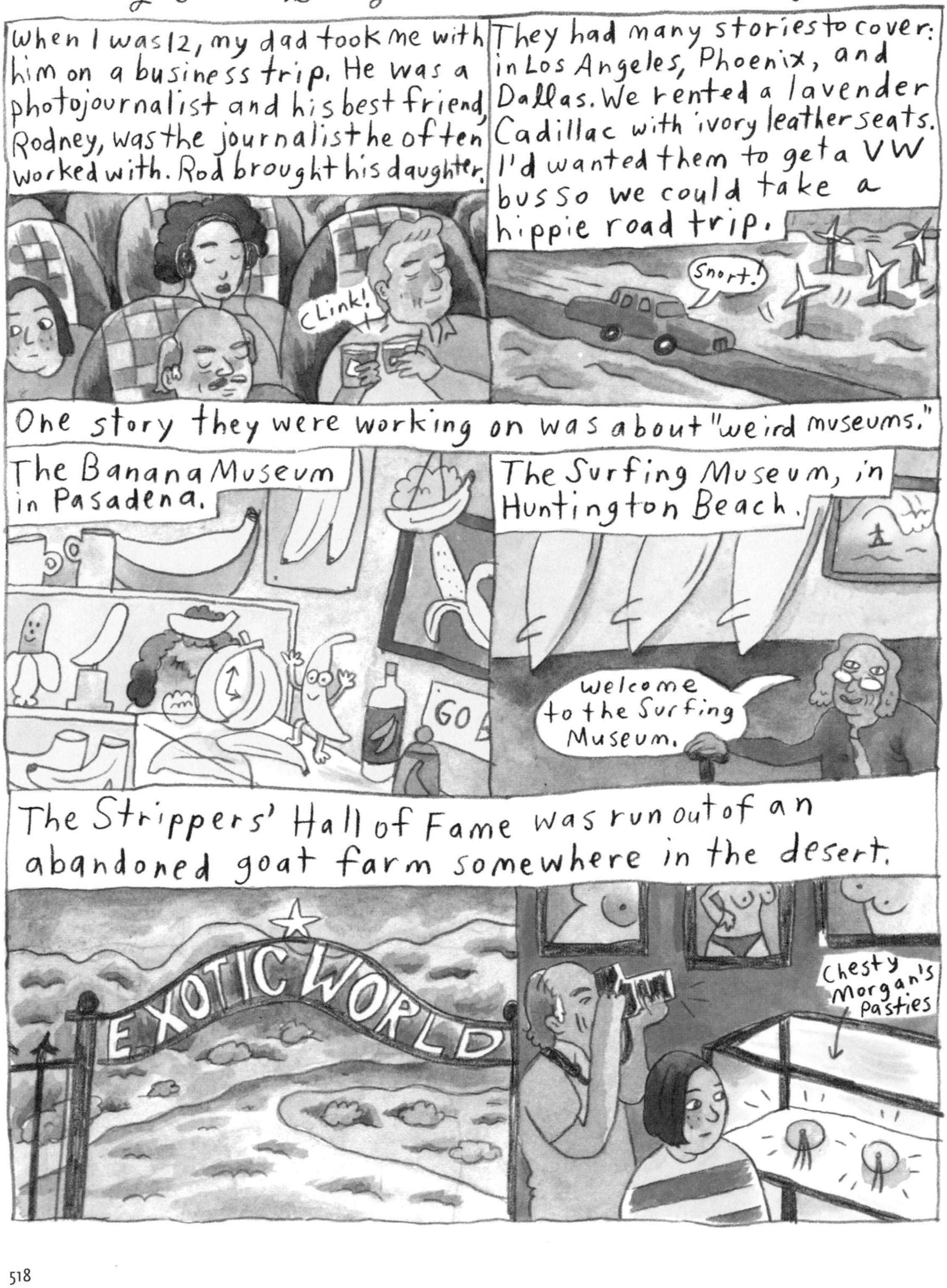
When I was 12, my dad took me with him on a business trip. He was a photojournalist and his best friend, Rodney, was the journalist he often worked with. Rod brought his daughter.
Clink!
They had many stories to cover: in Los Angeles, Phoenix, and Dallas. We rented a lavender Cadillac with ivory leather seats. I'd wanted them to get a VW bus so we could take a hippie road trip.
Snort!
One story they were working on was about "weird museums."
The Banana Museum in Pasadena.
The Surfing Museum, in Huntington Beach.
Welcome to the Surfing Museum.
The Strippers' Hall of Fame was run out of an abandoned goat farm somewhere in the desert.
EXOTIC WORLD
Chesty Morgan's pasties

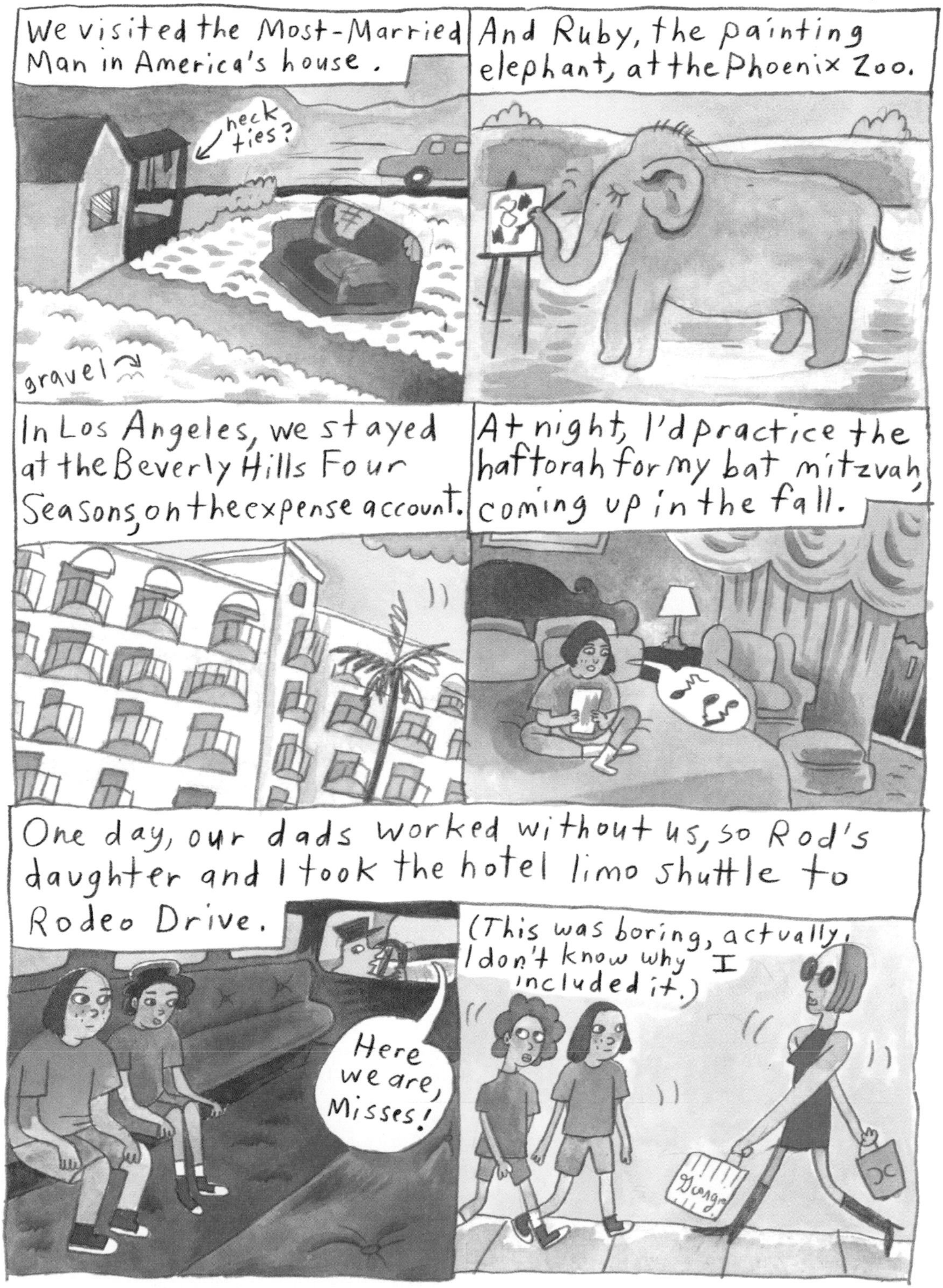
We visited the Most-Married Man in America's house.
heck ties?
gravel
And Ruby, the painting elephant, at the Phoenix Zoo.
In Los Angeles, we stayed at the Beverly Hills Four Seasons, on the expense account.
At night, I'd practice the haftorah for my bat mitzvah, coming up in the fall.
One day, our dads worked without us, so Rod's daughter and I took the hotel limo shuttle to Rodeo Drive.
Here we are, Misses!
(This was boring, actually, I don't know why I included it.)

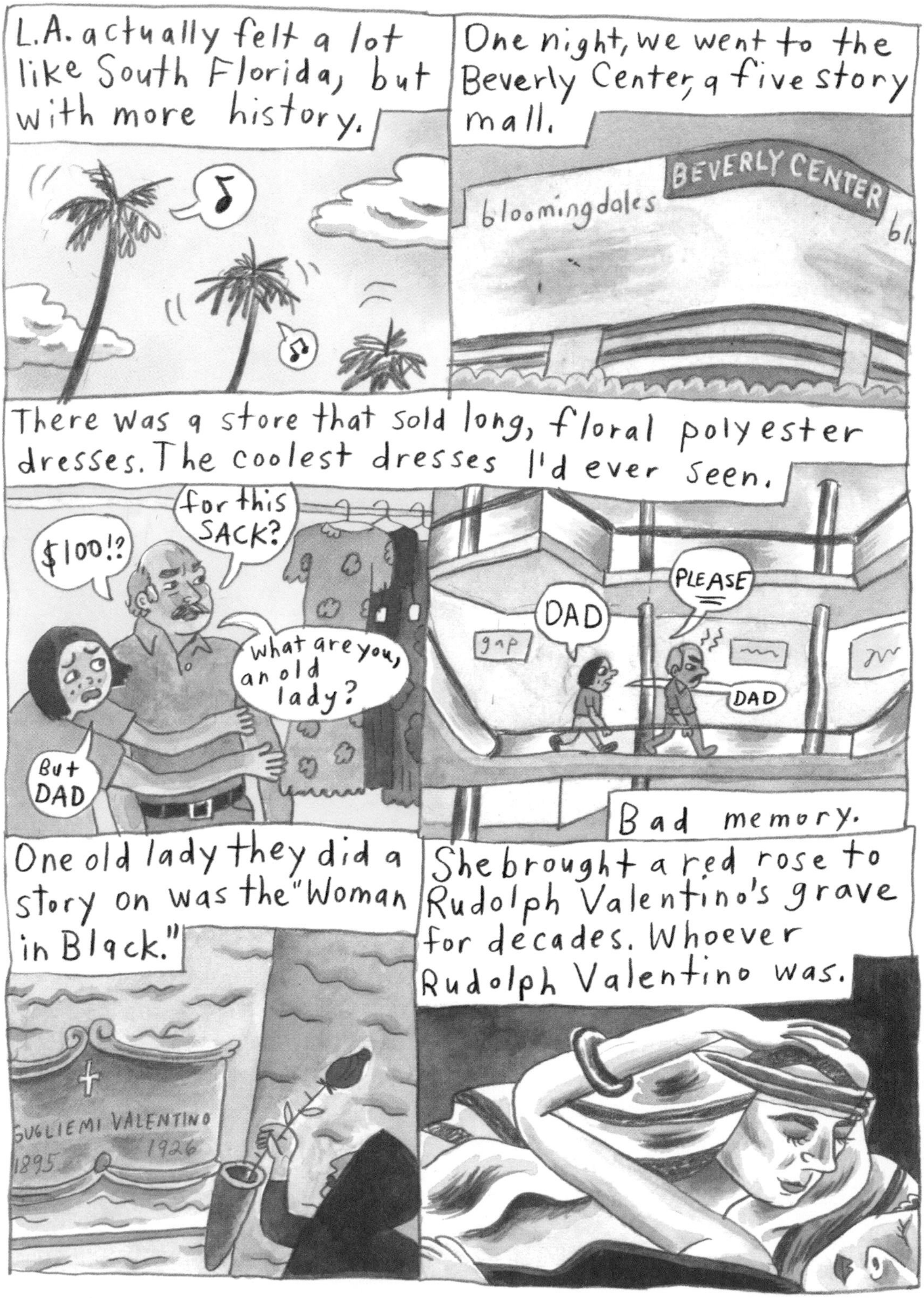
L.A. actually felt a lot like South Florida, but with more history.
One night, we went to the Beverly Center, a five story mall.
BEVERLY CENTER
bloomingdales
There was a store that sold long, floral polyester dresses. The coolest dresses I'd ever seen.
$100!?
for this SACK?
what are you, an old lady?
But DAD
DAD
PLEASE
gap
DAD
Bad memory.
One old lady they did a story on was the "Woman in Black."
GUGLIEMI VALENTINO
1895 1926
She brought a red rose to Rudolph Valentino's grave for decades. Whoever Rudolph Valentino was.

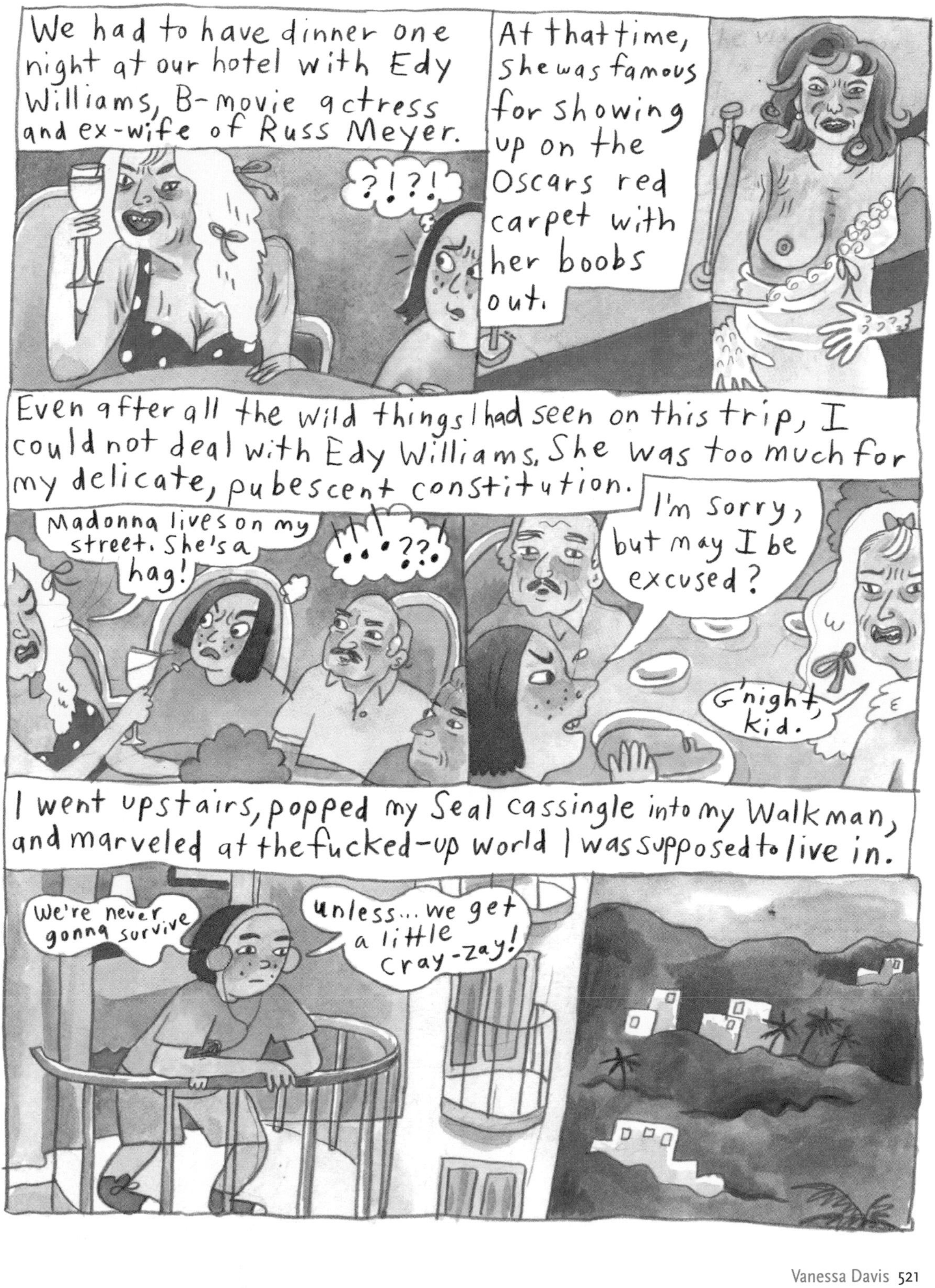
We had to have dinner one night at our hotel with Edy Williams, B-movie actress and ex-wife of Russ Meyer.
?!?!
At that time, she was famous for showing up on the Oscars red carpet with her boobs out.
Even after all the wild things I had seen on this trip, I could not deal with Edy Williams. She was too much for my delicate, pubescent constitution.
Madonna lives on my street. She's a hag!
...??!
I'm sorry, but may I be excused?
G'night, kid.
I went upstairs, popped my Seal cassingle into my Walkman, and marveled at the fucked-up world I was supposed to live in.
We're never gonna survive
unless... we get a little cray-zay!

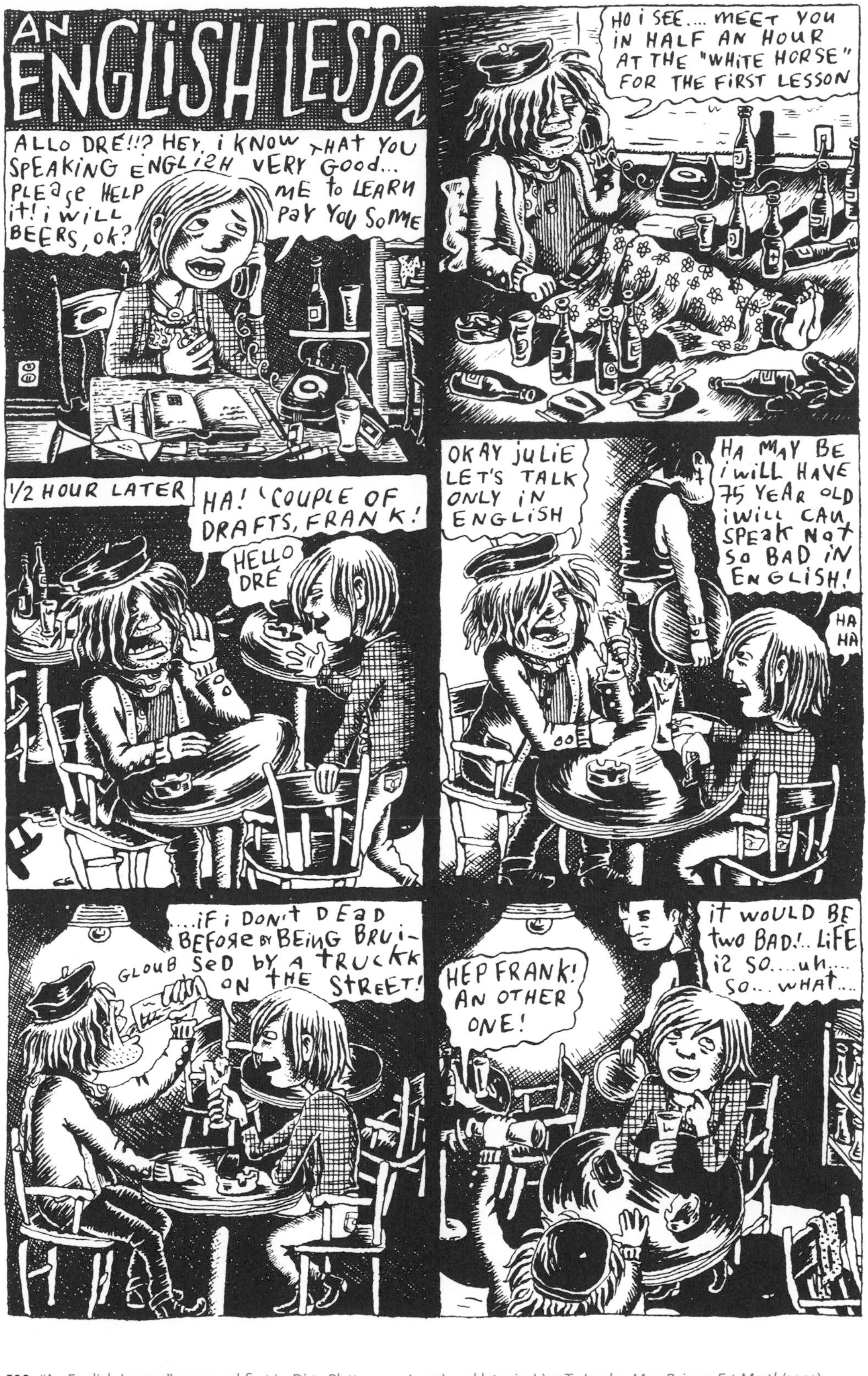
AN ENGLiSH LESSON
ALLO DRE!!? HEY, i KNOW THAT YOU SPEAKiNG ENGLiSH VERY Good... PLEaSE HELP ME to LEARN it! i WiLL PAY YOU SoMME BEERS, OK?
HO i SEE.... MEET YOU IN HALF AN HOUR AT THE "WHiTE HORSE" FOR THE FiRST LESSON
1/2 HOUR LATER
HA! 'COUPLE OF DRAFTS, FRANK!
HELLO DRÉ
OKAY JULiE LET'S TALK ONLY iN ENGLiSH
HA MAY BE i WiLL HAVE 75 YEAR OLD i WiLL CAN SPEAK NOT So BAD IN ENGLiSH!
HA HA
...iF i DON'T DEaD BEFORE BY BEiNG BRUi-SED BY A TRUCKK ON THE STREET!
GLOUB
HEP FRANK! AN OTHER ONE!
iT WOULD BE TWO BAD!.. LiFE iS SO....uh.... SO... WHAT...

 "An English Lesson" appeared first in *Dirty Plotte* no. 2 (1991) and later in *Lève Ta Jambe, Mon Poisson Est Mort!* (1993).

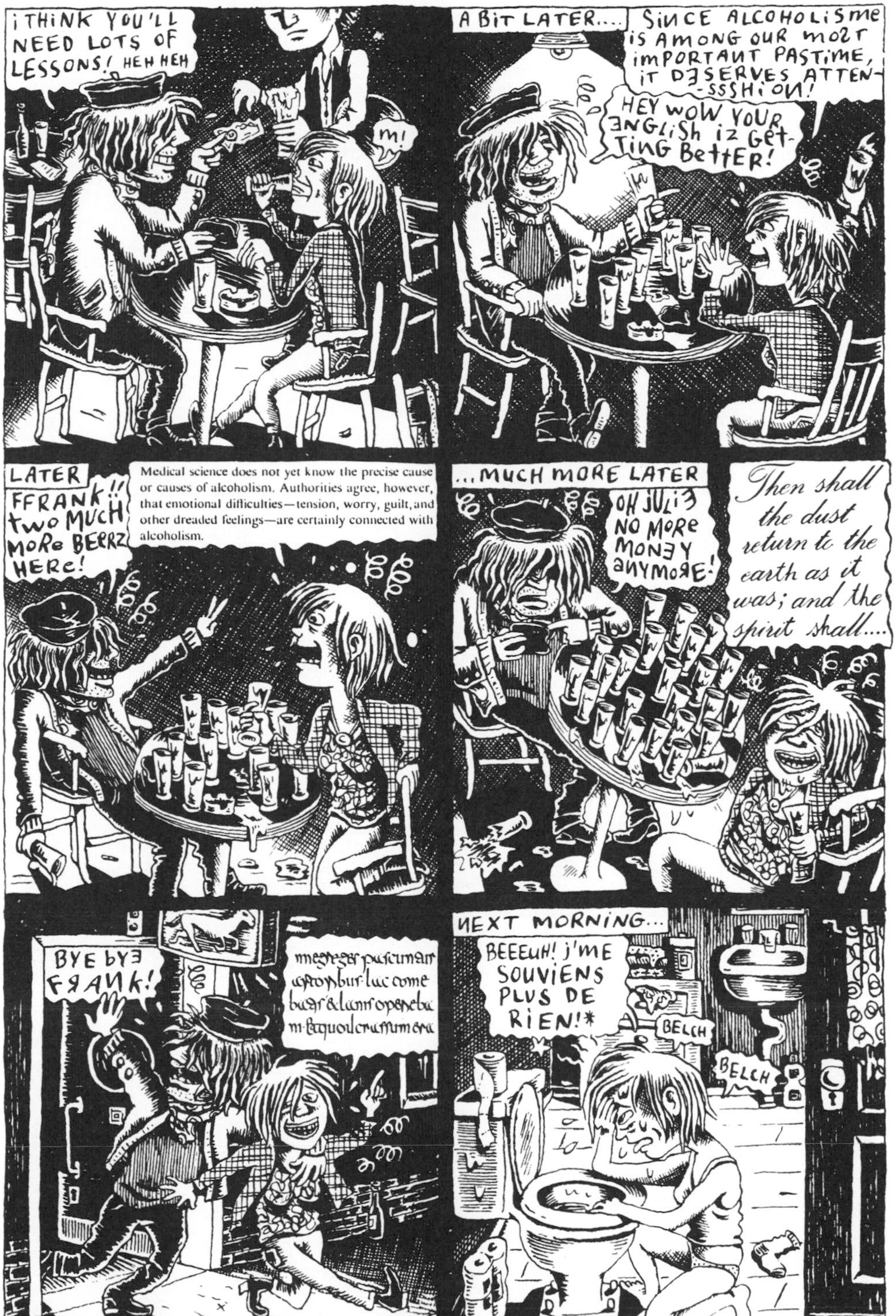
i THINK YOU'LL NEED LOTS OF LESSONS! HEH HEH
m!
A BIT LATER....
SINCE ALCOHOLISME IS AMONG OUR MOST IMPORTANT PASTIME, IT DESERVES ATTEN--SSSHION!
HEY WOW YOUR ENGLISH IZ GETTING BETTER!
LATER
FFRANK!! TWO MUCH MORE BERRZ HERE!
Medical science does not yet know the precise cause or causes of alcoholism. Authorities agree, however, that emotional difficulties—tension, worry, guilt, and other dreaded feelings—are certainly connected with alcoholism.
...MUCH MORE LATER
OH JULIE NO MORE MONEY ANYMORE!
Then shall the dust return to the earth as it was; and the spirit shall....
BYE BYE FRANK!
NEXT MORNING...
BEEEUH! j'ME SOUVIENS PLUS DE RIEN!*
BELCH
BELCH
END
BY JULIE DOUCET 1990
*"ARGHRGH i CAN'T REMEMBER ANYTHING.."

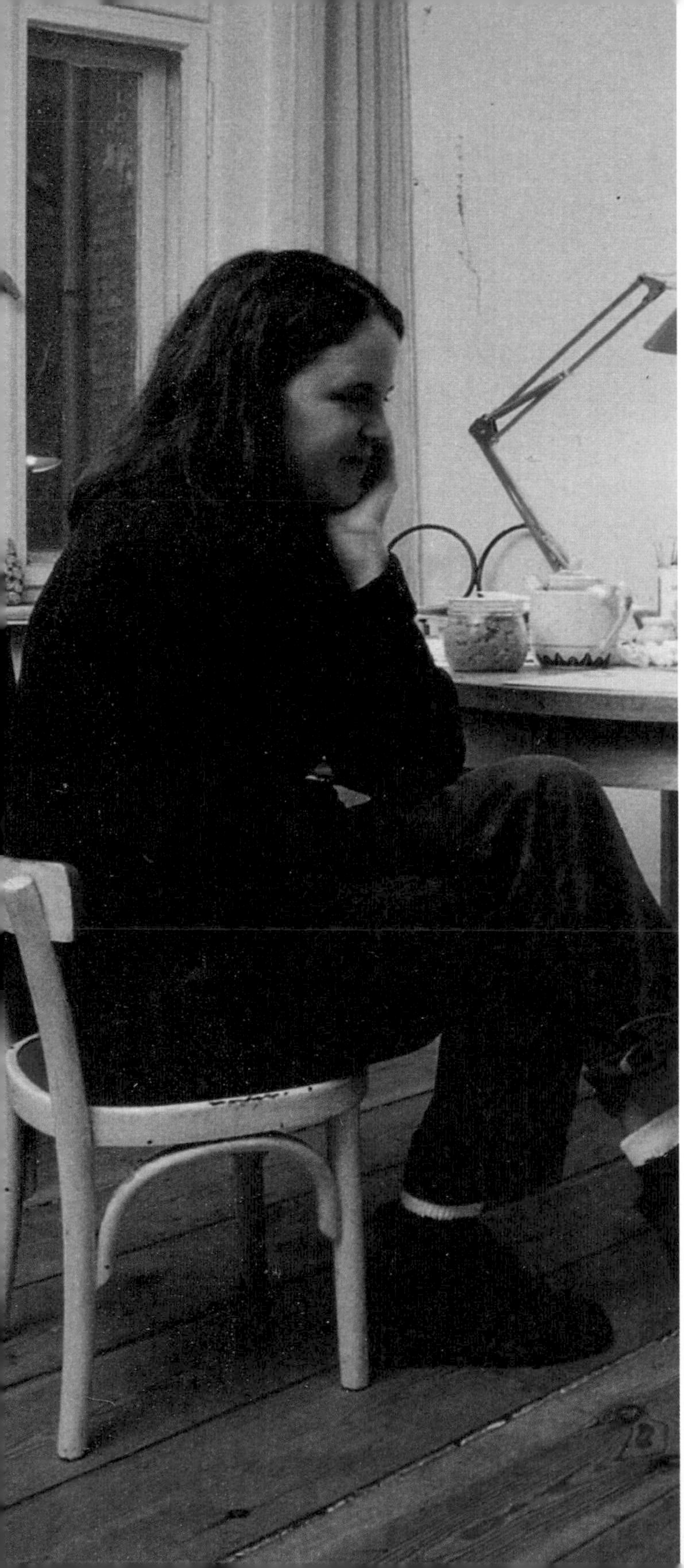

Paris, 1990: Jacques Noël, bookseller at Un Regard Moderne, pulled a little photocopied fanzine out of his stacks for me. He knew my tastes and thought I might like it. It was by a young Québécois artist I'd never heard of. Her name was Julie Doucet, and he was right—I liked it instantly. Her drawing style spoke to me the moment I saw it. Sébastien Morlighem, the French publisher who had published that book, gave me Julie's address. I wrote her right away for more information. I received a parcel with copies of her self-published *Dirty Plotte* and *Mini-Plotte*. I was in awe. She was grungy, funny, she talked about herself, she drew her dreams! It corresponded surprisingly well with what our fledgling group was thinking about: it was time for comics to talk about real life. After I put together the one and only issue of the magazine *Labo* (Futuropolis) in January 1990, a different publishing house began taking shape in Paris. It would be called L'Association. Our discovery of Julie had come at just the right time. In November 1990, we released our first publication, *Logique de guerre comix*, in the style of American underground comix. It featured Julie with a syringe nightmare story. Julie was the first person we'd published from outside our group, and it was all the better that she was neither male nor from France. We began planning the first L'Association books, to be released in January 1991 for the next Angoulême festival. There were three on our list: a collection of unpublished pieces by Dupuy & Berbérian, a pre-OuBaPian collaboration between Trondheim and me, and a *Dirty Plotte* compilation to be titled *Charming Periods*. In the end, only the first two made that Angoulême. Julie's book—renamed *Ciboire de Criss!*—eventually came out in 1996. Julie was now busy with her "real" comic, the first issue of which was scheduled for release in January 1991. And she was no longer self-publishing: a Montreal-based publisher, also founded in 1990, was going to bring out *Dirty Plotte* as a standard comic. That publisher was Drawn & Quarterly.

—J.C. Menu, cartoonist, co-founder of L'Association, publisher of L'Apocalypse

JULIE'S SACRED PLOTTE

an appreciation by Deb Olin Unferth

The first D+Q issue of *Dirty Plotte* included an anatomical drawing of one—with the clitoris, pubis, and labia labeled in Chinese characters and the word *plotte* scribbled adolescently beside it in Doucet's hand, in case anyone wasn't sure what one was. The sly title alone embodied the content: Doucet's playful, fierce grin at sexual violence, her mash of broken English and slangy French, and her long-armed reach into the female subconscious. She is one of the greats, an invincible underground cartoonist raised on *RAW* and still numbered among the most innovative and courageous of her ilk.[1]

Dirty Plotte is a dream journal, a rant, a vision, a memoir. Julie grows a penis and rapes a woman on the sidewalk. Julie stomps through the city like Godzilla, menstrual blood leaking from her underpants and drowning fleeing citizens. Julie as frog, as exotic dancer, as Popeye. At first glance the comics seem absurdly cramped, heavily inked with incongruous imagery and butchered perspectives: slender heels beside old work boots, misshapen heads, twisting legs, things curving that aren't supposed to be curving. Sometimes the clutter disperses the energy of the page, each panel shooting off into several disparate storylines. Other times it gathers the energy and thrusts it back to the main attraction (Julie) and whatever fantasy she is playing out, be it wishful thinking or paranoid delusion, in a vomit of tomboyish femininity.

When your eyes do settle on an image, it's usually a drawing of Julie. She looks crazy and rumpled and frantic—but also endearing and naive, even sexy. Julie kicks the human heads that have emerged apocalyptically out of the ground. Julie is stabbed in the eye with a syringe. Out of nowhere we skid to a stop on a calm, civilized Julie: there she is on the cover of issue five, in four portraits, her hair falling gently around her smooth face, her full lips ready for kisses. It feels like we're taking a long breath. But a few pages later she upends herself and becomes Julie the old skinny hag with missing teeth and torn clothing. The caption reads, "The day I can't take it anymore."

It is such a relief to read these comics after a long day of confronting a world obsessed with uniformity. Sameness is all around me and within me, tamping me down. Every day I am charged with being the thing I said I was, which is to say a lot like everyone else, and with being it more and more. Doucet, with each incarnation, grants herself contradiction and multiplicity. The comics feel uniquely her, like a burst of Julie, like a can of Julie with the top off, an exuberant, irrepressible expression of her, scrawled with her markings. In one comic she graffities a wall in her own panel, "Julie was here" (as if we might forget).

She's not doing it to be cute or rebellious. Yes, an unprecedented number of stories take place in the bathroom. An impressive number are about tampons, penises, breasts, boogers, blood—especially menstrual blood, but also blood dripping from razor blades or from her own body as she slices it ("self portrait in a possible situation"). But hilarious as they are, there are no cheap jokes in the bathroom. This is high comedy. She is exploring those aspects of humanhood, especially womanhood, that are out of our control. She records the moment we become unknown to ourselves: when we orgasm, when we dream, when we bleed. Penises and tampons are tinged with mysterious meaning, objects to laugh at and fear. And no human act is safe from Doucet. We weave in and out of the state of non-being all the time. Her four-panel comic "Do-It-Yourself: Laugh!" shows a woman going from a state of calm self-possession in instruction panel A to the laugh in panel D, a look of derangement and self-absence, the opposite of Munch's existential *Scream*. The reader slowly stops laughing.

Doucet's comics attempt to capture that realm of sacred nonexistence: not to disturb it or demystify it, but to reveal it. These fleeting states are minor versions of Doucet's singular loss of control. Her epilepsy runs through the comics as an undercurrent and a threat. "It's all very mysterious," she says in her *Dangerous Drawings* interview. "I just cease to exist for what could be days, hours or two seconds—as far as I know!" At any moment Julie, in or out of the comic, might fall to the ground groaning, pull her own hair, rip

---

1   *This despite the fact that she gave up drawing a decade ago. Doucet and Patti Smith, we want to ask them both the same question: why did you leave? (Though by instinct we know why.)*

her clothes, roll around at the feet of innocent bystanders. People will run from her. It is her birthright. In fact, she talks about drawing her early comics in similar terms: "so unconscious, so directly my mind on paper." The most urgent parts of her are what she can't see or know. This may be why her work feels like a search, why it has such gravity amid the humour, and why the line of continuity between us and her feels so direct and complete.

To my untrained eye, Doucet's work reminds me of medieval paintings with its brutalized scales and perspectives, strings of narrative unrolling over the page in a shrewdly haphazard clutter. In place of gold leaf and halos, she gives us crowded black lines and her own sacred objects: her stove-top espresso maker, her empty beer bottles, her inks, brushes, cat, and those giant Doucet eyes. It's Julie at the drawing table again and again, Julie grinning perversely at the reader, Julie tearing up a page ("AWW FFUCK SHHIT OFF!! AZWTKK!"), Julie saying she can't do it anymore, it's just too hard to fill a whole comic book, knives laid out among her pens. She is trying to get it right, draw that controlled, uncontrollable thing (herself) amid her collapse of junk and hand it, bloody and squalling, to us.

I didn't see Doucet's work until 2006, so I missed those early, bloody days. I was living in the exact middle of the country in the exact middle of my life, and somehow I'd been assigned to teach the comics class, though I knew little about comics. I ordered a pile of books (Ware, Moore, McCloud…) and the students turned up on the first day with a book I hadn't ordered or even heard of. By error the bookstore had gotten Doucet's dream journal, *My Most Secret Desire*. I don't know how it happened. The students held the book up for me to see. The colour of the hardback was the deepest shade of the girliest princess pink—at once ridiculous and demanding. On the slipcover were three Julies drawn by Julie, all weeping. Their boobs and nipples were outlined, their noses big and red: sex and absurdity, a self-presentation of cartoon sorrow and femininity. Warner Brothers, Doucet-style. All I had to do was see the cover to know this cartoonist had stepped into my subconscious and found me cringing and giggling in a corner. I reached for the book with twitching fingers. I read the first page.

Deb Olin Unferth is the author of Minor Robberies, Vacation, and Revolution, which was a National Book Critics Award finalist. Her work has appeared in Harper's, the New York Times, McSweeney's, the Believer, the Boston Review, Esquire, and other magazines.

Dirty Plotte no. 7 by Julie Doucet: "Robert the Elevator Operator Goes Back Home"— there's no plot here. It's just a man walking home. A man with a nose so long it droops down like a small elephant trunk— a trunk with little hairs sprouting all over it—walks home from work, arrives at a tiny home, kneels down, unlocks the door, and crawls in. For eighteen crowded freak-filled panels. I remember being repulsed but charmed by this new way of drawing noses when Julie introduced it as her new innovation/obsession in the previous issue of *Dirty Plotte*. And that combination of charm and repulsion is key to the comics of Julie Doucet. But this strip also reads as a refutation of the gender-switching party girl piss-and-menstrual-blood underground cartoonist persona that had made Julie famous. Julie's art has always been restless and here she's not giving us the pleasure of voyeurism at all. The entirety of this strip is one of comics' all-time most gorgeous stylists showing off that she can draw better than everybody else.
—*Tom Devlin*

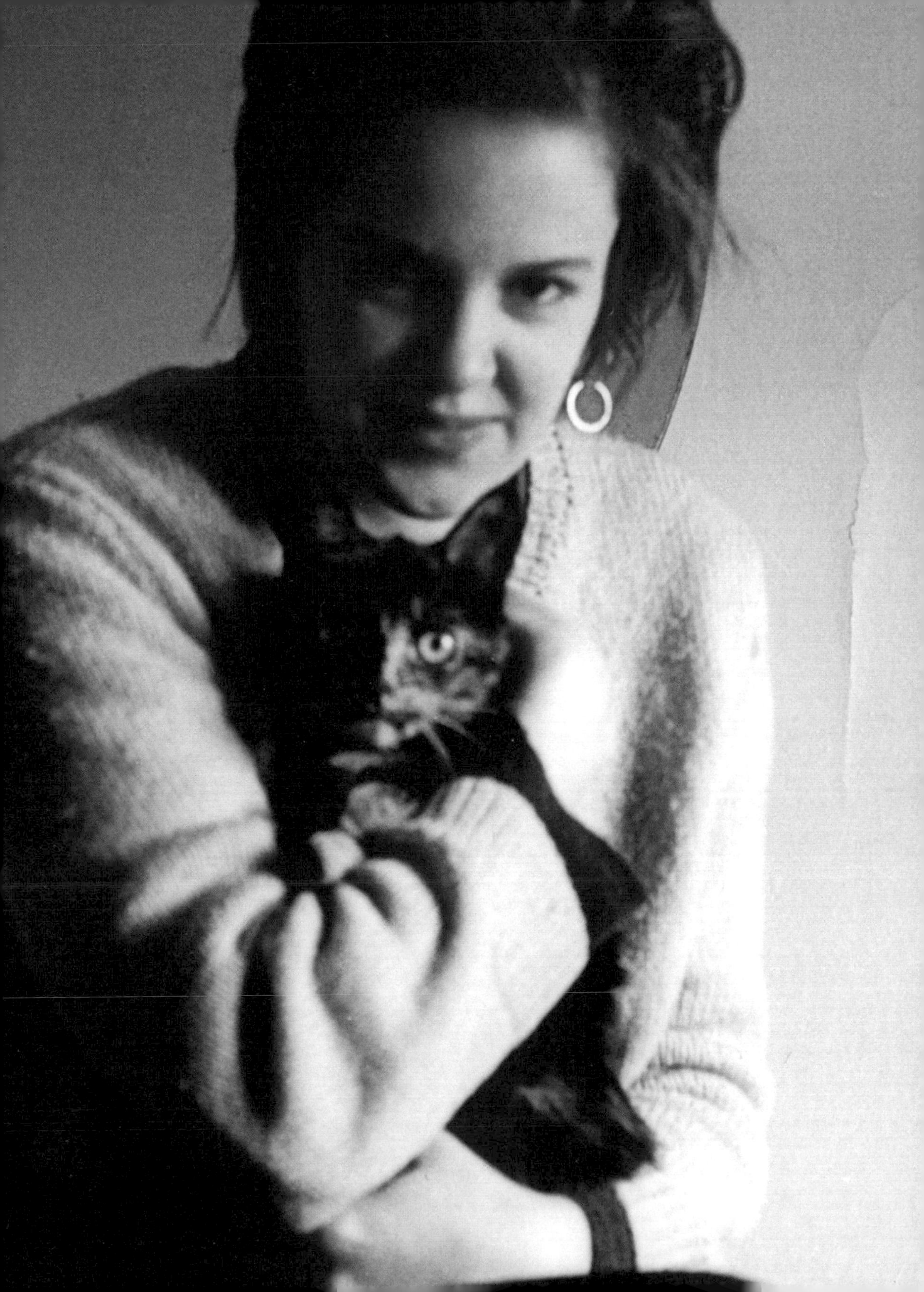

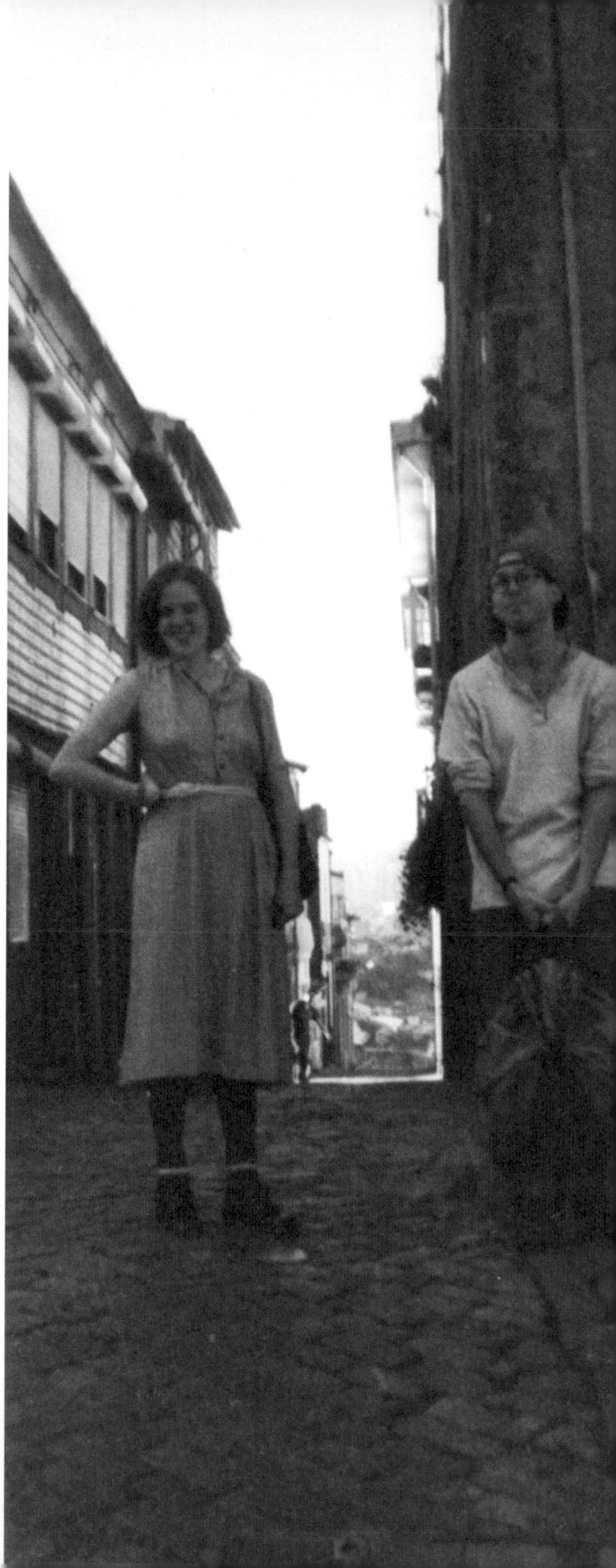

I discovered *Dirty Plotte* at Legends, a small comic store in Victoria, BC (they are still there, by the way). I was fifteen, visiting my father for the first time in over ten years. I felt some sort of an earthquake going through me: not only was this comic made by an awesome lady, it was made by someone who came from Quebec, whom I had never heard of before. A parallel world about home, a world away from home. The following summer I sent Julie a letter in Berlin with a minicomic of my own. One day, I came home from school and there was a postcard from her in the mail. It was like a miracle taking place in my sad suburb of Montreal. A surrealistic moment. In her postcard Julie said that she had heard of me through Simon Bossé, that he had told her I had gotten him to silkscreen a cover for my next comic with money I had borrowed from my dad. She was excited to get mail from a young girl living in Quebec, a rare kind of letter, she said.

She mentioned coming to Montreal soon, that there would be an art opening at Le Cheval Blanc, a tavern. She asked "Will they still let you in if you are underage but don't drink?" That day I went to the tavern to meet Julie. By that point I had made friends with a few people in the minicomics scene, so I had people to hang out with. My clothes and hair were crazy that day. I looked like a candy raver. My pants were so huge and fuzzy. I had a paper bag full of cinnamon lips I had gotten from a dépanneur nearby. I offered Julie one. It was pretty awkward—my whole getup was basically screaming *I am still a baby!*

In the couple years that followed, Julie moved back to Montreal and she and I became friends for real. I feel hesitant to say more than that because I see her as one of the most important people in my life. I hope that if some teenager got in touch with me now about how much they love what I do I would be as friendly about it as she was to me.—***Geneviève Castrée***

DIRTY PLOTTE #1

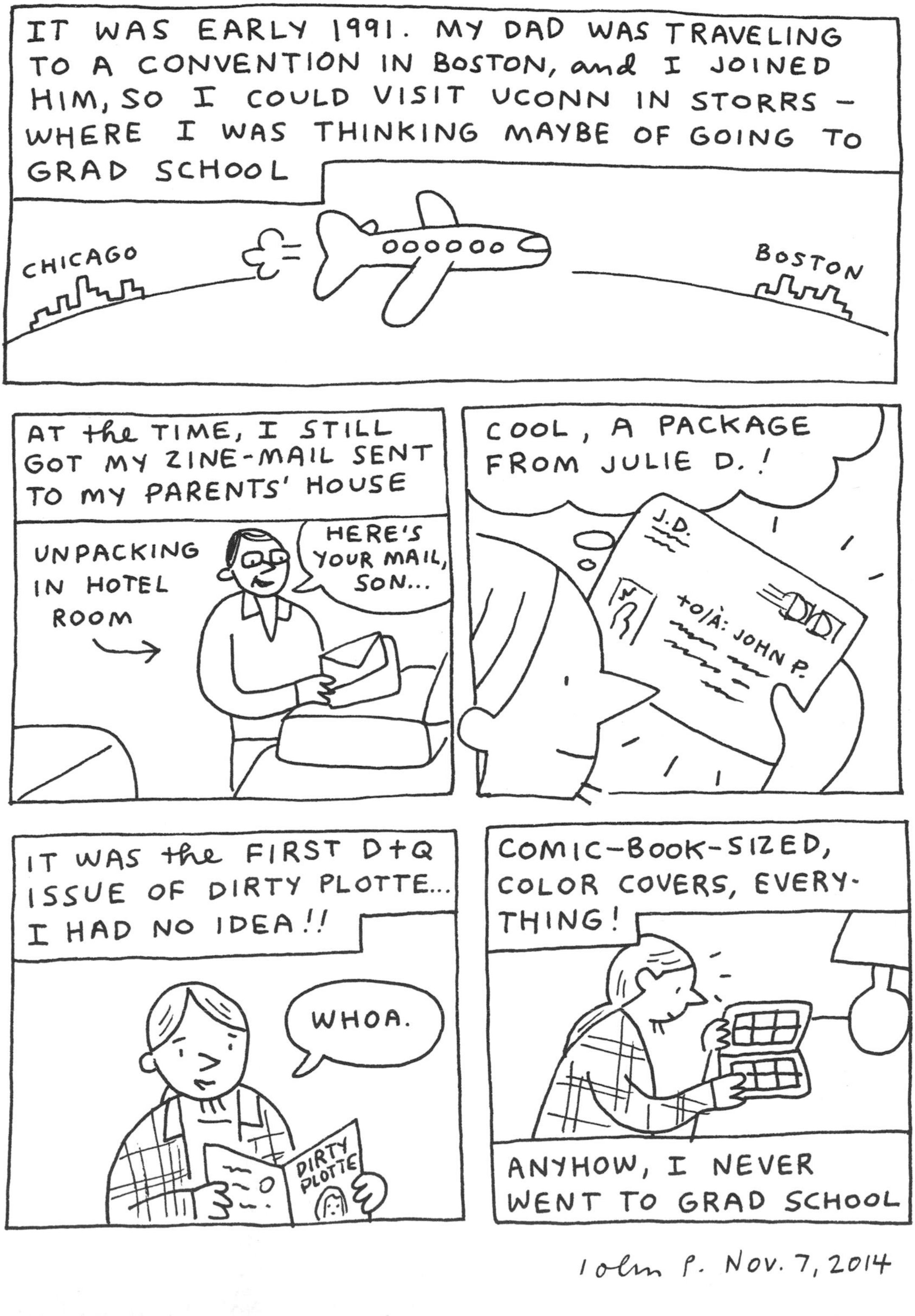
IT WAS EARLY 1991. MY DAD WAS TRAVELING TO A CONVENTION IN BOSTON, and I JOINED HIM, SO I COULD VISIT UCONN IN STORRS – WHERE I WAS THINKING MAYBE OF GOING TO GRAD SCHOOL
CHICAGO
BOSTON
AT the TIME, I STILL GOT MY ZINE-MAIL SENT TO MY PARENTS' HOUSE
UNPACKING IN HOTEL ROOM
HERE'S YOUR MAIL, SON...
COOL, A PACKAGE FROM JULIE D.!
J.D.
TO/À: JOHN P.
IT WAS the FIRST D+Q ISSUE OF DIRTY PLOTTE... I HAD NO IDEA!!
WHOA.
DIRTY PLOTTE
COMIC-BOOK-SIZED, COLOR COVERS, EVERYTHING!
ANYHOW, I NEVER WENT TO GRAD SCHOOL
John P. Nov. 7, 2014

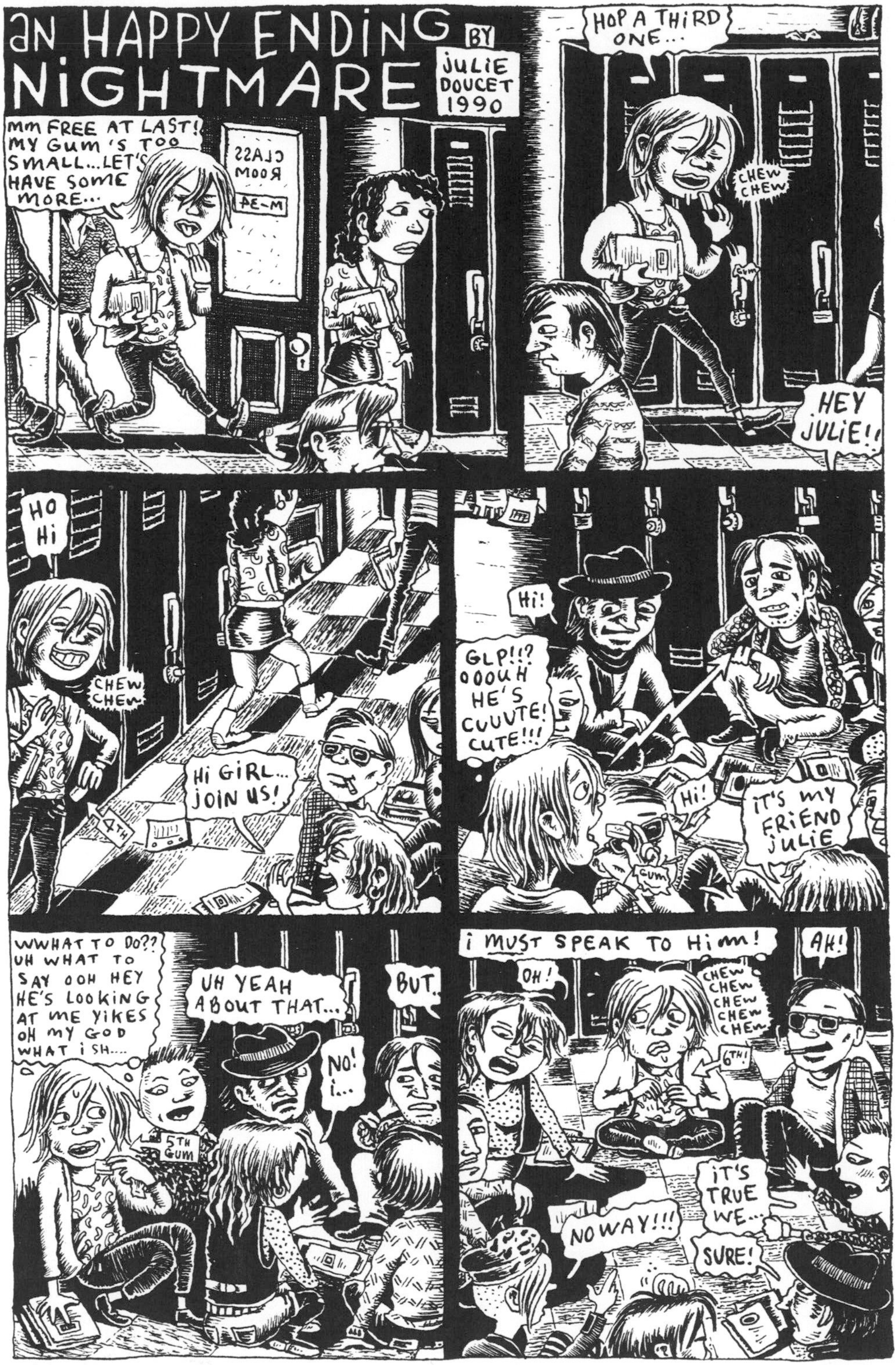

an HAPPY ENDING NIGHTMARE
BY JULIE DOUCET 1990
MM FREE AT LAST! MY GUM'S TOO SMALL...LET'S HAVE SOME MORE...
HOP A THIRD ONE...
CHEW CHEW
GUM
HEY JULIE!!
HO HI
CHEW CHEW
HI GIRL... JOIN US!
4TH
HI!
GLP!!? OOOUH HE'S CUUUTE! CUTE!!!
HI!
IT'S MY FRIEND JULIE
GUM
WWHAT TO DO?? UH WHAT TO SAY OOH HEY HE'S LOOKING AT ME YIKES OH MY GOD WHAT I SH....
UH YEAH ABOUT THAT...
BUT..
NO! I...
5TH GUM
I MUST SPEAK TO HIM!
AH!
OH!
CHEW CHEW CHEW CHEW CHEW
6TH!
IT'S TRUE WE...
NO WAY!!!
SURE!

 "An Happy Ending Nightmare" appeared first in *Dirty Plotte* no. 3 (1991) and later in *My Most Secret Desire* (1995).

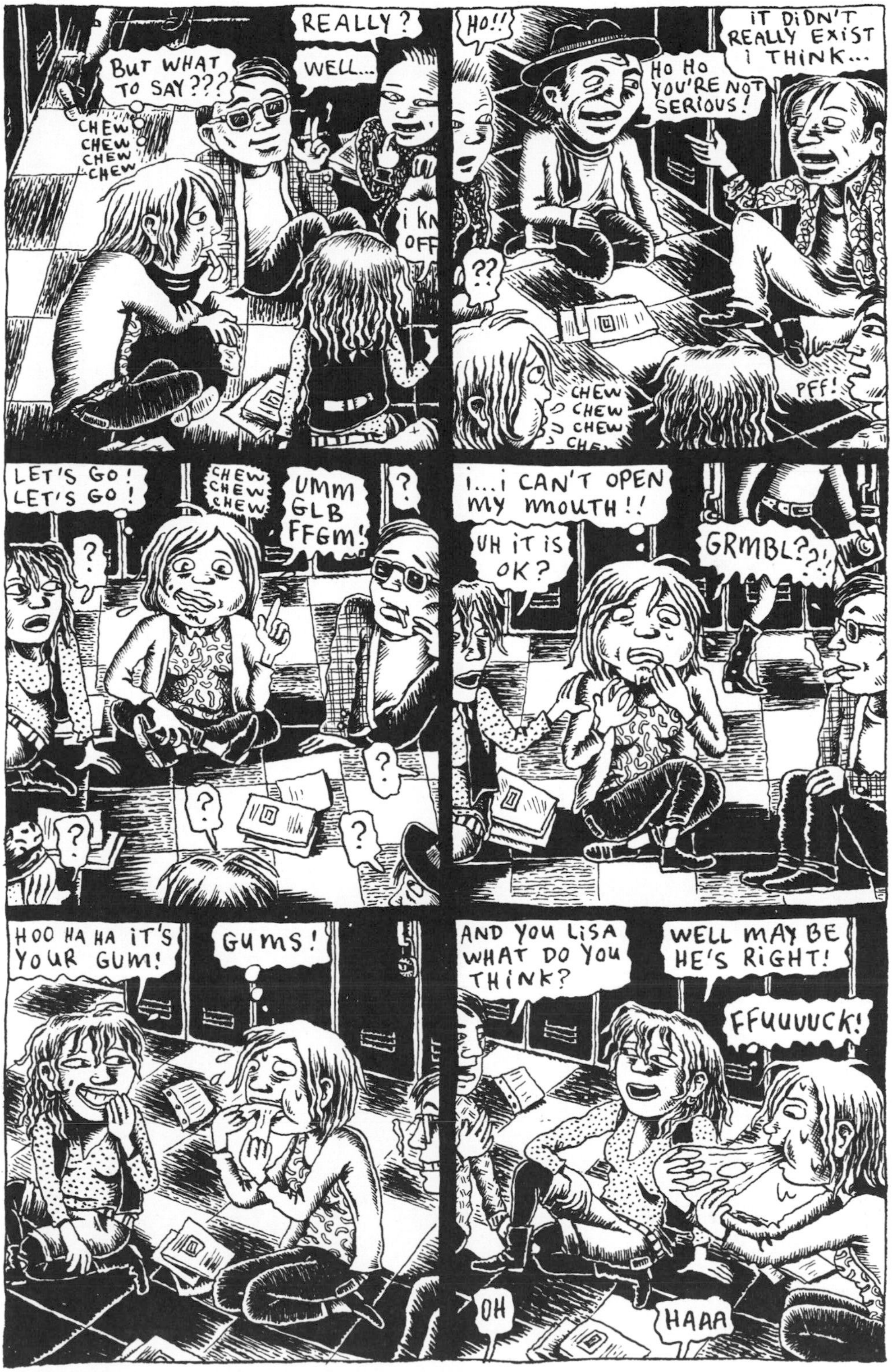
REALLY?
BUT WHAT TO SAY???
WELL...
CHEW CHEW CHEW CHEW
HO!!
IT DIDN'T REALLY EXIST I THINK...
HO HO YOU'RE NOT SERIOUS!
??
CHEW CHEW CHEW
PFF!
LET'S GO! LET'S GO!
CHEW CHEW CHEW
UMM GLB FFGM!
?
?
?
?
?
?
I... I CAN'T OPEN MY MOUTH!!
UH IT IS OK?
GRMBL?!?!
HOO HA HA IT'S YOUR GUM!
GUMS!
AND YOU LISA WHAT DO YOU THINK?
WELL MAYBE HE'S RIGHT!
FFUUUUCK!
OH
HAAA

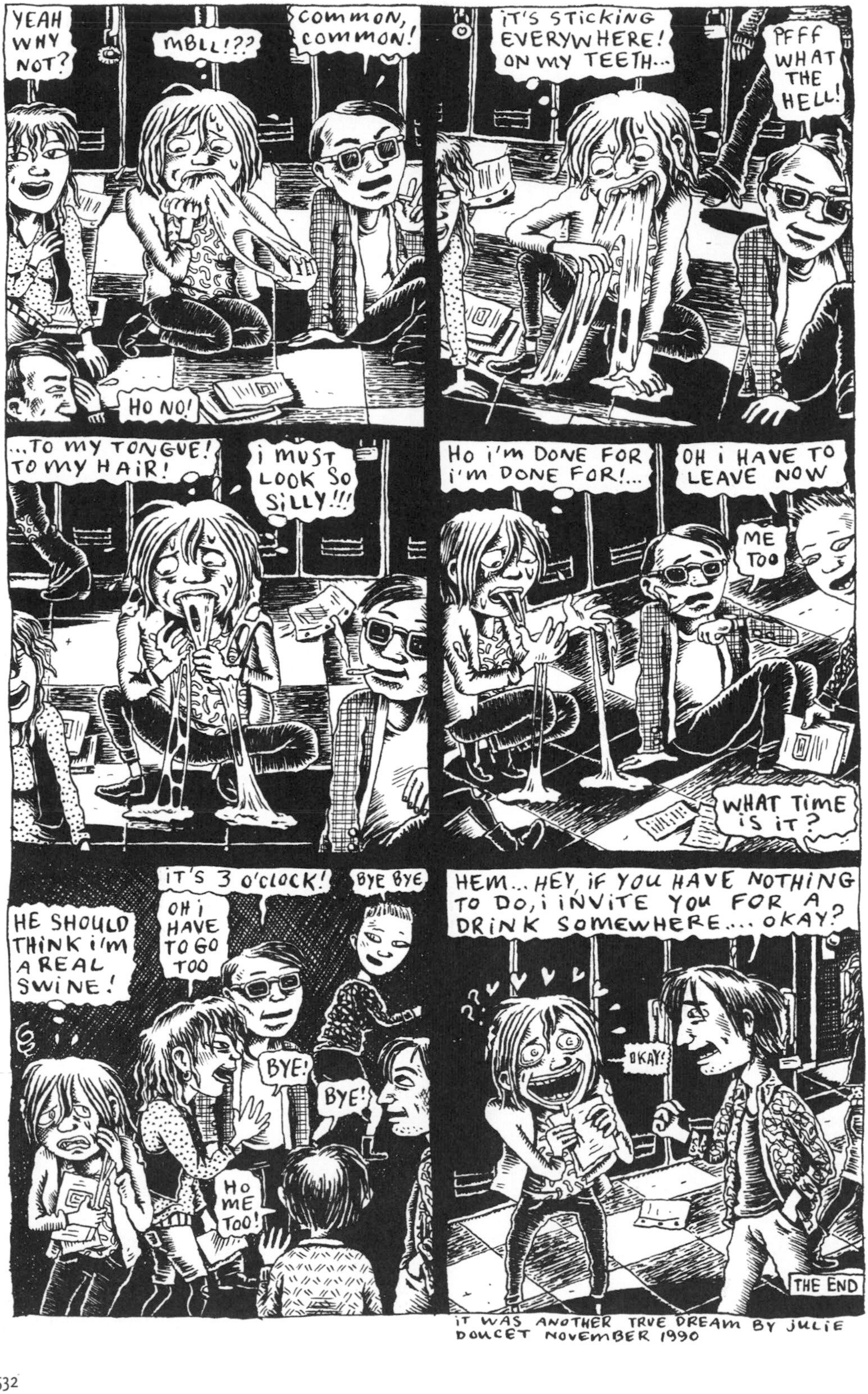
YEAH WHY NOT?
MBLL!??
COMMON, COMMON!
HO NO!
iT'S STiCKiNG EVERYWHERE! ON MY TEETH...
PFFF WHAT THE HELL!
...TO MY TONGUE! TO MY HAIR!
i MUST LOOK SO SiLLY!!!
Ho i'm DONE FOR i'm DONE FOR!...
OH i HAVE TO LEAVE NOW
ME TOO
WHAT TIME iS iT?
HE SHOULD THiNK i'm A REAL SWiNE!
iT'S 3 O'CLOCK!
OH i HAVE TO GO TOO
BYE BYE
BYE!
BYE!
Ho ME TOO!
HEM... HEY, iF YOU HAVE NOTHiNG TO DO, i iNViTE YOU FOR A DRiNK SOMEWHERE... OKAY?
OKAY!
THE END

iT WAS ANOTHER TRUE DREAM BY JULiE DOUCET NOVEMBER 1990

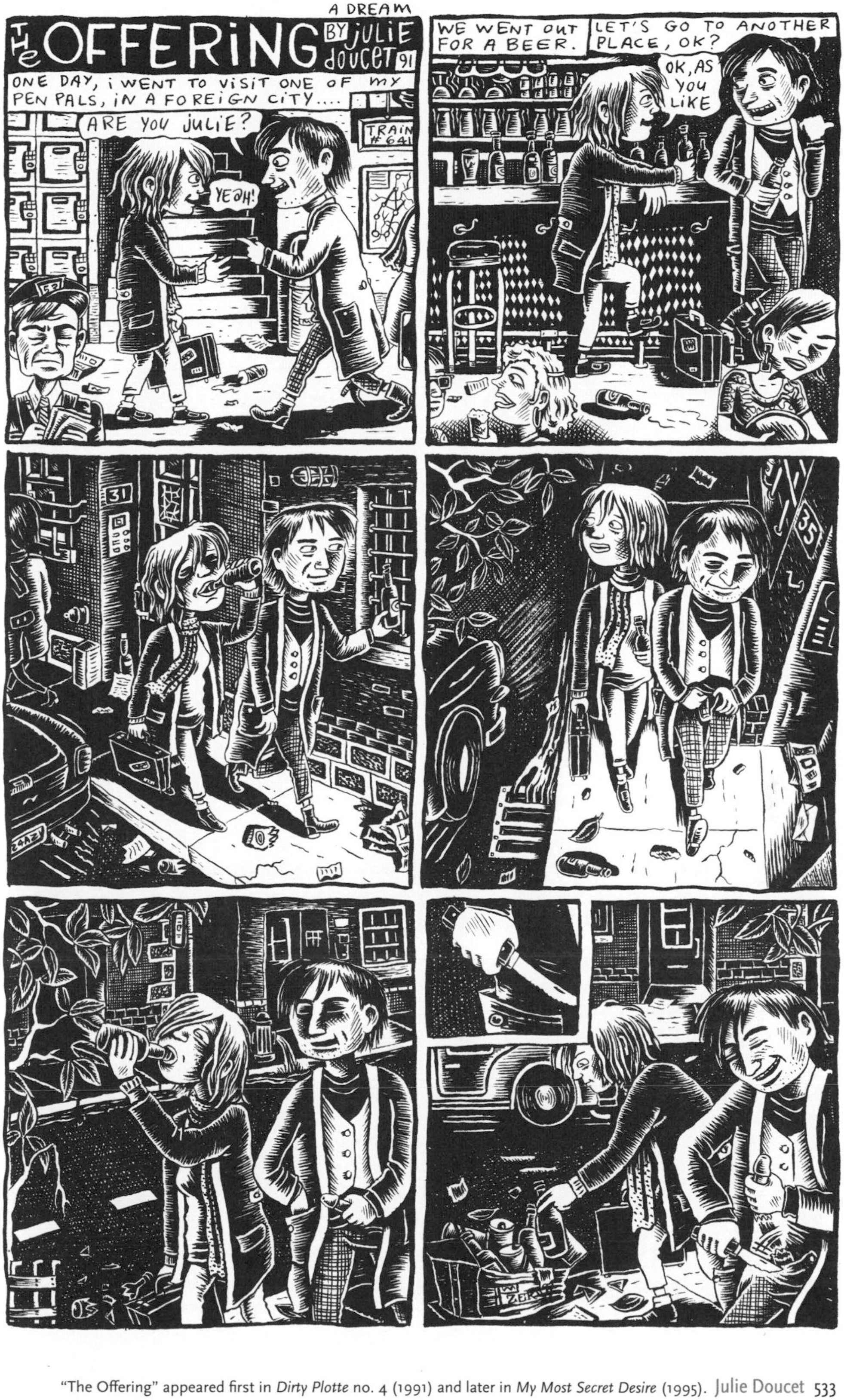
THE OFFERING
A DREAM BY julie doucet 91
ONE DAY, i WENT TO VISIT ONE OF MY PEN PALS, iN A FOREIGN CITY....
ARE YOU JULIE?
YEAH!
TRAIN #641
WE WENT OUT FOR A BEER.
LET'S GO TO ANOTHER PLACE, OK?
OK, AS YOU LIKE
31
35

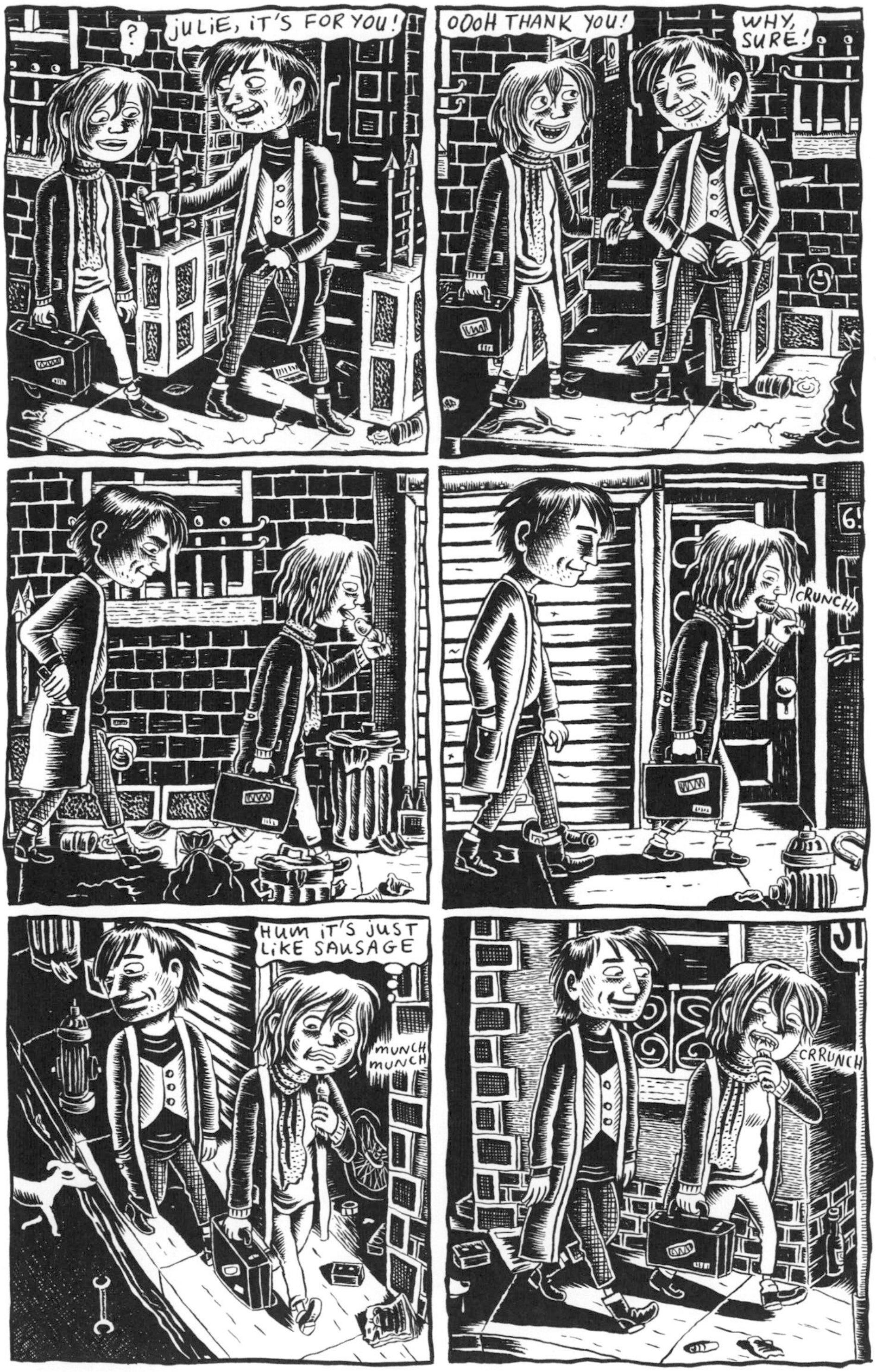
?
JULIE, IT'S FOR YOU!
OOOH THANK YOU!
WHY, SURE!
CRUNCH!
HUM IT'S JUST LIKE SAUSAGE
MUNCH MUNCH
CRRUNCH

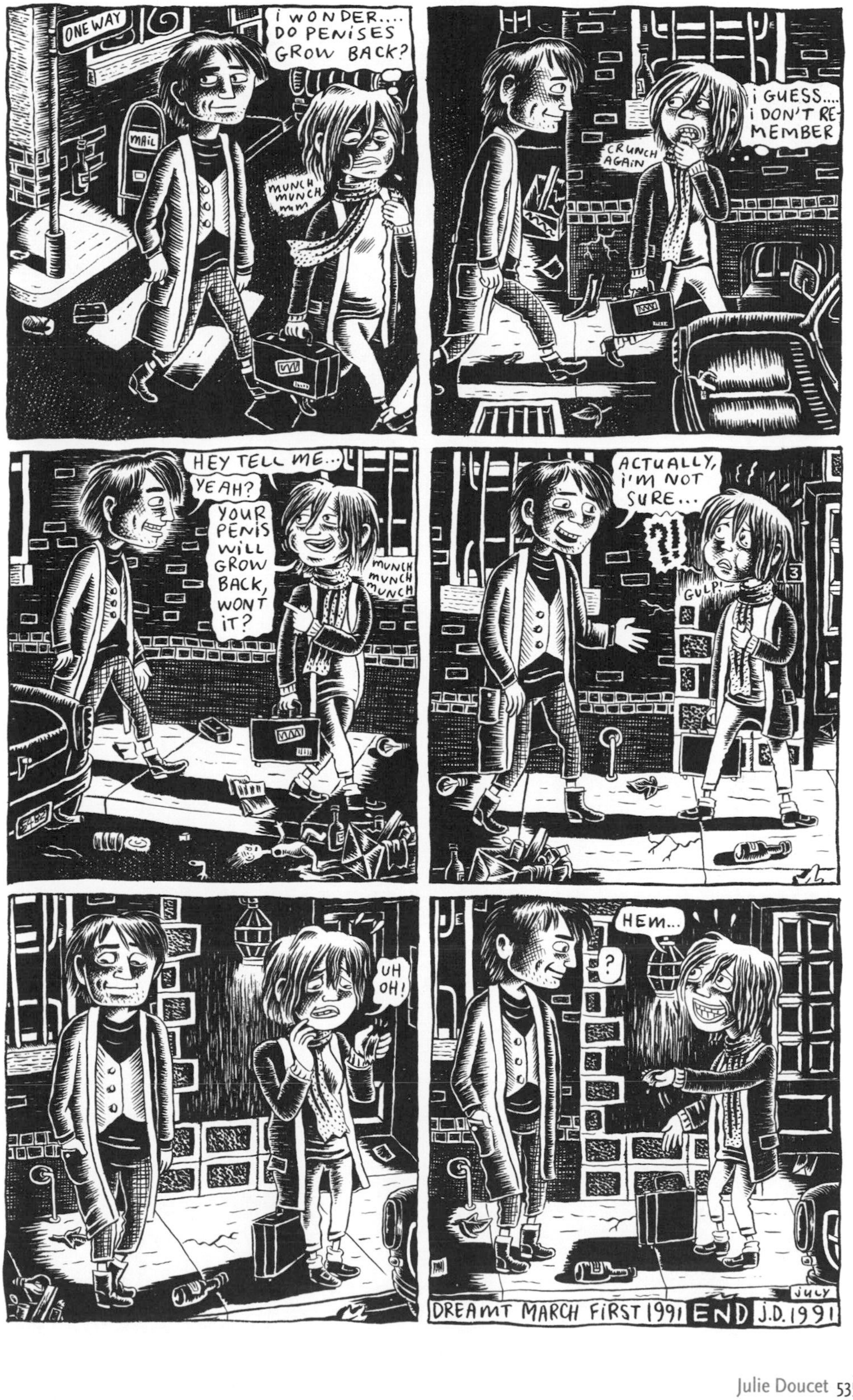
ONE WAY
i WONDER.... DO PENiSES GROW BACK?
MAIL
MUNCH MUNCH mm
i GUESS.... i DON'T RE-MEMBER
CRUNCH AGAiN
HEY TELL ME...
YEAH?
YOUR PENiS WiLL GROW BACK, WONT iT?
MUNCH MUNCH MUNCH
ACTUALLY, i'M NOT SURE...
?!!
GULP!
3
UH OH!
HEM...
?
JULY
DREAMT MARCH FiRST 1991 END J.D. 1991

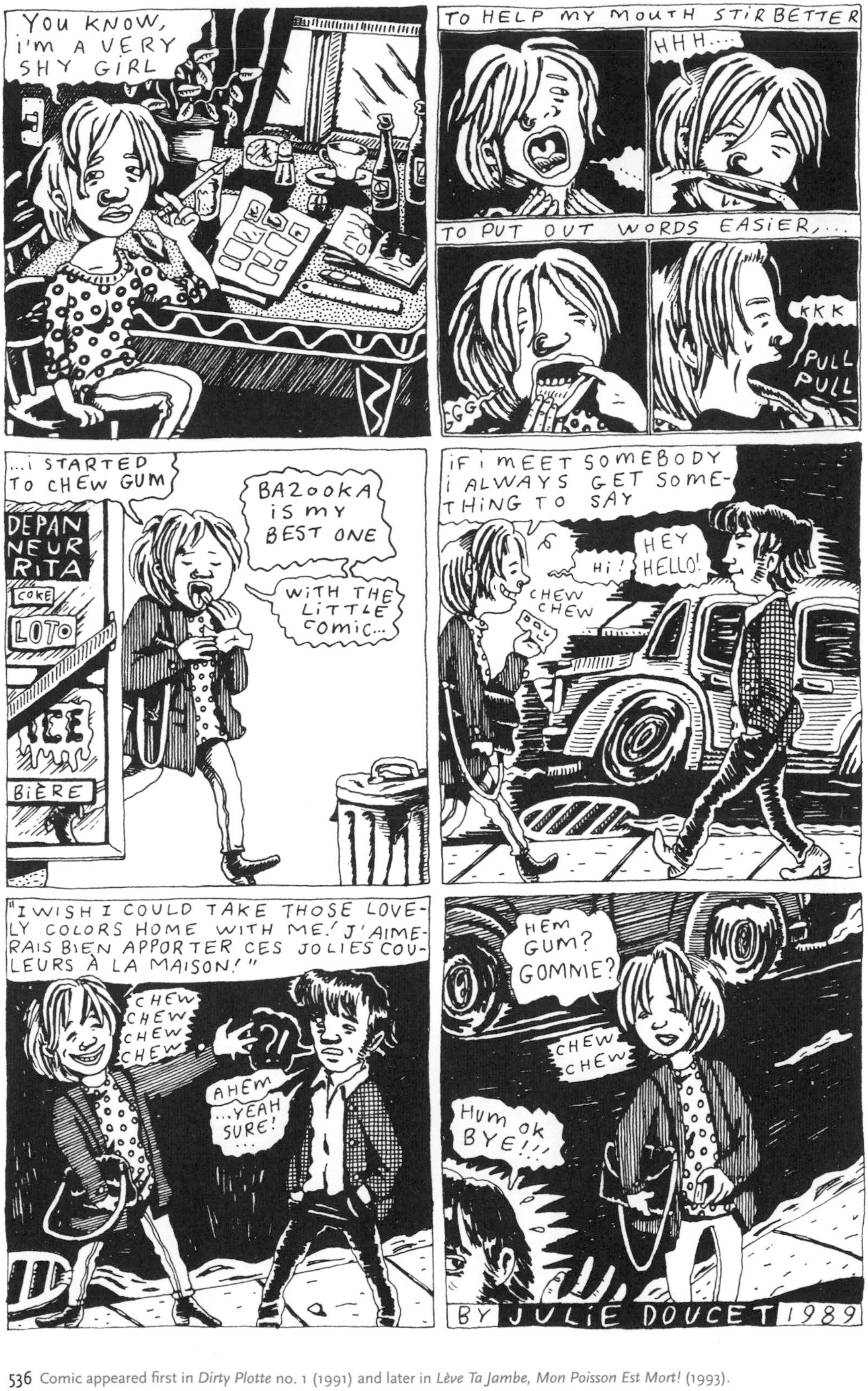
YOU KNOW, I'M A VERY SHY GIRL
TO HELP MY MOUTH STIR BETTER
HHH....
TO PUT OUT WORDS EASIER,...
GG
KKK
PULL PULL
...I STARTED TO CHEW GUM
DEPANNEUR RITA
COKE
LOTO
ICE
BIÈRE
BAZOOKA IS MY BEST ONE
WITH THE LITTLE COMIC...
IF I MEET SOMEBODY I ALWAYS GET SOMETHING TO SAY
HI!
HEY HELLO!
CHEW CHEW
"I WISH I COULD TAKE THOSE LOVELY COLORS HOME WITH ME!' J'AIMERAIS BIEN APPORTER CES JOLIES COULEURS À LA MAISON!"
CHEW CHEW CHEW CHEW
?!
AHEM ...YEAH SURE! ...
HEM GUM? GOMMIE?
CHEW CHEW
HUM OK BYE!!!
BY JULIE DOUCET 1989

Comic appeared first in *Dirty Plotte* no. 1 (1991) and later in *Lève Ta Jambe, Mon Poisson Est Mort!* (1993).

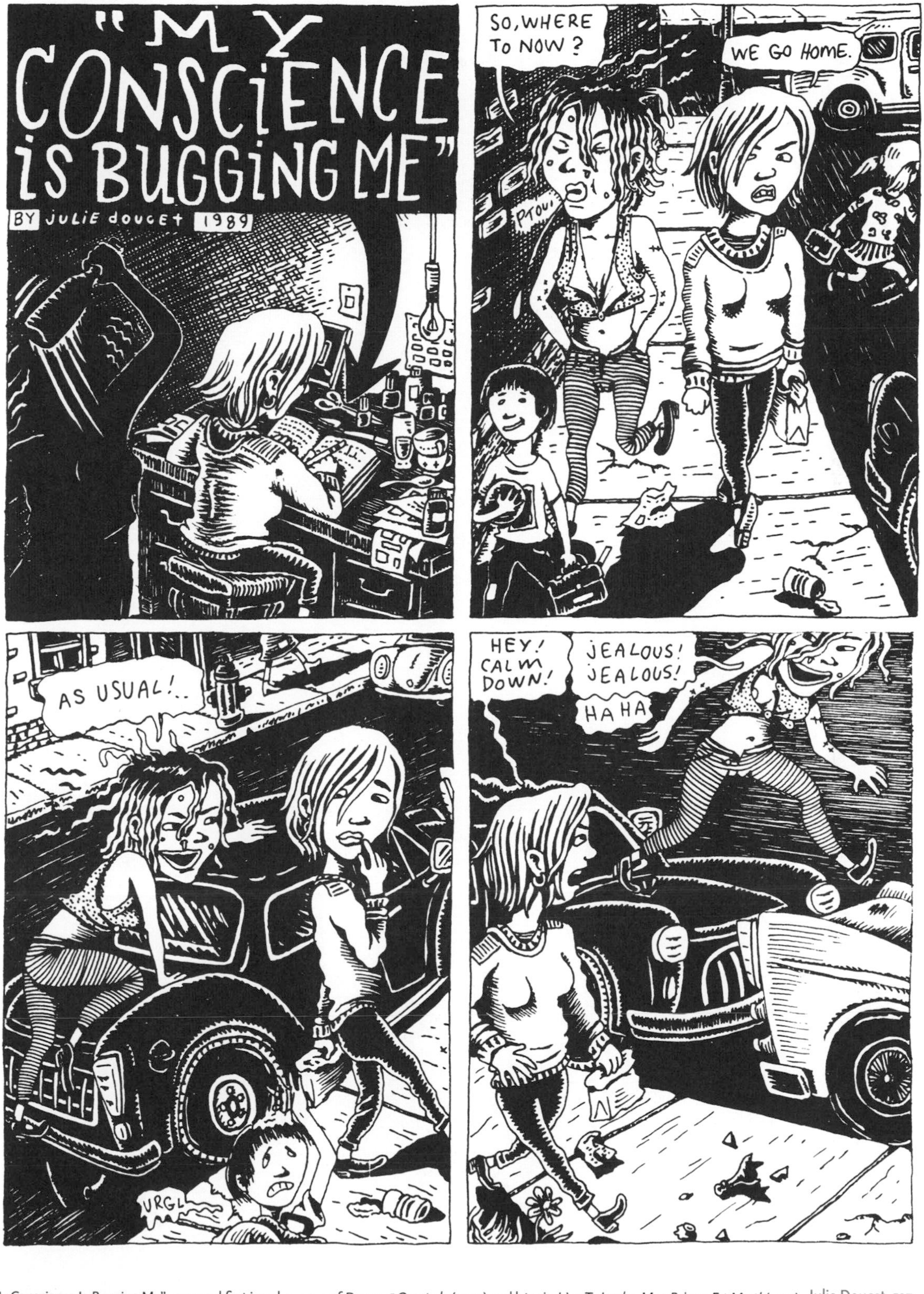
"MY CONSCIENCE IS BUGGING ME"
BY JULIE DOUCET 1989
SO, WHERE TO NOW?
WE GO HOME.
PTOUI
AS USUAL!..
URGL
HEY! CALM DOWN!
JEALOUS! JEALOUS!
HA HA

"My Conscience Is Bugging Me" appeared first in vol. 1, no. 2 of *Drawn & Quarterly* (1990) and later in *Lève Ta Jambe, Mon Poisson Est Mort!* (1993).

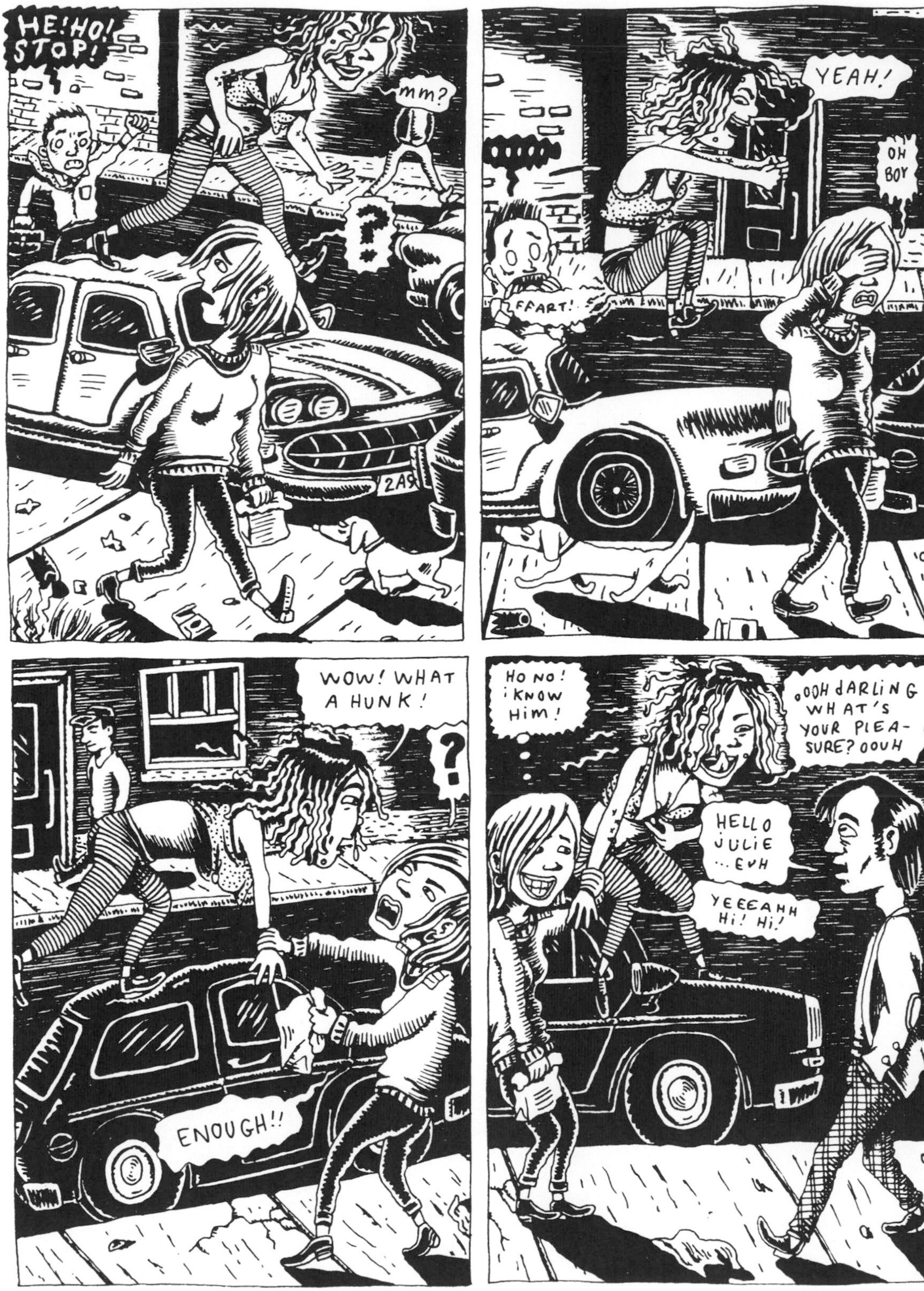
HE! HO! STOP!
mm?
?
YEAH!
OH BOY
FFART!
WOW! WHAT A HUNK!
?
ENOUGH!!
HO NO! I KNOW HIM!
OOOH DARLING WHAT'S YOUR PLEA-SURE? OOUH
HELLO JULIE ...EUH
YEEEAHH Hi! Hi!

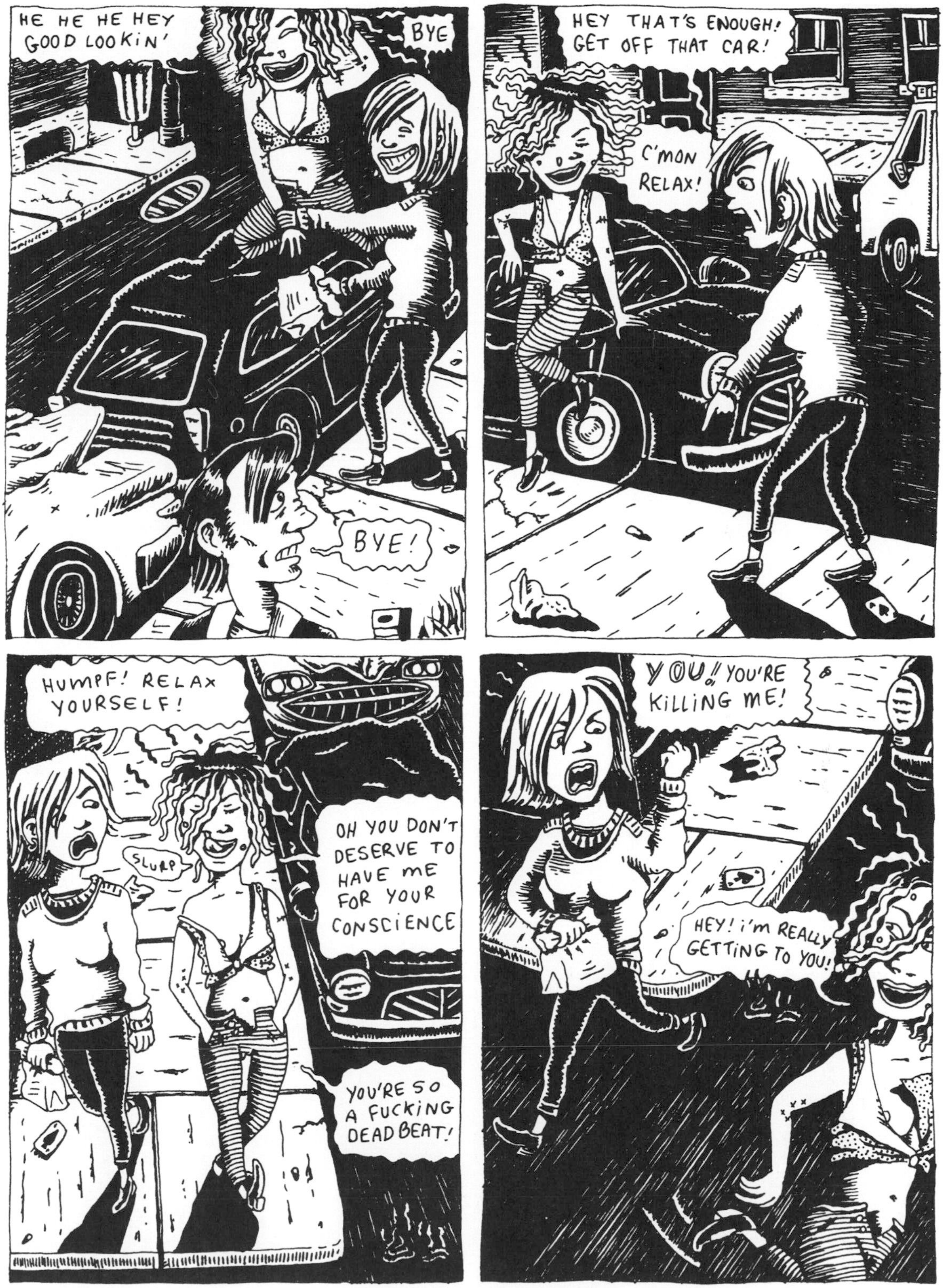
HE HE HE HEY GOOD LOOKIN'
BYE
BYE!
HEY THAT'S ENOUGH! GET OFF THAT CAR!
C'MON RELAX!
HUMPF! RELAX YOURSELF!
SLURP
OH YOU DON'T DESERVE TO HAVE ME FOR YOUR CONSCIENCE
YOU'RE SO A FUCKING DEADBEAT!
YOU!! YOU'RE KILLING ME!
HEY! I'M REALLY GETTING TO YOU!

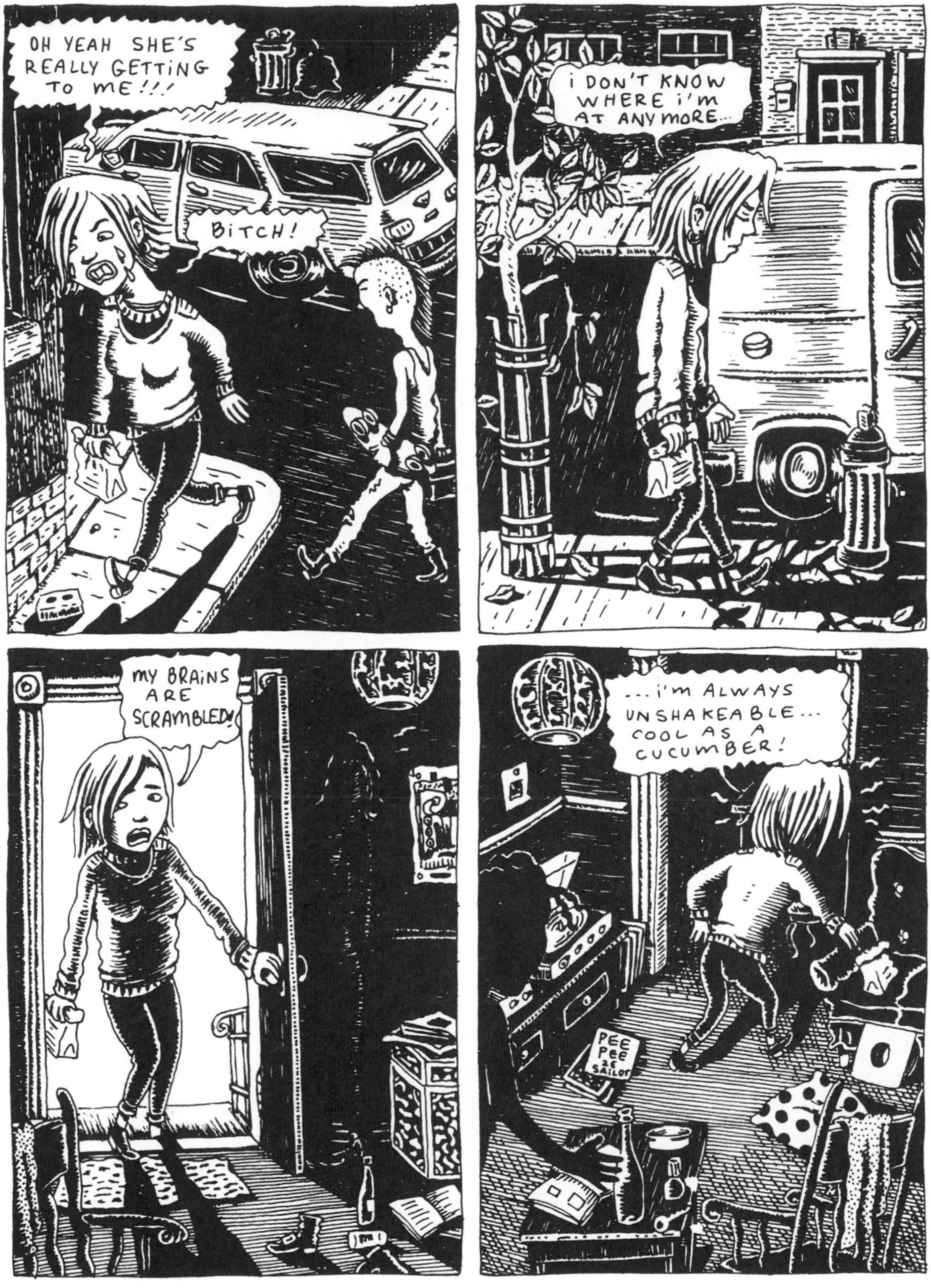
OH YEAH SHE'S REALLY GETTING TO ME!!!
BITCH!
i DON'T KNOW WHERE i'm AT ANYMORE...
MY BRAINS ARE SCRAMBLED!
...i'm ALWAYS UNSHAKEABLE... COOL AS A CUCUMBER!
PEE PEE

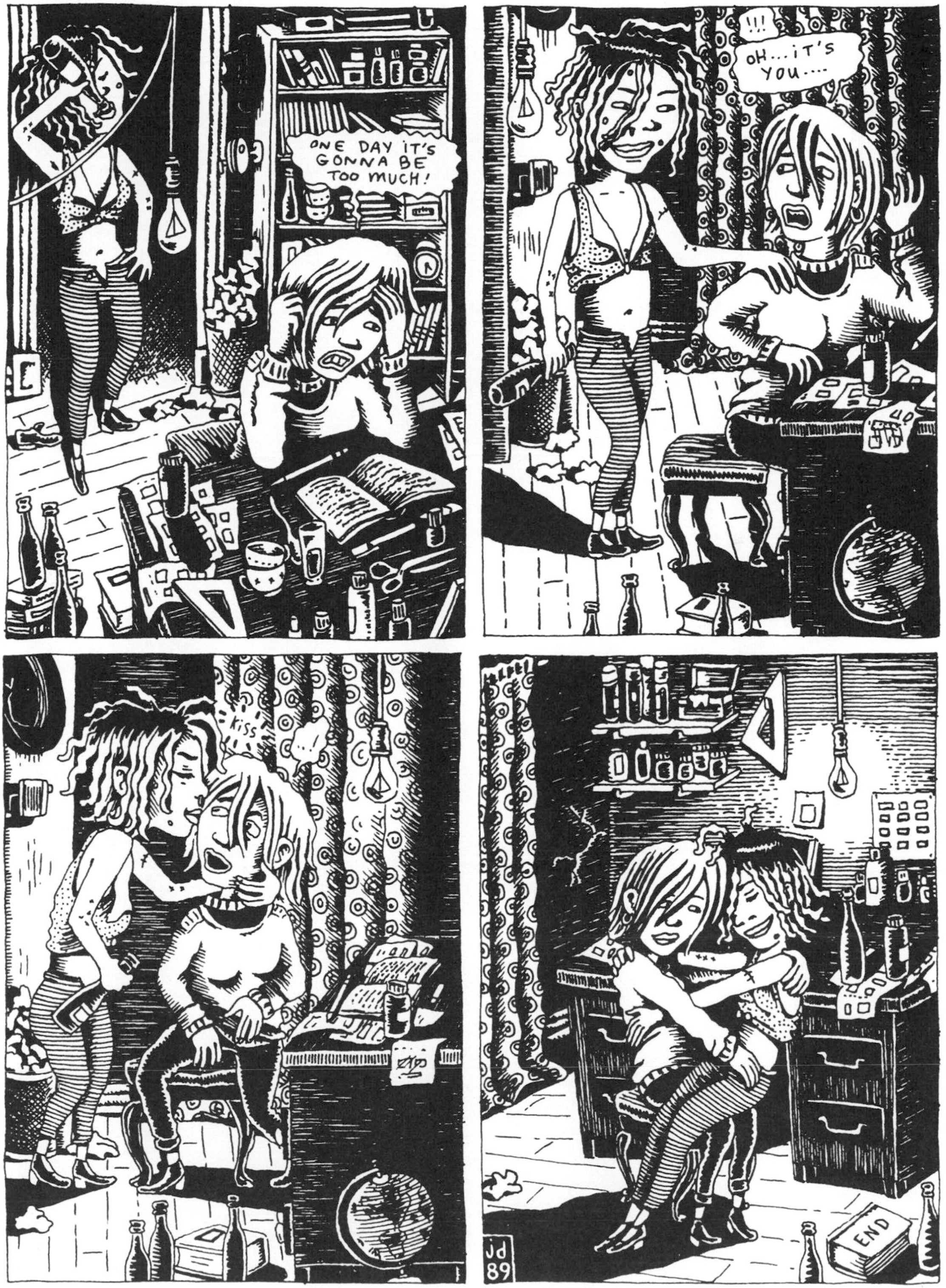
ONE DAY IT'S GONNA BE TOO MUCH!
!!!
OH... IT'S YOU....
KISS
...
JD 89
END

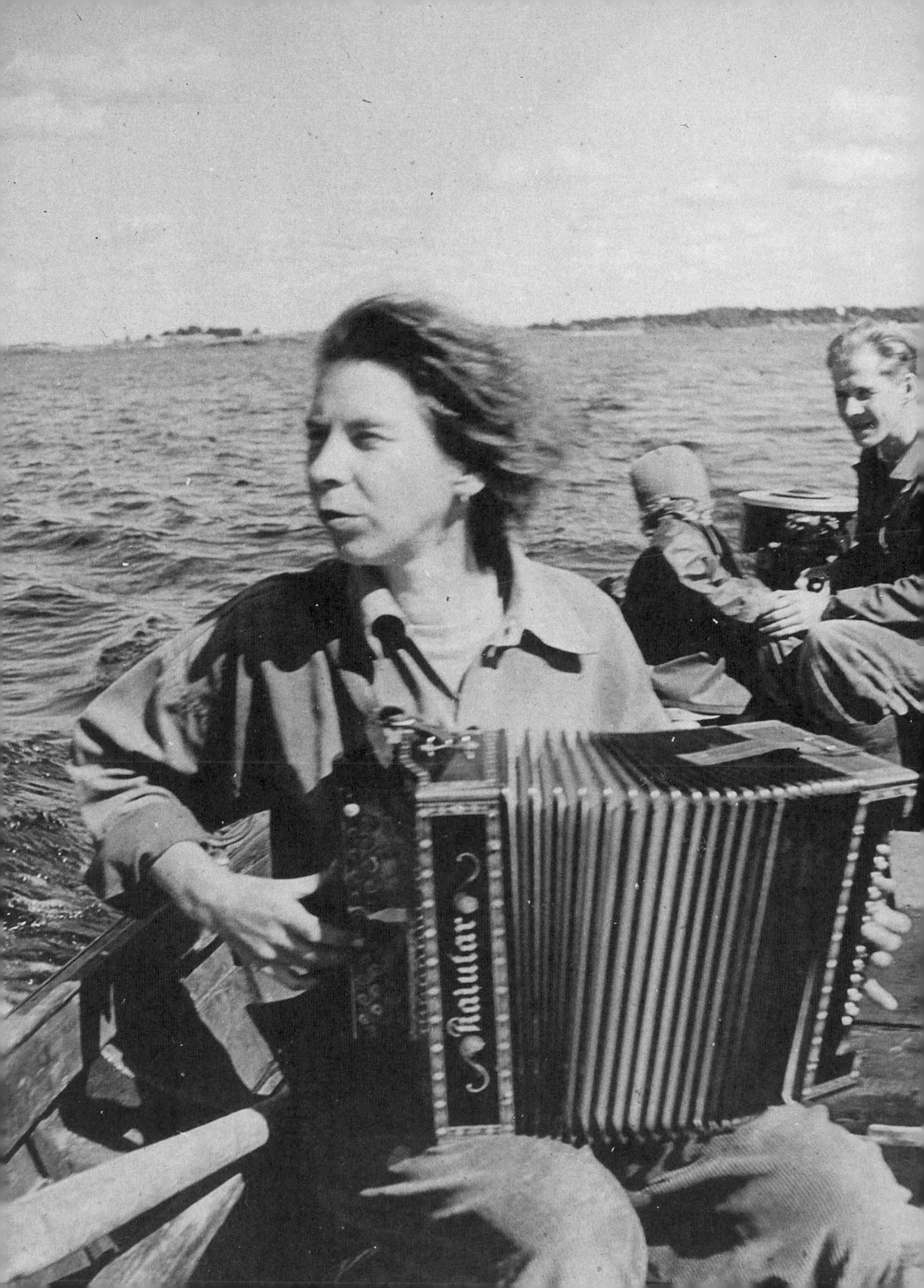

A RIGHT SIZED DREAM

an appreciation of Tove Jansson by Sheila Heti

One day my mother—who immigrated from Hungary forty years ago—was visiting my apartment. She noticed that on the fridge my boyfriend and I had taped a large picture of Charlie Brown, which we had torn from the pages of the *New Yorker*. It was just Charlie Brown standing there with his hands at his sides. Upon seeing the picture she stopped and said, "What a nice boy! Who is it?" The remarkable thing wasn't only discovering that my mother was probably the only person living in North America who had never encountered Charlie Brown, but that upon seeing him for the first time, she immediately liked him, felt sympathy and tenderness. Until that moment, I had not fully understood the power of comics: I had never witnessed so starkly what a perfect line can summon. A line drawn with love can make us as vulnerable as what the line depicts. Whatever cynicism I had about how commerce creates familiarity creates conditioned responses create "love," it crumbled in that instant. An artist's love for what they create is what creates love.

The first time I encountered Tove Jansson's *Moomin* strips, I had the same feeling as my mother: What a nice boy! (Or whatever sort of creature Moomin is—a creature from a tender dream.) There is such vulnerability in his eyebrows, in his little round tummy, in the way he doesn't have a mouth, in the babyish slope of the bottom of his face.

It was strange, then, to learn that Jansson's first drawing of Moomin was an attempt to draw "the ugliest creature imaginable" after a fight with her brother about Immanuel Kant. (She sketched this proto-Moomin on the wall of their outhouse at a country cottage.) The creature became plumper and friendlier in time, and his world filled out in such warm tones that it is hard not to be wistful for the life of a Moomintroll: what a sweet, happy family Moomin has! A mother who takes care of people in a quiet sort of way, a father who loves adventure, and a girlfriend with an ankle bracelet. There are friends and odd creatures always coming and going. Money is sometimes a problem for the Moomin clan, but never so much as when they have too much of it. Competing boy-creatures can also pose a problem, as Moomin's girlfriend sometimes falls in love with one, but she never loves them for any longer than a few consecutive strips. Moomin is open like a child, jealous like a teenager, and fretful like an old man. He is curious and trepidatious. And it is hard not to feel open and fretful and curious and trepidatious when moving through his puzzling (and yet ultimately safe) world.

Tove Jansson was the most successful Finnish illustrator and writer of children's books of her day, and she was the most widely read Finn abroad. She began her life as an artist early—she had her first drawing published at fifteen. She drew political cartoons for the lefty magazine *Garm* and published three Moomin books between 1945 and 1948 (when she was in her mid-thirties), hoping to write something innocent and sweet to counter the despairs of World War II. Around this time, she broke an engagement with a man and fell in love with the (female) artist Tuulikki Pietilä, who would become her partner and artistic collaborator for the rest of her life. In addition to her children's books and comic strips, which have been translated into almost fifty languages, Jansson wrote eleven novels and story collections for an adult audience. She continued to live and work in Helsinki, the city of her birth, her entire life, summering with her partner on the island Klovharu. She died in 2001 at the age of eighty-six. Pietilä outlived her by eight years.

One of my favourites of Jansson's long strips—which she drew for a London paper in the late fifties, finally handing the strip over to her brother because the daily grind left little time for her other work, and which are collected in the five volumes of *Moomin: The Complete Tove Jansson Comic Strip*—involves the Moomin clan visiting the Riviera, where all but Moominmamma fall in love with the high life. They temporarily become rich and everything feels glamorous. Mamma is the only one who knows that this is not a better life for them, and she makes a home within a four-poster bed, placing drapes around its sides, instead of letting them stretch out through the majestic hotel room; she

Tove Jansson with her brother Per Olov. The child between them is likely a young Sophia Jansson. Photo: Lars Jansson (late 1960s). © Moomin Characters™

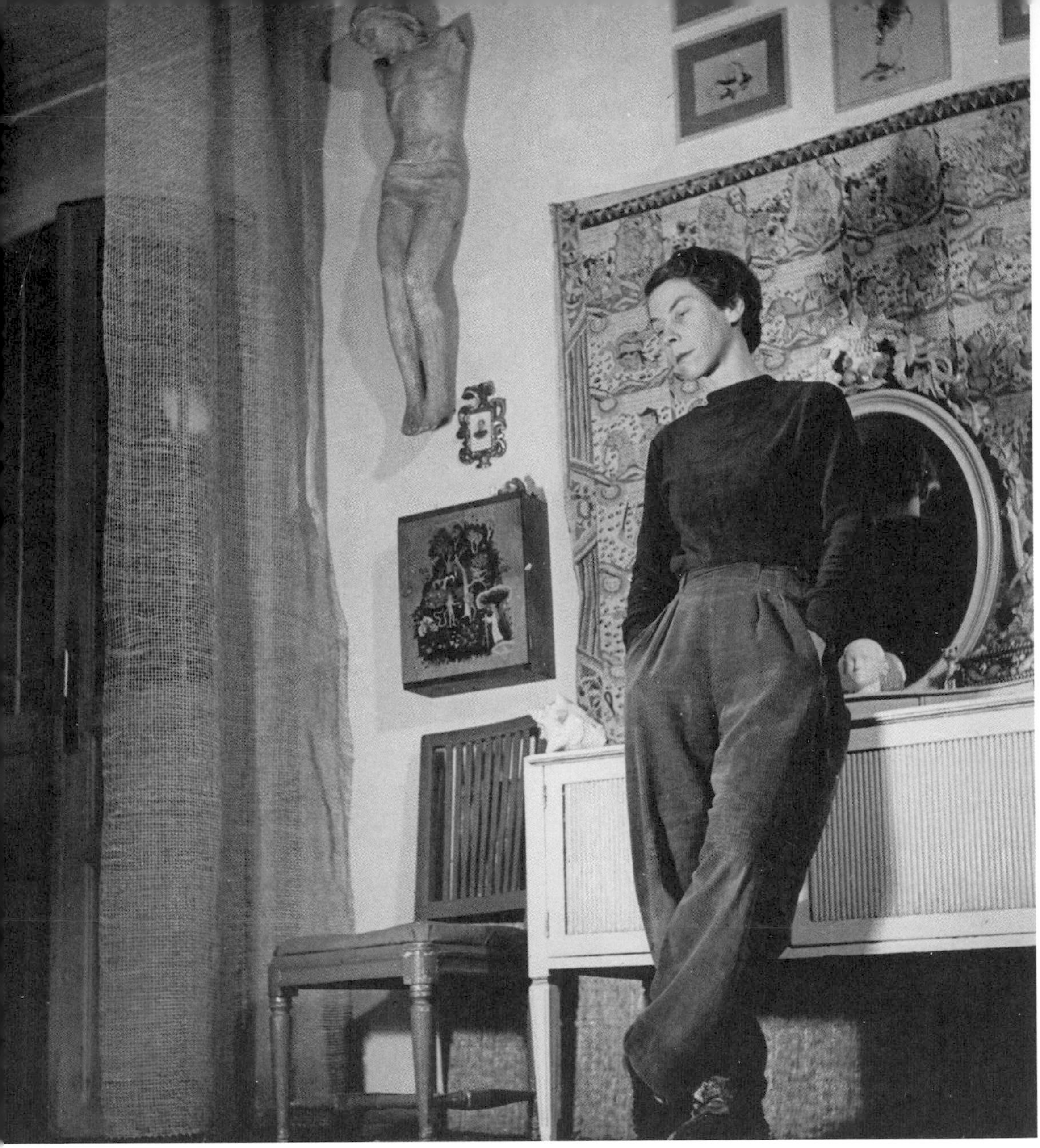

Tove Jansson moved into her turret studio in 1944, having a strong painter identity at the time. Photo: Per Olov Jansson. ©Moomin Characters™

I attribute my childhood obsession with the end of the world to Tove Jansson books. The Moomin family was always barely surviving a meteorite, or a giant wave, or endless winter—just cataclysm after cataclysm. Even the darkest children's literature rarely treats the end of the world as more than an abstract threat, and I remember appreciating the concreteness of Tove Jansson's disasters; *Moomin and the Comet* in particular had those eerie scenes of ants marching in prophetic formations, and a walk through a nightmare wasteland where the ocean used to be. Now that I'm grown and draw comics for a living, I could easily talk forever about every aspect of this perfect strip, but what still stands out is that it was the first apocalyptic literature I ever read. If I end up having a kid, and they're as neurotic and doom-obsessed as I was, I'm glad to be able to show them an age-appropriate vision of armageddon.

—***Sam Alden, cartoonist of*** **It Never Happened Again**

 (Right) An homage to Rembrandt, this painting depicts the seriousness with which Tove took her career. Oil on canvas, 1941. ©Moomin Characters™

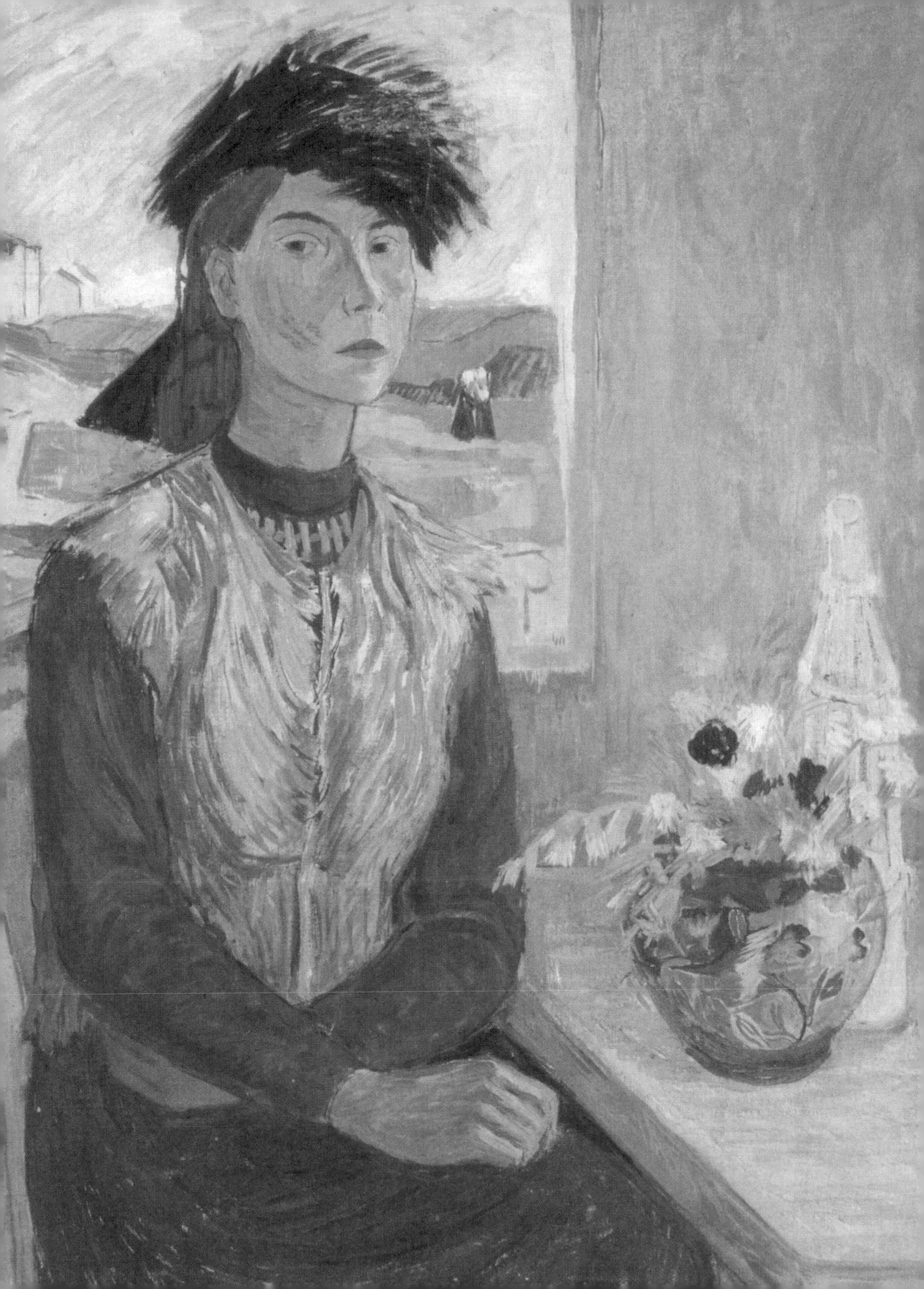

then tries to convince them that the most suitable thing would be to live under a canoe, and sets up house there. A rich creature, a dilettante artist, is taken with their way of life and tries it out—"How wonderful! I've never before met REAL bohemians!"—and for a spell, he feels so free. But in the end, the chilliness of life beneath the canoe and the absence of warm coffee in the morning sadden him, and he returns to his wealth. "Anyway," he says, "I have suffered for my art. How my friends will admire me."

At last the Moomin clan heads home, with Mamma saying to her family, "Admit high life got a bit tiresome." They agree but still reminisce about the finer moments. The beauty of this story is not in any high moralism, nor any insistence that one life (a bohemian one) is better than another (a life of luxury). Instead, Jansson suggests that everyone may have a life to which they are most suited, in which they can be most happy (maybe not completely happy, but happy enough) and that once they have found it, the only things that result from trying to be even happier are absurd and humiliating capers that return them exactly to where they were before. It's a simple sentiment, and a beautiful and rarely spoken one, so at odds with either a stern asceticism or a giddy consumerism. More like: everyone lives in their own dream, and the happiest are satisfied with a dream that's the right size.

It's a sentiment she expressed differently in *Garm* with a cartoon of Adolf Hitler as a wailing, diapered infant being offered slices of cake by Chamberlain and other world leaders—the slices labeled with the names of luckless European states—in an attempt to stop his tyrannical tears. Hitler's dream was wholly the wrong size. Kant-Moomin could have been peering unhappily from the corner.

It seems Jansson understood all babies—the innocent and the corrupt.

Jansson's life remained pretty much the same from the age of fifteen on: she lived in one place, she did artistic work—just as she saw her parents do in the house where she grew up—she had one big relationship, never had children, and always summered by the sea. She carried Moomin with her for many years. But even if she did dream herself a life of exactly the right size, even if she hadn't lived through the Second World War, it couldn't have been a life without its complications.

Of course, everyone dreams that a simple life is possible—if not for oneself, then for other people. We all wonder why hassles and problems constantly arise. In this, the genius *Moomin* strip is highly instructive: problems arise because a) people want to make improvements; b) there is a lot to be scared of; c) some people want adventure; d) others are too blithe and don't care enough for your feelings; and e) people make messes out of things about which they are too romantic. The *Moomin* strips are the opposite of a mess. Perhaps because Moomin began as the ugliest of creatures, Jansson could draw him lovingly, but without romance.

Sheila Heti is the author of six books, including the novels* How Should a Person Be? *and* Ticknor. *Her work has been translated into more than a dozen languages, and her writing has appeared in* McSweeney's, n+1, Harper's, *the* Believer, *the* London Review of Books, *the* New York Times, *and other places.

Tove and Lars Jansson. ©Moomin Characters™

Lars Jansson is an interesting case in international comics. He was a published writer from an early age. He's from a family of artists. His father was a sculptor, his mother a well-known graphic designer, his older brother a photographer, and his sister, Tove, well, she became the most internationally famous artist that Finland ever produced. Tove became something of a national celebrity with her illustration and children's books, but it was *Moomin*, her comic strip, that brought her international fame. These comics freed her from the various freelance jobs that she needed to pay the bills, but they soon became a creative albatross. She wanted out. Within a couple of years of *Moomin*'s launch, Tove brought Lars in to help with the scripts—he'd been helping with the translation right from the start. Lars saw the day-to-day grind that his sister endured and formulated a plan. While he had never spent any time drawing, he taught himself to be a cartoonist—in secret—and then presented his work to Tove. Upon seeing Lars's efforts, Tove immediately resigned from the strip. Lars wrote and drew *Moomin* for the next fifteen years.

—Tom Devlin

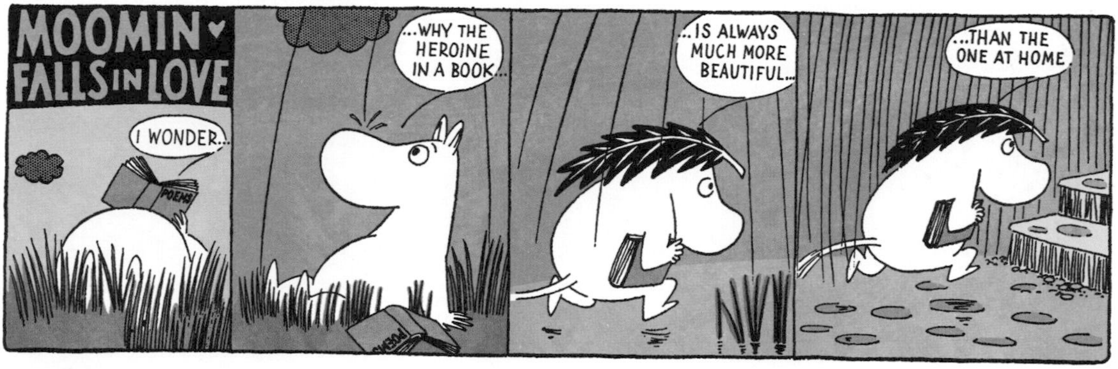
MOOMIN FALLS IN LOVE
I WONDER...
POEMS
...WHY THE HEROINE IN A BOOK...
POEMS
...IS ALWAYS MUCH MORE BEAUTIFUL...
...THAN THE ONE AT HOME.

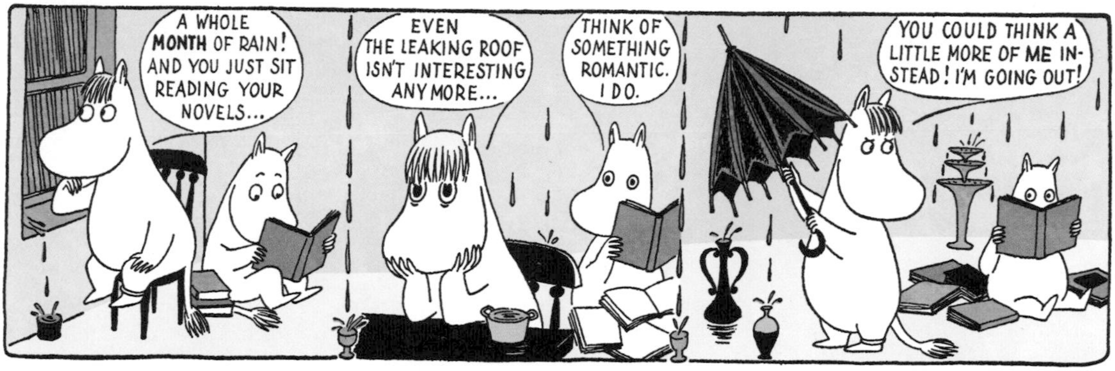
A WHOLE MONTH OF RAIN! AND YOU JUST SIT READING YOUR NOVELS...
EVEN THE LEAKING ROOF ISN'T INTERESTING ANY MORE...
THINK OF SOMETHING ROMANTIC. I DO.
YOU COULD THINK A LITTLE MORE OF ME INSTEAD! I'M GOING OUT!

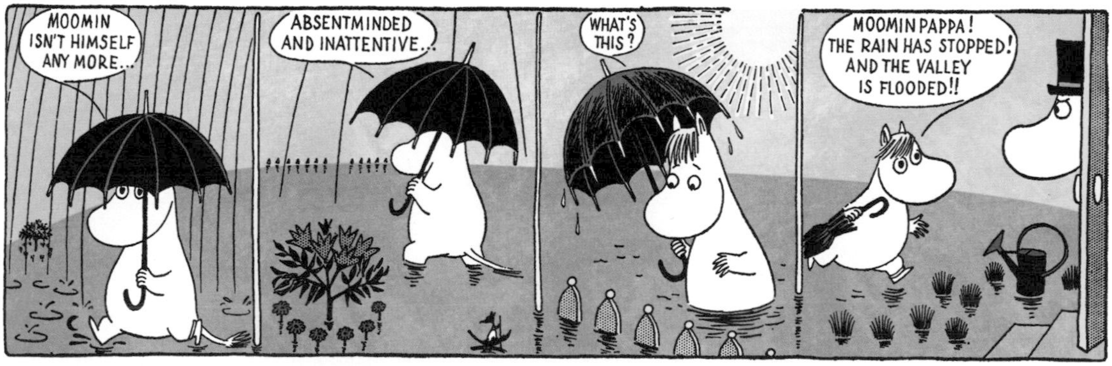
MOOMIN ISN'T HIMSELF ANY MORE...
ABSENTMINDED AND INATTENTIVE...
WHAT'S THIS?
MOOMINPAPPA! THE RAIN HAS STOPPED! AND THE VALLEY IS FLOODED!!

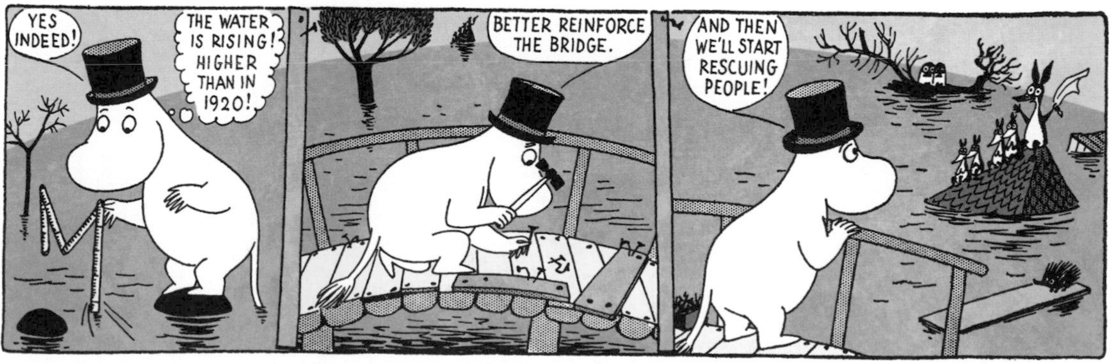
YES INDEED!
THE WATER IS RISING! HIGHER THAN IN 1920!
BETTER REINFORCE THE BRIDGE.
AND THEN WE'LL START RESCUING PEOPLE!

These strips appeared first in the *London Evening News* (1954) and later in colour in D+Q's *Moomin Falls in Love* (2013). Tove Jansson

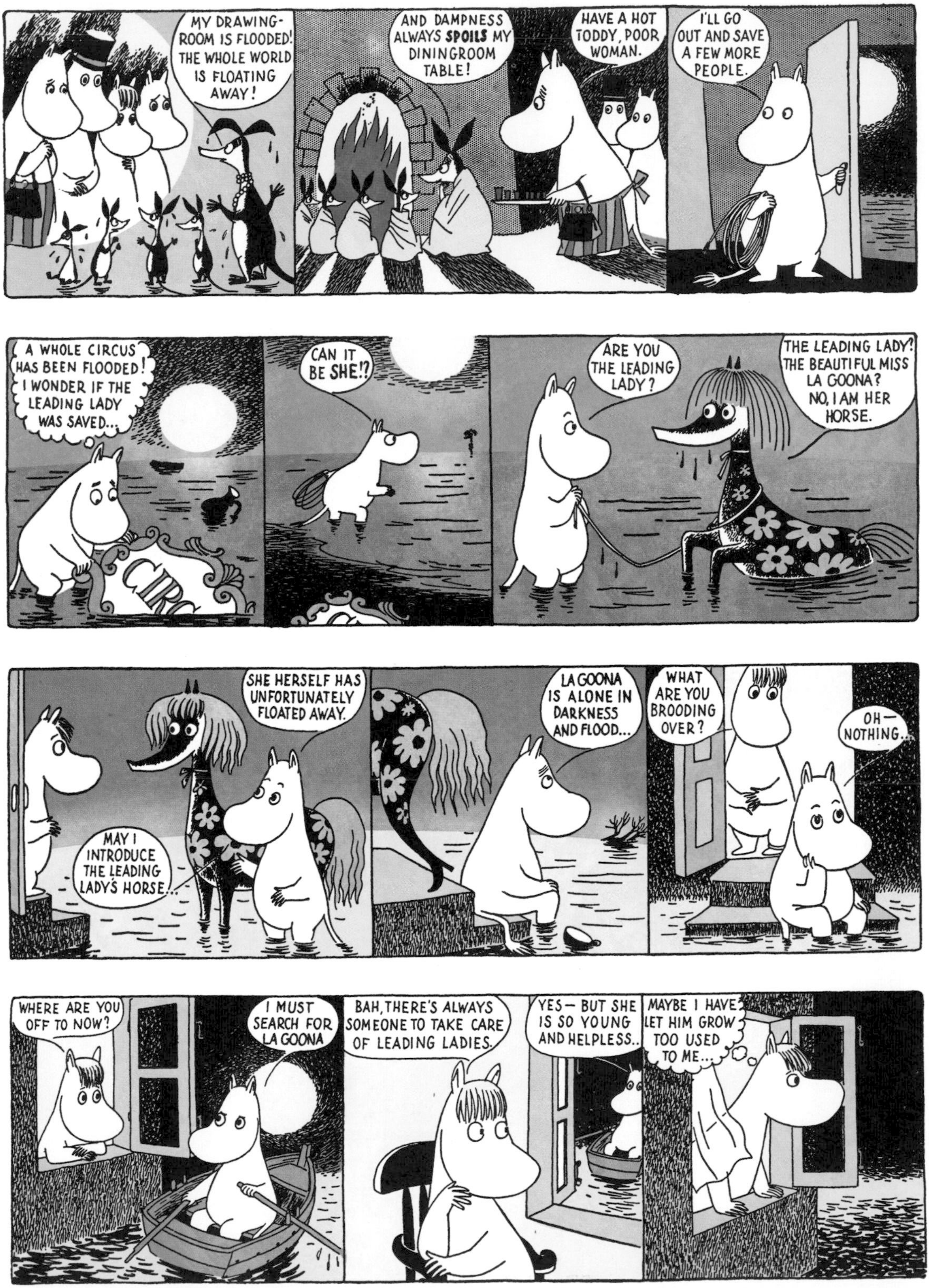
MY DRAWING-ROOM IS FLOODED! THE WHOLE WORLD IS FLOATING AWAY!
AND DAMPNESS ALWAYS **SPOILS** MY DININGROOM TABLE!
HAVE A HOT TODDY, POOR WOMAN.
I'LL GO OUT AND SAVE A FEW MORE PEOPLE.
A WHOLE CIRCUS HAS BEEN FLOODED! I WONDER IF THE LEADING LADY WAS SAVED...
CIRC
CAN IT BE **SHE**!?
ARE YOU THE LEADING LADY?
THE LEADING LADY? THE BEAUTIFUL MISS LA GOONA? NO, I AM HER HORSE.
SHE HERSELF HAS UNFORTUNATELY FLOATED AWAY.
MAY I INTRODUCE THE LEADING LADY'S HORSE...
LA GOONA IS ALONE IN DARKNESS AND FLOOD...
WHAT ARE YOU BROODING OVER?
OH— NOTHING...
WHERE ARE YOU OFF TO NOW?
I MUST SEARCH FOR LA GOONA
BAH, THERE'S ALWAYS SOMEONE TO TAKE CARE OF LEADING LADIES.
YES— BUT SHE IS SO YOUNG AND HELPLESS..
MAYBE I HAVE LET HIM GROW TOO USED TO ME...

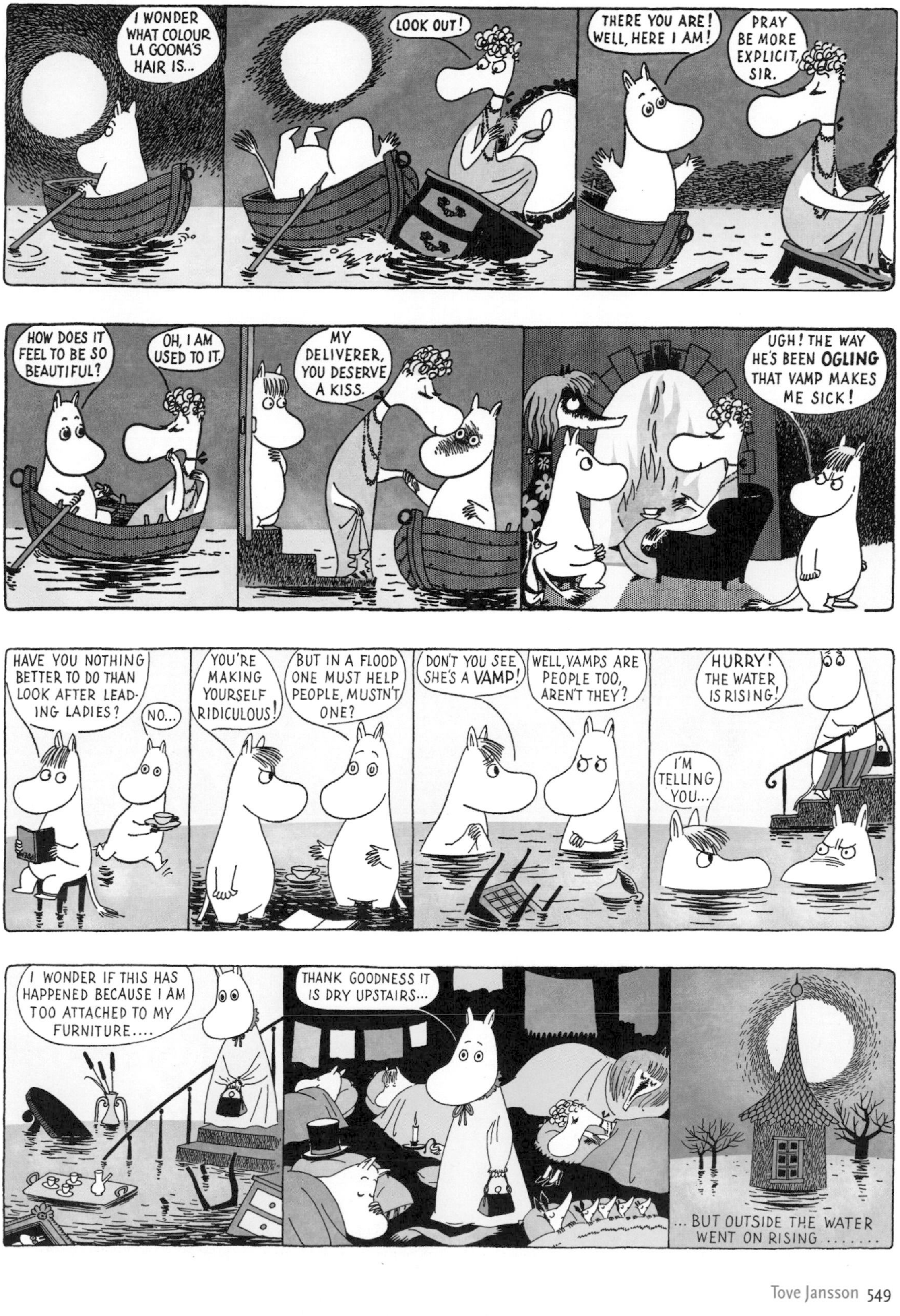
I WONDER WHAT COLOUR LA GOONA'S HAIR IS...
LOOK OUT!
THERE YOU ARE! WELL, HERE I AM!
PRAY BE MORE EXPLICIT, SIR.
HOW DOES IT FEEL TO BE SO BEAUTIFUL?
OH, I AM USED TO IT.
MY DELIVERER, YOU DESERVE A KISS.
UGH! THE WAY HE'S BEEN OGLING THAT VAMP MAKES ME SICK!
HAVE YOU NOTHING BETTER TO DO THAN LOOK AFTER LEADING LADIES?
NO...
YOU'RE MAKING YOURSELF RIDICULOUS!
BUT IN A FLOOD ONE MUST HELP PEOPLE, MUSTN'T ONE?
DON'T YOU SEE SHE'S A VAMP!
WELL, VAMPS ARE PEOPLE TOO, AREN'T THEY?
HURRY! THE WATER IS RISING!
I'M TELLING YOU...
I WONDER IF THIS HAS HAPPENED BECAUSE I AM TOO ATTACHED TO MY FURNITURE....
THANK GOODNESS IT IS DRY UPSTAIRS...
... BUT OUTSIDE THE WATER WENT ON RISING.......

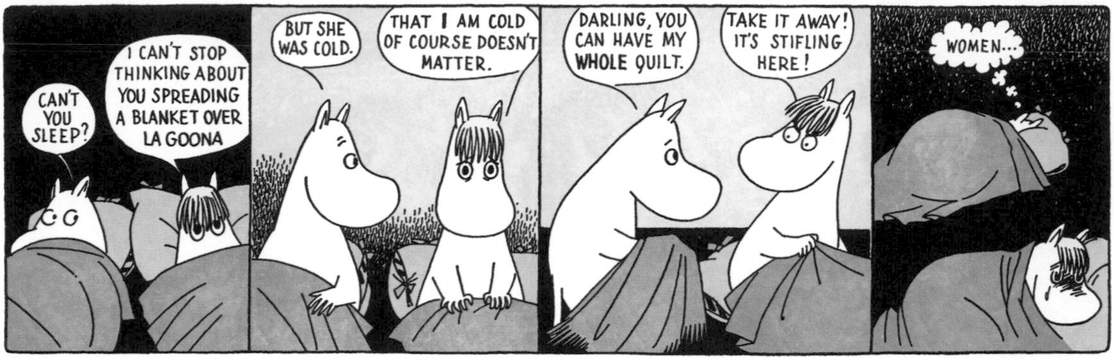
CAN'T YOU SLEEP?
I CAN'T STOP THINKING ABOUT YOU SPREADING A BLANKET OVER LA GOONA
BUT SHE WAS COLD.
THAT I AM COLD OF COURSE DOESN'T MATTER.
DARLING, YOU CAN HAVE MY WHOLE QUILT.
TAKE IT AWAY! IT'S STIFLING HERE!
WOMEN...

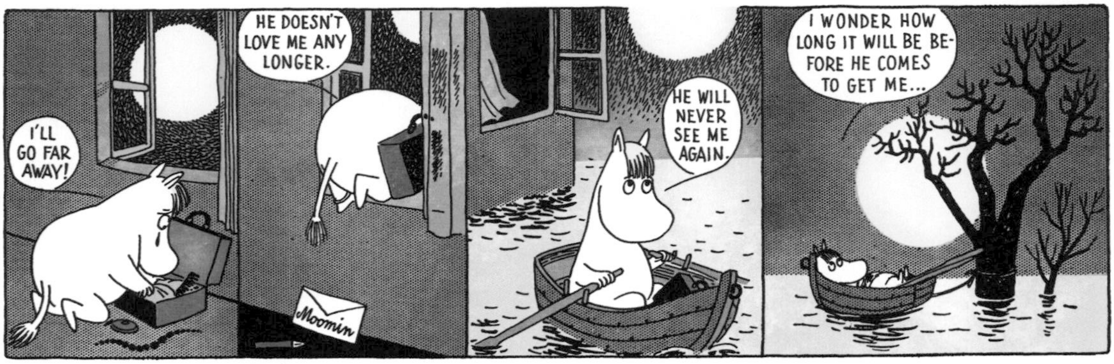
I'LL GO FAR AWAY!
HE DOESN'T LOVE ME ANY LONGER.
Moomin
HE WILL NEVER SEE ME AGAIN.
I WONDER HOW LONG IT WILL BE BEFORE HE COMES TO GET ME...

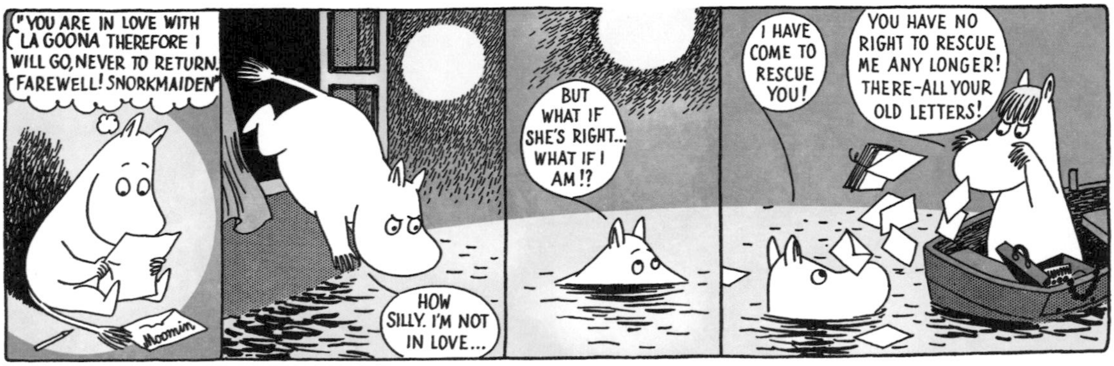
"YOU ARE IN LOVE WITH LA GOONA THEREFORE I WILL GO, NEVER TO RETURN. FAREWELL! SNORKMAIDEN"
Moomin
HOW SILLY. I'M NOT IN LOVE...
BUT WHAT IF SHE'S RIGHT... WHAT IF I AM!?
I HAVE COME TO RESCUE YOU!
YOU HAVE NO RIGHT TO RESCUE ME ANY LONGER! THERE-ALL YOUR OLD LETTERS!

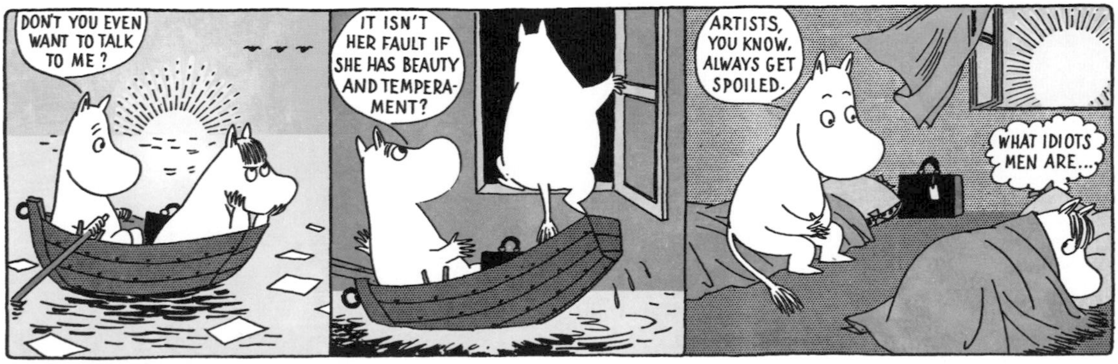
DON'T YOU EVEN WANT TO TALK TO ME?
IT ISN'T HER FAULT IF SHE HAS BEAUTY AND TEMPERAMENT?
ARTISTS, YOU KNOW, ALWAYS GET SPOILED.
WHAT IDIOTS MEN ARE...

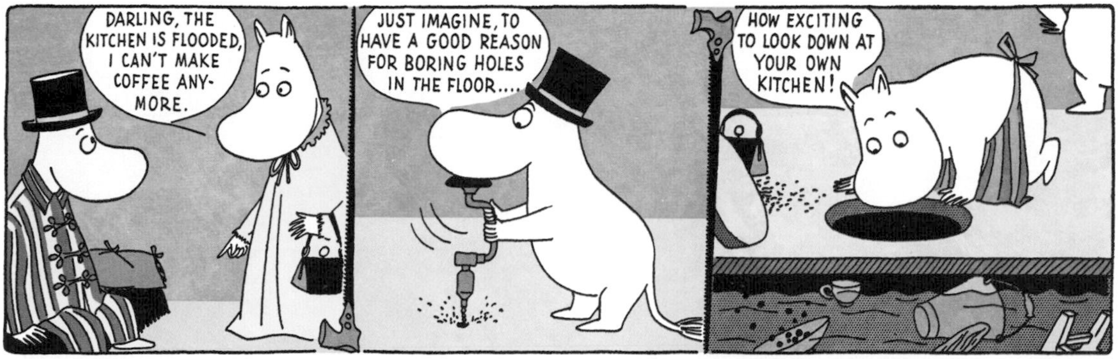
DARLING, THE KITCHEN IS FLOODED, I CAN'T MAKE COFFEE ANY-MORE.
JUST IMAGINE, TO HAVE A GOOD REASON FOR BORING HOLES IN THE FLOOR....
HOW EXCITING TO LOOK DOWN AT YOUR OWN KITCHEN!

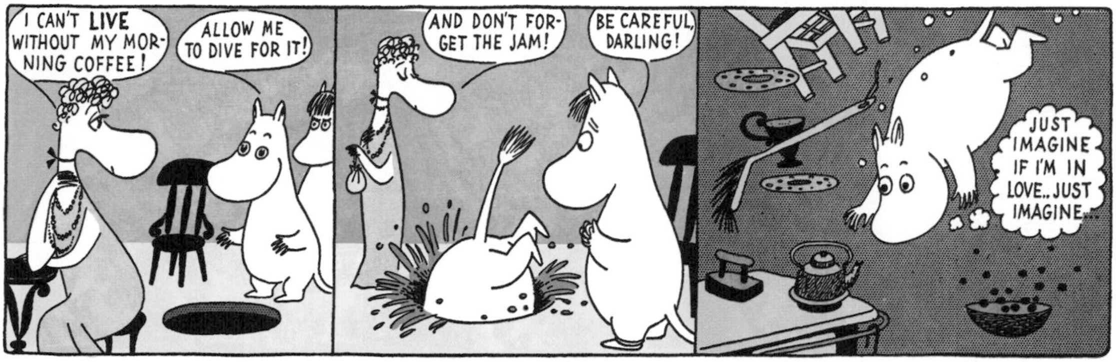
I CAN'T **LIVE** WITHOUT MY MOR-NING COFFEE!
ALLOW ME TO DIVE FOR IT!
AND DON'T FOR-GET THE JAM!
BE CAREFUL, DARLING!
JUST IMAGINE IF I'M IN LOVE.. JUST IMAGINE...

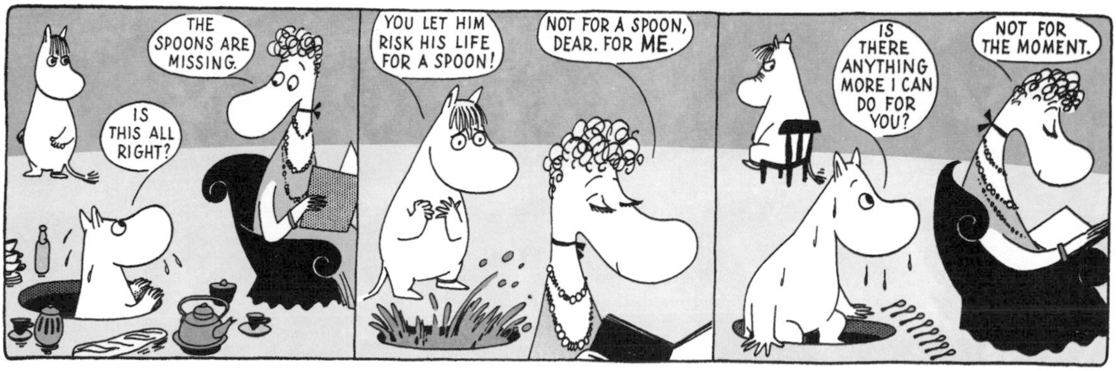
THE SPOONS ARE MISSING.
IS THIS ALL RIGHT?
YOU LET HIM RISK HIS LIFE FOR A SPOON!
NOT FOR A SPOON, DEAR. FOR **ME**.
IS THERE ANYTHING MORE I CAN DO FOR YOU?
NOT FOR THE MOMENT.

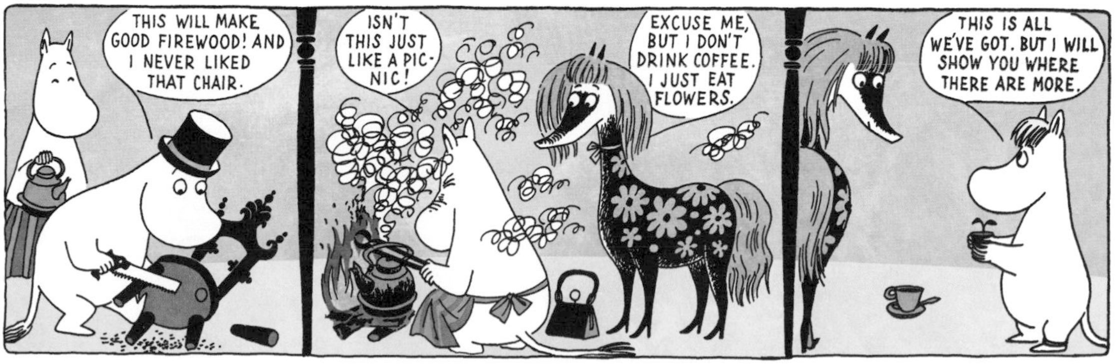
THIS WILL MAKE GOOD FIREWOOD! AND I NEVER LIKED THAT CHAIR.
ISN'T THIS JUST LIKE A PIC-NIC!
EXCUSE ME, BUT I DON'T DRINK COFFEE. I JUST EAT FLOWERS.
THIS IS ALL WE'VE GOT. BUT I WILL SHOW YOU WHERE THERE ARE MORE.

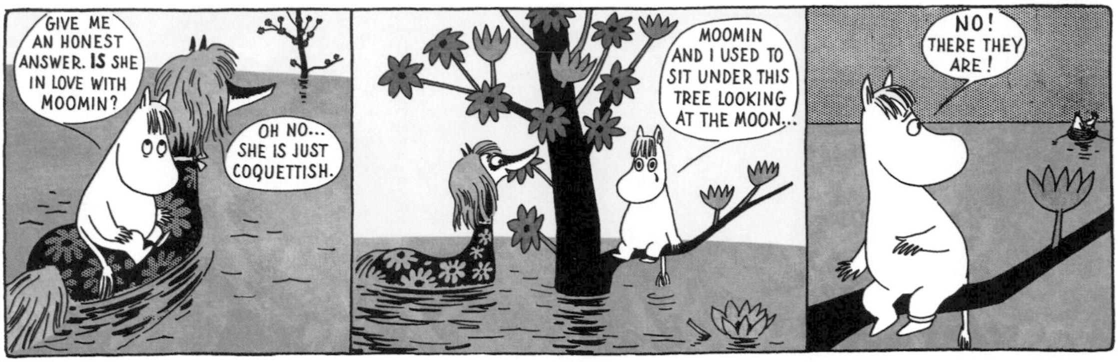
GIVE ME AN HONEST ANSWER. IS SHE IN LOVE WITH MOOMIN?
OH NO... SHE IS JUST COQUETTISH.
MOOMIN AND I USED TO SIT UNDER THIS TREE LOOKING AT THE MOON...
NO! THERE THEY ARE!

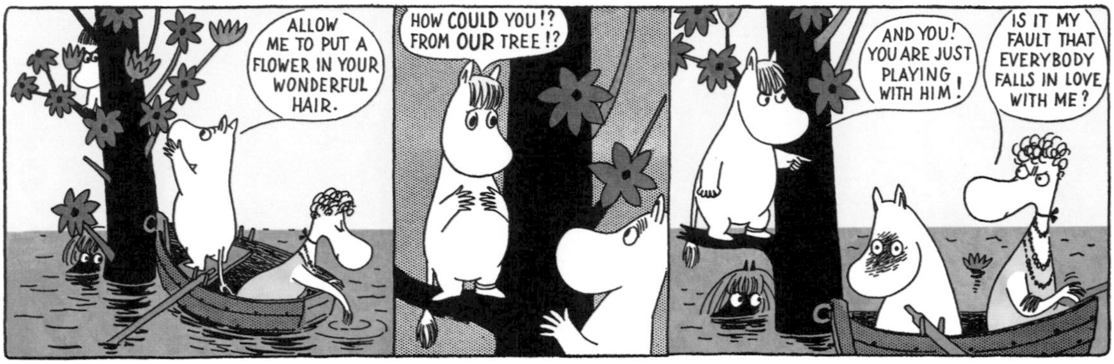
ALLOW ME TO PUT A FLOWER IN YOUR WONDERFUL HAIR.
HOW COULD YOU!? FROM OUR TREE!?
AND YOU! YOU ARE JUST PLAYING WITH HIM!
IS IT MY FAULT THAT EVERYBODY FALLS IN LOVE WITH ME?

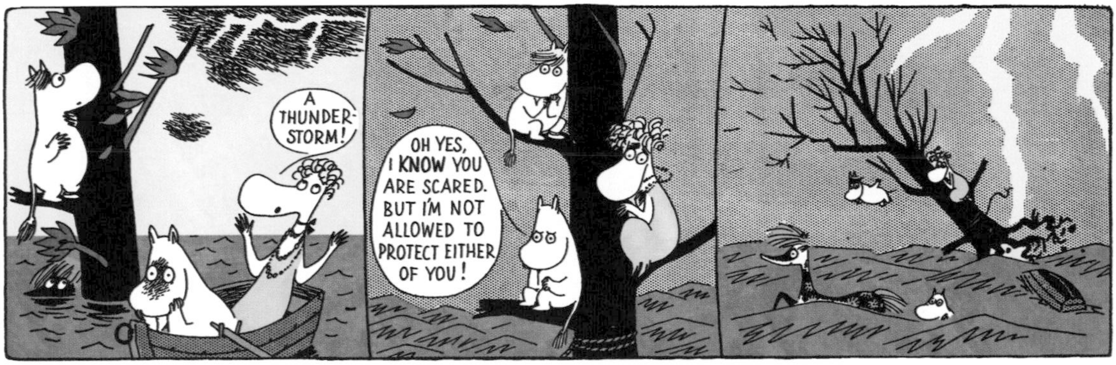
A THUNDER-STORM!
OH YES, I KNOW YOU ARE SCARED. BUT I'M NOT ALLOWED TO PROTECT EITHER OF YOU!

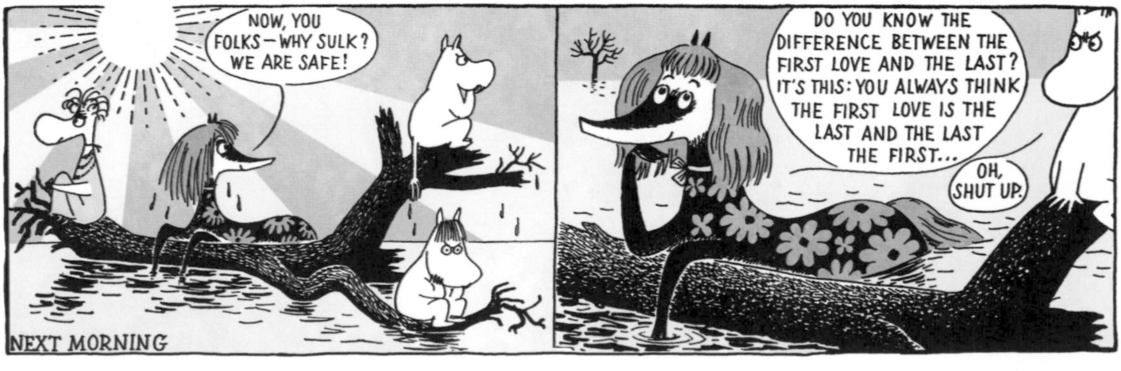
NOW, YOU FOLKS—WHY SULK? WE ARE SAFE!
NEXT MORNING
DO YOU KNOW THE DIFFERENCE BETWEEN THE FIRST LOVE AND THE LAST? IT'S THIS: YOU ALWAYS THINK THE FIRST LOVE IS THE LAST AND THE LAST THE FIRST...
OH, SHUT UP.

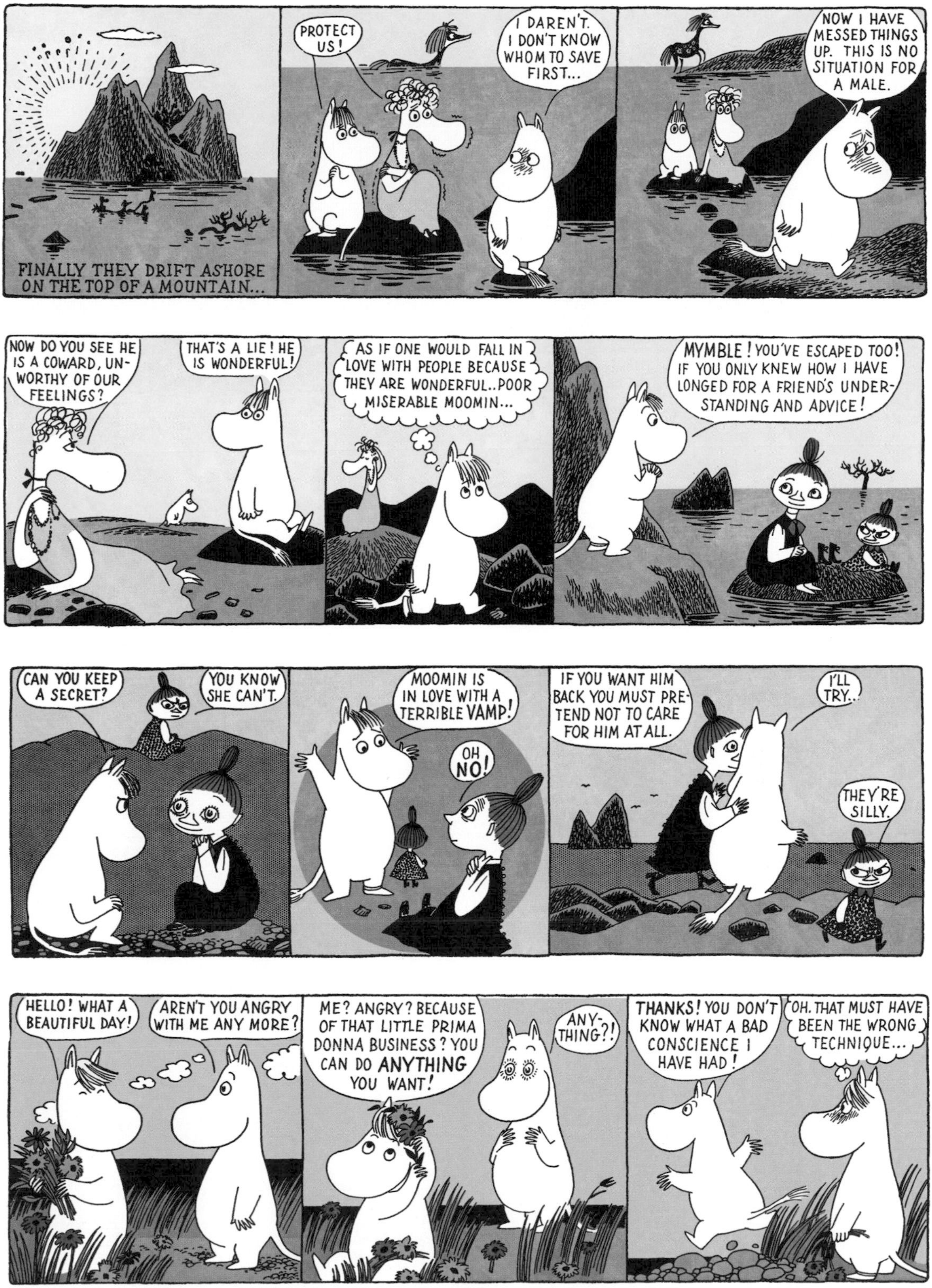

FINALLY THEY DRIFT ASHORE ON THE TOP OF A MOUNTAIN...
PROTECT US!
I DAREN'T. I DON'T KNOW WHOM TO SAVE FIRST...
NOW I HAVE MESSED THINGS UP. THIS IS NO SITUATION FOR A MALE.
NOW DO YOU SEE HE IS A COWARD, UNWORTHY OF OUR FEELINGS?
THAT'S A LIE! HE IS WONDERFUL!
AS IF ONE WOULD FALL IN LOVE WITH PEOPLE BECAUSE THEY ARE WONDERFUL.. POOR MISERABLE MOOMIN...
MYMBLE! YOU'VE ESCAPED TOO! IF YOU ONLY KNEW HOW I HAVE LONGED FOR A FRIEND'S UNDERSTANDING AND ADVICE!
CAN YOU KEEP A SECRET?
YOU KNOW SHE CAN'T.
MOOMIN IS IN LOVE WITH A TERRIBLE VAMP!
OH NO!
IF YOU WANT HIM BACK YOU MUST PRETEND NOT TO CARE FOR HIM AT ALL.
I'LL TRY..
THEY'RE SILLY.
HELLO! WHAT A BEAUTIFUL DAY!
AREN'T YOU ANGRY WITH ME ANY MORE?
ME? ANGRY? BECAUSE OF THAT LITTLE PRIMA DONNA BUSINESS? YOU CAN DO ANYTHING YOU WANT!
ANYTHING?!
THANKS! YOU DON'T KNOW WHAT A BAD CONSCIENCE I HAVE HAD!
OH. THAT MUST HAVE BEEN THE WRONG TECHNIQUE...

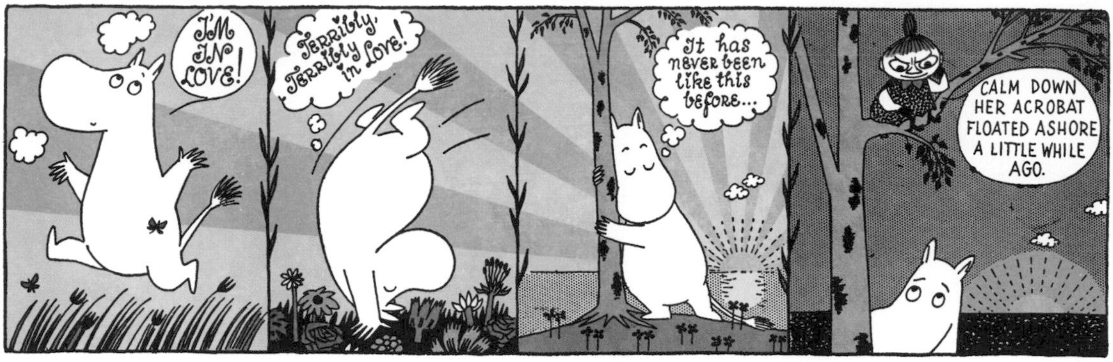
I'M IN LOVE!
Terribly, terribly in love!
It has never been like this before...
CALM DOWN HER ACROBAT FLOATED ASHORE A LITTLE WHILE AGO.

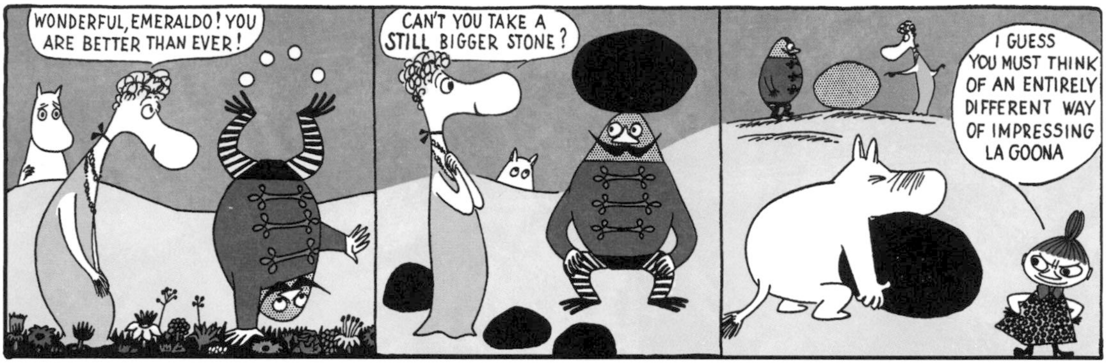
WONDERFUL, EMERALDO! YOU ARE BETTER THAN EVER!
CAN'T YOU TAKE A **STILL** BIGGER STONE?
I GUESS YOU MUST THINK OF AN ENTIRELY DIFFERENT WAY OF IMPRESSING LA GOONA

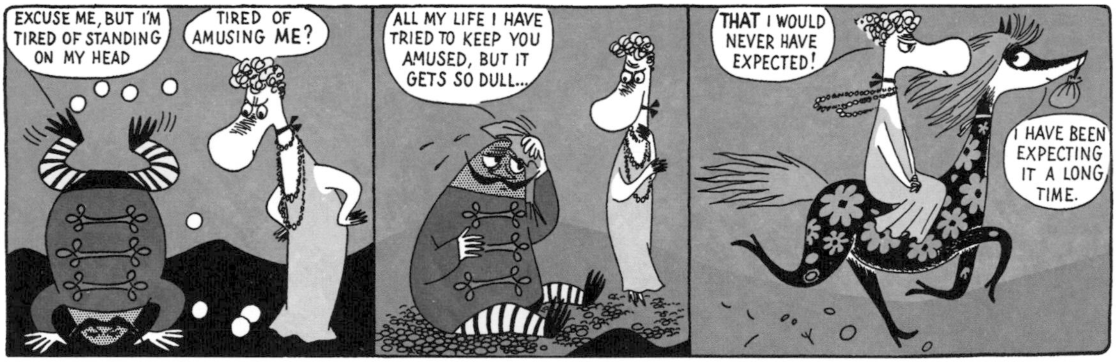
EXCUSE ME, BUT I'M TIRED OF STANDING ON MY HEAD
TIRED OF AMUSING **ME**?
ALL MY LIFE I HAVE TRIED TO KEEP YOU AMUSED, BUT IT GETS SO DULL...
THAT I WOULD NEVER HAVE EXPECTED!
I HAVE BEEN EXPECTING IT A LONG TIME.

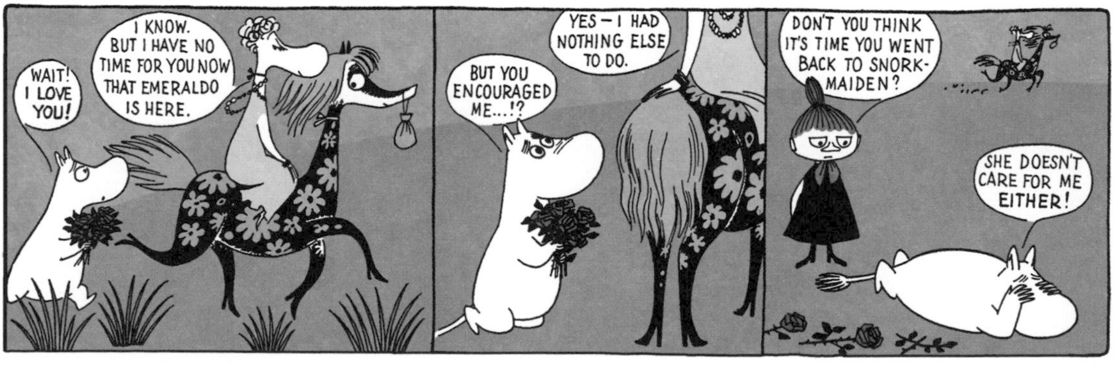
WAIT! I LOVE YOU!
I KNOW. BUT I HAVE NO TIME FOR YOU NOW THAT EMERALDO IS HERE.
BUT YOU ENCOURAGED ME...!?
YES — I HAD NOTHING ELSE TO DO.
DON'T YOU THINK IT'S TIME YOU WENT BACK TO SNORK-MAIDEN?
SHE DOESN'T CARE FOR ME **EITHER**!

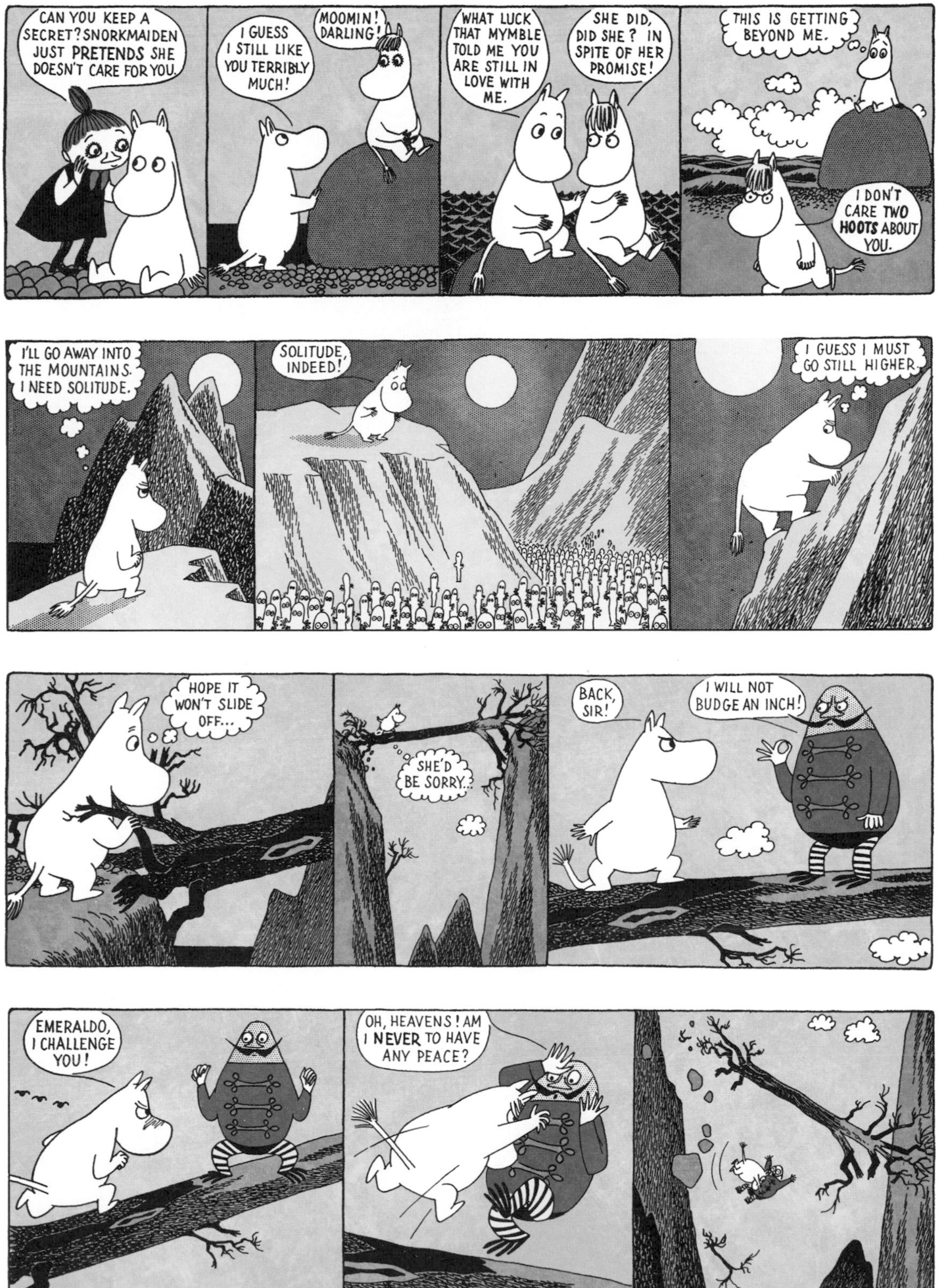
CAN YOU KEEP A SECRET? SNORKMAIDEN JUST PRETENDS SHE DOESN'T CARE FOR YOU.
I GUESS I STILL LIKE YOU TERRIBLY MUCH!
MOOMIN! DARLING!
WHAT LUCK THAT MYMBLE TOLD ME YOU ARE STILL IN LOVE WITH ME.
SHE DID, DID SHE? IN SPITE OF HER PROMISE!
THIS IS GETTING BEYOND ME.
I DON'T CARE TWO HOOTS ABOUT YOU.
I'LL GO AWAY INTO THE MOUNTAINS. I NEED SOLITUDE.
SOLITUDE, INDEED!
I GUESS I MUST GO STILL HIGHER.
HOPE IT WON'T SLIDE OFF...
SHE'D BE SORRY...
BACK, SIR!
I WILL NOT BUDGE AN INCH!
EMERALDO, I CHALLENGE YOU!
OH, HEAVENS! AM I NEVER TO HAVE ANY PEACE?

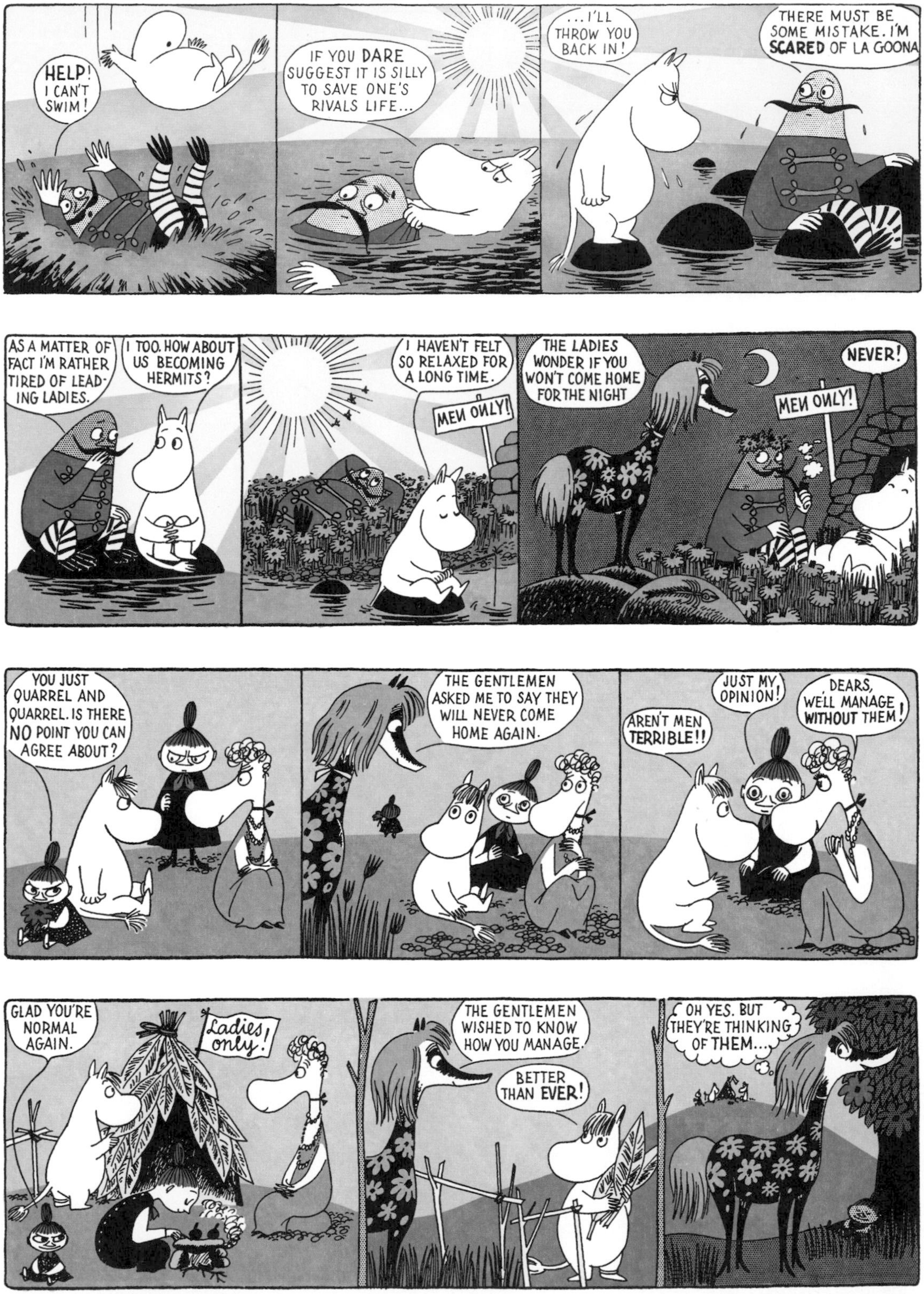
HELP! I CAN'T SWIM!
IF YOU DARE SUGGEST IT IS SILLY TO SAVE ONE'S RIVALS LIFE...
...I'LL THROW YOU BACK IN!
THERE MUST BE SOME MISTAKE. I'M SCARED OF LA GOONA
AS A MATTER OF FACT I'M RATHER TIRED OF LEADING LADIES.
I TOO. HOW ABOUT US BECOMING HERMITS?
I HAVEN'T FELT SO RELAXED FOR A LONG TIME.
MEN ONLY!
THE LADIES WONDER IF YOU WON'T COME HOME FOR THE NIGHT
NEVER!
MEN ONLY!
YOU JUST QUARREL AND QUARREL. IS THERE NO POINT YOU CAN AGREE ABOUT?
THE GENTLEMEN ASKED ME TO SAY THEY WILL NEVER COME HOME AGAIN.
AREN'T MEN TERRIBLE!!
JUST MY OPINION!
DEARS, WE'LL MANAGE WITHOUT THEM!
GLAD YOU'RE NORMAL AGAIN.
Ladies only!
THE GENTLEMEN WISHED TO KNOW HOW YOU MANAGE.
BETTER THAN EVER!
OH YES. BUT THEY'RE THINKING OF THEM...

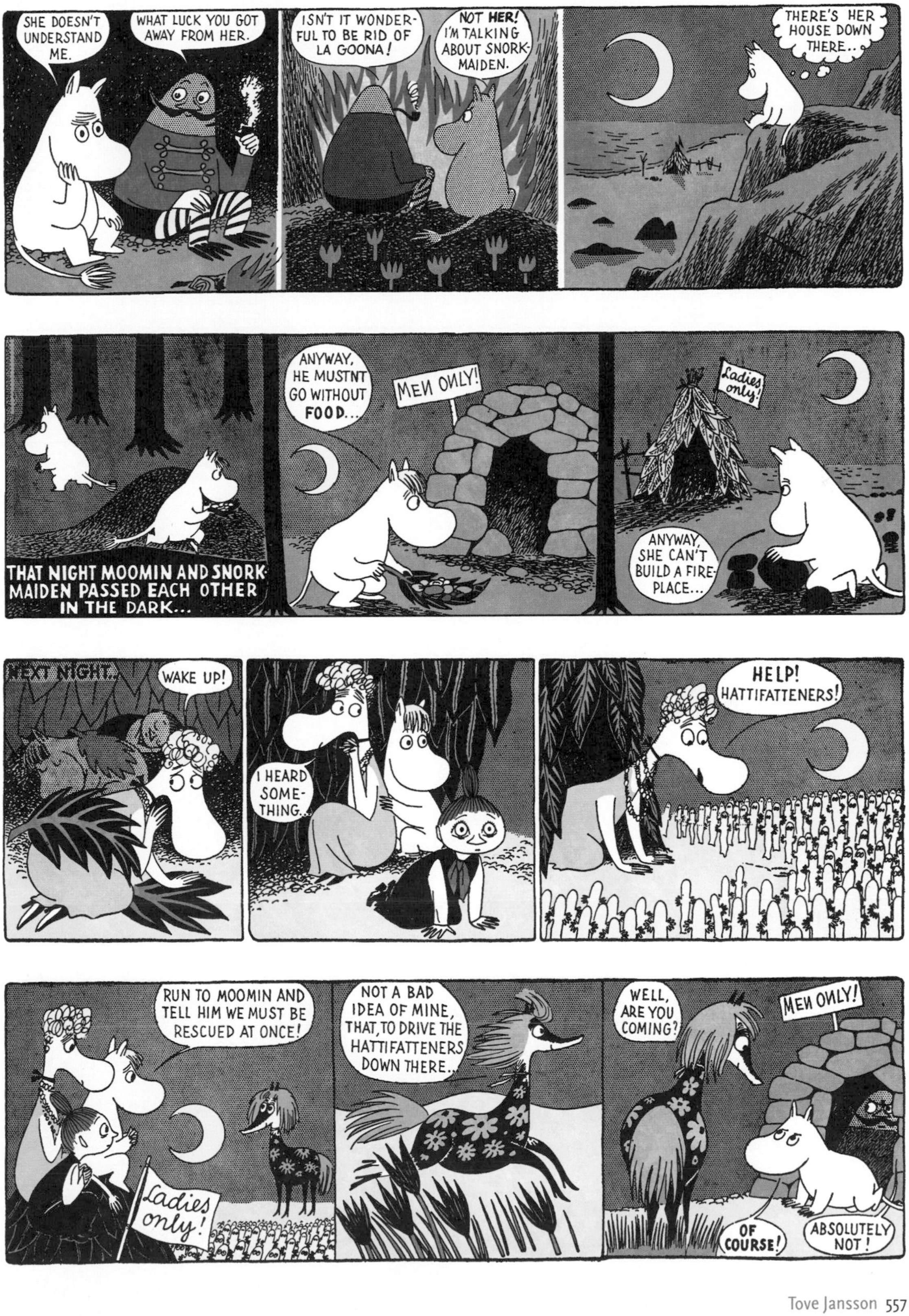
SHE DOESN'T UNDERSTAND ME.
WHAT LUCK YOU GOT AWAY FROM HER.
ISN'T IT WONDERFUL TO BE RID OF LA GOONA!
NOT HER! I'M TALKING ABOUT SNORKMAIDEN.
THERE'S HER HOUSE DOWN THERE..
THAT NIGHT MOOMIN AND SNORKMAIDEN PASSED EACH OTHER IN THE DARK...
ANYWAY, HE MUSTNT GO WITHOUT FOOD...
MEN ONLY!
Ladies only!
ANYWAY, SHE CAN'T BUILD A FIREPLACE...
NEXT NIGHT..
WAKE UP!
I HEARD SOMETHING...
HELP! HATTIFATTENERS!
RUN TO MOOMIN AND TELL HIM WE MUST BE RESCUED AT ONCE!
Ladies only!
NOT A BAD IDEA OF MINE, THAT, TO DRIVE THE HATTIFATTENERS DOWN THERE..
WELL, ARE YOU COMING?
MEN ONLY!
OF COURSE!
ABSOLUTELY NOT!

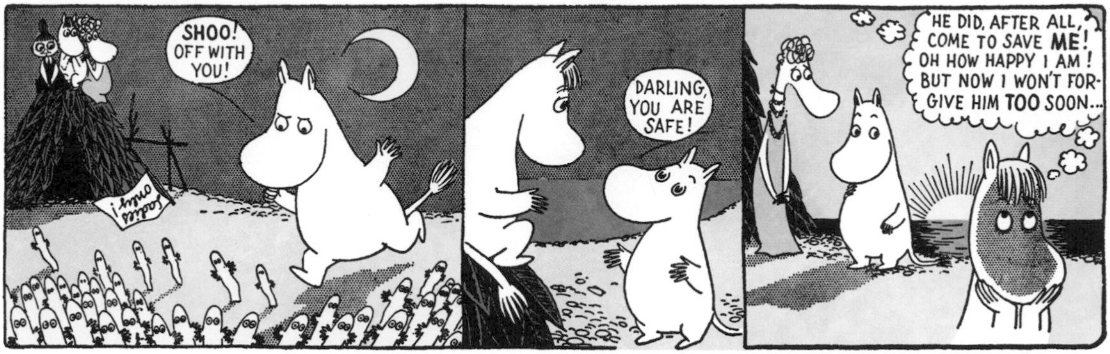
SHOO! OFF WITH YOU!
DARLING, YOU ARE SAFE!
HE DID, AFTER ALL, COME TO SAVE ME! OH HOW HAPPY I AM! BUT NOW I WON'T FORGIVE HIM TOO SOON...

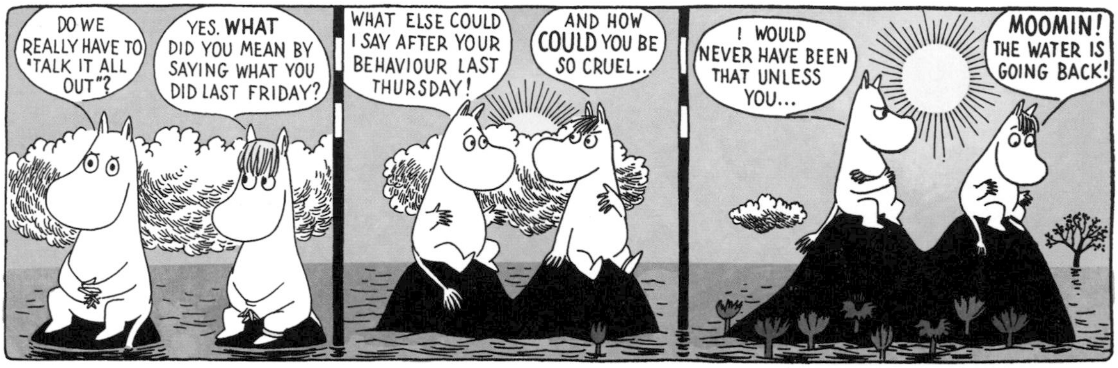
DO WE REALLY HAVE TO "TALK IT ALL OUT"?
YES. WHAT DID YOU MEAN BY SAYING WHAT YOU DID LAST FRIDAY?
WHAT ELSE COULD I SAY AFTER YOUR BEHAVIOUR LAST THURSDAY!
AND HOW COULD YOU BE SO CRUEL...
I WOULD NEVER HAVE BEEN THAT UNLESS YOU...
MOOMIN! THE WATER IS GOING BACK!

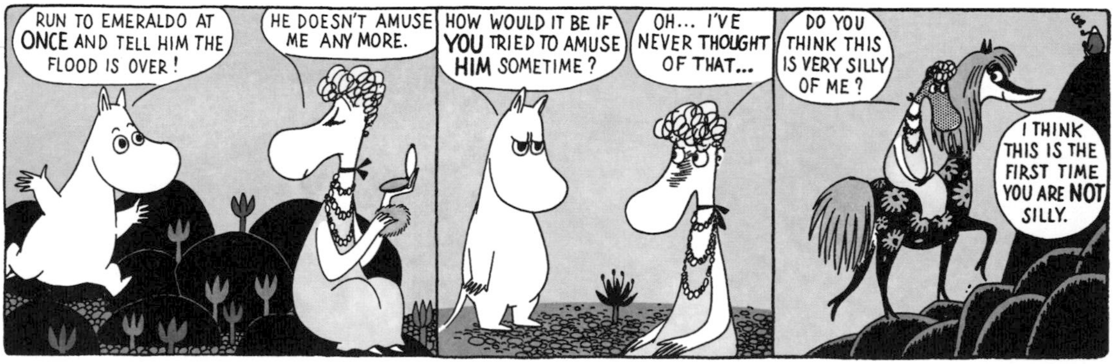
RUN TO EMERALDO AT ONCE AND TELL HIM THE FLOOD IS OVER!
HE DOESN'T AMUSE ME ANY MORE.
HOW WOULD IT BE IF YOU TRIED TO AMUSE HIM SOMETIME?
OH... I'VE NEVER THOUGHT OF THAT...
DO YOU THINK THIS IS VERY SILLY OF ME?
I THINK THIS IS THE FIRST TIME YOU ARE NOT SILLY.

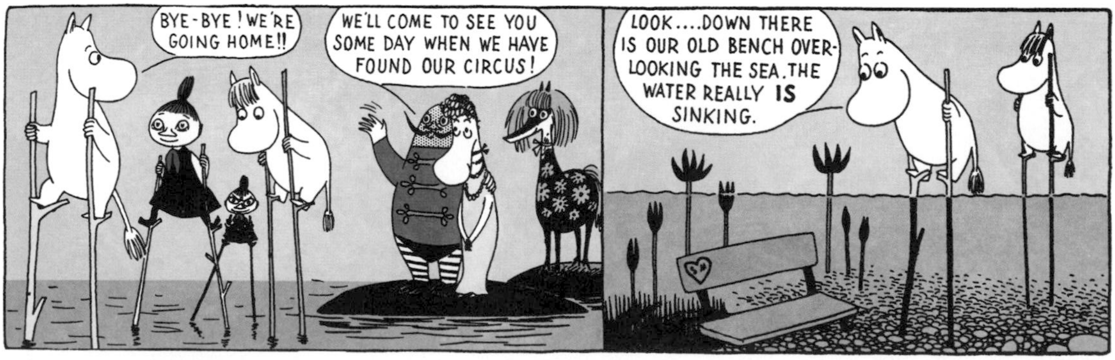
BYE-BYE! WE'RE GOING HOME!!
WE'LL COME TO SEE YOU SOME DAY WHEN WE HAVE FOUND OUR CIRCUS!
LOOK....DOWN THERE IS OUR OLD BENCH OVERLOOKING THE SEA. THE WATER REALLY IS SINKING.

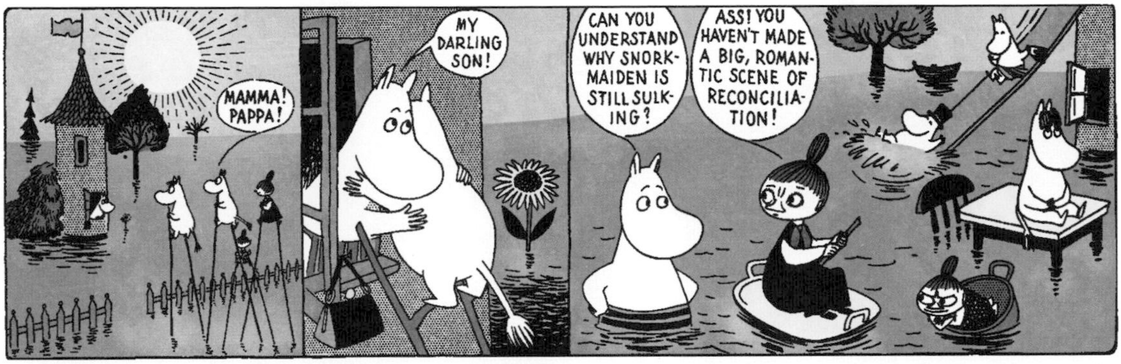
MAMMA! PAPPA!
MY DARLING SON!
CAN YOU UNDERSTAND WHY SNORK-MAIDEN IS STILL SULK-ING?
ASS! YOU HAVEN'T MADE A BIG, ROMAN-TIC SCENE OF RECONCILIA-TION!

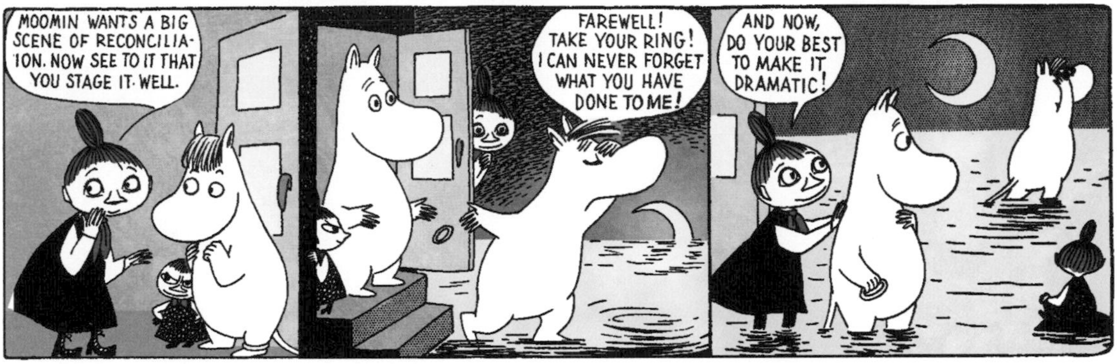
MOOMIN WANTS A BIG SCENE OF RECONCILIA-TION. NOW SEE TO IT THAT YOU STAGE IT WELL.
FAREWELL! TAKE YOUR RING! I CAN NEVER FORGET WHAT YOU HAVE DONE TO ME!
AND NOW, DO YOUR BEST TO MAKE IT DRAMATIC!

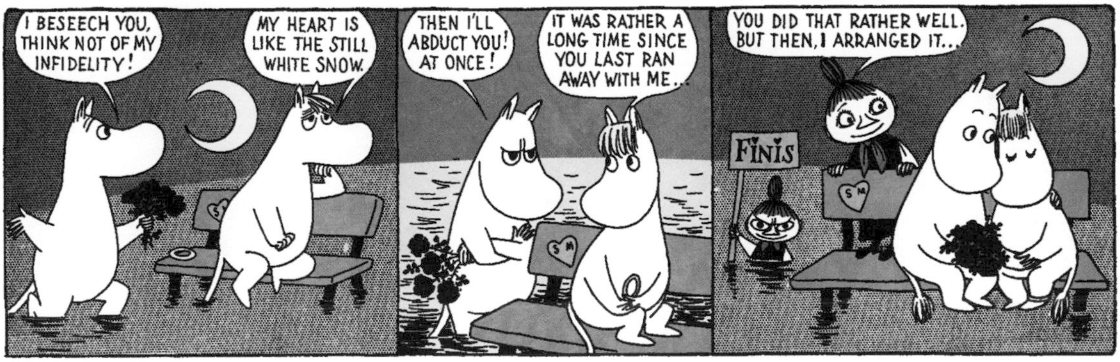
I BESEECH YOU, THINK NOT OF MY INFIDELITY!
MY HEART IS LIKE THE STILL WHITE SNOW.
THEN I'LL ABDUCT YOU! AT ONCE!
IT WAS RATHER A LONG TIME SINCE YOU LAST RAN AWAY WITH ME...
YOU DID THAT RATHER WELL. BUT THEN, I ARRANGED IT...
FINIS

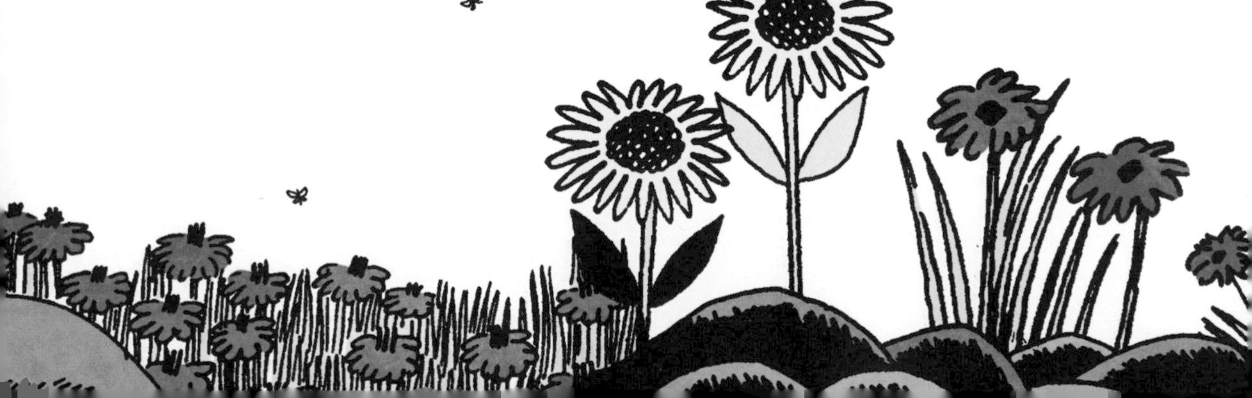

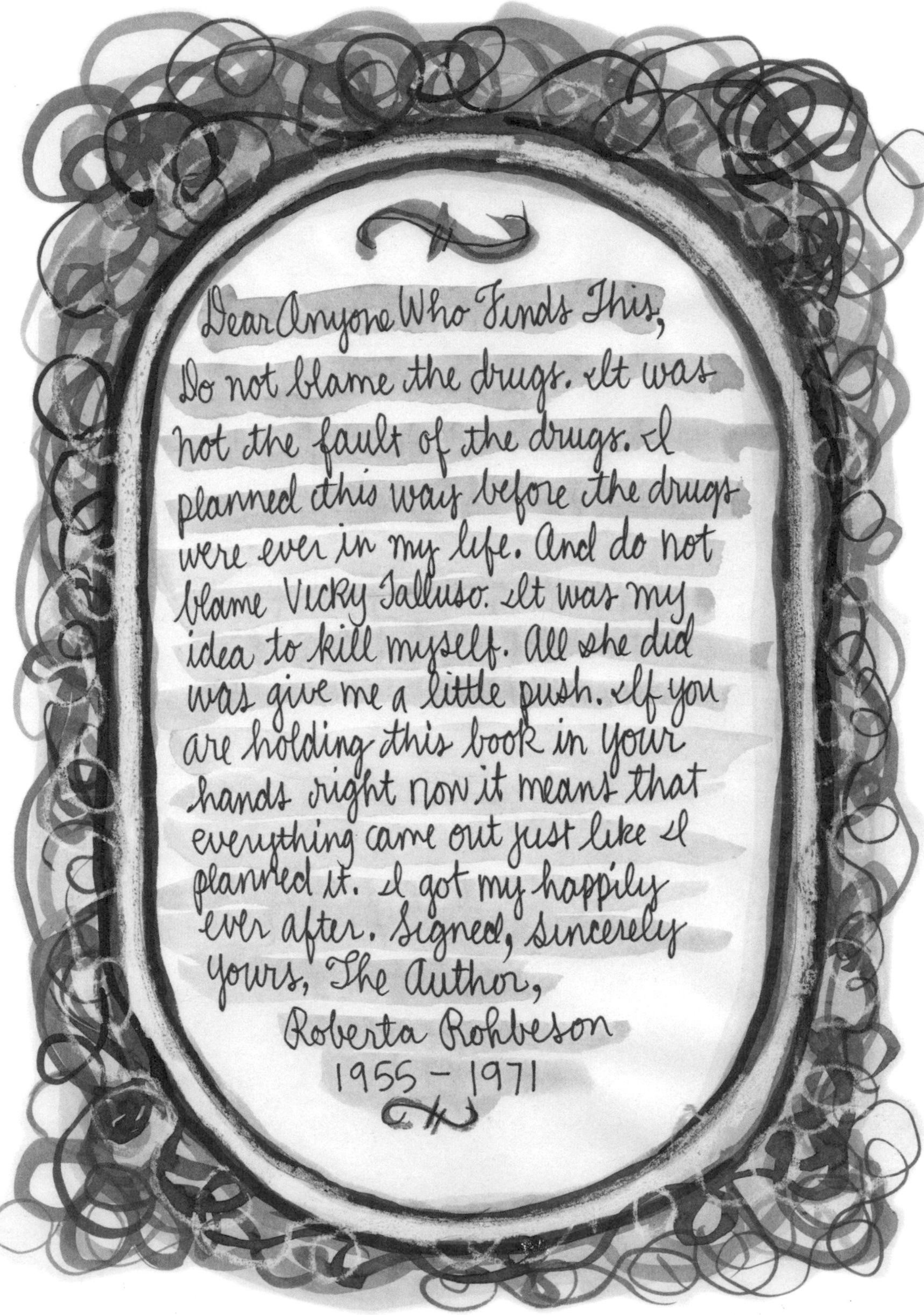
Dear Anyone Who Finds This,
Do not blame the drugs. It was
not the fault of the drugs. I
planned this way before the drugs
were ever in my life. And do not
blame Vicky Talluso. It was my
idea to kill myself. All she did
was give me a little push. If you
are holding this book in your
hands right now it means that
everything came out just like I
planned it. I got my happily
ever after. Signed, sincerely
yours, The Author,
Roberta Rohbeson
1955 – 1971

 Excerpt from Lynda Barry's *Cruddy* (Simon & Schuster, 1999), which was originally written by hand before being transcribed to text for publication.

This is the first picture of Roberta and Julie that I drew— this is when I thought they were Edna and Lucy. I thought I was writing a second book with the same characters that were in *The Good Times are Killing Me*. It took me a while to realize they were two completely different girls.
—*Lynda Barry*

Where did I read that Lynda had "drawn" all of *Cruddy* with a brush—writing it out in looping cursive on sheets of yellow paper? Maybe she told me this in person when I fannishly professed my love of that work as we rushed to a panel at a convention? As we were putting the finishing touches on the twenty-fifth anniversary book, it occurred to me that maybe Lynda was too busy to make the final *final* deadline and I should try another approach. Would she have any of these mythical pages of *Cruddy*? I confess, I've long held the idea that maybe someday we could publish the complete facsimile manuscript (impossible) but probably just so I could see the actual pages. A package arrived in the mail from Lynda. "These are the booklets I drew Cruddy in, I've got a ton of them. Enjoy!" read a Post-it note.—*Tom Devlin*

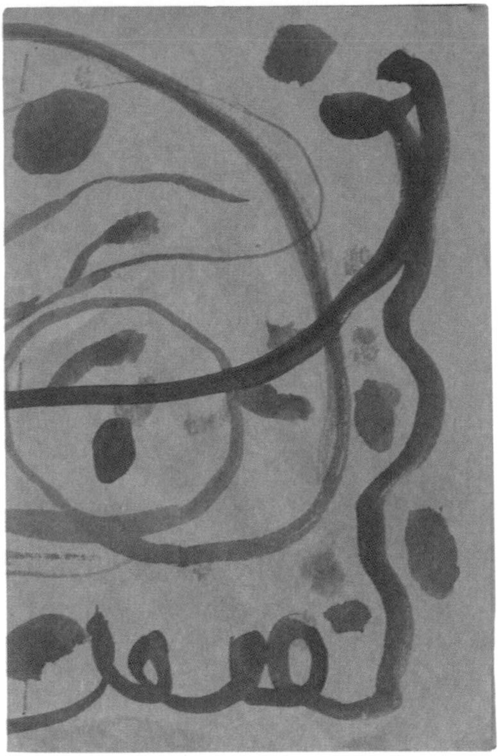

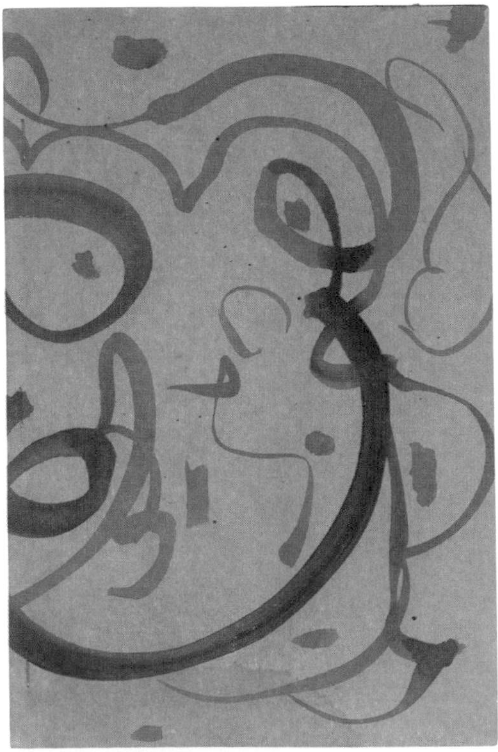

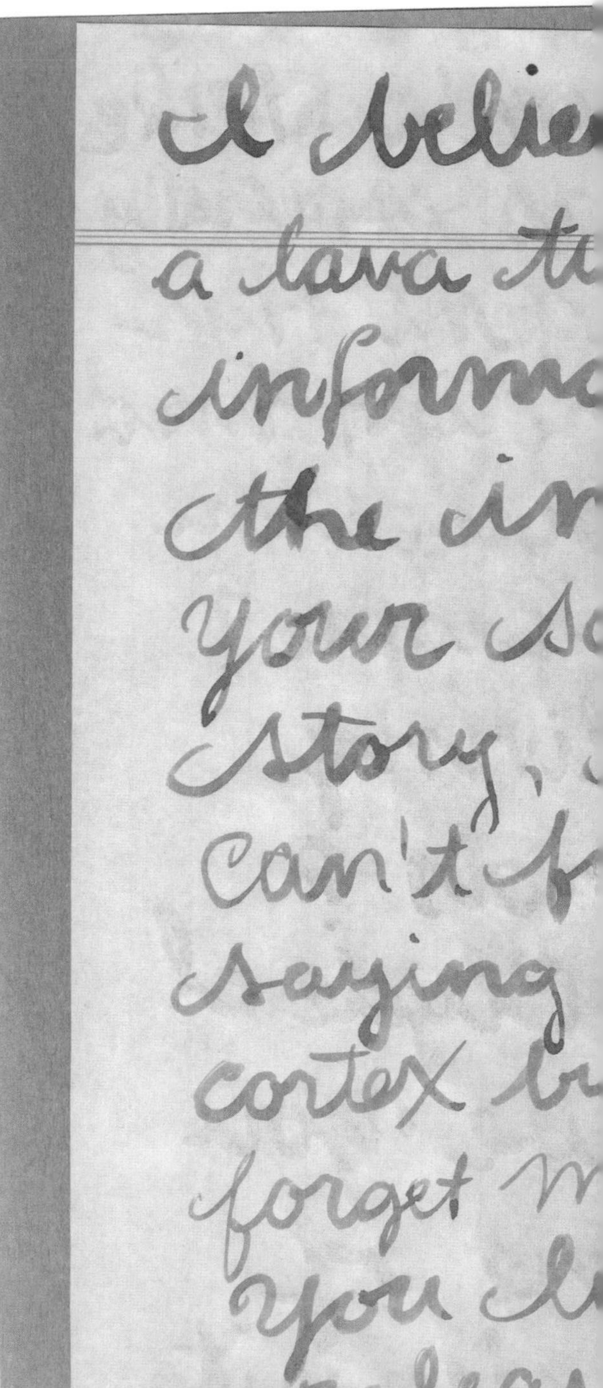
I belie
a lava th
informa
the in
your so
story,
Can't f
saying
cortex b
forget m
you l
releas

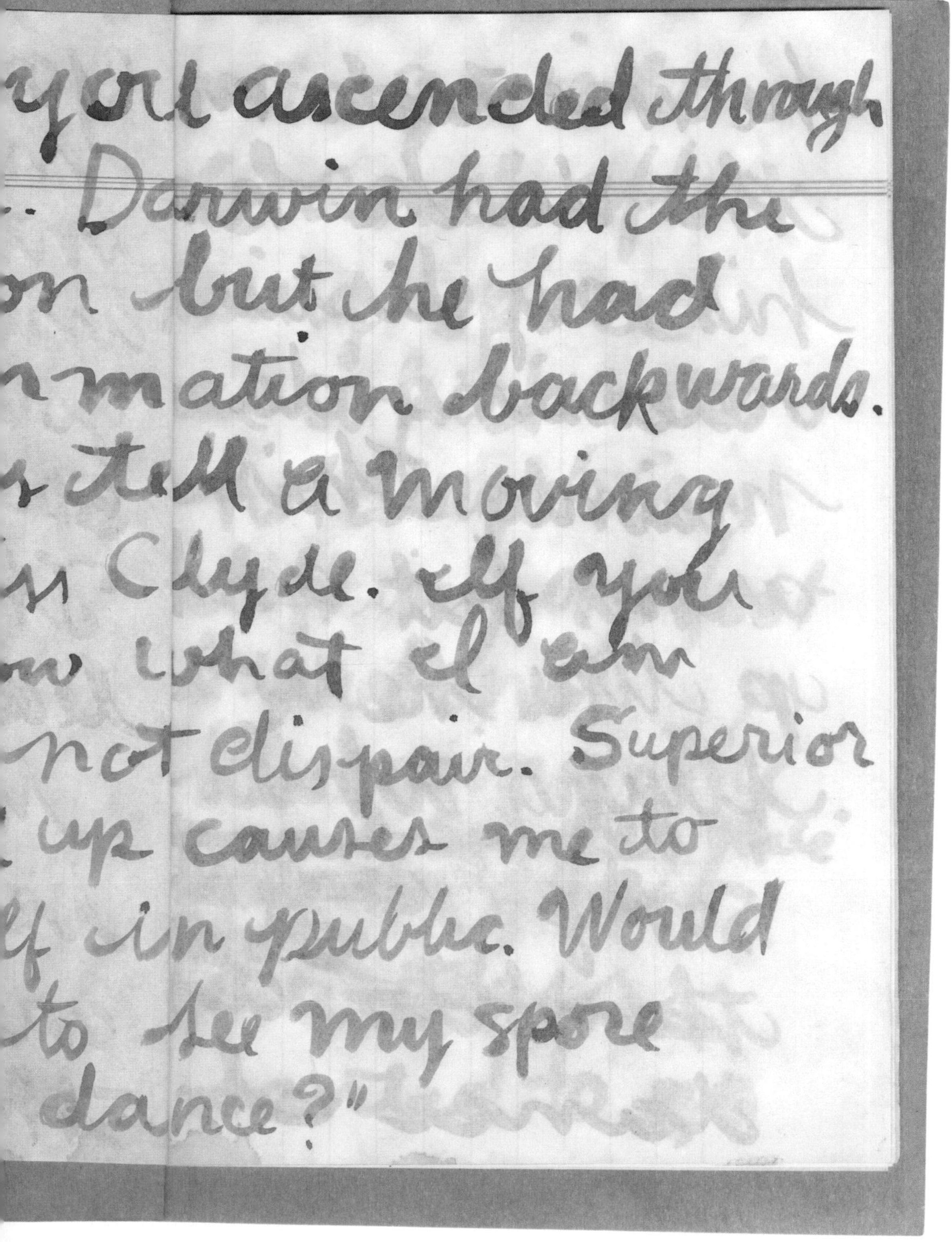
you ascended through
.. Darwin had the
on but he had
rmation backwards.
s still a moving
ss Clyde. If you
ow what I am
not dispair. Superior
up causes me to
lf in public. Would
to see my spore
dance?"

16/219 Molecules and evidence
are a hard thing to
get rid of. The blood
on the turtles hand
was crusted brown.
The man floated in
the resevoir for three
days before they found
him. I have been
floating for thirteen
years going on fourteen.
I saw a rich lady
once while I was

16/220 walking in one of the
towns the father left
me in after we pulled
out of the Knocking
Hammer before the
5:30 came Curving
the corner. The lady
had a gold locket [redacted]
on a long gold chain.
It had a cross made
of real pearls on it
and I rember thinking
about how big it

16/221 was. How you could hide
a lot [redacted] of evidence
in it, proof of who you
were incase the buzzards
got you first, because
sometimes that happens.
The lady with the
golden chain told me
I looked too serious
for a kid my age.
She said [redacted]

16/222 "When
I was your age, I felt
like I was at play
in the fields of the
Lord."
The turtle sat up.
He said, "Did you ask
her who mows the
grass in the fields
of the Lord?"
The bush spoke. "She
didn't mean anything
by it" the bush said.
"She was only trying

to be nice."

"Fore!" shouted one of the pastel peanut men and we heard the high whip of his club sounding so close I jumped.

"Them," said the turtle, pointing toward the whipping sound. "They're at play in the fields of the lord. And I want to get in

there."

"Can't we talk about something else?" said the bush. "I'm starting to ride on a bummer."

The Turtle's very pink eyes glowed at me. "Do you know the Bible Edna?"

"Hey," said the bush. "I asked her that first."

And the Turtle told about how Moses

dragged his people in circles around the desert until all the ones who were born slaves died off because Moses believed that people who were born slaves could never stop thinking and acting like slaves and they would never be any good at golf."

Vicky's enraged

head pushed itself out of the bush. "Where?! Where does it say that in the bible turtle because it doesn't say that in the Bible because golf wasn't even invented yet."

"Golf," said the Turtle closing his eyes and laying back down, "Has always been among

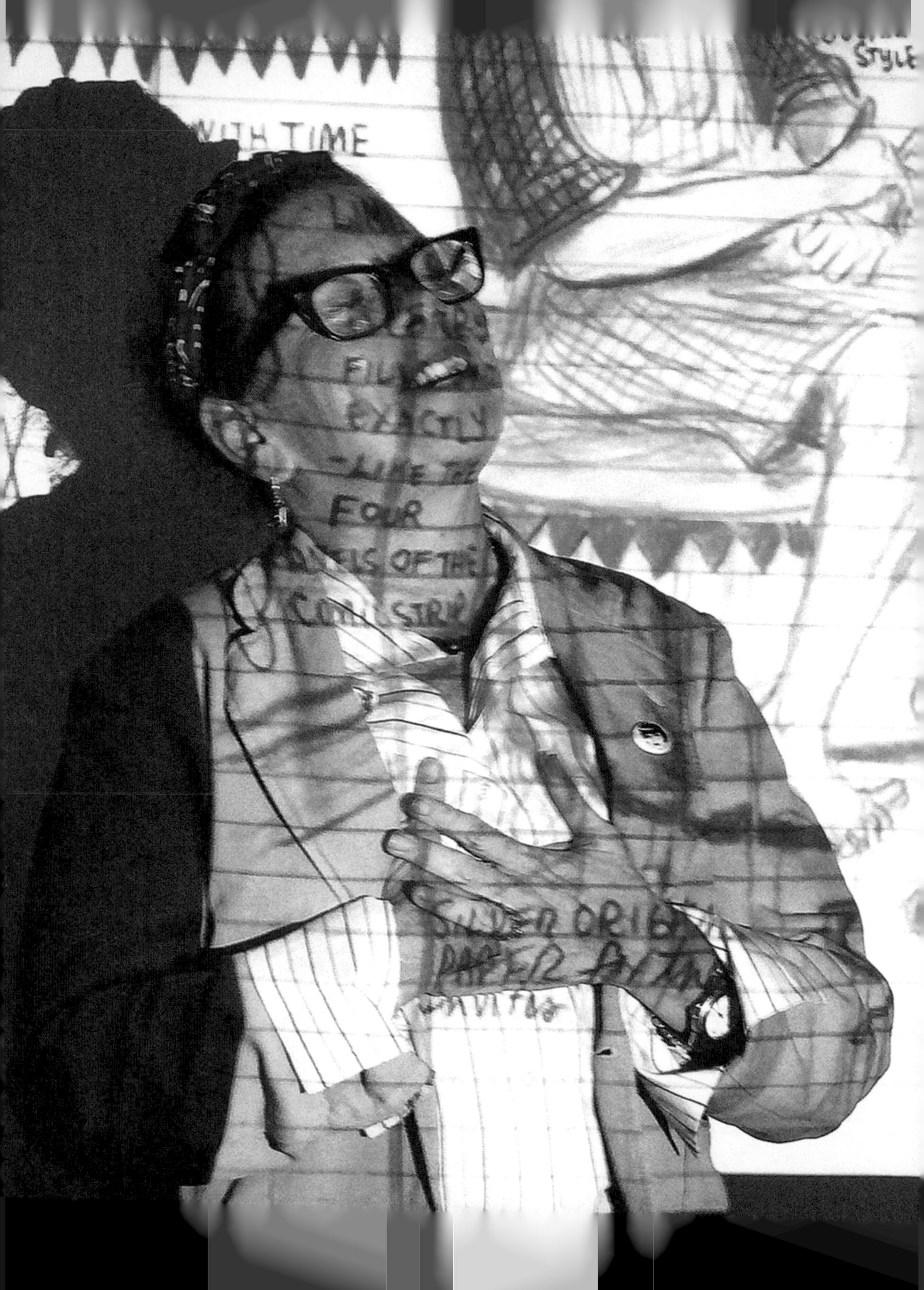
STYLE
WITH TIME
EXACTLY
FOUR

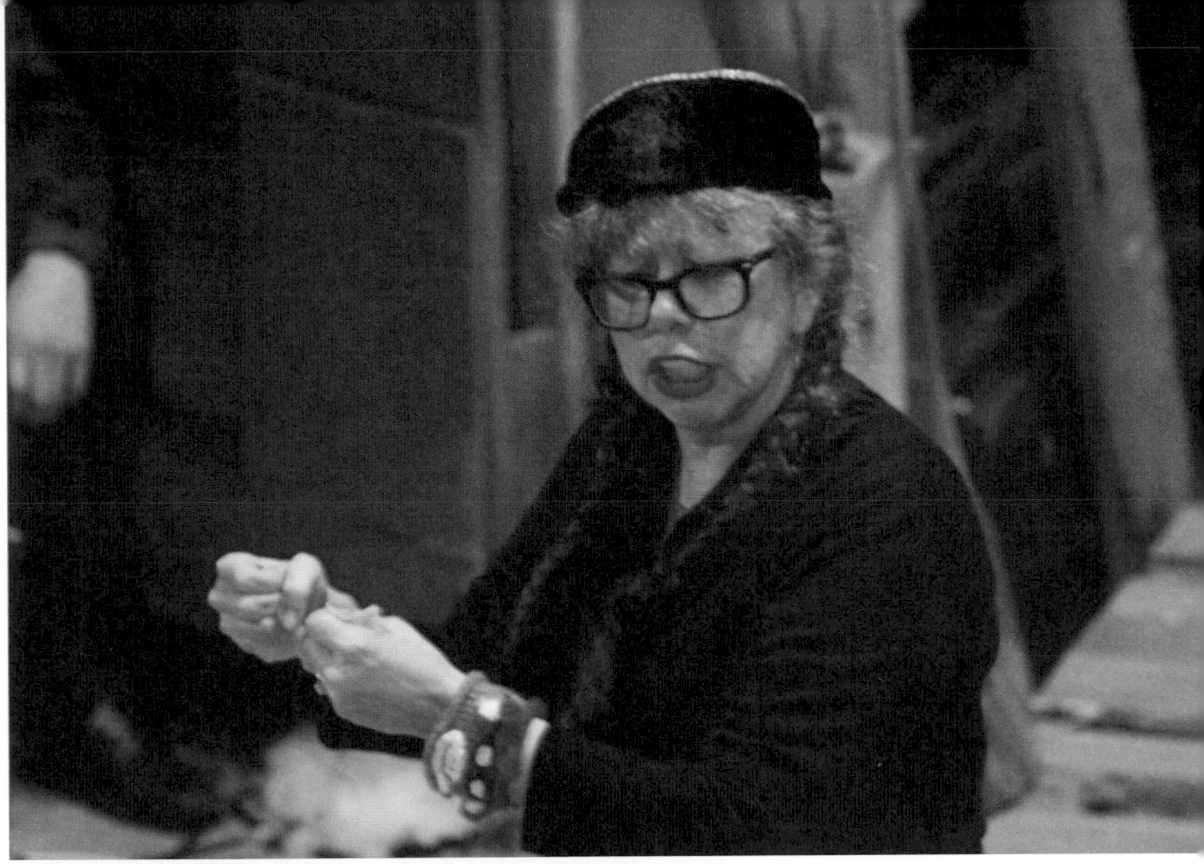

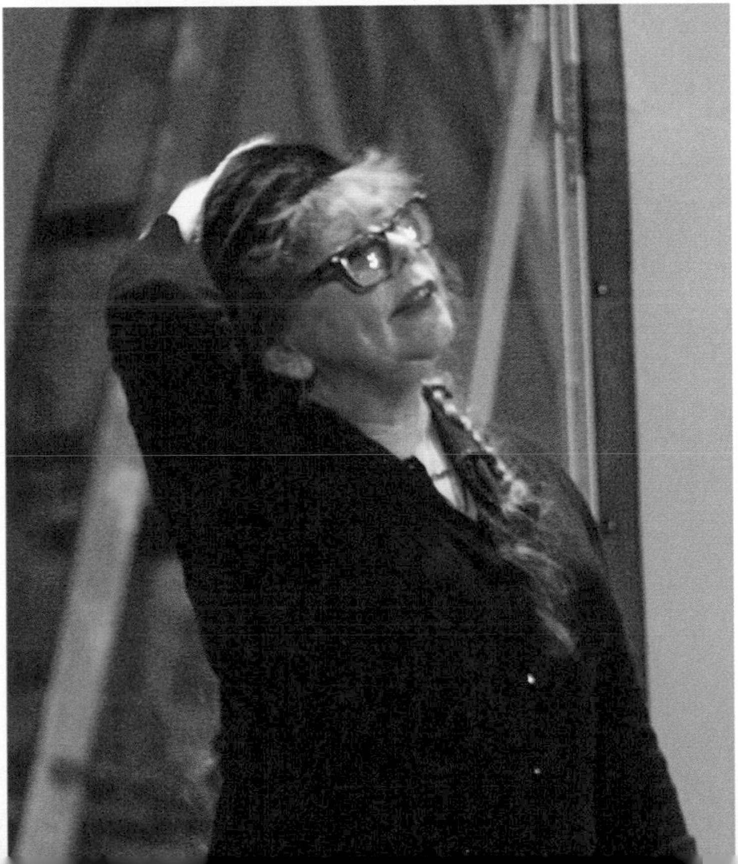

(Left) Lynda Barry at the Booksmith, San Francisco. Photo: Chris Anthony Diaz & Graham Willcox (2008). (Right) Lynda Barry in Montreal. Photos: Marilis Cardinal (2011).

The Freddie Stories was one of the first graphic novels I'd ever read that threw down the gauntlet for the true power of storytelling in comics. I figured it might be a *Garfield*-esque book from the packaging, but Barry's writing and drawing were so pitch-perfect, so humane and specific, that I was sucked in for life. Whereas a lot of cartoonists create this distance between the subject and the audience through sterile lines and pared-down words, *The Freddie Stories* gave me a visceral reaction. I felt Freddie's pain and joy, I saw the world through his lens because of Barry's carefully crafted drawings and writing. To this day I hope the darkness has left him and he's found somewhere to be free.

—***Lauren Weinstein***

I met Lynda in the 1970s, when she was a student, only a few years after I started teaching at Evergreen. She enrolled in Images, a program that I was teaching with Mark, a philosopher. In the class students had to produce five images each week in any single visual medium. Lynda made drawings. My plan was to review her work with her, carefully, for one hour each week. We assumed the drawings themselves would speak to us, tell us what might be next, and then there would be an evolution of visual ideas and skill. Lynda was very serious, never missed a meeting, and always brought five carefully rendered images.

For the first five weeks she made small drawings of a cactus. We studied these as if they might describe the meaning of the universe. While some faculty stressed keeping to a topic, we encouraged seeing from a variety of views. Lynda, instead, had the cactus growing slightly from one image to the next. She would point out the extraordinary shift that I could barely discern. She was concerned that the cactus would soon leave the page, and mid-quarter she changed the focus of her work to lamp cords plugged into the wall, knotted, curled, or hanging. (While she never discussed this at the time, I learned many years later that the lamp cords illustrated her notions about love.) Her seriousness, dedication, and acceptance of the program theme, "Make your *own* images," inspired others to do the same, and the result was authentic and personal work made by the entire class. It wasn't only doing her own work that influenced others. She saw everyone's images as live things that spoke to her, and she had no trouble telling people what their images said to her: this one seemed hungry and another was very noisy.

I worked with Lynda in other contexts and knew that her drawings needed to be seen outside of the college. She worked independently in Seattle while still a student and was published in the *Seattle Sun*. How marvelous and deserved is the attention and respect she now enjoys. Over the past thirty or so years we have become friends and she recently appeared in a drawing I was making, wearing the very same expression of serious attention that I saw on her face when she was my student.

—Marilyn Frasca is a visual artist whose work has been exhibited all over the United States in museums and galleries. Frasca is a faculty emerita at the Evergreen State College, where she has taught since 1973. Lynda Barry routinely name-checks Marilyn as the single most influential creative force in her life.

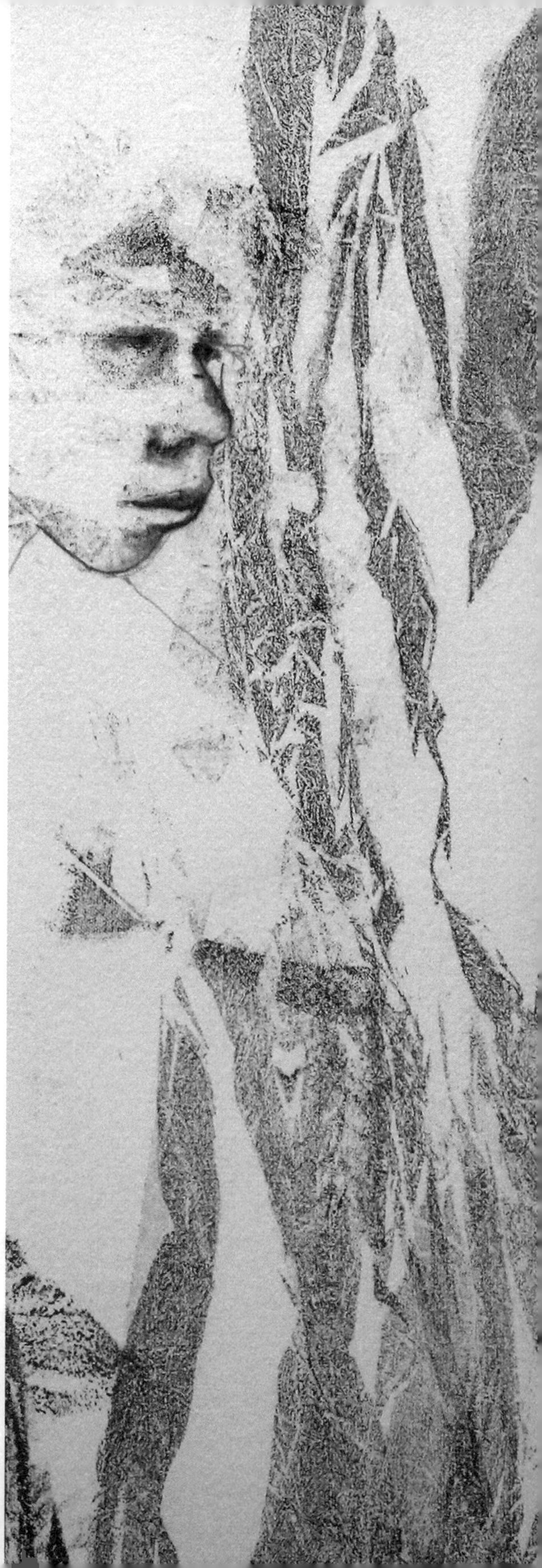

 Drawing of Lynda Barry by Marilyn Frasca (2013).

STILL TASTING PERFECT

an appreciation of Lynda Barry by Hillary Chute

My mother brought home Lynda Barry's *The Good Times Are Killing Me*—the novel that ends with images of Barry's lovingly handcrafted portraits of musicians like Jimmie Rodgers—when I was twelve. I read the book repeatedly over the next several years. It felt like a magical object to me, with its square, electric-blue cover dotted with colourful spirals and its unusual format as an episodic story about girls my age, with chapter titles like "My Disappointment" and "My Record Player," capped out by a suite of musicians appearing in multimedia collage. (I later found out that Lynda made the beautiful tin frames that enclose the portraits—and the house on the book's cover—out of roofing material.) Some years later, my creative writing teacher, the poet Bruce Smith, assigned our high school class Lynda's comic strip "The Red Comb," from her 1988 collection *Down the Street*. I was so struck by it that I taped the photocopy of the four-panel strip to the door of my bedroom. This must have seemed weird, since the strip is about some kind of abuse we never see but which feels present, but I felt awed by the storytelling. Lynda is peerless at offering a world in which trouble is never skirted but levity can remain; her work is the opposite of one-note. "Writing believable fiction in comics," Chris Ware affirms, "in many ways, I believe, started with her."

Maybe Lynda is the reason I have built a career on writing about comics: my strong responses to her work at twelve and seventeen (and again at twenty-two, when I became obsessed with the adorable, hilarious way she draws people dancing) surely imprinted on me in some deep way. "Everybody knows a bad influence," "The Red Comb" begins. "On our street it was Kenny Watford who could whistle so loud." Like in her novels, the voices in "The Red Comb" hail you—"everybody"—and you do not want to leave them, no matter what. And as my teacher recognized in assigning a comic strip as a model for how a story works, Barry's comics have a richness that springs from the way their expressive, uninhibited voices combine with her striking narrative economy. I have now spent, in my own teaching, many entire class periods discussing just these four panels with college students. Barry's are among the most musical comics I know—they have strong, discernible beats and rhythms in their structure as well as in their lilting sentences, with their kid mellifluousness that propels you through the frames.

It is safe to say that Lynda Barry has not hit a false note in her entire career. And she has produced a lot of different kinds of work—novels, plays, comics, audio recordings like *The Lynda Barry Experience*—and guilelessly created new aesthetic categories for decades, from a deck of cards comics colouring book (*Naked Ladies*) to "autobifictionalography" (*One! Hundred! Demons!*) to activity books like Drawn & Quarterly's *What It Is* and *Picture This* and now *Syllabus*, about her recent courses at the University of Wisconsin–Madison. I have learned many things about comics and life from Lynda Barry (I have also been her student twice in her Writing the Unthinkable class). Her work inflects a lot of my own language: her characters, from Marlys to Roberta/Clyde, have seeped into my life. Things I have seamlessly incorporated into my lexicon that come straight out of the world of her comics include the exclamation "dang!"; "cream" to indicate punishment; and the assessment "still tasting perfect" to describe old candy found under the porch (yes, this comes up often). I feel about her books the way the kid in the *One! Hundred! Demons!* chapter "Magic Lanterns" feels about his (lost) stuffed toy: they are many things to me, including profoundly comforting. When I recently got lice I immediately contacted Lynda; who could forget her masterpiece "Head Lice and My Worst Boyfriend," the opener to *One! Hundred! Demons!*? But what I mean is actually something formal and non-topical: her books provide a world of humour, of reflection, of mourning, of pathos that never fails to grab me and absorb me into *playing back*, to use one of Lynda's Winnicottian formulations from *What It Is*: "I believe a kid who is playing is not alone. There is something brought alive during play, and this something, when played with, seems to play back." In *Down the Street* she even has a double spread that simply announces "PLAY" and swarms with drawings of labelled everyday objects: "an interesting stick"; "a shoe box"; "a horse shoe"; "a flashlight." The sense of promise in the everyday pervades Lynda's work.

Lynda's work is about play, and it also enacts play. The line in particular plays back—it feels active, vital, alive (she doesn't pencil, the line is spontaneous). More than any other cartoonist I can think of, Lynda's work is about handwriting. She points out that hands are the original digital devices. "I'm the opposite of a snob when it comes to reading something," she told me once in an interview. "I'll read anything that has handwriting, and it's really hard for me to be bored or unhappy when I'm reading comics. I even love stuff that, you know, when you're reading it, you might think, this isn't really working…I never think of that. I think drawing, writing, handwriting, drawing." Lynda's line is most usually these days made with a brush: she paints her comics, as she explains in *One! Hundred! Demons!*. Her comics and her collages, which combine word and image, make clear the *visual voice* in the line—and how different visual voices come from different implements. She explained that she painted her novel *Cruddy* with a brush after trying to write it on a computer and failing. She dried the pages with a hairdryer. And even though it eventually appeared typeset, that Barry even handwrites her prose work shows how crucial handwriting is not only as an aesthetic effect but also as a creative practice. In Barry's comics and activity books, handwriting will change even in the space of one word, moving from script to capital letters. This is all a way of making readers look at words, in addition to images, as marks made by a body—at making them encounter comics language. In her collages, the mark as an abstract visual and the mark as a word sometimes blur: we are not always supposed to be able to decipher the words in the handwriting of an elderly woman with palsy that Lynda collages into her pages in *What It Is*, but rather to appreciate it as the perseverance and fragile beauty of mark-making.

Lynda's work has all the texture and the gravitas of avant-garde experiment, but it is profoundly unpretentious. She has a preternatural ability to capture the cadences of how real people speak—and how *creatively* real people, especially kids, speak to each other (she suggested once this ability to listen may have come from growing up in a bilingual family where the adults didn't teach the kids how to speak the language they spoke to each other). As Dave Eggers put it, reviewing *The! Greatest! Of! Marlys!* in the *New York Times*, Barry is "as good a chronicler of adolescence as we've had." And Barry has worked across different media her entire career, for instance as a painter and a cartoonist in the 1980s, despite the singularity of one format and the reproducibility of the other.

When her gallerist told her, "Don't ever tell anyone that you're watching TV while you're making paintings," Barry decided to quit showing in galleries ("For the rich people they need it to be this sort of *deep experience*, and they're sort of buying the talisman of the experience, so the idea that you're watching Phil Donahue…" she explained). That changed in 2014 when she had a show at Adam Baumgold Gallery in New York—Everything: Part 1, based on pages from her Drawn & Quarterly collection of her earliest work from the late 1970s and early 1980s. Barry's democratic desire to demystify the way art works, and to reveal it as something available to the non-expert, the non-professional, is directly connected to her innovation of form and format. In *One! Hundred! Demons!*, she explicitly tells readers exactly which tools she used to create the book and even where one could buy them—and she also points out "I will try ANY PAPER!" She painted *One! Hundred! Demons!* on yellow legal paper and even on paper bags.

The huge positive response that book elicited—after almost twenty-five years of publishing, it was her first to claim any kind of autobiographical content, and her first to explicitly ask, "Come on! Don't you want to try it?"—led to her genre-breaking comics-and-collage activity books, *What It Is* and *Picture This*, which combine actual writing exercises with rare and rich snippets from Barry's life as a child and adult artist. These books are unclassifiable, like a lot of her work is, but all the more powerful for inhabiting themselves as *weird objects*, like a lot of her work always has. Who knew activity books could be so narrative, so meditative, so evocative, and so haunting? Barry's activity books, which ask questions like "What is an image?" hearken back to her early days when her comics were first sold by Printed Matter, the New York City institution that sells artist-made books: each page is individually collaged, its own graphic unit and artwork.

Barry's comic strip *Ernie Pook's Comeek* ("Pook" rhymes with "book"; it comes from an in-joke with her brother) ran from 1979 to 2008; it was at one point syndicated in sixty papers nationally. She's authored nineteen books. Throughout thirty-five years of trends and movements in publishing, Barry's work has remained timeless because she is so impervious to fashion and the codification of comics tastes and has stuck to making new kinds of work even during fallow periods between publishers. That she is back *so* big time right now, reinventing the field again, is thrilling; she even managed, in the uptight world of academia to which I also belong, to earn herself the bang-up position of professor of interdisciplinary creativity at the Wisconsin Institute for Discovery at UW–Madison (*how amazing is that title?*). As Nick Hornby said—and I will add that this applies across all of the forms in which she works—Barry is "one of America's very best contemporary writers." Plus, she has been known to drink with me in the morning.

Hillary Chute is an associate professor of English at the University of Chicago and the author of Graphic Women: Life Narrative and Contemporary Comics *and* Outside The Box: Interviews with Contemporary Cartoonists, *and the associate editor of Art Spiegelman's* MetaMaus. *She has written for numerous academic periodicals, as well as for* Artforum *and* Bookforum.

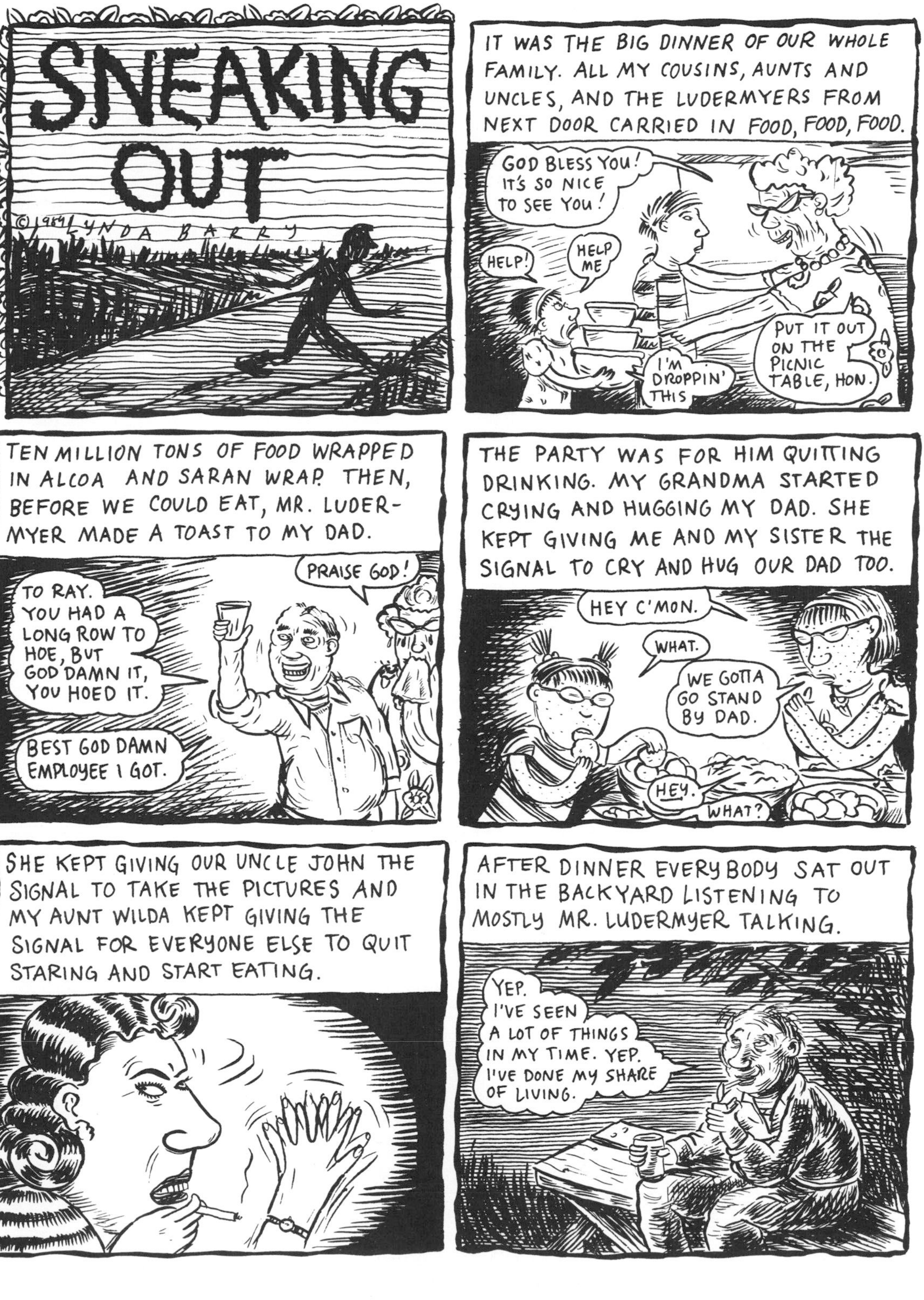
SNEAKING OUT
©1984 LYNDA BARRY
IT WAS THE BIG DINNER OF OUR WHOLE FAMILY. ALL MY COUSINS, AUNTS AND UNCLES, AND THE LUDERMYERS FROM NEXT DOOR CARRIED IN FOOD, FOOD, FOOD.
GOD BLESS YOU! IT'S SO NICE TO SEE YOU!
HELP!
HELP ME
I'M DROPPIN' THIS
PUT IT OUT ON THE PICNIC TABLE, HON.
TEN MILLION TONS OF FOOD WRAPPED IN ALCOA AND SARAN WRAP. THEN, BEFORE WE COULD EAT, MR. LUDERMYER MADE A TOAST TO MY DAD.
PRAISE GOD!
TO RAY. YOU HAD A LONG ROW TO HOE, BUT GOD DAMN IT, YOU HOED IT.
BEST GOD DAMN EMPLOYEE I GOT.
THE PARTY WAS FOR HIM QUITTING DRINKING. MY GRANDMA STARTED CRYING AND HUGGING MY DAD. SHE KEPT GIVING ME AND MY SISTER THE SIGNAL TO CRY AND HUG OUR DAD TOO.
HEY C'MON.
WHAT.
WE GOTTA GO STAND BY DAD.
HEY.
WHAT?
SHE KEPT GIVING OUR UNCLE JOHN THE SIGNAL TO TAKE THE PICTURES AND MY AUNT WILDA KEPT GIVING THE SIGNAL FOR EVERYONE ELSE TO QUIT STARING AND START EATING.
AFTER DINNER EVERYBODY SAT OUT IN THE BACKYARD LISTENING TO MOSTLY MR. LUDERMYER TALKING.
YEP. I'VE SEEN A LOT OF THINGS IN MY TIME. YEP. I'VE DONE MY SHARE OF LIVING.

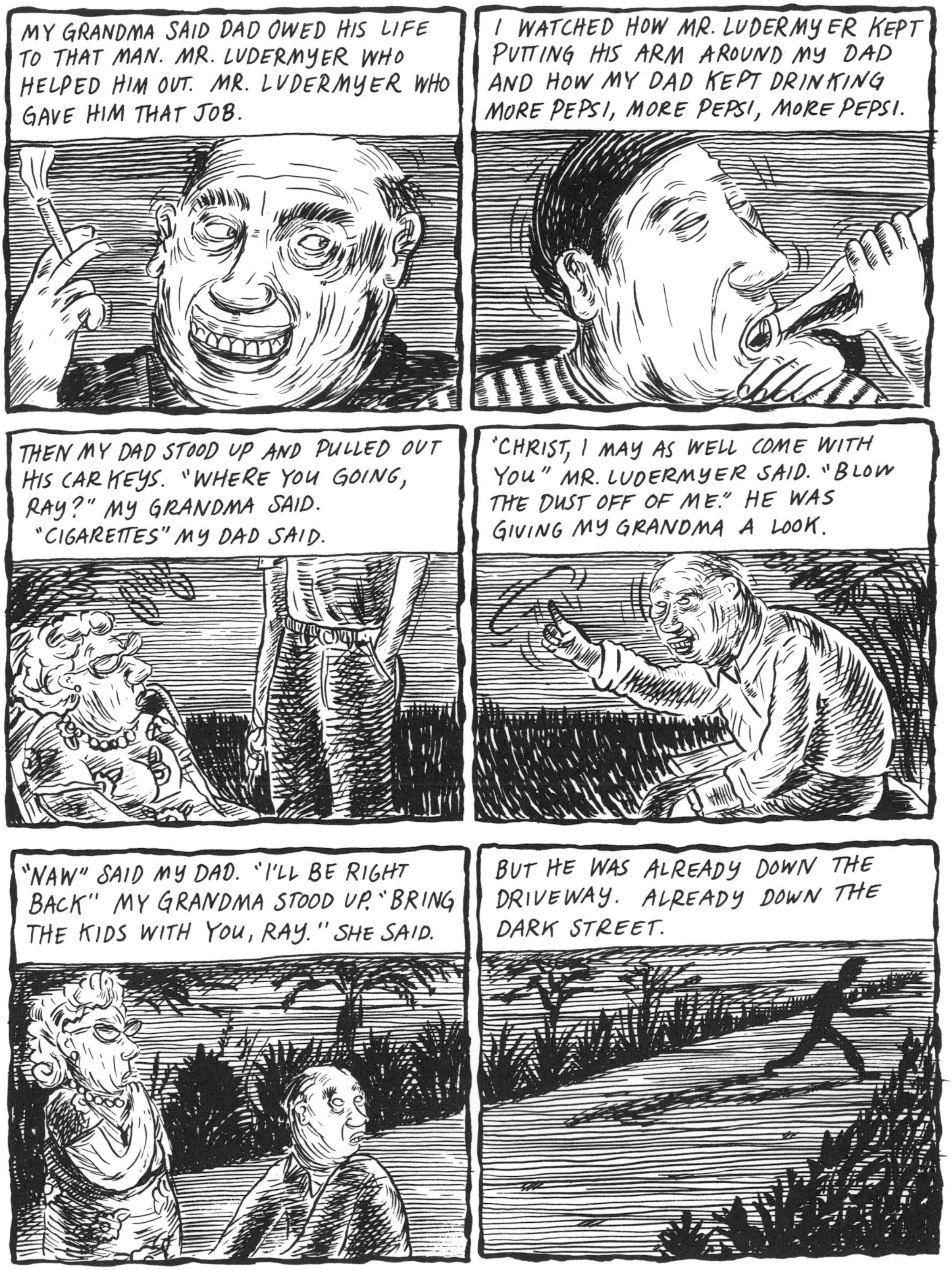
MY GRANDMA SAID DAD OWED HIS LIFE TO THAT MAN. MR. LUDERMYER WHO HELPED HIM OUT. MR. LUDERMYER WHO GAVE HIM THAT JOB.
I WATCHED HOW MR. LUDERMYER KEPT PUTTING HIS ARM AROUND MY DAD AND HOW MY DAD KEPT DRINKING MORE PEPSI, MORE PEPSI, MORE PEPSI.
THEN MY DAD STOOD UP AND PULLED OUT HIS CAR KEYS. "WHERE YOU GOING, RAY?" MY GRANDMA SAID. "CIGARETTES" MY DAD SAID.
"CHRIST, I MAY AS WELL COME WITH YOU" MR. LUDERMYER SAID. "BLOW THE DUST OFF OF ME." HE WAS GIVING MY GRANDMA A LOOK.
"NAW" SAID MY DAD. "I'LL BE RIGHT BACK" MY GRANDMA STOOD UP. "BRING THE KIDS WITH YOU, RAY." SHE SAID.
BUT HE WAS ALREADY DOWN THE DRIVEWAY. ALREADY DOWN THE DARK STREET.

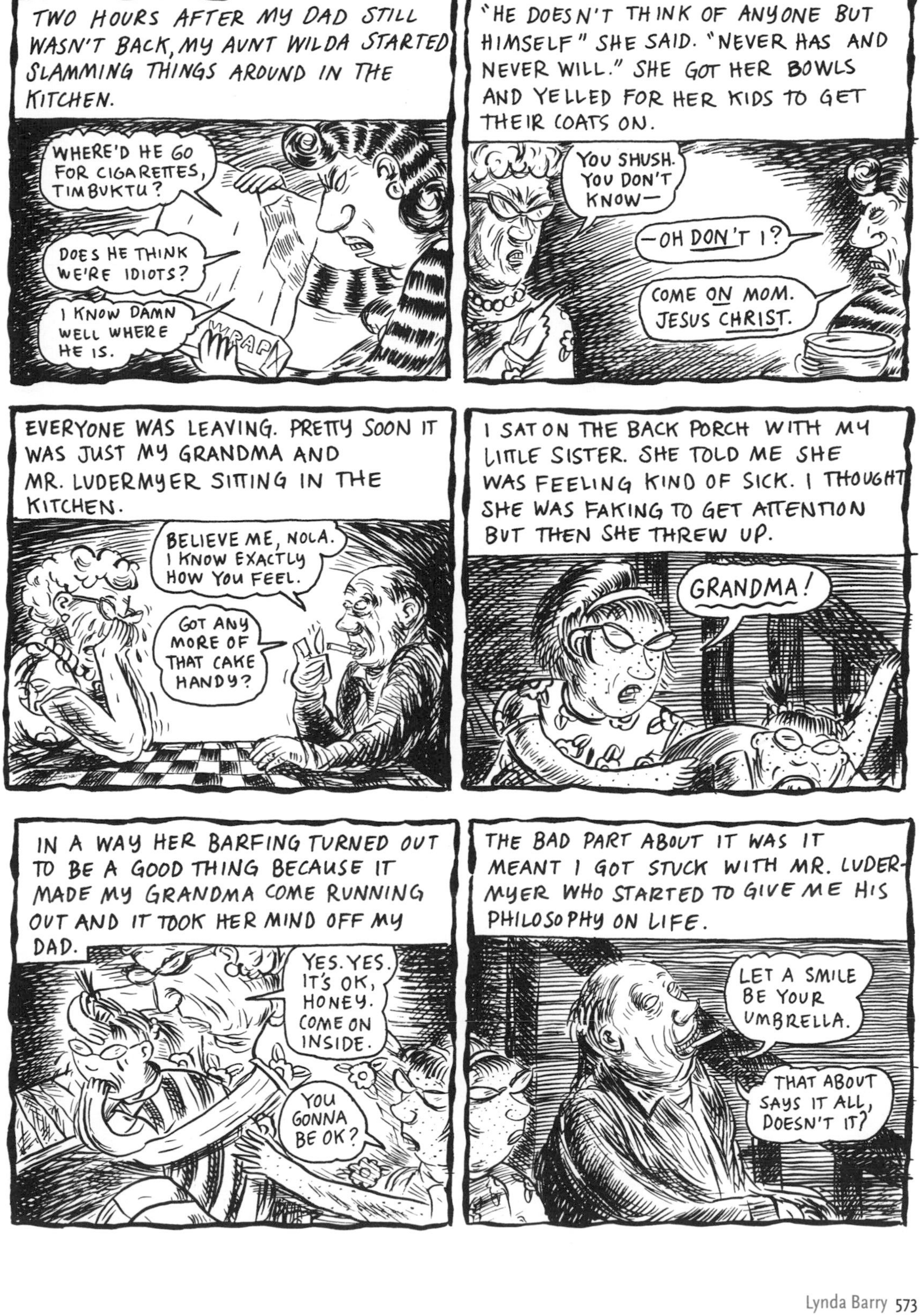
TWO HOURS AFTER MY DAD STILL WASN'T BACK, MY AUNT WILDA STARTED SLAMMING THINGS AROUND IN THE KITCHEN.
WHERE'D HE GO FOR CIGARETTES, TIMBUKTU?
DOES HE THINK WE'RE IDIOTS?
I KNOW DAMN WELL WHERE HE IS.
WRAP
"HE DOESN'T THINK OF ANYONE BUT HIMSELF" SHE SAID. "NEVER HAS AND NEVER WILL." SHE GOT HER BOWLS AND YELLED FOR HER KIDS TO GET THEIR COATS ON.
YOU SHUSH. YOU DON'T KNOW—
—OH DON'T I?
COME ON MOM. JESUS CHRIST.
EVERYONE WAS LEAVING. PRETTY SOON IT WAS JUST MY GRANDMA AND MR. LUDERMYER SITTING IN THE KITCHEN.
BELIEVE ME, NOLA. I KNOW EXACTLY HOW YOU FEEL.
GOT ANY MORE OF THAT CAKE HANDY?
I SAT ON THE BACK PORCH WITH MY LITTLE SISTER. SHE TOLD ME SHE WAS FEELING KIND OF SICK. I THOUGHT SHE WAS FAKING TO GET ATTENTION BUT THEN SHE THREW UP.
GRANDMA!
IN A WAY HER BARFING TURNED OUT TO BE A GOOD THING BECAUSE IT MADE MY GRANDMA COME RUNNING OUT AND IT TOOK HER MIND OFF MY DAD.
YES. YES. IT'S OK, HONEY. COME ON INSIDE.
YOU GONNA BE OK?
THE BAD PART ABOUT IT WAS IT MEANT I GOT STUCK WITH MR. LUDERMYER WHO STARTED TO GIVE ME HIS PHILOSOPHY ON LIFE.
LET A SMILE BE YOUR UMBRELLA.
THAT ABOUT SAYS IT ALL, DOESN'T IT?

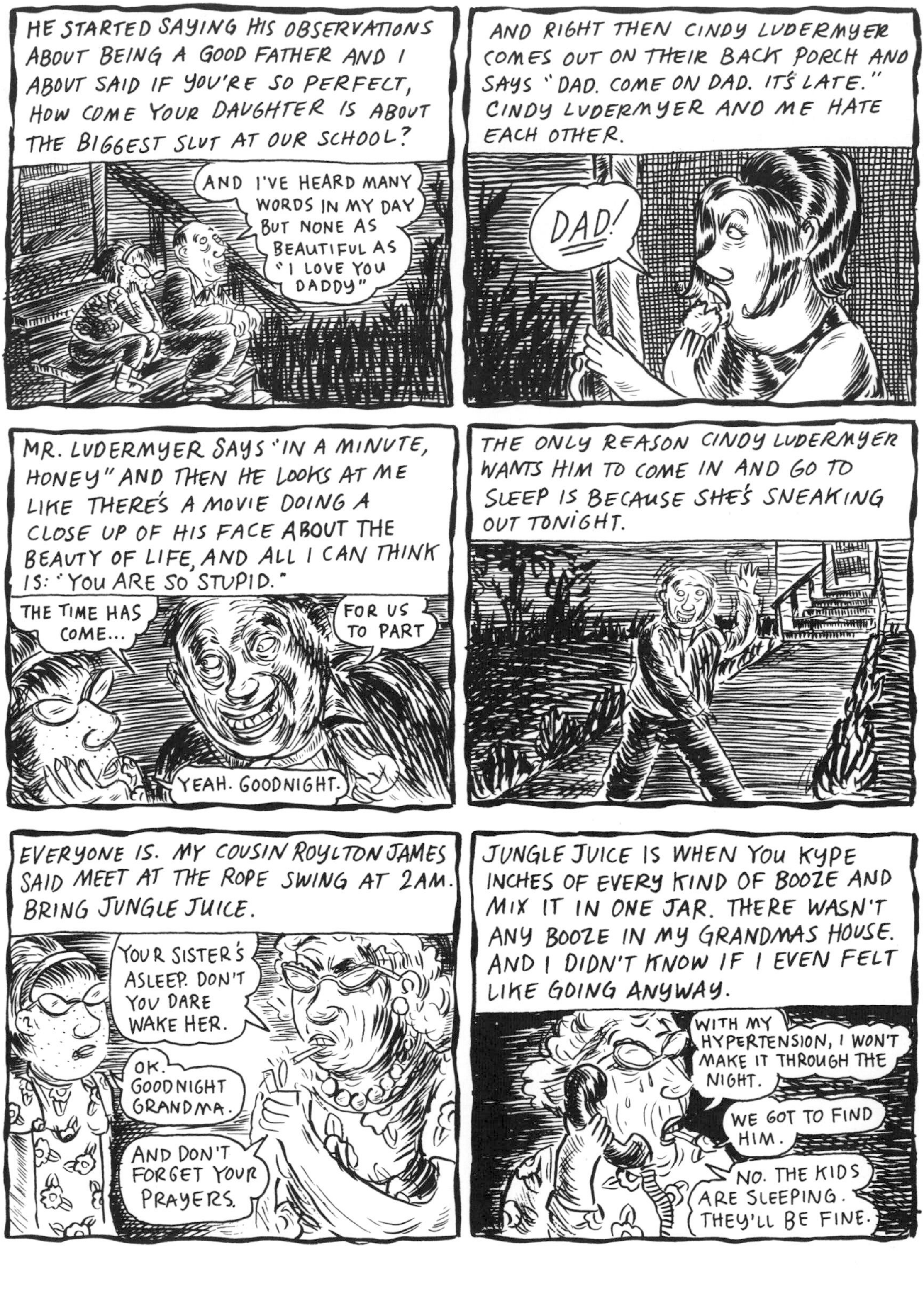
HE STARTED SAYING HIS OBSERVATIONS ABOUT BEING A GOOD FATHER AND I ABOUT SAID IF YOU'RE SO PERFECT, HOW COME YOUR DAUGHTER IS ABOUT THE BIGGEST SLUT AT OUR SCHOOL?
AND I'VE HEARD MANY WORDS IN MY DAY BUT NONE AS BEAUTIFUL AS "I LOVE YOU DADDY"
AND RIGHT THEN CINDY LUDERMYER COMES OUT ON THEIR BACK PORCH AND SAYS "DAD. COME ON DAD. IT'S LATE." CINDY LUDERMYER AND ME HATE EACH OTHER.
DAD!
MR. LUDERMYER SAYS "IN A MINUTE, HONEY" AND THEN HE LOOKS AT ME LIKE THERE'S A MOVIE DOING A CLOSE UP OF HIS FACE ABOUT THE BEAUTY OF LIFE, AND ALL I CAN THINK IS: "YOU ARE SO STUPID."
THE TIME HAS COME...
FOR US TO PART
YEAH. GOODNIGHT.
THE ONLY REASON CINDY LUDERMYER WANTS HIM TO COME IN AND GO TO SLEEP IS BECAUSE SHE'S SNEAKING OUT TONIGHT.
EVERYONE IS. MY COUSIN ROYLTON JAMES SAID MEET AT THE ROPE SWING AT 2AM. BRING JUNGLE JUICE.
YOUR SISTER'S ASLEEP. DON'T YOU DARE WAKE HER.
OK. GOODNIGHT GRANDMA.
AND DON'T FORGET YOUR PRAYERS.
JUNGLE JUICE IS WHEN YOU KYPE INCHES OF EVERY KIND OF BOOZE AND MIX IT IN ONE JAR. THERE WASN'T ANY BOOZE IN MY GRANDMAS HOUSE. AND I DIDN'T KNOW IF I EVEN FELT LIKE GOING ANYWAY.
WITH MY HYPERTENSION, I WON'T MAKE IT THROUGH THE NIGHT.
WE GOT TO FIND HIM.
NO. THE KIDS ARE SLEEPING. THEY'LL BE FINE.

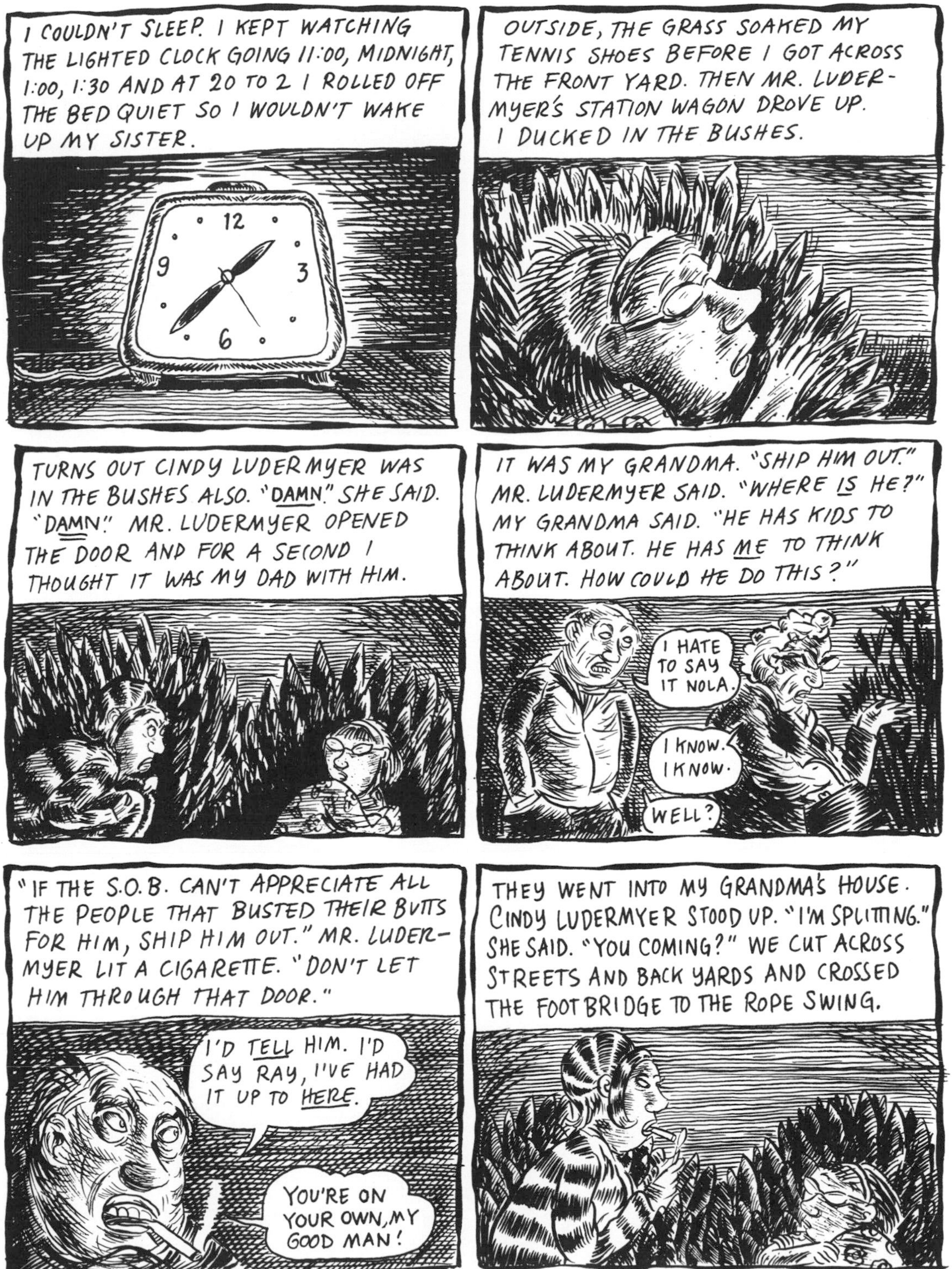
I COULDN'T SLEEP. I KEPT WATCHING THE LIGHTED CLOCK GOING 11:00, MIDNIGHT, 1:00, 1:30 AND AT 20 TO 2 I ROLLED OFF THE BED QUIET SO I WOULDN'T WAKE UP MY SISTER.
12
9
3
6
OUTSIDE, THE GRASS SOAKED MY TENNIS SHOES BEFORE I GOT ACROSS THE FRONT YARD. THEN MR. LUDERMYER'S STATION WAGON DROVE UP. I DUCKED IN THE BUSHES.
TURNS OUT CINDY LUDERMYER WAS IN THE BUSHES ALSO. "DAMN." SHE SAID. "DAMN." MR. LUDERMYER OPENED THE DOOR AND FOR A SECOND I THOUGHT IT WAS MY DAD WITH HIM.
IT WAS MY GRANDMA. "SHIP HIM OUT." MR. LUDERMYER SAID. "WHERE IS HE?" MY GRANDMA SAID. "HE HAS KIDS TO THINK ABOUT. HE HAS ME TO THINK ABOUT. HOW COULD HE DO THIS?"
I HATE TO SAY IT NOLA.
I KNOW. I KNOW.
WELL?
"IF THE S.O.B. CAN'T APPRECIATE ALL THE PEOPLE THAT BUSTED THEIR BUTTS FOR HIM, SHIP HIM OUT." MR. LUDERMYER LIT A CIGARETTE. "DON'T LET HIM THROUGH THAT DOOR."
I'D TELL HIM. I'D SAY RAY, I'VE HAD IT UP TO HERE.
YOU'RE ON YOUR OWN, MY GOOD MAN!
THEY WENT INTO MY GRANDMA'S HOUSE. CINDY LUDERMYER STOOD UP. "I'M SPLITTING." SHE SAID. "YOU COMING?" WE CUT ACROSS STREETS AND BACK YARDS AND CROSSED THE FOOTBRIDGE TO THE ROPE SWING.

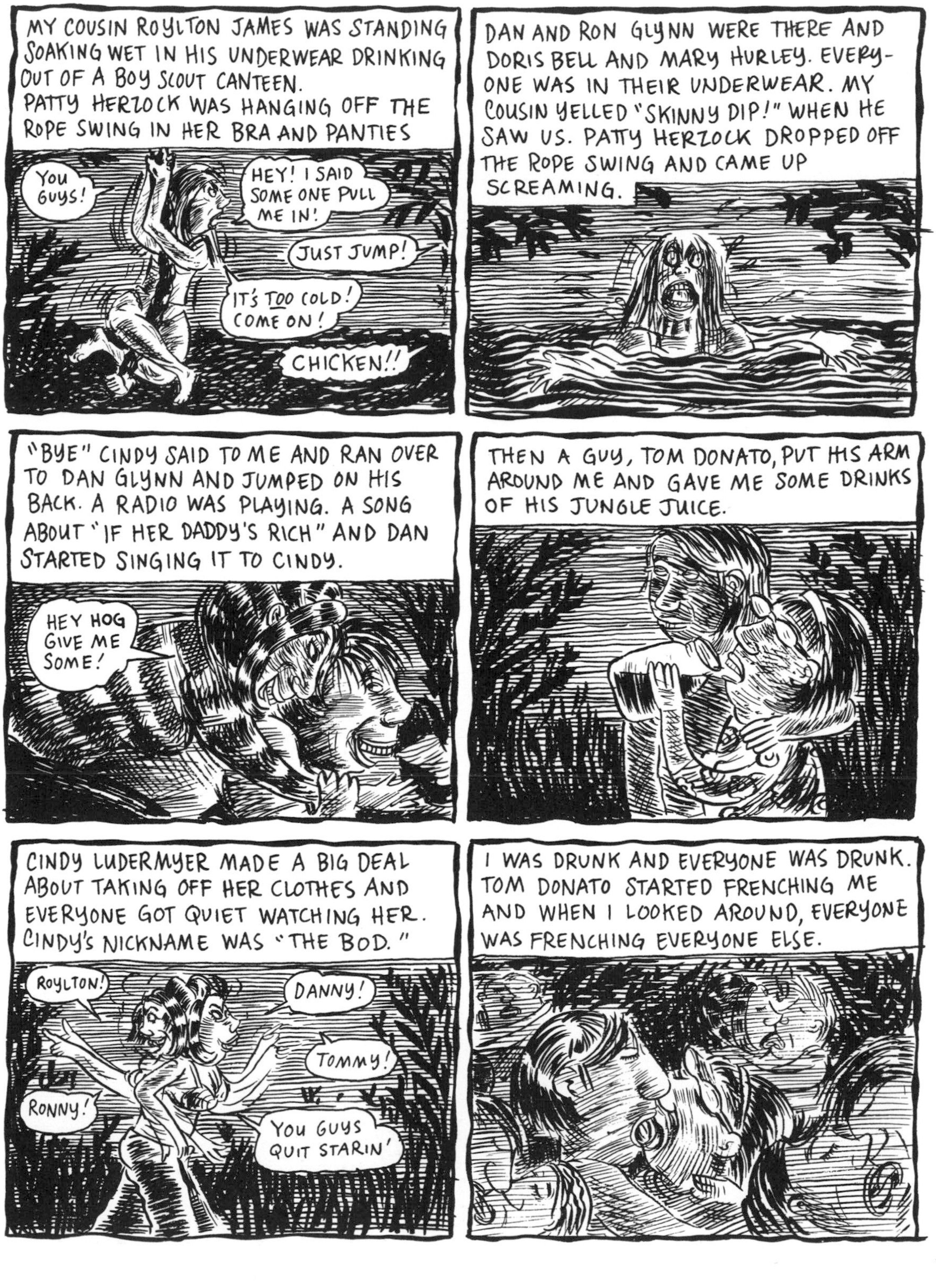
MY COUSIN ROYLTON JAMES WAS STANDING SOAKING WET IN HIS UNDERWEAR DRINKING OUT OF A BOY SCOUT CANTEEN.
PATTY HERZOCK WAS HANGING OFF THE ROPE SWING IN HER BRA AND PANTIES
YOU GUYS!
HEY! I SAID SOME ONE PULL ME IN!
JUST JUMP!
IT'S TOO COLD! COME ON!
CHICKEN!!
DAN AND RON GLYNN WERE THERE AND DORIS BELL AND MARY HURLEY. EVERY-ONE WAS IN THEIR UNDERWEAR. MY COUSIN YELLED "SKINNY DIP!" WHEN HE SAW US. PATTY HERZOCK DROPPED OFF THE ROPE SWING AND CAME UP SCREAMING.
"BYE" CINDY SAID TO ME AND RAN OVER TO DAN GLYNN AND JUMPED ON HIS BACK. A RADIO WAS PLAYING. A SONG ABOUT "IF HER DADDY'S RICH" AND DAN STARTED SINGING IT TO CINDY.
HEY HOG GIVE ME SOME!
THEN A GUY, TOM DONATO, PUT HIS ARM AROUND ME AND GAVE ME SOME DRINKS OF HIS JUNGLE JUICE.
CINDY LUDERMYER MADE A BIG DEAL ABOUT TAKING OFF HER CLOTHES AND EVERYONE GOT QUIET WATCHING HER. CINDY'S NICKNAME WAS "THE BOD."
ROYLTON!
DANNY!
TOMMY!
RONNY!
YOU GUYS QUIT STARIN'
I WAS DRUNK AND EVERYONE WAS DRUNK. TOM DONATO STARTED FRENCHING ME AND WHEN I LOOKED AROUND, EVERYONE WAS FRENCHING EVERYONE ELSE.

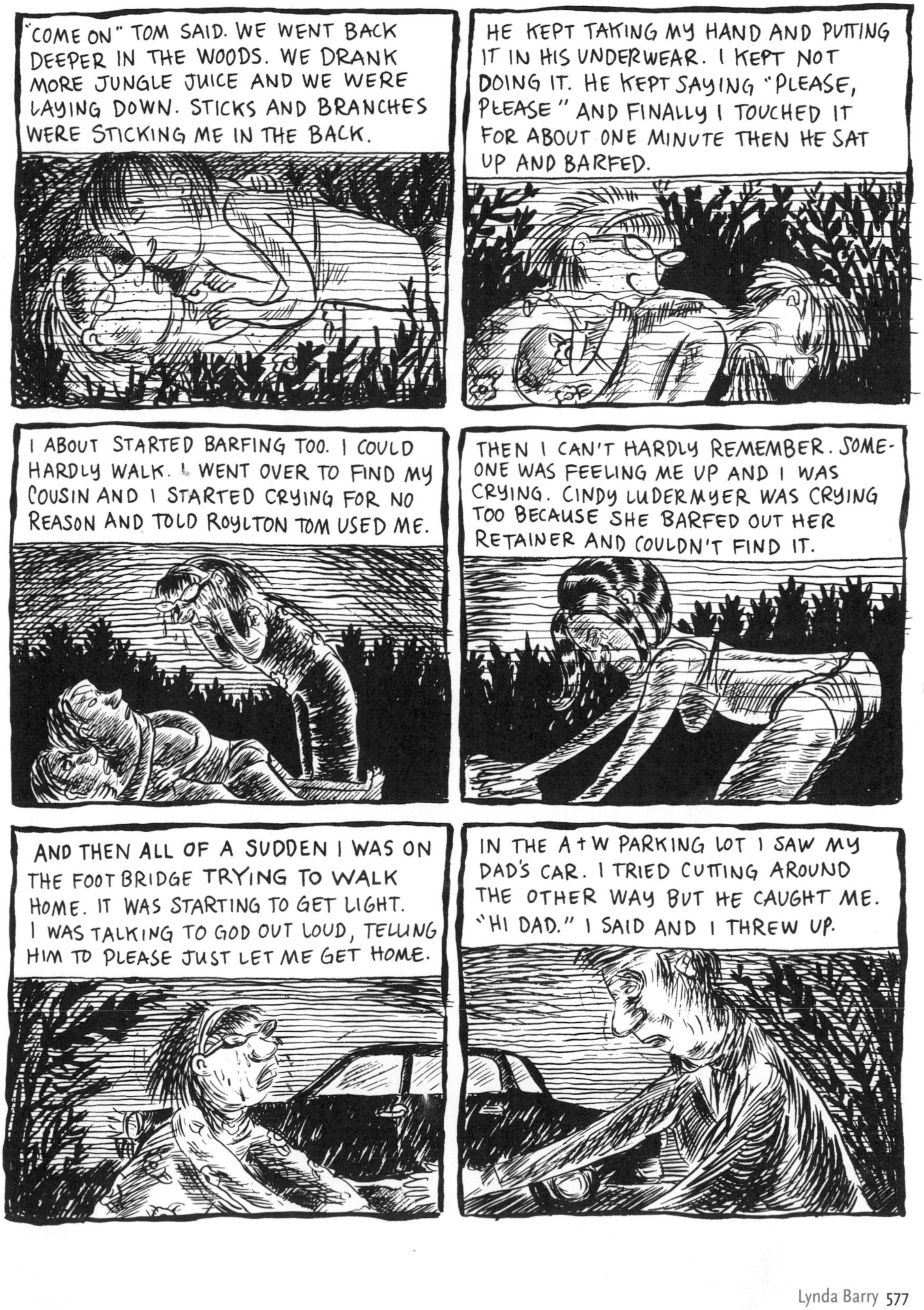
"COME ON" TOM SAID. WE WENT BACK DEEPER IN THE WOODS. WE DRANK MORE JUNGLE JUICE AND WE WERE LAYING DOWN. STICKS AND BRANCHES WERE STICKING ME IN THE BACK.
HE KEPT TAKING MY HAND AND PUTTING IT IN HIS UNDERWEAR. I KEPT NOT DOING IT. HE KEPT SAYING "PLEASE, PLEASE" AND FINALLY I TOUCHED IT FOR ABOUT ONE MINUTE THEN HE SAT UP AND BARFED.
I ABOUT STARTED BARFING TOO. I COULD HARDLY WALK. I WENT OVER TO FIND MY COUSIN AND I STARTED CRYING FOR NO REASON AND TOLD ROYLTON TOM USED ME.
THEN I CAN'T HARDLY REMEMBER. SOMEONE WAS FEELING ME UP AND I WAS CRYING. CINDY LUDERMYER WAS CRYING TOO BECAUSE SHE BARFED OUT HER RETAINER AND COULDN'T FIND IT.
AND THEN ALL OF A SUDDEN I WAS ON THE FOOT BRIDGE TRYING TO WALK HOME. IT WAS STARTING TO GET LIGHT. I WAS TALKING TO GOD OUT LOUD, TELLING HIM TO PLEASE JUST LET ME GET HOME.
IN THE A+W PARKING LOT I SAW MY DAD'S CAR. I TRIED CUTTING AROUND THE OTHER WAY BUT HE CAUGHT ME. "HI DAD." I SAID AND I THREW UP.

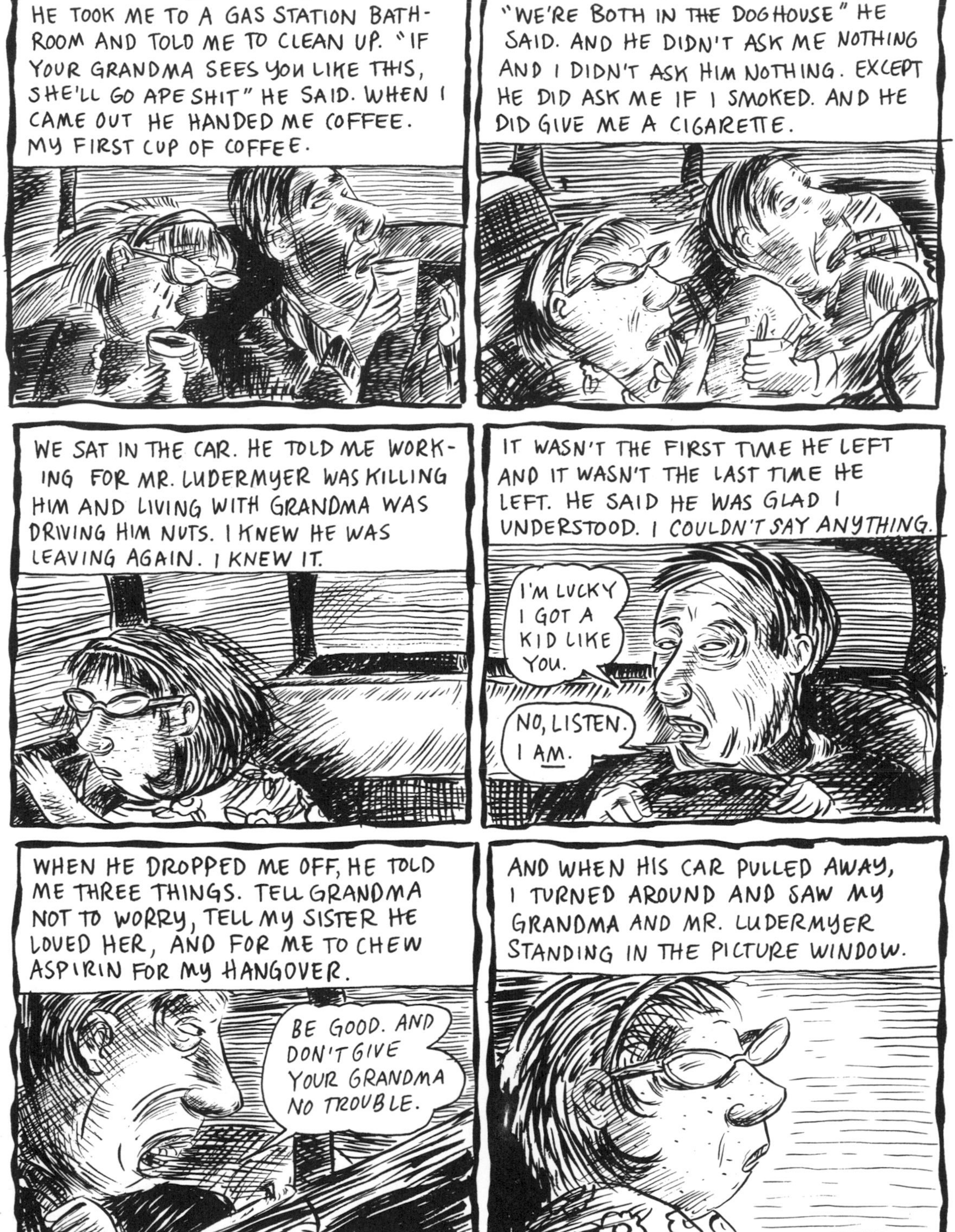
HE TOOK ME TO A GAS STATION BATHROOM AND TOLD ME TO CLEAN UP. "IF YOUR GRANDMA SEES YOU LIKE THIS, SHE'LL GO APE SHIT" HE SAID. WHEN I CAME OUT HE HANDED ME COFFEE. MY FIRST CUP OF COFFEE.
"WE'RE BOTH IN THE DOGHOUSE" HE SAID. AND HE DIDN'T ASK ME NOTHING AND I DIDN'T ASK HIM NOTHING. EXCEPT HE DID ASK ME IF I SMOKED. AND HE DID GIVE ME A CIGARETTE.
WE SAT IN THE CAR. HE TOLD ME WORKING FOR MR. LUDERMYER WAS KILLING HIM AND LIVING WITH GRANDMA WAS DRIVING HIM NUTS. I KNEW HE WAS LEAVING AGAIN. I KNEW IT.
IT WASN'T THE FIRST TIME HE LEFT AND IT WASN'T THE LAST TIME HE LEFT. HE SAID HE WAS GLAD I UNDERSTOOD. I COULDN'T SAY ANYTHING.
I'M LUCKY I GOT A KID LIKE YOU.
NO, LISTEN. I AM.
WHEN HE DROPPED ME OFF, HE TOLD ME THREE THINGS. TELL GRANDMA NOT TO WORRY, TELL MY SISTER HE LOVED HER, AND FOR ME TO CHEW ASPIRIN FOR MY HANGOVER.
BE GOOD. AND DON'T GIVE YOUR GRANDMA NO TROUBLE.
AND WHEN HIS CAR PULLED AWAY, I TURNED AROUND AND SAW MY GRANDMA AND MR. LUDERMYER STANDING IN THE PICTURE WINDOW.

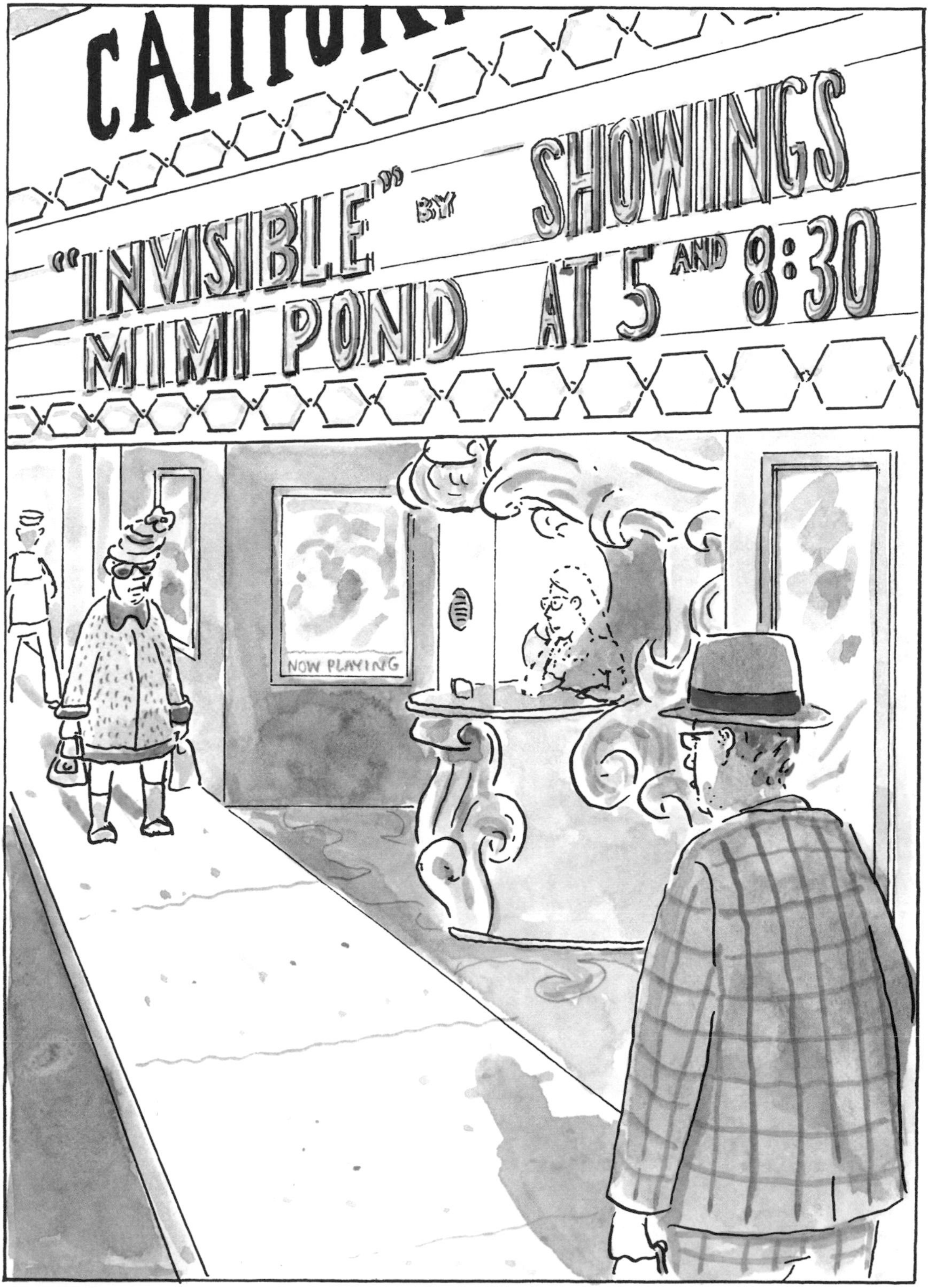
CALIFORN
"INVISIBLE" BY MIMI POND
SHOWINGS AT 5 AND 8:30
NOW PLAYING

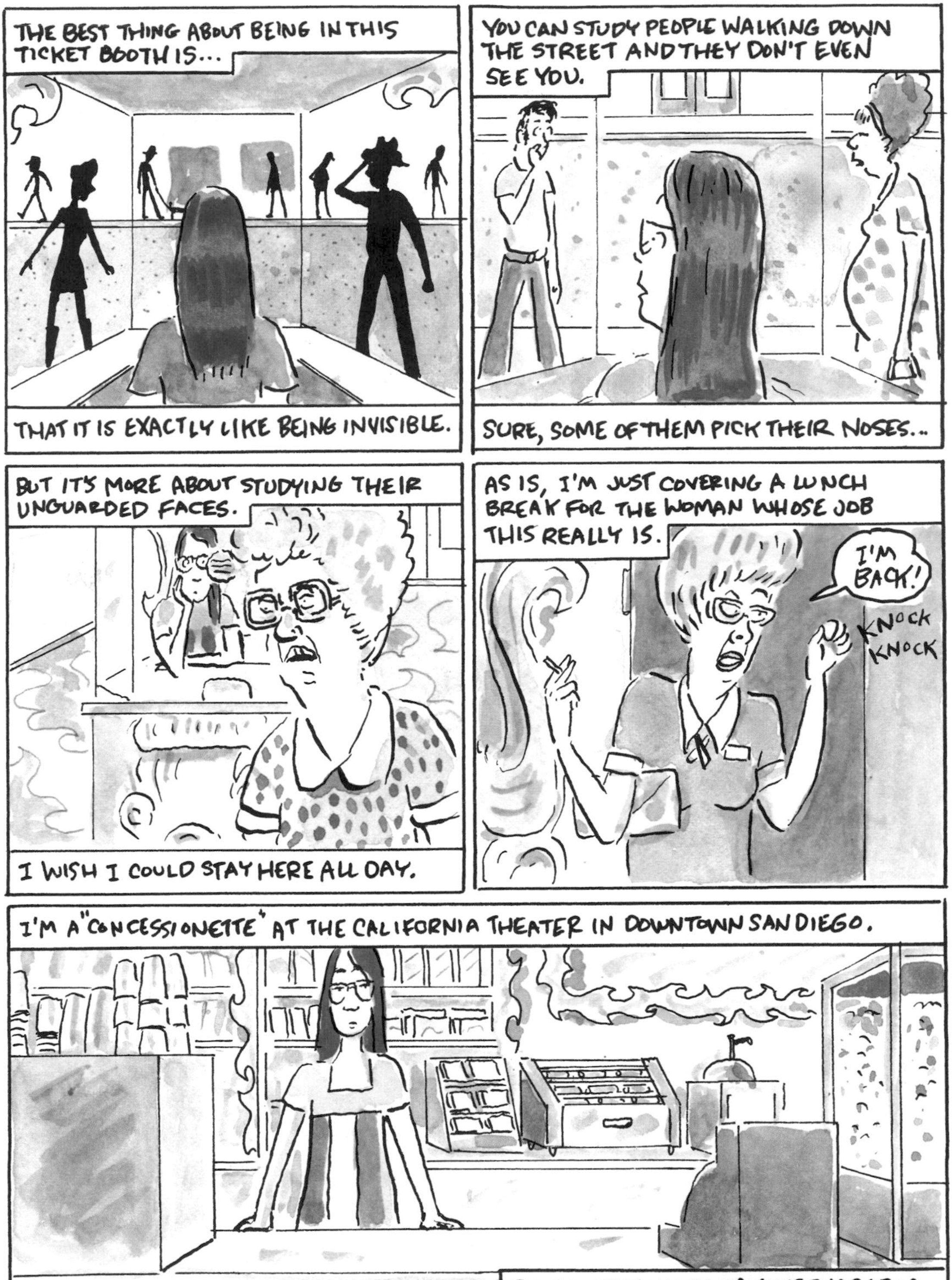

THE BEST THING ABOUT BEING IN THIS TICKET BOOTH IS...
THAT IT IS EXACTLY LIKE BEING INVISIBLE.
YOU CAN STUDY PEOPLE WALKING DOWN THE STREET AND THEY DON'T EVEN SEE YOU.
SURE, SOME OF THEM PICK THEIR NOSES...
BUT IT'S MORE ABOUT STUDYING THEIR UNGUARDED FACES.
I WISH I COULD STAY HERE ALL DAY.
AS IS, I'M JUST COVERING A LUNCH BREAK FOR THE WOMAN WHOSE JOB THIS REALLY IS.
I'M BACK!
KNOCK KNOCK
I'M A "CONCESSIONETTE" AT THE CALIFORNIA THEATER IN DOWNTOWN SAN DIEGO.
THAT JUST MEANS I WORK THE SNACK BAR.

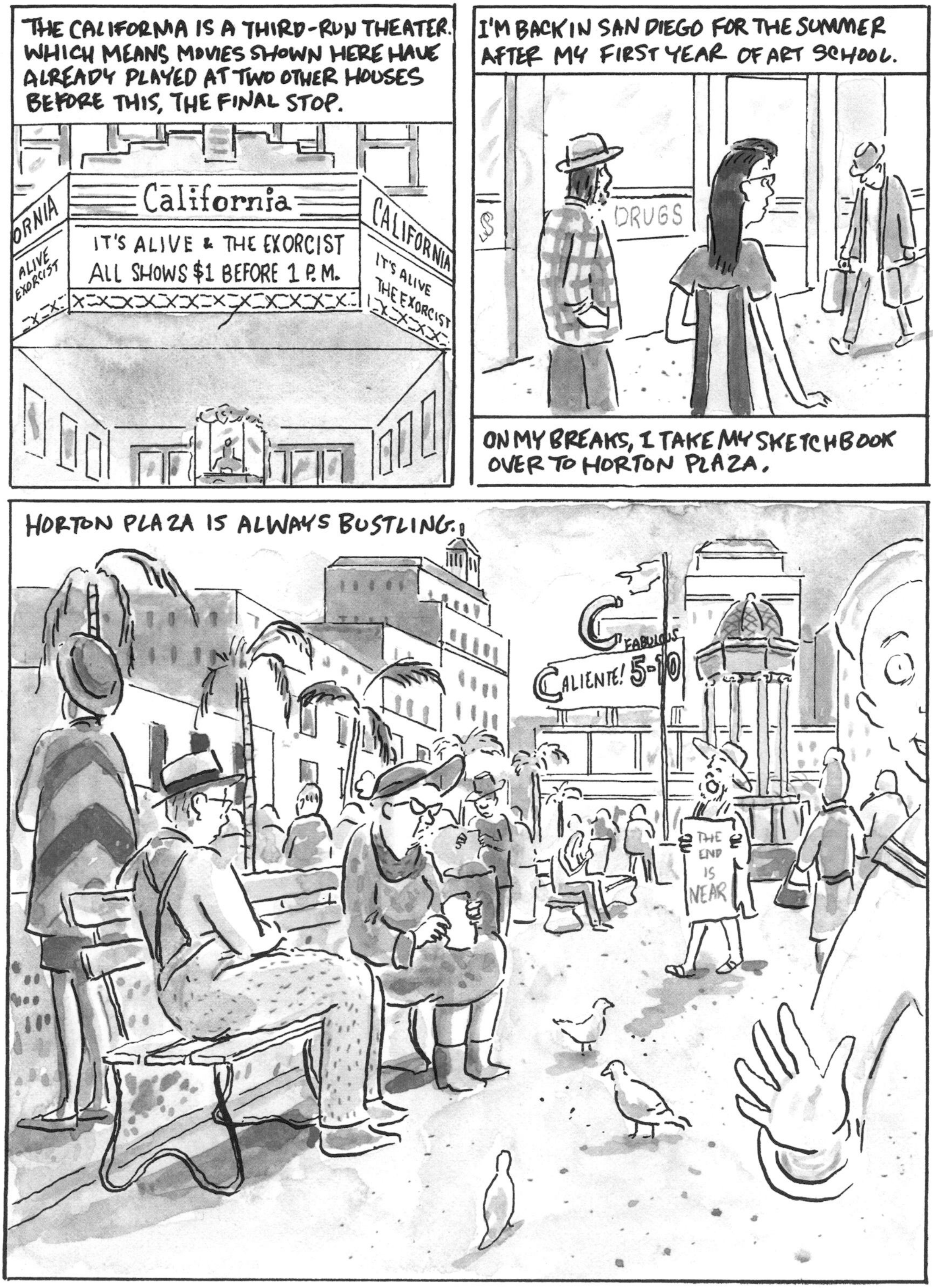
THE CALIFORNIA IS A THIRD-RUN THEATER. WHICH MEANS MOVIES SHOWN HERE HAVE ALREADY PLAYED AT TWO OTHER HOUSES BEFORE THIS, THE FINAL STOP.
California
IT'S ALIVE & THE EXORCIST
ALL SHOWS $1 BEFORE 1 P.M.
ORNIA
ALIVE
EXORCIST
CALIFORNIA
IT'S ALIVE
THE EXORCIST
I'M BACK IN SAN DIEGO FOR THE SUMMER AFTER MY FIRST YEAR OF ART SCHOOL.
DRUGS
ON MY BREAKS, I TAKE MY SKETCHBOOK OVER TO HORTON PLAZA.
HORTON PLAZA IS ALWAYS BUSTLING.
FABULOUS
CALIENTE! 5-10
THE END IS NEAR

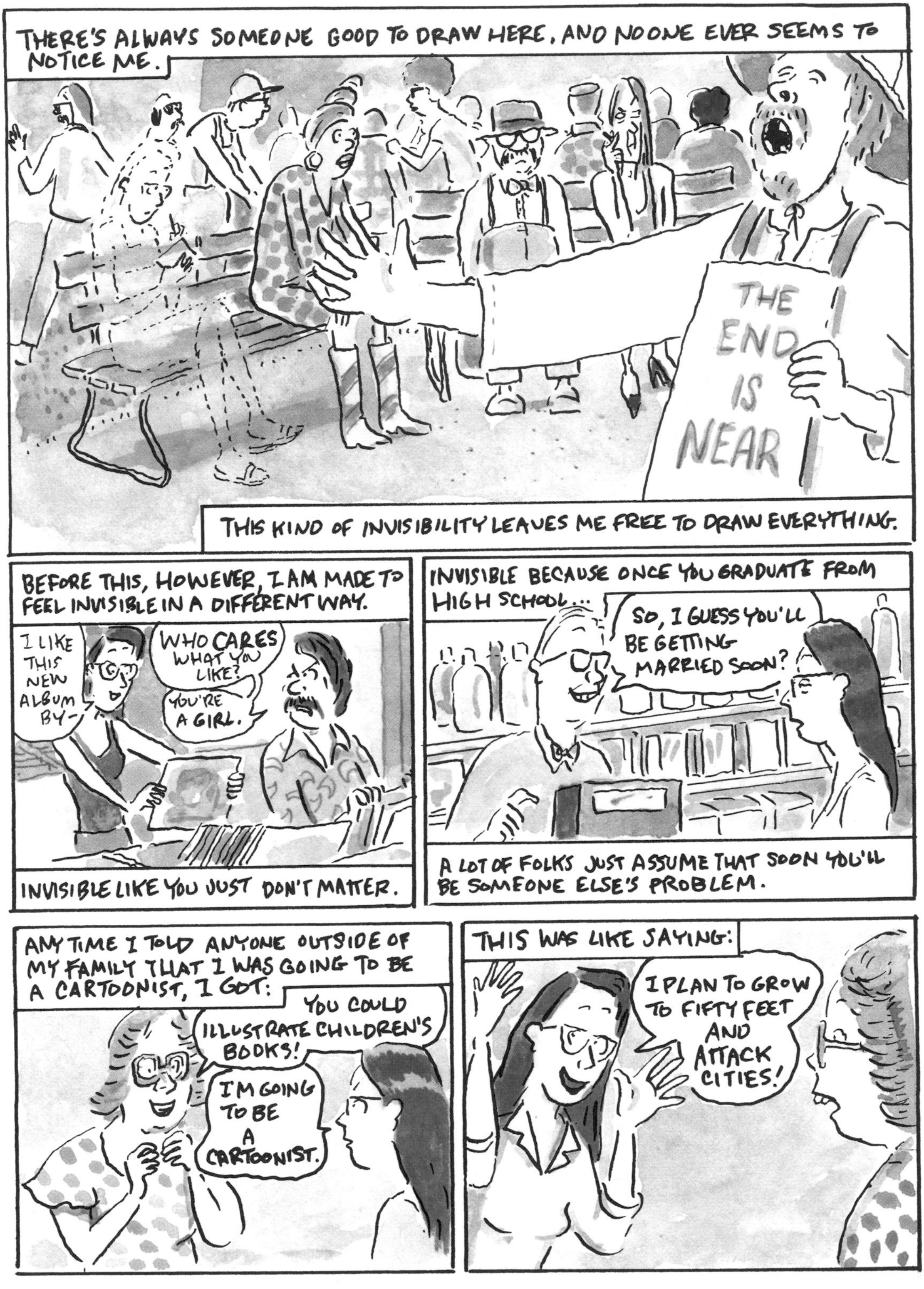
THERE'S ALWAYS SOMEONE GOOD TO DRAW HERE, AND NO ONE EVER SEEMS TO NOTICE ME.
THE END IS NEAR
THIS KIND OF INVISIBILITY LEAVES ME FREE TO DRAW EVERYTHING.
BEFORE THIS, HOWEVER, I AM MADE TO FEEL INVISIBLE IN A DIFFERENT WAY.
I LIKE THIS NEW ALBUM BY-
WHO CARES WHAT YOU LIKE?
YOU'RE A GIRL.
INVISIBLE LIKE YOU JUST DON'T MATTER.
INVISIBLE BECAUSE ONCE YOU GRADUATE FROM HIGH SCHOOL...
SO, I GUESS YOU'LL BE GETTING MARRIED SOON?
A LOT OF FOLKS JUST ASSUME THAT SOON YOU'LL BE SOMEONE ELSE'S PROBLEM.
ANY TIME I TOLD ANYONE OUTSIDE OF MY FAMILY THAT I WAS GOING TO BE A CARTOONIST, I GOT:
YOU COULD ILLUSTRATE CHILDREN'S BOOKS!
I'M GOING TO BE A CARTOONIST.
THIS WAS LIKE SAYING:
I PLAN TO GROW TO FIFTY FEET AND ATTACK CITIES!

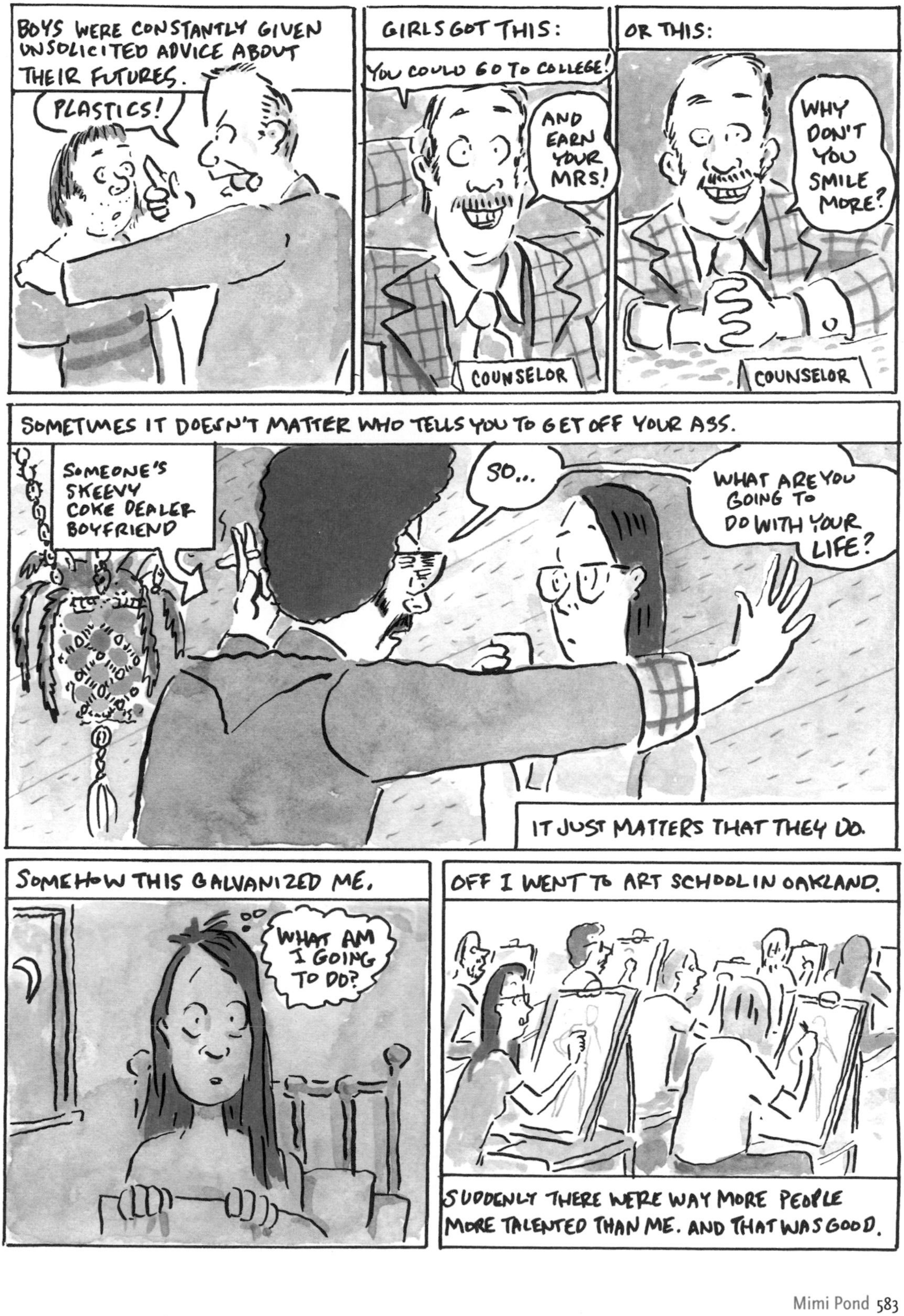
BOYS WERE CONSTANTLY GIVEN UNSOLICITED ADVICE ABOUT THEIR FUTURES.
PLASTICS!
GIRLS GOT THIS:
YOU COULD GO TO COLLEGE!
AND EARN YOUR MRS!
COUNSELOR
OR THIS:
WHY DON'T YOU SMILE MORE?
COUNSELOR
SOMETIMES IT DOESN'T MATTER WHO TELLS YOU TO GET OFF YOUR ASS.
SOMEONE'S SKEEVY COKE DEALER BOYFRIEND
SO...
WHAT ARE YOU GOING TO DO WITH YOUR LIFE?
IT JUST MATTERS THAT THEY DO.
SOMEHOW THIS GALVANIZED ME.
WHAT AM I GOING TO DO?
OFF I WENT TO ART SCHOOL IN OAKLAND.
SUDDENLY THERE WERE WAY MORE PEOPLE MORE TALENTED THAN ME. AND THAT WAS GOOD.

BUT NOW I WAS BACK HOME FOR THE SUMMER, LOOKING FOR WORK.

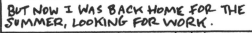

CAFETERIA

I FIGURED ONE MINIMUM-WAGE JOB WAS AS GOOD AS ANOTHER.

THIS REALLY HAPPENED. HOW DO WE KNOW YOU WON'T JUST RUN OFF AND GET MARRIED?

WELL, YEAH, BECAUSE YOU WOULD HAVE INVESTED SO MUCH IN TRAINING ME TO SCOOP MASHED POTATOES...

THE OTHER THING THAT HAPPENED WAS THAT I GOT TO MEET MY IDOL.

... NEON BUZZIN', TELEPHONE'S RINGIN', IT'S YOUR SECOND COUSIN... ♪

MAYBE I WASN'T TOM WAITS FAN #1, BUT I WAS PROBABLY TOM WAITS FAN #34.

I'D BECOME OBSESSED WITH HIM AFTER SEEING HIM PERFORM AT THE 1974 SAN DIEGO STATE FOLK FESTIVAL.

... AND THE STEAM HEAT IS DRIPPIN' OFF THE WALL... ♪

HE WAS SINGING ABOUT THE SAME STUFF I WAS TRYING TO DRAW...

WOOLWORTH'S RHINESTONE DIAMOND EARRINGS AND A SIDEWAYS GLANCE ♪

GRITTY, URBAN REALITY.

AND HE WAS ACTUALLY FROM SAN DIEGO!

♪ NOW THE WAITRESS SAYS... EGGS AND SAUSAGE... ♪

UP UNTIL THEN, IT SEEMED LIKE NO ONE EXCITING COULD COME FROM MY TOWN.

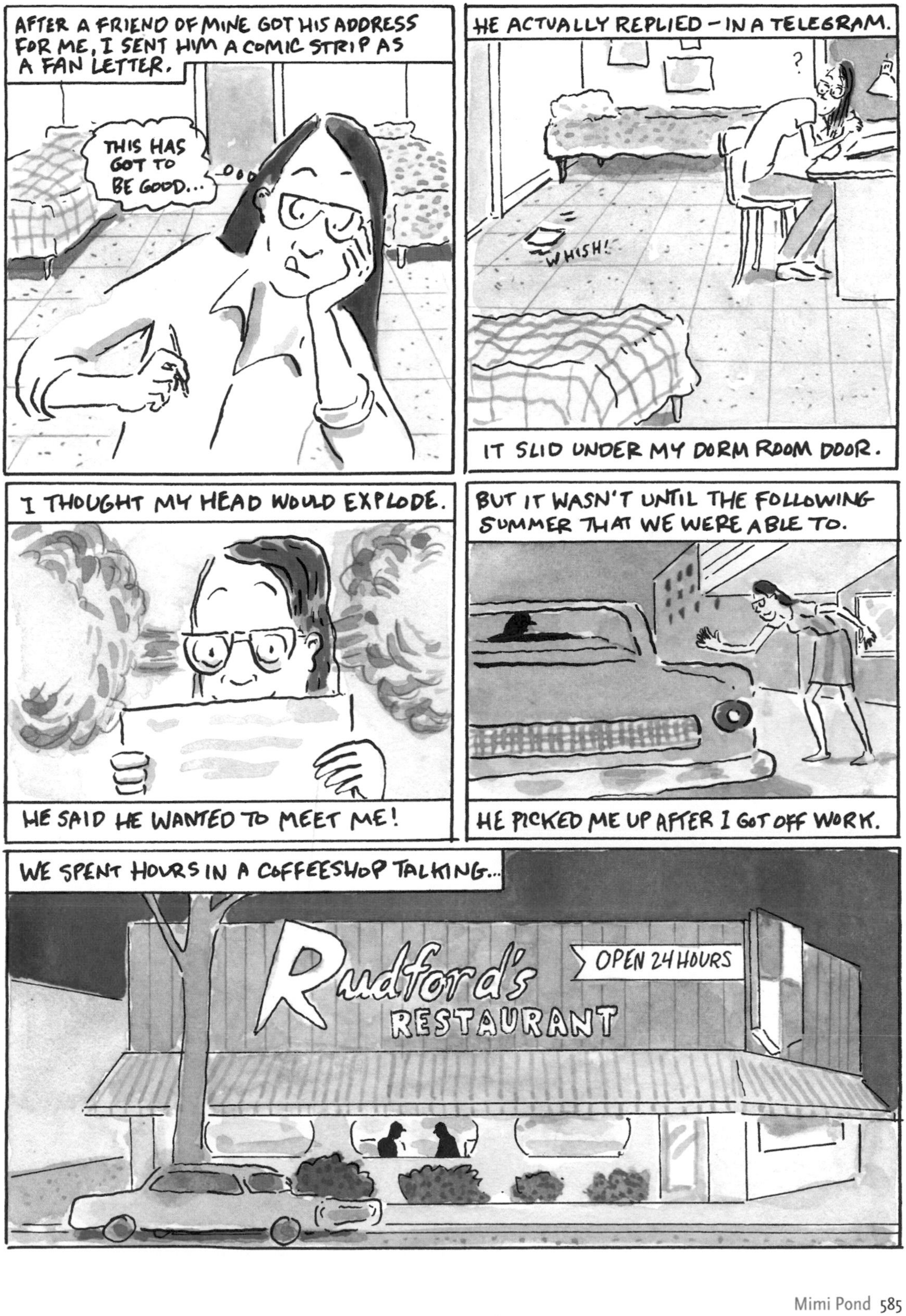
AFTER A FRIEND OF MINE GOT HIS ADDRESS FOR ME, I SENT HIM A COMIC STRIP AS A FAN LETTER.
THIS HAS GOT TO BE GOOD...
HE ACTUALLY REPLIED – IN A TELEGRAM.
?
WHISH!
IT SLID UNDER MY DORM ROOM DOOR.
I THOUGHT MY HEAD WOULD EXPLODE.
HE SAID HE WANTED TO MEET ME!
BUT IT WASN'T UNTIL THE FOLLOWING SUMMER THAT WE WERE ABLE TO.
HE PICKED ME UP AFTER I GOT OFF WORK.
WE SPENT HOURS IN A COFFEESHOP TALKING...
Rudford's
RESTAURANT
OPEN 24 HOURS

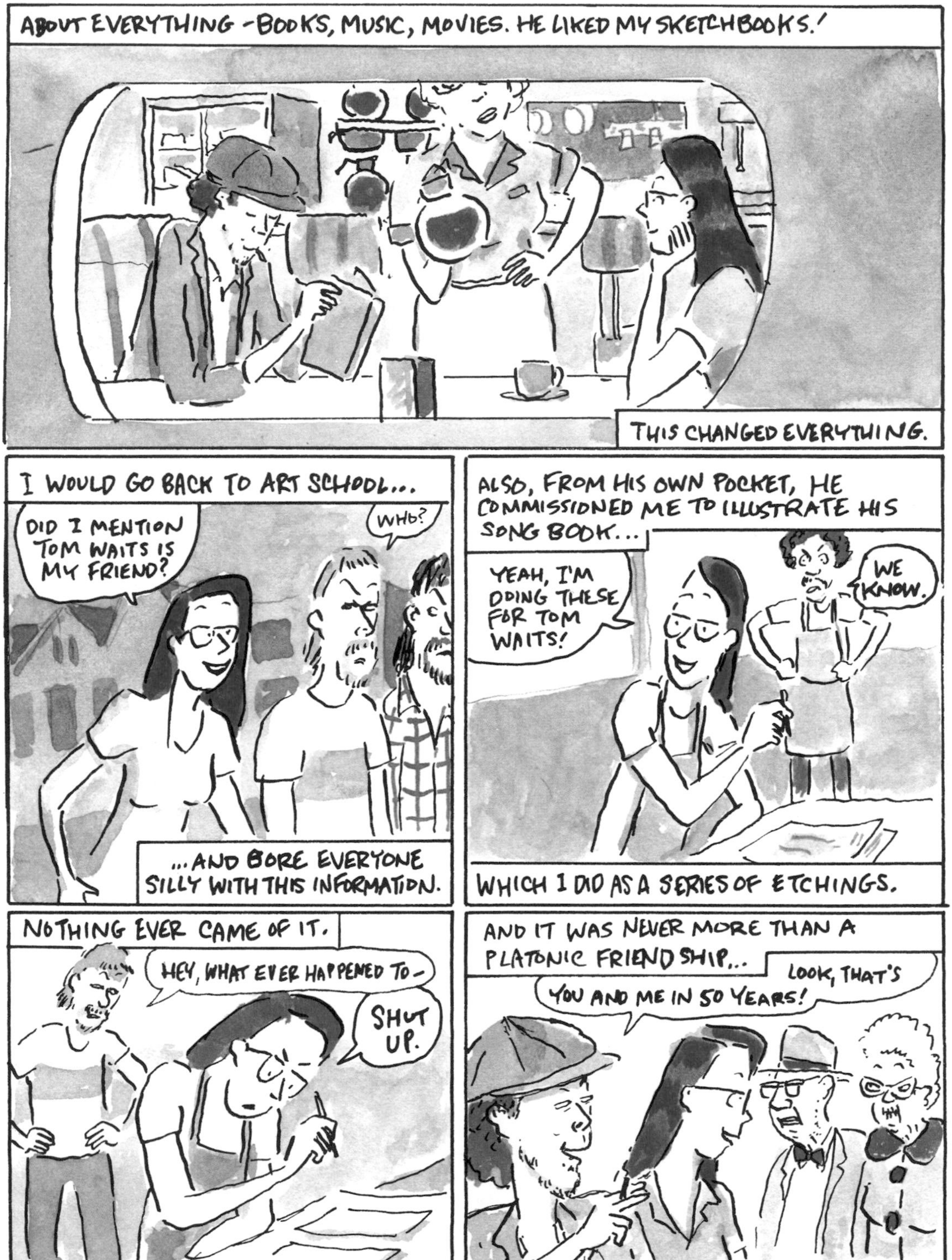
ABOUT EVERYTHING - BOOKS, MUSIC, MOVIES. HE LIKED MY SKETCHBOOKS!
THIS CHANGED EVERYTHING.
I WOULD GO BACK TO ART SCHOOL...
DID I MENTION TOM WAITS IS MY FRIEND?
WHO?
...AND BORE EVERYONE SILLY WITH THIS INFORMATION.
ALSO, FROM HIS OWN POCKET, HE COMMISSIONED ME TO ILLUSTRATE HIS SONG BOOK...
YEAH, I'M DOING THESE FOR TOM WAITS!
WE KNOW.
WHICH I DID AS A SERIES OF ETCHINGS.
NOTHING EVER CAME OF IT.
HEY, WHAT EVER HAPPENED TO-
SHUT UP.
I DON'T KNOW WHY, EXACTLY.
AND IT WAS NEVER MORE THAN A PLATONIC FRIENDSHIP...
LOOK, THAT'S YOU AND ME IN 50 YEARS!
FOR WHICH I AM GRATEFUL NOW.

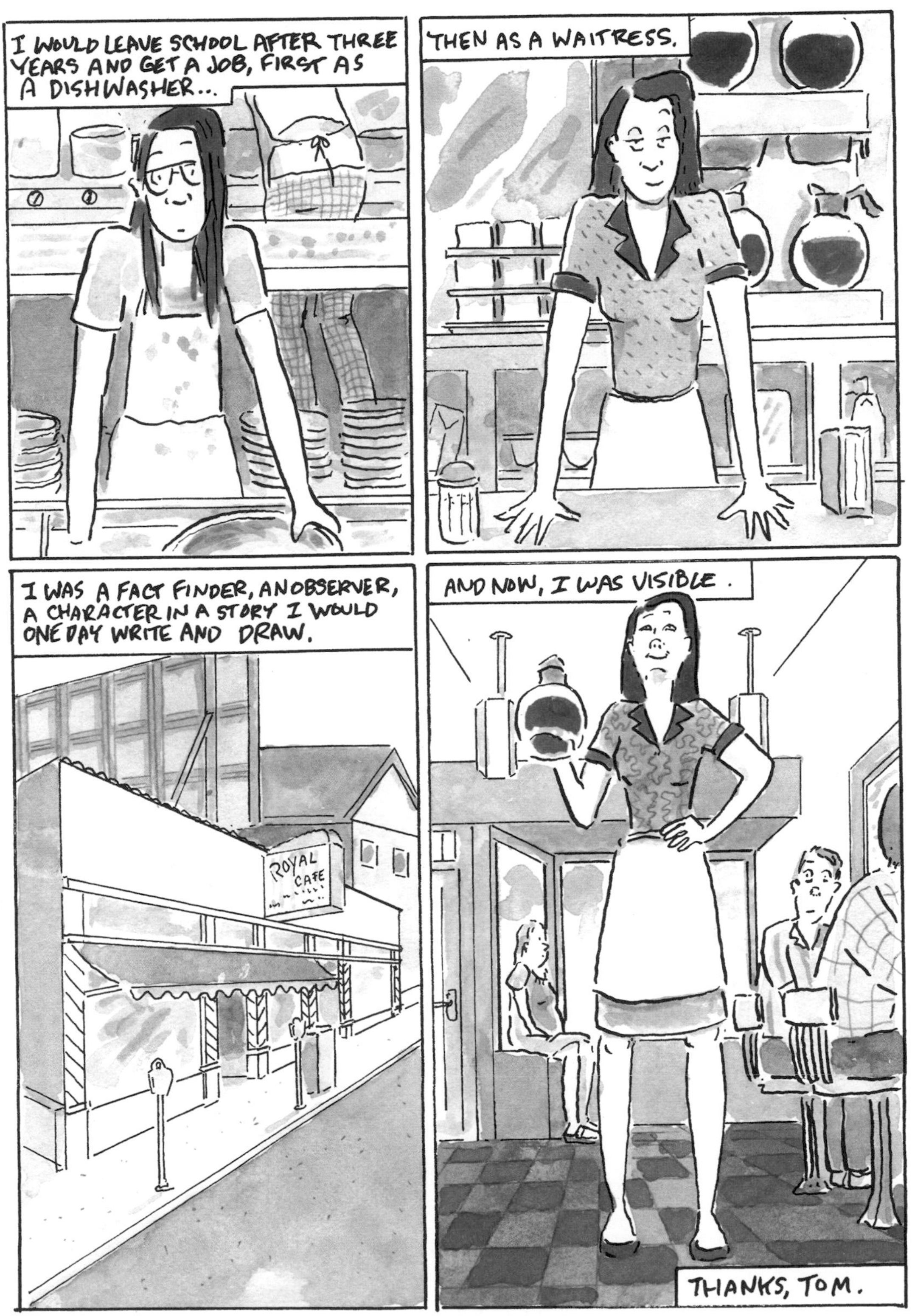
I WOULD LEAVE SCHOOL AFTER THREE YEARS AND GET A JOB, FIRST AS A DISHWASHER...
THEN AS A WAITRESS.
I WAS A FACT FINDER, AN OBSERVER, A CHARACTER IN A STORY I WOULD ONE DAY WRITE AND DRAW.
ROYAL CAFE
AND NOW, I WAS VISIBLE.
THANKS, TOM.

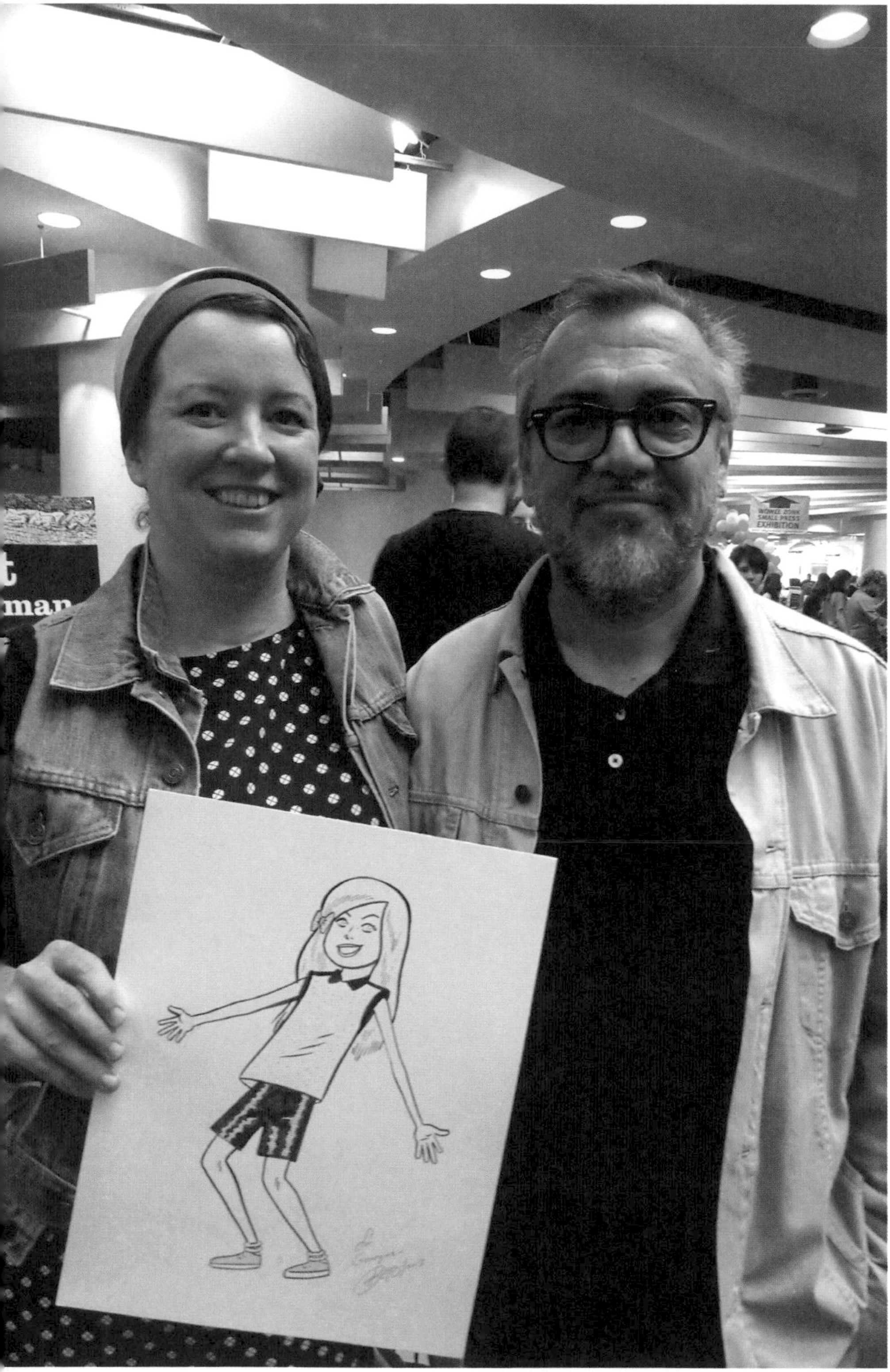
SMALL PRESS
EXHIBITION

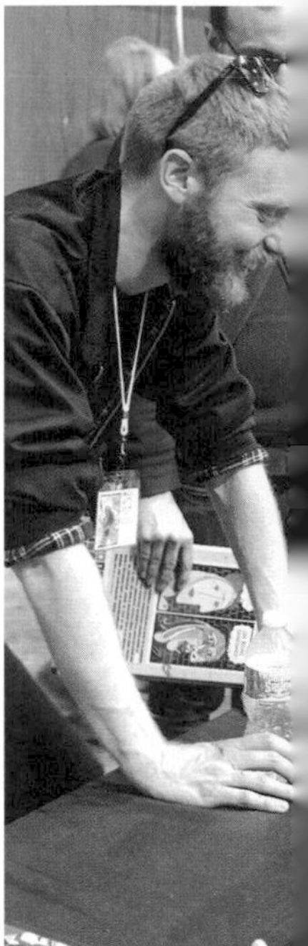

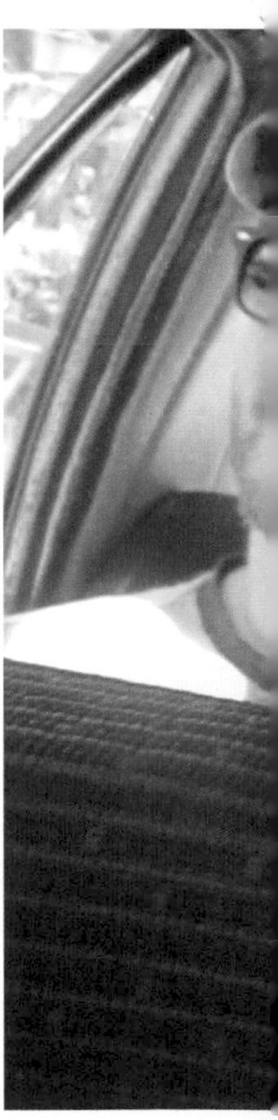

 (Left) Peggy Burns & Gilbert Hernandez at Toronto Comic Arts Festival (2013). (Top centre) Brecht Vandenbroucke & Art Spiegelman at MoCCA Fest (201

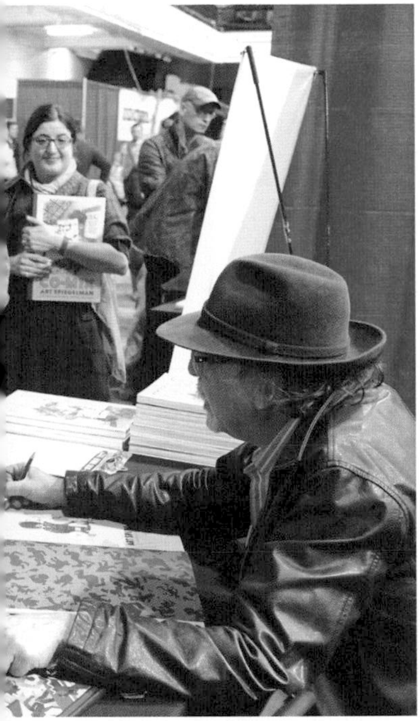

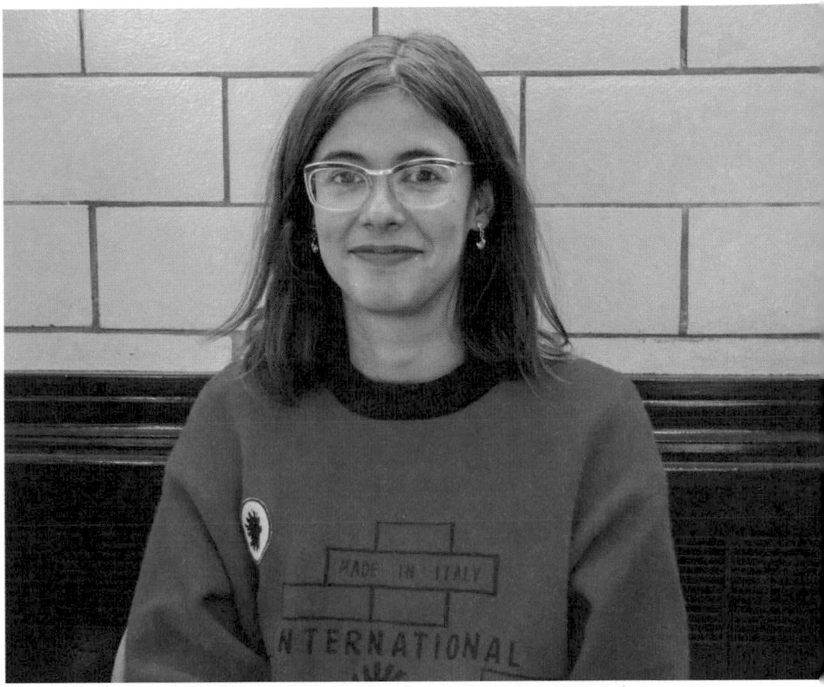
MADE IN ITALY
NTERNATIONAL

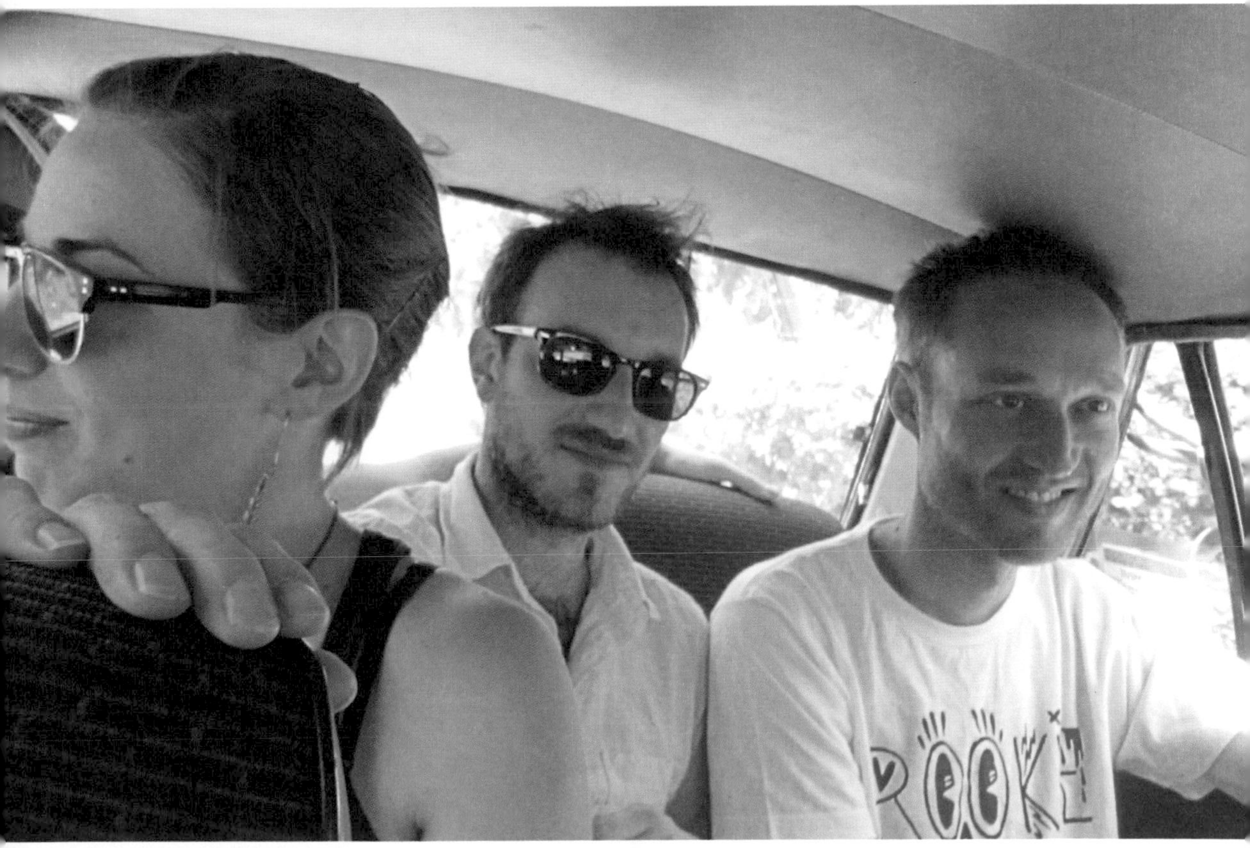

p) Aisha Franz at Comics Arts Brooklyn. Photo: Jody Culkin (2014). (Bottom) Florent Ruppert, Sarah Glidden, Jérôme Mulot & Anders Nilsen in Colombia (2012).

KATE BEATON

an appreciation by Margaret Atwood

Recently I was being interviewed about my books, comic-book superheroes, Shakespeare's history plays, vampires, revenge murders done with fossils in the Arctic, and other such closely related matters. In the midst of a particularly acrobatic subject leap, I found myself saying to the interviewer, "I think you would like this."

"This" was *Hark! A Vagrant*, a collection of comic strips by Kate Beaton. How many people have I recommended it to? Quite a lot. Very few things in recent years have made me laugh so much in the bathroom.

Wherein lies the *Vagrant*'s peculiar charm?

The girl can draw, for one thing. But it's more than that.

Beaton began life—well, not life, but late-adolescent life—as a history and English student, if I've got the story right. Then she kind of wandered into the comics, because, being a doodler, and being from Canada where people make fun of everything, and being from Nova Scotia where they do it even more, though maybe not as much as the Newfoundlanders, she naturally enough started making fun of the revered classics and the famous historical figures and events she was studying. As one does.

Let she who has never drawn arms and a moustache on the picture of the Venus de Milo in her Latin book cast the first rubber eraser. I cherish to this day my brother's high school copy of Jane Austen's *Pride and Prejudice*. In one of the illustrations, Mr. Darcy (swoon) is proposing to Elizabeth Bennet (yay), and my brother added word balloons above their heads so he is saying "'Grrr!'" and she is saying "'Eek!'" Which sums it all up, in a minimalist, warped, bathetic kind of way.

Thus do great comic-strip careers begin. Usually during the high school years, when we (for one, or several) used to put on skits about Hamlet in which the hero was called Omelette, and when my mother (b. 1909) related that her generation did the same, only the target was Sir Walter Scott's "Young Lochinvar," performed with a broomstick steed. L.M. Montgomery had something similar in mind when she had Anne (she of the gables) re-enacting Tennyson's "Lady of Shalott," only the barge sinks. The Greeks were making similar fun of their own revered

myths during the classical age, which was indeed the way Gilbert and Sullivan began in *The Gods Grown Old*. There's just something about a heroic-looking anything that makes you long, at least at times, to stick a tiny pin in its balloon.

My own Canadian generation was well acquainted with (for instance) Max Ferguson's Rawhide Little Theatre on the radio, whose rendition of *Wuthering Heights* gave it a whole new dimension, with Heathcliff intoning, "I must go out on the moors again, / To the lonely moors and the sky, / And all I want is a sharp stick, / To poke in Edgar Linton's eye."

Not to mention Wayne and Shuster, whose take on Julius Caesar is unforgettable: "I want a martinus." Bartender: "You mean martini." "If I'd wanted two I'd have asked for them." (You see? Unforgettable, because, hey, I haven't forgotten it.)

My brother wandered off into neuroscience and a major comic artist was lost to the world, but Kate Beaton's pals egged her on because they loved what she was doing. Who but a po-faced, dour, humourless, puffed-up Malvolio type would not?

Of course, in order to burlesque a work of literature or an historic event, you have to know it and, in some sense, love it—or at least understand its inner workings. Kate Beaton doesn't talk down to her audience, no matter how much fun she's poking: she assumes we've read the books and have at least a passing acquaintance with the historical figures and events she's redrawing. Nor is her intent malevolent: she does not intend to destroy her targets, merely to see them from, well, a different angle. The beheading of Mary, Queen of Scots, was tragic from one point of view, but farcical from another: her red wig came off, her little dog ran up underneath the skirts of the now headless corpse. There's a burping-in-church aspect to Beaton's approach. It doesn't demolish the church, but it does add another dimension.

Which are my favourites? Beaton hasn't yet (to my knowledge) done a *Pride and Prejudice*—it's harder to do this kind of thing with a work that's already comic—but her *Jane Eyre* is a thing of beauty and a joy forever. She knows her Victorian memes very well indeed—I speak as a former

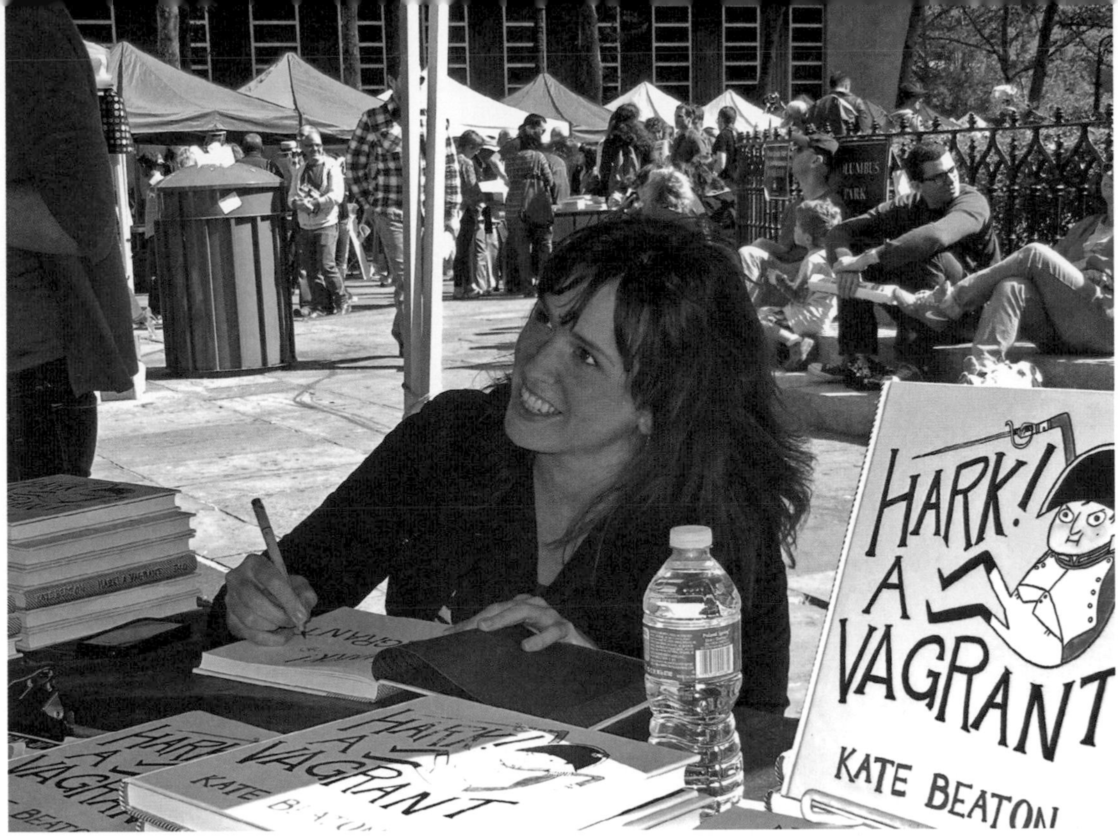
HARK!
A
VAGRANT
KATE BEATON

Victorianist—and the hero reduced by wounds or blindness or both to a state in which the heroine can get him under nursely control is not unique to Charlotte Brontë. Beaton's last *Jane Eyre* strip shows a decrepit Mr. Rochester. Jane says, "Oh Mr. Rochester you are uglier than ever and blind and crippled… and we are equals now that I am totally superior to you! Now I can LOVE you!" To which Rochester replies, "Golly. That's perfect." Arrow into the bull's eye. As it were.

In her footnote—for Beaton is in the habit of adding footnotes when the fancy takes her—she comments, "In the various essays out there titled 'In Defense of Mr. Rochester,' we are to understand that keeping a nutty wife in your attic was a reasonable alternative to the asylums of the day. Fair enough. However, after much consideration, we the jury still find Mr. Rochester to be a creepy wife-hiding weirdo. We know Jane is coming back to him eventually, but we really wish Bertha could make a break for it." As she does, sort of, in Jean Rhys's masterpiece on the subject, *Wide Sargasso Sea*. Which Beaton must have read or I'm a monkey's aunt.

Equally wondrous is Beaton's *Dracula*, which zeroes in on the Victorian distrust of excess sexiness in women, among other features. And that brings us to an up-to-date feature of Beaton's work, which is her wicked neo-feminism. Nobody gets away with much in this department, including Charles Dickens, whose penchant for dumb, innocent, sexless young ingénues is duly skewered. ("So hot!") Then there's *Crime and Punishment* and *The Great Gatsby* and the French revolution and "Anne of Sleeves" (she of the gables, what did I tell you) and Nancy Drew and—because Beaton takes on memes of all kinds, comic-book ones included—"Sexy Batman," a very tough Wonder Woman, and a tiny, perfect little strip in which Wolverine is becoming domesticated and scratching up the furniture, and has to be shooed away with a rolled-up newspaper, looking woefully forlorn.

So there you have it. Wide-ranging, spot-on, delightfully drawn, and laugh-in-the-bathroom-making. It's a rich plum pudding; don't read it all at once. What will Beaton do next? Will her youthful high spirits continue to generate these outside-the-lines hijinks and surreal juxtapositions? Let us hope so. I, for one, am Constant Reader.

Margaret Atwood is the author of over sixty books of poetry, children's literature, fiction, and non-fiction, including* The Handmaid's Tale, Oryx and Crake, *and* The Blind Assassin *(for which she won the Booker Prize.) Her work has been translated into more than forty languages.

Kate Beaton at Brooklyn Book Festival. Photo: Calvin Reid (2011).

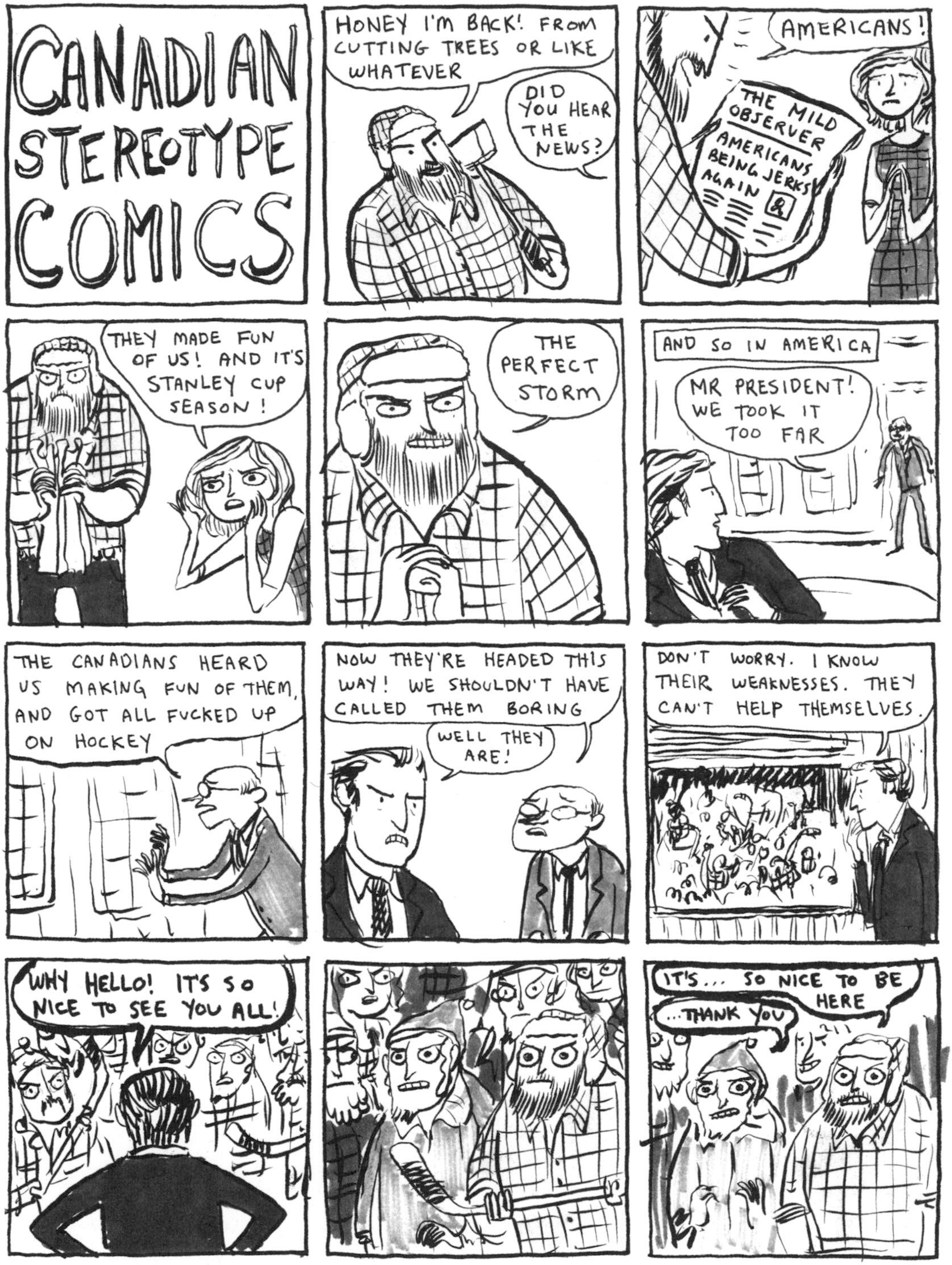
CANADIAN STEREOTYPE COMICS
HONEY I'M BACK! FROM CUTTING TREES OR LIKE WHATEVER
DID YOU HEAR THE NEWS?
AMERICANS!
THE MILD OBSERVER
AMERICANS BEING JERKS AGAIN
THEY MADE FUN OF US! AND IT'S STANLEY CUP SEASON!
THE PERFECT STORM
AND SO IN AMERICA
MR PRESIDENT! WE TOOK IT TOO FAR
THE CANADIANS HEARD US MAKING FUN OF THEM, AND GOT ALL FUCKED UP ON HOCKEY
NOW THEY'RE HEADED THIS WAY! WE SHOULDN'T HAVE CALLED THEM BORING
WELL THEY ARE!
DON'T WORRY. I KNOW THEIR WEAKNESSES. THEY CAN'T HELP THEMSELVES.
WHY HELLO! IT'S SO NICE TO SEE YOU ALL!
IT'S... SO NICE TO BE HERE
...THANK YOU

Canadian stereotypes are either hilarious and amazing or stupid and embarrassing, depending on whom you ask. But I can't help myself. I love our silly stereotypes. Anyone who gets upset because too many people think their country is exceedingly polite needs to rethink their priorities. I want to apologize to anyone who is offended by that statement.

 These strips first appeared on harkavagrant.com and were later collected by D+Q in *Hark! A Vagrant* (2011).

GREAT GATSBYS

Everyone has to read *The Great Gatsby* in high school because it's the best example of constructing a novel with themes and symbols, like legos, only not legos but the American Dream and the eyes of Dr. T.J. Eckleburg. Fifteen-year-olds can really get behind an essay on what the green light means, which is good, because they sure as heck won't relate to any of the characters, who are all huge jerks with enough money to be wasted most of the time on top of being miserable.

DREAM GIRL

I'M IN LOVE WITH DAISY
YEAH, I GUESS SHE IS HOT AND RICH
AND HIGH CLASS
IT'S NOT THAT! IT'S HER PERSONALITY
EXCEPT WHEN SHE'S VAIN AND SHALLOW
WHICH, GRANTED, IS MOST OF THE TIME

LIKE TOM'S A GOOD FATHER

DAISY! WHERE IS OUR DAUGHTER?
HUH?
OUR BABY
WHAT BABY

IN THE VALLEY OF ASHES

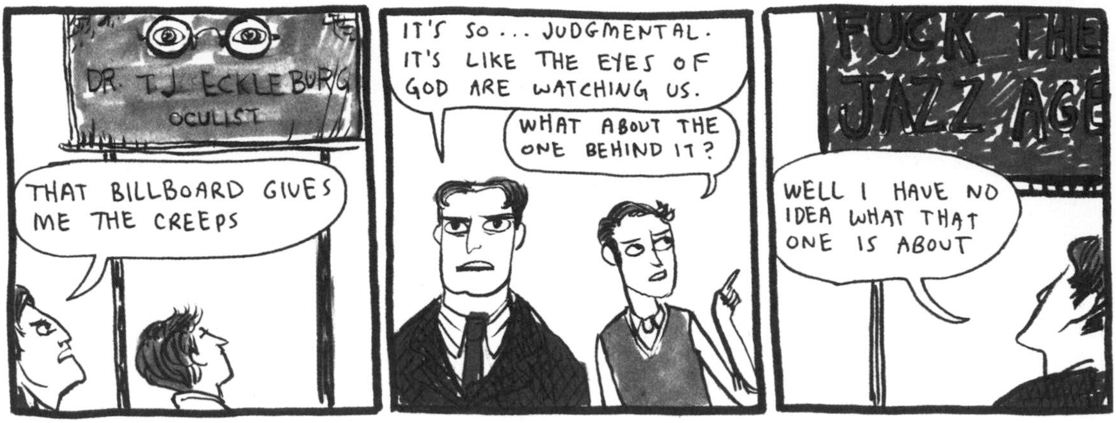

DR. T.J. ECKLEBURG
OCULIST
THAT BILLBOARD GIVES ME THE CREEPS
IT'S SO ... JUDGMENTAL. IT'S LIKE THE EYES OF GOD ARE WATCHING US.
WHAT ABOUT THE ONE BEHIND IT?
FUCK THE
JAZZ AGE
WELL I HAVE NO IDEA WHAT THAT ONE IS ABOUT

GREEN LIGHT

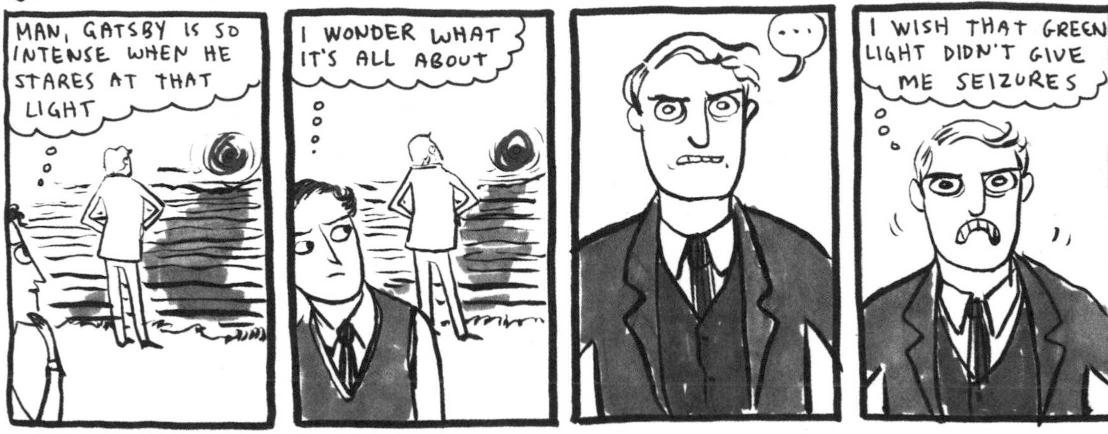

MAN, GATSBY IS SO INTENSE WHEN HE STARES AT THAT LIGHT
I WONDER WHAT IT'S ALL ABOUT
...
I WISH THAT GREEN LIGHT DIDN'T GIVE ME SEIZURES

THE REAL JAY GATSBY

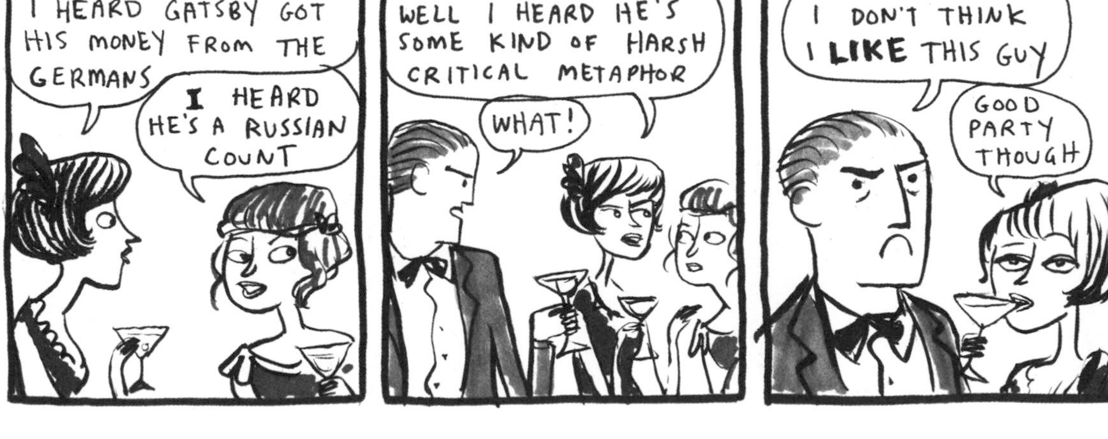

I HEARD GATSBY GOT HIS MONEY FROM THE GERMANS
I HEARD HE'S A RUSSIAN COUNT
WELL I HEARD HE'S SOME KIND OF HARSH CRITICAL METAPHOR
WHAT!
I DON'T THINK I **LIKE** THIS GUY
GOOD PARTY THOUGH

THAT'S PRETTY OLD

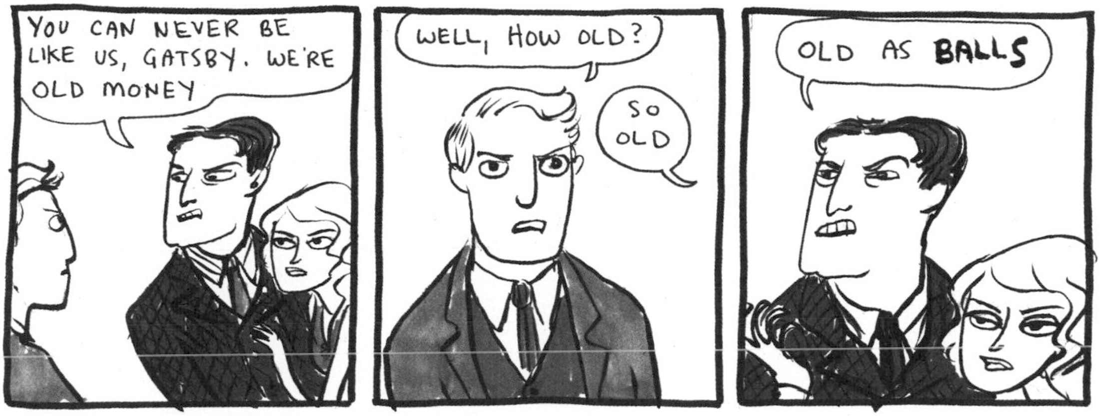
YOU CAN NEVER BE LIKE US, GATSBY. WE'RE OLD MONEY
WELL, HOW OLD?
SO OLD
OLD AS BALLS

LATER SHE DUMPS HIM

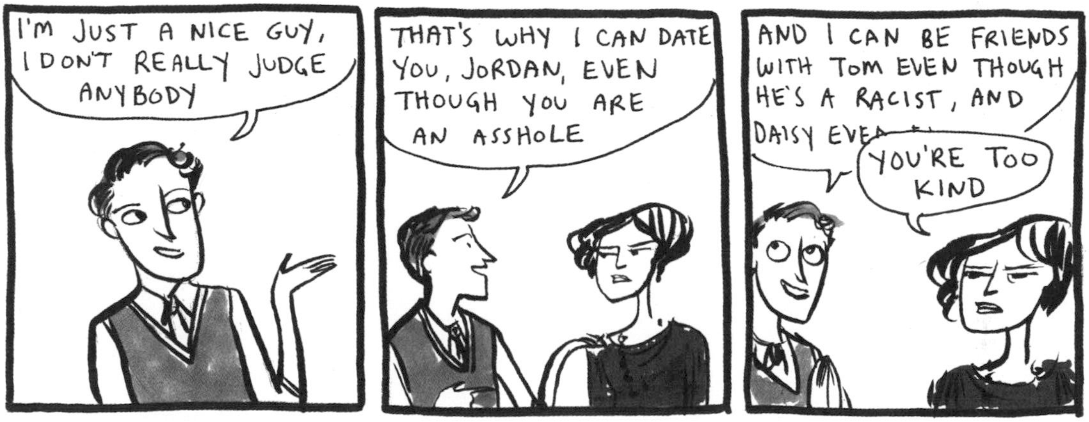
I'M JUST A NICE GUY, I DON'T REALLY JUDGE ANYBODY
THAT'S WHY I CAN DATE YOU, JORDAN, EVEN THOUGH YOU ARE AN ASSHOLE
AND I CAN BE FRIENDS WITH TOM EVEN THOUGH HE'S A RACIST, AND DAISY EVE
YOU'RE TOO KIND

JUST AS GOOD THE SECOND TIME

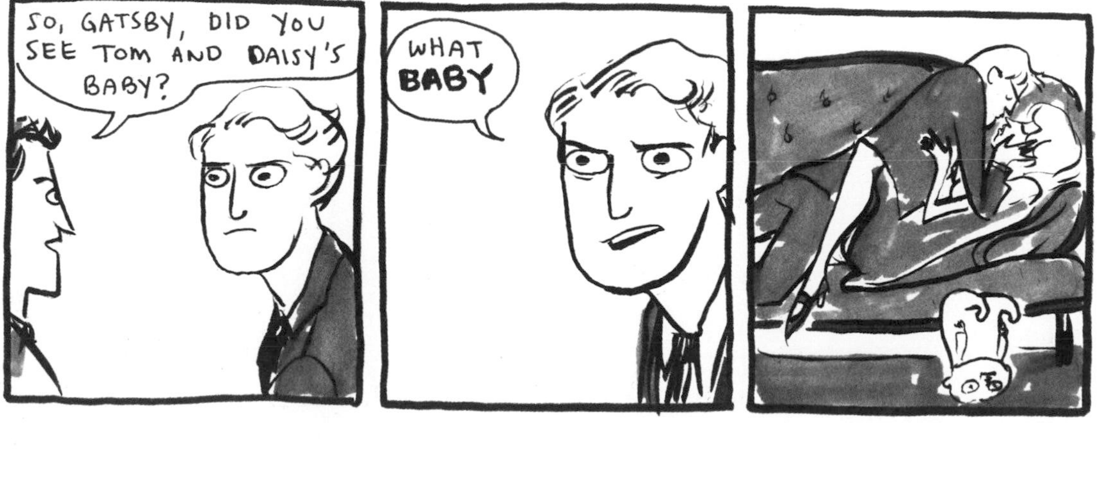
SO, GATSBY, DID YOU SEE TOM AND DAISY'S BABY?
WHAT BABY

RASKOLNIKOV

Ah, the disenchanted young people of today, letting the things they read go to their heads. Folly of youth! It's everything your father warned you about when you said you were getting a philosophy degree. Why couldn't you just get a trade in plumbing? Everyone needs a plumber sooner or later! Now you've gone and embarrassed yourself by killing a few people for your new principles. What on earth are we going to tell the neighbours?

IT'S SO HARD TO BE BETTER THAN EVERYONE
OH YOU NEEDY, RAGGED, DISGUSTING POOR PEOPLE
MAYBE I LOVE THEM
POOR OLD MAN
SPARE SO CHANG
NO!! MAYBE I HATE THEM
EFF OFF

THE AWFUL DEED
STUPID OLD WOMAN
THIS DOESN'T FEEL LIKE SILVER
BUT CAN I REALLY KILL HER?
NAPOLEON, HELP ME
ehh
SWEET AXE BRO, GONNA KILL SOMEONE?
NICE

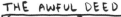

THROW THEM OFF THE TRAIL

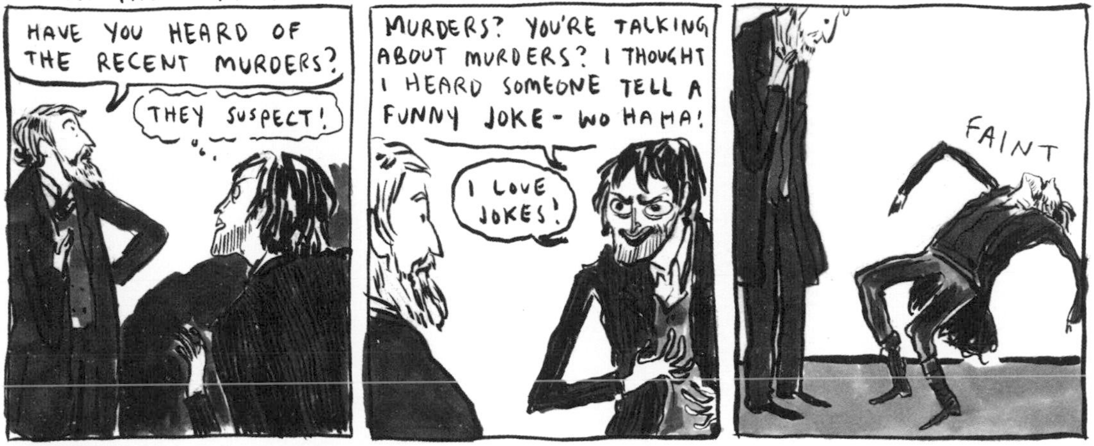
HAVE YOU HEARD OF THE RECENT MURDERS?
THEY SUSPECT!
MURDERS? YOU'RE TALKING ABOUT MURDERS? I THOUGHT I HEARD SOMEONE TELL A FUNNY JOKE - WO HAHA!
I LOVE JOKES!
FAINT

BLUNT SIDE OF THE AXE BUT OH WELL

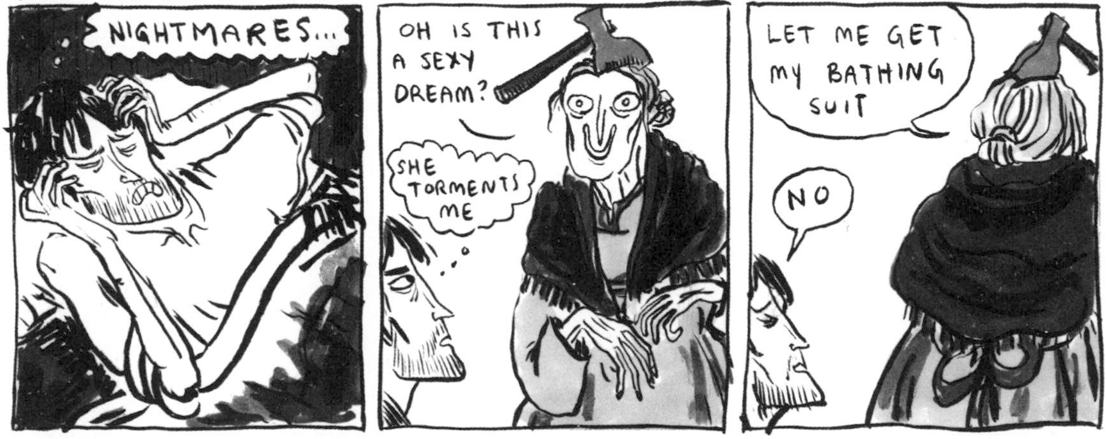
NIGHTMARES...
OH IS THIS A SEXY DREAM?
SHE TORMENTS ME
LET ME GET MY BATHING SUIT
NO

RAZUMIKHIN MY ONLY FRIEND

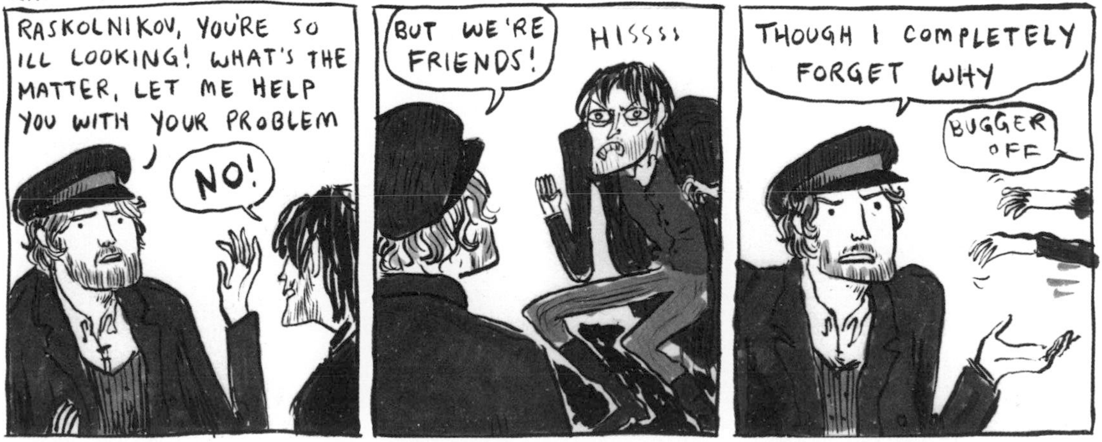
RASKOLNIKOV, YOU'RE SO ILL LOOKING! WHAT'S THE MATTER, LET ME HELP YOU WITH YOUR PROBLEM
NO!
BUT WE'RE FRIENDS!
HISSSS
THOUGH I COMPLETELY FORGET WHY
BUGGER OFF

GOREYS

Edward Gorey made many a nice book in his day and, on top of this, designed many a nice book cover. We're going to do a little exercise with some of them. You take a book, and then you guess what the story inside of it is based on the info you get from the cover. Because, you know, that's just how books work.

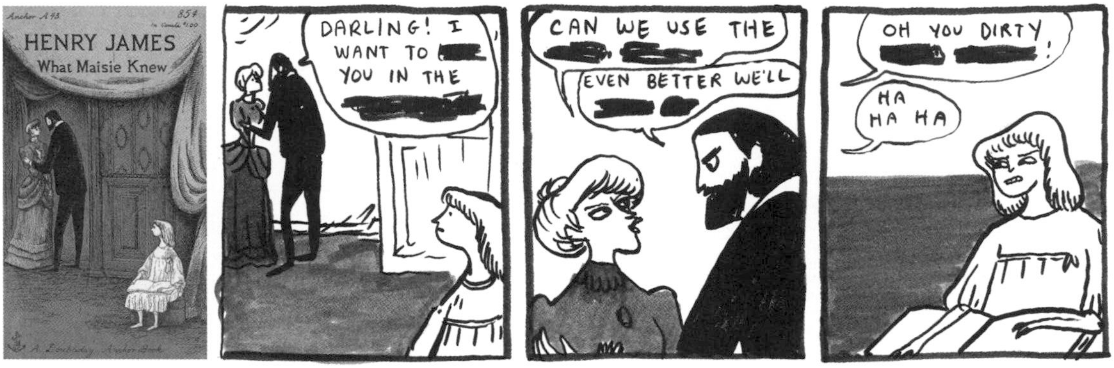
HENRY JAMES
What Maisie Knew
DARLING! I WANT TO [redacted] YOU IN THE [redacted]
CAN WE USE THE [redacted]
EVEN BETTER WE'LL [redacted]
OH YOU DIRTY [redacted]!
HA HA HA

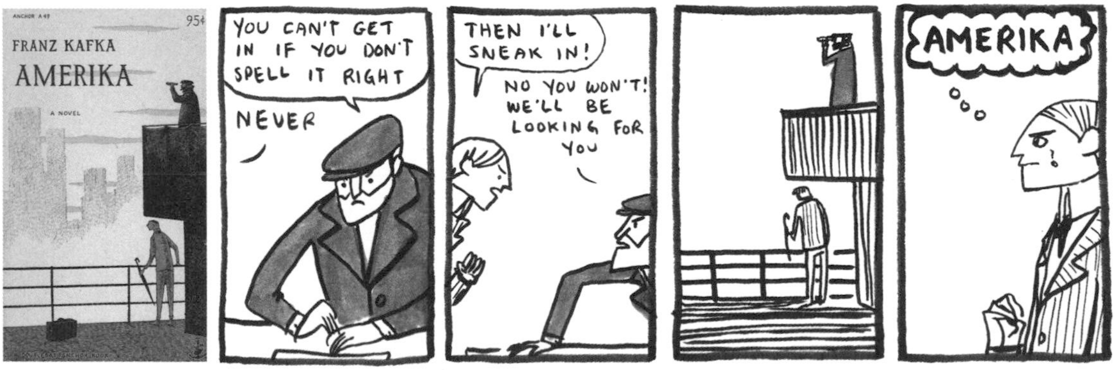
ANCHOR A49
95¢
FRANZ KAFKA
AMERIKA
A NOVEL
YOU CAN'T GET IN IF YOU DON'T SPELL IT RIGHT
NEVER
THEN I'LL SNEAK IN!
NO YOU WON'T! WE'LL BE LOOKING FOR YOU
AMERIKA

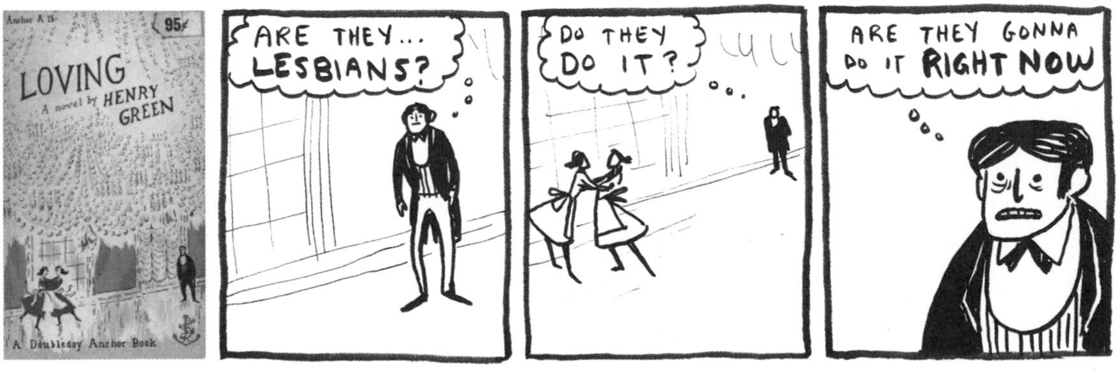
95¢
LOVING
A novel by HENRY GREEN
A Doubleday Anchor Book
ARE THEY... LESBIANS?
DO THEY DO IT?
ARE THEY GONNA DO IT RIGHT NOW

THE AUTOBIOGRAPHY OF WILLIAM BUTLER YEATS
WHEN WILLIAM BUTLER YEATS WAS BORN HE WAS A GIANT BIRD!!
CRAAA
EVERYONE WAS LIKE WHOAA BUT THEN HE WROTE SOME POEMS
CRAAAH
THESE ARE PRETTY GOOD
THE WANDERER
A NOVEL BY ALAIN-FOURNIER
THERE I CAME UPON AN ENCHANTED WOOD
AND THE MAGICAL SLUTS OF THE FOREST
HELLO
HI
OH WHAT AN ADVENTU WE
GRANDPA'S STORIES ARE NOT TO BE LISTENED TO
TRUE TALES FROM THE ANNALS OF CRIME AND RASCALITY BY ST. CLAIR McKELWAY
COME LET ME TELL YOU A TALE OF CRIME AND RASCALITY
COME ... CLOSER
MY WALLET!
Anchor A-210
Selections from the Writings of KIERKEGAARD
Translated by Lee M. Hollander
A Doubleday Anchor Book
KIERKEGAARD

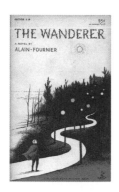

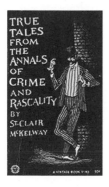

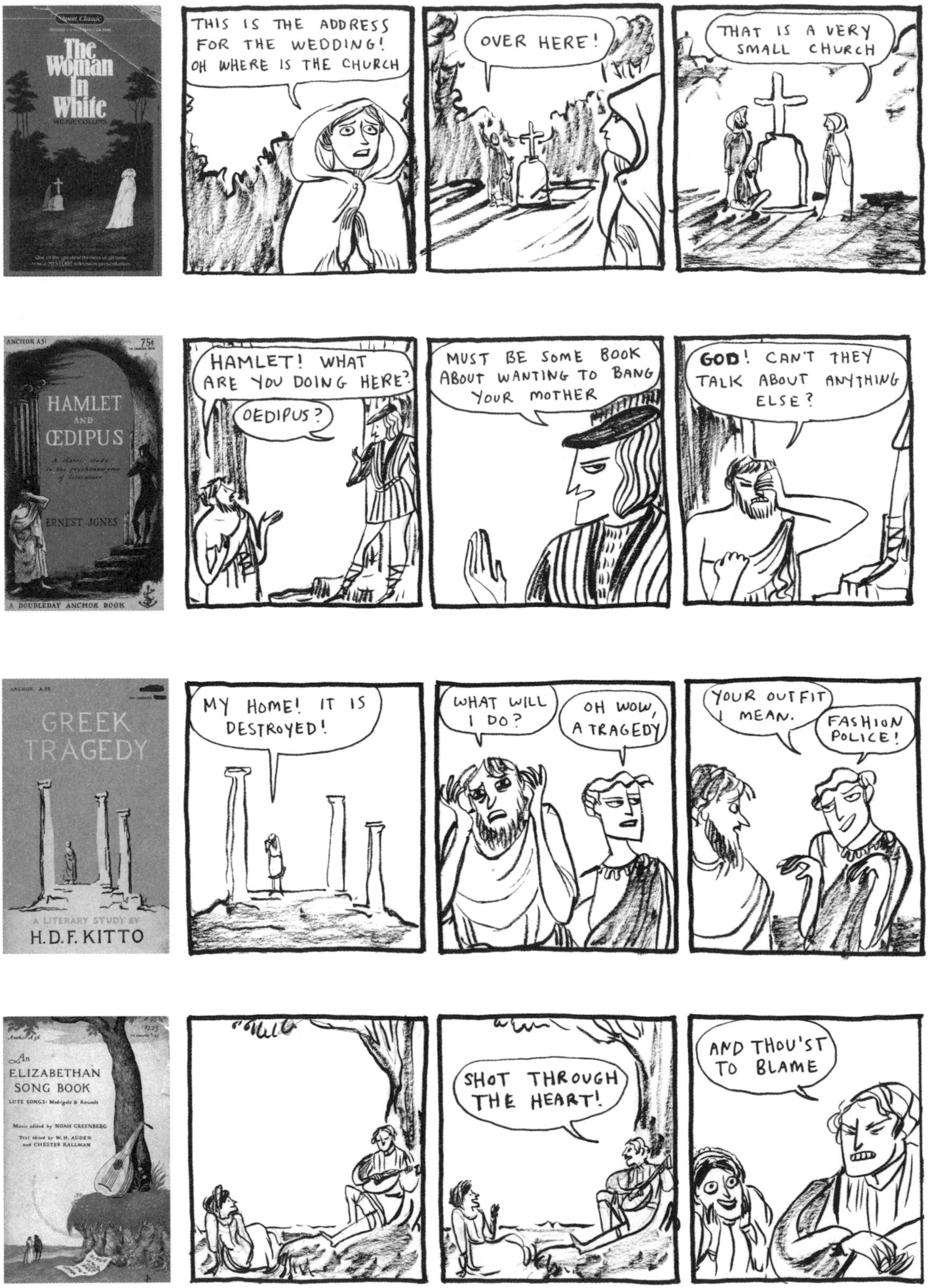
Signet Classic
The Woman In White
WILKIE COLLINS
THIS IS THE ADDRESS FOR THE WEDDING! OH WHERE IS THE CHURCH
OVER HERE!
THAT IS A VERY SMALL CHURCH
ANCHOR A31
75¢
HAMLET AND ŒDIPUS
ERNEST JONES
A DOUBLEDAY ANCHOR BOOK
HAMLET! WHAT ARE YOU DOING HERE?
OEDIPUS?
MUST BE SOME BOOK ABOUT WANTING TO BANG YOUR MOTHER
GOD! CAN'T THEY TALK ABOUT ANYTHING ELSE?
ANCHOR A38
GREEK TRAGEDY
A LITERARY STUDY BY
H.D.F. KITTO
MY HOME! IT IS DESTROYED!
WHAT WILL I DO?
OH WOW, A TRAGEDY
YOUR OUTFIT I MEAN.
FASHION POLICE!
An ELIZABETHAN SONG BOOK
LUTE SONGS: Madrigals & Rounds
Music edited by NOAH GREENBERG
Text edited by W. H. AUDEN and CHESTER KALLMAN
SHOT THROUGH THE HEART!
AND THOU'ST TO BLAME

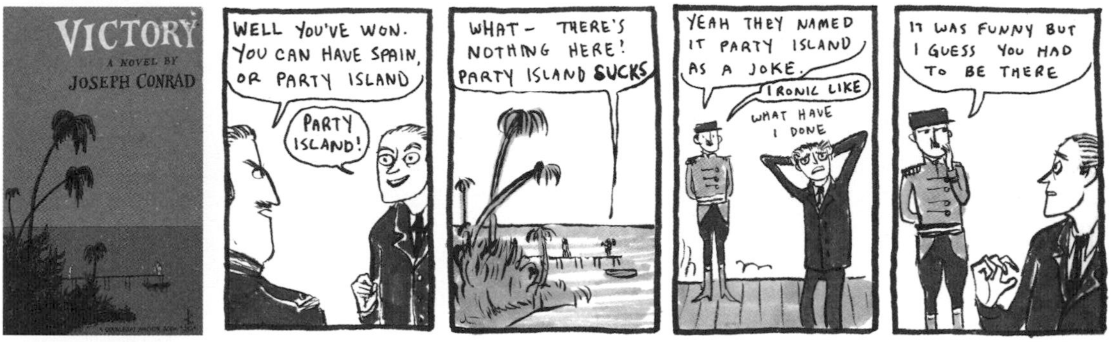
VICTORY
A NOVEL BY
JOSEPH CONRAD
WELL YOU'VE WON. YOU CAN HAVE SPAIN, OR PARTY ISLAND
PARTY ISLAND!
WHAT - THERE'S NOTHING HERE! PARTY ISLAND SUCKS
YEAH THEY NAMED IT PARTY ISLAND AS A JOKE.
IRONIC LIKE
WHAT HAVE I DONE
IT WAS FUNNY BUT I GUESS YOU HAD TO BE THERE

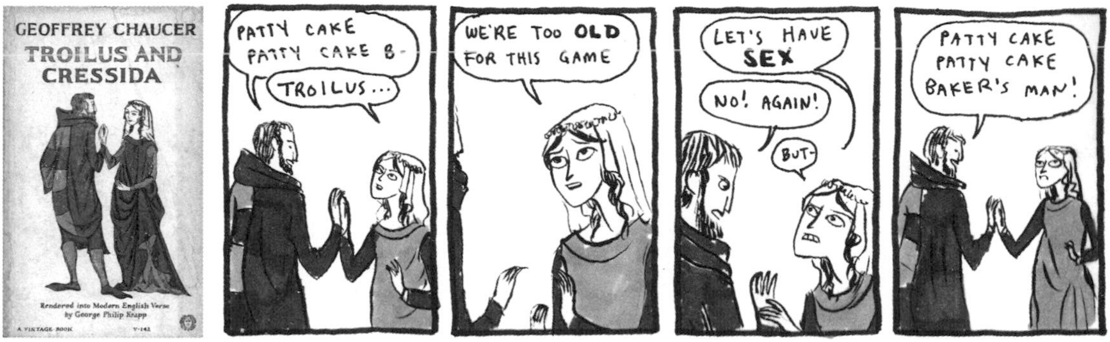
GEOFFREY CHAUCER
TROILUS AND CRESSIDA
Rendered into Modern English Verse by George Philip Krapp
A VINTAGE BOOK
V-142
PATTY CAKE PATTY CAKE B-
TROILUS...
WE'RE TOO OLD FOR THIS GAME
LET'S HAVE SEX
NO! AGAIN!
BUT-
PATTY CAKE PATTY CAKE BAKER'S MAN!

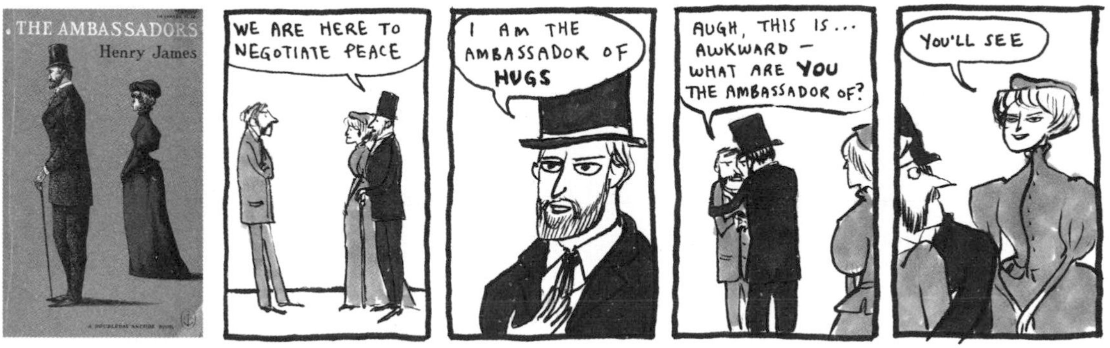
THE AMBASSADORS
Henry James
WE ARE HERE TO NEGOTIATE PEACE
I AM THE AMBASSADOR OF HUGS
AUGH, THIS IS... AWKWARD - WHAT ARE YOU THE AMBASSADOR OF?
YOU'LL SEE

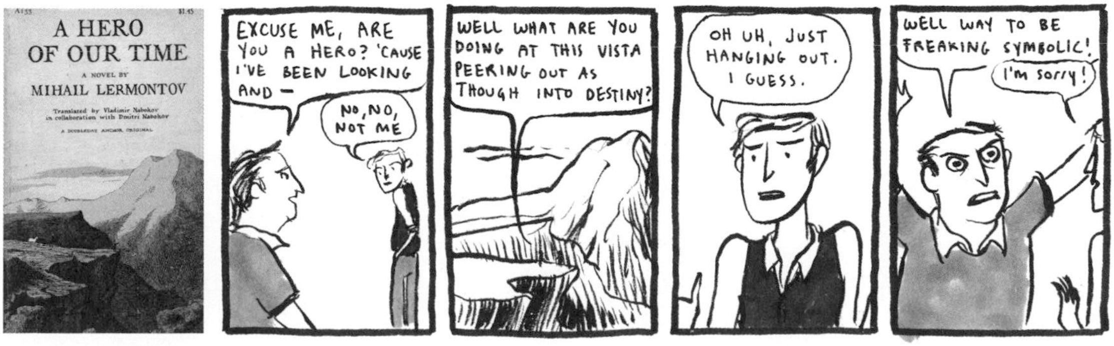
A HERO OF OUR TIME
A NOVEL BY
MIHAIL LERMONTOV
Translated by Vladimir Nabokov in collaboration with Dmitri Nabokov
EXCUSE ME, ARE YOU A HERO? 'CAUSE I'VE BEEN LOOKING AND -
NO, NO, NOT ME
WELL WHAT ARE YOU DOING AT THIS VISTA PEERING OUT AS THOUGH INTO DESTINY?
OH UH, JUST HANGING OUT. I GUESS.
WELL WAY TO BE FREAKING SYMBOLIC!
I'M SORRY!

JANE EYRE

What the heck is happening out on those moors? Is it like when you're out in your boat for too long and you start to lose it, and you think you see a beautiful mermaid, but it's really a manatee? Then you've made out with it and you don't know why? We only want Jane to be happy though, because she had a pretty rough go in life and she's a smart cookie. We'll let her have Mr. Rochester because she loves him, even though he might be a manatee.

GOOD TO BE UGLY

YOU EXAMINE ME, MISS EYRE, DO YOU THINK ME HANDSOME?

NO SIR

WELL GOOD! BECAUSE YOU'RE UGLY TOO

GOOD THEN WE ARE BOTH UGLY

THE SOLUTION

SO I LOCKED MY WIFE IN THE ATTIC AND SLEPT MY WAY THROUGH EUROPE SPENDING HER FORTUNE

IT WAS HARD. IT WAS I WHO SUFFERED

JANE DO YOU THINK I HAD A **CHOICE**

DO YOU?

THEN I FOUND THIS SELF-HELP BOOK

BIGAMY ~THE~ ANSWER TO ALL YOUR PROBLEMS

WHAT WERE YOU THINKING

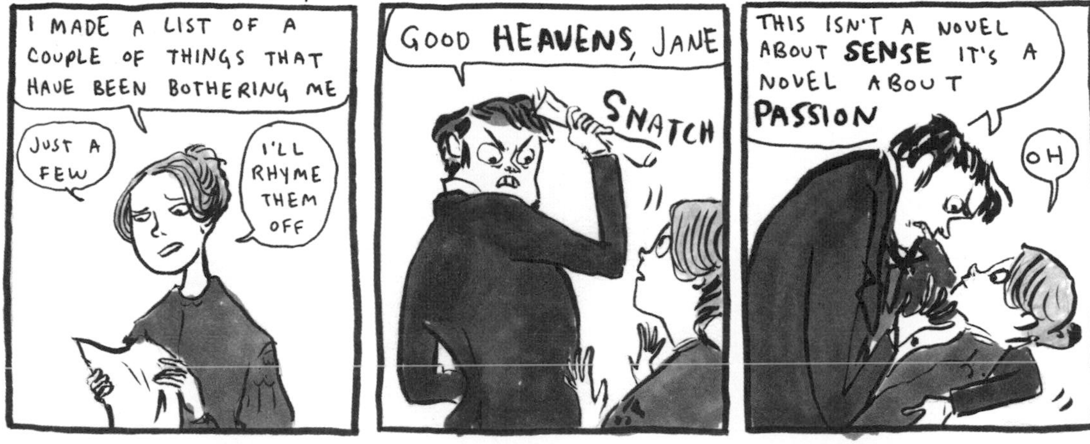
I MADE A LIST OF A COUPLE OF THINGS THAT HAVE BEEN BOTHERING ME
JUST A FEW
I'LL RHYME THEM OFF
GOOD HEAVENS, JANE
SNATCH
THIS ISN'T A NOVEL ABOUT SENSE IT'S A NOVEL ABOUT PASSION
OH

TRUEST DECLARATION

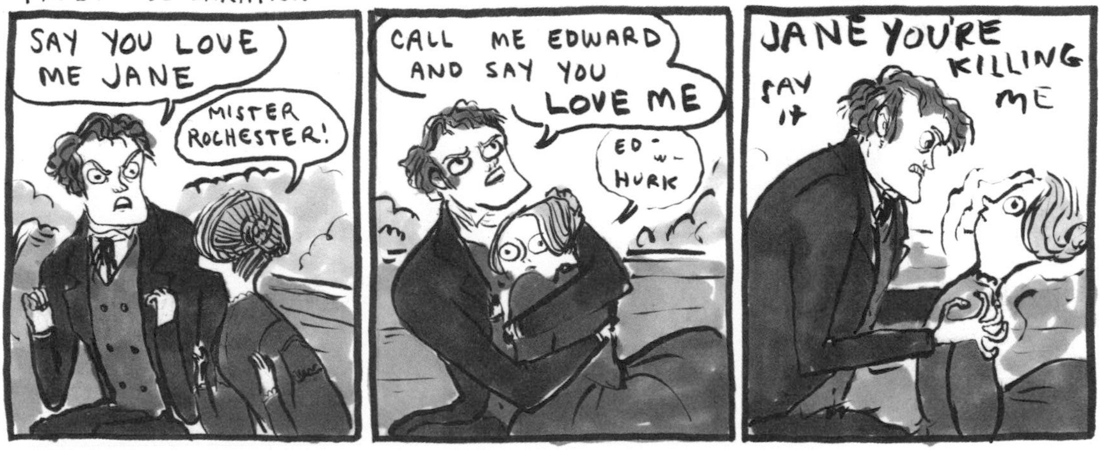
SAY YOU LOVE ME JANE
MISTER ROCHESTER!
CALL ME EDWARD AND SAY YOU LOVE ME
ED-W-HURK
JANE YOU'RE KILLING ME
SAY IT

JEALOUSY

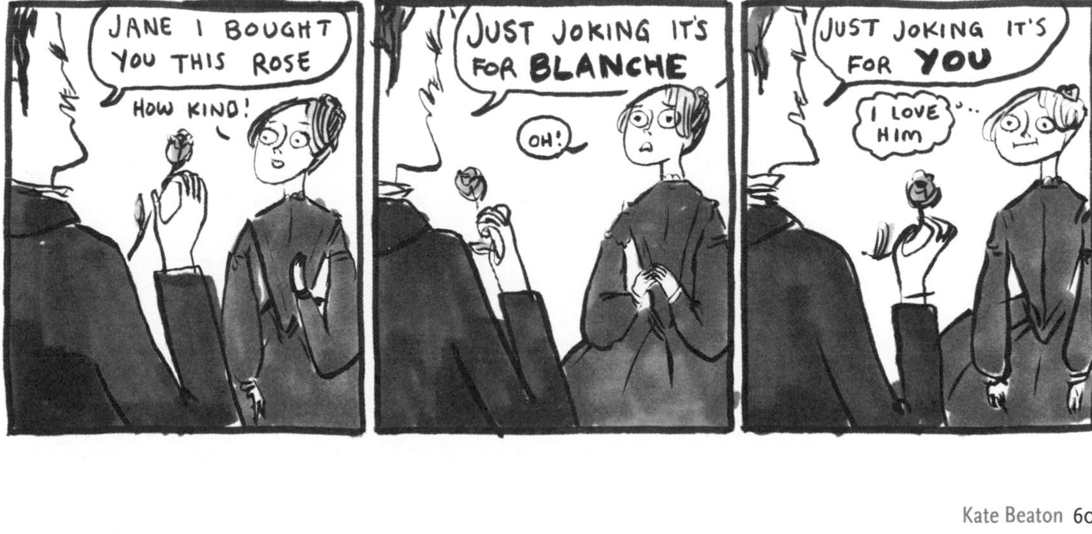
JANE I BOUGHT YOU THIS ROSE
HOW KIND!
JUST JOKING IT'S FOR BLANCHE
OH!
JUST JOKING IT'S FOR YOU
I LOVE HIM

the osteopath

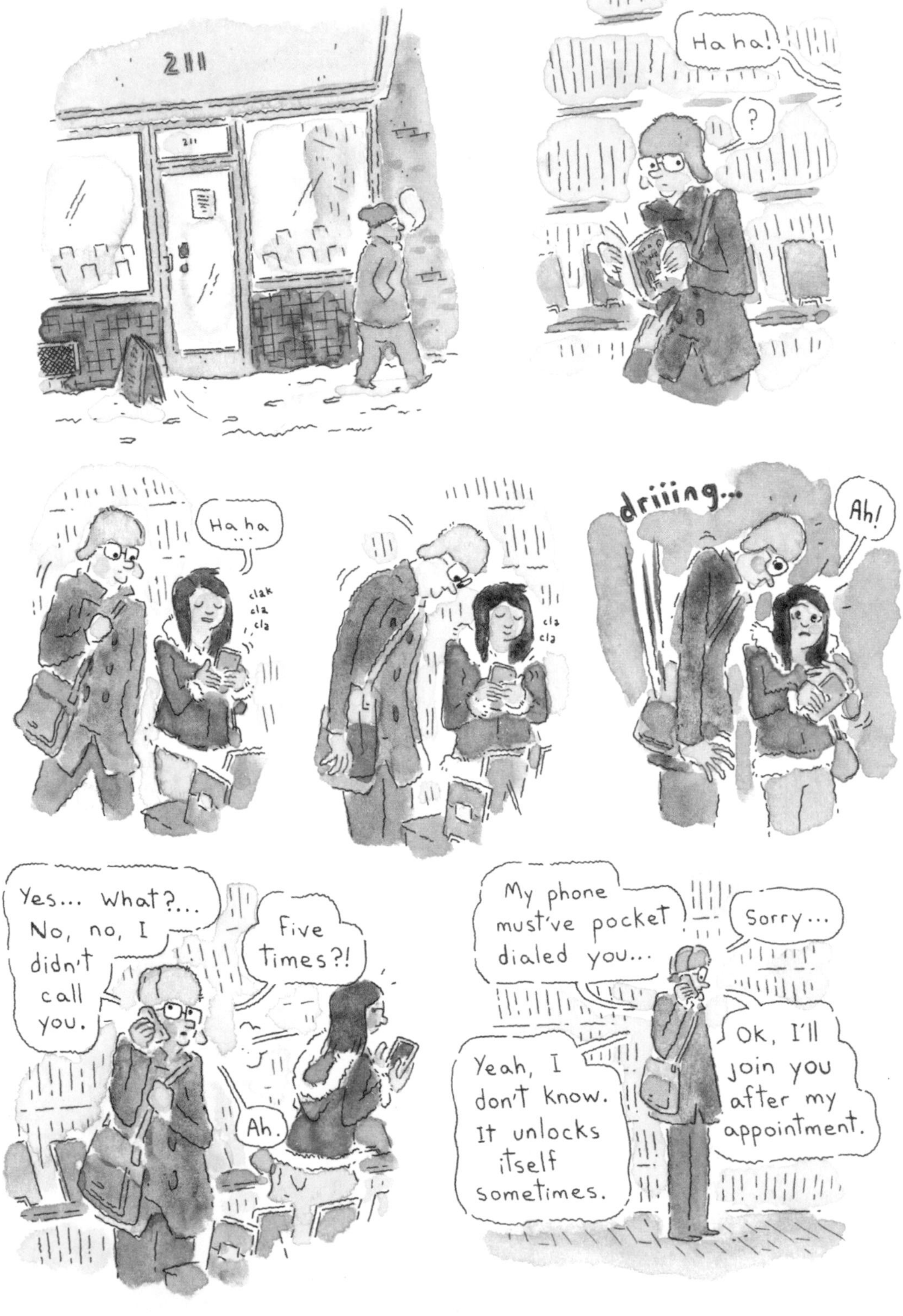

211
211
Ha ha!
?
Ha ha ...
clak cla cla
cla cla
driiing...
Ah!
Yes... What?... No, no, I didn't call you.
Five times?!
Ah.
My phone must've pocket dialed you...
Sorry...
Yeah, I don't know. It unlocks itself sometimes.
Ok, I'll join you after my appointment.

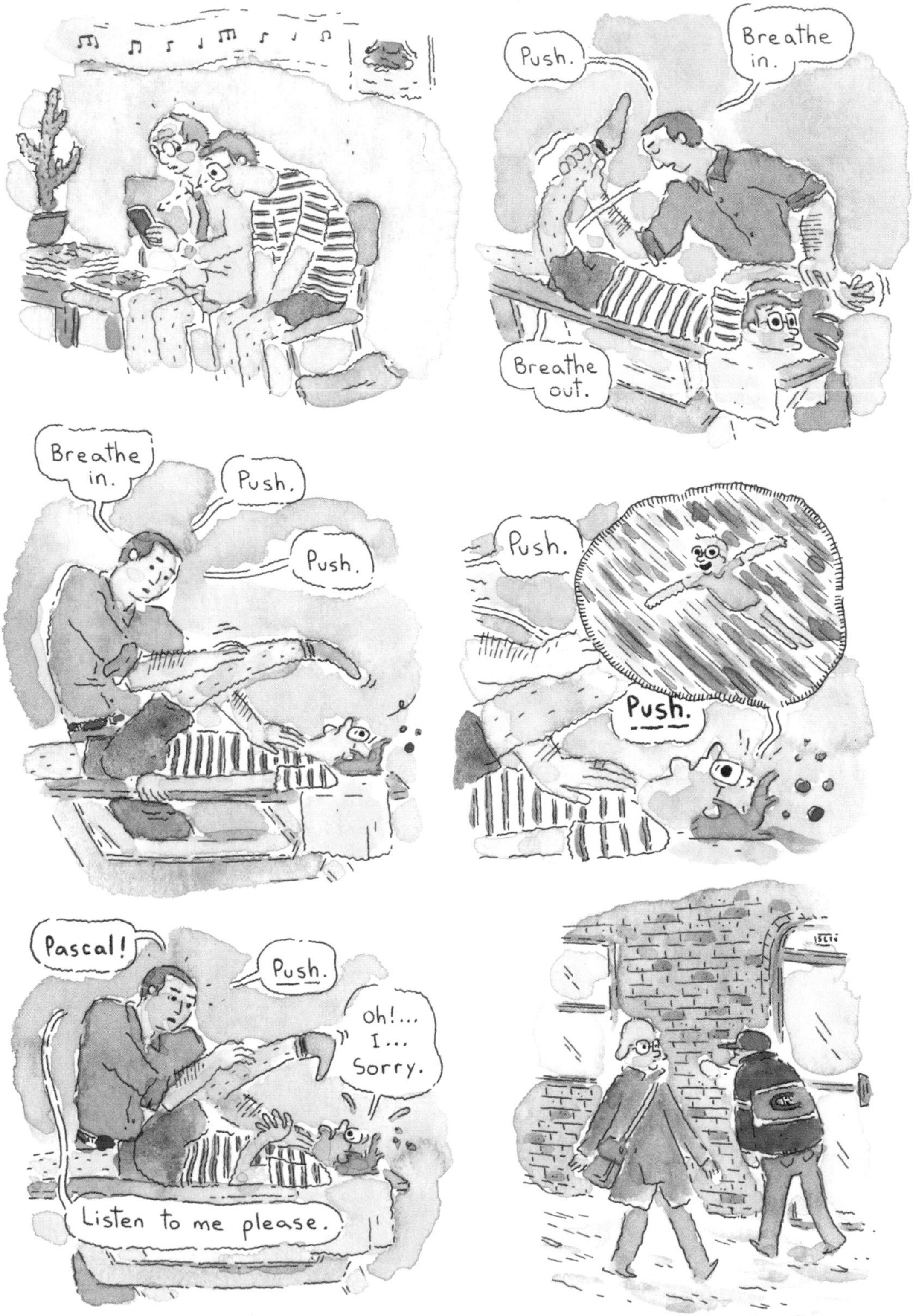
Push.
Breathe in.
Breathe out.
Breathe in.
Push.
Push.
Push.
Push.
Pascal!
Push.
Oh!... I... Sorry.
Listen to me please.

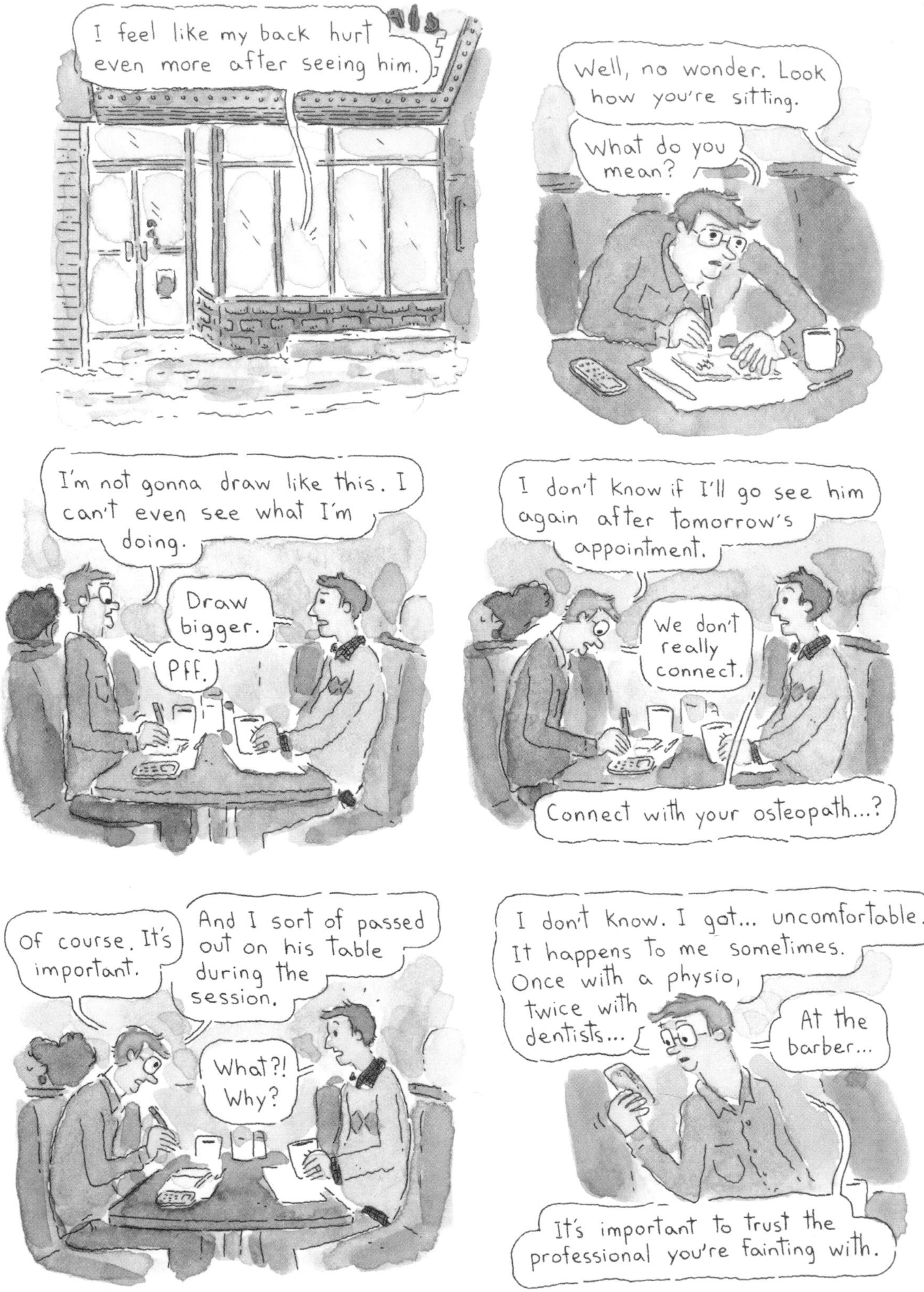
I feel like my back hurt even more after seeing him.
Well, no wonder. Look how you're sitting.
What do you mean?
I'm not gonna draw like this. I can't even see what I'm doing.
Draw bigger.
Pff.
I don't know if I'll go see him again after tomorrow's appointment.
We don't really connect.
Connect with your osteopath...?
Of course. It's important.
And I sort of passed out on his table during the session.
What?! Why?
I don't know. I got... uncomfortable. It happens to me sometimes. Once with a physio, twice with dentists...
At the barber...
It's important to trust the professional you're fainting with.

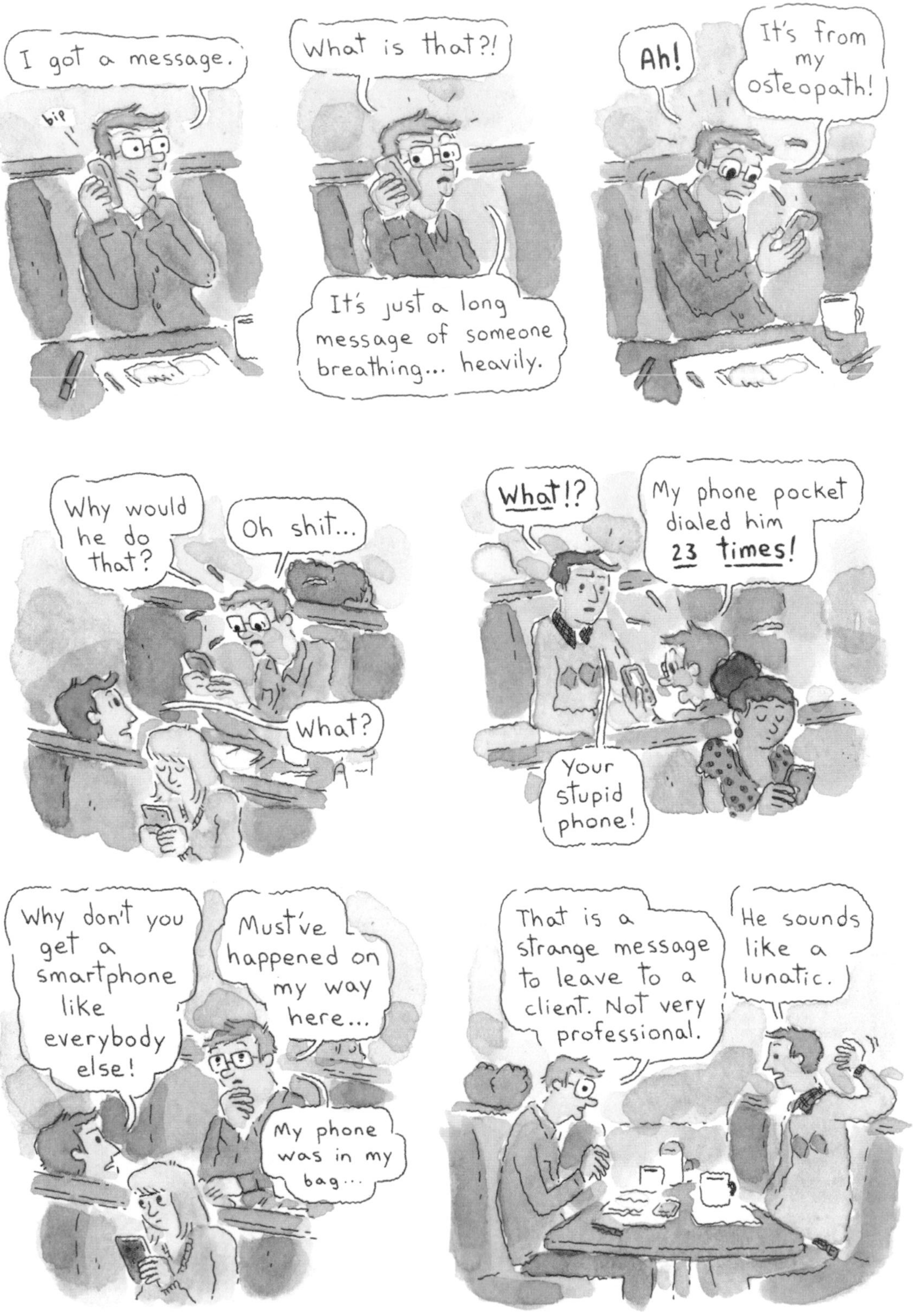

bip
I got a message.
What is that?!
It's just a long message of someone breathing... heavily.
Ah!
It's from my osteopath!
Why would he do that?
Oh shit...
What?
What!?
My phone pocket dialed him 23 times!
Your stupid phone!
Why don't you get a smartphone like everybody else!
Must've happened on my way here...
My phone was in my bag...
That is a strange message to leave to a client. Not very professional.
He sounds like a lunatic.

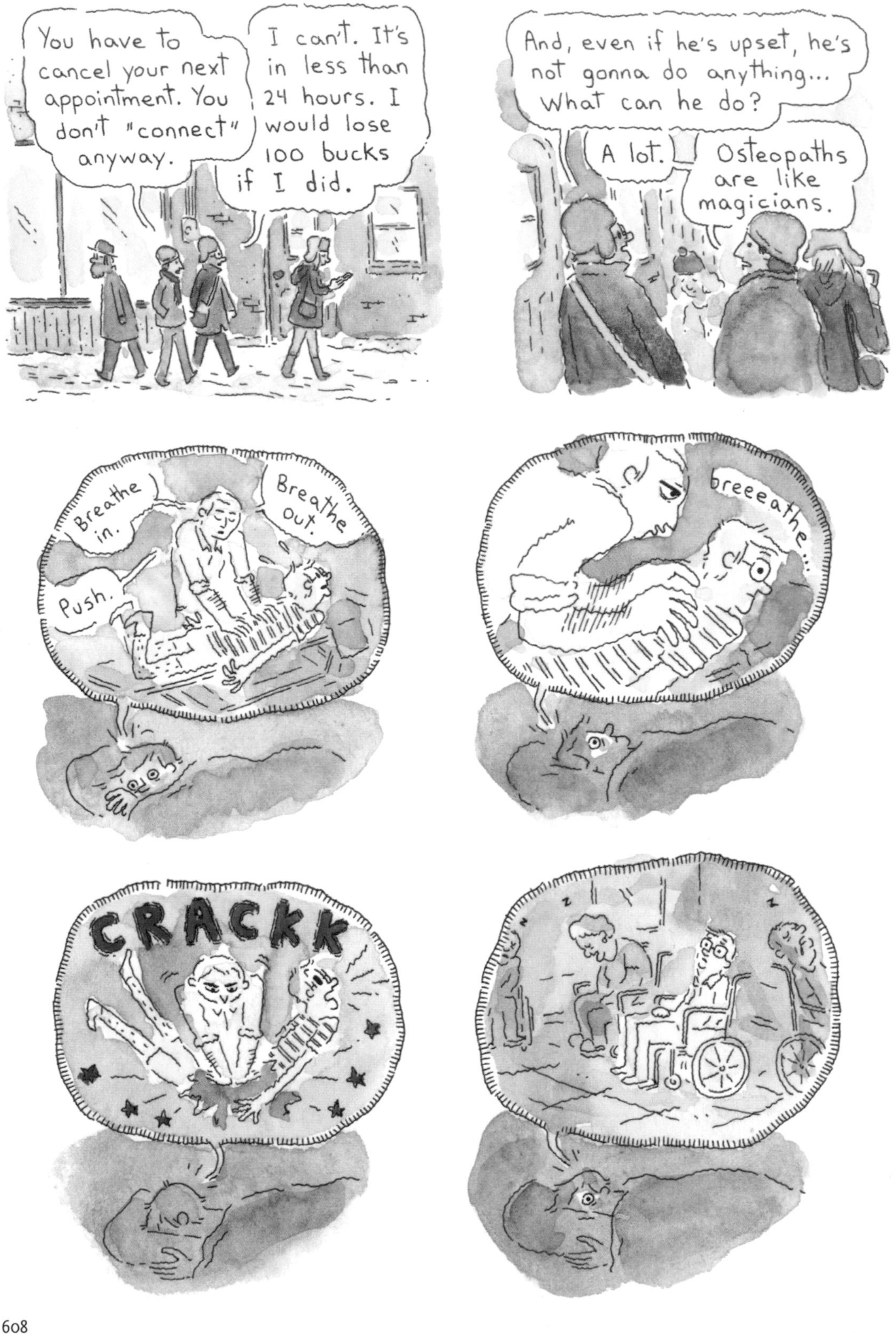
You have to cancel your next appointment. You don't "connect" anyway.
I can't. It's in less than 24 hours. I would lose 100 bucks if I did.
And, even if he's upset, he's not gonna do anything... What can he do?
A lot.
Osteopaths are like magicians.
Breathe in.
Breathe out.
Push.
breeeathe...
CRACKK

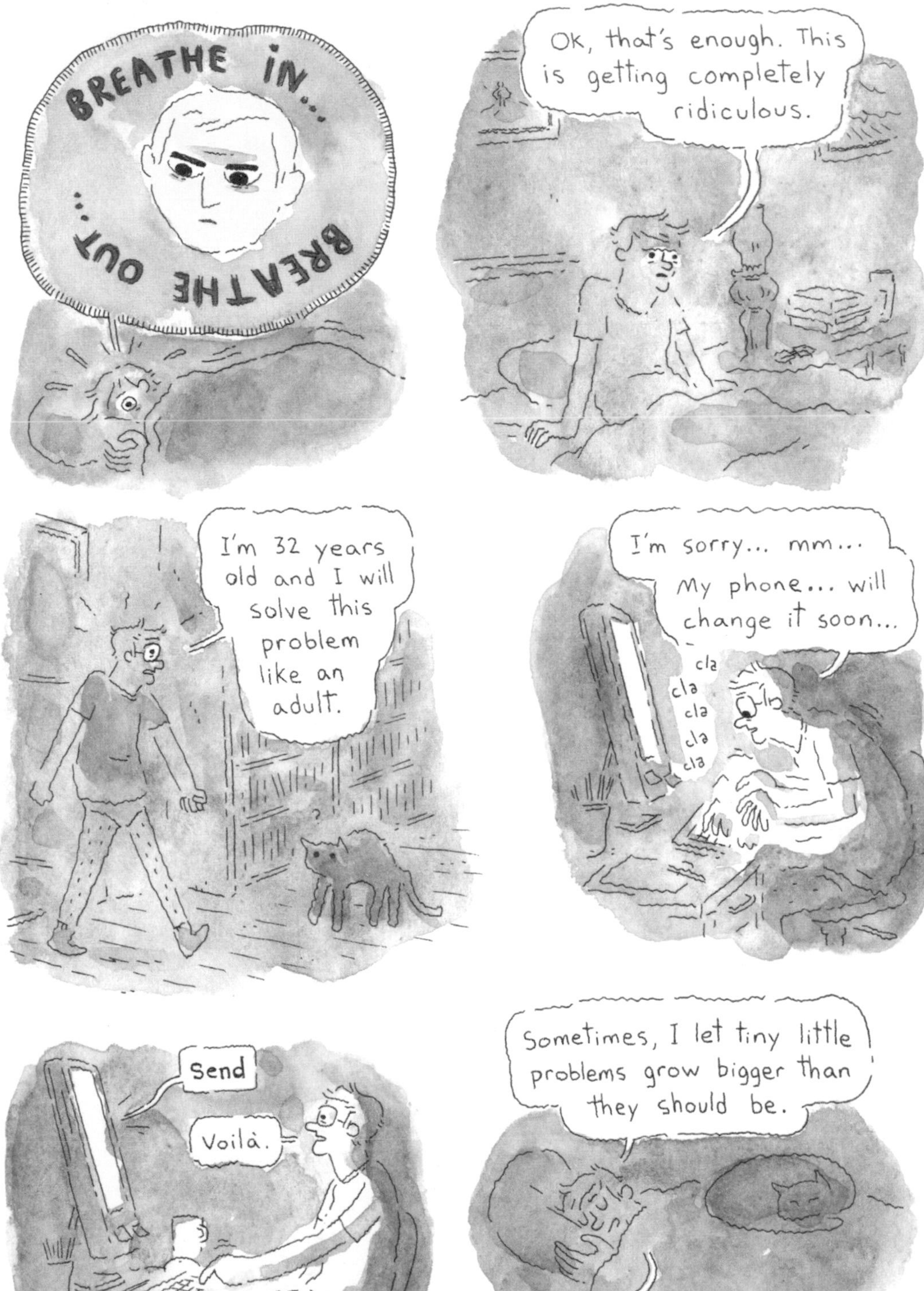
BREATHE IN...
...BREATHE OUT...
Ok, that's enough. This is getting completely ridiculous.
I'm 32 years old and I will solve this problem like an adult.
I'm sorry... mm... My phone... will change it soon...
cla cla cla cla cla
Send
Voilà.
Sometimes, I let tiny little problems grow bigger than they should be.
It's just 23 stupid pocket dialed phone calls. Who cares!

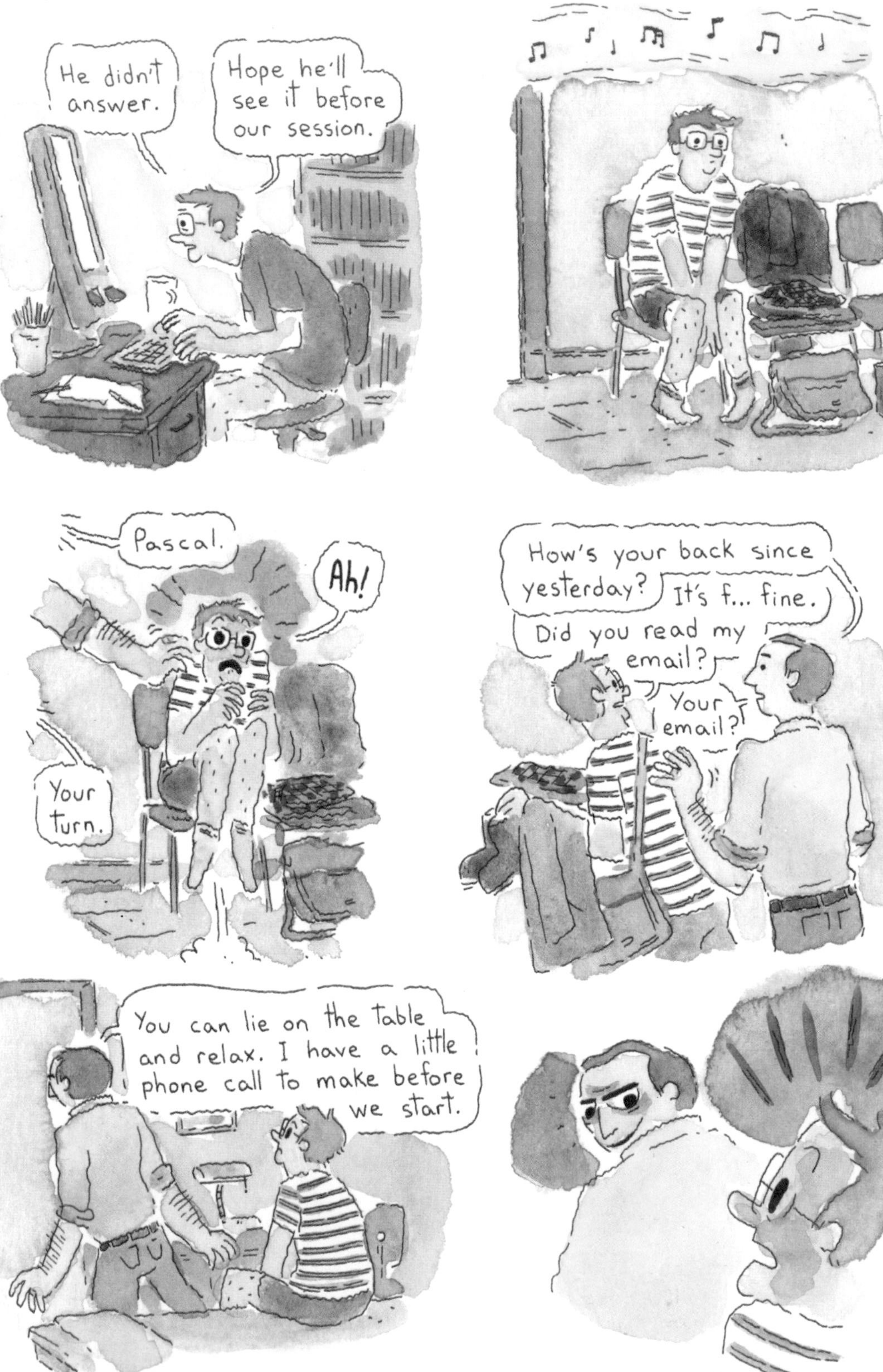
He didn't answer.
Hope he'll see it before our session.
Pascal.
Ah!
Your turn.
How's your back since yesterday?
It's f... fine.
Did you read my email?
Your email?
You can lie on the table and relax. I have a little phone call to make before we start.

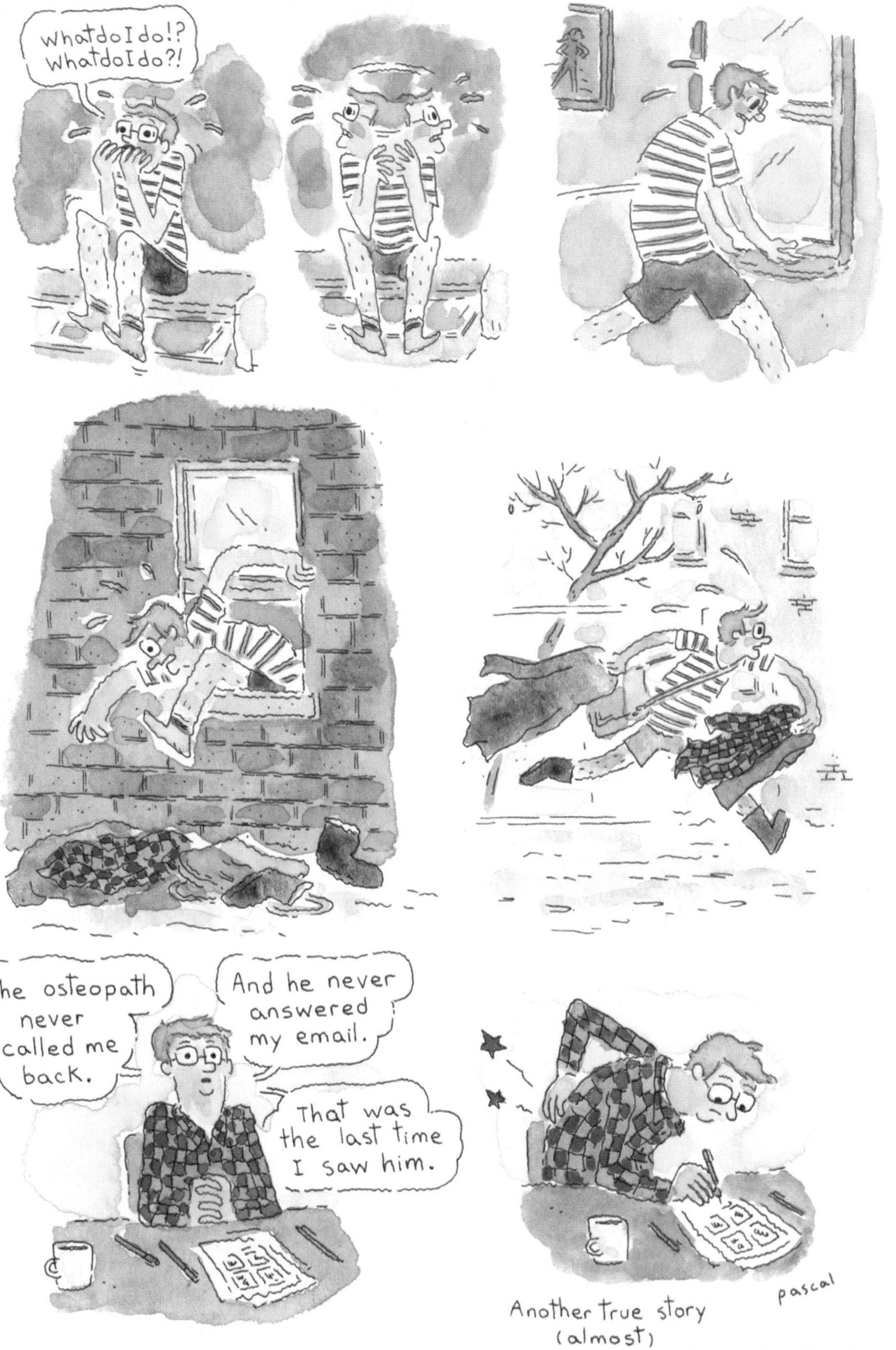
WhatdoIdo!? WhatdoIdo?!
The osteopath never called me back.
And he never answered my email.
That was the last time I saw him.
pascal
Another true story (almost)

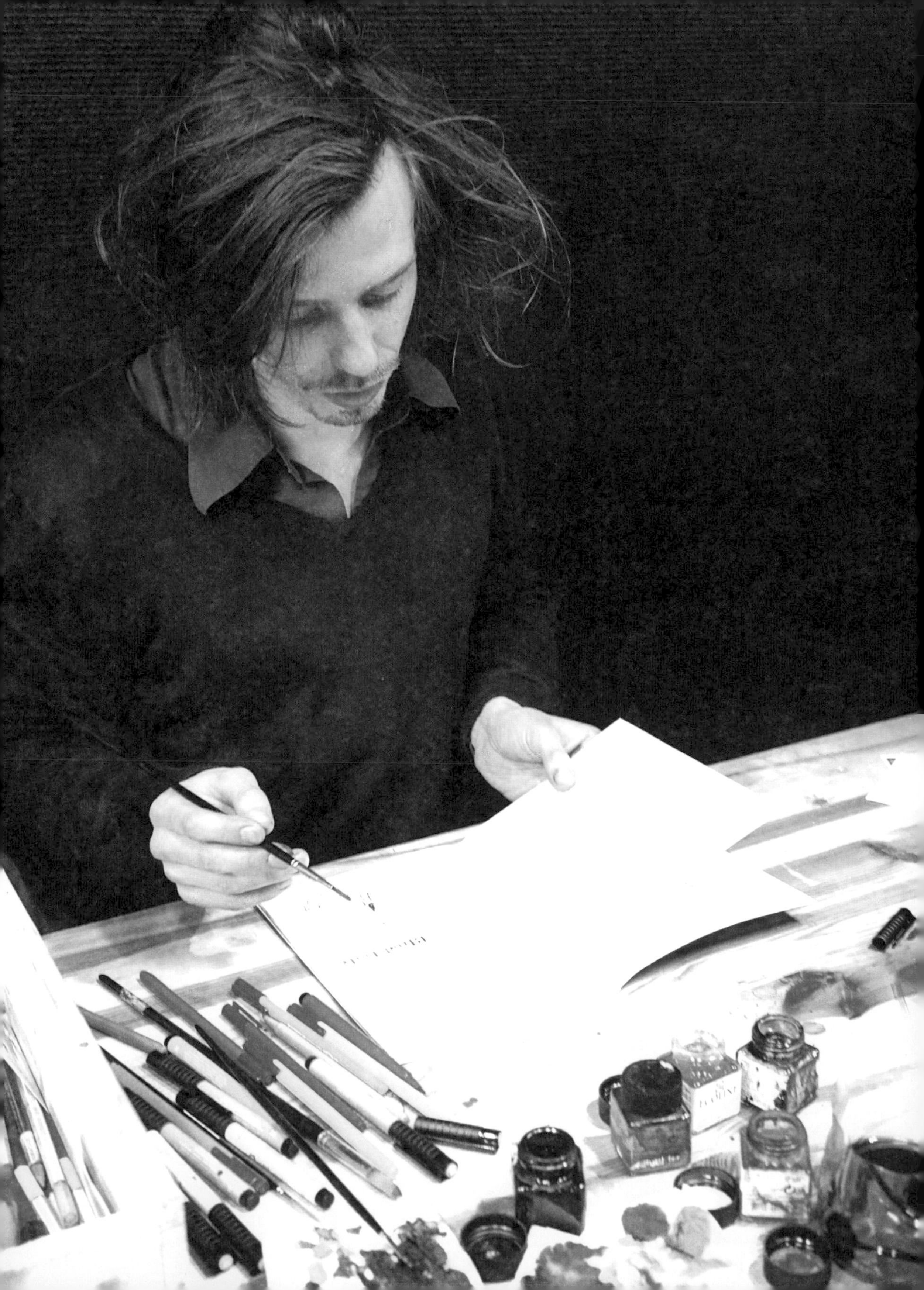

Brecht Evens is fluent in comics. It's like he breathes his paintings onto the page. His pacing feels effortless, his characters naive in just the right way, or full of themselves in equal parts.

When *The Wrong Place* came out, I was so fascinated by it that I scoured the web to figure out where this man had come from. He wasn't much older than me. How had he possibly made this thing? Did he study comics, or do Belgian children simply spring forth with an innate understanding of the medium? I had to know, but I didn't have to dig very deep. Ever the gentleman, Brecht had left a timeline of past work up on his website. There I discovered, my god, he used to draw in black and white. He had an awkward high-fantasy comics phase. He even had an awkward stoner comics phase! His early work looked nothing like his current stuff, but here was proof that he had drawn his ass off, learning the craft inside out. Damn. There was a lot of work ahead of me. I'd never even drawn a stoner comic.

Brecht has the fluency to which I aspire. Here is an artist who takes playfulness seriously, who I doubt will ever stop exploring. I feel privileged to ride along. Privileged, awestruck, and still more than a little jealous.

***—Sophie Yanow, cartoonist of* War of Streets and Houses**

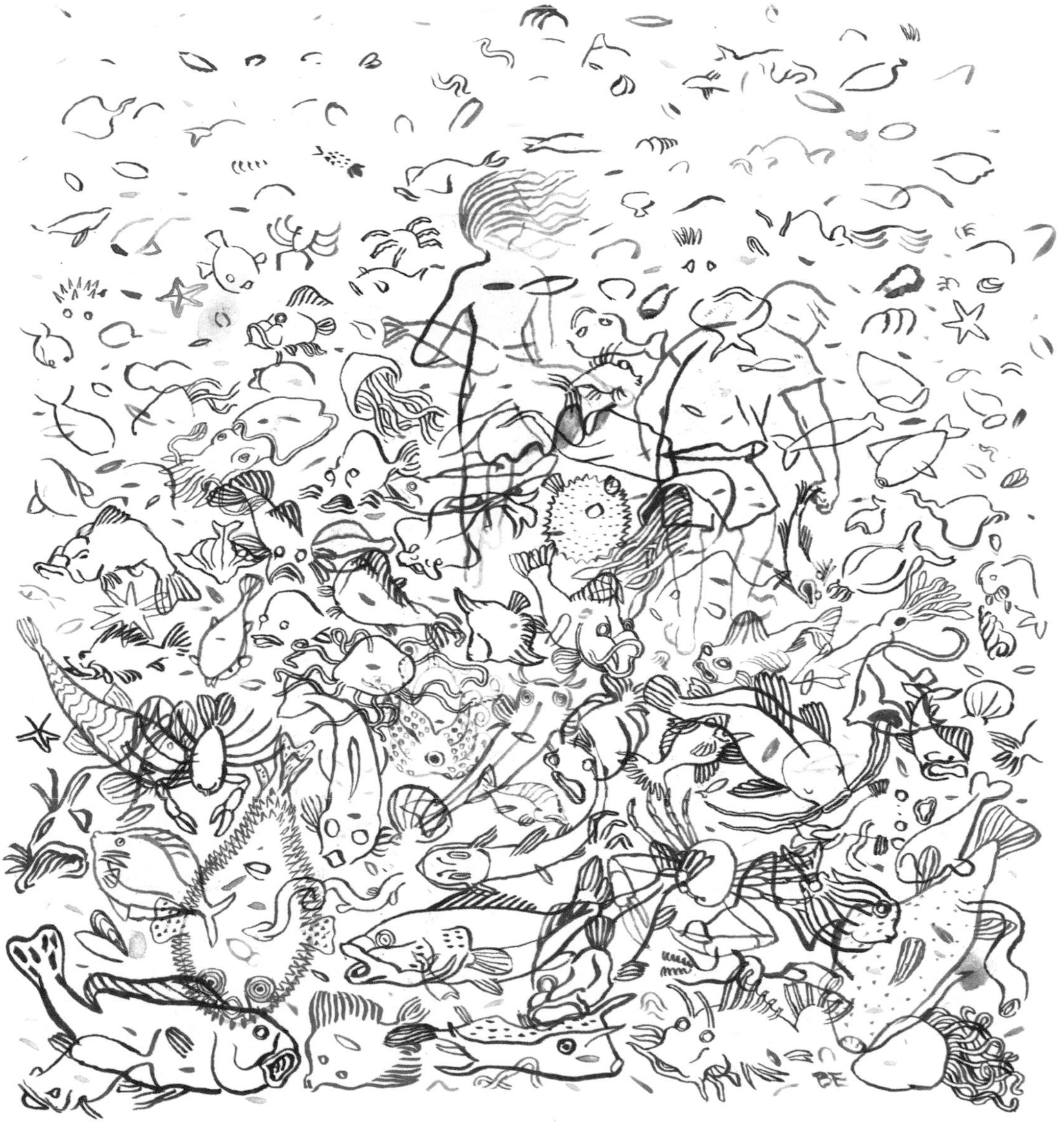

(Left) Brecht Evens in Angoulême (2013).

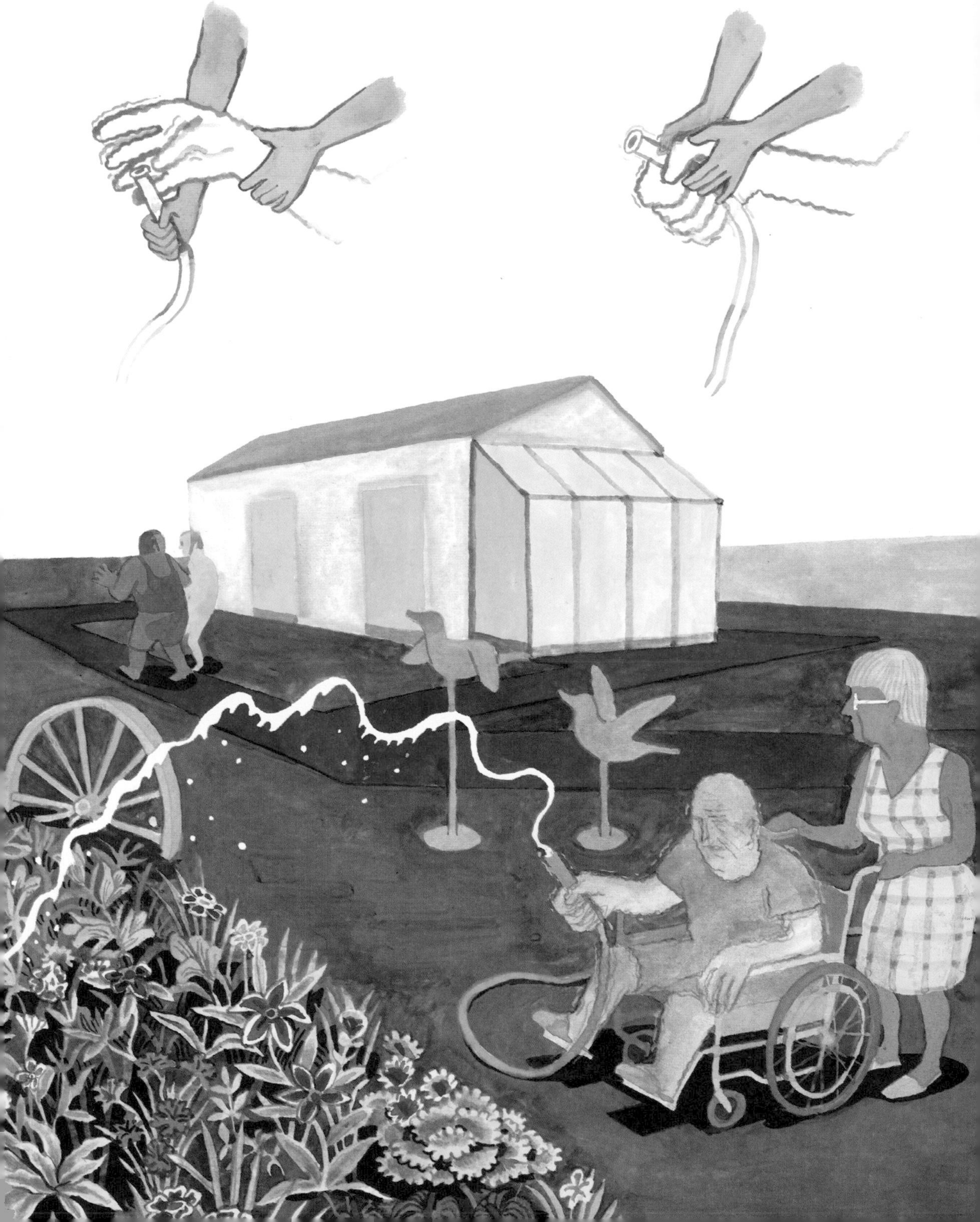

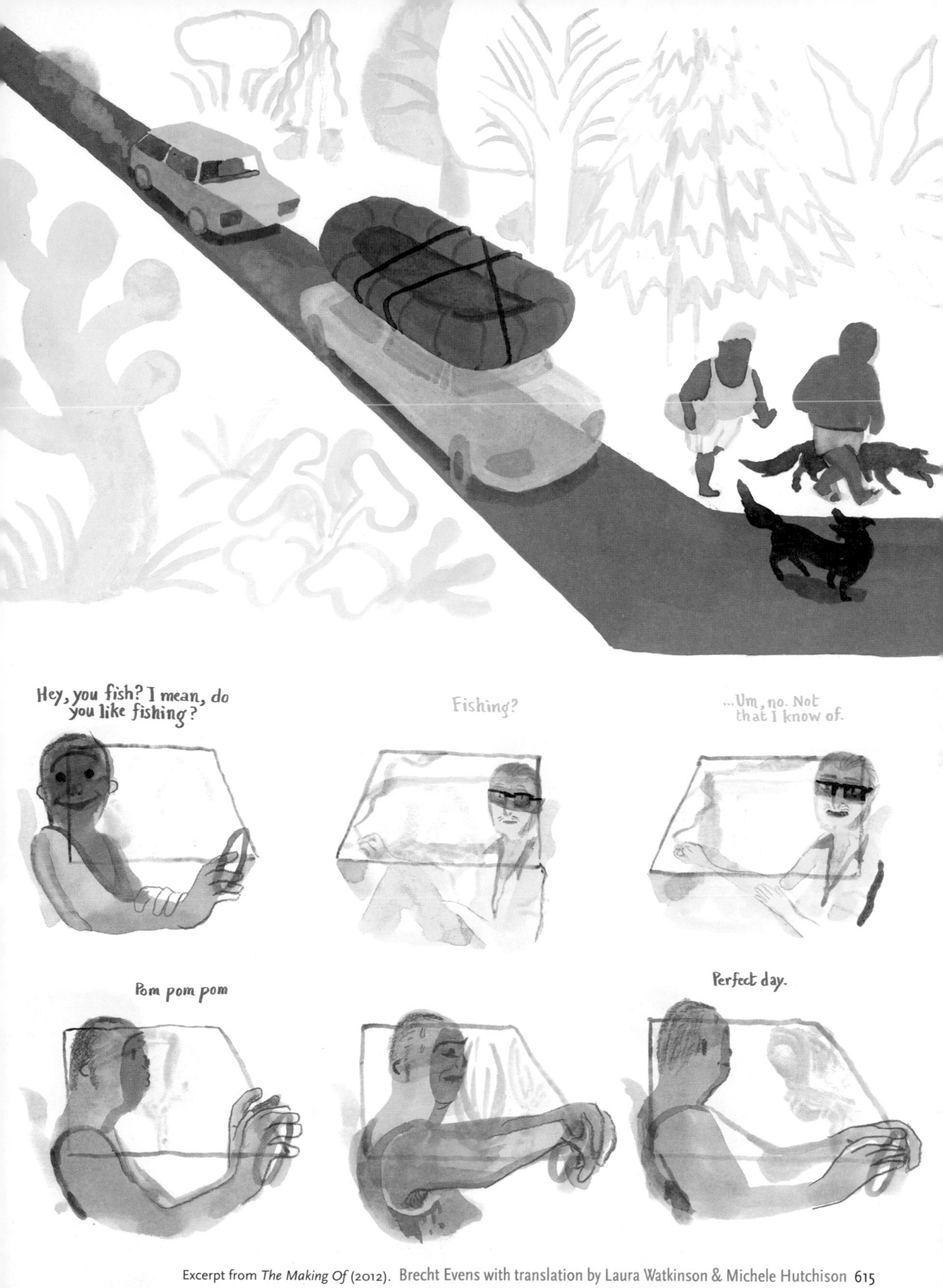
Hey, you fish? I mean, do you like fishing?
Fishing?
...Um, no. Not that I know of.
Pom pom pom
Perfect day.

Excerpt from *The Making Of* (2012). Brecht Evens with translation by Laura Watkinson & Michele Hutchison

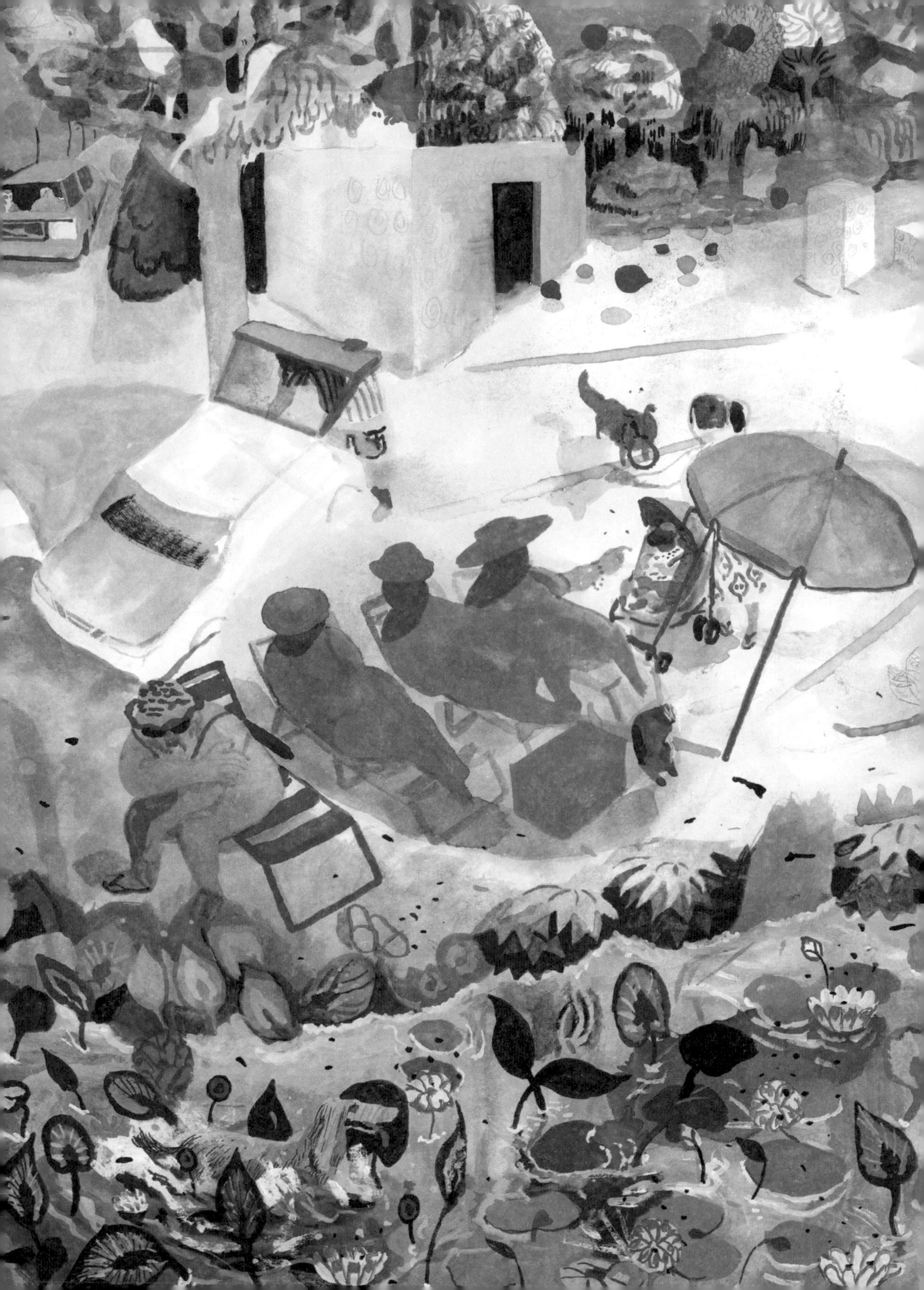

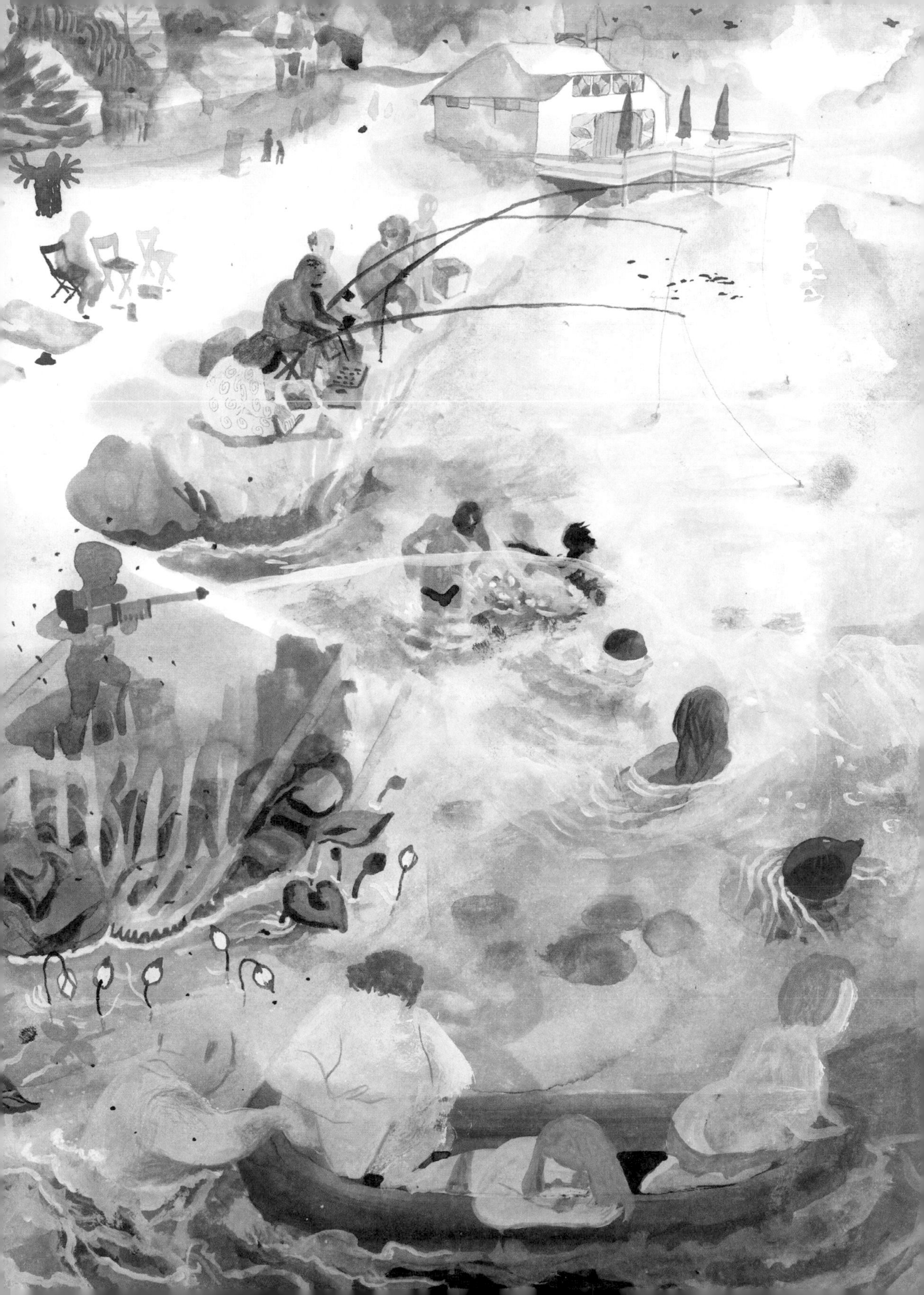

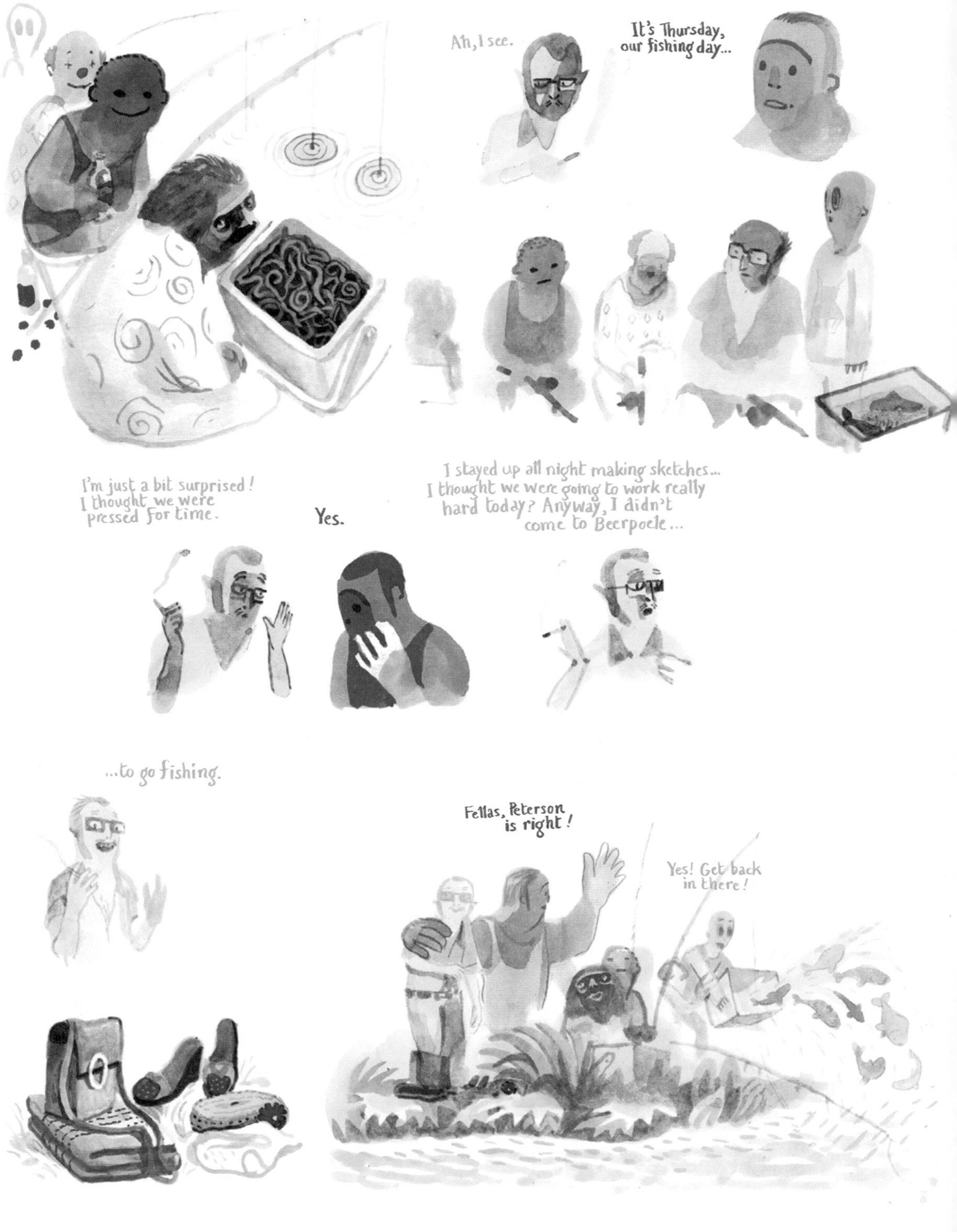

Ah, I see.
It's Thursday, our fishing day...
I'm just a bit surprised! I thought we were pressed for time.
Yes.
I stayed up all night making sketches... I thought we were going to work really hard today? Anyway, I didn't come to Beerpoele...
...to go fishing.
Fellas, Peterson is right!
Yes! Get back in there!

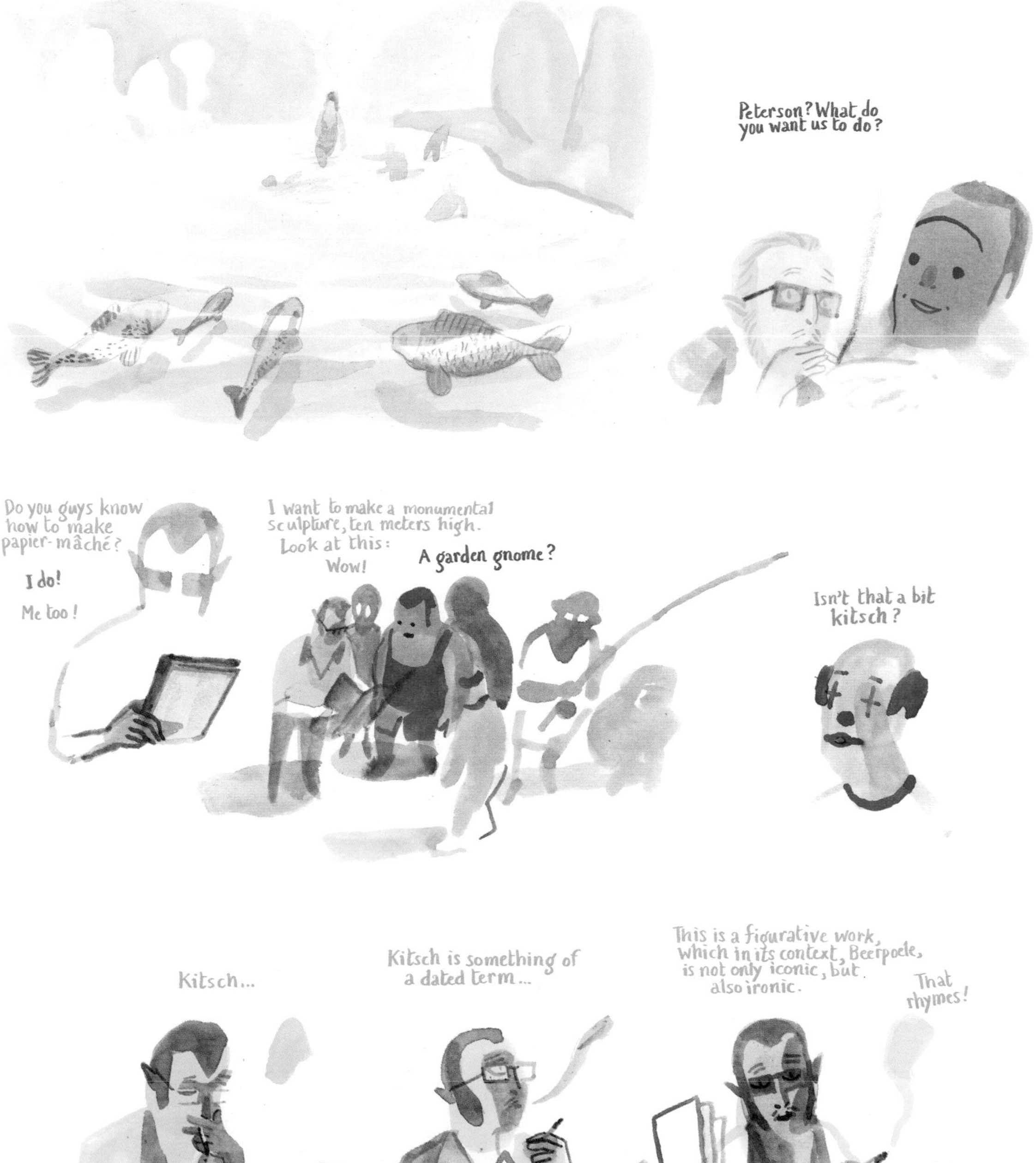
Peterson? What do you want us to do?
Do you guys know how to make papier-mâché?
I do!
Me too!
I want to make a monumental sculpture, ten meters high.
Look at this:
Wow!
A garden gnome?
Isn't that a bit kitsch?
Kitsch...
Kitsch is something of a dated term...
This is a figurative work, which in its context, Beerpoele, is not only iconic, but also ironic.
That rhymes!

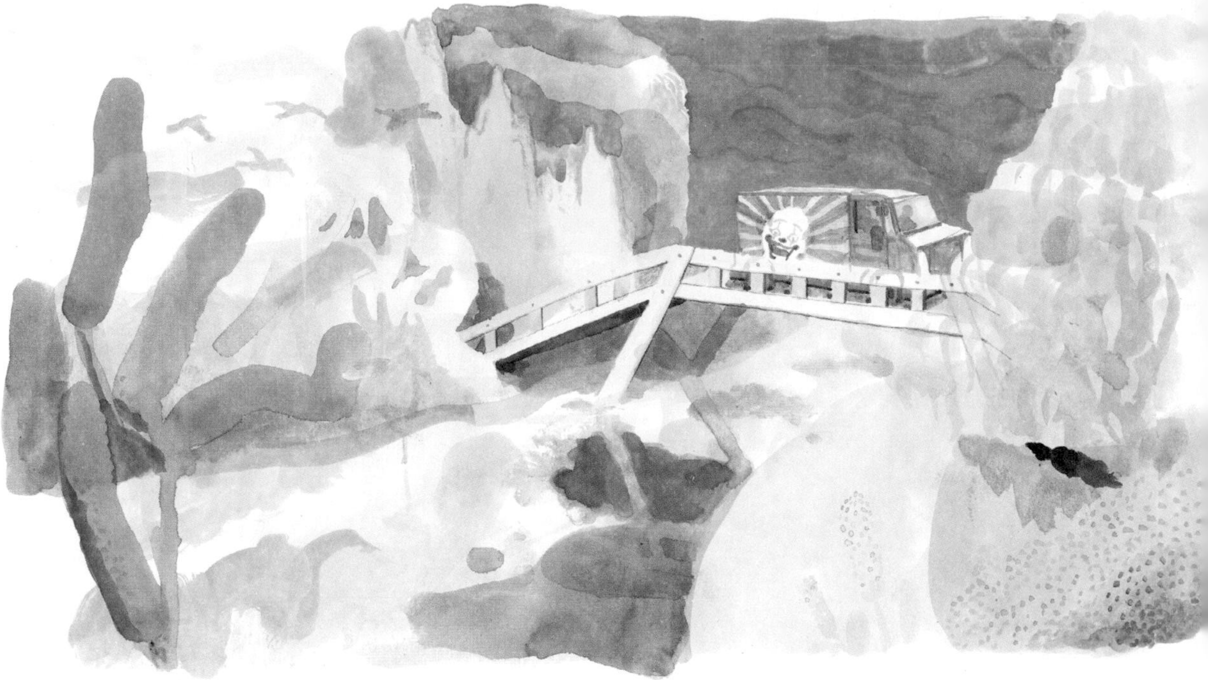

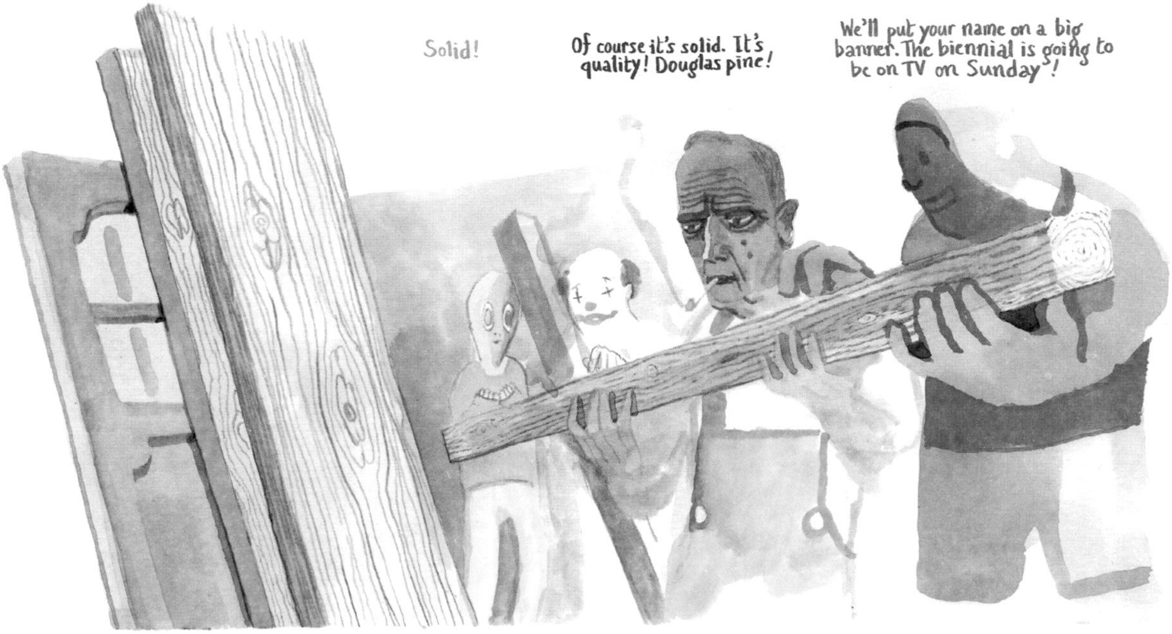
Solid!
Of course it's solid. It's quality! Douglas pine!
We'll put your name on a big banner. The biennial is going to be on TV on Sunday!

If you look at the sun for a moment, then look away, you can see all these little balls.
Oh yes!
That's great, guys!
Yes. Yes!
I think we've got everything we need to start!
From now on, we're not going to aim low and end up low, but aim high and...
BLUE
RE
YEL
ALKYD BLACK

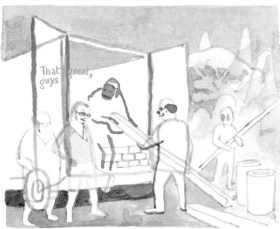

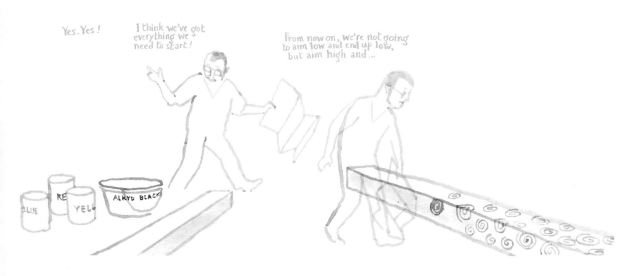

Oji Suzuki's atmospheric drawings remind me of the thick, bold lines of the Rider-Waite tarot deck by Pamela Colman Smith. Like Suzuki, Smith was inspired by the flat picture planes of Japanese woodblock prints. Like that tarot deck, Suzuki tells ambiguous, nuanced stories as clearly and bluntly as possible. Characters straggle the night. A woman visits a floating head. A boy walks between raindrops to stay dry. It's always raining. Also similarly to the tarot, the book easily recalls personal experiences in the reader. I was a teenager in Nagoya, Japan (where Suzuki grew up), and everyone was paranoid about the rain being acidic there. The rumour was that your hair would fall out if you were in the rain too long. *A Single Match* makes me remember these things. I've read it many times. Usually if you can't read the words in a foreign comic, it's better...you can imagine the content as more interesting than it truly is. *A Single Match* is one of the rare non-English comics that became more compelling after you could actually read it.

***—Dash Shaw, cartoonist of* Bottomless Belly Button, Doctors, *and* Cosplayers.**

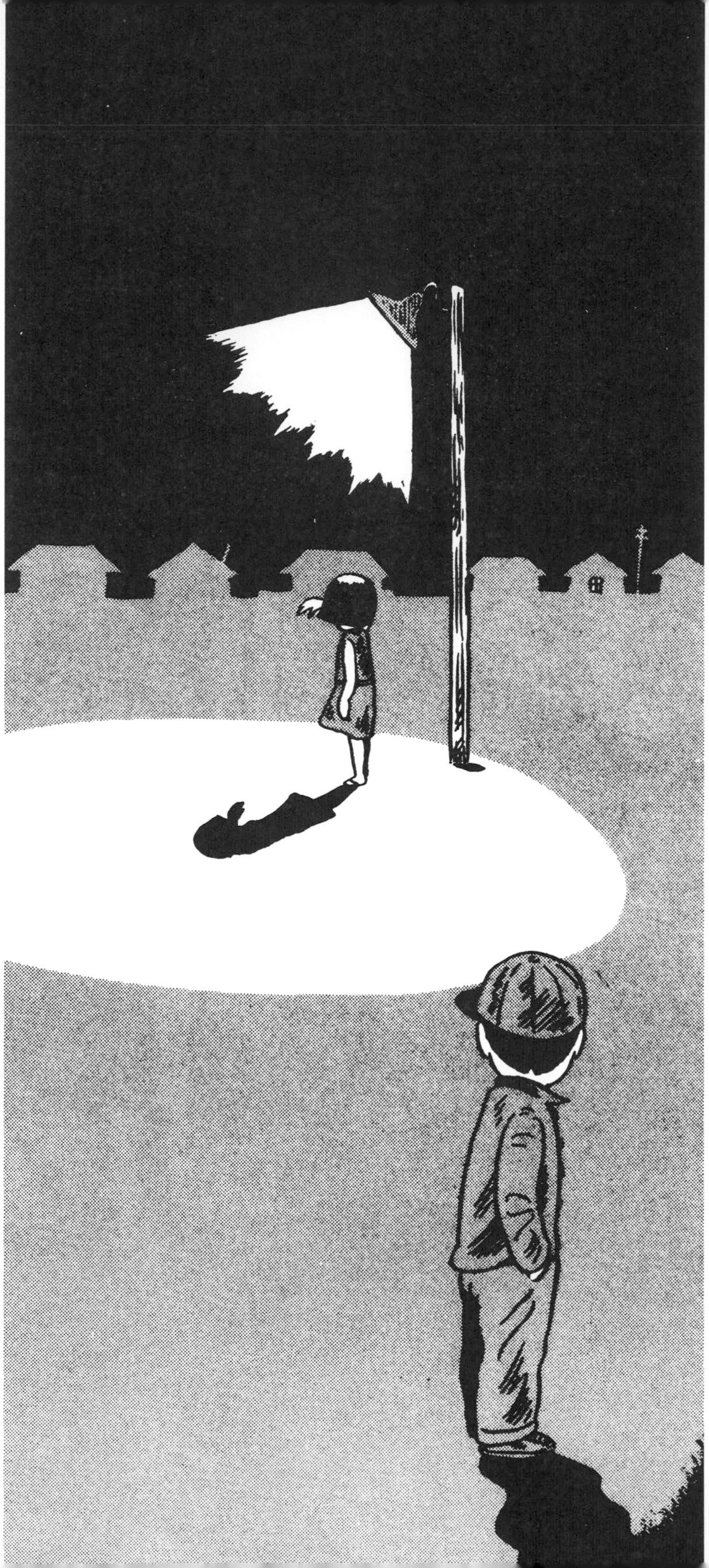

Image from *A Single Match* (2010).

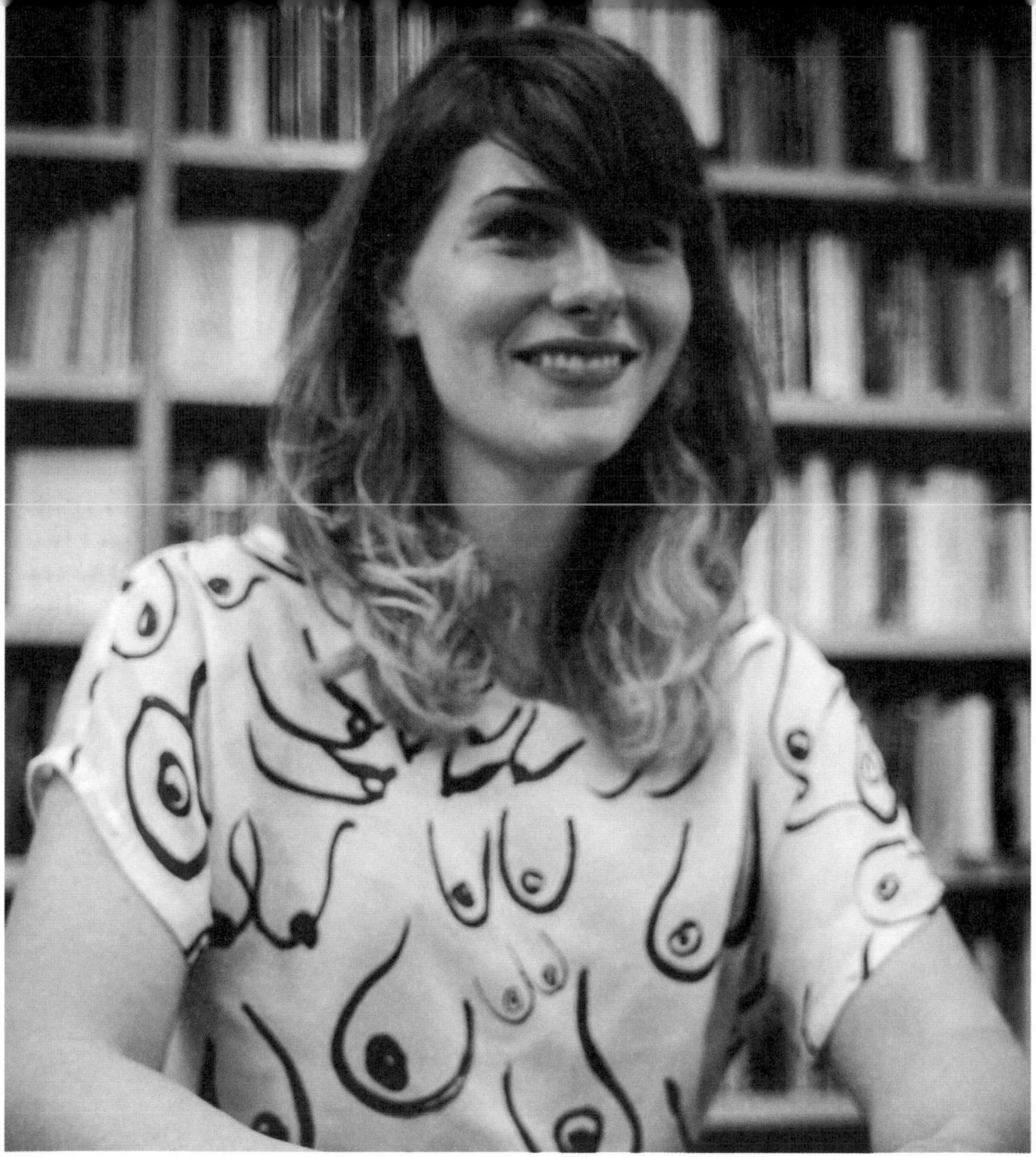

Lisa Hanawalt's comics are particularly close to my heart because they were some of the first that I picked up on my own, without an older sibling's recommendation or Drawn & Quarterly's guiding publishing hand. Working at the Librairie D+Q, I felt like I learned about Lisa Hanawalt at the same time that the rest of the world did. I picked up her gross, beautiful comics and laughed and cringed and loved them from the first issue of *I Want You*. I followed her to the pages of the *Believer*, to her website, to the *Hairpin*. There was something about the self-aware way she wrote twenty-something anxiety, about her hilarious depictions of the disgusting things our bodies do, about her comfort with anthropomorphized (but stylish) lizard people. I showed it to everyone. Some people got weirded out. I liked that. I kept talking about Lisa's work. For months I kept *My Dirty Dumb Eyes* on our living room coffee table. I'd come home to people reading it and laughing. Thanks for all the butts, Lisa.

—Julia Pohl-Miranda

Lisa Hanawalt at Pegasus Books. Photo: Chris Anthony Diaz & Graham Willcox (2013).

SURREALISM, CHEERY RESIGNATION, OR LITERATURE ITSELF

an appreciation of Tom Gauld by Tom Spurgeon

Tom Gauld's comics whisper. They force you to lean in. They are insistent and still and never impose.

The drawings themselves are finely textured on the page, courtesy of a cross-hatching style that is the way the Scottish cartoonist's work is most like that of the late, great Edward Gorey—though not the sole way. Many of Gauld's comics feel like pieces of cloth moved across a smooth, cold board, the last-ditch attempt to communicate between a cold narrator and an unmoved audience. His narratives are filled with objects that absorb rather than refract: mouldy books, outcroppings of rock, seedy neighbourhoods, and decaying buildings. Gauld knows how to employ white space to isolate and diminish the force of a character on the page, establishing a baseline volume of those figures relative to the world. They matter only to themselves; they lack import; they move over and about his landscapes like intruders. Gauld's figure drawing, never settled, smooths and simplifies the persons portrayed until they carry with them little life beyond those broad strokes Gauld deigns to share and make real. Some of Tom Gauld's comics lack words of any kind; others dole out text sparingly. They hold our attention without demanding it in a public, outward way.

Tom Gauld was born in Aberdeenshire, Scotland, in 1976. This puts the illustrator and cartoonist between two vital generations of comics makers. He was preceded to market by the last of the continuity cartoonists: underground, overground, indie, alternative, and post-alternative self-identifiers who knew their place in a continuum of creation with the ultimate aim of widespread mainstream acceptance and the legitimacy that might come with it. Succeeding Gauld are a legion of still-developing newer cartoonists empowered to self-publish by online tools, readers with access to nearly every important comic ever published, completely untethered from a standard canon. A comics reader from Tom Gauld's generation might read a *Watchmen*, or a *Maus*, or the first series in an orgy of "serious" *Batman* comics, but they don't feel compelled to like them. They are their own creatures. They are in between.

Gauld attended school to study illustration. He prefers to be called a cartoonist and an illustrator; those younger might prefer the former, and those older, the latter—value sets that don't apply to him. Gauld has become so adept at shaping some of the more toned-down, modest choices he may make in terms of the drawing itself that they generate additional power on the page, power you would not expect of them otherwise.

Partly as a result of that skill with images, Gauld makes very fine short comics, even what one might call summary comics. They are there to communicate a specific effect, a focused message, as cleanly and clearly as possible. He has a panelist's skill when it comes to finding the right moment in time to present for maximum effect. His is a significant catalogue of head-holding moments; he draws interesting shoulders. Tom Gauld has an eye for the tools of comics making that allows him to see elements like captions, word balloons, text, and panel arrangement as both component parts and disruptive elements of comics creation. He makes aesthetic choices with his lettering denied the less thoughtful, to significant effect in his longer narratives. His second book with Drawn & Quarterly, the collection *You're All Just Jealous of My Jetpack*, may be the most perfectly named comics work of the last thirty years for how it strikes Gauld's unique power to get at breaks within norms for cartoon effect. If the dominant mode of comic-book making is a constant, cinematic exaggeration, Gauld's best short works are like a series of shoebox panoramata. The pages could be accompanied by percussion.

Gauld began as a self-publisher. As a student he started a publishing imprint with the illustrator and cartoonist Simone Lia. I think Gauld is more practical for this experience, but also open to greater possibility. While several cartoonists in the publishing environment created by the rise of Chris Ware can demand flourishes and sizing and paper stock that best flatter and enhance the comics being made, Gauld regularly evinces the notion that this is a two-way street, that limitations on the page can become enhancers of mood, that the assignment on hand can shape the art in a primary way, not to be fought but engaged. Tom Gauld's

 (Right) Tom Gauld signing *Goliath* at San Diego Comic-Con, where he was a special guest (2013).

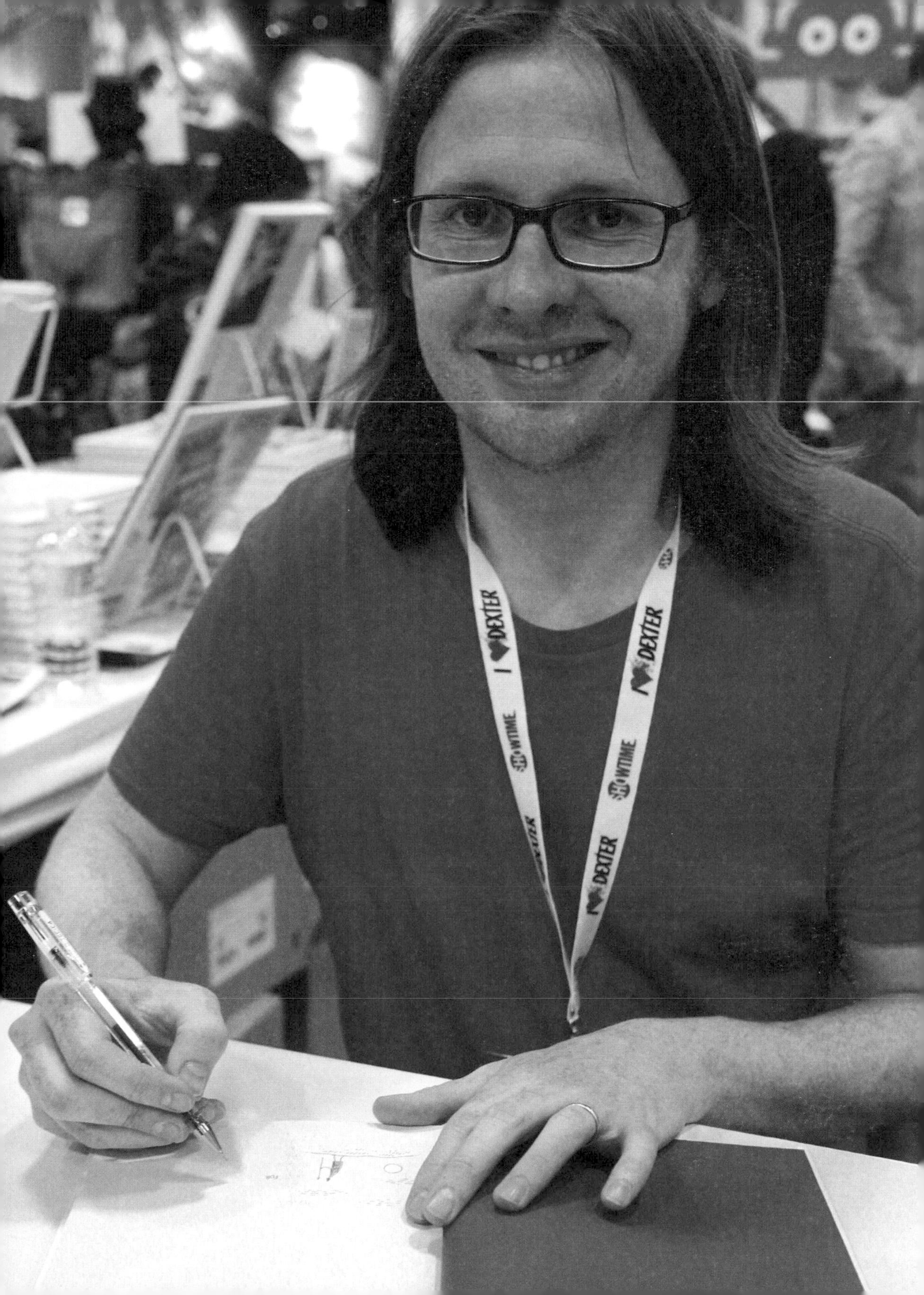
DEXTER

In 2013 I went to Comic-Con with D+Q. One night, Tracy and Julia took me and Lisa Hanawalt out to a bar. We were chatting (about comics I imagine, though it may have been a shirt Lisa had bought with drawings of boobs on it) when we were interrupted by two slightly drunk young men. One said to me, "Hey man, we just wanted to know what you've done to get these three chicks to yourself." I can't exactly remember what I replied but in a perfect world it would have been, "All you need to know, sir, is that I am a Cartoonist."—***Tom Gauld***

work can be unassuming because there's little in the way of a fiery ego being housed or hosted or presented; it can hit harder for all the ways he incorporates all of the elements available to him. Gauld may be the only cartoonist of significance working right now for whom a single change in his résumé might have made him a different cartoonist.

Gauld's great work with Drawn & Quarterly is *Goliath*, a work whose fate I wonder about had it not been that particular publishing partnership in effect. Settling on the Goliath story, Gauld found emotional resonance in the human embodiment of one of his misused hulks from comics past. More suited to administrative work, Goliath of Gath gets pulled into a drama based solely on his perceived physical talents. It's not much in the way of self-direction for a character to abandon, but it has dramatic effect. Goliath becomes that much more isolated, more withdrawn, almost comically or even operatically so. The one companion forced upon Goliath is unable to truly connect with him due to age and a very different kind of self-awareness. His questions reinforce Goliath's role and thus his isolation.

What makes *Goliath* different from everything else in Gauld's work to date is the David character, a terrifying embodiment of a completely sideways reality, so foreign to Goliath that the fundaments of that reality, the lines and words, are executed in an altered fashion. A more Gauldian ending might have been Goliath in the desert on his own, interminably. No such luck this time around. Then again, that particularly potency to Gauld's work lingers over the concluding elements to Goliath. When Goliath is killed, the reader may experience a moment of personal sadness, but it's also possible to have seen the character as dead from the start—pulled from his own station and understanding of the world into a historical pageant that's even less human than the quiet, nondescript existence he'd previously enjoyed. Goliath became a supporting player in King David's story by being denied the lead in his own. He has been dead for several pages, cast out of his own story like the stone Goliath drops in an early scene.

The one great alteration to the reading experience provided by *You're All Just Jealous of My Jetpack* is that it encourages an engaged cover-to-cover reading. You might choose not to, just as you might choose to read the clipped online versions in the *Guardian* dozens at a time. *Jetpack* is a series of significant moments connected by recurring Gauldian interests: surrealism, or cheery resignation, or literature itself. The fact that a bit of humour can be had from nearly any situation provides a lot of the strips with a surge of good feeling that I'm not sure would be the same were they consumed at the pace at which they were published. It's almost as if our proximity to the moment is what makes events cheerful rather than desperate. If humour is classically held to be "tragedy + time," Gauld's second book with Drawn & Quarterly seems to suggest that space has something to say there, too.

Tom Gauld is a key figure for Drawn & Quarterly moving forward as a publishing entity. No one in his half-group of cartoonists better conforms to that combination of literary ambition and idiosyncratic picture-making central to the publisher, the values evinced by the titanic cartoonists of the publisher's first decade. Unlike some of the younger cartoonists currently published by Drawn & Quarterly, Gauld seems to have intersecting interests with almost none of the current landscape, now that a small group of printmakers and art-book publishers have come and gone. I would not be surprised to learn that Gauld is one of the most popular cartoonists in the history of the publisher, or if he remained so moving forward. Hopefully D+Q will continue to provide a platform for his readers to see existing work differently, and for the artist to get at some of his primary concerns using an alternate set of tools and emphases. Tom Gauld is very close to the heart of what this great publisher does, whether that heart beats more forcefully at the centre of the company or off and to the side.

Tom Spurgeon is a critic and journalist who writes extensively about comics on his website, the* Comics Reporter. *He was the editor of the* Comics Journal *from 1994–1999. He has won three Eisner Awards for Best Comics-Related Periodical/Journalism. He most famously wrote the unpublished history of Fantagraphics.

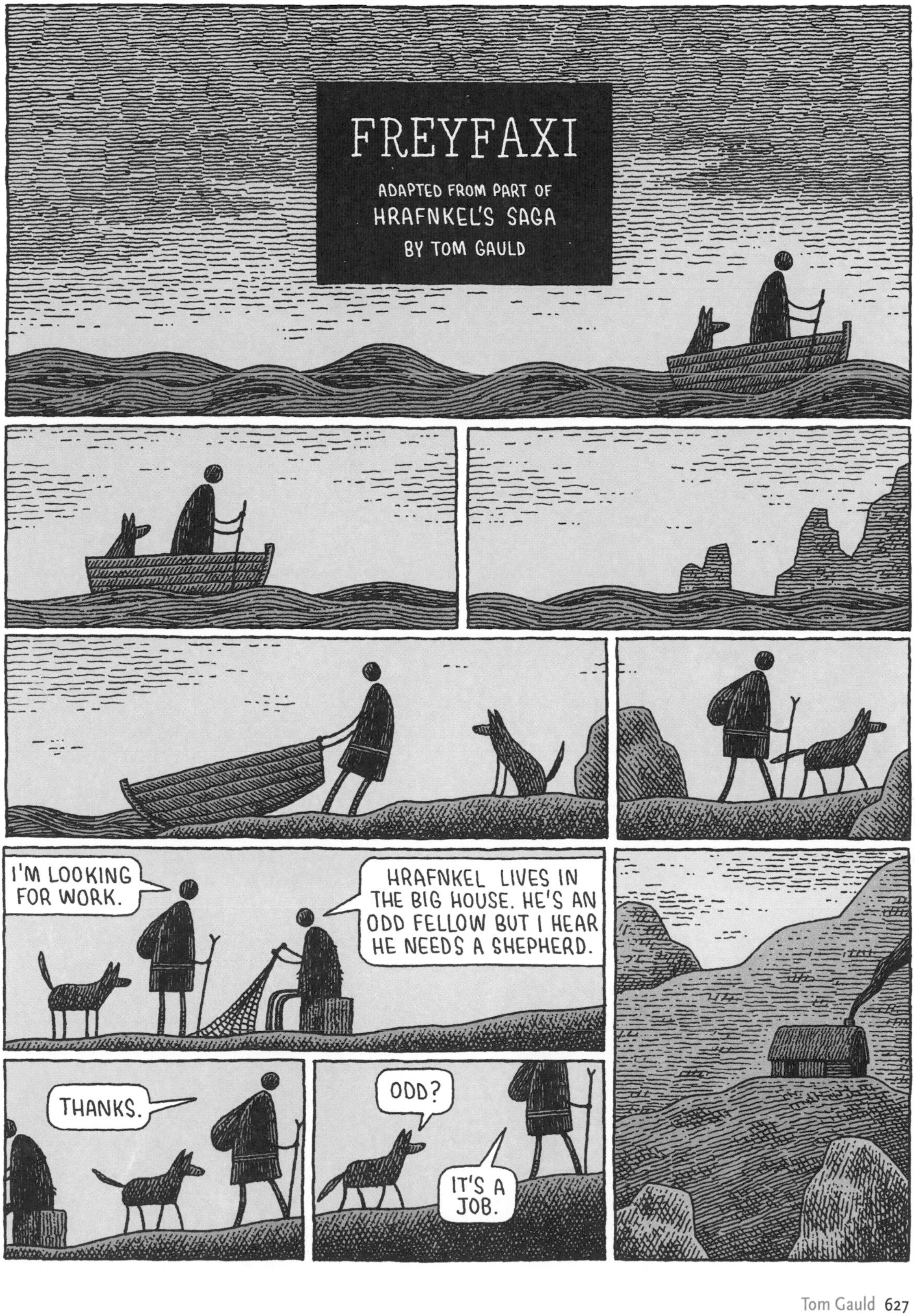
FREYFAXI
ADAPTED FROM PART OF
HRAFNKEL'S SAGA
BY TOM GAULD
I'M LOOKING FOR WORK.
HRAFNKEL LIVES IN THE BIG HOUSE. HE'S AN ODD FELLOW BUT I HEAR HE NEEDS A SHEPHERD.
THANKS.
ODD?
IT'S A JOB.

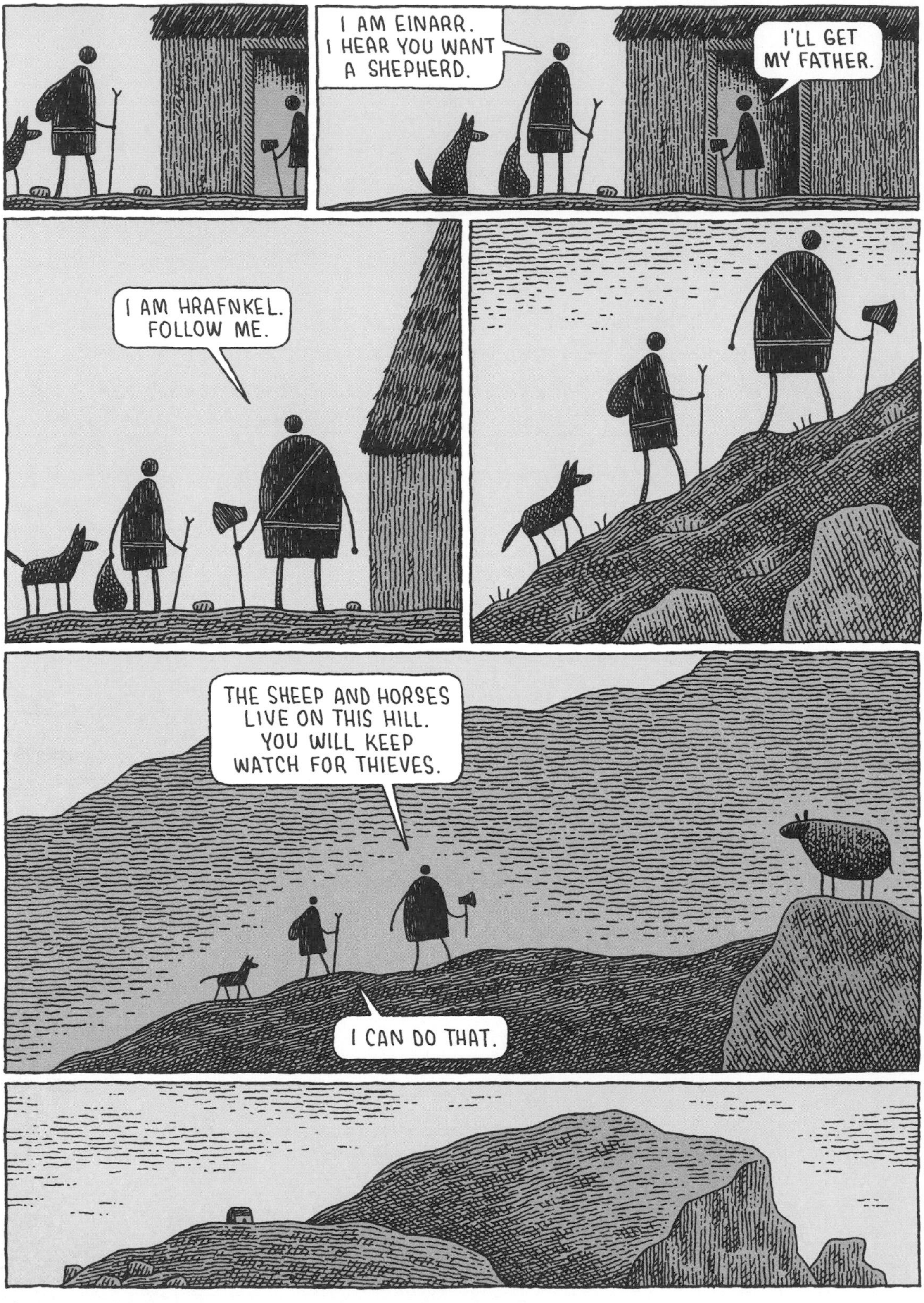
I AM EINARR. I HEAR YOU WANT A SHEPHERD.
I'LL GET MY FATHER.
I AM HRAFNKEL. FOLLOW ME.
THE SHEEP AND HORSES LIVE ON THIS HILL. YOU WILL KEEP WATCH FOR THIEVES.
I CAN DO THAT.

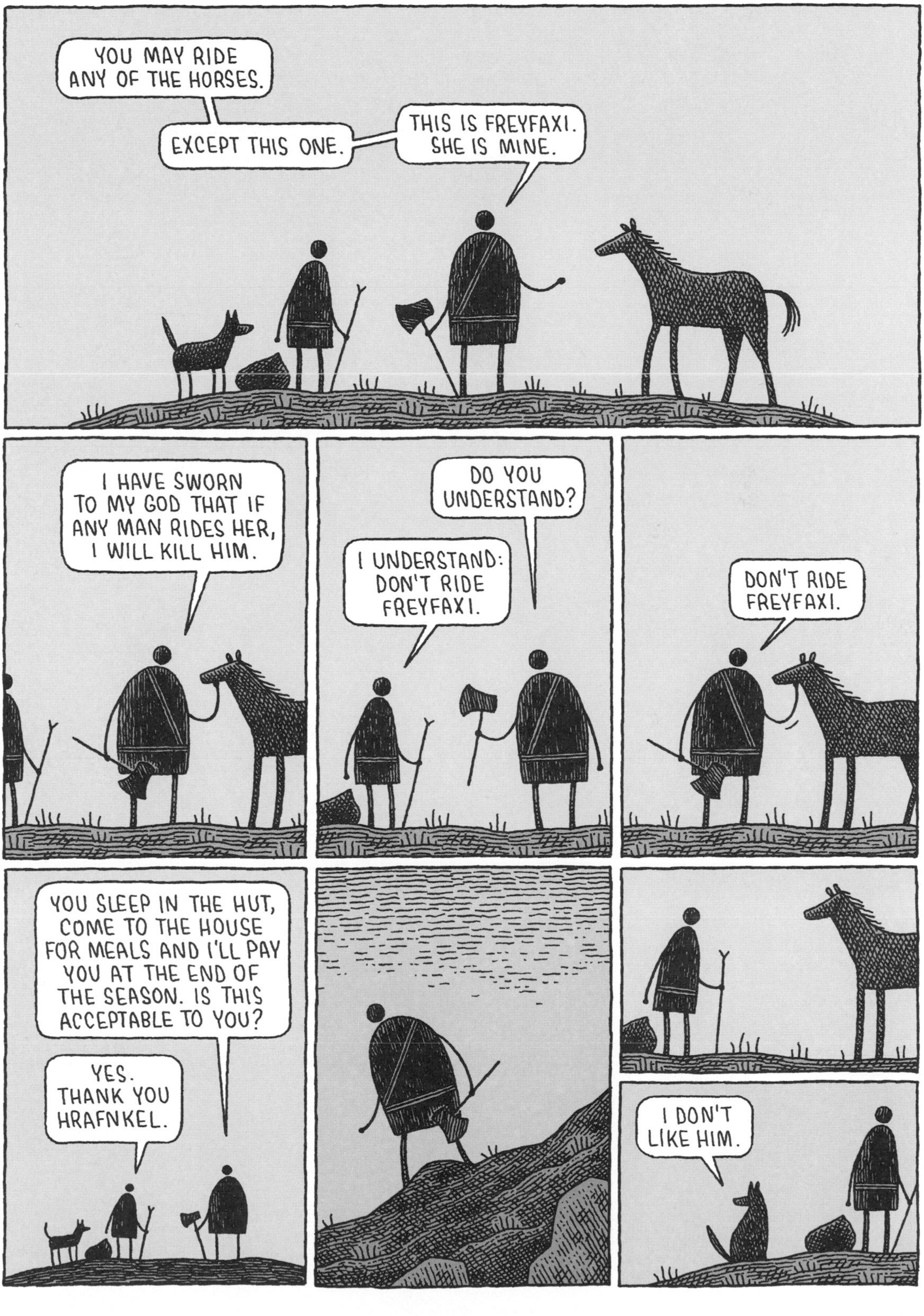

YOU MAY RIDE ANY OF THE HORSES.
EXCEPT THIS ONE.
THIS IS FREYFAXI. SHE IS MINE.
I HAVE SWORN TO MY GOD THAT IF ANY MAN RIDES HER, I WILL KILL HIM.
DO YOU UNDERSTAND?
I UNDERSTAND: DON'T RIDE FREYFAXI.
DON'T RIDE FREYFAXI.
YOU SLEEP IN THE HUT, COME TO THE HOUSE FOR MEALS AND I'LL PAY YOU AT THE END OF THE SEASON. IS THIS ACCEPTABLE TO YOU?
YES. THANK YOU HRAFNKEL.
I DON'T LIKE HIM.

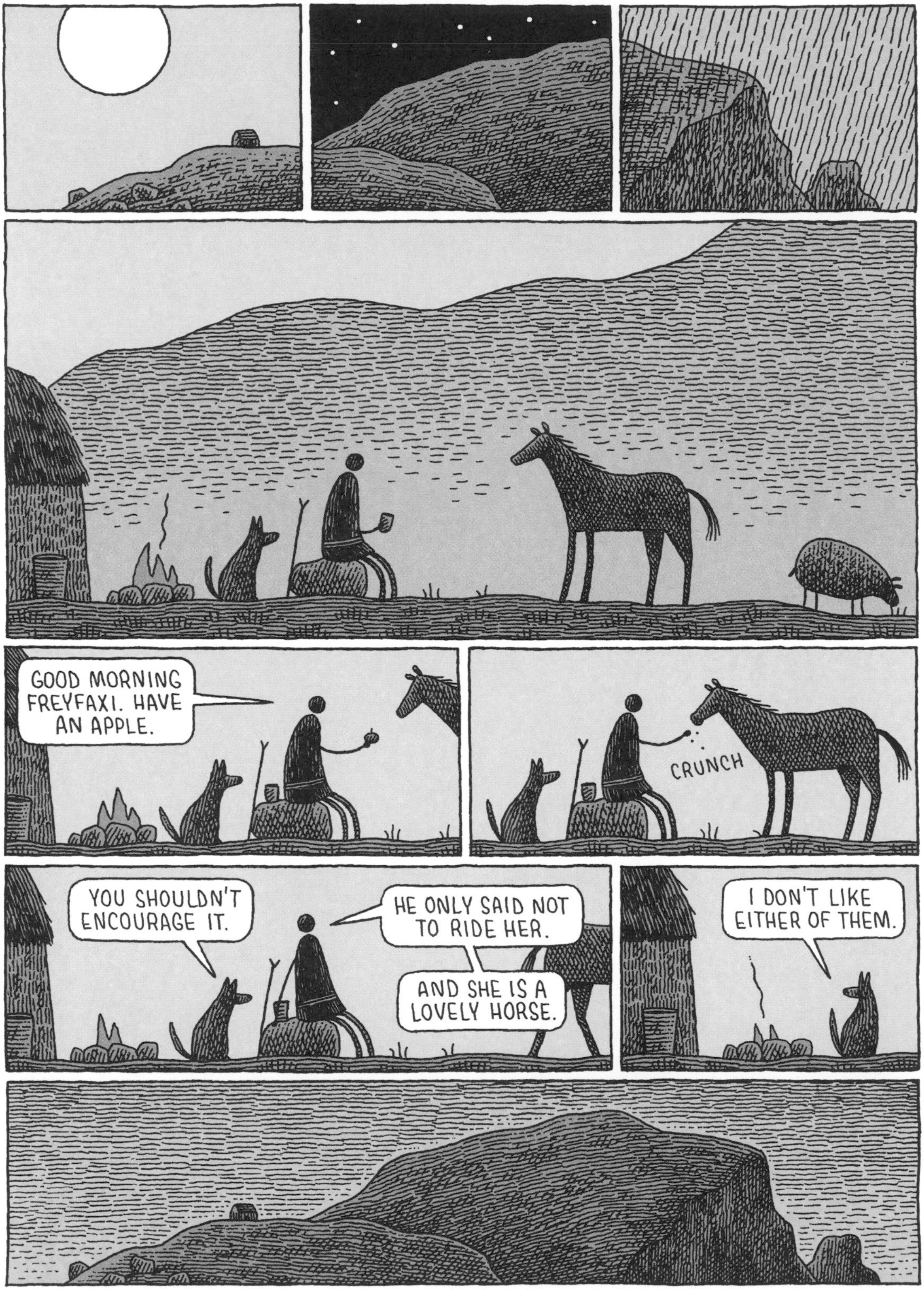
GOOD MORNING FREYFAXI. HAVE AN APPLE.
CRUNCH
YOU SHOULDN'T ENCOURAGE IT.
HE ONLY SAID NOT TO RIDE HER.
AND SHE IS A LOVELY HORSE.
I DON'T LIKE EITHER OF THEM.

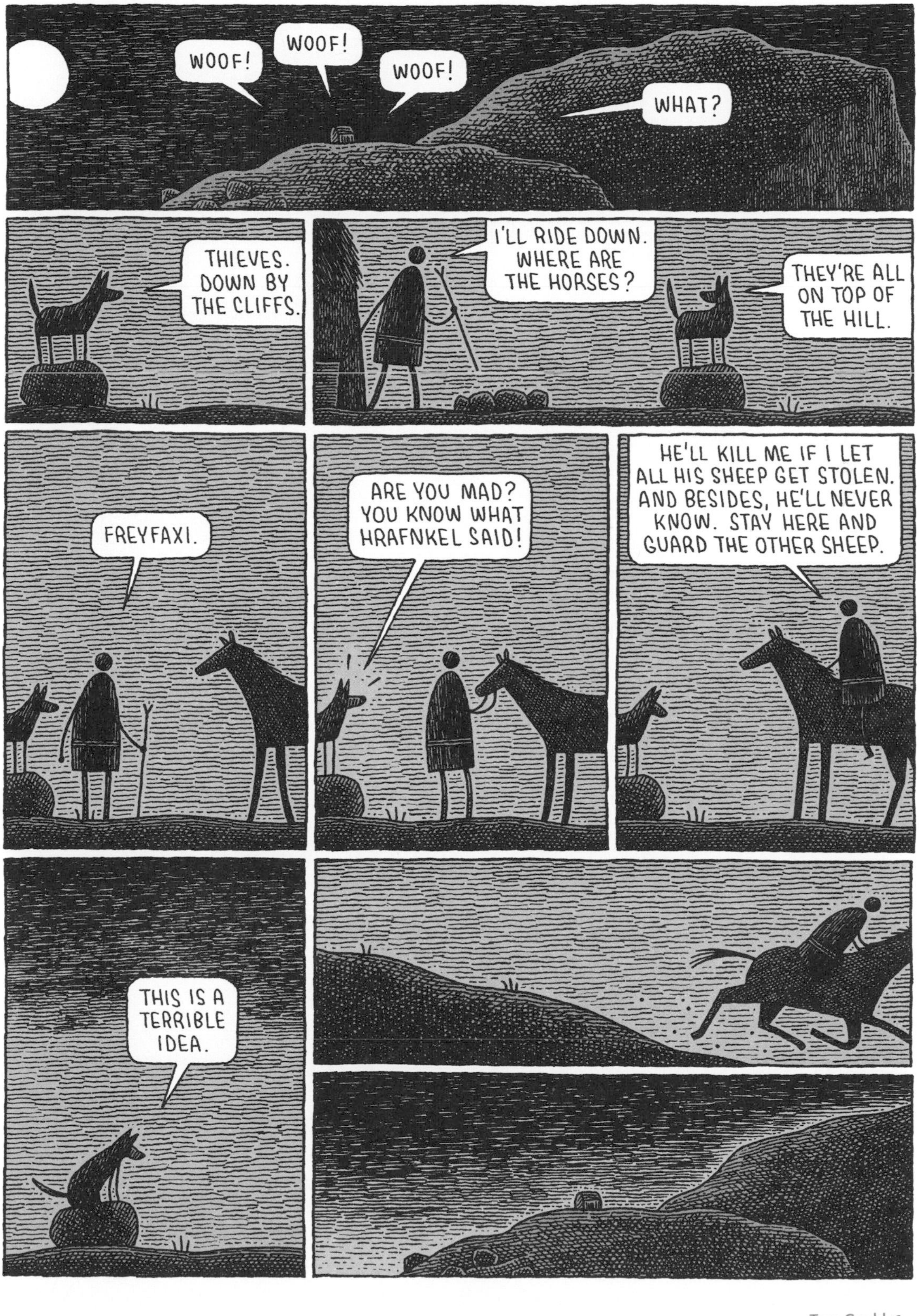
WOOF!
WOOF!
WOOF!
WHAT?
THIEVES. DOWN BY THE CLIFFS.
I'LL RIDE DOWN. WHERE ARE THE HORSES?
THEY'RE ALL ON TOP OF THE HILL.
FREYFAXI.
ARE YOU MAD? YOU KNOW WHAT HRAFNKEL SAID!
HE'LL KILL ME IF I LET ALL HIS SHEEP GET STOLEN. AND BESIDES, HE'LL NEVER KNOW. STAY HERE AND GUARD THE OTHER SHEEP.
THIS IS A TERRIBLE IDEA.

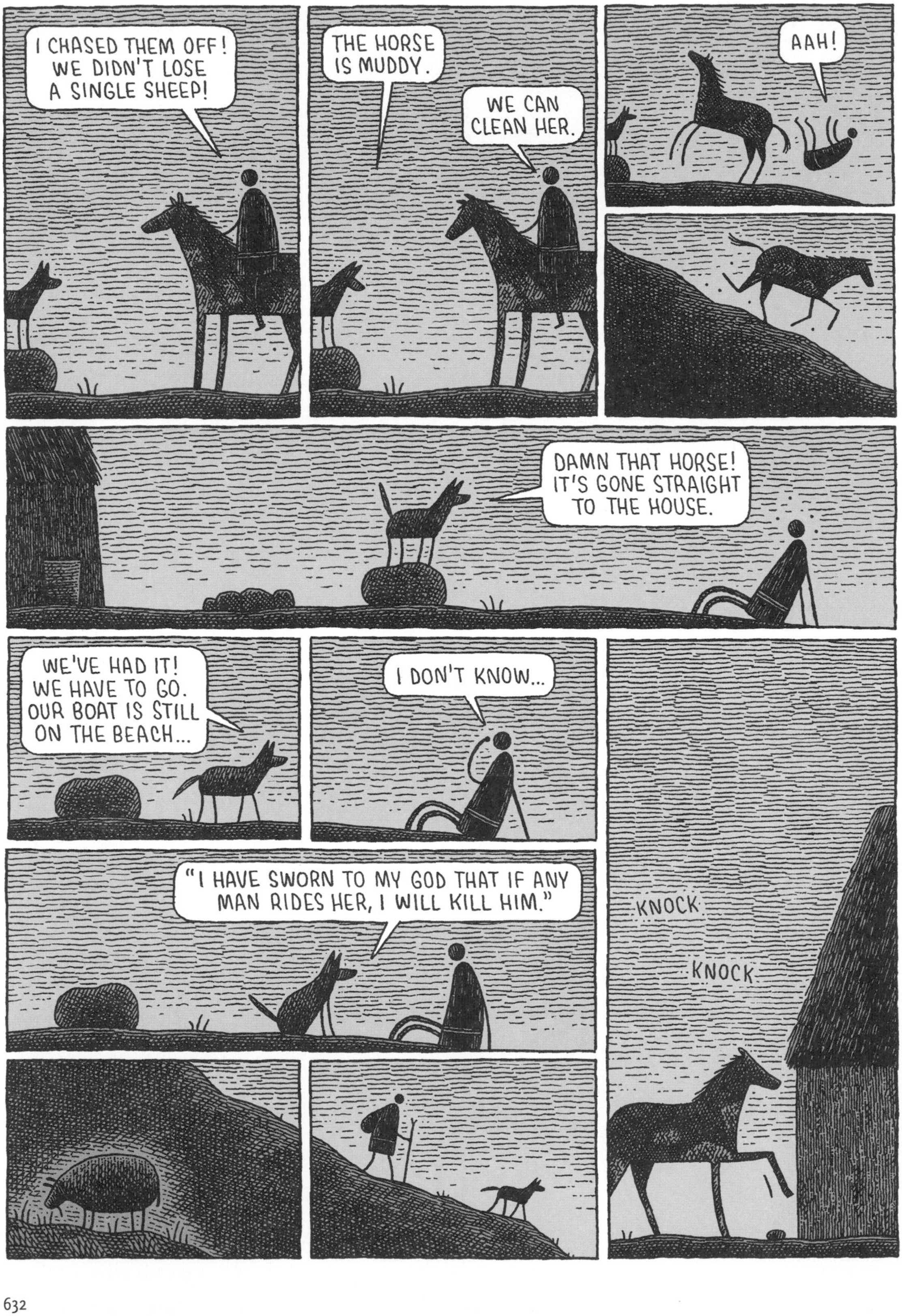
I CHASED THEM OFF! WE DIDN'T LOSE A SINGLE SHEEP!
THE HORSE IS MUDDY.
WE CAN CLEAN HER.
AAH!
DAMN THAT HORSE! IT'S GONE STRAIGHT TO THE HOUSE.
WE'VE HAD IT! WE HAVE TO GO. OUR BOAT IS STILL ON THE BEACH...
I DON'T KNOW...
"I HAVE SWORN TO MY GOD THAT IF ANY MAN RIDES HER, I WILL KILL HIM."
KNOCK
KNOCK

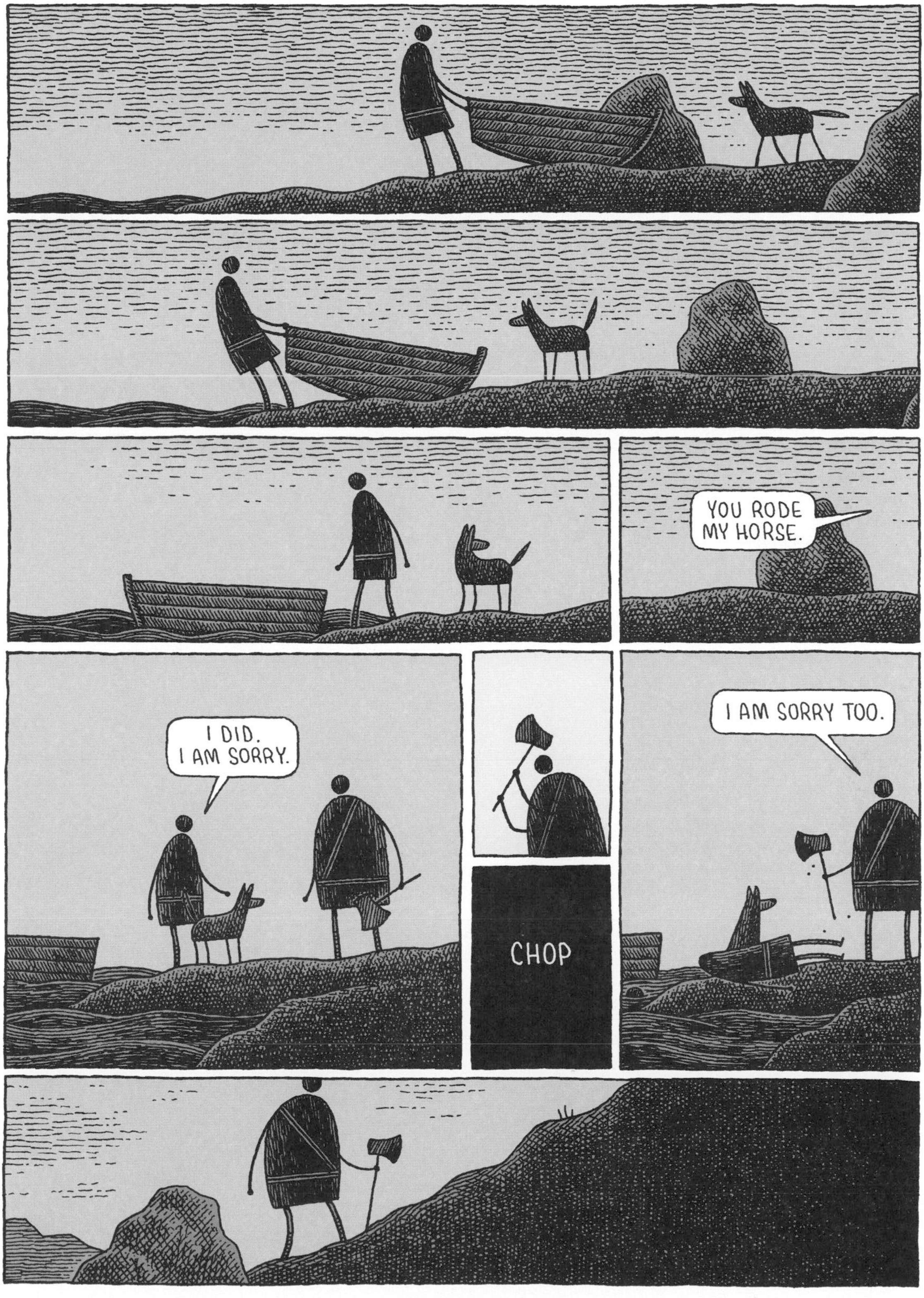
YOU RODE MY HORSE.
I DID. I AM SORRY.
CHOP
I AM SORRY TOO.

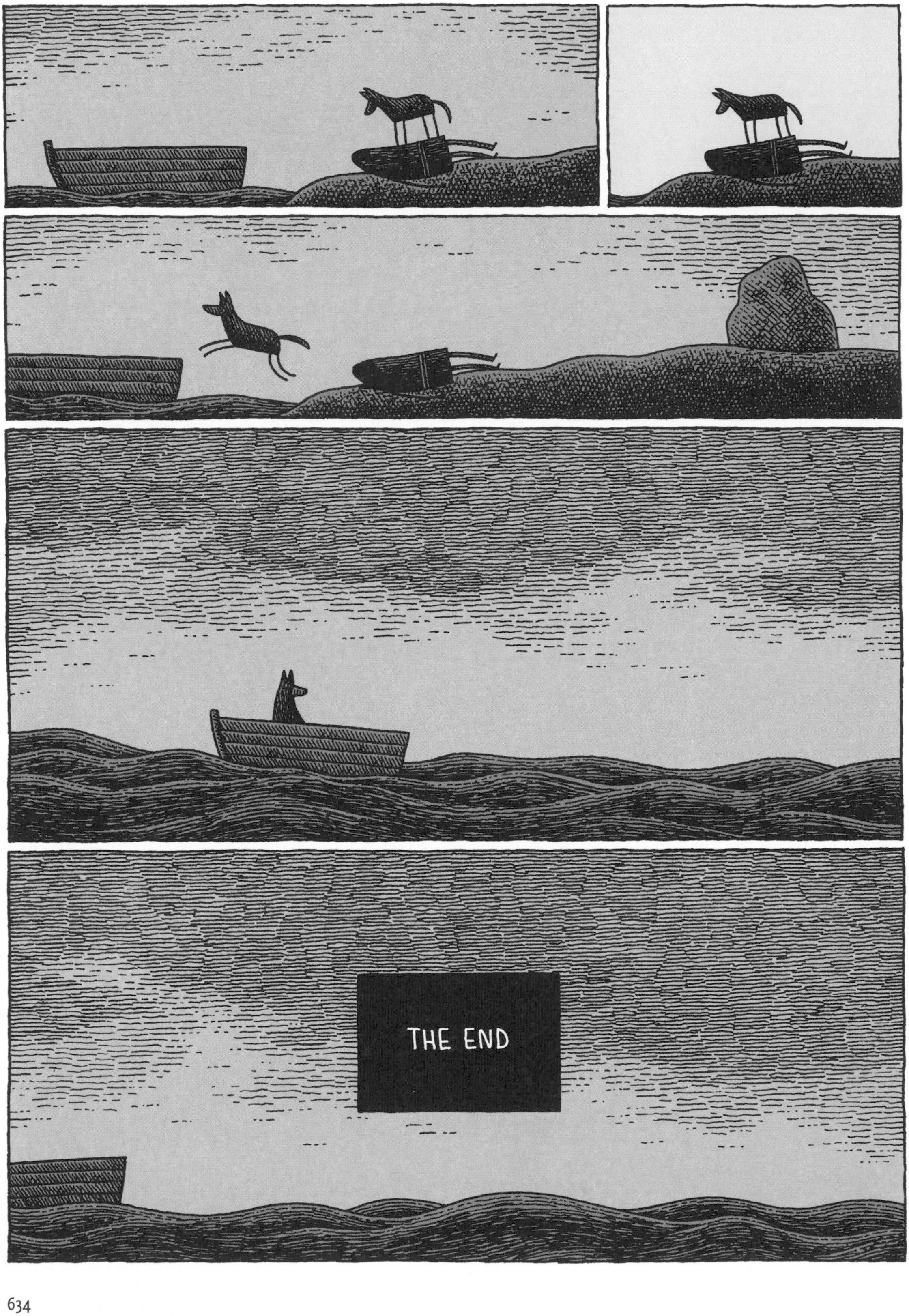
THE END

THE LUCKY BASTARD

OH GOD!
AAAAAAHH!
GOODNESS ! I SEEM TO HAVE SURVIVED UNSCATHED.
NOW, WHERE'S MY... AH, THERE'S MY SUITCASE.
WELL, WHADDAYA KNOW-- MY MODEL SHIP'S OKAY TOO !
TH-- THAT'S MY MODEL SHIP, MISTER !
NO LAD, THIS ONE'S YOURS.
AWWW...

It's hard to fathom that such a time ever existed, but yes, there was one brief period when Joe Matt was a prolific cartoonist. With his cartooning output sadly all but dried up these days (believe it or not, the thirteen pages that follow this represent his entire body of "new" material over the past decade), it's quite a challenge to hearken back to a time when Joe was producing work at a steady clip. And no, I'm not referring to his thirteen-issue stint on *Peepshow*. The Joe Matt "jam" sketchbooks occupied much of his time throughout the mid-1990s and the early 2000s. For much of this period Joe carried a sketchbook in hand when meeting cartoonist friends, and this sketchbook was reserved for the sole purpose of collaborative comic strips. Joe would

Panels one, four, seven: Joe Matt. Panels two, five, eight: Chester Brown. Panels three, six, nine: Seth.

start one panel and then the next person would follow, each making up the story as they went along. In the early days, Joe's partners were primarily Chester Brown and Seth. Then, as Joe began to travel to conventions, the circle widened to include other D+Q cartoonists like Adrian Tomine and Julie Doucet. Occasionally Joe even managed to corner people like Will Eisner, Gilbert Shelton, and Matt Groening and get their contributions. At one point in the early 2000s I visited Joe in Los Angeles, and there he was, sitting down with musician Aimee Mann at the neighbourhood Starbucks, both swapping panels in an ongoing jam strip. Even his mother dutifully obliged, although I can only find one example of their collaboration. And what has become of these "jam" sketchbooks? With the exception of a limited-run, self-published, photocopied version from 1998, much of this material has never been collected. A Google search turns up little beyond a handful of relevant examples. Sadly, it appears that this period in Joe Matt's career is all but forgotten. We've searched high and low, and we've managed to locate this one prime example of a "jam" strip in a dark corner in Peter Birkemoe's basement.—***Chris Oliveros***

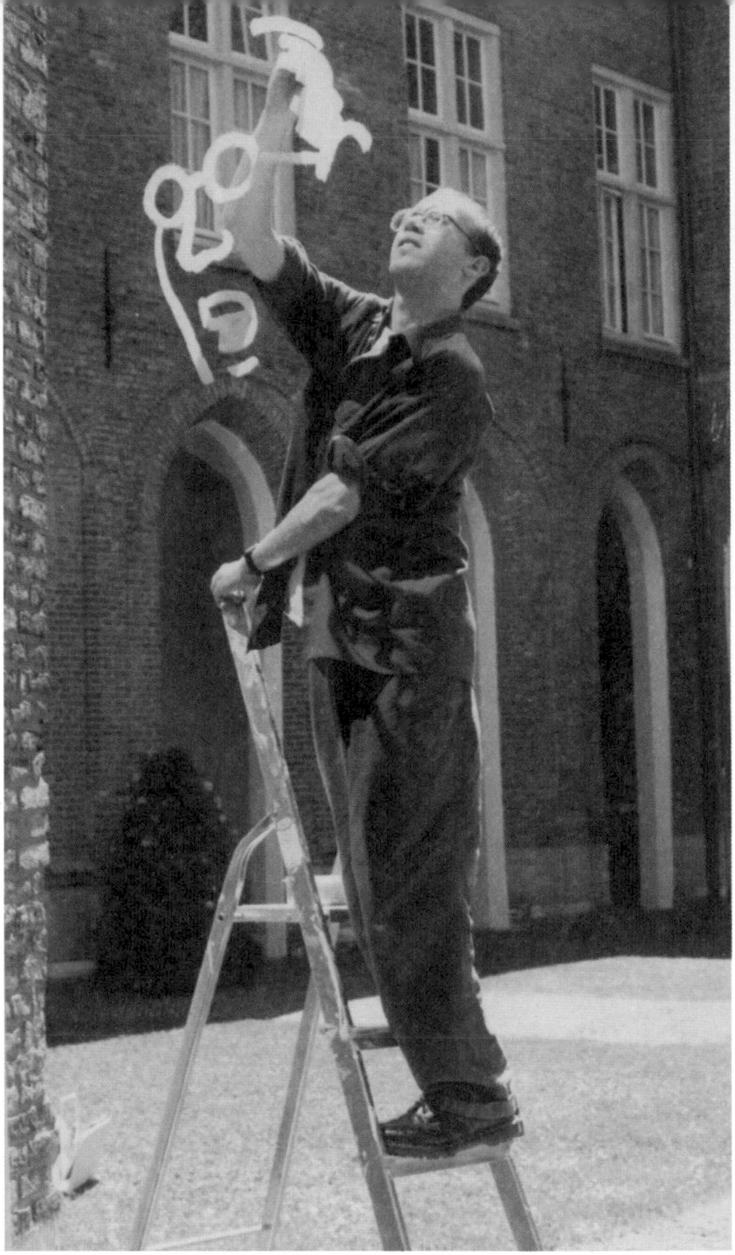

The first issue of the *Spent* story arc came out right before I entered high school (I was still in grade seven or eight, I think). It was the first issue of *Peepshow* I'd ever read. The final issue of the arc came out about eight years later, very shortly after I'd dropped out of college. I remember thinking about how much my life had changed in the time between *Spent* starting and *Spent* finishing. It spanned a lot of my "milestones." I'd started high school, graduated high school, started college, left college, drawn my first comic, had my first art show, got published for the first time, played my first concert, had my first kiss, lost my virginity, got my first job, got fired from my first job, had my first girlfriend, had my first breakup, watched my parents break up, got black hairy tongue syndrome, etc. But each new *Peepshow* release would let me check in on the always reliable Joe Matt—still the same, still editing porn and peeing into jars and jacking off in his room. It was very comforting, almost like an anchor, except the anchor was covered in semen.—***Michael DeForge***

 Joe prepping for the D+Q exhibition in Haarlem, Netherlands (1996).

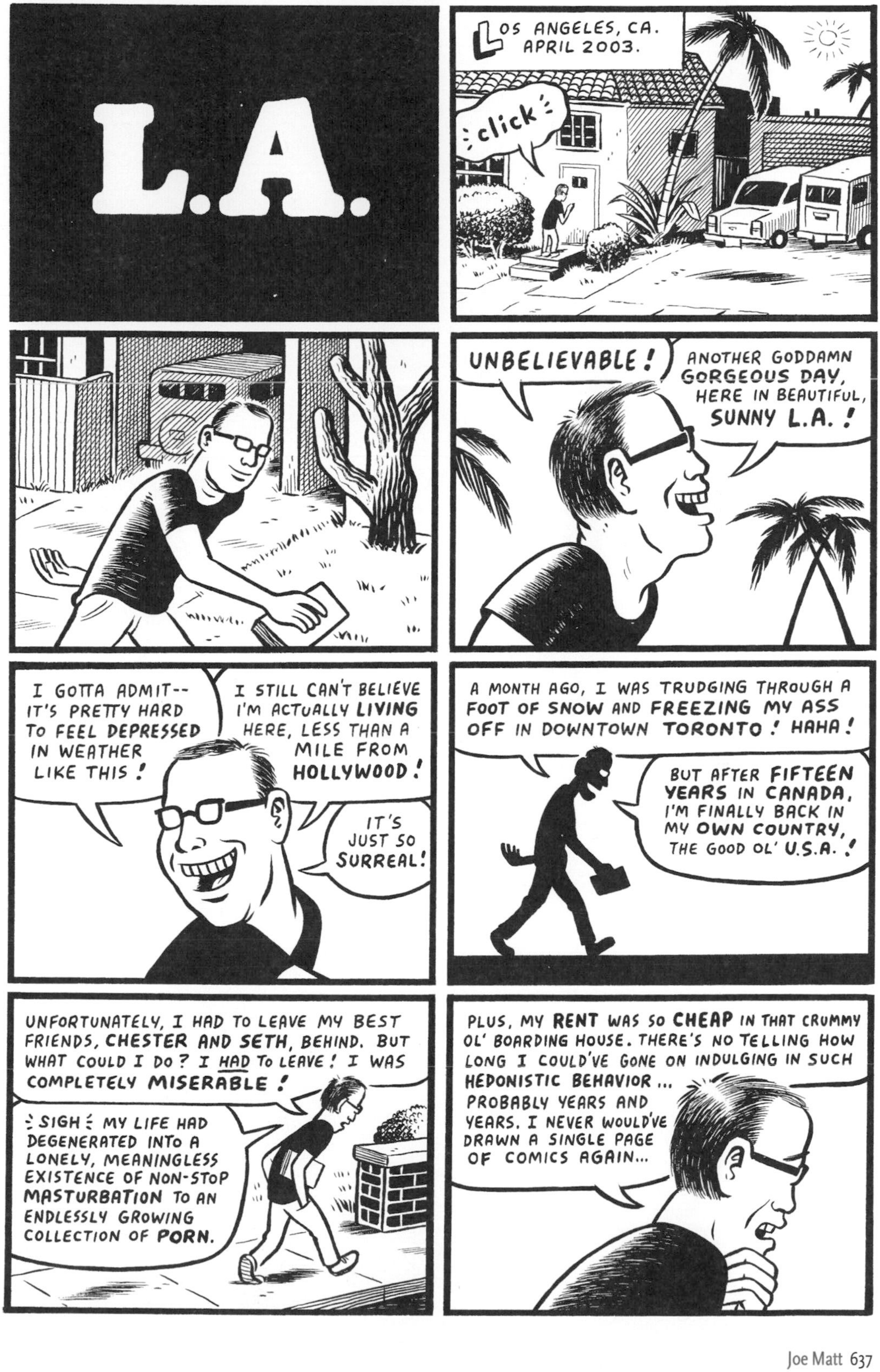
L.A.
LOS ANGELES, CA. APRIL 2003.
click
UNBELIEVABLE!
ANOTHER GODDAMN GORGEOUS DAY, HERE IN BEAUTIFUL, SUNNY L.A.!
I GOTTA ADMIT-- IT'S PRETTY HARD TO FEEL DEPRESSED IN WEATHER LIKE THIS!
I STILL CAN'T BELIEVE I'M ACTUALLY LIVING HERE, LESS THAN A MILE FROM HOLLYWOOD!
IT'S JUST SO SURREAL!
A MONTH AGO, I WAS TRUDGING THROUGH A FOOT OF SNOW AND FREEZING MY ASS OFF IN DOWNTOWN TORONTO! HAHA!
BUT AFTER FIFTEEN YEARS IN CANADA, I'M FINALLY BACK IN MY OWN COUNTRY, THE GOOD OL' U.S.A.!
UNFORTUNATELY, I HAD TO LEAVE MY BEST FRIENDS, CHESTER AND SETH, BEHIND. BUT WHAT COULD I DO? I HAD TO LEAVE! I WAS COMPLETELY MISERABLE!
SIGH MY LIFE HAD DEGENERATED INTO A LONELY, MEANINGLESS EXISTENCE OF NON-STOP MASTURBATION TO AN ENDLESSLY GROWING COLLECTION OF PORN.
PLUS, MY RENT WAS SO CHEAP IN THAT CRUMMY OL' BOARDING HOUSE. THERE'S NO TELLING HOW LONG I COULD'VE GONE ON INDULGING IN SUCH HEDONISTIC BEHAVIOR...
PROBABLY YEARS AND YEARS. I NEVER WOULD'VE DRAWN A SINGLE PAGE OF COMICS AGAIN...

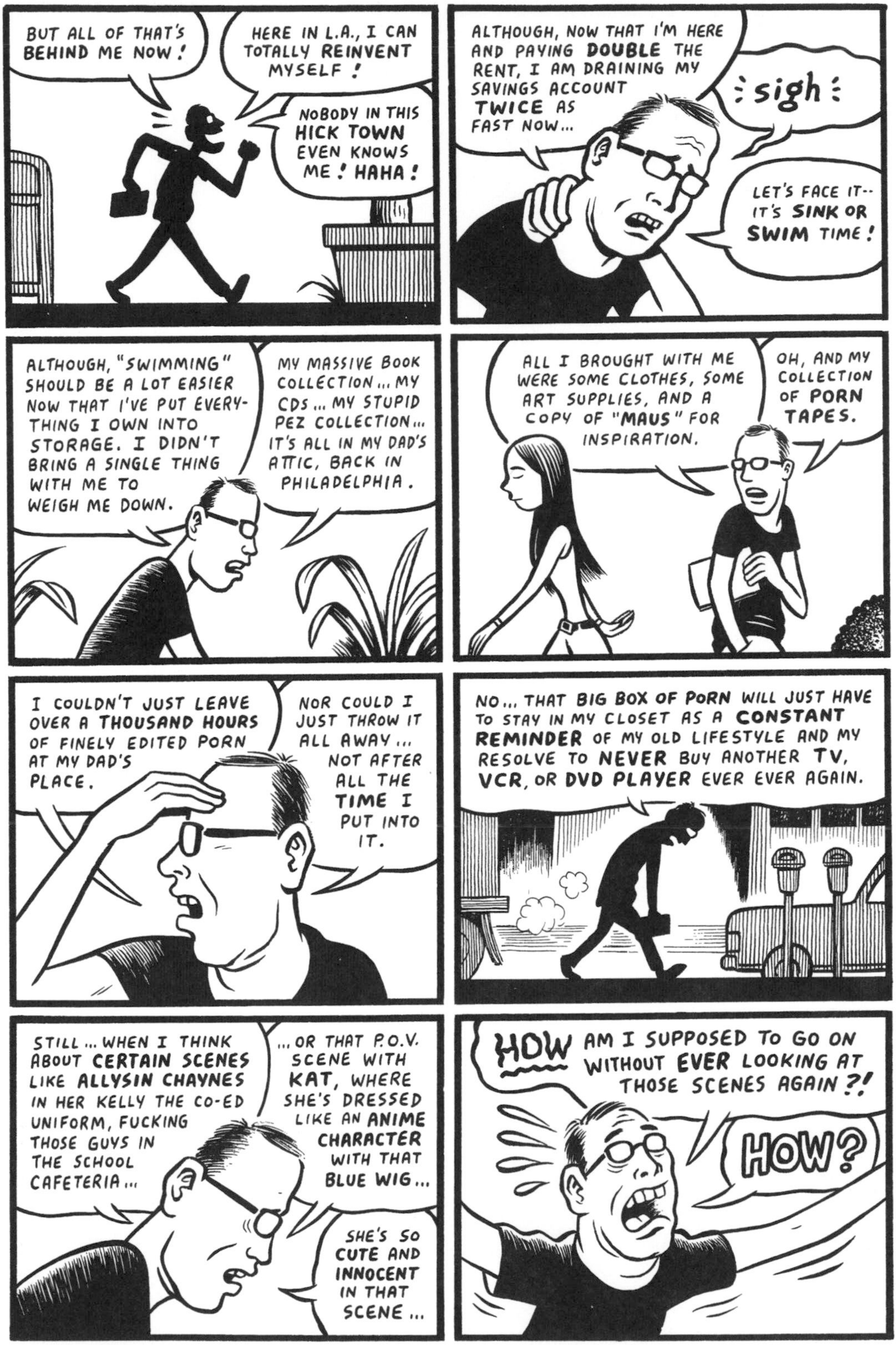
BUT ALL OF THAT'S BEHIND ME NOW!
HERE IN L.A., I CAN TOTALLY REINVENT MYSELF!
NOBODY IN THIS HICK TOWN EVEN KNOWS ME! HAHA!
ALTHOUGH, NOW THAT I'M HERE AND PAYING DOUBLE THE RENT, I AM DRAINING MY SAVINGS ACCOUNT TWICE AS FAST NOW...
sigh
LET'S FACE IT-- IT'S SINK OR SWIM TIME!
ALTHOUGH, "SWIMMING" SHOULD BE A LOT EASIER NOW THAT I'VE PUT EVERYTHING I OWN INTO STORAGE. I DIDN'T BRING A SINGLE THING WITH ME TO WEIGH ME DOWN.
MY MASSIVE BOOK COLLECTION... MY CDS... MY STUPID PEZ COLLECTION... IT'S ALL IN MY DAD'S ATTIC, BACK IN PHILADELPHIA.
ALL I BROUGHT WITH ME WERE SOME CLOTHES, SOME ART SUPPLIES, AND A COPY OF "MAUS" FOR INSPIRATION.
OH, AND MY COLLECTION OF PORN TAPES.
I COULDN'T JUST LEAVE OVER A THOUSAND HOURS OF FINELY EDITED PORN AT MY DAD'S PLACE.
NOR COULD I JUST THROW IT ALL AWAY... NOT AFTER ALL THE TIME I PUT INTO IT.
NO... THAT BIG BOX OF PORN WILL JUST HAVE TO STAY IN MY CLOSET AS A CONSTANT REMINDER OF MY OLD LIFESTYLE AND MY RESOLVE TO NEVER BUY ANOTHER TV, VCR, OR DVD PLAYER EVER EVER AGAIN.
STILL... WHEN I THINK ABOUT CERTAIN SCENES LIKE ALLYSIN CHAYNES IN HER KELLY THE CO-ED UNIFORM, FUCKING THOSE GUYS IN THE SCHOOL CAFETERIA...
...OR THAT P.O.V. SCENE WITH KAT, WHERE SHE'S DRESSED LIKE AN ANIME CHARACTER WITH THAT BLUE WIG...
SHE'S SO CUTE AND INNOCENT IN THAT SCENE...
HOW AM I SUPPOSED TO GO ON WITHOUT EVER LOOKING AT THOSE SCENES AGAIN?!
HOW?

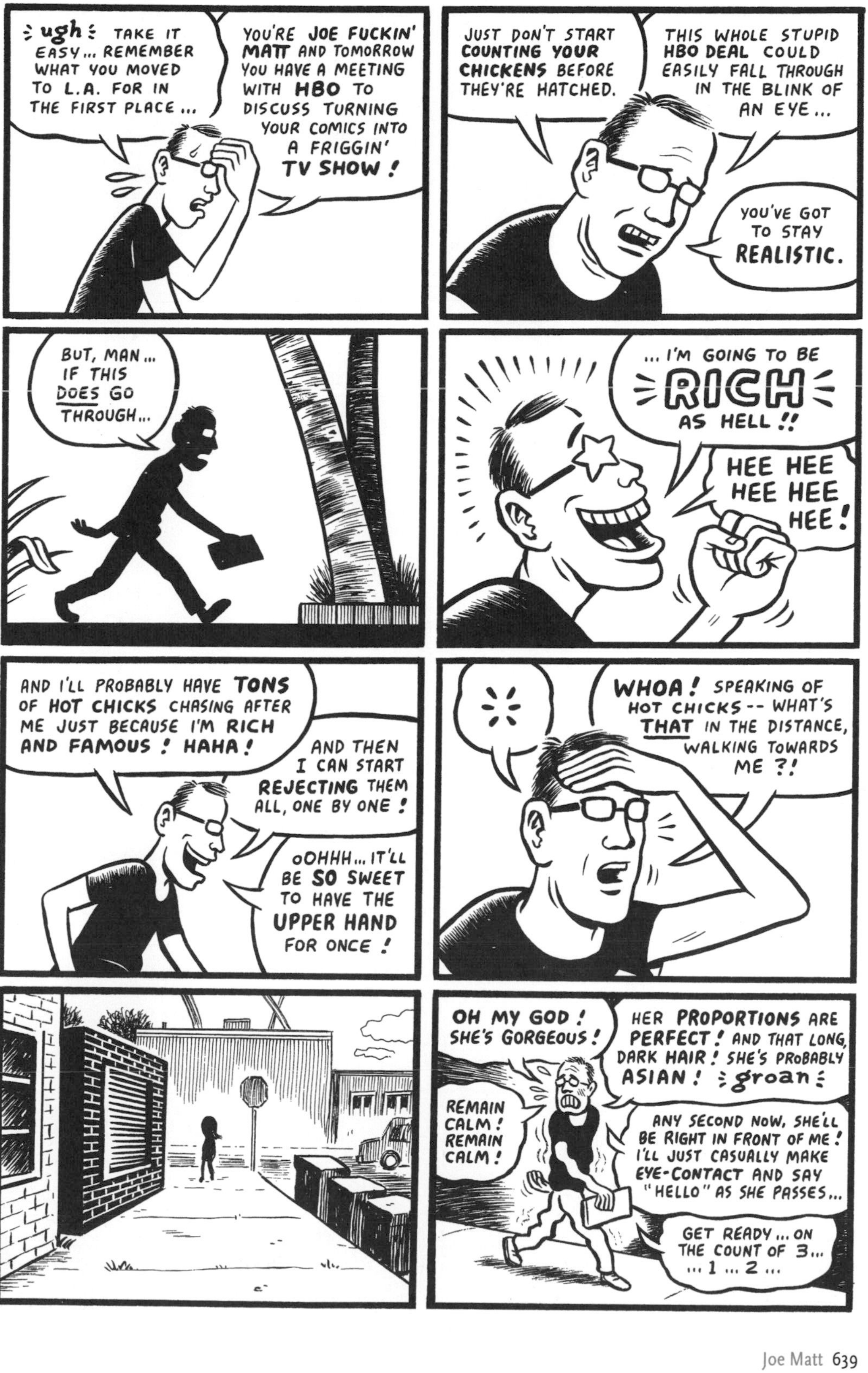

ugh TAKE IT EASY... REMEMBER WHAT YOU MOVED TO L.A. FOR IN THE FIRST PLACE...
YOU'RE JOE FUCKIN' MATT AND TOMORROW YOU HAVE A MEETING WITH HBO TO DISCUSS TURNING YOUR COMICS INTO A FRIGGIN' TV SHOW!
JUST DON'T START COUNTING YOUR CHICKENS BEFORE THEY'RE HATCHED.
THIS WHOLE STUPID HBO DEAL COULD EASILY FALL THROUGH IN THE BLINK OF AN EYE...
YOU'VE GOT TO STAY REALISTIC.
BUT, MAN... IF THIS DOES GO THROUGH...
... I'M GOING TO BE RICH AS HELL!!
HEE HEE HEE HEE HEE!
AND I'LL PROBABLY HAVE TONS OF HOT CHICKS CHASING AFTER ME JUST BECAUSE I'M RICH AND FAMOUS! HAHA!
AND THEN I CAN START REJECTING THEM ALL, ONE BY ONE!
oOHHH... IT'LL BE SO SWEET TO HAVE THE UPPER HAND FOR ONCE!
WHOA! SPEAKING OF HOT CHICKS -- WHAT'S THAT IN THE DISTANCE, WALKING TOWARDS ME?!
OH MY GOD! SHE'S GORGEOUS!
HER PROPORTIONS ARE PERFECT! AND THAT LONG, DARK HAIR! SHE'S PROBABLY ASIAN! groan
REMAIN CALM! REMAIN CALM!
ANY SECOND NOW, SHE'LL BE RIGHT IN FRONT OF ME! I'LL JUST CASUALLY MAKE EYE-CONTACT AND SAY "HELLO" AS SHE PASSES...
GET READY... ON THE COUNT OF 3... ...1 ...2 ...

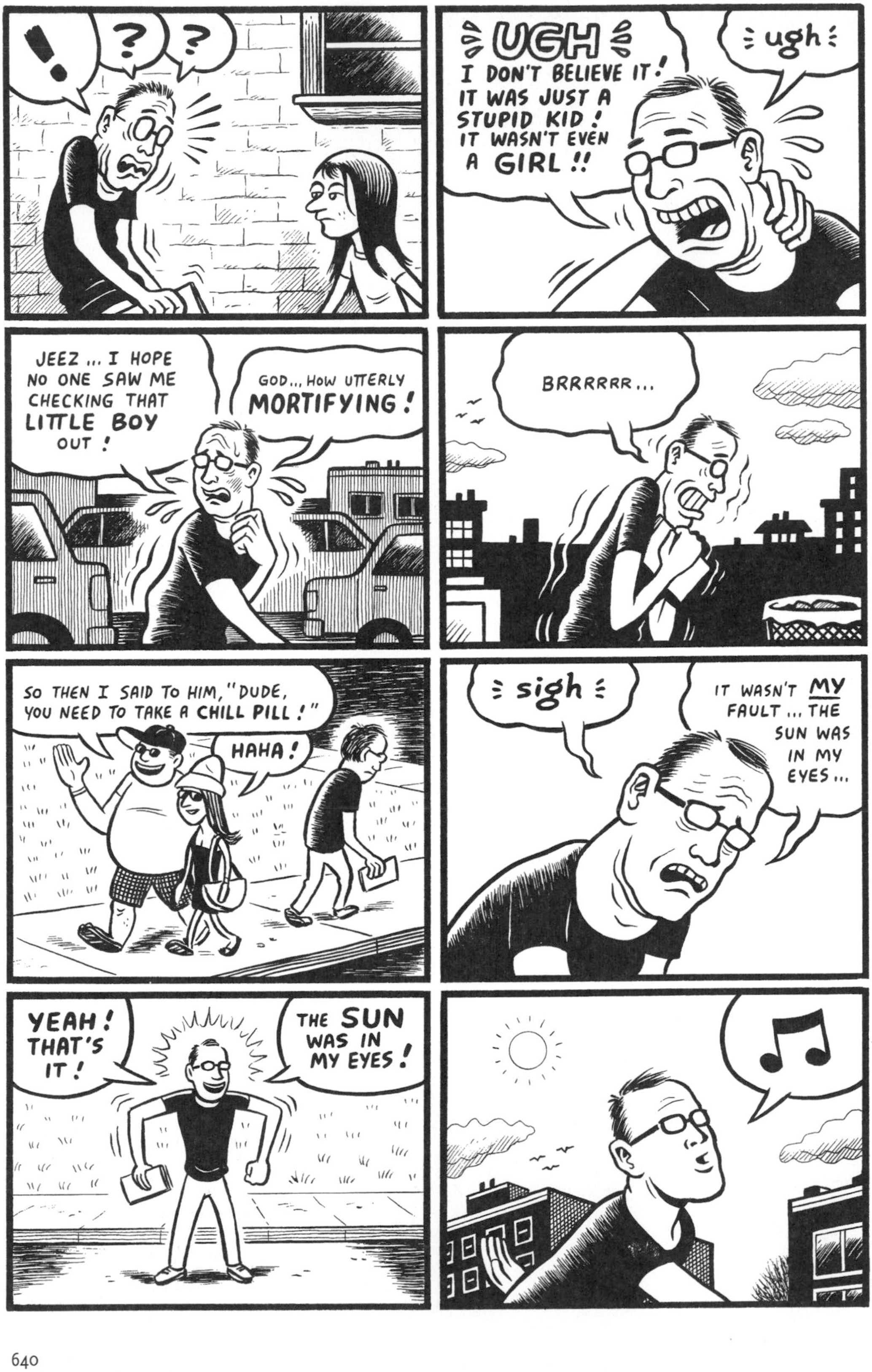
!
?
?
UGH
I DON'T BELIEVE IT! IT WAS JUST A STUPID KID! IT WASN'T EVEN A GIRL!!
ugh
JEEZ ... I HOPE NO ONE SAW ME CHECKING THAT LITTLE BOY OUT!
GOD ... HOW UTTERLY MORTIFYING!
BRRRRRR ...
SO THEN I SAID TO HIM, "DUDE, YOU NEED TO TAKE A CHILL PILL!"
HAHA!
sigh
IT WASN'T MY FAULT ... THE SUN WAS IN MY EYES ...
YEAH! THAT'S IT!
THE SUN WAS IN MY EYES!

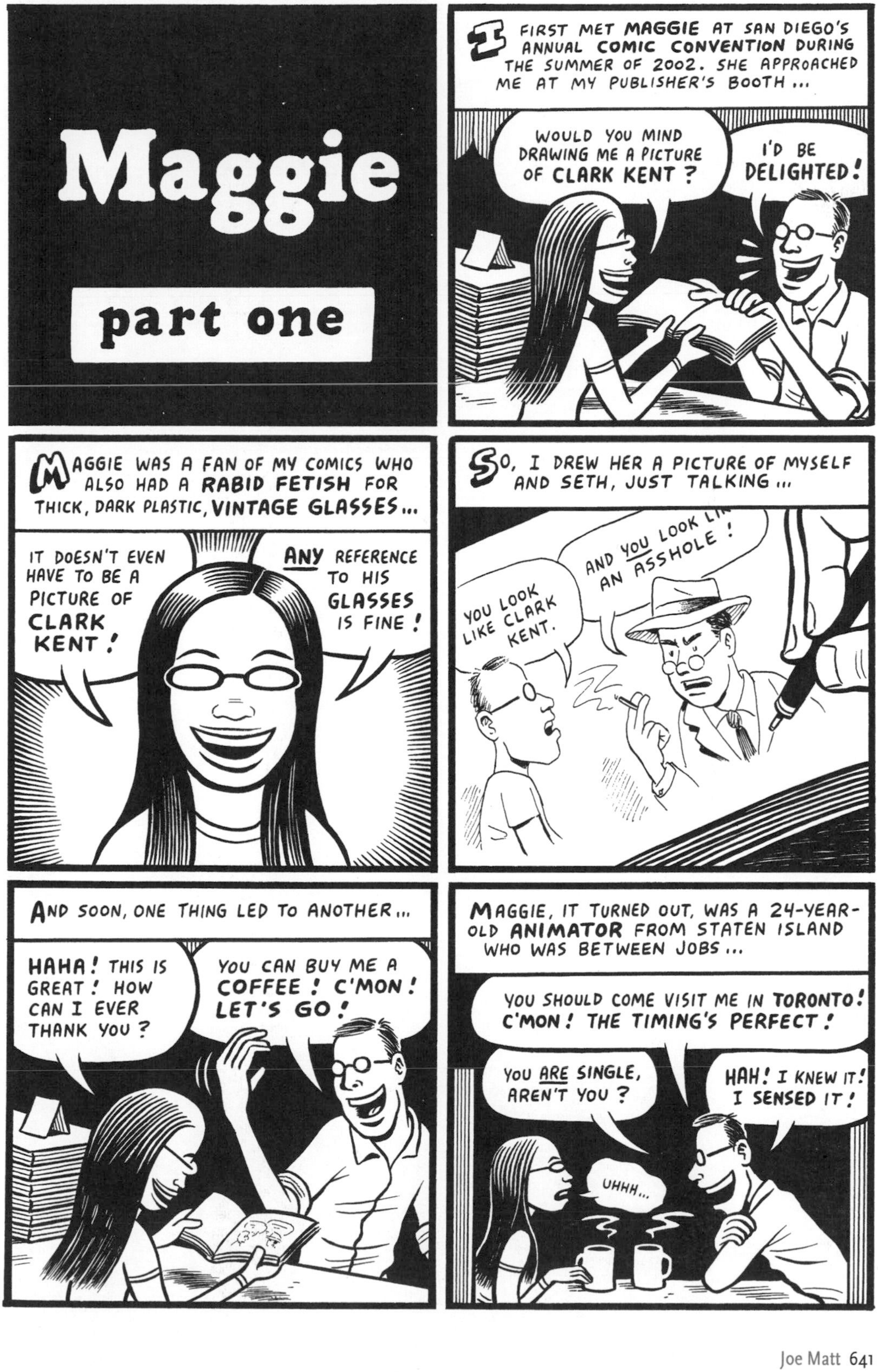
Maggie
part one
I FIRST MET MAGGIE AT SAN DIEGO'S ANNUAL COMIC CONVENTION DURING THE SUMMER OF 2002. SHE APPROACHED ME AT MY PUBLISHER'S BOOTH...
WOULD YOU MIND DRAWING ME A PICTURE OF CLARK KENT?
I'D BE DELIGHTED!
MAGGIE WAS A FAN OF MY COMICS WHO ALSO HAD A RABID FETISH FOR THICK, DARK PLASTIC, VINTAGE GLASSES...
IT DOESN'T EVEN HAVE TO BE A PICTURE OF CLARK KENT!
ANY REFERENCE TO HIS GLASSES IS FINE!
SO, I DREW HER A PICTURE OF MYSELF AND SETH, JUST TALKING...
YOU LOOK LIKE CLARK KENT.
AND YOU LOOK LI AN ASSHOLE!
AND SOON, ONE THING LED TO ANOTHER...
HAHA! THIS IS GREAT! HOW CAN I EVER THANK YOU?
YOU CAN BUY ME A COFFEE! C'MON! LET'S GO!
MAGGIE, IT TURNED OUT, WAS A 24-YEAR-OLD ANIMATOR FROM STATEN ISLAND WHO WAS BETWEEN JOBS...
YOU SHOULD COME VISIT ME IN TORONTO! C'MON! THE TIMING'S PERFECT!
YOU ARE SINGLE, AREN'T YOU?
UHHH...
HAH! I KNEW IT! I SENSED IT!

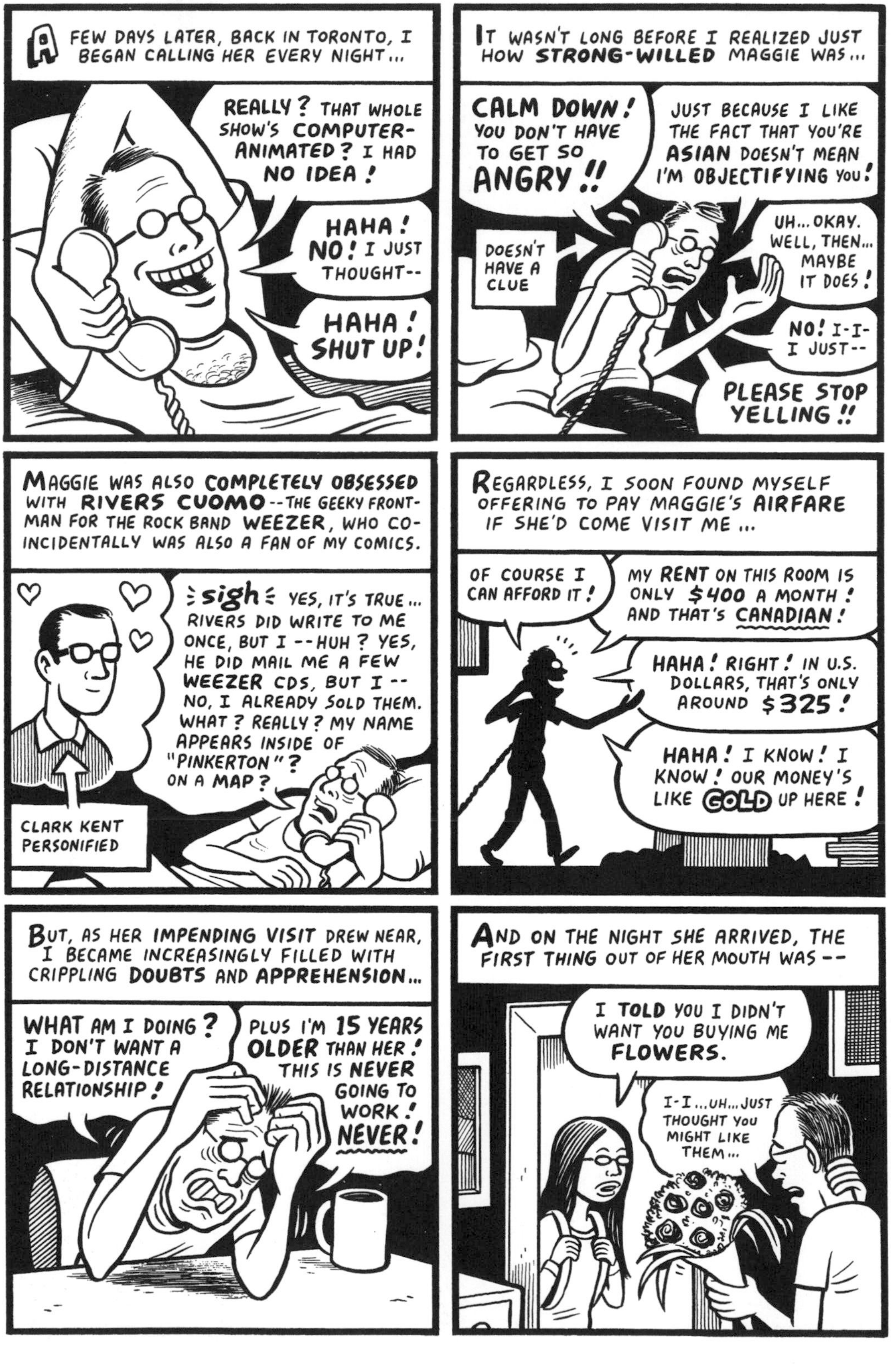
A FEW DAYS LATER, BACK IN TORONTO, I BEGAN CALLING HER EVERY NIGHT...
REALLY? THAT WHOLE SHOW'S COMPUTER-ANIMATED? I HAD NO IDEA!
HAHA! NO! I JUST THOUGHT--
HAHA! SHUT UP!
IT WASN'T LONG BEFORE I REALIZED JUST HOW STRONG-WILLED MAGGIE WAS...
CALM DOWN! YOU DON'T HAVE TO GET SO ANGRY!!
JUST BECAUSE I LIKE THE FACT THAT YOU'RE ASIAN DOESN'T MEAN I'M OBJECTIFYING YOU!
DOESN'T HAVE A CLUE
UH... OKAY. WELL, THEN... MAYBE IT DOES!
NO! I-I-I JUST--
PLEASE STOP YELLING!!
MAGGIE WAS ALSO COMPLETELY OBSESSED WITH RIVERS CUOMO--THE GEEKY FRONT-MAN FOR THE ROCK BAND WEEZER, WHO CO-INCIDENTALLY WAS ALSO A FAN OF MY COMICS.
sigh YES, IT'S TRUE... RIVERS DID WRITE TO ME ONCE, BUT I --HUH? YES, HE DID MAIL ME A FEW WEEZER CDS, BUT I -- NO, I ALREADY SOLD THEM. WHAT? REALLY? MY NAME APPEARS INSIDE OF "PINKERTON"? ON A MAP?
CLARK KENT PERSONIFIED
REGARDLESS, I SOON FOUND MYSELF OFFERING TO PAY MAGGIE'S AIRFARE IF SHE'D COME VISIT ME...
OF COURSE I CAN AFFORD IT!
MY RENT ON THIS ROOM IS ONLY $400 A MONTH! AND THAT'S CANADIAN!
HAHA! RIGHT! IN U.S. DOLLARS, THAT'S ONLY AROUND $325!
HAHA! I KNOW! I KNOW! OUR MONEY'S LIKE GOLD UP HERE!
BUT, AS HER IMPENDING VISIT DREW NEAR, I BECAME INCREASINGLY FILLED WITH CRIPPLING DOUBTS AND APPREHENSION...
WHAT AM I DOING? I DON'T WANT A LONG-DISTANCE RELATIONSHIP!
PLUS I'M 15 YEARS OLDER THAN HER! THIS IS NEVER GOING TO WORK! NEVER!
AND ON THE NIGHT SHE ARRIVED, THE FIRST THING OUT OF HER MOUTH WAS--
I TOLD YOU I DIDN'T WANT YOU BUYING ME FLOWERS.
I-I...UH...JUST THOUGHT YOU MIGHT LIKE THEM...

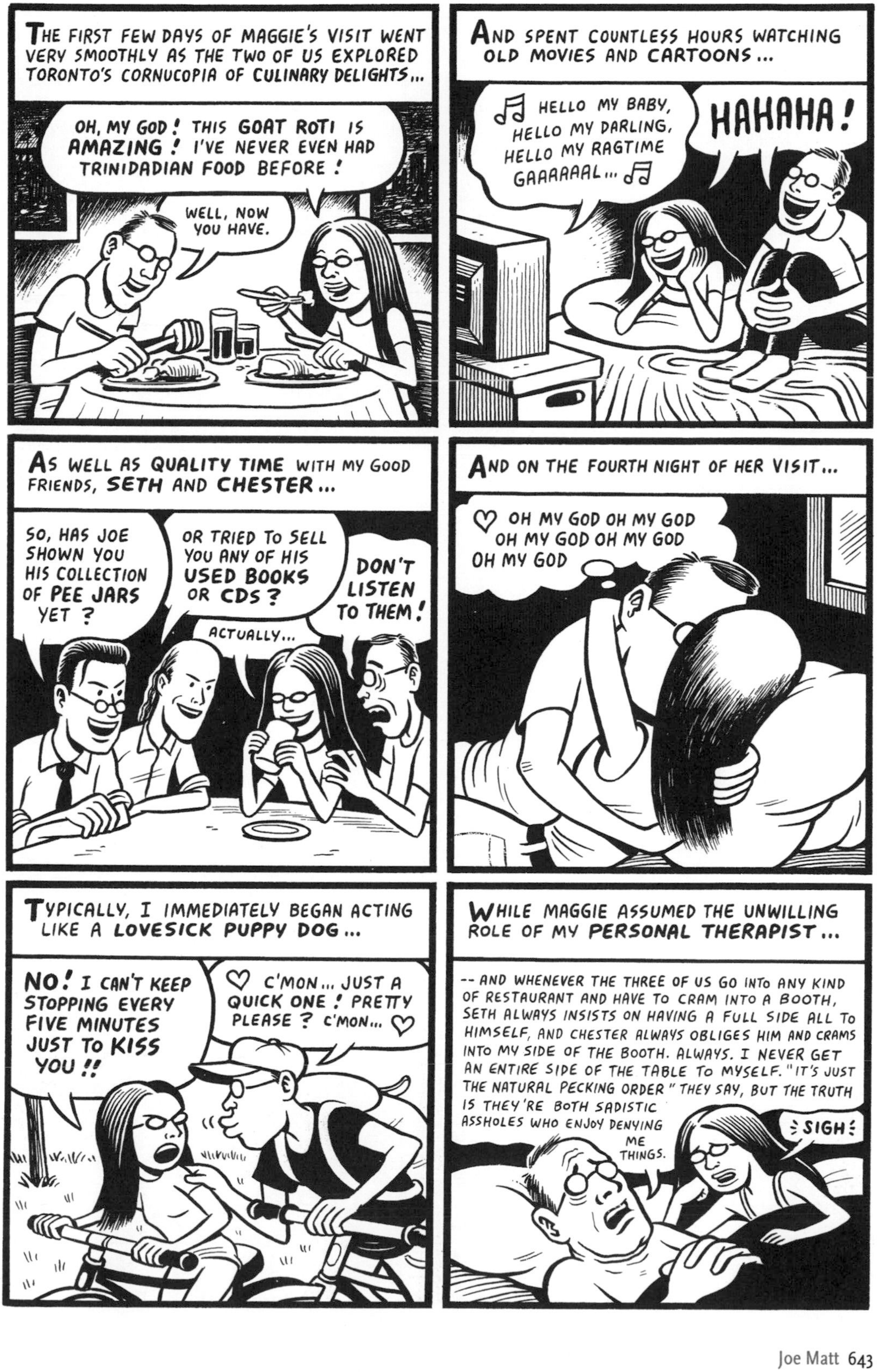
THE FIRST FEW DAYS OF MAGGIE'S VISIT WENT VERY SMOOTHLY AS THE TWO OF US EXPLORED TORONTO'S CORNUCOPIA OF CULINARY DELIGHTS...
OH, MY GOD! THIS GOAT ROTI IS AMAZING! I'VE NEVER EVEN HAD TRINIDADIAN FOOD BEFORE!
WELL, NOW YOU HAVE.
AND SPENT COUNTLESS HOURS WATCHING OLD MOVIES AND CARTOONS...
♫ HELLO MY BABY, HELLO MY DARLING, HELLO MY RAGTIME GAAAAAAL... ♫
HAHAHA!
AS WELL AS QUALITY TIME WITH MY GOOD FRIENDS, SETH AND CHESTER...
SO, HAS JOE SHOWN YOU HIS COLLECTION OF PEE JARS YET?
OR TRIED TO SELL YOU ANY OF HIS USED BOOKS OR CDS?
DON'T LISTEN TO THEM!
ACTUALLY...
AND ON THE FOURTH NIGHT OF HER VISIT...
♡ OH MY GOD OH MY GOD OH MY GOD OH MY GOD OH MY GOD
TYPICALLY, I IMMEDIATELY BEGAN ACTING LIKE A LOVESICK PUPPY DOG...
NO! I CAN'T KEEP STOPPING EVERY FIVE MINUTES JUST TO KISS YOU!!
♡ C'MON... JUST A QUICK ONE! PRETTY PLEASE? C'MON... ♡
WHILE MAGGIE ASSUMED THE UNWILLING ROLE OF MY PERSONAL THERAPIST...
-- AND WHENEVER THE THREE OF US GO INTO ANY KIND OF RESTAURANT AND HAVE TO CRAM INTO A BOOTH, SETH ALWAYS INSISTS ON HAVING A FULL SIDE ALL TO HIMSELF, AND CHESTER ALWAYS OBLIGES HIM AND CRAMS INTO MY SIDE OF THE BOOTH. ALWAYS. I NEVER GET AN ENTIRE SIDE OF THE TABLE TO MYSELF. "IT'S JUST THE NATURAL PECKING ORDER" THEY SAY, BUT THE TRUTH IS THEY'RE BOTH SADISTIC ASSHOLES WHO ENJOY DENYING ME THINGS.
SIGH

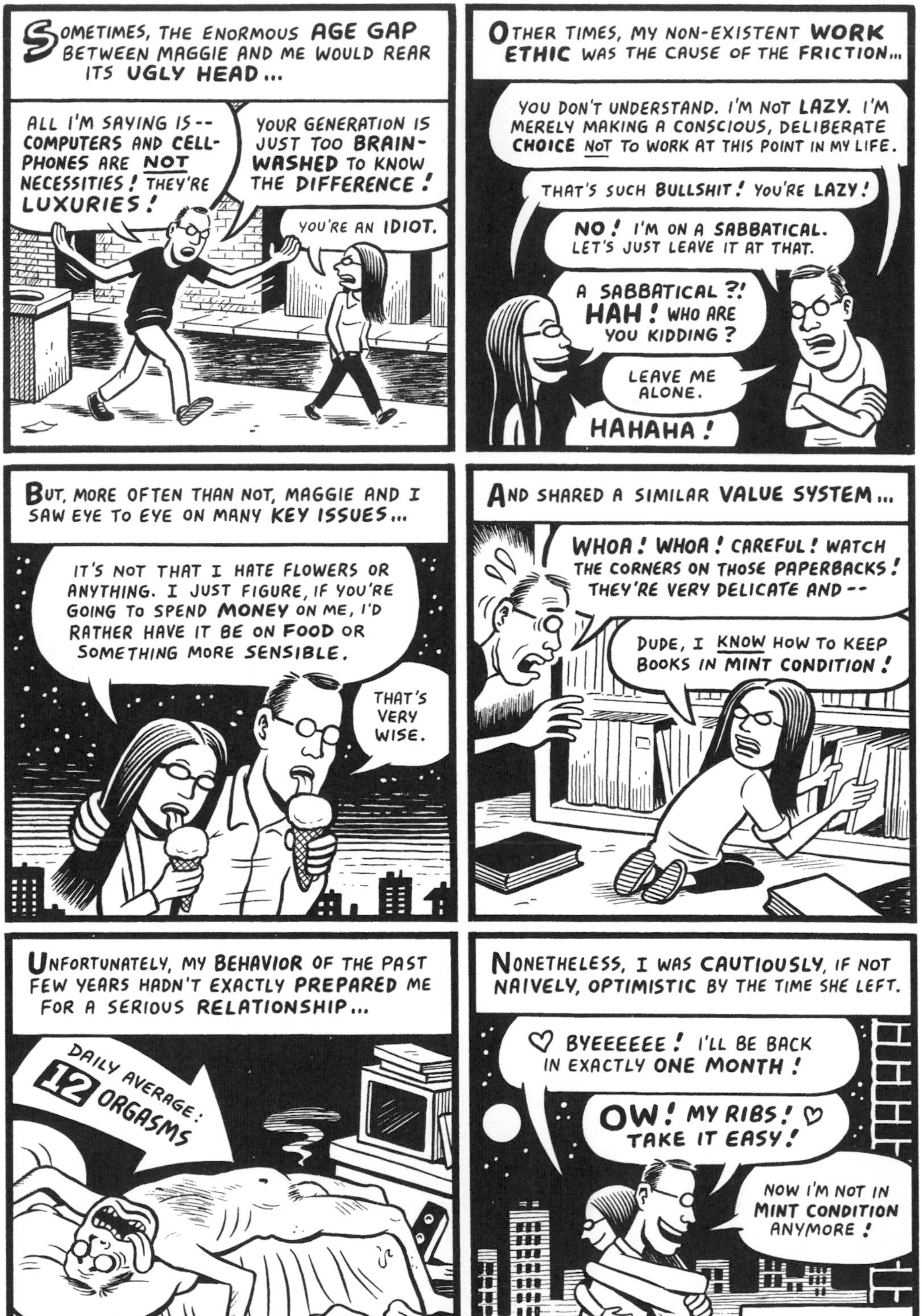
SOMETIMES, THE ENORMOUS AGE GAP BETWEEN MAGGIE AND ME WOULD REAR ITS UGLY HEAD...
ALL I'M SAYING IS -- COMPUTERS AND CELL-PHONES ARE NOT NECESSITIES! THEY'RE LUXURIES!
YOUR GENERATION IS JUST TOO BRAIN-WASHED TO KNOW THE DIFFERENCE!
YOU'RE AN IDIOT.
OTHER TIMES, MY NON-EXISTENT WORK ETHIC WAS THE CAUSE OF THE FRICTION...
YOU DON'T UNDERSTAND. I'M NOT LAZY. I'M MERELY MAKING A CONSCIOUS, DELIBERATE CHOICE NOT TO WORK AT THIS POINT IN MY LIFE.
THAT'S SUCH BULLSHIT! YOU'RE LAZY!
NO! I'M ON A SABBATICAL. LET'S JUST LEAVE IT AT THAT.
A SABBATICAL?! HAH! WHO ARE YOU KIDDING?
LEAVE ME ALONE.
HAHAHA!
BUT, MORE OFTEN THAN NOT, MAGGIE AND I SAW EYE TO EYE ON MANY KEY ISSUES...
IT'S NOT THAT I HATE FLOWERS OR ANYTHING. I JUST FIGURE, IF YOU'RE GOING TO SPEND MONEY ON ME, I'D RATHER HAVE IT BE ON FOOD OR SOMETHING MORE SENSIBLE.
THAT'S VERY WISE.
AND SHARED A SIMILAR VALUE SYSTEM...
WHOA! WHOA! CAREFUL! WATCH THE CORNERS ON THOSE PAPERBACKS! THEY'RE VERY DELICATE AND --
DUDE, I KNOW HOW TO KEEP BOOKS IN MINT CONDITION!
UNFORTUNATELY, MY BEHAVIOR OF THE PAST FEW YEARS HADN'T EXACTLY PREPARED ME FOR A SERIOUS RELATIONSHIP...
DAILY AVERAGE: 12 ORGASMS
NONETHELESS, I WAS CAUTIOUSLY, IF NOT NAIVELY, OPTIMISTIC BY THE TIME SHE LEFT.
♡ BYEEEEEE! I'LL BE BACK IN EXACTLY ONE MONTH!
OW! MY RIBS! ♡ TAKE IT EASY!
NOW I'M NOT IN MINT CONDITION ANYMORE!
TO BE CONTINUED...

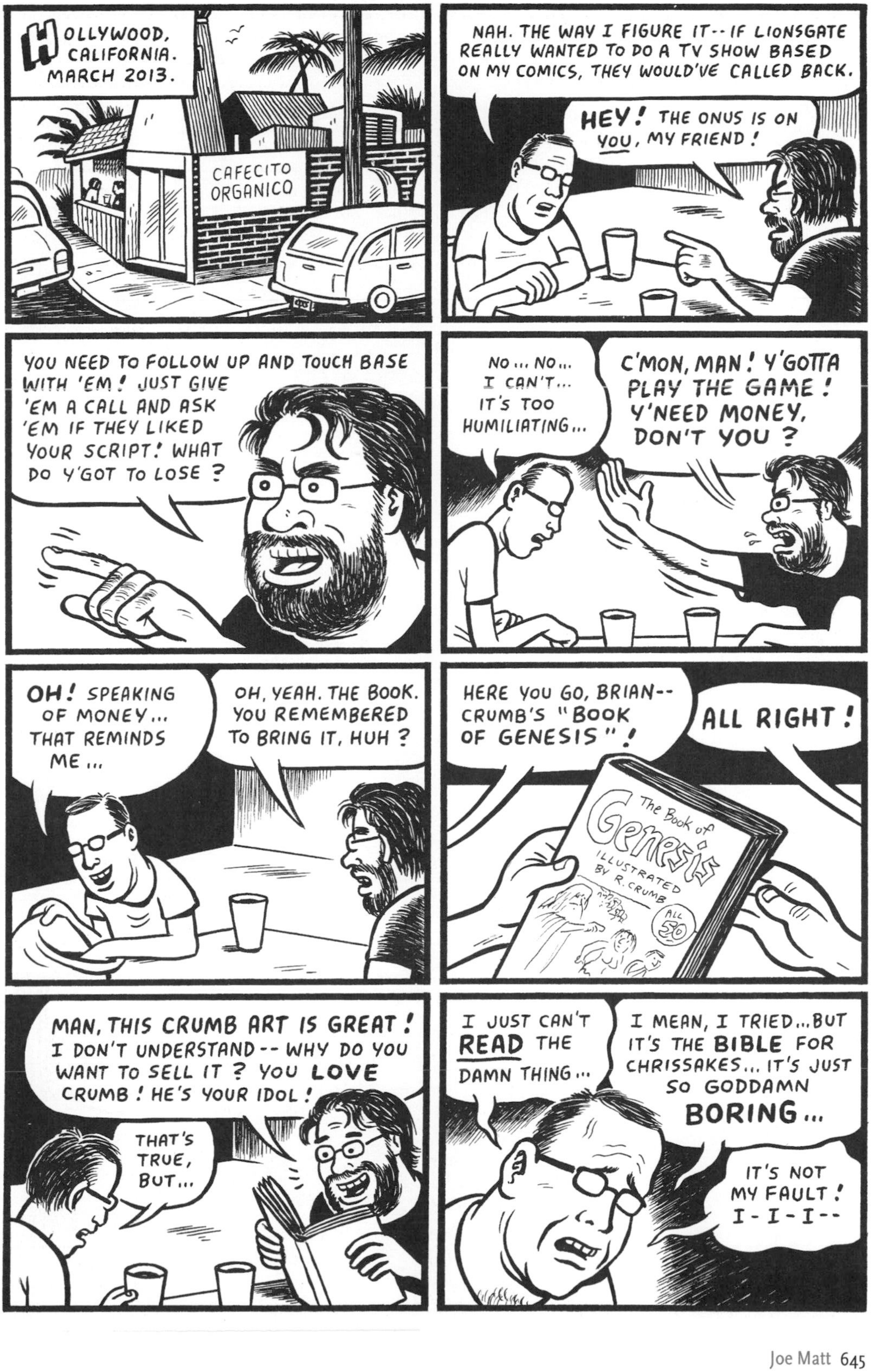
HOLLYWOOD, CALIFORNIA. MARCH 2013.
CAFECITO ORGANICO
NAH. THE WAY I FIGURE IT -- IF LIONSGATE REALLY WANTED TO DO A TV SHOW BASED ON MY COMICS, THEY WOULD'VE CALLED BACK.
HEY! THE ONUS IS ON YOU, MY FRIEND!
YOU NEED TO FOLLOW UP AND TOUCH BASE WITH 'EM! JUST GIVE 'EM A CALL AND ASK 'EM IF THEY LIKED YOUR SCRIPT! WHAT DO Y'GOT TO LOSE?
NO... NO... I CAN'T... IT'S TOO HUMILIATING...
C'MON, MAN! Y'GOTTA PLAY THE GAME! Y'NEED MONEY, DON'T YOU?
OH! SPEAKING OF MONEY... THAT REMINDS ME...
OH, YEAH. THE BOOK. YOU REMEMBERED TO BRING IT, HUH?
HERE YOU GO, BRIAN-- CRUMB'S "BOOK OF GENESIS"!
ALL RIGHT!
The Book of Genesis ILLUSTRATED BY R. CRUMB
ALL 50
MAN, THIS CRUMB ART IS GREAT! I DON'T UNDERSTAND -- WHY DO YOU WANT TO SELL IT? YOU LOVE CRUMB! HE'S YOUR IDOL!
THAT'S TRUE, BUT...
I JUST CAN'T READ THE DAMN THING...
I MEAN, I TRIED... BUT IT'S THE BIBLE FOR CHRISSAKES... IT'S JUST SO GODDAMN BORING...
IT'S NOT MY FAULT! I - I - I --

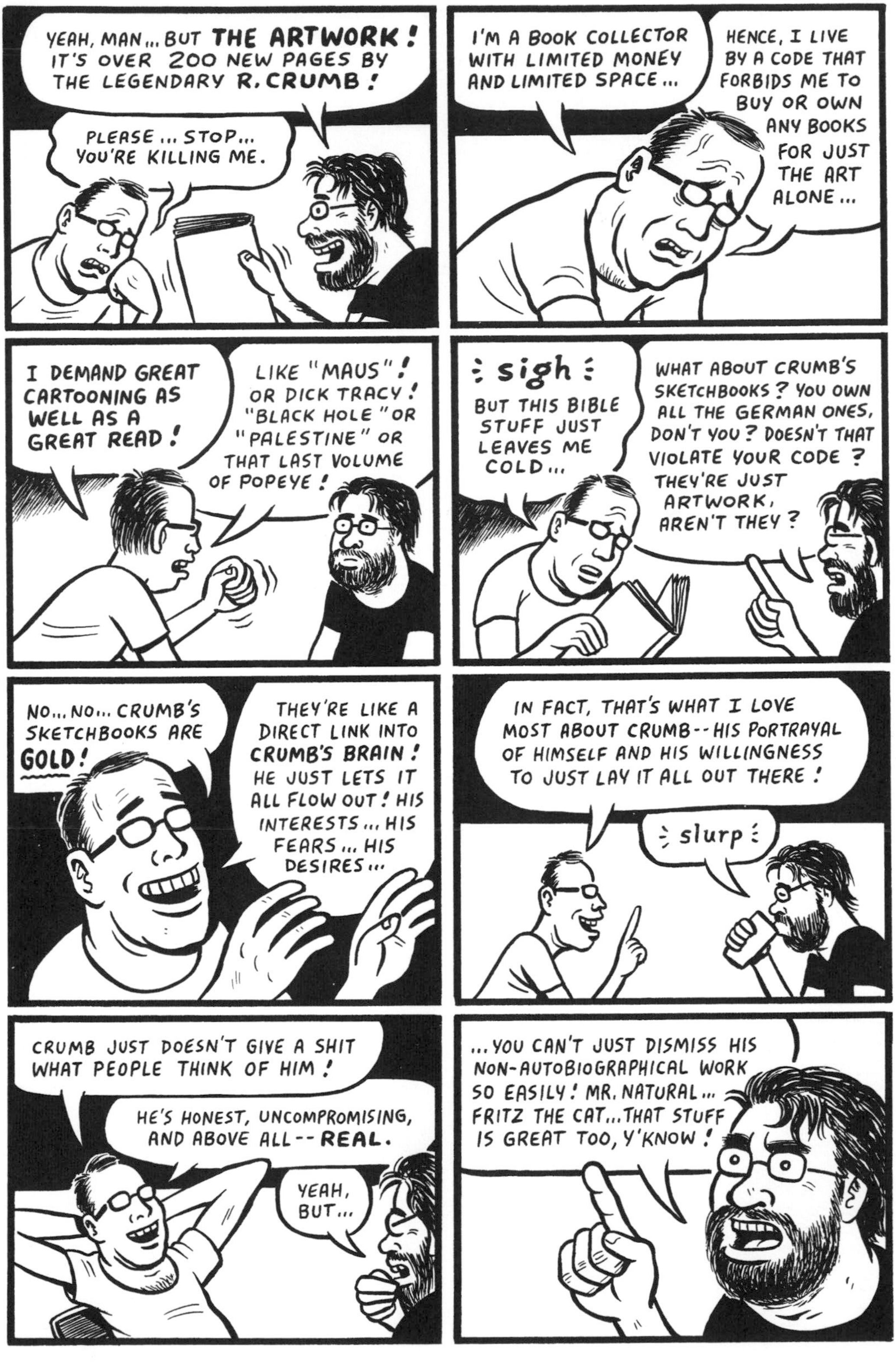
YEAH, MAN... BUT THE ARTWORK! IT'S OVER 200 NEW PAGES BY THE LEGENDARY R. CRUMB!
PLEASE... STOP... YOU'RE KILLING ME.
I'M A BOOK COLLECTOR WITH LIMITED MONEY AND LIMITED SPACE...
HENCE, I LIVE BY A CODE THAT FORBIDS ME TO BUY OR OWN ANY BOOKS FOR JUST THE ART ALONE...
I DEMAND GREAT CARTOONING AS WELL AS A GREAT READ!
LIKE "MAUS"! OR DICK TRACY! "BLACK HOLE" OR "PALESTINE" OR THAT LAST VOLUME OF POPEYE!
sigh
BUT THIS BIBLE STUFF JUST LEAVES ME COLD...
WHAT ABOUT CRUMB'S SKETCHBOOKS? YOU OWN ALL THE GERMAN ONES, DON'T YOU? DOESN'T THAT VIOLATE YOUR CODE? THEY'RE JUST ARTWORK, AREN'T THEY?
NO... NO... CRUMB'S SKETCHBOOKS ARE GOLD!
THEY'RE LIKE A DIRECT LINK INTO CRUMB'S BRAIN! HE JUST LETS IT ALL FLOW OUT! HIS INTERESTS... HIS FEARS... HIS DESIRES...
IN FACT, THAT'S WHAT I LOVE MOST ABOUT CRUMB--HIS PORTRAYAL OF HIMSELF AND HIS WILLINGNESS TO JUST LAY IT ALL OUT THERE!
slurp
CRUMB JUST DOESN'T GIVE A SHIT WHAT PEOPLE THINK OF HIM!
HE'S HONEST, UNCOMPROMISING, AND ABOVE ALL--REAL.
YEAH, BUT...
...YOU CAN'T JUST DISMISS HIS NON-AUTOBIOGRAPHICAL WORK SO EASILY! MR. NATURAL... FRITZ THE CAT... THAT STUFF IS GREAT TOO, Y'KNOW!

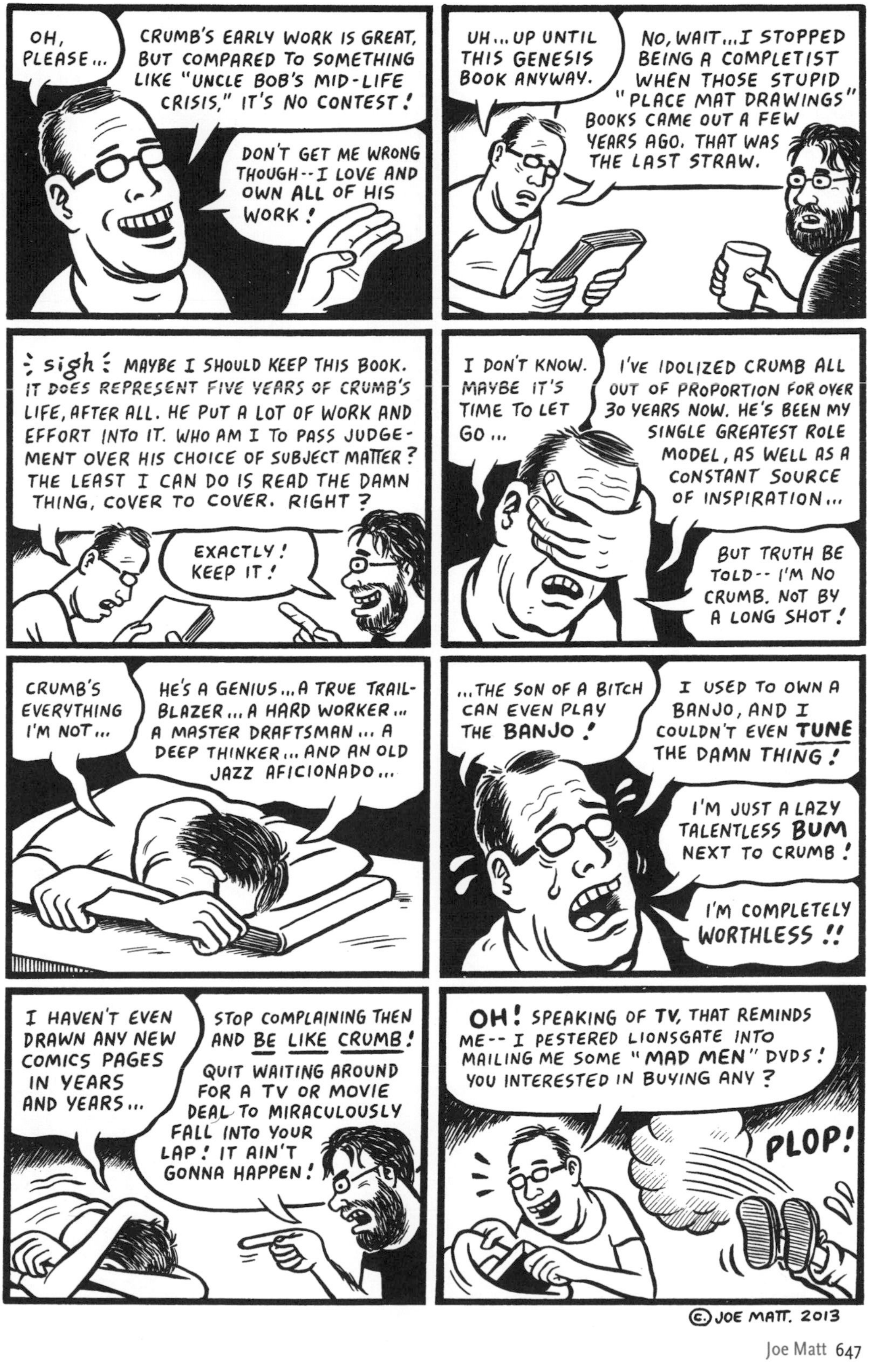
OH, PLEASE...
CRUMB'S EARLY WORK IS GREAT, BUT COMPARED TO SOMETHING LIKE "UNCLE BOB'S MID-LIFE CRISIS," IT'S NO CONTEST!
DON'T GET ME WRONG THOUGH--I LOVE AND OWN ALL OF HIS WORK!
UH... UP UNTIL THIS GENESIS BOOK ANYWAY.
NO, WAIT... I STOPPED BEING A COMPLETIST WHEN THOSE STUPID "PLACE MAT DRAWINGS" BOOKS CAME OUT A FEW YEARS AGO. THAT WAS THE LAST STRAW.
sigh MAYBE I SHOULD KEEP THIS BOOK. IT DOES REPRESENT FIVE YEARS OF CRUMB'S LIFE, AFTER ALL. HE PUT A LOT OF WORK AND EFFORT INTO IT. WHO AM I TO PASS JUDGEMENT OVER HIS CHOICE OF SUBJECT MATTER? THE LEAST I CAN DO IS READ THE DAMN THING, COVER TO COVER. RIGHT?
EXACTLY! KEEP IT!
I DON'T KNOW. MAYBE IT'S TIME TO LET GO...
I'VE IDOLIZED CRUMB ALL OUT OF PROPORTION FOR OVER 30 YEARS NOW. HE'S BEEN MY SINGLE GREATEST ROLE MODEL, AS WELL AS A CONSTANT SOURCE OF INSPIRATION...
BUT TRUTH BE TOLD--I'M NO CRUMB. NOT BY A LONG SHOT!
CRUMB'S EVERYTHING I'M NOT...
HE'S A GENIUS... A TRUE TRAIL-BLAZER... A HARD WORKER... A MASTER DRAFTSMAN... A DEEP THINKER... AND AN OLD JAZZ AFICIONADO...
...THE SON OF A BITCH CAN EVEN PLAY THE BANJO!
I USED TO OWN A BANJO, AND I COULDN'T EVEN TUNE THE DAMN THING!
I'M JUST A LAZY TALENTLESS BUM NEXT TO CRUMB!
I'M COMPLETELY WORTHLESS!!
I HAVEN'T EVEN DRAWN ANY NEW COMICS PAGES IN YEARS AND YEARS...
STOP COMPLAINING THEN AND BE LIKE CRUMB!
QUIT WAITING AROUND FOR A TV OR MOVIE DEAL TO MIRACULOUSLY FALL INTO YOUR LAP! IT AIN'T GONNA HAPPEN!
OH! SPEAKING OF TV, THAT REMINDS ME--I PESTERED LIONSGATE INTO MAILING ME SOME "MAD MEN" DVDS! YOU INTERESTED IN BUYING ANY?
PLOP!

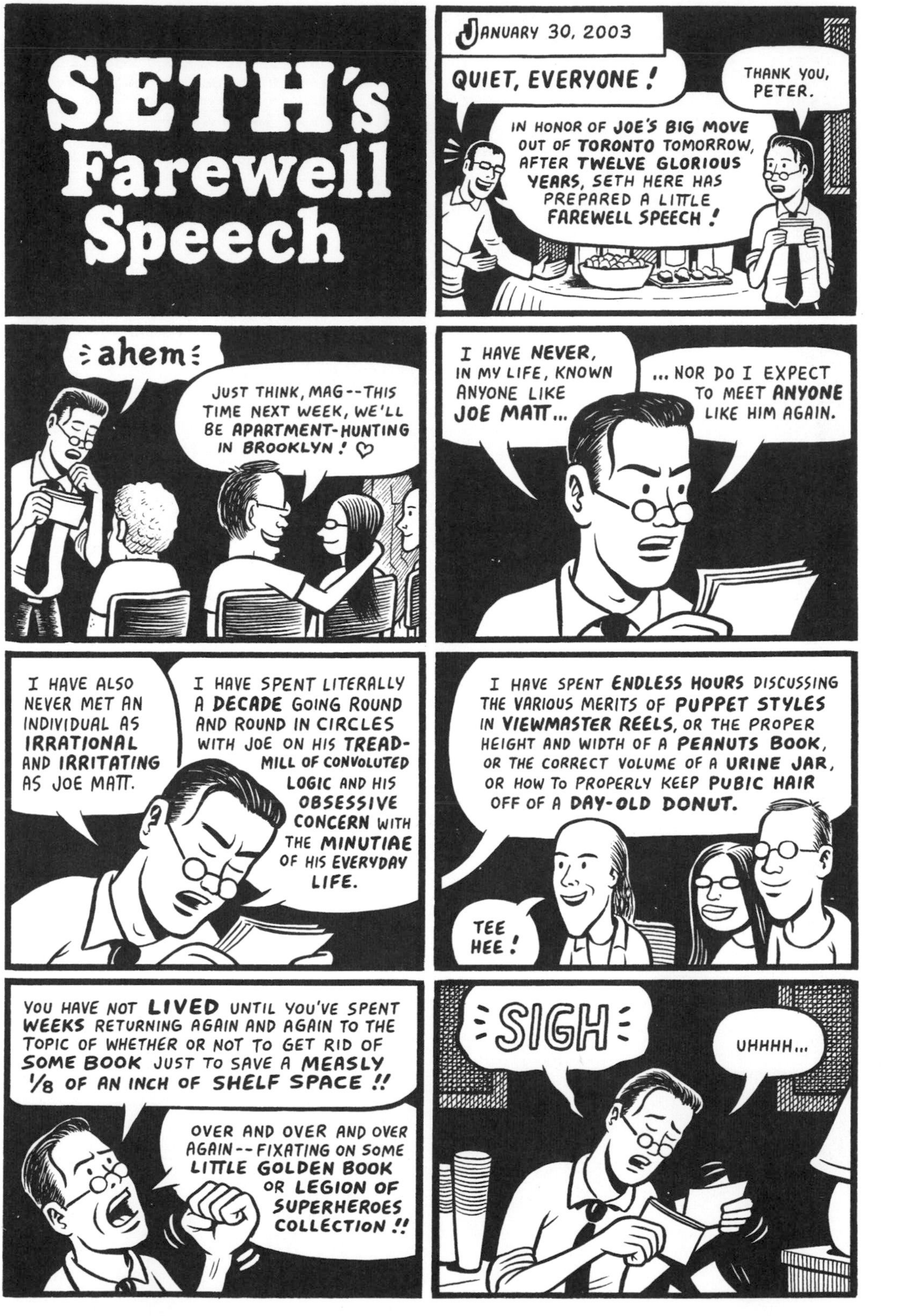
SETH's Farewell Speech
JANUARY 30, 2003
QUIET, EVERYONE!
THANK YOU, PETER.
IN HONOR OF JOE'S BIG MOVE OUT OF TORONTO TOMORROW, AFTER TWELVE GLORIOUS YEARS, SETH HERE HAS PREPARED A LITTLE FAREWELL SPEECH!
ahem
JUST THINK, MAG--THIS TIME NEXT WEEK, WE'LL BE APARTMENT-HUNTING IN BROOKLYN! ♡
I HAVE NEVER, IN MY LIFE, KNOWN ANYONE LIKE JOE MATT...
...NOR DO I EXPECT TO MEET ANYONE LIKE HIM AGAIN.
I HAVE ALSO NEVER MET AN INDIVIDUAL AS IRRATIONAL AND IRRITATING AS JOE MATT.
I HAVE SPENT LITERALLY A DECADE GOING ROUND AND ROUND IN CIRCLES WITH JOE ON HIS TREAD-MILL OF CONVOLUTED LOGIC AND HIS OBSESSIVE CONCERN WITH THE MINUTIAE OF HIS EVERYDAY LIFE.
I HAVE SPENT ENDLESS HOURS DISCUSSING THE VARIOUS MERITS OF PUPPET STYLES IN VIEWMASTER REELS, OR THE PROPER HEIGHT AND WIDTH OF A PEANUTS BOOK, OR THE CORRECT VOLUME OF A URINE JAR, OR HOW TO PROPERLY KEEP PUBIC HAIR OFF OF A DAY-OLD DONUT.
TEE HEE!
YOU HAVE NOT LIVED UNTIL YOU'VE SPENT WEEKS RETURNING AGAIN AND AGAIN TO THE TOPIC OF WHETHER OR NOT TO GET RID OF SOME BOOK JUST TO SAVE A MEASLY 1/8 OF AN INCH OF SHELF SPACE!!
OVER AND OVER AND OVER AGAIN--FIXATING ON SOME LITTLE GOLDEN BOOK OR LEGION OF SUPERHEROES COLLECTION!!
SIGH
UHHHH...

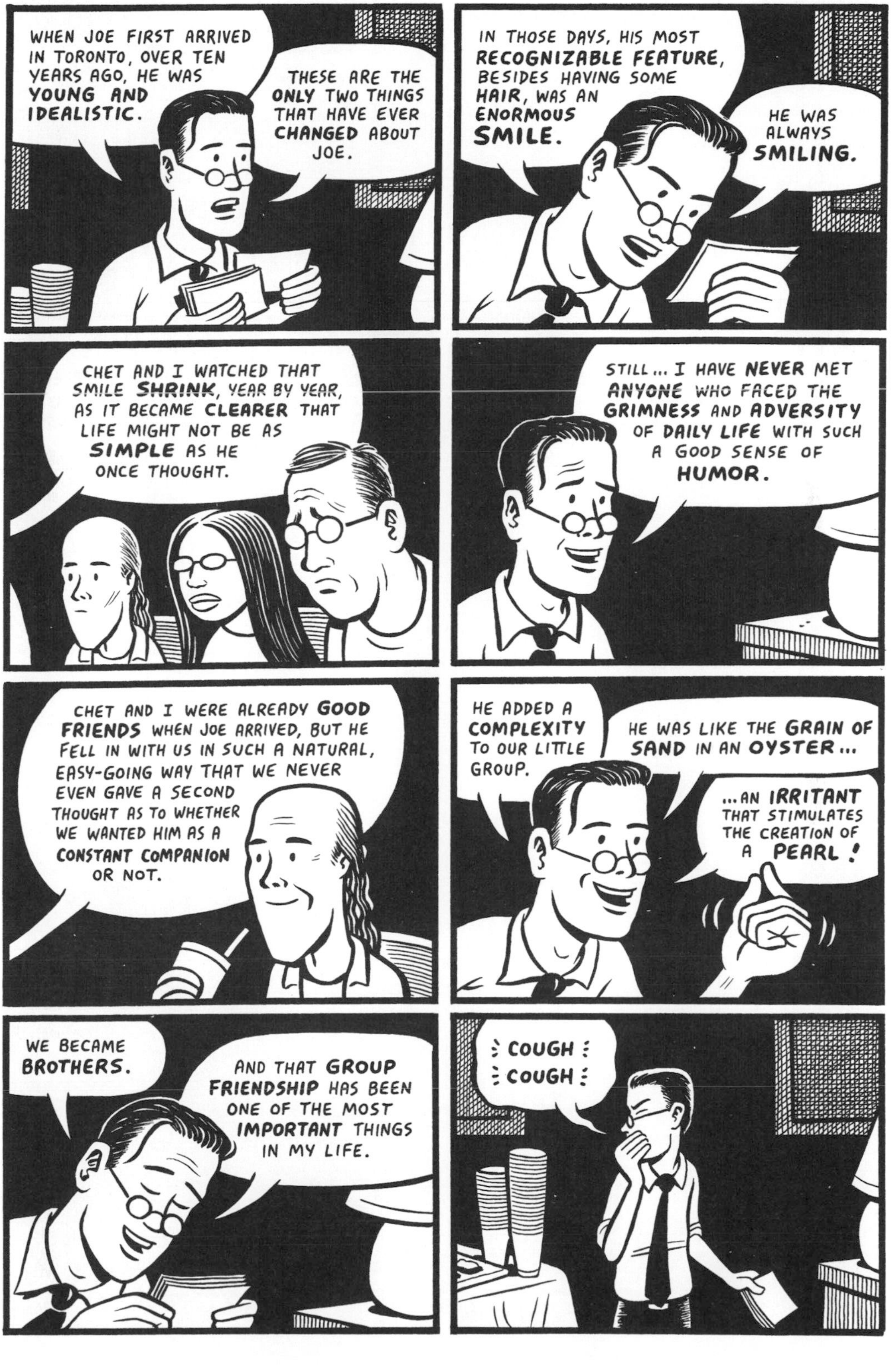
WHEN JOE FIRST ARRIVED IN TORONTO, OVER TEN YEARS AGO, HE WAS YOUNG AND IDEALISTIC.
THESE ARE THE ONLY TWO THINGS THAT HAVE EVER CHANGED ABOUT JOE.
IN THOSE DAYS, HIS MOST RECOGNIZABLE FEATURE, BESIDES HAVING SOME HAIR, WAS AN ENORMOUS SMILE.
HE WAS ALWAYS SMILING.
CHET AND I WATCHED THAT SMILE SHRINK, YEAR BY YEAR, AS IT BECAME CLEARER THAT LIFE MIGHT NOT BE AS SIMPLE AS HE ONCE THOUGHT.
STILL ... I HAVE NEVER MET ANYONE WHO FACED THE GRIMNESS AND ADVERSITY OF DAILY LIFE WITH SUCH A GOOD SENSE OF HUMOR.
CHET AND I WERE ALREADY GOOD FRIENDS WHEN JOE ARRIVED, BUT HE FELL IN WITH US IN SUCH A NATURAL, EASY-GOING WAY THAT WE NEVER EVEN GAVE A SECOND THOUGHT AS TO WHETHER WE WANTED HIM AS A CONSTANT COMPANION OR NOT.
HE ADDED A COMPLEXITY TO OUR LITTLE GROUP.
HE WAS LIKE THE GRAIN OF SAND IN AN OYSTER ...
... AN IRRITANT THAT STIMULATES THE CREATION OF A PEARL!
WE BECAME BROTHERS.
AND THAT GROUP FRIENDSHIP HAS BEEN ONE OF THE MOST IMPORTANT THINGS IN MY LIFE.
COUGH
COUGH

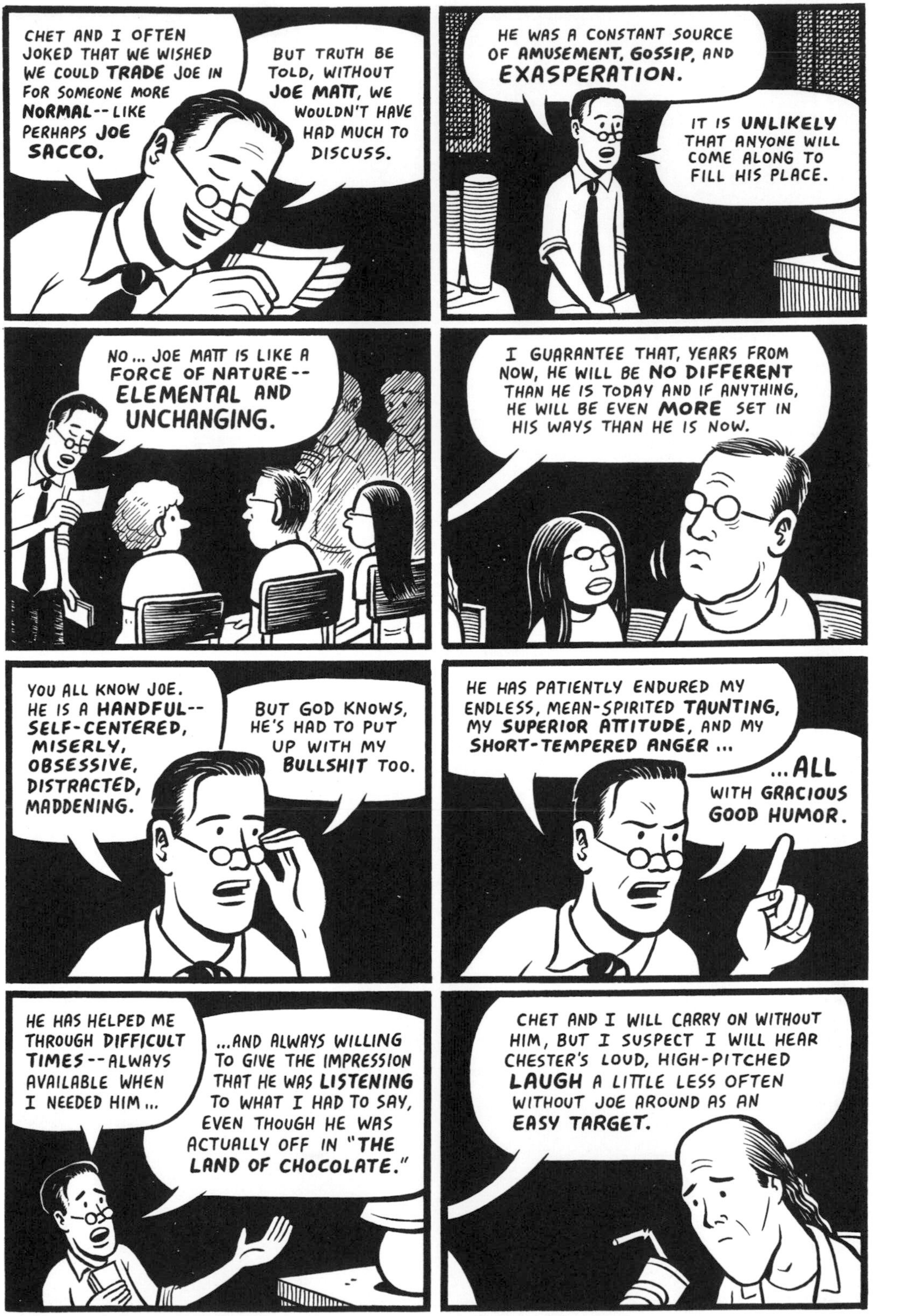
CHET AND I OFTEN JOKED THAT WE WISHED WE COULD TRADE JOE IN FOR SOMEONE MORE NORMAL--LIKE PERHAPS JOE SACCO.
BUT TRUTH BE TOLD, WITHOUT JOE MATT, WE WOULDN'T HAVE HAD MUCH TO DISCUSS.
HE WAS A CONSTANT SOURCE OF AMUSEMENT, GOSSIP, AND EXASPERATION.
IT IS UNLIKELY THAT ANYONE WILL COME ALONG TO FILL HIS PLACE.
NO... JOE MATT IS LIKE A FORCE OF NATURE--ELEMENTAL AND UNCHANGING.
I GUARANTEE THAT, YEARS FROM NOW, HE WILL BE NO DIFFERENT THAN HE IS TODAY AND IF ANYTHING, HE WILL BE EVEN MORE SET IN HIS WAYS THAN HE IS NOW.
YOU ALL KNOW JOE. HE IS A HANDFUL--SELF-CENTERED, MISERLY, OBSESSIVE, DISTRACTED, MADDENING.
BUT GOD KNOWS, HE'S HAD TO PUT UP WITH MY BULLSHIT TOO.
HE HAS PATIENTLY ENDURED MY ENDLESS, MEAN-SPIRITED TAUNTING, MY SUPERIOR ATTITUDE, AND MY SHORT-TEMPERED ANGER...
...ALL WITH GRACIOUS GOOD HUMOR.
HE HAS HELPED ME THROUGH DIFFICULT TIMES--ALWAYS AVAILABLE WHEN I NEEDED HIM...
...AND ALWAYS WILLING TO GIVE THE IMPRESSION THAT HE WAS LISTENING TO WHAT I HAD TO SAY, EVEN THOUGH HE WAS ACTUALLY OFF IN "THE LAND OF CHOCOLATE."
CHET AND I WILL CARRY ON WITHOUT HIM, BUT I SUSPECT I WILL HEAR CHESTER'S LOUD, HIGH-PITCHED LAUGH A LITTLE LESS OFTEN WITHOUT JOE AROUND AS AN EASY TARGET.

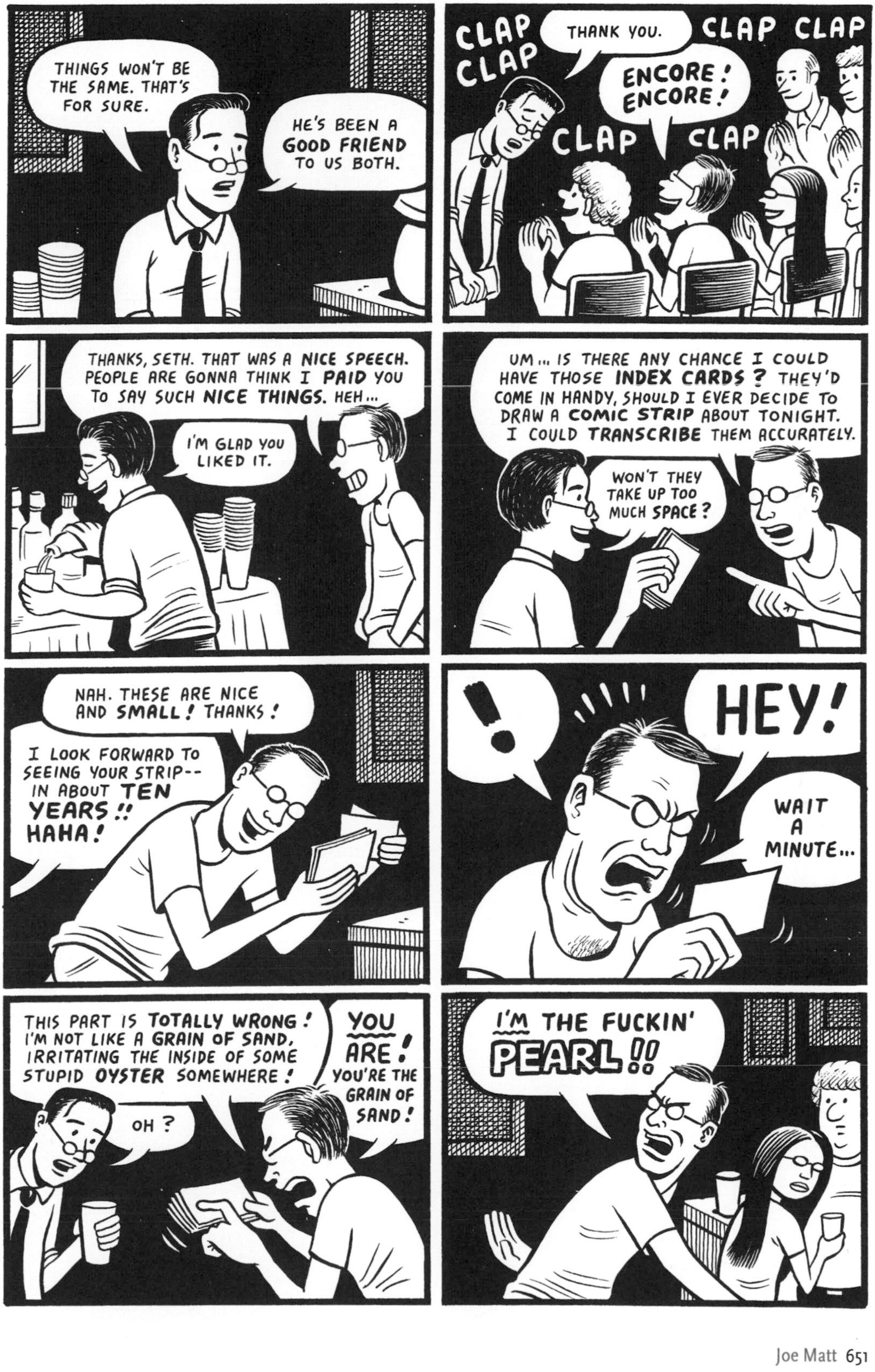
THINGS WON'T BE THE SAME. THAT'S FOR SURE.
HE'S BEEN A GOOD FRIEND TO US BOTH.
CLAP CLAP
THANK YOU.
CLAP CLAP
ENCORE! ENCORE!
CLAP
CLAP
THANKS, SETH. THAT WAS A NICE SPEECH. PEOPLE ARE GONNA THINK I PAID YOU TO SAY SUCH NICE THINGS. HEH...
I'M GLAD YOU LIKED IT.
UM... IS THERE ANY CHANCE I COULD HAVE THOSE INDEX CARDS? THEY'D COME IN HANDY, SHOULD I EVER DECIDE TO DRAW A COMIC STRIP ABOUT TONIGHT. I COULD TRANSCRIBE THEM ACCURATELY.
WON'T THEY TAKE UP TOO MUCH SPACE?
NAH. THESE ARE NICE AND SMALL! THANKS!
I LOOK FORWARD TO SEEING YOUR STRIP-- IN ABOUT TEN YEARS!! HAHA!
!
HEY!
WAIT A MINUTE...
THIS PART IS TOTALLY WRONG! I'M NOT LIKE A GRAIN OF SAND, IRRITATING THE INSIDE OF SOME STUPID OYSTER SOMEWHERE!
YOU ARE! YOU'RE THE GRAIN OF SAND!
OH?
I'M THE FUCKIN' PEARL!!

It seems longer than twenty-five years ago when I first heard from—and of—Chris Oliveros. He was about to leave art school (SVA, I believe), and was thinking of starting up an alternative comics anthology somewhat similar to the one I had just resigned from editing, called *Weirdo*, and was asking me for some advice.

Weirdo was started by the legendary cartoonist Robert Crumb and ran throughout the 1980s. Originally edited by Crumb, it was later managed by me and, after me, Crumb's wife, Aline Kominsky-Crumb, though Robert always had a huge presence in the magazine, and thus it was always thought of as his magazine.

Editing *Weirdo*, as well as working with my all-time favourite artist, was an exciting and valuable experience, but also a taxing one. The pay was chicken feed, for one thing, and hardly compensated for the nightmare that is dealing with some of the more temperamental and insecure contributors. As a result, I'm pretty sure the loudest piece of advice I gave Chris was *don't do it*. Do *anthing else* instead! But he sounded pretty determined, so I hope that what other bits of advice I gave him proved to be helpful.

Chris also asked me to contribute to the first issue of what he had already decided to call *Drawn & Quarterly*. I had my own one man anthology running at the time, and thus had little time to contribute to other publications, but offered him a one-page strip I had lying around—a typically overexaggerated piece of nonsense featuring a hyperactive brat named Girly-Girl. Chris agreed to run the piece, but when I actually saw the first issue it was hard not to notice that Chris's sensibilities were far more refined and subdued than my own. As a result I felt like I "ruined" his magazine with my own loud, garish "artwork" and silently decided not to darken his door with any more submissions.

This is not to suggest that I had a problem with Chris's sensibility—in fact, D+Q quickly became the home of many of my favourite cartoonists, and their output these past twenty-five years has been second to none. And it took almost that many years before I worked up the nerve to pitch a book idea to him—albeit one that I assumed would be well suited to his line. Thankfully he agreed, and I must say that it's quite an honour and a privilege to be working with him again—only this time sans Girly-Girl!

—Peter Bagge

P.S: YES, I GREW UP IN THE 'BURBS. WHAT WHITE KID DIDN'T?

CHRIS,

GLAD YOU LIKED THE MINI-COMIC I SENT YOU, AND THAT YOU'RE ALSO GONNA GO AHEAD W/ D+Q IN SPITE OF THE MONEY SITUATION.

YOU MIGHT AS WELL TRY NEWSTAND DISTRIBUTORS + BOOK-STORES, BUT KEEP IN MIND THAT THEY'RE NO BETTER—AND IN MANY WAYS WORSE—THAN THE COMIC MARKET. YOU'LL FIND THEY'LL EXPECT A LOT FROM YOU, WHILE THEY'LL DO LITTLE FOR YOU IN RETURN.

AT THE SAME DON'T EVER GIVE UP HAMMERING AWAY AT THE DIRECT-SALES PEOPLE. YES, WE ALL KNOW THEY SUCK, BUT THEY'RE NOT HOPELESS, + IT TAKES A WHILE FOR A NEW PUBLISHER TO CARVE A LIL' NICHE FOR HIMSELF.

M. DOUGAN'S ADDRESS: 129 WARREN AVE. N., SEATTLE, WA, 98109. APT. H.

LATER —PETER B.

 Letter from Peter Bagge to Chris Oliveros (1990).

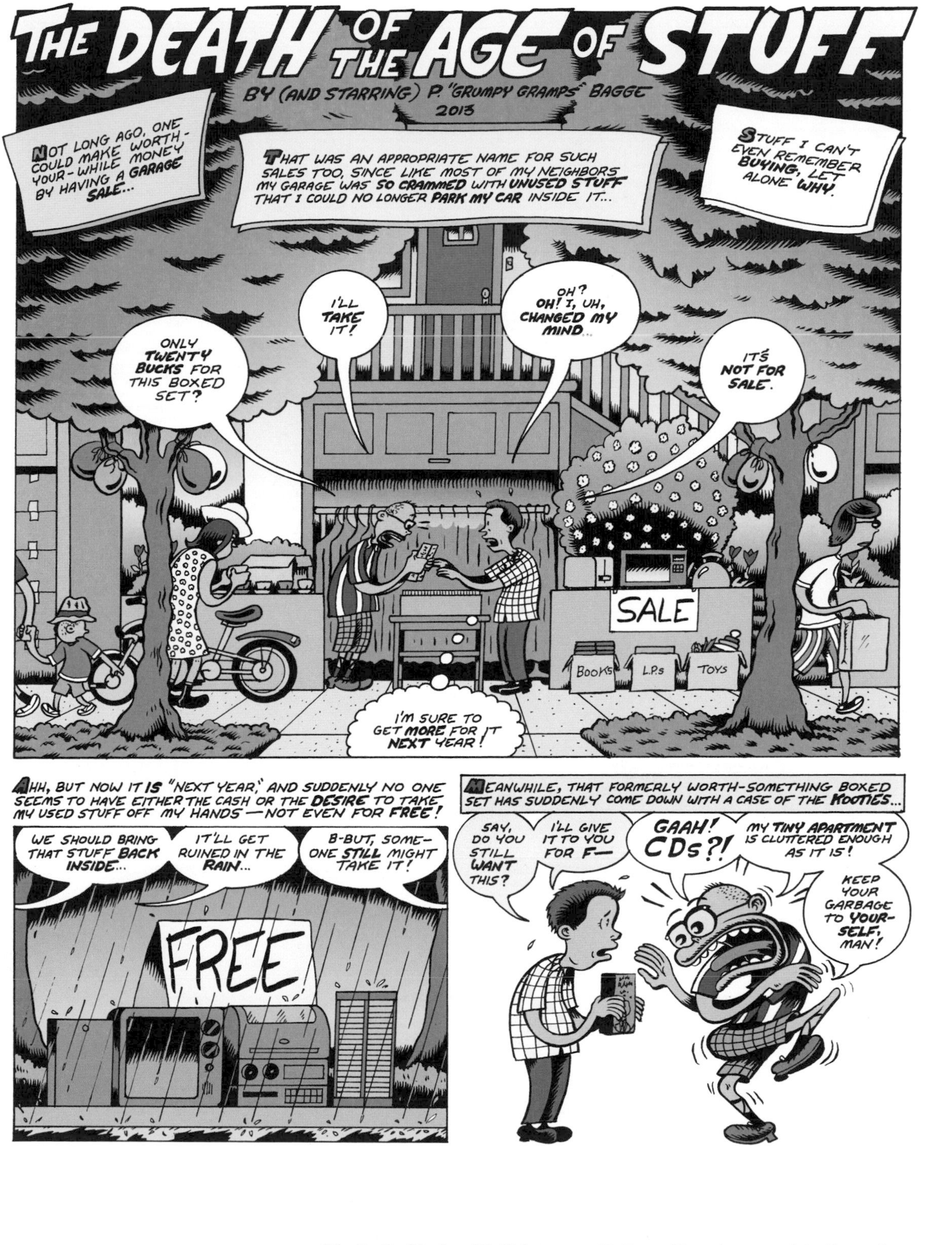
THE DEATH OF THE AGE OF STUFF
BY (AND STARRING) P. "GRUMPY GRAMPS" BAGGE 2013
NOT LONG AGO, ONE COULD MAKE WORTH-YOUR-WHILE MONEY BY HAVING A GARAGE SALE...
THAT WAS AN APPROPRIATE NAME FOR SUCH SALES TOO, SINCE LIKE MOST OF MY NEIGHBORS MY GARAGE WAS SO CRAMMED WITH UNUSED STUFF THAT I COULD NO LONGER PARK MY CAR INSIDE IT...
STUFF I CAN'T EVEN REMEMBER BUYING, LET ALONE WHY.
ONLY TWENTY BUCKS FOR THIS BOXED SET?
I'LL TAKE IT!
OH? OH! I, UH, CHANGED MY MIND...
IT'S NOT FOR SALE.
SALE
BOOKS
L.P.s
TOYS
I'M SURE TO GET MORE FOR IT NEXT YEAR!
AHH, BUT NOW IT IS "NEXT YEAR," AND SUDDENLY NO ONE SEEMS TO HAVE EITHER THE CASH OR THE DESIRE TO TAKE MY USED STUFF OFF MY HANDS — NOT EVEN FOR FREE!
WE SHOULD BRING THAT STUFF BACK INSIDE...
IT'LL GET RUINED IN THE RAIN...
B-BUT, SOME-ONE STILL MIGHT TAKE IT!
FREE
MEANWHILE, THAT FORMERLY WORTH-SOMETHING BOXED SET HAS SUDDENLY COME DOWN WITH A CASE OF THE KOOTIES...
SAY, DO YOU STILL WANT THIS?
I'LL GIVE IT TO YOU FOR F—
GAAH! CDs?!
MY TINY APARTMENT IS CLUTTERED ENOUGH AS IT IS!
KEEP YOUR GARBAGE TO YOUR-SELF, MAN!

"The Death of the Age of Stuff" first appeared in *Reason* (November 2013).

Of course, I myself have less need for stuff these days. For one thing, my entire family downloads or streams **all** of our entertainment needs off of the **internet**...

> Want to watch **another** episode of "The Walking Dead"?

> Nah. Six straight hours of exploding zombies is my **limit**.

> Beautiful day out

> ♫..treasure... that... is... what... you... are...

Nice knowin' ya, record and video stores!

And what we do buy we purchase online, even **groceries**...

> Look! I'm **food shopping** in my PJs!

> Let's see, do I want **ripe** bananas, or "slightly green"?

> I'm told Amazon's a bad company to work for...

> But they're so **cheap!**

> And we have "Amazon Prime"!

> *oof*!

Sorry, local grocery stores!

While every day someone invents a **new app** that eliminates the need for yet another **middleman**...

> This new app makes it possible for me to do my own taxes...

> What'll they think of **next**?

So long, accountants, travel agents, realtors, etc....

In fact, there's **countless** ways to save money via the net...

> There's a local yoga studio that specializes in **back pain**...

> Here, I'll give you their **number**...

> I'll just search for yoga back stretches on **YouTube** instead! Problem **solved!**

> Okay.

My apologies, yoga instructors everywhere!

Then there's the many ways this new technology has made my job **so much easier**: scanners, photoshop, email, file sharing, etc....

> I used to have to package and haul literally **everything** I drew to this place back in the day...

> And I'd wait in line **forever!**

> The P.O. looks **empty** these days, though.

UNITED STATES POST OFFICE

Adios, U.S. Post Office!

While this new economy has been a **boon** for some, it also has almost **obliterated** entire industries, while putting a big dent in **others**...

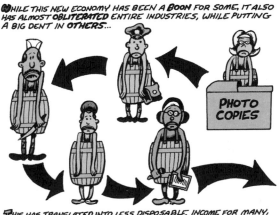

PHOTO COPIES

This has translated into less disposable income for many, meaning even **less demand for stuff**, which in turn affects more **livelihoods**...

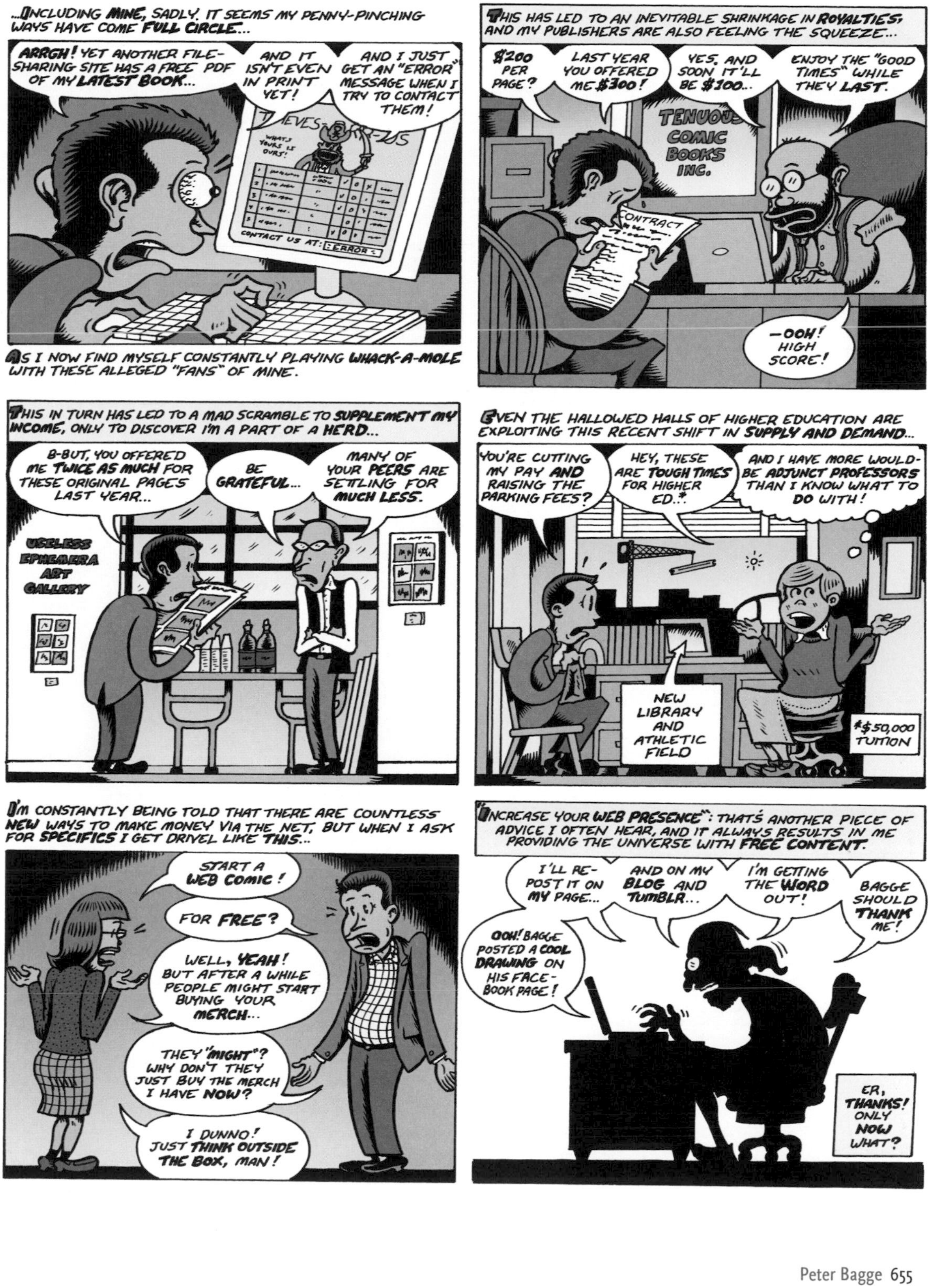
...INCLUDING MINE, SADLY. IT SEEMS MY PENNY-PINCHING WAYS HAVE COME FULL CIRCLE...
ARRGH! YET ANOTHER FILE-SHARING SITE HAS A FREE PDF OF MY LATEST BOOK...
AND IT ISN'T EVEN IN PRINT YET!
AND I JUST GET AN "ERROR" MESSAGE WHEN I TRY TO CONTACT THEM!
WHAT'S YOURS IS OURS!
CONTACT US AT: ERROR
AS I NOW FIND MYSELF CONSTANTLY PLAYING WHACK-A-MOLE WITH THESE ALLEGED "FANS" OF MINE.
THIS HAS LED TO AN INEVITABLE SHRINKAGE IN ROYALTIES, AND MY PUBLISHERS ARE ALSO FEELING THE SQUEEZE...
$200 PER PAGE?
LAST YEAR YOU OFFERED ME $300!
YES, AND SOON IT'LL BE $100...
ENJOY THE "GOOD TIMES" WHILE THEY LAST.
COMIC BOOKS INC.
CONTRACT
—OOH! HIGH SCORE!
THIS IN TURN HAS LED TO A MAD SCRAMBLE TO SUPPLEMENT MY INCOME, ONLY TO DISCOVER I'M A PART OF A HERD...
B-BUT, YOU OFFERED ME TWICE AS MUCH FOR THESE ORIGINAL PAGES LAST YEAR...
BE GRATEFUL...
MANY OF YOUR PEERS ARE SETTLING FOR MUCH LESS.
USELESS EPHEMERA ART GALLERY
EVEN THE HALLOWED HALLS OF HIGHER EDUCATION ARE EXPLOITING THIS RECENT SHIFT IN SUPPLY AND DEMAND...
YOU'RE CUTTING MY PAY AND RAISING THE PARKING FEES?
HEY, THESE ARE TOUGH TIMES FOR HIGHER ED..*
AND I HAVE MORE WOULD-BE ADJUNCT PROFESSORS THAN I KNOW WHAT TO DO WITH!
NEW LIBRARY AND ATHLETIC FIELD
*$50,000 TUITION
I'M CONSTANTLY BEING TOLD THAT THERE ARE COUNTLESS NEW WAYS TO MAKE MONEY VIA THE NET, BUT WHEN I ASK FOR SPECIFICS I GET DRIVEL LIKE THIS...
START A WEB COMIC!
FOR FREE?
WELL, YEAH! BUT AFTER A WHILE PEOPLE MIGHT START BUYING YOUR MERCH...
THEY "MIGHT"? WHY DON'T THEY JUST BUY THE MERCH I HAVE NOW?
I DUNNO! JUST THINK OUTSIDE THE BOX, MAN!
"INCREASE YOUR WEB PRESENCE": THAT'S ANOTHER PIECE OF ADVICE I OFTEN HEAR, AND IT ALWAYS RESULTS IN ME PROVIDING THE UNIVERSE WITH FREE CONTENT.
I'LL RE-POST IT ON MY PAGE...
AND ON MY BLOG AND TUMBLR...
I'M GETTING THE WORD OUT!
BAGGE SHOULD THANK ME!
OOH! BAGGE POSTED A COOL DRAWING ON HIS FACE-BOOK PAGE!
ER, THANKS! ONLY NOW WHAT?

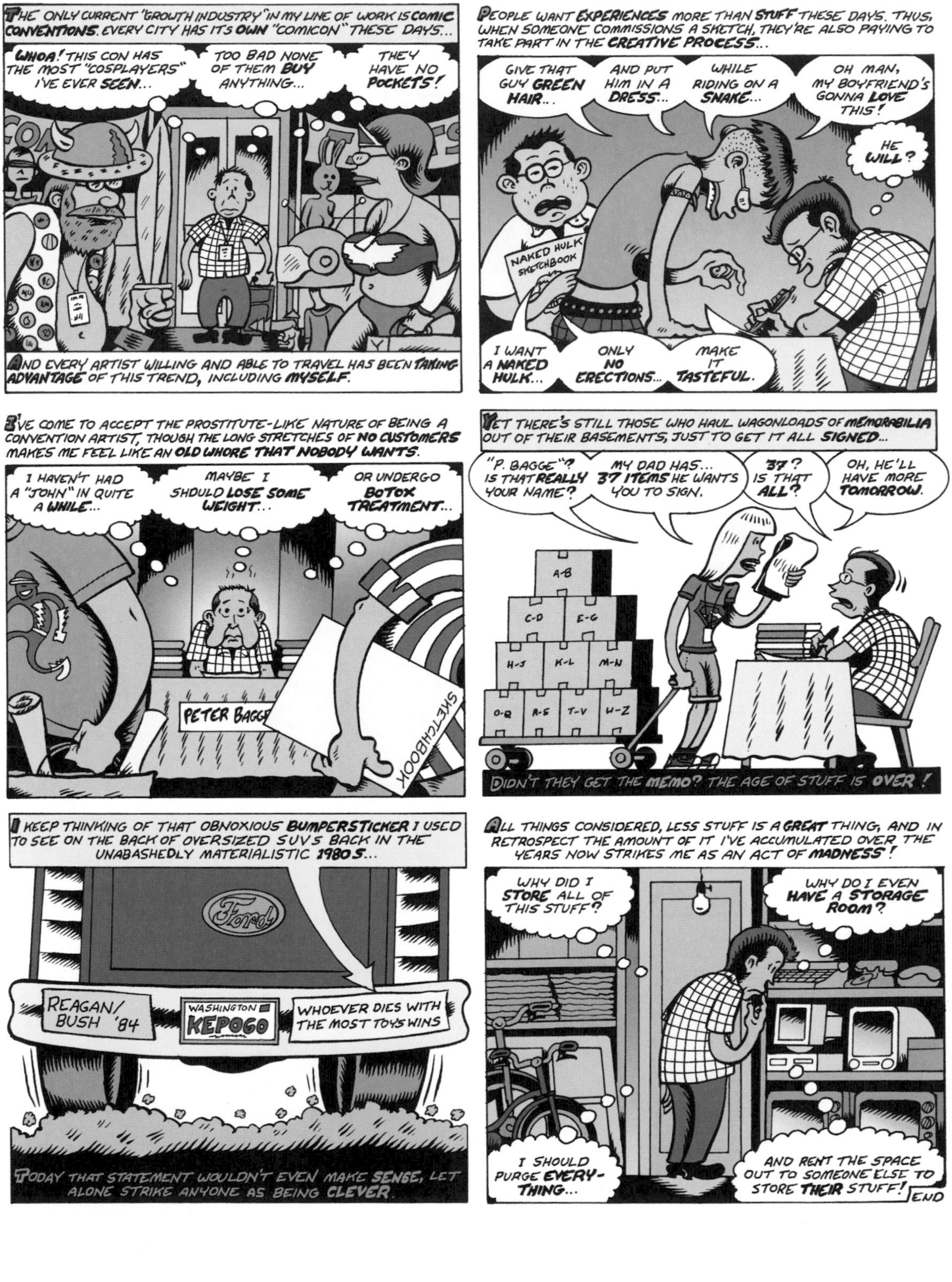
THE ONLY CURRENT "GROWTH INDUSTRY" IN MY LINE OF WORK IS COMIC CONVENTIONS. EVERY CITY HAS ITS OWN "COMICON" THESE DAYS...
WHOA! THIS CON HAS THE MOST "COSPLAYERS" I'VE EVER SEEN...
TOO BAD NONE OF THEM BUY ANYTHING...
THEY HAVE NO POCKETS!
AND EVERY ARTIST WILLING AND ABLE TO TRAVEL HAS BEEN TAKING ADVANTAGE OF THIS TREND, INCLUDING MYSELF.
PEOPLE WANT EXPERIENCES MORE THAN STUFF THESE DAYS. THUS, WHEN SOMEONE COMMISSIONS A SKETCH, THEY'RE ALSO PAYING TO TAKE PART IN THE CREATIVE PROCESS...
GIVE THAT GUY GREEN HAIR...
AND PUT HIM IN A DRESS...
WHILE RIDING ON A SNAKE...
OH MAN, MY BOYFRIEND'S GONNA LOVE THIS!
HE WILL?
NAKED HULK SKETCHBOOK
I WANT A NAKED HULK...
ONLY NO ERECTIONS...
MAKE IT TASTEFUL.
I'VE COME TO ACCEPT THE PROSTITUTE-LIKE NATURE OF BEING A CONVENTION ARTIST, THOUGH THE LONG STRETCHES OF NO CUSTOMERS MAKES ME FEEL LIKE AN OLD WHORE THAT NOBODY WANTS.
I HAVEN'T HAD A "JOHN" IN QUITE A WHILE...
MAYBE I SHOULD LOSE SOME WEIGHT...
OR UNDERGO BOTOX TREATMENT...
PETER BAGGE
SKETCHBOOK
YET THERE'S STILL THOSE WHO HAUL WAGONLOADS OF MEMORABILIA OUT OF THEIR BASEMENTS, JUST TO GET IT ALL SIGNED...
"P. BAGGE"? IS THAT REALLY YOUR NAME?
MY DAD HAS... 37 ITEMS HE WANTS YOU TO SIGN.
37? IS THAT ALL?
OH, HE'LL HAVE MORE TOMORROW.
A-B
C-D
E-G
H-J
K-L
M-N
O-Q
R-S
T-V
W-Z
DIDN'T THEY GET THE MEMO? THE AGE OF STUFF IS OVER!
I KEEP THINKING OF THAT OBNOXIOUS BUMPERSTICKER I USED TO SEE ON THE BACK OF OVERSIZED SUVS BACK IN THE UNABASHEDLY MATERIALISTIC 1980S...
Ford
REAGAN/ BUSH '84
WASHINGTON KEPOGO
WHOEVER DIES WITH THE MOST TOYS WINS
TODAY THAT STATEMENT WOULDN'T EVEN MAKE SENSE, LET ALONE STRIKE ANYONE AS BEING CLEVER.
ALL THINGS CONSIDERED, LESS STUFF IS A GREAT THING, AND IN RETROSPECT THE AMOUNT OF IT I'VE ACCUMULATED OVER THE YEARS NOW STRIKES ME AS AN ACT OF MADNESS!
WHY DID I STORE ALL OF THIS STUFF?
WHY DO I EVEN HAVE A STORAGE ROOM?
I SHOULD PURGE EVERY-THING...
AND RENT THE SPACE OUT TO SOMEONE ELSE TO STORE THEIR STUFF!
END

LIFE, LOVE, AND AFRICAN MISADVENTURES IN ABOUET & OUBRERIE'S AYA

an appreciation by Calvin Reid

Marguerite Abouet and Clément Oubrerie's *Aya: Life in Yop City* and *Love in Yop City* are irresistible works. Initially that's because of Aya, the heroine of Abouet's story: an ever-so-sensible young Ivorian woman who is delightful, smart, and sharp tongued. She talks common sense to her parents, offers generally unsolicited but sage advice to her friends, and tries to do the right thing in tough situations. But I also connected immediately with Aya's urban setting, youth-focused sensibility, and comic dissection of Africa's evolving social and political classes. I'm a black American who grew up in the 1960s, and throughout college I was heavily influenced by black nationalism and pan-Africanism as much as the civil rights movement. I also happen to have immediate relatives (by marriage) from Liberia and Sierra Leone—not Ivory Coast, but two West African countries nonetheless. I was lucky enough to have visit Lagos, Nigeria, in the late 1970s, a city that provides a vivid sense of connection to Abouet's presentation of Abidjan of those years. For me, especially, Abouet's story, Aya's story, is irresistibly readable, but it's an engaging social comedy attractive to anyone. It is an enduring tale of modern African post-colonial development, wise as well as entertaining for its comic portrayal of life in Yop City, a neighbourhood in Ivory Coast's capital city of Abidjan, in the late 1970s, a time of unprecedented economic and political stability in the country's history.

The Aya series is a fictional slice of life designed to entertain while carrying details of Abouet's memories of life in Ivory Coast. Abouet starts with Aya's family. Her father, Ignace, is a capable manager at an Ivorian brewery who nevertheless mismanages his personal and family life. Fanta, Aya's mother and nobody's fool, rallies the women of Yop City to confront the periodic foolishness of the men. Then there are Aya's friends. Adjoua is a key character in a series of boy/girl shenanigans and hookups that proceed, like a cascade of dominoes, to an unexpected pregnancy and the comic revelation of the true identity of her child's father. Through Adjoua, Abouet plunges the reader into the irresistible world of Yop City.

Aya is a charming series with a teen pregnancy at its core, but it's more than a record of teen misbehaviour and personal failings. It's a story about the unexpected consequences of, and the redemptive social responses to, the acts of the young (and old) people Abouet creates. Indeed, the more dubious (and humourous) the schemes and behaviours Abouet's characters engage in, the more we see the depth of her characterizations when it's time for them to face the music.

Bintou is another of Aya's friends. A young Yop City hottie and party girl, Bintou is also something of an Ivorian Lucille Ball, bouncing comically from one self-inflicted train wreck of a relationship to another. Yet she is also a devoted friend to Adjoua (despite their interest in the same man), no matter the two girls' Betty and Veronica–like rivalry over Mamadou, the "skirt chaser" as Abouet labels him. Mamadou is another apparently dubious character whose stature seems to grow as we get to know him. And of course there's Hervé, the slow but sure dimwit turned successful mechanic that all the girls avoid—at least at first. Like all of Abouet's characters, Hervé, who can't read or write when we first meet him, grows in complexity and nuance, developing far beyond our initial comic reactions as Abouet's story reveals new facets of his personality and circumstances. (Abouet's women, by the way, shine with their antics, often in response to the men's clueless declaration of some traditional male privilege—like taking a second wife.)

These are just a few of the key characters that make these books so special. And don't let me neglect the superb artwork of Oubrerie, who depicts Abouet's army of Yop City characters in expressive cartoon line drawing that primes the narrative for comedy while carefully documenting the details of Ivorian city life. Oubrerie's lively drawings and splendid colour visually delineate a very funny Yop City mash-up, hybrid culture and street life. It's a cultural life animated by modern urbanity and French post-colonialism, along with the still-powerful social mores of traditional African village life, now extended into city life to hilarious effect.

Rooted in the details of Abouet's life growing up in Ivory Coast, the Aya books spin that life into a very perceptive and funny African soap opera. Abouet's graphic novels offer delightful comic misadventures with a keen eye for the social complexity of modern urban African life.

Calvin Reid is a senior news editor for **Publishers Weekly** *and the coeditor of* **Publishers Weekly's Comics World.**

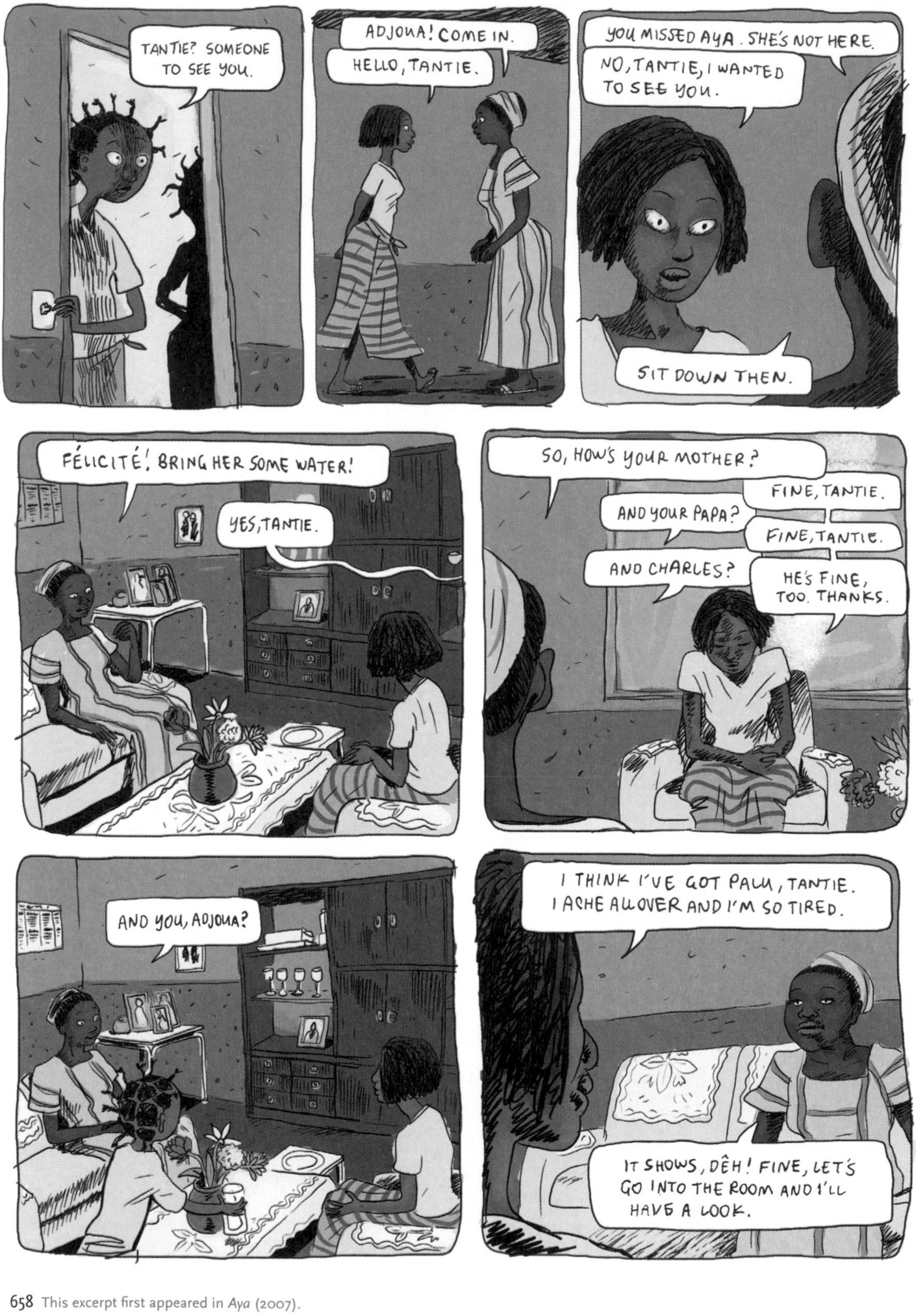
TANTIE? SOMEONE TO SEE YOU.
ADJOUA! COME IN.
HELLO, TANTIE.
YOU MISSED AYA. SHE'S NOT HERE.
NO, TANTIE, I WANTED TO SEE YOU.
SIT DOWN THEN.
FÉLICITÉ! BRING HER SOME WATER!
YES, TANTIE.
SO, HOW'S YOUR MOTHER?
FINE, TANTIE.
AND YOUR PAPA?
FINE, TANTIE.
AND CHARLES?
HE'S FINE, TOO. THANKS.
AND YOU, ADJOUA?
I THINK I'VE GOT PALU, TANTIE. I ACHE ALL OVER AND I'M SO TIRED.
IT SHOWS, DÊH! FINE, LET'S GO INTO THE ROOM AND I'LL HAVE A LOOK.

 This excerpt first appeared in *Aya* (2007).

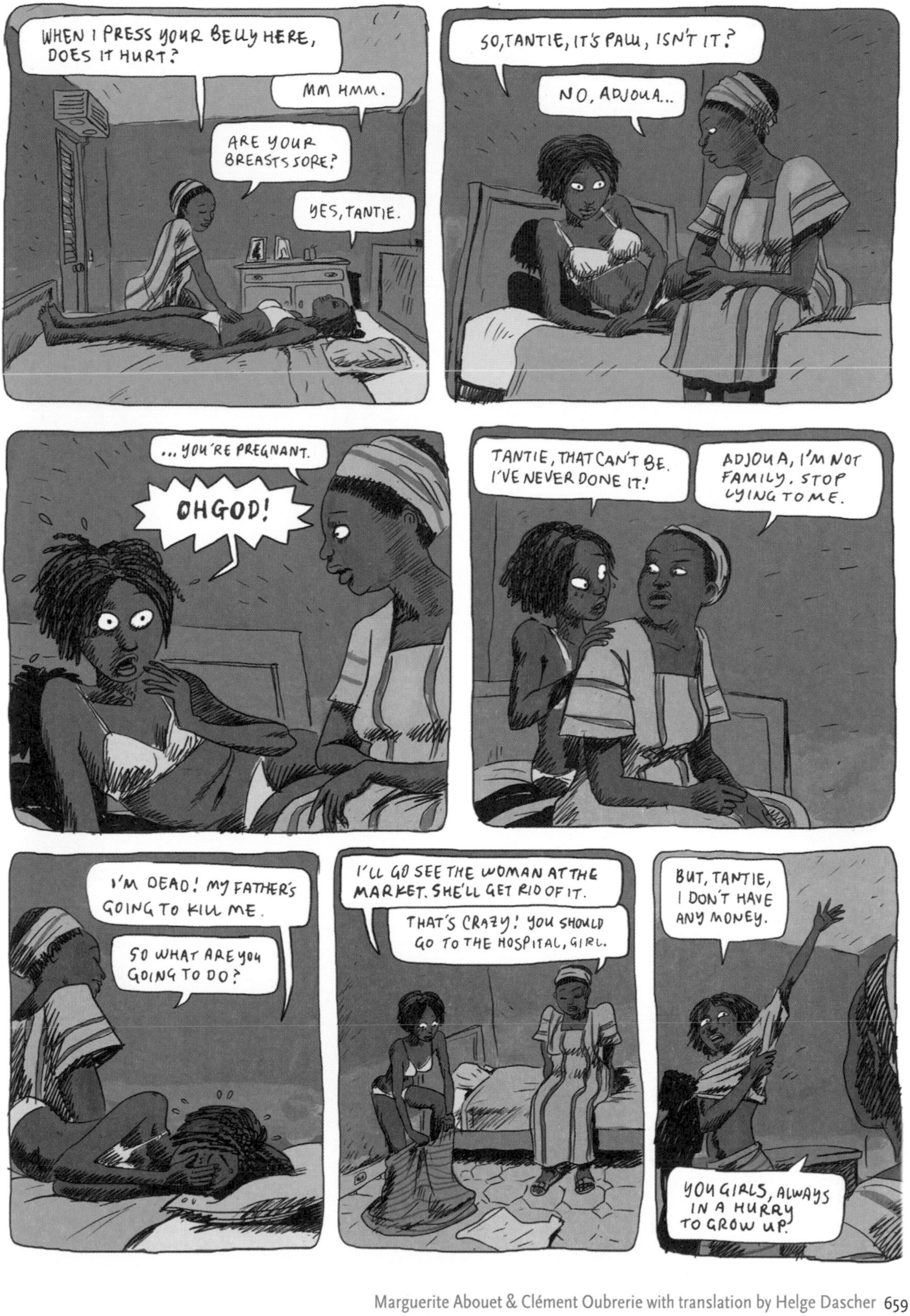
WHEN I PRESS YOUR BELLY HERE, DOES IT HURT?
MM HMM.
ARE YOUR BREASTS SORE?
YES, TANTIE.
SO, TANTIE, IT'S PALU, ISN'T IT?
NO, ADJOUA...
... YOU'RE PREGNANT.
OHGOD!
TANTIE, THAT CAN'T BE. I'VE NEVER DONE IT!
ADJOUA, I'M NOT FAMILY. STOP LYING TO ME.
I'M DEAD! MY FATHER'S GOING TO KILL ME.
SO WHAT ARE YOU GOING TO DO?
I'LL GO SEE THE WOMAN AT THE MARKET. SHE'LL GET RID OF IT.
THAT'S CRAZY! YOU SHOULD GO TO THE HOSPITAL, GIRL.
BUT, TANTIE, I DON'T HAVE ANY MONEY.
YOU GIRLS, ALWAYS IN A HURRY TO GROW UP.

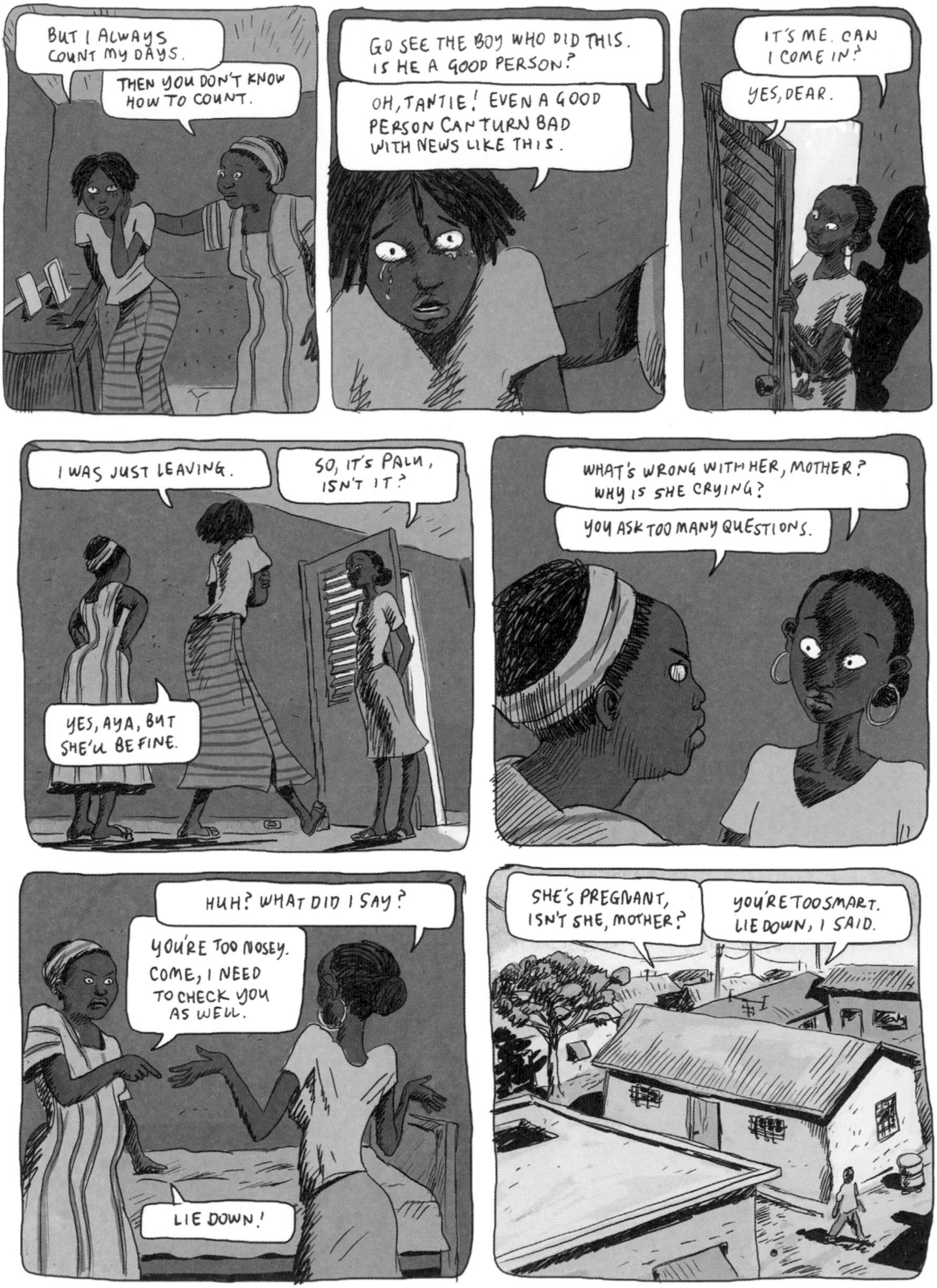
BUT I ALWAYS COUNT MY DAYS.
THEN YOU DON'T KNOW HOW TO COUNT.
GO SEE THE BOY WHO DID THIS. IS HE A GOOD PERSON?
OH, TANTIE! EVEN A GOOD PERSON CAN TURN BAD WITH NEWS LIKE THIS.
IT'S ME. CAN I COME IN?
YES, DEAR.
I WAS JUST LEAVING.
SO, IT'S PALU, ISN'T IT?
YES, AYA, BUT SHE'LL BE FINE.
WHAT'S WRONG WITH HER, MOTHER? WHY IS SHE CRYING?
YOU ASK TOO MANY QUESTIONS.
HUH? WHAT DID I SAY?
YOU'RE TOO NOSEY. COME, I NEED TO CHECK YOU AS WELL.
LIE DOWN!
SHE'S PREGNANT, ISN'T SHE, MOTHER?
YOU'RE TOO SMART. LIE DOWN, I SAID.

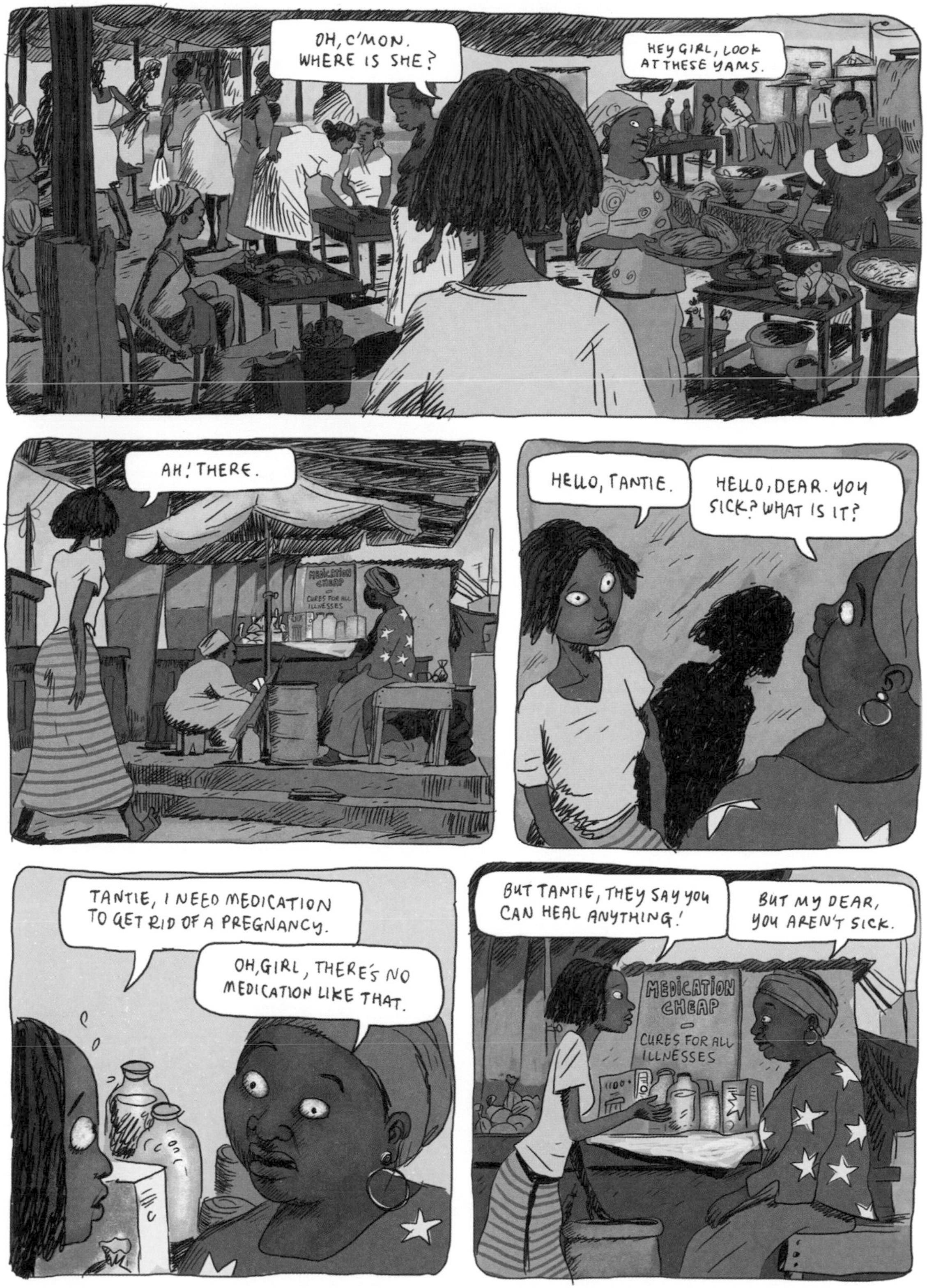
OH, C'MON. WHERE IS SHE?
HEY GIRL, LOOK AT THESE YAMS.
AH! THERE.
MEDICATION CHEAP
CURES FOR ALL ILLNESSES
HELLO, TANTIE.
HELLO, DEAR. YOU SICK? WHAT IS IT?
TANTIE, I NEED MEDICATION TO GET RID OF A PREGNANCY.
OH, GIRL, THERE'S NO MEDICATION LIKE THAT.
BUT TANTIE, THEY SAY YOU CAN HEAL ANYTHING!
BUT MY DEAR, YOU AREN'T SICK.
MEDICATION CHEAP
CURES FOR ALL ILLNESSES

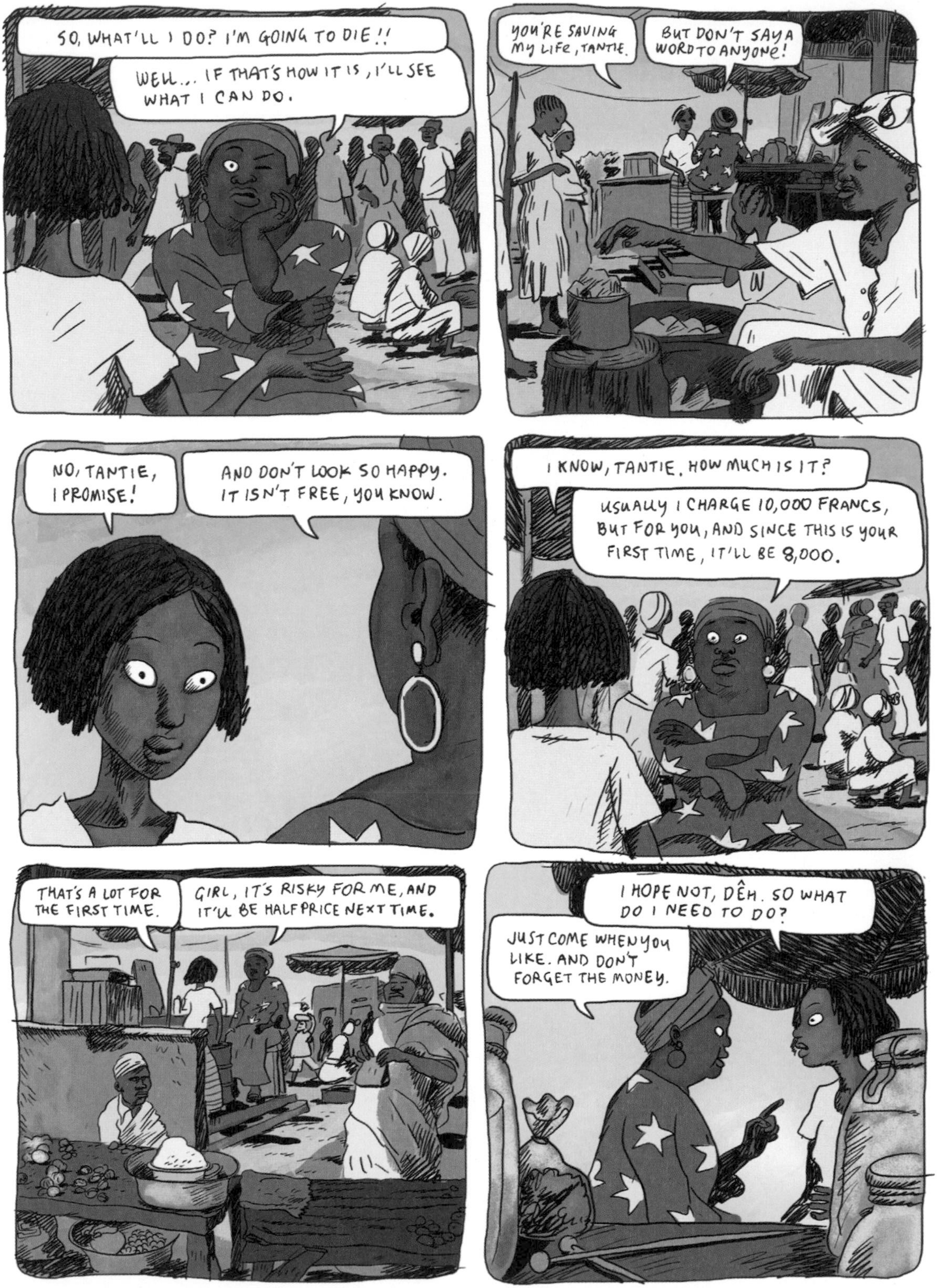
SO, WHAT'LL I DO? I'M GOING TO DIE!!
WELL... IF THAT'S HOW IT IS, I'LL SEE WHAT I CAN DO.
YOU'RE SAVING MY LIFE, TANTIE.
BUT DON'T SAY A WORD TO ANYONE!
NO, TANTIE, I PROMISE!
AND DON'T LOOK SO HAPPY. IT ISN'T FREE, YOU KNOW.
I KNOW, TANTIE. HOW MUCH IS IT?
USUALLY I CHARGE 10,000 FRANCS, BUT FOR YOU, AND SINCE THIS IS YOUR FIRST TIME, IT'LL BE 8,000.
THAT'S A LOT FOR THE FIRST TIME.
GIRL, IT'S RISKY FOR ME, AND IT'LL BE HALF PRICE NEXT TIME.
I HOPE NOT, DÊH. SO WHAT DO I NEED TO DO?
JUST COME WHEN YOU LIKE. AND DON'T FORGET THE MONEY.

The next day, my father left on his first tour of the country.

WELL, FANTA, LOOKS LIKE I'M OFF. IS EVERYTHING IN MY BAG?

YES, IGNACE, IT'S ALL THERE.

AYA, KEEP AN EYE ON THE KIDS, OK?

MM HM.

AND I DON'T WANT YOU FOOLING AROUND.

YOU TOO, AND DON'T FORGET TO CALL HOME!

HOW COULD I FORGET TO CALL MY DEAR WIFE?

SURE, AND DON'T DRIVE TOO FAST.

DON'T KILL YOURSELF!

AND BRING BACK LOTS OF GIFTS.

OK, AYA, GO TIDY UP THE ROOM.

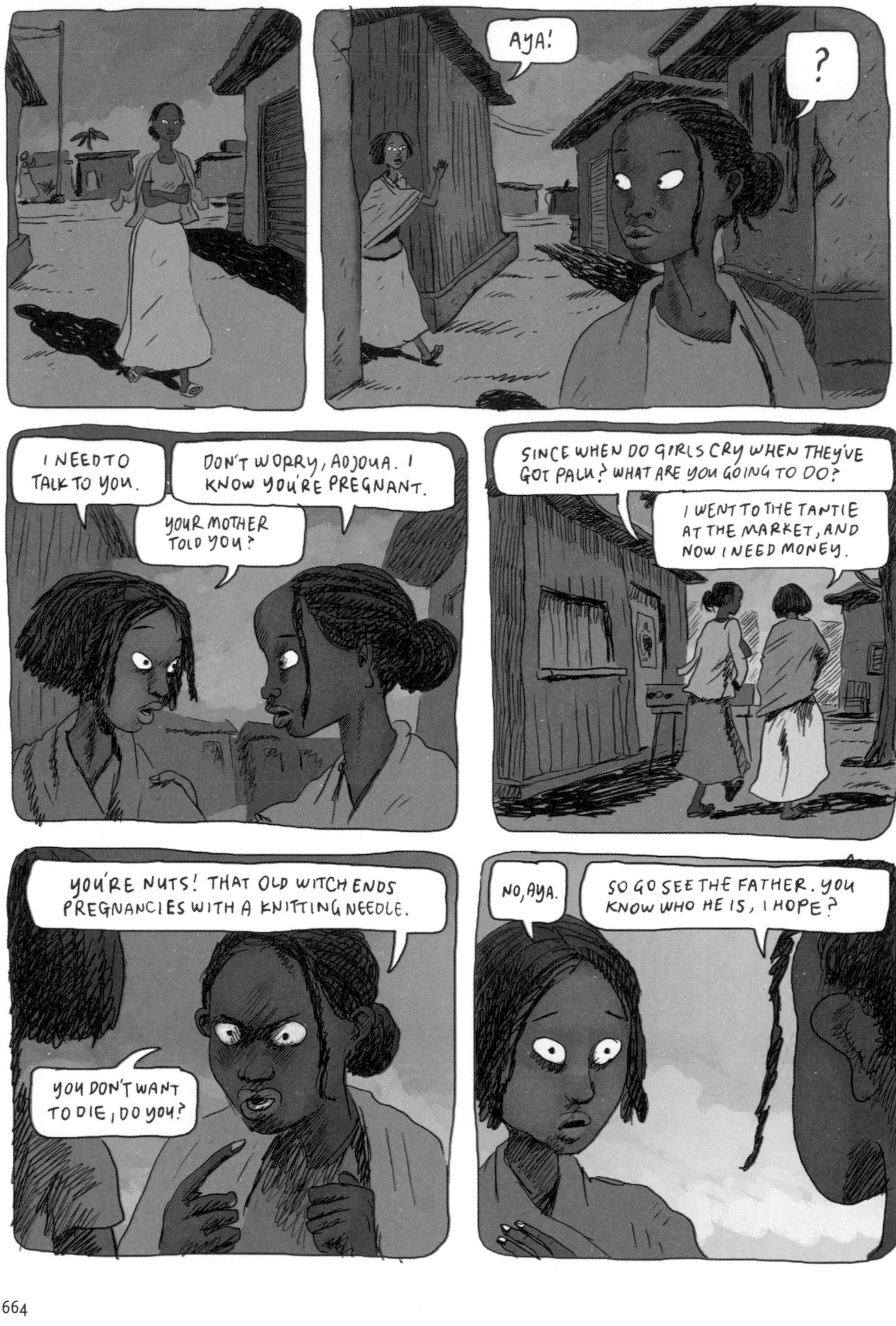
AYA!
?
I NEED TO TALK TO YOU.
DON'T WORRY, ADJOUA. I KNOW YOU'RE PREGNANT.
YOUR MOTHER TOLD YOU?
SINCE WHEN DO GIRLS CRY WHEN THEY'VE GOT PALU? WHAT ARE YOU GOING TO DO?
I WENT TO THE TANTIE AT THE MARKET, AND NOW I NEED MONEY.
YOU'RE NUTS! THAT OLD WITCH ENDS PREGNANCIES WITH A KNITTING NEEDLE.
YOU DON'T WANT TO DIE, DO YOU?
NO, AYA.
SO GO SEE THE FATHER. YOU KNOW WHO HE IS, I HOPE?

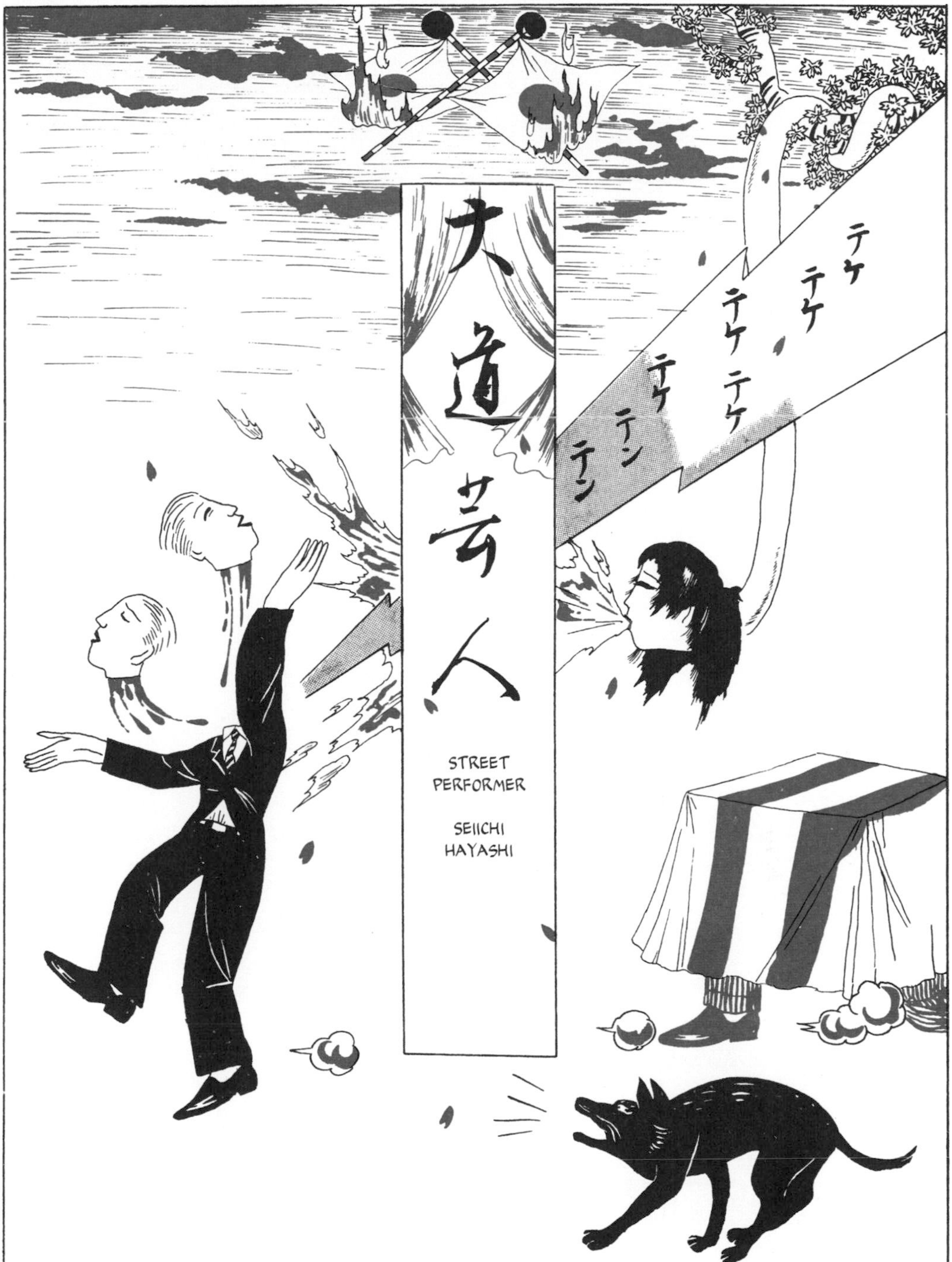
大道芸人
テケ テケ テケ テケ テン テン
STREET PERFORMER
SEIICHI HAYASHI

SFX: TICKY TICKY TICKY TICKY TIN TIN

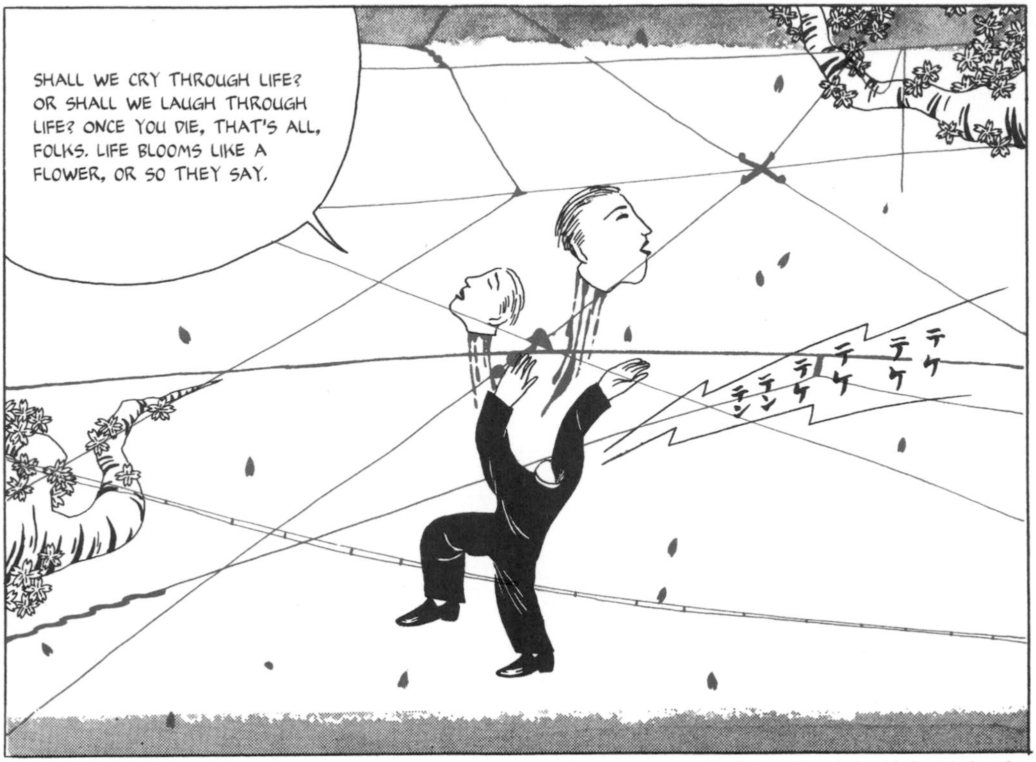
SHALL WE CRY THROUGH LIFE? OR SHALL WE LAUGH THROUGH LIFE? ONCE YOU DIE, THAT'S ALL, FOLKS. LIFE BLOOMS LIKE A FLOWER, OR SO THEY SAY.
テケテケテケテケテンテン

SFX: TICKY TICKY TICKY TICKY TIN TIN

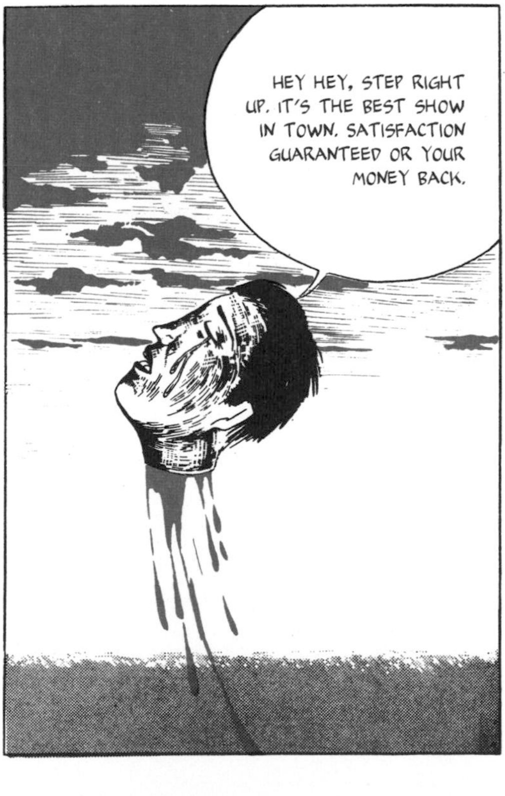
HEY HEY, STEP RIGHT UP. IT'S THE BEST SHOW IN TOWN. SATISFACTION GUARANTEED OR YOUR MONEY BACK.

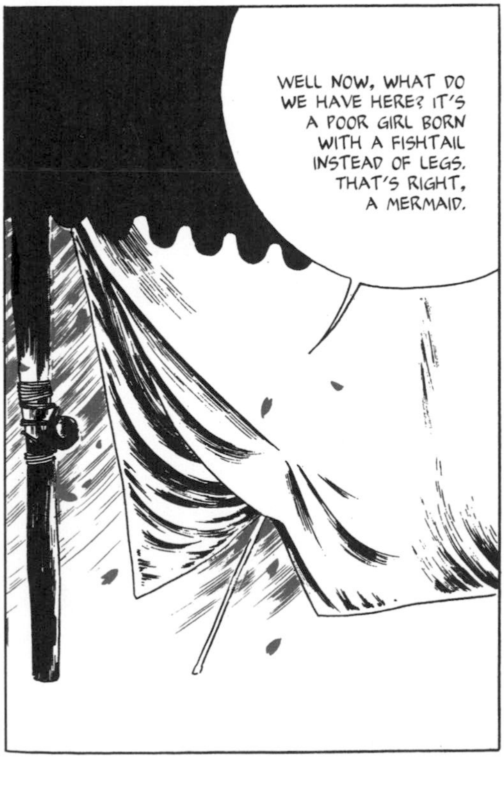
WELL NOW, WHAT DO WE HAVE HERE? IT'S A POOR GIRL BORN WITH A FISHTAIL INSTEAD OF LEGS. THAT'S RIGHT, A MERMAID.

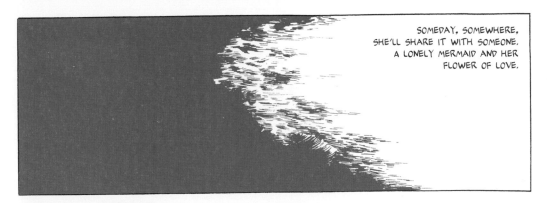

SOMEDAY, SOMEWHERE, SHE'LL SHARE IT WITH SOMEONE. A LONELY MERMAID AND HER FLOWER OF LOVE.

I SEE IT!

IT REALLY IS!

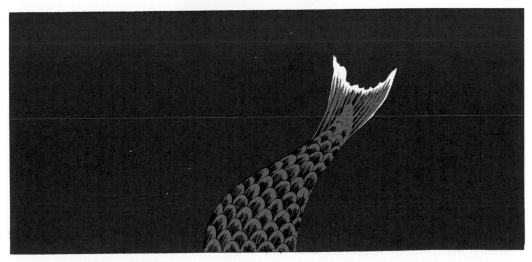

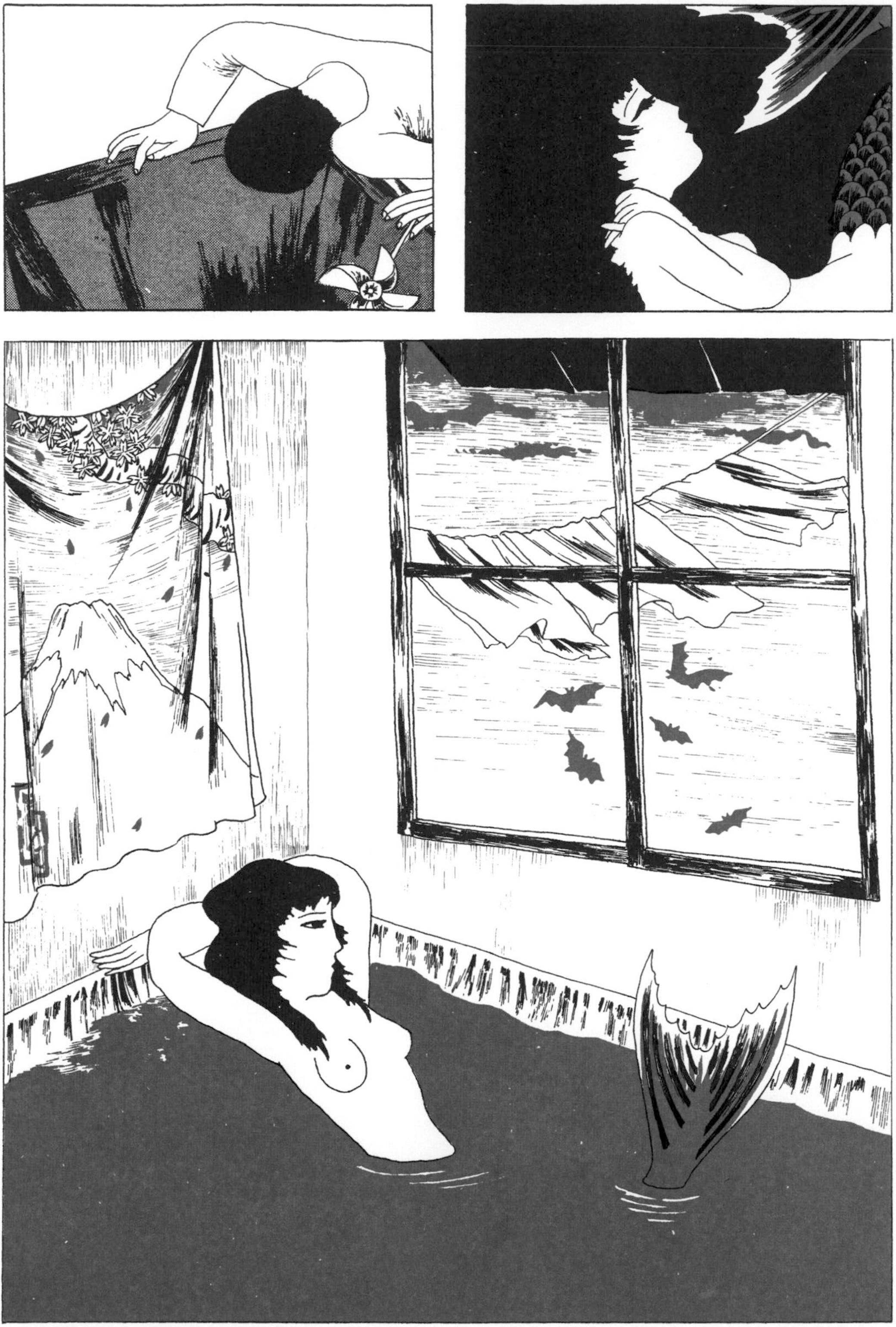

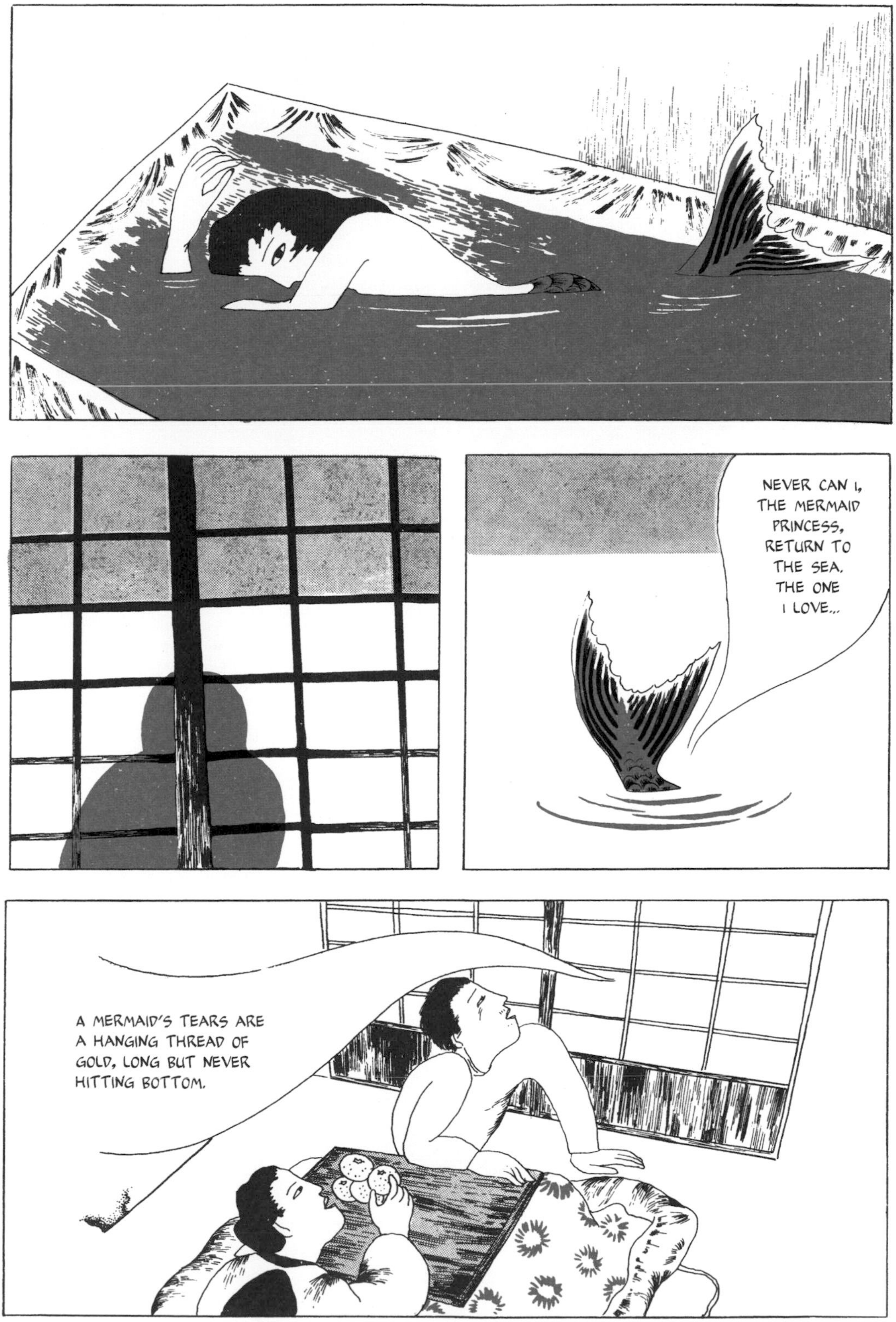
NEVER CAN I, THE MERMAID PRINCESS, RETURN TO THE SEA, THE ONE I LOVE...
A MERMAID'S TEARS ARE A HANGING THREAD OF GOLD, LONG BUT NEVER HITTING BOTTOM.

I WAS WRONG TO HAVE GIVEN BIRTH TO SUCH A GIRL.

TV: THE WORD "TOMORROW" IS WRITTEN WITH THE CHARACTERS "A BRIGHT DAY"

SHE WOULD
BE SO MUCH
HAPPIER WERE
SHE DEAD...

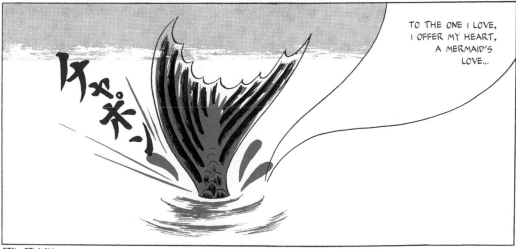

TO THE ONE I LOVE,
I OFFER MY HEART,
A MERMAID'S
LOVE...

SFX: SPLASH

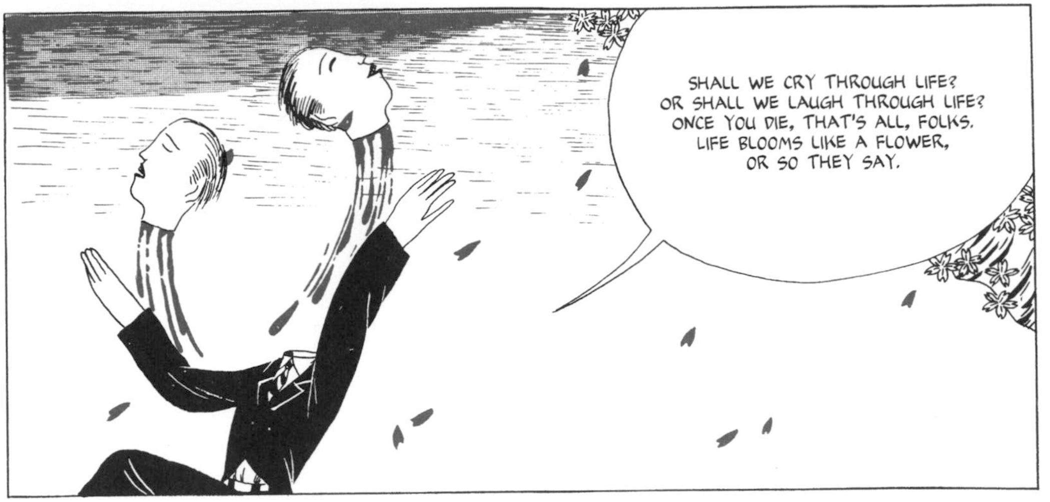
SHALL WE CRY THROUGH LIFE? OR SHALL WE LAUGH THROUGH LIFE? ONCE YOU DIE, THAT'S ALL, FOLKS. LIFE BLOOMS LIKE A FLOWER, OR SO THEY SAY.

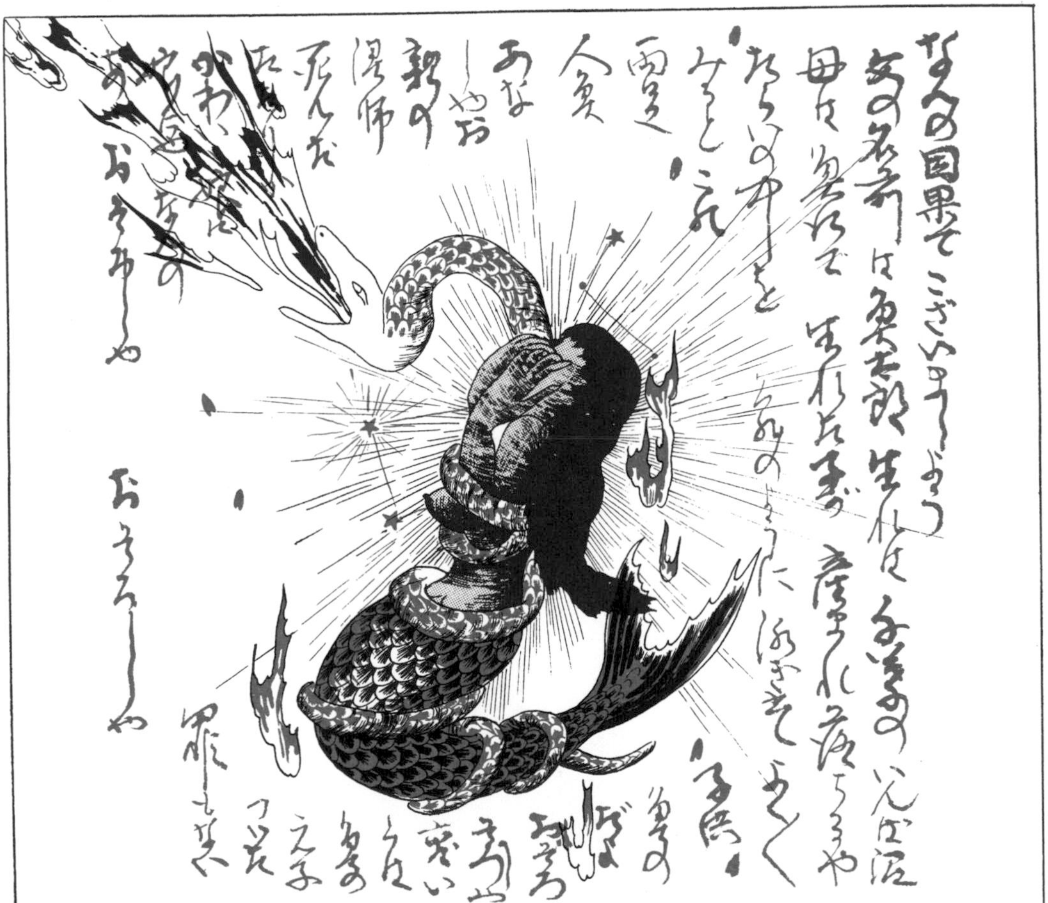

WHAT KARMA HAS BROUGHT THIS FATE? WAS IT BECAUSE HER FATHER WAS NAMED UOTARŌ, FISH BOY? WAS IT BECAUSE HE WAS BORN IN INBANUMA, A TOWN IN CHIBA NAMED AFTER A MARSH? WAS IT BECAUSE HER MOTHER WAS NAMED UOE, FISH BAY? WHATEVER THE REASON, THEIR DAUGHTER WAS BORN IN A WELL AND POPPED OUT SWIMMING LIKE A FISH. LOOK, LOOK CLOSELY AT THE CHILD'S LEGS. LIKE A FISH'S THEY ARE. SHE'S A MERMAID. SO HORRIBLE, HOW HORRIBLE. HER PARENTS WERE FISHERMEN. WAS THIS PUNISHMENT FOR THEIR TRADE? HAS THEIR SWEET DAUGHTER BEEN MADE TO BEAR THE CURSE OF SOME FISH THEY ONCE KILLED? SHE IS INNOCENCE ITSELF. SO HORRIBLE, HOW HORRIBLE.

FINDING PIPPI

an appreciation by Tom Devlin

When Peggy and I were invited to Helsinki we were pretty excited to not only visit Tove Jansson's home (!!!!) but go to the Marimekko Outlet as well. We didn't really consider much else. What? We love designer fabric! Did I know that I would be taking a sauna with *Pearls Before Swine*'s Stephan Pastis? I did not. Everyone was wonderful and very relaxed (more on this later). I had a chance to meet some old internet friends like Juhani Tolvanen, biographer and friend of Tove. We were invited to go mushroom picking in the Finnish forest—well, actually we were told we should have come two days earlier to go mushroom picking, but I'm looking on the bright side here. We took meetings and missed an onstage interview. (Everyone was so relaxed that they forgot to tell us we had an interview. And they didn't seem to care that much when we missed it!) Of course, this is a very long lead-up to Pippi Longstocking and we're even in the "wrong" Scandinavian country (though there is a Swedish-speaking minority in Finland—the Janssons were part of that minority, actually). After one of my meetings, the woman I was meeting with took me back out to the book tent to browse. She showed me some excellent (but obvious) titles and we chatted. I dug through some boxes and spotted something interesting. "Is this old?" I asked. The drawing and the colouring certainly seemed to suggest that it was. "It is," she replied. "These are reprints of vintage Pippi comics written by Astrid Lindgren." To me, this seemed impossible. Everyone in the world had heard of Pippi. How could these comics have been passed over? I immediately bought all three volumes (imagining that many, many more were coming).

Later that night, at the festival bar, Peg and I were having one last beer before catching our flight home. I asked an editor from a different Finnish company if he knew these comics. He did. "They are not so good," he said. In my head, I thought, "This can't be true. They're beautiful. They look hilarious." We left the party and caught our flight home. At home I immediately Googled Ingrid Vang Nyman. I was completely unfamiliar with her but her story was fascinating (I won't repeat it here because it's documented in the comics and online). As it turns out, there were not many, many more volumes (only the three), and as it turns out,

that editor could not have been more wrong. These comics are what you hope for in an adaptation. The original writer brings her wit and magic and the illustrator brings a beautiful idiosyncratic style to the comics. It's a great disappointment that there were only these three volumes of comics from the pair and that Ingrid never did comics again. The sequences in which Pippi puts out a fire (because the firefighters aren't quick enough) and has a tug-of-war with her dad (both using their teeth) are two of my all-time favourite scenes in all of comics.

Over the past thirty years I've translated scores of books from the Nordic languages, but the most fun project has been working with Drawn & Quarterly on Astrid Lindgren's Pippi Longstocking comics. I've always been a big fan of Pippi, but I wasn't familiar with these comics, which were originally published in Swedish children's magazines in the 1950s, so I was delighted to receive an email from Tom Devlin in 2011 telling me that he had recently discovered the Pippi comics, newly repackaged and republished in Sweden. And now he was looking for a translator to bring them into English. Was I interested? Yes!

And thus began a lively three-year collaboration with Tom and his colleagues. As the translator, I had to fit the English words into the limited spaces, which was not as easy as I expected and occasionally required some real wrestling with the language. I also had to make sure the dialogue would sound right to modern-day children, without veering too far from the original tone and intent of the Swedish. And translating humour is always challenging. Pippi had to sound as quirky and feisty and funny in English as she does in Swedish.

Working on these comic has been a joy, and I'm thrilled to see the three volumes now available in English. As Pippi herself might say: Hooray for Drawn & Quarterly!

—*Tiina Nunnally, preeminent translator of Scandanavian languages in English. Her many awards and honors include the PEN/BOMC Translation Prize for her work on Sigrid Undset's* Kristin Lavransdatter.

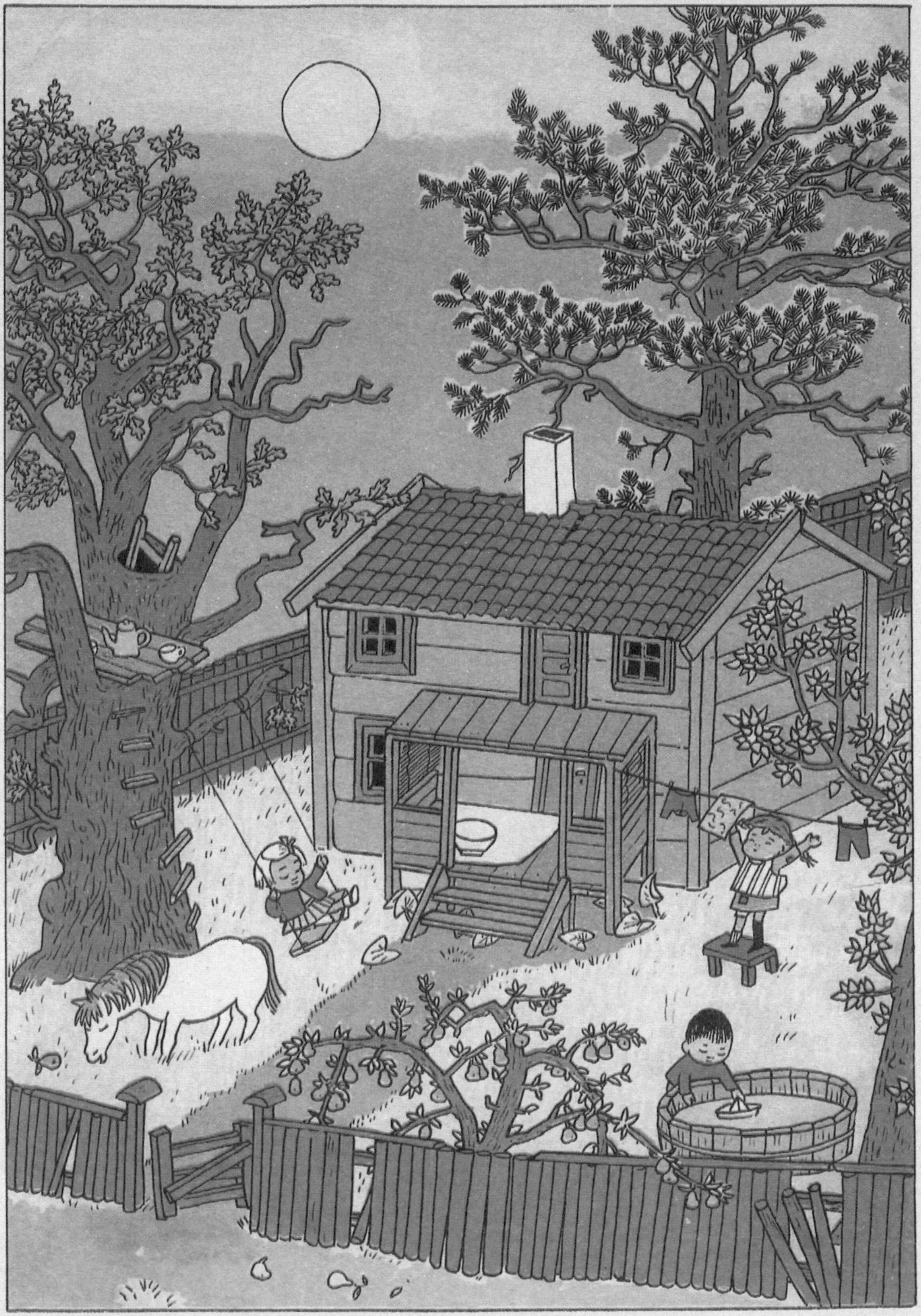

 From the Swedish magazine *Allers* where excerpts of Pippi novels were serialized in the 1940s. Ingrid Vang Nyman provided new illustrations.

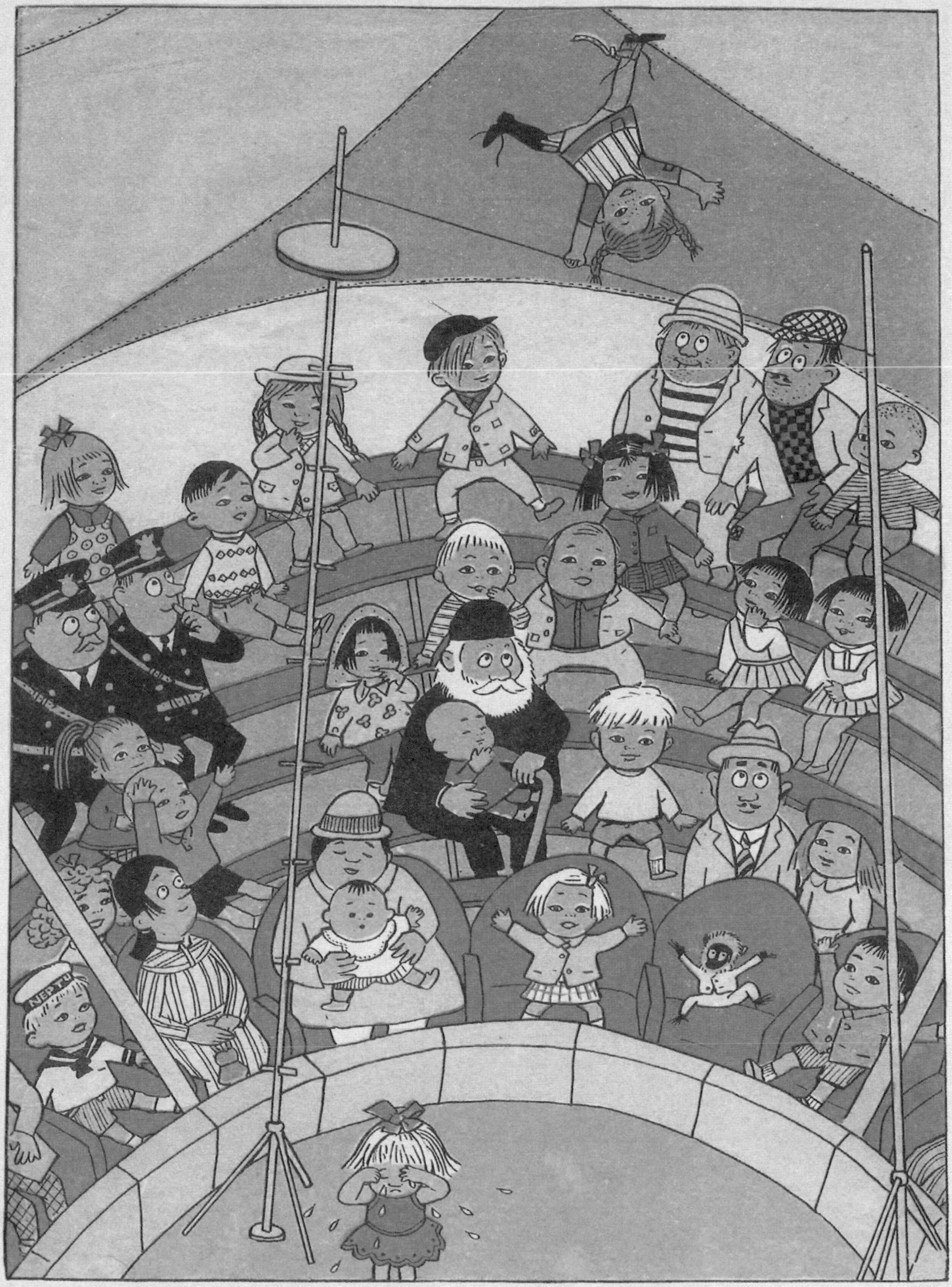

PIP & QUACK

THE EXPERTS

ON EVERYTHING

By Anouk Ricard

Today:

How to be an actor

On the stage and on the screen!

Hey there, Quack, have you memorized the lines I wrote?

Yes.

But it wasn't easy.

All right, here goes!

?

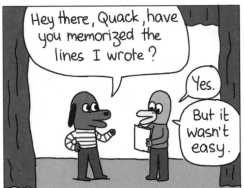

What the hell are you doing outside?

THEATRE

It says here: "Character comes in from out front."

That means off stage, down there!

Okay.

676

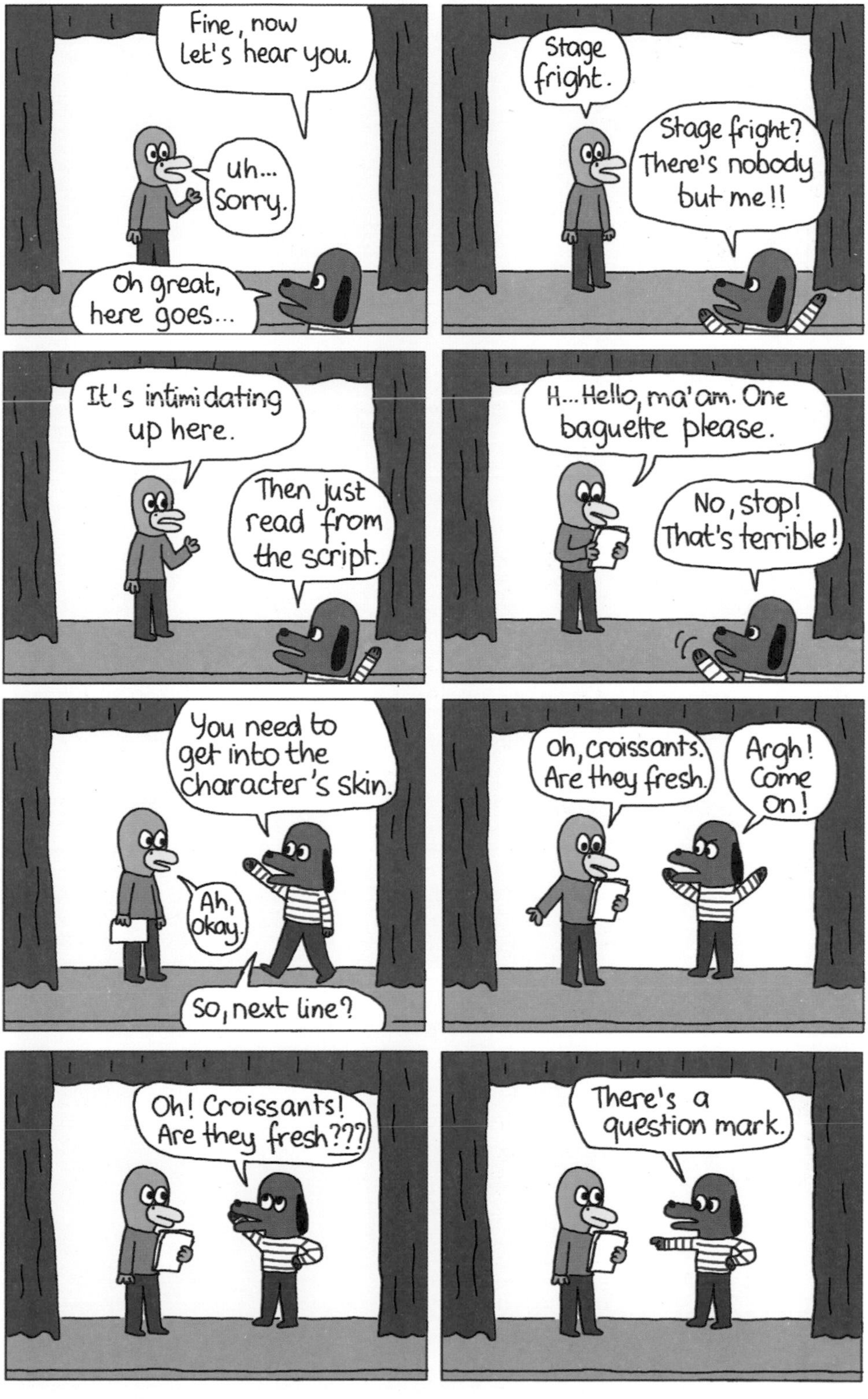
Fine, now Let's hear you.
uh... Sorry.
Oh great, here goes...
Stage fright.
Stage fright? There's nobody but me!!
It's intimidating up here.
Then just read from the script.
H... Hello, ma'am. One baguette please.
No, stop! That's terrible!
You need to get into the character's skin.
Ah, Okay.
So, next line?
Oh, croissants. Are they fresh.
Argh! Come on!
Oh! Croissants! Are they fresh???
There's a question mark.

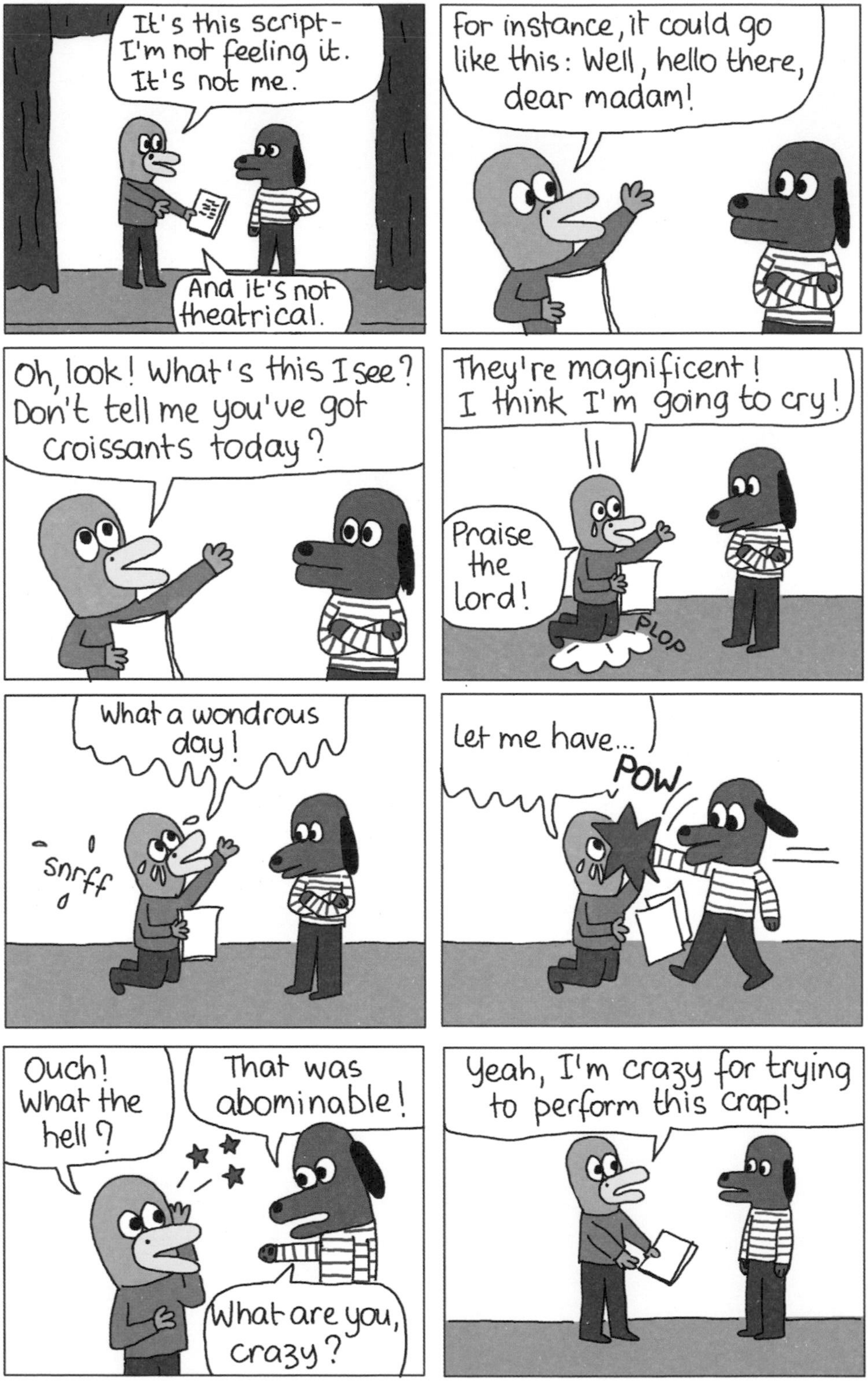
It's this script- I'm not feeling it. It's not me.
And it's not theatrical.
For instance, it could go like this: Well, hello there, dear madam!
Oh, look! What's this I see? Don't tell me you've got croissants today?
They're magnificent! I think I'm going to cry!
Praise the lord!
PLOP
What a wondrous day!
snrff
Let me have...
POW
Ouch! What the hell?
That was abominable!
What are you, crazy?
Yeah, I'm crazy for trying to perform this crap!

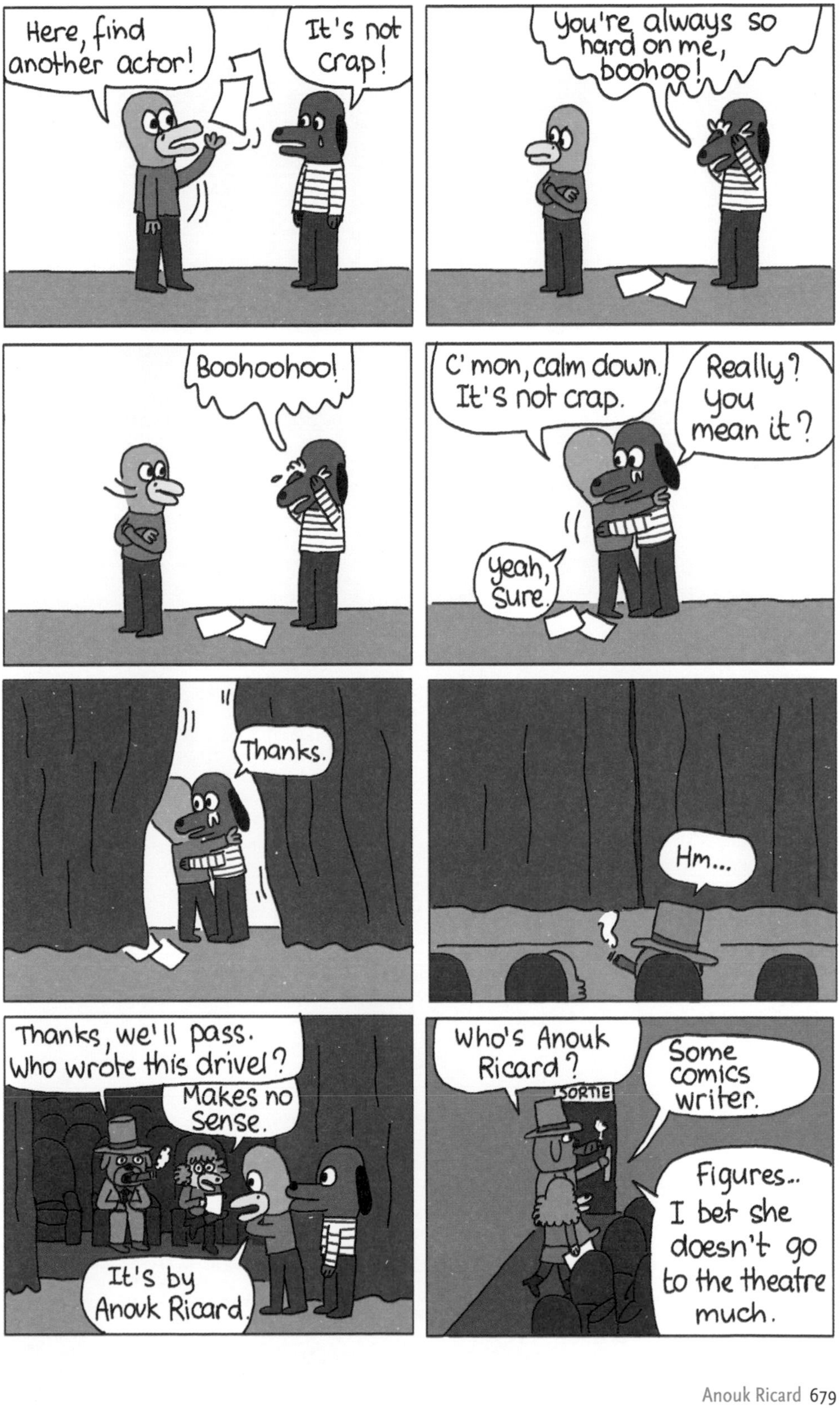
Here, find another actor!
It's not crap!
You're always so hard on me, boohoo!
Boohoohoo!
C'mon, calm down. It's not crap.
Really? You mean it?
Yeah, sure.
Thanks.
Hm...
Thanks, we'll pass. Who wrote this drivel?
Makes no sense.
It's by Anouk Ricard.
Who's Anouk Ricard?
SORTIE
Some comics writer.
Figures.. I bet she doesn't go to the theatre much.

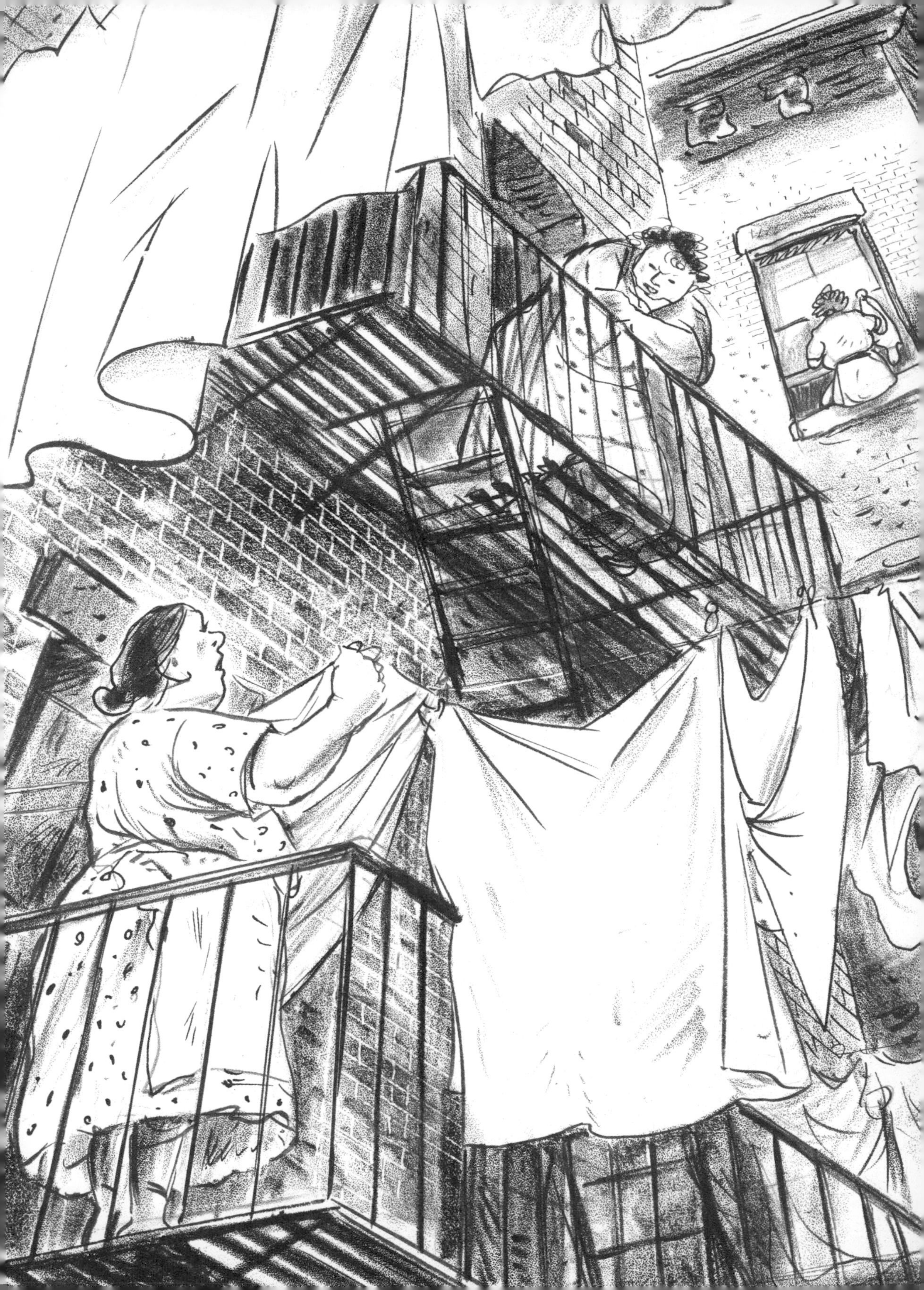

METROPOLITAN MAN

an appreciation of Denys Wortman by James Sturm

Denys Wortman's first ambition was to become a painter. In 1906, he began studying at the New York School of Fine and Applied Art where his classmates included George Bellows, Rockwell Kent, and Edward Hopper. Despite struggling with his canvases, he met with some success, exhibiting a painting in the seminal 1913 Armory Show. It wasn't until 1924, when he took over *Metropolitan Movies*, a comics feature in the pages of the *New York World* newspaper, that Wortman found his true calling.

Wortman produced over nine thousand drawings for *Metropolitan Movies* (later syndicated as *Everyday Movies*) over a thirty-year span. His drawings were held in high esteem by cartoonists, fine artists, and museum curators, as well as the poor and working-class men and women that were both the focus of his work and the majority of his sizeable audience. He was compared to Hogarth, Daumier, and Renoir.

On the surface, Wortman's drawings look casually rendered, but further study reveals masterful compositions teeming with closely observed visual details—a historian's treasure trove. The architectural flourishes of a building's entryway, the latest office equipment, and merchandise crowding the shelves of a pharmacy ground the drawing in a specific time and place. The prices of a rose from a subway peddler in 1937 (two cents), a hamburger in 1940 (ten cents), or twelve lessons at a beauty salon in 1943 ($47.95) bring the era's economic reality home.

Though he was talented and prolific, Wortman's work was never recognized by art historians. It has fared only slightly better among cartooning aficionados who celebrate great comics for one or more of the following reasons: exceptional artwork, memorable characters, and outstanding narratives or humour.

Wortman's art is exceptional but is best appreciated before reduction. Most daily newspaper cartoonists like Milt Gross and Ernie Bushmiller (with whom Wortman shared a studio) worked with reproduction in mind. They drew in pen and ink and eliminated extraneous details, resulting in images that were visually more aggressive, bridging the gap between drawing and graphic design.

Wortman drew with lithographic crayons, black carbon pencil, and ink on eleven-by-seventeen-inch (or larger) coquille board—a bristol board with a finely pebbled textured surface designed to aid halftone reproduction. When substantially shrunk for publication, the drawings' luminous and subtle tonal shifts were seriously compromised, especially when printed on cheap newsprint. Only a few history-of-cartooning books have ever reprinted a Wortman panel, and the quality of reproduction is quite poor.

Metropolitan Movies had a few recurring characters like Mopey Dick and the Duke and Mrs. Rumpel, but no one that became renowned like Prince Valiant or Little Orphan Annie. For the most part, Wortman presented anonymous New Yorkers in slice-of-life tableaux. The real star of *Metropolitan Movies* was the city itself.

Although many of Wortman's cartoons are funny, humour was not his primary goal. For the single-panel cartoonist, the joke or idea is the organizing principle for the drawing's formal structure, but with most of Wortman's work, the drawing operates independently of the caption. Wortman often drew his images first, with no text in mind. He relied upon his wife, Hilda Renbold Wortman, readers of *Metropolitan Movies*, and a few select collaborators to supply many of the captions (he disliked the term "gag"). "I don't try to be funny," he said, "I try to draw contemporary life."

In addition to providing captions, Hilda took thousands of photos that Denys used as reference for his drawings. It is hard to imagine Wortman creating so many drawings at such a high level of verisimilitude without his wife's contributions.

Wortman continued to paint throughout his life—and often in good company. Throughout the 1940s and 1950s, Reginald Marsh, Thomas Hart Benton, and Guy Pène du Bois made their way to Wortman's Martha's Vineyard home to paint and enjoy one another's company.

Now is an opportune time for Wortman to emerge from the gap between art and comics because the distinction between these two has never been less pronounced. Although Wortman's newspaper panels did not cause him to be remembered as a towering figure in American cartooning, his original drawings certainly make a case for him as an important twentieth-century artist.

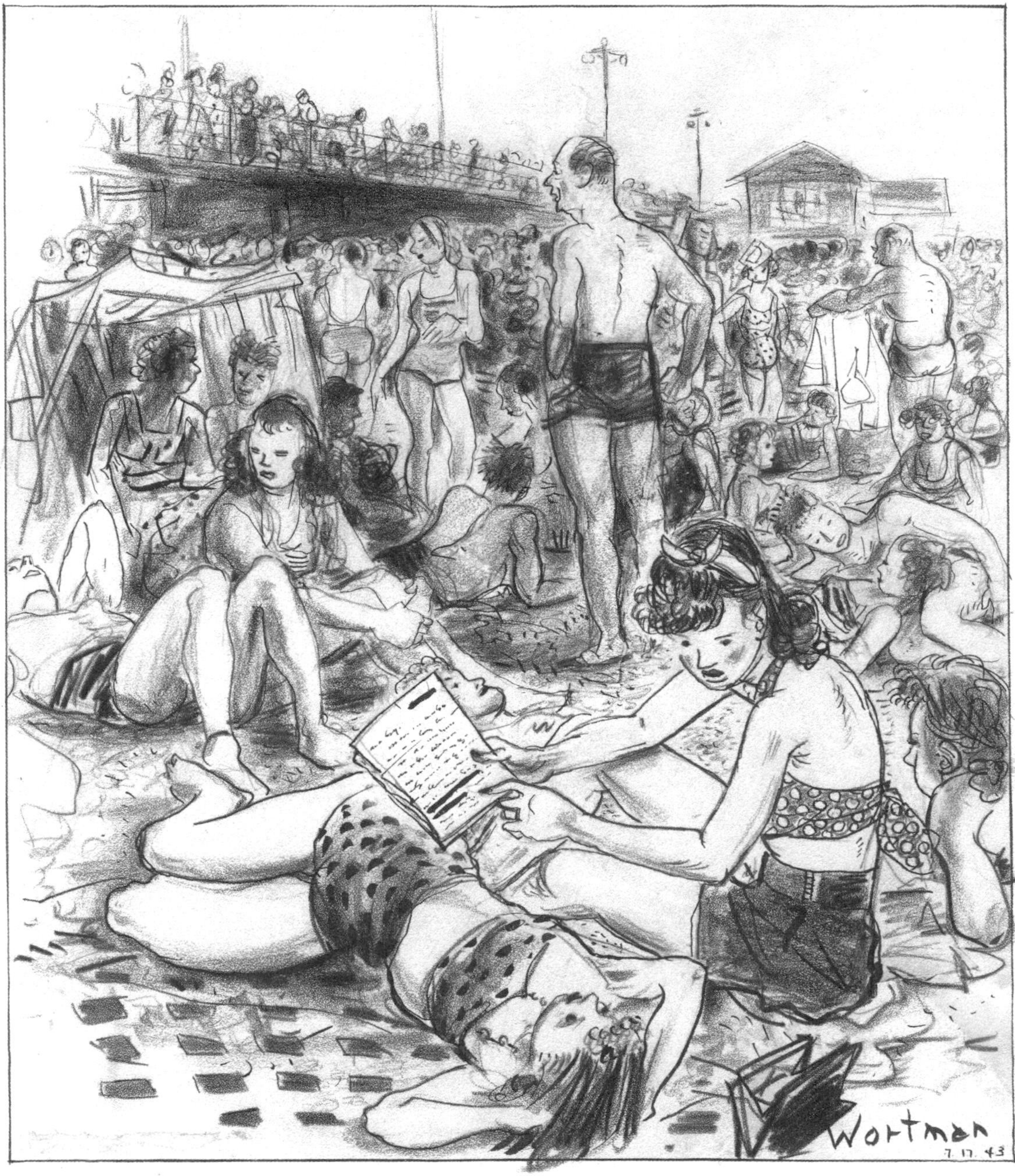
Wortman
7.17.43

"Look what the censors did to this letter I got from Joe. I'm sure he said he loved me a coupla times in there where they've blacked it out."

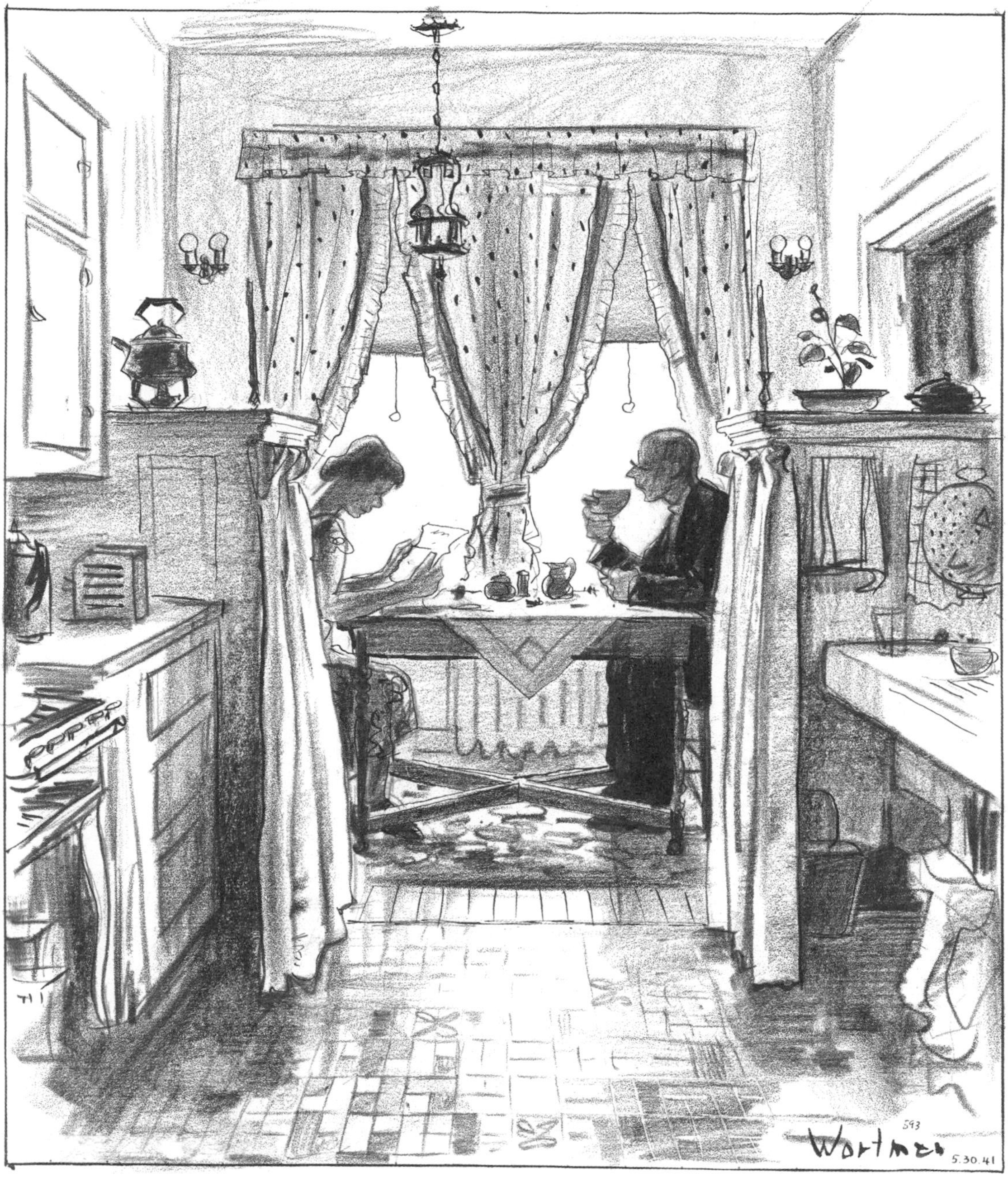
Wortman
5.30.41

"It's from the Browns. I wrote her I had a lot of gossip to tell her, and now we're invited for the weekend at their bungalow—just as I figured."

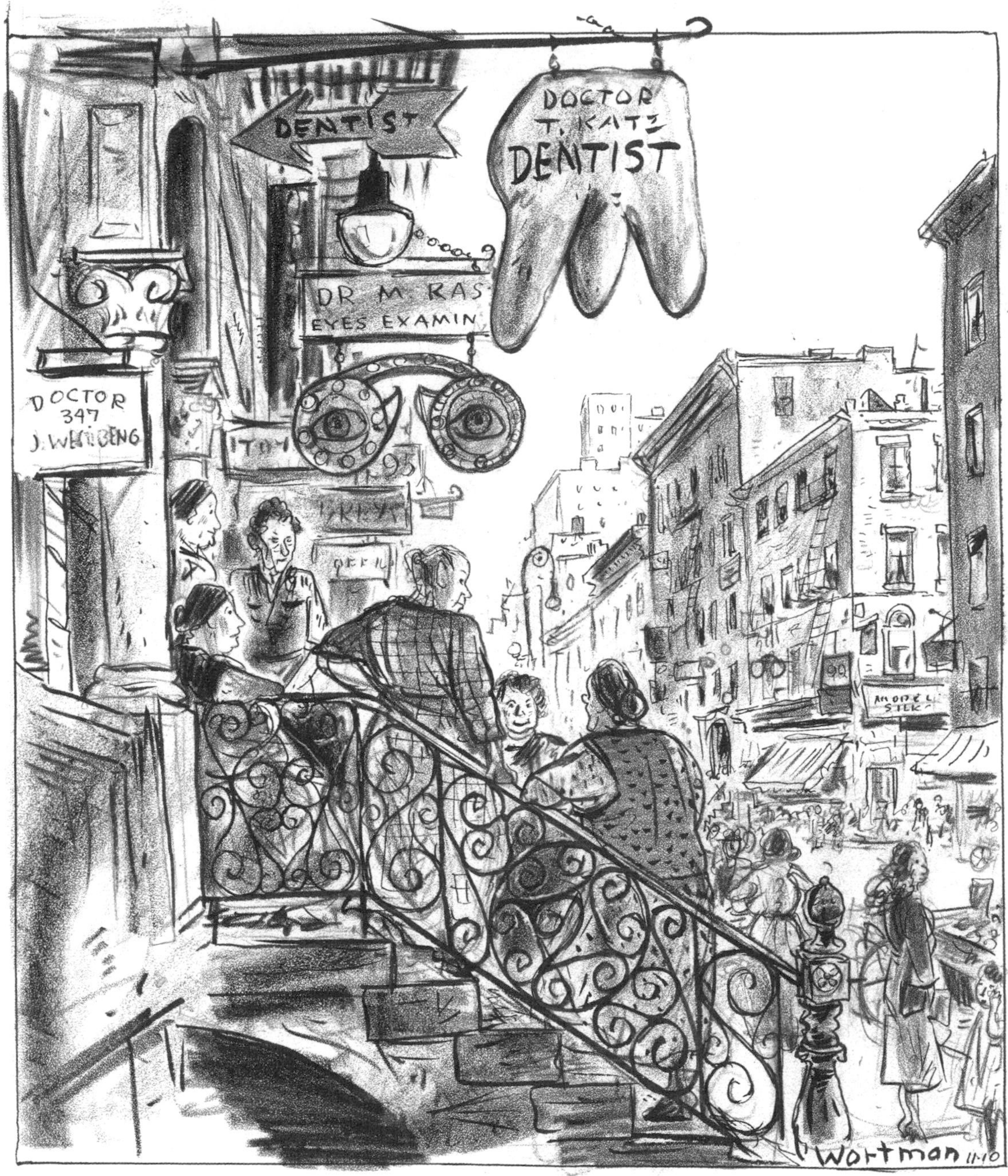
DENTIST
DOCTOR
T. KATZ
DENTIST
DR M. RAS
EYES EXAMIN
DOCTOR
347
Wortman

"One of my daughters is married; the other could have been many times except she wants a title—a doctor or a dentist."

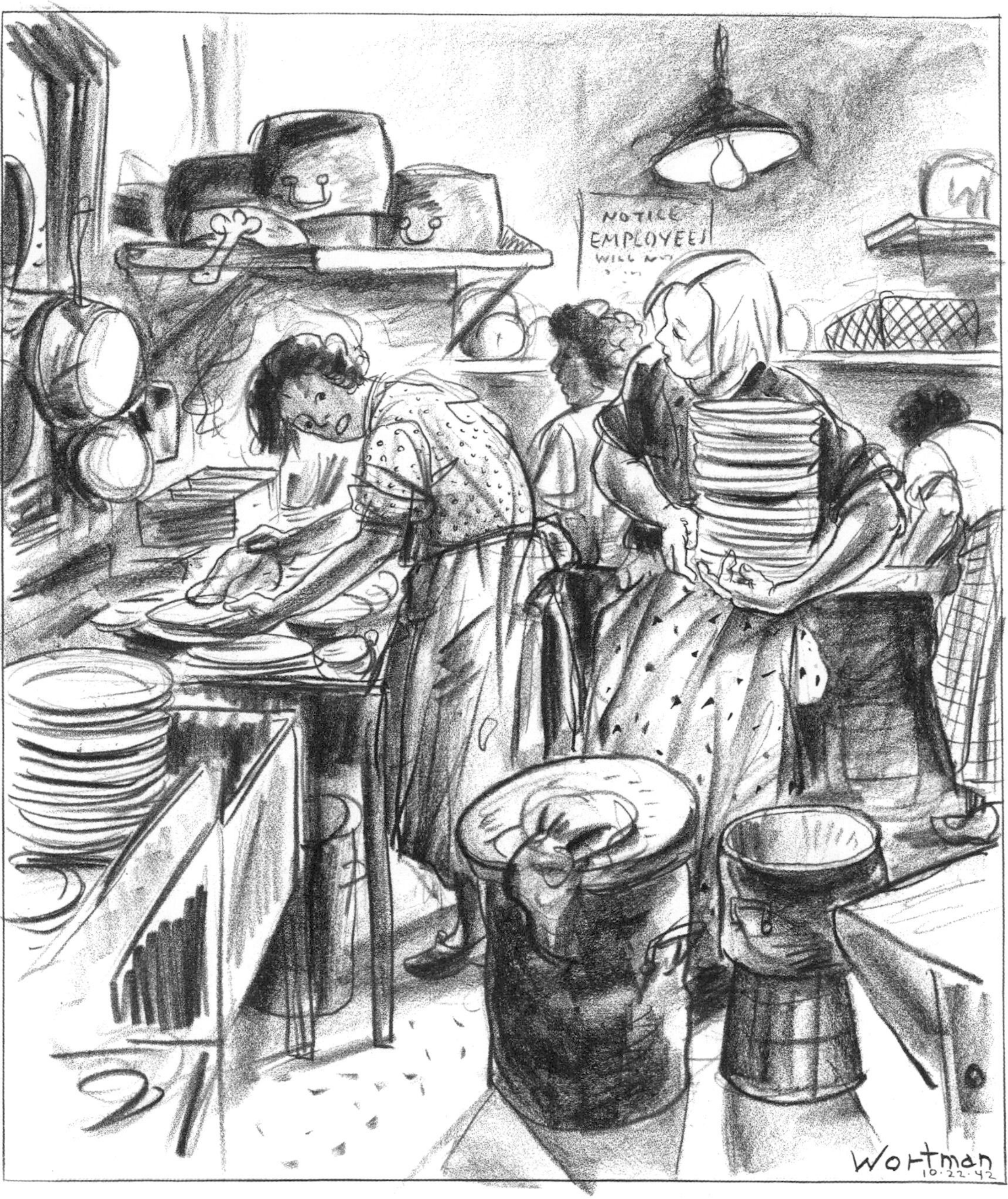
NOTICE
EMPLOYEES
WILL NOT
Wortman
10·22·42
"When I get married I'm gonna have all paper plates."

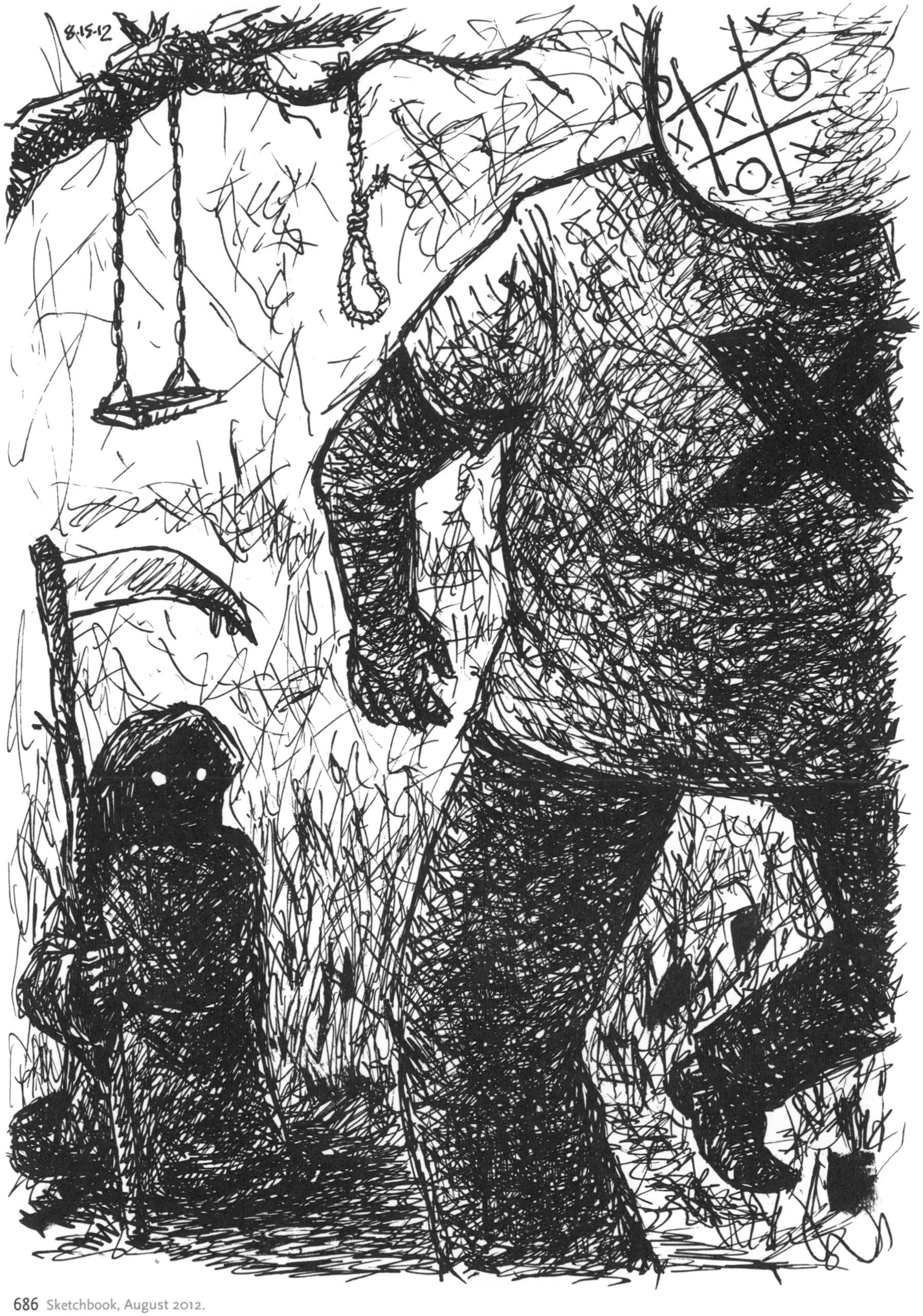
8.15.12

 Sketchbook, August 2012.

ART SPIEGELMAN

an appreciation by Rina Zavagli

I've known Art Spiegelman for more than twenty years—we're old friends. Art and Françoise Mouly, his collaborator and wife, have vacationed frequently in Paris and in Tuscany with me and Lorenzo Mattotti, my collaborator and husband. We met a few years after the publication of the first part of *Maus*, a work that revolutionized comics and became a success worldwide. In January 2011, Art was awarded the Grand Prix at Angoulême. He asked me to curate the retrospective exhibition he had to organize for the following year, and through that experience, our friendship and my admiration for him only grew.

Art worried about the exhibition from the start, initially perceiving the honour as an obligation. For all the prestige of the event, the prospect of having to oversee it weighed on him. And more than anything, with the recent publication of a new edition of *Breakdowns* (2008) and *MetaMaus* (2011), which marked the twenty-fifth anniversary of the first volume of *Maus*, he wasn't crazy about the idea of sifting through his archives and revisiting his own work yet again.

But Art is passionate about comics, and he has a way of transmitting that passion to those who work with him. Detail oriented, he wanted to continue with an idea we had used in 2009 when he finally agreed to let Galerie Martel in Paris hold an exhibition and sale of his work. The concept was to shed light on his creative process—the laboratory of someone who has spent a long career racking his mind to come up with new ways of making comics and telling stories. I think we succeeded. The two of us went through his entire body of work, from *RAW*, the magazine he put out with Françoise Mouly, to his *New Yorker* covers, and of course his masterpiece, *Maus*.

We looked through hundreds of breakdowns, sketches, and studies to select the ones that best represent his vision of drawing and of what he thinks comics should be. I discovered all the steps that go into the making of his work. Art is highly critical of his production and demanding of himself. In creating *Maus*, for instance, he sometimes made as many as twenty preparatory sketches before settling on a final drawing.

Working with Art on his retrospective exhibition gave me new insights into the work of this fascinating artist. It was

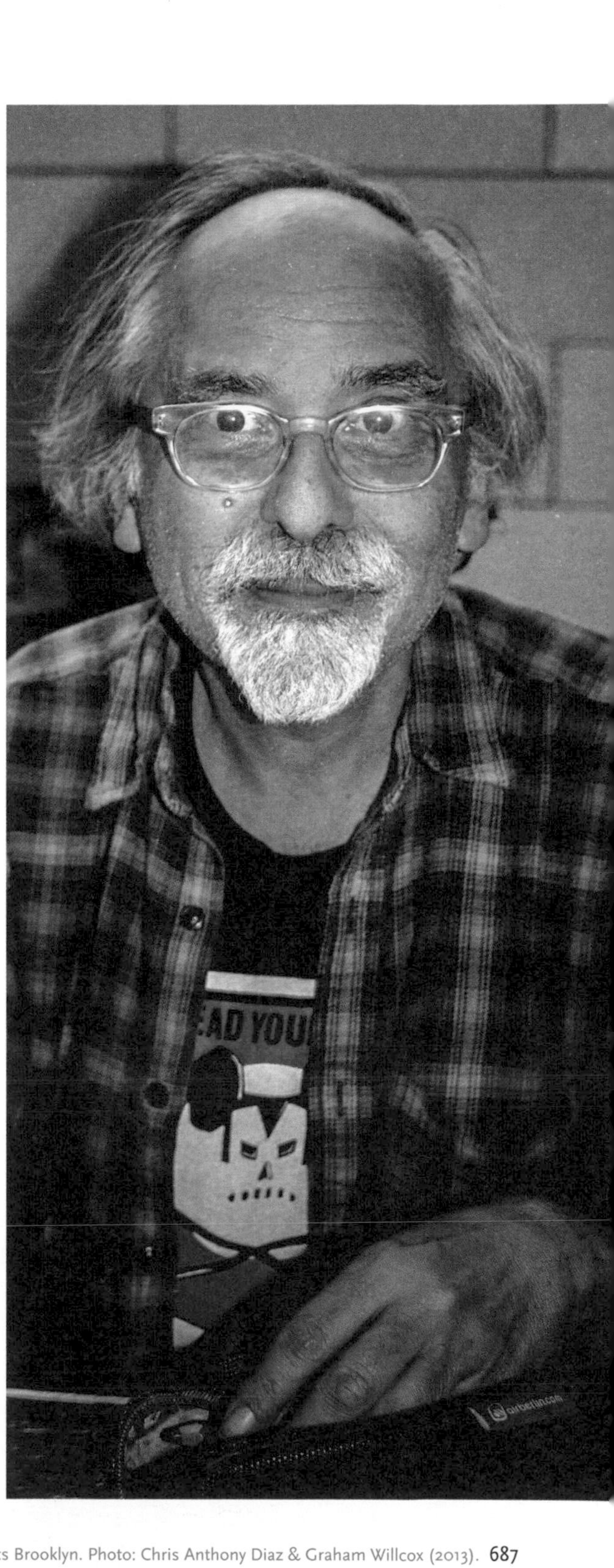

Art Spiegelman at Comic Arts Brooklyn. Photo: Chris Anthony Diaz & Graham Willcox (2013).

also an opportunity for us to compare our methods and share experiences while strengthening the ties that already existed between us. Art has a great and self-deprecating sense of humour, and his generosity is matched by a boundless curiosity.

Art lives through and for comics. I've always been fascinated by his deep and sincere love for the medium and its history, of which he's a real connoisseur. It's a passion bordering on obsession. Comics are always at the heart of his work and his approach to the world. Everything refers back to the language of comics. He is interested in many things, notably other forms of art, but the means of expression he favours remains sequential art. Comics are how he talks to his readers. Over the years, this abiding passion has let him enrich the medium of comics and leave his mark on its history.

Another thing I've always admired about this exceptional artist is his integrity. After *Maus* came out, Art was repeatedly approached with offers to make his bestseller into a movie, or to tap the very real and probably substantial merchandising potential of his work. He just turned the offers down, systematically and emphatically.

The exhibition CO-MIX: A Retrospective of Comics, Graphics, and Scraps opened at the Cité internationale de

---

This essay is as much a confession as it is an appreciation. I once believed that Art's drawing skills were subpar. I was introduced to this opinion by none other than Art Spiegelman himself. "I have the hands of a butcher," he's said on more than one occasion. I believed him because it was convenient for me to do so.

Looking back, this notion seems utterly absurd, especially given the fact that Art was my guiding light as a young cartoonist. I moved to New York City in 1989 with the hopes of figuring out how to make a graphic novel. In college I did a daily comic strip for the school newspaper. Though I loved working on a strip, after a few years the format felt limiting. I tried to create a graphic novel but had no clue as to how to do so.

There were no schools to study this and only one cartoonist that I knew of working in the long form to even emulate. I had started reading the serialized chapters of *Maus* in the pages of *RAW*. On the back cover of one of the issues was an advertisement for the School of Visual Arts. I sent off for their catalogue and saw Art's name listed as an instructor.

By the time I arrived at SVA, Art had stopped teaching and was wrestling with the success of the first volume of *Maus* while simultaneously trying to finish the second. I did manage to get an internship at *RAW*, and one of my duties in the pre–desktop scanner era was to operate that giant stat camera and shoot original art for publication. One afternoon my supervisor, Bob Sikoryak, handed me a binder full of plastic sleeves— chapter ten of *Maus*—to shoot. For several hours, the red glow of the darkroom became my classroom. With each page I pulled out to shoot, there beneath it was the previous draft, and beneath that page an earlier draft, and so on. It was both sobering and exhilarating to consider how much planning and thought went into crafting each page.

Being exposed to Art's working method, I started to realize that cartooning is less like the drawing I was taught in school—a spontaneous act of discovery or straight-up rendering—and more a meticulous process of codifying marks into an idiosyncratic visual alphabet. Art's "alphabet" combined expressive mark-making with the precision of an engineer. Given the content and scope of *Maus*, anything less would not do.

I began to understand cartooning as choreographed doodles that have to dance with all the other formal elements of the page (word balloons, text, panel borders, etc.) with the intention of being read as a singular performance.

Now when I hear Art's assertion that he can't draw, it is like listening to someone bemoan their inability to properly work a wood stove while having discovered groundbreaking ways of applying thermodynamic energy. But in my twenties, when I struggled mightily with my drawing, I related all too well to Art's "hands of a butcher" comment (and if you've ever seen my large, fleshy hands you can see why that comment was especially pertinent). I took solace in the belief that if Art was able to accomplish what he did with his "butcher hands," then there was hope for me too. Art became my patron saint for cartoonists who couldn't draw. He gave me hope that however much I struggled with my work, I still had a shot at making a decent comic despite my crippling limitations.

la bande dessinée in Angoulême. It has since travelled to the prestigious Centre Pompidou in Paris, the Museum Ludwig in Cologne, Germany, the Vancouver Art Gallery in Canada, and the Jewish Museum in New York. Its last stop will be at the Art Gallery of Ontario in Toronto, Canada. I'm delighted that I was able to work on the show and, in this way, help bring Art's substantial body of work and extraordinary contribution to comics to the attention of the art world at large.

Rina Zavagli, curator of CO-MIX, A Retrospective of Comics, Graphics, and Scraps.

Perhaps Art should be the patron saint for cartoonists who struggle? Ultimately isn't it the struggle against one's limitations, knowing there is a good chance that things could go south at any moment, that allows someone the best chance of creating something special? I think of Art's sketchbook drawings as missives from an artist who is courageous enough to station himself on the outer edge of his ability. This is where the most possibilities lie. Art's sketchbooks are a vaudevillian kaleidoscope of popular culture, personal obsessions, and historical perils in which he is trying to impose some meaning and structure (and find some humour) in an absurd and cruel world.

On many individual pages you can see Art cooking with the language of comics, using familiar ingredients (a banana, Uncle Sam, etc.), while infusing his recipe with varying concentrations of playfulness and desperation to see if he can't concoct something entirely new. Other drawings look like Art is just trying to get his crazy, incomprehensible self out of his head and onto the paper so he can get to know it better. The purpose of the dense scrawl of some doodles seems to be first and foremost to fill space and avoid being consumed by a void.

Taken as a whole, Art's drawings give the feeling that there are stakes involved: something at risk, something to be discovered, even if the artist himself bemoans his lack of skill for the expedition he has undertaken. There's a restless, impatient quality that gives each drawing a sense of urgency. However it is parsed, the work feels alive, and if this isn't what constitutes "good drawing," I don't know what does. Sorry I sold you short, Art! —*James Sturm*

2/8

Dear Chris

Thanks a lot for D+Q and the PLAYBOY (I had just bought Chester Brown's book a day or so before and will gladly pass this one on in the hopes of making new converts). I like your 'zines a lot and am fascinated by the fact that Canada has become such a hotbed of vital comix activity.

I'm a big fan of Julie's work and I can probably be bullied into giving a quote but would appreciate being left off the hook only because I've had to write so _many_ damn blurbs recently. I dunno.

Anyway, Please keep up the Good Work.

all the best
— art

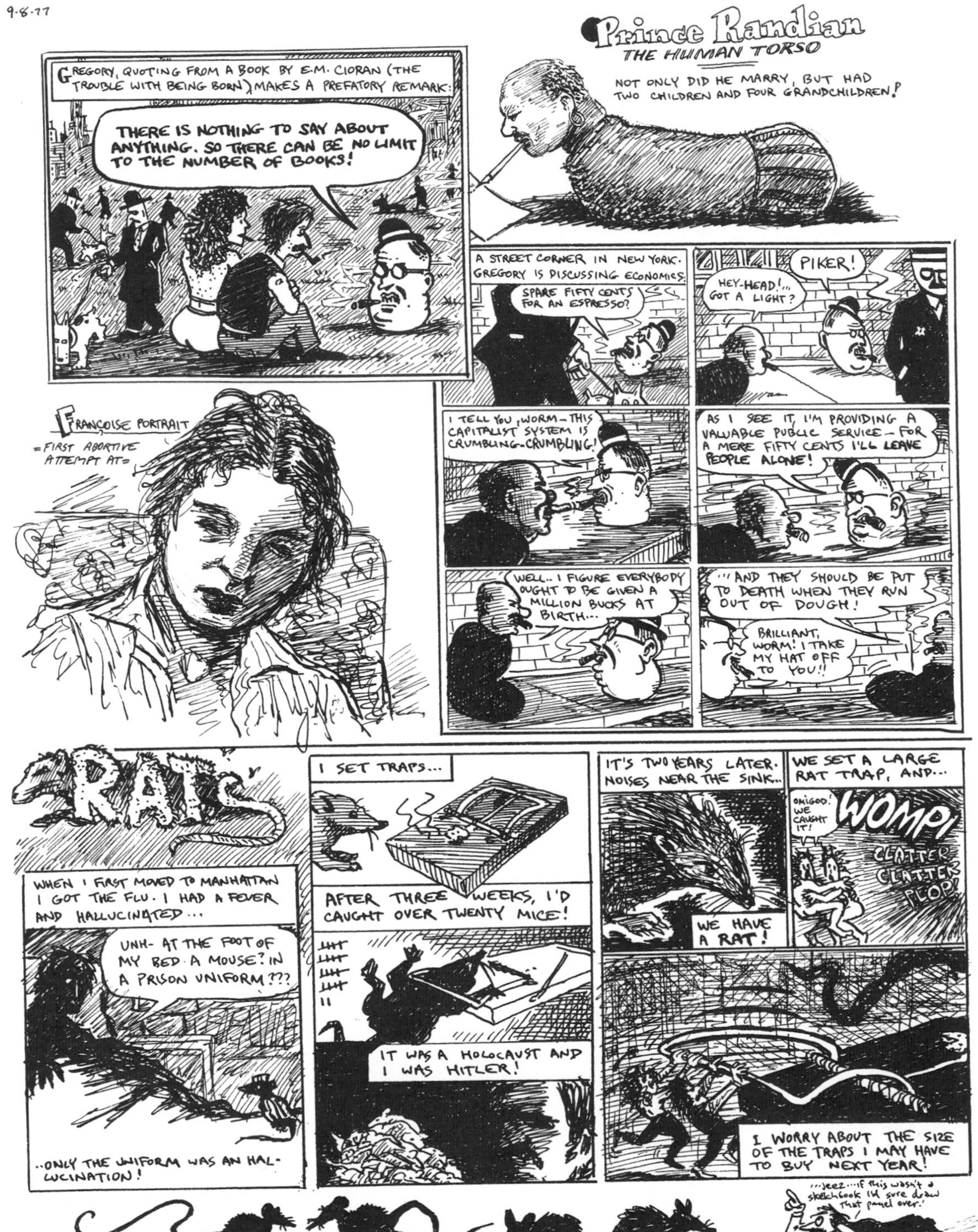
9.8.77
GREGORY, QUOTING FROM A BOOK BY E.M. CIORAN (THE TROUBLE WITH BEING BORN) MAKES A PREFATORY REMARK:
THERE IS NOTHING TO SAY ABOUT ANYTHING. SO THERE CAN BE NO LIMIT TO THE NUMBER OF BOOKS!
Prince Randian
THE HUMAN TORSO
NOT ONLY DID HE MARRY, BUT HAD TWO CHILDREN AND FOUR GRANDCHILDREN!
FRANÇOISE PORTRAIT
=FIRST ABORTIVE ATTEMPT AT=
A STREET CORNER IN NEW YORK. GREGORY IS DISCUSSING ECONOMICS.
SPARE FIFTY CENTS FOR AN ESPRESSO?
PIKER!
HEY-HEAD!... GOT A LIGHT?
I TELL YOU, WORM-THIS CAPITALIST SYSTEM IS CRUMBLING-CRUMBLING!
AS I SEE IT, I'M PROVIDING A VALUABLE PUBLIC SERVICE-FOR A MERE FIFTY CENTS I'LL LEAVE PEOPLE ALONE!
WELL.. I FIGURE EVERYBODY OUGHT TO BE GIVEN A MILLION BUCKS AT BIRTH...
...AND THEY SHOULD BE PUT TO DEATH WHEN THEY RUN OUT OF DOUGH!
BRILLIANT, WORM! I TAKE MY HAT OFF TO YOU!!
RATS
WHEN I FIRST MOVED TO MANHATTAN I GOT THE FLU. I HAD A FEVER AND HALLUCINATED...
UNH- AT THE FOOT OF MY BED A MOUSE? IN A PRISON UNIFORM???
..ONLY THE UNIFORM WAS AN HALLUCINATION!
I SET TRAPS...
AFTER THREE WEEKS, I'D CAUGHT OVER TWENTY MICE!
IT WAS A HOLOCAUST AND I WAS HITLER!
IT'S TWO YEARS LATER. NOISES NEAR THE SINK..
WE HAVE A RAT!
WE SET A LARGE RAT TRAP, AND...
OMIGOD! WE CAUGHT IT!
WOMP!
CLATTER CLATTER PLOP!
I WORRY ABOUT THE SIZE OF THE TRAPS I MAY HAVE TO BUY NEXT YEAR!
...jeez...if this wasn't a sketchbook I'd sure draw that panel over!

690 Sketchbook, September 1977.

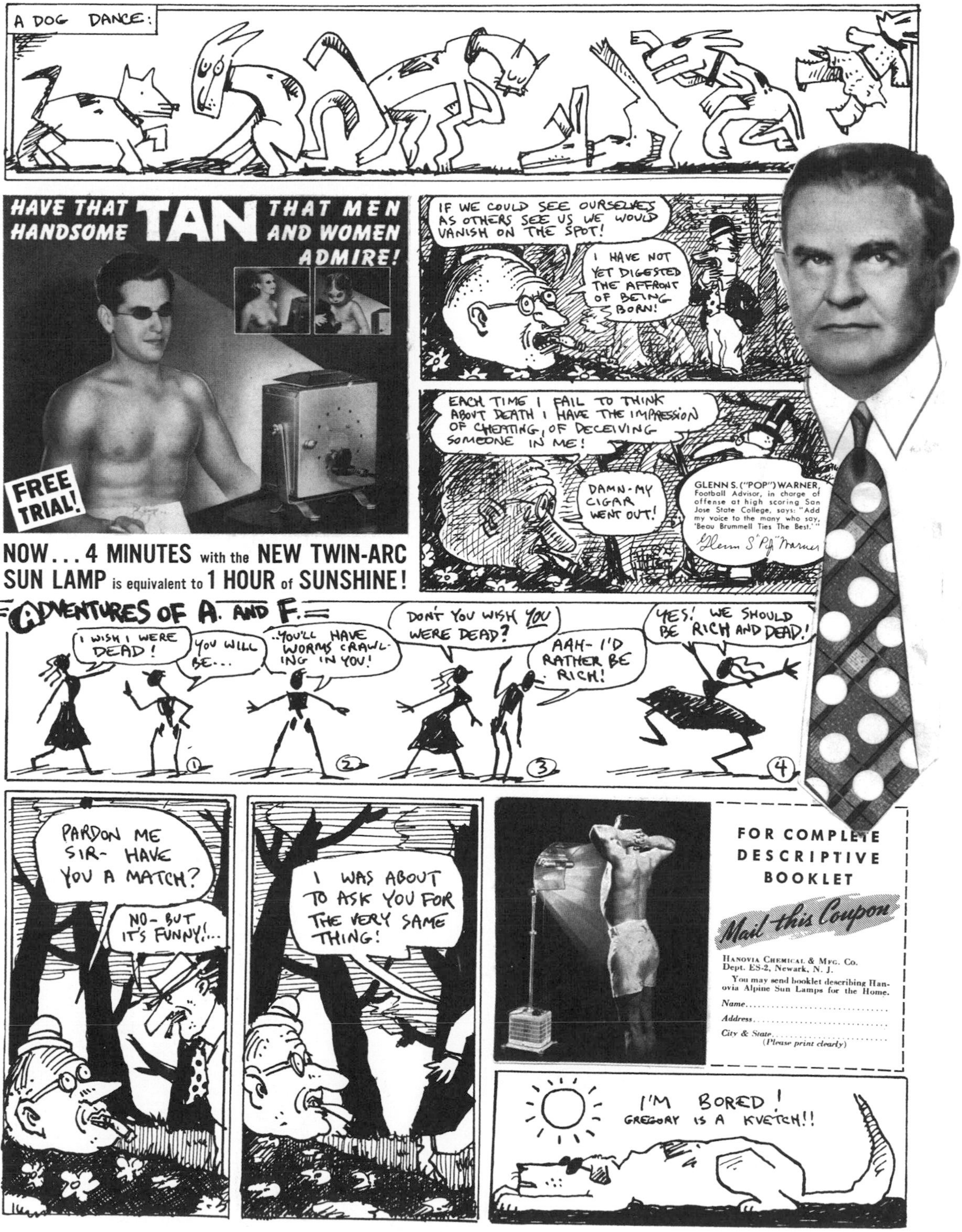
A DOG DANCE:
HAVE THAT HANDSOME TAN THAT MEN AND WOMEN ADMIRE!
FREE TRIAL!
NOW... 4 MINUTES with the NEW TWIN-ARC SUN LAMP is equivalent to 1 HOUR of SUNSHINE!
IF WE COULD SEE OURSELVES AS OTHERS SEE US WE WOULD VANISH ON THE SPOT!
I HAVE NOT YET DIGESTED THE AFFRONT OF BEING BORN!
EACH TIME I FAIL TO THINK ABOUT DEATH I HAVE THE IMPRESSION OF CHEATING, OF DECEIVING SOMEONE IN ME!
DAMN-MY CIGAR WENT OUT!
GLENN S. ("POP") WARNER, Football Advisor, in charge of offense at high scoring San Jose State College, says: "Add my voice to the many who say, 'Beau Brummell Ties The Best.'"
Glenn S. "Pop" Warner
ADVENTURES OF A. AND F.
I WISH I WERE DEAD!
YOU WILL BE...
..YOU'LL HAVE WORMS CRAWLING IN YOU!
1
2
DON'T YOU WISH YOU WERE DEAD?
AAH- I'D RATHER BE RICH!
3
YES! WE SHOULD BE RICH AND DEAD!
4
PARDON ME SIR- HAVE YOU A MATCH?
NO- BUT IT'S FUNNY!...
I WAS ABOUT TO ASK YOU FOR THE VERY SAME THING!
FOR COMPLETE DESCRIPTIVE BOOKLET
Mail this Coupon
HANOVIA CHEMICAL & MFG. Co. Dept. ES-2, Newark, N. J.
You may send booklet describing Hanovia Alpine Sun Lamps for the Home.
Name
Address
City & State
(Please print clearly)
I'M BORED! GREGORY IS A KVETCH!!

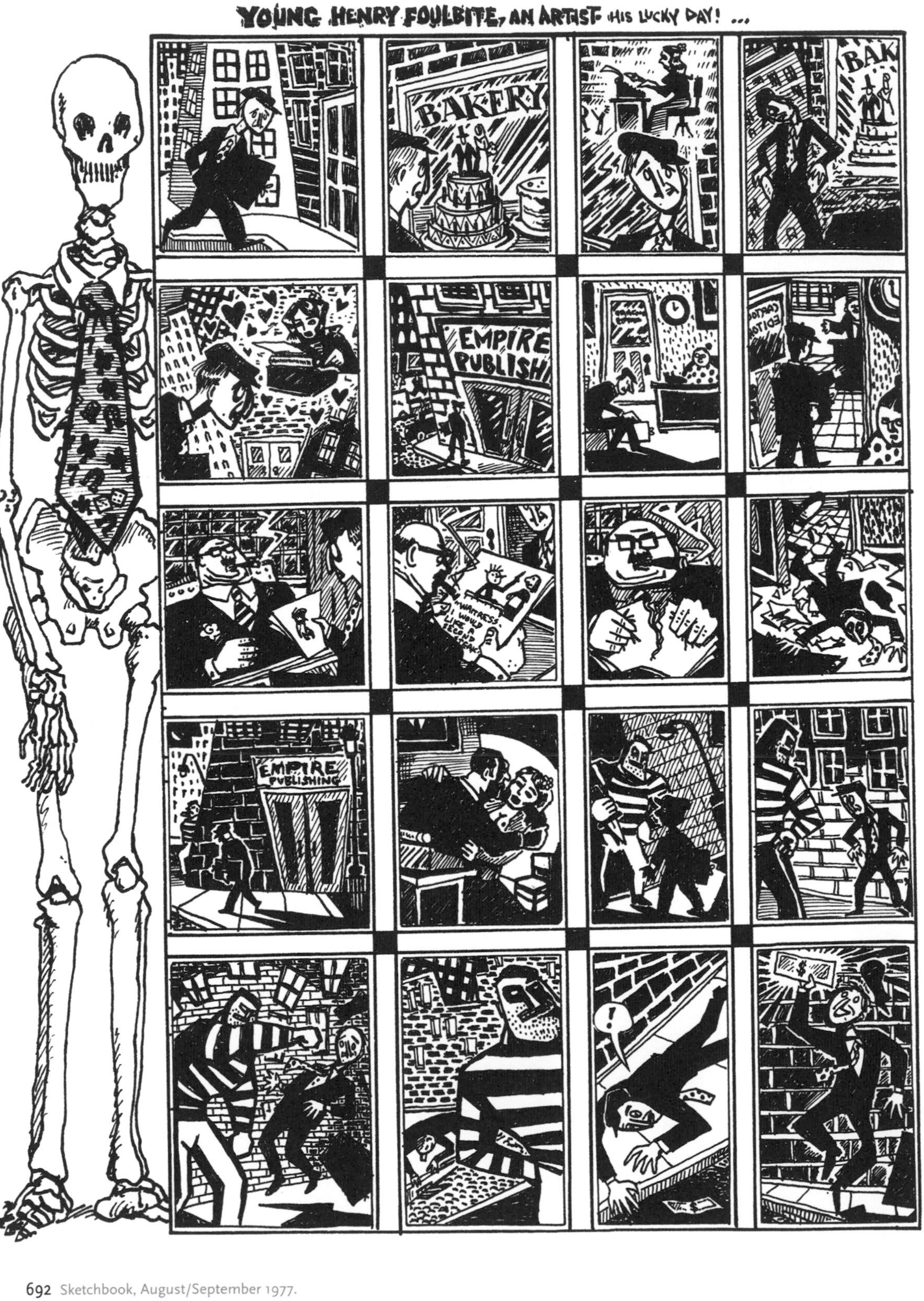
YOUNG HENRY FOULBITE, AN ARTIST HIS LUCKY DAY! ...
BAKERY
BAK
EMPIRE
PUBLISH
"WAITRESS:
I WOULD
LIKE A
SECOND
EMPIRE
PUBLISHING
!

 Sketchbook, August/September 1977.

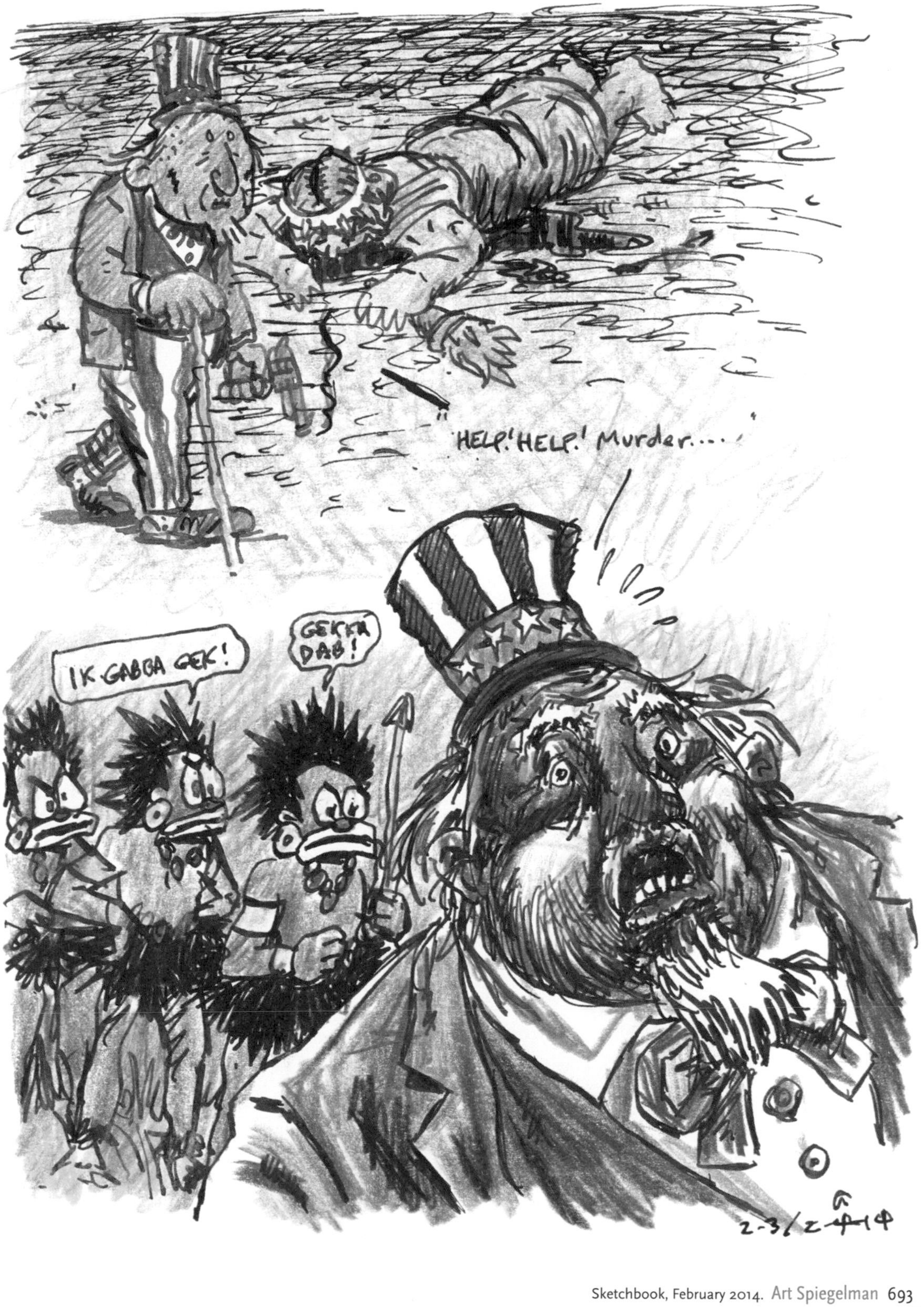
"HELP! HELP! Murder...."
IK GABBA GEK!
GEKKA DAB!

Sketchbook, February 2014. Art Spiegelman

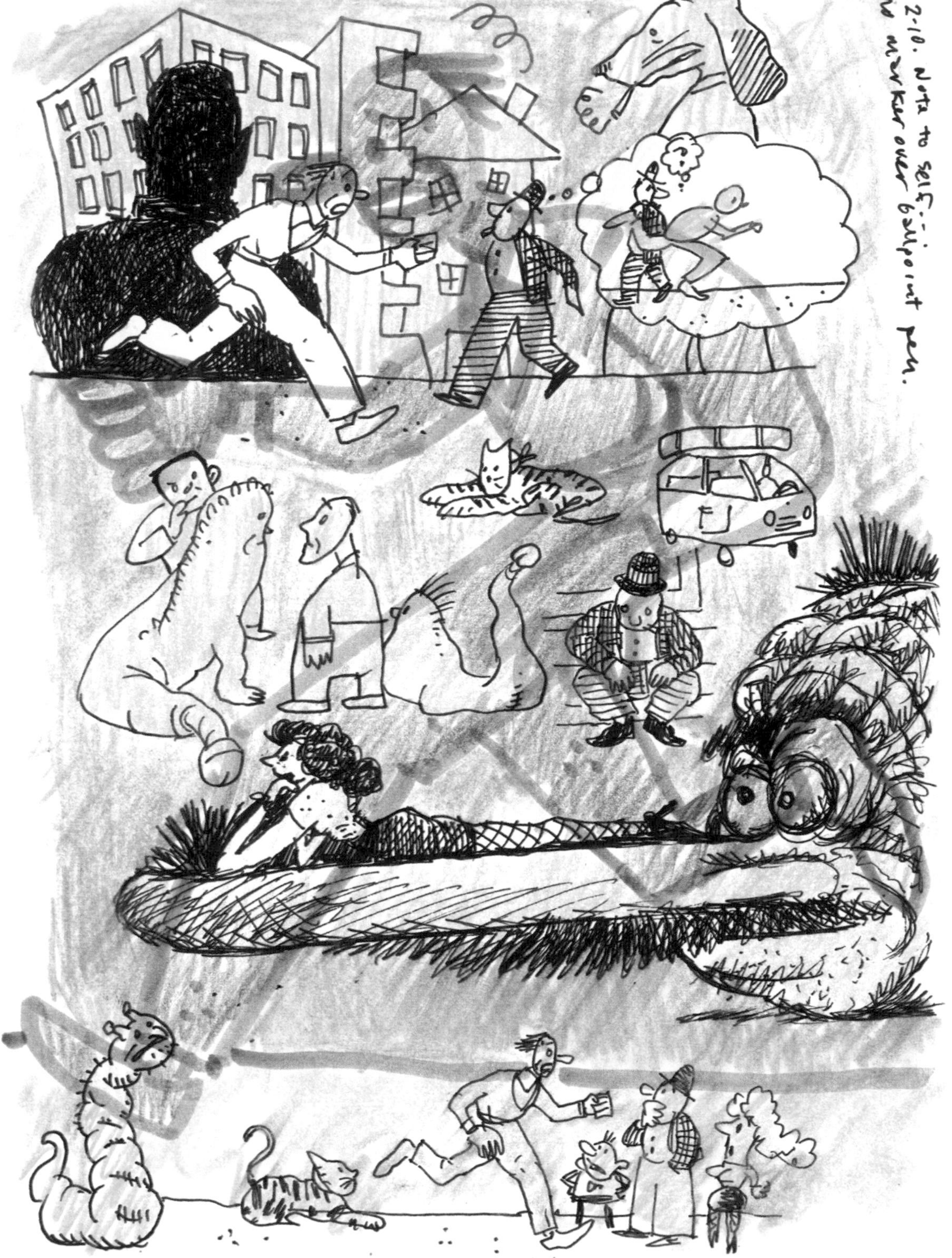
2-10. Note to self:
no marker over ballpoint pen.

 (Left) Sketchbook, February 2014. (Right) Sketchbook, November 2012.

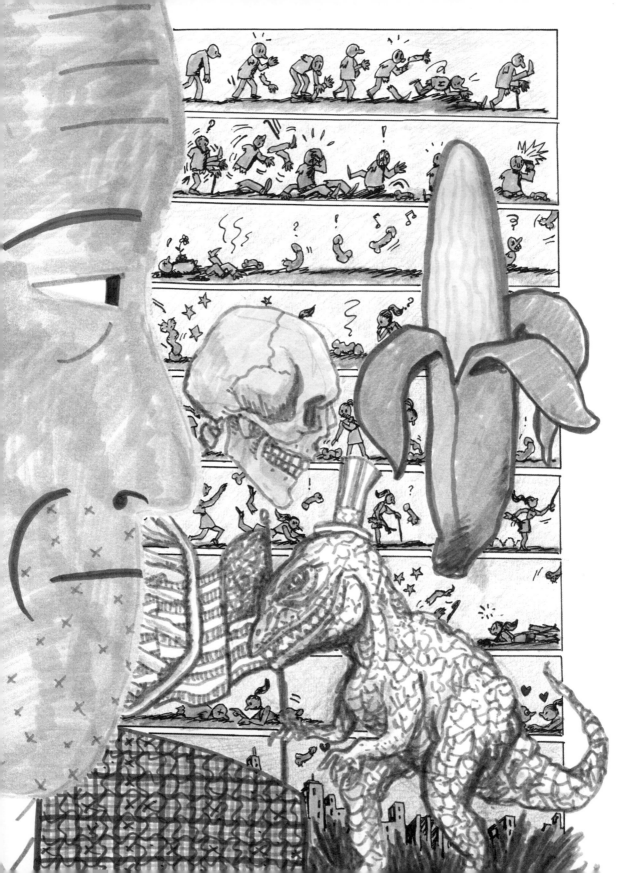

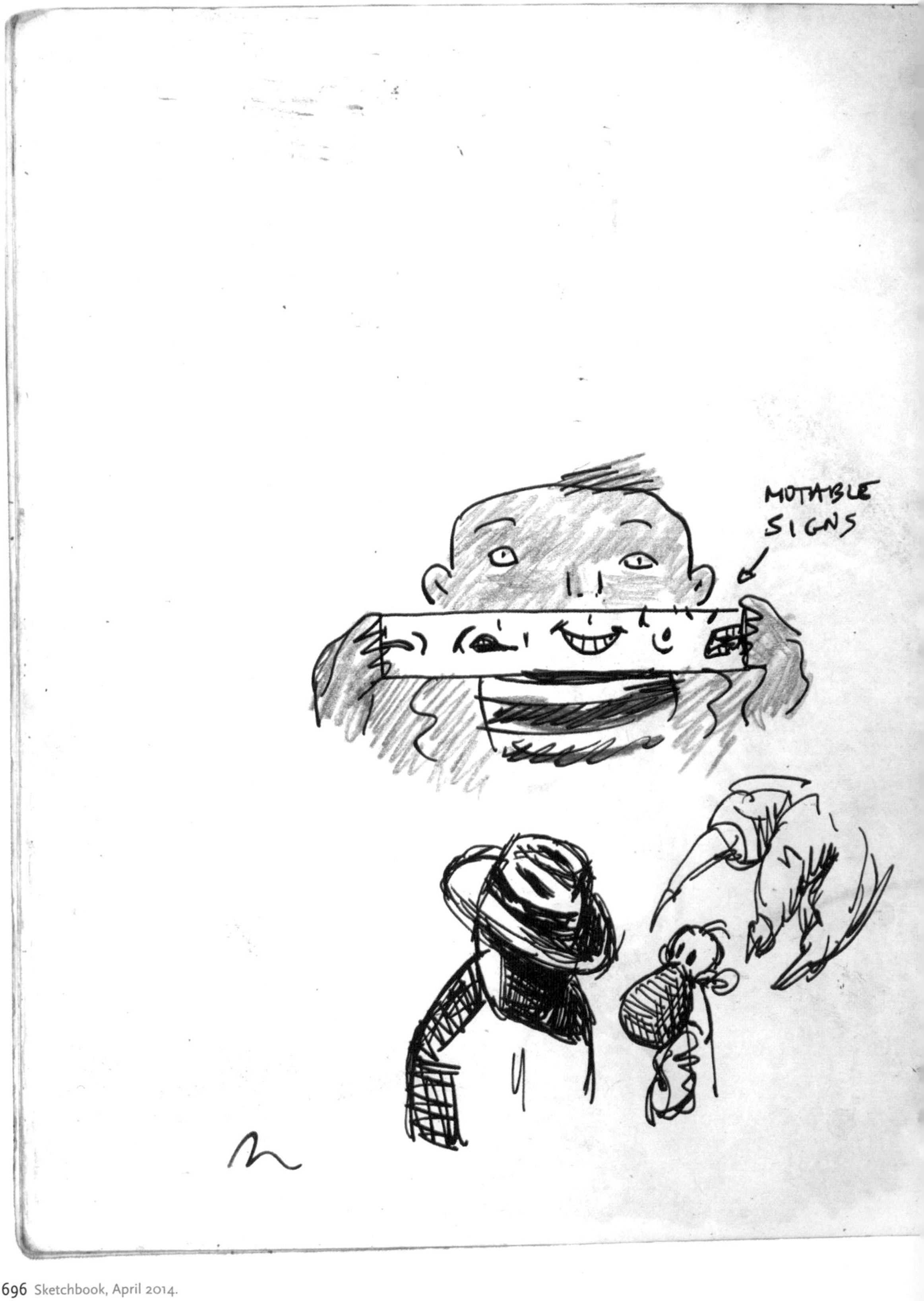
MUTABLE
SIGNS

 Sketchbook, April 2014.

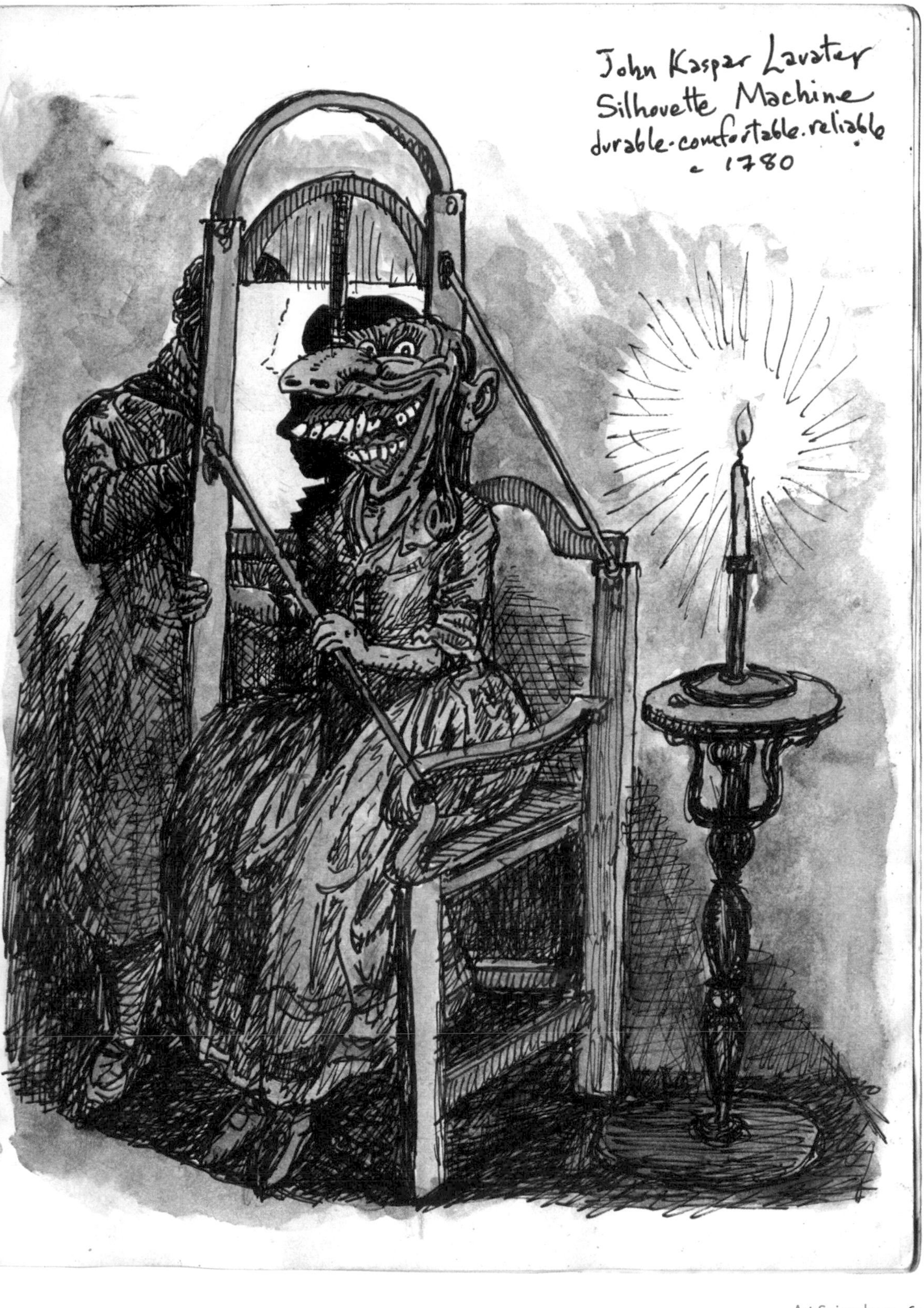
John Kaspar Lavater
Silhouette Machine
durable-comfortable-reliable
c 1780

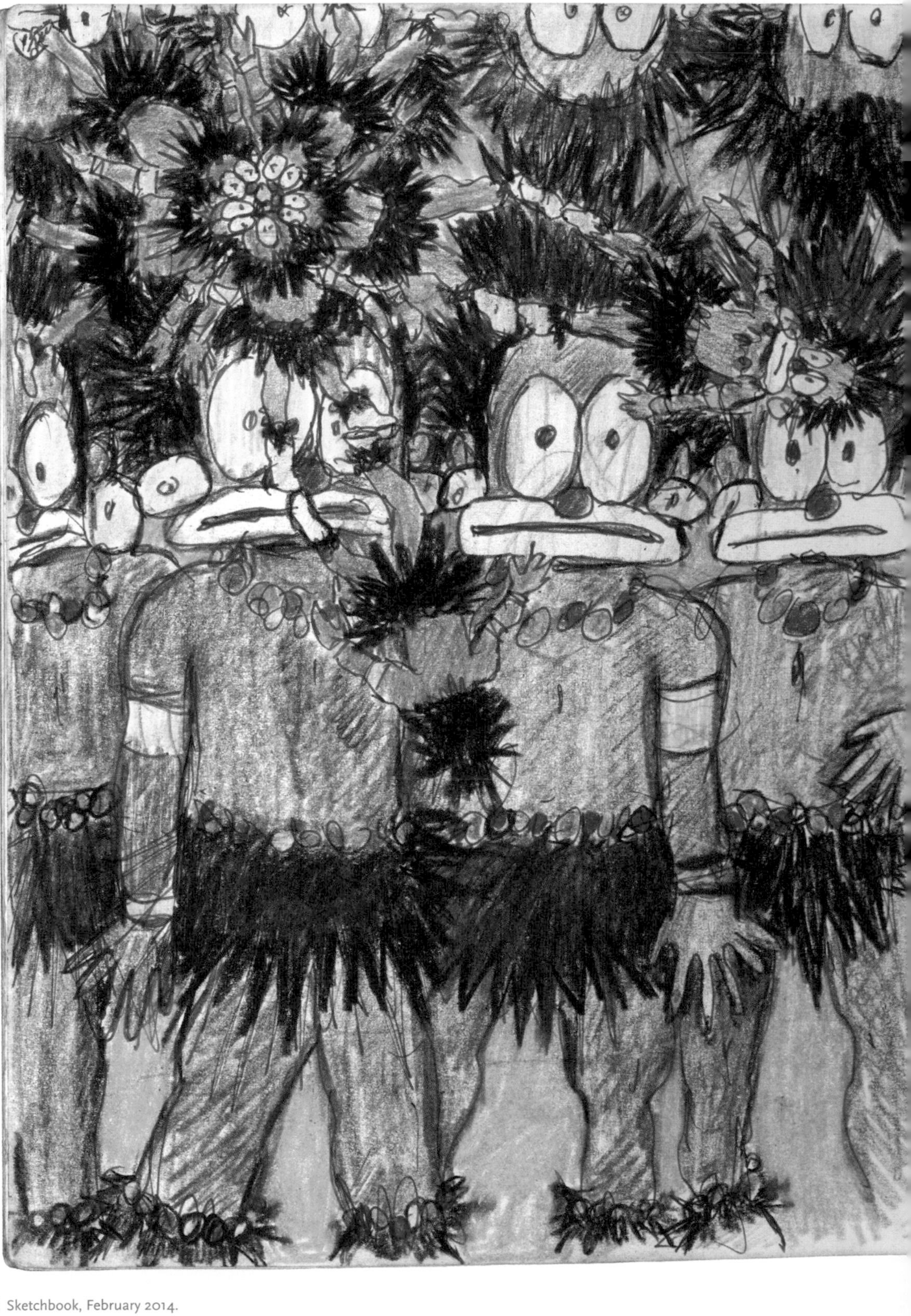

 Sketchbook, February 2014.

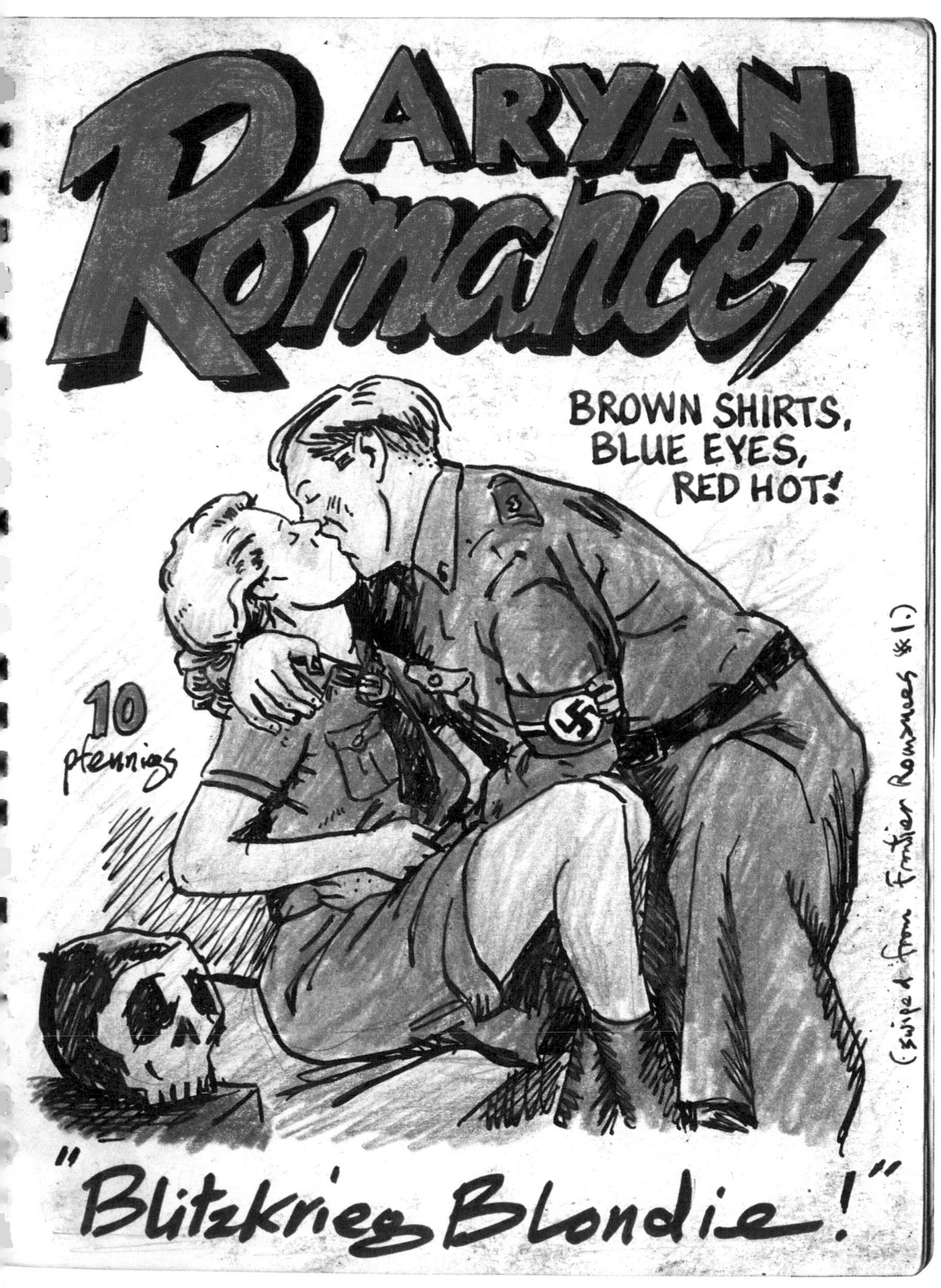
ARYAN
Romances
BROWN SHIRTS,
BLUE EYES,
RED HOT!
10
pfennigs
(swiped from Frontier Romances #1.)
"Blitzkrieg Blondie!"

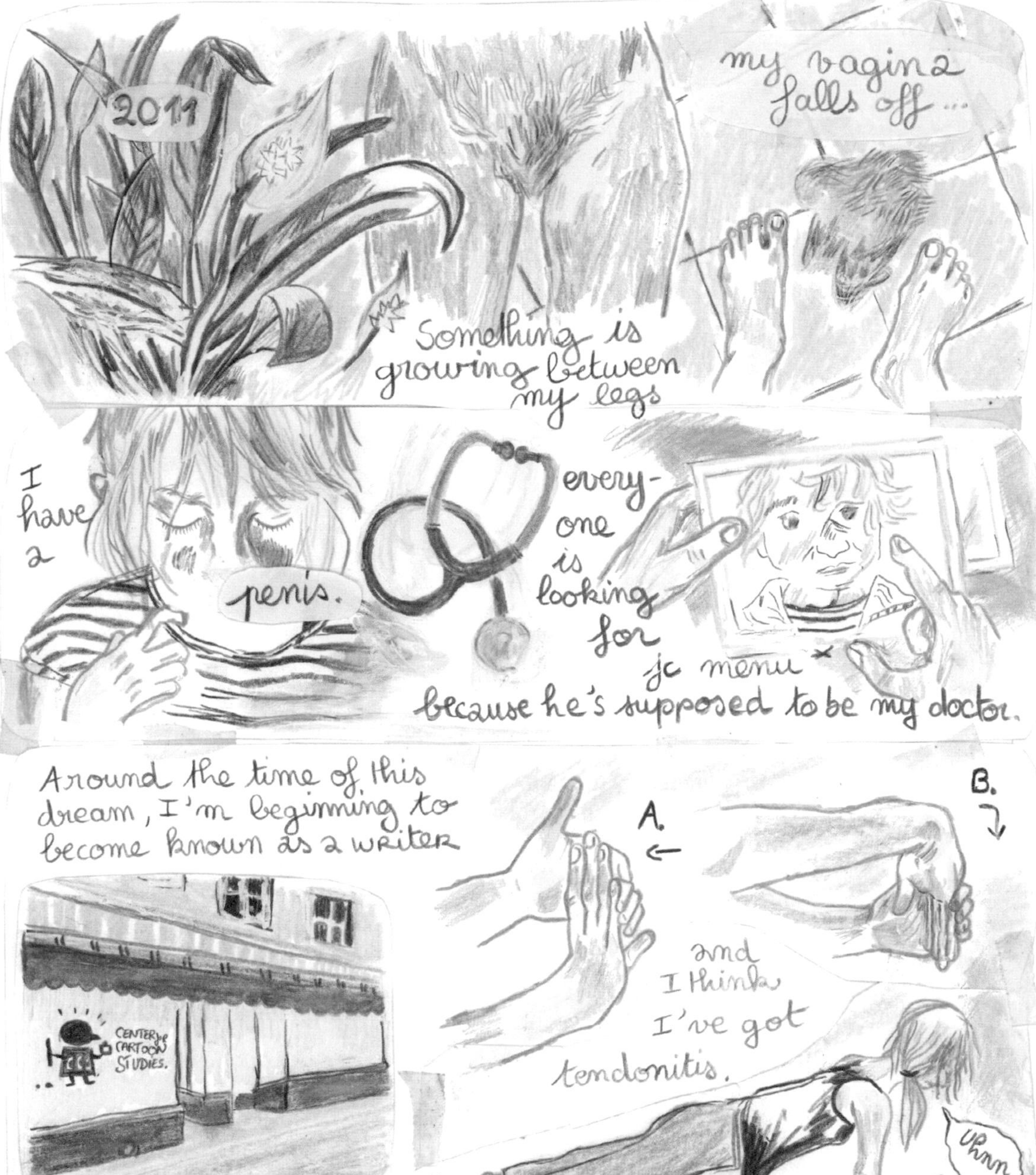
2011
Something is growing between my legs
my vagina falls off...
I have a
penis.
everyone is looking for
jc menu*
because he's supposed to be my doctor.
Around the time of this dream, I'm beginning to become known as a writer
CENTER for CARTOON STUDIES.
(I'm a fellow at the Center for Cartoon Studies)
A.
B.
and I think I've got tendonitis.
Uhnn...
* jc menu - founder and long-time editor of l'Association, the renowned independent French comics publisher.

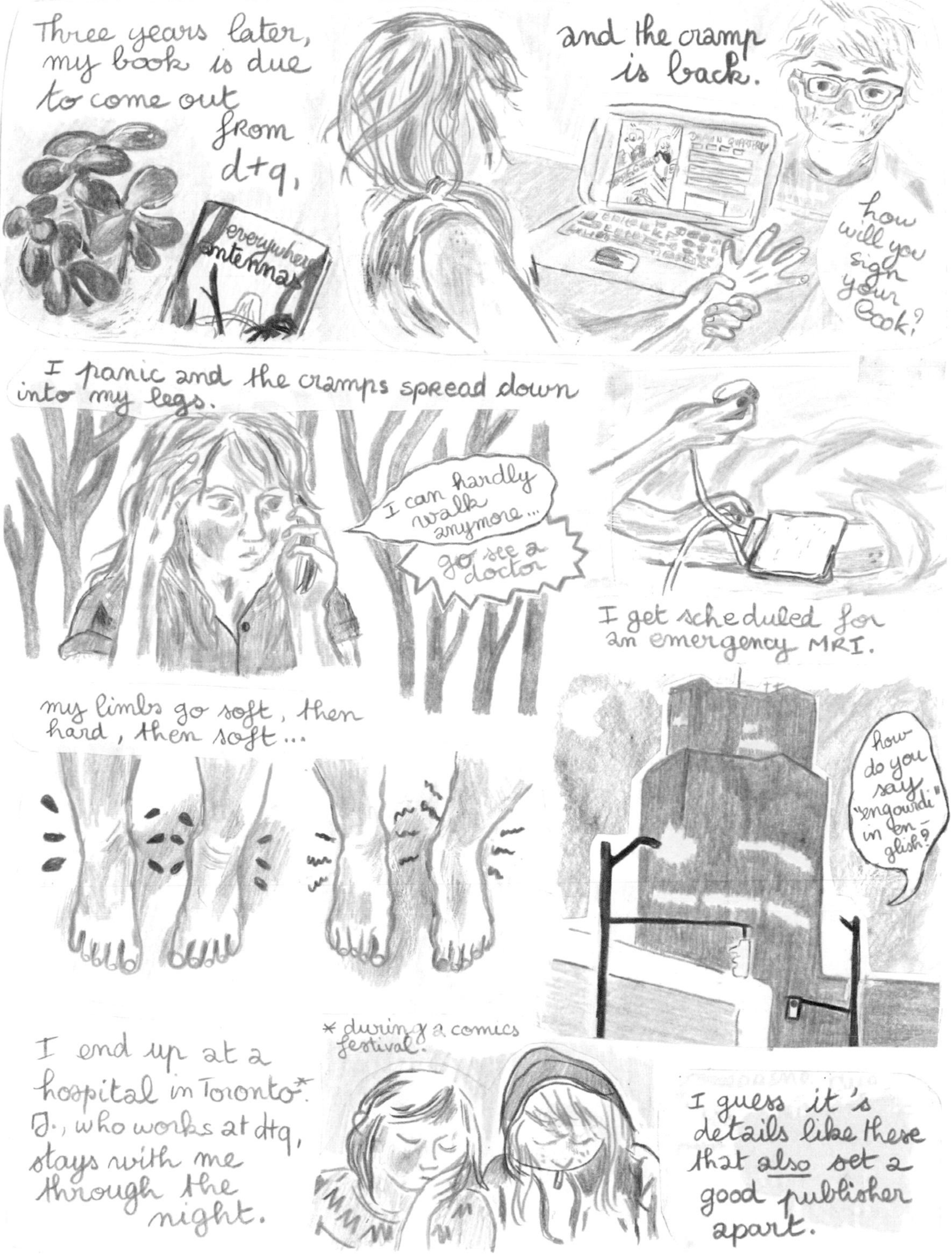
Three years later, my book is due to come out from d+q,
everywhere antennas
and the cramp is back.
how will you sign your book?
I panic and the cramps spread down into my legs.
I can hardly walk anymore...
go see a doctor
I get scheduled for an emergency MRI.
my limbs go soft, then hard, then soft...
how do you say "engourdi" in English?
I end up at a hospital in Toronto*. J., who works at d+q, stays with me through the night.
* during a comics festival.
I guess it's details like these that also set a good publisher apart.

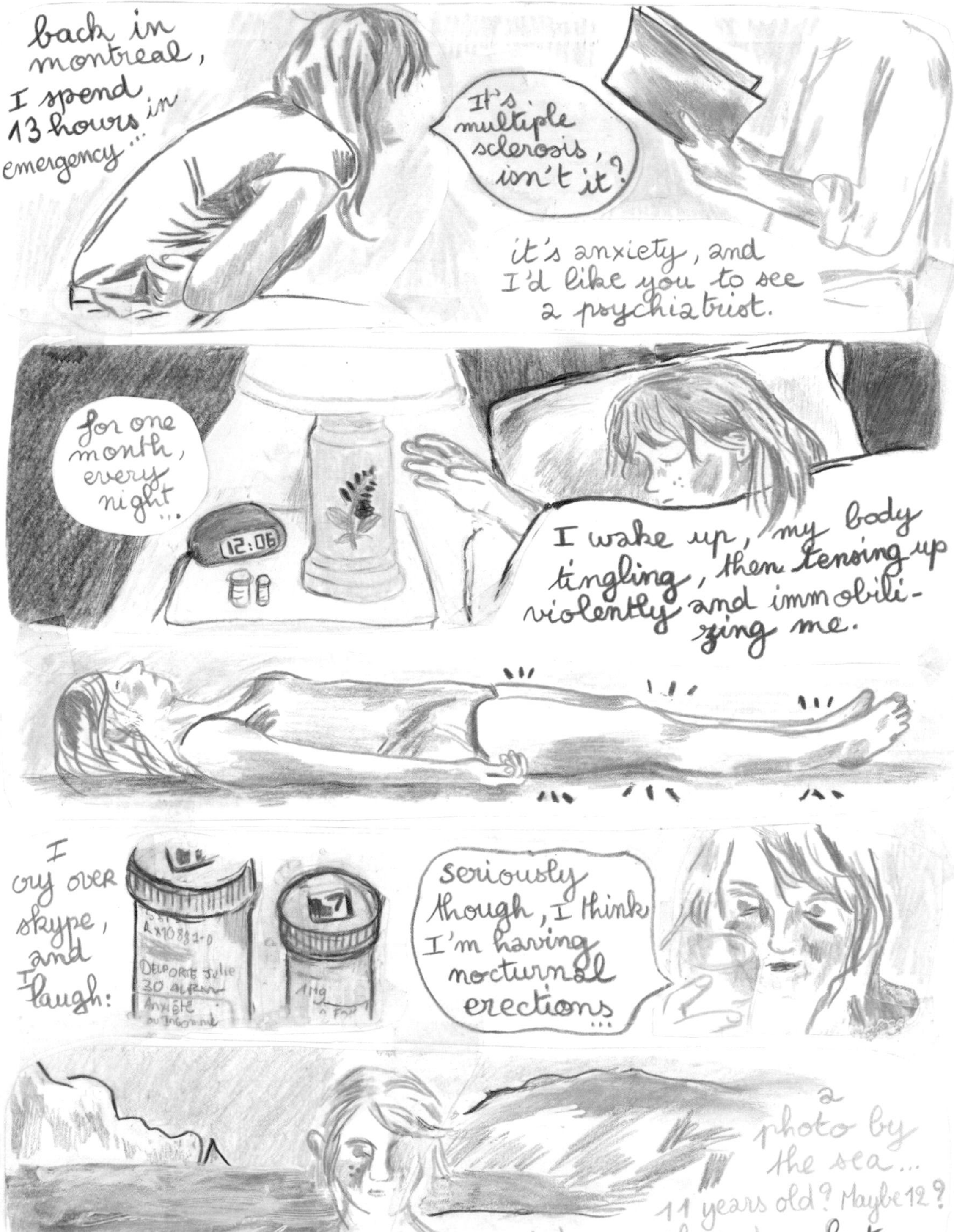
back in montreal, I spend 13 hours in emergency…
It's multiple sclerosis, isn't it?
it's anxiety, and I'd like you to see a psychiatrist.
for one month, every night…
12:06
I wake up, my body tingling, then tensing up violently and immobilizing me.
I cry over skype, and I laugh:
seriously though, I think I'm having nocturnal erections…
a photo by the sea…
11 years old? Maybe 12?
It's me already, but I don't have breasts.

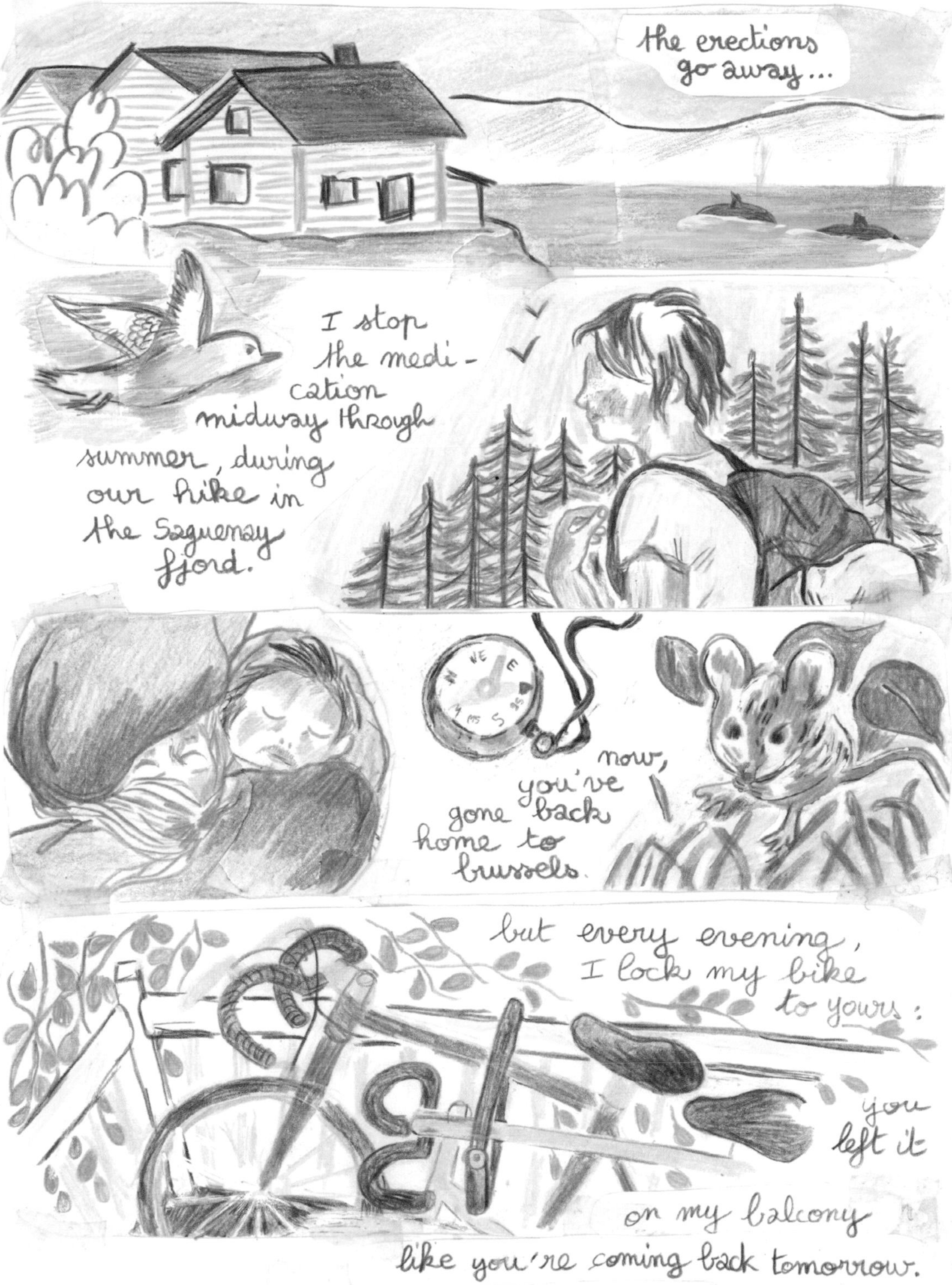
the erections go away...
I stop the medi-cation midway through summer, during our hike in the Saguenay fjord.
now, you've gone back home to brussels.
but every evening, I lock my bike to yours:
you left it
on my balcony
like you're coming back tomorrow.

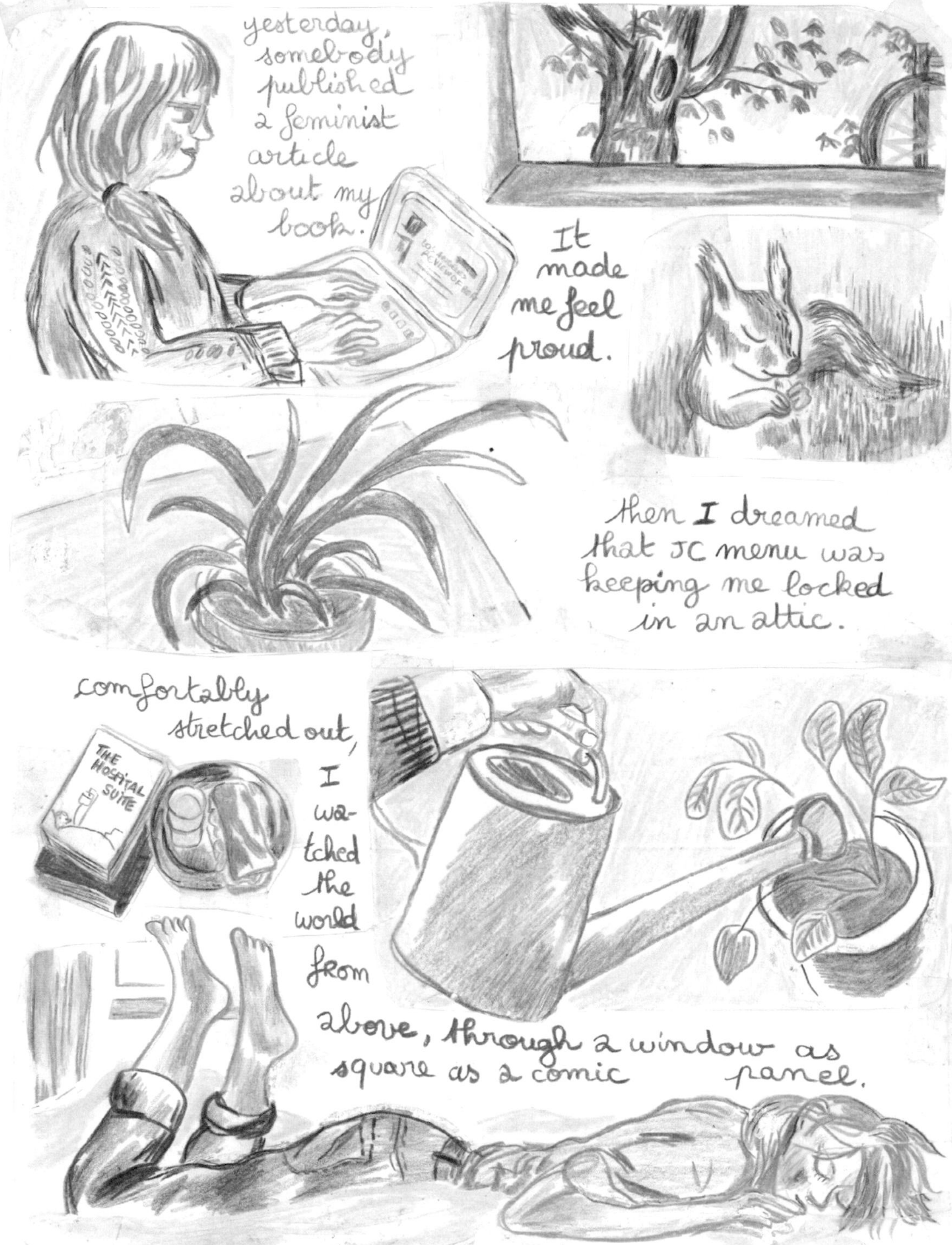
yesterday, somebody published a feminist article about my book.
It made me feel proud.
then I dreamed that JC menu was keeping me locked in an attic.
comfortably stretched out,
THE HOSPITAL SUITE
I watched the world from
above, through a window as square as a comic panel.

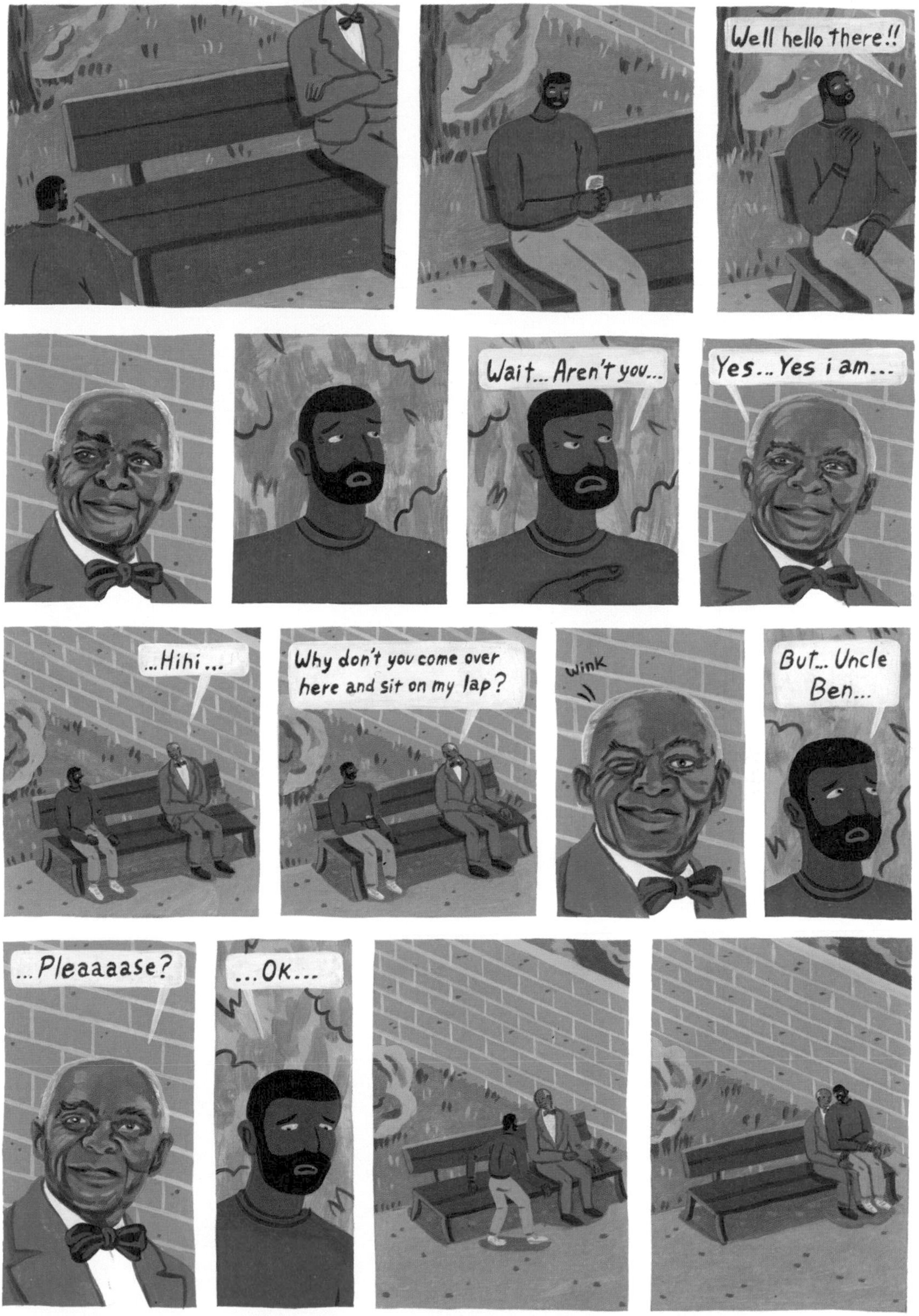
Well hello there!!
Wait... Aren't you...
Yes... Yes i am...
...Hihi...
Why don't you come over here and sit on my lap?
wink
But... Uncle Ben...
...Pleaaaase?
...Ok...

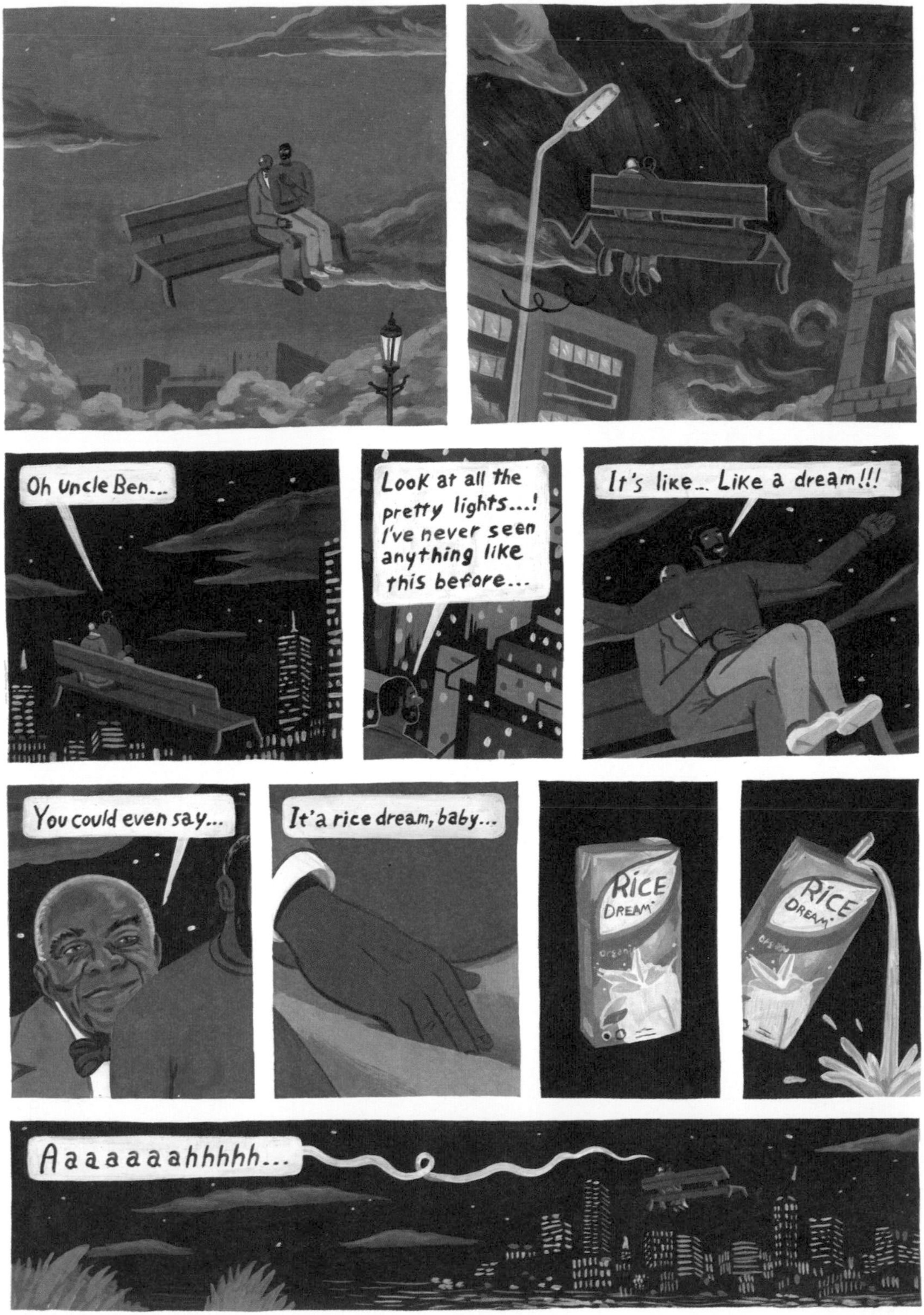
Oh uncle Ben...
Look at all the pretty lights...! I've never seen anything like this before...
It's like... Like a dream!!!
You could even say...
It'a rice dream, baby...
RICE DREAM
RICE DREAM
Aaaaaaahhhhh...

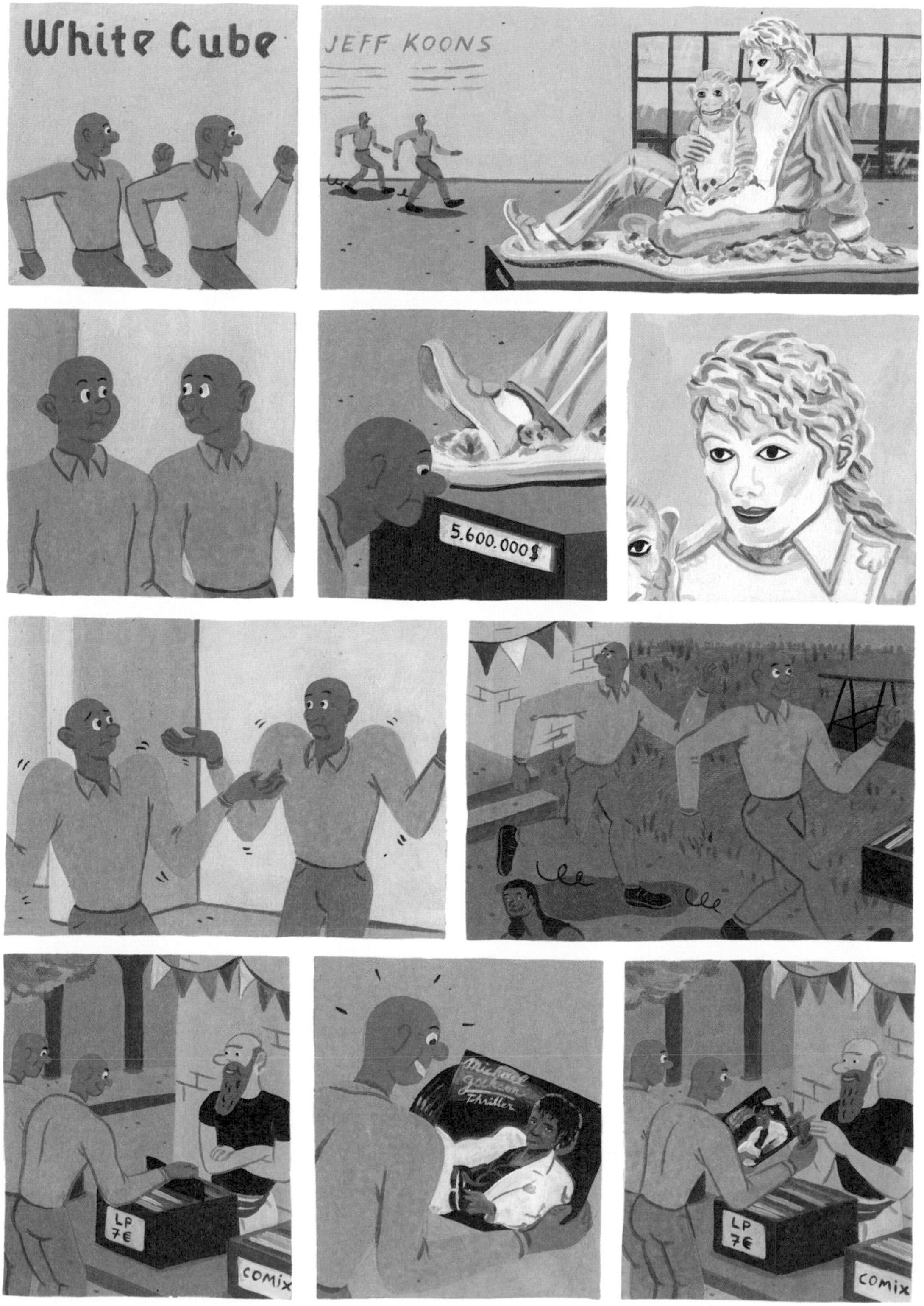
White Cube
JEFF KOONS
5.600.000$
Michael Jackson Thriller
LP 7€
COMIX
LP 7€
COMIX

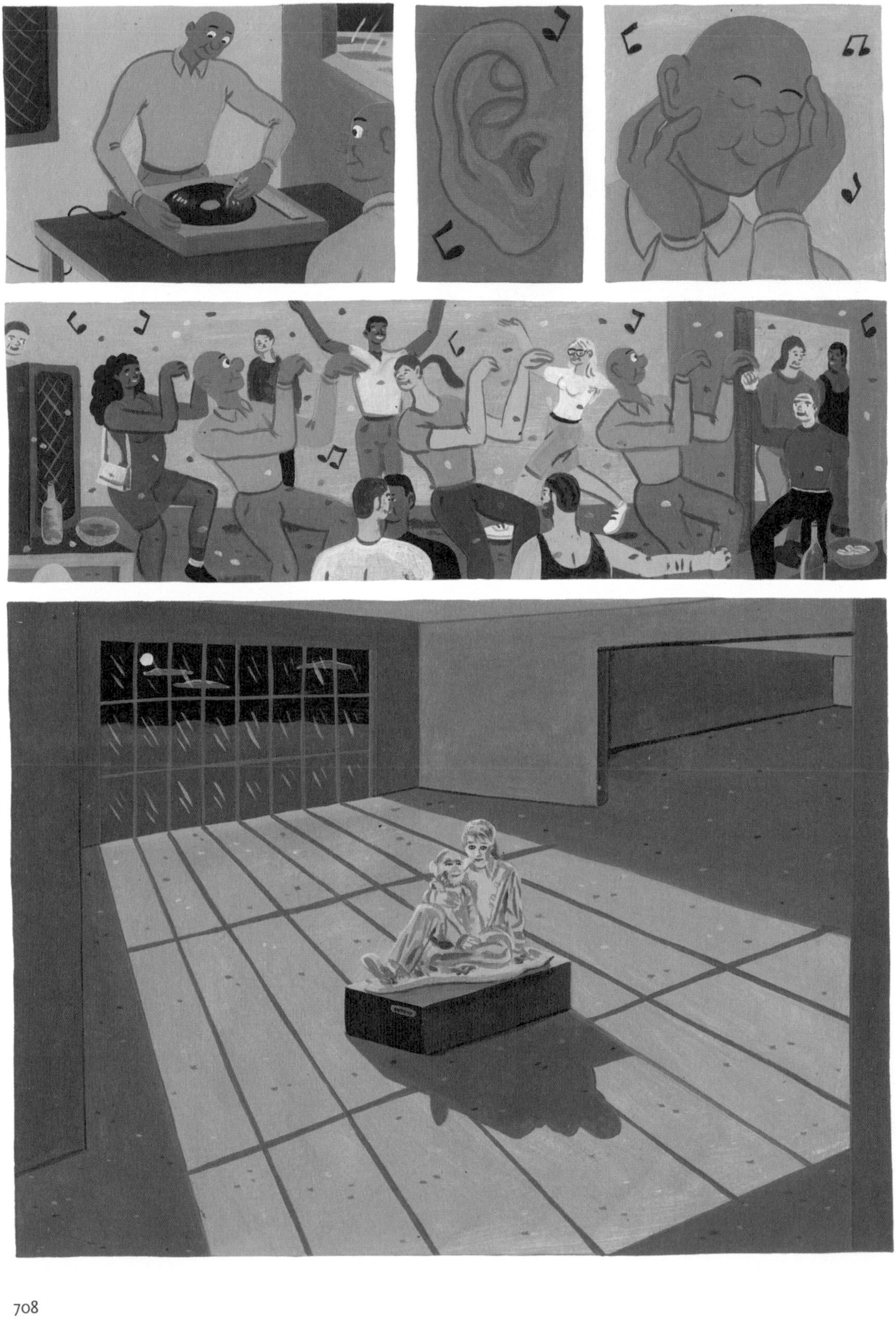

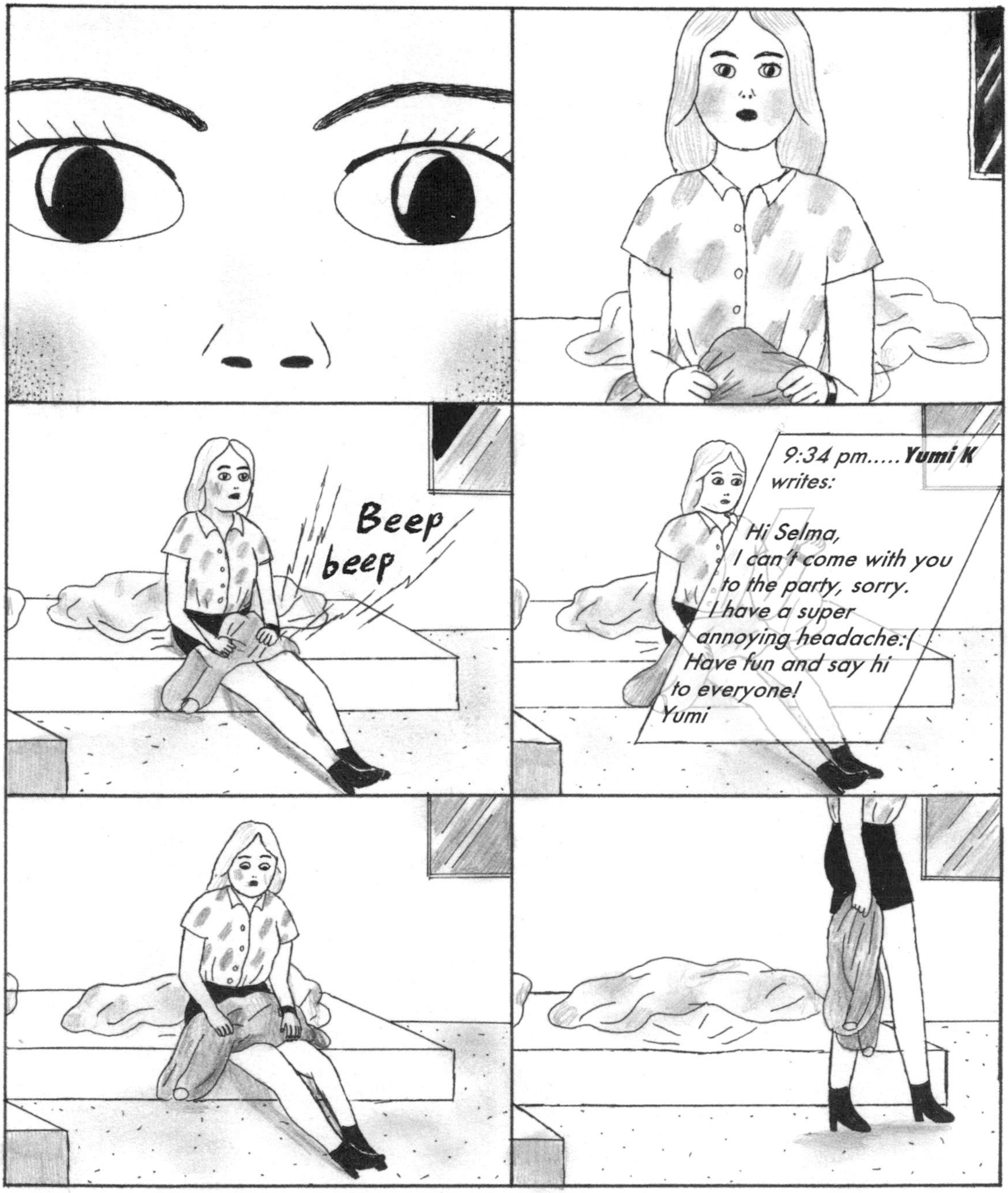
Beep beep
9:34 pm.....**Yumi K** writes:
Hi Selma,
I can't come with you to the party, sorry.
I have a super annoying headache:(
Have fun and say hi to everyone!
Yumi

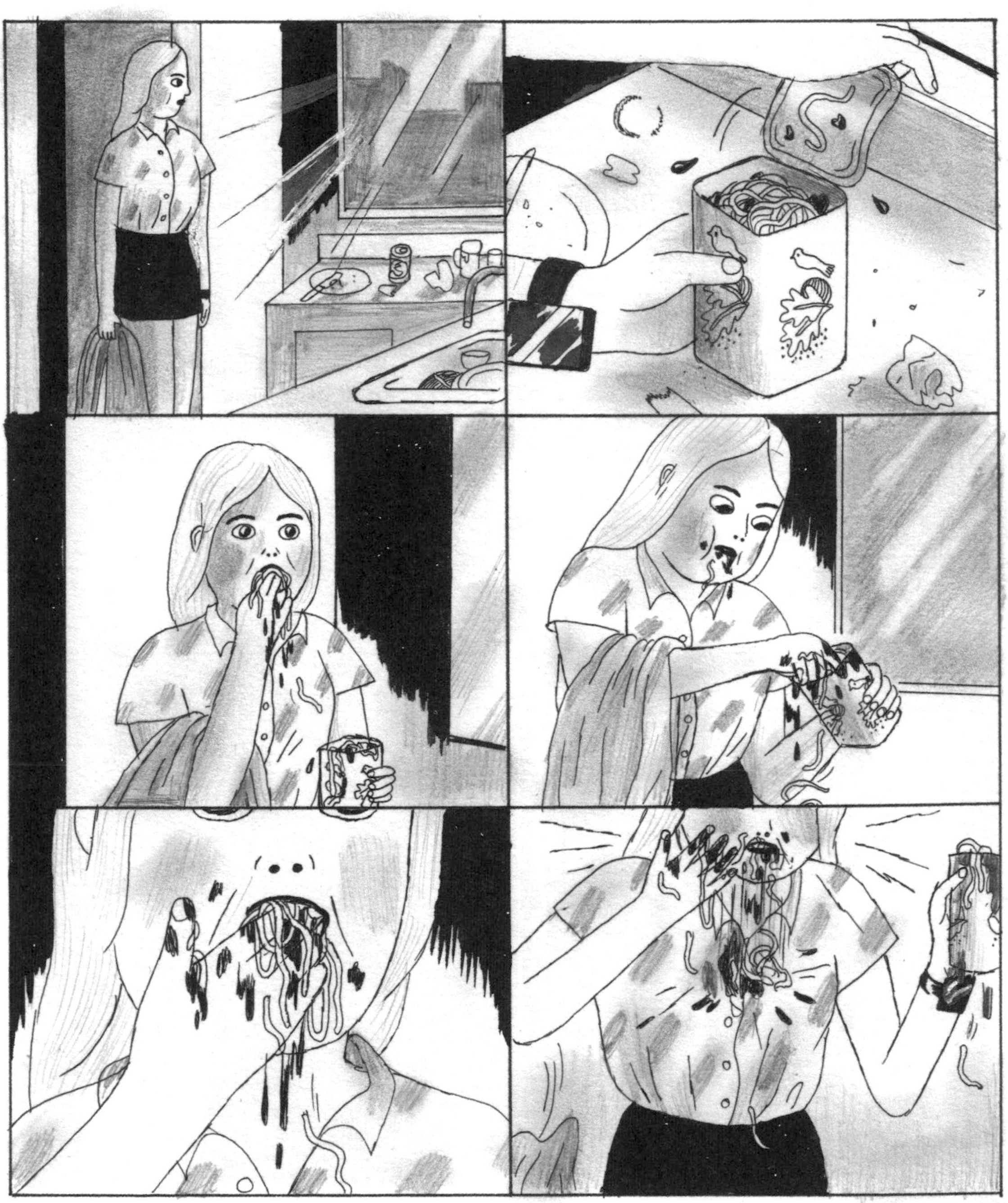

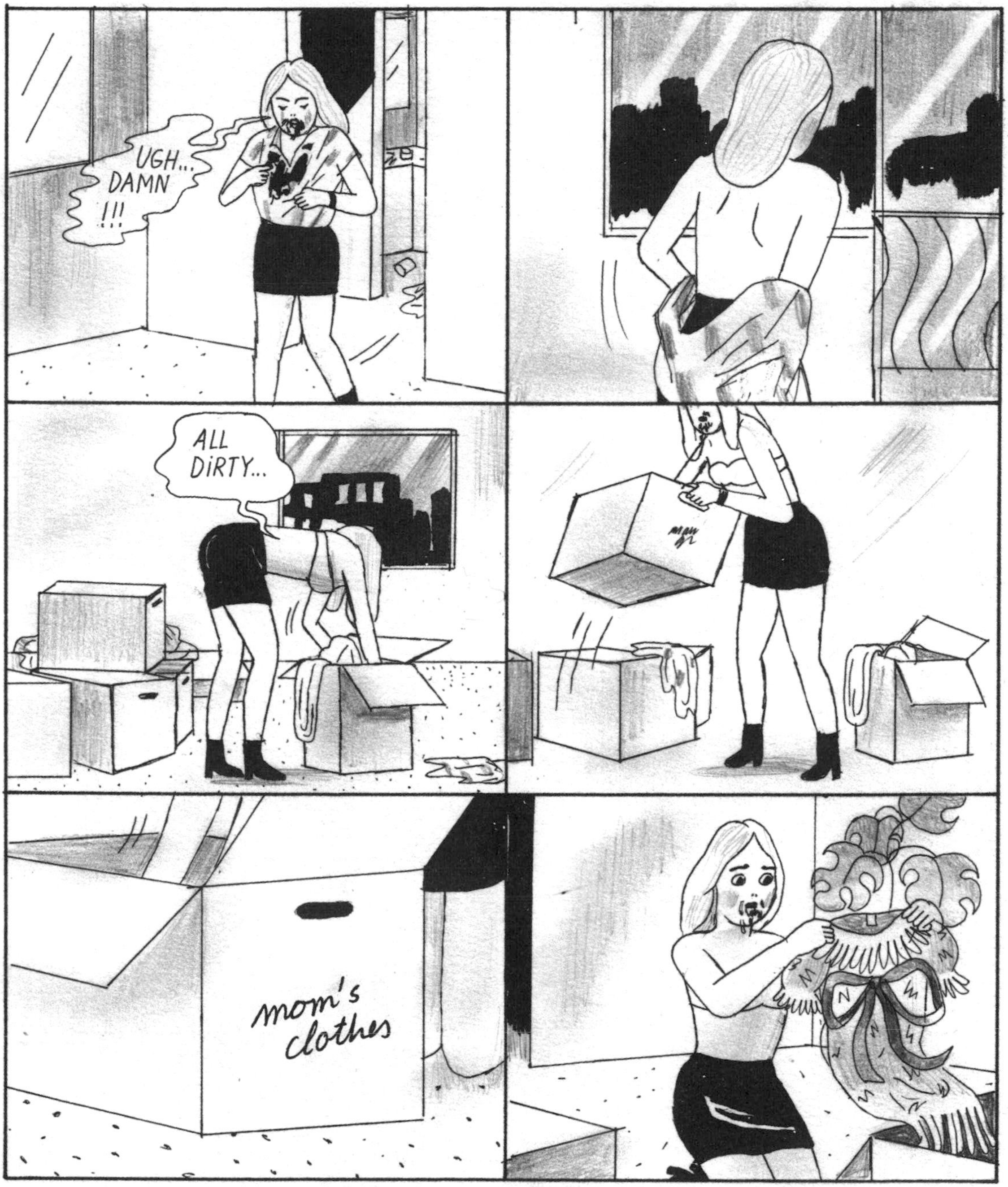
UGH... DAMN !!!
ALL DiRTY...
mom's clothes

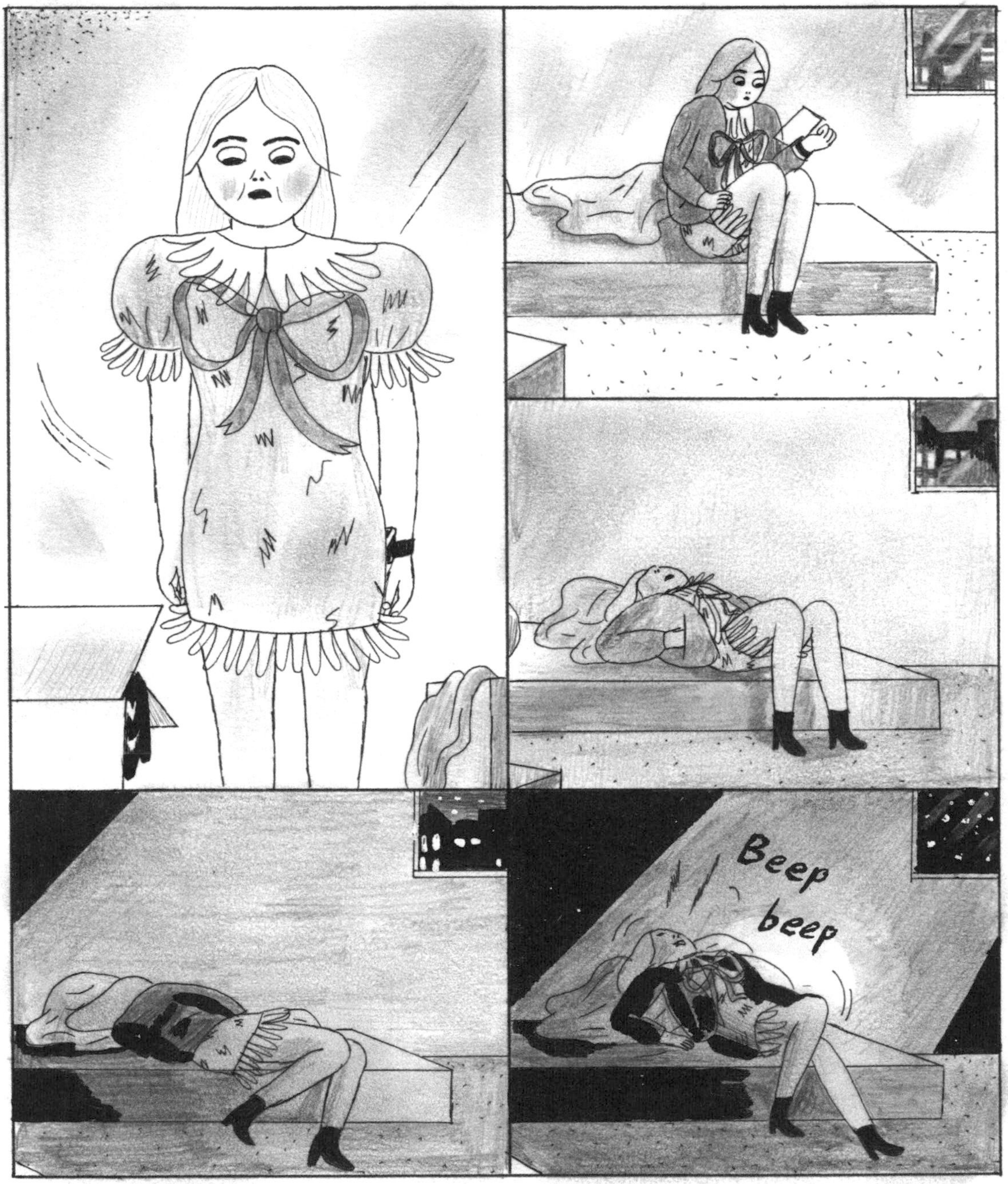
Beep
beep

THINGS TO DO ON YOUR TWO DAYS OFF DURING A comics festival IN COLOMBIA

SARAH GLIDDEN

MAKE A PLAN TO TRAVEL WITH THREE PEOPLE WHO YOU WANT TO PLAY IT COOL IN FRONT OF FOR DIFFERENT REASONS.

PEGGY BURNS: ASSOCIATE PUBLISHER OF D+Q, YOUR FAVORITE COMICS PUBLISHER. YOU WANT HER TO TAKE A LOOK AT THE BOOK YOU ARE WORKING ON BUT DON'T DARE ASK.

FRAN LOPEZ: CARTOONIST FROM ARGENTINA WHO YOU JUST MET A FEW DAYS AGO AND HAVE A CRUSH ON.

ANDERS NILSEN: DOESN'T EVERYONE WANT ANDERS TO THINK THEY'RE COOL?

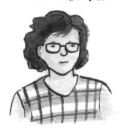

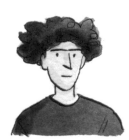

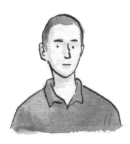

TAKE A TAXI TO SALENTO, A SMALL TOWN IN THE MIDDLE OF COLOMBIAN COFFEE COUNTRY.

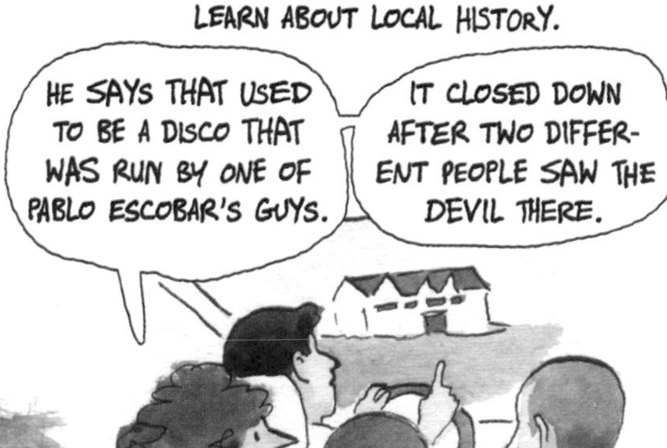

IS THIS WHERE JUAN VALDEZ IS FROM?

LEARN ABOUT LOCAL HISTORY.

HE SAYS THAT USED TO BE A DISCO THAT WAS RUN BY ONE OF PABLO ESCOBAR'S GUYS.
IT CLOSED DOWN AFTER TWO DIFFERENT PEOPLE SAW THE DEVIL THERE.

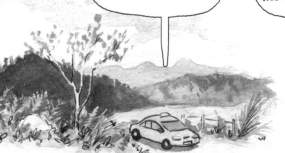

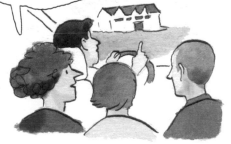

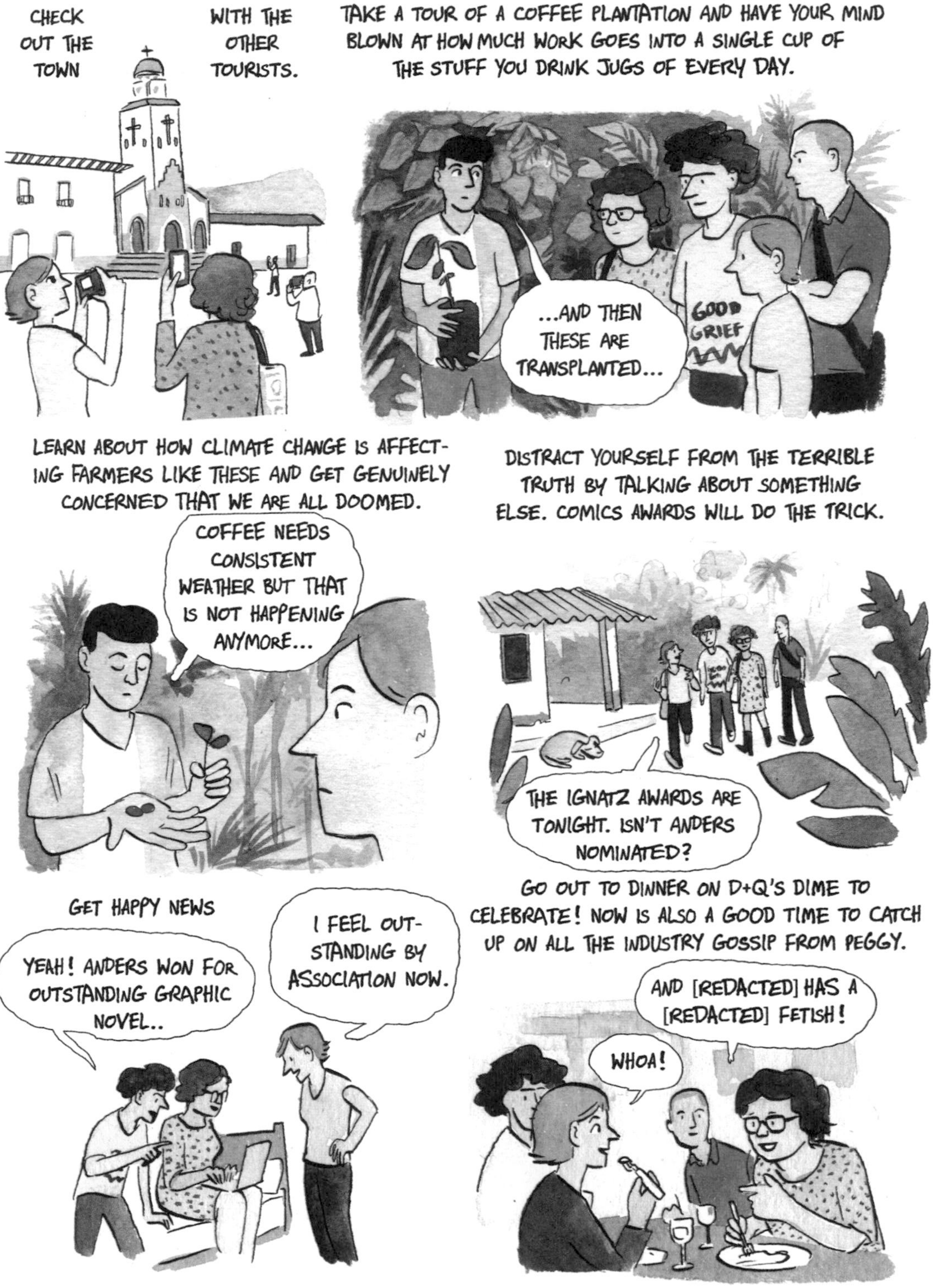
CHECK OUT THE TOWN
WITH THE OTHER TOURISTS.
TAKE A TOUR OF A COFFEE PLANTATION AND HAVE YOUR MIND BLOWN AT HOW MUCH WORK GOES INTO A SINGLE CUP OF THE STUFF YOU DRINK JUGS OF EVERY DAY.
...AND THEN THESE ARE TRANSPLANTED...
GOOD GRIEF
LEARN ABOUT HOW CLIMATE CHANGE IS AFFECTING FARMERS LIKE THESE AND GET GENUINELY CONCERNED THAT WE ARE ALL DOOMED.
COFFEE NEEDS CONSISTENT WEATHER BUT THAT IS NOT HAPPENING ANYMORE...
DISTRACT YOURSELF FROM THE TERRIBLE TRUTH BY TALKING ABOUT SOMETHING ELSE. COMICS AWARDS WILL DO THE TRICK.
THE IGNATZ AWARDS ARE TONIGHT. ISN'T ANDERS NOMINATED?
GET HAPPY NEWS
YEAH! ANDERS WON FOR OUTSTANDING GRAPHIC NOVEL..
I FEEL OUT-STANDING BY ASSOCIATION NOW.
GO OUT TO DINNER ON D+Q'S DIME TO CELEBRATE! NOW IS ALSO A GOOD TIME TO CATCH UP ON ALL THE INDUSTRY GOSSIP FROM PEGGY.
AND [REDACTED] HAS A [REDACTED] FETISH!
WHOA!

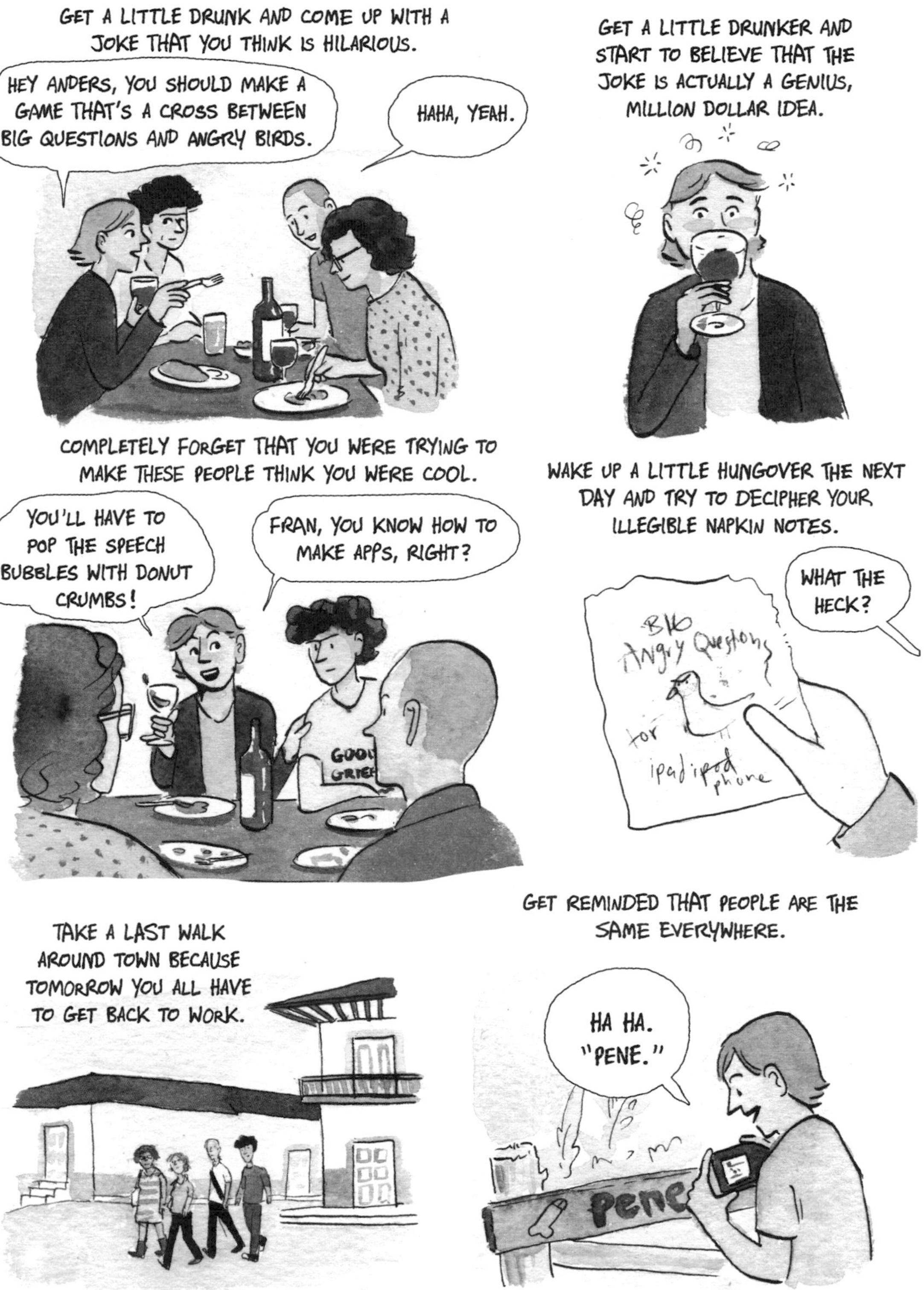
GET A LITTLE DRUNK AND COME UP WITH A JOKE THAT YOU THINK IS HILARIOUS.
HEY ANDERS, YOU SHOULD MAKE A GAME THAT'S A CROSS BETWEEN BIG QUESTIONS AND ANGRY BIRDS.
HAHA, YEAH.
GET A LITTLE DRUNKER AND START TO BELIEVE THAT THE JOKE IS ACTUALLY A GENIUS, MILLION DOLLAR IDEA.
COMPLETELY FORGET THAT YOU WERE TRYING TO MAKE THESE PEOPLE THINK YOU WERE COOL.
YOU'LL HAVE TO POP THE SPEECH BUBBLES WITH DONUT CRUMBS!
FRAN, YOU KNOW HOW TO MAKE APPS, RIGHT?
WAKE UP A LITTLE HUNGOVER THE NEXT DAY AND TRY TO DECIPHER YOUR ILLEGIBLE NAPKIN NOTES.
WHAT THE HECK?
BIG
Angry Questions
for
ipad ipod
phone
TAKE A LAST WALK AROUND TOWN BECAUSE TOMORROW YOU ALL HAVE TO GET BACK TO WORK.
GET REMINDED THAT PEOPLE ARE THE SAME EVERYWHERE.
HA HA. "PENE."
Pene

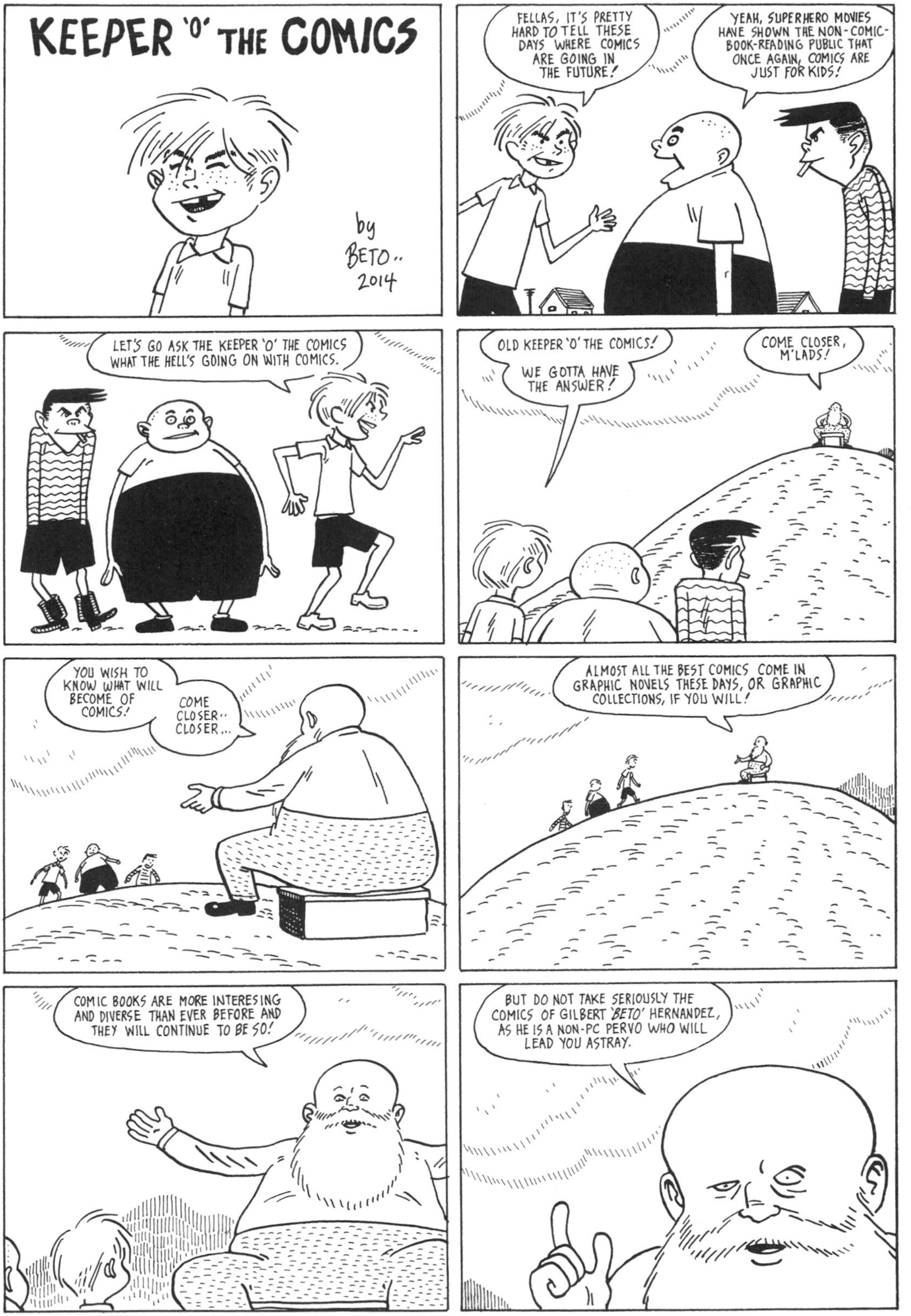
KEEPER 'O' THE COMICS
by BETO.. 2014
FELLAS, IT'S PRETTY HARD TO TELL THESE DAYS WHERE COMICS ARE GOING IN THE FUTURE!
YEAH, SUPERHERO MOVIES HAVE SHOWN THE NON-COMIC-BOOK-READING PUBLIC THAT ONCE AGAIN, COMICS ARE JUST FOR KIDS!
LET'S GO ASK THE KEEPER 'O' THE COMICS WHAT THE HELL'S GOING ON WITH COMICS.
OLD KEEPER 'O' THE COMICS!
WE GOTTA HAVE THE ANSWER!
COME CLOSER, M'LADS!
YOU WISH TO KNOW WHAT WILL BECOME OF COMICS!
COME CLOSER.. CLOSER...
ALMOST ALL THE BEST COMICS COME IN GRAPHIC NOVELS THESE DAYS, OR GRAPHIC COLLECTIONS, IF YOU WILL!
COMIC BOOKS ARE MORE INTERESING AND DIVERSE THAN EVER BEFORE AND THEY WILL CONTINUE TO BE SO!
BUT DO NOT TAKE SERIOUSLY THE COMICS OF GILBERT 'BETO' HERNANDEZ, AS HE IS A NON-PC PERVO WHO WILL LEAD YOU ASTRAY.

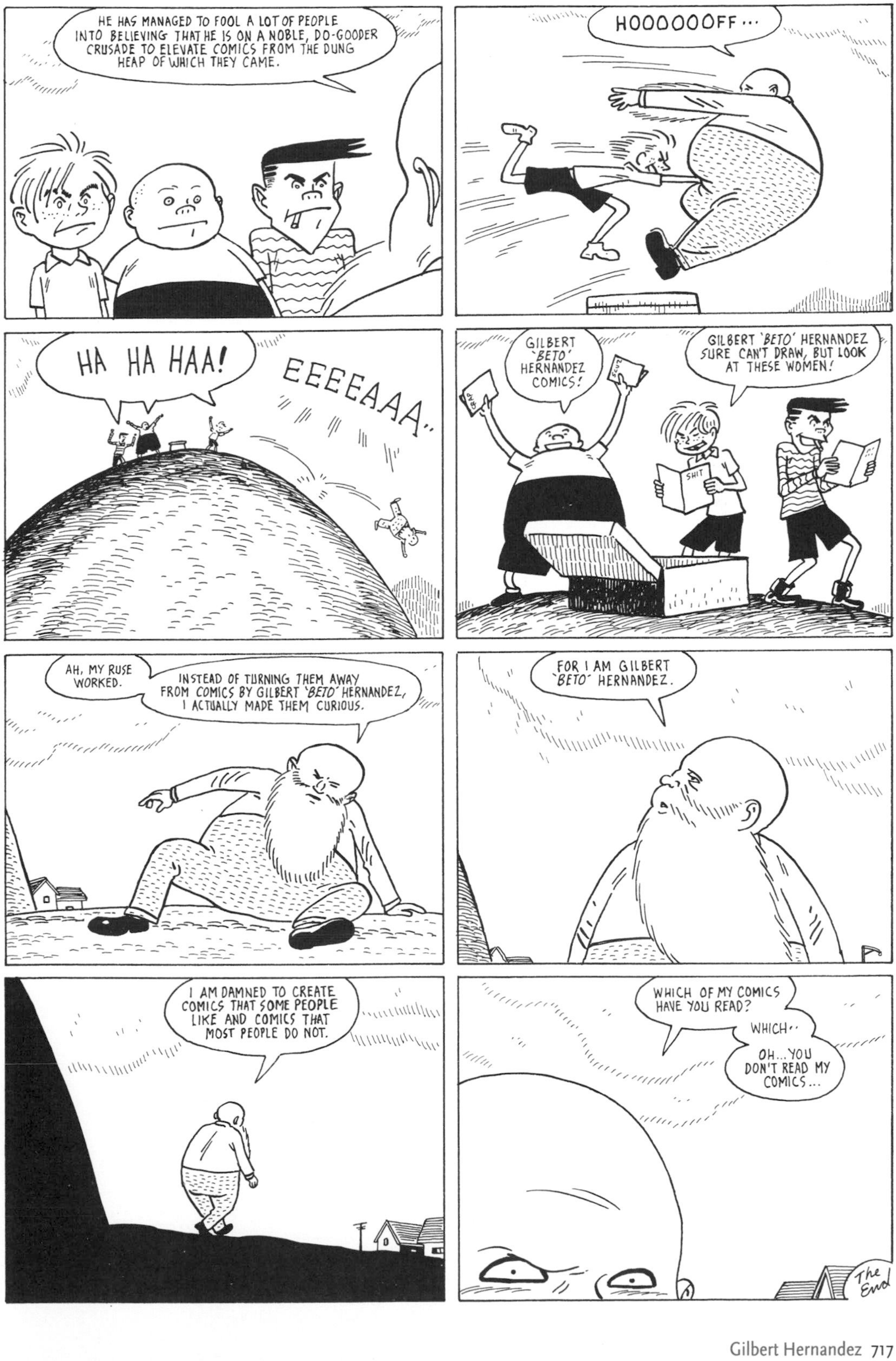
HE HAS MANAGED TO FOOL A LOT OF PEOPLE INTO BELIEVING THAT HE IS ON A NOBLE, DO-GOODER CRUSADE TO ELEVATE COMICS FROM THE DUNG HEAP OF WHICH THEY CAME.
HOOOOOOFF...
HA HA HAA!
EEEEAAAA..
GILBERT 'BETO' HERNANDEZ COMICS!
GILBERT 'BETO' HERNANDEZ SURE CAN'T DRAW, BUT LOOK AT THESE WOMEN!
SHIT
AH, MY RUSE WORKED.
INSTEAD OF TURNING THEM AWAY FROM COMICS BY GILBERT 'BETO' HERNANDEZ, I ACTUALLY MADE THEM CURIOUS.
FOR I AM GILBERT 'BETO' HERNANDEZ.
I AM DAMNED TO CREATE COMICS THAT SOME PEOPLE LIKE AND COMICS THAT MOST PEOPLE DO NOT.
WHICH OF MY COMICS HAVE YOU READ?
WHICH..
OH... YOU DON'T READ MY COMICS...
The End

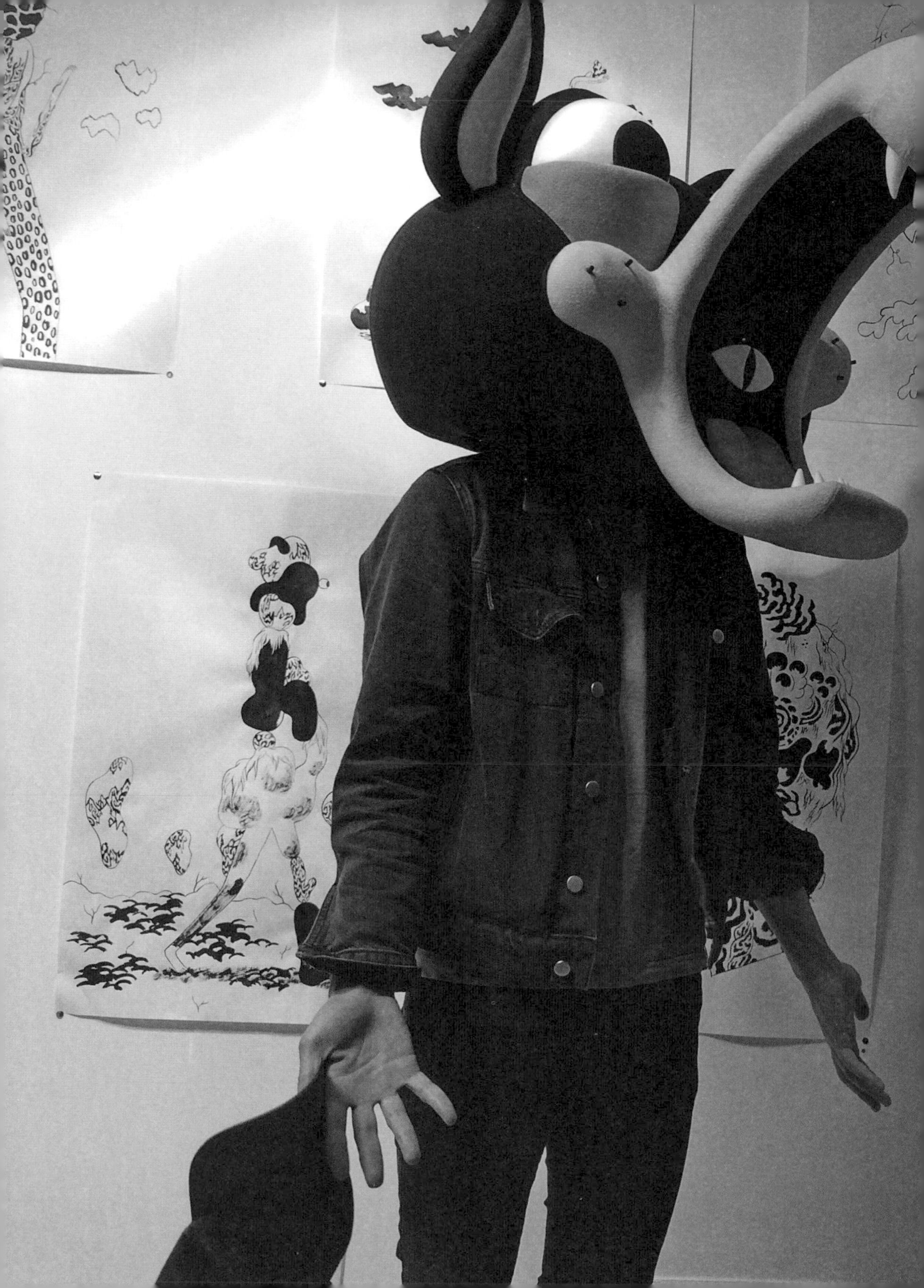

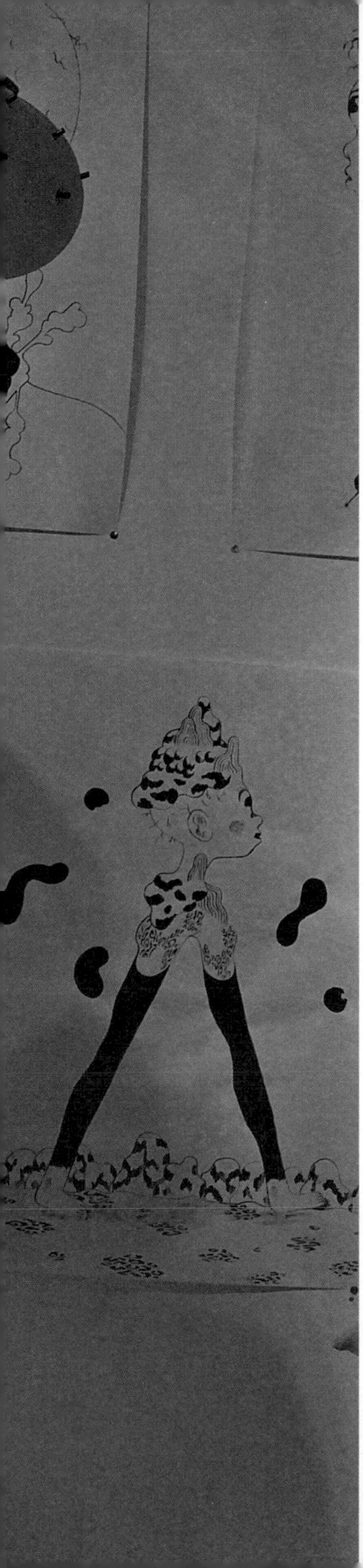

(Left) Michael DeForge wearing a mascot head of *Ant Colony*'s dog spider at the opening of his show at Weird Things in Toronto. Made by Phil Woollam. Photo: Annie Koyama (2014).

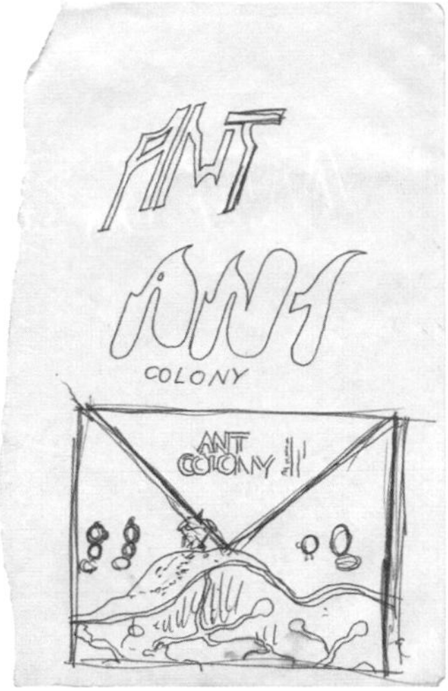
ANT
ANT
COLONY
ANT COLONY

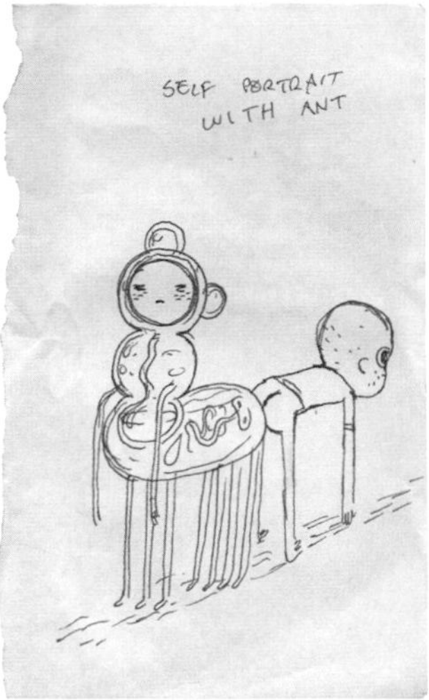
SELF PORTRAIT
WITH ANT

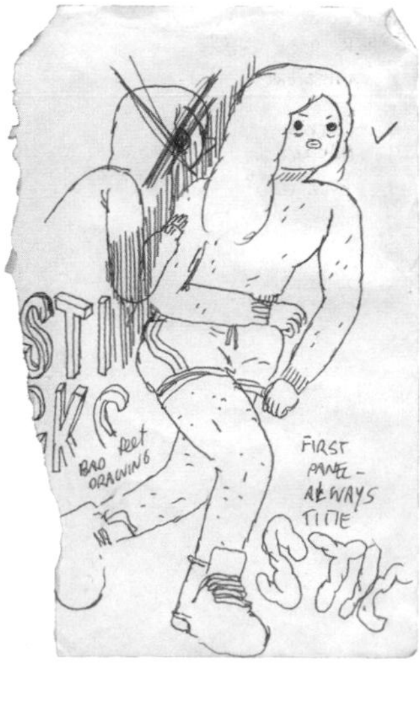
BAD feet DRAWING
FIRST PANEL - ALWAYS TITLE

At this point in his somewhat young career, a lot of hyperbole has been thrown around concerning Michael DeForge. He has been described as "the best new cartoonist of his generation," "the greatest talent to come along in twenty years," and in possession of "the highest pompadour in the Toronto area." A lot of this has dissipated as Michael has consistently produced comic story after comic story and book collection after book collection—two collections for Drawn & Quarterly, the beautiful, funny, nasty *Ant Colony* and the melancholy, terrifying *First Year Healthy*; and two collections for his primary publisher, Koyama Press, *Very Casual* and *A Body Beneath*, not to mention his ongoing *Lose* series. This hyperbole distracts from the fact that DeForge just might be (New Hyperbole Alert) the most restless and ambitious comics creator since Dan Clowes created *Eightball*. Michael is, like Clowes, such a distinctive stylist that other cartoonists are immediately pulled into his orbit, and this causes people to overlook the fact that, in both Michael's and Dan's cases, there's a writerly ambition that outstrips their graphic talents. Each new issue of *Lose* practically makes the previous issue obsolete as Michael stretches and grows as a writer. This isn't meant to downplay his talent as an actual drawer or diminish his abilities in combining words and pictures—they're prodigious. It's more about focusing on the feeling that DeForge's writing has a searching quality. The phrases are tight and descriptive, the dialogue hangs with the tentativeness of real speech.

—Tom Devlin

"Originals" from *Ant Colony* and *Sticks Angelica*.

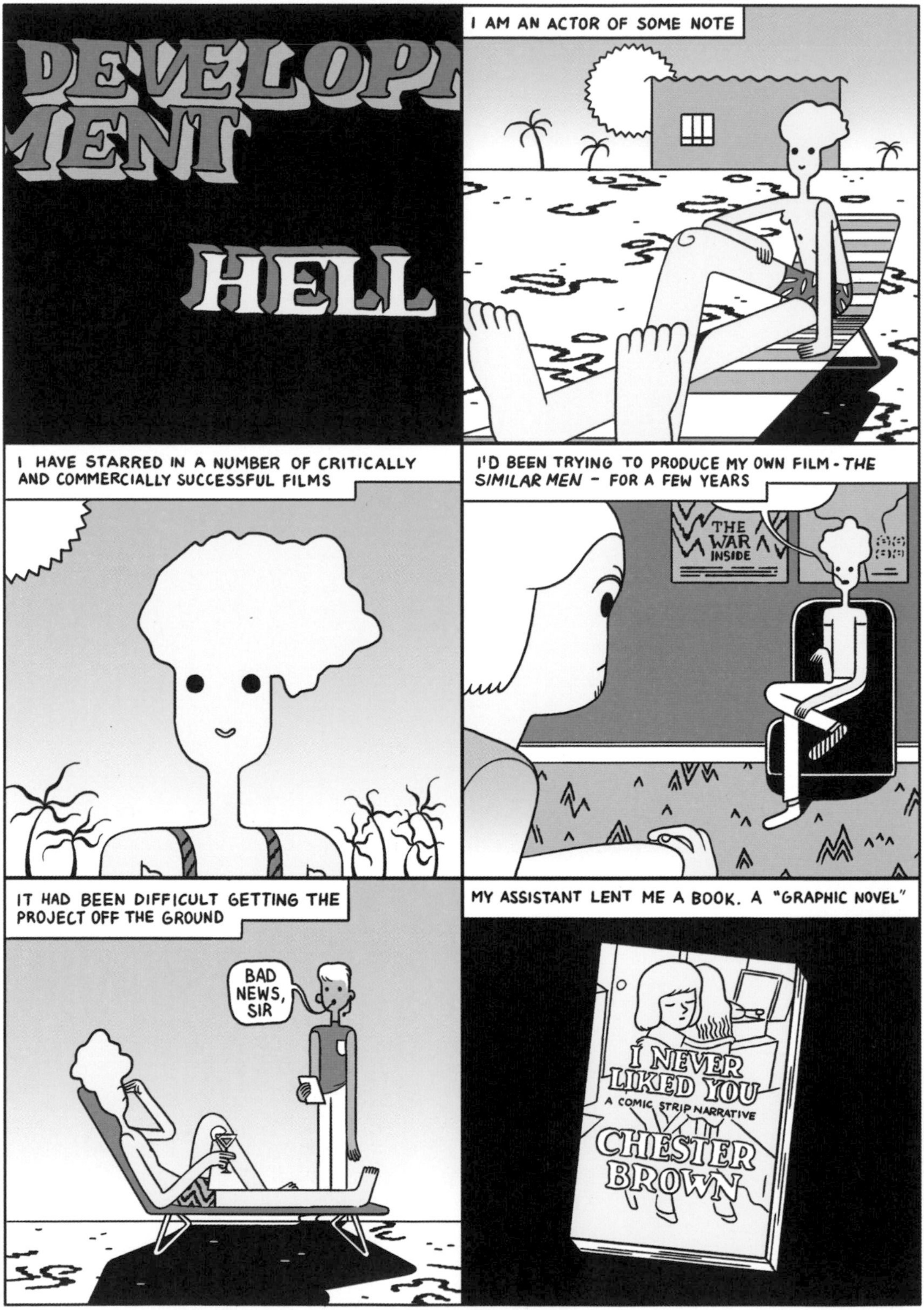
DEVELOPM
MENT
HELL
I AM AN ACTOR OF SOME NOTE
I HAVE STARRED IN A NUMBER OF CRITICALLY AND COMMERCIALLY SUCCESSFUL FILMS
I'D BEEN TRYING TO PRODUCE MY OWN FILM - *THE SIMILAR MEN* - FOR A FEW YEARS
THE WAR INSIDE
IT HAD BEEN DIFFICULT GETTING THE PROJECT OFF THE GROUND
BAD NEWS, SIR
MY ASSISTANT LENT ME A BOOK. A "GRAPHIC NOVEL"
I NEVER LIKED YOU
A COMIC STRIP NARRATIVE
CHESTER BROWN

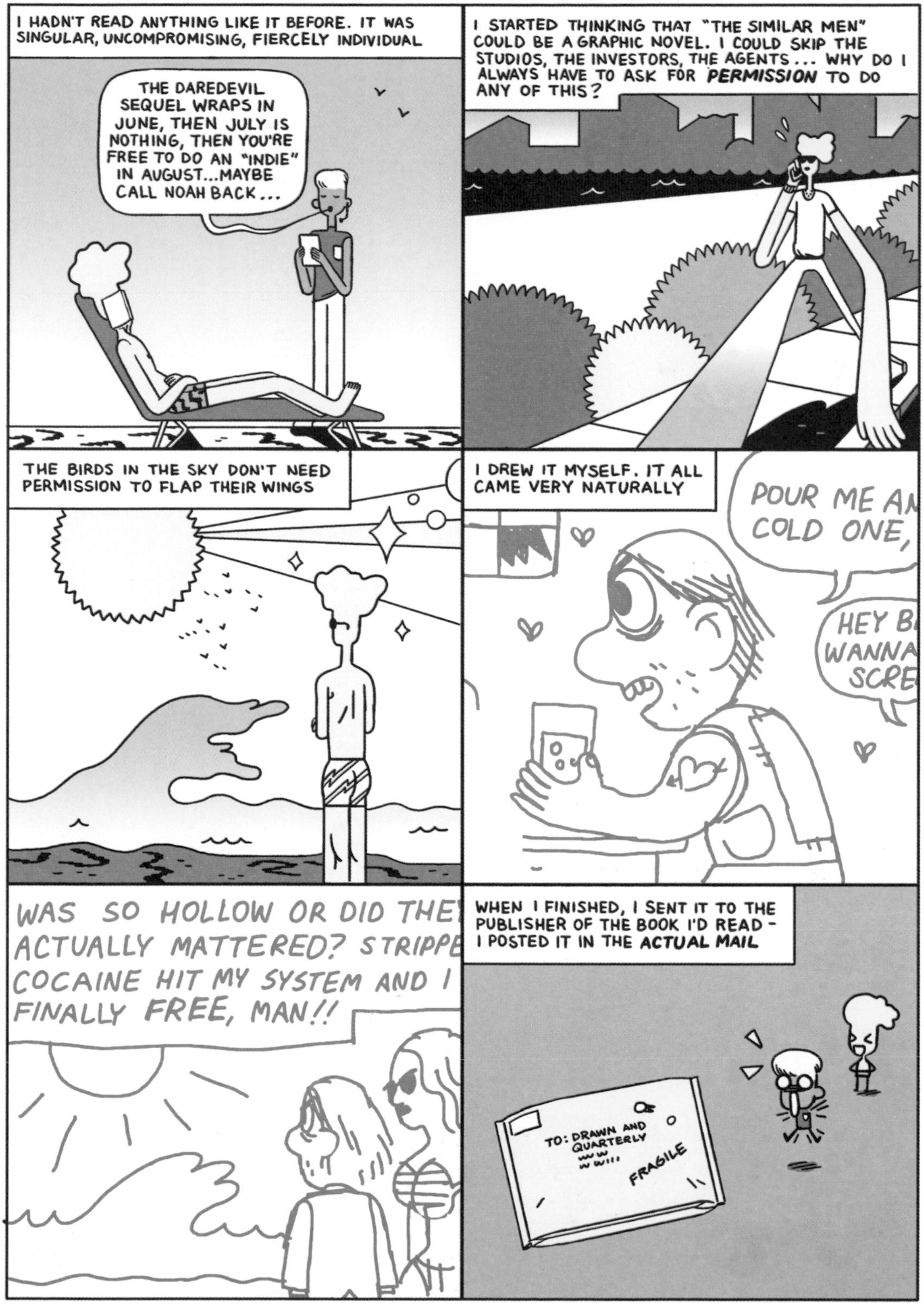
I HADN'T READ ANYTHING LIKE IT BEFORE. IT WAS SINGULAR, UNCOMPROMISING, FIERCELY INDIVIDUAL
THE DAREDEVIL SEQUEL WRAPS IN JUNE, THEN JULY IS NOTHING, THEN YOU'RE FREE TO DO AN "INDIE" IN AUGUST...MAYBE CALL NOAH BACK...
I STARTED THINKING THAT "THE SIMILAR MEN" COULD BE A GRAPHIC NOVEL. I COULD SKIP THE STUDIOS, THE INVESTORS, THE AGENTS... WHY DO I ALWAYS HAVE TO ASK FOR PERMISSION TO DO ANY OF THIS?
THE BIRDS IN THE SKY DON'T NEED PERMISSION TO FLAP THEIR WINGS
I DREW IT MYSELF. IT ALL CAME VERY NATURALLY
POUR ME A
COLD ONE,
HEY B
WANNA
SCRE
WAS SO HOLLOW OR DID THE
ACTUALLY MATTERED? STRIPPE
COCAINE HIT MY SYSTEM AND I
FINALLY FREE, MAN!!
WHEN I FINISHED, I SENT IT TO THE PUBLISHER OF THE BOOK I'D READ - I POSTED IT IN THE ACTUAL MAIL
TO: DRAWN AND QUARTERLY
FRAGILE

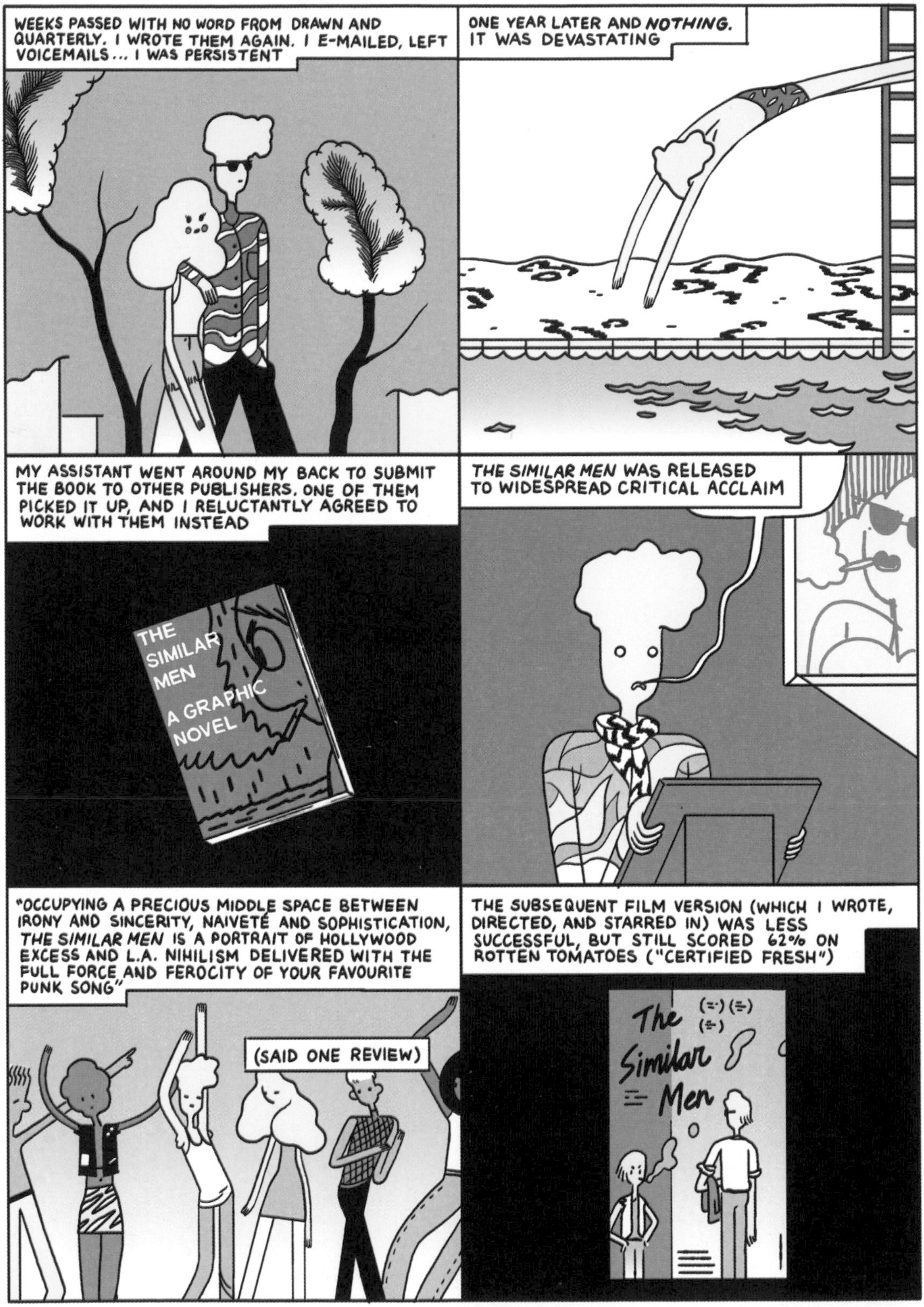
WEEKS PASSED WITH NO WORD FROM DRAWN AND QUARTERLY. I WROTE THEM AGAIN. I E-MAILED, LEFT VOICEMAILS... I WAS PERSISTENT
ONE YEAR LATER AND NOTHING. IT WAS DEVASTATING
MY ASSISTANT WENT AROUND MY BACK TO SUBMIT THE BOOK TO OTHER PUBLISHERS. ONE OF THEM PICKED IT UP, AND I RELUCTANTLY AGREED TO WORK WITH THEM INSTEAD
THE SIMILAR MEN A GRAPHIC NOVEL
THE SIMILAR MEN WAS RELEASED TO WIDESPREAD CRITICAL ACCLAIM
"OCCUPYING A PRECIOUS MIDDLE SPACE BETWEEN IRONY AND SINCERITY, NAIVETÉ AND SOPHISTICATION, THE SIMILAR MEN IS A PORTRAIT OF HOLLYWOOD EXCESS AND L.A. NIHILISM DELIVERED WITH THE FULL FORCE AND FEROCITY OF YOUR FAVOURITE PUNK SONG"
(SAID ONE REVIEW)
THE SUBSEQUENT FILM VERSION (WHICH I WROTE, DIRECTED, AND STARRED IN) WAS LESS SUCCESSFUL, BUT STILL SCORED 62% ON ROTTEN TOMATOES ("CERTIFIED FRESH")
The Similar Men

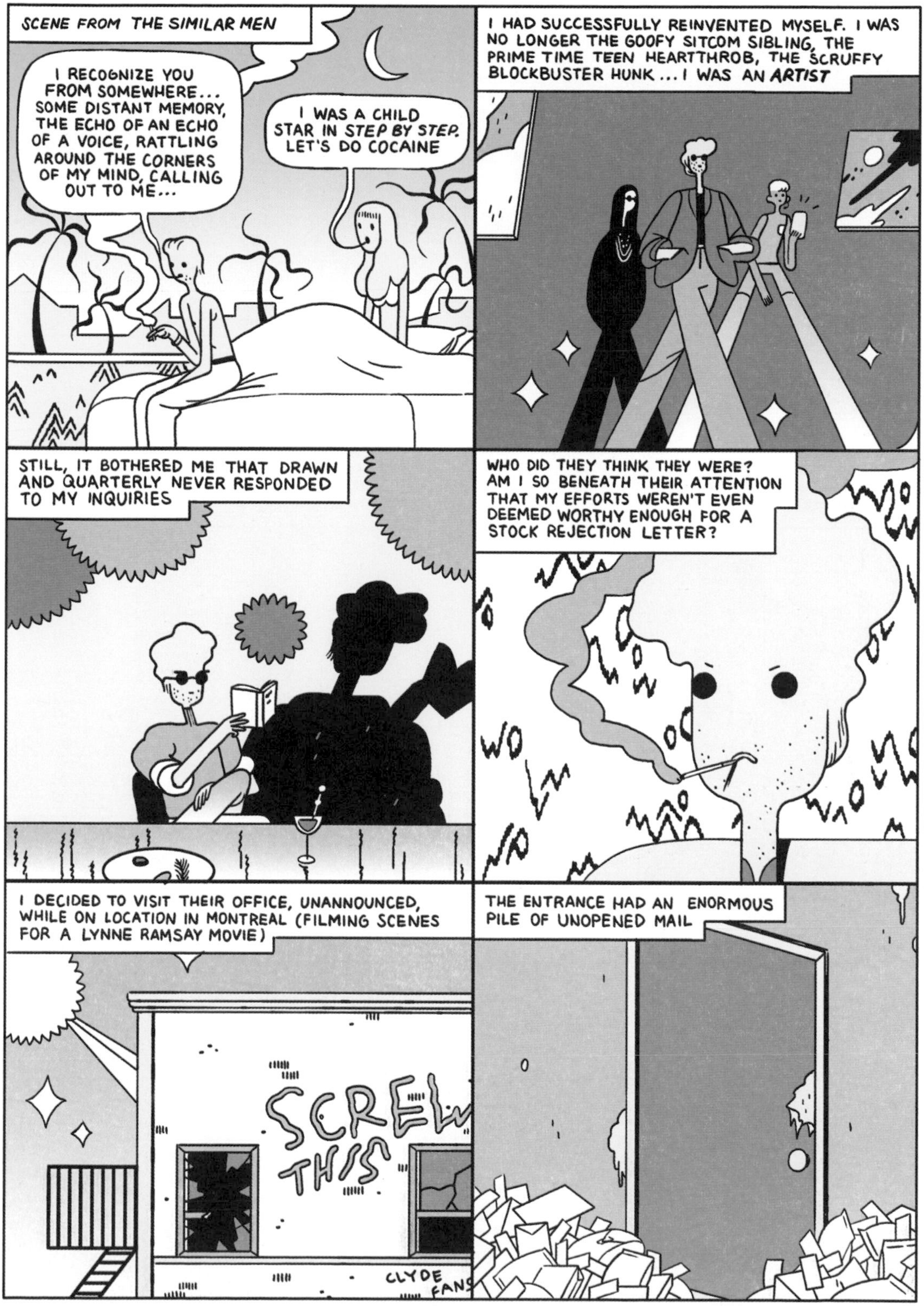
SCENE FROM THE SIMILAR MEN
I RECOGNIZE YOU FROM SOMEWHERE... SOME DISTANT MEMORY, THE ECHO OF AN ECHO OF A VOICE, RATTLING AROUND THE CORNERS OF MY MIND, CALLING OUT TO ME...
I WAS A CHILD STAR IN STEP BY STEP. LET'S DO COCAINE
I HAD SUCCESSFULLY REINVENTED MYSELF. I WAS NO LONGER THE GOOFY SITCOM SIBLING, THE PRIME TIME TEEN HEARTTHROB, THE SCRUFFY BLOCKBUSTER HUNK ... I WAS AN ARTIST
STILL, IT BOTHERED ME THAT DRAWN AND QUARTERLY NEVER RESPONDED TO MY INQUIRIES
WHO DID THEY THINK THEY WERE? AM I SO BENEATH THEIR ATTENTION THAT MY EFFORTS WEREN'T EVEN DEEMED WORTHY ENOUGH FOR A STOCK REJECTION LETTER?
I DECIDED TO VISIT THEIR OFFICE, UNANNOUNCED, WHILE ON LOCATION IN MONTREAL (FILMING SCENES FOR A LYNNE RAMSAY MOVIE)
SCREW THIS
CLYDE FANS
THE ENTRANCE HAD AN ENORMOUS PILE OF UNOPENED MAIL

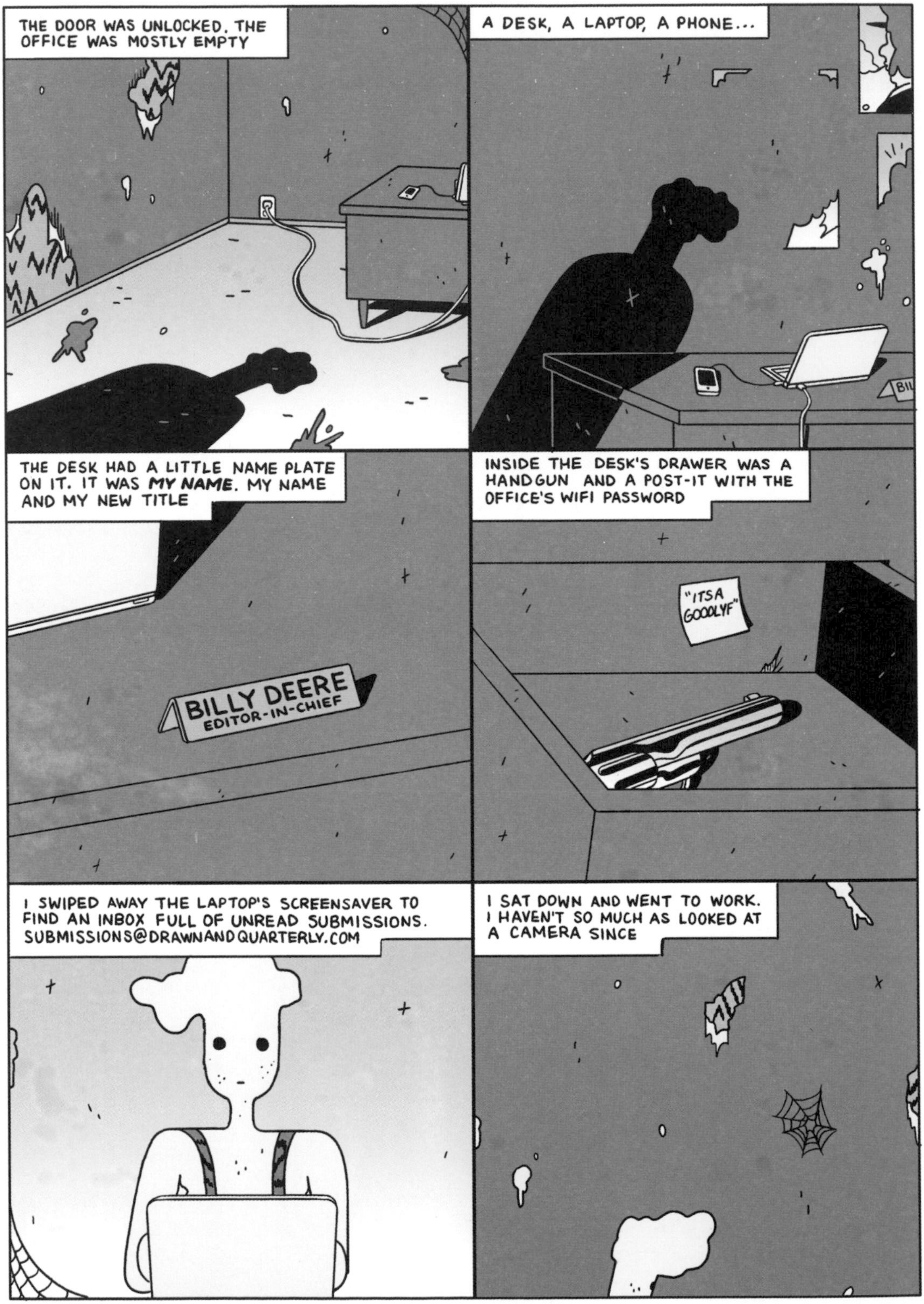
THE DOOR WAS UNLOCKED. THE OFFICE WAS MOSTLY EMPTY
A DESK, A LAPTOP, A PHONE...
THE DESK HAD A LITTLE NAME PLATE ON IT. IT WAS **MY NAME**. MY NAME AND MY NEW TITLE
BILLY DEERE
EDITOR-IN-CHIEF
INSIDE THE DESK'S DRAWER WAS A HANDGUN AND A POST-IT WITH THE OFFICE'S WIFI PASSWORD
"ITSA GOOOLYF"
I SWIPED AWAY THE LAPTOP'S SCREENSAVER TO FIND AN INBOX FULL OF UNREAD SUBMISSIONS. SUBMISSIONS@DRAWNANDQUARTERLY.COM
I SAT DOWN AND WENT TO WORK. I HAVEN'T SO MUCH AS LOOKED AT A CAMERA SINCE

THE EVER-AMAZING SHIGERU MIZUKI

an appreciation by Frederik L. Schodt

In the last quarter century, manga and anime have stormed through the world's consciousness. In Japan, Shigeru Mizuki has been a nationally revered artist for decades, but in North America he did not receive much attention until 2011, when Drawn & Quarterly began publishing his works in translation. Mizuki stands at the top of the manga pyramid in Japan today, having outlived nearly all his contemporaries and received a long list of awards. Yet he is firmly planted in Japanese culture and doesn't fit easily into a single globalized commercial category.

Mizuki was born Shigeru Mura in 1922 and raised in Sakaiminato, on Japan's western seacoast. As a child he exhibited a precocious drawing ability, but if we are to believe his self-deprecating recollections, he was not a good student. A local woman—NonNonBa, or "Auntie NonNon"—befriended him and helped him develop a passionate interest in the spirit world, especially in local tales of *yōkai*. Sometimes translated as goblins and ghosts, in the animistic world view of Japanese people, yōkai can resemble the trolls of northern Europe, for they are closely linked with local natural phenomena and objects.

Today Japan is in the midst of a yōkai boom, with yōkai-themed manga, anime, video games, toys, candy, and even wristwatches now on the market. And no one has contributed more to this boom than Mizuki, who is often referred to as a yōkai artist and researcher. By far his most popular manga series is the spooky-sounding *GeGeGe no Kitarō*, created in 1960 and first animated for television in 1968. Today, in the minds of most young Japanese, it is probably safe to say that Mizuki's yōkai characters and his stories have supplanted many of the original folk tales and

legends that inspired them. It would be hard to exaggerate their popularity.

Mizuki began drawing professionally right after the war, as an illustrator for the *kamishibai* ("paper plays") and *kashihonya* (pay library) markets. He made his first hit in the latter with *Rocketman*, in 1957, at the ripe old age of thirty-three. When these markets were later absorbed into the mainstream Tokyo manga market, his versatility helped him make the successful transition, and he won an award in 1965 for his hit *Terebi-kun* (TV kid), about a boy who could enter his TV.

The route by which Mizuki became an artist was hardly direct. As a young man, he was drafted into the Imperial Army in 1943 and sent to Rabaul, on the island of New Britain, in today's Papua New Guinea. It was one of the worst places to be an infantryman, for when Japan began losing the war they were largely cut off from the homeland, headquarters essentially abandoning them to their fate in the jungle, condemning them to starvation, disease, bombing, and—since surrender was not an option—death in *banzai* suicide charges. Mizuki lost his left arm in an Allied bombing raid and developed both malaria and dysentery, but he survived. And in the process he developed a strong attachment to the natives of New Guinea, who helped him through his illness and injuries, and introduced him to the natural world. His experiences reinforced his belief in the spirit world and gave him further courage to take his own path in life.

Because of his injuries, after the war Mizuki was limited in the type of work that he could do, but luckily he could eke out a living by drawing. And while his yōkai manga and those in other genres subsequently have brought him fame and fortune, it is his stories about World War II, Japan's

Shōwa era, and his depiction of his own horrendous experiences that have earned him an unassailable niche in the pantheon of manga greats. His 1973 *Sōin Gyokusai Seyo* (*Onward Towards Our Noble Deaths* in English) is among the most powerful manga ever created.

What is the secret of Mizuki's success? He creates fascinating and diverse stories, and—as is highlighted here with two shorts—often juxtaposes simple cartoony characters with realistic backgrounds. Readers quickly sense that his stories are created by someone fearless yet quirky, with a deeply human worldview. It is no coincidence that on Twitter today, fans are fond of tweeting eccentric quotations from Mizuki, such as his admonition to "be lazy."

Reflecting Mizuki's status these days, two hugely popular live-action television series about him have been screened—one in 1991–92 about his relationship with his childhood spiritual mentor, NonNonBa, and one in 2010, based on a book by his wife. And in his hometown of Sakaiminato, he has nearly been deified. A local train line is named after his yōkai characters and decorated with their images. There is even a Mizuki Road, where the street is lined with scores of bronze statues of his yōkai characters, a museum dedicated to him, and stores selling Mizuki- and yōkai-themed trinkets. Over two million tourists visit each year.

Frederik L. Schodt is an award-winning author of numerous non-fiction books on Japan and a well-known translator. In 2009, he received the Order of the Rising Sun, Gold Rays with Rosette, for his work. His latest book is* Professor Risley and the Imperial Japanese Troupe: How an American Acrobat Introduced Circus to Japan—and Japan to the West *(Stone Bridge Press).

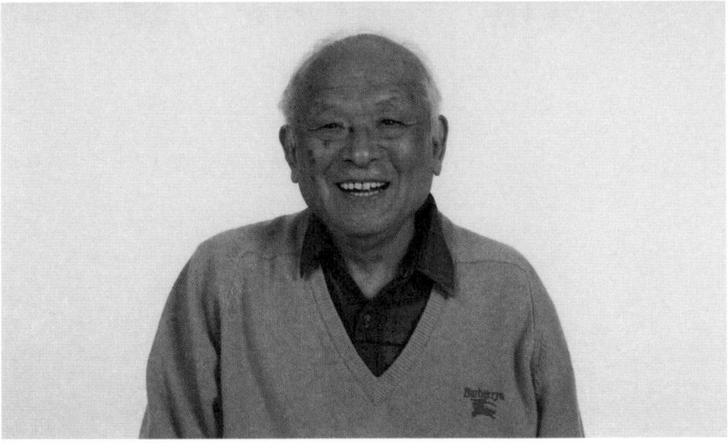

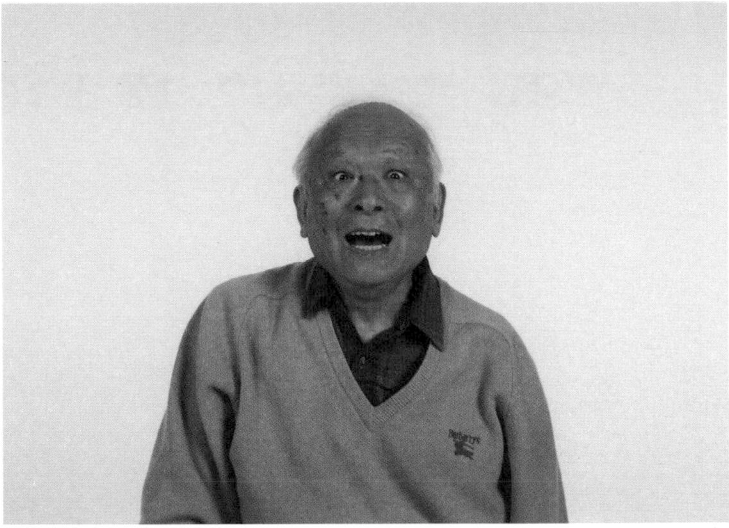

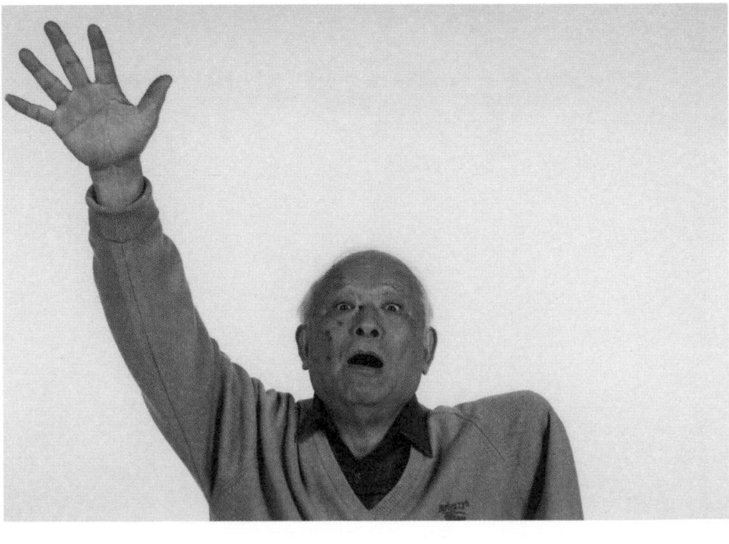

A decade ago, at a friend's bar in Osaka, I drunkenly declared that I would make it my holy mission to translate Shigeru Mizuki's works and bring his wonders to the West. It was a crime that this rare genius was so unknown. I decided to remedy that.

It was love at first sight when I discovered Shigeru Mizuki and his yōkai world at the massive Toyland in the basement of Umeda Station in Osaka, Japan. I had come in search of Godzilla and Ghibli but found something better—a huge display showcasing a barrage of strangeness: a one-eyed boy in a striped vest, a walking eyeball, a cat girl, a living wall, a one-footed umbrella with a lolling tongue and a single eye. It was a menagerie of beasts and monsters beyond the wildest nightmares of Godzilla and his *daikaiju* brethren. I was hooked. If it had been a movie, the scene would have gone soft focus with romantic background music, or maybe a dramatic upsweep as Man Discovers Destiny. But at the time I had no idea what they were. Or who was the mind behind them.

Almost immediately, I began collecting and reading as many of Shigeru Mizuki's works as I could. The deeper I dove into his comics—and simultaneously the more language and culture I absorbed—the more I realized he is an integral cornerstone of modern Japan. Shigeru Mizuki is Japan's Walt Disney, Jack Kirby, Will Eisner, Charles Addams, Mike Mignola, Epicurus, and Howard Zinn all embodied in a single, living human. (That part is important—at ninety-two years old, Mizuki is a true "living legend.") Like Disney, he is a beloved figure who shaped the dreams and imagination of a country. Like Kirby, he created an unparalleled body of work spanning every genre of comic-book art and influenced every artist to follow. Like Eisner, he passionately drove comic art to maturity with the *gekiga* movement and his own war autobiographies. Like Addams, he gave a familiar, melancholy face to the darker side of life. Like Mignola, he deeply mined the world's folklore and made it contemporary and alive. Like Epicurus, he is a profound philosopher who espouses that there is nothing so sweet in life as happiness and the simple pleasures being alive brings. Like Zinn, he is an unrepentant, unforgiving historian who refuses to let the powerful obfuscate the shameful actions of their country. By virtue of his long life and experience, Mizuki is a vital link to the past. With both his yōkai and his war stories, he bridges Japan's history to the modern age. Without him, Japan would literally be a different country. And a much less interesting place.

Having spent the last few years translating his works, I know Mizuki better than I ever imagined. I get inside his head. I know how he phrases things, his sense of humour and his sadness. I fought his battles with him in Rabaul. I discovered oddly shaped deities on the side of the road with him and peered into the mystical lands of the gods and monsters called yōkai. I looked through his eyes at the mystery and wonder of the world. I've seen the absolute joy he finds in the most mundane things, like a McDonald's hamburger or an autumn snack. I maintain he is one of the most unique and interesting people to ever come out of Japan. And I hope by my retelling his stories to you, you get to experience him too.

—*Zack Davisson, translator, writer, and scholar of Japanese folklore.*

HANPIDON

It was definitely in Kumamoto Prefecture, and about twenty years ago, that I went to see Hanpidon. I didn't know what to make of him at first. I remember he had a stone statue that looked something like a rice field *kami** that got mixed up with a kami of fortune. He was an odd one, that's for sure! Even Hanpidon didn't seem to know what he was. The look on his face made me think he was some kind of senile yōkai.** Anyways, he looked unreliable for a kami. Still, someone had set a single fish before him as an offering.

The people of the village that Hanpidon watched over were friendly enough, and we engaged in some lighthearted chat while I visited. It seemed like a peaceful place, with few woes. It made me wonder if Hanpidon was a better kami than I gave him credit for. It isn't wise to mock folk beliefs, after all. There are mysteries and enigmas in this world. Believe me, I know.

In Kyushu—and everywhere in Japan—there are kami and beliefs unique to those places. Hanpidon is one of these. And a charming one at that.

**In the native folklore religion Shinto, kami refers to a numinous spiritual energy that exists in all living things and sometimes takes the form of specific entities. It is often translated as "god," although a less specific term like "deity" or "spirit" might be closer. The Force from Star Wars is based off of kami beliefs.*

***Yōkai translates literally as "mysterious phenomenon" and can be used as a generic term for Japan's native folkloric monsters.*

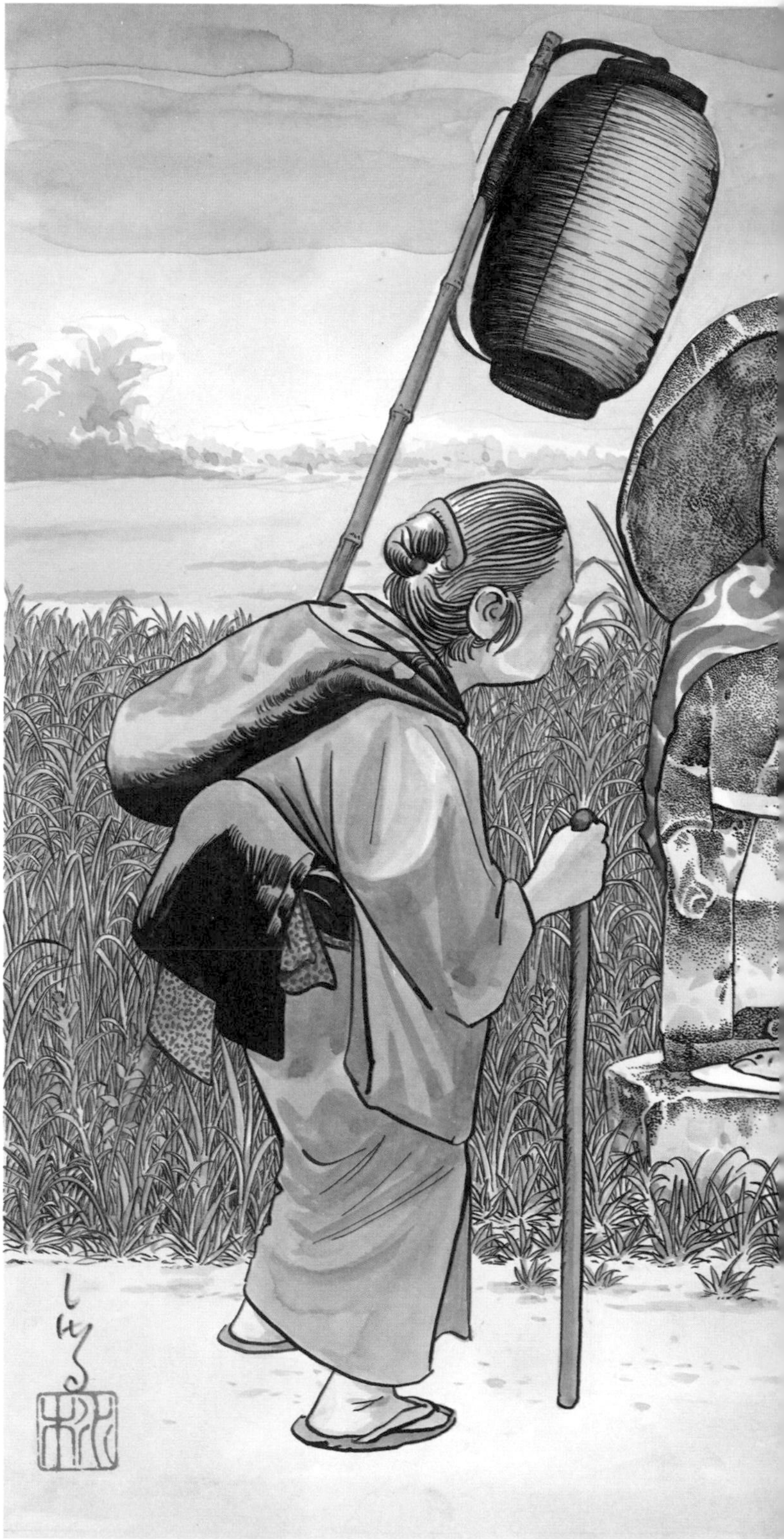

 Excerpt from *Yōkai Encyclopedia* (1992). It is one of dozens of entertaining and educational non-manga works that Mizuki has created.

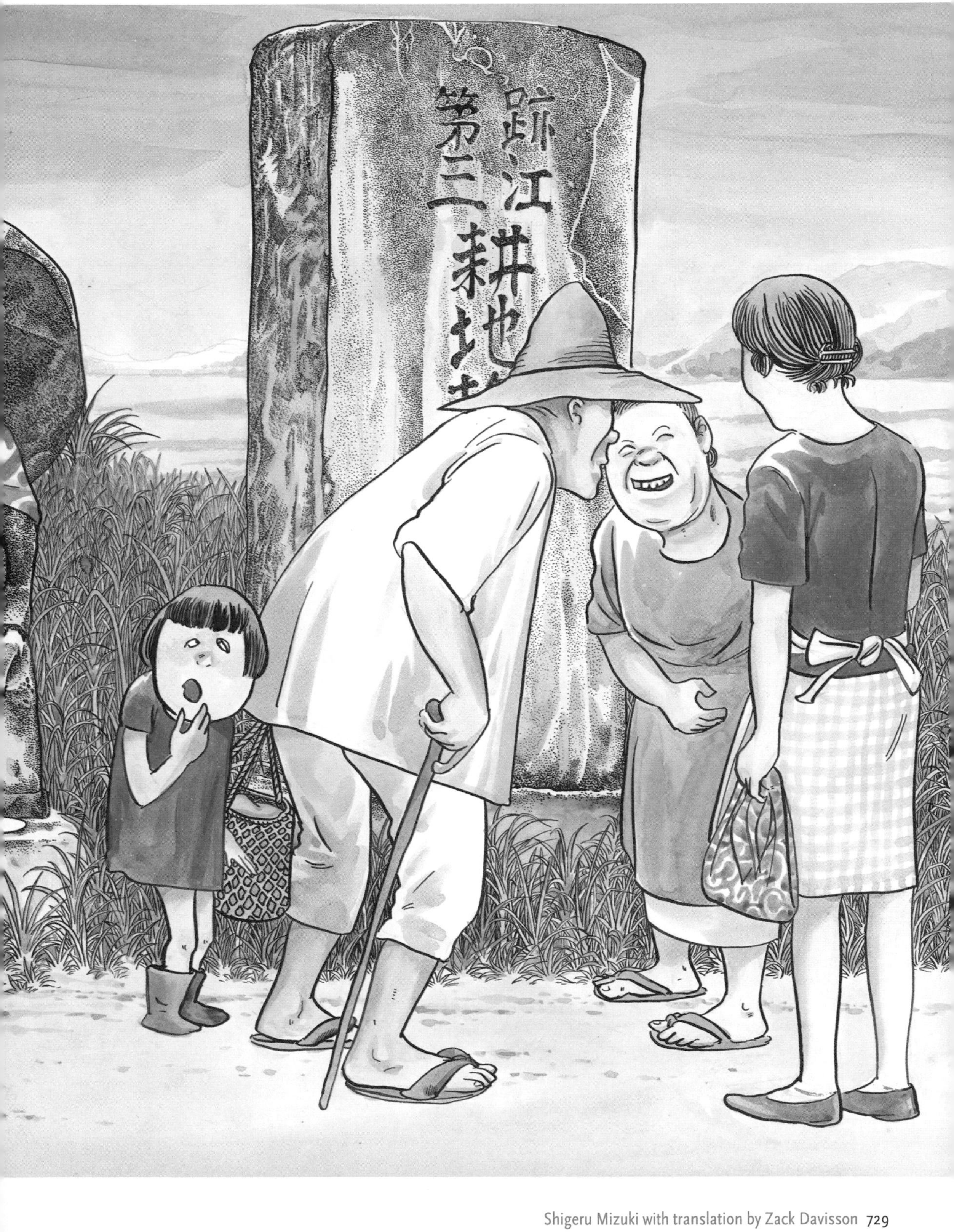
第二耕地

DŌTSŪ SAMA: THE HONOURABLE DŌTŌ

These yōkai—no, I should say kami—are known by many names across Japan. In Shimane Prefecture they are called *tonbai*. In Hiroshima Prefecture they are known as *tobyō*. Whatever you call them, they are a type of divine snake. *Dōtō sama* are small snakes, with black bodies ringed in amber and white necks and heads. They straddle the spectrum between yōkai and kami and are perhaps better called *yōkaigami*. They curse and possess human beings and can only be expelled by rites of exorcism. These exorcisms are vigorous affairs, performed by the young shrine maidens called *miko*.

Long ago, I saw a dōtō shrine in Kasaoka city, Okayama Prefecture. It looked like a village of tiny stone houses made for little faerie folk. I was amazed. Piled on an altar in the middle of this miniature village was a pile of eggs, an offering to the divine snakes of their favourite food. Since olden times, snakes have been the natural enemies of rats, and having snakes around was an advantage. Gratitude and respect to these snakes gradually changed to worship, and at some point in time the snakes were accorded divine prestige and power. A religion formed around them. In time, humans began to imagine that this mystical might could be turned against them, and that the snakes could curse as well as cure. They raised shrines to pacify the snake kami. Whether they have true power or not, I wasn't going to tempt them. I left an egg as an offering before I departed.

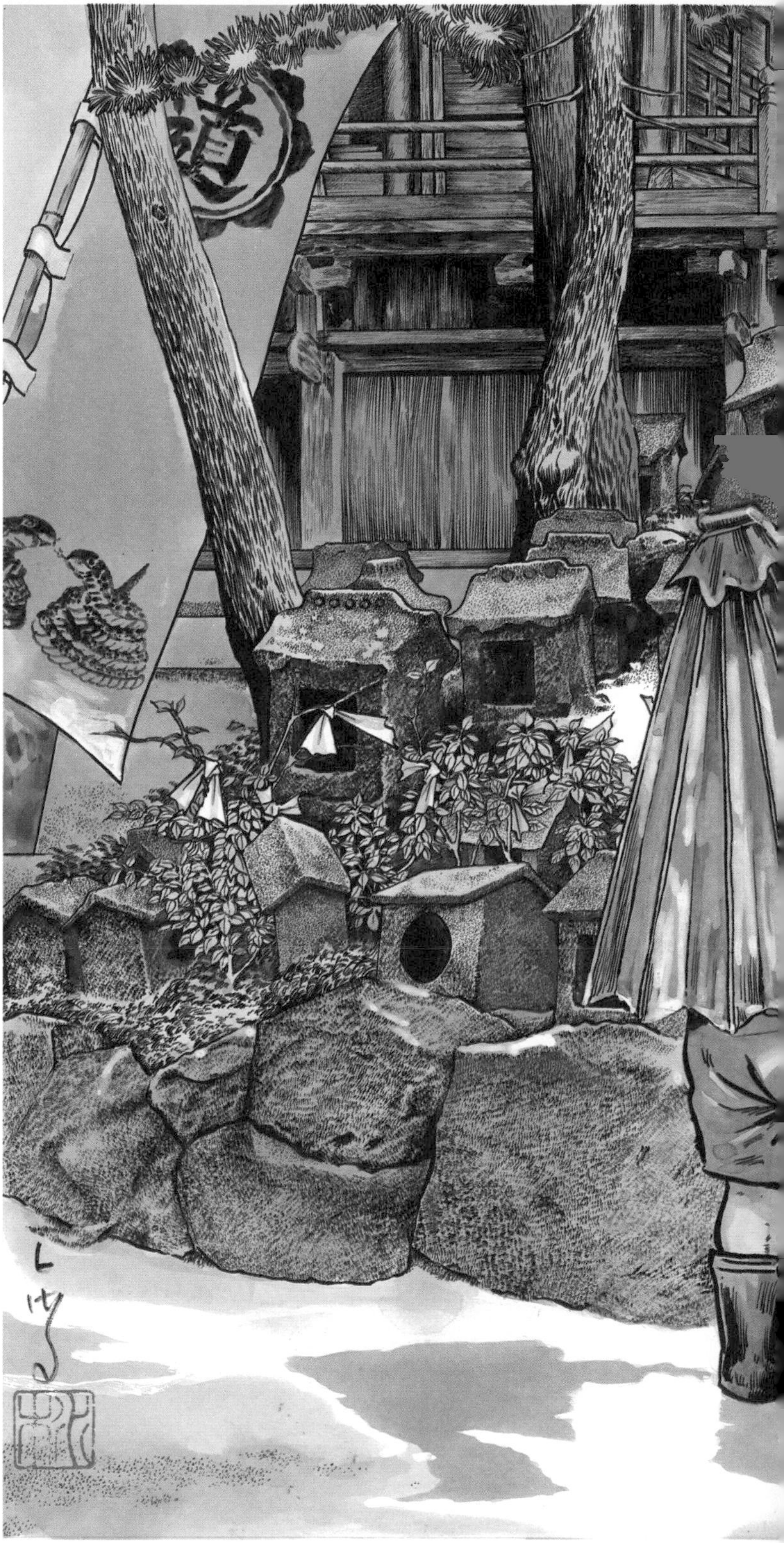

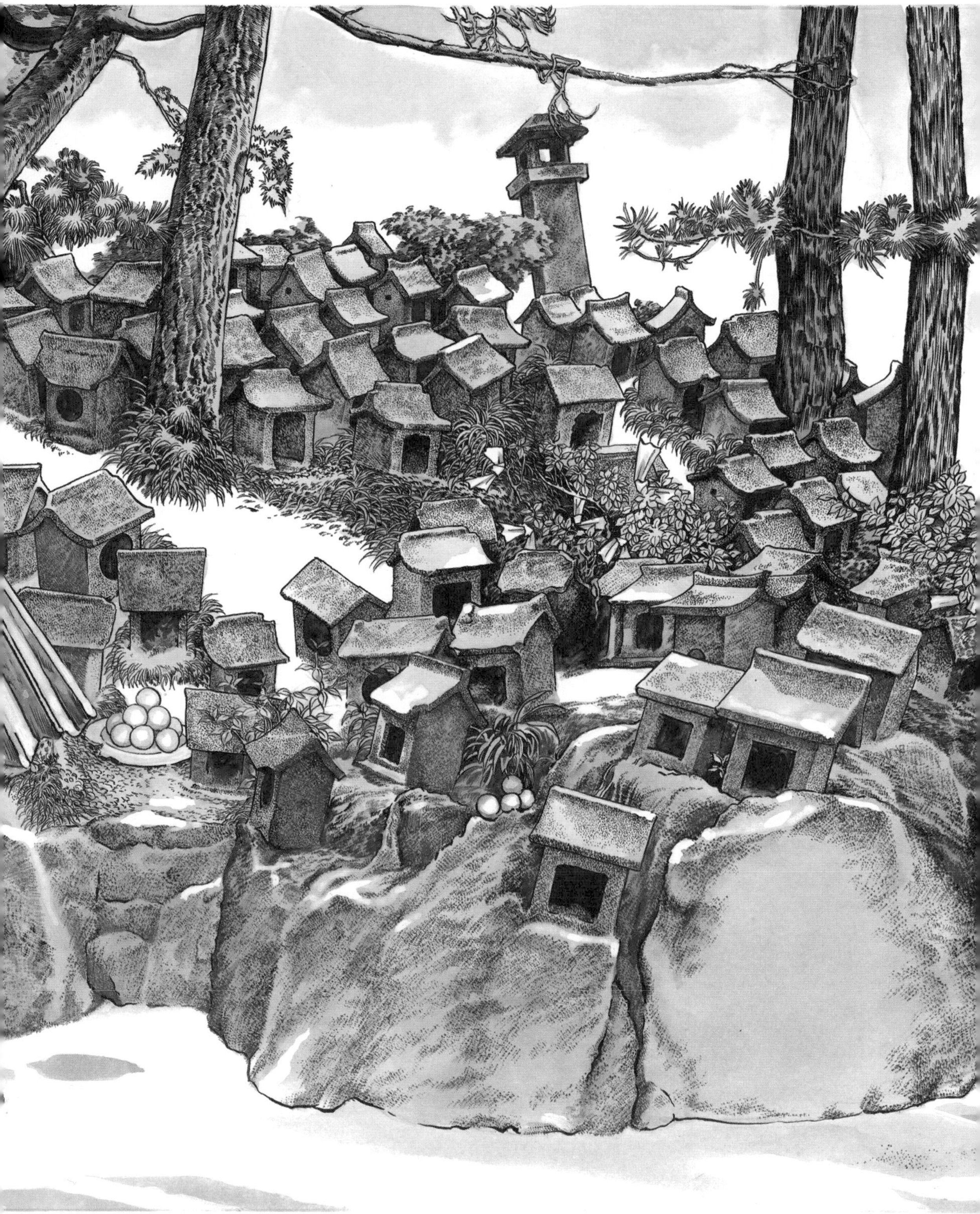

IYADANI SAN: THE DWELLERS OF IYADANI

There is a temple in Kagawa Prefecture called Iyadani-ji. It is said that when people die, their souls come to rest in this temple. The temple is old, and there is an eerie sensation about the place. It feels as if it is filled with the spirits of the dead, and each blow of the wind is a touch of their hands. It sent shivers up my spine.

There are cliffs near the temple, carved by yōkai winds to resemble faces. They look like half-completed Buddhist statuary. There are so many. Although, given the nature of the nearby temple, perhaps they are the faces of the dead, each soul in the temple doing its best to render its own monument. Either way, it feels like a place not meant for the living.

Children and families come to this temple about twice a year and call the names of their dead relatives. It is said that they come when called. Having been to this temple, and having felt the presence of the unknown, I believe this to be true.

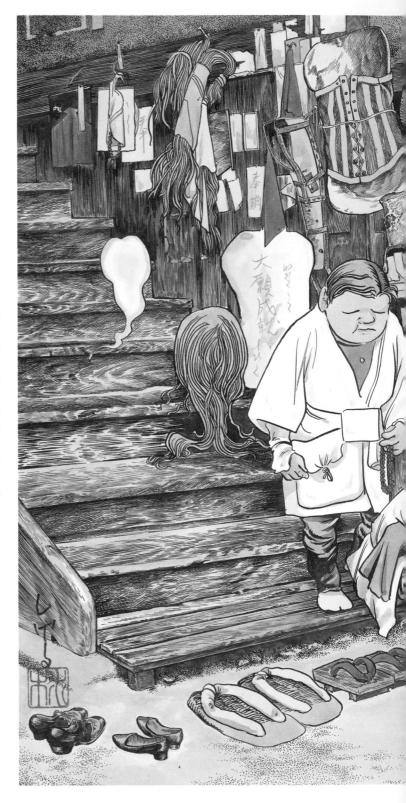

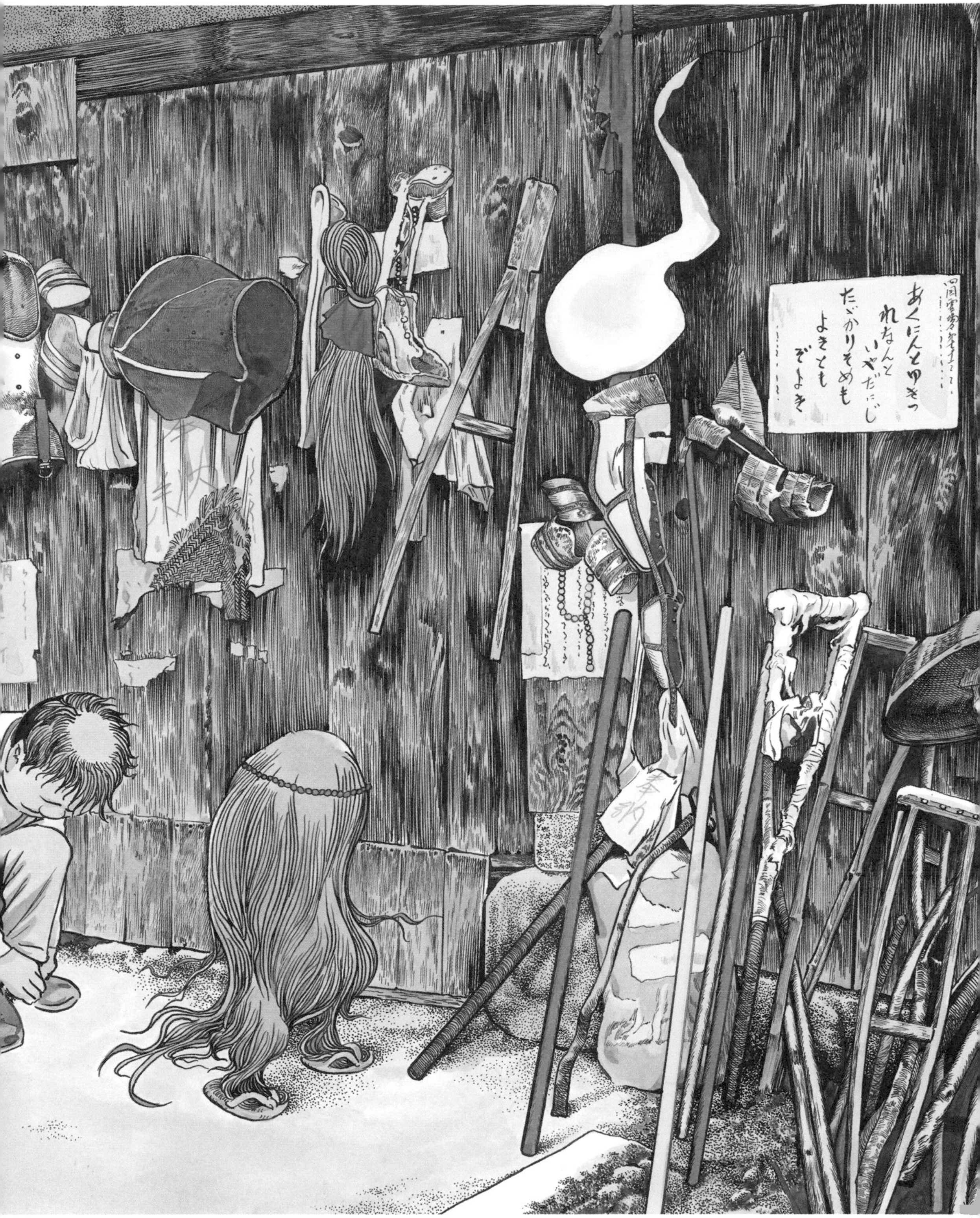
あくにんとゆきつ
れなんと
いやだにじ
たゞかりそめも
よきとも
ぞよき

JIZO DŌ: THE JIZO HALL

About twenty years ago, I went to visit a Jizo* hall in Kanaki, in Aomori Prefecture. When I arrived, there were no services going on. The doors were shut, but I cracked them open and peeked inside. There were all sorts of Jizo statues—a Jizo wearing a military cap; a Jizo dressed in a school uniform; every sort of Jizo you could imagine. It was deathly quiet. All of those unearthly Jizos were standing still, as if at attention. I couldn't say why, but I was frozen in fear. It was as if they were neither living nor dead, neither statues nor gods. They were something unexplainable. All I can say is they exuded what people refer to as "spiritual power."

Just then I was spotted by the caretaker. Realizing I was intruding, I made to leave, but the caretaker stopped me. He reprimanded me, saying, "Your fate has brought you here for a reason. You cannot leave yet." I knew he was correct. I stayed a while longer to learn what lessons the Jizos had to teach me.

**In Japanese Buddhism, Jizo is the deity of children and compassion for the dead. He guards the entrance to hell and rescues children from limbo. Japan is filled with Jizo statues. Parents often dress the Jizos up in clothing as an offering, praying for protection for the spirits of their dead children. In this story, the Jizo in the military cap would be a prayer for a child killed in a war, and the student's uniform would be from parents who lost their child while still a student.*

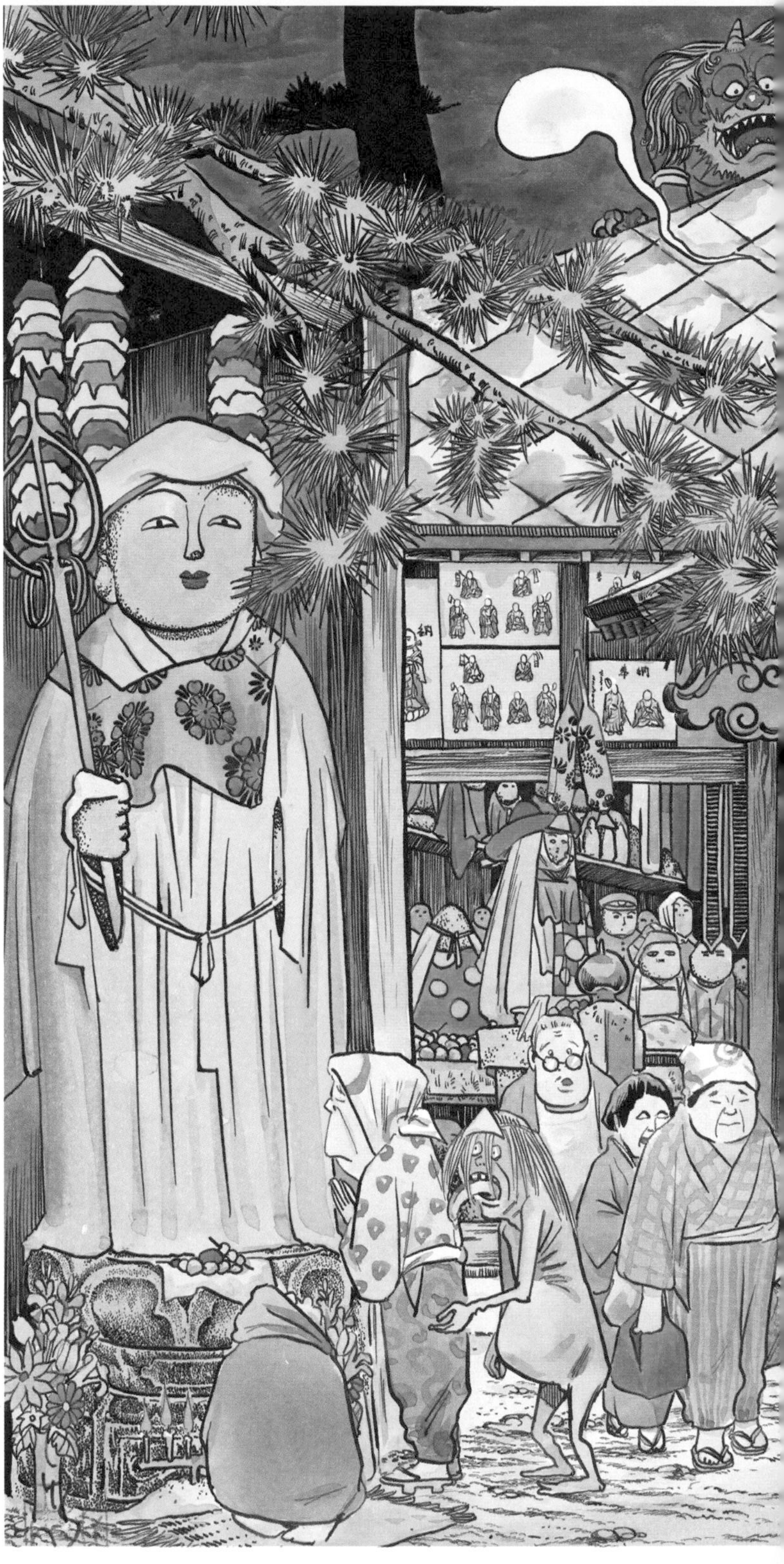

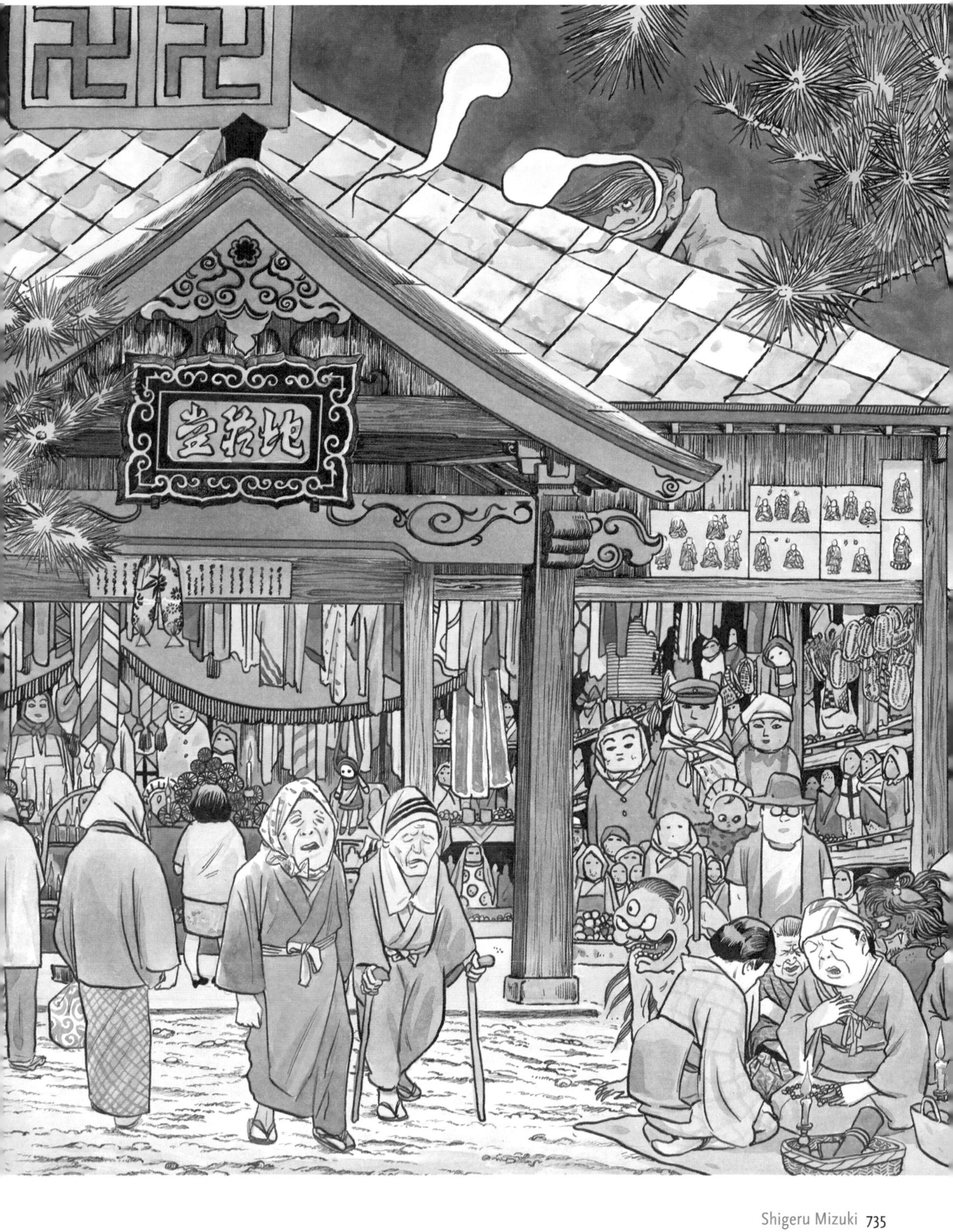

TEASHI NO KAMI: THE HAND-AND-FOOT GOD

If you travel around Japan, you will discover many mysterious kami dedicated to specific illnesses. For example, I have met a kami of tooth decay and a kami of headaches. Another was the hand-and-foot kami, purported to heal illness and injuries related to hands and feet. I discovered this hand-and-foot kami in northern Akita Prefecture, in Wakami city. I was amazed to see a giant mound of stone and wooden tablets, all in the shape of hands and feet. I discovered that people suffering from an affliction in their extremities would either commission or carve a stone or wooden tablet, write their name on it, then place it here as an offering. There were so many it looked like a mountain of limbs. It was almost impossible to see the true shape of the shrine buried underneath, but I wanted to know. I tried peeking through the gaps and saw a small stone dwelling that looked like a miniature temple. However, I couldn't see what was inside.

In Okayama Prefecture, there is a kami of feet called Ashi Osama (the great god of feet). At that shrine, people also make their prayers by offering stone or wooden votive tablets in the shape of feet. The shrine is in an isolated village called Kamigyobu in the Atetsu region. Many who would benefit from the kami's assistance are unable to make the trek, so a system has been established so you can send in a foot-shaped tablet with your name on it. Others will make the pilgrimage for you and set your offering before the kami.

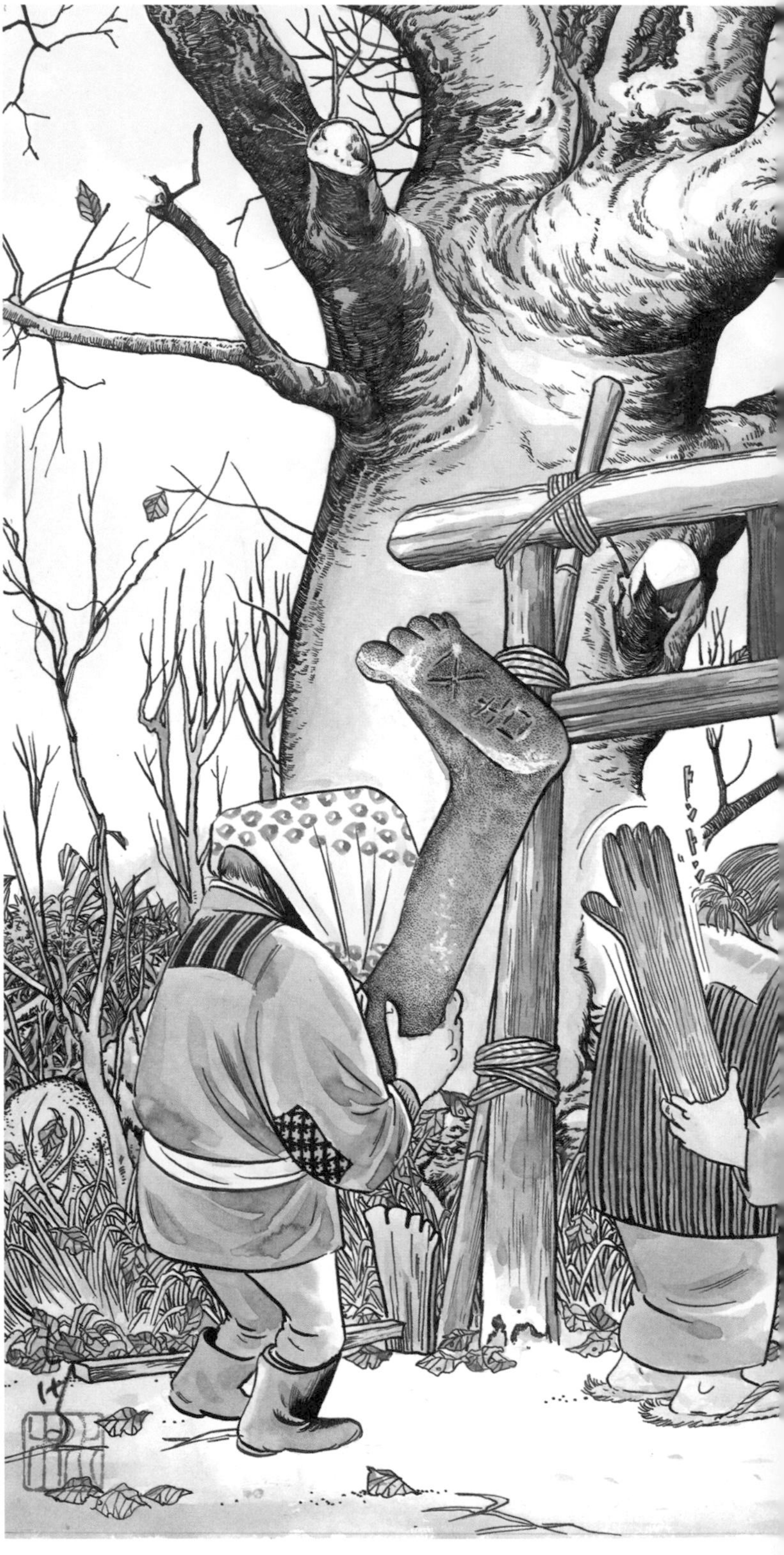

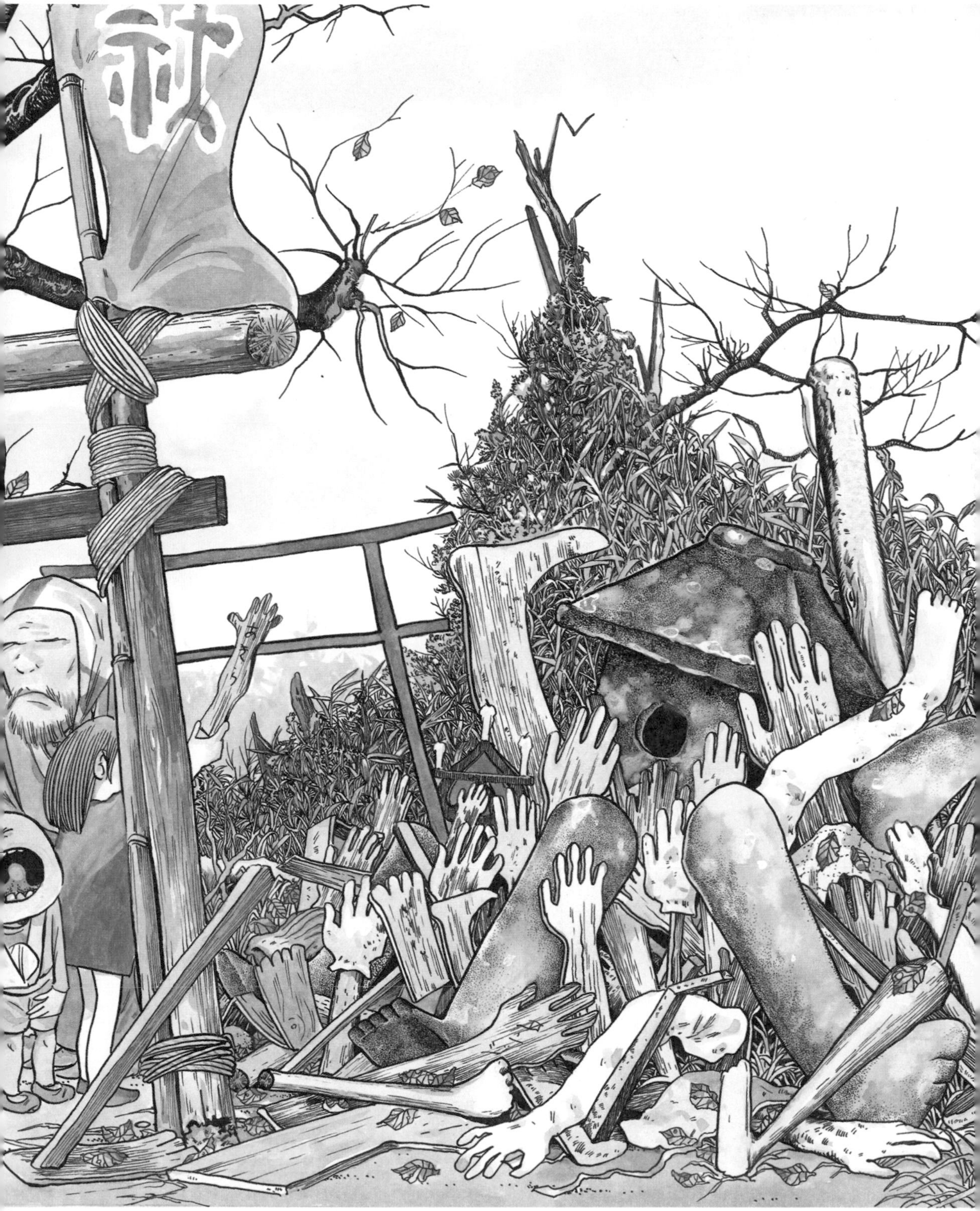

DAKITSUKI BASHIRA: THE HUGGING PILLAR

In the suburbs of Aizuwakamatsu, there is a temple called Eryō-ji that is home to a thousand-armed Kannon* statue. Near the statue is a massive pillar called the *dakitsuki bashira*—the hugging pillar. The elderly wrap their arms around it and pray, "Let me leave this life without pain and suffering, like a leaf falling gently from a tree when its time is done." So many people have hugged this pillar and prayed throughout the years that it is polished to a smooth and lustrous black.

Another pillar near the statue of the Kannon is covered in combs tangled with women's hair. There is an old saying in Japan that "a woman's hair is her life," and these women were offering their precious hair as a sacrifice to Kannon, praying for her mercy. Seeing these twin pillars, I was stunned, unable to speak or move. For more than a thousand years these pillars had been polished by human bodies seeking relief from their sufferings. There was something numinous there, something that could not be seen but could definitely be felt. I was filled with wonder at the ponderous mysteries of life. Without a doubt, there is more to this world than what we can touch and see, even if I don't know what that is.

**In Japanese Buddhism, Kannon is the goddess of mercy. She is imported from India and China, as are all Japanese Buddhist deities. Kannon comes in several forms, such as the thousand-armed Kannon of this story. This Kannon manifested innumerable arms so that she could offer a helping hand to everyone in need. In India, Kannon was male.*

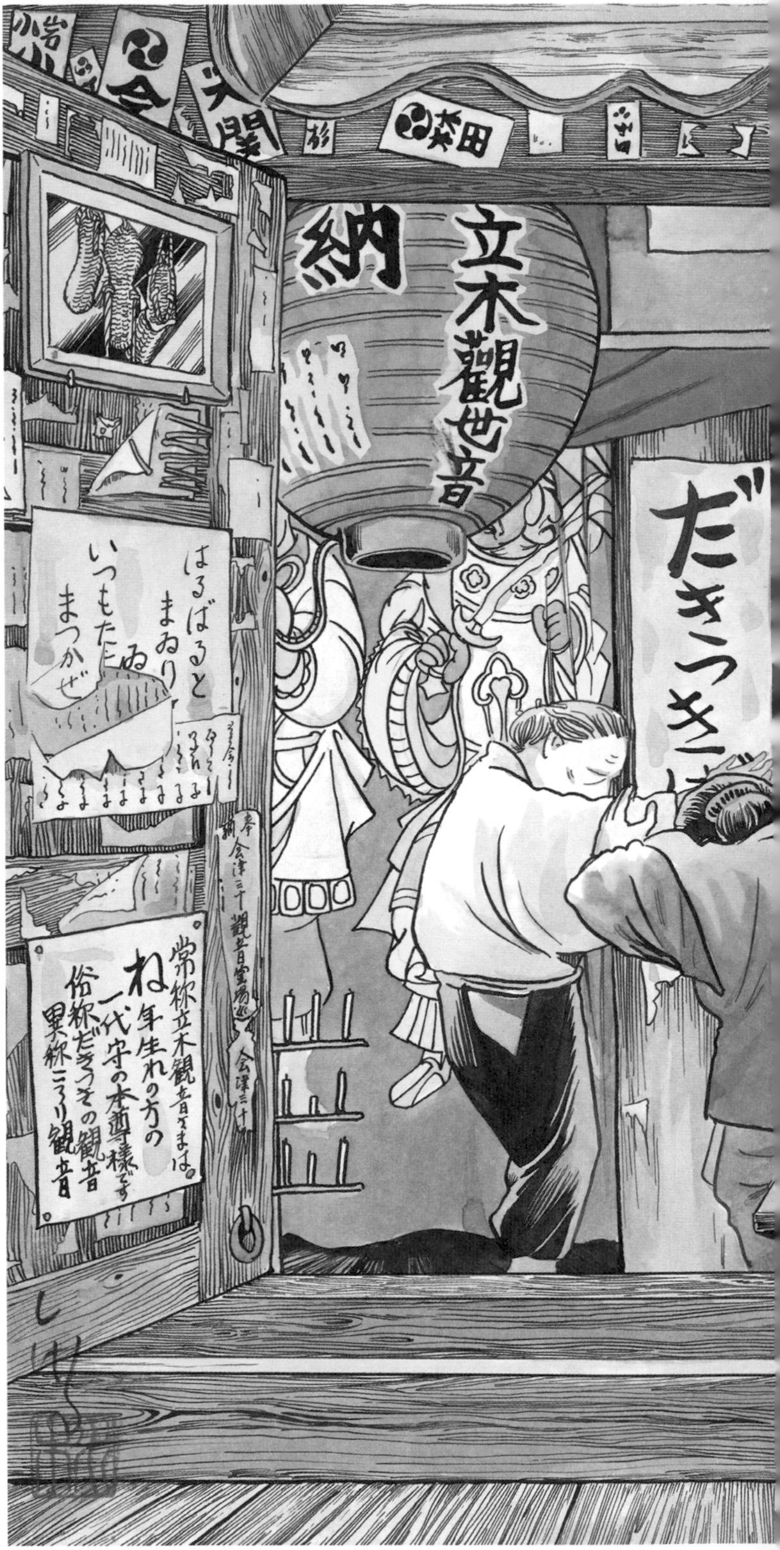

立木觀世音
納
はるばると
まゐりぬ
いつもたえ
まつかぜ
常称立木観音さまは
ね年生れの方の
一代守の本尊様です
俗称だきつきの観音
異称ニヲリ観音
会津三十
だきつき

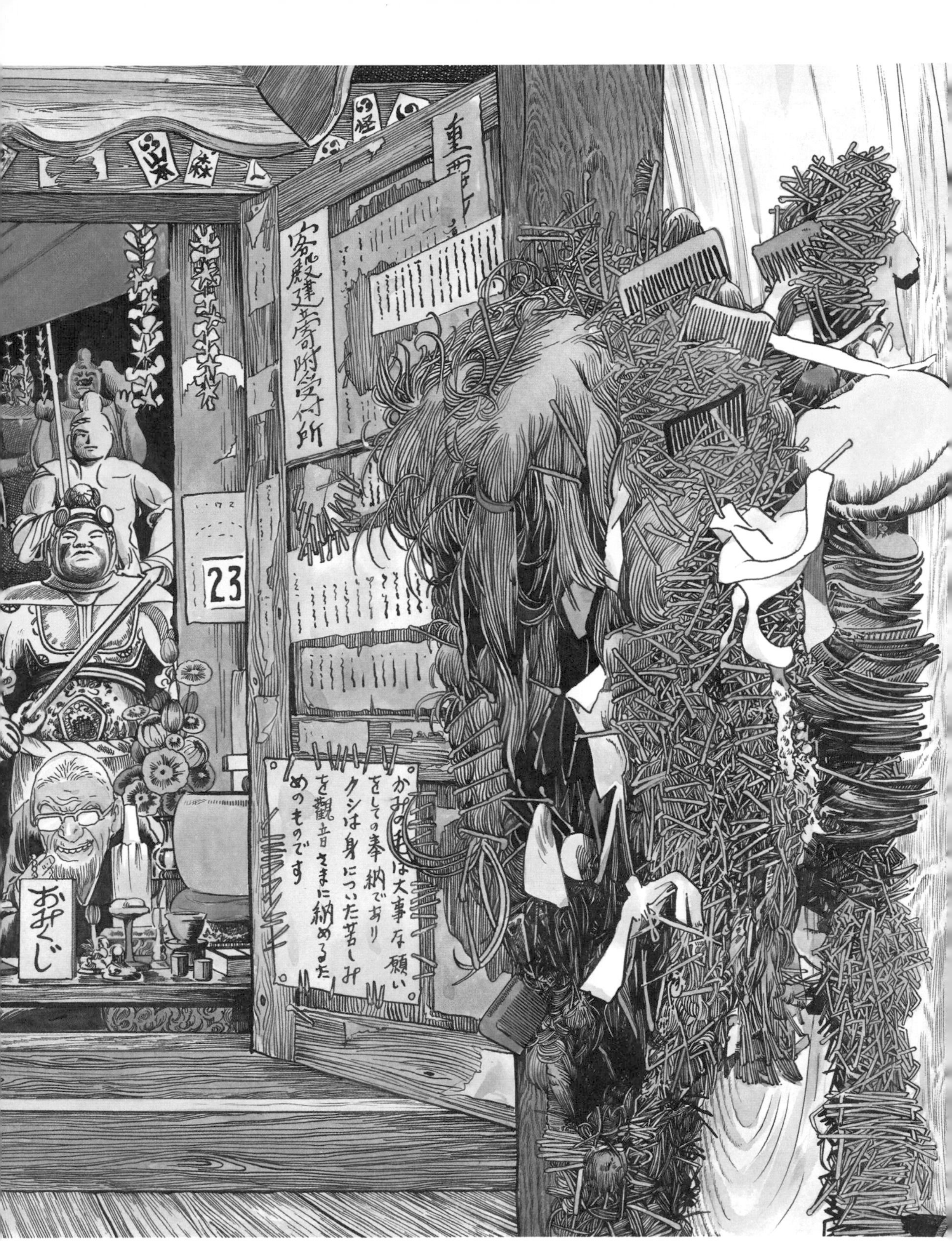
客殿建立寄附受付所
23
かみの毛は大事な願いをしての奉納でありクシは身についた苦しみを観音さまに納めるためのものです
おみくじ

OSHIKKO SAMA: THE HONOURABLE OSHIKO

Around Shōwa 20 (1965), I went to see a strange artifact called *oshikko sama* I had heard was enshrined in a dwelling in Namagi, Aomori Prefecture. The place resembled some sort of bizarre ironworks. Tucked in a corner of the building was oshikko sama. I was announced as "some professor from Tokyo University here to look at oshikko sama." The old man of the house gingerly produced the idol, which looked like a pair of entwined *kappa*, male and female. He explained, "This whole region used to be swampland. Oshikko pulled *shirikodama** out of many little boys and girls." I thought that sounded plausible. This lowland region was exactly the kind of place where you would have found kappa in olden times.

In the Tohoku region up north, in Tsugaru-heiya, many shrines remain dedicated to oshikko and *suiko*, large kappa known as "water tigers." These *kappa oyabun*** have been enshrined as kami to prevent little children from drowning. This is not an ancient belief: the practice comes from the Meiji period and began at Jitsuso-ji Temple, in Kituzkuri, Tsugaru-heiya.

**Literally "small anus ball," this is a magical ball believed to hide just inside the human digestive tract near the liver. Kappa treasure this ball and reach up through the anus to pull it out, thus killing their victims.*

***The term "oyabun" is used in the yakuza gangster world to indicate a boss or capo. All kappa oyabun report to the Dragon King who lives in a palace under the ocean and rules all water-dwelling yōkai.*

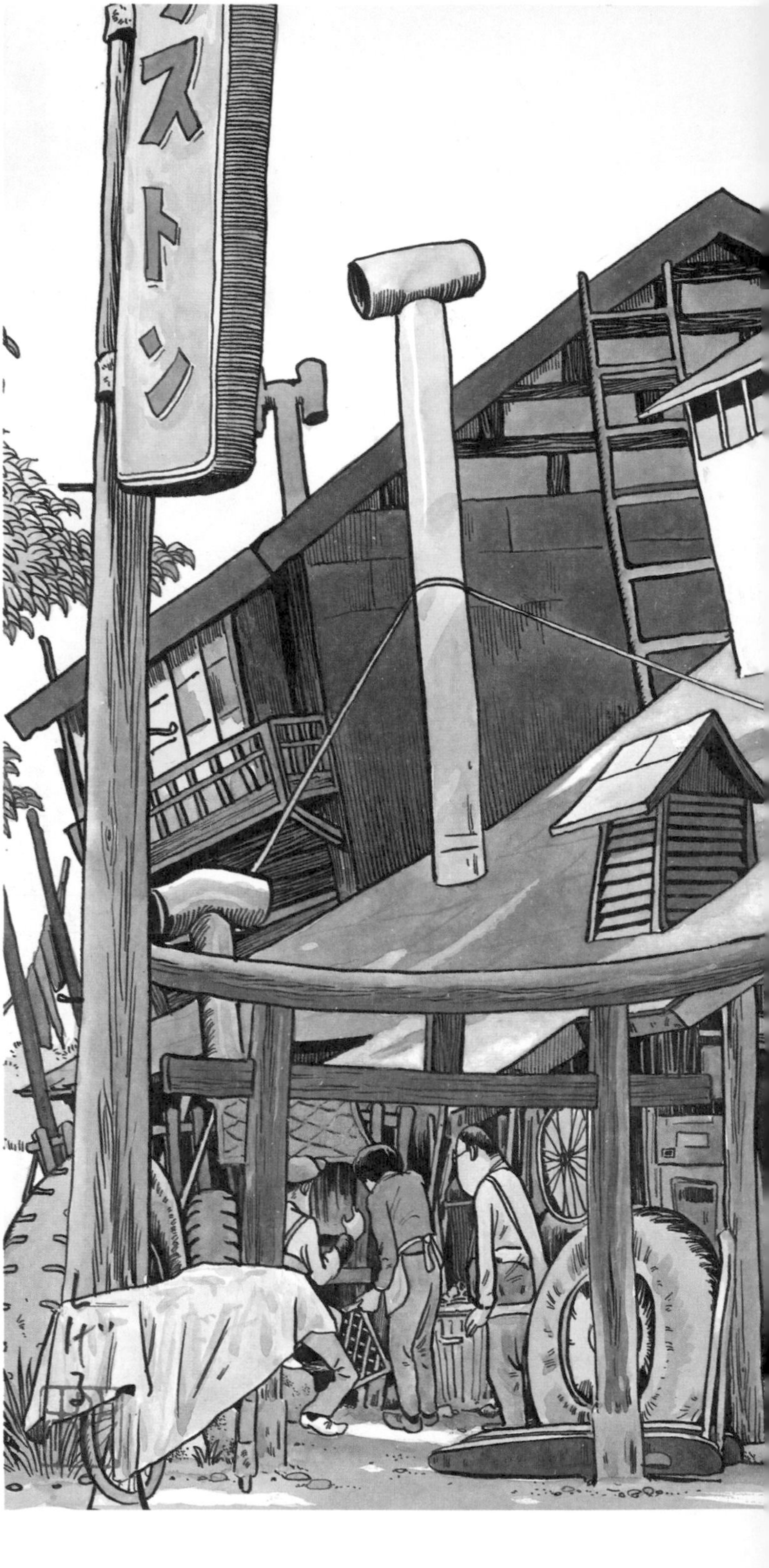
ストン

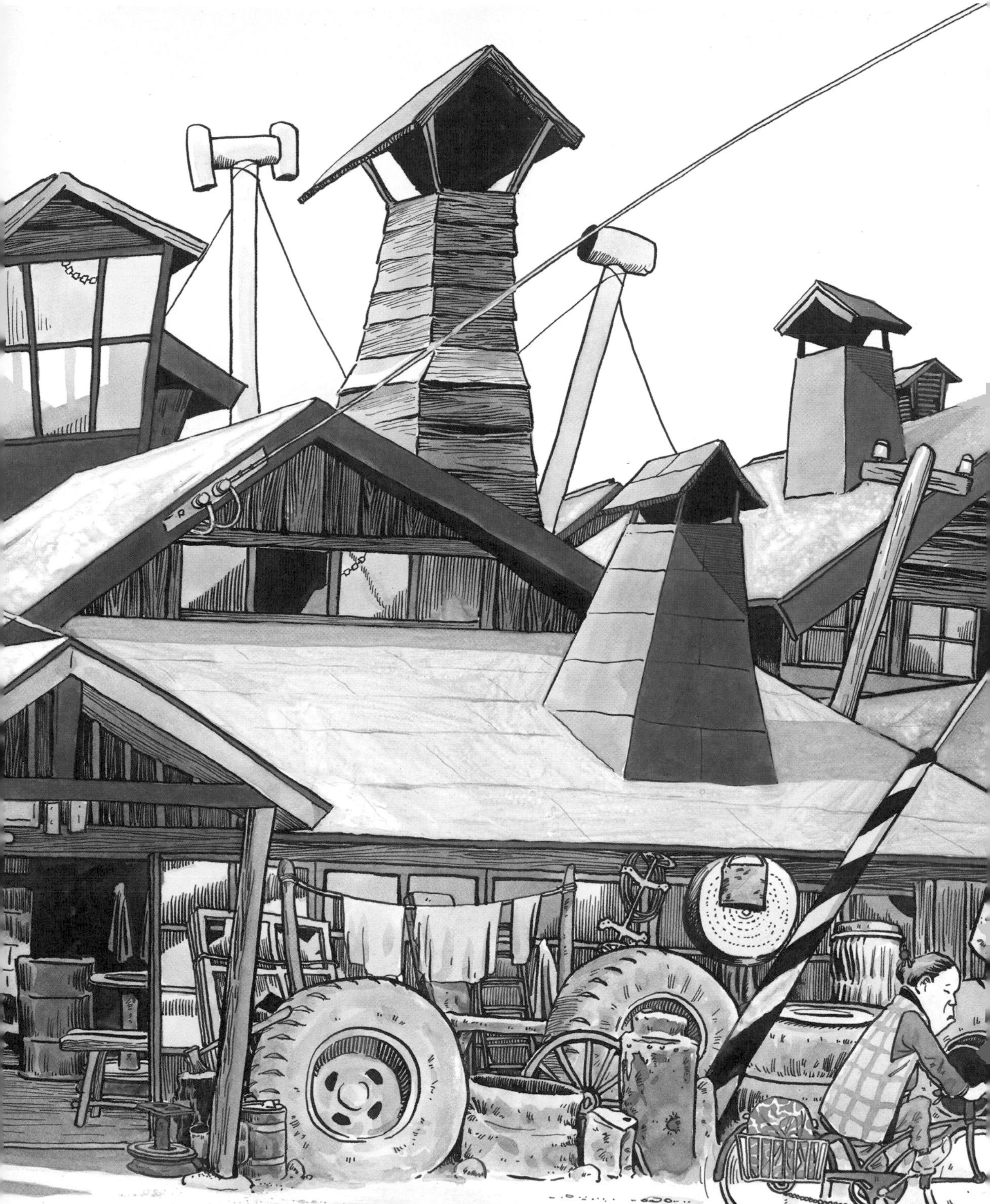

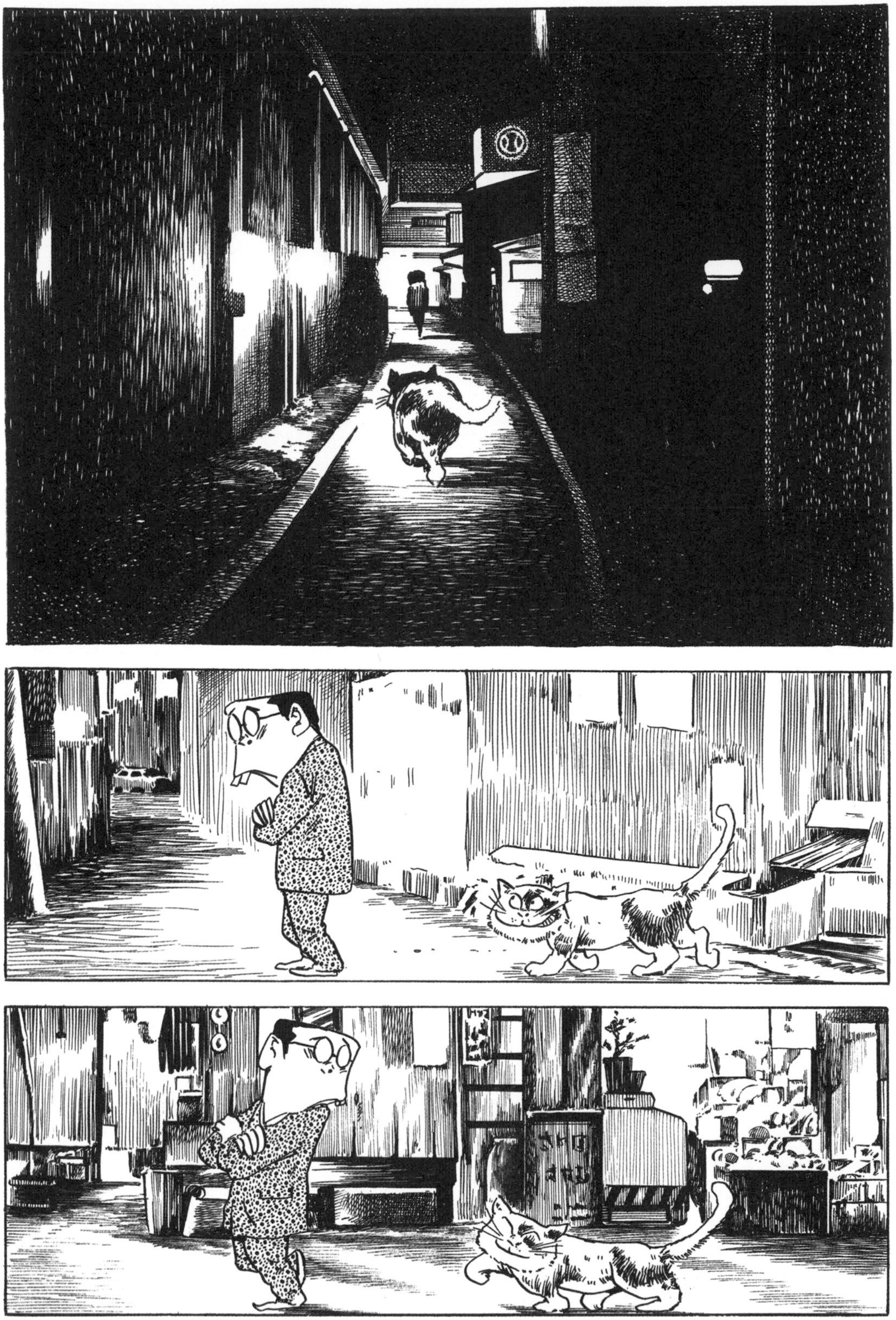

 "Cold Case" originally appeared in a series of shorts titled *Silent Shock* that ran in *Gendai Manga* magazine (1970).

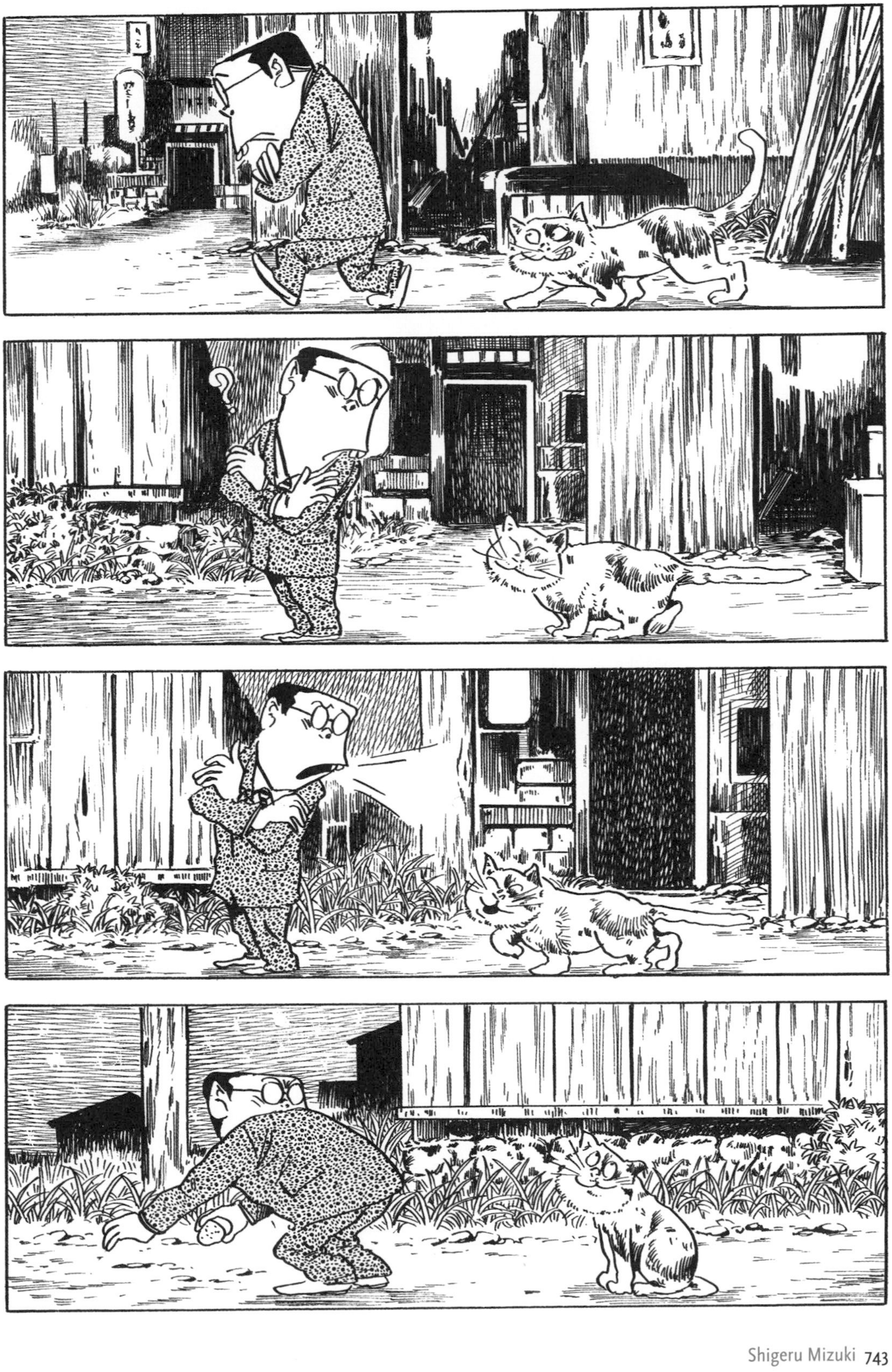

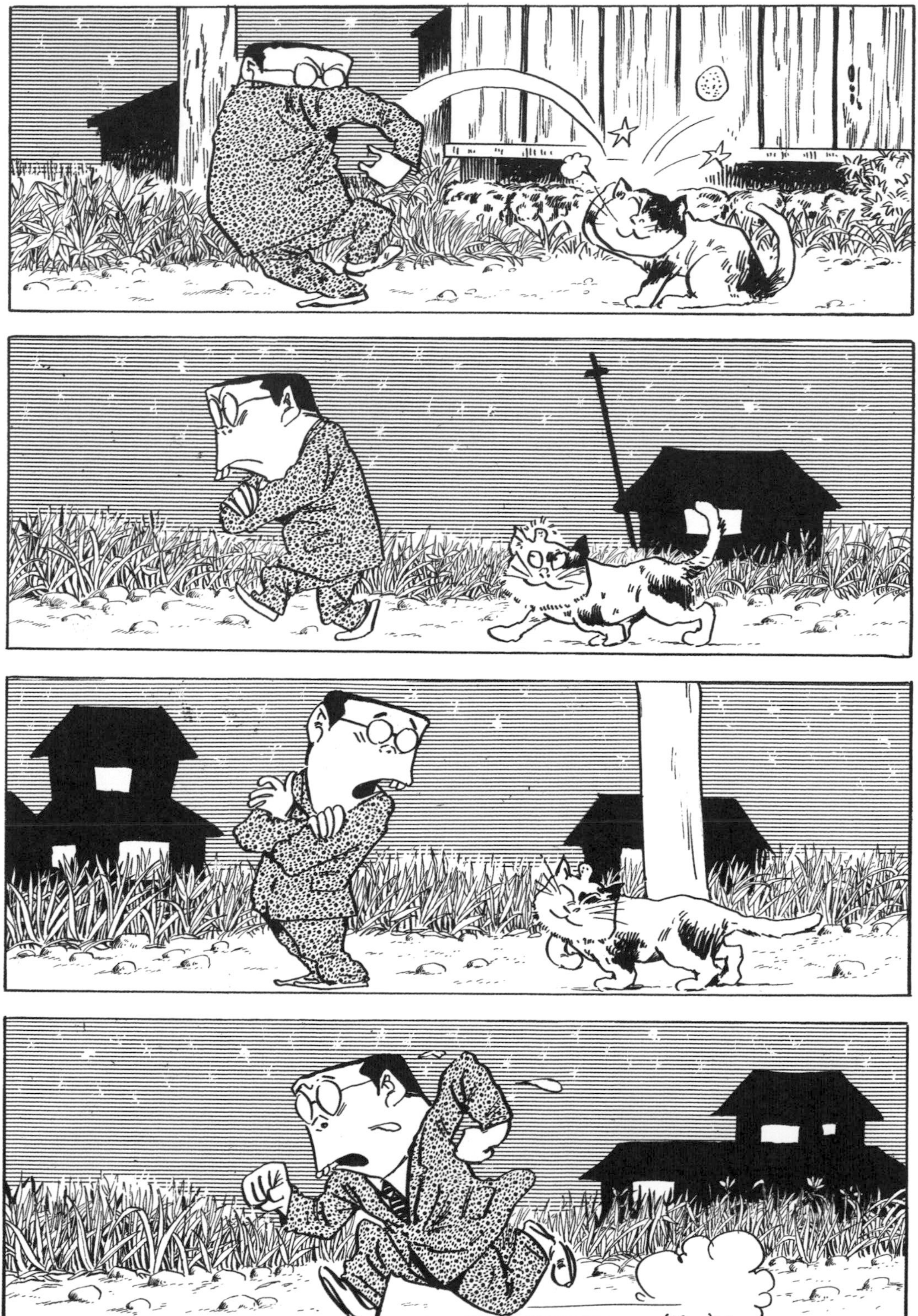

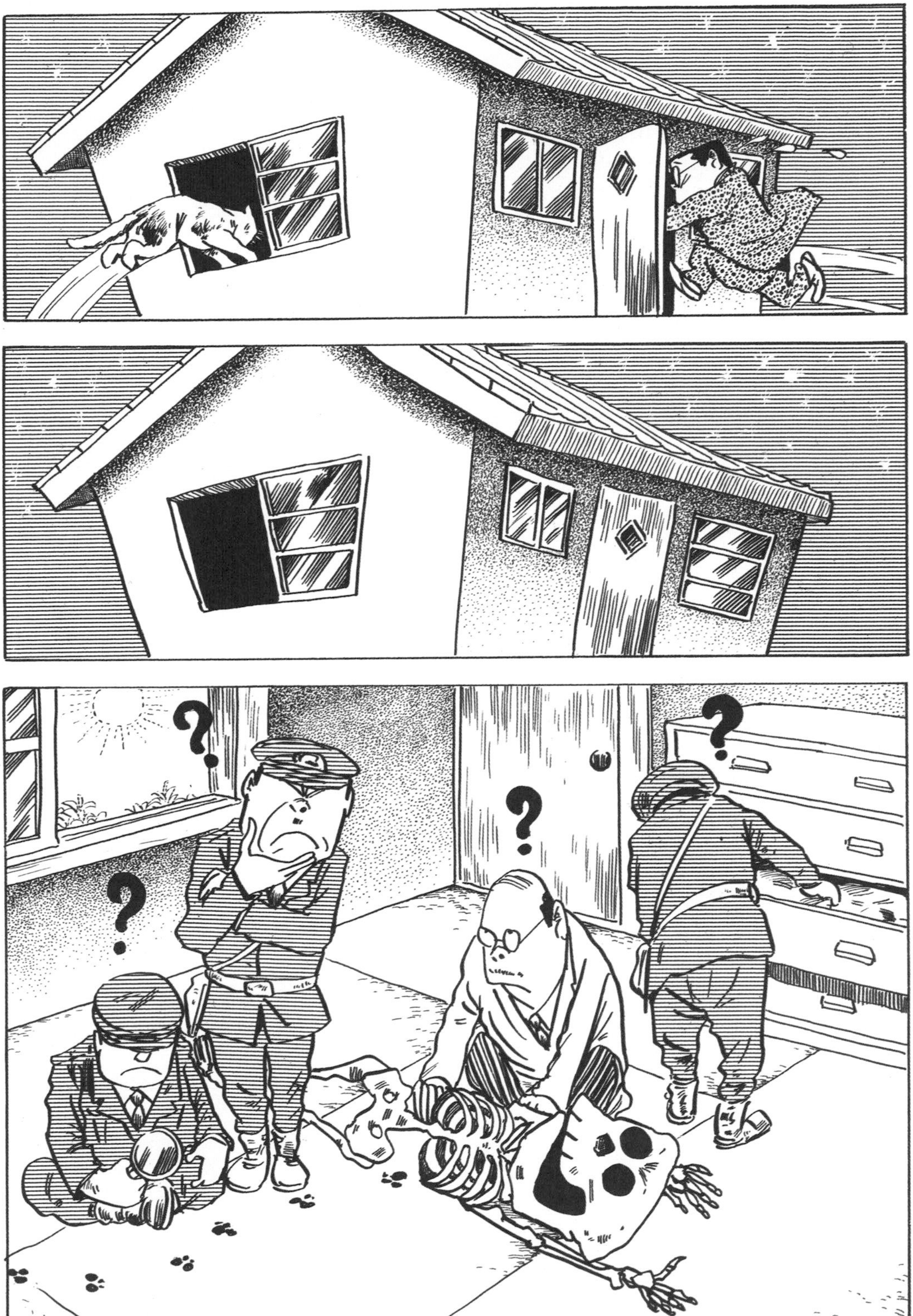

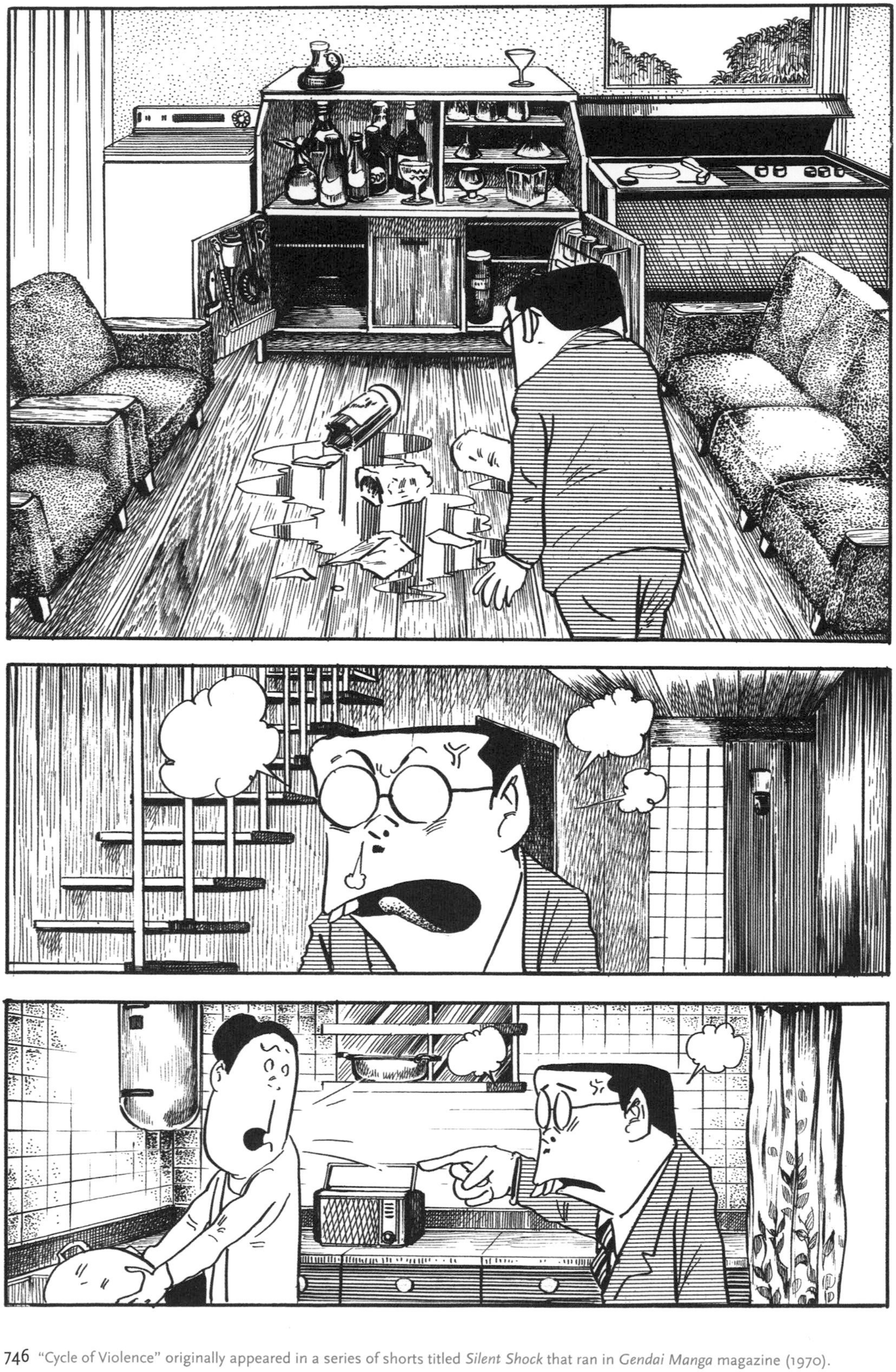

 "Cycle of Violence" originally appeared in a series of shorts titled *Silent Shock* that ran in *Gendai Manga* magazine (1970).

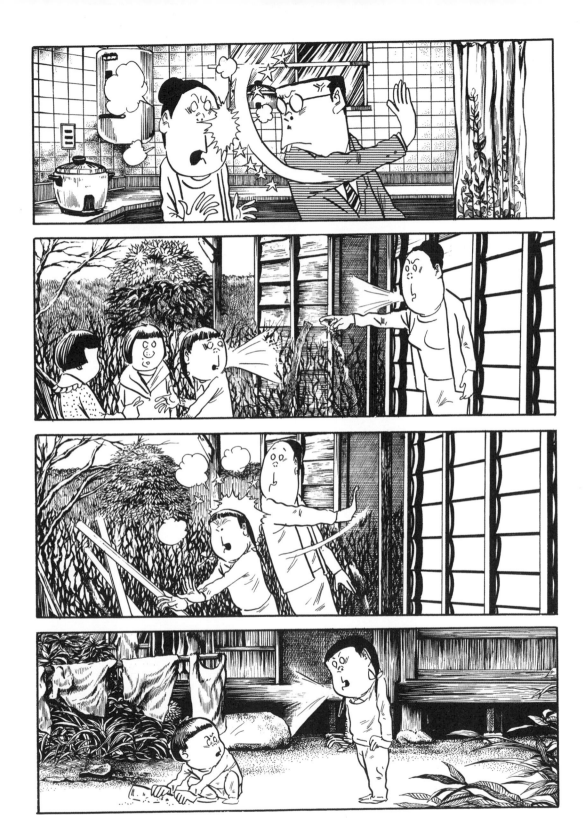

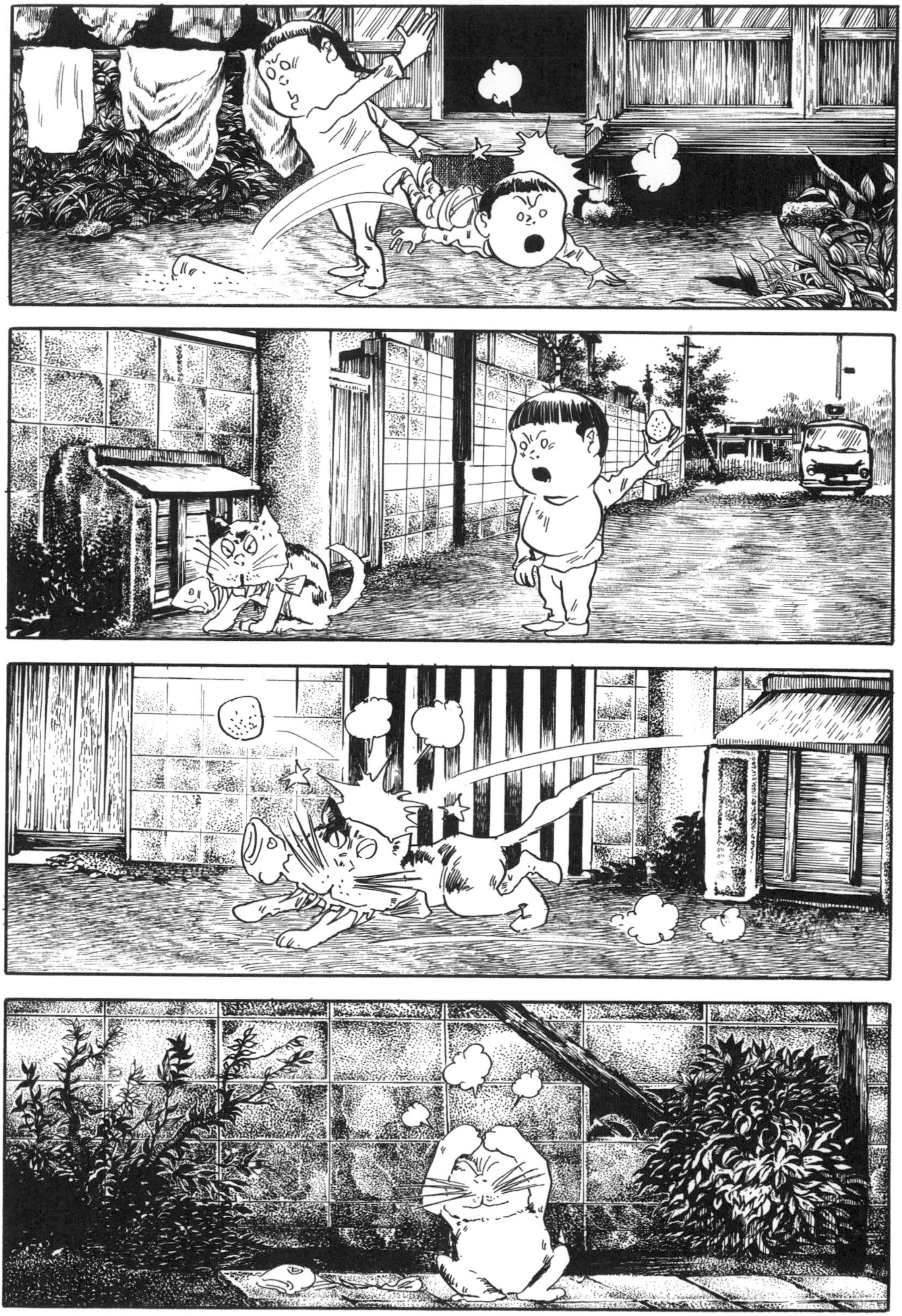

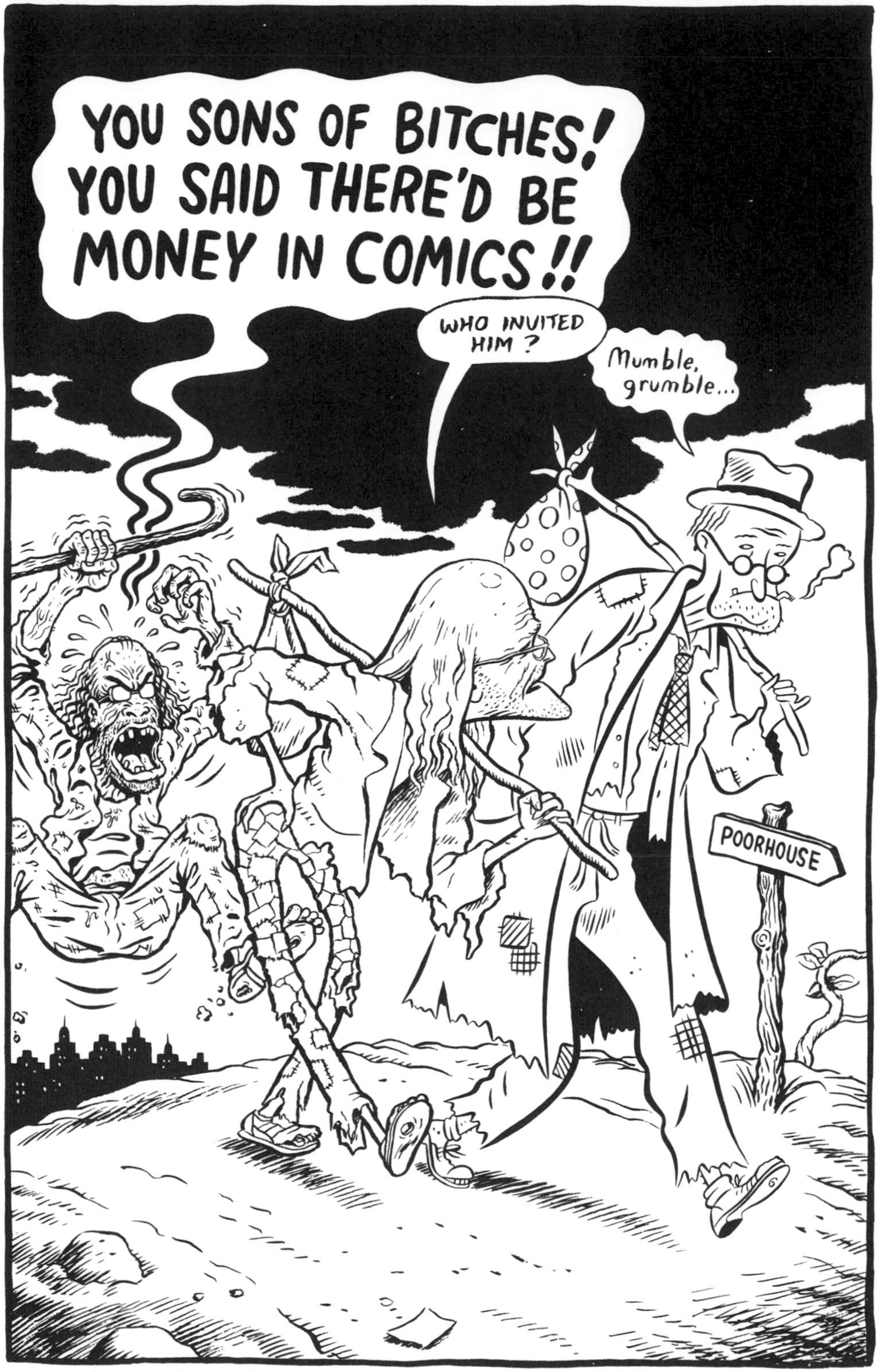
YOU SONS OF BITCHES! YOU SAID THERE'D BE MONEY IN COMICS!!
WHO INVITED HIM?
Mumble, grumble...
POORHOUSE

Joe Matt FIFTY YEARS DOWN THE ROAD SETH

D+Q CONTRIBUTORS *1990–present*

MARGUERITE ABOUET

Marguerite was born in Abidjan, Ivory Coast, in 1971. *Aya* was her first comic. It won the first book prize at the Angoulême Comics Festival and was made into an animated film. She is also the writer of the comic book series *Akissi*.

With Clément Oubrerie: *Aya* (Feb 2007); *Aya of Yop City* (Sept 2008); *Aya: The Secrets Come Out* (Sept 2009); *Aya: Life in Yop City* (Sept 2012); *Aya: Love in Yop City* (Feb 2013)

SONJA AHLERS

Sonja was born in 1971. She was nominated for the prestigious Sobey Art Award and lives in Whitehorse, Canada. She also writes poetry and regularly exhibits visual art and installation work.

The Selves (June 2010), *Rookie Yearbook One* (Sept 2012), *Rookie Yearbook Two* (Oct 2013)

AMBER ALBRECHT

Amber grew up in a seaside town on the west coast of Canada. She received her BFA from Concordia University in 2005. She works primarily in the mediums of drawing and printmaking.

Idyll (May 2012)

FRANÇOIS AVRIL

François was born in 1961 in Paris. He has illustrated over twenty books since 1985, several of which were collaborations with other cartoonists like Charles Berbérian and Philippe Petit-Roulet.

With Philippe Petit-Roulet: "63, Rue de la Grange aux Belles," *Drawn & Quarterly* vol. 2, no. 1 (Aug 1994)

DAVID B.

Pierre-François Beauchard was born on February 9, 1959. Using the pen name

David B., he is the author of the acclaimed graphic novel *Epileptic*. He is also a co-founder of the great French independent comics publisher L'Association.

Babel vol. 1 (Oct 2004)

PETER BAGGE

Peter was born December 11, 1957, in Peekskill, NY, and now lives in Seattle. He got his start in comics in the R. Crumb–edited magazine *Weirdo*. His comics *Neat Stuff* and *Hate* helped define the modern era of alternative comics.

"Girly-Girl and Her Pal Chuckie-Boy," *Drawn & Quarterly* no. 1 (April 1990); *Woman Rebel: The Margaret Sanger Story* (Oct 2013)

T. EDWARD BAK

Bak was born in Denver, CO, in 1970. He is currently working on a comics biography of Georg Steller. He lives in Portland, OR.

"Untitled," *Drawn & Quarterly Showcase* vol. 5 (Aug 2008)

ANNE BARAOU

Anne was born in Bordeaux in 1965. She is a member of OuBaPo.

With Pascale Bougeault: inside back cover, *Drawn & Quarterly* no. 10 (Dec 1992)

LYNDA BARRY

Lynda was born in Seattle in 1956. She has worked as a painter, cartoonist, writer, illustrator, playwright, editor, commentator, and teacher, and found that they are very much alike. She lives in Wisconsin, where she is a Discovery Fellow and assistant professor of interdisciplinary creativity at the Image Lab at University of Wisconsin–Madison.

What It Is (May 2008); *Picture This* (Nov 2010); *Blabber Blabber Blabber: Everything Volume One* (Oct 2011); *The Freddie Stories* (Jan 2013); *One! Hundred! Demons!* ebook (April 2014); *Syllabus: Notes from an Accidental Professor* (Oct 2014)

STANISLAS BARTHÉLÉMY

Stanislas was born in 1961 in Rennes, France. He has drawn graphic novels and children's books in France since 1986. He is one of the founding members of the seminal French publishing house L'Association.

With José-Louis Bocquet and Jean-Luc Fromental: "The Adventures of Hergé," *Drawn & Quarterly Anthology* vol. 4 (July 2001); *The Adventures of Hergé* (Nov 2011)

HERVÉ "BARU" BARULEA

Baru was born in 1947 in Nancy, France. He won the prestigious Alph-Art award for the best original French-language comic for *L'Autoroute du Soleil* (Casterman).

"The Road to America," *Drawn & Quarterly* vol. 2, no. 4 (Dec 1995); "The Road to America," *Drawn & Quarterly* vol. 2, no. 5 (April 1996); "The Road to America," *Drawn & Quarterly* vol. 2, no. 6 (June 1997); *Road to America* (March 2002)

CLARA BAYLISS

Clara collaborated with David Collier on a handful of semi-autobiographical comic strips in the early 1990s.

With David Collier: "Roommate World," *Drawn & Quarterly* no. 3 (Jan 1991); "From the Wires of the Associated Press," *Drawn & Quarterly* no. 4 (March 1991); "Liquid," *Drawn & Quarterly* no. 6 (October 1991); "Another Job Story," *Drawn & Quarterly* no. 7 (March 1992); "Those Tenacious Teens!" *Drawn & Quarterly* no. 9 (July 1992); "Liquid," *The Best of Drawn & Quarterly* (Dec 1993)

KATE BEATON

Kate was born in Mabou, Cape Breton, in 1983. She appeared on the comics scene in 2007 with her webcomic *Hark! A Vagrant*. She has become one of the most influential contemporary cartoonists of the new millennium.

***Hark! A Vagrant* (Sept 2011)**

GABRIELLE BELL

Gabrielle was born in England in 1976 and raised in California. The title story of her book *Cecil and Jordan in New York* was adapted for the anthology film *Tokyo!* by Michel Gondry. She lives in New York.

"Felix," *Drawn & Quarterly Showcase* vol. 4 (June 2006); *Lucky* vol. 1 (Nov 2006); *Lucky* vol. 2, no. 1 (May 2007); *Lucky* vol. 2, no. 2 (May 2008); *Cecil and Jordan in New York* (March 2009)

MARC BELL

Marc and his twin sister, Marcie, were born in London, Ontario, in 1971. He has produced hundreds of minicomics and six books.

***The Stacks* (Dec 2004); *Illusztraijuns for Brain Police* (Oct 2008); *Hot Potatoe* (Nov 2009); *Pure Pajamas* (Sept 2011)**

CHARLES BERBÉRIAN

Charles was born in 1959 in Baghdad and spent his childhood in Baghdad, Beirut, Lebanon, and later, in Paris. In his twenties, he began a collaboration with Philippe Dupuy that continued until recently. Together, they were awarded the 2008 Lifetime Achievement Award at the Angoulême Comics Festival.

With Philippe Dupuy: "Monsieur Jean," *Drawn & Quarterly* vol. 2, no. 4 (Dec 1995); "A Trip to Lisbon," *Drawn & Quarterly* vol. 2, no. 6 (June 1997); "Monsieur Jean," *Drawn & Quarterly Anthology* vol. 3 (May 2000); "Monsieur Jean," *Drawn & Quarterly Anthology* vol. 5 (Aug 2003); *Get a Life* (July 2006); *Maybe Later* (July 2006)

ANNE D. BERNSTEIN

Anne is a writer, story editor, and illustrator who has worked on the animated series *Daria*, and was at one time head writer for MTV Animation. Anne created the cover art for D+Q's very first publication.

Cover and "Out of Control Fantasy Comics," *Drawn & Quarterly* no. 1 (April 1990); "Tis the Grimaces" and "The Luckville Nearly New Shop," *Drawn & Quarterly* no. 2 (Oct 1990); "Househunting," *Drawn & Quarterly* no. 3 (Jan 1991); "The Neck," *Drawn & Quarterly* no. 9 (July 1992)

ROXANNA BIKADOROFF

Roxanna was born in Montreal. She has worked for over twenty-five years as an illustrator for numerous publications including the *New Yorker* and the *Walrus*.

With Maurice Vellekoop and Fiona Smyth: *Fabulous Babes* no. 1 (July 1995)

LEE BINSWANGER

Lee moved from Maryland to San Francisco in 1979, partly to see first-hand what was going on with the underground comix scene. In 1980, she sold two single-panel cartoons to the humour magazine *National Lampoon*, then found her way into the newly revived *Wimmen's Comix* in the mid-eighties. She submitted work to *Wimmen's* up to the last issue in 1991.

"The Cat, the Mouse, the Girl, and Her Groceries: A True Story," *Drawn & Quarterly* no. 8 (April 1992)

PASCAL BLANCHET

Born in Trois-Rivières, Quebec, in 1980, Pascal has worked as a full-time illustrator since 2004. In 2007, he designed the Drawn & Quarterly bookstore logo and the sign, which still hangs in the front window at 211 Bernard West in the Mile End neighbourhood.

***White Rapids* (Oct 2007); *Baloney* (Feb 2009)**

R.O. BLECHMAN

Oscar Robert Blechman was born in 1930 in Brooklyn, NY. He is an animator, illustrator, and cartoonist. His first graphic novel, *The Juggler of Our Lady*, was published in 1953.

***Talking Lines* (Sept 2009)**

1990

***Drawn & Quarterly* no. 1:** cover, Anne D. Bernstein; inside front cover, Marisa Gelfusa; inside back cover, John Oliveros; back cover, Joe Matt; "Girly-Girl and Her Pal Chuckie-Boy," Peter Bagge; "Out of Control Fantasy Comics," Anne D. Bernstein; "A Dear John Letter from Your Dog on Moving Day," Philip Fine and John Oliveros; "Seven-Second Stories," Robert Leighton; "Three Guys Hard Up on Their Luck," Mailly; "Drawing," Ruth Martinez; "AutoMatt," Joe Matt; "Life After Three Card Monte," Chris Oliveros; "Thermal Dynamics," John Oliveros; "Christmas 1,000,000 B.C.," Alice Sebold and J.D. King; "U.S. Violent Americans," Dennis Worden *(April)*

***Drawn & Quarterly* no. 2:** cover, J.D. King; inside covers, Luc Giard; back cover, Joe Matt; "The Grimaces" and "The Luckville Nearly New Shop," Anne D. Bernstein; "My Conscience Is Bugging Me" and "Robbery," Julie Doucet; "Tuesday, 3:00–3:30: Angst," Philip Fine and John Oliveros; "Doody Doll," Drew Friedman; "The Beastniks," J.D. King; "'E' Emcees Squares," Robert Leighton; "Still Hard Up on His Luck," Mailly; "True-life Stories," Ida Marx; "AutoMatt," Joe Matt; "End Eviction Fears" and "Mean Woman Blues," Carel Moiseiwitsch; "Fake Ads," Anthony Mostrom; "Credo" and "Gloom," Richard Sala; "Foolbert Sturgeon's Cartoon Club," Foolbert Sturgeon; "Friday Night," James Sturm; "The Strange Case of Ross Brown," Dennis Worden *(Oct)*

1991

***Dirty Plotte* no. 1,** Julie Doucet *(Jan)*

***Drawn & Quarterly* no. 3:** cover, Joe Matt; inside front cover, "Zebra," Carel Moiseiwitsch; inside back cover, Eve Damie; back cover, "Mass Denial," Mary Fleener; "Crazy Comix," David Abu Bacha; "Roommate World," Clara Bayliss and David Collier; "Househunting," Anne D. Bernstein; "I'm Home, Working," Rena Cohen and Yayo; "The Fatal Kiss" and "Maybe I Don't Really Exist," Julie Doucet; "The Journey of Ticoune and Marco" and "The Mask," Luc Giard; "AutoMatt," Joe Matt; "Apples and Oranges," Ida Marx; "Untitled," Bernie Mireault;

"The Conspiracy Nuts," Anthony Mostrom; "Magic Marker Comics," John Oliveros; "One of the Wonders of the World," Richard Sala; "The Early Adventures of Paddy Booshwah," Foolbert Sturgeon; "Signs of the Times," James Sturm; "Freak Scene," Carol Swain; "Real Men," Colin Upton; "I'm Having Chest Pains," Wayno *(Jan)*

***Dirty Plotte* no. 2,** Julie Doucet *(March)*

***Drawn & Quarterly* no. 4:** cover and front matter, Chester Brown; logo design, Michel Rabagliati; back cover, "The Boob," Joe Matt; "From the Wires of the Associated Press," Clara Bayliss and David Collier; "At Night," Julie Doucet; "The Creepy Guy Syndrome" and "Black Cherry," Michael Dougan; "Do I Look Like I Work Here?" Mary Fleener; "This Is My House," Luc Giard; "The Mutual Admiration Society," Sebastian Hassinger and Bernie Mireault; "Fly in Your Eye," Patrick Jenkins; "AutoMatt," Joe Matt; "We Hold These Truths to Be Self Evident," Carel Moiseiwitsch; "Don't Talk to Strangers," R.W. Rowland; "A Newlywed's Heartache," Richard Sala; "Why?" Seth; "The Further Adventures of Paddy Booshwah," Foolbert Sturgeon; "Crazey Ole' Hound in 'Ring,'" James Sturm; "'B' Movie," Carol Swain; "Color My Day," Carol Tyler; "Homoman," Maurice Vellekoop *(March)*

***Palookaville* no. 1,** Seth *(April)*

***Drawn & Quarterly* no. 5:** cover, Richard Sala; back cover, "Jefferson," Seth; "The Gross-out Contest," David Abu Bacha and Bernie Mireault; "There's More to Drawing These Comic Strips," David Collier; "An Happy Ending Nightmare," Julie Doucet; "The Extreme Generation," Mary Fleener; "My Father" and "Diane," Luc Giard; "Sexaholics Anonymous," Joe Matt; "Priapic Alphabet," Carel Moiseiwitsch; "Mr. Pig Nose Goes for a Walk," Jeannie Pappas; "The Somnambulist," Richard Sala; "I'm OK/You're Not," Fiona Smyth; "Lullaby of Broadway 1991," Maurice Vellekoop *(June)*

***Dirty Plotte* no. 3,** Julie Doucet *(July)*

***Yummy Fur* no. 25,** Chester Brown *(July)*

***Palookaville* no. 2,** Seth *(Sept)*

***Dirty Plotte* no. 4,** Julie Doucet *(Oct)*

BLUTCH

Blutch was born Christian Hincker in Strasbourg, France, in 1967. He is considered one of the most famous French cartoonists and was discovered by a contest organized by the monthly magazine *Fluide Glacial.*

"Fist to Fist," *Drawn & Quarterly Anthology* vol. 3 (May 2000); "The Boxer," *Drawn & Quarterly Anthology* vol. 4 (July 2001)

JOSÉ-LOUIS BOCQUET

José-Louis was born in Neuilly-sur-Seine, France, in 1962. At age thirteen, he launched his own magazine, called *Bizu*. He moved to Bois-de-la-Roche in 1990.

With Stanislas Barthélémy and Jean-Luc Fromental: "The Adventures of Hergé," *Drawn & Quarterly Anthology* vol. 4 (July 2001); *The Adventures of Hergé* (Nov 2011)

ARIEL BORDEAUX

Ariel was born in Philadelphia in 1968 and grew up in Massachusetts. Her well-regarded 1990s minicomic, *Deep Girl*, was recently collected as a graphic novel. She lives in Rhode Island with her husband and their son.

***No Love Lost* (April 1997)**

KIT BOSS

Kit is a producer and writer on the cult-favourite TV show *Bob's Burgers*.

With Michael Dougan: "Chicken Stories," *Drawn & Quarterly* no. 8 (April 1992)

PASCALE BOUGEAULT

Pascale was born in Bourges, France, in 1958. She studied art history and architecture and has worked as a librarian.

With Anne Baraou: inside back cover, *Drawn & Quarterly* no. 10 (Dec 1992)

CLARE BRIGGS

(1875–1930) Clare was one of the great documenters of late-nineteenth-and early-twentieth-century American life as seen in his many newspaper strips—*When a Feller Needs a Friend, The Days of Real Sport*, and others.

With Wilbur D. Nesbit: *Oh Skin-Nay!: The Days of Real Sport* (March 2007)

RAYMOND BRIGGS

Raymond was born in 1934. He has written one of the most affecting graphic novels of all time—*When the Wind Blows*.

***Gentleman Jim* (July 2008)**

MATT BROERSMA

Matt grew up in South Texas. He has pursued various careers, including a period as a bartender and lounge singer in Japan. He lives in England.

"The Mummy," *Drawn & Quarterly Showcase* vol. 3 (Aug 2005)

CHESTER BROWN

Chester was born in Montreal, Canada, on May 16, 1960, and grew up in the nearby suburb of Chateauguay. At nineteen, he moved to Toronto where he began self-publishing his minicomic *Yummy Fur*, which was eventually reprinted and turned into a series by Canadian publisher Vortex. The first Vortex issue sold well enough that Chester quit his day job and began working full-time as a cartoonist.

Cover and front matter, *Drawn & Quarterly* no. 4 (March 1991); *Yummy Fur* no. 25 (July 1991); *Yummy Fur* no. 26 (Oct 1991); *Yummy Fur* no. 27 (Jan 1992); *Yummy Fur* no. 28 (May 1992); *Yummy Fur* no. 29 (Aug 1992); *The Playboy* (Dec 1992); *Yummy Fur* no. 30 (April 1993); *Yummy Fur* no. 31 (Sept 1993); *Yummy Fur* no. 32 (Jan 1994); *Underwater* no. 1 (Aug 1994); *I Never Liked You* (Nov 1994); *Underwater* no. 2 (Dec 1994); *Underwater* no. 3 (May 1995); *Underwater* no. 4 (Sept 1995); *Underwater* no. 5 (Feb 1996); *Underwater* no. 6 (May 1996); *Underwater* no. 7 (Aug 1996); *Underwater* no. 8 (Dec 1996); *Underwater* no. 9 (April 1997); *Underwater* no. 10 (June 1997); *Underwater* no. 11 (Oct 1997); *The Little Man: Short Strips, 1980–1995* (April 1998); *Louis Riel* no. 1 (Jan 1999); *Louis Riel* no. 2 (Sept 1999); *Louis Riel* no. 3 (Dec 1999); *Louis Riel* no. 4 (May 2000); *Louis Riel* no. 5 (Sept 2000); *Louis Riel* no. 6 (May 2001); *I Never Liked You* (new edition, April 2002); *Louis Riel* no. 7 (June 2002); *Louis Riel* no. 8 (Oct 2002); *Louis Riel* no. 9 (Feb 2003); Louis Riel: A Comic-Strip Biography (Sept 2003); *Ed the Happy Clown* no. 1 (Feb 2005); *Ed the Happy Clown* no. 2 (May 2005);

Ed the Happy Clown no. 3 (Aug 2005); *Ed the Happy Clown* no. 4 (Nov 2005); *Ed the Happy Clown* no. 5 (Jan 2006); *Ed the Happy Clown* no. 6 (March 2006); *Ed the Happy Clown* no. 7 (May 2006); *Ed the Happy Clown* no. 8 (July 2006); *The Little Man: Short Strips, 1980–1995* (new edition, Aug 2006); *Ed the Happy Clown* no. 9 (Sept 2006); *Paying for It* (May 2011); *Ed the Happy Clown* (new edition, June 2012); *The Playboy: A Comic-Strip Memoir* (new edition, May 2013); *Louis Riel: Tenth Anniversary Edition* (Oct 2013)

JEFFREY BROWN

Jeffrey was born in 1975. He first came to prominence with his masterpiece *Clumsy*. More recently, he has created a series of humorous and bestselling Star Wars tie-ins.

"Untitled," *Drawn & Quarterly Showcase* vol. 2 (April 2004)

ED BRUBAKER

Ed was born in 1966. He started drawing alternative comics with his series *Purgatory U.S.A.* but became famous with his work for major publishers DC and Marvel. He has won Eisner Awards on four separate occasions.

With Jason Lutes: *The Fall* (Feb 2001)

GENEVIÈVE CASTRÉE

Geneviève was born in Quebec in 1981. She has known she would be a cartoonist since the age of nine. She entered the Montreal underground scene while she was still a teenager. She draws, makes small sculptures out of porcelain, and plays music under the name Ô PAON. She lives in the Pacific Northwest.

"We're Wolf," *Drawn & Quarterly Showcase* vol. 3 (Aug 2005); *Susceptible* (Feb 2013)

MARTIN CENDREDA

Martin was born and raised in Los Angeles. He's worked on the animated television shows *The Problem Solverz* and *BoJack Horseman*.

"Dog Days," *Drawn & Quarterly Showcase* vol. 4 (June 2006)

GRAHAM CHAFFEE

Graham wrote the graphic novels *Good Dog* and *The Big Wheels*.

"Johnny and Babe," *Drawn & Quarterly* vol. 2, no. 3 (May 1995)

ALBERT CHARTIER

(1912–2004) Albert was probably the most renowned Québécois cartoonist and illustrator of the mid-twentieth century, best known for having created the comic strip *Onésime*.

"Albert Chartier: A Retrospective," *Drawn & Quarterly Anthology* vol. 5 (Aug 2003)

MICHAEL CHO

Michael was born in South Korea and moved to Canada at the age of six. He lives in a nice house in Toronto.

Back Alleys and Urban Landscapes (June 2012)

LAURENT CILLUFFO

Laurent's geometric, carefully constructed drawings have graced the pages of numerous print outlets ranging from the *Boston Globe* to the *Los Angeles Times*. His tiny spot drawings have been published frequently in the pages of the *New Yorker*.

Covers and endpapers, *Drawn & Quarterly* vol. 2, no. 5 (April 1996)

DANIEL CLOWES

Daniel was born in 1961 in Chicago. In 1989, he started the comic series *Eightball*, where his seminal graphic novel *Ghost World* was originally serialized. He lives in Oakland, CA, with his wife and son.

Wilson (April 2010); *The Death-Ray* (Oct 2011)

SANTIAGO COHEN

Santiago was born in Mexico in 1954. He has illustrated numerous children's books and created the graphic novel *The Fifth Name*.

"Letter to Papa," *Drawn & Quarterly* no. 8 (April 1992); "House of Angels," *Drawn & Quarterly* no. 9 (July 1992); front cover and inside front cover, *Drawn & Quarterly* no. 10 (Dec 1992); "Life Cycle" and "House of Angels," *The Best of Drawn & Quarterly* (Dec 1993)

Drawn & Quarterly no. 6: cover, Mary Fleener; inside back cover, "Music," Maurice Vellekoop; back cover, "How to Be Cheap," Joe Matt; "Liquid," Clara Bayliss and David Collier; "A Stubborn Flower," Julie Doucet; "A Miracle on East Third Street," Michael Dougan; "The Statuette," Luc Giard; "Walking on the Moon," Ida Marx; "AutoMatt," Joe Matt; "Sh-Boom," Carel Moiseiwitsch; "Barney's Dream," R.W. Rowland; "Night Sky," Seth; "The Faithless," Fiona Smyth; "The New Adventures of Jesus," Foolbert Sturgeon; "Why I'm A-Gin Southern Min!" Carol Tyler; "A Heterosexual's Guide to Gay Cruising," Maurice Vellekoop (Oct) *Yummy Fur* no. 26, Chester Brown (Oct)

1992

Yummy Fur no. 27, Chester Brown *(Jan)*
Peepshow no. 1, Joe Matt *(Feb)*
Drawn & Quarterly no. 7: cover and inside cover, Pierre Lefebvre and Luc Giard; inside back cover, Bernie Mireault; front matter, Diane Obomsawin; "Another Job Story," Clara Bayliss and David Collier; "Whipped-Up in Wichita," Lloyd Dangle; "Le Baiser," Julie Doucet; "Where the Boys Are," Michael Dougan; "Night of the Oh-So-Very Dead," Dennis P. Eichhorn and Fiona Smyth; "The Yin Yang Man," Mary Fleener; "Talkin' Nineties," Roberta Gregory; "Time-Bomb," Richard Sala; "Some Things I Think You Should Know About Joe Matt," Seth; "8 Pillars of Gay Culture," Maurice Vellekoop *(March)*
Drawn & Quarterly no. 8: cover, Daniel Clowes; inside front cover, "Day of Crabby Art," Maurice Vellekoop; inside back cover, "Can I Ever Tell the Truth About These Trees?" Pierre Lefebvre and Luc Giard; back cover, "Parallel Universe," Maurice Vellekoop; "The Cat, the Mouse, the Girl, and Her Groceries: A True Story," Lee Binswanger; "Letter to Papa," Santiago Cohen; "Chicken Stories," Michael Dougan and Kit Boss; "Speak Up!" Dennis P. Eichhorn and Carol Swain; "That Time of the Month," Roberta Gregory; "I Can't Say What Hit Me," Pierre Lefebvre and Luc Giard; "Like Everyday," Mailly; "Professional Training," Marti; "Camera Obscura" and "The Darkened Room,"

Carel Moiseiwitsch; "On My Day Off,"
Joe Sacco; "Interrupted," Fiona Smyth; "Pie
Kids," Carol Tyler; "Advertising Feature,"
Maurice Vellekoop; "The Meek,"
Gig Wailgum (April)

Slutburger no. 3, Mary Fleener (April)

Dirty Plotte no. 5, Julie Doucet (May)

Peepshow no. 2, Joe Matt (May)

Yummy Fur no. 28, Chester Brown (May)

Drawn & Quarterly no. 9: front cover
and "A Folk Tale," Seth; inside front cover
and "A Brief History of Civilisation," David
Mazzucchelli; back cover, Peter Kuper;
front matter, J.D. King; "Those Tenacious
Teens!" Clara Bayliss and David Collier;
"The Neck," Anne D. Bernstein; "House of
Angels," Santiago Cohen; "My Dad in
Tucson," Lloyd Dangle; "Kentucky Fried
Funeral," Michael Dougan; "Going Steady
in the Seventh Grade," Debbie Drechsler;
"That Night" and "Stevenson Has Found
Another Letter," Pierre Lefebvre and Luc
Giard; "Barcelona," Marti; "Notes from
the Ledge," Carel Moiseiwitsch; "Art
Fantasy," Maurice Vellekoop (July)

Yummy Fur no. 29, Chester Brown (Aug)

Slutburger no. 1, Mary Fleener (Oct)

Peepshow no. 3, Joe Matt (Nov)

Drawn & Quarterly no. 10: front cover
and inside front cover, Santiago Cohen;
front matter, Seth; inside back cover, Anne
Baraou and Pascale Bougeault; back cover,
"Soap Brought to You by Supra-Galaxy," and
"The Secret Life of Gloria Badcock," Maurice
Vellekoop; "Visitors in the Night" and "Making
Friends," Debbie Drechsler; "Within Three
Seconds" and "Claudia," Marti; "Horror in
the Henhouse," John Mullen and Michael
Dougan; "Fate," Francisco Torres Linhart;
"The Old Nazi Guy," Vincent (Dec)

The Playboy, Chester Brown (Dec)

1993

Dirty Plotte no. 6, Julie Doucet (Jan)

Slutburger no. 2, Mary Fleener (Feb)

Peepshow no. 4, Joe Matt (April)

Yummy Fur no. 30, Chester Brown (April)

Dangle no. 1, Lloyd Dangle (May)

MAREK COLEK

Marek is a Toronto-based animator and illustrator. He collaborates with Pat Shewchuk under the name Tin Can Forest.

With Pat Shewchuk: Pohadky (Oct 2008)

DAVID COLLIER

David was born in 1963 in Windsor, Ontario. He has been in the Canadian Army and currently lives in Hamilton, Ontario.

"There's More to Drawing These Comic Strips," *Drawn & Quarterly* no. 5 (June 1991); *Just the Facts: A Decade of Comics Essays* (Oct 1998); *Humphrey Osmond: Psychedelic Pioneer* (Dec 1998); *Surviving Saskatoon* (July 2000); *Portraits from Life* (March 2001); *Collier's* vol. 2, no. 1 (Feb 2002); *The Hamilton Sketchbook* (June 2002); *Collier's* vol. 2, no. 2 (March 2003); *The Frank Ritza Papers* (Sept 2004) **With Clara Bayliss:** "Roommate World," *Drawn & Quarterly* no. 3 (Jan 1991); "From the Wires of the Associated Press," *Drawn & Quarterly* no. 4 (March 1991); "Liquid," *Drawn & Quarterly* no. 6 (Oct 1991); "Another Job Story," *Drawn & Quarterly* no. 7 (March 1992); "Those Tenacious Teens!" *Drawn & Quarterly* no. 9 (July 1992); "Liquid," *The Best of Drawn & Quarterly* (Dec 1993)

SEAN T. COLLINS

Sean is a comics writer and pop culture journalist who often writes for national magazines like *Rolling Stone* and *Wired*.

R. CRUMB

Robert was born in 1943 in Philadelphia. He rose to prominence in the underground comics scene when his work appeared in *Zap* in 1968. Much of his work appeared in the magazine he founded, *Weirdo* (1981–1993).

Waiting for Food (March 2004)

LLOYD DANGLE

Lloyd was the cartoonist of the long-running comic strip *Trouble Town* from 1988–2011. He now does commercial work and lives in New York.

"Whipped-Up in Wichita," *Drawn & Quarterly* no. 7 (March 1992); "My Dad in Tucson," *Drawn & Quarterly* no. 9 (July 1992); *Dangle* no. 1 (new edition, May 1993); *Dangle* no. 2 (new edition, May 1993); *Dangle* no. 3 (new edition, Jan 1994); *Dangle* no. 4 (new edition, Dec 1995)

VANESSA DAVIS

Vanessa was born in 1978 in West Palm Beach, FL. She is an exceptional cook. She currently lives in Los Angeles.

Make Me a Woman (Sept 2010)

MICHAEL DEFORGE

Michael was born in 1987 and grew up in Ottawa, Ontario. After a few years of experimenting with short strips and zines, he created *Lose* no. 1, his first full-length comic. He lives in Toronto.

Ant Colony (Jan 2014); *First Year Healthy* (Jan 2015)

ERIK DE GRAAF

Erik has worked as a graphic designer in Holland since the 1980s. In the early 2000s he started writing and drawing comics.

Endpapers and "Game," *Drawn & Quarterly Showcase* vol. 2 (April 2004)

GUY DELISLE

Guy was born in Quebec City in 1966. He is best known for his "stranger-in-a-strange-land" travelogues that he created traveling with his wife who worked as an administrator for Doctors Without Borders. *Jerusalem* won the Best Book Prize at the Angoulême Comics Festival. He lives in the south of France with his family.

Pyongyang: A Journey in North Korea (Sept 2005); *Shenzhen: A Travelogue from China* (Oct 2006); *Aline and the Others* (Dec 2006); *Albert and the Others* (Feb 2008); *Burma Chronicles* (Sept 2008); *Jerusalem: Chronicles from the Holy City* (April 2012); *A User's Guide to Neglectful Parenting* (June 2013); *Even More Bad Parenting Advice* (Aug 2014)

JACQUES DE LOUSTAL

Jacques was born in 1956 in Neuilly-Sur-Seine. He goes by the pen name "Loustal." He has published over sixty comics, art books, and illustrated titles.

With Jean-Luc Fromental: "The Ghost of Whitechapel," *Drawn & Quarterly* vol. 2, no. 2 (Dec 1994)

JULIE DELPORTE

Julie was born in Saint-Malo, France, in 1983. She has been a fellow at the Center for Cartoon Studies. She lives in Montreal.

Everywhere Antennas (May 2014)

JULIE DOUCET

Julie was born in 1965 in the Montreal suburb of Saint-Lambert. She started publishing her minicomics in the late 1980s and became the first cartoonist with a solo title for Drawn & Quarterly. She quit drawing comics to explore other art forms but readers still ask her if she's "working on anything these days."

"My Conscience is Bugging Me" and "Robbery," *Drawn & Quarterly* no. 2 (Oct 1990); *Dirty Plotte* no. 1 (Jan 1991); "The Fatal Kiss" and "Maybe I Don't Really Exist," *Drawn & Quarterly* no. 3 (Jan 1991); *Dirty Plotte* no. 2 (March 1991); "At Night," *Drawn & Quarterly* no. 4 (March 1991); "An Happy Ending Nightmare," *Drawn & Quarterly* no. 5 (June 1991); *Dirty Plotte* no. 3 (July 1991); *Dirty Plotte* no. 4 (Oct 1991); "A Stubborn Flower," *Drawn & Quarterly* no. 6 (Oct 1991); "Le Baiser," *Drawn & Quarterly* no. 7 (March 1992); *Dirty Plotte* no. 5 (May 1992); *Dirty Plotte* no. 6 (Jan 1993); *Dirty Plotte* no. 7 (Sept 1993); *Lève Ta Jambe, Mon Poisson Est Mort* (Oct 1993); "So...Your Place or Mine?" and "At Night Coming Home," *The Best of Drawn & Quarterly* (Dec 1993); *Dirty Plotte* no. 8 (Feb 1994); *Dirty Plotte* no. 9 (April 1995); *My Most Secret Desire* (Sept 1995); *Dirty Plotte* no. 10 (Dec 1996); *Dirty Plotte* no. 11 (Sept 1997); *Dirty Plotte* no. 12 (Aug 1998); *My New York Diary* (May 1999); *The Madame Paul Affair* (Aug 2000); *Long Time Relationship* (July 2001); *Lady Pep* (Dec 2004); *365 Days: A Diary* (Jan 2008)

MICHAEL DOUGAN

Michael was born in East Texas and was a mainstay of comics anthologies throughout the 1980s into the '90s. He is the author of two books: *East Texas: Tales from Behind the Pine Curtain* and *I Can't Tell You Anything*.

"The Creepy Guy Syndrome" and "Black Cherry," *Drawn & Quarterly* no. 4 (March 1991); "A Miracle on East Third Street," *Drawn & Quarterly* no. 6 (Oct 1991); "Where the Boys Are," *Drawn & Quarterly* no. 7 (March 1992); "Kentucky Fried Funeral," *Drawn & Quarterly* no. 9 (July 1992); "Black Cherry" and "The Creepy Guy Syndrome," *The Best of Drawn & Quarterly* (Dec 1993)

With Kit Boss: "Chicken Stories," *Drawn & Quarterly* no. 8 (April 1992)

With John Mullen: "Horror in the Henhouse," *Drawn & Quarterly* no. 10 (Dec 1992)

DEBBIE DRECHSLER

Debbie was born in 1953 in Champaign, IL. She currently lives in Santa Rosa, CA, with her husband and dog.

"Going Steady in the Seventh Grade," *Drawn & Quarterly* no. 9 (July 1992); "Visitors in the Night" and "Making Friends," *Drawn & Quarterly* no. 10 (Dec 1992); "Visitors in the Night" and "Constellations," *The Best of Drawn & Quarterly* (Dec 1993); *Nowhere* no. 1 (Oct 1996); *Nowhere* no. 2 (May 1997); *Nowhere* no. 3 (Nov 1997); *Nowhere* no. 4 (July 1998); *Nowhere* no. 5 (April 1999); *The Summer of Love* (July 2002; new edition, June 2003)

ERIC DROOKER

Eric illustrated the wordless graphic novels *Flood!* and *Blood Song*. He is a frequent cover artist for the *New Yorker*.

"Eleanor," *Drawn & Quarterly* vol. 2, no. 2 (Dec 1994)

MICHAEL DUMONTIER

Michael was born in 1974 in Winnipeg. He is a co-founder of the influential Winnipeg art collective, Royal Art Lodge. Since the dissolution of the collective, Dumontier and fellow co-founder Neil Farber continue to work and create art together. They both reside in Winnipeg.

With Neil Farber: *Constructive Abandonment* (May 2011); *Animals with Sharpies* (June 2013)

PHILIPPE DUPUY

Philippe was born in Paris in 1960. He published his first comic twenty years later. Almost all of his work until recently has been in collaboration with Charles Berbérian.

Haunted (March 2008)

With Charles Berbérian: "Monsieur Jean," *Drawn & Quarterly* vol. 2, no. 4 (Dec 1995); "A Trip to Lisbon,"

Dangle no. 2, Lloyd Dangle *(May)*
Palookaville no. 3, Seth *(June)*
Dirty Plotte no. 7, Julie Doucet *(Sept)*
Slutburger no. 4, Mary Fleener *(Sept)*
Yummy Fur no. 31, Chester Brown *(Sept)*
Lève Ta Jambe, Mon Poisson Est Mort, Julie Doucet *(Oct)*
Peepshow no. 5, Joe Matt *(Oct)*
Palookaville no. 4, Seth *(Dec)*
The Best of Drawn & Quarterly: covers and endpapers, "8 Pillars of Gay Culture," "Homoman," "Music," and "Night Job," Maurice Vellekoop; front and end matter, "Life Cycle," and "House of Angels," Santiago Cohen; "Liquid," Clara Bayliss and David Collier; "So...Your Place or Mine?" and "At Night Coming Home," Julie Doucet; "Black Cherry" and "Creepy Guy Syndrome," Michael Dougan; "Visitors in the Night" and "Constellations," Debbie Drechsler; "A Dear John Letter from Your Dog on Moving Day," Philip Fine and John Oliveros; "The Extreme Generation," Mary Fleener; "My Father's a Brain Specialist," Luc Giard; "Talkin' Nineties," Roberta Gregory; "Geometrical Beastniks," J.D. King; "(@!#¡%)," Peter Kuper; "Claudia" and "Within Three Seconds," Marti; "My Darkest Secret" and "Aug. 16, 1989," Joe Matt; "A Brief History of Civilisation," David Mazzucchelli; "Sh-Boom," Carel Moiseiwitsch; "Credo," Richard Sala; "Night Sky," "A Folk Tale," and "Why?" Seth; "Fate," Francisco Torres Linhart; "Why I'm A-Gin Southern Min!" Carol Tyler; "The Strange Case of Ross Brown," Dennis Worden *(Dec)*

1994
Yummy Fur no. 32, Chester Brown *(Jan)*
Dangle no. 3, Lloyd Dangle *(Jan)*
Dirty Plotte no. 8, Julie Doucet *(Feb)*
Peepshow no. 6, Joe Matt *(April)*
Palookaville no. 5, Seth *(May)*
Drawn & Quarterly vol. 2, no. 1: covers and endpapers, Seth; "63, Rue de la Grange aux Belles," Avril and Petit-Roulet; "Personals," Marcellus Hall; "It Was the War of the Trenches," Jacques Tardi;

"The Hannah Story," Carol Tyler; "The Same Old Story," Maurice Vellekoop *(Aug)*
Underwater **no. 1,** Chester Brown *(Aug)*
I Never Liked You, Chester Brown *(Nov)*
Palookaville **no. 6,** Seth *(Nov)*
Drawn & Quarterly **vol. 2, no. 2:** covers, endpapers, and "Rates of Exchange," David Mazzucchelli; "Eleanor," Eric Drooker; "The Ghost of Whitechapel," Jacques de Loustal and Jean-Luc Fromental; "It Was the War of the Trenches," Jacques Tardi; "More Than Coincidence?" Maurice Vellekoop *(Dec)*
Underwater **no. 2,** Chester Brown *(Dec)*

1995

Peepshow **no. 7,** Joe Matt *(March)*
Dirty Plotte **no. 9,** Julie Doucet *(April)*
Optic Nerve **no. 1,** Adrian Tomine *(April)*
Palookaville **no. 7,** Seth *(April)*
Drawn & Quarterly **vol. 2, no. 3:** covers and endpapers, J.D. King; "Johnny and Babe," Graham Chaffee; "Bicycle Thief," Pentti Otsamo; "It Was the War of the Trenches," Jacques Tardi; "Side Door Lover," Maurice Vellekoop *(May)*
Underwater **no. 3,** Chester Brown *(May)*
Fabulous Babes **no. 1,** Maurice Vellekoop, Fiona Smyth, and Roxanna Bikadoroff *(July)*
Peepshow **no. 8,** Joe Matt *(July)*
Flowers, Nelson Hagood and Anthony Baker *(Aug)*
My Most Secret Desire, Julie Doucet *(Sept)*
Slutburger **no. 5,** Mary Fleener *(Sept)*
Underwater **no. 4,** Chester Brown *(Sept)*
Optic Nerve **no. 2,** Adrian Tomine *(Nov)*
Dangle **no. 4,** Lloyd Dangle *(Dec)*
Drawn & Quarterly **vol. 2, no. 4:** cover and endpapers, Josh Gosfield; "The Road to America," Baru; "Monsieur Jean," Dupuy and Berbérian; "Sof' Boy," Archer Prewitt; "Good Grief!" Seth; "Gone," Carol Tyler; "A Day in the Life of Pierre Pouffé," Maurice Vellekoop *(Dec)*
Palookaville **no. 8,** Seth *(Dec)*

1996

Underwater **no. 5,** Chester Brown *(Feb)*
Drawn & Quarterly **vol. 2, no. 5:** covers and

Drawn & Quarterly **vol. 2, no. 6 (June 1997); "Monsieur Jean,"** ***Drawn & Quarterly Anthology*** **vol. 3 (May 2000); "Monsieur Jean,"** ***Drawn & Quarterly Anthology*** **vol. 5 (Aug 2003);** ***Get a Life*** **(July 2006);** ***Maybe Later*** **(July 2006)**

DENNIS P. EICHHORN

Dennis was born in 1945 in Deer Lodge, MT. He has written comics that have been illustrated by nearly every practising underground cartoonist from 1985 through 1990. He lives in Bremerton, WA.

With Fiona Smyth: "Night of the Oh-So-Very Dead," ***Drawn & Quarterly*** **no. 7 (March 1992)**
With Carol Swain: "Speak Up!" ***Drawn & Quarterly*** **no. 8 (April 1992)**

BRECHT EVENS

Brecht was born in 1986 in Belgium. He studied illustration in Gent and is now a cartoonist and painter in Paris. His first book won a prize for "audacity" at the Angoulême Comics Festival.

The Wrong Place **(Nov 2010);** ***The Making Of*** **(Aug 2012)**

NEIL FARBER

Neil was born in Winnipeg in 1975. He was a founding member of the Royal Art Lodge with Marcel Dzama amd Michael Dumontier. He still collaborates regularly with Michael.

With Michael Dumontier: ***Constructive Abandonment*** **(May 2011);** ***Animals with Sharpies*** **(June 2013)**

PHILIP FINE

Philip was born in Ontario in 1963 and grew up in Chomedey, Quebec, one street over from Chris Oliveros. He now lives in Montreal, one street over from Tom and Peggy. He works as a writer and editor for CBC Radio in Montreal.

With John Oliveros: "A Dear John Letter from Your Dog on Moving Day," ***Drawn & Quarterly*** **no. 1 (April 1990); "Tuesday, 3:00–3:30: Angst,"** ***Drawn & Quarterly*** **no. 2 (Oct 1990); "A Dear John Letter from Your Dog on Moving Day,"** ***The Best of Drawn & Quarterly*** **(Dec 1993)**

MARY FLEENER

Mary was born in 1951. She is one of the most personally entertaining of the second-generation cartoonists. She lives in San Diego.

"Mass Denial," ***Drawn & Quarterly*** **no. 3 (Jan 1991); "Do I Look Like I Work Here?"** ***Drawn & Quarterly*** **no. 4 (March 1991); "The Extreme Generation,"** ***Drawn & Quarterly*** **no. 5 (June 1991); cover,** ***Drawn & Quarterly*** **no. 6 (Oct 1991); "The Yin Yang Man,"** ***Drawn & Quarterly*** **no. 7 (March 1992);** ***Slutburger*** **no. 3 (April 1992);** ***Slutburger*** **no. 1 (Oct 1992);** ***Slutburger*** **no. 2 (Feb 1993);** ***Slutburger*** **no. 4 (Feb 1993); "The Extreme Generation,"** ***The Best of Drawn & Quarterly*** **(Dec 1993);** ***Slutburger*** **no. 5 (Sept 1995)**

MATTHEW FORSYTHE

Matt was born in Toronto in 1976. He was the lead designer on *Adventure Time* at Cartoon Network and he has also illustrated children's books, including the award-winning *My Name is Elizabeth!*

Ojingogo **(Feb 2009);** ***Jinchalo*** **(Feb 2012)**

AISHA FRANZ

Aisha was born in Fürth, Germany, in 1984 and was named after an elephant from TV. She currently lives in Berlin, where she's part of the comics collective the Treasure Fleet.

Earthling **(Nov 2014)**

DON FREEMAN

(1908–1978) Don, born in San Diego, was an American printmaker, cartoonist, and children's book author. He is best known for his book *Corduroy*. Don was also a jazz musician.

Skitzy: The Story of Floyd W. Skitzafroid **(Dec 2008)**

DREW FRIEDMAN

Drew was born in 1958 in New York. He was first published in *RAW* in 1980 and has since gone on to have his comics and illustrations published by virtually every major print outlet in North America, from the *Wall Street Journal* to *MAD* magazine.

"Doody Doll," ***Drawn & Quarterly*** **no. 2 (Oct 1990)**

JEAN-LUC FROMENTAL

Jean-Luc was born in Tunisia in 1950. His work has routinely appeared in the celebrated French comics magazine *Métal Hurlant*.

With Jacques de Loustal: "The Ghost of Whitechapel," *Drawn & Quarterly* vol. 2, no. 2 (Dec 1994)

With José-Louis Bocquet and Stanislas Barthélémy: "The Adventures of Hergé," *Drawn & Quarterly Anthology* vol. 4 (July 2001); *The Adventures of Hergé* (Nov 2011)

ANNELI FURMARK

Anneli was born in 1962 in Vallentuna, Sweden. She won the Urhunden (a Swedish comics award) twice: in 2005 for the album *Amatörernas Afton* and in 2008 for *Jamen Förlåt Da.*

"Inland," *Drawn & Quarterly Showcase* vol. 5 (Aug 2008)

JOHN GALLANT

(1917–2011) John was born in Prince Edward Island. He collaborated with his son Seth on a memoir of his childhood.

With Seth: *Bannock, Beans and Black Tea: Memories of a Prince Edward Island Childhood in the Great Depression* (May 2004)

MIGUEL GALLARDO

Miguel was part of the first wave of cartoonists to emerge in the post-Franco period in Spain in the late 1970s. He co-created the popular character Makoki before moving on to autobiographical comics in the 1990s and early 2000s.

"Red, Blue and Black," *Drawn & Quarterly* vol. 2, no. 6 (June 1997)

TOM GAULD

Tom was born in Aberdeen, Scotland, in 1976. He grew up in an actual castle or part of a dilapidated castle. He studied illustration at Edinburgh College of Art. He lives in London, England, with his partner and two daughters.

Goliath (Feb 2012); *You're All Just Jealous of My Jetpack* (April 2013)

TAVI GEVINSON

Tavi was born in 1996 in Oak Park, IL. She created her fashion blog *Style Rookie*

at age eleven. She is editor-in-chief of *Rookie* magazine.

Rookie Yearbook One (Sept 2012); *Rookie Yearbook Two* (Oct 2013)

LUC GIARD

Luc was born in 1956 in Saint-Hyacinthe, Quebec. He likes drawing Tintin. He lives in Montreal.

Inside cover, *Drawn & Quarterly* no. 2 (Oct 1990); "The Journey of Ticoune and Marco" and "The Mask," *Drawn & Quarterly* no. 3 (Jan 1991); "This Is My House," *Drawn & Quarterly* no. 4 (March 1991); "My Father" and "Diane," *Drawn & Quarterly* no. 5 (June 1991); "The Statuette," *Drawn & Quarterly* no. 6 (Oct 1991); "My Father's a Brain Specialist," *The Best of Drawn & Quarterly* (Dec 1993); *A Village Under My Pillow* (April 2005)

With Pierre Lefebvre: cover and inside cover, *Drawn & Quarterly* no. 7 (March 1992); "I Can't Say What Hit Me," *Drawn & Quarterly* no. 8 (April 1992); "That Night" and "Stevenson Has Found Another Letter," *Drawn & Quarterly* no. 9 (July 1992)

PASCAL GIRARD

Pascal was born in Jonquière, Quebec, in 1981. He began filling his notebook with drawings on his very first day of school and never stopped. Since he was unable to rid himself of this habit, he naturally decided to make it his career and become a cartoonist. He lives in Montreal and is good friends with Tom and Peggy's son, Woody.

Nicolas (Feb 2009); *Bigfoot* (Dec 2010); *Reunion* (April 2011); *Petty Theft* (May 2014)

SARAH GLIDDEN

Sarah was born in 1980 in Boston, MA, and studied painting at Boston University. Her first graphic novel, *How to Understand Israel in 60 Days or Less*, has been translated into French, German, Spanish, Italian, and Dutch.

Rolling Blackouts (forthcoming)

JOSH GOSFIELD

Josh worked for ten years as art director for *New York* magazine before embarking on a

endpapers, Laurent Cilluffo; "The Road to America," Baru; "The Dead of Winter," Debbie Drechsler; "Fishing," Pentti Otsamo; "Dora the Living Doll," Maurice Vellekoop (April)

Peepshow no. 9, Joe Matt (April)

Underwater no. 6, Chester Brown (May)

Palookaville no. 9, Seth (June)

Optic Nerve no. 3, Adrian Tomine (Aug)

Underwater no. 7, Chester Brown (Aug)

It's a Good Life, If You Don't Weaken, Seth (Sept)

32 Stories: The Complete Optic Nerve Mini-Comics, Adrian Tomine (Oct)

Nowhere no. 1, Debbie Drechsler (Oct)

Dirty Plotte no. 10, Julie Doucet (Dec)

Underwater no. 8, Chester Brown (Dec)

1997

No Love Lost, Ariel Bordeaux (April)

Optic Nerve no. 4, Adrian Tomine (April)

Underwater no. 9, Chester Brown (April)

Nowhere no. 2, Debbie Drechsler (May)

Palookaville no. 10, Seth (May)

Drawn & Quarterly vol. 2, no. 6: covers, endpapers, and "Orpheus," Max; "The Road to America," Baru; "A Trip to Lisbon," Dupuy and Berbérian; "Red, Blue and Black," Miguel Gallardo; "Late Summer Sun," Jason Lutes; "Tout Va Bien," Francisco Torres Linhart; "Waiting" and "Artwork," Maurice Vellekoop (June)

Underwater no. 10, Chester Brown (June)

Peepshow no. 10, Joe Matt (July)

The Poor Bastard, Joe Matt (Aug)

Dirty Plotte no. 11, Julie Doucet (Sept)

Palookaville no. 11, Seth (Oct)

Sleepwalk and Other Stories, Adrian Tomine (Oct)

Sof' Boy and Friends no. 1, Archer Prewitt (Oct)

Underwater no. 11, Chester Brown (Oct)

Vellevision, Maurice Vellekoop (Nov)

Nowhere no. 3, Debbie Drechsler (Nov)

1998

Berlin no. 4, Jason Lutes (Feb)

Optic Nerve no. 5, Adrian Tomine (Feb)

Soba: Stories from Bosnia, Joe Sacco (Feb)

The Little Man: Short Strips, 1980–1995, Chester Brown (April)

Palookaville no. 12, Seth *(May)*
Peepshow no. 11, Joe Matt *(June)*
Hundreds of Feet Below Daylight, James Sturm *(July)*
Nowhere no. 4, Debbie Drechsler *(July)*
Dirty Plotte no. 12, Julie Doucet *(Aug)*
Sof' Boy and Friends no. 2, Archer Prewitt *(Aug)*
The Extended Dream of Mr. D no. 1, Max *(Sept)*
Just the Facts: A Decade of Comics Essays, David Collier *(Oct)*
Berlin no. 5, Jason Lutes *(Dec)*
Humphrey Osmond: Psychedelic Pioneer, David Collier *(Dec)*

1999

Louis Riel no. 1, Chester Brown *(Jan)*
Homunculus: A Picture Novella in Six Parts, Pentti Otsamo *(Jan)*
The Extended Dream of Mr. D no. 2, Max *(Jan)*
Berlin no. 1, Jason Lutes *(Feb)*
Optic Nerve no. 6, Adrian Tomine *(Feb)*
Nowhere no. 5, Debbie Drechsler *(April)*
My New York Diary, Julie Doucet *(May)*
The Extended Dream of Mr. D no. 3, Max *(May)*
Palookaville no. 13, Seth *(July)*
Berlin no. 6, Jason Lutes *(Aug)*
Louis Riel no. 2, Chester Brown *(Sept)*
Drawn & Quarterly Year 2000 Calendar *(Sept)*
Louis Riel no. 3, Chester Brown *(Dec)*
The Extended Dream of Mr. D, Max *(Dec)*

2000

Peepshow: The Cartoon Diary of Joe Matt, Joe Matt *(March)*
Berlin no. 7, Jason Lutes *(April)*
Peepshow no. 12, Joe Matt *(April)*
Drawn & Quarterly Anthology vol. 3: covers and endpapers, Chris Ware; "Fist to Fist," Blutch; "Monsieur Jean," Dupuy and Berbérian; "Gasoline Alley," Frank King; "The Peasant and the Snake," Mark Lang; "Safety Instructions," Jason Little; "Two Stories," Franco Matticchio; "The Other One," Harry Mayerovitch; "The Shepherd," Pentti Otsamo; "Paul: Apprentice Typographer," Michel Rabagliati; "Sketchbook," Seth; "Dostoyevsky Comics," R. Sikoryak *(May)*
Louis Riel no. 4, Chester Brown *(May)*

successful illustration career, a highlight being his iconic Malcolm X cover for the *New Yorker*.
Cover and endpapers, *Drawn & Quarterly* vol. 2, no. 4 (Dec 1995)

ROBERTA GREGORY

Roberta was born in 1953 in Los Angeles, CA. She drew the comic book *Naughty Bits* for several years and is one of the most important female cartoonists from the second-generation underground.
"Talkin' Nineties," *Drawn & Quarterly* no. 7 (March 1992); "That Time of the Month," *Drawn & Quarterly* no. 8 (April 1992); "Talkin' Nineties," *The Best of Drawn & Quarterly* (Dec 1993)

STEVEN GUARNACCIA

Steven is an illustrator, designer, and associate professor of illustration at Parsons The New School for Design.
Covers and endpapers, *Drawn & Quarterly Anthology* vol. 4 (July 2001)

MARCELLUS HALL

Marcellus was born in Minneapolis. He has had dual careers, working simultaneously as a musician and an illustrator. He's fronted several bands.
"Personals," *Drawn & Quarterly* vol. 2, no. 1 (Aug 1994)

LISA HANAWALT

Lisa grew up in Palo Alto, CA. In 2008, Lisa self-published *Stay Away From Other People*, establishing her comic-making style of funny illustrated lists and anthropomorphized animals. She lives in Los Angeles and is the character designer for *BoJack Horseman*.
***My Dirty Dumb Eyes* (May 2013)**

SAMMY HARKHAM

Sammy was born in Los Angeles in 1980. He splits his time between the US and Australia. He is the founding editor of the influential comics anthology *Kramers Ergot*.
"Somersaulting," *Drawn & Quarterly Showcase* vol. 3 (Aug 2005); *Crickets* no. 1 (Jan 2006); *Crickets* no. 2 (Jan 2008)

SEIICHI HAYASHI

Seiichi was born on March 7, 1945, in Manchuria, China. He is one of the most prominent avant-garde cartoonists of the 1960s and '70s in Japan.
***Red Colored Elegy* (July 2008)**

JEET HEER

Jeet is a journalist who has written for the *National Post*, *Boston Globe*, and others. He has written extensively on comics and contributed essays to the *Walt & Skeezix*, *Krazy & Ignatz*, and *Little Orphan Annie* archival series.
***Oh, Skin-Nay!: The Days of Real Sport* (March 2007); *Walt & Skeezix: Book One, 1921–1922* (June 2005); *Walt & Skeezix: Book Two, 1923–1924* (Aug 2006); *Walt & Skeezix: Book Three, 1925–1926* (Oct 2007); *Walt & Skeezix: Book Four, 1927–1928* (April 2010); *Walt & Skeezix: Book Five, 1929–1930* (Dec 2011); *Walt Before Skeezix* (June 2014)**

GILBERT HERNANDEZ

Gilbert was born in 1957 in Oxnard, CA, a middle child in a family of six children. Alongside his brothers Jaime and Mario, Gilbert co-created and contributed to the acclaimed comic-book series *Love and Rockets*.
***Marble Season* (April 2013); *Bumperhead* (Sept 2014)**

PABLO HOLMBERG

Pablo was born in 1979 in Buenos Aires, Argentina. Pablo's comics have been serialized each week on his website since 2004.
***Eden* (Aug 2010)**

TOM HORACEK

Tom draws a gag comic called *Foolish Mortals*.
***All We Ever Do Is Talk About Wood* (Nov 2008)**

DYLAN HORROCKS

Dylan was born in 1966 and lives in Auckland, New Zealand, with his wife and two teenage sons. He has written and drawn the comic-book series *Pickle* (Black Eye) and *Atlas* (Drawn & Quarterly).
***Atlas* no. 1 (Sept 2001); *Hicksville* (March 2002); *Atlas* no. 2 (Feb 2006); *Atlas* no. 3 (Dec 2006); *Hicksville* (new edition, Jan 2010)**

KEVIN HUIZENGA

Kevin was born in 1977 in Harvey, IL, and spent most of his childhood in South Holland, IL, near Chicago. He lives in St. Louis, MO.

"Glenn Ganges," *Drawn & Quarterly Showcase* vol. 1 (Sept 2003); *Or Else* no. 1 (Oct 2004); *Or Else* no. 2 (Jan 2005); *Or Else* no. 3 (Aug 2005); *Or Else* no. 4 (March 2006); *Curses* (Dec 2006); *Or Else* no. 5 (Oct 2008); *The Wild Kingdom* (Aug 2010); *Gloriana* (June 2012)

LAURENCE HYDE

(1914–1987) Laurence was born in England and later immigrated to Canada. He was a wood engraver, designer, and filmmaker—and wrote and illustrated books for adults and children.

***Southern Cross: A Novel of the South Seas* (Oct 2007)**

IGORT

Igort was born Igor Tuveri in 1958, in Sardinia. He is a cartoonist and illustrator as well as the publisher of Coconino Press.

***5 Is the Perfect Number* (Nov 2003)**

LARS JANSSON

(1926–2000) Lars became a published author at sixteen. He taught himself how to draw when he replaced his older sister, Tove, on the *Moomin* comic strip.

***Moomin: The Complete Tove Jansson Comic Strip* vol. 3 (Sept 2008); *Moomin: The Complete Tove Jansson Comic Strip* vol. 4 (May 2009); *Moomin: The Complete Tove Jansson Comic Strip* vol. 5 (July 2010); *Moomin: The Complete Lars Jansson Comic Strip* vol. 6 (May 2011); *Moomin: The Complete Lars Jansson Comic Strip* vol. 7 (Sept 2012); *Moomin: The Complete Lars Jansson Comic Strip* vol. 8 (Oct 2013); *Moomin: The Complete Lars Jansson Comic Strip* vol. 9 (July 2014)**

TOVE JANSSON

(1914–2001) Tove was a legendary Finnish children's book author, artist, and creator of the Moomins. The Moomins are featured in children's books, comic strips, theatre, opera, film, radio, theme parks, and TV.

***Moomin: The Complete Tove Jansson Comic Strip* vol. 1 (Nov 2006); *Moomin: The Complete Tove Jansson Comic Strip* vol. 2 (Oct 2007); *Moomin: The Complete Tove Jansson Comic Strip* vol. 3 (Sept 2008); *Moomin: The Complete Tove Jansson Comic Strip* vol. 4 (May 2009); *The Book About Moomin, Mymble and Little My* (Oct 2009); *Moomin: The Complete Tove Jansson Comic Strip* vol. 5 (July 2010); *Who Will Comfort Toffle?* (Sept 2010); *Moominvally Turns Jungle* (Oct 2012); *Moomin's Winter Follies* (Oct 2012); *Moomin Builds a House* (March 2013); *Moomin Falls in Love* (March 2013); *Moomin and the Comet* (Oct 2013); *Moomin and the Sea* (Oct 2013); *Moomin and the Golden Tail* (Feb 2014); *Moomin's Desert Island* (Feb 2014); *Moomin on the Riviera* (Sept 2014); *Moomin: The Deluxe Anniversary Edition* (Oct 2014)**

KEITH JONES

Keith is a fine artist, Canadian doodler, and cartoonist. He briefly owned a hot dog restaurant in Toronto.

***Bacter-Area* (Jan 2005); *Catland Empire* (June 2010)**

MIRIAM KATIN

Miriam was born in Hungary during World War II. She later immigrated to Israel and then the US, where she worked on *Daria* and other shows for MTV and Disney.

***We Are On Our Own: A Memoir* (May 2006); *Letting It Go* (March 2013)**

SUSUMU KATSUMATA

(1943–2007) Susumu got his start in *Garo*, and became an award-winning *manga-ka*.

***Red Snow* (Nov 2009)**

KERASCOËT

Kerascoët is the pen name of husband-wife team Marie Pommepuy and Sébastien Cosset. They live in France.

With Fabien Vehlmann: *Beautiful Darkness* (Feb 2014)

J.D. KING

J.D.'s comics career bridged between the first and second generations of underground cartoonists. He is primarily known as an illustrator.

Cover and "The Beastniks," *Drawn & Quarterly* no. 2 (Oct 1990); front matter, *Drawn & Quarterly* no. 9 (July 1992); "Geometrical Beastniks," *The Best*

***Palookaville* no. 14,** Seth *(May)*
***Optic Nerve* no. 7,** Adrian Tomine *(June)*
***Surviving Saskatoon*,** David Collier *(July)*
***The Madame Paul Affair*,** Julie Doucet *(Aug)*
***Louis Riel* no. 5,** Chester Brown *(Sept)*
***Paul in the Country*,** Michel Rabagliati *(Oct)*
***Berlin* no. 8,** Jason Lutes *(Dec)*

2001

***Berlin: City of Stones*,** Jason Lutes *(Feb)*
***The Fall*,** Ed Brubaker and Jason Lutes *(Feb)*
***Portraits from Life*,** David Collier *(March)*
***Louis Riel* no. 6,** Chester Brown *(May)*
***Palookaville* no. 15,** Seth *(May)*
***Palookaville* no. 1,** Seth *(tenth anniversary edition, June)*
***Drawn & Quarterly Anthology* vol. 4:** covers and endpapers, Steven Guarnaccia; "The Boxer," Blutch; "The Adventures of Hergé," José-Louis Bocquet, Jean-Luc Fromental, and Stanislas Barthélémy; "Oh, To Celebrate!" Miriam Katin; "Gasoline Alley," Frank King; "Poster Gallery," Harry Mayerovitch; "We Must Know We Will Know," Ron Regé, Jr.; "Bleeding Tree," Nicolas Robel; "Little Pearl," R. Sikoryak *(July)*
***Long Time Relationship*,** Julie Doucet *(July)*
***The Golem's Mighty Swing*,** James Sturm *(July)*
***Atlas* no. 1,** Dylan Horrocks *(Sept)*
***Optic Nerve* no. 8,** Adrian Tomine *(Sept)*
***Jar of Fools*,** Jason Lutes *(Sept)*
***Vernacular Drawings*,** Seth *(Dec)*

2002

***Collier's* vol. 2, no. 1** (also known as Dennis Coté Was Good and Bad), David Collier *(Feb)*
***Peepshow* no. 13,** Joe Matt *(Feb)*
***Hicksville*,** Dylan Horrocks *(March)*
***Road to America*,** Baru *(March)*
***I Never Liked You*,** Chester Brown *(new edition, April)*
***Summer Blonde*,** Adrian Tomine *(May)*
***Berlin* no. 9,** Jason Lutes *(June)*
***Louis Riel* no. 7,** Chester Brown *(June)*
***The Hamilton Sketchbook*,** David Collier *(June)*
***The Summer of Love*,** Debbie Drechsler *(July)*
***Fair Weather*,** Joe Matt *(Aug)*
***Paul Has a Summer Job*,** Michel Rabagliati *(Aug)*
***Louis Riel* no. 8,** Chester Brown *(Oct)*

2003

Louis Riel **no. 9,** Chester Brown *(Feb)*

Palookaville **no. 16,** Seth *(Feb)*

Collier's **vol. 2, no. 2,** David Collier *(March)*

Waiting for Food, R. Crumb *(March)*

Berlin **no. 10,** Jason Lutes *(April)*

The Summer of Love, Debbie Drechsler *(new edition, June)*

Drawn & Quarterly Anthology **vol. 5:** covers and endpapers, Dupuy and Berbérian; "Pictures and Conversations," introduction by Alberto Manguel, illustration by Jan Van der Veken; "Albert Chartier: A Retrospective," Albert Chartier; "Monsieur Jean," Dupuy and Berbérian; "Way to Go," Harry Mayerovitch; "Jamilti," Rutu Modan; "Paul in the Metro," Michel Rabagliati; "The Crypt of Brontë," R. Sikoryak; "Kept," Yoshihiro Tatsumi; *(Aug)*

The ACME Novelty Datebook **vol. 1,** Chris Ware *(Aug)*

Drawn & Quarterly Showcase **vol. 1:** front cover, endpapers, and "87 blvd. des Capucines," Nicolas Robel; back cover and "Glenn Ganges," Kevin Huizenga *(Sept)*

Louis Riel: A Comic-Strip Biography Chester Brown *(Sept)*

5 Is the Perfect Number, Igort *(Nov)*

The Fixer: A Story from Sarajevo, Joe Sacco *(Dec)*

2004

Optic Nerve **no. 9,** Adrian Tomine *(Jan)*

Dogs and Water, Anders Nilsen *(March)*

Way to Go, Harry Mayerovitch *(March)*

Drawn & Quarterly Showcase **vol. 2:** covers and "Life During Wartime," Pentti Otsamo; "Untitled," Jeffrey Brown; endpapers and "Game," Erik De Graaf *(April)*

Bannock, Beans and Black Tea: Memories of a Prince Edward Island Childhood in the Great Depression, Seth and John Gallant *(May)*

Sof' Boy and Friends **no. 3,** Archer Prewitt *(May)*

Scrapbook: Uncollected Work, 1990–2004, Adrian Tomine *(June)*

Clyde Fans Book One, Seth *(July)*

Palookaville **no. 17,** Seth *(Sept)*

The Frank Ritza Papers, David Collier *(Sept)*

of Drawn & Quarterly **(Dec 1993)**
With Alice Sebold: "Christmas 1,000,000 B.C." ***Drawn & Quarterly*** **no. 1 (April 1990)**

FRANK KING

(1883–1969) One of the pioneering giants of American newspaper comics, Frank was born in Cashton, WI. He joined the staff of the *Chicago Tribune* in 1909. After creating a string of minor hits, he made his lasting mark in 1919 with *Gasoline Alley,* which became one of the most widely syndicated and read strips in North America until King's death in 1969. He spent most of his life in Chicago and Florida.
Walt & Skeezix: Book One, 1921–1922 **(June 2005);** ***Walt & Skeezix: Book Two, 1923–1924*** **(Aug 2006);** ***Walt & Skeezix: Book Three, 1925–1926*** **(Oct 2007);** ***Walt & Skeezix: Book Four, 1927–1928*** **(April 2010);** ***Walt & Skeezix: Book Five, 1929–1930*** **(Dec 2011);** ***Walt Before Skeezix*** **(June 2014)**

PETER KUPER

Peter was born in 1958 in Summit, NJ. He is known as an autobiographical and political cartoonist. He briefly drew a comic called *Bleeding Heart.*
Back cover, ***Drawn & Quarterly*** **no. 9 (July 1992); "(@!#¡%),"** ***The Best of Drawn & Quarterly*** **(Dec 1993)**

MARK LANG

Mark was born in Red Deer, Alberta, in 1966. He now lives in Montreal. He is a three-time recipient of the Elizabeth Greenshields Foundation Grant. His paintings can be found in private and corporate collections in Canada, the US, and abroad.
"The Peasant and the Snake," ***Drawn & Quarterly Anthology*** **vol. 3 (May 2000)**

EMILIE LE HIN-SINGH

Emilie is a translator and publicist who works extensively with prestigious art comics publisher Éditions Cornélius.

PIERRE LEFEBVRE

Pierre is the editor-in-chief of *Liberté.*
With Luc Giard: cover and inside cover, ***Drawn & Quarterly*** **no. 7 (March 1992); "I Can't Say What Hit Me,"** ***Drawn & Quarterly*** **no. 8 (April 1992); "That Night" and "Stevenson Has Found Another Letter,"** ***Drawn & Quarterly*** **no. 9 (July 1992)**

ROBERT LEIGHTON

Robert was born in 1960. He is a regular contributor to the *New Yorker.* He has written for Comedy Central and Nickelodeon.
"Seven-Second Stories," ***Drawn & Quarterly*** **no. 1 (April 1990); "'E' Emcees Squares,"** ***Drawn & Quarterly*** **no. 2 (Oct 1990)**

ASTRID LINDGREN

(1907–2002) Astrid was the creator of one of Sweden's most iconic fictional characters, Pippi Longstocking. The Pippi books have been translated into more than sixty languages.
With Ingrid Vang Nyman: ***Pippi Moves In*** **(Oct 2012);** ***Pippi Fixes Everything*** **(Sept 2013);** ***Pippi Won't Grow Up*** **(Nov 2014)**

JASON LITTLE

Jason was born in 1970 in Binghamton, NY. He has published two graphic novels about his character Bee.
"Safety Instructions," ***Drawn & Quarterly Anthology*** **vol. 3 (May 2000)**

AMY LOCKHART

Amy is a filmmaker, animator, and artist. Her animations have screened at festivals nationally and internationally, including the Ann Arbor Film Festival and International Animation Festival in Hiroshima, Japan. She teaches at OCAD in Toronto.
Dirty Dishes **(Jan 2010)**

JASON LUTES

Jason was born in New Jersey in 1967. He currently lives in Vermont with his partner and two children and teaches at the Center for Cartoon Studies.
"Late Summer Sun," ***Drawn & Quarterly*** **vol. 2, no. 6 (June 1997);** ***Berlin*** **no. 4 (Feb 1998);** ***Berlin*** **no. 5 (Dec 1998);** ***Berlin*** **no. 1 (new edition, Feb 1999);** ***Berlin*** **no. 6 (Aug 1999);** ***Berlin*** **no. 7 (April 2000);** ***Berlin*** **no. 8 (Dec 2000);** ***Berlin: City of Stones*** **(June 2000);** ***Berlin*** **no. 9 (June 2002);** ***Berlin*** **no. 10**

(April 2003); *Jar of Fools* (Sept 2001); *Berlin* no. 11 (Jan 2005); *Berlin* no. 12 (Dec 2005); *Berlin* no. 13 (Aug 2007); *Berlin* no. 14 (Dec 2007); *Berlin* no. 15 (March 2008); *Berlin* no. 16 (June 2008); *Berlin: City of Smoke* (Aug 2008); *Berlin* no. 17 (Nov 2010); *Berlin* no. 18 (Jan 2012)
With Ed Brubaker: *The Fall* (Feb 2001)

BRAD MACKAY

Brad is a freelance journalist and a co-founder of the Doug Wright Awards. His writing on comics (and other subjects) has appeared in the *Globe and Mail, Toronto Star, Ottawa Citizen, CBC, Toronto Life,* and *Quill & Quire.*

The Collected Doug Wright, Volume One: Canada's Master Cartoonist (May 2009); *Nipper 1963–1964* (Oct 2010); *Nipper 1965–1966* (Sept 2011); *Nipper 1967–1968* (Dec 2012)

ALBERTO MANGUEL

Alberto was born in 1948 in Buenos Aires. He is a translator, essayist, novelist, and editor.
With Jan Van der Veken: Introduction ("Pictures and Conversations"), *Drawn & Quarterly* vol. 5 (Aug 2003)

MARTI

Marti was born in Barcelona in 1956. His most famous series is *The Cabbie* (1982).
"Professional Training," *Drawn & Quarterly* no. 8 (April 1992); "Barcelona," *Drawn & Quarterly* no. 9 (July 1992); "Within Three Seconds" and "Claudia," *Drawn & Quarterly* no. 10 (Dec 1992); "Within Three Seconds" and "Claudia," *The Best of Drawn & Quarterly* (Dec 1993)

RUTH MARTINEZ

Ruth was one of the initial people who answered the plea for submissions in the *New York Press.*
"Drawing," *Drawn & Quarterly* no. 1 (April 1990)

JOE MATT

Joe was born in Philadelphia in 1963. By his own account, he was a spoiled, selfish, and unpleasant child with a bedwetting problem, who also happened to be obsessed with

collecting comics. He currently lives and avoids work in Los Angeles.
Back cover and "AutoMatt," *Drawn & Quarterly* no. 1 (April 1990); back cover and "AutoMatt," *Drawn & Quarterly* no. 2 (Oct 1990); cover and "AutoMatt," *Drawn & Quarterly* no. 3 (Jan 1991); back cover ("The Boob") and "AutoMatt," *Drawn & Quarterly* no. 4 (March 1991); "Sexaholics Anonymous," *Drawn & Quarterly* no. 5 (June 1991); back cover ("How to Be Cheap") and "AutoMatt," *Drawn & Quarterly* no. 6 (Oct 1991); *Peepshow* no. 1 (Feb 1992); *Peepshow* no. 2 (May 1992); *Peepshow* no. 3 (Nov 1992); *Peepshow* no. 4 (April 1993); *Peepshow* no. 5 (Oct 1993); "My Darkest Secret" and "Aug. 16, 1989," *The Best of Drawn & Quarterly* (Dec 1993); *Peepshow* no. 6 (April 1994); *Peepshow* no. 7 (March 1995); *Peepshow* no. 8 (July 1995); *Peepshow* no. 9 (April 1996); *Peepshow* no. 10 (July 1997); *The Poor Bastard* (Aug 1997); *Peepshow* no. 11 (June 1998); *Peepshow: The Cartoon Diary of Joe Matt* (new edition, March 2000); *Peepshow* no. 12 (April 2000); *Peepshow* no. 13 (Feb 2002); *Fair Weather* (Aug 2002); *Peepshow* no. 14 (Oct 2006); *Spent* (May 2007)

FRANCO MATTICCHIO

Franco was born in 1957 in Varese, Italy. He made his debut as an illustrator in 1979 on the third page of the *Corriere della Sera.*
"Two Stories," *Drawn & Quarterly Anthology* vol. 3 (May 2000)

MAX

Spanish cartoonist Max was born Francesc Capdevila. He has published two books, *Bardin the Superrealist* and *Vapor,* with Fantagraphics.
Covers, endpapers, and "Orpheus," *Drawn & Quarterly* vol. 2, no. 6 (June 1997); *The Extended Dream of Mr. D* no. 1 (Sept 1998); *The Extended Dream of Mr. D* no. 2 (Jan 1999); *The Extended Dream of Mr. D* no. 3 (May 1999); *The Extended Dream of Mr. D* (Dec 1999)

HARRY MAYEROVITCH

(1910–2004) Harry had many careers during his lifetime. He was an architect, artist, illustrator, author, and cartoonist. He died in his sleep on his ninety-fourth birthday, two weeks after the release of his final book.

Babel vol. 1, David B. (Oct)
Or Else no. 1, Kevin Huizenga (Oct)
Above and Below, James Sturm (Dec)
Lady Pep, Julie Doucet (Dec)
The Stacks, Marc Bell (Dec)

2005

Bacter-Area, Keith Jones (Jan)
The Chronicles of Lucky Ello, Peter Thompson (Jan)
Berlin no. 11, Jason Lutes (Jan)
Or Else no. 2, Kevin Huizenga (Jan)
Ed the Happy Clown no. 1, Chester Brown (Feb)
A Village Under My Pillow, Luc Giard (April)
Ed the Happy Clown no. 2, Chester Brown (May)
Free Comic Book Day—Adventures of Paul, Michel Rabagliati (May)
Paul Moves Out, Michel Rabagliati (May)
Satiro-Plastic: The Sketchbook of Gary Panter, Gary Panter (June)
Walt & Skeezix: Book One, 1921–1922, Frank King (June)
War's End: Profiles from Bosnia 1995–1996, Joe Sacco (June)
Drawn & Quarterly Showcase vol. 3: covers and "We're Wolf," Geneviève Castrée; endpapers and "Somersaulting," Sammy Harkham; "The Mummy," Matt Broersma (Aug)
Ed the Happy Clown no. 3, Chester Brown (Aug)
Or Else no. 3, Kevin Huizenga (Aug)
Baghdad Journal: An Artist in Occupied Iraq, Steve Mumford (Sept)
Big Questions #7: Dinner and a Nap, Anders Nilsen (Sept)
Pyongyang: A Journey in North Korea, Guy Delisle (Sept)
The Push Man and Other Stories, Yoshihiro Tatsumi (Sept)
Optic Nerve no. 10, Adrian Tomine (Oct)
Palookaville no. 18, Seth (Oct)
Perfect Example, John Porcellino (Oct)
Ed the Happy Clown no. 4, Chester Brown (Nov)
Berlin no. 12, Jason Lutes (Dec)
Wimbledon Green: The Greatest Comic Book Collector in the World, Seth (Dec)

2006

Crickets no. 1, Sammy Harkham *(Jan)*

Ed the Happy Clown no. 5, Chester Brown *(Jan)*

Fallen Angel, Nicolas Robel *(Jan)*

Atlas no. 2, Dylan Horrocks *(Feb)*

Big Questions #8: Theory and Practice, Anders Nilsen *(Feb)*

Ed the Happy Clown no. 6, Chester Brown *(March)*

Or Else no. 4, Kevin Huizenga *(March)*

A Nut at the Opera, Maurice Vellekoop *(April)*

The Awake Field, Ron Regé, Jr. *(April)*

Ed the Happy Clown no. 7, Chester Brown *(May)*

Free Comic Book Day—Monsieur Jean, Dupuy and Berbérian *(May)*

We Are On Our Own: A Memoir, Miriam Katin *(May)*

Drawn & Quarterly Showcase vol. 4: covers, endpapers, and "Won't Be Licked," Dan Zettwoch; "Felix," Gabrielle Bell; "Dog Days," Martin Cendreda *(June)*

Ed the Happy Clown no. 8, Chester Brown *(July)*

Get a Life, Philippe Dupuy and Charles Berbérian *(July)*

Maybe Later, Philippe Dupuy and Charles Berbérian *(July)*

Skibber Bee Bye, Ron Regé, Jr. *(July)*

The Little Man: Short Strips, 1980–1995, Chester Brown *(new edition, Aug)*

Walt & Skeezix: Book Two, 1923–1924, Frank King *(Aug)*

Abandon the Old in Tokyo, Yoshihiro Tatsumi *(Sept)*

Big Questions #9: The Lost and Found, Anders Nilsen *(Sept)*

Ed the Happy Clown no. 9, Chester Brown *(Sept)*

Shenzhen: A Travelogue from China, Guy Delisle *(Sept)*

Peepshow no. 14, Joe Matt *(Oct)*

Don't Go Where I Can't Follow, Anders Nilsen *(Nov)*

Lucky vol. 1 Gabrielle Bell *(Nov)*

Moomin: The Complete Tove Jansson Comic Strip vol. 1, Tove Jansson *(Nov)*

"The Other One," *Drawn & Quarterly Anthology* vol. 3 (May 2000); "Poster Gallery," *Drawn & Quarterly Anthology* vol. 4 (July 2001); "Way to Go," *Drawn & Quarterly Anthology* vol. 5 (Aug 2003); *Way to Go* (March 2004)

DAVID MAZZUCCHELLI

David was born 1960 and lives in Manhattan. He teaches comic-book storytelling at the School of Visual Arts. He is best known for his books *City of Glass* (in collaboration with Paul Karasik) and *Asterios Polyp*.

Inside front cover and "A Brief History of Civilisation," *Drawn & Quarterly* no. 9 (July 1992); "A Brief History of Civilisation," *The Best of Drawn & Quarterly* (Dec 1993); covers, endpapers, and "Rates of Exchange," *Drawn & Quarterly* vol. 2, no. 2 (Dec 1994)

SERAH-MARIE MCMAHON

Serah-Marie is the founder of *WORN Fashion Journal* and a freelance creative director. In 2010, she was nominated for a National Magazine Award for Best Cover of the Year. She lives in Toronto.

***The WORN Archive: A Fashion Journal about the Art, Ideas, and History of What We Wear* (April 2014)**

BERNIE MIREAULT

Bernie is a Montreal cartoonist known for his comics series *MacKenzie Queen* and *The Jam* as well as being a bit player in Joe Matt's early comics.

"Untitled," *Drawn & Quarterly* no. 3 (Jan 1991); inside back cover, *Drawn & Quarterly* no. 7 (March 1992)
With Sebastian Hassinger: "The Mutual Admiration Society," *Drawn & Quarterly* no. 4 (March 1991)
With David Abu Bacha: "The Gross-Out Contest," *Drawn & Quarterly* no. 5 (June 1991)

SHIGERU MIZUKI

Shigeru was born in 1922 and lives in Tokyo, Japan. He is a specialist in stories of yōkai and is considered a master of the genre. He is arguably the most famous living cartoonist in Japan.

***Onward Towards Our Noble Deaths* (April 2011); *NonNonBa* (May 2012); *Kitaro* (Aug 2013); *Showa 1926–1939: A History of Japan* (Nov 2013); *Showa 1939–1944: A History of Japan* (June 2014); *Showa 1944–1953: A History of Japan* (Nov 2014)**

RUTU MODAN

Rutu was born in 1966 in Tel Aviv, where she still resides. In her twenties, she edited the Israeli edition of *MAD* magazine. She has won two Eisner Awards for her graphic novels *Exit Wounds* and *The Property*.

"Jamilti," *Drawn & Quarterly Anthology* vol. 5 (Aug 2003); *Exit Wounds* (June 2007); *Jamilti and Other Stories* (Sept 2008); *The Property* (May 2013)

CAREL MOISEIWITSCH

Carel is an activist and visual artist who has exhibited internationally. She taught drawing at the Emily Carr Institute of Art and Design and was a freelance editorial illustrator for the *Vancouver Sun* and the *Province* for over a decade. She lives in Vancouver, BC.

"End Eviction Fears" and "Mean Woman Blues," *Drawn & Quarterly* no. 2 (Oct 1990); inside cover ("Zebra"), *Drawn & Quarterly* no. 3 (Jan 1991); "We Hold These Truths to Be Self Evident," *Drawn & Quarterly* no. 4 (March 1991); "Priapic Alphabet," *Drawn & Quarterly* no. 5 (June 1991); "Sh-Boom," *Drawn & Quarterly* no. 6 (Oct 1991); "Camera Obscura" and "The Darkened Room," *Drawn & Quarterly* no. 8 (April 1992); "Notes from the Ledge," *Drawn & Quarterly* no. 9 (July 1992); "Sh-Boom," *The Best of Drawn & Quarterly* (Dec 1993)

JULIE MORSTAD

Julie graduated from the Alberta College of Art and Design in 2004 with a BFA. She is an award-winning illustrator and lives in Vancouver with her family, where she teaches at Emily Carr.

***Milk Teeth* (Nov 2007); *The Wayside* (Oct 2012)**

STEVE MUMFORD

Steve was born in 1960 and lives in New York. Typically he works in large, realist oil paintings, as well as watercolour on paper. He is best known for his depiction of scenes from the on-going American wars in Iraq and Afghanistan.

***Baghdad Journal: An Artist in Occupied Iraq* (Sept 2005)**

WILBUR D. NESBIT

(1871–1927) Wilbur was born in Nenia, OH. He was a noted newspaper humorist.

With Clare Briggs: *Oh Skin-Nay!: The Days of Real Sport* (March 2007)

ANDERS NILSEN

Anders was born in 1973. He began self-publishing in 1999 by photocopying drawings and comics from his sketchbooks and stapling them together into a minicomic called *Big Questions*. He currently teaches at MCAD in Minneapolis.

***Dogs and Water* (Nov 2004); *Big Questions no. 7: Dinner and a Nap* (Sept 2005); *Big Questions no. 8: Theory and Practice* (Feb 2006); *Big Questions no. 9: The Lost and Found* (Sept 2006); *Don't Go Where I Can't Follow* (Nov 2006); *Dogs and Water* (new edition, May 2007); *Big Questions no. 10: The Hand That Feeds* (Oct 2007); *Big Questions no. 11: Sweetness and Light* (Nov 2008); *Big Questions no. 12: A Young Crow's Guide to Hunting* (July 2009); *Big Questions no. 13: A House That Floats* (Oct 2009); *Big Questions no. 14: Title and Deed* (May 2010); *Big Questions no. 15: The Sweet Taste of Victory* (Dec 2010); *Big Questions* (Aug 2011); *Don't Go Where I Can't Follow* (new edition, Dec 2012); *Rage of Poseidon* (Oct 2013)**

CHRISTIAN NORTHEAST

Christian lives with his wife and two daughters in Ontario. His work has appeared in the *New Yorker*, *Nickelodeon*, *GQ*, *Time*, *McSweeney's*, and the *New York Times*.

***Prayer Requested* (July 2009)**

ADRIAN NORVID

Adrian was born in London, England, in 1959. He is currently a fine arts professor at Concordia University and lives in Montreal.

***Nogoodniks* (Aug 2011)**

DIANE OBOMSAWIN

Diane was born in 1959. She spent the first twenty years of her life in France. After studying graphic design, she came to Canada in 1983 and turned her attention to painting, comics, and animation. She lives in Montreal.

***Kaspar* (March 2009); *On Loving Women* (Feb 2014)**

JOHN OLIVEROS

John was born in 1963 and lives in Montreal. He is the older brother of Chris Oliveros.

Inside back cover and "Thermal Dynamics," *Drawn & Quarterly* no. 1 (April 1990); "Magic Marker Comics," *Drawn & Quarterly* no. 3 (Jan 1991)
With Philip Fine: "A Dear John Letter from Your Dog on Moving Day," *Drawn & Quarterly* no. 1 (April 1990); "Tuesday, 3:00–3:30: Angst," *Drawn & Quarterly* no. 2 (Oct 1990); "A Dear John Letter from Your Dog on Moving Day," *The Best of Drawn & Quarterly* (Dec 1993)

JOE OLLMANN

Joe was raised on a Christmas tree farm. He won the Doug Wright Award for Best Book in 2007 for *This Will All End in Tears*. He lives in Hamilton, Ontario, with his wife and son.

***Mid-Life* (March 2011)**

PENTTI OTSAMO

Pentti was born in 1967 and lives in Maaninka, Finland. He's known for portraying everyday life in a clear style.

"Bicycle Thief," *Drawn & Quarterly* vol. 2, no. 3 (May 1995); "Fishing," *Drawn & Quarterly* vol. 2, no. 5 (April 1996); *Homunculus: A Picture Novella in Six Parts* (Jan 1999); "The Shepherd," *Drawn & Quarterly Anthology* vol. 3 (May 2000); "Life During Wartime," *Drawn & Quarterly Showcase* vol. 2 (April 2004)

CLÉMENT OUBRERIE

Clément is an award-winning illustrator and animator. Most recently, he is the artist of the French comic-book series *Pablo*.

With Marguerite Abouet: *Aya* (Feb 2007); *Aya of Yop City* (Sept 2008); *Aya: The Secrets Come Out* (Sept 2009); *Aya: Life in Yop City* (Sept 2012); *Aya: Love in Yop City* (Feb 2013)

GARY PANTER

Gary was born in 1950 in Texas. In the 1970s, he defined the influential punk ratty style. He is most culturally famous for being the set designer on *Pee-wee's Playhouse*. He lives in Brooklyn, NY.

***Satiro-Plastic: The Sketchbook of Gary Panter* (June 2005)**

Aline and the Others, Guy Delisle *(Dec)*
***Atlas* no. 3,** Dylan Horrocks *(Dec)*
Curses, Kevin Huizenga *(Dec)*

2007

Aya, Marguerite Abouet and Clément Oubrerie *(Feb)*
One Eye, Charles Burns *(Feb)*
Oh Skin-Nay!: The Days of Real Sport, Clare Briggs and Wilbur D. Nesbit *(March)*
***Optic Nerve* no. 11,** Adrian Tomine *(March)*
Dogs and Water, Anders Nilsen *(new edition, May)*
Free Comic Book Day—Lynda Barry Sampler, Lynda Barry *(May)*
James Sturm's America: God, Gold, and Golems, James Sturm *(May)*
King-Cat Classix, John Porcellino *(May)*
***Lucky* vol. 2, no. 1,** Gabrielle Bell *(May)*
Spent, Joe Matt *(May)*
Exit Wounds, Rutu Modan *(June)*
Joseph, Nicolas Robel *(July)*
***Berlin* no. 13,** Jason Lutes *(Aug)*
Big Questions #10: The Hand That Feeds, Anders Nilsen *(Oct)*
***Moomin: The Complete Tove Jansson Comic Strip* vol. 2,** Tove Jansson *(Oct)*
Shortcomings, Adrian Tomine *(Oct)*
Southern Cross: A Novel of the South Seas, Laurence Hyde *(Oct)*
Walt & Skeezix: Book Three, 1925–1926, Frank King *(Oct)*
White Rapids, Pascal Blanchet *(Oct)*
Milk Teeth, Julie Morstad *(Nov)*
***Berlin* no. 14,** Jason Lutes *(Dec)*
***The ACME Novelty Datebook* vol. 2,** Chris Ware *(Dec)*

2008

365 Days: A Diary, Julie Doucet *(Jan)*
***Crickets* no. 2,** Sammy Harkham *(Jan)*
Albert and the Others, Guy Delisle *(Feb)*
***Palookaville* no. 19,** Seth *(Feb)*
***Berlin* no. 15,** Jason Lutes *(March)*
Fire Away, Chris von Szombathy *(March)*
Haunted, Philippe Dupuy *(March)*
Paul Goes Fishing, Michel Rabagliati *(March)*
Free Comic Book Day—Gekiga Manga Sampler,

Seiichi Hayashi and Yoshihiro Tatsumi *(May)*
Good-Bye, Yoshihiro Tatsumi *(May)*
***Lucky* vol. 2, no. 2**, Gabrielle Bell *(May)*
What It Is, Lynda Barry *(May)*
***Berlin* no. 16**, Jason Lutes *(June)*
Against Pain, Ron Regé, Jr. *(July)*
Gentleman Jim, Raymond Briggs *(July)*
Red Colored Elegy, Seiichi Hayashi *(July)*
***Drawn & Quarterly Showcase* vol. 5**: covers and "Untitled," Amanda Vähämäki; endpapers and "Inland," Anneli Furmark; "Untitled," T. Edward Bak *(Aug)*
Aya of Yop City, Marguerite Abouet and Clément Oubrerie *(Sept)*
Berlin: City of Smoke, Jason Lutes *(Sept)*
Burma Chronicles, Guy Delisle *(Sept)*
Jamilti and Other Stories, Rutu Modan *(Sept)*
***Moomin: The Complete Tove Jansson Comic Strip* vol. 3**, Tove Jansson *(Sept)*
Illusztraijuns for Brain Police, Marc Bell *(Oct)*
***Or Else* no. 5**, Kevin Huizenga *(Oct)*
Pohadky, Marek Colek and Pat Shewchuk *(Oct)*
All We Ever Do Is Talk About Wood, Tom Horacek *(Nov)*
Big Questions #11: Sweetness and Light, Anders Nilsen *(Nov)*
Skitzy: The Story of Floyd W. Skitzafroid, Don Freeman *(Dec)*

2009
Baloney, Pascal Blanchet *(Feb)*
Nicolas, Pascal Girard *(Feb)*
Ojingogo, Matthew Forsythe *(Feb)*
Cecil and Jordan in New York, Gabrielle Bell *(March)*
Kaspar, Diane Obomsawin *(March)*
A Drifting Life, Yoshihiro Tatsumi *(April)*
The Bun Field, Amanda Vähämäki *(April)*
32 Stories: The Complete Optic Nerve Mini-Comics Box Set Adrian Tomine *(May)*
Free Comic Book Day—Nancy and Melvin Monster, John Stanley *(May)*
George Sprott: 1894–1975, Seth *(May)*
***Moomin: The Complete Tove Jansson Comic Strip* vol. 4**, Tove Jansson *(May)*
The Collected Doug Wright, Volume One: Canada's Master Cartoonist, Doug Wright *(May)*
The John Stanley Library: Melvin

PHILIPPE PETIT-ROULET

Philippe was born in Paris. He has illustrated twenty books since the early 1980s and has frequently collaborated with other writers and artists, including François Avril.

With François Avril: "63, Rue de la Grange aux Belles," *Drawn & Quarterly* vol. 2, no. 1 (Aug 1994)

MIMI POND

Mimi has created comics for the *Los Angeles Times, Seventeen* magazine, *National Lampoon*, and many other publications. She has also written for television: her credits include the first full-length episode of *The Simpsons* and, come on, *Designing Women*. She lives in Los Angeles, CA.

***Over Easy* (April 2014)**

JOHN PORCELLINO

John has been self-publishing his minicomic *King-Cat Comics and Stories* since 1989. He's run a small-press distribution business called Spit and a Half as a sideline for most of this time. He is the focus of the recent documentary *Root Hog or Die*. He lives in South Beloit, IL.

***Perfect Example* (Oct 2005); *King-Cat Classix* (May 2007); *Map of My Heart* (Oct 2009); *The Hospital Suite* (Sept 2014)**

ARCHER PREWITT

Archer was born in 1963. He is an active musician in the independent music scene in Chicago, IL, most often associated with the bands the Sea and Cake and the Coctails.

"Sof' Boy," *Drawn & Quarterly* vol. 2, no. 4 (Dec 1995); *Sof' Boy and Friends* no. 1 (Oct 1997); *Sof' Boy and Friends* no. 2 (Aug 1998); *Sof' Boy and Friends* no. 3 (May 2004)

MICHEL RABAGLIATI

Michel was born in 1961. He started drawing comics in his forties, after working as a graphic designer for many years. He cites the art style of European comics *Spirou and Fantasio, Asterix*, and Hergé's Adventures of Tintin as influences upon his work. He lives in Montreal.

Logo design, *Drawn & Quarterly* no. 4 (March 1991); "Paul: Apprentice Typographer," *Drawn & Quarterly Anthology* vol. 3 (May 2000); *Paul in the Country* (Oct 2000); *Paul Has a Summer Job* (Aug 2002); "Paul in the Metro," *Drawn & Quarterly Anthology* vol. 5 (Aug 2003); *Paul Moves Out* (May 2005); *Paul Goes Fishing* (March 2008)

BRIAN RALPH

Brian was born in 1973 in Metuchen, NJ. He attended the Rhode Island School of Design and became a member of the influential artist collective Fort Thunder. He was a long-standing contributor to *Giant Robot* magazine and is currently teaching sequential art at Savannah College of Art and Design.

***Daybreak* (Sept 2011); *Cave-In* (Feb 2013); *Reggie-12* (Aug 2013)**

RON REGÉ, JR.

Ron was born in 1969 in Plymouth, MA. He has been drawing comics since 1986, often under the series title *Yeast Hoist*. He performs music under the name Discombobulated Ventriloquist. He lives in Los Angeles.

"We Must Know We Will Know," *Drawn & Quarterly Anthology* vol. 4 (July 2001); *The Awake Field* (April 2006); *Skibber Bee Bye* (July 2006); *Against Pain* (July 2008)

ANOUK RICARD

Anouk was born in 1970. She has created comics for children and adults, as well as stop-motion animation. She lives in Strasbourg, France.

***Anna & Froga: Wanna Gumball?* (June 2012); *Anna & Froga: I Dunno, What Do You Want to Do?* (Aug 2013); *Benson's Cuckoos* (June 2014); *Anna & Froga: Thrills, Spills, and Gooseberries* (Nov 2014)**

NICOLAS ROBEL

Nicolas was born in 1974. He and his family emigrated to Switzerland when he was three years old. He graduated in visual communication from the École supérieure des arts visuels in Geneva, Switzerland. Nicolas runs the small art comics publishing house B.ü.l.b. He lives in Geneva, Switzerland.

"Bleeding Tree," *Drawn & Quarterly* vol. 4 (July 2001); "87 blvd. des Capucines," *Drawn & Quarterly Showcase* vol. 1 (Sept 2003); *Fallen Angel* (Jan 2006); *Joseph* (July 2007)

SEAN ROGERS

Sean writes about comics for the *Globe and Mail*, and has published in the *Walrus*, the *Comics Journal*, and elsewhere. He contributed the afterword to the anniversary edition of Chester Brown's *Louis Riel*, and edited the special comics issue of *Descant*.

JOE SACCO

Joe was born in Malta in 1960. He took a two-decade break from his important humour work to write political novels, most recently *Footnotes in Gaza* and *The Great War*. He lives in Portland, OR.

"On My Day Off," *Drawn & Quarterly* no. 8 (April 1992); *Soba: Stories from Bosnia* (Feb 1998); *The Fixer: A Story from Sarajevo* (Dec 2003); *War's End: Profiles from Bosnia 1995–1996* (June 2005); *The Fixer and Other Stories* (Oct 2009)

IMIRI SAKABASHIRA

Imiri was born in 1964. He is part of the Japanese underground manga generation centring around publications like *Garo* and *AX*.

The Box Man (Jan 2010)

RICHARD SALA

Richard's comics have appeared in *RAW* and he has published several books. He is the author of the series *Evil Eye* and the recent graphic novels *In a Glass Grotesquely* and *Delphine*. He lives in Berkeley, CA.

"Credo" and "Gloom," *Drawn & Quarterly* no. 2 (Oct 1990); "One of the Wonders of the World," *Drawn & Quarterly* no. 3 (Jan 1991); "A Newlywed's Heartache," *Drawn & Quarterly* no. 4 (March 1991); cover and "The Somnambulist," *Drawn & Quarterly* no. 5 (June 1991); "Time-Bomb," *Drawn & Quarterly* no. 7 (March 1992); "Credo," *The Best of Drawn & Quarterly* (Dec 1993)

JEAN-MARIE "MAILLY" SAULI

Mailly, a French cartoonist, was living in New York when he answered the *New York Press* ad for submissions for the first anthology.

"Three Guys Hard Up On Their Luck," *Drawn & Quarterly* no. 1 (April 1990); "Still Hard Up on His Luck," *Drawn & Quarterly* no. 2 (Oct 1990); "Like Everyday," *Drawn & Quarterly* no. 8 (April 1992)

SETH SCRIVER

Seth directed the animated film *Asphalt Watches* (2013) with Shayne Ehman. It won the Best Canadian First Feature Film at the Toronto International Film Festival. He lives in Toronto, Ontario.

Stooge Pile (March 2010)

ALICE SEBOLD

Alice has published three novels: *Lucky* (1999), *The Lovely Bones* (2002), and *The Almost Moon* (2007). But it's safe to say she will be best remembered for her collaborative comic with J.D. King in *Drawn & Quarterly* no. 1.

With J.D. King: "Christmas 1,000,000 B.C.," *Drawn & Quarterly* no. 1 (April 1990)

SETH

Seth was born in 1962 in Ontario. He is the cartoonist behind the comic-book series *Palookaville*, which started as a pamphlet comic and is now a semi-annual hardcover. His comics have appeared in everything. He lives in Guelph, Ontario, with his wife.

"Why?" *Drawn & Quarterly* no. 4 (March 1991); *Palookaville* no. 1 (April 1991); back cover ("Jefferson"), *Drawn & Quarterly* no. 5 (June 1991); *Palookaville* no. 2 (Sept 1991); "Night Sky," *Drawn & Quarterly* no. 6 (Oct 1991); "Some Things I Think You Should Know About Joe Matt," *Drawn & Quarterly* no. 7 (March 1992); cover and "A Folk Tale," *Drawn & Quarterly* no. 9 (July 1992); front matter, *Drawn & Quarterly* no. 10 (Dec 1992); *Palookaville* no. 3 (June 1993); *Palookaville* no. 4 (Dec 1993); "Night Sky," "A Folk Tale," and "Why?" *The Best of Drawn & Quarterly* (Dec 1993); *Palookaville* no. 5 (May 1994); covers and endpapers, *Drawn & Quarterly* vol. 2, no. 1 (Aug 1994); *Palookaville* no. 6 (Nov 1994);

Monster vol. 1, John Stanley (May)

Big Questions #12: A Young Crow's Guide to Hunting, Anders Nilsen (July)

Prayer Requested, Christian Northeast (July)

Aya: The Secrets Come Out, Marguerite Abouet and Clément Oubrerie (Sept)

Masterpiece Comics, R. Sikoryak (Sept)

Talking Lines, R. O. Blechman (Sept)

The John Stanley Library: Nancy vol. 1, John Stanley (Sept)

Big Questions #13: A House That Floats, Anders Nilsen (Oct)

Map of My Heart, John Porcellino (Oct)

The Book About Moomin, Mymble and Little My, Tove Jansson (Oct)

The Fixer and Other Stories, Joe Sacco (Oct)

Hot Potatoe, Marc Bell (Nov)

Red Snow, Susumu Katsumata (Nov)

2010

Dirty Dishes, Amy Lockhart (Jan)

Hicksville, Dylan Horrocks (new edition, Jan)

The Box Man, Imiri Sakabashira (Jan)

The John Stanley Library: Thirteen Going on Eighteen, John Stanley (Jan)

Market Day, James Sturm (March)

Stooge Pile, Seth Scriver (March)

The John Stanley Library: Melvin Monster vol. 2, John Stanley (March)

Black Blizzard, Yoshihiro Tatsumi (April)

Indoor Voice, Jillian Tamaki (April)

Walt & Skeezix: Book Four, 1927–1928, Frank King (April)

Wilson, Daniel Clowes (April)

Big Questions #14: Title and Deed, Anders Nilsen (May)

Free Comic Book Day—Yow! The John Stanley Library, John Stanley (May)

Catland Empire, Keith Jones (June)

The Selves, Sonja Ahlers (June)

Moomin: The Complete Tove Jansson Comic Strip vol. 5, Tove Jansson (July)

Eden, Pablo Holmberg (Aug)

The John Stanley Library: Nancy vol. 2, John Stanley (Aug)

The Wild Kingdom, Kevin Huizenga (Aug)

Make Me a Woman, Vanessa Davis (Sept)

The John Stanley Library: Tubby,

John Stanley (Sept)
Who Will Comfort Toffle?
Tove Jansson (Sept)
Nipper 1963–1964, Doug Wright (Oct)
Palookaville no. 20, Seth (Oct)
Berlin no. 17, Jason Lutes (Nov)
Denys Wortman's New York: Portrait of the City in the 1930s and 1940s, James Sturm, Brandon Elston, and Denys Wortman (Nov)
Picture This, Lynda Barry (Nov)
The ACME Novelty Library: Lint (no. 20), Chris Ware (Nov)
The Native Trees of Canada, Leanne Shapton (Nov)
The Wrong Place, Brecht Evens (Nov)
Bigfoot, Pascal Girard (Dec)
Big Questions #15: The Sweet Taste of Victory, Anders Nilsen (Dec)

2011

A Single Match, Oji Suzuki (Jan)
Scenes from an Impending Marriage, Adrian Tomine (Feb)
Mid-Life, Joe Ollmann (March)
The John Stanley Library: Melvin Monsters vol. 3, John Stanley (March)
Onward Towards Our Noble Deaths, Shigeru Mizuki (April)
Reunion, Pascal Girard (April)
Constructive Abandonment, Michael Dumontier and Neil Farber (May)
Free Comic Book Day—John Stanley's Summer Fun, John Stanley (May)
Moomin: The Complete Lars Jansson Comic Strip vol. 6, Lars Jansson (May)
Paying for It, Chester Brown (May)
The Klondike, Zach Worton (May)
Big Questions, Anders Nilsen (Aug)
Nogoodniks, Adrian Norvid (Aug)
Daybreak, Brian Ralph (Sept)
Hark! A Vagrant, Kate Beaton (Sept)
Nipper 1965–1966, Doug Wright (Sept)
Optic Nerve no. 12, Adrian Tomine (Sept)
Pure Pajamas, Marc Bell (Sept)
The John Stanley Library: Nancy vol. 3, John Stanley (Sept)
Blabber Blabber Blabber: Everything Volume One, Lynda Barry (Oct)

Palookaville no. 7 (April 1995); "Good Grief," *Drawn & Quarterly* vol. 2, no. 4 (Dec 1995); *Palookaville* no. 8 (Dec 1995); *Palookaville* no. 9 (June 1996); *It's a Good Life, If You Don't Weaken* (Sept 1996); *Palookaville* no. 10 (May 1997); *Palookaville* no. 11 (Oct 1997); *Palookaville* no. 12 (May 1998); *Palookaville* no. 13 (July 1999); "Sketchbook," *Drawn & Quarterly Anthology* vol. 3 (May 2000); *Palookaville* no. 14 (May 2000); *Palookaville* no. 15 (May 2001); *Palookaville* no. 1 (tenth anniversary edition, June 2001); *Vernacular Drawings* (Dec 2001); *Palookaville* no. 16 (Feb 2003); *Clyde Fans Book One* (July 2004); *Palookaville* no. 17 (Sept 2004); *Palookaville* no. 18 (Oct 2005); *Wimbledon Green: The Greatest Comic Book Collector in the World* (Dec 2005); *Palookaville* no. 19 (Feb 2008); *George Sprott: 1894–1975* (May 2009); *Palookaville* no. 20 (Oct 2010); *The Great Northern Brotherhood of Canadian Cartoonists* (Oct 2011); *Palookaville* no. 21 (Oct 2013)
With John Gallant: *Bannock, Beans and Black Tea: Memories of a Prince Edward Island Childhood in the Great Depression* (May 2004)

LEANNE SHAPTON

Leanne was born in 1973. She has been an art director for the op-ed page at the *New York Times*. She is the author of several books, including the National Book Critics Award winner *Swimming Studies*. She lives in New York City.
***The Native Trees of Canada* (Nov 2010); *Sunday Night Movies* (Oct 2013)**

PAT SHEWCHUK

Pat is a Toronto-based animator and illustrator. She collaborates with Marek Colek under the name Tin Can Forest.
With Marek Colek: *Pohadky* (Oct 2008)

R. SIKORYAK

Bob was born in 1964. His comics and illustrations have appeared in the *New Yorker*, *RAW*, the *Onion*, *GQ*, and *MAD*. He teaches at Parsons The New School for Design and at the Center for Cartoon Studies. He lives in New York City with his wife.
"Dostoyevsky Comics," *Drawn & Quarterly Anthology* vol. 3 (May 2000); "Little Pearl," *Drawn & Quarterly Anthology* vol. 4 (July 2001); "The Crypt of Brontë," *Drawn & Quarterly Anthology* vol. 5 (Aug 2003); *Masterpiece Comics* (Sept 2009)

FIONA SMYTH

Fiona was born in 1964. She's a painter, muralist, animator, cartoonist, and illustrator. She lives in Toronto, Ontario.
"I'm OK / You're Not," *Drawn & Quarterly* no. 5 (June 1991); "The Faithless," *Drawn & Quarterly* no. 6 (Oct 1991); "Interrupted," *Drawn & Quarterly* no. 8 (April 1992)
With Dennis P. Eichhorn: "Night of the Oh-So-Very Dead," *Drawn & Quarterly* no. 7 (March 1992)
With Maurice Vellekoop and Roxanna Bikadoroff: *Fabulous Babes* no. 1 (July 1995)

ART SPIEGELMAN

Art was born in 1948 in Stockholm, Sweden. He was the first comics artist to win the Pulitzer Prize, which he received for his groundbreaking bestseller *Maus*. He lives in New York City.
***Co-Mix: A Retrospective of Comics, Graphics, and Scraps* (Sept 2013)**

JOHN STANLEY

(1914–1993) John is most famous for his scripts for the Little Lulu comics produced by Dell and is considered by many comics historians to be the most consistently funny and idiosyncratic comic-book writer to ever work in comics.
***The John Stanley Library: Melvin Monster* vol. 1 (May 2009); *The John Stanley Library: Nancy* vol. 1 (Sept 2009); *The John Stanley Library: Thirteen Going on Eighteen* (Jan 2010); *The John Stanley Library: Melvin Monster* vol. 2 (March 2010); *The John Stanley Library: Nancy* vol. 2 (Aug 2010); *The John Stanley Library: Tubby* (Sept 2010); *The John Stanley Library: Melvin Monster* vol. 3 (March 2011); *The John Stanley Library: Nancy* vol. 3 (Sept 2011); *The John Stanley Library: Nancy* vol. 4 (June 2013)**

LESLIE STEIN

Leslie draws the comic *Eye of the Majestic Creature* and plays in the band Prince Rupert's Drops.

FOOLBERT STURGEON

Foolbert Sturgeon is the pen name of cartoonist Frank Stack. He was born in 1937 in Houston, TX. He is credited with publishing the first underground comic, *The Adventures of Jesus*, in 1962.

"Foolbert Sturgeon's Cartoon Club," *Drawn & Quarterly* no. 2 (Oct 1990); "The Early Adventures of Paddy Booshwah," *Drawn & Quarterly* no. 3 (Jan 1991); "The Further Adventures of Paddy Booshwah," *Drawn & Quarterly* no. 4 (March 1991); "The New Adventures of Jesus," *Drawn & Quarterly* no. 6 (Oct 1991)

JAMES STURM

James was born in New York City in 1965. He is the founder of the National Association of Comics Art Educators (NACAE) as well as the co-founder of the Center for Cartoon Studies. He lives in Vermont with his wife and daughters.

"Friday Night," *Drawn & Quarterly* no. 2 (Oct 1990); "Signs of the Times," *Drawn & Quarterly* no. 3 (Jan 1991); "Crazy Ole' Hound in 'Ring,'" *Drawn & Quarterly* no. 4 (March 1991); *Hundreds of Feet Below Daylight* (July 1998); *The Golem's Mighty Swing* (July 2001); *Above and Below* (Dec 2004); *James Sturm's America: God, Gold, and Golems* (May 2007); *Market Day* (March 2010); *Denys Wortman's New York: Portrait of the City in the 1930s and 1940s* (Nov 2010)

OJI SUZUKI

Oji was born in 1949. Besides being a cartoonist, he has produced short films and has written and drawn children's books. He lives in Tokyo.

A Single Match (Jan 2011)

CAROL SWAIN

Carol was born in 1962 in London, England. She created the brilliant comic series *Way-Out Strips* the same year D+Q was born.

"Freak Scene," *Drawn & Quarterly* no. 3 (Jan 1991); "'B' Movie," *Drawn & Quarterly* no. 4 (March 1991) With Dennis P. Eichhorn: "Speak Up!" *Drawn & Quarterly* no. 8 (April 1992)

JILLIAN TAMAKI

Jillian was born in Ottawa and grew up in Calgary, Alberta. She has received numerous awards for the graphic novels *Skim* and *This One Summer*, which she co-created with her cousin Mariko. Jillian has taught illustration at the New York City School of Visual Arts and OCAD. She lives in Toronto.

Indoor Voice (April 2010); *SuperMutant Magic Academy* (April 2015)

JACQUES TARDI

Jacques was born in 1946 in France. He won the Grand Prix in Angoulême in 1985 and is considered one of France's master cartoonists.

"It Was the War of the Trenches," *Drawn & Quarterly* vol. 2, no. 1 (Aug 1994); "It Was the War of the Trenches," *Drawn & Quarterly* vol. 2, no. 2 (Dec 1994); "It Was the War of the Trenches," *Drawn & Quarterly* vol. 2, no. 3 (May 1995)

YOSHIHIRO TATSUMI

Yoshihiro was born in 1935 in Osaka. He has been drawing comics professionally since he was a teenager. He is currently finishing his follow-up to *A Drifting Life*. He lives in Japan with his wife.

"Kept," *Drawn & Quarterly Anthology* vol. 5 (Aug 2003); *The Push Man and Other Stories* (Sept 2005); *Abandon the Old in Tokyo* (Sept 2006); *Good-Bye* (May 2008); *A Drifting Life* (April 2009); *Black Blizzard* (April 2010); *Fallen Words* (May 2012)

PETER THOMPSON

Peter was born in 1970. He lives in Ontario.

The Chronicles of Lucky Ello (Jan 2005)

ADRIAN TOMINE

Adrian was born in Sacramento, CA, in 1974. Adrian began self-publishing his comic-book series *Optic Nerve* when he was sixteen. He lives in Brooklyn with his wife and daughters.

Optic Nerve no. 1 (April 1995); *Optic Nerve* no. 2 (Nov 1995); *Optic Nerve* no. 3 (Aug 1996); *32 Stories: The Complete Optic Nerve Mini-Comics* (Oct 1996); *Optic Nerve* no. 4 (April 1997); *Sleepwalk and Other Stories* (Oct 1997); *Optic Nerve* no. 5 (Feb 1998); *Optic Nerve* no. 6 (Feb 1999); *Optic Nerve* no. 7 (June 2000); *Optic Nerve* no. 8 (Sept 2001); *Summer Blonde* (May 2002); *Optic Nerve* no. 9 (Jan 2004);

The Death-Ray, Daniel Clowes *(Oct)*
The Great Northern Brotherhood of Canadian Cartoonists, Seth *(Oct)*
The Adventures of Hergé, Stanislas Barthélémy, José-Louis Bocquet, and Jean-Luc Fromental *(Nov)*
Walt & Skeezix: Book Five, 1929–1930, Frank King *(Dec)*

2012

Berlin no. 18, Jason Lutes *(Jan)*
Goliath, Tom Gauld *(Feb)*
Jinchalo, Matthew Forsythe *(Feb)*
Jerusalem: Chronicles from the Holy City, Guy Delisle *(April)*
Fallen Words, Yoshihiro Tatsumi *(May)*
Free Comic Book Day—Moomin Color Special, Tove Jansson *(May)*
Idyll, Amber Albrecht *(May)*
NonNonBa, Shigeru Mizuki *(May)*
Anna & Froga: Want a Gumball? Anouk Ricard *(June)*
Back Alleys and Urban Landscapes, Michael Cho *(June)*
Birdseye Bristoe, Dan Zettwoch *(June)*
Ed the Happy Clown, Chester Brown *(new edition, June)*
Gloriana, Kevin Huizenga *(June)*
Beethoven Birthday Party: A 2013 Hark!
A Vagrant Calendar, Kate Beaton *(Aug)*
The Making Of, Brecht Evens *(Aug)*
There She Blows: A 2013 Hark! A Vagrant Literary Calendar, Kate Beaton *(Aug)*
Aya: Life in Yop City, Marguerite Abouet and Clément Oubrerie *(Sept)*
Moomin: The Complete Lars Jansson Comic Strip vol. 7, Lars Jansson *(Sept)*
Rookie Yearbook One, Tavi Gevinson *(Sept)*
Moominvalley Turns Jungle, Tove Jansson *(Oct)*
Moomin's Winter Follies, Tove Jansson *(Oct)*
New York Drawings, Adrian Tomine *(Oct)*
Pippi Moves In, Astrid Lindgren and Ingrid Vang Nyman *(Oct)*
The Wayside, Julie Morstad *(Oct)*
Multi-Story Building Model, Chris Ware *(Nov)*
Don't Go Where I Can't Follow, Anders Nilsen *(new edition, Dec)*
Nipper 1967–1968, Doug Wright *(Dec)*

2013

The Freddie Stories, Lynda Barry *(Jan)*
Aya: Love in Yop City, Marguerite Abouet and Clément Oubrerie *(Feb)*
Cave-In, Brian Ralph *(Feb)*
Susceptible, Geneviève Castrée *(Feb)*
Letting It Go, Miriam Katin *(March)*
Moomin Builds a House, Tove Jansson *(March)*
Moomin Falls in Love, Tove Jansson *(March)*
Marble Season, Gilbert Hernandez *(April)*
You're All Just Jealous of My Jetpack, Tom Gauld *(April)*
Free Comic Book Day—Marble Season, Gilbert Hernandez *(May)*
Free Comic Book Day—Pippi Longstocking Color Special, Astrid Lindgren and Ingrid Vang Nyman *(May)*
My Dirty Dumb Eyes, Lisa Hanawalt *(May)*
The Playboy: A Comic-Strip Memoir, Chester Brown *(new edition, May)*
The Property, Rutu Modan *(May)*
Animals with Sharpies, Michael Dumontier and Neil Farber *(June)*
A User's Guide to Neglectful Parenting, Guy Delisle *(June)*
The John Stanley Library: Nancy vol. 4, John Stanley *(June)*
Optic Nerve no. 13, Adrian Tomine *(July)*
Anna & Froga: I Dunno, What Do You Want to Do? Anouk Ricard *(Aug)*
Kitaro, Shigeru Mizuki *(Aug)*
Reggie-12, Brian Ralph *(Aug)*
Co-Mix: A Retrospective of Comics, Graphics, and Scraps, Art Spiegelman *(Sept)*
Pippi Fixes Everything, Astrid Lindgren and Ingrid Vang Nyman *(Sept)*
Louis Riel: Tenth Anniversary Edition, Chester Brown *(Oct)*
Moomin and the Comet, Tove Jansson *(Oct)*
Moomin and the Sea, Tove Jansson *(Oct)*
Moomin: The Complete Lars Jansson Comic Strip vol. 8, Lars Jansson *(Oct)*
Palookaville no. 21, Seth *(Oct)*
Rage of Poseidon, Anders Nilsen *(Oct)*
Rookie Yearbook Two, Tavi Gevinson *(Oct)*

Scrapbook: Uncollected Work, 1990–2004 **(June 2004);** ***Optic Nerve*** **no. 10 (Oct 2005);** ***Optic Nerve*** **no. 11 (March 2007);** ***Shortcomings*** **(Oct 2007);** ***32 Stories: The Complete Optic Nerve Mini-Comics Box Set*** **(May 2009);** ***Scenes from an Impending Marriage*** **(Feb 2011);** ***Optic Nerve*** **no. 12 (Sept 2011);** ***New York Drawings*** **(Oct 2012);** ***Optic Nerve*** **no. 13 (July 2013);** ***New York Postcards*** **(April 2014)**

FRANCISCO TORRES LINHART

Francisco is a cartoonist and illustrator. He lives in Spain.

"Fate," ***Drawn & Quarterly*** **no. 10 (Dec 1992); "Fate,"** ***The Best of Drawn & Quarterly*** **(Dec 1993); "Tout Va Bien,"** ***Drawn & Quarterly*** **vol. 2, no. 6 (June 1997)**

LEWIS TRONDHEIM

Lewis was born Laurent Chabosy in Fontainebleau, France, in 1964. He has written and drawn over one hundred comic books including the popular series *Dungeon* (NBM).

CAROL TYLER

Carol was born in 1951. She is the author of the three-book series *You'll Never Know*. She lives in Cincinnati, OH, with her husband.

"Color My Day," ***Drawn & Quarterly*** **no. 4 (March 1991); "Why I'm A-Gin Southern Min!"** ***Drawn & Quarterly*** **no. 6 (October 1991); "Pie Kids,"** ***Drawn & Quarterly*** **no. 8 (April 1992); "Why I'm A-Gin Southern Min!"** ***The Best of Drawn & Quarterly*** **(Dec 1993); "The Hannah Story,"** ***Drawn & Quarterly*** **vol. 2, no.1 (Aug 1994); "Gone,"** ***Drawn & Quarterly*** **vol. 2, no. 4 (Dec 1995)**

COLIN UPTON

Colin was born in 1960 in Winnipeg, Manitoba. He lives in Vancouver and has been involved in the small-press comics scene since the late 1980s.

"Real Men," ***Drawn & Quarterly*** **no. 3 (Jan 1991)**

AMANDA VÄHÄMÄKI

Amanda was born in 1981 in Finland. She grew up wandering around forests and lakes.

Drawn & Quarterly Showcase **vol. 5 (Aug 2008);** ***The Bun Field*** **(April 2009)**

BRECHT VANDENBROUCKE

Brecht Vandenbroucke is a Belgian cartoonist and illustrator. He has worked for numerous periodicals, including the *New York Times*.

White Cube **(March 2014)**

JAN VAN DER VEKEN

Jan was born in 1975 in Ghent, Belgium. His illustrations have appeared in the *New York Times*, *Nobrow*, and the *New Yorker*.

With Alberto Manguel: Introduction ("Pictures and Conversations"), ***Drawn & Quarterly*** **vol. 5 (Aug 2003)**

INGRID VANG NYMAN

(1916–1959) Ingrid was a noted Danish children's book illustrator, as well as the original illustrator of the Pippi chapter books.

With Astrid Lindgren: ***Pippi Moves In*** **(Oct 2012);** ***Pippi Fixes Everything*** **(Sept 2013);** ***Pippi Won't Grow Up*** **(Nov 2014)**

FABIEN VEHLMANN

Fabien was born in 1972. He has been nominated for awards at the Angoulême Comics Festival numerous times.

With Kerascoët: ***Beautiful Darkness*** **(Feb 2014)**

MAURICE VELLEKOOP

Maurice was born in 1964. His work has appeared in publications such as *Time*, *GQ*, and *Vogue*. He lives on magical Toronto Island.

"Homoman," ***Drawn & Quarterly*** **no. 4 (March 1991); "Lullaby of Broadway,"** ***Drawn & Quarterly*** **no. 5 (June 1991); inside back cover ("Music") and "A Heterosexual's Guide to Gay Cruising,"** ***Drawn & Quarterly*** **no. 6 (Oct 1991); "8 Pillars of Gay Culture,"** ***Drawn & Quarterly*** **no. 7 (March 1992); inside front cover ("Day of Crabby Art"), back cover ("Parallel Universe"), and "Advertising Feature,"** ***Drawn & Quarterly*** **no. 8 (April 1992); "Art Fantasy,"** ***Drawn & Quarterly*** **no. 9 (July 1992); back cover, "Soap Brought to You by Supra-Galaxy," and "The Secret Life of Gloria Badcock,"** ***Drawn & Quarterly*** **no. 10 (Dec 1992); covers, endpapers, "8 Pillars of Gay Culture," "Homoman," "Music," and "Night Job,"** ***The Best of Drawn & Quarterly*** **(Dec 1993); "The Same Old Story,"** ***Drawn & Quarterly*** **vol. 2, no. 1 (Aug 1994); "More Than Coincidence?"** ***Drawn & Quarterly*** **vol. 2, no. 2 (Dec 1994); "Side Door Lover,"**

Drawn & Quarterly vol. 2, no. 3 (May 1995); "A Day in the Life of Pierre Pouffe," *Drawn & Quarterly* vol. 2, no. 4 (Dec 1995); "Dora the Living Doll," *Drawn & Quarterly* vol. 2, no. 5 (April 1996); "Waiting" and "Artwork," *Drawn & Quarterly* vol. 2, no. 6 (June 1997); *Vellevision* (Nov 1997); *A Nut at the Opera* (April 2006) With Fiona Smyth and Roxanna Bikadoroff: *Fabulous Babes no. 1* (July 1995)

CHRIS VON SZOMBATHY

Chris was born in 1980. His artwork has appeared in galleries in Vancouver, Los Angeles, San Francisco, Barcelona, Madrid, London, and Manchester. He lives in Vancouver, BC.
Fire Away (March 2008)

KEVIN "GIG" WAILGUM

Kevin attended the School of Visual Arts in New York. He is the creator of Santa Clops. He lives in Connecticut.
"The Meek," *Drawn & Quarterly* no. 8 (April 1992)

CHRIS WARE

Chris was born Franklin Christenson Ware in 1967 in Omaha, NE. He has self-published several issues of his own magazine called the *Ragtime Ephemeralist*. His 2012 book, *Building Stories*, has won numerous awards, including the *Los Angeles Times* Book Prize. He lives in Oak Park, IL.
Covers and endpapers, *Drawn & Quarterly Anthology vol. 3* (May 2000); *The ACME Novelty Datebook vol. 1* (Aug 2003); *The ACME Novelty Datebook vol. 2* (Dec 2007); *The ACME Novelty Library no. 20* (*Lint*) (Nov 2010); *The Multi-Story Building Model* (Nov 2012)

WAYNO

Wayno is a Pittsburgh-based cartoonist and illustrator active since the late 1980s. He is the creator of the acclaimed *Beer Nutz* series.
"I'm Having Chest Pains," *Drawn & Quarterly no. 3* (Jan 1991)

DENNIS WORDEN

Dennis was born in Los Angeles and started cartooning in 1981. He is the creator and cartoonist of *Stickboy*.

"U.S. Violent Americans," *Drawn & Quarterly* no. 1 (April 1990); "The Strange Case of Ross Brown," *Drawn & Quarterly* no. 2 (Oct 1990); "The Strange Case of Ross Brown," *The Best of Drawn & Quarterly* (Dec 1993)

DENYS WORTMAN

(1887–1958) For thirty years, Denys drew the comic strip *Metropolitan Movies*. He also displayed work in the infamous Armory Show in 1913.
With James Sturm and Brandon Elston: *Denys Wortman's New York: Portrait of the City in the 1930s and 1940s* (Nov 2010)

ZACH WORTON

Zach was born in the wilds of Saskatchewan. He spends his time collecting knick-knacks and geegaws, writing more than he has time to draw, and playing music with his two bands, Apeshit Simians and Zorton and the Cannibals. He lives in Toronto.
The Klondike (April 2011)

DOUG WRIGHT

(1917–1983) *Doug Wright's Family*, aka *Nipper*, ran for more than thirty-five years in magazines and newspapers across Canada and the US.
The Collected Doug Wright, Volume One: Canada's Master Cartoonist (May 2009); *Nipper 1963–1964* (Oct 2010); *Nipper 1965–1966* (Sept 2011); *Nipper 1967–1968* (Dec 2012)

YAYO

Yayo is the pen name of Diego Herrara, a Montreal-based children's book artist and magazine illustrator.
With Rena Cohen: "I'm Home, Working," *Drawn & Quarterly no. 3* (Jan 1991)

DAN ZETTWOCH

Dan was born in 1977 in Louisville, KY— the birthplace of Muhammad Ali and the cheeseburger. He lives in St. Louis.
Covers, endpapers, and "Won't Be Licked," *Drawn & Quarterly Showcase vol. 4* (June 2006); *Birdseye Bristoe* (June 2012)

Sunday Night Movies, Leanne Shapton *(Oct)*
Woman Rebel: The Margaret Sanger Story, Peter Bagge *(Oct)*
Showa 1926–1939: A History of Japan, Shigeru Mizuki *(Nov)*

2014
Ant Colony, Michael DeForge *(Jan)*
Beautiful Darkness, Fabien Vehlmann and Kerascoët *(Feb)*
Moomin and the Golden Tail, Tove Jansson *(Feb)*
Moomin's Desert Island, Tove Jansson *(Feb)*
On Loving Women, Diane Obomsawin *(Feb)*
White Cube, Brecht Vandenbroucke *(March)*
New York Postcards, Adrian Tomine *(April)*
One! Hundred! Demons! Lynda Barry *(ebook edition, April)*
Over Easy, Mimi Pond *(April)*
The WORN Archive: A Fashion Journal about the Art, Ideas, and History of What We Wear, Serah-Marie McMahon *(April)*
Everywhere Antennas, Julie Delporte *(May)*
Free Comic Book Day—Showa: A History of Japan, Shigeru Mizuki *(May)*
Petty Theft, Pascal Girard *(May)*
Benson's Cuckoos, Anouk Ricard *(June)*
Showa 1939–1944: A History of Japan, Shigeru Mizuki *(June)*
Walt Before Skeezix, Frank King *(June)*
Moomin: The Complete Lars Jansson Comic Strip vol. 9, Lars Jansson *(July)*
Even More Bad Parenting Advice, Guy Delisle *(Aug)*
Bumperhead, Gilbert Hernandez *(Sept)*
Moomin on the Riviera, Tove Jansson *(Sept)*
The Hospital Suite, John Porcellino *(Sept)*
Moomin: The Deluxe Anniversary Edition, Tove Jansson *(Oct)*
Syllabus: Notes from an Accidental Professor, Lynda Barry *(Oct)*
Anna & Froga: Thrills, Spills, and Gooseberries, Anouk Ricard *(Nov)*
Earthling, Aisha Franz *(Nov)*
Pippi Won't Grow Up, Astrid Lindgren and Ingrid Vang Nyman *(Nov)*
Showa 1944–1953: A History of Japan, Shigeru Mizuki *(Nov)*

D+Q STAFF *1989–present*

CHRIS OLIVEROS *editor-in-chief* 1989–present

MARINA LESENKO *copy editor* 1989–2003 *translator* 2010 *store employee* 2007

TRAIE PAYNE *office assistant* 2001–2002 *store employee* 2007–2008

ELIZABETH WALKER *publicist* 2002–2003

PEGGY BURNS *publicity director* 2003–2008 *associate publisher* 2008–present

REBECCA ROSEN *intern* 2003–2004 *production assistant* 2004–2008 *production manager* 2008–2010

TOM DEVLIN *production manager* 2004–2008 *creative director* 2008–present

JAMIE QUAIL *intern* 2004 *publicity coordinator* 2005–2008

JESSICA CAMPBELL *intern* 2006–2007 *publicity assistant* 2007–2008
publicity coordinator 2008–2010 *design manager* 2010–2012

ALISON NATURALE *intern* 2007 *production assistant* 2008

JAMIE SALOMON *accountant* 2007–2009

KIT MALO *operations director* 2008–2009

JULIA POHL-MIRANDA *intern* 2008–2009 *store employee* 2009–2011
publicity & marketing assistant 2011–2012 *editorial & marketing manager* 2012–present

CLAIRE BENNETT *publicity assistant* 2009–2010

ANN CUNNINGHAM *business manager* 2009–2012 *finance director* 2012–present

TRACY HURREN *intern* 2010 *production manager* 2010–2012 *managing editor* 2012–present

MARIE-JADE MENNI *intern* 2011 *store employee* 2011–2013 *production assistant* 2013–present

ALEXANDRA AUGER *marketing assistant* 2013–present *store employee* 2014

MARCELA HUERTA *intern* 2014 *store employee* 2014 *production assistant* 2015–present

CLAUDIA EVE BEAUCHESNE *intern* 2007 *store employee* 2007–2008

MATT SHANE *store employee* 2007–2009

RORY SEYDEL *intern* 2007 *store manager* 2008–2011

JULIEN CECCALDI *store employee* 2008–2013

ELIF SAYDAM *store employee* 2008–2009

AMBER ALBRECHT *store employee* 2009–2010

YANIYA LACHARITE *store employee* 2009–2010

CHANTALE POTIE *store employee* 2009–2012

FIONA DUNCAN *intern* 2010 *store employee* 2010–2012

JASON GRIMMER *retail and events director* 2011–present

HELEN CHAU BRADLEY *store employee* 2012–present *events coordinator* 2014–2015

ALESHIA JENSEN *store employee* 2012–present *events coordinator* 2013–present

EMILY BELANGER *intern* 2013 *store employee* 2013

JULIE DELPORTE *store employee* 2013–present

KIRA MAE POIRIER *store employee* 2013–present

SAELAN TWERDY *store employee* 2013–present

DAPHNE BEAUDOIN–PILON *store employee* 2014–present

ALYSSA FAVREAU *intern* 2012 *store employee* 2014–present

KATE LEWIS *store employee* 2014–present

INDEX

Thanks to all of the cartoonists, writers, translators, and photographers who provided original material exclusive to this book; to all of our friends and colleagues who contributed photos, anecdotes, or artwork that we couldn't fit into the book; to our incredibly patient copy editor Kathleen Fraser; to all of our wonderful and invaluable interns over the years, and especially our interns who worked on this book, Sara Paoletti and Alison Vanderkruyk.

Special thanks to all the translators, editors, and letterers who have worked on our books over the years: Jocelyne Allen, Peter Blegvad, Jessica Cohen, Helge Dascher, Zack Davisson, Brandon Elston, Ray Fenwick, Ioana Georgescu, Sophie Hannah, Asaf Hanuka, Tim Hensley, Rhian Heppleston, Ryan Holmberg, Michele Hutchison, John Kuramoto, Marina Lesenko, Jesse Mishory, Taro Nettleton, Tiina Nunnally, Yuji Oniki, Dirk Rehm, Geneviève Scott, Kate Sibbald, Noah Stollman, Adrian Tomine, Rich Tommasso, Laura Watkinson, Akemi Wegmüller, and Chris Ware.

Thank you to all D+Q employees, past and present, and most of all, to every Drawn & Quarterly author. We are honoured to have published your work.

D+Q thanks the companies we work with every day to create and sell our books: Regina Ang from TWP; the one and only Scott Lavelle from Imago; retailers and festivals around the world; our foreign rights agent, Samantha Haywood of the Transatlantic Agency; our foreign publishers; our warehouse, Transport Specialties International; our distributors, Macmillan, Raincoast, Diamond, and PGUK; and especially Spenser Lee and everyone at Farrar, Straus and Giroux.

Chris Oliveros thanks Marina Lesenko, Rafael Oliveros, Peggy Burns, and Peter Birkemoe.

And lastly, thank you to the Government of Quebec—in particular the Jeunes Volontaires program—and the Government of Canada. Drawn & Quarterly acknowledges the financial contribution of the Government of Canada through the Canada Book Fund and the Canada Council for the Arts for our publishing activities and for support of this edition.

Thank you to Helge Dascher for translating numerous comics and essays in this book, including the following short texts: Jean-Louis Gauthey (page 37), Diane Obomsawin (page 71), Jean-Christophe Menu (page 524), and Rina Zavagli (page 687).

Unless otherwise noted on page, all writing, comics, and illustrations in this book are appearing here for the first time, with the exceptions of Guy Delisle's "Just for Me," Archer Prewitt's Sof' Boy comics, and Rutu Modan's "The Rosa Luxemburg Mystery," which are appearing here for the first time in English.

drawnandquarterly.com. First hardcover edition: May 2015. Printed in China. 10 9 8 7 6 5 4 3 2 1

Library and Archives Canada Cataloguing in Publication: *Drawn & Quarterly: Twenty-five years of contemporary cartooning, comics, and graphic novels* / Tom Devlin, editor. ISBN 978-1-77046-199-4 (bound). 1. Drawn & Quarterly (Firm)—History. 2. Comic books, strips, etc.—Publishing—Québec (Province)—Montréal—History. I. Devlin, Tom, editor. Z483.D73D73 2015   070.509714'28   C2014-907017-9

Published in the USA by Drawn & Quarterly, a client publisher of Farrar, Straus and Giroux. Published in Canada by Drawn & Quarterly, a client publisher of Raincoast Books. Published in the United Kingdom by Drawn & Quarterly, a client publisher of Publishers Group UK.

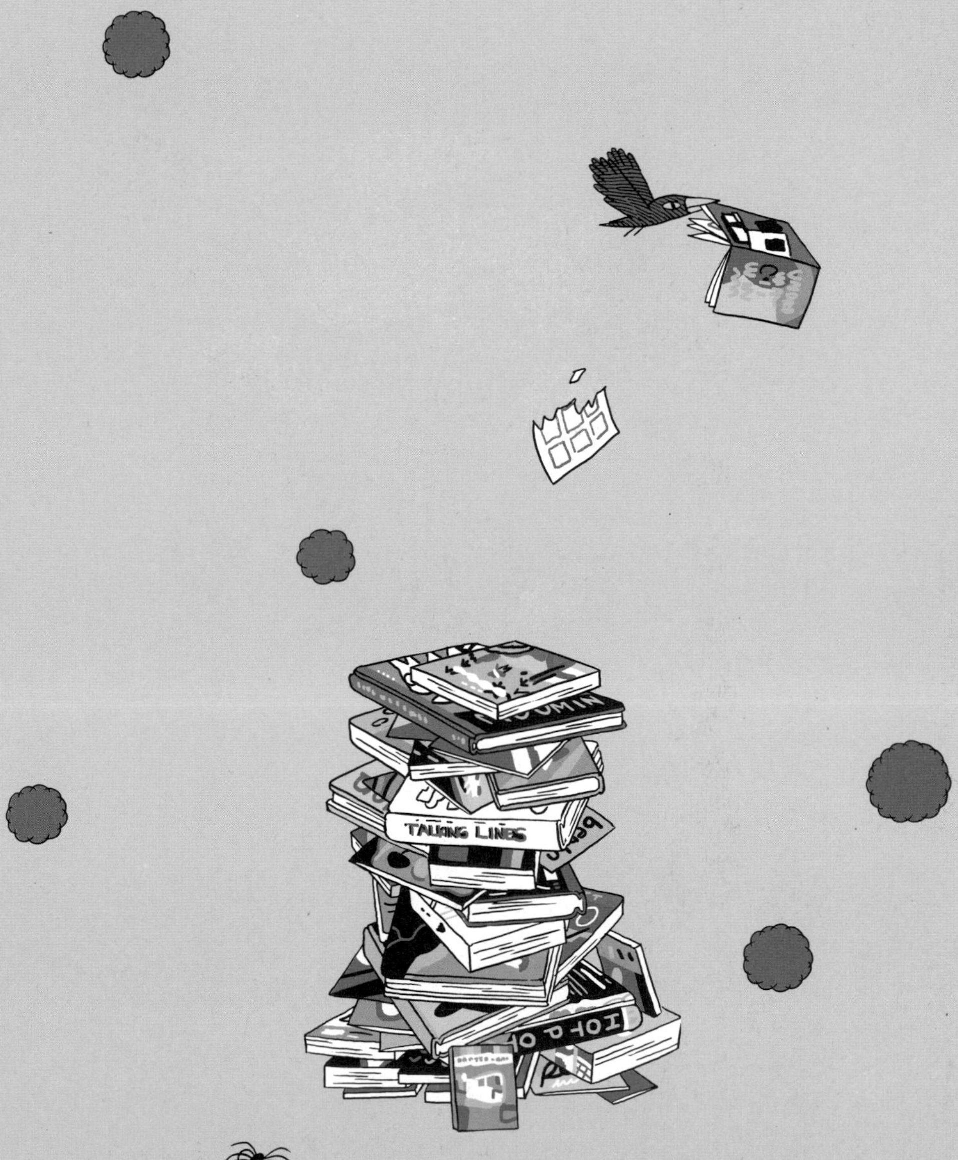
TALKING LINES

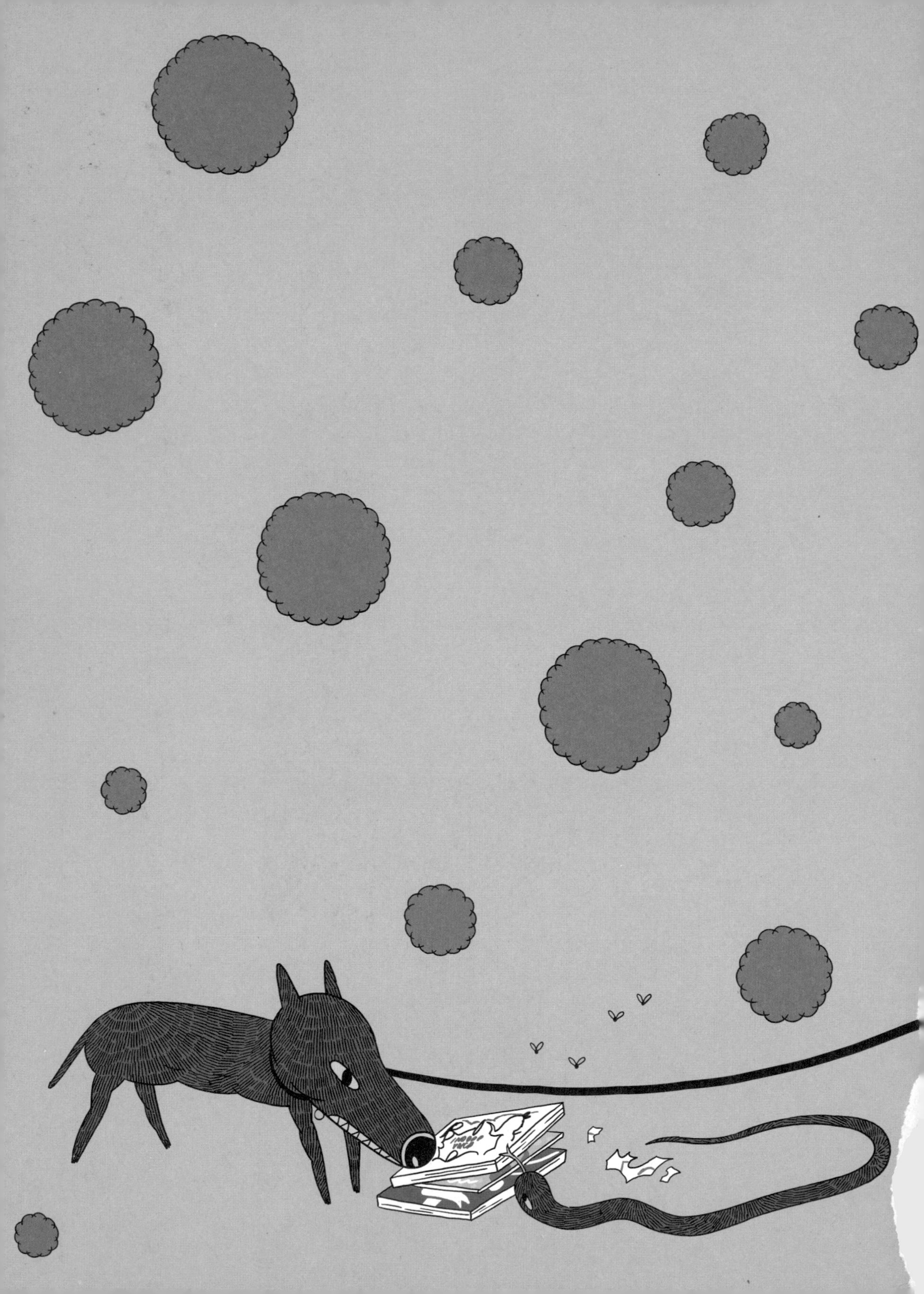